ROSTER OF NORTH CAROLINIANS

IN CONFEDERATE NAVAL SERVICE

[Confederate States Navy & Marine Corps]

Abstracted and Compiled by LTC Sion H. Harrington III, United Army (Retired)
(Former Military Collection Archivist, Archives and Records Section, Division of Historical Resources,
North Carolina Department of Cultural Resources, Raleigh, North Carolina)
(Project Initiated 2004)

Copyright 2004 by LTC (Ret.) Sion H. Harrington III
— All Rights Reserved —

www.scuppernongpress.com

Roster of North Carolinians in Confederate Naval Service
by LTC (Ret.) Sion H. Harrington III

©2021 The Scuppernong Press

First Printing

The Scuppernong Press
PO Box 1724
Wake Forest, NC 27588
www.scuppernongpress.com

Cover and book design by Frank B. Powell, III

About the cover. An engraving of the CSS *Shenandoah* while in port at Melbourne, Australia in 1864. *From the Library of Congress.*

All rights reserved. Printed in the United States of America.

No part of this book may be reproduced or transmitted in any form or by any means, electronic or mechanical, including photocopying, recording, or by any information and storage and retrieval system, without written permission from the publisher.

International Standard Book Number ISBN 978-1-942806-36-3

Library of Congress Control Number: 2021917995

TABLE OF CONTENTS

Introduction iii

Roster (In Alphabetical Order) 1

Appendices:

  I. Notes on Roster Entries 351

II. Bibliography: Citation Abbreviations for Works Cited
    (with full citation in right column) 351

III. Bibliography: Full Citations for Works Cited
    (with abbreviated citations in right column) 364

IV. Rank/Rates and Special Terms mentioned in the Roster 376

V. Confederate Ships and Floating Batteries Mentioned in the Roster 379

VI. Confederate Naval Stations, Yards, and Activities Mentioned in the Roster 399

VII: Interesting Tidbits from *The Roster of North Carolinians
    in Confederate Naval Service* 400

Index 409

First Confederate Naval Jack

INTRODUCTION
to
Roster of North Carolinians in Confederate Naval Service
by
LTC Sion H. Harrington III, United States Army (Retired))

This work has been a true labor of love during the decade and a half I have worked on it. I have always enjoyed the challenge of historical research and this book provided plenty of challenging opportunities. This roster is in no way meant to detract from the brave service of the men who fought in the Confederate infantry, artillery, cavalry, or any other land-based service. My own great-great grandfathers are counted among these stalwart men. It is simply to add to the body of knowledge about those from North Carolina who served and defended their State and new nation, just as "some" of their ancestors of 1776 did eighty-five years before. Were these men alive today they would no doubt wonder why the act of secession in 1776 is celebrated today, while the secession of 1860-61 is demonized. The circumstances were quite similar and the institution of slavery, which seems to be the "hot button" issue of the latter war flourished during both. It is indeed an intellectually puzzling question further muddied by hypocrisy and double standards of our current "Zeitgeist."

The genesis for this book came when I realized there was no extensive or reliable listing of sailors and marines who served in Confederate naval forces, especially for those from my native North Carolina. My primary reason for delving into such a relatively obscure topic of the War Between the States was sparked when I realized there was little in the way of a roster on the men who served in Confederate naval forces, especially those from North Carolina. I felt very strongly that these men had done their duty and deserved to be recognized like their compatriots who fought in the infantry artillery and cavalry arms of the army. My mission was to rectify that shortcoming and my goal became to make this roster the most comprehensive collection of information pertaining to North Carolinians who served in Confederate Naval service published to date.

The standard resources for service from North Carolina during the War Between the States were consulted but yielded limited results. It was then I discovered two gentlemen whose seminal work in identifying Confederate sailors and marines was truly an inspiration. In an Internet search, I discovered the massive collection of records compiled by Mr. Terry Foenander of Australia. Yes, I was amazed, too, that someone from Australia had devoted so much of his life to preserving the memories and service of the South's sailors and marines but thankfully he had. Mr. Foenander was most helpful in my endeavor. Sadly, he passed away only a few years ago. God rest his soul.

Another gentleman who has been of tremendous assistance is Mr. R. Bruce Long. His work on the war in coastal North Carolina and especially in identifying the members of the "North Carolina Navy" and the "North Carolina Squadron" early in the war filled a critical gap in the roster. I am very much indebted to this outstanding historian for his willingness to share his extensive research with me.

Perhaps the best way to describe this roster is by explaining what it is not. As hard as I tried to make it so, I cannot claim it is a comprehensive list of all North Carolinians who served the Confederacy on, or near, the water. It is this author's humble attempt to document a group of men all too often under appreciated and superficially treated by historians of the conflict. North Carolina men and boys serving in the land forces were well documented by the North Carolina Department of Cultural Resources' on-going multi-volume series *North Carolina Troops, 1861 – 1865: A Roster*. The fact that North Carolina naval personnel had no such annotated roster was sufficient justification for me to develop such a roster. It is my hope that by preserving and publishing the names and such service information as could be found that the Tar Heels who served the Confederate naval service may receive the recognition they so richly deserve.

In compiling the roster, I have made every attempt to be as accurate and comprehensive as possible, but it is neither totally complete nor infallible. It is and always will be a work in progress since additional information will no doubt come to light in the future. It represents nearly two decades of research in a variety of sources ranging from primary to secondary published works to, in a couple of instances, anecdotal family stories. As with any work it is left to the reader to assign their own level of credibility to the sources and the information gleaned from them. If there are gaps or erroneous information, I assure the reader it was not by design.

No county of residence or even state of residence could be confirmed for some sailors or marines. They were included in the roster based on the sources cited or other clues. Likewise, sources listed for some entries may appear weak on legitimacy, but they are included to ensure that any North Carolinian who available information indicates "probably" or "may" have performed Confederate naval service is not omitted. Again, I leave it to the readers' discretion to determine the level of trustworthiness they allocate.

The reader will notice some entries contain contradictory information. This is due to differences in information found in the sources quoted. For example, an entry may state a man "enlisted at Camp Holmes near Raleigh," whereas another source may indicate he "enlisted in Wilmington" on such and such a date which also tends to vary. This could be the result of a man having been initially enrolled for naval service in Raleigh at one of the two major Camps of Instruction where newly enlisted or conscripted men normally received their first military training. The sailor or marine-to-be may well have not taken the oath for naval service until he arrived in Wilmington and reported for training aboard the "receiving ship" where he was given his initial naval familiarization training.

Some entries are longer than others reflecting the amount of information available. Since there is considerably more information available on the better-known men and higher-ranking individuals, no effort has been made in this roster to treat those men in detail. There are, however, some longer entries on famous as well as lesser-known men whose life and service were of particular interest.

In some cases, the information for two men was found to be so similar as to suspect they were perhaps one in the same. Where there was no way to distinguish between them, both entries were included in the hope that one day information would come to light that would bring clarity to the situation.

Two notations found often in the roster are those related to men coming into the naval service from the army and records indicating an individual being reported as having "run" on such and such a date. The latter is an obvious reference to men taking "French leave" as desertion was sometimes called in the Nineteenth Century. Quite a few are listed as having "run" in February of 1862 after the disastrous battles on and around Roanoke Island and later in Elizabeth City. It is likely a goodly number of these men re-enlisted or were conscripted into either the navy or army as time went by and the Conscript Law caught up with them.

The issue of transfers from the army sheds light on both conditions in the field and how these men were initially perceived by their new navy or marine comrades. At least four hundred and seventeen Tar Heels transferred from the Army to the Navy. Since very few of the army transfers possessed any degree of seaman skills, they were invariably assigned as Landsmen. As the term implies, these were "land men" rather than "sea men" who were given the least skilled duties to perform. Likewise, marines normally lacked any nautical skills and were equally despised by the sailors who had to do the hard, skilled work of running a ship. One advantage the Landsman had over the marine was that, in time, he might learn just enough seamanship to be perceived as "useful" aboard ship by the sailors.

A considerable number of men were temporarily transferred to the Navy for short periods of service or received permission from the Army to permanently transfer to naval service. At least four hundred and seventeen North Carolinians switched from the Army to the Navy. In former Confederate Navy officer Captain William Harwar Parker's book about his career as a naval officer from 1841 to 1865, published in 1883, can be found this rather telling quote regarding those received from the army. "Occasionally we got a man from the Army and we kept a bathing arrangement on the wharf where all recruits were bathed, and their clothes well boiled before being allowed to come on board." This comment was no doubt addressing the lice with which too many soldiers having to live outdoors twenty-four hours a day, seven days a week and with little chance to bath or wash their clothing regularly had to contend. Had they been allowed on board the close confines of a ship without this "delousing" effort, the disease-caring critters could have rapidly spread and caused a great deal of mischief among the crew, thus reducing their efficiency and endangering their health. Although initially somewhat humiliating, in time I am sure the soldiers-turned-sailors appreciated being rid of the aggravating pests.

Among the nearly three thousand North Carolina men and boys listed in this roster as having served in either the North Carolina Navy, Confederate States Navy, or both, or Confederate States Marine Corps are the names of several of special note, for either good or bad. For these I refer the reader to Appendix VII: THE ODD, THE STRANGE, AND THE NOTEWORTHY: NOTES ON NORTH CAROLINIANS IN CONFEDERATE NAVAL SERVICE.

The Confederate States Navy was never large. It was constantly short of ships, personnel, especially skilled mariners, and all types of equipment and supplies from food to cannons. Compared to the number of men provided to the Army, North Carolina's contribution to the South's relatively small navy of approximately three thousand seems unimpressive. But in the light of evidence, this number spread over four years was anything but unimpressive. According to *Life in Jefferson Davis' Navy* (Tomblin), by 1864, at the peak of the Confederate States Navy's strength she had only seven hundred and fifty-three officers and four thousand four hundred and fifty enlisted men on duty! Others had served during the three years preceding and either been killed in action or died of wounds, died of disease, transferred to the Army, or simply deserted…Our state's contribution was significant.

Although no North Carolinians were discovered to have served in the tiny Confederate States Revenue Service, ninety-eight men from our state did serve in the small regiment-sized Confederate States Marine Corps. The Confederate Marines were established on March 16, 1861 by an act of the Confederate States Congress. Its force establishment was set at forty-six officers and nine hundred and forty-four enlisted men, for a total of nine hundred and ninety. This figure was very slightly increased later. Manning difficulties plagued the Confederate States Marine Corps throughout its existence. By October 30, 1864, the Corps consisted of a mere five hundred and thirty-nine men, spread out over several ships and stations. Unless one lived in or near a major United States Navy base or station, it is unlikely the average Southerner would have known much if anything about the marines. And, with the tendency of local men to enlist together and the army being a known commodity, it is no surprise few Tar Heels rushed to enlist in the Confederate Marine Corps, or Navy.

Two North Carolinians became officers in the Confederate Marine Corps. Lieutenant John DeBerniere Roberts was born in North Carolina but reared in South Carolina and served from that state. Lieutenant Francis Hawkes Cameron was born in Orange County, North Carolina and served throughout the war. He became the adjutant general of North Carolina from 1893 – 1896. Among the ninety-one enlisted marines from North Carolina were some thirty-two who were "enlisted" from among conscripts in 1864 at Camp Holmes near Raleigh. One of those placed in the Confederate Marine Corps was Henry Hunter Bowen of Washington County, North Carolina. In a letter home to his wife, Henry wrote that he and his compatriots ere to be placed in the "meareans" [marines] to serve on a steamer in Charleston Harbor. He seemed satisfied with his assigned branch of service as he wrote to his wife that he had been told they "have the finest clothing and best to eat …" The letters written during his service in the Confederate States Marine Corps were donated to the State Archives of North Carolina by the widow of Mr. John Oden of Beaufort County, North Carolina. It was Mr. Oden's wish that this rare and valuable correspondence be preserved in the State Archives. When evaluated, the eighteen letters of Henry Hunter Bowen written between 1864 and 1865 and the one from his brother, George Washington Bowen, a fellow "mearean," written on the back of one of Henry's, were found to be the largest collection of enlisted Confederate Marine correspondence known to exist! Given the minuscule size of the Confederate States Marine Corps, these letters most certainly are extremely rare and valuable.

With the fall of Fort Fisher and Wilmington after two hard-fought battles, the sailors and marines who manned the fort and ancillary stations joined those whose ships or stations had to be abandoned in the face of Sherman's advancing army. These men performed commendable service as "web-footed" infantry in the last few weeks of the war. Most noteworthy was their defense as the "rear guard" of General Robert E. Lee's army as it evacuated the lines around Richmond and Petersburg and headed west in the hopes of escaping the ever-tightening noose of the seemingly inexhaustible supply of Union soldiers. Many North Carolina naval personnel were in Company F, Naval Battalion, with General Custis Lee's Division. These and other sailors and marines-turned infantry fought valiantly at the Battle of Sailor's Creek [Saylor's Creek] which was fought on April 6, 1865 near Farmville, Virginia, giving other Confederate units time to cross Sailor's and Little Sailor's Creeks to relative, if temporary, safety. This violent action which included savage hand-to-hand combat is said to have been the last "major" engagement of the Confederate Army of Northern Virginia.

Rare is the historian who can produce any work worthy of its paper without the help of others, and so it is with this roster. I wish to acknowledge the invaluable assistance of those who helped make this roster possible. I will not attempt to list here every person or resource consulted in compiling this roster since a comprehensive list of those resources utilized can be found at the end of the roster. I have already mentioned the incredible assistance received from Terry Foenander and R. Bruce Long. No amount of thanks would be sufficient to express the appreciation and admiration I have for these two men and their contribution to preserving the memories of those North Carolinians who served their state and the Confederacy in the naval forces.

However, I must make mention of a few to whom I owe a debt of gratitude. I offer special thanks to Josh Howard, former employee of the Research Branch, North Carolina Department of Cultural Resources, Raleigh, North Carolina, for his invaluable assistance in locating entries for this roster. Likewise, I extend my heartfelt thanks to the personnel of the Search Room of the Archives and Records Section of the State Archives of North Carolina, in particular Dr. Larry Odzak, Dennis Daniels, and Susan Woodson, and William (Bill) Brown and Dr. Boyd Cathey, the current and former Archives Registrars. To my former Military Collection intern (Summer of 2004) at the Archives, Kaitlin Hocutt, a big thank you for your yeoman work in helping me gather and enter materials. Other employees of the North Carolina Department of Cultural Resources to whom I am indebted include Matthew Brown, former editor of the *North Carolina Troops, 1861 – 1865: A Roster* series, and his able assistant editor Dr. Michael Coffey. I also wish to thank Mrs. Allison Hall Thurman and Mrs. Tomoko Cole for their research assistance. Andrew Duppstadt of North Carolina Historic Sites was particularly helpful and supportive. To Jesse R. (Dick) Lankford, James O. Sorrell and Steve Massengill, my former supervisors, and Dr. Jeffrey Crowe, the former Deputy Secretary of Archives and History, North Carolina Department of Cultural Resources, I offer my most humble thanks for allowing me the privilege of achieving one of my childhood dreams: to work for the North Carolina State Archives!

And last, but certainly not least, I thank the dearest, most important person in my life, my wife with whom I have shared the happiest fifty-one years of my life. Without her support and patience in allowing me to sit for hours on end typing and researching while she sat somewhat neglected, this roster could never have been completed.

Since beginning the *"Roster of North Carolinians in Confederate Naval Service"* project in late 2003, I have experienced a great many hours of pleasurable research and writing. It is my hope this roster will be as useful to the public as it has been fun for me to compile. If I have overlooked anyone who aided me in its creation, please know it was not intentional and accept my sincere apologies with the knowledge that your assistance is deeply appreciated.

Abbott, John (North Carolina?)
Landsman, CSS ARCTIC, Cape Fear River, North Carolina, 1863.
[Source(s): Foenander; ORN 2, 1, 279]

Abernathy, James Robert (Gaston County, North Carolina)
Private, Confederate States Army//Confederate States Navy. Abernathy enlisted at age 39 on September 3, 1864, in Company D [Source "North Carolina Troops" shows Company B], 28th Regiment, North Carolina Troops. He transferred to Confederate States Navy on April 3, 1864. He was officially transferred by Special Order #89 dated April 16, 1864.
[Source(s): NCT, VIII; Foenander; Card File; Cloninger]

Abernathy, John (North Carolina)
Private, Confederate States Marine Corps. A worker at the Confederate States Navy Yard, Charlotte, North Carolina who was likely one of the circa three hundred workmen armed, equipped, and formed into one of three companies of "Marines" for defense purposes in late 1864 or early 1865. He may have been a member of the one company detailed to accompany Confederate Major General Joseph Wheeler as his unit escorted the wife and family of President Jefferson Davis, some government officials, and the gold of the Confederate Treasury south as they attempted to escape Union capture.
[Source: SHSP (Vol. 40); "Char. Obs.," April 3, 1910 and June 5, 1910; "Char. News," June 5, 1910]

Adams, James A. (Craven County, North Carolina)
Sergeant, Confederate States Army//Landsman, Confederate States Navy. Adams resided in Craven County, North Carolina, where he enlisted at age 21 on May 27, 1861, for the war, in Company F, 2nd Regiment North Carolina Troops. He entered the unit as a Sergeant but was a Private when he transferred to the Confederate States Navy in December 1861. Born in 1840, he died on January 13, 1865, and was buried in Oakwood Cemetery, Raleigh, Wake County, North Carolina.
[Source(s): Card File; NPS; NCT, III; Stepp, "Burials"]

Adams, James H.
4th Sergeant [?], Confederate States Navy. Adams was born in 1840 and died on January 13, 1865. He is buried in Grave #421 of the Confederate Section of Oakwood Cemetery, Raleigh, North Carolina.
[Source(s): "Oakwood Cemetery," Raleigh, North Carolina].

Adams, William (Beaufort County, North Carolina)
[NOTE: Possibly same as William Adams, Gunner's Mate, q.v.]
Landsman, Confederate States Navy. Adams was born in England in 1821. He resided as a sailor in Beaufort County, North Carolina, where he enlisted on November 6, 1861 [October 21, 1861, per "MR, III"] at age 40 as a Private, Company C, 40th Regiment, North Carolina Troops (3rd Regiment, North Carolina Artillery). He was listed as present or accounted for until he was transferred to the Confederate States Navy on May 5, 1862. Though his death date is unknown, he is buried at Bethel Baptist Church, Orange County, North Carolina.
[Source(s): NA, RG 109; Card File; MR, III; North Carolina Troops, I; Stepp, "Burials;" Foenander]

Adams, William (Beaufort County,
North Carolina.) [NOTE: Possibly same as William Adams, Born in England, q.v.]
Gunner's Mate, Confederate States Navy. Previous service aboard CSS NORTH CAROLINA.
[Source(s): ORN, 2, 1, pp. 293, 295-296; MR, 4, 443]

Adams, William C. (No County listed)
[NOTE: Possibly same as William Adams, Gunner's Mate, or William Adams, born in England, q.v.; see enlistment date] Landsman, Confederate States Navy. Adams enlisted on December 21, 1863 at Raleigh for the war. He served aboard the CSS ARCTIC, 1863.
[Source(s): NA, RG 109; Card File; Foenander]

Adcock, Benjamin F. (Chatham County, North Carolina)
Private, Confederate States Army//Confederate States Navy. Born in 1839, Adcock enlisted at age 23 [Source "Foenander" gives age as "20" and date as July 15, 1862] on April 19, 1862 for the war in Company D, 61st

Regiment, North Carolina Troops. The Roll of Honor indicates that he was transferred to the 26th Regiment, North Carolina Troops, on an unspecified date. However, records of the 26th Regiment do not indicate that he served therein. Source "NCT, III" states he "may have served later as a Private in 2nd Company E, 2nd Regiment, North Carolina Troops." A "Benjamin F. Adcock" enlisted in Wake County, North Carolina, at "age 20" on July 15, 1862 for the war in 2nd Company E, 2nd Regiment, North Carolina State Troops and served until he transferred to the Confederate States Navy on April 5, 1864.
[Source(s): Card File; Lane Society; NCT, III; Foenander]

Adcock, R. J. (County unknown)
Private, Confederate States Marine Corps. Prisoner of War records indicate he was captured at Fort Fisher on January 15, 1865, and confined at Point Lookout, Maryland, until released on June 3, 1865, on taking the Oath of Allegiance to the United States. Unit listed on records as "20 N. C. Marines or Company B, 3 Bat. NORTH CAROLINA."
[Source(s): NA, RG 109; Card File]

Adkins, J. N. ["J. M."] (Brunswick County, North Carolina)
Pilot, Confederate States Navy. Adkins served aboard the Blockade Runner "Ella and Annie." An application for pension, filed on July 5, 1909 by his widow, Susan Adkins, age 84, listed her post office as Southport, Brunswick County, North Carolina, and states he enlisted on or about June 15, 1861.
[Source(s): McElroy; Clark, p.357, Vol. 5, North Carolina Regiment 1861-1865; Card File; Pensions (North Carolina)]

Adkins, James N. (County unknown)
[May Be same as J.N. Adkins,
q.v.] Quartermaster, Confederate States Navy. Adkins served in the crew of the CSS CASWELL. Born on August 15, 1825 and died on February 9, 1881, he was buried in the Old Cemetery at Southport, North Carolina.
[Source(s): Gravestone Records, v. 8, p. 60; Card File; Stepp, "Burials"]

Agnew, _____
3rd Assistant Engineer, North Carolina Navy.
[Source: NCS]

Agnew, R. S. (County unknown)
Captain, North Carolina Navy. Agnew signed a State of North Carolina voucher for pay covering the period from April 29, 1861 to May 20, 1861, received July 12, 1861 as "Captain NORTH CAROLINA Engineers," and for pay from May 20 to July 1, 1861 received of Major A. M. Lewis July 12, 1861 as 2nd Assistant Engineer, NORTH CAROLINA Navy. He appears on a reference card as Captain, North Carolina Engineers, in service of the state as of May 1, 1861 under Colonel Ellwood Morris, Engineer-in-Chief, North Carolina Engineers.
[Source(s): NA, RG 109; Card File]

Aikens [Akin, Akins], Robert H. (North Carolina)
Ordinary Seaman, Confederate States Navy. Aikens enlisted on June 5, 1863 at Wilmington for the war. An "R. Akins (CSN) was admitted to the Confederate General Hospital No. 4, Wilmington, North Carolina on June 27, 1863 with "diarrh" and assigned to ward/bed number 3/39 and listing his post office as "Mot. Creek" [There was a "Mott Creek" listed in Onslow County and a "Motts Creek" listed in New Hanover County, North Carolina]. He was discharged on July 10, 1863. Aikens served aboard the ironclad CSS NORTH CAROLINA, Cape Fear River, North Carolina, 1864 [A "Robert Aiken, Burke County, North Carolina" served aboard the CSS NORTH CAROLINA]. Though no "Robert H. Aikens" was found, an "R. H. Aikens" was listed in the Cleveland County, North Carolina 1860 census.
[Source(s): Foenander; ORN 2, 1, 294 – 296; Census (NC), 1860; NC Gaz; NA, RG 45; Card File]

Aikman, Robert (Burke County, North Carolina)
Master's Mate, Confederate States Navy. Aikman served in Louisiana waters in 1865.
[Source(s): McElroy; MR, 4, p. 443]

Airs, Robert E. (Washington County, North Carolina)
Private, Confederate States Army//Confederate States Navy. Resided in Washington County, North Carolina where he enlisted as a Private at age 28 on June 24, 1861 in Company G, 1st Regiment, North Carolina State Troops.

Present or accounted for until discharged on February 3, 1862 upon transfer to the Confederate States Navy (January 1862 per MR, I).
[Source(s): Card File; NCT, III; Foenander; MR, I]

Albright, Nicholas (County unknown) (North Carolina?)
Landsman, Confederate States Navy. Enlisting on March 1, 1864, at Raleigh, for the war, Albright served aboard the CSS ARCTIC, Cape Fear River, North Carolina, 1863.
[Source(s): NA, RG 45; Card File; Foenander]

Alderman, H. (County unknown)
Landsman, Confederate States Navy. Assigned from Raleigh, North Carolina, to Battery Brooke, James River, Virginia, October 1864.
[Source(s): Foenander; ORN 1, 10, 805; www.http://membres.multimania.fr/confederatestatearmy/repertoire/p/0p.html]

Alderman, Ira H. (Alamance County, North Carolina)
Private, Confederate States Army/Confederate States Navy. Residing in Alamance County, North Carolina, Alderman enlisted at age 26 on October 1, 1862, in Forsyth County, North Carolina, as a Private in Company F, 28th Regiment, North Carolina Troops [per Source: S.O. # 89]. North Carolina Pension records indicate he was wounded at Fredericksburg, Chancellorsville, and Gettysburg. He transferred to Confederate States Navy on August 3, 1864 and served as a Landsman aboard the CSS VIRGINIA II, James River Squadron, Virginia, 1864-1865.
[Source(s): North Carolina Troops, VIII; Foenander; ORN 2, 1, 311; Card File; S.O. # 89]

Alderman, J. (County unknown)
Landsman, Confederate States Navy. Alderman was assigned from Raleigh, North Carolina, to Battery Brooke, James River, Virginia, October 1864. [ORN 1, 10, 805]
[Source(s): www.http://membres.multimania.fr/confederatestatearmy/repertoire/p/0p.html; ORN 1, 10, 805; Foenander]

Aldred, Joseph [Sampson County, North Carolina]
Landsman, Confederate States Navy. Aldred served aboard the CSS ARCTIC, Cape Fear River, North Carolina, 1863. He is probably the same as "J. Aldred" that was admitted on February 17, 1864, to Confederate General Military Hospital #4, Wilmington, North Carolina, for "fistula." He was transferred to the Smallpox Hospital on March 1, 1864. His post office was listed as Clinton, North Carolina.
[Source(s): Foenander; ORN 2, 1, 278; H and P Records]

Aldrich, Joseph (Guilford County and Sampson County, North Carolina)
Landsman, Confederate States Navy. Aldrich enlisted on January 25, 1864, at Raleigh, North Carolina, for the war. His name appears on Registers of Confederate States Army General Military Hospital Number 4, Wilmington, North Carolina, which states he was admitted February 17, 1864, with "fistula" and transferred to the Smallpox Hospital on March 1, 1864. His post office was given on the registers as Jamestown and Clinton, North Carolina.
[Source(s): NA, RG 109; Card File]

Aldrich, William (born Rhode Island//resided Rowan County, North Carolina)
Seaman, Confederate States Navy. In 1860, Aldrich resided as a machinist, with his wife Rachel and son, in Salisbury, Rowan County, North Carolina. He enlisted in the Confederate States Navy at Camp Holmes, Raleigh, North Carolina, on March 7, 1864, for the war. He was described as age 43; eyes, hazel; hair, dark; complexion, dark; height, 5 feet 9½ inches; place of birth, Rhode Island; occupation machinist. In 1880, he is shown as a railroad machinist residing with his wife in Wilmington, North Carolina.
[Source(s): NA, RG 45; Card File; Census (North Carolina), 1860 & 1880; Foenander]

Aldrich, William
Confederate States Navy. Aldrich is listed as a supernumerary aboard the ironclad sloop CSS NORTH CAROLINA, Cape Fear River, North Carolina, 1864 [NOTE: May be same as "William Aldrich, born in Rhode Island," q.v.]).
[Source(s): Foenander; ORN 2, 1, 295 & 297]

Aldridge [Aldredge], William Newton (Lenoir County, North Carolina)
Confederate States Navy. (NOTE: Name also shown as "W.U. Aldrich"). Aldridge was born in Lenoir County, North

Carolina, on July 10, 1844, the son of Jessie and Emanitha Aldridge. In 1860, he resided with his parents in Jefferson County, Florida, as a farm laborer. He enlisted at Monticello, Florida, July 1861, in Company H, 3rd Florida Infantry. On his Florida pension application, he claimed to have been overstrained on a forced march in Kentucky in October 1862, and was subsequently transferred to the Confederate States Navy, where he served as a Landsman aboard the CSS CHATTAHOOCHEE, beginning May 4, 1864. He also served aboard the ironclad floating battery, CSS GEORGIA (also known as the STATE OF GEORGIA and LADIES' RAM), Savannah Squadron, Georgia, 1864. He further deposed that toward the end of the war he was attached to Company K, 10th Florida Infantry, and was paroled at Appomattox, April 9, 1865. He married D. A. C. Mansfield at Hillsborough, County, Florida, November 15, 1885. Aldridge worked as a farmer after the war, dying in Tampa, Florida, on March 30, 1921.
[Source(s): Foenander]

Alexander, George
Seaman, Confederate States Navy.
Per payroll, bounty, clothing, and small stores records, Alexander served as a Seaman aboard the CSS BEAUFORT from September 1861 - March 1862. His name appears on the North Carolina Squadron payroll for the 1st quarter of 1862 (Dec. 1, 1861 - April 15, 1862). He transferred to the James River Squadron on April 15, 1862.
[Source: NCCWSP]

Alexander, Joseph Wilson (Lincoln County, North Carolina)
Lieutenant, Confederate States Navy. Born in Lincoln County, North Carolina, Alexander served as a Lieutenant in the United States Navy from September 21, 1853 until he resigned his commission in 1861. He commanded the North Carolina Ship (NCS) RALEIGH, later the CSS, RALEIGH, in North Carolina waters, July 22, 1861-1862, participating in the Battle of Roanoke Island on February 7-8, 1862. On March 3, 1862, Alexander was ordered detached from Flag Officer French Forrest to report to Buchanan for duty, joining the James River Squadron, April 15, 1862. In the Battle of Hampton Roads, Virginia, March 8-9, 1862, serving as the tug supporting the CSS VIRGINIA, for which it was commended by the Confederate States Congress. He was commissioned by the Confederate States Congress from North Carolina as a First Lieutenant, Confederate States Navy, October 23, 1862 [Both sources "Foenander" and "Fold3, USN Resignees" give date as July 18, 1861], to rank from October 2, 1862, he served aboard the CSS VIRGINIA (MERRIMAC), "1861" [sic]. Alexander served as First Lieutenant and executive officer aboard the CSS ATLANTA in Georgia waters in 1862 – 1863; was captured at Wassaw Sound, Georgia, by the USS WEEHAWKIN, June 17, 1863, off Savannah and taken as a Prisoner of War to Fort Lafayette, New York Harbor, New York, thence to Fort Warren, Boston, Massachusetts, on July 4, 1863. He escaped on August 19, 1863 but was recaptured and confined at Portland Gaol, and subsequently returned to Fort Warren, September 7, 1863. He was paroled on September 28, 1864 at City Point, Virginia, and exchanged on October 18, 1864, and sent to Richmond. While a Prisoner of War, he was promoted on June 2, 1864 to First Lieutenant, Provisional Confederate States Navy, to rank from January 6, 1864. Circa November 1864, Alexander was ordered to report to Confederate Army Lieutenant General William J. Hardee, Commander of the Department of South Carolina, at Charleston, South Carolina, for special "torpedo" duty under Isaac N. Brown, CSN. He later served aboard the CSS VIRGINIA II until detached on December 19, 1864 and ordered to command the CSS BEAUFORT, in Virginia waters, 1864-1865. He was taken sick in February 1865 and sent to the hospital. After the war, he returned to his home in Lincolnton, North Carolina.
[Source(s): McElroy; Clark, Vol. IV, p. 735; Register; Card File; Journal; Foenander; NCS; ONWR; Fold3, USN Resignees]

Alexander, M. S. (County unknown)
Confederate States Navy. Alexander enlisted on June 13, 1864, in Raleigh, for the war.
[Source(s): NA, RG 45; Card File]

Alexander, Telemacus H. C. (Mecklenburg County, North Carolina)
Seaman [Landsman], Confederate States Navy. Alexander enlisted on April 25, 1864 in Raleigh, for the war. His name appears on a roll of Prisoners of War at Point Lookout, Maryland, which gives his place and date of capture as Burkeville [Virginia], April 6, 1865. He arrived at Point Lookout prison on April 14, 1865 from City Point, Virginia. Alexander took the Oath of Allegiance to the United States on June 23, 1865, at Point Lookout, Maryland. The oath gives his place of residence as Mecklenburg County, North Carolina. His description was as follows: complexion, fair; hair, flaxy; eyes, dark blue; height, 5 feet 6 ¾ inches.
[Source(s): NA, RG 109; NA, RG 45; Card File]

Allen, Alment A. (County unknown)
Landsman, Confederate States Navy. Allen enlisted on October 16, 1863, in Wilmington, North Carolina, for the war. Crewmember, CSS NEUSE as of March - October 1864.
[Source(s): NA, RG 45; Card File; NEUSE Roster; CMACSSN]

Allen, Charles J. (Caswell County)
Confederate States Navy. Allen's application for pension filed on July 6, 1909, at age 83, listed his post office as Milton, Caswell County, North Carolina. It states he enlisted in the Confederate States Navy on or about May 1, 1864. The application for a pension was approved.
[Source(s): Pensions (North Carolina); Card File]

Allen, Gabriel (Washington County, North Carolina)
Private, Confederate States Army//Ordinary Seaman, Confederate States Navy. Allen resided in Washington County, North Carolina, where he enlisted at age 28 on June 28, 1861, for the war, in Company G, 1st Regiment, North Carolina Troops. He is listed as present or accounted for until discharged on February 2 [3, per source NCT, III], 1862 upon transfer to the Confederate States Navy, where he served aboard the CSS VIRGINIA, Hampton Roads, Virginia, 1862.
[Source(s): Card File; North Carolina Troops, III; Foenander]

Allen, George C. (North Carolina?)
Landsman, Confederate States Navy. Allen served aboard the ironclad CSS RALEIGH, in North Carolina and Virginia waters, 1862 - 1864.
[Source(s): Foenander; ORN 2, 1, 302]

Allen, George S.
Captain's Clerk, Confederate States Navy.
Appointed Captain's Clerk on July 18, 1861, Allen served aboard the CSS VIRGINIA in that year. He served in that position aboard the NCS EDWARDS per its July – September 1861 payroll and aboard the NCS FORREST per its muster roll of October 30, 1861. Allen served as a Captain's Clerk aboard the NCS ELLIS from January – May 1862 per a logbook entry dated November 1, 1861 and payroll records for the period. Allen resigned on January 19, 1862.
[Source: NCCWSP]

Allen, George W. (County unknown)
Landsman, Confederate States Navy. Allen enlisted on May 27, 1864, in Raleigh, North Carolina, for the war.
[Source(s): NA, RG 45; Card File]

Allen, G. P. (North Carolina?)
Landsman, Confederate States Navy. Allen served aboard the CSS ARCTIC, Cape Fear River, North Carolina, 1863.
[Source(s): Foenander; ORN 2, 1, 278]

Allen, James F. (County unknown)
Landsman, Confederate States Navy. Allen enlisted on February 11, 1864, in Raleigh, North Carolina, for the war. He served aboard the CSS RALEIGH in North Carolina and Virginia waters, 1862 – 1864.
[Source(s): NA, RG 45; Card File; Foenander; ORN 2, 1, 302]

Allen, Jesse Q. (County unknown)
Landsman, Confederate States Navy. Allen enlisted on May 27, 1864, in Raleigh, North Carolina, for the war.
[Source(s): NA, RG 45; Card File]

Allen, John (County unknown)
Landsman, Confederate States Navy. Allen enlisted on April 13, 1864, in Kinston, North Carolina, for three years or the war. May be the "John Allen" who served aboard the CSS NEUSE as of March – October 1864.
[Source(s): NA, RG 45; Card File; NEUSE Roster; CMACSSN]

Allen, John H. (North Carolina?)
Surgeon's Steward, Confederate States Navy. Allen served aboard the CSS ARCTIC, Cape Fear River, North Carolina, 1863, and in the same rating aboard the CSS RALEIGH in North Carolina and Virginia waters, 1864.
[Source(s): Foenander; ORN 2, 1, 278 & 301]

Allen, William B. (North Carolina)
Private, Confederate States Army; Confederate States Navy. His obituary in *Confederate Veteran* magazine (page 35, January 1901 issue) states he served in Company A, 22nd Regiment, North Carolina Troops prior to volunteering "from the ranks to go as a gunner on the Confederate gunboats, finally being assigned to the *Alabama*, and was with her when she went down in front of Cherbourg, he being one of the few saved after a swim of six miles." [Editor's NOTE: No record is found of his serving in the Confederate Navy, Company A, 22nd Regiment, North Carolina Troops, or any other North Carolina regiment].
[Source(s): *Confederate Veteran* (January 1901)]

Allen, W.G. (North Carolina?)
Landsman, Confederate States Navy. Allen served aboard the CSS YADKIN, Wilmington, North Carolina, 1864.
[Source(s): Foenander; ORN 2, 1, 313]

Allen, William [G. L.?] (County unknown)
Landsman, Confederate States Navy. Allen enlisted on March 1, 1864, in Raleigh, North Carolina.
[Source(s): NA, RG 45; Card File]

Allin, John (Forsyth County, North Carolina)
Confederate States Navy. Allin's name appears on a register of Confederate States Army General Military Hospital Number 4, Wilmington, North Carolina dated August 29, 1864, that gives his disease as "February Typh." And states that he was returned to duty September 7, 1864 and furloughed September 10, 1864. His post office as was listed as Winston. May be same as "john Allen" who served aboard the CSS NEUSE, March – April 1864 [q.v.].
[Source(s): NA, RG 109; Card File; NEUSE Roster]

Alley, P.E. (Rockingham County, North Carolina)
Confederate States Navy. Alley enlisted in the Confederate States Navy August 2, 1863 in Wilson County, North Carolina, or Wilmington, North Carolina.
[Source(s): MR, 4, p. 446]

Almond, Green (Stanly County, North Carolina)
Private, Confederate States Army/Confederate States Navy. Born to Martin and Mary Almond in 1841, in Stanly County, North Carolina, Almond resided and enlisted there at age 23 on September 7, 1861, as a Private in Company K, 28th Regiment, North Carolina Troops. He was wounded in the right foot at Chancellorsville, Virginia, on May 3, 1863, and returned to duty on an unspecified date. He transferred to the Confederate States Navy on April 10, 1864.
[Source(s): Card File; North Carolina Troops, VIII; Foenander; Census (North Carolina), 1860]

Alred [Aldred], Shubel (Forsyth County, North Carolina)
Landsman, Confederate States Navy. Born 1846, the son of Walter and Nancy "Aldred," in Guilford County, North Carolina, Alred enlisted on March 21, 1864 in Raleigh, for the war. Another record states he was conscripted on March 18, 1864 [while another gives the date as March 17, 1864], at age 18, from Colonel Mastin's 71st Regiment, North Carolina Militia, from Forsyth County, North Carolina. Alred served as a Landsman aboard the CSS ALBEMARLE, and at Halifax Station, 1864. He deserted on March 25 [probably 1865] and was described as follows: eyes, dark; hair, dark; height, 5 feet 9 ½ inches; place of birth, Guilford County, North Carolina; occupation, miner.
[Source(s): NA, RG 45; Card File; Foenander; Roster, 71st Regiment, North Carolina; Census (North Carolina), 1860]

Alt (Ault), Charles
Seaman, Confederate States Navy.
Alt served as a Seaman aboard the NCS EDWARDS per shipping articles he signed on July 25, 1861. He served as a Seaman aboard the NCS FORREST per that ship's muster roll dated October 30, 1861, and as a Gunner's Mate for the ship payroll period for the 1st quarter of 1862. Alt served aboard the CSS Virginia in 1862 and appears on its final payroll as a Seaman. He appears on receiving ship UNITED STATES payroll ending March 31, 1862.
[Source: NCCWSP]

Anderson, A. S. (County unknown)
Seaman, Confederate States Navy. His name appears on a muster roll of Seamen unattached to Regiments of Naval

Brigade, Army of Tennessee, paroled at Greensboro, North Carolina, 1865.
[Source(s): NA, RG 109; Card File]

Anderson, D. W. (County unknown)
Landsman, Confederate States Navy. Anderson enlisted on July 25, 1864, in Raleigh, North Carolina, for the war.
[Source(s): NA, RG45; Card File]

Anderson, E. (Wilkes County, North Carolina)
Private, Confederate States Army/Confederate States Navy. Residing in Wilkes County, North Carolina, Anderson enlisted at age 30 on April 1, 1863, for the war, as a Private in Company B, 55th Regiment, North Carolina Troops. He transferred to the Confederate States Navy on or about April 15, 1864.
[Source(s): Card File; NCT, XIII; Foenander]

Anderson, Frank (North Carolina?)
Seaman, Confederate States Navy. Anderson served in the North Carolina Squadron [SEE NOTE #3] aboard the CSS BEAUFORT, September 1861 - April 1862, operating in North Carolina and Virginia waters. He served aboard the CSS RALEIGH, as of April 1862.
[Source(s): Foenander; ORN 2, 1, 281; NCCWSP]

Anderson, J. H. (North Carolina?)
Captain's Steward, Confederate States Navy. Anderson served aboard the CSS NORTH CAROLINA, Cape Fear River, North Carolina, 1864.
[Source(s): Foenander; ORN 2, 1, 294 - 296]

Anderson, John W. (Brunswick County, North Carolina, or New Hanover County, North Carolina)
Pilot, Confederate States Navy. Anderson served aboard the Blockade Runner the "Mary Celeste," and as a crewman aboard the CSS NORTH CAROLINA. His name appears on a register of Confederate States Army General Military Hospital Number 4, Wilmington, North Carolina, dated July 21, 1862, giving his disease as "cholera morbus," and stating that he was returned to duty on July 22, 1862. His post office is listed on the register as Wilmington. Source "Foenander" lists a "John W. Anderson," who served as a Quartermaster aboard the wooden side-wheeled steamer CSS CASWELL, the CSS ARCTIC, and on the Wilmington Station, North Carolina 1861 - 1863. Per source "WDJ" (August 13, 1864), Anderson died on August 7, 1864 of unknown causes.
[Source(s): McElroy; MR, 4, p. 443; NA, RG 109; Card File; Foenander; "WDJ" (Aug. 8, 1864)]

Anderson, Jefferson (Cumberland County, North Carolina)
Confederate States Navy/Private, Company A, Naval Battalion. His name appears on a roll of Prisoners of War at Point Lookout, Maryland, stating that he was captured at High Bridge [Virginia] on April 6, 1865, and sent from City Point, Virginia, to Point Lookout on April 14, 1865. He was released on June 23, 1865 upon taking the Oath of Allegiance to the United States The oath gives his place of residence as Cumberland County, North Carolina. His description was as follows: complexion, fair; hair, light; eyes, grey; height, 5 feet 5 ¾ inches.
[Source(s): NA, RG 109; Card File]

Anderson, John T. (Camden County, North Carolina)
Private, Confederate States Army//Landsman, Confederate States Navy. Anderson served initially in Captain W. A. Duke's Independent Company, the Jonesboro Guards, raised at the courthouse in Camden County, North Carolina, May 30-31, 1861. Nearly the entire company was captured at the Battle of Hatteras Inlet, though seven men were in camp sick the day of the battle and apparently escaped capture. There is no indication that Anderson was among those taken prisoner. With his company virtually non-existent, it was apparently disbanded, and he was assigned to 1st Company I, 32nd Regiment, North Carolina Troops, in September 1861. He reported for duty on February 20, 1862 and was present or accounted for until the company was disbanded on April 12, 1862. He enlisted as a Private in Company A, 56th Regiment, North Carolina Troops, in Camden County, North Carolina, at age 22 on May 2, 1862, for the war. He was hospitalized in Goldsboro, North Carolina, on August 24, 1862, but returned to duty in September-October 1862. He was reported present until May 22, 1863, when captured at the Battle of Second Gum Swamp, North Carolina. Sent to New Bern, North Carolina, he was paroled and transferred to City Point, Virginia, where he was received on May 28, 1863, for exchange. He returned to duty prior to July 1, 1863. Anderson was reported present until he transferred to the Confederate States Navy in April 1864 and [per source "Foenander"] served as a Landsman aboard the CSS ALBEMARLE, and at Halifax Station, 1864. [Source "Driver" claims a "John T. Anderson," born circa 1840 in Prince George's County, Maryland, enlisted initially in Company A, 56th

Regiment, North Carolina Troops. He states he later enlisted in Company F, 4th Battalion (Naval), Virginia Local Defense Troops, Richmond, Virginia, on July 27, 1864, at age 18, but was shown as age 20 on an August 4, 1864 unit roll (Virginia?). He surrendered in April 1865, at Colfax, Guilford County, North Carolina. On his Pension Application dated June 9, 1926, he is listed as a "Carpenter, age 71, Norfolk, res[idence]. 32 years." He was alive in Norfolk, Virginia, per a postwar roster] [NOTE: This may be a different man].
[Source(s): Card File; North Carolina Troops, IX and XIII; Long; Driver; ORN 2, 1, 274; Foenander]

Anderson, M. J.
Landsman, Confederate States Navy. Anderson enlisted on May 3, 1864 in Raleigh for the war.
[Source(s): NA, RG 45; Card File]

Anderson, R. (North Carolina?)
1st Class Fireman, Confederate States Navy. Anderson served aboard the CSS YADKIN, Wilmington, North Carolina, 1864.
[Source(s): Foenander; ORN 2, 1, 313]

Anderson, Thomas (Cumberland County, North Carolina) [NOTE: May be same as "Thomas J. Anderson," q.v.]
Confederate States Navy. Anderson served as a crewman aboard the CSS NORTH CAROLINA.
[Source(s): Oates; MR, 4, p. 433]

Anderson, Thomas J. [NOTE: May be same as "Thomas Anderson," q.v.]
Seaman, Confederate States Navy. Anderson enlisted on June 5, 1863, in Wilmington, North Carolina, for the war.
[Source(s): NA, RG 45; Card File; Foenander]

Anderson, William (County unknown)
Gunner, Confederate States Navy. Anderson was a Gunner aboard the CSS NORTH CAROLINA "in Wilmington Harbor." He died on 10/2/63 in Farmer's Hotel, Wilmington, North Carolina of unknown causes.
[Source(s): Josh Howard; "WDJ" (October 14, 1863)]

Andrews, Charles (County unknown)
Seaman or 1st Class Fireman, Confederate States Navy. Andrews served aboard the CSS RALEIGH in North Carolina and Virginia waters, 1862 – 1864, and eventually promoted to 1st Class Fireman. Transferred to James River Squadron 15 April 1862. Served at Drewry's Bluff as 2nd class fireman as early as 1 April 1863. He was attached to Semmes' Naval Brigade when it surrendered in April 1865. He was paroled at Greensboro, North Carolina on April 26, 1865. His name appears on a muster roll of Seamen unattached to regiments of the Naval Brigade, Army of Tennessee paroled at Greensboro, North Carolina, 1865.
[Source(s): NA, RG 109; Card File; ORN 2, 1, 301; M1091; Foenander; NCCWSP]

Andrews, Charles (County unknown)
Seaman or 1st Class Fireman, Confederate States Navy. Andrews served aboard the CSS RALEIGH in North Carolina and Virginia waters, 1862 – 1864, and eventually promoted to 1st Class Fireman. Transferred to James River Squadron 15 April 1862. Served at Drewry's Bluff as 2nd class fireman as early as 1 April 1863. He was attached to Semmes' Naval Brigade in April 1865 was surrendered and paroled at Greensboro, North Carolina, April 26, 1865. His name appears on a muster roll of Seamen unattached to regiments of the Naval Brigade, Army of Tennessee paroled at Greensboro, North Carolina, 1865.
[Source(s): NA, RG 109; Card File; ORN 2, 1, 301; M1091; Foenander; NCCWSP]

Andrews, John (North Carolina?)
Seaman, Confederate States Navy. Andrews served aboard the CSS CASWELL, a wooden side-wheeled steamer, which operated as a tender on the Wilmington Station, North Carolina). Andrews served during or between the period July 1861 to June 1862.
[Source(s): Foenander; ORN 2, 1, 282]

Anthony, James G. (Halifax County, North Carolina)
Second Lieutenant, Confederate States Army//Landsman, Confederate States Navy. Anthony was born in Halifax County, North Carolina, where he enlisted at age 26 on April 23, 1861 for twelve months service in Company G, 41st Regiment, North Carolina Troops (3rd Regiment, North Carolina Cavalry). Mustered in as a Corporal, Anthony was appointed Second Lieutenant to rank from November 11, 1861. Present or accounted for through April 1862

when he resigned. He was conscripted on April 2, 1864, at Camp Holmes, from Colonel Bell's 35th Regiment, North Carolina Militia, Halifax County, North Carolina. His description was as follows: Age, 29; eyes, black; hair, dark; complexion, florid; height, 5 feet 6 ½ inches; place of birth, Halifax; occupation, farmer.
[Source(s): NA, RG 45; North Carolina Troops, II; Card File; Roster, 35th Regiment, North Carolina Militia]

Anthony, J. G. (County unknown) [NOTE: May be same as "James G. Anthony, q.v.]
Landsman, Confederate States Navy. Anthony enlisted on April 4, 1864, in Raleigh, North Carolina, for the war.
[Source: NA, RG 45; North Carolina Troops, II; Card File; Roster, 35th Regiment, North Carolina Militia]

Armstrong, A. (North Carolina)
Landsman, Confederate States Navy. Records indicate he was a Prisoner of War, captured in Jackson Hospital, Richmond, Virginia, on April 3, 1865. He escaped from the hospital on April 19, 1865. [NOTE: May be same as "Alexander Armstrong" or "Arthur Armstrong," q.v.]
[Source(s): H and P Records]

Armstrong, Alexander ("Alex") (Washington County, North Carolina)
Landsman, Confederate States Navy. Armstrong was born in 1843 and died in 1909. He was buried in the Episcopal Cemetery [Hollywood Cemetery], Elizabeth City, Pasquotank County, North Carolina.
[Source(s): WCL; Card File; Gravestone Records, v. 3, p. 198; Stepp, "Burials;" Darden]

Armstrong, Arthur (County unknown)
Landsman, Confederate States Navy. Armstrong enlisted on October 5, 1863 at Camp Holmes [near Raleigh, North Carolina].
[Source(s): NA, RG 45; Card File]

Arnold, James (County unknown)
Landsman, Confederate States Navy. Arnold enlisted on June 19, 1863, in Wilmington, North Carolina, for the war.
[Source(s): NA, RG 45; Card File]

Arnold, Joseph H. (Craven County, North Carolina)
Confederate States Navy. Listed as a Craven County, North Carolina, "day laborer" in the 1860 North Carolina Census, Arnold enlisted as a Private "for the war," in Company B, 10th Regiment (1st Regiment, North Carolina Artillery) at the age of 28 on June 13, 1861. He was captured at Fort Macon, April 26, 1862, and paroled until exchanged in August 1862. He was appointed Corporal on May 1, 1863. He transferred to the Confederate States Navy on September 3, 1863, but the order was revoked on December 4, 1863. Arnold was later detailed on engineer duty in Goldsboro. He was age 30 in 1864. A "J. H. Arnold" served aboard the CSS NEUSE as of March – October 1864 [q.v.].
[Source(s): North Carolina Troops, I; Census (NC), 1860; "Hill; Foenander; NEUSE Roster; CMACSSN]

Ashe, Dr. Alexander Swann (North Carolina)
Assistant Surgeon, Confederate States Navy. Ashe was born in North Carolina in 1839 and was living in the Colvin's Creek Community of New Hanover County, North Carolina and working as a doctor in 1860. He may have moved to Georgia prior to the War Between the States where he married Amaryllis Pride Hall on June 27, 1860 in Knoxville, Georgia. He is said to have served as an Assistant Surgeon aboard the CSS RALEIGH on the Richmond Station circa 1861 - 1862. He died on June 27, 1866 in Galveston, Texas at age 27.
[Source(s): Census (NC), 1860; NCCWSP; www.ashefamily.info/ashefamily/4188.htm]

Atkins, A. S. (County unknown)
Landsman, Confederate States Navy. Atkins enlisted on February 11, 1864 in Raleigh, North Carolina, for the war, and served aboard the CSS RALEIGH in North Carolina and Virginia waters, 1862 – 1864
[Source(s): NA, RG 445; Card File; Foenander]

Atkinson, W. J. (County unknown)
Landsman, Confederate States Navy. Atkinson enlisted on June 8, 1864, in Raleigh, North Carolina, for the war.
[Source(s): Card File]

Ausley, J. F. (Moore [later, Lee] County)
Confederate States Navy. Ausley's application for pension was filed on July 3, 1911, at 78, listing his post office

as Sanford, Lee County. On the application he states he enlisted on or about January 10, 1862. His application for pension was approved. Born April 19, 1833; died December 20, 1911, buried at Goldston Methodist Church, Chatham County, North Carolina.
[Source(s): Pension (North Carolina); Card File; Stepp, "Burials"]

Autry [Autrey], D. R. (County unknown)
Landsman, Confederate States Navy. Autry enlisted on June 11, 1864, in Raleigh, North Carolina, for the war, and served aboard the CSS ARCTIC and CSS ALBEMARLE, Cape Fear River, and on the Halifax Station, Halifax, North Carolina 1863 - 1864.
[Source(s): Foenander; NA, RG 45; Card File; ORN 2, 1, 274 & 279]

Avent, James T. [or "J"] (Nash County, North Carolina)
Sergeant, Confederate States Army//Landsman, Confederate States Navy. Avent was born in 1830 in Griffin, Nash County, North Carolina, where he lived as a farmer prior to enlisting on December 13, 1861, as a Sergeant in Company B, 13th Battalion, North Carolina Troops. He served later in Colonel Wright's 32nd Regiment, North Carolina Militia, from Nash County, from which he was conscripted at age 33 on March 7, 1864 at Camp Holmes [near Raleigh, North Carolina], and served in the Confederate States Navy. He served as a Landsman aboard the CSS ALBEMARLE and on the Halifax Station, 1864. After the war, Avent married in Nash County, and resided there as a farmer, with his wife Margaret, and children. His description was as follows: Age, 33; eyes, hazel; hair, light; complexion, fair; height, 5 feet 7 ½ inches; place of birth, Nash County; occupation, farmer. [NOTE: A "James T. Avent of Nash County, North Carolina, enlisted as a Sergeant in Company B, 13th Battalion, North Carolina Infantry, on December 13, 1861, for the war. Present or accounted for through December 1862. No further record].
[Source(s): NA, RG 45; Foenander; Roster, 32nd Regiment, North Carolina Militia; Card File; North Carolina Troops, V]

Avent [Avant], James W. (Nash County, North Carolina)
Landsman, Confederate States Navy ["Company B, Hunter's Navy Battalion"]. Avent was conscripted on March 7, 1864 at Camp Holmes [near Raleigh, North Carolina] from Colonel Wright's 32nd Regiment, North Carolina Militia, from Nash County. His description was as follows: Age, 24; eyes, hazel; hair, dark; complexion, dark; height 5 feet, 7 ½ inches; place of birth, Nash County; occupation, farmer. His name appears on a roll of Prisoners of War at Point Lookout, Maryland, that states he was captured at Evans Farm [Virginia] on April 6, 1865, and was sent from City Point, Virginia, to Point Lookout, Maryland, on April 14, 1865. Avent was released on June 22, 1865 upon taking the Oath of Allegiance to the United States. Said oath listed his place of residence as Nash County, North Carolina, and gave his description as follows: complexion, dark; hair, black; eyes, hazel; height, 5 feet, 6 ¾ inches.
[Source(s): NA, RG 45; NA, RG 109; Roster, 32nd Regiment, North Carolina Militia; Card File]

Avera, William H. (County unknown)
Landsman, Confederate States Navy. Avera enlisted on March 24, 1864, in Raleigh, North Carolina, for the war.
[Source(s): NA, RG 45; Card File]

Avera, Willis H. (Johnston County, North Carolina)
Landsman, Confederate States Navy. Avera was born in Johnston County, North Carolina, and enlisted from there at age 19 on March 18, 1864, in the Confederate States Navy at Camp Holmes [near Raleigh, North Carolina]. Was enlisted from Colonel Heath's 41st Regiment, North Carolina Militia, from Johnston County. His description was as follows: Age 19; eyes, blue; hair, dark; complexion, fair; height, 5 feet, 7 ½ inches; place of birth, Johnston County; occupation, farmer. Avera served aboard the CSS ALBEMARLE, and on the Halifax Station, 1864.
[Source(s): Foenander; NA, RG 45; Card File; Roster, 41st Regiment, North Carolina Militia]

Avereit, James T. (County unknown)
Confederate States Navy. Avereit's name appears on a list of conscripts "in yard at Halifax," June 9, 1864.
[Source(s): NA, RG 45; Card File]

Avent [Avert], James W. (Nash County, North Carolina)
Landsman, Confederate States Navy. Born in Nash County, North Carolina, and enlisted there at age 24 in the Confederate States Navy. One source states he name appears on a list of conscripts "in yard at Halifax," June 9, 1864. He served as a Landsman aboard the CSS ALBEMARLE, and on the Halifax Station, 1864.
[Source(s): NA, RG 45; Card File; Foenander]

Aycock, A. S. (County unknown)
Landsman, Confederate States Navy. Aycock enlisted on August 17, 1864, in Raleigh, North Carolina, for the war.
[Source(s): NA, RG 45; Card File]

Aycock (Aycoke, Aycocke), Ambrose (Franklin County, North Carolina)
Private, Confederate States Army//Landsman, Confederate States Navy. Born about 1825, the son of R. and Sally Aycock, in Warren County, North Carolina, Aycock resided in Franklin County, North Carolina, as a farmer where he enlisted at age 37 on May 20, 1861 in Company G. 15th Regiment, North Carolina Troops. He was present or accounted for until discharged on August 20, 1862, by reason of being over age. He was conscripted on March 2, 1864 [another source says "enlisted March 24, 1864 at Raleigh for the war"] at Camp Holmes [near Raleigh, North Carolina] from Colonel Thomas' 40th Regiment, North Carolina Militia, from Franklin County, North Carolina. His name appears on a list of conscripts for the Confederate States Navy "in yard at Halifax, June 9, 1864." He served as a Landsman aboard the CSS ALBEMARLE, and on the Halifax Station, 1864. His description was as follows: Age, 40; eyes, grey; hair, dark; complexion, dark; height, 5 feet 8 inches; place of birth, Warren County, North Carolina; occupation, farmer. Aycock resided as a farmer, in 1880, with his wife May, at Sandy Creek Township, Franklin County, North Carolina.
[Source(s): NA, RG 45; Card File; Foenander; Census (NC), 1880; Roster, 40th Regiment, North Carolina Militia; North Carolina Troops, V and Addenda]

Bagwell [Bagnell], G. Ross (Robeson County, North Carolina)
Landsman, Confederate States Navy. Source "Foenander" lists a "C. R. Bagnell" as having served aboard the CSS ARCTIC, Cape Fear River, North Carolina, as of 1863. Another source states Bagwell enlisted on August 10, 1864, in Raleigh, North Carolina, for the war. He was born on November 15, 1838, died on March 5, 1904, and was buried at Hayes Chapel Christian Church, Wake County, North Carolina.
[Source(s): NA, RG 45; Card File; Stepp, "Burials;" Foenander; ORN 2, 1, 279]

Bailey, J.J. (North Carolina?) [NOTE: May be same as "Thomas J. Bailey, q.v.]
Seaman, Confederate States Navy. Bailey served aboard the CSS North Carolina, Cape Fear River, North Carolina, 1864.
[Source(s): Foenander; ORN 2, 1, 296.]

Bailey, Thomas J. (North Carolina?)
[NOTE: May be same as "J. J. Bailey, q.v.]
Landsman, Confederate States Navy. Served aboard the CSS NORTH CAROLINA, Cape Fear River, North Carolina, 1864.
[Sources(s): Foenander; ORN 2, 1, 294 & 295]

Bailey, Richard (Perquimans County, North Carolina)
Private, Confederate States Army// Confederate States Navy. Bailey resided and enlisted in Perquimans County, North Carolina, at age 29 on April 28, 1862, for the war, in Company F, 11th Regiment, North Carolina Troops. He was present or accounted for until transferred to the Confederate States Navy on April 1, 1864.
[Source(s): Card File; North Carolina Troops, V]

Bain, A. W.
Captain's Clerk, Confederate States Navy.
Bain was appointed a Captain's Clerk on December 5, 1861 and served aboard the CSS BEAUFORT as a member of the North Carolina Squadron, participating in the Battle of Hampton Roads, March 8 – 9, 1862. He transferred to the James River Squadron on April 15, 1862 and was appointed a Paymaster's Clerk on October 29, 1862. Bain served on the Confederate Cruiser CSS FLORIDA, 1862 – 1863, at Drewry's Bluff, 1863 – 1864, and aboard the CSS CHICKAMAUGA in 1864. Records indicate he was again appointed as a Paymaster's Clerk on September 10, 1864, likely for his service aboard the CSS CHICKAMAUGA.
[Source: NCCWSP]

Bairgess, D. B. (Randolph County, North Carolina)
> Confederate States Navy. Bairgess' name appears on a Register of General Hospital Number 4 and 5, Wilmington, North Carolina, under the heading of "Men furloughed from General Hospitals, Wilmington, North Carolina" dated September 22, 1863, giving place of residence as Franklinville, Randolph County, North Carolina. It states he was furloughed for 30 days and gives his disease as "debility from continued fever — sick 8 weeks."
> [Source(s): NA, RG 109; Card File]

Baker, Daniel (Moore County, North Carolina)
> Confederate States Navy. Baker enlisted in the Confederate States Navy at age 18 in September 1864. He was captured in April 1865 under "Eurel" [Ewell] near Dentonville [Virginia]. Ewell surrendered about 6,000 that day. He was imprisoned at Newport News, Virginia, until he took the Oath of Allegiance on or about July 1, 1865.
> [Source(s): Card File; Tennessee Pension Applications, R.D. 1788]

Baker, F (?) M. (Moore County, North Carolina)
> Private, Confederate States Navy [Naval Battalion]. Baker was captured at Farmville, Virginia, in April 1865, and took the Oath of Allegiance at Newport News, Virginia, on June 26, 1865.
> [Source(s): H and P Records]

Baker, James (Robeson County, North Carolina)
> Confederate States Navy. A pension application made on August 1, 1913, by his widow, Ann Baker, age 84, listed her post office as Rowland, Robeson County, North Carolina. It states he enlisted in the Confederate States Navy on or about May 20, 1861. The application for pension was approved.
> [Source(s): Pensions (North Carolina); Card file]

Baker, James L. (County unknown)
> Landsman, Confederate States Navy. Baker enlisted on June 24, 1864, in Raleigh, North Carolina, for the war.
> [Source(s): NA, RG 45; Card File]

Baker, John (County unknown)
> Ordinary Seaman, Confederate States Navy. Baker enlisted on June 1, 1863, in Wilmington, North Carolina, for the war.
> [Source(s): Card File; NA, RG 45]

Baker, John C. (Mecklenburg County, North Carolina)
> Private, Confederate States Army// Confederate States Navy. Baker was born, resided in and enlisted in Mecklenburg County, North Carolina, on June 12, 1861, at age 21, as a Private, Company B, 13th Regiment, North Carolina Troops. He was present or accounted for until he transferred to the Confederate States Navy on February 26, 1862, for duty on the CSS VIRGINIA (CSS MERRIMAC).
> [Source(s): Card File; North Carolina Troops, V; MR, I; Foenander]

Baker, William (Brunswick County, North Carolina)
> Pilot, Confederate States Navy. Baker was born in Brunswick County, North Carolina, on November 3, 1841. He enlisted in the Confederate States Navy in Wilmington, North Carolina, in the summer of 1861, and served as a pilot on board the CSS RALEIGH and CSS ARCTIC, from 1861 to 1864. He was captured aboard the CSS ARCTIC, near Fort Fisher, North Carolina, about February 1865, and imprisoned at Macon, North Carolina, until the end of the war. A letter from Washington, D.C., dated August 11, 1914, from Superintendent W. S. Thompson (of the Navy Department, Library & Naval War Records), noted that "Pilots in the service of the Confederate Navy did not come under the heading of 'enlisted men,' but held distinctive appointments as 'pilots,' frequently made by Commanders of fleets or single vessels." Baker married Ms. Virginia McDonald in Charleston, South Carolina, on February 3, 1880. He died in Nassau County, Florida, on May 22, 1915.
> [Source(s): Foenander]

Baldwin, Kelly (County unknown)
> Landsman, Confederate States Navy. Baldwin enlisted on August 17, 1864, in Raleigh, North Carolina, for the war.
> [Source(s): Card File; NA, RG 45]

Ball, Lemuel (Currituck County, North Carolina?)
> Seaman/Boatswain's Mate, Confederate States Navy. Ball's record is one of a series of contradictory records. Source

NCCWSP indicate he shipped as a Seaman on board the side-wheel steam tug CSS ELLIS on August 3, 1862 at Canal Bridge, Coinjock, Currituck County, North Carolina. Records indicate Ball served as a Boatswain's Mate aboard the CSS ELLIS from "November 1, 1861 through early 1862" as a member of the North Carolina Squadron. In another contradiction, some records show he was paid for service on the CSS Ellis from "August 3, 1861 through February 7, 1863." His name appears on a payroll of receiving ship CSS UNITED STATES ending March 31, 1862]. Other records show he was superannuated for rations at Drewry's Bluff, Virginia from May 12, 1862 through May 24, 1862. Ball's name is found on a CSS VIRGINIA clothing list at Drewry's Bluff on July 20, 1862. He was paid at Drewry's Bluff for the period May 13, 1862 through September 13, 1862. Ball's name appears on the final payroll of the CSS VIRGINIA as a Seaman for the period April 1, 1862 through September 13, 1862.
[Source(s): Foenander; ORN 1, 6, 781 & 2, 1, 285 & 309; NCCWSP]

Ball, Samuel (Beaufort County, North Carolina)
Confederate States Marine Corps. Ball's name appears on a roll of Prisoners of War at Point Lookout, Maryland, stating that he was captured at Farmville, April 6, 1865, confined at Point Lookout on April 14, 1865, and released on taking the Oath of Allegiance to the United States on June 24, 1865. His Oath of Allegiance states that he resided in Beaufort County, North Carolina, and gives his description as follows: complexion, fair; hair, dark brown; eyes, blue; height, 5" 7."
[Source(s): Card File; NA, RG 109; NCT, Doc. #0185, p.1; Donnelly]

Ball, Thomas M. (Iredell County, North Carolina)
1st Sergeant, Confederate States Army//Landsman, Confederate States Navy. Ball resided in Iredell County, North Carolina, where he was by occupation a farmer prior to enlisting there at age 24 in Company H, 4th Regiment, North Carolina State Troops. He mustered in as a Corporal, and was wounded at South Mountain, Maryland, on September 1, 1862. He rejoined the company prior to May 3, 1863 when he was wounded in the head and/or hand at Chancellorsville, Virginia. Promoted to Sergeant on October 1, 1863, he was present or accounted for until transferred to the Confederate States Navy on December 30, 1863. Ball served as a Landsman aboard the CSS ARCTIC and CSS RALEIGH, 1863 - 1864, and was aboard the CSS BOMBSHELL when that vessel was captured by Union gunboats in Albemarle Sound, North Carolina, on May 5, 1864. He was transferred, the same day, from the USS CERES to the USS SASSACUS, and thence to the steamer USS LOCKWOOD, on May 10, on which he was transported to the prison at Point Lookout, Maryland, on May 17, 1864 [One source indicates he was "confined at Fort Monroe, Virginia, until transferred to Point Lookout, Maryland"]. Transferred to the prison at Elmira, New York, on August 15, 1864, he was confined there until released upon taking the Oath of Allegiance to the United States between June 16 and 19, 1865 [One source gives date as "June 16."] The Oath lists his place of residence as Statesville, North Carolina and gives his description as follows: complexion, fair; hair, dark; eyes, blue; height, 6 feet 2 ½ inches. In 1880, Ball resided as a farmer with his wife Mary J. Ball and six children at Union Grove, Iredell County, North Carolina
[Source(s): Card File; NA, RG 109; NCT, IV; Census (NC), 1880; Foenander]

Ball, William E. (Pasquotank County [?], North Carolina)
Seaman, Confederate States Navy. Born in North Carolina in1840, Ball is shown as a mariner, residing in a boarding house at Elizabeth City, Pasquotank County, North Carolina, on the 1860 North Carolina Census. He served as Seaman aboard the side-wheeled steam tug CSS ELLIS (which operated in North Carolina waters), 1861 - 1862.
[Source(s): ORN 1, 6, 781 & 2, 1, 285; Census (NC), 1860; Foenander; NCCWSP]

Ball, William Erasmus [Erosmus] (Granville County, North Carolina)
Landsman, Confederate States Navy. Born in 1825, Ball resided in 1860 as a farmer with his wife, Ann Mitchell Ball, and four children, at Fork Creek district, Granville County, North Carolina. He enlisted on March 31, 1864 [Source "Foenander" lists date as "21 or 30"], in Raleigh, North Carolina, for the war, while another record states he was conscripted on March 30, 1864 at Camp Holmes (near Raleigh, North Carolina) from Colonel Dolby's 43rd Regiment, North Carolina Militia, Granville County, North Carolina. His description was as follows: Age, 42; eyes, gray; hair, dark; complexion, fair; height, 5 feet 11 ½ inches; place of birth, Granville County, North Carolina; occupation, farmer. He served aboard the CSS ALBEMARLE and on the Halifax Station in 1864. One record indicates he was mortally wounded on May 15, "1863" [probably 1864] in North Carolina. An application for pension filed on July 6, 1885 by his widow, Ann Ball, age 60, residence listed as Wilton, Granville County, North Carolina, states he enlisted in Halifax, North Carolina, on or about March 1864, and served on the CSS ALBEMARLE. It further states he came home sick and died, May 15, "1863." An application for pension was filed on July 1, 1901 by his widow, Ann M. Ball, age 70, listing her post office as Wilton, Granville County, North Carolina. The application states her husband died during the war, but no date is shown. The application was

approved.
[Source(s): Foenander; NA, RG 45; Pensions (North Carolina); Roster, 43rd Regiment, North Carolina Militia; Card File; NCCWSP]

Ballance, J. W.
Landsman, Confederate States Navy.
He served aboard the NCS ELLIS as a Landsman in 1862. Captured in the action at Elizabeth City, Ballance was carried to Roanoke Island where he was paroled on February 12, 1862 and returned to Elizabeth City. He served as a member of the North Carolina Squadron.
[Source: NCCWSP]

Ballance, John W. (Currituck County, North Carolina)
Private, Confederate States Army//Quarter Gunner; Landsman, Confederate States Navy. Born in 1835 in Currituck County, North Carolina, Balance resided in Pasquotank County, North Carolina, as a mariner. He enlisted as a Private in Company A, 8th Regiment, North Carolina State Troops, at age 26 on July 22, 1861. Captured at Roanoke Island, February 8, 1862, Balance was paroled at Elizabeth City on February 21, 1862 and exchanged at Aiken's Landing, James River, Virginia November 10, 1862. He transferred to the Confederate States Navy on January 20, 1863 [another source states he was a Seaman who "enlisted February 9, 1863 at Wilmington for three years or the war"]. Ballance served aboard the receiving ship CSS ARCTIC, 1863, as a Seaman, as Captain of the Foretop and Quarter Gunner aboard the CSS NORTH CAROLINA in early to mid-1864, and as a Quarter Gunner aboard the CSS TALLAHSSEE, late 1864. He is buried in Episcopal Cemetery [Hollywood Cemetery], Elizabeth City Pasquotank County, North Carolina.
[Source(s): ORN, 2, 1, 279, 294-296; NCT, IV; MR, IV; Gravestone Records, v. 3, p. 201; Stepp, "Burials;" MR, I; Foenander]

Ballance, Levin [Levy, Levi] (Currituck County, North Carolina)
Private, Confederate States Army//Ordinary Seaman, Confederate States Navy. Born about 1843 in the Court House District of Currituck County, North Carolina, Ballance was the foster son of Peter and S. Parker Ballance. He resided in Currituck County as a farmer until enlisting on August 19, 1861, at the age of 19, in Company B, 8th Regiment, North Carolina State Troops. A company muster roll indicates that he transferred to the Confederate States Navy on October 13, 1861, where he served as an Ordinary Seaman aboard the CSS SEA BIRD. The Roll of Honor states he was killed in action, aboard that vessel, off Roanoke Island, on February 10, 1862 [Source "NCT, IV" incorrectly shows his date of death as February 7, 1862].
[Source(s): ORN, I, 6, p.596; SEA BIRD; NA, RG 45; NCT, IV; Census (NC), 1850; Foenander; NCCWSP]

Balt, John (County unknown)
"Naval Department." "Killed on the Tarboro' Branch Railroad on Wednesday the 18th inst., two men, named JOHN BALT and C.C. GASKINS. They belonged to the Naval Department at Wilmington. Their bodies were brought to Rocky Mount and interred as decently as circumstances would admit."
[Source(s): Card File; "Daily Confed." (5/23/64)]

Bancroft, Henry (North Carolina?)
Seaman, Confederate States Navy. Bancroft served aboard the side-wheeled steamer CSS WINSLOW in North Carolina waters from July through November 1861.
[Source(s): Foenander; ORN 2, 1, 312; NCCWSP]

Banks, David (County unknown)
Confederate States Navy. Banks' name appears on a roll of non-commissioned officers and privates employed on extra duty at Wilmington, North Carolina, during the month of August 1864, shown serving as a "Mate Steamer." Contains remarks: "Over age. Age 51. Able Bodied." No rank or organization given.
[Source(s): Card File; NA, RG 109]

Banks, John S. (North Carolina)
Confederate States Navy. Born in North Carolina; appointed from Florida. Assistant Paymaster, on April 22, 1862. Appointed Assistant Paymaster, Provisional Confederate States Navy, June 2, 1864. Served on steamers CSS MASSACHUSETTS [NOTE: No such Confederate ship has been found], CSS MAUREPAS and CSS PONTCHARTRAIN, Jackson Station, 1862. CSS PALMETTO STATE, Charleston Station, 1862 – 1864.
[Source(s): Register; Officer, 1861-65; Foenander; ONWR]

Banks, Thomas (North Carolina?)
Landsman, Confederate States Navy. Banks served aboard the CSS ARCTIC, Cape Fear River, North Carolina, 1863, and aboard the steam gunboat CSS RALEIGH, [in] North Carolina and Virginia waters, 1864.
[Source(s): Foenander; ORN 2, 1, 278 & 302.]

Barber, John (Perquimans County, North Carolina)
Confederate States Navy. Barber deserted on June 15, 1863 from Wilmington, North Carolina.
[Source(s): "Absentees"]

Barber, Simon (Simeon; Semen) (Johnston County, North Carolina)
Landsman, Confederate States Navy. Barber's name appears on a list of conscripts "on Egypt Mills" dated June 9, Conscripted on March 18, 1864 at Camp Holmes from Colonel Heath's 41st Regiment, North Carolina Militia, Johnston, County, North Carolina. Description as follows: Age, 38; eyes, blue; hair, dark; complexion, florid; height, 5 feet 7 ½ inches; place of birth, Johnston County, North Carolina; occupation, farmer. Another record states he "Enlisted March 24, 1864 at Raleigh for the war."
[Source(s): Card File; NA, RG 45; Roster, 41st Regiment, North Carolina Militia]

Barber, W. C.
Confederate States Navy (Civilian?). Per source "WDJ" (April 24, 1863), Barber drowned after falling overboard from the steamboat "Grist" in Wilmington Harbor (no record found of a CSS GRIST). It is unknown whether Barber was in the Navy or a civilian possibly performing service for the Navy. There was no date of death listed, but it was presumably in April 1863.
[Source(s): "WDJ" (Apr. 24, 1863)]

Barbob, Anthony (County unknown)
Confederate States Navy. Barbob served in the Confederate Navy running steamships between Nassau and Charleston, SC.
[Source(s): Card File; Shuford Chapt., UDC]

Barco, Caleb (Washington County, North Carolina)
Private, Confederate States Army//Carpenter, Confederate States Navy. Born in Washington County, North Carolina, the son of Luke Barco and Nancy Gamiel, Barco resided as a fisherman in Currituck County, North Carolina, prior to enlisting there as a Private at age 21 on August 6, 1861, for the war, in Company B, 8th Regiment, North Carolina State Troops. Private, Company B, 8th Regiment, North Carolina State Troops]. He was present or accounted for until transferred to the Confederate States Navy on or about January 10, 1863, where he served as a Carpenter on board the CSS ARCTIC, and a Coxswain aboard the CSS NORTH CAROLINA, 1864. Prisoner of war records indicate he was captured at Harper's Farm, Virginia, on April 6, 1865 and confined at Point Lookout, Maryland, on April 13, 1865, where he remained until released after taking the Oath of Allegiance to the United States on June 23, 1865. Oath of Allegiance gives place of residence as Currituck County, North Carolina. Description as follows: complexion, dark; hair, black; eyes, blue; height, 5' 6 ½." He married Mrs. Martha Jane (Forbes) Russell on November 9, 1873 and worked as a farm laborer and fisherman in Dare County, North Carolina. Listed as "Hispanic" in John O'Donnell-Rosales book, HISPANIC CONFEDERATES.
[Source(s): Foenander; North Carolina Troops, IV; MR, 4, p. 443; NA, RG 109; H and P Records]

Barger, Allen (Catawba County, North Carolina)
Private, Confederate States Army//Landsman, Confederate States Navy. Born in 1840, Barger resided in Catawba County, North Carolina, where he enlisted at age 22 on March 15, 1862 as a Private in Company C, 28th Regiment, North Carolina Troops. Captured at Hanover Court House, Virginia, on May 27, 1862, he was confined at Fort Monroe, Virginia, and at Fort Columbus, New York Harbor. Barger was exchanged at Aiken's Landing, James River, Virginia, on August 5, 1862. Listed as present or accounted for until he transferred to the Confederate States Navy on April 3, 1864. He died in 1910 and was buried at St. Stephens Lutheran Church, Catawba County, North Carolina.
[Source(s): Card File; Stepp, "Burials;" North Carolina Troops, VIII; Foenander; S.O. # 89; Foenander]

Barham, R. H. (possibly from Bertie or Northampton County, North Carolina)
Private, Confederate States Army//Confederate States Navy. Enlisted as a Private in Company H, 19th Regiment, North Carolina Troops (1st Regiment, North Carolina Cavalry). Barham transferred to the Confederate States Navy on September 3, 1863. No further record.
[Source(s): Card File; North Carolina Troops, II; Foenander]

Barkadoo, F. (Resident of Beaufort County, North Carolina)
Private, Company D, Confederate States Marine Corps. Barkadoo served on the CSS TENNESSEE and was captured at the Battle of Mobile Bay, August 5, 1864. He was a prisoner of war on Ship Island, Mississippi, from October 28, 1864.
[Source(s): North Carolina Troops, Doc. #0299; Card File]

Barker, Solomon (Perquimans County, North Carolina)
Confederate States Navy. Barker deserted on June 15, 1863 from Wilmington, North Carolina.
[Source(s): "Absentees"]

Barlow, T. W. (County unknown)
Landsman, Confederate States Navy. Barlow enlisted on June 6, 1864 in Raleigh, North Carolina, for the war.
[Source(s): Card file; NA, RG 45]

Barnard, A. J. (North Carolina?)
Seaman, Confederate States Navy. Barnard served aboard the CSS BEAUFORT, September 1861 - April 1862, in North Carolina and Virginia waters. He appears on the North Carolina Squadron's payroll for the 1st quarter of 1862 (December 1, 1861 - December 10, 1861). Barnard was discharged by order of Flag Officer French Forrest on December 10, 1861.
[Source(s): Foenander; ORN 2, 1, 281; NCCWSP]

Barnes, Leonard (Washington County, North Carolina)
Private, Confederate States Army//Confederate States Navy. Barnes resided in Washington County, North Carolina, where he enlisted at age 22 on June 24, 1861 as a Private in Company G [One source says "C"], 1st Regiment, North Carolina State Troops. He was present or accounted for until discharged on February 3, 1862 after being transferred to the Confederate States Navy.
[Source(s): Card File; North Carolina Troops, III; Foenander]

Barnett, James (Currituck County, North Carolina)
Seaman, Confederate States Navy. Born in Tyrrell County, North Carolina; Barnett resided in Currituck County, North Carolina. He was by occupation a sailor prior to his enlistment at age 18 on August 1, 1861 in Company B, 8th Regiment, North Carolina State Troops. He was shown as present or accounted for until he transferred to the Confederate States Navy on or about January 10, 1863.
[Source(s): North Carolina Troops, IV]

Barnett (Barnette), James Jennet(te)
(Source "Foenander" gives his middle name as "Nennette"), Jr. (Tyrrell [or Hyde County] County, North Carolina)
Private, Confederate States Army//Seaman and Officer's Steward, Confederate States Navy//Private, Company A, Naval Battalion. Barnette was born at Stumpy Point, Tyrrell County, North Carolina, August 14, 1844 [Note: Source NCCWSP gives month as "April"], the son of James Jennette Barnette, Sr., and Mary Elizabeth O'Brien. He resided in Currituck County, North Carolina as a sailor at the time of his enlistment there on August 1, 1861, at age 18, as a Private in Company B, 8th Regiment, North Carolina State Troops. Barnette was captured at Roanoke Island, North Carolina, and paroled, February 12, 1862. He was listed as present or accounted for until transferred to the Confederate States Navy on or about January 10, 1863. He served as an Officer's Steward aboard the CSS ARCTIC and the CSS SEA BIRD. Source NCCWSP states he served from at least July 1861 through February 1862 on detached duty aboard the CSS SEA BIRD. Seaman Barnett was captured in the Battle of Elizabeth City and carried to Roanoke Island where he was paroled on February 12, 1862 and returned to Elizabeth City. Source NCCWSP states his name appears on a payroll of the North Carolina Squadron for the period December 1, 1861 through April 15, 1862, on which date he is listed as "on parole." Barnett was captured at High Bridge [Virginia], April 6, 1865, and arrived at City Point, Virginia, April 14, 1865. His name appears as a signee to an Oath of Allegiance to the United States, subscribed and sworn to at Point Lookout, Maryland, on June 23, 1865, giving place of residence as Hyde County, North Carolina. Released on June 23, his description was as follows: complexion, fair; hair; light brown; eyes, blue; height, 5 feet, 8 ¼ inches. Barnett was born on August 14, 1844. His first marriage was to Salome J. Dailey, May 9, 1869, at Hyde County, North Carolina, and his second was to Olive Frances Gray, March 17, 1889, at Buxton, North Carolina. His post-war occupations included fisherman, house carpenter, mechanic, and shipyard watchman. Barnett(e) died in Buxton, Dare County, North Carolina, on March 4, 1937 and was buried at Quidley Cemetery, Dare County, North Carolina.
[Source(s): North Carolina Troops, IV; Foenander; NCCWSP; Card file; NA, RG 109; Stepp, "Burials;" H and P Records; NCCWSP]

Barnhill, Robert H. (Pender County, North Carolina)
"N. S." [rate as per North Carolina pension application], Confederate States Navy. Born in 1826, Barnhill served in the Confederate States Navy. He resided post-war (1880) as a farmer with his wife, Elizabeth J. Barnhill, and five children, in Lincoln, Pender County, North Carolina. His pension claim filed July 1, 1907 at age 80, listing his post office as Rocky Point, Pender County, North Carolina. His approved application states he was in the Navy and enlisted in August 1862. There was a pension claim filed on July 1, 1912, by his widow, Elizabeth Barnhill, age 85, listing her post office as Rocky Point, Pender County, North Carolina
[Source(s): Card File; Pensions (North Carolina); Foenander]

Barrett, James (Tyrrell County, North Carolina)
Confederate States Navy. Barrett enlisted in the Confederate States Navy in Wilmington, North Carolina.
[Source(s): MR, 4, p. 444]

Barrington, Jesse S. (Craven County, North Carolina)
Corporal, Confederate States Army//Confederate States Navy. Barrington resided in Craven County, North Carolina until he enlisted as a Private at age 28 on November 21, 1861 in Company K, 31st Regiment, North Carolina Troops. Captured at Roanoke Island, North Carolina on February 8, 1862, he was paroled in Elizabeth City, North Carolina on February 21, 1862. Barrington returned to duty on or about September 12, 1862. He was promoted to Corporal between May – August 1864 and was present or accounted for until September 1864 when he was reported Absent Without Leave. Source "Card File" indicates naval service.
[Source(s): Card File; NCT, Vol. VII]

Barron, Benjamin A.
Ordinary Seaman, Confederate States Navy.
Served as an Ordinary Seaman from January 1, 1862 - January 1, 1862. He was promoted to Gunner's Mate on January 2, 1862. He was demoted to Ordinary Seaman on February 12, 1862. His name appears on the North Carolina Squadron payroll for the 1st quarter of 1862 (January 1, 1862 - March 28, 1862) but is listed as having "run" as of a payroll ending on February 28, 1862. [Source: NCCWSP]

Barron, Caleb (County unknown)
Seaman, Confederate States Navy. Barron enlisted on January 18, 1863 in Wilmington, North Carolina, for the war.
[Source(s): Card File; NA, RG 45]

Barron, Samuel, Sr.
Flag officer, Confederate States Navy.
Born in and appointed from Virginia, Barron served as a Captain in the Virginia Navy on May 26, 1861 to rank from April 23, 1861. He was appointed to the rank of Captain, Confederate States Navy on June 11, 1861 [One source gives the date as October 23, 1862, to rank from March 26, 1861]. He commanded the naval defenses of North Carolina and Virginia during July 1861 and was captured while commanding at Fort Hatteras on August 29, 1861. He was paroled on September 25, 1861. In 1863 he commanded the defenses of the Cumberland and Tennessee Rivers. Barron served as the Flag Officer commanding Confederate naval forces in Europe, 1863-64. A contradictory piece of information indicates he was promoted to the rank of Captain, Provisional Navy, on June 2, 1864 to rank from May 13, 1863. He resigned his commission as a Flag Officer on February 28, 1865 while serving abroad.
[Source(s): McElroy; CR, p.302, Vol. 5, North Carolina Regiment 1861-1865; NCCWSP]

Bartlett, H. (County unknown)
Seaman, Confederate States Navy ["North Carolina"]. Bartlett's name appears on a register of Confederate States Army Hospital No. 11, Charlotte, North Carolina, giving complaint as "asthma" and date of admission as April 7, 1865.
[Source(s): Card File; NA, RG 109]

Bartlett, John
Seaman, Confederate States Navy.
Per muster and payroll records,
Bartlett served as a Seaman aboard the NCS JUNALUSKA from June 18, 1861 - August 20, 1861.
[Source: NCCWSP]

Barton, George H. [W.] (New Hanover County, North Carolina)
Ordinary Seaman, Confederate States Navy. Barton enlisted in the Confederate States Navy in Wilmington, North Carolina, on September 29, 1863, for the war. He served as an Ordinary Seaman aboard the CSS ARCTIC, 1863.
[Source(s): MR, 4, p. 444; NA, RG 45; Foenander; St. Amand]

Barton, John (County unknown)
Landsman, Seaman, Confederate States Navy.
Barton enlisted on June 1, 1864 in Halifax or Plymouth, North Carolina, "for the war." Per shipping and payroll records, Barton served as a Seaman aboard the CSS EDWARDS from July 25, 1861 - September 1861.
[Source(s): Card File; NA, RG 45; NCCWSP]

Barwick, Andrew Jackson (Wayne County, North Carolina)
Landsman, Confederate States Navy ("NORTH CAROLINA Navy"). Born in North Carolina in August 1845, Barwick enlisted in the Confederate States Navy on February 7, 1863 [another source says "1862"] at Wilmington, North Carolina, for the war. He served as a Landsman aboard the CSS ARCTIC, Cape Fear River, North Carolina, 1863, and as an Ordinary Seaman, Seaman, and then Coxswain aboard the CSS NORTH CAROLINA and CSS TALLAHASSEE, 1864. Attached to Semmes' Naval Brigade, April 1865, Barwick surrendered and was paroled at Greensboro, North Carolina, on April 26, 1865. He married "Eliza Ann" in 1875, and by 1880, lived as a farmer with her and their two sons in Indian Springs, Wayne County, North Carolina. A pension claim filed on July 28, 1912 at age 69, lists no post office, but he was living in Duplin County, North Carolina. The pension request was disallowed. A second pension application filed August 3, 1922 at age 78, listing post office as Mount Olive [Wayne County, North Carolina] was approved. He died sometime after 1910, while residing at Wolfscrape, Duplin County, North Carolina. An application for pension was filed on June 19, 1924 by his widow, Eliza Ann Barwick, age 67, listing her post office as Mt. Olive, "Duplin Company" [sic] [Wayne County], North Carolina. His wife drew a pension for his service.
[Source(s): MR, 4, p. 443; UDC, MC of Svc.; Pensions (North Carolina); NA, RG 45; Census (NC), 1880, 1900, and 1910; Foenander]

Basco, Solomon (County unknown)
Ordinary Seaman, Confederate States Navy. Basco enlisted on June 1, 1863 in Wilmington, North Carolina for the war.
[Source(s): Card File; NA, RG 45]

Bass, A. O. (County unknown)
Landsman, Confederate States Navy. Bass enlisted on April 11, 1864 in Raleigh, North Carolina, for the war.
[Source(s): Card File; NA, RG 45]

Batchelor, Newton J. (Franklin County, North Carolina)
Landsman ["Private"], Confederate States Navy ["Naval Battalion"]. Batchelor enlisted on July 28, 1864 in Raleigh, North Carolina, for the war. Prisoner of war records indicate he was captured at Harper's Farm [Virginia] on April 6, 1865, and confined at Point Lookout, Maryland, from April 14, 1865, until released after taking the Oath of Allegiance to the United States on June 24, 1865. The oath gave his residence as Franklin County, North Carolina, and his description as follows: Complexion, light; hair, brown; eyes, hazel; height, 5 feet, 8 ¾ inches.
[Source(s): Card File; NA, RG 45; NA, RG 109]

Bateman, Hardy (North Carolina)
Landsman, Confederate States Navy. Bateman served aboard the CSS BEAUFORT, September 1861 - April 1862, in North Carolina and Virginia waters. Source NCCWSP states he was born in North Carolina in 1832 and lived in the Washington District of Beaufort County, North Carolina where he worked as a fisherman [per the North Carolina Census, 1860]. He served aboard the CSS BEAUFORT from circa September through December 1861 and was a member of the North Carolina Squadron from December 1, 1861 through January 8, 1862. Bateman received a discharge on January 8, 1862.
[Source(s): Foenander; ORN 2, 1, 281; NCCWSP; Census (NC), 1860]

Bates, Benjamin H. (New Hanover County, North Carolina)
Assistant Engineer [3rd Engineer], Confederate States Navy. Bates enlisted in New Hanover County, North Carolina, on September 1, 1861, for twelve months, as a Private in 1st Company A, 36th Regiment, North Carolina Troops (2nd

North Carolina Artillery), and was appointed to the rank of Corporal in May 1863 [Source "Foenander" gives date as "January or February 1864]. He was detailed as a Machinist on the Wilmington and Manchester Railroad on October 19, 1863 and reported as absent "detailed" when transferred to 2nd Company I, 10th Regiment, North Carolina States Troops (1st Regiment, North Carolina Artillery) in November 1863. Bates was promoted to Assistant Engineer in and transferred to the Confederate States Navy in May or June 1864 and served aboard the CSS RALEIGH and CSS YADKIN, Wilmington Station, North Carolina, 1864. He was attached, as a Lieutenant to Semmes' Naval Brigade in April 1865, and was surrendered and paroled at Greensboro, North Carolina, April 26, 1865.
[Source(s): Card File; North Carolina Troops, I; Foenander]

Batten, O. D.
Landsman, Confederate States Navy. Batten enlisted on October 5, 1863 at Camp Holmes [Raleigh, North Carolina], for the war.
[Source(s): Card File; NA, RG 45]

Battle, Richard Henry, Sr. (Edgecombe County, North Carolina)
Acting Master's Mate, Confederate States Navy. Battle was born about 1846 in and appointed from North Carolina. [Source "Foenander" states his obituary indicates he entered the Confederate States Navy as a Midshipman, but existing records only show his rank as Acting Master's Mate (warranted August 15, 1863) at Edward's Ferry, North Carolina]. Commissioned from Edgecombe, County, North Carolina as an Acting Master's Mate on August 15, 1863, Battle was appointed an Acting Master's Mate, Provisional Navy, on June 2, 1864. He served at Edward's Ferry, North Carolina and on board the CSS ARCTIC, Wilmington Station, 1863-1864. [One source gives his birth date as February 15, 1807(?)]. Battle worked as a travelling salesman after the war, marrying Isabella (maiden name unknown) in 1889. They lived in Denver, Colorado, until moving to Atlanta, Georgia, about 1905. He never applied for a Confederate pension stating to his wife that he "didn't fight for pay." He worked for the Cudahy Packing Company and, later, the American Tobacco Company. Battle died in February 1917, at his residence, 288 East North Avenue, Atlanta, Georgia, after he was hit by a streetcar. His widow, Mrs. Isabella Battle, filed for a Confederate pension under his name from Fulton County, Georgia. [One source gives his death date as November 22, 1882, and that he is buried in Oakwood Cemetery, Raleigh, North Carolina]. [NOTE: Conflicting information may indicate two men by the same name].
[Source(s): Register; MR, 4, p. 404 and 448; Thorpe Roster; Stepp, "Burials;" Foenander]

Bauldree (Baldree), Frederick (North Carolina)
Landsman, Confederate States Navy. Bauldree (Baldree) was born in North Carolina, in 1827 (1870). Census shows his birthplace as Florida). He joined the Confederate States Navy for three years or the war, serving as a Landsman aboard the CSS CHATTAHOOCHEE, as of May 4, 1864 and later aboard the ironclad floating battery CSS GEORGIA, Savannah Squadron, 1864. His personal description showed he had hazel eyes, dark hair, dark complexion, and stood 5 feet 6 inches tall. Later, he served aboard the CSS ISONDIGA and the CSS CHICORA, Charleston Squadron. In his post-war years, Bauldree worked as a wheelwright and carpenter, respectively. In 1880, he resided with his wife, Martha, and four children, at Oak Grove, Liberty County, Florida.
[Source(s): Foenander; ORN 1, 17, 701 and 2, 1, 283 & 287]

Baum, Thomas T. (Currituck County, North Carolina)
Ordinary Seaman, Confederate States Navy. Born in North Carolina in 1846, he served on board the CSS SEA BIRD from circa July 1861 through February 1862. His name appears on a payroll of the North Carolina Squadron covering the period from December 1, 1861 – April 15, 1862. Captured at Roanoke Island, North Carolina, he was paroled in February 1862 [Source NCCWSP states he appears on a payroll dated 15 April 1862 as "on parole;" and may have served in Company A, 8th North Carolina Regiment, though his name does not appear in that unit in the North Carolina Troops series]. Following the war, Baum resided (1880) as a sailor with his wife, Emily, and five children, at Atlantic, Currituck County, North Carolina.
[Source(s): Foenander; Census (NC), 1880; NCT, Vol. IV; NCCWSP]

Bean, Jonathan (County unknown)
Landsman, Confederate States Navy. Bean enlisted on June 22, 1863 in Wilmington, North Carolina, for the war. He served as a Landsman aboard the CSS ARCTIC, Cape Fear River, North Carolina, 1863, and aboard the CSS RALEIGH in North Carolina and Virginia waters, 1864.
[Source(s): Foenander; Card File; NA, RG 45]

Beard, A. (County unknown) [NOTE: May be same as "Abram Beard," q.v.]
Landsman, Confederate States Navy. Beard enlisted on October 19, 1863 at Camp Holmes [Raleigh, North Carolina], and served as a Landsman, CSS ARCTIC, Cape Fear River, North Carolina, 1863.
[Source(s): Card File; Foenander]

Beard, Able (Watauga County, North Carolina)
Seaman [Landsman], Confederate States Navy. Hospital records indicate he was admitted to Confederate States Army General Military Hospital Number 4 in Wilmington, North Carolina, on December 15, 1863 with "febris typhoides" and died on December 24, 1863. Records indicate his post office as Sugar Grove, North Carolina. He was buried in Oakdale Cemetery, Wilmington, New Hanover, North Carolina, in the Confederate mass grave.
[Source(s): Card File; NA, RG 109; Stepp, "Burials"]

Beard, Abram (Watauga County, North Carolina)
Landsman, Confederate States Navy. Beard enlisted on October 19, 1863 in Wilmington, North Carolina, for the war. Source MR lists an "Abram Brown" who enlisted in the Confederate States Navy on October 1, 1862 in Wilmington, North Carolina.
[Source(s): Card File; NA, RG 45; MR, IV, 445]

Beard, James (County unknown)
[NOTE: May be same as "James S. Beard" and "T. S. Beard," q.v.)
Landsman, Confederate States Navy. Beard enlisted on October 30, 1863 in Raleigh, North Carolina, for the war.
[Source(s): Card File; NA, RG 45]

Beard, James S. (County unknown)
[NOTE: May be same as "James Beard" and "T. S. Beard," q.v.)
Landsman, Confederate States Navy. Beard enlisted on November 1, 1863 in Wilmington, North Carolina, for the war. Source "MR" shows his enlistment as under the name "J. S. Beard." He served as a Landsman aboard the CSS ARCTIC, Cape Fear River, North Carolina, 1863.
[Source(s): Card File; NA, RG 45; Foenander; MR, IV, 445]

Beard, T. S. (Cumberland County, North Carolina) [NOTE: May be same as "James Beard" and "James S. Beard," q.v.)
Confederate States Navy. Beard enlisted in Wilmington, North Carolina.
[Source(s): MR, IV, 445]

Beasley, James W.
Ordinary Seaman, Confederate States Navy.
Per bounty, muster, clothing, and payroll records, Beasley served aboard the CSS RALEIGH from January 16, 1862 – April 15, 1862. His name appears on the North Carolina Squadron payroll for the 1st quarter of 1862 (March 4, 1862 - April 15, 1862). He served at Drewry's Bluff as an Ordinary Seaman from April 1, 1863 - June 30, 1863.
[Source: NCCWSP]

Beasley, Joseph W. (Currituck County, North Carolina)
Seaman and Ordinary Seaman, Confederate States Navy//Corporal, Company F, 2nd Regiment, Naval Brigade, Confederate States Navy. Beasley enlisted on March 4, 1862 and served as a crewman on board the CSS RALEIGH in Virginia waters, 1862-1864. His name appears as a signee to a Parole of Prisoners of War headed, "Office [of] Provost Marshal, Dist. of East. Va., April 27, 1865," on which his county of residence was given as Currituck, North Carolina. Beasley filed for a pension on July 1, 1907, age 68, listing post office as Knotts Island, Currituck County, North Carolina. The pension request was approved.
[Source(s): Card File; NA, RG 109; Pensions (North Carolina); Foenander]

Beasley, N. (County unknown)
Landsman, Confederate States Navy. Beasley enlisted on October 5, 1863 at Camp Holmes [Raleigh, North Carolina].
[Source(s): Card File; NA, RG 45]

Beasley, Robert B. (Granville County, North Carolina)
Corporal, Confederate States Army//Landsman, Confederate States Navy. Beasley was born and lived in Granville County, North Carolina, as a farmer prior to enlisting at age 26 on June 5, 1861 in Company E, 23rd Regiment,

North Carolina Troops (13th Regiment, North Carolina Volunteers). He was mustered in as a Corporal and present or accounted for until discharged on August 4, 1862 after providing a substitute. Another record indicates he was "Conscripted March 30, 1864 at Camp Holmes from Colonel Dolby's 43rd Regiment, North Carolina Militia, Granville County, North Carolina. His description was as follows: Age, 28; eyes, blue; hair, dark; complexion, fair; height, 5 feet 6 ½ inches; place of birth, Granville County, North Carolina; occupation, farmer]. He later served in the Confederate States Navy.
[Source(s): Card File; NA, RG 45; Roster, 43rd Regiment, North Carolina Militia; North Carolina Troops, VII and VII Addendum; Foenander]

Beasley (Barclay), Stephen (North Carolina)
Seaman, Confederate States Navy.
Beasley was born in North Carolina in 1842. He resided in the North Banks District of Currituck County, North Carolina where he worked as a waterman. He may have served in Company A, 8th Regiment, North Carolina Troops. Muster records indicate he served as a Seaman aboard the CSS SEA BIRD from July 1861- February 1862. Beasley received a partial payment on February 18, 1862 at Gosport Navy Yard following the sinking of the SEA BIRD at the Battle of Elizabeth City on February 10, 1862. His name appears on a North Carolina Squadron payroll for the 1st quarter of 1862 (December 1, 1861 - April 15, 1862). He was captured at Roanoke Island, North Carolina, and paroled in February 1862. He was listed as "on parole" per a payroll dated April 15, 1862. Records indicate Beasley transferred to the James River Squadron on the same date.
[Source(s): Foenander; 1860 Census (NC); NCCWSP]]

Beaty, David (North Carolina?)
Landsman, Confederate States Navy. Beaty served aboard the CSS ARCTIC, Cape Fear River, North Carolina, 1863.
[Source(s): Foenander]

Beaumaster, Henry (also Hendrick Bowmaster)
Ordinary Seaman, Captain's Steward, Officer's Steward, Confederate States Navy.
Per the shipping articles he signed on July 25, 1861, Beaumaster served as an Ordinary Seaman aboard the CSS EDWARDS. He was listed as a Captain's Steward on this ship per its payroll for July - September 1861. He transferred to the CSS ELLIS on October 31, 1861 and served as an Officer's Steward per payroll and logbook entries from November 2, 1861 - the 1st quarter of 1862.
[Source: NCCWSP]

Beck, D. (County unknown)
Landsman, Confederate States Navy. Beck enlisted on June 11, 1864 in Raleigh, North Carolina, for the war. A September 25, 1864 letter requesting a transfer from Charleston, South Carolina (CSS INDIAN CHIEF) to either Halifax or Kinston, North Carolina, to North Carolina Governor Zebulon B. Vance, is signed by D. Beck, D. M. Faust, R. Tripp, and J. C. Tripp. Apparently, the transfer was not within Vance's ability to grant. Letter states that all four were "Soldiers in Colonel Mallet's [Mallett's] battalion and desired when we entered the navy to serve in North Carolina but were not permitted to do so."
[Source(s): Card File; NA, RG 45; Vance Papers]

Beckwith, Albert G. (Chatham County, North Carolina)
Confederate States Navy. Born in 1825, Beckwith enlisted on April 15, 1864 in Raleigh, North Carolina, for the war. His pension application filed on July 6, 1903 at age 76, listed his post office as "Ascend," Chatham County, North Carolina. The application states he enlisted in April 1864 in Charleston, SC, and served aboard the CSS CHICORA at Charleston, SC. Beckwith resided (1880) as a farmer, with his wife, Lois, and four children, at Williams, Chatham County, North Carolina.
[Source(s): Foenander; Card File; Pensions (North Carolina); NA, RG 45; Census (NC), 1880]

Beels (Beals), Wilson (Camden County, North Carolina)
Sergeant, Confederate States Army//Confederate States Navy. Born in North Carolina in 1830, he served previously as a Corporal in Captain G. G. Luke's Independent Company before being assigned as a Corporal to 1st Company H, 32nd Regiment, North Carolina Troops, in September 1861, while a Prisoner of War at Fort Columbus, New York Harbor, or Fort Warren, Boston Harbor, Massachusetts. He was paroled at Fort Warren, Boston Harbor, on January 30, 1862, and transferred for exchange. Present or accounted for until the company was disbanded on April 2, 1862.

Beels enlisted as a Private in Camden County, North Carolina, for the war, at age 33 on April 22, 1862, in Company A, 56th Regiment, North Carolina Troops. Mustered in as a Sergeant, he was reduced to the ranks on September 30, 1862. Reported present through December 1863, and detailed on hospital duty at Weldon, North Carolina, in January-February 1864. Beels transferred to the Confederate States Navy on or about April 6, 1864 and served as a Landsman on the CSS ALBEMARLE, and at Halifax Station, 1864. As of 1880, he resided as a farm hand with his wife Julia and one daughter at Shiloh, Camden County, North Carolina.
[Source(s): Card File; North Carolina Troops, IX and XIII; Foenander; Census (NC), 1880]

Beercraft, Henry (North Carolina?)
Landsman, Seaman, Master-at-Arms, Confederate States Navy.
Beercraft served aboard the CSS FANNY in North Carolina waters circa September - December 1861 and May 1862. By March 1862 he was serving aboard the CSS RALEIGH in North Carolina and Virginia waters, 1862 – 1864. Source NCCWSP indicates Beercraft's name appears on a North Carolina Squadron payroll for the 1st quarter of 1862 (December 1, 1861 - April 15, 1862). He transferred to the James River Squadron on April 15, 1862 and served at Drewry's Bluff as a Master-at-Arms (April 1, 1863 - June 30, 1863, per payroll records. He is listed on a payroll as having served as a Master-at-Arms aboard the CSS RALEIGH, November 16, 1863 - 15 December 15, 1863 as a member of the James River Squadron.
[Source(s): Foenander; NCCWSP]

Beer(s), Charles O. (New Hanover County, North Carolina [?])
Seaman, Confederate States Navy [?]. Born in New York, in 1834, Beers died on March 24, 1905, and was buried in Oakdale Cemetery, Wilmington, North Carolina. Source "*Oakdale*, Davis" states Beers first appears in the 1880 North Carolina Census in Columbus County, and was still listed there on the 1900 Census, living with his nephew Francis B. Gault. He was apparently initially buried at Lake Waccamaw but removed to Oakdale on September 20, 1949 to a lot owned by F. B. Gault. No evidence of his service in the Confederate States Navy was found other than the Oakdale Cemetery entry.
[Source(s): Stepp, "Burials;" *Oakdale*, Davis; Foenander]

Beery, Benjamin Washington (Brunswick County, North Carolina)
Captain, Confederate States Navy. Born in Brunswick County, North Carolina, December 12, 1822 and reared in Wilmington, North Carolina. Beery died on April 24, 1892 [Source "Stepp"]. Source "*Oakdale*, Davis" quotes the *Wilmington Messenger* newspaper of April 20, 1892 saying he died a day or more before the 20th]. A citizen of Wilmington from his youth, Beery married Ann Eliza Williams of New Hanover County, North Carolina Oct 13, 1843. Mr. Beery was noted for his strength of body and mind, and was successful in his business, ship building, and with his brother, William Beery, owned a shipyard across the Cape Fear River on Eagle's Island, opposite the city of Wilmington, North Carolina. There they specialized in pilot boats, schooners, side wheel steamers, and brigs. A portion of his time was also devoted to the wrecking business on the dangerous coast of North Carolina. Early in the war he rigged out the steam tug "Mariner" at his own expense for a privateering expedition. It was commissioned by President Davis on July 14, 1861. He was commissioned a "Captain" and placed in command of a Wilmington crew, among whom were such men as Benjamin Flanner and Sam Potter and was successful in bringing several prizes into port and turning them over to the Confederate Government. This work, however, was soon abandoned as his services were needed by the Confederate Government to build war vessels. The Beery Shipyard was converted into a Navy Yard. His yard built the ironclad CSS NORTH CAROLINA, the steamer CSS YADKIN (the flagship of Commodore Lynch who commanded the fleet protecting the Cape Fear River and the city of Wilmington), and several other dispatch, tug, and gunboats, etc. The Navy yard did service during the entire war until the fall of Fort Fisher just before the evacuation of Wilmington when Captain Beery set fire to the building, ways, and machinery to prevent the Federals from using the yard. Captain Beery continued building merchant vessels many years after the war on the site of the old Navy yard. He died in 1892 at the age of 70 at the residence of his daughter and son-in-law Colonel Roger Moore, of Wilmington, North Carolina. His other daughters were Mrs. J.A. Fore and Mrs. W.A. Willson of Charlotte and Wilmington, North Carolina.
[Source(s): McElroy; Card File; Labree; Stepp, "Burials;" *Oakdale*, Davis; "Messenger," 4/20/1892]

Beery [Berry], Whitford (Whiteford) Robert (New Hanover County, North Carolina)
Landsman, Confederate States Navy. Beery was born in Wilmington, North Carolina, in1844 [1843, per source "Foenander"], the son of Samuel and F.M. Beery (or Berry). He enlisted in New Hanover County, North Carolina, on April 16, 1861, as a Private in 1st Company C, 36th Regiment, North Carolina Troops (2nd Regiment, North Carolina Artillery) and was detailed on special duty at the Confederate States Shipyard, Wilmington, North Carolina, on April 24, 1862. On November 4, 1863, he was transferred to Company C, 13th Battalion North Carolina Light

Artillery while still on detail at Wilmington in exchange for Savage, Lewis T. [P.] (q.v.). His name appears on a Muster Roll for March-April 1864 on Company C, 13th Battalion, North Carolina Light Artillery with the remark, "Transferred to C. S. Navy March 21 [1864], in exchange for L. T. Savage [q.v.]." He was exchanged by Special Order #67, Paragraph 2, A & IGO, dated March 21, 1864. Another source states he enlisted in the Confederate States Navy on March 28, 1864 at Kinston for three years or the war. May be the "W. R. Beery" that served on the CSS NEUSE as of March – April 1864. He appears on a roll of Prisoners of War as a Deserter captured March 14, 1865 and sent to either New Berne or Kinston. In 1880, he resided as a sailor with his wife, Susan C. Berry and five children, in Wilmington, New Hanover County, North Carolina. Buried Oakdale Cemetery, Wilmington, New Hanover County, North Carolina.
[Source(s): Card File; NA, RG 45; Stepp, "Burials;" Census (NC), 1880; Foenander; H and P Records; NA, RG 109; North Carolina Troops, I; NEUSE Roster]

Beeson, William (County unknown)
Ordinary Seaman, Confederate States Navy. Beeson enlisted on June 5, 1863 in Wilmington, North Carolina, for the war.
[Source(s): Card File; NA, RG 45]

Begley, Jacob (County unknown)
Confederate States Navy(?). Bagley signed an Oath of Allegiance to the United States at Wilmington, North Carolina, on March 4, 1865, giving is age as 37 and residence as New Orleans, LA. Name also appears on a list of persons who have taken the oath at Wilmington, North Carolina, showing residence as New Hanover County, North Carolina. [NOTE: No other evidence this man served with North Carolina Troops. See Compiled Military Service Record of Begley, Jacob, Private, Company C, 4th Battalion, Louisiana Infantry].
[Source(s): NA, RG 109; Card File]

Belanger, William (Martin County, North Carolina)
Private, Confederate States Army//Ordinary Seaman, Confederate States Navy. Belanger resided in Martin County, North Carolina, where he enlisted as a Private at age 26 on June 24, 1861 for the war in Company H, 1st Regiment, North Carolina State Troops. He was present or accounted for until discharged in Richmond, Virginia, on February 3, 1862 upon transfer to the Confederate States Navy, where he served as an Ordinary Seaman aboard the CSS VIRGINIA, Hampton Roads, Virginia, 1862.
[Source(s): Card File; Doc. #0397; North Carolina Troops, III; Foenander]

Belcher, James (North Carolina?)
Ordinary Seaman, Confederate States Navy. Belcher served aboard the CSS ALBEMARLE, and on Halifax Station, 1864.
[Source(s): Foenander; ORN 2, 1, 274]

Bell, Abram [Abraham] (County unknown) (North Carolina?)
Seaman, Confederate States Navy. Bell enlisted on February 11, 1864 in Wilmington, North Carolina, for the war, and served aboard the CSS ARCTIC, Cape Fear River, North Carolina, 1863.
[Source(s): Foenander; Card File; NA, RG 45; ORN 2, 1, 278]

Bell, Ivey Prescott (New Hanover County, North Carolina)
Confederate States Navy (?). "Served as Foreman of Construction, Department of Shipyard of the Cape Fear River, making gunboats, launches, etc., under control of the Confederate States Government." Bell was born on April 2, 1814, died on November 18, 1868, and was buried in Oakdale Cemetery, Wilmington, North Carolina.
[Source(s): Card File; UDC, Cape Fear; Stepp, "Burials"]

Bell, James (North Carolina?)
Seaman, Confederate States Navy. Bell served aboard the CSS ARCTIC, Cape Fear River, North Carolina, 1863, and as a Seaman aboard the CSS CASWELL (a wooden side wheeled steamer which operated as a tender on the Wilmington Station, North Carolina). He served circa July 1861 to June 1862.
[Source(s): Foenander; ORN 2, 1, 279.]

Bell, J. C. (County unknown)
Confederate States Navy. Bell enlisted on June 13, 1864 in Raleigh, North Carolina, for the war.
[Source(s): Card File; NA, RG 45]

Bell, John (County unknown)
> Ordinary Seaman, Confederate States Navy. Bell enlisted on March 6, 1863 in Wilmington, North Carolina, for three years. He served as an Ordinary Seaman aboard the CSS ARCTIC, Cape Fear River, North Carolina, 1863. In 1864, he served, as an Ordinary Seaman and Captain of the Maintop aboard the CSS NORTH CAROLINA, Cape Fear River.
> [Source(s): Card File; NA, RG 45; Foenander]

Bell, Joseph J. (Brunswick County, North Carolina[?])
> Confederate States Navy. Bell enlisted on February 10, 1863.
> [Source(s): Edge]

Bell, Ottoway
> 1st Class Boy, NCS WINSLOW. One of seven African American crew members aboard the NCS WINSLOW. Bell is thought to have been a free man.
> [Source(s): NCS]

Bell, William (Brunswick County, North Carolina)
> Quartermaster, Confederate States Navy. Bell enlisted in the Confederate States Navy in Wilmington, North Carolina, and served on the Wilmington Station, 1862-1864. A "William Bell" served as a Quarter Gunner aboard the CSS ARCTIC in 1862.
> [Source(s): MR, 4, p. 444; Foenander]

Bell, William Baker (Brunswick County, North Carolina)
> Pilot, Confederate States Navy. Bell was born in Brunswick County, North Carolina, on November 3, 1841. He enlisted in the Confederate States Navy in Wilmington, North Carolina, in the summer of 1861. He served as a Pilot on the CSS RALEIGH and the CSS ARCTIC from 1861 to 1864. He was captured aboard the CSS ARCTIC near Fort Fisher, North Carolina, about February 1865 and was imprisoned at Macon, North Carolina until the end of the war. In a letter dated at Washington, D.C., August 11, 1914, from Superintendent W.S. Thompson (of the Navy Department, Library & Naval War Records), it is noted that "Pilots in the service of the Confederate Navy did not come under the heading of 'enlisted men,' but held distinctive appointments as 'pilots,' frequently made by Commanders of fleets or single vessels;' married Virginia McDonald at Charleston, South Carolina, February 3, 1880; died at Nassau County, Florida, May 22, 1915.
> [Source(s): Foenander]

Bellamy, Marsden (New Hanover County (?), North Carolina)
> Private, Confederate States Army//Assistant Paymaster, Confederate States Navy. The brother of William James Harriss Bellamy (q.v.), Marsden Bellamy was born on January 14, 1843 in Marion, South Carolina. He enlisted in Halifax County, North Carolina, on October 16, 1861, for twelve months, in the "Scotland Neck Mounted Riflemen" (Company G, 41st Regiment, North Carolina Troops [3rd North Carolina Cavalry]). He was detailed as an Assistant Commissary of Subsistence at Kinston, North Carolina, on November 27, 1863. Bellamy was present or accounted for through February 1864. He was commissioned by the Confederate States Congress from North Carolina in the Provisional Confederate Navy on June 2, 1864 as an Assistant Paymaster and served aboard the CSS RICHMOND in the James River Squadron in Virginia waters, 1864. Bellamy resided as a lawyer with his wife Harriet H. Bellamy and five children in Wilmington, North Carolina, in 1880. He died on December 1, 1909 and was buried at the Oakdale Cemetery, Wilmington, North Carolina.
> [Source(s): McElroy; Ellis; Wayne Carver (Wilmington, North Carolina); Card File; CMH; Stepp, "Burials;" North Carolina Troops, II; Foenander]

Bellamy, William James Harriss (New Hanover County, North Carolina)
> Private, Confederate States Army/Landsman, Confederate States Navy. Brother of Marsden Bellamy (q.v.), William James Harriss Bellamy was born on September 6, 1844, in New Hanover County, North Carolina. He resided there as a 17-year-old student prior to enlisting on August 20, 1861 at Camp Wyatt, for the war, as a Private in Company I, 18th Regiment, North Carolina Troops. Bellamy was present or accounted for until wounded in the shoulder and knee at Gaines' Mill, Virginia, June 27, 1862. He was discharged on July 16, 1862, by reason of being underage. Bellamy enlisted in the Confederate States Navy on June 22, 1863 in Wilmington, North Carolina, but provided a substitute the next day and returned to the University of North Carolina at Chapel Hill. He died on November 18, 1911, and was buried in Oakdale Cemetery, Wilmington, New Hanover County, North Carolina.
> [Source(s): Card File; NA, RG 45; CMH; Stepp, "Burials;" North Carolina Troops, VI; Foenander; CMH (North Carolina, Vol. IV)]

Bene, Jonathan (County unknown)
Confederate States Navy. Bene enlisted on November 20, 1863 in Raleigh, North Carolina, for the war.
[Source(s): Card File; NA, RG 45]

Bennet, Henry
Captain's Steward, Confederate States Navy.
Bennet served aboard the CSS FORREST as a Captain's Steward per that ship's muster roll ending October 30, 1861.
[Source: NCCWSP]

Bennett, Hardy Kirving (Sampson County, North Carolina)
Private, Confederate States Army//Confederate States Navy(?). Bennett served initially in Captain William Devane's Independent Company, North Carolina Troops before transferring as a Private to Company A, 61st Regiment, North Carolina Troops on or about September 5, 1862. Reported present or accounted for through April 1864, Bennett was captured at Globe Tavern, Virginia on August 19, 1864 and confined at Point Lookout, Maryland. Paroled at Point Lookout on March 17, 1865, he was received for exchange at Boulware's Wharf, James River, Virginia on March 19, 1865. Source "Card File" indicates naval service.
[Source(s): Card File; NCT, Vol. XIV]

Bennett, James (County unknown)
(Likely same as "James J. Barnette," q. v.)
Confederate States Navy. [SEE: Private; Company B, 8th Regiment, North Carolina State Troops].
[Source(s): Card File]

Bennett, Josiah (County unknown)
Confederate States Navy. [SEE: Corporal; Company K, 31st Regiment, North Carolina Troops].
[Source(s): Card File]

Bensell (Bensel), Joseph W. (Brunswick County(?), North Carolina) [NOTE: See Bensell, Joseph W. that died 1872]
Pilot, Confederate States Navy. Bensell served aboard the Blockade runner "City of Petersburg." He was lost at sea on December 11, 1862, aged 46 years. His marker is in Old Southport Cemetery, Southport, North Carolina.
[Source(s): McElroy; Card File; "Chronicles"]

Bensell, Joseph W. (Brunswick County(?), North Carolina) [NOTE: see Bensell, Joseph W. that died 1862]
Captain, North Carolina Navy. Bensell died on December 1, 1872, and was buried in Southport Cemetery, Brunswick County, North Carolina.
[Source(s): Stepp, "Burials"]

Benthall, Robert
Confederate States Navy.
Discharged from the CSS FORREST by order of Flag Officer French on January 17, 1862.
[Source: NCCWSP]

Benton, A. J. (North Carolina)
Landsman, Confederate States Navy. Benton enlisted on November 30, 1863 in Raleigh, North Carolina, for the war. Another record says he enlisted on December 5, 1863 at Wilmington for the war. Benton served as a Landsman aboard the CSS ARCTIC, Cape Fear River, North Carolina, 1863, and aboard the CSS RALEIGH in North Carolina and Virginia waters, 1864.
[Source(s): Card File; NA, RG 45; Foenander]

Benton, Charles P. (B.) (County unknown)
Landsman, Confederate States Navy. Benton enlisted on December 5, 1863 in Wilmington, North Carolina, for the war. A "C. P. Benton" enlisted on November 30, 1863 as a Landsman in Raleigh, North Carolina, for the war. Benton served aboard the CSS ARCTIC, Cape Fear River, North Carolina, 1863, and aboard the CSS RALEIGH [in] North Carolina and Virginia waters, 1864.
[Source(s): Card File; NA, RG 45; Foenander]

Benton, John (North Carolina?)
Seaman, Boatswain's Mate, Confederate States Navy.
Per payroll records, Benton served as a Seaman aboard the CSS EDWARDS from July - September 1861 and aboard the CSS FORREST as a Seaman per its muster roll dated October 30, 1861. He transferred to the CSS CURLEW on September 30, 1861 where he served as a Seaman through November 20, 1861. Payroll records indicate he served as a Boatswain's Mate aboard the CSS CURLEW through the 1st quarter of 1862. His name appears on the payroll of the receiving ship UNITED STATES ending March 31, 1862. Benton served aboard the CSS ALBEMARLE in May 1864, and on the Halifax Station in 1864. He was highly praised by his commander, James W. Cooke, for his actions aboard the CSS ALBEMARLE on May 5, 1864.
[Source(s): Foenander; NCCWSP]

Benton, Moses (New Hanover County, North Carolina[?])
Landsman, Confederate States Navy. Benton was born on February 8, 1849, and enlisted on December 5, 1863 in Wilmington, North Carolina, for the war. He served on the CSS ARCTIC, Cape Fear River, North Carolina, 1863, on the crew of the CSS CASWELL, and aboard the CSS RALEIGH in North Carolina and Virginia waters, 1864. He died in 1880 and was buried in Martindale-Biddle Cemetery south of Wilmington, New Hanover County, North Carolina, a short distance from the River Road. Another record lists a "Moses Benton" who enlisted on November 30, 1863 as a Landsman in Raleigh, North Carolina, for the war.
[Source(s): Card File; Gravestone Records, v. 8, p. 61; NA, RG 45; Stepp, "Burials;" Foenander]

Benton, Robert (North Carolina?)
Second Class Fireman, Confederate States Navy. Benton served aboard the CSS SEA BIRD as a 2nd Class Fireman. His name appears on the North Carolina Squadron payroll for the 1st quarter of 1862 with the notation "run 1 December 1861."
[Source(s): Foenander; ORN 2, 1, 306; NCCWSP]

Benton, W. A. (County unknown)
Landsman, Confederate States Navy. Benton enlisted on November 30, 1863 in Raleigh, North Carolina, for the war, and served aboard the CSS RALEIGH in North Carolina and Virginia waters, 1862 – 1864.
[Source(s): Card File; NA, RG 45; Foenander]

Benton, W. H. (North Carolina?)
Landsman, Confederate States Navy. Benton served aboard the CSS ARCTIC, Cape Fear River, North Carolina, 1863.
[Source(s): Foenander; ORN 2, 1, 277]

Berganus, Thomas (County unknown)
Confederate States Navy. Berganus enlisted on December 10, 1863 in Raleigh, North Carolina, for the war.
[Source(s): Card File; NA, RG 45]

Berry, W. R. (North Carolina?)
Confederate States Navy. Name appears on the March-October 1864 roster of the CSS NEUSE.
[Source: CMACSSN]

Bessent, Thomas (County unknown)
Landsman, Confederate States Navy. Bessent enlisted on August 17, 1864 in Raleigh, North Carolina, for the war.
[Source(s): Card File; NA, RG 45]

Best, Joseph (Currituck County, North Carolina)
Private, Confederate States Army//Officer's Steward, Confederate States Navy. Best was born in Currituck County, North Carolina, where he lived as a sailor, prior to enlisting as a Private in Company B, 8th Regiment, North Carolina State Troops, at age 27 on August 6, 1861. He was listed as present or accounted for until he transferred to the Confederate States Navy on January 10, 1863. He served as a Carpenter on the receiving ship CSS ARCTIC, and as an Officer's and Wardroom Steward on the CSS NORTH CAROLINA and the CSS TALLAHASSEE in 1864. He enlisted again in the army on April 1, 1864, as a Private in Company I, 17th Regiment, North Carolina Troops (2nd Organization). Best was present or accounted for through October 1864. He married Penelope "Penny" Baum, February 1, 1872, in Currituck County, North Carolina.
[Source(s): ORN, 2, 1, 279, 293, 295 and 296; North Carolina Troops, IV and VI; MR, IV; Card File; NA, RG 45; Foenander; North Carolina Troops IV & VI]

Best, Joseph (County unknown)
> [NOTE: May be same as Joseph Best, Currituck County, North Carolina]
> Seaman, Confederate States Navy. Best enlisted on January 18, 1863 in Wilmington, North Carolina for three years.
> [Source(s): Card File; NA, RG 45]

Best, T. H. (County unknown)
> Landsman, Confederate States Navy. Best enlisted on April 22, 1864 in Raleigh, North Carolina for the war.
> [Source(s): Card File; NA, RG 45]

Bethea, J. A. (County unknown)
> Confederate States Navy. Bethea enlisted on June 24, 1864 in Raleigh, North Carolina, for the war.
> [Source(s): Card File; NA, RG 45]

Bethea, James K. (North Carolina)
> Ordinary Seaman, Confederate States Navy. Bethea enlisted on September 9, 1863 in Wilmington, North Carolina, for the war, and served aboard the CSS ARCTIC at Wilmington, North Carolina. Bethea was admitted to the Confederate General Hospital No. 4, Wilmington, North Carolina on November 20, 1863 with "Bronch. Acute" and assigned to ward/bed number 6/99 and listing his post office as "Rocky Creek." No release date was listed.
> [Source(s): Card File; NA, RG 45; Foenander; St. Amad; MR, IV, 444; Hosp. (No. 4), Wilm.]

Betts, John W. (Wake County, North Carolina)
> Landsman, Confederate States Navy/Company F, 2nd Regiment, Naval Brigade. Born on November 10, 1846, Betts worked as a clerk and office man before enlisting in April 1864 in Company B, 70th Regiment, North Carolina Troops (Junior Reserves) and went to the Navy as a Landsman on the steamer CSS FREDERICKSBURG. His name appears on a roll of officers and men who, absent from their commands, have reported to the Commandant, Post of Greensboro, North Carolina, and were paroled at Greensboro, North Carolina, on May 1, 1865. He filed a claim for a pension on July 1, 1912 at age 66, listing his post office as Neuse, Wake County, North Carolina. The application was approved. Betts filed an application for admission to the Soldier's Home on August 1, 1913 at age 67 and was admitted on May 27, 1915. He died on August 5, 1918 at the Soldier's Home, Raleigh, North Carolina, of "Uraemic Poison Contributory Chronic Nephristis." A widower, he was buried at Old Stone burying ground (Wake County, North Carolina) beside his mother. His father was Calvin Betts (born in Wake County); mother, Sallie W. Stone (born in Granville County).
> [Source(s): Card File; Soldier's Home; Pensions (North Carolina); NA, RG 109; Stepp, "Burials"]

Beveridge, B.
> Quartermaster, Confederate States Navy. Beveridge served aboard the CSS ALBEMARLE, and on Halifax Station, 1864.
> [Source(s): Foenander; ORN 2, 1, 274]

Biggs, Robert W. (Cumberland County, North Carolina)
> Landsman, Confederate States Navy. Biggs enlisted October 22, 1863 in Wilmington, North Carolina. Another record records his enlistment as October 29, 1863 at Camp Holmes [Raleigh, North Carolina], while yet another lists his enlistment as November 1, 1863 at Wilmington, North Carolina, for the war. He served aboard the CSS RALEIGH in North Carolina and Virginia waters, 1862 – 1864. Biggs' name appears on a register of Confederate States Army General Military Hospital Number 4, Wilmington, North Carolina, which states that he was admitted on February 13, 1864, with "scorbutus" and returned to duty on April 13, 1864. Post office listed as Fayetteville, North Carolina.
> [Source(s): MR, 4, p. 445; Card File; NA, RG 45; Foenander]

Bigham, William B. R. (Haywood County, North Carolina)
> Landsman, Confederate States Navy. Bigham enlisted on June 20, 1864 in Raleigh, North Carolina, for the war. His name appears on a record of paroled prisoners, Provost Marshal's Office, Middle Military Department, dated April 22, 1865, which states that he surrendered at Manchester, Virginia, April 15, 1865, and took the Oath of Allegiance on April 18, 1865. He was sent to Knoxville, Tennessee. Bigham's former residence was listed on the record as Haywood County, North Carolina.
> [Source(s): Card File; NA, RG 45; NA, RG 109]

Bill, G. B. ("North Carolina," born in Maine)
Confederate States Navy. Bill's name appears on a report of deserters received from the enemy. Report states he was born in Maine and gives his last residence as "North Carolina." Description as follows: Age, 55; eyes, blue; hair, gray; complexion, dark; height, 5 feet 10 inches. He was listed as received within Confederate States lines on February 18, 1865(?). Report carries the remark, "Taken the oath and discharged."
[Source(s): Card Files; NA, RG 109]

Billings, _____
Steward, Confederate States Navy. Billings served as a Steward aboard the CSS NORTH CAROLINA.
[Source(s): YOPP]

Birdsey, S. R. (County unknown)
Landsman, Confederate States Navy. Birdsey enlisted on November 10, 1863 in Wilmington, North Carolina, for the war. Another record shows him as enlisting on November 4, 1863 at Raleigh, North Carolina, for the war.
[Source(s): Card File; NA, RG 45]

Bishop, Charles H. (Beaufort County, North Carolina)
Private, Company B, Confederate States Marine Corps. Born December 15, 1844, Bishop resided in Beaufort County, North Carolina until his enlistment in the Confederate States Marine Corps where he served at Drewry's Bluff. Captured at Farmville, Virginia, April 6, 1865, his name appears as a signee to an Oath of Allegiance to the United States, subscribed and sworn to at Point Lookout, Maryland, June 24, 1865. Description as follows: Complexion fair; hair light; eyes hazel; height 5 feet 7 inches. He died on September 18, 1877 and was buried in the cemetery of the First Presbyterian Church, Washington, Beaufort County, North Carolina.
[Source(s): Lauderdale; North Carolina Troops, Doc.#0185, p.1 and 0299; NA; Card File; Stepp, "Burials;" Foenander]

Bishop, Reuben
Ordinary Seaman, Confederate States Navy. Bishop served aboard the CSS RALEIGH in North Carolina and Virginia waters, 1862-1864.
[Source(s): Foenander; ORN 2, 1, 302]

Bishop, Richard (Guilford County, North Carolina) (or, Randolph County, North Carolina)
Bishop enlisted in the Confederate States Navy on 15 August 1863 in Wilmington, North Carolina. A pension claim filed on July 1, 1901 by his widow, Nell, age 73, listed her post office as Randleman, Randolph County, North Carolina. There is no indication the pension was approved. Her pension application states he "drowned in the Cape Fear River" while in service (body not found).
[Source(s): MR, 4, p. 444; Card File; Pensions (North Carolina); Foenander]

Bishop, Thomas J. (New Hanover County, North Carolina)
First Class Boy, Confederate States Navy. Bishop enlisted in the Confederate States Navy in Wilmington, North Carolina. Source "Foenander" states he served as a First-Class Boy aboard the CSS ARCTIC in 1863. His name appears on a register of Confederate States Army General Military Hospital Number 4, Wilmington, North Carolina, being admitted on December 15, 1863, with "febris continua," and returned to duty on January 20, 1864. Post office listed as Wilmington, North Carolina.
[Source(s): MR, 4, p. 444; NA, RG 109; Card File; *ORN* 2, 1; Foenander; St. Amand]

Bishop, W. T. (Mecklenburg County, North Carolina)
Artificer, Confederate States Army//Artificer, Confederate States Navy. Bishop enlisted for the war in Mecklenburg County, North Carolina, on May 29, 1861 in Company C, 9th Regiment, North Carolina Troops (1st Regiment, North Carolina Cavalry). He mustered in as a Private and was appointed Artificer, September-October 1863. Present or accounted for until transferred to the Confederate States Navy by Special Order #113, Paragraph IV, Army of Northern Virginia, April 25, 1864.
[Source(s): Card File; NA, RG 109; North Carolina Troops, II; Foenander (New Hanover County, North Carolina) "Captain," Engineer/Confederate States Navy. Born in Dunfermline, Scotland on January 13, 1826 and immigrated to this country in July 1850. Located first in Concord, New Hampshire, thence to Detroit, Michigan, and later to Cincinnati, Ohio. Settled in Wilmington, North Carolina, about the time of the outbreak of the War Between the States, where he took charge of the Clarendon Iron Works, which made arms for the Confederacy. Before the close of the war, Bissett made five trips through the blockade on board the ship HANSER, serving as her Engineer. He was captured by the enemy on his last trip and imprisoned at Philadelphia. He spent a year in Iowa, returning to

Wilmington in 1867 where he resumed his position with the Clarendon Iron Works. He resigned in 1868 to accept the position as master machinist in the shops of the Atlantic Coast Line in Wilmington.
[Source(s): Card File; "Messenger," 3/25/1900]

Black, Alexander (Beaufort County, North Carolina)
Private, Confederate States Army//Seaman/Captain of the Hold, Confederate States Navy. Born in Scotland, Black resided in Beaufort County, North Carolina, as a sailor at the time he enlisted at age 30 on December 15, 1861 [October 21, 1861, per "MR, III"], as a Private in Company C, 40th Regiment, North Carolina Troops (3rd Regiment, North Carolina Artillery). He transferred to the Confederate States Navy on May 8, 1862 and served as a Seaman on the receiving ship CSS ARCTIC, August 1862, CSS NORTH CAROLINA, and CSS TALLAHASSEE, 1864, as Captain of the Hold.
[Source(s): ORN, 1, 23, 703; ORN 2, 1, 293, 295-296; North Carolina Troops, I; NA, RG 109; Card File; Foenander; MR, III]

Black, W. A. (County unknown)
Landsman, Confederate States Navy. Black enlisted on June 10, 1864 in Raleigh, North Carolina, for the war.
[Source(s): NA, RG 45; Card File]

Black, William M. (Gaston County, North Carolina)
Confederate States Army//Confederate States Navy. Born on August 24, 1844, Black enlisted in the Confederate States Navy on May 1, 1863. His post-war Gaston County, North Carolina pension application states that he had prior infantry service and had received a thigh wound (unit unknown). He died on January 7, 1918 and was buried in the Castanea Presbyterian Church Cemetery, Lucia, Gaston County, North Carolina.
[Source(s): Pensions (North Carolina); Foenander; Cloninger]

Blacknall, George (Granville County, North Carolina)
Surgeon, Confederate States Navy. Born on September 13, 1804 in Granville County, North Carolina, Blacknall attended medical school at the Department of Medicine, University of Pennsylvania. He entered the United Navy as a Surgeon's Mate on January 3, 1828. Rated as a Passed Assistant Surgeon on March 3, 1835, Blacknall was promoted to the rank of Surgeon on February 9, 1837. In 1860, he resided with his wife Emma and four daughters, in Norfolk, Virginia, until his resignation from the United Navy as a Surgeon on May 7, 1861. Appointed Surgeon in the Virginia Navy in May 1861 and served in the Naval hospital at Portsmouth, Virginia. He was appointed a Surgeon from North Carolina on June 14, 1861. He died at Gosport Navy Yard on January 20, 1862 [another source states January 21], and was buried at Cedar Grove Cemetery, Portsmouth, Virginia.
[Source(s): McElroy; Register; Card File; Driver; OCSN; Foenander; CWDTS; ONWR]

Blake, James (North Carolina?)
Seaman, Confederate States Navy. Blake served aboard the CSS ARCTIC, 1863.
[Source(s): Foenander; ORN 2, 1, 276]

Blake, Joseph Davidson (Mecklenburg County. North Carolina)
Lieutenant, Confederate States Navy. Born in 1831, in Charlotte, North Carolina, Blake was a graduate of the United Naval Academy, Annapolis, Maryland. He served in the Navy, from September 9, 1847, until his resignation as a Lieutenant, February 5, 1862. Blake was appointed from North Carolina as a First Lieutenant, Confederate States Navy, on February 23, 1862, and served on the CSS GAINES, Mobile Squadron, 1862 [Source "Fold3, USN Resignees" gives date as February 25, 1862]. His name appears on the Prescription Books of Hospital, from Steamer GAINES, Confederate States Navy, which indicates that he was admitted on June 13, 1862, with "subluxatio sprained wrist." Discharged [from hospital] on June 16, 1862. His hospital entry was annotated with: "age 31, North Carolina." Blake was on sick leave for an unspecified time during 1862. His name appears on the Prescription Books of Hospital, Steamer GAINES, Confederate States Navy, which indicate he was admitted on August 31, 1862 with "catarrah" and discharged on August 28, 1862. He was admitted again on August 30, 1862, with "catarrah" and granted leave of absence on September 2, 1862. Admitted for third time on October 31, 1862 with "phthisis pulmonalis" and was "condemned by medical survey and relieved from duty November 3, 1862." His age was given on books as 31 with remark: "NORTH CAROLINA" Blake was appointed a First Lieutenant, Provisional Confederate States Navy, on June 2, 1864, to rank from January 6, 1864. He served at Drewry's Bluff, Virginia, "1863-1864" (?). He died on July 5, 1864 at age 33 while on sick leave in Charlotte, North Carolina, after contracting tuberculosis [consumption] while in the service. He is buried in Old Settler's Cemetery [First Presbyterian Church], Charlotte, North Carolina.

[Source(s): Register; McElroy; Card File; NA, RG 109; "WD," July 2, 1864; "CW-E," April 19, 1979; Stepp, "Burials;" Journal; OCSN; Foenander; ONWR; Fold3, USN Resignees]

Blalock, W. A. (County unknown)
Landsman, Confederate States Navy. Blalock enlisted on April 13, 1864 in Raleigh, North Carolina, for the war.
[Source(s): NA, RG 45; Card File]

Bleker, T. W. (or L. W.) (County unknown)
Seaman, Confederate States Navy. Bleker enlisted on June 13, 1864 in Raleigh, North Carolina, for the war.
[Source(s): Card File; NA, RG 45]

Blivens, H. (County unknown)
Confederate States Navy. Blivens' name appears on a list of conscripts "in yard at Halifax" June 9, 1864.
[Source(s): Card File; NA, RG 45]

Bloodworth, Benjamin T. (Pender County, North Carolina)
Confederate States Navy. Bloodworth enlisted in the Confederate States Navy in June 1862. He filed a claim for pension on June 22, 1901 at age 64, listing his post office as Burgaw, Pender County, North Carolina. His pension request was approved. His application of July 7, 1902 states he enlisted in May 1862, and that he was never wounded. A subsequent application dated July 6, 1906 states he enlisted in 1861.
[Source(s): Card File; "Pensions (North Carolina);" Foenander]

Bloom, J. F.
Landsman, Confederate States Navy. Bloom was assigned from Raleigh, North Carolina, to Battery Brooke, James River, Virginia, October 1864.
[Source(s): Foenander]

Bloom (Blum), William (Cabarrus County, North Carolina)
Carpenter's Mate, Confederate States Navy. Bloom served aboard the CSS NORTH CAROLINA, Cape Fear River, 1864. Source "Cruse" states he enlisted in Mecklenburg County, North Carolina, but was probably a resident of Cabarrus County, North Carolina. He served as a Carpenter's Mate aboard the CSS NORTH CAROLINA, Cape Fear River, North Carolina, 1864.
[Source(s): MR, 4, p. 448; Foenander; Cruse]

Blount (Blunt), Miles (Craven County, North Carolina)
Corporal, Confederate States Army//Confederate States Navy. Born in 1838 in Craven County, North Carolina, Blount resided and worked as a shingle maker in "Russels" until he enlisted at age 22 on May 27, 1861 for the war in Company F, 2nd Regiment, North Carolina State Troops. He was mustered in as a Corporal. Wounded at Fredericksburg, Virginia, on December 13, 1862, Blount was present or accounted for until he transferred to the Confederate States Navy on September 3, 1863. He served as a Landsman aboard the ironclad ram CSS PALMETTO STATE, Charleston Harbor, South Carolina, 1863-1864. He is also shown on a muster roll as having served on the CSS ALBEMARLE and on the Halifax Station, July-September 1864. In 1880, he resided as a shingle maker with his wife Louisa and four children at George, Colleton County, South Carolina.
[Source(s): Card File; North Carolina Troops, III; Foenander]

Blount, Sherman J. [A.?] (Sampson County, North Carolina)
Private, Confederate States Army//Confederate States Navy(?). Blount served initially with Captain William Devane's Independent Company, North Carolina Troops. He transferred to Company A, 61st Regiment, North Carolina Troops on or about September 5, 1862 and was listed as present or accounted for through August 31, 1864. He was reported sick in the hospital at Charleston, South Carolina on October 3, 1863, with a return to duty noted as November – December 1863. He was again hospitalized on February 22, 1864 with an "abscessus." Blount was transferred on March 17, 1864 to an unspecified unit (perhaps within the same regiment). He returned to duty prior to May 1, 1864 and was wounded in the side at the Battle of the Crater in Virginia near Petersburg on July 30, 1864. He was reported present or accounted for during the period September – October 1864 on duty at regimental headquarters (duty not specified). Blount was killed at the Battle of Bentonville between March 19 – 21, 1865. Source "Card File" indicates naval service.
[Source(s): Card File; NCT, Vol. XIV]

Blum (Blume), Frank L.
Midshipman, Confederate States Navy. Born on August 3, 1847, in Winston-Salem, North Carolina, Blum served as a Midshipman aboard the side wheeled steamer CSS PATRICK HENRY, James River, Virginia, 1864. He married in 1875 and resided in 1880 with his wife, Martha, and daughter, Maddin, as a notion dealer in Nashville, Davidson County, Tennessee. He was still residing in Nashville, as a general broker, in 1910.
[Source(s): Foenander; ORN 2, 1, 300]

Bobbitt, John Thomas (Possibly Orange or Vance [Durham] County, North Carolina)
Landsman, Confederate States Navy. Per the 1860 Granville County, North Carolina, Census, John T. Bobbitt was born May 1845, and had brothers George T. (born 1849) and Walton C. (born 1860). He enlisted on June 8, 1864 in Raleigh, North Carolina, for the war. Bobbitt married Laura F. Smith on October 3, 1888 in Durham, North Carolina. He died on September 18, 1921 at Roanoke, Virginia. Bobbitt was a successful real estate agent. His brother George W. (?) Bobbitt "lived on the home place in Fishing Creek until about 1885."
[Source(s): Card File; NA, RG 45; Census (NC), 1860]

Bodenhamer, W. A. (County unknown)
Landsman, Confederate States Navy. Bodenhamer enlisted on June 24, 1864 in Raleigh, North Carolina, for the war.
[Source(s): Card File; NA, RG 45]

Boell, Eramus (County unknown)
Confederate States Navy. Boell's name appears on a list of conscripts in the "yard at Halifax" June 9, 1864.
[Source(s): Card File; NA, RG 45]

Boggs, Spence [Spruce M. C.] (Cleveland County, North Carolina)
Private, Company B, Confederate States Marine Corps. Boggs enlisted on October 6, 1864 in Raleigh. He served on the Charleston, SC, station as a Private of the Marine guard on board the ironclad CSS COLUMBIA to February 7, 1865. Source "McLeod, August 30, 1874" states he was a good "cook." Boggs transferred to the CSS INDIAN CHIEF on February 8, 1865. He was captured at Harper's Farm, Virginia, on April 6, 1865, and his name appears as a signee to an Oath of Allegiance to the United States, subscribed and sworn to at Point Lookout, Maryland on June 23, 1865. His place of residence was given on the Oath as Cleveland County, North Carolina. Description as follows: Complexion fair; hair brown; eyes gray; height 5 feet 4 ½ inches.
[Source(s): NA; North Carolina Troops, Doc. # 0185, p. 1, and 0299; Card File; McLeod, August 30, 1874; Donnelly; Donnelly-ENL]

Bolles, Lewis
Confederate States Navy. Bolls enlisted in the Confederate States Navy in Wilmington, North Carolina.
[Source(s): MR, 4, p. 444; St. Amand]

Bolling, James (County unknown)
Landsman, Confederate States Navy. Bolling enlisted on November 13, 1863 in Wilmington, North Carolina, for the war.
[Source(s): Card File; NA, RG 45]

Bolt, John (Beaufort County, North Carolina)
Seaman, Confederate States Navy//Private, Confederate States Army//Seaman, Confederate States Navy. Bolt was born in England about 1827, and resided in 1860, with his wife Sarah and two children, as a Seaman in Washington, Beaufort County, North Carolina. He enlisted in Beaufort County, North Carolina, on May 10, 1861, age 35, as a Private in Company I, 3rd Regiment, North Carolina State Troops, and transferred to the Confederate States Navy on January 22, 1862. He re-enlisted in the Confederate States Army in Craven Company, North Carolina, on February 9, 1862, at age 36, as a Corporal in Company C, 61st Regiment, North Carolina Troops. He was reported as present in November-December 1862. He transferred back to the Confederate States Navy on January 15 ["16," per sources "Foenander," "North Carolina Troops', and "Beaufort County Sailors"], 1863 at Wilmington, North Carolina, for three years or the war. Bolt was admitted into Confederate General Hospital No. 4, Wilmington, North Carolina on January 27, 1863 with "Bronch. Acute" and assigned to ward/bed number 4/13, listing his post office as Washington [Beaufort County], North Carolina. He returned to duty on February 17, 1863. He served as a Seaman aboard the CSS ARCTIC and as Captain of the Forecastle on the CSS NORTH CAROLINA, 1864.
[Source(s): MR, I & IV; Card File; NA, RG 45; NA, RG 109; Foenander; "Beaufort County Sailors;" North Carolina Troops, III & XIV; ORN 2, 1, pp. 279, 293 & 295; Census (North Carolina), 1860; Hosp. (No. 4), Wilm.]

Boner, Joseph William (Forsyth County, North Carolina)
Landsman, Confederate States Navy. Boner enlisted on July 16, 1864 in Raleigh, North Carolina, for the war. Born August 30, 1798, he died on April 23, 1874, buried Salem Cemetery, Forsyth County, North Carolina.
[Source(s): NA, RG 45; Card File; Stepp, "Burials"]

Bonham, R. H. (North Carolina)
Confederate States Navy. Bonham served as a Private in Company H, 19th Regiment, North Carolina Troops (2nd North Carolina Cavalry). He transferred to the Confederate States Navy by command of the Confederate Secretary of War, Special Order No. 209, dated at Richmond, September 3, 1863, and was ordered to report to flag officer J.R. Tucker at Charleston, South Carolina.
[Source(s): Foenander]

Booth, E. G.
Assistant Surgeon, Confederate States Navy.
Served as an Assistant Surgeon aboard the CSS BEAUFORT. He transferred to the James River Squadron on April 15, 1862.
[Source: NCCWSP]

Booze, Solomon (Stokes County, North Carolina)
Landsman [Another record says he enlisted as a Seaman], Confederate States Navy. Booze enlisted in the Confederate States Navy on October 9, 1863 in Wilmington, North Carolina [Other records indicate he enlisted on October 12, 1863, at Camp Holmes, near Raleigh, North Carolina].
[Source(s): MR, 4, p. 444; Card File; NA, RG 45]

Bordsey, S. R. (North Carolina?)
Landsman, Confederate States Navy. Bordsey served aboard the CSS ARCTIC, Cape Fear River, North Carolina, 1863.
[Source(s): Foenander; ORN 2, 1, 277]

Bosburgh, Joseph (County unknown)
Confederate States Navy. Bosburgh was a crewman on the Confederate States Steamer LEE. His name appears on a Register of Confederate States Army General Military Hospital Number 4 in Wilmington, North Carolina, dated October 5, 1863, which gives his disease as "feb int quot" and states that he was returned to duty October 18, 1863. His post office was listed as Wilmington, North Carolina.
[Source(s): Card File; NA, RG 109]

Boswell, R. S. (County unknown)
Seaman, Confederate States Navy. Boswell enlisted on June 15, 1864 in Raleigh, North Carolina, for the war.
[Source(s): Card File; NA, RG 45]

Boswell, U. F. (County unknown)
Landsman, Confederate States Navy. Boswell enlisted on August 3, 1864 in Raleigh, North Carolina, for the war.
[Source(s): Card File; NA, RG 45]

Boswell, W.F. (North Carolina?)
Landsman, Confederate States Navy. Boswell served aboard the CSS NORTH CAROLINA, Cape Fear River, North Carolina, 1864.
[Source(s): Foenander; ORN 2, 1, 297]

Boudinot, William Elias (Chatham County, North Carolina)
Captain, Confederate States Navy. Born 1817, Boudinot was a graduate of the United Naval Academy at Annapolis. He served in the United Navy during the Mexican War. He "was serving as a master on the 74-gun ship OHIO… with the rank of lieutenant" at the outbreak of the Civil War. Resigning his commission, he joined the Confederate States Navy as a Captain. After the war, he lived in Pittsboro, Chatham County, North Carolina, until he passed away at about age 72 a few days prior to March 19, 1889, leaving "a wife but no children." He was buried at St. Bartholomew's Episcopal Church. "His active brain first originated the signal service and if his suggestions had been heeded it would have been adopted years before the war." He was adopted very early in life by Dr. Fred. J. Hill.
[Source(s): Card File; "DR," March 19, 1889; Lane Society]

Bouidin [Bouldin(?)], William Elias (Chatham County, North Carolina [?])
Assistant Surgeon, Confederate States Navy. Born October 17, 1817, Bouidin died on March 15, 1889, and was buried in the cemetery at St. Bartholomew's Episcopal Church, Chatham County, North Carolina.
[Source(s): Stepp, "Burials"]

Bow, Michael (County unknown)
Private, Confederate States Marine Corps. Bow was born in 1833, wounded in the bowels and captured at Fort Fisher on January 15, 1865, and died on January 17, 1865. He was buried in the Confederate Mass Grave, Oakdale Cemetery, Wilmington, New Hanover County, North Carolina.
[Source(s): "Daily Confed." (2/18/65); Card File; Stepp, "Burials"]

Bowden (Boyden), Jeremiah (Jerry)
(North Carolina?) ("Colored")
[Cabin] Boy, Confederate States Navy.
Bowden, listed as a "Colored boy," was captured at Roanoke Island, North Carolina, and paroled, February 1862.
[Source(s): Foenander; NCCWSP]

Bowen, George Washington (Washington County, North Carolina)
Private, Company E, Confederate States Marine Corps [another source says "Navy"]. Born on December 30, 1844 [Source "Donnelly" states 1833], Bowen enlisted ["conscripted with his brother Henry H. Bowen, q.v." (Editor's note)] in Raleigh, North Carolina, on October 6, 1864. He served on the Charleston, SC, station as a Private in the Marine guard aboard the ironclad, CSS COLUMBIA, to February 7, 1865, and was transferred to CSS INDIAN CHIEF on February 8, 1865. Captured at Harper's Farm, Virginia, on April 6, 1865, he was a prisoner of war at Libby Prison as of April 10, 1865, but was subsequently sent to Point Lookout, Maryland, where he was released on June 23, 1865. He married Mary Elizabeth Oden who as a widow applied for a pension on July 6, 1903, stating her husband enlisted in the Confederate States Marine Corps at Charleston, SC, circa October 9, 1864, and served aboard the CSS CHARLESTON, CSS INDIAN CHIEF, and CSS COLUMBIA. She was born June 28, 1841 and died March 14, 1930. George died June 21, 1898 [Sources "Donnelly" and "Foenander" state July 21, 1898] and both he and wife are buried in the Bowen Family Cemetery, on his home place, "on the right side of Rt. 32 just after crossing into Washington County, North Carolina, from Beaufort County, North Carolina."
[Source(s): Donnelly-RL; Donnelly-ENL; Lauderdale; North Carolina Troops, Doc.# 0299; Oden; Card File; UDC, MC of Svc.; Stepp, "Burials;" "Beaufort County Sailors;" Donnelly; Foenander]

Bowen, Henry Hunter (Washington County, North Carolina)
Private, Confederate States Marine Corps. Bowen was born on February 11, 1823 and lived on the northern Beaufort County-Washington County, North Carolina line. At age 41 he was conscripted and sent first to Camp Holmes near Raleigh. Bowen was soon transferred to Charleston, South Carolina, to the receiving ship CSS INDIAN CHIEF as a Marine recruit for the ironclad CSS COLUMBIA upon its completion. A letter to his wife dated October 10, 1864, from Charleston is reprinted in "Donnelly-RL," p. 151-152. Two of his brothers, William H. Bowen and Langley R. Bowen, were members of the Confederate States Marine Corps. He died on February 11, 1907 and was buried in the Bowen Family Cemetery, Washington County, North Carolina.
[Source(s): Donnelly-RL, p.151; Oden; Stepp, "Burials"]

Bowen, Langley (Washington County, North Carolina)
Confederate States Marine Corps. Brother of William H. and Henry Hunter Bowen, Langley Bowen lived on the northern Beaufort County-Washington County, North Carolina line.
[Source(s): Oden]

Bowen, Samuel M.
Engineer, North Carolina Navy.
Served aboard the NCS ALBEMARLE (not the ironclad CSS ALBEMARLE of 1864).
[Source: NCS]

Bowen, Timothy T. (New Hanover County, North Carolina)
Ordinary Seaman [Seaman], Confederate States Navy. Bowen enlisted in the Confederate States Navy in Wilmington, North Carolina on August 23, 1863 [another record gives the date as September 5, 1863 while another source lists it as 1862]. He was born on May 2, 1822 and died on September 23, 1902. He was buried in Mt. Holly Baptist Church Cemetery on Highway 117, in Pender County, North Carolina, between Wallace and Burgaw, North

Carolina. His widow, Isabella Bowen, filed a claim for a pension on July 6, 1903 at age 74 listing her post office as South Washington, Pender County, North Carolina. The pension was approved.
[Source(s): MR, 4, p. 444; Card File; Pension (North Carolina); NA, RG 45; Gravestone Records, v. 8, p. 44; Stepp, "Burials;" St. Amand; Foenander]

Bowen, William (Beaufort County, North Carolina)
Confederate States Navy. Bowen enlisted in Beaufort County, North Carolina, on June 26, 1861 at age 28 as a Private in Company G, 19th Regiment, North Carolina Troops (2nd Regiment, North Carolina Cavalry). He transferred to the Confederate States Navy on February 1, 1862.
[Source(s): North Carolina Troops, II; "Beaufort County Sailors"]

Bowen, William H. (Beaufort County, North Carolina)
Private, Confederate States Marine Corps. The brother of Langley and Henry Hunter Bowen [Source Donnelly-ENL adds a brother George], Bowen lived on the northern Beaufort County-Washington County, North Carolina line until he enlisted in Raleigh, North Carolina, on October 6, 1864. Bowen served on the Charleston Station as a Private of Marines on board the ironclad CSS COLUMBIA to February 7, 1865, when he transferred to the Confederate States Receiving Ship INDIAN CHIEF on February 8, 1865. He was captured and confined at Libby Prison, Richmond, Virginia on April 10, 1865, and reported to the Provost Marshal at Washington, DC, as of April 17, 1865. Bowen was furnished transportation to Elizabethtown, Essex County, New York. One source shows him as a deserter.
[Sources: Oden; Donnelly-ENL; North Carolina Troops, Doc.# 0299; Card File; Donnelly]

Bowers, Moses (County unknown)
Landsman, Confederate States Navy. Bowers enlisted on October 5, 1863 at Camp Holmes near Raleigh, North Carolina.
[Source(s): Card File; NA, RG 45]

Bowie, G.C. (North Carolina?)
Landsman, Confederate States Navy. Bowie served aboard the CSS ARCTIC, Cape Fear River, North Carolina, 1863.
[Source(s): Foenander; ORN 2, 1, 279]

Bowling, James (North Carolina?)
Landsman, Confederate States Navy. Bowling served aboard the CSS ARCTIC, Cape Fear River, North Carolina, 1863.
[Source(s): Foenander; ORN 2, 1, 277]

Bowling, Thomas (New Hanover County, North Carolina)
Seaman, Confederate States Navy. Bowling enlisted in the Confederate States Navy in Wilson, North Carolina, and served aboard the CSS ARCTIC, 1863. His name appears on a register of Confederate States Army General Military Hospital Number 4, Wilmington, North Carolina, as being admitted on January 2, 1864, with "pneumonia" and returned to duty February 23, 1864. His post office was listed as Wilmington, North Carolina, on the hospital register. Source "MR" gives place of enlistment as Wilmington, North Carolina.
[Source(s): Card File; NA, RG 109; MR, 4, p. 444; Foenander; St. Amand]

Bowman, William C. (North Carolina)
Ordinary Seaman, Confederate States Navy. Born in North Carolina, Bowman served as an Ordinary Seaman at age 18 aboard the CSS ATLANTA, 1863. He is possibly the same person listed in Source "Foenander" as "William C. Bowman" who enlisted in Winnsboro, Louisiana, on August 8, 1861, as a Private in Company C, 4th Battalion, Louisiana Infantry. He was transferred to the Confederate States Navy on December 15, 1862.
[Source(s): Foenander]

Boyd, J. J. (North Carolina?)
Landsman, Confederate States Navy.
Boyd served aboard the CSS FANNY in North Carolina waters, circa September - December 1861 and May 1862.
[Source(s): Foenander; ORN 2, 1, 285]

Boyd, Thomas S. (Currituck County, North Carolina)
Private, Confederate States Army//Landsman, Confederate States Navy.
Born in Philadelphia, Pennsylvania, Boyd lived as a plasterer until he enlisted in Currituck County, North Carolina,

at age 26 on May 13, 1861 in Company L, 17th Regiment, North Carolina Troops (1st Organization). He was present or accounted for until transferred to the Confederate States Navy on or about July 28, 1861. Per muster and payroll records, he served as a Landsman aboard the CSS FANNY from October 8, 1861 - December 12, 1861. Boyd received a partial payment on February 13, 1862 at the Gosport Navy Yard following the burning of the CSS FANNY at Elizabeth City on February 10, 1862. His name appears on the payroll of the North Carolina Squadron for the 1st quarter of 1862 (December 1, 1861 - February 28, 1862, on which date he is listed as having "run."
[Source(s): Card File; North Carolina Troops, VI; Foenander; NCCWSP]

Boydon (Bowden), Jeremiah (North Carolina?)
1st Class Boy, Confederate States Navy. Boydon served aboard the side-wheeled steamer CSS WINSLOW in North Carolina waters in July 1861 and the CSS SEA BIRD from July 1861 –February 1862. He was captured in the Battle of Elizabeth City on February 10, 1862 and carried to Roanoke Island where he was paroled on February 12, 1862 and returned to Elizabeth City. His name appears on the North Carolina Squadron payroll for the 1st quarter of 1862 (December 1, 1861 - April 15, 1861, on which date he is listed as "on parole."
[Source(s): Foenander; ORN 2, 1, 312; NCCWSP]

Boyer, Thomas (North Carolina?)
Ordinary Seaman, Confederate States Navy. Boyer served aboard the CSS NORTH CAROLINA, Cape Fear River, North Carolina, 1864.
[Source(s): Foenander; ORN 2, 1, 294-296]

Boyer, W. W. (North Carolina?)
Ordinary Seaman, Confederate States Navy. Boyer served aboard the CSS NORTH CAROLINA, Cape Fear River, North Carolina, 1864.
[Source(s): Foenander; ORN 2, 1, 294 & 295]

Boykin, Abraham (County unknown)
1st Sergeant, Confederate States Army//Confederate States Navy. Boykin initially served in Captain William Devane's Independent Company, North Carolina Troops until he transferred on or about September 5, 1862 to Company A, 61st Regiment, North Carolina Troops, later serving in Company G, 61st Regiment, North Carolina Troops. He was reported absent sick November – December 1862. Boykin returned to duty January – February 1863 and was reported on May 8, 1863 as absent on detached service as a picket guard at Hilton Ferry near Wilmington, North Carolina. He rejoined the regiment in July – August 1863 and was transferred to Company G of his regiment with the rank of 1st Sergeant on September 26, 1863. He was listed as present through December 31, 1863. Given a thirty-day on April 5, 1864, Boykin returned to duty prior to July 16, 1864 when he was "killed … by a Yankee sharp shooter [sic]" near Petersburg, Virginia. It was said of him, "He was always in the front rank, pressing on fearlessly to death or victory" ("Wilmington Weekly Journal," September 22, 1864). Source "Card File" lists an "Abraham Boykin" as having performed naval service.
[Source(s): Card File; NCT, Vol. XIV; WWJ (September 22, 1864)]

Boykin, Thomas J. (North Carolina)
Purser, Confederate Stats Navy.
[Source(s), Josh Howard; CN Subj. Files (Fold3)]

Boyle, Patrick (New Hanover County, North Carolina)
Landsman, Confederate States Navy. Boyle enlisted on September 28, 1863 at Camp Holmes, near Raleigh, North Carolina.
[Source(s): Card File; NA, RG 45]

Bracy, Samuel P. (North Carolina)
Landsman, Confederate States Navy. Bracy was born in North Carolina in 1846, the son of Samuel and Anne Bracy. In 1860, he resided with his parents in Robeson County, North Carolina. He served as a Landsman in the Confederate States Navy, was captured (date and place unknown), confined, died and was buried at Point Lookout, Maryland.
[Source(s): Foenander]

Bradley, B. (Wayne County, North Carolina)
Landsman, Confederate States Navy. Bradley enlisted in the Confederate States Navy on October 15, 1863 in Wilson, North Carolina [another source states he enlisted on October 26, 1863 in Wilmington; another source states

he enlisted on October 21 at Camp Holmes, near Raleigh, North Carolina]. Bradley served aboard the CSS ARCTIC, Cape Fear River, North Carolina, 1863.
[Source(s): MR, 4, p. 445; Card File; NA, RG 45; Foenander]

Bradley, John (North Carolina?)
Private, Confederate States Marine Corps. Bradley served in Company B, Confederate States Marine Corps, aboard the receiving ship CSS ARCTIC, Cape Fear River, North Carolina, April-June 1864.
[Source(s): Foenander; ORN 2, 1, 280 & 316]

Bradley (Braddy), Reubin A. (R. A.) (Brunswick County, North Carolina)
Private, Confederate States Army//Confederate States Navy. Born in Brunswick County, North Carolina, Bradley lived there as a farmer until he enlisted in New Hanover County, North Carolina at age 20 on July 23, 1861 in Company C, 8th Regiment., North Carolina State Troops for the war. Captured at Roanoke Island, North Carolina on February 8, 1862, he was paroled in Elizabeth City, North Carolina on February 21, 1862, and exchanged in August 1862. Bradley was present or accounted for until captured on the Weldon Railroad near Petersburg, Virginia on August 19, 1864. Taken initially as a prisoner of war to Point Lookout Prison in Maryland, he was later sent to Aikens Landing, James River, Virginia where he was received on September 18, 1864 for exchange. He was furloughed from the hospital in Richmond, Virginia on September 28, 1864.
[Source(s): Card File; NCT, Vol. IV]

Bradshaw, T. F. (County unknown)
[May be same as Theodore F. Bradshaw, q.v.]
Landsman, Confederate States Navy. Bradshaw enlisted on June 10, 1864 in Raleigh, North Carolina, for the war.
[Source(s): Card File; NA, RG 45]

Bradshaw, Theodore F. (Alamance County, North Carolina)
Confederate States Navy. Bradshaw enlisted on July 1, 1862. His widow, E. J. Bradshaw, filed a claim for pension on June 22, 1901 at age 74, listing her post office as Swepsonville, Alamance County, North Carolina. The pension application was approved and states he developed rheumatism and chronic diarrhea in January 1865 "and was never well again." He died in July 1866. Despondent states that Bradshaw was in the Navy and that his last commander was General Ewell.
[Source(s): Card File; Pensions (North Carolina)]

Brady, John [Probably Moore County, North Carolina]
Private, Confederate States Marine Corps. Brady served in Company B, Confederate States Marine Corps, aboard the CSS NORTH CAROLINA, Cape Fear River, North Carolina, 1864, and aboard the CSS RALEIGH, in North Carolina and Virginia waters, 1864. He was also later stationed 1 at Drewry's Bluff, Virginia, 1864. He is probably the same "Brady" that was mentioned by William McLeod (q.v.) in his letter of August 30, 1874, as being with his group of Confederate States Marines.
[Source(s): Foenander; ORN 2, 1, 296, 297, 302 & 314; McLeod, August 30, 1874; Donnelly]

Bragg, _____ (County unknown)
(North Carolina?)
Seaman, Confederate States Navy. Bragg was killed in action, possibly when his ship, the CSS SEA BIRD, was rammed and sunk by rhe USS COMMODORE PERRY in February 1862 at Elizabeth City, North Carolina.
[Source(s): ORN, Series I, Vol. 6, p.596]

Bragg, David (County unknown)
Landsman, Confederate States Navy. Bragg enlisted on June 10, 1864 in Raleigh, North Carolina, for the war.
[Source(s): Card File; NA, RG 45]

Bragg, William (North Carolina?)
Seaman, Confederate States Navy.
Bragg served AS A Seaman aboard the side-wheeled steamer CSS WINSLOW in North Carolina waters, July 1861 - February 1862. He was serving as a Seaman aboard the CSS SEA BIRD in February 1862. His name appears on the North Carolina Squadron payroll for the 1st quarter of 1862 (December 1, 1861 - February 14, 1862). He was mortally wounded on February 10, 1861 at the Battle of Elizabeth City, North Carolina and died on February 14, 1862 aboard USS COMMODORE PERRY.
[Source(s): Foenander; ORN 2, 1, 312; NCCWSP]

Bragg, Z (?) (Craven County, North Carolina)
>Private, Confederate States Navy. Bragg's name appears on a register of refugees and rebel deserters of the Provost Marshal General, Washington, DC, received on April 8, 1865, and sent to Fort Monroe [Virginia]. He took the Oath of Allegiance [no date] and was furnished transportation to New Bern, North Carolina.
>[Source(s): H and P Records]

Braisden, Brantley (County unknown)
>Landsman, Confederate States Navy. Braisden enlisted on January 6, 1864 in Raleigh, North Carolina, for the war. He served aboard the CSS ARCTIC, Cape Fear River, North Carolina, 1863.
>[Source(s): Foenander; Card File; NA, RG 45]

Branch, Thomas (Bladen County, North Carolina)
>Landsman, Confederate States Navy. Branch enlisted on April 18, 1864 in Raleigh, North Carolina [NOTE: His pension application states he enlisted in Charleston, South Carolina], for the war, and served in Charleston. His pension claim, filed on July 6, 1908 at age 62, listed his post office as Parkersburg, "Bladen" [Sampson?], County, North Carolina. The request for pension was disapproved.
>[Source(s): Card File; Pensions (North Carolina); NA, RG 45]

Brand (Brandt), A.R. (North Carolina?)
>Confederate States Navy. Brand served as a Fireman in the Confederate States Navy aboard the CSS BOMBSHELL. He was captured aboard the vessel during the engagement at Albemarle Sound, North Carolina, on May 5, 1864, and imprisoned in Elmira Prison, New York, where he died on January 4, 1865, of typhoid fever. He was buried at Woodlawn National Cemetery, 1825 Davis Street, Elmira, New York 14901, Section Confederate States Army, Site 1263.
>[Source(s): Foenander; ORN 1, 9, 746]

Brantley, H. A. (born in North Carolina)
>Coxswain, "Coast Guard and Confederate States Navy." Born in North Carolina in 1816, Brantley enlisted on October 15, 1861 and March 3, 1863 in Captain A. B. Noyes Coast Guard Company at St. Marks, Wakulla County, Florida. He possibly served in the Confederate States Navy aboard the CSS SPRAY.
>[Source(s): www.Confederate States Navyavy.org/stmarks.htm]

Brantley, William H. (Beaufort County, North Carolina)
>Ordinary Seaman, Confederate States Navy. Brantley enlisted on June 5,1863, in Wilmington, North Carolina, for the war, and served as a crewman aboard the CSS NORTH CAROLINA.
>[Source(s): MR, 4, p. 443; Card File; NA, RG 45; Foenander]

Branton, D. (County unknown)
>Ordinary Seaman, Confederate States Navy. Branton enlisted on June 5, 1863 in Wilmington, North Carolina, for the war.
>[Source(s): Card File; NA, RG 45]

Braswell, George W. (Johnston County, North Carolina)
>Confederate States Navy. Braswell was born in North Carolina, 1825, probably in Johnston County. He served as a Landsman and Ordinary Seaman aboard the CSS ARCTIC, 1863, and the CSS NORTH CAROLINA, Wilmington, 1864. In 1880, he resided as a farmer with his wife Keziah ("Kizzie") and six children at Boon Hill, Johnston County, North Carolina. His widow, Kizzy Braswell, age 71, filed a claim for his pension on June 27, 1901, listing her post office as Pine Level, Johnston, North Carolina. Her request for a pension was disapproved.
>[Source(s): MR, 4, p. 443; Card File; Pension (North Carolina); RCWV; Foenander]

Braswell, J. T. (North Carolina?)
>Landsman, Confederate States Navy. Braswell served aboard the CSS ARCTIC, Cape Fear River, North Carolina, 1863.
>[Source(s): Foenander; ORN 2, 1, 279]

Brawley, W. H.
>Ordinary Seaman, Confederate States Navy. Brawley served aboard the CSS NORTH CAROLINA, Cape Fear River, North Carolina, 1864.
>[Source(s): Foenander; ORN 2, 1, 297]

Braxton, Counsel (County unknown)
Landsman, Confederate States Navy. Braxton enlisted on March 1, 1864 in Raleigh, North Carolina, for the war.
[Source(s): Card File; NA, RG 45]

Braxton, D. (County unknown)
Confederate States Navy. Personal papers of Colonel Joseph Thompson, 49th Regiment, North Carolina Militia, state that he arrested D. Braxton, a deserter from the Camp of Instruction and returned him to Fort Holmes on June 23, 1863.
[Source(s): Card File; NA, RG 109]

Breedlove, Anderson (County unknown)
Landsman, Confederate States Navy. Breedlove enlisted on April 20, 1864 in Raleigh, North Carolina, for the war. A "Private A. Breedlove" of the Confederate States Naval Battalion was admitted to 2nd Division of Depot Field Hospital, "5th A. C. A. of P., City Point," Virginia, diagnosis: "VS L knee." Note says age 20.
[Source(s): Card File; NA, RG 45; H and P Records]

Breedlove, Isaiah Paschall (Granville County, North Carolina)
Landsman, Confederate States Navy. Breedlove was born on July 22, 1835 (Source "Foenander" lists date as 1847). His name appears on a list of conscripts in the "yard at Halifax" on June 9, 1864 [Another source states he enlisted February 1864 in Halifax, North Carolina, at the age of 28, while another source states he enlisted on March 31, 1864 in Raleigh]. Still another source lists an "I. B. Breedlove" as conscripted on March 31, 1864 at Camp Holmes from Colonel Dolby's 43rd Regiment, North Carolina Militia, Granville County, North Carolina. His pension application states he was a crew member on the CSS ALBEMARLE in February 1864. His description is given as follows: Age, 28; eyes, blue; hair, light; complexion, fair; height, 5 feet 8 ½ inches; place of birth, Granville County, North Carolina; occupation, farmer. In 1880, he resided as a farmer with his wife Celestia and four children at Oxford Township, Granville County, North Carolina. Breedlove filed a claim for pension on July 7, 1902 at age 67, listing his post office as Stovall, Granville County, North Carolina. The pension application was approved. Born on July 22, 1835, he died October 9, 1913, and was buried at Salem United Methodist Church, Oxford, North Carolina.
[Source(s): Card File; NA, RG 45; Pensions (North Carolina); Roster, 43rd Regiment, North Carolina Militia; Stepp, "Burials;" Foenander]

Brendle [Brendal(?), Brindle], Michael Alanson (Stokes County, North Carolina)
[NOTE: Source "NCT" lists middle initial as "E"]
Private, Confederate States Army/Confederate States Navy. Brendle was born on September 9, 1827, in Stokes County, North Carolina. In 1850 "M.E. Brendal" lived as a farmer in Forsyth County, North Carolina, with his wife, Julia (married January 2, 1850). On February 1, 1855 "Alason" Brendle married Susan Panther, Barry County, Missouri (tombstone record). Brendle enlisted on April 30, 1862 [Source "North Carolina Troops" gives enlistment date as March 18, 1862], at age 36, in Company D, 53rd Regiment, North Carolina Troops. He was reported present July-August 1862, but [per source "North Carolina Troops"] deserted on September 10, 1862. An "M.E. Brindle" is listed as a Private, Confederate States Navy, April and July 1864, assigned to the CSS ARCTIC, as "#139 Landsman." His name appears on a roll of those paroled at Greensboro, May 16, 1865. In 1880, he and his wife Susan were in Johnson County, Missouri, living with his daughter and son-in-law, Sarah Anne and James Oscar Young, in the town of Holden. In 1900, Brendle was listed as a widower in Red River County, Texas, receiving a pension for his service in Company D, 53rd Regiment, North Carolina Troops, and his two years aboard the ship "Articahoy" [ARCTIC?] in the Confederate States Navy. He died on March 5, 1902 (Red River or Lamar County, Texas?). He was 5'7" tall.
[Source(s): Card File; http://freepages.genealogy.rootsweb.com/~brendelforum/DescMichaelAlansonBrendel.htm; North Carolina Troops, XIII]

Brennan, Michael (North Carolina?)
Confederate States Navy. Brennen served as a crew member aboard the CSS BOMBSHELL and was captured aboard that vessel during the engagement at Albemarle Sound, North Carolina, on May 5, 1864. He was transferred the same day from the USS CERES to the USS SASSACUS, and thence to the USS LOCKWOOD, on May 10, 1864. He was transported to the prison at Point Lookout where he remained until released on June 27, 1865.
[Source(s): Foenander; ORN 1, 9, 746]

Brent, George Lee
Chief Clerk, Confederate States Navy. Brent was born in North Carolina, and appointed a Chief Clerk from Virginia, in the Office of Orders and Detail, Confederate States Navy Department, Richmond, Virginia, where he served

from 1863-1864. He attended an official court of inquiry as Recorder looking into the conduct of Commander John K. Mitchell, for his actions relating to the fall of New Orleans, in April 1862. Said court convened in Richmond, Virginia, in January 1864.
[Source(s): Foenander; ORN 1, 18, 318]

Brewer, A. (Mecklenburg County, North Carolina)
Private, Confederate States Marine Corps. A worker in the Confederate States Navy Yard, Charlotte, North Carolina, 1862-1865, Brewer "served in one of three companies of 'Marines', North Carolina Local Defense Troops, stationed there (Source: Driver)." Most of these workers came from the Gosport Navy Yard in Norfolk, Virginia, in 1862, following its evacuation by Confederate forces.
[Source(s): Driver]

Brewer, Thomas (Franklin County, North Carolina)
Landsman, Confederate States Navy. Brewer enlisted on February 27, 1864 in Raleigh, North Carolina, for the war, and served as a Landsman aboard the CSS ARCTIC, Cape Fear River, North Carolina, 1863. His name appears on a Register of Confederate States Army General Military Hospital Number 4, Wilmington, North Carolina, as being admitted on March 23, 1864 with "bronchitis acuta," post office listed as Louisburg, North Carolina. He returned to duty on June 12, 1864 and was "furloughed from Navy 30 days." He may be the same "Thomas Brewer" that served aboard the CSS NORTH CAROLINA, Cape Fear River, North Carolina, 1864.
[Source(s): Card File; Pensions (North Carolina); NA, RG 109]

Brewer, W. T. (Franklin County, North Carolina)
Landsman, Confederate States Navy/Naval Battalion. Brewer enlisted in 1862 in the Confederate States Navy. He was captured at Harper's Farm [Virginia] on April 6, 1865. His name appears on an Oath of Allegiance to the United States subscribed and sworn to at Point Lookout, Maryland, June 23, 1865, giving his residence as Franklin County, North Carolina. His description was as follows: complexion, florid; hair, auburn; eyes, grey; height, 5' 9 ¼." Brewer applied for a Confederate pension from Clark County, Arkansas. His widow Mary Blunt Brewer, age 70, applied for a pension, which was approved on September 18, 1929, on which she listed her post office as Franklin County, North Carolina. Mrs. Brewer claimed her husband served on an unnamed Confederate ironclad gunboat and was [also] on the CSS NORTH CAROLINA. She further stated that he was imprisoned at Point Lookout, Maryland, until released on June 23, 1865 Pension application deponent A. H. Dorsey (q.v.) claimed to have served with Breedlove.
[Source(s): Card File; Pensions (North Carolina); Foenander; H and P Records]

Bridgers [Bridges], J. F. (Robeson County, North Carolina)
Landsman, Confederate States Navy. Bridgers enlisted on July 14, 1864 in Raleigh, North Carolina, for the war. Another source states that Bridgers enlisted on July 6, 1864 and served at the Charleston Navy Yard. He filed for a pension on June 29, 1901 at age 73, listing his post office as being in Robeson County, North Carolina. Pension approved.
[Source(s): Card File; NA, RG 45; Pensions (North Carolina); Foenander]

Briggs, Charles (born in North Carolina)
Confederate States Army/Confederate States Navy. Briggs, unmarried, resided in New Orleans, Louisiana, where he worked as a sailor prior to enlisting at Camp Moore, Louisiana on July 22, 1861, at age 26, in Company A, 10th Louisiana Infantry. He was promoted to Sergeant on an unknown date and transferred to the Confederate States Navy on January 1, 1864.
[Source(s): Foenander; Booth 1, p. 115]

Briggs, J. S. (North Carolina/Tennessee)
Ordinary Seaman, Seaman, Confederate States Navy.
Born in North Carolina, Briggs was living in Tennessee as a Cooper when he enlisted in the Confederate States Navy on April 8, 1864. He served as Seaman and ordinary Seaman aboard the CSS Chattahoochee, 1864. He was transferred from the floating battery CSS GEORGIA, Savannah Squadron in September 1864 to the naval station at Wilmington, North Carolina. Briggs received a slight contusion of the knee during the Battle of Fort Fisher on December 25 [December 24, 1864, per source "FSW" (12/24/64].
[Sources: ORN 1, 17, 700 and 2, 1, 283; Confederate Navy subject file N - Personnel; NA - Complements, rolls, lists of persons, etc.; CSS Alabama - CSS Neuse, page 575; Foenander; Daily Confed. (1/2/65); 1860 Census (TN); "FSW" (12/24/64)].

Briggs, R. W. (Cumberland County, North Carolina)
Seaman, Confederate States Navy. Briggs enlisted in the Confederate States Navy on October 22, 1863, and served aboard the CSS ARCTIC, Cape Fear River, North Carolina, 1863
[Source(s): MR, IV, 445; Foenander]

Briggs, William H. (probably from New Hanover County, North Carolina)
Private, Confederate States Army//Seaman (?), Confederate States Navy. Briggs enlisted in New Hanover County, North Carolina, at age 27, on October 1, 1861 as a Private in Captain William C. Howard's Cavalry Company for twelve months. He was present or accounted for until "transferred to Naval Service April 11, 1862," where he served aboard the CSS ARCTIC, Cape Fear River, North Carolina, 1863
[Source(s): North Carolina Troops, II; Foenander]

Bright, Joseph (North Carolina?)
Private, Confederate States Marine Corps. Source "Foenander" states he served aboard the CSS NORTH CAROLINA, Cape Fear River, North Carolina, 1864, and later aboard the CSS BOMBSHELL, aboard which he was captured at Albemarle Sound, North Carolina, May 5, 1864. He was transferred, the same day, from the USS CERES to the USS SASSACUS, thence to the USS LOCKWOOD on May 10, 1864. He was later transported to an unnamed prisoner of war facility.
[Source(s): ORN 1, 9, 746 and 2, 1, 297; Foenander]

Bright, Washington
Confederate States Navy or Marine Corps(?). Bright was detailed to the Navy Yard, Charlotte, North Carolina, from Gosport Navy Yard, Norfolk, Virginia.
[Source(s): Driver]

Brigman (Brigham), E. (Richmond County, North Carolina)
Landsman, Confederate States Navy. Brigman enlisted in the Confederate States Navy on September 10, 1863 in Wilson, North Carolina. Other sources list an "E. Brigman" enlisting on October 21, 1863 at Camp Holmes, and on October 26, 1863 at Wilmington, North Carolina, for the war. Brigman served aboard the CSS ARCTIC, Cape Fear River, North Carolina, 1863
[Source(s): Foenander; MR, 4, p. 445; Card File; NA, RG 45]

Brindle [Brendle], Michael E. (Forsyth County, North Carolina)
Ordinary Seaman [another source says "Landsman"], Confederate States Navy. Brindle enlisted in the Confederate States Navy on October 10, 1863 in Wilson, North Carolina [another source says October 12, 1863 at Camp Holmes, near Raleigh, North Carolina]. Source "MR" states he enlisted in Wilmington, North Carolina.
[Source(s): MR, 4, p. 444; Card File; NA, RG 45]

Brinkman, Thomas W. (Brunswick County, North Carolina [?])
Pilot, Confederate States Navy. Brinkman served aboard the blockade runner "*Condor*." Born circa 1840, he died on December 11, 1872, and was buried in Southport, Brunswick County, North Carolina).
[Source(s): McElroy; Card File; Stepp, "Burials"]

Britt, B. L. (Johnston [?], County, North Carolina)
Landsman, Confederate States Navy. Britt enlisted on November 29, 1863 in Raleigh, North Carolina, for the war. He may be the same "B. Britt" that served aboard the CSS ARCTIC, Cape Fear River, North Carolina, 1863
[Source(s): Card File; NA, RG 45; Foenander]

Britt, James H. (Halifax County, North Carolina)
Steward, Confederate States Navy. Britt's name appears as a signee to an Oath of Allegiance to the United States, subscribed and sworn to at Fort Warren, Boston Harbor, Massachusetts, on June 15, 1863. The oath states that he was a Steward on the Steamer "R. E. LEE," and gives his place of residence as Halifax, North Carolina. His description was as follows: complexion, light; hair: [INCOMPLETE. SEE ORIGINAL CARD]

Britt, John (County unknown)
Landsman, Confederate States Navy. Britt enlisted on December 29, 1863 in Raleigh, North Carolina, for the war. He served aboard the CSS NORTH CAROLINA, Cape Fear River, North Carolina, 1864
[Source(s): Foenander; Card File; NA, RG 45]

Britt, U. (County unknown) [May BE SAME AS URIAH P. BRITT, q.v.]
Landsman, Confederate States Navy. Britt enlisted on March 30, 1864 in Raleigh, North Carolina, for the war.
[Source(s): Card File; NA, RG 45]

Britt, Uriah P. (Johnston County, North Carolina) [May BE SAME AS U. BRITT, q.v.]
Private, Confederate States Army//Landsman, Confederate States Navy. Britt was conscripted on July 16, 1862 at Camp Holmes [near Raleigh] from Colonel Woodall's 117th Regiment, North Carolina Militia from Johnston County, North Carolina. A descriptive Roll describes him as follows: age as 21; eyes, hazel; hair, light; complexion, fair; place of birth, Johnston County, North Carolina; occupation, farmer. Source "North Carolina Troops, VII" lists a "Uriah P. Britt" that enlisted in March 186[5] for the war. He was captured near Petersburg, Virginia on April 2, 1865 and confined at Point Lookout, Maryland, until released on June 24, 1865, after taking the Oath of Allegiance. Britt may have previously served as a Landsman in the Confederate States Navy
[Source(s): Card File; NA, RG 45; Roster, 117th Regiment, North Carolina Militia; North Carolina Troops, VII and VII Addendum; Foenander]

Bromley, George T.
Seaman, Confederate States Navy.
Per muster and payroll records, Bromley serve aboard the CSS JUNALUSKA from June 18, 1861 - August 1861. He is listed on payroll records of the CSS CURLEW from the 1st quarter of 1862 - November 20, 1862. His name appears on the payroll of the North Carolina Squadron for the 1st quarter of 1862 from August 20, 1861 - January 3, 1862. [Source: NCCWSP]

Bronson, Josiah (Camden County, North Carolina)
Private, Confederate States Army/Confederate States Navy. Bronson was born in Camden County, North Carolina, where he lived as a mariner. He enlisted in Pasquotank County, North Carolina, on July 5, 1861, at age 25, as a Private in Company A, 17th Regiment, North Carolina Troops (1st Organization). National Archives records erroneously indicate he may have served in 1st Company B, 32nd Regiment, North Carolina Troops. He transferred to the Confederate States Navy on October 6, 1861.
[Source(s): North Carolina Troops, VI (addendum) and IX; Foenander]

Bronson, Julian J. (County unknown)
Landsman, Confederate States Navy. Bronson enlisted on July 21, 1864 in Raleigh, North Carolina, for the war.
Sources: Card File; NA, RG 45]

Brookbank (Brookland), Thomas (County unknown)
Seaman, Confederate States Navy. Brookbank enlisted on June 15 [18], 1864 in Raleigh, North Carolina, for the war.
[Source(s): Card File; NA, RG 45; Duke Papers]

Brooks, Alexander (Stanly County, North Carolina)
First Lieutenant, Confederate States Army/Confederate States Navy. Brooks was born and resided as a farmer in Stanly County, North Carolina, where he enlisted at age 28 in Company H, 42nd Regiment, North Carolina Troops. Appointed a First Lieutenant on March 25, 1862, he resigned prior to June 30, 1862, which resignation was accepted on an unspecified date. He later served in the North Carolina Militia and was conscripted on March 12, 1864 at Camp Holmes, North Carolina, [near Raleigh] from Colonel "Cimpson's" ["Simpson?"] 83rd Regiment, North Carolina Militia, Stanly County, North Carolina. Description given as follows: Age, 30; eyes, grey; hair, dark; complexion, fair; height, 6 feet ½ inch; place of birth, Stanly County, North Carolina; occupation, farmer. Another source lists Andrew Alexander Brooks" as a "First Lieutenant, Confederate States Navy," with reference to "Company H, 42nd Regiment, North Carolina Troops [83rd Regiment, North Carolina Militia]," while another source lists him as "enlisted" March 14, 1864 in Raleigh, North Carolina, for the war. He died before April 5, 1864, in Weldon, North Carolina, of disease. His wife's name was T. C. Brooks.
[Source(s): Card File; NA, RG 45; Roster, 83rd Regiment, North Carolina M; North Carolina Troops, X; Foenander; Pensions (North Carolina)]

Brooks, J. (County unknown)
Landsman, Confederate States Navy. Brooks died on April 15, 1864 at or near Weldon, North Carolina. He was buried in the Confederate Cemetery, Halifax, Halifax County, North Carolina.
[Source(s): Card File; North Carolina Troops, Doc. #0314-91; Stepp, "Burials"]

Brooks, James D. (County unknown)
Landsman, Confederate States Navy. Brooks enlisted on August 10, 1864 in Raleigh, North Carolina, for the war. A "J. D. Brooks" served as a Landsman aboard the CSS ARCTIC, Cape Fear River, North Carolina, 1863.
[Source(s): Card File; NA, RG 45; ORN 2, 1, 279; Foenander]

Broom, Ellerson L. (Union County, North Carolina)
Private, Confederate States Army//Confederate States Navy. Broom was born in North Carolina, about 1834, and resided in Union County, North Carolina, at the time of his enlistment at age 19 on May 3, 1861, as a Private in Company B, 15th Regiment, North Carolina Troops. He was present or accounted for until wounded in the head at Fredericksburg, Virginia, on December 13, 1862. Broom was returned to duty in January-February 1863 and was present or accounted for until he transferred to the Confederate States Navy on April 1, 1864. He resided as a farmer, in 1870, with his wife, Tarley and two children, at Monroe, Union County, North Carolina
[Source(s): North Carolina Troops, V; Census (North Carolina), 1870; Foenander]

Brosell, George W. (County unknown)
Landsman, Confederate States Navy. Brosell enlisted on October 13, 1863 at Camp Holmes [near Raleigh].
[Source(s): Card File; NA, RG 45]

Brower, Allen (New Hanover County, North Carolina) [Source "North Carolina Troops, III" gives county as Washington]
Corporal, Confederate States Army//Confederate States Navy. Brower resided in Washington County, North Carolina, where he enlisted at age 30 on June 24, 1861, for the war, in Company G, 1st Regiment, North Carolina State Troops. Mustered in as a Corporal, he was present or accounted for until discharged on February 3, 1862 upon transfer to the Confederate States Navy.
[Source(s): Card File; North Carolina Troops, III; Foenander]

Brower, Emsey H. (Randolph County, North Carolina)
Ship's Corporal, Confederate States Navy. Born circa 1834 in Randolph County, North Carolina, Brower resided in Bladen County, North Carolina prior to enlisting in the Confederate States Navy in Norfolk, Virginia, 1861. He was assigned to the CSS CONFEDERATE STATES. He also served as Ship's Corporal aboard the CSS VIRGINIA, March 1862. Brower re-enlisted for the war on March 25, 1862, and was "transferred April 1, 1862," but source does not state where [Driver].
[Source(s): Driver]

Brown, Amos
Seaman, 1st Class Fireman, Confederate States Navy.
Brown served as a Seaman aboard the CSS CORA as of December 31, 1861, per payroll records. Promoted to 1st Class Fireman on January 1, 1862, his name appears on the payroll of the North Carolina Squadron for the 1st quarter of 1862 from December 31, 1861 - March 31, 1862.
[Source: NCCWSP]

Brown, H. Augustus (New Hanover County, North Carolina)
Private, Confederate States Navy. Brown served aboard the Confederate States Navy steamer EUGENIE. His name appears on a Register of Confederate States Army General Military Hospital Number 4, Wilmington, North Carolina, being admitted October 15, 1863 with "feb con com." He returned to duty on October 21, 1863. His post office was listed as Wilmington, North Carolina. An "H. Brown" served as a Landsman aboard the CSS ARCTIC, Cape Fear River, North Carolina, 1863. May be the "A. H. Brown" that served aboard the CSS NEUSE as of March – October 1964.
[Source(s): Card File; NA, RG 109; Foenander; ORN 2, 1, 277; NEUSE Roster; CMACSSN]

Brown, Henry (Johnston County, North Carolina)
Landsman, Confederate States Navy. Brown enlisted on October 19, 1863 in Wilmington, North Carolina, for the war. Source MR lists a "Henry Brown" as enlisting on October 19, 1863 at Camp Holmes, near Raleigh, North Carolina.
[Source(s): Card File; NA, RG 45; MR, IV, 444; RCWV]

Brown, Jacob (Rowan County, North Carolina)
Private, Confederate States Army//Confederate States Navy. Born in Rowan County, North Carolina, Brown resided as a laborer in Rockingham County, North Carolina, where he enlisted on May 3, 1861 [May 10, 1861, per

source MR, I] at age 21 as a Private in Company H, 13th Regiment, North Carolina Troops. Brown was present or accounted for until he transferred to the Confederate States Navy, for duty aboard the CSS MERRIMAC (CSS VIRGINIA), February 19, 1862 [Source MR, I showed the date as October 29, 1861]. A "J.C.C. Brown" served as a Landsman aboard the CSS ARCTIC, Cape Fear River, North Carolina, 1863. [ORN 2, 1, 279.]
[Source(s): Card File; Foenander; MR, I; North Carolina Troops, V; ORN 2, 1, 279]

Brown, James E. (North Carolina?)
Seaman, Confederate States Navy. Brown served aboard the CSS FANNY circa September - December 1861 and May 1862. He received a partial payment on February 13, 1862 at Gosport Navy Yard following the burning of the CSS FANNY at Elizabeth City on February 10, 1862. His name appears on the North Carolina Squadron payroll for the 1st quarter of 1862 (December 1, 1861 - March 31, 1862). He is listed as having "run" as of March 31, 1862.
[Source(s): Foenander; ORN 2, 1, 285; NEUSE Roster; NCCWSP]

Brown, J. J. (I.) (North Carolina?)
Seaman, Confederate States Navy. Brown served aboard the CSS BEAUFORT, September 1861 – March [April?] 1862, in North Carolina and Virginia waters. He received a partial payment on February 13, 1862 at Gosport Navy Yard following his efforts in manning Fort Cobb at the Battle of Elizabeth City on February 10, 1862. He appears on the payroll of the receiving ship ending March 31, 1862. Payroll records indicate he served with the North Carolina Squadron from at least the 1st quarter of 1862 from January 10, 1862 - April 15, 1862. He transferred to the James River Squadron on April 15, 1862. Brown may be the "James I. Brown" that served aboard the CSS NEUSE March – October 1865.
[Source(s): Foenander; ORN 2, 1, 281; NEUSE Roster; CMACSSN]

Brown, John
Boatswain's Mate, Confederate States Navy.
Brown shipped for a year aboard CSS RALEIGH on August 21, 1861 and served through at least the 1st quarter of 1862. He appears on the North Carolina Squadron payroll for the 1st quarter of 1862. He is listed as having "run" on a payroll ending February 21, 1862. [Source: NCCWSP]

Brown, John P. (Mecklenburg County, North Carolina)
Landsman, Confederate States Navy. Brown enlisted on October 31, 1863 in Wilmington, North Carolina. Another source lists his enlistment as November 5, 1863 at Wilmington, North Carolina, for the war, while another source states he enlisted November 2, 1863 at Raleigh, North Carolina, for the war. Brown served aboard the CSS ARCTIC, Cape Fear River, North Carolina, 1863
[Source(s): MR, 4, p. 445; Card File; NA, RG 45; Foenander]

Brown, John R. (Sampson County, North Carolina)
Landsman, Confederate States Navy (Private, Naval Battalion). Brown enlisted on July 16, 1864 in Raleigh, North Carolina, for the war. Another source states he enlisted July 4, 1864 at Charleston, SC, and served under Commodore Tucker at Charleston, SC. His name appears as a signature to an Oath of Allegiance to the United States subscribed and sworn to at Point Lookout, Maryland, June 24, 1865. His place of residence was given on the Oath as Sampson County, North Carolina. Description as follows: complexion, fair; hair, light brown; eyes, hazel; height, 5 feet 4 inches. His application for a pension filed on June 22, 1907 at age 61, and listing post office as Clinton, Sampson County, North Carolina, was "Disapproved." He filed another pension claim July 25, 1908 at age 62, listing his post office as Roseboro, Sampson County, North Carolina which was also "Disallowed." Brown filed yet another claim on July 13, 1909 in which he states he enlisted on July 5, 1864. This application was approved.
[Source(s): Card File; NA, RG 45; NA, RG 109; Pensions (North Carolina); Foenander]

Brown, John Somner (Meriwether County, Georgia)
Private/Confederate States Army//Confederate States Navy. Brown was born and enlisted in Meriwether County, Georgia, on September 16, 1861, as a Private in Company E, 2nd North Carolina Battalion, Infantry (NOTE: Source "Georgia Roster" says he enlisted in (New) Company A, 60th Regiment, Georgia Volunteer Infantry). He worked as a mechanic prior to enlistment. Captured at Roanoke Island, North Carolina, on February 8, 1862, Brown was paroled at Elizabeth City, North Carolina, on February 21, 1862. Appointed a musician, December 15, 1862, he transferred to the Confederate States Navy on April 23, 1864 (Source "Georgia Roster" states April 5, 1864). He was listed in Pike Company, Georgia, per 1870 Georgia Census.
[Source(s): Card File; North Carolina Troops, III; "Georgia Roster;" Census (GA), 1870]

Brown, Joseph (County unknown)
Seaman, Confederate States Navy. Brown enlisted on May 23, 1863 in Wilmington, North Carolina, for the war.
[Source(s): Card File; NA, RG 45]

Brown, Marshall (New Hanover County, North Carolina)
Private, Confederate States Army//Lieutenant, Confederate States Navy. Brown resided in New Hanover County, North Carolina, and had pre-war service in the United Revenue Service. He enlisted on March 27, 1862 as a Private in Company C, 1st Battalion, North Carolina Heavy Artillery. He transferred to the Confederate States Navy on March 10, 1863, and was appointed a Lieutenant, Confederate States Navy, for the war, on February 26, 1863. He served at the Wilmington station and aboard the CSS CHARLESTON at the Charleston station, 1863. Brown resigned his commission on November 13, 1863.
[Source(s): McElroy; Register; Card File; NA, RG 109; MR, IV; OCSN; Foenander; North Carolina Troops, I; ONWR]

Brown, Nelson (New Hanover County, North Carolina)
Seaman, Confederate States Navy. Brown enlisted in the Confederate States Navy on January 10, 1863 in Wilmington, North Carolina, for three years or the war. He served as a crewman on board the CSS ARCTIC, 1863, and the CSS NORTH CAROLINA, 1864.
[Source(s): MR, 4, p. 443; Card File; NA, RG 45; ORN 2, 1; Foenander]

Brown, Robert W. (North Carolina)
Assistant Paymaster, Confederate States Navy. Brown was nominated from North Carolina on April 4, 1862 and commissioned as a naval officer by the Confederate States Congress, 1862.
[Source(s): McElroy; Card File; Journal; OCSN; Foenander; ONWR; "Officers, January 1, 1864"]

Brown, Samuel N. (New Hanover County, North Carolina)
Private, Confederate States Army//Landsman, Confederate States Navy. Born in New Hanover County, North Carolina, Brown lived there as a mariner prior to enlisting there on April 15, 1861, at age 21 as a Private in Company I, 18th Regiment, North Carolina Troops. He was listed as present or accounted for until he transferred to the Confederate States Navy on January 12, 1862. Brown served as a Landsman aboard the CSS CURLEW through the 1st quarter of 1862. He appears on the payroll of the receiving ship UNITED STATES ending on March 31, 1862.
[Source(s): Card File; North Carolina Troops, VI; Foenander; NCCWSP]

Brown, Timothy
Ordinary Seaman, CSS ARCTIC, 1863. Is likely the same as "Timothy Brown" served as ordinary Seaman aboard the *CSS Neuse*, North Carolina, 1864.
[Source(s): *ORN* 2, 1, 276; Foenander; CN Subj. File, p. 1232; CMSCSSN]

Brown, William (Beaufort County, North Carolina)
Private, Confederate States Army//Confederate States Navy. Brown enlisted on June 26, 1861 at age 28 in Beaufort County, North Carolina, as a Private in Company G, 19th Regiment, North Carolina Troops (2nd Regiment, North Carolina Cavalry). He was listed as present or accounted for until he transferred to the Confederate States Navy on February 1, 1862.
[Source(s): North Carolina Troops, II; "Beaufort County Sailors;" Foenander]

Brown, William (Pasquotank County, North Carolina)
Private, Confederate States Army//Confederate States Navy. Born in Pasquotank County, North Carolina, Brown resided there as a farmer prior to enlisting "for the war" at age 23 on July 24, 1861 as a Private in Company A, 8th Regiment, North Carolina State Troops. Captured at Roanoke Island on February 8, 1862, he was paroled at Elizabeth City, North Carolina, on February 21, 1862, and exchanged in August 1862. He is listed as present or accounted for until he transferred to the Confederate States Navy on January 9, 1863.
[Source(s): North Carolina Troops, IV; "Beaufort County Sailors;" Foenander]

Brown, William (Beaufort County, North Carolina)
Private, Confederate States Army//Seaman, Confederate States Navy. Brown enlisted in Beaufort County, North Carolina, at age 28 on June 26, 1861 for the war in Company G, 19th Regiment, North Carolina Troops (2nd Regiment, North Carolina Cavalry). He is listed as present of accounted for until transferred to the Confederate

States Navy on February 1, 1862. One source gives transfer date as January 18, 1863 at Wilmington, North Carolina.
[Source(s): Card File; NA, RG 45]

Brown, William (North Carolina?)
Private, Confederate States Marine Corps.
Brown served in Company C, Confederate States Marine Corps. He was stationed aboard the receiving ship CSS ARCTIC, Cape Fear River, North Carolina, April - June 1864, and later aboard the CSS RALEIGH, in North Carolina and Virginia waters, 1864.
[Source(s): Foenander; ORN 2, 1, 280, 302 & 316]

Brown, William
Seaman, Quartermaster, Confederate States Navy.
Brown served aboard the CSS BEAUFORT per its payroll for September - November 1861. He was ordered discharged by order of Flag Officer French Forrest from the CSS FORREST on December 10, 1861. He appears on the payrolls of the North Carolina Squadron for the 1st quarter of 1862 (December 1, 1861 - December 10, 1861) and February 7, 1862 - April 15, 1862. Per bounty, clothing, and muster records, Brown served as a Seaman aboard the CSS RALEIGH from January 16, 1862 – April 1862. He transferred to the James River Squadron on April 15, 1862 and appears as a Quartermaster serving aboard the CSS RALEIGH with the James River Squadron from October 1 - December 15, 1862. According to payroll records, he was stationed at Drewry's Bluff as a Quartermaster from April 1, 1863 - June 30, 1863. He is listed on the November 16 - December 15, 1863 payroll of the James River Squadron.
[Source: NCCWSP]

Brown, Wyatt M.
North Carolina Navy.
Brown is listed by source DH Hill as one of the first officers commissioned in the North Carolina Navy. Served at Hatteras.
[Source(s): DH Hill; NCS]

Browning, Anthony L. (County unknown)
Private, Confederate States Army//Confederate States Navy. Born in Brunswick County, North Carolina, Browning resided there as a carpenter until he enlisted in Company F, 8th Regiment, North Carolina State Troops in New Hanover County, North Carolina at age 41 on August 19, 1861 for the war. Captured at Roanoke Island, North Carolina on February 8, 1862, he was paroled in Elizabeth City, North Carolina on February 21, 1862, and exchanged in August 1862. He was listed as present or accounted for until he died in the hospital in Richmond, Virginia o July 21, 1864 of pneumonia. Source "Card File" indicated naval service.
[Source(s): Card File; NCT, Vol. IV]

Bruce, John
Seaman, Confederate States Navy.
Bruce was serving aboard the CSS SEA BIRD by February 1862. He was captured in the Battle of Elizabeth City and was carried to Roanoke Island. His name appears on the North Carolina Squadron payroll for the 1st quarter of 1862 (January 1, 1862 - February 12, 1862). Bruce is listed as having "run" as of the February 12, 1862 payroll. He took the Oath of Allegiance to the United States at Roanoke Island on February 12, 1862.
[Source: NCCWSP]

Bruner, Josephus (Possibly same as "Joseph Bruner") (County unknown)
Confederate States Navy. Bruner enlisted on March 15, 1864 in Wilmington, North Carolina, for the war. Joseph Brunner (surname also shown as Bruner) served as a Landsman aboard the CSS RALEIGH, in North Carolina and Virginia waters, 1864. He also served as a Surgeon's Steward aboard the CSS North Carolina, Cape Fear River, North Carolina, 1864.
[Source(s): Card File; NA, RG 45; Foenander; ORN 2, 1, 294, 296 & 301]

Bryan, John (New Hanover County, North Carolina)
Ordinary Seaman, Confederate States Navy. Bryan enlisted on November 5, 1863 in Wilmington, North Carolina, for the war. He served aboard the CSS ARCTIC, 1863.
[Source(s): MR, 4, p. 445; Card File; NA, RG 45; St. Amand; Foenander]

Bryan, William Henry (Bladen County, North Carolina)
Landsman ("Private"), Confederate States Navy. Bryan was born on January 31, 1839 and enlisted on April 8, 1862 at age 23 (another source indicates that a "William H. Bryan" enlisted on April 25, 1864). He was discharged on or about May 26, 1865. He died on October 26, 1912, and was buried in the William H. Bryan Cemetery, near Bladenboro, Bladen County, North Carolina.
[Source(s): Card File; UDC, Bladen Starlets; NA, RG 45; Stepp, "Burials"]

Bryant, Alfred McL. (Sampson County, North Carolina)
Private, Confederate States Army//Confederate States Navy. Bryant resided in Sampson County, but enlisted in Duplin County, North Carolina, on March 28, 1862, for the war, in Company F, 20th Regiment, North Carolina Troops. He was listed as present or accounted for until he transferred to the Confederate Navy Department at Wilmington, North Carolina, on May 15, 1862.
[Source(s): Card File; North Carolina Troops, VI; Foenander]

Bryant, L. H. (North Carolina?)
Landsman, Confederate States Navy. Bryant served aboard the CSS ARCTIC, Cape Fear River, North Carolina, 1863.
[Source(s): Foenander; ORN 2, 1, 279.]

Buchanan, Jonathan (County unknown)
2nd Class Fireman, Confederate States Navy. Buchanan enlisted on October 15, 1863 in Wilmington, North Carolina, for the war. A "John Buchanan" served as a 2nd Class Fireman aboard the CSS ARCTIC, 1863, and aboard the CSS NORTH CAROLINA, Cape Fear River, North Carolina, 1864.
[Source(s): Card File; NA, RG 45; Foenander; ORN 2, 1, 276, 294, 295 & 297]

Buckman, Charles G. (County unknown)
Landsman, Confederate States Navy. Buckman enlisted on April 20, 1864 in Raleigh, North Carolina, for the war.
[Source(s): Card File; NA, RG 45]

Buckner, Jesse (County unknown)
Landsman, Confederate States Navy. Buckner enlisted on January 20, 1864 in Raleigh, North Carolina, for the war. He served aboard the CSS RALEIGH in North Carolina and Virginia waters, 1862 – 1864.
[Source(s): Card File; NA, RG 45; ORN 2, 1, 302; Foenander]

Buie, Gilbert E. (Cumberland County, North Carolina)
Confederate States Navy. Buie appears on a roll of Prisoners of War at Point Lookout, Maryland, which states he was captured at Burkeville, Virginia, on April 6, 1865, and confined at Point Lookout, Maryland, on April 14, 1865. He was released on taking the Oath of Allegiance to the United States on June 23, 1865. Place of residence given on Oath as Cumberland County, North Carolina. Description as follows: complexion, dark; hair, dark brown; eyes, blue; height, 5 feet 5 ½ inches. Born on November 2, 1832, Buie died on July 28, 1910, and was buried at Big Rockfish Presbyterian Church, Cumberland County, North Carolina.
[Source(s): Card File; NA, RG 109; Stepp, "Burials"]

Bullock, Henry A. (Granville County, North Carolina)
Private, Confederate States Army//Confederate States Navy. Bullock was born about 1826 in Granville County, North Carolina, where he resided as a farmer until he enlisted there at age 36 on February 24, 1862 as a Private in Company E, C. Mustered in as a Corporal, he was reduced to the ranks on July 16, 1862. He was hospitalized at Richmond, Virginia, on September 28, 1862, with a gunshot wound to the thigh. Place and date of wounding not reported. Bullock was returned to duty prior to December 13, 1862, when he was wounded in the thigh at Fredericksburg, Virginia. Returned to duty in May-June 1863, Bullock was present or accounted for until he transferred to the Confederate States Navy on or about April 15, 1864.
[Source(s): Card File; North Carolina Troops, XI; Foenander]

Burbage, Thomas J. (North Carolina?)
Acting Master, Confederate States Navy. Burbage served aboard the CSS ALBEMARLE, and on the Wilmington station, North Carolina, 1863 - 1864.
[Source(s): Foenander; ORN 2, 1, 274 & 323]

Burch (Berch), D. Z. (North Carolina)
    Confederate States Navy. Listed as "Navy," Burch was admitted to the Confederate General Hospital No. 4, Wilmington, North Carolina on July 17, 1862 with "Febris Typhoid" and assigned to ward/bed number 3/8 and listing his post office as "Cedar Grove" [Source NC Gaz lists a "Cedar Grove" in Orange County, North Carolina].
    [Source(s): NC Gaz; Hosp. (No. 4), Wilm.]

Burgess, Daniel B. (Randolph County, North Carolina)
    Ordinary Seaman, Confederate States Navy. Burgess enlisted in the Confederate States Navy "Heavy Artillery" on June 5, 1863 (Another source gives the date as "July 15, 1862," while source "Foenander" gives the year as 1864) in Wilmington, North Carolina, for the war. He was a crewmember on the steamer CSS NORTH CAROLINA. His name appears on a Register of Confederate States Army General Military Hospital Number 4, Wilmington, North Carolina, dated June 27, 1863, giving his disease as "diarrh" and assigning him to ward 3, bed 41. Hospital records list his office as "Franklinsville." He was wounded by shrapnel in the inner side of his right thigh on April 1, 1865 near Culpepper Courthouse, Virginia. His name appears on a roll of Prisoners of War at Point Lookout, Maryland, which states that he was captured at Burkesville, Virginia, April 6, 1865, and confined at Point Lookout, Maryland, April 14, 1865, until released on taking the Oath of Allegiance to the United States on June 23, 1865. The oath gives his place of residence as Randolph County, North Carolina. His description was given as follows: complexion, fair; hair, brown; eyes, blue; height, 5 feet 7 ¼ inches. He filed a claim for pension on July 1, 1912 at age 81, listing his post office as Ramseur, Randolph County, North Carolina. Approval not indicated.
    [Source(s): MR, 4, p. 443; Card File; NA, RG 45; NA, RG 109; Pensions (North Carolina); Foenander; Hosp. (No. 4), Wilm.]

Burgess, M. [Mitchell?] (possibly Mecklenburg County, North Carolina)
    Seaman, Confederate States Navy. Burgess enlisted on June 13, 1864 in Raleigh, North Carolina, for the war. An "M. Burgess," with the annotation "North Carolina," is buried in the Seaman's Burial Ground, Ashley River, Charleston, SC, with his date of death listed as December 3, 1864. North Carolina Confederate Pension records contain an application for pension made under the name of a "Mitchell Burgess," Mallett's Battalion (Camp Guards), who died in 1864. There was no information listed on where he died, or to verify that he was in the Confederate States Navy.
    [Source(s): Card File; NA, RG 45; SBG; North Carolina Pensions]

Burgess, William (Camden County, North Carolina)
    Private, Confederate States Army//Confederate States Navy. Burgess was born in Camden County, North Carolina, where he worked as a mariner prior to enlisting in Pasquotank County, North Carolina, at age 22 on September 24, 1861, for the war, in Company I, 5th Regiment, North Carolina State Troops. He transferred to the Confederate States Navy on or about October 21, 1862. He is listed as a Seaman aboard the CSS ALBEMARLE, and later served on the Halifax Station, July-September 1864.
    [Source(s): Card File; North Carolina Troops, IV; Foenander]

Burke, William (North Carolina?)
    Seaman, Confederate States Navy. Burke served aboard the CSS VIRGINIA and was wounded in the Battle of Hampton Roads, during the action of March 8 – 9, 1862.
    [Source(s): Foenander; ORN 2, 1, 310]

Burnes, M.E. (North Carolina?)
    Landsman, Confederate States Navy. Burnes served aboard the CSS ARCTIC, Cape Fear River, North Carolina, 1863.
    [Source(s): Foenander; ORN 2, 1, 278]

Burnett, Henery [Henry?] (North Carolina?)
    Landsman, Confederate States Navy.
    Burnett enlisted on July 16, 1864 in Raleigh, North Carolina, for the war.
    [Source(s): Card File; NA, RG 45]

Burnett [Burnet], James (Wilson County, North Carolina)
    Seaman ("Private"), Confederate States Navy (Confederate States Naval Battalion). Burnett enlisted on January 12, 1863 in Wilmington, North Carolina, for three years or the war. His name appears on a role of Prisoners of War at Point Lookout, Maryland, which states he was captured April 6, 1865 in Wake County, North Carolina, and

confined at Point Lookout, Maryland, April 14, 1865. Burnett was released on June 24, 1865 upon taking the Oath of Allegiance to the United States. The oath states that he resided in Wilson County, North Carolina. His description was as follows: complexion, fair; eyes, blue; height, 5 feet 8 ¾ inches.
[Source(s): Card File; NA, RG 45; NA, RG 109]

Burnett, N. (Chatham County, North Carolina)
Landsman, Confederate States Navy. Burnett served aboard the CSS ARCTIC, Cape Fear River, North Carolina, 1863.
[Source(s): Foenander; ORN 2, 1, 278]

Burney, William A. (Guilford County, North Carolina)
Landsman, Confederate States Navy. Burney enlisted on October 16, 1863 (or, October 26, 1863) in Wilmington, North Carolina. Another source states he enlisted October 21, 1863 at Camp Holmes [near Raleigh]. He served aboard the CSS ARCTIC, Cape Fear River, North Carolina, 1863.
[Source(s): MR, 4, p. 444; Card File; NA, RG 45; Foenander]

Burns, Bennett (Chatham County, North Carolina)
Confederate States Navy [Source "To Bear Arms" lists him as "Marine, Confederate States Navy"]. Burns was born in 1826 and lived as a blacksmith at Little Buffalo Creek, Chatham County, North Carolina [Source "Foenander" states he resided as a laborer, in 1850, with his wife, Mary, and daughter, at Lower Regiment, Chatham County, North Carolina]. He enlisted in the Confederate States Navy on October 1, 1863 in Charleston, South Carolina, and served aboard the CSS PALMETTO STATE. When Charleston was evacuated on February 18, 1865, Burns joined the Confederate Army and Navy personnel retreating northward to North Carolina. He surrendered to the occupying Union forces on April 24, 1865 at Avent's Ferry, North Carolina. Burns lived near Moncure, Chatham County, North Carolina. He applied for a Confederate pension from Chatham County, North Carolina
[Source(s): Pensions (North Carolina); Lane Society; To Bear Arms; Foenander]

Burns, Edward (New Hanover County, North Carolina)
3rd Corporal, Confederate States Army//Confederate States Navy. Burns resided in New Hanover County, North Carolina, where he enlisted at age 25 on June 24, 1861, for the war, in Company E, 1st Regiment, North Carolina State Troops. Mustered in as Corporal, he was reduced to the ranks on August 26, 1861. Burns was listed as present or accounted for until transferred to the Confederate States Navy on February 3, 1862.
[Source(s): Card File; North Carolina Troops, III; Foenander]

Burns, William E. (County unknown)
Landsman, Confederate States Navy. Burns enlisted on February 27, 1864 in Raleigh, North Carolina, for the war.
[Source(s): Card File; NA, RG 45]

Burnside, John (County unknown)
Landsman, Confederate States Navy. Burnside enlisted on June 11, 1864 in Raleigh, North Carolina, for the war.
[Source(s): Card File; NA, RG 45]

Burr, Horace C. (Born in North Carolina)
Acting Master's Mate [Master], Confederate States Navy. Born in North Carolina in November 1838, Burr was the son of Horace and Mary Jane Burr, with whom he resided in Wilmington, North Carolina in 1850. He was appointed from North Carolina and served aboard the CSS ARCTIC and CSS YADKIN on the Wilmington Station, 1862-1864, ranking as an Acting Master's Mate [Master]. Later, he was appointed an Acting Master's Mate (Provisional Navy) on June 2, 1864. He surrendered on April 14, 1865, at Farmville, Virginia, where he was paroled the same day. Burr married in 1876 and lived in Illinois after the war. In 1900, he resided as a credit manager in the furniture business in Omaha, Nebraska with his wife, Helen, and two sons. A "Horace C. Burr" died on June 11, 1877, and was buried in Oakdale Cemetery, Wilmington, New Hanover County, North Carolina. This was probably the father.
[Source(s): Register; Stepp, "Burials;" Foenander]

Burr, Louis Jennings
Blockade Runner (probably a Civilian). Per source "WDJ" September 7, 1864, Burr died aboard the steamer "Flamingo" (a blockade runner) at St. Georges, Bermuda on August 27, 1864. He was aged 17 and apparently serving on the vessel.
[Source(s): "WDJ" (Sept. 7, 1864); Josh Howard]

Burrus, George W.
>Pilot, Confederate States Navy. Burrus served aboard the blockade runner "Hebe."
>[Source(s): McElroy]

Burriss, Joseph N [A.]. (New Hanover County, North Carolina)
>Private, Confederate States Army//Seaman, Confederate States Navy. Born about 1833, Burriss enlisted in New Hanover County, North Carolina, at age 33, on October 1, 1861 for twelve months, in Captain William C. Howard's Cavalry Company (North Carolina Local Defense Troops). He was present or accounted for until "transferred to Naval Service April 11, 1862." Burris served as a Seaman on the CSS ARCTIC, 1863. In 1880, he resided as a Pilot with his wife, Mary, and three children, at Smithville, Brunswick County, North Carolina.
>[Source(s): North Carolina Troops, II; Foenander; ORN 2, 1, 277]

Burroughs, Thomas G. (North Carolina?)
>Confederate States Navy. Burroughs served on the CSS NORTH CAROLINA, at New Inlet, North Carolina, and is listed as having deserted October 9, 1863. He was taken aboard the USS SHENANDOAH, off Beaufort, North Carolina, and later sent to Hampton Roads, Virginia, for further questioning. [NOTE: His father, _____ Burroughs, was captured aboard the blockade runner, "Merrimac," off of New Inlet, North Carolina, in July 1863, and took the Oath of Allegiance. He served the Union Navy as a pilot aboard the USS MINNESOTA and USS SHOKOKON, but later deserted back to the Confederacy.
>[Source(s): Foenander; ORN 1, 9, 132, 137, 235]

Burris, Thomas
>Seaman, Confederate States Navy. Burris served aboard the CSS ARCTIC, Cape Fear River, North Carolina, 1863.
>[Source(s): Foenander; ORN 2, 1, 279]

Burrow, W. P. (also Burrows)
>Engineer, Confederate States Navy.
>Burrows served as an Engineer aboard the CSS EDWARDS from July - September 1861. Muster records show he was serving as an Engineer aboard the CSS FORREST as of October 30, 1861. He was transferred to the CSS ELLIS on an unknown date.
>[Source: NCCWSP]

Burrus, J. N. [NOTE: May be same as "Joseph N. Burriss, q.v.]
>Pilot, Confederate States Navy. Burrus served aboard the blockade runner "Hansa."
>[Source(s): McElroy]

Burrus, T. J. [Note: May be same as "Thomas Burrus"]
>Pilot, Confederate States Navy. Burrus served aboard the blockade runner "Let Her Be."
>[Source(s): McElroy]

Burrus, Thomas [Note: May be same as "T. J. Burrus"]
>Pilot, Confederate States Navy. Burrus served aboard the blockade runner "Banshee."
>[Source(s): McElroy]

Burruss, Edward T. (Born in North Carolina)
>Pilot, Confederate States Navy. Burruss served He was born in North Carolina in October 1836 and appointed a Pilot in the Confederate States Navy. He served aboard the blockade runner "Let Her Rip," the CSS TALLAHASSEE (renamed CSS OLUSTEE, and later CSS CHAMELEON), Wilmington Station, North Carolina, 1864. In 1880, he resided as a Pilot with his wife Mary M., and four children, in Smithville Township, Brunswick County, North Carolina. In 1900, he resided as a watchman in Wilmington, North Carolina.
>[Source(s): McElroy; Census (N C), 1880; Census (North Carolina), 1900; Foenander]

Burton, George W.
>Confederate States Navy. Burton enlisted in the Confederate States Navy on June 15, 1864, Raleigh, North Carolina.
>(Source: Duke Papers)

Butler, William (Wayne County, North Carolina)
>Landsman, Confederate States Navy. Butler enlisted in February 1863 and served aboard the CSS ARCTIC, Cape Fear River, North Carolina, 1863, and later aboard the CSS NEUSE in Kinston, North Carolina. He applied for

a Confederate pension from Wayne County, North Carolina. His widow, Susan Mary Butler, later applied for a pension from the same county.
[Source(s): "News-Argus" [Goldsboro, North Carolina], September 10, 2008; ORN 2, 1, 278; Pensions (North Carolina); Foenander]

Butt, Hayward
Seaman, Confederate States Navy. Butt enlisted from Wilson, North Carolina in 1861, and served aboard Confederate States gun boat CSS PALMETTO STATE. His widow, Mrs. Hayward Butt, and son, Dr. Hayward Butt, resided in Wilson, North Carolina after the war.
[Source(s): McElroy]

Butt, Josiah W.
Seaman, Quartermaster, Confederate States Navy.
Per muster records, Butt served as a Seaman aboard the CSS SEA BIRD from July – November 1861. He was promoted to Quartermaster on January 13, 1862. Captured in the Battle of Elizabeth City and carried to Roanoke Island, he was paroled there on February 12, 1862 and returned to Elizabeth City. He received partial payment on February 18, 1862 at Gosport Navy Yard following the sinking of the CSS SEA BIRD at Elizabeth City on February 10, 1862. He appears on a payroll of the North Carolina Squadron for the 1st quarter of 1862 (October 23, 1861 - April 15, 1862) whereon he is listed as "on parole" as of April 15, 1862.
[Source: NCCWSP]

Byrd, Richard W.
Master's Mate, Confederate States Navy.
Appointed to the rank of Master's Mate on September 4, 1861, he served aboard the CSS BEAUFORT from September. - November 1861. Records indicate he was dismissed on December 1, 1861.
[Source: NCCWSP

Cabel, John (County unknown)
Confederate States Navy (possibly). A "John Cabel," whose grave marker is annotated with "North Carolina," is buried in the Seaman's Burial Ground, Ashley River, Charleston, SC, date of death listed as October 26, 1864.
[Source(s): SBG]

Cable, I. R. (County unknown)
Landsman, Confederate States Navy. Cable enlisted on June 10, 1864 in Raleigh, North Carolina, for the war.
[Source(s): Card File; NA, RG 45]

Cable (Coble), Jerry O. (Alamance County, North Carolina)
Landsman, Confederate States Navy. Born in North Carolina in 1843, Cable enlisted in June 1863 [another source says February 4, 1864], in Raleigh, North Carolina, for the war], and served as a Landsman aboard the CSS ARCTIC. He married about 1871 and resided, in 1880, as a wagon maker, with his wife, Frances, and son Thomas, at Gibsonville, Guilford County, North Carolina. On July 1, 1901, he applied for a Confederate pension from Alamance County, North Carolina, stating he was "in the navy service." In a subsequent application filed on July 7, 1902 at age 63, he listed his post office as Elon College, Alamance County, North Carolina. This pension, which was approved, stated he served under "Captain Poindexter" in the Gulf of Mexico, and as a "Fireman" on the blockade runner "Chicamauga" [sic]. It further indicated that he fell and his left foot was crushed by a piston rod. His occupation, in 1910, was shown as that of blacksmith in a roper shop. Cable's widow, Frances E. Cable, applied for a widow's pension from the same county.
[Source(s): Card File; Pension (North Carolina); NA, RG 45; Foenander]

Cable, John (Alamance County, North Carolina [?]))
Landsman, Confederate States Navy. Cable enlisted on December 17, 1863 in Raleigh, North Carolina, for the war. Born June 1, 1812, he died on February 6, 1878, and was buried at Shallow Ford Christian Church, Alamance County, North Carolina.
[Source(s): Card File; NA, RG 45; Stepp, "Burials"]

Cahall (Cahal), George C. [B.] (Rockingham County, North Carolina)
Seaman, Confederate States Navy. Cahall enlisted on June 15, 1864 at Camp Holmes, Raleigh, North Carolina, for the war. His pension application states his knee, hips, and shoulder were dislocated on April 6, 1865 (circumstances not explained). He filed a claim for admission to Soldier's Home [Raleigh] on June 19, 1899, at age 76, which listed his post office as Rockingham, Rockingham County, North Carolina (Approval status not shown). He was described as a farmer, 5 feet 5/12 inches in height, fair complexion, Captured and confined at Point Lookout, Maryland, until released on June 24, 1865.
[Source(s): Card File; Pensions (North Carolina); NA, RG 45]

Cahoon, Doctrine (Washington County, North Carolina)
Confederate States Navy.
[Source(s): WCL; Darden]

Cahoon (Cahoone), James (Hyde County, North Carolina)
Master's Mate, Quartermaster/Confederate States Navy. Born in Hyde County, North Carolina, Cahoon resided as a Seaman in Beaufort County, North Carolina, where he enlisted on May 10, 1861, age 26, "for the war" in Company I, 3rd Regiment, North Carolina State Troops. He transferred to the Confederate States Navy on January 29, 1862, and served as a Seaman on the CSS RALEIGH, as early as March 25, 1862 - April 1862 [Note: Source NCCWSP says he was promoted to Quartermaster on February 8, 1862, and that his name appears on a payroll of the North Carolina Squadron covering the period from February 1862 - April 15, 1862]. Source NCCWSP states Cahoon transferred to the James River Squadron on April 15, 1862 and served at Drewry's Bluff as a Quartermaster from April 1, 1863 - June 30, 1863. He served as a Master's Mate at Richmond, Virginia, November 16, 1863 – December 15, 1865.
[Source(s): Card File; North Carolina Troops, III; "Beaufort County Sailors;" ORN 2, 1, pp.301 & 322; MR, I; Foenander; NCCWSP]

Cahoon, Turner (Beaufort County, North Carolina)
Confederate States Navy. Cahoon resided and enlisted in Beaufort County, North Carolina, on November 25, 1861, at age 31, as a Private in Company C, 40th Regiment, North Carolina Troops (3rd Regiment, North Carolina Artillery). He transferred to Confederate States Navy on May 8, 1862.
[Source(s): Card File; "Beaufort County Sailors;" North Carolina Troops, I]

Cahoon, W.J. (Washington County, North Carolina)
Landsman, Confederate States Navy. Cahoon served on the floating battery, CSS ARCTIC, Cape Fear River, North Carolina, and on the steam gunboat CSS YADKIN, Wilmington, North Carolina, 1864.
[Source(s): WCL; OR (Navy), Series II, Vol. I, p.279; Darden; *ORN* 2, 1, 279 & 313]

Cahoun (Cahoon), Thomas T.
Seaman, Confederate States Navy. Cahoon served aboard the CSS ARCTIC, August 1862.
[Source(s): Foenander; ORN 1, 23, 703 and 2, 1, 276.]

Cain (Kain), James Harrison (Davie County, North Carolina)
Private, Confederate States Marine Corps [Some sources list him as a Landsman or Seaman, Confederate States Navy]. Born April 14, 1845, Cain enlisted in the Home Guard where he served for 15 months. He was enlisted into the Confederate States Navy at Plymouth, North Carolina, "by Capt. Worley" on July 27, 1864 at age 18, and served aboard the CSS ALBEMARLE until it was sunk. Source "Hasty and Winfree" states that the Cain Family file in the Davie County Library states James H. Cain and the Gunner were the only two survivors of the 60-man crew of the CSS ALBEMARLE to escape. According to the story, these two men later rigged a "torpedo" in the ALBEMARLE's gun room, which had remained above water, in order to deny the ship to the enemy. After rigging the gun room for destruction, the two swam ashore with a few possessions, including Cain's revolver. [NOTE: no extensive damage to the gun deck is readily visible on a postwar photograph of the CSS ALBEMARLE, which was raised post-war]. Source "North Carolina Troops" records indicate Cain was a member of the Confederate States Marine Corps who enlisted at Plymouth, North Carolina, on "June" 27, 1864. Per hospital muster rolls, he was attached as a patient on January 23, 1865 to General Hospital #6, Fayetteville, North Carolina, January 23-February 21, 1865 (another source gives dates of the muster rolls as February 21 and February 28, 1865), where he received a 60-day furlough on February 21, 1865 to return to his home at Clarksville, Davie County, North Carolina. A source states he served a total of nine months in the "Confederate States Navy." His pension claim filed June 24, 1926, at age 81, listing his post office as Mocksville, Davie County, North Carolina, was approved. A pension claim filed June 3, 1933 by

his widow, E. A. Cain, age 87 was also approved. Her post office was listed as Mocksville, Davie County, North Carolina. He died on August 28, 1932, and was buried at Eaton's Baptist Church, Davie County, North Carolina. His daughter was Mrs. G. M. Kirkman, Post office Box 530, Greensboro, North Carolina
[Source(s): McElroy; North Carolina Troops, Doc.# 0185, p. 2, and 0299; NA; Card File; Stepp, "Burials;" Pensions (North Carolina); Hasty and Winfree]

Calder, Samuel (Richmond County, North Carolina)
Landsman, Confederate States Navy. Calder enlisted on September 10, 1863 [another source gives the date as October 19, 1863] in Wilmington, North Carolina, in the Confederate States Navy, and served aboard the CSS ARCTIC. His name appears on a register of Confederate States Army General Military Hospital Number 4, Wilmington, North Carolina, as being admitted on December 7, 1863 with "debilitas," and returned to duty March 21, 1864. His post office was given on the register as Laurinburg, North Carolina.
[Source(s): MR, 4, p. 445; Card File; NA, RG 109; NA, RG 45; Richmond County Soldiers; Foenander]

Caldwell, M. W. (County unknown)
Landsman, Confederate States Navy. Caldwell enlisted on April 25, 1864 in Raleigh, North Carolina, for the war.
[Source(s): Card File; NA, RG 45]

Caldwell, W. L. (County unknown)
Landsman, Confederate States Navy. Caldwell enlisted on June 11, 1864 in Raleigh, North Carolina, for the war.
[Source(s): card File; NA, RG 45]

Calhoon, O. C. (County unknown)
Landsman, Confederate States Navy. Calhoon enlisted on June 8, 1864 in Raleigh, North Carolina, for the war.
[Source(s): Card File; NA, RG 45]

Cameron, Alexander Hamilton "Ham" (Moore County, North Carolina)
Private, Confederate States Marine Corps. Cameron was born on March 28, 1835 in Moore County, North Carolina. He entered service at Camp Holmes, North Carolina, near Raleigh, and was assigned to Company A, Confederate States Marine Corps. He arrived in Charleston, SC, on Sunday, November 6, 1864, with a group of North Carolina conscripts and reported aboard the CSS INDIAN CHIEF, for drill and instruction as a Marine. He served aboard the CSS CHICORA and the ironclad ram CSS COLUMBIA, in Charleston, South Carolina. Per source "McLeod, August 30, 1874," Cameron left the unit [deserted?] at Jonesboro, North Carolina, on the march to Richmond. He married Margaret Cole on November 30, 1865; and, died in Moore County, North Carolina on March 7, 1890.
[Source(s): Foenander; "Citizen News-Record," July 8, 1987; Davis, November 17, 1864]

Cameron, Francis Hawkes (Orange County, North Carolina)
First Lieutenant, Company A, Confederate States Marine Corps. Born June 1, 1838 in Hillsborough, North Carolina, he reportedly entered the United States Coast Survey in 1855 and was stationed in Brooklyn, New York, where he was at the outbreak of the war. Unofficial sources state he declined a commission in the United States Army. Running the blockade to Savannah, Georgia, he traveled to Montgomery, Alabama, and offered his services to the Confederacy. Per source "Evans," Cameron was commissioned as a Lieutenant in the Confederate States Army and served under General Braxton Bragg at Pensacola, Florida. While there, he performed the "perilous duty of blockading the channel under the guns of the Federal forts." He became violently ill in June of 1861 and returned home to recuperate. Former United States Congressman (1847-1853) and Confederate Congressman A. W. Venable (1862-1864) recommended him for a commission to President Jefferson Davis in August of 1861, referring to him as lately in the United States Coast Survey and a Master's Mate in the United States Navy. Approved, Cameron was appointed from North Carolina as a Second Lieutenant in the Confederate States Marine Corps on September 20, 1861. He joined Company A, Confederate States Marine Corps, at Savannah, Georgia, on October 2, 1861, and is reported to have served under Commodore Tattnall along the South Carolina and Georgia coasts aboard the CSS HUNTRESS, Savannah Squadron flagship CSS SAVANNAH, and the CSS FINGAL (later renamed the CSS ATLANTA), as well as having participated in the engagement at Port Royal, South Carolina, (November 1861) and other engagements. Cameron was nominated in the Confederate Senate for First Lieutenant, Confederate States Marine Corps, on December 7, 1861, confirmed on December 13, 1861, and promoted on October 10, 1862. Cameron was serving on board the CSS HUNTRESS (1861-1862) at Charleston, South Carolina, when ordered back to Savannah, Georgia, on January 15, 1862, to which he reported three days later. He accompanied his company to Camp Beall, Drewry's Bluff, James River Squadron, Virginia, in the spring of 1862, where he remained on duty until April 1965, serving as Acting Assistant Quartermaster and Acting Assistant Commissary of Subsistence

for the Marine battalion [Source "Foenander" gives dates as "1863-1864"]. He is said to have been involved in the organization of a Masonic fraternity, James River Lodge, No. 206, at Drewry's Bluff, in October 1863. He participated actively in the defeat of the Federal fleet during its attack on Drewry's Bluff and in the Seven Days campaign. In May of 1864, he helped repulse Federal General Benjamin Butler's advance on the cities of Richmond and Petersburg in support of General Grant's campaign against General Robert E. Lee's forces. In this action, Lieutenant Cameron commanded the left wing of the Confederate skirmish line. He is said to have commanded Camp Beall for several months at some point prior to its evacuation. During the retreat in April 1865, Cameron fought as part of the rear guard. Avoiding capture on April 6th, at Sailor's Creek, Cameron was involved in the Army's last battle at Appomattox Court House, Virginia, on April 9, 1865 before it was forced to yield to superior numbers and surrender. He was paroled May 13, 1865, in Richmond, Virginia. Back in his native state, he took a patriotic interest in the reformation of the North Carolina militia, in which he served as Captain of Company A, First Regiment, North Carolina State Guard from 1877 to 1878. From 1879 to 1891, Cameron served as Inspector-General with the rank of Colonel, and from 1893 to 1897 as the state's Adjutant-General with the rank of Brigadier-General. Cameron is said to have been a resident of Norfolk, Virginia, in 1882. He was in the insurance business in Richmond, Virginia, [and, per source "Evans," also in North Carolina] during the last three years of his life. He died on March 30, 1900 in Richmond, Virginia, and was buried at St. Matthew's Episcopal Church, Hillsborough, North Carolina.
[Source(s): Confederate States Marine Corps Officer Burials, Donnelly-RL, Register, McElroy; North Carolina Troops, Doc.# 0299; Gravestone Records, v. 3, p. 150; Card File; Stepp, "Burials;" Journal; OCSN; Foenander; Donnelly-ENL; Donnelly-BS; Evans; ONWR]

Cameron, J. B. (New Hanover County, North Carolina)
Confederate States Navy. Cameron's name appears on a register of Confederate States Army General Military Hospital Number 4, Wilmington, North Carolina, dated March 16, 1864, which lists his disease as "vulnus incism." Lists his post office is listed as Wilmington, New Hanover County, North Carolina.
[Source(s): Card File; NA, RG 109]

Cameron, John B. (Moore County, North Carolina) [NOTE: Same as John B. Moore?]
Confederate States Navy. Born June 5, 1845, Cameron died on May 25, 1929, and was buried in Johnson Grove Cemetery, Moore County, North Carolina.
[Source(s): Stepp, "Burials"]

Campbell, David M. (Iredell County, North Carolina)
Landsman, Confederate States Navy. Campbell enlisted on June 13, 1864, in Raleigh, North Carolina, for the war. His name appears on a roll of prisoners of war at Point Lookout, Maryland which states that he was captured at Burkeville [Virginia] on April 6, 1865, and confined at Point Lookout, Maryland, on April 14, 1865. He was released on June 24, 1865after taking the Oath of Allegiance, which gives his place of residence as Iredell County, North Carolina. Description as follows: complexion, dark; hair, dark brown; eyes, hazel; height, 6 feet ¼ inch. Campbell died on April 20, 1914 and was buried in the cemetery of Society Hill Baptist Church, Iredell County, North Carolina.
[Source(s): Card File; NA, RG 109; NA, RG 45; Stepp, "Burials"]

Campbell, William (Rutherford County, North Carolina)
Confederate States Navy. Campbell enlisted on October 14, 1863, in Wilmington, North Carolina in the Confederate States Navy.
[Source(s): MR, 4; BRGS]

Campbell, William (County unknown)
[May be the same as WILLIAM CAMPBELL, Rutherford County, North Carolina, q. v.)
Landsman, Confederate States Navy. Campbell enlisted on October 26, 1863 [Source "Foenander" lists his enlistment date as October 14, 1863], in Wilmington, North Carolina [another source says "Camp Holmes"], for the war. He served aboard the CSS ARCTIC, Cape Fear River, North Carolina, 1863, and aboard the CSS RALEIGH, in North Carolina and Virginia waters, 1864.
[Source(s): Card File; NA, RG 45; Foenander]

Cannon, B. (New Hanover County, North Carolina)
Confederate States Navy. Cannon's name appears on a register of Confederate States Army General Military Hospital Number 4, Wilmington, North Carolina, dated August 4, 1862 giving his disease as "vulnus incism." His

post office was listed as Wilmington, North Carolina.
[Source(s): Card File; NA, RG 109]

Cannon, Ezaria (County unknown)
Landsman, Confederate States Navy. Cannon enlisted on February 4, 1864, in Raleigh, North Carolina, for the war.
[Source(s): Card File; NA, RG 45]

Cannon, J. C. (County unknown)
Ordinary Seaman, Confederate States Navy. Cannon enlisted for the war on June 13, 1863, in Wilmington, North Carolina.
[Source(s): Card File; NA, RG 45]

Cannon, James W.
Seaman, Confederate States Navy. Cannon enlisted from North Carolina in 1861 and served aboard the Confederate States receiving ship CSS INDIAN CHIEF. He transferred in 1863 to the Confederate States submarine CSS HUNLEY and was subsequently drowned in Charleston Harbor.
[Source(s): McElroy; Card File]

Cannon, John (North Carolina?)
1st Class Fireman, Confederate States Navy. Cannon served aboard the wooden side-wheeled tender CSS CASWELL, Wilmington Station, North Carolina, between July 1861 and June 1862. He later served aboard the CSS ARCTIC, Cape Fear River, North Carolina, 1862 -1863.
[Source(s): Foenander]

Cannon (Gannon), John B. (New Hanover County, North Carolina)
Seaman, Confederate States Navy. Cannon served aboard the CSS NORTH CAROLINA, 1864. His name appears on a register of Confederate States Army General Military Hospital Number 4, Wilmington, North Carolina, as having been admitted on March 18, 1864 with "vulnus incism." He was returned to duty on June 17, 1864. His post office was listed as Wilmington, North Carolina.
[Source(s): Card File; NA, RG 109; Foenander]

Canter, Francis (County unknown)
Seaman, Confederate States Navy. Canter enlisted on September 29, 1863 in Wilmington, North Carolina, for the war.
[Source(s): card File; NA, RG 45]

Cardwell, John H. (Wilkes County, North Carolina)
Private, Confederate States Army//Landsman, Confederate States Navy. Cardwell resided in Wilkes County, North Carolina, where he enlisted at age 18 on November 3, 1862, for the war, as a Private in Company K, 53rd Regiment, North Carolina Troops. He was reported present on surviving company muster rolls through February 1864 and transferred to the Confederate States Navy on or about April 5, 1864. His name appears on a Roll of Prisoners of War captured in Hospitals, Richmond, Virginia dated April 3, 1865. Cardwell appears on a register of patients for Jackson Hospital, Richmond, Virginia, dated April 8, 1865. His name in the Jackson Hospital register entry for May 28, 1865, carried the remark, "Turned over to Pro. Marshal April 21, 1865." [One source in annotated with "See Company F, 52nd Regiment, North Carolina Troops," though Cardwell does not appear on that unit's rolls].
[Source(s): Card File; NA, RG 109; North Carolina Troops, XIII]

Carey, Jim
Ordinary Seaman, North Carolina Navy.
NCS WINSLOW. Slave of Master Patrick McCarrick, and one of seven African American crew members aboard the NCS WINSLOW.
[Source(s): NCS]

Carlton, Morgan (County unknown)
Landsman, Confederate States Navy. Carlton enlisted on September 28, 1863, at Camp Holmes [near Raleigh, North Carolina], for the war.
[Source(s): Card File; NA, RG 45]

Carman, Jacob C. (North Carolina?)
>Ordinary Seaman, Confederate States Navy. Carman served aboard the CSS NORTH CAROLINA, Cape Fear River, North Carolina, 1864.
>[Source(s): Foenander]

Carmine(s), Joseph (Chowan County, North Carolina)
>Private, Confederate States Army//Confederate States Navy. Carmine resided in Chowan County, North Carolina, where he enlisted at age 20 on May 18, 1861 (May 10, 1861 per MR) for the war in Company A, 1st Regiment, North Carolina State Troops. He was per MRs listed as present of accounted for until he transferred to the Confederate States Navy on February 1, 1862. He served as an Ordinary Seaman aboard the CSS VIRGINIA, Hampton Roads, Virginia, 1862.
>[Source(s): Card File; MR, I; North Carolina Troops, III; Foenander]

Carney, John C. (New Hanover County, North Carolina)
>Confederate States Navy//Private, Confederate States Army. Carney served aboard the Confederate States Steamer CSS NORTH CAROLINA. Special Order #164/11, Adjutant & Inspector General's Office, states that he was to be transferred to Company K, ___ N. C., Artillery [Source "North Carolina Troops, I" lists a "John N. Carney" [q.v.] who enlisted in Company K, 10th Regiment, North Carolina Troops (1st Regiment, North Carolina Artillery) on July 19, 1863, for the war, from New Hanover County, North Carolina.
>[Source(s): Card File; NA, RG 109; North Carolina Troops, I]

Carney, John N. (New Hanover County, North Carolina)
>Ordinary Seaman, Confederate States Navy. Carney enlisted on June 5, 1863, in Wilmington, North Carolina, for the war. He deserted on October 26, 1863.
>[Source(s): Card File; NA, RG 45; North Carolina Troops, I]

Carpenter, Joseph (Cleveland County, North Carolina)
>Confederate States Navy. Carpenter enlisted on August 27, 1863, in Wilmington, North Carolina in the Confederate States Navy.
>[Source(s): MR, 4; BRGS]

Carpenter, Joseph (County unknown)
>Landsman, Confederate States Navy. Carpenter enlisted on October 26, 1863 [another source says October 21, 1863 at Camp Holmes] in Wilmington, North Carolina, for the war. He served aboard CSS ARCTIC, 1863.
>[Source(s): Card File; NA, RG 45; Foenander]

Carr, Samuel M. (Franklin County, North Carolina)
>Confederate States Army//"Private," Confederate States Navy. Carr was born in Franklin County, North Carolina and resided in Wake County as a carpenter. He enlisted in Wake County on March 1, 1862 at age 25 in Company C, 47th Regiment, North Carolina Troops. He was reported in the hospital at Petersburg, Virginia during January – February 1863, returning to duty between March – April 1863. He was captured at Gettysburg between July 3 – 5, 1863 and was hospitalized at Gettysburg with an unspecified illness or wound. He was sent as a prisoner of war to Fort Delaware prison arriving there on or about July 9, 1863. Carr was released on or about March 18, 1864 after taking the Oath of Allegiance and joining the United Navy. Source "Card File" lists him as having Confederate Naval service.
>[Source(s): Card File; NCT, Vol. XI]

Carrence, John J.
>Seaman, North Carolina Navy.
>Served as a Seaman aboard the NCS SEA BIRD per the ship's muster roll covering July - November 1861. He transferred from the NCS FORREST on September 30, 1861 [NOTE: there is no reference to when he transferred to the NCS FORREST or to what vessel or station he went upon leaving the NCS FORREST]. His name appears on North Carolina Squadron payroll for the 1st quarter of 1862. He was discharged on December 1, 1861
>[Source: NCCWSP]

Carroll, John W. (County unknown)
>Landsman, Confederate States Navy. Carroll enlisted on April 11, 1864, in Kinston, North Carolina, for three years or the war. May be the "J. W. Carroll" that served aboard the CSS NEUSE as of March – April 1864.
>[Source(s): Card File; NA, RG 45; NEUSE Roster; CMACSSN]

Carroll, Page C. (Orange County, North Carolina)
    Confederate States Navy. Born in North Carolina about 1834, the son of Alsey and Betsy Carroll, Page C. Carroll resided as a farm laborer in Orange County, North Carolina, in 1860. Enlisting on August 6, 1863, in Wilmington, North Carolina, Carroll served as an Ordinary Seaman aboard the CSS ARCTIC in 1863. His name appears on Registers of Confederate States Army General Military Hospital Number 4, Wilmington, North Carolina, as being admitted on September 4, 1863, with "debility." His post office was given as "Universe [sic][University] Station, North Carolina" [NOTE: probably Chapel Hill, North Carolina]
    [Source(s): MR, 4, p. 445; Card File; NA, RG 109; Foenander; Census (North Carolina), 1860]

Carroll, Thomas (New Hanover County, North Carolina)
    Second Class Fireman, Confederate States Navy. Carroll served aboard the CSS CASWELL, Wilmington Station, North Carolina, sometime between July 1861 and June 1862. He later served aboard the CSS ARCTIC, Cape Fear River, North Carolina, in 1863. In 1864, he was a 1st Class Fireman on the ironclad sloop CSS NORTH CAROLINA, Cape Fear River, North Carolina. His name appears on a register of Confederate States Army General Military Hospital Number 4, Wilmington, North Carolina, dated July 29, 1862, which gives his disease as "febris remit," and his post office as Wilmington, North Carolina.
    [Source(s): Card File; NA, RG 109; Foenander]

Carson, Andrew J. (Pasquotank County, North Carolina)
    Private, Confederate States Army//Ordinary Seaman, Seaman, Confederate States Navy. Born in Norfolk, Virginia, Carson was a machinist by occupation prior to enlisting in Pasquotank County, North Carolina, at age 23, on May 4, 1861, as a Private in Company L, 17th Regiment, North Carolina Troops (1st Organization). He was present or accounted for until transferred to the Confederate States Navy on or about October 14, 1861. He served as an Ordinary Seaman, later promoted to Seaman, aboard the CSS CURLEW circa November 20, 1861 and appears on a North Carolina Squadron payroll for the period December 8, 1861 - January 3, 1862.
    [Source(s): Card File; North Carolina Troops, VI; NCCWSP]

Carter, Francis
    Confederate States Navy. Carter enlisted in Wilmington, North Carolina in the Confederate States Navy.
    [Source(s): MR, IV, 445]

Carter, James M. (Wayne County, North Carolina)
    Confederate States Navy. A claim for pension was filed on June 18, 1901, by Carter's widow, Julia A. Carter, age 62. It listed her post office as Goldsboro, Wayne County, North Carolina. The pension application states he enlisted in Captain Ingraham's company and served with him at Battery Brooke on the James River in Virginia. It further stated that the company was commanded by "St. B…(?)" at the end of the war.
    [Source(s): Card File; Pensions (North Carolina)]

Carter, Jesse A. (Warren County, North Carolina)
    Landsman, Confederate States Navy. Born on January 3, 1842, Carter enlisted on March 30, 1864, in Raleigh, North Carolina, for the war [another source says he "appears on a list of conscripts 'in yard at Halifax, June 9, 1864'"]. Yet, another source says he enlisted March 27, 1864 at Camp Holmes [near Raleigh, North Carolina] from Colonel Johnson's 34th Regiment, North Carolina Militia, Halifax County, North Carolina. Description as follows: age, 20; eyes, hazel; hair, dark; complexion, fair; height, 5 feet 10 inches; place of birth, Warren County, North Carolina; occupation, farmer. He is said to have served as a Landsman aboard the CSS ALBEMARLE. Carter died on August 10, 1914 (?).
    [Source(s): Card File; NA, RG 45; Roster, 34th Regiment, North Carolina Militia]

Carter, , Jonathan Hanby (Surry County, North Carolina)
    Lieutenant, Confederate States Navy. Born near Mt. Airy, Stokes County, North Carolina, on January 1, 1823, Carter was appointed to the naval school that became the United States Naval Academy as a Midshipman on March 12, 1840. He graduated as a Passed Midshipman on July 11, 1846, number 46 of 47 in the first graduating class of the Naval Academy. He was detailed upon graduation to special duty at the Naval Observatory, Georgetown, DC (where one source states "ill feelings" developed between him and Secretary of War Jefferson Davis over some unexplained "social affair"). Carter served during the Mexican War, for which his widow Henrietta G. Tompkins Carter later received a small pension ($8.00 a month) from the United States Government. He served on Commodore Perry's expedition to Japan, and later with Commander Cadwalader Ringgold's expedition to map the Bering Straits and western Pacific for the whaling industry. Carter received promotion to "Master" on March 1, 1855 and to Lieutenant on September 14, 1855. He resigned as Lieutenant, United States Navy, after 21 years of service, on April 25, 1861.

He was appointed a First Lieutenant in the Confederate States Navy from North Carolina sometime after May of 1861 [Source "Fold3, USN Resignees" gives date as April 27, 1861]. His initial duties were as an officer on the staff of Major General Leonidas Polk, and later as Aide-de-Camp to General John C. Pemberton with specific duty in the area of naval construction. Promoted to First Lieutenant on October 23, 1862, to rank from October 2, 1862, Carter was subsequently promoted to First Lieutenant Provisional Navy, June 2, 1864, to rank from January 6, 1864. He served on the CSS GENERAL POLK, New Orleans Station, Mississippi defenses, 1861 – 1862, and on the Jackson Station, 1862. He supervised construction of ironclads, including the CSS MISSOURI, which he later commanded and surrendered. He served on the Red River defenses, 1863 – 1865. Another source states he was a "First Lieutenant, commanding the defences [sic] of La in 1863-65." Carter was assigned to some unspecified special duty in 1864 and surrendered on May 26, 1865 [Source "Margaret Carter" states he surrendered with the CSS MISSOURI at Galveston, Texas, on June 3, 1865]. Paroled on June 7, 1865, he died on March 7, 1884 at Edgefield Courthouse, South Carolina, and is buried in the local Baptist church cemetery [Another source erroneously states Shirley, Virginia, 1887]. Physical description: "Approximately" 5 feet 6 inches tall, light hair, grey eyes, and fair complexion.
[Source(s): McElroy; Card File; "Margaret Carter;" Journal; ONWR; Fold3, USN Resignees]

Carter, Michael (Sampson County, North Carolina)
Confederate States Navy. Carter enlisted at age 26 on March 11, 1862 [date given as November 11, 1862, per source "North Carolina Troops, I"] in 2nd Company A, 36th Regiment, North Carolina Troops (2nd Regiment, North Carolina Artillery). He transferred to the Confederate States Navy in February 1863. Carter appears on a Roll of Prisoners of War paroled at Gainesville, Alabama, June 30, 1865, giving place of residence as NORTH CAROLINA
[Source(s): Card File; NA, RG 109; MR, II; North Carolina Troops, I; Foenander]

Carter, Samuel H. (Randolph County, North Carolina)
Private, Confederate States Army//Landsman, Confederate States Navy. Carter resided in Randolph County, North Carolina, where he enlisted at age 23 on June 18, 1861, as a Private in Company L, 22nd Regiment, North Carolina Troops. Records indicate he had a "finger shot off by accident" at Fredericksburg, Virginia, August 28, 1861, and that he returned to duty on an unspecified date. Carter was listed as a deserter on September 15, 1863; however, he apparently returned to duty on an unspecified date. He transferred to the Confederate States Navy on or about April 3, 1864, per Special Order No. 89, and served aboard the CSS PATRICK HENRY. Born June 19, 1837, Carter died on February 12, 1917, and was buried at Oakgrove Methodist Church, Randolph County, North Carolina.
[Source(s): Card File; Stepp, "Burials;" North Carolina Troops, VII; Foenander]

Cartwill, J. (Wilkes County, North Carolina)
"Private," Confederate States Navy. Cartwill's name appears as a signature to an Oath of Allegiance to the United States subscribed and sworn to at Newport News, Virginia, on June 14, 1865. Place of residence given on Oath as Wilkes County, North Carolina. Description as follows: complexion, fair; hair, light; eyes, blue; height, 5 feet 9 inches. Oath also carries the remark: "Captured Richmond April 3."
[Source(s): Card File; NA, RG 109]

Cartwright, Jesse (Camden County, North Carolina)
Confederate States Army //Seaman, Confederate States Navy// Confederate States Army. Cartwright was born circa 1837 in Camden County, North Carolina and lived there as a farmer in 1860. Sources "Card File" and "NCT, Vol. XV" reference his having served in Company D, 1st Regiment, North Carolina Infantry (Union), United States Army. His name appears on the rolls of Company C, 68th Regiment, North Carolina Troops, Confederate States Army, stating he enlisted from Camden County, North Carolina on August 31, 1863 for the war. Cartwright's name appears on a bounty payroll list dated February 11, 1864. Cartwright transferred to the Confederate States Navy on May 10, 1864. However, Clothing Lists, Small Stores, and Payroll records quoted in source NCCWSP indicate he served as a Seaman aboard the CSS RALEIGH circa September 2, 1861 through at least the first quarter of 1862.
[Source(s): Card File; NCCWSP; NCT, Vols. III and XV]

Casey [Caldwell], Caswell (Currituck County, North Carolina)
Private, Confederate States Army//Landsman, Ordinary Seaman, North Carolina Navy (later, Confederate States Navy). Casey was born in Norfolk, Virginia, and worked as mechanic until he enlisted at age 17 in Currituck County, North Carolina, on May 13, 1861 as a Private in Company E, 17th Regiment, North Carolina Troops (1st organization). He was present or accounted for until he transferred to the North Carolina Navy (later, Confederate States Navy) prior to July 28, 1861. Records quoted by source NCCWSP indicate he served as a Landsman aboard the CSS FANNY from circa October 8, 1861 through December 12, 1861. Casey received a partial payment on February 13, 1862 at Gosport following the burning of the FANNY at Elizabeth City, North Carolina on February

10, 1862. His name appears on a payroll for the North Carolina Squadron covering the period from December 1, 1861 through 28 February 28, 1862. Payroll records indicate he served as an Ordinary Seaman aboard the CSS NANSEMOND with the James River Squadron from at least October 7, 1863 through December 15, 1863.
[Source(s): Card File; North Carolina Troops, VI; NCCWSP]

Casey, J. W. (Sampson County, North Carolina)
Confederate States Army//Confederate States Navy. Casey enlisted in the Confederate States Army on May 9, 1861. He transferred to the Confederate States Navy in May 1862.
[Source(s): MR, III]

Casey, James W. (Craven County, North Carolina)
Private, Confederate States Army//Confederate States Navy. Casey was born in Craven County, North Carolina, and resided as a carpenter in Sampson County, North Carolina, where he enlisted on May 9, 1861, at age 22, as a Private in Company F, 20th Regiment, North Carolina Troops. He was present or accounted for until he transferred to the Confederate Navy Department at Wilmington, May 15, 1862.
[Source(s): Foenander; MR, II; North Carolina Troops, VI]

Cashwell, G. [Same as "Giles Cashwell"]
Landsman, Confederate States Navy. Cashwell served aboard the CSS ARCTIC, Cape Fear River, North Carolina, 1863.
[Source(s): Foenander; ORN 2, 1, 278]

Cashwell, Giles (County unknown)
Landsman, Confederate States Navy. Cashwell enlisted on February 4, 1864 in Raleigh, North Carolina, for the war. A "J. Cashwell," whose headstone is annotated with "North Carolina Naval Hospital," is buried in the Seaman's Burial Ground, Ashley River, Charleston, SC, date of death listed as November 17, 1864.
[Source(s): Card File; NA, RG 45]

Cassidy (Cassiday), Henry C. (New Hanover County, North Carolina)
Private, Confederate States Army//Confederate States Navy. Cassidy enlisted at age 18 as a Private on November 9, 1861, in New Hanover County, North Carolina, in Company I, 18th Regiment, North Carolina Troops. He was listed as present or accounted for until "detached to work on gunboats" at Wilmington, North Carolina, on May 1, 1862. Source "MR, II" states he transferred to Confederate States Navy in 1863. A company muster roll dated January-February 1864 states that he "deserted and ran the blockade to Nassau."
[Source(s): MR, II; North Carolina Troops, VI]

Casy, Clarence
Passed Midshipman, Confederate States Navy. Casy was wounded slightly in the right leg at Fort Fisher, December 24, 1864.
[Source(s): Card File; "Daily Confed." (1/2/65)]

Caudle, D. F. (Yadkin County, North Carolina)
Confederate States Navy. Caudle enlisted on July 19, 1863 in Wilmington, North Carolina in the Confederate States Navy.
[Source(s): MR, 4, p. 445; Casstevens]

Cauler, Samuel (County unknown)
Confederate States Navy. Cauler enlisted on October 19, 1863 at Camp Holmes [near Raleigh, North Carolina].
[Source(s): Card File; NA, RG 45]

Cecil, H. H. [North Carolina??? Same as "William H. Cecil" (?) q.v.]
Landsman, Confederate States Navy. Cecil served aboard the steam gunboat CSS Yadkin, Wilmington, North Carolina, 1864.
[Source(s): Foenander; ORN 2, 1, 313]

Cecil, William H. (County unknown)
Landsman, Confederate States Navy. Cecil enlisted on March 1, 1864 in Raleigh, North Carolina, for the war.
[Source(s): Card File; NA, RG 45]

Certain [Centane], Edward S. [G?] (New Hanover County, North Carolina)
Seaman, Confederate States Navy. Born in Craven County, North Carolina, about 1843, Certain enlisted in New Hanover Company, North Carolina, on July 3, 1861, as a Private in Company E, 10th Regiment, North Carolina Troops (1st Regiment, North Carolina Artillery). He transferred to the Confederate States Navy on May 5, 1862 and served as an Ordinary Seaman, CSS ARCTIC, and as a crewman, CSS NORTH CAROLINA, Wilmington, North Carolina, Station, 1862-1864. Certain appears on a Roll of Prisoners of War at Point Lookout, Maryland, which states that he was captured near Fayetteville, North Carolina, March 10, 1865 and confined at Point Lookout, Maryland, on March 30, 1865. He was released on May 15, 1865 after taking the Oath of Allegiance to the United States on which his place of residence was given as Wilmington, North Carolina. Occupation: Seaman.
[Source(s): MR, 4, p. 443; Card File; NA, RG 109; Foenander; North Carolina Troops, I; ORN, 1 & 2; St. Amand; Census (NC), 1860; Foenander]

Cervantes (Servantes), Antonio
North Carolina Navy.
Cervantes was a crewman aboard the prize "Transit" captured by NCS WINSLOW. He was pressed into North Carolina Navy service at New Bern by Lieutenant Commanding Thomas Crossan, North Carolina Navy. His name appears on the July - November 1861 muster roll of NCS SEA BIRD as an Ordinary Seaman. Per the ship's February 20, 1862 "Overcoat List," Cervantes was billed for an overcoat after his discharge on January 4, 1862.
[Source: NCCWSP]

Chadwick, Samuel B., Jr. (Carteret County, North Carolina)
Confederate States Army//Confederate States Navy. Chadwick resided as a mariner prior to enlisting in Company A, 1st Battalion, North Carolina Heavy Artillery in Carteret County, North Carolina, at age 25, on June 10, 1861, for the war. On parole after his capture at Fort Macon, North Carolina, on April 26, 1862, he was exchanged in August 1862. Chadwick was detailed for service on the blockade runner "Kate" on November 11, 1862. He was listed as absent on detailed service through May-June 1863 when he was reported as a deserter.
[Source(s): North Carolina Troops, I]

Chalk, William (Pasquotank County, North Carolina)
Ordinary Seaman, North Carolina Navy (?), Confederate States Navy. Chalk was born in North Carolina circa 1820 and resided in Pasquotank County as a wheelwright as of 1860. He served aboard the CSS BEAUFORT from at least January 16, 1862 through March 1862. On February 13, 1862 he received a partial pay at the Gosport Navy Yard in Norfolk, Virginia following the Battle of Elizabeth City on February 10, 1862. He served with the North Carolina Squadron from at least January 6, 1862 through April 15, 1862, and with the James River Squadron on April 15, 1862.
[Source(s): Census (NC), 1860; NCCWSP]

Chamberlain, Edward
Acting Master, North Carolina Navy.
Chamberlain served as an Acting Master aboard the CSS JUNALUSKA [per ship's muster roll]. His name appears on a CSS JUNALUSKA payroll covering the June 18, 1861 - August 20, 1861.
[Source: NCCWSP; North Carolina Archives]

Chambers, William H.
Private, Confederate States Army//Seaman, North Carolina Navy, Confederate States Navy.
Chambers was born in Perquimans County, North Carolina where he lived as a farmer prior to enlisting there as a Private in Company I, 17th Regiment, North Carolina Troops at age 20 on May 8, 1861. He transferred to North Carolina Navy (later, Confederate States Navy) prior to July 30, 1861. He shipped for one year as a Seaman aboard the NCS RALEIGH on August 31, 1861 where he served from that date until at least April 1862. His name appears on the North Carolina Squadron payroll covering the 1st quarter of 1862 and a subsequent one covering the period from February 21, 1862 - April 15, 1862. He transferred to the James River Squadron on April 15, 1862.
[Source: NCCWSP]

Chambers, W. H. (Perquimens County, North Carolina)
Private, Confederate States Army//Confederate States Navy. Born in Perquimens County, North Carolina, Chambers lived there as a sailor prior to enlisting at age 36 on June 1, 1861 as a Private in Company I, 17th Regiment, North Carolina Troops (1st Organization). He is listed as present or accounted for until he transferred to the Confederate States Navy prior to July 30, 1861, where he served as a Seaman aboard the CSS RALEIGH.
[Source(s): Card File; North Carolina Troops, XIV; Foenander]

Chambers, William H. (Perquimans County, North Carolina)
Seaman, Confederate States Navy. Chambers was born in Perquimans County, North Carolina circa 1841, where he lived as a farmer prior to enlisting at age 20 as a Private in Company I, 17th North Carolina Regiment (1st organization) on May 8, 1861. He transferred to the Confederate States Navy prior to July 30, 1861, shipping for 1 year aboard the CSS RALEIGH on August 31, 1861. He served as a Seaman aboard the RALEIGH from at least September 1861 through April 1862. Chambers' name appears on a payroll of the North Carolina Squadron covering the period from February 21, 1862 through April 15, 1862 at which time he transferred to the James River Squadron.
[Source: NCCWSP]

Chamblee, William H. (Wake County, North Carolina)
Private, Confederate States Army//Confederate States Navy. Born Wake County, North Carolina, Chamblee resided there as a farmer until he enlisted in Company K, 14th Regiment, North Carolina Troops, at age 21, at Camp Bragg, Virginia, on June 24, 1861. He was mustered as a Private and promoted to Corporal on April 26, 1862 but reduced to ranks on July 1, 1862. Chamblee was listed as present or accounted for until wounded and captured at Chancellorsville, May 1-3, 1863. He was paroled on or about June 30, 1863 and rejoined his company prior to January 1, 1864. Chamblee was present or accounted for until he transferred to the Confederate States Navy on or about April 5, 1864.
[Source(s): Card File; North Carolina Troops, Vol. V]

Chapman, John (Burke County, North Carolina)
Seaman [Landsman], Confederate States Navy. Born on September 27, 1836, Chapman enlisted on January 15, 1863 at Wilmington, North Carolina, for three years or the war; died August 27, 1927, buried Salem Methodist Church, Burke County, North Carolina.
[Source(s): Card File; NA, RG 45; Stepp, "Burials"]

Chapman, John (Beaufort County, North Carolina) [NOTE: May be same a John Chapman, Craven County, NC, q.v.]
Corporal, Confederate States Army//Confederate States Navy. Born in New York, Chapman resided in Beaufort County, North Carolina, as a Seaman where he enlisted at age 24 on May 10, 1861 [MR, I states May 16, 1861], as a Private in Company I, 3rd Regiment, North Carolina State Troops. Mustered in as a Private, he was promoted to Corporal in November-December 1862. He transferred to the Confederate States Navy on January 29, 1862.
[North Carolina Troops, III; "Beaufort County Sailors;" MR, I; Foenander; North Carolina Troops, XIV]

Chapman, John (Craven County, North Carolina) [NOTE: May be same a John Chapman, Beaufort Company, NC, q.v.]
Private, Confederate States Army//Confederate States Navy. Born in New York, Chapman was a pre-war sailor residing and enlisting in Craven County, North Carolina, on February 9, 1862, at age 24, as a Private, Company C, 61st Regiment North Carolina Troops. He was promoted to Corporal sometime in November or December 1862 and transferred to the Confederate States Navy on January 16, 1863 (see previous entry, which may be the same person).
[Source(s): North Carolina Troops, XIV; Foenander]

Chapman, John [NOTE: May be same as either the John Chapman of Beaufort County, or the John Chapman from Craven County, North Carolina, q.v.]
Seaman, Confederate States Navy. Chapman served on the CSS ARCTIC, Cape Fear River, North Carolina, 1863.
[Source(s): Foenander; MR, I]

Cheatham, James (Alamance County, North Carolina)
Landsman, Confederate States Navy. Cheatham enlisted on October 24, 1863 in Wilmington, North Carolina, for three years or the war. Other sources give his enlistment as October 29, 1863 at Camp Holmes (near Raleigh, North Carolina), and November 1, 1863 in Wilmington.
[Source(s): MR, 4, p. 445; Card File; NA, RG 45]

Cheek, James M. (Harnett County, North Carolina)
Confederate States Army//Confederate States Navy. Cheek enlisted in Company A, 1st Battalion, North Carolina Artillery, in New Hanover County, North Carolina, on May 13, 1862, for the war. He was detailed in the Engineer Department at Wilmington on March 23, 1863 and attached to a gunboat on May 6, 1863. Cheek died in Wilmington, North Carolina on July 9, 1864 of disease.
[Source(s): North Carolina Troops, I]

Cherry, E. S. (Beaufort County, North Carolina)
Private, Confederate States Marine Corps. [Listed on National Archives records as "Navy Batt. or Marine Corps"].

Cherry's name appears on a roll of Prisoners of War at Newport News, Virginia, which states that he was captured on April 6, 1865, on the South Side Railroad, "near Farmville, Virginia." He was confined at Newport News, Virginia, on April 16, 1865. His Oath of Allegiance to the United States was subscribed and sworn to at Newport News, Virginia, on June 30, 1865, giving his residence as Beaufort County, North Carolina. Description: Complexion light; hair dark; eyes black; height 5 feet 6 inches.
[Source(s): North Carolina Troops, Doc. # 0185, p. 1; NA; Card File]

Childs, Charles (County unknown)
Ordinary Seaman, Confederate States Navy. Childs enlisted on December 21, 1863 in Raleigh, North Carolina, for the war.
[Source(s): Card File; NA, RG 45]

Childs, Charles C.
Landsman, Confederate States Navy. Childs served aboard the CSS ARCTIC, Cape Fear River, North Carolina, 1863. In 1864, he served as an Ordinary Seaman aboard the CSS NORTH CAROLINA, Cape Fear River, North Carolina [NOTE: May be same as "Charles Childs," q.v.].
[Source(s): Foenander; ORN 2, 1, 277, 294 & 295]

Chinnis, Samuel R. (Brunswick County, North Carolina)
Lieutenant, Confederate States Army//First Lieutenant, Confederate States Navy. Chinnis was born in Brunswick County, North Carolina, and resided in Columbus County, North Carolina as a farmer prior to enlistment at age 31. He was appointed a First Lieutenant in Company K, 51st Regiment, North Carolina Troops on March 22, 1862. He was present or accounted for until July-August 1862 when he was reported absent sick. Chinnis rejoined the company in November-December 1862 and was present or accounted for until he resigned on September 15, 1863 in order to "join the Navy." He was admitted into Confederate General Hospital No. 4, Wilmington, North Carolina on September 7, 1863 with "Hemmord" and assigned to ward/bed number 8/221 and listing his post office as "Wilmington." He was discharged on September 18, 1863. His resignation was accepted on October 1, 1863. Source "North Carolina Troops, XII" mentioned no service in the Confederate States Navy.
[Source(s): Card File; North Carolina Troops, XII; Hosp. (No. 4), Wilm.]

Churton, William (County unknown)
Seaman, Confederate States Navy. Churton enlisted on June 13, 1863 in Wilmington, North Carolina, for the war.
[Source(s): Card File; NA, RG 45]

Claiborne, George Weldon (North Carolina)
Assistant Surgeon, Confederate States Navy. Claiborne was born in and appointed from North Carolina as Assistant Surgeon for the war on July 15, 1863 by the Confederate Congress [another source gives the date as August 21, 1863], and served on the Richmond Station, 1863. He was commissioned Assistant Surgeon for the war, January 7, 1864, to rank from August 31, 1863. Claiborne served aboard the partial ironclad, CSS Huntsville ["CSS HUNTERSVILLE"?], Mobile Squadron, Alabama, 1863-1864. He was appointed Assistant Surgeon, Provisional Navy, on June 2, 1864. He surrendered at Mobile, Alabama, and was paroled on May 10, 1865.
[Source(s): Register, McElroy; Card File; Foenander; ONWR; Register]

Claiborne, Welborne [Weldon] G. [May be same as Claiborne, George W.]
Assistant Surgeon, Confederate States Navy. Claiborne enlisted in 1863 from North Carolina and was commissioned by the Confederate States Congress.
[Source(s): Card File]

Clanahan, A. (North Carolina?) (May be same as "A. McClanahan/McClennehan" q.v.)
Confederate States Navy. Name appears on the March-October 1864 roster of the CSS NEUSE.
[Source: CMACSSN]

Clapp, Anderson (Alamance County, North Carolina)
Private, Confederate States Army//Confederate States Navy. The son of Tobias and Peggy Clapp, and a pre-war farmer, Clapp married in 1854. He enlisted there at age 32 on February 28, 1862 in Company K, 47th Regiment, North Carolina Troops. He was reported as present January-March 1864 and transferred to the Confederate States Navy on or about April 3, 1864. He resided with his wife, Lucinda, in Alamance County, in 1910. [Source(s): S.O. # 89; North Carolina Troops, XI; Foenander; Card File; Census (North Carolina), 1850 and 1910]

Clapp, Isaac (Alamance County, North Carolina)
Private, Confederate States Army//Landsman, Confederate States Navy. Born in Alamance County, North Carolina, Clapp lived there as a farmer until he enlisted in Alamance County on July 17, 1862, at age 22, as a Private in Company F, 53rd Regiment, North Carolina Troops. He was reported present in September 1862-February 1863. He was captured at Gettysburg, Pennsylvania, on or about July 4 or 5, 1863, and confined at Fort Delaware, Delaware, on or about July 9, 1863. Paroled at Fort Delaware on July 30, 1863, he was received at City Point, Virginia, on August 1, 1863, for exchange. He was received at City Point, Virginia, August 1, 1863, for exchange. Clapp transferred to the Confederate States Navy on April 23, 1864 and served as a Landsman on the CSS VIRGINIA II, 1864-1865. Records of the Federal Provost Marshal indicate that he was paroled at Greensboro on May 24, 1865, giving his unit as Company F, 53rd Regiment, North Carolina Troops.
[Source(s): Foenander; Card File; North Carolina Troops XIII; ORN 2, 1, 311]

Clapp, J. (North Carolina?) [NOTE: May be same as "J. Clapp" of Guilford County, q.v.] Landsman, Confederate States Navy. Clapp served aboard the CSS ARCTIC, Cape Fear River, North Carolina, 1863.
[Source(s): Foenander; ORN 2, 1, 277]

Clapp, J. (Guilford County, North Carolina) [NOTE: May be same as "J. Clapp" CSS ARCTIC, q.v.]
Landsman, Confederate States Navy. Clapp enlisted in the Confederate States Navy on October 16, 1863 in Wilmington, North Carolina. Another source states he enlisted October 19, 1863 at Camp Holmes [near Raleigh, North Carolina]. Still another source says he enlisted October 19, 1863 at Wilmington, North Carolina, for the war.
[Source(s): MR, 4, p. 445; Card File; NA, RG 45]

Clapp (Clap), William (Moore County, North Carolina)
Private, Confederate States Marine Corps. A resident of Moore County, North Carolina, Clapp was sent to Camp Holmes, near Raleigh, North Carolina, where he received instruction for a short time, and was then sent to Charleston where he served in the Confederate States Marine Corps. He served aboard the CSS INDIAN CHIEF, for further drill and instruction as a Marine. He later served aboard the CSS CHICORA, Charleston Station. A letter of James C. Davis, November 17, 1864, states the group from Camp Holmes, of which "Clap (Clapp)" was a part, arrived aboard the CSS INDIAN CHIEF, Charleston, SC, on Sunday, November 6, 1864, and was designated to serve aboard the ironclad CSS CHICORA.
[Source(s): Davis, November 17, 1864; Foenander]

Clark, Henry E. (County unknown)
Landsman, Confederate States Navy. Clark enlisted on May 3, 1864 in Raleigh, North Carolina, for the war.
[Source(s): Card File; NA, RG 45]

Clark, James D. (Bertie County, North Carolina)
Confederate States Navy. "Company C (?)." Clark filed a claim for a pension on November 2, 1921 at age 82, listing his post office as Colerain, Bertie County, North Carolina. The pension request was approved. His widow Magnolia Clark, age 60, whom he married prior to 1880, filed her initial pension request in 1925 and a claim for increase in pension on August 6, 1936. She listed her post office as Windsor, North Carolina. Approval status not shown.
[Source(s): Card File; Pensions (North Carolina); Foenander]

Clark, Nat (County unknown)
Landsman, Confederate States Navy. Clark enlisted on April 25, 1864 at Halifax or Plymouth, North Carolina, for the war.
[Source(s): Card File; NA, RG 45]

Clark, William (County unknown)
Landsman, Confederate States Navy. Clark enlisted on September 28, 1863 at Camp Holmes [near Raleigh, North Carolina] for the war.
[Source(s): Card File; NA, RG 45]

Clark, William H. W. (Barbados//Pasquotank County, North Carolina)
Private, Confederate States Army//Confederate States Navy. Born in Bridgetown, Barbados, Clark enlisted in Pasquotank Company, North Carolina, at age 21 on May 4, 1861 in Company L, 17th Regiment, North Carolina Troops (1st Organization). He was present or accounted for until he transferred to the Confederate States Navy on

October 4, 1861. He served as a Seaman aboard the CSS CURLEW from circa October 4, 1861 through the first quarter of 1862. Clark appears on a payroll record ending March 31, 1862 of the receiving ship CSS UNITED STATES.
[Source(s): Card File; North Carolina Troops, VI]; NCCWSP

Class (Claus?), William (County unknown)
Landsman, Confederate States Navy. Class enlisted June 10, 1864 in Raleigh, North Carolina, for the war.
[Source(s): Card File; NA, RG 45]

Clayton, Daniel (Stanly County, North Carolina)
Landsman, Confederate States Navy. Clayton enlisted in the Confederate States Navy on August 24, 1863 in Wilmington, North Carolina. Another source states he enlisted on September 11, 1863 at Camp Holmes [near Raleigh, North Carolina] for the war. Still another source states he enlisted on September 22, 1863 in Wilmington, North Carolina, for the war.
[Source(s): MR, 4, p. 445; Card File; NA, RG 45]

Clayton, James (Duplin County, North Carolina)
Private, Confederate States Army//Confederate States Navy. Born in England, Clayton resided in Duplin County, North Carolina, as a sailor, until he enlisted as a substitute in New Hanover County, North Carolina, on July 6, 1862, at age 36, as a Private in Company G, 61st Regiment, North Carolina Troops. He was reported sick in the hospital at Wilson, North Carolina on December 17,1862 and transferred to the Confederate States Navy on February 17, 1863 where he served as a Seaman on board the CSS ARCTIC in 1863.
[Source(s): Foenander; North Carolina Troops XIV; ORN 2, 1, 276]

Clayton, James (Stanly County, North Carolina)
1st Class Fireman [Landsman], Confederate States Navy. Clayton enlisted in the Confederate States Navy on August 24, 1863 in Wilmington, North Carolina. Another source states he enlisted on January 21, 1863 in Wilmington, North Carolina, for three years or the war, while another source states he enlisted on September 22, 1863 in Wilmington, North Carolina, for the war. A "James Clayton" enlisted on September 11, 1863 at Camp Holmes [near Raleigh, North Carolina] for the war. He died on June 1, 1864, and was buried in Oakdale Cemetery, in the Confederate mass grave, Wilmington, New Hanover County, North Carolina. SEE Company G, 61st Regiment, North Carolina Troops.
[Source(s): MR, 4, p. 445; Card File; NA, RG 45; Stepp, "Burials"]

Clayton, R. H. (County unknown)
Ordinary Seaman, Confederate States Navy. Clayton enlisted on April 12, 1864 in Kinston, North Carolina, for three years or the war. Served aboard the CSS NEUSE as of the ship's March – October 1864 muster rolls.
[Source(s): Card File; NA, RG 45; NEUSE Roster; CMACSSN]

Clegg, Edward B. (Franklin County, North Carolina)
Private, Confederate States Marine Corps. Enlisted in the Confederate States Marine Corps on November 1, 1864 at Raleigh, North Carolina, at about the age of 19. Served at Charleston, SC, where he contracted measles on or about November 28, 1864. Hospitalized in Charlotte, North Carolina, for measles from April 7 –April 14, 1865. Paroled at Charlotte, North Carolina, May 4, 1865. Filed a claim for a pension on June 7, 1913, age 68, Post Office Franklinton, Franklin County. Claim approved.
[Pensions (North Carolina); Card File; Donnelly-ENL]

Clement, J. K. (County unknown)
Landsman, Confederate States Navy. Clement enlisted on June 1, 1864 in Raleigh, North Carolina, for the war.
[Source(s): Card File; NA, RG 45]

Clements, George W. (Washington County, North Carolina)
Seaman, Confederate States Navy. Clements enlisted in Washington County, North Carolina, on September 16, 1862, for the war, in Company K, 41st Regiment, North Carolina Troops (3rd Regiment, North Carolina Cavalry). Present of accounted for until he transferred to the Confederate States Navy on March 23, 1864. Another source states he entered the Confederate States Navy on April 12, 1864 at Halifax or Plymouth, North Carolina for the war.
[Source(s): WCL; Card File; NA, RG 45; North Carolina Troops, II]

Clemmons, A. B. [NOTE: May be the same as George Clemments, q.v.]
Landsman, Confederate States Navy. Clemmons enlisted on October 5, 1863 at Camp Holmes [near Raleigh, North Carolina]. Another source states he enlisted on October 11, 1863 in Wilmington, North Carolina, for the war.
[Source(s): Card File; NA, RG 45]

Clemmons, A. P. (Brunswick County, North Carolina)
Confederate States Navy. Clemmons enlisted in the Confederate States Navy on August 24, 1863 in Wilmington, North Carolina.
[Source(s): MR, 4, p. 445]

Clemmons [Clements], J. H. (Brunswick County, North Carolina)
Landsman, Confederate States Navy. Born in Smithville (North Carolina) on February 21, 1831, Clemmons served as a crewman aboard the CSS NORTH CAROLINA. [NOTE: Source "Foenander" states he served as a Quartermaster, CSS NORTH CAROLINA, 1864]. Clemmons filed a claim for pension on July 3, 1911 at age 79, listing his post office as Southport, North Carolina. Said pension request was approved. He resided as a farmer with his wife, Jane, and five sons (eldest son born 1858), at Lockwood's Folly, Brunswick County, North Carolina, in 1880. He died on August 29, 1914, and was buried in Old Southport Cemetery, Southport, Brunswick County, North Carolina.
[Source(s): MR, 4, p. 443; Card File; Pensions (North Carolina); Gravestone Records, v.6 p. 308; Stepp, "Burials;" Foenander; Census (NC), 1880]

Clemmons, Josephus
Confederate States Navy. Born in North Carolina, about 1820, Clemmons served as a pilot in the Confederate States Navy beginning on December 30, 1862. He served aboard the CSS BALTIC, Mobile Squadron, Alabama, 1863. He "resided as a pilot with his wife, Margaret, at Tatemville, Baldwin County, Alabama, in 1880. He was involved in an accident in October 1896. After taking the steamer USS MIAMI out over the Mobile bar, and on leaving this vessel in heavy seas, he fell off the ladder into his son's yawl. He was taken to his home and attended by a doctor who found no bones broken, but Clemmons had received internal injuries. At that time Clemmons had been on the Mobile bar for sixty years and was thought to be the oldest pilot in the United States [Foenander]."
[Source(s): Foenander]

Clifford, Green B. (Forsyth County, North Carolina)
Landsman, Confederate States Navy. Clifford enlisted on June 8, 1864 in Raleigh, North Carolina, for the war. A claim for pension filed by his widow, Louisa J. Davis, age 71, on June 10, 1904, listed her post office as Forsyth County, North Carolina, was disallowed. Clifford was killed on the retreat from Richmond, Virginia, April 6, 1865. She married Clifford on November 2, 1854 and S. B. Davis on December 26, 1870. Deponent J. [Jacob] F. Coon stated that he and Green Clifford joined "a Detachment of Cavalry at Morganton, North Carolina, commanded by Robert Vance and sometime after joining his company with Major McLean's Battalion went to and beyond Asheville and were engaged in fighting deserters and Yankees," thence to Tennessee with Longstreet and later to Virginia with Lee's Army. "Clifford, I, and others joined the Navy and remained with the Navy under the command of Commodore Tucker at Charleston, SC, and Drewry's Bluff below Richmond until the evacuation of Richmond when we retreated with the Army, on the retreat Green B. Clifford was killed by a shell at or near Burkesville, Virginia, on April 6th, 1865. I was near him and saw him killed..." His widow Louisa J. Clifford Davis' pension application lists Clifford's enlistment in the Navy as November 1, 1864, and states he had prior service in a "Conscript Battalion."
[Source(s): Card File; Pensions (North Carolina); NA, RG 45]

Clinton, Michael
Landsman, Confederate States Navy. Clinton enlisted on April 11, 1864 at Kinston, North Carolina, for three years or the war. Served aboard the CSS NEUSE as of the ship's March – October 1864 muster rolls.
[Source(s): Card File; NA, RG 45; NEUSE Roster; CMACSSN]

Cloninger, Emanuel (Gaston County, North Carolina) (NOTE: Source "Howard" lists name as "Edward").
Private, Confederate States Army//Confederate States Navy. Born on October 22, 1840 in Gaston County, North Carolina, Cloninger was the son of Jonas and Sarah Cloninger. He resided in the county as a farmer until he enlisted on October 6, 1861 at age 20 in Company H, 37th Regiment, North Carolina Troops. Captured at Fredericksburg, Virginia, on December 13, 1862, he was exchanged on or about December 17, 1862, and returned to duty in February 1863. Per source "Cloninger," he married his wife, "Elizabeth C." in 1863 [Other sources give the date as 1864]. He transferred to the Confederate States Navy on or about April 10, 1864. Cloninger married in 1865, and

resided as a farmer with his wife, Elizabeth, at Dallas Township, Gaston County, North Carolina, in 1910. He died in Durham County, North Carolina, on December 1, 1924 and was buried in the Cloninger Cemetery, Dallas, Gaston County, North Carolina.
[Source(s): Card File; North Carolina GENWEB, www.ncgenweb.us/nccivwar/rosters/37coh.htm; Howard; North Carolina Troops, IX; Foenander; Cloninger]

Clonts, J. Garrison (Burke County, North Carolina)
Confederate States Navy. Clonts was shown as a shoemaker, in 1900, with his wife and child, residing at Silver Creek Township, Burke County, North Carolina. Clonts' initial application for pension, dated June 29, 1901, states he enlisted on August 20, 1863 and served on the Wilmington station. His second application, dated June 22, 1903, states he enlisted on December 20, 1863 and served aboard the CSS NORTH CAROLINA under Captain Poindexter. His widow Elminor [Elmina] Giles Clonts, whom he married in Burke County, North Carolina, on February 23, 1865, filed an application for pension on July 15, 1915 in which she stated he enlisted on May 1, 1863 and that he died on December 31, 1914.
[Source(s): Pensions (North Carolina); Foenander]

Clontz, Jacob S. (Burke County, North Carolina [?])
Landsman, Confederate States Navy. Born October 15, 1831, Clontz died on December 31, 1914, and was buried at Glen Alpine Methodist Church, Burke County, North Carolina.
[Source(s): Stepp, "Burials"]

Clontz [Clonts; Clouts], James Garrison (Burke County, North Carolina)
Landsman ("Private"), Confederate States Navy. Clontz enlisted on August 19, 1863 in Wilmington, North Carolina. His name appears on a register of Confederate States Army General Military Hospital Number 4, Wilmington, North Carolina, stating he was admitted on January 7, 1864 with "rheumatismus chronicus" and returned to duty on May 24, 1864. His post office was listed as Morganton, North Carolina. He appears on Registers of Confederate States Army General Military Hospital Number 4, Wilmington, North Carolina, which states that he was admitted on September 4, 1863 with "debility" and returned to duty on December 4, 1863, post office listed as Morganton, Burke County, North Carolina. Clontz is shown as a shoemaker in 1900 with his wife and child residing at Silver Creek Township, Burke County, North Carolina. His initial application for pension, at age 65, dated June 29, 1901, listing his post office as Glen Alpine, Burke County, North Carolina, states he enlisted on August 20, 1863, and that he served on the Wilmington Station. The application was approved. His second application, dated June 22, 1903, states he enlisted on December 20, 1863 and that he served aboard the CSS NORTH CAROLINA under Captain Poindexter. His widow Elminor [Elmina] Giles Clonts of Burke County, North Carolina, whom he married in Burke County, North Carolina, on February 23, 1865, filed an application for a pension on July 15, 1915 at age 73, which was approved, in which she stated he enlisted on May 1, 1863 and that he died on December 31, 1914. Attached to the application was a pass dated January 22, 1865, Headquarters, 3rd Military District, Wilmington, North Carolina, to Morganton, North Carolina, good for two days. A notation on his card in the files of the North Carolina Troops Project states, "Navy Warship N. C. [CSS NORTH CAROLINA?].
[Source(s): MR, 4, p. 445; Card File; NA, RG 45; NA, RG 109; Pensions (North Carolina)]

Clopton, Joseph (Franklin County, North Carolina)
Landsman, Confederate States Navy. Clopton enlisted on October 24, 1863 [another source says October 26, 1863 at Camp Holmes] in Wilmington, North Carolina.
[Source(s): MR, 4, p. 445; Smithwick; Card File; NA, RG 45]

Close, John E. (Guilford County, North Carolina)
Private, Confederate States Army//First Class Fireman, Confederate States Navy. Born in Guilford County, North Carolina, in 1839, the son of James and Jane Close, Close resided in Guilford County, North Carolina, as a machinist until he enlisted in Lincoln County, North Carolina, at age 21 on April 25, 1861 for six months as a Private in Company K, 1st Regiment, North Carolina Infantry (6 months, 1861). He was listed as present or accounted for until mustered out November 12-13, 1861. He enlisted in the Confederate States Navy on March 1, 1864 in Raleigh, North Carolina, for the war and served as a First-Class Fireman on the CSS ALBEMARLE and at Halifax Station, 1864. Another source states he was conscripted on March 19, 1864 at Camp Holmes [near Raleigh, North Carolina] from Colonel Coble's 68th Regiment, North Carolina Militia from Guilford County, North Carolina. Description: age, 23; eyes, gray; hair, red; complexion, florid; height, 5 feet 7 inches; place of birth, Guilford County, North Carolina; occupation, machinist.
[Source(s): Card File; NA, RG 45; Roster, 68th Regiment, North Carolina Militia]

Clounts [Clonts; Clontz], Jeremiah (Mecklenburg County, North Carolina).
Corporal, Company C, Confederate States Marine Corps. A "Jeremiah Clonts" enlisted as a Private in Company B, 15th Regiment, North Carolina Troops on June 24, 1861 from Union County, North Carolina. He was discharged in August 1862. A J. G. Clonts" enlisted in the Confederate States Navy from Burke County, North Carolina, on August 19, 1863. Another source states he enlisted on October 6, 1864 in Raleigh, North Carolina (Source Donnelly-ENL gives location as "probably at Charleston, SC"). He served as a member of the Marine guard aboard the CSS COLUMBIA, Charleston, South Carolina, from October 6, 1864 – February 8, 1865. Clounts transferred to the CSS INDIAN CHIEF on February 8, 1865 and was later captured at Harper's Farm, Virginia, April 6, 1865, and confined at Point Lookout on April 15, 1865. He was released upon signing an Oath of Allegiance from Point Lookout, Maryland, June 24, 1865, giving his address as Mecklenburg County, North Carolina. Description: Complexion fair; hair brown; eyes gray; height 5 feet 10 ½ inches. A Jeremiah "Clontz" died suddenly in Mecklenburg County, North Carolina, on January 27, 1870, according to "Southern Home," dated February 10, 1870. Source "McLeod, August 30, 1874" states he died "three years ago [i.e. ca. 1871]. Source Donnelly-ENL states "This last [man] might well have transferred to the Marine Corps" but this may well be in error (see roster entry James G. Clontz).
[Source(s): McLeod, August 30, 1874; Donnelly; NA; North Carolina Troops, Doc. # 0185, p. 1 and 0299; Card File; Donnelly-ENL]

Clouts, J. G. (Burke County, North Carolina)
Confederate States Navy. Clouts enlisted on August 19, 1863 in Wilmington, North Carolina.
[Source(s): MR, IV, 445]

Cloyd, I. M. (County unknown)
Ordinary Seaman, Confederate States Navy. Cloyd enlisted on June 22, 1863 in Wilmington, North Carolina, for the war.
[Source(s): Card File; NA, RG 45]

Cobb, J. T. (Johnston County, North Carolina)
Confederate States Navy. Cobb enlisted on October 14, 1864 from Johnston County, North Carolina. He was in service at Drewry's Bluff, Virginia, "and made a good soldier. He came through the war alright and yet lives in the town of Smithfield where he has resided since the war and made a success in business."
[Source(s): RCWV]

Cobb, W. H. (County unknown)
Landsman, Confederate States Navy. Cobb enlisted on January 6, 1864 in Wilmington, North Carolina, for the war. He served as a Seaman and Ship's Steward aboard the CSS ARCTIC, Cape Fear River, North Carolina, 1863, and was attached to Semmes' Naval Brigade, April 1865. He surrendered and was paroled at Greensboro, North Carolina, April 26, 1865.
[Source(s): card File; NA, RG 45; Foenander]

Coble, J. O. (Alamance County, North Carolina)
Confederate States Navy. Coble filed a claim for pension on July 1, 1901 at age 63, listing his post office as Elon College, Alamance County, North Carolina. The claim was disallowed.
[Source(s): Card File; Pensions (North Carolina)]

Coble, James (Alamance County, North Carolina)
Private, Confederate States Army//Confederate States Navy. Coble enlisted on May 21, 1861 at age 18 in Alamance County, North Carolina, in Company H, 15th Regiment, North Carolina Troops (5th Regiment, North Carolina Volunteers) as a Private. He was present or accounted for until transferred to Company G, 44th Regiment, North Carolina Troops, on July 1, 1863, in exchange for Private John M. Davidson. Reportedly transferred to the Confederate States Navy on or about April 1, 1864, no evidence was found by the North Carolina Troops roster staff of his naval service.
[Source(s): Card File; North Carolina Troops, V and X]

Coble, John (["Rock Creek"], _____ County, North Carolina)
Seaman, Confederate States Navy. Registers of Confederate States Army General Military Hospital Number 4, Wilmington, North Carolina, record that he was admitted March 1, 1864 with "vulnus sclopeticum" and returned to duty March 21, 1864. His post office was listed as Rock Creek [no county listed].
[Source(s): Card File; NA, RG 109]

Cobler, Robert (Rockingham County, North Carolina)
> Private, Confederate States Army//Confederate States Navy. Born in North Carolina, in 1833, the son of Elijah and Hilary Cobler, Cobler enlisted in Rockingham County, North Carolina on September 1, 1861 in Company I, 13th Regiment, North Carolina Troops. He was listed as present or accounted or until he transferred to the Confederate States Navy on April 16, 1864.
> [Source(s): Card File; North Carolina Troops, V; Foenander]

Cochran (Cockran), John J. (Cabarrus County, North Carolina)
> Landsman, Confederate States Navy. Cochran enlisted April 25, 1864 in Raleigh, North Carolina, for the war [Source "Pensions (North Carolina)" states he enlisted in Rowan County, North Carolina], in Company D, 34th Regiment, North Carolina Troops. He was discharged in Virginia (possibly due to an injury to his leg) in 1862, was conscripted around the first of April 1864 in Charlotte, North Carolina, and enlisted in the Navy in Raleigh with an officer that was there for recruits. He served in the Navy at Charleston, South Carolina. His claim for a pension, filed June 8, 1901 at age 64, listed his post office as Glass, Cabarrus Company, North Carolina. The pension was approved. Cochran's application for admittance to the Soldier's Home in Raleigh was made on April 8, 1905. He was born in 1837 and died on June 27, 1931 [Source "Stepp" – March 6, 1908], and was buried at Bethphage Presbyterian Church Cemetery, Cabarrus County, North Carolina.
> [Source(s): Card File; Pension (North Carolina); NA, RG 45; Gravestone Records, v.12, p.173]

Cockrell, J. V. (County unknown)
> Landsman, Confederate States Navy. Having served as a Landsman aboard the CSS ARCTIC, Cape Fear River, North Carolina, in 1863, Cockrell's name appears on a Roll of Prisoners of War at Newport News, Virginia, which states that he was captured at Farmville, Virginia, April 6, 1865.
> [Source(s): Card File; NA, RG 109; Foenander]

Coggin, William M. (N.?)
> Assistant Surgeon, Confederate States Navy. Appointed from North Carolina, Coggin was nominated as an Assistant Surgeon, Provisional Navy, November 1864. His name is found on list of paroled prisoners of war who took the amnesty oath on May 11, 1865, in Richmond, Virginia.
> [Source(s): Register, McElroy; ONWR]

Coggins (Cogins), Thomas (Edgecombe County, North Carolina)
> Private, Confederate States Army// Landsman, Confederate States Navy. Coggins was born in Lawrence, Edgecombe County, North Carolina, in 1840, where he resided as a farmer and enlisted on May 8, 1861 [Source MR, I, gives the date as May 1, 1861], at age 21 as a Private in Company G, 13th Regiment North Carolina Troops. He was listed as present or accounted for until he transferred to the Confederate States Navy on February 20, 1862 [Source MR, I, gives the date as February 10, 1862]. Coggins served as a Landsman aboard the CSS VIRGINIA, 1862.
> [Source(s): Card File; North Carolina Troops, V; ORN 2, 1, 309; Census (North Carolina), 1860; North Carolina VR; MR, I; Foenander]

Cole, H. M. (County unknown)
> Landsman, Confederate States Navy. Cole enlisted on October 25, 1864 in Raleigh, North Carolina, for the war. He served as a Landsman aboard the CSS ARCTIC, Cape Fear River, North Carolina, in 1863. In 1864, he served aboard the CSS NORTH CAROLINA, on the Cape Fear River.
> [Source(s): Card File; NA, RG 45; Foenander]

Cole, Thomas (Moore County, North Carolina)
> Private, Naval Battalion, Confederate States Navy. His name appears as a signature to an Oath of Allegiance to the United States, subscribed and sworn to at Point Lookout, Maryland, June 24, 1863. His place of residence was given on the Oath as Moore County, North Carolina. Description: complexion, light; hair, brown; eyes, gray; height, 5 feet 9 inches.
> [Source(s): Card File; NA, RG 109]

Cole, William (New Hanover County, North Carolina)
> Landsman (another source states Ordinary Seaman), Confederate States Navy. Cole enlisted on October 8, 1863 in Wilmington, North Carolina, and served aboard the CSS ARCTIC. Another source states he enlisted on October 12, 1863 at Camp Holmes [near Raleigh, North Carolina]. Source "Foenander" lists a "William Cole" as a Carpenter's

Mate, CSS ALBEMARLE, and Halifax Station, 1864, per *ORN* 2, 1, page 274.
[Source(s): MR, 4, p. 445; Card File; NA, RG 45; Foenander; St. Amand; ORN 2, 1]

Coleman, David
Lieutenant, North Carolina Navy. Coleman is listed by source DH Hill as one of the first officers commissioned in the North Carolina Navy. On May 25, 1861, the ship "Fairfield," apparently chartered in Virginia prior to her purchase and renamed the "Ellis," was reported as carrying guns to Hatteras and Ocracoke under the command of Lieutenant David Coleman. An 1861 resolution by the General Assembly of North Carolina complimented Coleman on his naval skills, qualifications, and service to the Navy of the State of North Carolina and recommended him for the Confederate States Navy.
[Source(s): DH Hill; Resolutions (GA of North Carolina; NCS]

Coleman, John Henry (Rockingham County, North Carolina)
Private, Confederate States Army/Landsman, Confederate States Navy. Born on August 14, 1839 in Rockingham County, North Carolina, Coleman resided as a blacksmith prior to enlisting there at age 22 on February 27, 1862 as a Private in Company E, 45th Regiment, North Carolina Troops. He was listed as present or accounted for until wounded at Gettysburg, Pennsylvania, July 1-3, 1863. Coleman returned to duty in November-December 1863 and was present or accounted for until transferred to the Confederate States Navy on or about April 10, 1864. Coleman died on May 1, 1910, and was buried at Holt's Chapel, Guilford County, North Carolina.
[Source(s): Card File; Stepp, "Burials;" North Carolina Troops, XI]

Coley, James J. (Nash County, North Carolina)
Landsman (per another source "Ordinary Seaman"), Confederate States Navy. Coley enlisted in the Confederate States Navy from Nash County, North Carolina on October 19, 1863 at Camp Holmes [near Raleigh, North Carolina]. Another source states that he enlisted on October 19, 1863 in Wilmington, North Carolina, for the war.
[Source(s): MR, 4, p. 445; McElroy; Card File; NA, RG 45]

Coley, Samuel (Possibly from North Carolina).
Two Samuel Coleys are found in the 1860 Census of North Carolina: One from Stanly County, born in 1818, and one from Granville County, born about 1845. Source "FSW" (12/24/64) lists him as having been wounded by splinters in the face at the First Battle of Fort Fisher, December 24, 1864.
[Source(s): "FSW" (12/24/64); Census (NC), 1860].

Colie, James W. (Lenoir County, North Carolina)
Confederate States Navy. Born in New York in March 1835, Colie served at the "Navy yard at Wilmington," Confederate States Navy. He filed a claim for a pension on June 15, 1901 at age 67, listing his post office as Kinston, Institute Township, Lenoir County, North Carolina, where he resided with his two sons as a house carpenter. His claim was disallowed.
[Source(s): Card File; Pensions (North Carolina); Foenander]

Coll, J. N. M. (county unknown)
Confederate States Navy. Coll enlisted on January 2, 1864 in Raleigh, North Carolina, for the war.
[Source(s): card File; NA, RG 45]

Collins [Colins], Henry (New Hanover County, North Carolina)
Confederate States Navy. Collins served as a crewman aboard the CSS NORTH CAROLINA. There are several men named "Henry Collins" from several sources with ties to North Carolina service, all of whom "may" be the same man. Sources Foenander and ORN state that "Henry Collins" served as Captain of Forecastle, CSS ARCTIC, CSS NORTH CAROLINA, and CSS TALLAHASSEE, 1864; "Henry Collings (Collins?)," Seaman, CSS ARCTIC, 1862-1863; "Henry Collins," Seaman, CSS CASWELL (a side-wheeled tender in Wilmington, on service sometime between July 1861 and June 1862.
[Source(s): MR, 4, p. 443; St. Amand; Foenander]

Collins, John (Lenoir County, North Carolina)
Confederate States Navy. Collins enlisted in Lenoir County, North Carolina, in 1st Company A, 36th Regiment, North Carolina Troops, on October 12, 1863, for three years. He was present or accounted for until he transferred to 2nd Company I, 10th Regiment, North Carolina Troops (1st Regiment, North Carolina Artillery) in November 1863. Collins transferred to the Confederate States Navy, March-April 1864.
[Source(s): Card File; North Carolina Troops, I]

Collins, John (New Hanover County, North Carolina?)

Ordinary Seaman, Confederate States Navy/Private, Confederate States Marine Corps. Born about 1819, Collins served in the "Armoury Guards" just before the war. He enlisted as an Ordinary Seaman in the Confederate States Navy in Wilmington, North Carolina, in 1863. He served on board the ram CSS RALEIGH, and later transferred to Company C, Confederate States Marine Corps, 1864, as a Private. He was stationed aboard the receiving ship CSS ARCTIC and aboard the CSS RALEIGH, Cape Fear River, North Carolina, 1864–1865. Captured at Fort Fisher, January 15, 1865, he was sent as a prisoner of war to Point Lookout, Maryland, where he remained until the end of the war. Collins resided as a laborer in Dayton, Ohio, in the 1880's. He applied for entry to the R.E. Lee Camp 1, Confederate Soldiers' Home, Richmond, Virginia.
[Source(s): Foenander; ORN 2, 1, 280, 302 & 316]

Collins, Philip

Seaman, Quartermaster, North Carolina Navy.
Collins served as a Seaman aboard the NCS EDWARDS per his shipping articles dated July 25,1861. He is listed as a Quartermaster aboard the NCS FORREST as of that ship's muser roll dated October 30, 1861. Collins' name appears as a Quartermaster on the NCS FORREST payroll list covering the 1st quarter of 1862]. He is said to have served aboard the CSS VIRGINIA.
[Source: NCCWSP]

Colly, Samuel [Unknown] [North Carolinian?]

Seaman, Confederate States Navy. Colly was listed as slightly wounded by splinters in the back of the leg, slight contusion of the back from the explosion of a gun, Fort Fisher, December 25, 1864.
[Source(s): Daily Confed. (1/2/65); Daily Confed. (12/25/64)]

Colter, Michael (County unknown)

Ordinary Seaman, Confederate States Navy. Colter enlisted on January 15, 1863 in Wilmington, North Carolina, for three years or the war.
[Source(s): Card File; NA, RG 45]

Compton, David

Ordinary Seaman, North Carolina Navy.
Compton served aboard the NCS RALEIGH and transferred to the James River Squadron on April 15, 1862
[Source: NCCWSP]

Comron, Richard R. (Onslow County, North Carolina)

Corporal, Confederate States Army//Confederate States Navy. Born in Onslow County, North Carolina, in 1834, the son of Hannah Comron, Comron worked as a clerk prior to enlisting in New Hanover County, North Carolina, in Company G, 18th Regiment, North Carolina Troops, as a Private at age 28 on August 30, 1861. Comron was present or accounted until reported absent without leave for the period May through October 1862. He was reported present for duty November-December 1862. Comron was promoted to Corporal on January 1, 1863 and listed as present or accounted for until he transferred to the Confederate States Navy on or about April 10. 1864.
[Source(s): Card File; Pensions (North Carolina); North Carolina Troops, VI]

Condon, Thomas (County unknown)

Landsman, Confederate States Navy. Condon enlisted on June 8, 1863 in Wilmington, North Carolina, for the war. He served as a Landsman on board the CSS NORTH CAROLINA and CSS TALLAHASSEE, Cape Fear River, North Carolina, 1864
[Source(s): Card File; NA, RG 45; Foenander]

Cone, J. B. (County unknown)

Confederate States Navy. A claim for pension filed on July 27, 1927 by Cone's widow, Sarah Cone of Bladen County, North Carolina (no post office listed) was approved.
[Source(s): Card File; Pensions (North Carolina)]

Conn (Cann), Dixon G. (Franklin County, North Carolina)

Sergeant, Confederate States Army//Master-at-Arms (Seaman), Confederate States Navy. Born in Franklin County, North Carolina on March 13, 1840, Conn enlisted from Chapel Hill, North Carolina, 1861, in Company D, 5th North Carolina Volunteers; Company I, 15th troops, Company K 32nd North Carolina Regiment, 1862. Discharged in 1863 because of wounds, Conn volunteered for the Confederate States Navy and served on board the CSS

INDIAN CHIEF and CSS PEE DEE at Cheraw, South Carolina. Another source states he enlisted on May 30, 1864 in Raleigh, North Carolina, for the war. He was taken prisoner on April 6, 1865 and confined at Craney Island. His name appears as signature to an Oath of Allegiance to the United States, subscribed and sworn to at Newport News, Virginia, June 14, 1865. His place of residence was given on the Oath as Franklin County, North Carolina. Description: complexion, fair; hair, dark; eyes, blue; height, 5 feet 8 inches. His Oath carries the remark, "captured at Farmville [Virginia] April 6." Conn died in 1921. One source erroneously stated that he "drowned in Charleston Harbor in 1863 on a trial trip of the C. S. Submarine "Hunley."
[Source(s): McElroy, with attached obituary; NA, RG 45; Card File; NA, RG 109]

Connell, Jerry (County unknown)
Ordinary Seaman, Confederate States Navy. Connell enlisted on June 1, 1863 in Wilmington, North Carolina, for three years or the war.
[Source(s): Card File; NA, RG 45]

Connelly, George A. (County unknown)
Landsman (Private), Confederate States Navy. Source "Foenander" states he "served as a Landsman, CSS ARCTIC, Cape Fear River, North Carolina, in 1863 (a "George A. Connoly," of the CSS RALEIGH, who served in North Carolina and Virginia waters, 1862 – 1864, may be the same person). His name appears on a register of Confederate States Army General Military Hospital Number 4, Wilmington, NORTH CAROLINA, being admitted March 31, 1864, with "fractura…" He was transferred to the Smallpox Hospital on April 21, 1864. His post office was given on the register as Fords, NORTH CAROLINA
[Source(s): Card File; NA, RG 109; ORN 2, 1, 278; Foenander]

Conner, Cornelius C. (Lenoir County, North Carolina)
Private, Confederate States Army//Landsman, Confederate States Navy. Connor enlisted in Lenoir County, North Carolina, on July 21, 1862 for the war as a substitute for Louis B. Cox in Company B, 63rd Regiment, North Carolina Troops (5th Regiment, North Carolina Cavalry). Connor was shown as present or accounted for until he transferred to the Confederate States Navy on April 21, 1864. He served as a Private in Company G, 2nd Regiment, Semmes' Naval Brigade, April 1865. He was surrendered and paroled at Greensboro, North Carolina, April 26, 1865.
[Source(s): North Carolina Troops, II; Foenander]

Connor, Thomas
Confederate States Navy. Connor enlisted in the Confederate States Navy in Wilmington, North Carolina.
[Source(s): St. Amand; MR, IV, 445]

Connour, Franklin
Landsman, Seaman, North Carolina Navy.
Connour served from January 10, 1862 -February 9, 1862 and was promoted to Seaman on February 10, 1862. His name appears on a North Carolina Squadron payroll covering the 1st quarter of 1862 from January 10, 1862 - March 26, 1862. He is listed as having "run" (a.k.a. deserted) per the payroll ending March 26, 1862.
[Source: NCCWSP]

Conroy, John (County unknown)
Confederate States Navy. Registers of Confederate States Army General Military Hospital Number 4, Wilmington, North Carolina, state that he was admitted August 29, 1863, with "frebris int" and returned to duty on September 1, 1863. His post office was given on the register as Wilmington, North Carolina. Conroy served aboard the steamer CSS PHANTOM.
[Source(s): Card File; NA, RG 109]

Conway, Edward
Ordinary Seaman, North Carolina Navy.
Conway served as an Ordinary Seaman aboard the NCS EDWARDS beginning with his shipping articles dated July 25, 1861 and going through at least September 1861. On September 17, 1861 he transferred to the receiving ship CSS UNITED STATES on detached duty. He served as an Ordinary Seaman aboard the NCS FORREST at least as early as October 30, 1861.
[Source: NCCWSP]

Cook, Edwin [May be same as the Edwin Cook listed below]
Seaman, North Carolina Navy "Battery." Cook was captured at Jetersville, Virginia, April 6, 1865 [another source gives place of capture as Richmond, Virginia]. Received from City Point, Virginia, on April 14, 1865 at Point Lookout, Maryland. Cook died on June 1, 1865 at Point Lookout, Maryland, of chronic diarrhea and was buried in the Confederate Cemetery there.
[Source(s): Purser]

Cook, Edwin (County unknown) [May be same as the Edwin Cook listed above].
Landsman, Confederate States Navy. Cook enlisted on June 11, 1864 in Raleigh, North Carolina, for the war.
[Source(s): Card File; NA, RG 45]

Cook, Harrison (Yadkin County, North Carolina)
Private, Confederate States Army//Landsman, Confederate States Navy. Cook resided in Yadkin County, North Carolina and enlisted at age 20 on October 17, 1862, for the war, as a Private in Company D, 44th Regiment, North Carolina Troops. Source "North Carolina Troops" states he deserted on November 16, 1862. Cook enlisted for the war in the Confederate States Navy on June 6, 1864 at Raleigh. Cook served as a Private in a naval battalion, with which he was captured. His name appears on a roll of Prisoners of War at Point Lookout, Maryland, which states that he was captured at Farmville, Virginia on April 6, 1865, confined at Point Lookout, Maryland on April 14, 1865 and released after taking the Oath of Allegiance to the United States on June 24, 1865. The Oath of Allegiance gives his place of residence as Yadkin County, North Carolina, and description as follows: Complexion light; hair brown; eyes grey; height 5'6.
[Source(s): Card File; NA, RG 109; NA, RG 45; NCT, Vol. X; Casstevens]

Cook, Thomas M. (Sampson County, North Carolina)
Private, Confederate States Army//Confederate States Navy. Cook was born in Sampson County and enlisted at age 44 in Duplin County, North Carolina on March 28, 1862 in Company K, 51st Regiment, North Carolina Troops. He was present or accounted for until September-October 1862 when he was listed as sick in the hospital at Goldsboro, North Carolina. On December 29, 1862 he was admitted to the hospital at Wilmington with pneumonia. He returned to duty on January 4, 1863 and was present or accounted for until he transferred to Company A, 15th Battalion (Lucas's), South Carolina Heavy Artillery on May 1, 1863. Though not specifically mentioned in *North Carolina Troops*, his naval service obviously came thereafter.
[Source(s): Card File; NCT, Vol. XII]

Cook, William (New Hanover County, North Carolina)
Private, Confederate States Army//Confederate States Navy. Cook resided and enlisted in New Hanover County, North Carolina, on May 27, 1861, at age 33, for the war in Company D, 3rd Regiment, North Carolina Troops. He transferred to the Confederate States Navy on May 16, 1862.
[Source(s): North Carolina Troops, III; Foenander; MR, I]

Cook, William [NOTE: May be same as William W. Cook, q.v.]
Seaman, Confederate States Navy. Cook served aboard the CSS ARCTIC, Cape Fear River, North Carolina, 1862 - 1863.
[Source(s): Foenander; *ORN* 1, 23, 703 and 2, 1, 279]

Cook, William W.
Officers' Steward, Confederate States Navy. Cook served aboard the screw steamer CSS FANNY operating in North Carolina waters as either a Seaman or Officer's Steward serving during the period September - December 1861 and May 1862. His name appears on a North Carolina Squadron payroll for the 1st quarter 1862 covering from December 1, 1861 - February 28, 1862. Cook was listed as having "run" (a.k.a. deserted) per the payroll ending February 28, 1862.
[Source(s): *ORN* 2, 1, 285; Foenander; NCCWSP]

Cooke, James Wallace (Craven County, North Carolina) [*North Carolina's highest ranking officer in the Confederate Navy*]
Lieutenant, North Carolina Navy//Captain, Confederate States Navy. Cooke was born to Thomas and Esther (Wallace) Cooke in Beaufort, North Carolina on August 23, 1812 [Source "Driver" states he was born on August 29, 1812]. In September of 1815, Cooke's father, a successful merchant, was lost at sea during a hurricane off the coast of North Carolina. James became an orphan the following year when his mother died of consumption. He and his younger sister were taken in by their uncle, Henry Marchant Cooke, also of Beaufort, North Carolina. Henry

M. Cooke, the Customs Collector at the port of Beaufort, obtained an appointment for fifteen-year-old James in the United States Navy as a Midshipman on April 1, 1828. He achieved Passed Midshipman status on June 14, 1834 and was promoted to Lieutenant on February 25, 1841. He was on the expedition with Commodore Perry that opened Japan. He resigned from the United States Navy, May 2 1861, as a lieutenant. Residing in Portsmouth, Virginia, Cooke enlisted in the Virginia Navy and was appointed to the rank of Commander on May 8, 1861. He was appointed First Lieutenant in the Confederate States Navy to rank from June 11, 1861. His assignments included the construction of Fort Powhatan on the James River, command of the naval batteries at Aquia Creek on the Potomac River, and Gosport Navy Yard, 1861-1862. He was with Lynch's Flotilla in Eastern North Carolina, and Lieutenant Commanding the NCS WELDON E. EDWARDS, July 25, 1861 through September 1861, the NCS FORREST in October 1861, the NCS ELLIS in North Carolina waters, circa October 30, 1861 through the 1st quarter of 1862, participating in the Battle off Cobb's Point battery, Roanoke Island, North Carolina, February 7-8, 1862, where his vessel was destroyed, and he was wounded in the leg and arm [NOTE: Source "Foenander" states wounded in the "right arm and captured"]. Cooke was captured at Elizabeth City, North Carolina on February 10, 1862 and paroled February 12, 1862 to his home in Portsmouth, Virginia. He went to Warrenton, North Carolina, until his exchange in September 1862. He was appointed Commander on August 25, 1862 to rank from May 17 [25], 1862, and Commander, Provisional Navy, June 2, 1864, to rank from May 13, 1863. He was promoted to Commander on September 17, 1862 and returned to North Carolina to serve on the Wilmington Station, 1862 – 1864, where he commanded the CSS BALTIC in 1863 and was placed in charge of building the naval defenses of Roanoke River and the CSS ALBEMARLE, 1863-1864. He commanded the CSS ALBEMARLE under Commander R. F. Pinkney, in the Confederate attack upon Plymouth, North Carolina, April 19, 1864, and the sinking of USS SOUTHFIELD, off Plymouth, North Carolina, April 19, 1864. He was promoted to Captain on June 10, 1864 for gallant and meritorious conduct while attacking the enemy's fleet on May 5, 1864 in the Albemarle Sound and placed in command of all Naval forces operating in the waters of North Carolina, until the end of the war. On detached service as of June 17, 1864, Cooke was paroled in Raleigh, North Carolina on May 12, 1865. [Source Booker states he was born in Portsmouth, Virginia]. Cooke returned home to Portsmouth, Virginia, where he died on June 21, 1869. He was buried in that city's Cedar Grove Cemetery.
[Source(s): Register, McElroy; MR, 4, p. 449; Officers, January 1, 1864; "Booker," p.81; Driver; Journal; *Reveille;* Foenander; CWDTS; ONWR; Fold3, USN Resignees; NCCWSP; Wikipedia]

Cooke, John (Surry County, North Carolina)
Ordinary Seaman, Confederate States Navy. Cooke enlisted on March 2, 1864 in Kinston for three years or the war. A "John Cook" appears on a Register of Pettigrew General Hospital No. 13, Raleigh, North Carolina, which states he was admitted September 16, 1864, with "delerium tremens" and returned to duty September 25, 1864. A "John Cook" served aboard the CSS NEUSE, March-October 1864. Post office given as Mt. Airy, North Carolina and county as Surry.
[Source(s): Card File; NA, RG 45, Card File; NA, RG 109; NEUSE Roster; CMACSSN]

Cooley, Lewis (Warren County, North Carolina)
Private, Confederate States Army//Confederate States Navy. Cooley resided in Warren County, North Carolina, where he enlisted at age 32 on July 22, 1861 for the war in Company E, 9th Regiment, North Carolina Troops (1st Regiment, North Carolina Cavalry). He was reported as "absent without leave since October 1, 1863" until reported "in arrest with charges" on November-December 1863 muster roll. Cooley transferred to the Confederate States Navy on April 25, 1864.
[Source(s): North Carolina Troops, II]

Coon, Jacob F. (Davie County, North Carolina)
Seaman, Confederate States Navy (Naval Bat.). Coon enlisted on June 13, 1864, in Raleigh for the war. His name appears on a roll of Prisoners of War at Point Lookout, Maryland, captured at Burkesville April 6, 1865 and confined until he took the Oath of Allegiance to the United States on June 24, 1865. Oath gives place of residence as Davie County, North Carolina, and description as follows: Complexion light; hair brown; eyes light blue; height 5 ft. 7.5 in. [See Green B. Clifford entry for additional information on the service of Jacob F. Coon].
[Source(s): Card File; NA, RG 109; Card File: NA, RG 45]

Cooper, James H. (New Hanover County)
Confederate States Navy. Registers of Confederate States Army General Military Hospital Number 4, Wilmington, North Carolina, dated February 25, 1863, indicate Cooper was admitted with "dysentery chronic" and assigned to ward 1. The Register states he was returned to duty March 13, 1863. His post office was given on the Register as Wilmington, North Carolina. Born circa 1825, Cooper died September 3, 1903 and was buried at Ephesus Baptist Church, Wake County, North Carolina.

[Source(s): Card File; NA, RG 109; Stepp, "Burials;" Hosp. (No. 4), Wilm.]

Cope, Joseph (County unknown)
Landsman, Confederate States Navy. Cope enlisted on August 12, 1864, in Raleigh for the war. He served as a Landsman aboard the CSS ARCTIC, Cape Fear River, North Carolina, 1863.
[Source(s): Card File; NA, RG 45; Foenander]

Copeland, Isaac (Surry County, North Carolina)
Private, Confederate States Army//Landsman, Confederate States Navy. Born in North Carolina in 1842, the son of Harden and Mary Copeland, Copeland resided and enlisted at age 20 in Surry County, North Carolina for twelve months as a Private in Company B, 2nd North Carolina Battalion (Infantry) at age 20 on September 18, 1861 for twelve months. Captured at Roanoke Island, North Carolina, on February 8, 1862, and paroled at Elizabeth City, North Carolina, on February 21, 1862. He was wounded and captured at Gettysburg, Pennsylvania, circa July 1-5, 1863. Copeland was transferred on July 14, 1863 from a hospital in Gettysburg to DeCamp General Hospital, David's Island, New York Harbor, where he remained until paroled and sent to City Point, Virginia, sometime between September 8-16, 1863, for exchange. Absent on parole through February 1864. Copeland transferred to the Confederate States Navy on April 5, 1864 and served as a coal heaver on board the CSS PATRICK HENRY and the ironclad CSS VIRGINIA II, James River Squadron, Virginia, 1864-1865. Never married, Copeland resided as a farmer in Dobson Township, Surry County, North Carolina, as of the time of the 1910 Census.
[Source(s): North Carolina Troops, III; Isaac Copeland Papers, North Carolina Archives; *ORN* 2, 1, 311; MR, IV; Census (North Carolina), 1910]

Core, John B. (Bladen County, North Carolina)
Landsman, Confederate States Navy. Born on August 31, 1845, Core enlisted on September 28, 1863, at Camp Holmes for the war. He died on February 15, 1914, and was buried in White Oak Baptist Church Cemetery, White Oak, North Carolina. First widow's application for pension from Sarah Core, dated July 27, 1927, stated John B. Core enlisted in Fayetteville, North Carolina, in the Confederate States Navy in 1862; and, that he died in 1913. She submitted a second application for increase, dated April 26, 1932 (no additional information).
[Source(s): Card File; NA, RG 45; Gravestone Records; Stepp, "Burials;" Pensions (North Carolina); Foenander]

Cornehlsen, J. H. W. (County Unknown) [Probably the same as J.H.N. Cornekelsen, q.v.]
Landsman, Confederate States Navy. Cornehlsen enlisted on November 3, 1863, in Wilmington for the war.
[Source(s): Card File; NA, RG 45]

Corneklsen, J. H. N. (County Unknown) [Probably the same as J.H.W. Cornehlsen, q.v.]
Landsman, Confederate States Navy. Corneklsen enlisted on October 30, 1863, in Raleigh for the war.
[Source(s): Card File; NA, RG 45]

Costin, Thomas (North Carolina[?])
Seaman, Confederate States Navy. Costin suffered a slight contusion of the back from the explosion of a gun at Fort Fisher, December 25, 1864. Source Census (NC), 1860 identifies two men who may be this sailor: Thomas W., Pasquotank County, North Carolina, born about 1839; and Thomas, New Hanover County, North Carolina, born about 1839.
[Source(s): Daily Confed. (1/2/65)]

Costin, William H. (New Hanover County, North Carolina)
Landsman, Confederate States Navy. Costin's name appears on a list of conscripts in the yard [at Halifax?] and then transferred to Wilmington, North Carolina, June 9, 1864. Card File and NA, RG 45 sources state he was conscripted on March 25, 1864 [Card File states he enlisted for the war on March 28, 1864 at Raleigh], at Camp Holmes from Colonel Strange's 22nd Regiment, North Carolina Militia of New Hanover County, North Carolina, and was described as age 44; eyes blue; hair light; height 5 feet 6 inches; place of birth: New Hanover County, North Carolina; occupation, mason.
[Source(s): Card File: NA, RG 45]

Costner, Joseph, Sr. (Gaston County, North Carolina)
Confederate States Navy. Costner enlisted in the Confederate States Navy and served at Wilmington, North Carolina, and Drewry's Bluff, Virginia. He served under Captain Poindexter, 1864-1865.
[Source(s): Gaston County Veterans; Cloninger]

Costner, Michael Henry (Gaston County, North Carolina)
Landsman, Confederate States Navy. Born January 26, 1821, Costner served as a Landsman aboard the CSS ARCTIC, Cape Fear River, North Carolina, 1863. He is said to have served in "Poindexter's Company," 1864 – 1865. His name appears on a roll of Prisoners of War at Point Lookout, Maryland, who arrived April 14, 1865, having been captured at Harpers Farm, April 6, 1865. He was released upon taking the Oath of Allegiance to the United States on June 24, 1865. The Oath lists his residence as Gaston County, North Carolina, and description as: complexion dark; hair brown; eyes gray; height 5 feet 7.5 inches. He died March 7, 1905, and was buried at Philadelphia Lutheran Church, Gaston County, North Carolina. Source "Cloninger" gives the place of burial as the Kostner Church Cemetery, Dallas, Gaston County, North Carolina.
[Source(s): NA, RG 109; Card File; Stepp, "Burials;" Foenander; Cloninger]

Course, William (Free Negro)
Officer's Steward, North Carolina Navy.
Course served aboard the NCS RALEIGH from circa September 2, 1861 – 1st quarter of 1862. He deserted in February 1862 and joined the United States Navy at Elizabeth City.
[Source: NCCWSP]

Cowell (Cowel), Benjamin B. (Currituck County, North Carolina).
Ordinary Seaman, Confederate States Navy. Cowell was born in Currituck County, North Carolina where he lived as a farmer before enlisting as a Private at age 18 on May 13, 1861 in Company E, 17th Regiment, North Carolina Troops (1st Organization). He transferred to the Confederate States Navy prior to July 28, 1861 and served as an Ordinary Seaman aboard the CSS CURLEW from circa November 20, 1861 through the first quarter of 1862. His name appears on a payroll ending March 31, 1862 for the receiving ship CSS UNITED STATES.
[Source: NCCWSP]

Cowell (Cowel), Benjamin B. (Currituck County, North Carolina)
"Private," Confederate States Navy. Born in Currituck County, North Carolina about 1843, Cowell lived there as a farmer until he enlisted in Currituck County at age 18 as a Private in Company E, 17th Regiment, North Carolina Troops (1st Organization), on May 13, 1861. He transferred to the Confederate States Navy prior to July 28, 1861 and served aboard the NCS CURLEW at least during the 1st quarter of 1862. His name appears on the payroll of the receiving ship CSS UNITED STATES covering the period ending May 31, 1862.
[Source(s): Card File; North Carolina Troops, VI; Foenander; NCCWSP]

Cowell, H. B. (may be Benjamin Cowell)
Landsman, Confederate States Navy. Landsman aboard the CSS FANNY as of October 8, 1861]
[Source: NCCWSP]

Cowan [Cowin], J. D. (Mecklenburg County, North Carolina)
Landsman, Confederate States Navy. Cowen enlisted on April 25, 1864, in Raleigh for the war. His Oath of Allegiance to the United States, sworn to at Newport News, Virginia, June 30, 1865, gives his description as: complexion dark; eyes gray; height 5 feet 7 inches. The Oath carried the remark, "Captured at Richmond April 3, 1865."
[Source(s): NA, RG 45; NA, RG 109; Card File]

Cox, B. G. (Randolph County, North Carolina)
Landsman, Confederate States Navy. Cox enlisted on October 20, 1863, in Wilmington, North Carolina, for the war. Card File entry listed enlistment date as October 26, 1863. NA RG 45 indicates enlistment as October 21, 1863, at Camp Holmes,
[Source(s): MR, 4, p. 445; NA, RG 45; Card File]

Cox, J. H. (County unknown)
Landsman, Confederate States Navy. Cox enlisted on November 22, 1863, in Wilmington, North Carolina, for the war. Another listing indicates enlistment on November 20, 1863, in Raleigh, North Carolina, for the war.
[Source(s): Card File; NA RG 45]

Cox, J. S. (County unknown)
Landsman, Confederate States Navy. Cox enlisted on August 29, 1864, in Raleigh, North Carolina, for the war.
[Source(s): Card File; NA RG 45]

Cox, R. T. (County unknown)
> Private, Confederate States Army//Confederate States Navy. Cox's place and date of enlistment in Company K, 8th Regiment, North Carolina State Troops are unknown. He was discharged on April 22, 1863 upon transfer to Confederate States Navy.
> [Source(s): Card File; North Carolina Troops, IV]

Crabtree, Caleb C.
> Confederate States Navy. Crabtree enlisted on March 15, 1864, at age 20, in the Confederate States Navy.
> [Source(s): Foenander]

Crabtree, Charles C. ["Caleb C."] (Wake County, North Carolina)
> Landsman, Confederate States Navy. Crabtree was born in Granville County, North Carolina, where he lived as a wheelwright prior to his conscription on March 15, 1864 [March 18, 1864, Raleigh, North Carolina], at Camp Holmes from Colonel Ivey's 38th Regiment, North Carolina Militia, Wake County, North Carolina. Description: age 20; eyes hazel; hair dark; complexion florid; height 5 feet 7 inches; place of birth Granville County, North Carolina; occupation wheelwright. Other records indicate his name appears on a list of conscripts in the yard at Halifax and then transferred to Wilmington, North Carolina, June 9, 1864.
> [Source(s): Card File; NA, RG 45; Foenander]

Craig, Charles William (Brunswick Company(?), North Carolina)
> Pilot (2nd Officer), Confederate States Navy ["North Carolina Navy" (see Stepp)]. Served aboard the blockade runner "Margaret and Jessie." Sprunt lists the ship as the "Margaret and Jennie" and states Craig was born August 13, 1837. He died on April 22, 1890 and was buried in Oakdale Cemetery, Wilmington, North Carolina. NA RG 109 states Craig appears on a roll of prisoners received at Fort Lafayette, New York Harbor on November 18, 1863, captured "on Str. Margaret and Jessie" ("blockade runner") about November 5, 1863. He appears on another list of prisoners confined at Fort Lafayette, New York Harbor, stating he was released February 8, 1864, "by order of Gen. Dix." He is said to have made 20 attempts to run the blockade, 18 of which were successful.
> [Source(s): McElroy; Chronicles; NA RG 109; Stepp, "Burials"]

Craig, James William "Jim Billy" (New Hanover County(?), North Carolina)
> Blockade Runner Pilot, Confederate States Navy[?]. Sprunt's Chronicles states he was born May 23, 1840, died July 11, 1914, and was buried in Oakdale Cemetery, New Hanover Company, Wilmington, North Carolina. Craig was the pilot of the "Lynx." He was twice captured and imprisoned at Old Point Comfort and Point Lookout, Maryland. Craig served as a witness on the pension application of Joseph H. Pepper (q.v.). In post-war years he served as an ordained Methodist minister and lived in Southport and Wilmington.
> [Source(s): Card File; Chronicles; Gravestone Records, v. 6, p. 308; Pensions (North Carolina); *Oakdale*, Davis]

Craig, William Pleasant "Pleas" (Buncombe County, North Carolina)
> Private, Confederate States Army//Landsman (other sources list him as a "Seaman"), Confederate States Navy. Craig worked as a shoemaker until he enlisted at age 22 in Zebulon B. Vance's Company F, 14th Regiment, North Carolina Troops, Confederate States Army, on May 3 [4], 1861. He transferred to the Confederate States Navy on February 18, 1862 by order of General Benjamin Huger for service on board the CSS VIRGINIA (MERRIMACK). He was reported as a Private on the July-August 1863 muster roll of Company C, 65th Regiment, North Carolina Troops (6th Regiment, North Carolina Cavalry) with the annotation, "absent without leave." Apprehended on an unspecified date, court-martialed, and sentenced to be shot, his sentence was suspended on September 12, 1864, after the intercession of North Carolina Governor Zebulon B. Vance. Craig was issued clothing on November 14, 1864.
> [Source(s): McElroy; Card File; Howard; North Carolina Troops, II & V; ORN 2, 1, 309; MR, I; Foenander]

Craig, T. W. (J. W.?) (County unknown)
> Pilot, Confederate States Navy. Craig served aboard the blockade runners "Lynox" and "Pet."
> [Source(s): McElroy; Card File]

Craig[e], William H. (Orange County, North Carolina)
> Seaman, Confederate States Navy. Craig was born in Chapel Hill, North Carolina, on November 30, 1840. He enlisted on June 13, 1864, in Raleigh, North Carolina, for the war. Source www.couchgenweb.com/arkansas/jackson/biog-c.htm states he enlisted in the Confederate States Navy in Charleston, South Carolina, but was transferred to the "heavy artillery" at Wilmington, North Carolina, where he remained until February 1864. He was then put in charge of an engineering corps and remained in that capacity until the close of the war. Surviving the war, Craig returned to Chapel Hill and re-entered the University of North Carolina. He later moved to Kenyon,

Arkansas where he became a prominent businessman and postmaster. [Source "North Carolina Troops, I (p. 446)" lists a "William H. Craig," farmer of Orange County, North Carolina, who enlisted at age 22 on March 11, 1862 for the war in 2nd Company G, 40th Regiment, North Carolina Troops (3rd Regiment, North Carolina Artillery), who died on July 13, 1862]
[Source(s): Card File; NA RG 45; www.couchgenweb.com/arkansas/jackson/biog-c.htm]

Crane, Samuel (North Carolina)
Ordinary Seaman, North Carolina Navy, Confederate States Navy. Born circa 1842 in North Carolina, Crane was living in the Coinjock District of Currituck County, North Carolina in 1860. He enlisted "for the war" aboard the CSS RALEIGH on August 24, 1861 and served aboard her from circa August 15, 1861 through April 15, 1862 as part of the North Carolina Squadron. He transferred to the James River Squadron on April 15, 1862 and served at Drewry's Bluff from April 1, 1863 through June 30, 1863 and probably longer.
[Sources: Census (NC), 1860; NCCWSP]

Crane, Thomas (probably Tyrrell County, North Carolina)
Seaman, Confederate States Navy. Crane shipped for 1 year aboard the CSS RALEIGH on September 8, 1861 as a Seaman from September 2 [?], 1861 through April 1862. His name appears on a payroll of the North Carolina Squadron covering from February 28, 1862 through April 15, 1862 on which date he transferred to the James River Squadron. Crane served at Drewry's Bluff as a Seaman from at least April 1, 1863 through 30 June 30, 1863.
[Source: NCCWSP]

Crapon, Marsden C. (Brunswick County, North Carolina)
Third Assistant Engineer, Confederate States Navy. Born circa 1835, Crapon resided as an engineer, in 1860, with his wife, Anna, in the Smithville district, Brunswick County, North Carolina. He was appointed from North Carolina and served aboard the CSS ELLIOTT, 1861; CSS CASWELL, Wilmington Station, 1861-1862. He died in 1862 at age 27.
[Source(s): Register; Purser; Census (North Carolina), 1860; Foenander]

Craven, E. J. V. (E. I. V.) (E. T. V) (Randolph County, North Carolina)
Landsman, Confederate States Navy. Craven enlisted in the Confederate States Navy on October 20, 1863 [or, October 26, 1863] in Wilmington, North Carolina; or [October 21, 1863 at Camp Holmes, Raleigh, North Carolina]. He served as a Seaman aboard the CSS ARCTIC, Cape Fear River, North Carolina, 1863.
[Source(s): MR, 4, p. 445; NA RG 45; Card File; Foenander]

Crawford, Charles D. (Beaufort County, North Carolina)
Confederate States Navy. Crawford resided in Beaufort County, North Carolina, where he enlisted as a Private in Company K, 41st Reg., North Carolina Troops (3rd Regiment, North Carolina Cavalry) on May 16, 1862. He was listed as present or accounted for until he transferred to the Confederate States Navy on December 26, 1863. His age was 25 in 1864. He served aboard the CSS NEUSE as of the ship's March - October 1864 muster rolls.
[Source(s): North Carolina Troops, II, p. 256; Census (NC), 1860; Hill; Card File; "Beaufort County Sailors;" Foenander; NEUSE Roster; CMACSSN]

Crawford, Charles H. (New Hanover County, North Carolina)
Private, Confederate States Army//Confederate States Navy. Crawford resided in New Hanover County, North Carolina, where he enlisted at age 33 on January 17, 1862 for the war in Company F, 3rd Regiment, North Carolina State Troops. He was listed as present or accounted for until transferred to the Confederate States Navy on April 13, 1864.
[Source(s): Card File; North Carolina Troops, III]

Crawford, Isham (County unknown)
Landsman, Confederate States Navy. Crawford enlisted on January 6, 1864, in Raleigh for the war. Served aboard the CSS NEUSE as of the ship's March – October muster rolls.
[Source(s): Card File; NA RG 45; NEUSE Roster; CMACSSN]

Crawford, T. D. (Beaufort County, North Carolina)
Second Lieutenant, Confederate States Navy. Hailing from Washington, North Carolina, his prisoner of war record indicates he was captured near Washington, North Carolina, on February 26 [February 24], 1865, and confined at Fort Pulaski, Georgia, Hilton Head, South Carolina, and Fort Delaware, Delaware, where he was released after taking the Oath of Allegiance on June 16, 1865. His place of residence on his Oath of Allegiance was listed as Pitt

County, North Carolina, and description: complexion light; hair red; eyes blue; height 6 feet. Information from "The State" and Clark's Regiments indicate Crawford was one of 111 North Carolina soldiers chosen at Fort Delaware, Delaware, and sent to Morris Island, Charleston Harbor, South Carolina, where he was confined under circumstances that exposed then to extreme hardship and to the fire of the Confederate garrison defending Charleston, September 7 – October 21, 1864 [NOTE: this information conflicts with his date of capture].
[Source(s): McElroy; Card File; NA RG 109; Clark, IV, pp. 721-724; "The State" (August 1982 and July 1982)]

Crews (Cruse), Robert T. (Granville County, North Carolina)
Landsman, Confederate States Navy. Crews was conscripted on March 30, 1864 [March 31, 1864], at Camp Holmes, from Colonel Dolby's 43rd Regiment, North Carolina Militia, Granville County, North Carolina. Description: Age 19; eyes hazel; hair dark; complexion fair; height 5 feet 4.5 inches. Crews was born on June 7, 1844 in Granville Co, North Carolina, where he lived as a farmer. He died on February 17, 1915, and was buried in Elmwood Cemetery, Granville County, North Carolina.
[Source(s): Card File; NA RG 45; Stepp, "Burials"]

Criswell, James (County unknown)
Landsman, Confederate States Navy. Criswell enlisted on May 11, 1864, in Raleigh, North Carolina, for the war.
[Source(s): Card File; NA RG 45]

Crocker, W. D. (County unknown)
Landsman, Confederate States Navy. Crocker enlisted on April 20, 1864, "at Halifax and Plymouth, North Carolina" for the war. Crocker died of disease at Elmira Prison as a Prisoner of War in March 1865. He was buried in Woodlawn Cemetery. Notations indicate he was a Seaman on the CSS ALBEMARLE.
[Source(s): Card File; NA RG 45; Josh Howard]

Cronin, James C.
Boatswain's Mate, Confederate States Navy.
Cronin enlisted at Camp Clark, Texas, for the war as a Private in Company B, 4th Texas Infantry on July 11, 1861. He was discharged per Special Order # 192, Adjutant & Inspector General's Office, paragraph 61 on October 28, 1861 to "work in another government branch." He was a Boatswain's Mate aboard the Receiving Ship CSS CONFEDERATE STATES from January 1, 1862 - January 9, 1862; a Boatswain's Mate aboard the CSS SEA BIRD from January 10, 1862 - February 9, 1862

Appears on North Carolina Squadron payroll for the 1st quarter of 1862 from January 10, 1862 – February 9, 1862; and was a Boatswain's Mate aboard the CSS VIRGINIA and manned Gun #3 during the Battle of Hampton Roads, March 8-9, 1862. His name appears on the payroll ending March 31, 1862 of the receiving ship CSS UNITED STATES. He appears on the CSS VIRGINIA's final payroll as a "boson's mate" (common abbreviation for Boatswain's Mate based on how the title was pronounced) for the period covering April 1, 1862 - June 30, 1862. Cronin served with the CSS VIRGINIA detachment at Drewry's Bluff per a July 20, 1862 Clothing Receipt Roll.

Cronin was one of the CSS VIRGINIA crewmen that volunteered for service on the CSS CHATTAHOOCHIE on August 1, 1862 and served on that ship through December 31, 1862 and from April 1, 1863 - June 12, 1863. Cronin was on board at the time of that ship's boiler explosion on May 27, 1863. On June 13, 1863 he transferred to the CSS SAVANNAH in the Savannah River Squadron and was appointed by the State of Georgia as a Boatswain on July 11, 1863.

He served aboard the CSS SAVANNAH (formerly the "Oconee") on the Savannah Station in 1863. He is listed as having been paid for service at the Charleston Naval Station for the period October 1, 1863 - October 31, 1863 and was on the CSS SAVANNAH on the Charleston Station in 1864. Cronin was named a Boatswain, Provisional Navy on June 2, 1864
[Source: NCCWSP]

Croom, Joseph T. (New Hanover County, North Carolina)
Confederate States Navy. Born in North Carolina in August 1825, Croom resided with his wife, Ella J., and three children in New Hanover County, North Carolina in 1860. His pension application filed on July 20, 1903, at age 77, listed his post office listed as Gritt, Pender County, North Carolina. Pension approved. He listed his enlistment date in the Navy as 1862.
[Source(s): Card File; Pensions (North Carolina); Census (North Carolina), 1860; Foenander]

Crossan, Alex
> 1st Class Boy, North Carolina Ship WINSLOW. Slave of ship commander Thomas Crossan, and one of seven African American crew members aboard the NCS WINSLOW.
> [Source(s): NCS]

Crossan, Thomas Morrow (Born 1819 in the North)
> Lieutenant, Confederate States Navy. Of Northern birth, Crossan married a lady from North Carolina. Upon the secession of North Carolina, Crossan cast his fortunes with her and served as a first commander of the CSS WINSLOW and afterwards as commander of the North Carolina blockade runner, "Ad-Vance." Listed by source DH Hill as one of the first officers commissioned as a Lieutenant in the North Carolina Navy. An 1861 resolution by the General Assembly of North Carolina complimented Crossan on his naval skills, qualifications, and service to the Navy of the State of North Carolina and recommended him for the Confederate States Navy. He died on October 16, 1865, and was buried in Somerville Cemetery, Warrenton, North Carolina.
> [Source(s): McElroy; Ellis; Card File; Stepp, "Burials;" DH Hill; Resolutions (GA of North Carolina)]

Crossan, William
> Seaman, NCS WINSLOW. Slave of ship commander Thomas Crossan, and one of seven African American crew members aboard the NCS WINSLOW.
> [Source(s): NCS]

Crossland, Sebastian T. (Cumberland County, North Carolina)
> Sergeant, Confederate States Army//Confederate States Navy (?). Crossland was born in Cumberland County, North Carolina where he resided as a farmer until enlisting as a Private at Camp Mangum near Raleigh at age 20 on December 2, 1861 in Company A, 35th Regiment, North Carolina Troops. Reported present or accounted for January - April 1862, he was promoted to Sergeant between March – April 1862. On January 21, 1864 he was transferred as a Private to Company C, 51st Regiment, North Carolina Troops in exchange for Corporal John E. Hussey. Reported present or accounted for through October 1864, Crossland was reported absent under arrest in Richmond, Virginia November – December 1864, no explanation given. He was reported in the hospital at Salisbury, North Carolina as of January 21, 1865 with an unspecified complaint. He returned to duty on February 5, 1865. Source "Card File" lists him as having performed naval service.
> [Source(s): Card File; NCT, Vol. VIII]

Crumpler, William E. (County unknown)
> Landsman, Confederate States Navy. Crumpler enlisted on June 6, 1864, in Raleigh for the war.
> [Source(s): Card File; NA RG 45]

Cullifer, Joseph (Washington County, North Carolina)
> Private, Confederate States Army//Confederate States Navy. Cullifer resided in Washington County, North Carolina where he enlisted at age 26 on June 24, 1861 for the war in the Company G, 1st Regiment, North Carolina State Troops. He was present or accounted for until discharged on February 3, 1862 upon transfer to the Confederate States Navy, where he served as an Ordinary Seaman aboard the CSS VIRGINIA, Hampton Roads, Virginia, 1862.
> [Source(s): Card File; North Carolina Troops, III; Foenander]

Cullington, James (Washington County, North Carolina)
> 4th Corporal, Confederate States Army//Confederate States Navy. Born about 1842, Cullington resided in Washington County, North Carolina, where he enlisted at age 19 on June 24, 1861 for the war in Company G, 1st Regiment, North Carolina State Troops. Mustered in as a Corporal, he was reduced to the rank of Private on November 15, 1861. Cullington was present or accounted for until discharged on February 3, 1862 upon transfer to the Confederate States Navy (January 1862 per MR). He served as Seaman aboard the CSS VIRGINIA, Hampton Roads, 1862, and later as Captain of the Forecastle on the CSS ALBEMARLE, and at Halifax Station, 1864. He was highly praised by his commander, James W. Cooke, for his actions aboard the CSS ALBEMARLE, May 5, 1864.
> [Source(s): Card File; North Carolina Troops, III; Foenander; MR, I]

Cummings, J. F. F. (County unknown)
> Landsman, Confederate States Navy. Cummings enlisted on August 12, 1864, in Raleigh, for the war.
> [Source(s): Card File; NA RG 45]

Cunningham, J. B. (Madison County, North Carolina)
> Confederate States Navy. A resident of Madison County, North Carolina, Cunningham served as a pilot aboard the CSS VIRGINIA, and participated in the engagement at Hampton Roads, Virginia, March 1862.
> [Source(s): Foenander]

Cunningham, John
> Seaman, Confederate States Navy. Cunningham enlisted in the Confederate States Navy in Wilmington, North Carolina, on September 9, 1863, for the war. He served aboard the CSS ARCTIC, 1863, and the CSS YADKIN, 1864.
> [Source(s): Card File; NA RG 45; Foenander; St. Amand].

Currance, John S. (may also be John J. Carrence)
> Seaman, North Carolina Navy, Confederate States Navy.
> Currence served as a Seaman aboard the NCS EDWARDS per his shipping articles dated July 25, 1861 and through September 1861. He filled the same role aboard the NCS FORREST at least as early as October 30, 1861.
> [Source: NCCWSP]

Currie, Archibald (Cumberland County, North Carolina)
> "Private," Confederate States Navy. Registers of Confederate States Army General Military Hospital Number 4, Wilmington, North Carolina, state he was admitted on March 31, 1864, with "febris remittens" and returned to duty on April 28, 1864. His post office was given on the registers as Dundarrach, North Carolina.
> [Source(s): Card File; NA RG 109]

Currie [Curry], Archibald A. (County unknown) [NOTE: May be same as Archibald Currie and /or "A. A. Curry"]
> Landsman, Confederate States Navy. Currie enlisted on January 25, 1864, in Raleigh, for the war.
> [Source(s): Card File; NA RG 45; Foenander]

Currie, John H.
> Landsman, Seaman, Confederate States Navy. Born in June 1833 [Source "Stepp" – 1834], Currie died on February 14, 1914, and was buried in the Confederate Section of Oakwood Cemetery, Raleigh, Wake County, North Carolina, Grave # 101. Currie is said to have served aboard the CSS ALBEMARLE.
> [Source(s): Oakwood; Stepp, "Burials"]

Curry ["Currie"?], A. A. (North Carolina?)
> Landsman, Confederate States Navy. Curry served aboard the CSS ARCTIC, Cape Fear River, North Carolina, 1863. In 1864, he served aboard the CSS NORTH CAROLINA, Cape Fear River, and the CSS RALEIGH, in North Carolina and Virginia waters.
> [Source(s): Foenander]

Curtis, H. W. (County unknown)
> Landsman, Confederate States Navy. Curtis enlisted on February 4, 1864, in Raleigh, for the war. He served as a Landsman aboard the CSS ARCTIC, Cape Fear River, North Carolina, 1863
> [Source(s): Card File; NA RG 45; Foenander]

Curtis, James Alexander (Alamance County, North Carolina)
> "Private," Confederate States Navy. Source "Pensions (North Carolina)" lists his home of record as Randolph County, North Carolina. An attachment to the application for pension of widow, Mary E. Curtis, states that "J. A. Curtis was employed at the first part of the war at Clapp's Foundry and Machine Works as a gun maker and when the gun shop was moved to Fayetteville, North Carolina, he was then working for the North Carolina Railroad Company at Company Shops in Alamance County, North Carolina. In 1864 he was conscripted and enlisted in Raleigh, North Carolina, and was assigned to the Navy and did service on a gun boat known as "Old Ironsides." He was later transferred to Petersburg and was sick in hospital at the end of the war." He appears on a roll of prisoners of war transferred from Libby Prison, Richmond, Virginia, to Newport News, Virginia, April 23, 1865, which state he was captured at Naval Hospital, Richmond, Virginia, on April 3, 1865. He signed an Oath of Allegiance at Newport News, Virginia, June 14, 1865. His place of residence was listed on the Oath as Alamance County, North Carolina. Description: complexion fair; hair dark; eyes dark; height 5 feet 6 inches. He died in 1923.
> [Source(s): Card File; NA RG 109; Pensions (North Carolina)]

Curtis, J. D. (County unknown)
    Ordinary Seaman, Confederate States Navy. Curtis enlisted on June 1, 1863, in Wilmington, North Carolina, for three years.
    [Source(s): Card File; NA RG 45]

Curtis, J. J. (Perquimans County, North Carolina)
    Confederate States Navy. Curtis deserted on June 20, 1863 from Smithville, North Carolina.
    [Source(s): "Absentees"]

Curtis, J. K. (County unknown)
    Landsman, Confederate States Navy. Curtis enlisted on May 18, 1864 in Raleigh, North Carolina, for the war.
    (Sources: Card File; NA RG 45]

Curtis, John M.
    Seaman, Confederate States Navy. Curtis enlisted from the State of North Carolina and served aboard the CSS VIRGINIA.
    [Source(s): McElroy; Merrimack; Card File]

Curtis, William R. (Gates County, North Carolina)
    Seaman and Captain of the After Guard, Confederate States Navy. Curtis served as a Seaman and Captain of the After Guard aboard the CSS NORTH CAROLINA, Cape Fear River, North Carolina, 1864.
    [Source(s): MR, 4, p. 443; Foenander]

Curtis, William R. (County unknown)
    (NOTE: May be same as W. R. Curtis)
    Ordinary Seaman, Confederate States Navy. Curtis enlisted on June 1, 1863 in Wilmington, North Carolina, for three years.
    [Source(s): Card File; NA RG 45]

Cussick, Thomas F. (also Cuprick)
    1st Class Fireman, North Carolina Navy, Confederate States Navy.
    A native of Ireland, Cussick was aged 25 working as a canal laborer prior signing on as a 2nd Class Fireman aboard the NCS WINSLOW per that ship's muster roll of July - November 1861. He was serving as a 1st Class Fireman on board the NCS SEA BIRD by February 1862. He participated and was captured in the Battle of Elizabeth City and was carried to Roanoke Island as a prisoner. His name appears on a payroll of the North Carolina Squadron for the 1st quarter of 1862 covering the period from December 1, 1861 – February 12, 1862. He was listed" per the payroll report ending February 12, 1862. He took the Oath of Allegiance to the United States on February 12, 1862 on Roanoke Island.
    [Source: NCCWSP]

Cuthbert, Elijah C. (Craven County, North Carolina)
    Confederate States Navy. Cuthbert served aboard the Steamer "Boston." His name appears on a register of prisoners of war at Military Prison, Camp Hamilton, Virginia, which states he was captured off Wilmington, North Carolina, July 8, 1864, by the federal gunboat USS FORT JACKSON and charged as a "Blockade Runner." He was confined at Camp Hamilton July 18, 1864, and sent to Point Lookout, Maryland, August 24, 1864. His name also appears on a roll of prisoners of war released at Point Lookout, Maryland, from May 12 to 14, 1865 on taking the Oath of Allegiance. His place of residence was given on the Oath of Allegiance as New Bern, North Carolina; occupation as Seaman.
    [Source(s): Card File' NA RG 109]

Dallas, James J. (Rockingham County, North Carolina)
    Seaman, Confederate States Navy. Dallas enlisted on June 18, 1864 in Raleigh for the war. The brother of Robert W. Dallas (q.v.), James died in 1894 in Rockingham County, North Carolina and was buried at the old Dallas Family Cemetery, Dallas Family home place, Rockingham County, North Carolina.
    [McElroy; NA, RG 45; Dallas; Stepp, "Burials"]

Dallas, Robert W. (Rockingham County, North Carolina)
Private, Confederate States Marine Corps or Landsman, Confederate States Navy. Family records indicate birth in 1820. He married Jane B. Travis in Pittsylvania County, Virginia, on December 20, 1841. Enlisted June 15, 1864, in Raleigh for the war. Other sources list him as either a Landsman, Confederate States Navy, Seaman, Confederate States Navy, or Private, Confederate States Marine Corps [Source Donnelly-ENL says "Marine Corps]. Appeared on a roll of prisoners of war at Point Lookout, Maryland, which stated he was captured at Harper's Farm on April 6, 1865, and confined at Point Lookout, Maryland, until released on June 11, 1865, on taking the Oath of Allegiance to the United States. Description: Complexion light; hair iron gray; eyes dark blue; height 5 feet 8 inches. Brother of James J. Dallas (q.v.). Died 1892 when run over by a train in Rocky Mount, North Carolina.
[Source(s): North Carolina Troops, Doc. # 0185, p. 1, and 0299; NA; Card File; McElroy; Dallas]

Dalton, Andrew J. (Wake County, North Carolina)
Confederate States Navy. A printer at the *Weekly Raleigh Register* (Raleigh, North Carolina) in 1861, Dalton is said to have participated in the bombardment of Fort Sumter in April 1861, and to have served in several other engagements in the early months of the war. He left his job as a printer to serve aboard the CSS VIRGINIA (MERRIMAC) and was wounded in the action of Saturday, March 8, 1862, at Hampton Roads, Virginia.
[Source(s): Foenander; "Weekly Raleigh Register" (March 12, 1862)]

Dalton, Hamilton Henderson (North Carolina/Mississippi)
Confederate States Navy. Born in Madison County, North Carolina, on May 19, 1835, the son of Robert Hunter and Jane Martin Henderson Dalton (brother of William Robert Dalton). Previous service in the United States Navy, as a Lieutenant, from October 1, 1851. He attempted to resign at the beginning of the war, but was refused, and imprisoned at Fort Warren, Massachusetts (1861). He was released and exchanged in January 1862. On December 30, 1861, he was appointed (possibly in absentia) as a Lieutenant, Confederate States Navy, from Mississippi, and served on the Mississippi River defenses; aboard the CSS LIVINGSTON, 1862; and the Jackson Station, Mississippi River defenses, 1862. Dalton married Margaret McMillan in Monroe County, Mississippi, on July 7, 1862. He was appointed First Lieutenant, Confederate States Navy on October 23, 1862, and First Lieutenant, Provisional Confederate States Navy, on June 2, 1864 to rank from January 6, 1864. Served aboard the CSS LIVINGSTON, , 1862; Jackson Station, 1862; CSS GEORGIA, Savannah Squadron, 1862-63; steamers CSS TUSCALOOSA and CSS BALTIC, Mobile Squadron, 1863; CSS CHATTAHOOCHEE, 1863; temporarily transferred to the Charleston Station, for defensive duties, in September 1863; attached to the Savannah Squadron, aboard the steamers CSS GEORGIA, CSS SAMPSON, and CSS SAVANNAH, 1863 - 1864; detached from the CSS SAVANNAH and ordered to the command of the stern-wheeled gunboat CSS ISONDIGA, Savannah squadron, June 30, 1864; returned to command of CSS SAVANNAH, in late 1864; later served aboard the CSS RICHMOND, James River Squadron, 1865; ordered to Mobile, Alabama, but failed to reach that station before the final surrender. After the war, Dalton resided in several places, including Birmingham, Alabama (as a wholesale lumber and coal merchant), St. Louis, Missouri, Los Angeles, California and Seattle, King County, State of Washington. He was married with one son, who is noted to have treated his father very badly, and "robbed him of nearly every cent he had in the world." His wife died some years before his death. Dalton was a member of the United Confederate Veterans and was admitted to the Robert E. Lee, Camp 1, Confederate Veterans' Home, Richmond, Virginia, in December of 1923. He died on October 20, 1924, and his remains were taken by relatives for burial at the family plot at St. Louis, Missouri.
[Source(s): Navy Gray; Foenander; ONWR]

Daly, James M. [North Carolina(?)]
Confederate States Navy. Landsman aboard the CSS ARCTIC, Cape Fear River, North Carolina, 1863, and the CSS RALEIGH, in North Carolina and Virginia waters, 1864.
[Source(s): Foenander; ORN 2, 1, 278 & 302]

Daly, John T. (Lenoir County, North Carolina)
Private, Confederate States Army//Confederate States Navy. Resided in Lenoir County, North Carolina, where he enlisted at age 18 on May 14, 1862, for the war, in Company A, 47th Regiment, North Carolina Troops. Captured at Gettysburg, Pennsylvania, July 1-4, 1863, he was hospitalized at David's Island, New York Harbor, on or about July 17, 1863. No reason was given for his hospitalization. Paroled at David's Island on an unspecified date, he was received at City Point, Virginia, on September 8, 1863, for exchange, and returned to duty on an unspecified date. Reported present in January-February 1864. He transferred to the Confederate States Navy on April 1, 1864.
[Source(s): McElroy; North Carolina Troops, XI; Foenander]

Daly, J. W.
> 1st Class Boy, Confederate States Navy. Enlisted at age 17 and served as a 1st Class Boy aboard the CSS NORTH CAROLINA, Cape Fear River, North Carolina, 1864.
> [McElroy; UDC, Kinston; Foenander]

Daniel, Jno. (Wayne County, North Carolina)
> Confederate States Navy. Name appears as signature to an Oath of Allegiance to the United States, subscribed and sworn to September 26, 1863. Place of residence given on oath as Goldsboro, North Carolina. Description: Complexion, dark; hair, brown; eyes, blue; height, 6 ft. 1 in.
> [McElroy; NA, RG 109]

Daniel, John T. (Currituck County, North Carolina)
> Private, Confederate States Army//Confederate States Navy. Born in Currituck County, North Carolina, where he resided as a sailor prior to enlisting there at age 16 on August 10, 1861, for the war, as a Private in Company B, 8th Regiment, North Carolina Troops. Captured at Roanoke Island, North Carolina, on February 8, 1862, and paroled at Elizabeth City, North Carolina, on February 21, 1862. Exchanged in August 1862. Present or accounted for until transferred to the Confederate States Navy on or about April 10, 1964.
> [Source(s): North Carolina Troops, IV; McElroy]

Daniel, Robert Heath (Edgecombe or Halifax County, North Carolina)
> Commissary and/or Surgeon's Steward, Confederate States Navy. Born in North Carolina, in April 1845, he enlisted in the Confederate States Navy at the age of 17, from Halifax, North Carolina, in 1861. Daniel served on board the CSS ALBEMARLE. He married on June 3, 1875 and resided as a merchant, in 1880, with his wife, Lucy Gary Daniel, and two children (eldest child born in 1877), at Halifax, Halifax County, North Carolina. He continued to reside at Halifax and was employed as enumerator and tax collector. He was still shown at this residence in 1920; his widow, Lucy later applied for a post war Confederate pension from Halifax County, North Carolina. Application for pension dated October 27, 1932 by his widow Lucy Gary Daniel at age 81, states he enlisted in 1865 in Halifax [1864?]. He was discharged in April [1865]. An application to join the United Daughters of the Confederacy states his military record as: "served in Confederate States Navy as Surgeon's Steward. He served under Captain Cook, Commander of the gun boat ALBEMARLE stationed at Halifax. He was Surgeon's Steward under Dr. Peck of Greens[boro], Alabama and Dr. [Forte(?)] of Warrenton, North Carolina." He was also said to have been involved in "the construction and operation of the Ram Albemarle." Daniel died on September 28, 1930 but was not drawing a pension at the time of his death. Daughters were Miss. Esther Daniel, Halifax, North Carolina and Mrs. H. R. Marshall, 511 Keenan St., Wilson, North Carolina.
> [Source(s): McElroy; Pensions (North Carolina); Foenander; Census (North Carolina) 1880]

Daniel, William S. (Alexander County, North Carolina)
> Landsman, Confederate States Navy. Born in North Carolina, about 1835, Daniel enlisted on November 15 [14], 1863, in Wilmington [Raleigh] for the war. Appears on a register of Confederate States Army General Military Hospital Number 4, Wilmington, North Carolina, being admitted March 23, 1864, with "pleuritis" and returned to duty May 7, 1864. Post office given on register as Taylorsville, North Carolina. Widow Clementine Daniel's June 25, 1912 application for pension states he "enlisted on October 15, 1862[;] transferred to the Navy and served on board the ship ARCTIC [;] Captain Pa [...?] [in] command. He was on duty on the Carolina coast from Wilmington, North Carolina, to Charleston, SC, stationed on Cape Fear River when not on duty."
> [Source(s): McElroy; NA, RG 445; NA, RG 109; NA, RG 45; Pensions (North Carolina); Foenander]

Daniels, Edward (New Hanover County, North Carolina)
> Crewman, Confederate States Navy. CSS NORTH CAROLINA.
> [Source(s): MR, 4, p. 443; St. Amand]

Daniels, Edward F. (Brunswick County, North Carolina)
> Confederate States Navy. Born in North Carolina about 1834, Daniels served in the Confederate States Navy as a Quartermaster and Pilot aboard the CSS CASWELL and CSS ARCTIC, Wilmington Station, 1861-1863. A pension request claim filed on July 5, 1909, by his widow, Sarah E. Daniels, at age 67, listed his post office as Southport, Brunswick County, North Carolina. Pension request was approved. In the application she states her husband enlisted in the Confederate States Navy on December 1, 1862. The witness on the application was John W. Galloway of Southport, North Carolina.
> [McElroy; Pensions (North Carolina; Foenander; ORN 1 & 2; Foenander]

Daniels, John Thomas, Sr. (Currituck County, North Carolina)
Confederate States Navy. Daniels was born in Currituck County, North Carolina, in February 1846, the son of Thomas Ros Daniels (1825 – 1855) and Celia T. Pugh (c. 1819 – 1849). He resided at the home of his grandmother, Sarah Daniel, in Currituck County as a sailor prior to enlisting there, on August 10, 1861, as a Private in Company B, 8th Regiment, North Carolina State Troops. He was captured at Roanoke Island, February 8, 1862, exchanged August 1862, and transferred to the Confederate States Navy on or about April 10, 1864. He served as an Ordinary Seaman aboard the CSS ALBEMARLE and at Halifax Station, late 1864. He married Mary "Polly" Wescott, circa 1870. In post war years, Daniels' occupations included sailor, farmer and fisherman. He is shown residing as a boatman and farmer with his wife and four children at Nags Head Township, Dare County, North Carolina, in 1880.
[Source(s): Foenander; North Carolina Troops IV; ORN 2, 1, 274; Census (NC), 1880]

Daniels, E.T.
Pilot, Confederate States Navy. Served aboard the blockade runner "Coquette."
[Source(s): McElroy]

Daniels, Jordan (Beaufort County, North Carolina)
Confederate States Marine Corps. Enlisted at Raleigh, North Carolina, on October 6, 1864 and served in Company F, Confederate States Marine Corps, on the Charleston, South Carolina, station. Served as a Private of the Marine guard on board the ironclad CSS COLUMBIA to February 7, 1865. Transferred to the CSS INDIAN CHIEF on February 8, 1865. Appears on a register of Confederate States Army General Hospital No. 11, Charlotte, North Carolina, being admitted on April 7, 1865. Disease listed as "phthisis." Captured at General Hospital #11, Charlotte, North Carolina, on April 13, 1865, and sent to another hospital on April 14, 1865. Daniels was paroled at Raleigh, North Carolina, May 6, 1865, and died circa April 1867. A pension claim was filed on June 28, 1901 by his widow, Polly Ann Daniels, age 65, POST OFFICE "Bumyon" [sic] (Bunyan), Beaufort County, North Carolina. The pension was approved. Per the 1860 Census of North Carolina, Daniels, age 27, lived at Longacre, Beaufort County, North Carolina, with his wife, age 32.
[Source(s): Pensions (North Carolina); North Carolina Troops, Doc.# 0299; NA; Card File; Census (NC), 1860]

Darcy, A.
Seaman, Confederate States Navy.
Darcy's name appears on a payroll of the North Carolina Squadron for the period covering the 1st quarter of 1862 from January 7, 1862 - February 28, 1862. He is listed as having "run" per the payroll ending February 28, 1862.
[Source: NCCWSP]

Darnel, Augustin[e] (Stokes County, North Carolina)
Private, Confederate States Army//Confederate States Navy. Darnel was born in Stokes County, North Carolina about 1824 and resided in Surry County, North Carolina where he lived as a farmer prior to enlisting there at age 35 on March 27, 1862, in Company E, 53rd Regiment, North Carolina Troops. He was discharged on May 24, 1862, by reason of being overage, but then re-enlisted in Company H, 53rd Regiment, North Carolina Troops in Stokes County, North Carolina on February 25, 1863. He transferred to the Confederate States Navy on or about April 10, 1864. His first application for a North Carolina Confederate Pension, dated June 22, 1907, gives his enlistment date as February 1862, and states that "after serving in the Army a while (Company E, 53rd Reg.)" he joined the Navy and was in the service on the "Patrick Henry" [CSS PATRICK HENRY] under Captain Parker when the war closed." Second application dated July 4, 1908 (no additional data). He resided as a farmer with his wife Sallie and two nephews at Pilot, Surry County, NC, in 1880. He died in Rutherford County, North Carolina, June 28, 1911.
[Source(s): Foenander; McElroy; Pensions (North Carolina); North Carolina Troops, XIII]

Darrack, David
Landsman, Confederate States Navy. Enlisted December 6, 1863. Name canceled with line on roll and carries the remark, "Deserted from camp."
[McElroy; NA, RG 45]

Dashiel, Julius C. (Pasquotank County, North Carolina)
Private, Confederate States Army//Landsman, Confederate States Navy. Born in Nansemond County, Virginia, Dashiel was a student prior to enlisting in Pasquotank County, North Carolina, at age 24 on April 23, 1861 as a Private in Company A, 17th Regiment, North Carolina Troops (1st Organization). Present of accounted for until he transferred to the Confederate States Navy on July 18, 1861.
[Source(s): McElroy; North Carolina Troops, VI]

Davenport, Snowden B. (Tyrrell County, North Carolina)
Private, Confederate States Army//Seaman, Confederate States Navy. Enlisted in Tyrrell County, North Carolina, on June 28, 1862 for the war in Company G, 1st Regiment, North Carolina State Troops. Present or accounted for until transferred to the Confederate States Navy on December 30, 1863. Davenport served as a Seaman aboard the CSS ARCTIC and as landsman aboard the CSS RALEIGH, 1864; captured aboard the CSS BOMBSHELL during the engagement at Albemarle Sound, North Carolina, May 5, 1 864, and transferred, the same day, from the USS CERES to the USS SASSACUS, then to the steamer USS LOCKWOOD, on May 10, 1864, for transportation to a prisoner of war facility.
[Source(s): McElroy; North Carolina Troops, III; Foenander]

Davidson, Sylvester
Ordinary Seaman, Confederate States Navy. Served as a Landsman aboard the CSS ARCTIC, Cape Fear River, North Carolina, 1863. He had further service as an Ordinary Seaman aboard the CSS RALEIGH, in North Carolina and Virginia waters, 1864.
[Source(s): Foenander; ORN 2, 1, 278 & 302]

Davidson, Wilbar (Wilbur) (Buncombe County, North Carolina)
Cadet/Midshipman/Second Lieutenant, Confederate States Navy. Served as a Midshipman in the Confederate States Naval School from Asheville, North Carolina. Served as a Midshipman aboard side wheeled steamer CSS PATRICK HENRY, James River, Virginia, 1864 (which served as the Confederate States Naval Academy). He served aboard the CSS VIRGINIA II, James River, Virginia, 1864-1865. At the end of the war, he was attached as Second Lieutenant to command Company E, 1st Regiment, Semmes' Naval Brigade, in April 1865. Davidson surrendered and was paroled at Greensboro, North Carolina, April 26, 1865. He is shown as one of the few members of the Association of Survivors of the Confederate States Navy, when they met up at Murphy's Hotel, in Richmond, Virginia, in May 1907.
[Source(s): McElroy; Foenander]

Davis, Abram
Seaman, Confederate States Navy. Enlisted January 1, 1864, in Wilmington for the war.
[McElroy; NA, RG 45]

Davis, Anson (Carteret County, North Carolina)
Confederate States Navy. Davis enlisted in the Confederate States Navy, was captured and enlisted in the Union Army, probably in Company G or H, 1st North Carolina Volunteers (US).
[Source(s): Salter]

Davis, B. M. (Wayne County, North Carolina)
Private(?), Confederate States Navy. Appears on a Roll of Prisoners of War paroled at Provost Marshal's Office at Goldsboro, North Carolina. Residence given as Wayne County, North Carolina.
[McElroy; NA, RG 109]

Davis, B. W.
Seaman, Confederate States Navy. Davis enlisted on April 15, 1864, in Kinston for three years or the war. While serving as a Seaman aboard the CSS BOMBSHELL, he was captured at Albemarle Sound, North Carolina, May 5, 1864. He was transferred the same day from the USS CERES to the USS SASSACUS, then to the steamer USS LOCKWOOD, on May 10, 1864, for transportation to a prisoner of war facility. Confined at Point Lookout, Maryland, he died there and is buried at the Point Lookout Cemetery.
[Source(s): Foenander; McElroy; NA, RG 45]

Davis, David A. [North Carolina (?)]
Seaman, Officers' Steward and Flag Officer's Cook, Confederate States Navy.
Served as an Officers' Steward aboard the CSS BEAUFORT; September 1861 - April 1862, operating in North Carolina and Virginia waters as part of the North Carolina Squadron. He served later as a Flag Officer's Cook aboard the steam gunboat CSS YADKIN, Wilmington, North Carolina in1864. His name appears on a payroll of the receiving ship CSS UNITED STATES ending March 31, 1862 and on the payroll of the North Carolina Squadron for the 1st quarter of 1862 covering from February 21, 1862 - April 15, 1862. Davis transferred to the James River Squadron on April 15, 1862. He served at Drewry's Bluff as Officer's Steward from April 1, 1863 - June 30, 1863.
[Source(s): Foenander; NCCWSP]

Davis, D. M.
Ordinary Seaman, Confederate States Navy. Enlisted April 12, 1864, in Kinston, North Carolina, for three years or the war. Served aboard the CSS NEUSE as of the ship's March – October 1864 muster roll.
[McElroy; NA, RG 45; NEUSE Roster; CMACSSN]

Davis, George W. (Carteret County, North Carolina)
First Lieutenant, Confederate States Army//Confederate States Navy. Davis enlisted October 16, 1861, in Company G, 40th North Carolina Infantry, and was appointed a First Lieutenant. He transferred to the Confederate States Navy "blockading service" and served as a Landsman aboard CSS SELMA. Captured at Mobile Bay, Alabama, August 5, 1864, he was sent aboard the USS PORT ROYAL, as a prisoner of war. Confined at Fort Warren, Boston Harbor, Massachusetts, Davis was exchanged on March 2, 1865. He married Carrie M. Smith, December 21, 1865, at Brunswick, North Carolina, and resided in Florida beginning in January 1888. He died on October 19, 1893 in Hancock County, Michigan (or October 1, 1903, in Louisiana).
[Source(s): Foenander; ORN 1, 21, 844]

Davis, George W. W. (New Hanover County, North Carolina [?])
Seaman, Confederate States Navy. Born August 24, 1844, Davis died on May 30, 1885, and was buried in Oakdale Cemetery, Wilmington, North Carolina.
[Source(s): Stepp, "Burials"]

Davis, Hiram A. [H. E. (?)] (Catawba County, North Carolina)
Third Lieutenant, Confederate States Army//Confederate States Navy. Born in Randolph County, North Carolina, about 1834, Davis resided in Catawba County, North Carolina, as a machinist or carpenter until he enlisted there at age 29 on October 31, 1861, as a Sergeant, in Company F, 38th Regiment, North Carolina Troops. He was elected Lieutenant on April 1, 1863. Present or accounted for through February 1864. Court-martialed, reason unknown, on or about April 9, 1864, he resigned on May 1, 1864, by reason of his desire to serve in the Confederate States Navy. His resignation was accepted on June 30, 1864 however there is no record of his service in the Navy [per source "North Carolina Troops," "[H]is letter of resignation is annotated by one of his superior officers who state that 3rd Lieutenant Davis was 'an inefficient officer.' No evidence was located that he served in the navy."]. He resided as a carpenter, in 1870, with his wife, Louisa and one son, at Clines Township, Catawba County, North Carolina. Davis filed an application for a pension on July 9, 1902, at the age of 61, listing his post office as Belhaven, Beaufort County, North Carolina. The application gives his enlistment date as April 1864, and states that he was injured in June 1864. He served in the Navy at Charleston, SC, working on the CSS INDIAN CHIEF, "a "parley (?) and receiving ship." He fell from the upper deck to the lower deck and severely damaged his back. His Captain was "Dosny" [or "Dosrng...(?)] and his Lieutenant was Ray. Said pension was approved. One source lists him as "wounded" [probably "injured"] at Charleston, SC, in 1864.
[Source(s): McElroy; Pensions (North Carolina); North Carolina Troops, I & X; Foenander]

Davis, Hosea E.
Landsman, Confederate States Navy. Enlisted May 27, 1864, at Raleigh for the war.
[McElroy; NA, RG 45]

Davis, Isaac A. (Bladen County, North Carolina)
Corporal, Confederate States Army//Landsman, Confederate States Navy. Born April 29, 1843, in Bladen County, North Carolina, and was a farmer there until he enlisted as a Private at age 18 at Camp Wyatt on September 27, 1861, in Company B, 18th Regiment, North Carolina Troops. Promoted to Corporal on October 22, 1862, Davis was present or accounted for until he transferred to Confederate States Navy on or about April 3, 1864. He died September 28, 1917 and was buried at Oak Grove Church, Bladen County, North Carolina.
[Source(s): North Carolina Troops, VI; McElroy; Foenander; S.O. #89; Stepp, "Burials"]

Davis, James C. (Moore County, North Carolina)
Private, Confederate States Marine Corps. A resident of Moore County, North Carolina, Davis served in the Confederate States Marine Corps. He was sent to Camp Holmes, where he was instructed for a short time, before being sent to Charleston for service aboard the CSS INDIAN CHIEF. He arrived there on Sunday, November 6, 1864, for further drill and instruction as a marine. He was later sent aboard the CSS CHICORA, Charleston Station. He wrote a letter to the editor of the *Fayetteville Observer*, dated November 17, 1864, describing his movements and activities on the CSS INDIAN CHIEF.
[Source(s): Davis, November 17, 1864; Foenander; Fay. Obs. (Nov., 24, 1864)]

Davis, Jeff (Moore County, North Carolina)
Confederate States Marine Corps. Mentioned in the April 24, 1871 letter of William McLeod (q.v.), former member of the Confederate States Marine Corps.
[Source(s): Donnelly; McLeod Ltr., April 24, 1871]

Davis, John (Wayne County, North Carolina)
Private, Confederate States Army//Landsman, Confederate States Navy. Leaving his pre-war occupation as a laborer, Davis enlisted in Cumberland County, North Carolina, on March 18, 1864, at age 18, in the Confederate States Navy. He served as a Landsman aboard the CSS ALBEMARLE, and at Halifax Station, 1864. Another source states Davis was conscripted on March 18, 1864, at Camp Holmes, from Colonel McCoy's 54th Regiment, North Carolina Militia, Cumberland County, North Carolina. Description: Eyes-gray; hair- light; complexion-fair; height-5ft. 3in; age 18; place of birth-Wayne [County, North Carolina]; occupation-laborer.
[Source(s): McElroy; NA, RG45; Roster, 54th Regiment, North Carolina Militia; Foenander]

Davis, John
Landsman, Confederate States Navy. Enlisted March 21, 1864, in Raleigh for war.
[McElroy, NA, RG 45]

Davis, Josiah C. (Mecklenburg County, North Carolina)
Private, Confederate States Army//Confederate States Navy. Born in Cocke County, Tennessee, Davis resided as a farmer and enlisted in Mecklenburg County, North Carolina on May 20, 1861 at age 23 as a Private in Company B, 13th Regiment, North Carolina Troops. Present or accounted for until he transferred to the Confederate States Navy on February 25, 1862 for duty on the CSS VIRGINIA (CSS MERRIMAC).
[Source(s): McElroy; North Carolina Troops, V; MR, I; Foenander]

Davis, L. M. (Alexander County, North Carolina) [NOTE: May be same as "L. M. Davis, Alexander County, enlisted June 13, 1864, q.v.]
Confederate States Navy. Enlisted August 1, 1863. Filed a claim for a pension on July 18, 1924, age 80, post office Hiddenite, Alexander County. The request was approved. Davis served in the Navy on the sloop of war CSS PEE DEE under the command of "Captain Johnson." Wounded by shellfire on July 4, 1864.
[Source(s): McElroy; Pensions (North Carolina)]

Davis, L. M. (Alexander County, North Carolina) [NOTE: May be same as "L. M. Davis, Alexander County, enlisted August 1, 1863, q.v.]
Confederate States Navy. Enlisted on June 13, 1864, in Raleigh, North Carolina, for the war. He applied for a post war Confederate pension from Alexander County, North Carolina.
[Source(s): McElroy; NA, RG 45; Foenander]

Davis, Samuel R. [North Carolina (?)]
Landsman, Confederate States Navy. Served aboard the steam gunboat CSS YADKIN, Wilmington, North Carolina, 1864.
[Source(s): Foenander; ORN 2, 1, 313]

Day, James L. [North Carolina (?)]
Seaman, Confederate States Navy. Day served aboard the CSS SEA BIRD as part of the North Carolina Squadron from July 1861 – March 1862. He was captured in the Battle of Elizabeth City on February 10, 1862, following the sinking of the CSS SEA BIRD, taken to Roanoke Island, North Carolina, paroled on February 12, 1862, and returned to Elizabeth City. He received a partial payment on February 18, 1862 at Gosport Navy Yard [NOTE: probably circa February 18, 1862]. His name appears on a North Carolina Squadron payroll for the 1st quarter of 1862 covering from December 1,1861 – April 15, 1862. He is listed as "on parole" on a payroll dated April 15, 1862.
[Source(s): Foenander; Scharf, 392; ORN 2, 1, 306; NCCWSP]

Day, L. S. (L. L.) (North Carolina)
Seaman, Pilot/Confederate States Navy. Day was born in North Carolina circa 1817 and resided in the 1st Ward of the town of New Bern, Craven County, North Carolina as a "Sea Captain." He served aboard the CSS SEA BIRD from July 1861 through 10 February 1862. His name appears on an 1862 North Carolina Squadron payroll as a Seaman from 1 December 1861 - 9 January 1862 and 19 February 1862 - 15 April 1862. On 10 January 1862 he was elevated to the position of "Pilot," and his name was moved to the officer roll. One source stated he later served as Pilot of the CSS APPOMATTOX. Day held the position for only one month since his ship was rammed and sunk

during the Battle of Elizabeth City, North Carolina on 10 February 1862. Day is listed as having received a partial payment on 18 February 1862 at Gosport Navy Yard, Norfolk, Virginia. The very next day, February 19, 1862, he was demoted and returned to enlisted status. [Source(s): Foenander; ORN 2, 1, 306; NCCWSP; Census (NC), 1860]

Dawkins, W. K. (Moore County, North Carolina)
Private, Confederate States Marine Corps. Enlisted at Raleigh, North Carolina, on October 6, 1864. [NOTE: Letter of James C. Davis, November 17, 1864, states the group from Camp Holmes, of which Dawkins was a part, arrived aboard the CSS INDIAN CHIEF, Charleston, South Carolina, on Sunday, November 6, 1864, and was designated to serve aboard the ironclad CSS CHICORA]. Served on the Charleston Station as a Private of the Marine guard on board the ironclad, CSS COLUMBIA. Deserted on January 5, 1865.
[Source(s): North Carolina Troops, Doc.# 0299; Card File; Davis, November 17, 1864]

Deal, Daniel [North Carolina (?)]
Landsman, Confederate States Navy. Served aboard the CSS ARCTIC, Cape Fear River, North Carolina, 1863.
[Source(s): Foenander; ORN 2, 1, 278.]

Deal, David (New Hanover County, North Carolina)
Seaman, Confederate States Navy. Registers of Confederate States Army General Military Hospital Number 4, Wilmington, North Carolina, state that he was admitted January 21, 1864, with "pneumonia" and returned to duty January 26, 1864. Post office given on register as Wilmington, North Carolina. No further records.
[Source(s): McElroy; NA, RG 109]

Deal [Deel], Sidney L. (Burke/Mecklenburg County, North Carolina)
Private, Confederate States Army//Landsman, Confederate States Navy. Born in Burke County, North Carolina, about 1842, Deal was by occupation a farmer prior to enlisting in Mecklenburg County, North Carolina, at age 21 on May 28, 1861, for the war, in Company D, 6th Regiment, North Carolina State Troops. Transferred to the Confederate States Navy, September 3, 1863, and ordered to report to Charleston, South Carolina, where he served as a Landsman on board the CSS CHICORA. He resided as a farmer, in 1870, with his wife Martha, at Morganton Township, Burke County, North Carolina.
[Source(s): McElroy; North Carolina Troops, IV; *ORN* 2, 1, 284; Foenander; Census (North Carolina), 1870; MR, I]

Dean, A. F. (County unknown)
Confederate States Marine Corps. Wounded ("concussion of brain") and captured at Fort Fisher on January 15, 1865.
[Source(s): "Daily Confed." (2/18/65); Card File]

Deanes (Deams), M. H [Possibly M. H. Deannis or Marclem Hines Dean] (Nash County, North Carolina)
Confederate States Navy. Registers of Confederate States Army Military Hospital Number 4, Wilmington, North Carolina, state that he was admitted June 27, 1863, with "rheum." and was returned to duty July 10, 1863. Post office given as Stan Hope [Nash County, NORTH CAROLINA?].
[Source(s): McElroy; NA, RG 109; Foenander]

Deannis, M. H. [Possibly M. H. Deanes (or Deams) or Marclem Hines Deans]
Confederate States Navy. Enlisted June 1, 1863, at Wilmington for the war.
[Source(s): McElroy; NA, RG 45]

Deans, M. H. (Mecklenburg County, North Carolina)
Crewman, Confederate States Navy. CSS NORTH CAROLINA.
[Source(s): MR, 4, p. 443]

Deans, Marcum (Marclem) Hines [DEANES, DEAMS, DEANNIS] (New Hanover County, North Carolina)
Confederate States Navy. Deans enlisted in 1863. A claim was filed by his widow, Mary A. Deans, age 60, post office Wilmington, New Hanover County, North Carolina on June 21, 1901. Approval not shown. Husband died in Wilmington near the close of the war.
[Source(s): McElroy; Pensions (North Carolina)]

Deaton, John L.
    Landsman, Confederate States Navy. Enlisted August 1, 1864, in Raleigh for the war. No further records.
    [Source(s): McElroy; NA, RG 45]

Debose (De'Bouse; De Bose; DeBowee), Richard F. [Pender County, North Carolina]
    Ordinary Seaman, Confederate States Navy. Enlisted in the Confederate States Navy on September 5, 1863, in Wilmington, North Carolina, for the war. One source lists his enlistment date at August 23, 1863. Registers of Confederate States Army General Military Hospital Number 4, Wilmington, North Carolina, state he was admitted on October 22, 1863, with "rheumatism chron," assigned to ward/bed 6/113. Records indicate he listed his post office as Moore's Creek, North Carolina. Source "Hosp. (No. 4), Wilm." Has a double entry for this man giving an alternate date of admission as December 22, 1863.
    [Source(s): McElroy; NA, RG 109; NA, RG 45; MR. 4, p. 445; St. Amand; Hosp. (No. 4), Wilm.]

Deel, David
    Landsman, Confederate States Navy. Enlisted January 11, 1864, in Raleigh for the war.
    [Source(s): McElroy; NA, RG 45]

Deese [Dees], John B.
    Landsman, Confederate States Navy. Enlisted July 21, 1864, in Raleigh for the war. Deese served as a Landsman aboard the CSS ARCTIC, Cape Fear River, North Carolina, 1863.
    [Source(s): Foenander; ORN 2, 1, 279; McElroy; NA, RG 45]

Dellinger, Charles (Lincoln County, North Carolina)
    Landsman, Confederate States Navy. Dellinger enlisted on February 6, 1864, in Raleigh for the war. He served as a Landsman aboard the CSS ARCTIC, Cape Fear River, North Carolina, 1863, the CSS RALEIGH, North Carolina and Virginia waters, 1864, and as a Private, Company F, Confederate States Naval Battalion. His name appears on a roll of Prisoners of War at Point Lookout, Maryland, which states that he was captured at Farmville April 6, 1865. Confined at Point Lookout, Maryland, April 14, 1865, he was released on June 26, 1865, on taking the Oath of Allegiance to the United States. The Oath gives his place of residence as Lincoln County, North Carolina, and description as follows: Complexion-dark; hair-black; eyes-hazel; height-5 ft. 9½ in.
    [Source(s): McElroy; NA, RG 109; NA, RG 45; Hoke Camp; Foenander; ORN 2, 1, 278 & 302]

Dellinger, George (Lincoln County, North Carolina)
    Landsman, Confederate States Navy (Private, Naval Battalion). Dellinger enlisted on February 6, 1864, in Raleigh for the war. He served as a Landsman aboard the CSS ARCTIC, Cape Fear River, North Carolina, 1863, and aboard the CSS RALEIGH, in North Carolina and Virginia waters, 1862 -1864. Later, he served as a Private, Company F, Confederate States Naval Battalion. His name appears on a roll of Prisoners of War at Point Lookout Maryland, which states that he was captured at Farmville on April 6, 1865, and confined at Point Lookout April 14, 1865. His Oath of Allegiance to the United States was subscribed and sworn to at Point Lookout, Maryland, June 26, 1865, giving his place of residence as Lincoln County, North Carolina, and description as follows: Complexion-dark; hair-black; eyes-hazel; height-5 ft. 6½ in.
    [Source(s): McElroy; NA, RG 109; NA, RG 45; Hoke Camp; Foenander; ORN 2, 1, 278 & 302]

Delly, John (Dolly, Dellay, Delley)
    Private, Confederate States Army//Seaman, Coxswain, Confederate States Navy.
    Delly enlisted at Camp Clark, Texas, for the war as a Private in Company B, 4th Texas Infantry. He was discharged October 28, 1861 per Special Order #192, Adjutant & Inspector General's Office 61, para 12 to "work in another government branch." He served on the Receiving Ship CONFEDERATE STATES from January 1, 1862 - January 9, 1862. Delly served in North Carolina Squadron as a Seaman, appearing on a payroll of the North Carolina Squadron for the 1st quarter of 1862 covering from January 10, 1862 - February 9, 1862. He served as a Coxswain aboard the CSS VIRGINIA and reenlisted for war on that ship on March 25, 1862 for which he received a $50 bonus. His name appears as a Seaman on the final payroll of the CSS VIRGINIA for the period April 1, 1862 - 30 September 30, 1862. Delly was superannuated for rations while serving at Drewry's Bluff, Virginia for the period May 12, 1862 - May 24, 1862. A Drewry's Bluff payroll for the period May 13, 1862 - June 30, 1863, shows Delly in service there. He served as a Quartermaster at Drewry's Bluff from December 6, 1863 - December 31, 1863, and as a Seaman aboard the CSS VIRGINIA II as a member of the James River Squadron, in 1864-65. He was in Jackson General Hospital, Richmond, Virginia as of April 8, 1865. He is listed as having deserted on April 19, 1865.
    [Source: NCCWSP]

Dement, A. Y.
   Landsman, Confederate States Navy. Enlisted September 28, 1863, at Camp Holmes for the war.
   [Source(s): McElroy; NA, RG 45]

Dennis, A. J.
   Confederate States Navy.
   Dennis' name appears on a CSS RALEIGH clothing and small stores lists which indicate he was aboard prior to September 2, 1861
   [Source: NCCWSP]

Dent, James O. (Rowan County, North Carolina)
   Private, Confederate States Army//Landsman/Seaman, Confederate States Navy (Company F, Confederate States Navy Battalion). Born about 1845, Dent enlisted on June 8, 1864, in Raleigh, North Carolina, for the war. His name appears on a roll of Prisoners of War at Point Lookout, Maryland, which states that he was captured at Harpers Farm April 6, 1865. Confined at Point Lookout on April 14, 1865, he was released on June 12, 1865. His Oath of Allegiance to the United States was subscribed and sworn to at Point Lookout, Maryland, June 12, 1865, giving his place of residence as Rowan County, North Carolina, and description as follows: Complexion-light; hair-light; eyes-light blue; height-5 ft. 3½ in. An alternate source gives home as "Cabarrus County, North Carolina." His application for a pension dated August 2, 1920, age 74, gives his enlistment date as December 15, 1864, and states he initially served in the Army's Company K, 1st Regiment, North Carolina Troops [NOTE: Does not appear in that unit in source *North Carolina Troops,* though widow's pension application states he enlisted (Army?) in 1862]. He transferred to the Confederate States Navy in Charleston, South Carolina, and served under "Captain Stowe" and "Captain Hines." His widow Martha Ann Dent filed an application for pension on June 19, 1933 stating that James O. Dent died March 14, 1922. Her subsequent application dated May 9, 1935 provided no additional information on his service.
   [Source(s): McElroy; NA, RG 109; NA, RG 45; Pensions (North Carolina); North Carolina Troops, III]

Denton, Joseph S. (Currituck County, North Carolina)
   Confederate States Navy. Enlisted August 25, 1861. Denton filed a claim for pension on July 1, 1901, age 58, giving his post office as Basco, Currituck County. His approved pension application states he served in the Confederate States Navy at Sandy Point, North Carolina, and was wounded on June 15, 1864 by a shell fragment that put out his right eye.
   [Source(s): McElroy; Pensions (NORTH CAROLINA)]

Derham, George
   Landsman, Confederate States Navy. Enlisted December 17, 1863, in Raleigh for the war.
   [Source(s): McElroy; NA, RG 45]

Desmukes (Dismukes), George W. (Chatham County, North Carolina)
   Private, Company C, Confederate States Marine Corps. Believed to have been one of 32 North Carolina conscripts sent to the Confederate naval station, Charleston, South Carolina, per Colonel Beall's report of October 30, 1864. A member of Company C, Confederate States Marine Corps, Desmukes' name appears on a roll of Prisoners of War at Point Lookout, Maryland, which states that he was captured at Farmville, Virginia, on April 6, 1865. He was confined at Point Lookout, Maryland, on April 14, 1865, and released on June 12, 1865 (one source says June 3, 1865). His Oath of Allegiance to the United States was subscribed and sworn to at Point Lookout, Maryland, on June 12, 1865. Oath gives place of residence as Chatham County, North Carolina. Description as follows: Complexion light; hair light brown; eyes blue; height 5 feet 8 inches.
   [Source(s): NA; North Carolina Troops, Doc.# 0299; Card File; Donnelly-ENL; Beall; Donnelly]

Dessman, James (Johnston County, North Carolina)
   Confederate States Navy. Dessman served aboard the steamer CSS EUGENIE. Registers of Confederate States Army General Military Hospital Number 4, Wilmington, North Carolina, state he was admitted October 7, 1863, with "enteritis" and returned to duty October 16, 1863. His post office was given as Clayton, North Carolina and Wilmington, North Carolina.
   [Source(s): McElroy; NA, RG 109]

Devine (Divine), James
   Seaman, Confederate States Navy.
   Devine's name appears on the North Carolina Squadron payroll for the 1st quarter of 1862 covering from January 10,

1862 - March 6, 1862. He received a partial payment on February 13, 1862 at Gosport Navy Yard which covered his service from January 10, 1862 - March 6, 1862. His name appears on the final North Carolina Squadron's payroll. Devine's name appears on the payroll ending March 31, 1862 for the receiving ship CSS UNITED STATES. He was reported as unfit for service by the Surgeon on March 5, 1862 and discharged from the receiving ship the next day.
[Source: NCCWSP]

Dewey, Oliver S.
North Carolina Navy. Listed by source D. H. Hill as one of the first officers commissioned as a "naval agent" in the North Carolina Navy.
[Source(s): DH Hill; NCS]

Dick, Edward L. (Guilford County, North Carolina)
Second Assistant Engineer and/or Paymaster's Clerk, Confederate States Navy. Born in 1837 in Greensboro, North Carolina, Dick was a former Third Assistant Engineer, United States Navy, and had served at Annapolis. At the outbreak of the war, he resigned his commission and enlisted in the Confederate States Navy. He appointed Second Assistant Engineer, August 19, 1864 (Source *ORN* 2, 1, 301 shows his rating as Paymaster's Clerk). Appointed Second Assistant Engineer Provisional Confederate States Navy, June 2, 1864. He served aboard the steamer CSS RALEIGH, Wilmington Station, 1863 – 1864. He later served aboard the CSS NANSEMOND, James River Squadron, 1864; the CSS FREDERICKSBURG and CSS NANSEMOND, James River Squadron, Virginia waters, 1863-1864 [?], as Assistant Engineer. Dick resided as a machinist, in 1880, at the residence of his brother, in North Platte, Lincoln County, Nebraska. He was unmarried. [; *Register1864*; *M1091*; *1880, Census.*]
[Source(s): McElroy; Foenander; *ORN* 1, 10, 766 and 2, 1, 301 & 323; Census (Neb.), 1880]

Diggs, W. Riley
Confederate States Navy. Former Private, Company B, 31st Regiment, North Carolina Troops. [NOTE: Per source "LocateGrave," a "W. Riley Diggs," Confederate States Army, died November 26, 1864, and is buried in Woodlawn Cemetery, Elmira, New York]
[Source(s): McElroy; North Carolina Troops; LocateGrave]

Dilen, John [Possibly John Dillan]
Confederate States Navy. Name appears as signature to an Oath of Allegiance to the United States, subscribed and sworn to at Point Lookout, Maryland on June 26, 1865. Place of residence given on Oath as Guilford County, North Carolina, and description as follows: Complexion-dark; hair-black; eyes-hazel; height-5 ft. 4¾ in.
[Source(s): McElroy; NA, RG 109]

Dillan, James
Landsman, Confederate States Navy. Enlisted October 5, 1863, at Camp Holmes for the war.
[Source(s): McElroy; NA, RG 45]

Dillan, John [Possibly DILEN, JOHN]
Landsman, Confederate States Navy. Enlisted October 5, 1863, at Camp Holmes for the war.
[Sources; McElroy; NA, RG 45

Dillard, Jesse (Guilford County, North Carolina)
Landsman, Confederate States Navy. Enlisted November 1 (or 5), 1863, in Wilmington, North Carolina for the war. Dillard served as a Landsman aboard the CSS ARCTIC, Cape Fear River, North Carolina, 1863.
[Source(s): McElroy; MR, 4, p. 445; NA, RG 45; *ORN* 2, 1, 277; Foenander]

Dillon [Dillion], Isaiah [Isiah] (Guilford County, North Carolina)
Landsman ["Gunner" per source Stepp, "Burials"], Confederate States Navy. Enlisted August 24, 1863/ October 10 (or 11) 1863, in Wilmington, North Carolina for the war. (One source indicates he enlisted October 12, 1863, at Camp Holmes, Raleigh, North Carolina). Dillon married Cynthia Wheeler in Guilford County, North Carolina on November 18, 1853. He died on May 6, 1864 and is buried in the Confederate Section of Oakwood Cemetery, Raleigh, North Carolina in grave # 422. His headstone shows his rank as "Gunner" and mentions service on board the CSS NEUSE. He served aboard the CSS NEUSE as of the ship's March – October 1864 muster roll.
[Source(s): McElroy, MR, 4, p. 445; Ellis; Oakwood; Hill; Marriage Bonds, North Carolina Archives; NA, RG 45; Stepp, "Burials;" NEUSE Roster; CMACSSN]

Dillon, Jesse
>Landsman, Confederate States Navy. Enlisted November 2, 1863, in Raleigh for the war.
>[Source(s): McElroy; NA, RG 45]

Dismukes (Desmukes), John Madison (Chatham County, North Carolina)
>Private, Confederate States Marine Corps ["Company C" per source Donnelly-ENL] [source "Foenander" lists him as Confederate States Navy]. Born in North Carolina, in 1845, the son of Charles and Martha B. Dismukes, he is believed to have been one of 32 North Carolina conscripts sent to the Confederate naval station, Charleston, South Carolina, per Colonel Beall's report of October 30, 1864. Enlisted in May 1864 and, per his 1909 pension application, served aboard the CSS INDIAN CHIEF at Charleston, South Carolina. Captured at Farmville, Virginia, April 6, 1865, he was sent as a Prisoner of War to Point Lookout, Maryland, from where he was released on taking the Oath of Allegiance on June 3, 1865. In 1880, he resided as a farmer with his wife Carrie, and their four children (eldest child born 1867), at the home of his parents, in Baldwin, Chatham County, North Carolina. Dismukes filed a pension claim on July 12, 1909, age 63, listing his post office as Pittsboro, Chatham County. Claim approved. His widow, Carrie E. Dismukes, age 66, post office Chatham County, filed a claim on July 14, 1913, which was approved.
>[Source(s): Foenander; McElroy; Pensions (North Carolina); Donnelly-ENL; Donnelly; Census (NC), 1880 and 1920; North Carolina Troops, Doc. # 0185, p. 1, and 0299; Card File]

Dixon, Duncan A. (Chowan County, North Carolina)
>Private, Confederate States Army//Midshipman, Confederate States Navy. Born in Mississippi in 1845, Dixon resided in Chowan County, North Carolina, where he enlisted at Orange Court House, Virginia, at age 16 on August 20, 1862, for the war, in Company A, 1st Regiment, North Carolina State Troops. Present of accounted for until he was discharged on June 28, 1863 [Source "Foenander" gives rank as "Midshipman" and date as "June 15, 1863"] upon receiving an appointment as Acting Midshipman, Confederate States Navy. Dixon served aboard the school ship CSS PATRICK HENRY, 1863, and later aboard the CSS SELMA, Mobile Squadron, 1863 – 1864. He was captured at Mobile Bay, Alabama, August 5, 1864, and sent aboard the USS PORT ROYAL as a prisoner of war. He escaped from New Orleans on October 14, 1864.
>[Source(s): McElroy; North Carolina Troops, III; Foenander; *ORN* 1, 21, 844]

Dixon, George W. (Beaufort County, North Carolina)
>Seaman, Confederate States Navy. Resided as a merchant in Washington, Beaufort County, North Carolina prior to the war. Served as a Seaman aboard the CSS SEABIRD from July through November 1861 and was serving aboard the CSS CURLEW as of the first quarter of 1862. He appears on a North Carolina Squadron payroll covering the from December 1, 1861 through January 19, 1862 [Sources: Census (NC), 1860; NCCWSP]

Dixon, Sylvester (Silvester) (Brunswick County, North Carolina)
>Landsman, Confederate States Navy.
>Born in North Carolina in 1835, Dixon resided as a mariner in Portsmouth, Carteret County, North Carolina at the time he enlisted on August 15, 1861 [Source NCCWSP states he shipped (i.e., enlisted, on July 25, 1861]. He served as a Landsman aboard the CSS EDWARDS (July 25, 1861) and the CSS VIRGINIA, Hampton Roads, Virginia, in 1862. He served as a Landman aboard the CSS FORREST during the first quarter of 1862 and his name appears on a roll of the receiving ship CSS UNITED STATES with an end date of March 31, 1862. His name appears on the final payroll of the CSS VIRGINIA covering from April 1, 1862 - July 31, 1862 as a Landsman. He filed a claim for a pension on June 12, 1901, at age 66, listing his post office as Supply, Brunswick County, North Carolina. Said application was approved. A pension application was filed on July 1, 1910 by his widow Brittania I. Dixon, age 70, listing her post office as Supply, Brunswick County. It provided no additional information on his service. Said application was approved.
>[Source(s): McElroy, Pensions (NORTH CAROLINA); Census (NC), 1860; Foenander; NCCWSP]

Dobson, John L.
>Landsman, Confederate States Navy. Enlisted May 11, 1864, in Raleigh for the war. A "John Dobson," identified as "North Carolina Naval Hospital," is buried in the Seaman's Burial Ground, Ashley River, Charleston, SC, date of death listed as October 24, 1864.
>[Source(s): McElroy; NA, RG 45; SBG]

Donlon [Dolan], Timothy (New Hanover County, North Carolina)
>Confederate States Navy. Born December 25, 1836, in Ireland, Donlon came to Wilmington in 1856 as a young man after having spent a few months in Connecticut. Said to have served aboard the CSS STONE [probably the

CSS STONO]. Appointed Superintendent of Oakdale Cemetery in 1862, his life's work until two years before his death. He was a charter member of Wilmington's Hibernian Society, organized in 1867, as well as the Howard Relief Volunteer Fire Company and Knights of Columbus. He died on June 1, 1916 at his home at 120 North 3rd St., Wilmington, North Carolina, and was buried at Oakdale Cemetery, Wilmington, North Carolina. Per Source "Star, 6/2/1916," he was aged 80 at his death and had celebrated his 79th birthday "last Christmas."
[Source(s): "Messenger," April 20, 1892; "Star," 6/2/1916; Foenander; PCNMC]

Doogan, Richard
Seaman, Confederate States Navy. Enlisted April 21, 1863, in Wilmington for three years or the war.
[Source(s): McElroy; NA, RG 45]

Dorsey, A. D. [A. H.] (Franklin County, North Carolina)
Confederate States Marine Corps. Listed as deponent on the North Carolina Confederate pension application of Isaiah P. Breedlove (q.v.). Dorsey's application for pension was filed on June 13, 1908 when he was 70 years old. He lived near Louisburg in Franklin County, North Carolina. He stated he enlisted on or about December 1861 and served in the Marine Corps at Drewry's Bluff, Fort Fisher (where he was wounded in the thigh), and at the evacuation of Petersburg where he was wounded in the head [NOTE: This was likely at or around the time of the Battle of Sailor's Creek].
[Source(s): Pensions (North Carolina) (see application of Isaiah P. Breedlove and A. D. Dorsey)]

Dorsey, Archibald
Landsman, Confederate States Navy. Born in North Carolina in May 1846, Dorsey served as a Landsman aboard the CSS ARCTIC, 1863, and as a Landsman aboard the CSS NORTH CAROLINA as of the 3rd Quarter, 1864. Dorsey married about 1869 and resided as a farmer, in 1900, with his wife, Saffrona, at Cedar Rock Township, Franklin County, North Carolina. [ORN 2, 1, 278 & 296; 1900 United States Census.]
[Source(s): Roster, CSS North Carolina, 3rd Qtr., 1864; Donnelly-ENL; Foenander; ORN 2, 1, 278 & 296; Census (North Carolina), 1900]

Dorsey [Dorsett; Dorsy], Archibald D. (Franklin County, North Carolina)
Private, Confederate States Marine Corps. Born in Franklin County, North Carolina. Believed to have been one of 32 North Carolina conscripts sent from Raleigh to the Confederate naval station, Charleston, South Carolina, per Colonel Beall's report of October 30, 1864. Served as a Private, Confederate States Marine Corps. Name appears as a signature to an Oath of Allegiance to the United States subscribed and sworn to at Point Lookout, Maryland, on June 12, 1865. Place of residence given on Oath as near Louisburg, Franklin County, North Carolina. Description: Complexion dark; hair brown; eyes hazel; height 5 feet 5 ¾ inches. Filed for a pension on June 13, 1908, age 70, POST OFFICE Louisburg, Franklin County, North Carolina, wherein he stated he enlisted in the Marine Corps at Fort Fisher in December 1861. Dorsey served at Fort Fisher, North Carolina, where he was wounded in the left thigh, and at Petersburg, Virginia, during its evacuation where he was wounded in the head.
[Source(s): North Carolina Troops, Doc. # 0185, p. 1, and 0299; NA; Kearney; Pensions (North Carolina); Card File; Beall; Donnelly-ENL]

Dorsey, Balden
Landsman, Confederate States Navy. Enlisted February 27, 1864, in Raleigh for the war.
[Source(s): McElroy; NA, RG 45]

Dosher, John Julius
Pilot, Confederate States Navy. Pilot of the Blockade Runner *North Heath*. Died September 16, 1892, aged 66 years. Buried in Old Southport Cemetery, Southport, North Carolina.
[Source(s): McElroy; Chronicles; Gravestone Records, v. 6, p. 307]

Dosher, Richard
Pilot, Confederate States Navy. Served aboard the Blockade Runner *Old Dominion*.
[Source(s): McElroy]

Doss, Ralph (Pasquotank County, North Carolina)
Confederate States Navy. Enlisted from Elizabeth City, North Carolina in Company C, 56th North Carolina Regiment. Transferred about February 1864 to the Confederate States Navy and served aboard the ram CSS ALBEMARLE.
[Source(s): McElroy, North Carolina Troops]

Dougherty, Daniel
Seaman, Confederate States Navy. Enlisted on November 20, 1863, in Wilmington for the war and served as a Landsman aboard the CSS ARCTIC, 1863. Likely the same man who served as a Quarter Gunner on board the CSS NORTH CAROLINA, Cape Fear River, North Carolina, 1864).
[Source(s): McElroy; NA, RG 45; *ORN* 2, 1, 277, 295, and 296]

Douglas [Douglass], J. A.
Seaman, Confederate States Navy. Douglas enlisted on June 13, 1864, in Raleigh for the war. His name appears on a Descriptive List of "rebel deserters" received January 26, 1865 [place received unknown] which states that he "escaped from Confed. Rec. Ship *Indian Chief,* Charleston Harbor, South Carolina, January 26, 1865." Place of birth and residence given as North Carolina, occupation Seaman and description as follows: Age-23; eyes-hazel; hair-dark; complexion-fair; height-5 ft. 8½ in. Also, appears on a list of deserters from the enemy turned over to Provost Marshal General Department of the South, to be furnished transportation to New York, New York per Steamer FULTON, February [?], 1865. List states that he came into the lines at Morris Island.
[Source(s): McElroy; NA, RG 45; NA, RG 109]

Douglas, William (Washington County, North Carolina)
Private, Confederate States Army//Confederate States Navy. Resided in Washington County, North Carolina, where he enlisted at age 25 on June 24, 1861 (June 28, 1861 per MR), for the war, in Company G, 1st Regiment, North Carolina State Troops. Present or accounted for until discharged on February 3, 1862 upon transfer to the Confederate States Navy.
[Source(s): McElroy; North Carolina Troops, III; Foenander]

Douglas [Douglass], William E.
Ordinary Seaman, Confederate States Navy. Enlisted November 22, 1863, in Wilmington for the war. Probably the same as "Wm. E." who enlisted on November 20, 1863, in Raleigh for the war. Ordinary Seaman aboard the CSS ARCTIC, 1863. He may be the same "William B. Douglass" that later served as an Ordinary Seaman on the steam gunboat CSS RALEIGH, North Carolina and Virginia waters, 1864.
[Source(s): McElroy; NA, RG 45; Foenander; ORN 1, 9, 746]

Dowds, Wm. H. (New Hanover County, North Carolina)
Ordinary Seaman, Confederate States Navy. Enlisted January 26, 1864, in Wilmington for the war. Name appears as signature to Oath of Allegiance to the United States subscribed and sworn to at Elmira, New York, May 17, 1865. Place of residence given on Oath as Wilmington, North Carolina, and description as follows: Complexion-dark; hair-dark; eyes-black; height-5 ft. 10 in. Probably the same as "W. H. Dowd," a crew member on the CSS BOMBSHELL when captured aboard said vessel during the engagement at Albemarle Sound, North Carolina, May 5, 1864.
[Source(s): McElroy; NA, RG 45; NA, RG 109; Foenander]

Dowdy, Adam (Currituck County, North Carolina)
Private, Confederate States Army// Confederate States Navy (?). Born in Currituck County, North Carolina where he resided as a sailor prior to enlisting for the war as a Private on August 6, 1861 at age 22 in Company B, 8th Regiment, North Carolina Troops. Captured at Roanoke Island, North Carolina, on an unspecified date and paroled, he was exchanged at Aiken's Landing on the James River in Virginia on November 10, 1862. Dowdy died on James Island, Charleston, South Carolina, on April 29, 1863 "of cholera." Although this soldier was transferred to the Confederate States Navy, it appears he died before his transfer took place.
[Source(s): McElroy; North Carolina Troops]

Dowdy [Doudy], Bannister (Currituck County, North Carolina)
Landsman/Seaman, Confederate States Navy. Dowdy was born in 1839 in North Carolina, the son of Thomas and Julia Dowdy (the brother of Major Dowdy, q.v.). He resided with his parents, in 1850, in the Poplar Branch District of Currituck County, NC as a farmer. He served as a Seaman, then Landsman, aboard the screw steamer CSS FANNY, 1861 - 1862. He was a member of the North Carolina Squadron from 1 December 1861 – 28 February 1862.
[Source(s): Foenander; ORN 2, 1, 285; Census North Carolina, 1850; Census (NC), 1860; NCCWSP]

Dowdy [Dowday], George W. (Currituck County, North Carolina).
Private, Confederate States Army//Seaman, North Carolina Navy, Confederate States Navy.
Born in Currituck County, North Carolina, where he resided as a farmer [Source "Foenander" gives occupation as "Seaman"] prior to enlisting there at age 24 on August 1, 1861, for the war, in Company B, 8th Regiment, North

Carolina State Troops. Dowdy transferred to the Navy circa July 1861. He served aboard the CSS SEA BIRD, from at least July 1861- February 1862. He was captured at the Battle of Elizabeth City, North Carolina on February 10, 1862. His name appears on the North Carolina Squadron payroll for the 1st quarter of 1862 covering from December 1, 1861 - April 15, 1862. Dowdy is listed as "on parole" as of April 15, 1862. [NOTE: This entry may pertain to two different men. One or more sources indicate he was "present or accounted for" as a member of the 8th Regiment, North Carolina Troops until captured at Cold Harbor, Virginia on June 1, 1864. He was confined at Point Lookout, Maryland until transferred to Elmira, New York, on July 12, 1864 and released on May 15, 1865 after taking the Oath of Allegiance].
[Source(s): North Carolina Troops, IV; Sea Bird; Scharf, p.391; *ORN* 2, 1, 306]

Dowdy (Dowday), Major (Currituck County, North Carolina)
Seaman, Confederate States Navy. Born in North Carolina in 1847, the son of Thomas and Julia Dowdy (brother of Bannister Dowdy, q.v.), Dowdy, a farmer, resided with his parents, in the Poplar Branch District of Currituck County, North Carolina. He shipped (i.e., enlisted) for one year on 8 September 1861 and served as a Seaman aboard the steam gunboat CSS RALEIGH from September 1861 through at least the first quarter of 1862. Payroll records indicate he served as part of the North Carolina Squadron from 21 February 1862 until 15 April 1862 when he was transferred to the James River Squadron. He resided as a farmer, in 1880, with his wife Lydia, and son John (born 1873), at Crawford, Currituck County, North Carolina.
[Source(s): Foenander: ORN 2, 1, 301; Census (North Carolina), 1850, 1860, and 1880; NCCWSP]

Dowdy, Bannister
Landsman, Seaman, Confederate States Navy.
Per the 1860 Census of North Carolina, Dowdy was born in North Carolina, ca. 1839, and resided as a farm laborer in the Poplar Branch District, Currituck County, North Carolina. He was the brother of Major Dowdy (q. v.). Per muster roll records, Bannister Dowdy served as a Seaman aboard the NCS FANNY from October 8, 1861 - December 12, 1861, and as a Landsman per the CSS FANNY'S payroll list dated December 20, 1861. His name appears on the North Carolina Squadron payroll for the 1st quarter of 1862 covering from December 1, 1861 - February 28, 1862.
[Source: NCWSP; NC Census (1860)]

Dowdy, Major (also Dowday)
Seaman, Confederate States Navy.
Born in North Carolina, circa 1843, Dowdy resided in the Poplar Branch District, Currituck Co., North Carolina. He was the brother of Bannister Dowdy (q. v.). Major Dowdy shipped on September 8, 1861 for one year as a Seaman aboard the CSS RALEIGH, though his name appears on clothing and small stores lists dated September 2, 1861. He appears as a Seaman aboard the RALEIGH on a small stores list, for October 1861. [NOTE: Source NCCWSP indicates Dowdy "Moved to Johnston's payroll February 21, 1862," but contains no further information. No ship by that name appears on the standard lists of Confederate ships]. Dowdy appears as a Seaman aboard the CSS RALEIGH on a payroll for the 1st quarter of 1862 and on a muster roll for April 1862. His name appears on the payroll of the North Carolina Squadron for the 1st quarter of 1862 from February 21, 1862 - April 15, 1862. Dowdy transferred to the James River Squadron on April 15, 1862.
[Source: NCCWSP; NC Census (1860)]

Downard, John (May be same as "J. W. Downward," q. v.]
Seaman, Gunner's Mate, Confederate States Navy. Previously served in the British Navy where he was awarded the Crimean medal. Downward served as a Seaman aboard the CSS BEAUFORT December 1, 1861. He was rated as a Gunner's Mate on December 11, 1861 and served aboard the CSS BEAUFORT from at least September 1861 through January 16, 1862. He received a partial payment at Gosport Navy Yard, Norfolk, Virginia on February 13, 1862 following duty as part of the garrison of Fort Cobb at Elizabeth City, North Carolina on February 10, 1862. He continued his service as a Gunner's Mate, on board the CSS BEAUFORT from circa February 1862 through March 1862]. His name appears on a payroll for the North Carolina Squadron payroll covering the period from December 1, 1861 through April 15, 1862. Downard transferred to the James River Squadron on April 15, 1862.
[Source: NCCWSP]

Downard, John
Seaman, Gunner's Mate, Confederate States Navy.
Downard previously served in the British Navy where he received the Crimean medal. He was serving as a Seaman aboard the CSS BEAUFORT as of December 1, 1861. He was rated as a Gunner's Mate, on December 11, 1861 and, per payroll, clothing, small stores, and bounty records, served in that position aboard the CSS BEAUFORT from

September – January 1862. He received a partial payment on February 13, 1862 at Gosport Navy Yard following his participation in manning Fort Cobb at the Battle of Elizabeth City on February 10, 1862. Downard's name appears on the North Carolina Squadron payroll for the 1st quarter of 1862 (December 1, 1861 - April 15, 1862). He transferred to the James River Squadron on April 15, 1862.
[Source: NCCWSP]

Downard (Downward), J. (John) W. (Lenoir County, North Carolina)
Confederate States Marine Corps [per his wife's North Carolina pension application]. Downward enlisted in the Spring of 1862 and served aboard the gunboat CSS NEUSE as of the ship's March – October 1864 muster rolls. A pension claim was filed on June 27, 1901 by his widow, Jane Downward, age 58, post office Kinston, Lenoir County. It was approved. His name appears as "John Downard" on "Muster Rolls of the Confederate Navy Department, Record Group 45, National Archives, Washington, DC."
[Source(s): McElroy; Pensions (NORTH CAROLINA); NEUSE Roster; CMACSSN]

Downs, Britton E. (Beaufort County, North Carolina)
Private, Confederate States Army//Ordinary Seaman, Confederate States Navy. Born in Beaufort County, North Carolina, circa 1837, where he resided as a farmer until he enlisted on May 22, 1861, at age 25, as a Private in Company K, 17th Regiment, North Carolina Troops (1st. Organization). He mustered out on or about March 26, 1862, on disbandment of the company. Downs enlisted in Confederate States Navy on June 5, 1863 in Wilmington for the war. Per S.O.#164/11, A&IGO, July 11, 1863 [Sources "washingtongrays" and "www.ncgenweb.us/nccivwar/rosters/10cok.htm" give date as July 19, 1863], he transferred from the CSS NORTH CAROLINA to Company K., 10th Regiment, North Carolina Troops (1st Regiment, North Carolina Artillery), but deserted on October 26, 1863. Downs resided as a farmer with his wife Alvania and six children in Chocowinity, Beaufort County, North Carolina, per 1880 United States Census. He was still residing there in 1890.
[Source(s): McElroy; NA, RG 109; NA, RG 45; North Carolina Troops, I & VI; "Beaufort County Sailors;" Foenander; Census (North Carolina)(Ancestry.com), 1880; www.thewashingtongrays.homestead.com; www.ncgenweb.us/nccivwar/rosters/10cok.htm]

Dowty, George (also Doudy)
Ordinary Seaman, Confederate States Navy.
Dowty served as an Ordinary Seaman aboard the CSS ELLIS per an entry in the ship's logbook dated November 1, 1861 and the payroll list for the ELLIS covering the period January - May 1861].
[Source: NCCWSP]

Doxey, G. T. (North Carolina)
Landsman, Confederate States Navy. Served as a Landsman aboard the CSS FANNY from at least October 8, 1861 through December 13, 1861. He received a partial payment on 13 February 13,1862 at Gosport Navy Yard following the burning of the CSS FANNY at Elizabeth City on February 10, 1862. His name appears on a payroll for the North Carolina Squadron from December 1, 1861 through February 28, 1862.
[Source: NCCWSP]

Doxey, Grandy B [T.] (Currituck County, North Carolina)
Private, Confederate States Army//Landsman, Seaman, Confederate States Navy. Born in Currituck County, North Carolina, where he lived as a farmer until enlisting there at age 21 on May 13, 1861 as a Private in Company E, 17th Regiment, North Carolina Troops (1st Organization). Present or accounted for until he transferred to the Confederate States Navy on or about November 1, 1861. He served in North Carolina waters as a Landsman aboard the CSS FANNY October 8, 1861 through December 12, 1861, and as a Seaman aboard the FANNY from December 13, 1861 through May 1862. His name appears on the North Carolina Squadron payroll for the 1st quarter of 1862 covering from December 1, 1861 - February 28, 1862. Doxey was listed as having "run" per the payroll ending February 28, 1862.
[Source(s): McElroy; NCCWSP; North Carolina Troops, VI; *ORN* 2, 1, 285; Foenander]

Doxey, H. B. (may be Haywood Doxey, q. v.)
Landsman, Confederate States Navy. CSS FANNY as of October 8, 1861.
[Source: NCCWSP]

Doxey, Haywood D. (Currituck County, North Carolina) (may be H. B. Doxey, q. v.)
Private, Confederate States Army//Landsman, Ordinary Seaman, Confederate States Navy.
Born in the Court House District of Currituck County, North Carolina, in 1840, the son of Latimore and Nancy

Doxey. He lived in Currituck County as a farmer until enlisting at Oregon Inlet at age 19 on July 28, 1861 as a Private in Company E, 17th Regiment, North Carolina Troops [1st Organization]). He enlisted on September 30, 1863, for the war, in Currituck County, North Carolina as a Private in Company G, 68th Regiment, North Carolina Troops and transferred to Company D, 59th Regiment, North Carolina Troops [4th Regiment, North Carolina Cavalry] in March 1864, joining the regiment at Petersburg, Virginia [Source North Carolina Troops, II, gives date as May 1, 1864]. Present or accounted for through October 1864, Doxey was reported as a "deserter" by the Provost Marshal's Office, Norfolk, Virginia on January 18, 1865. The date of his Confederate States Navy service is unknown. Per payroll records, he was serving as an Ordinary Seaman aboard the CSS CURLEW on November 20, 1861 and as a Landsman thereon during the 1st quarter of 1861. His name appears on the payroll of the receiving ship CSS UNITED STATES ending March 31, 1862. Doxey resided as a farmer in 1870 with his wife Chloe and four children in Crawford Township, Currituck County, North Carolina, and later as a merchant, with his third wife, Lettie (whom he married in 1890), in 1910, in Crawford Township. Doxey died in Crawford Township on December 25, 1922. [Source(s): McElroy; North Carolina Troops, II, VI and XV; Foenander; Census (North Carolina), 1870 and 1910; NCCWSP]

Doxey, Haywood (Though dates conflict, this may be the same as "Hayward D. Doxey," q. v.]
Ordinary Seaman, Landsman, Confederate States Navy. Born in the Court House
District of Currituck County, North Carolina circa 1841, Doxey was the brother of John Thomas Doxey (q. v.). He worked as a farmer prior to enlisting at age 19 as a Private in Company E, 17th Regiment, North Carolina Troops at Oregon Inlet on July 28, 1861. He transferred to the Confederate States Navy at an unspecified date and served as an Ordinary Seaman aboard the CSS CURLEW as early as November 20, 1861 and later as a Landsman aboard the same ship. He appears on a payroll of the receiving ship CSS UNITED STATES with an end date of March 31, 1862.
[Source: NCCWSP; Census (NC), 1860]

Doxey, John Thomas (Currituck County, North Carolina)
Private, Confederate States Army//Confederate States Navy. Born in Currituck County, North Carolina, the brother of Haywood Doxey (q. v.), where he lived as a farmer prior to enlisting at age 22 on July 28, 1861 at Oregon Inlet as a Private in Company E, 17th Regiment, North Carolina Troops (1st Organization). He transferred to the Confederate States Navy on an unspecified date and served as a Seaman aboard the CSS FANNY from circa October 8, 1861 through December 20, 1861. Payroll records of the North Carolina Squadron indicate he served with that unit from December 1, 1861 through February 28, 1862. He was listed as having "run" per the payroll ending February 28, 1862.
[Source(s): McElroy; North Carolina Troops, VI; NCCWSP]

Dozier (Dozia), Smith W. (Yadkin County, North Carolina)
Corporal, Confederate States Army//Confederate States Navy. Dozier was born in May 1842, in Yadkin County, North Carolina, the son of Dr. Nathan Bright and Olive Vestal Dozier, and brother of Nathan C. Dozier. He resided in Yadkin County, North Carolina, as a farmer with his parents prior to enlisting there at age 19 on August 13, 1861 as a Private in Company I, 28th Regiment, North Carolina Troops. Captured at Hanover Court House, Virginia, on May 27, 1862, Dozier was confined at Fort Monroe, Virginia, and Fort Columbus, New York Harbor. He was paroled and transferred to Aiken's Landing, James River, Virginia, where he was exchanged August 5, 1862. Promoted to Corporal, August 29, 1862, he transferred to the Confederate States Navy, April 3, 1864. He moved to Arkansas prior to 1880, and by 1900, was in Bellefonte Township, Boone County, Arkansas, where he resided as a grocer, with his two children. He is shown as a widower in 1900, still residing in Boone County in 1910.
[Source(s): Foenander; North Carolina Troops, 8,210; S.O. #89; Casstevens; North Carolina Troops, Vol. VIII; Census Ark.), 1880, 1900, and 1910]

Drake, Edward (also Doake)
Seaman, Confederate States Navy.
Drake served aboard the CSS BEAUFORT per a bounty list dated January 16, 1862 and a clothing list for March 1862. His name appears on the payroll of the North Carolina Squadron for the 1st quarter of 1862 covering from March 11, 1862 - April 15, 1862. He transferred to the James River Squadron on April 15, 1862.
[Source: NCCWSP]

Drake, Frank H. (North Carolina)
Confederate States Navy. Served aboard the CSS SUMTER under Raphael Semmes, 1861-1862. Left the Confederate States Navy service in 1862 in Liverpool, England and sailed to Australia using the 25 Pounds Sterling

he received from "Cornhill" magazine of London for a manuscript he sold them concerning his adventures on the CSS SUMTER. The article was published in the August 1862 issue. This article may be the first published about and by a Confederate States Navy enlisted sailor. Drake drowned in the Torrens River near Adelaide in 1867. Per his obituary, he was born in North Carolina and was by occupation, a printer and compositor.
[Source(s): Foenander]

Drake, Wade (Wake County, North Carolina)
Landsman, Confederate States Navy. Born in North Carolina, in 1843, Drake enlisted in the Confederate States Navy on October 17 (or 19), 1863 in Wilmington, North Carolina (or at Camp Holmes, Raleigh, North Carolina) for the war. He served as a Landsman aboard the CSS ARCTIC, Cape Fear River, North Carolina, 1863. He later served on the CSS RALEIGH in North Carolina and Virginia waters, 1864. He resided as a farmer, in 1880, with his wife, Martha J. (maiden name Wyett), and daughter Florance (born 1879), at Gold Hill, Rowan County, North Carolina.
[Source(s): McElroy; NA, RG 45; MR, 4, p. 445; *ORN* 2, 1, 277, 278 & 302; Foenander; Census (NC), 1880]

Drake, William Francis (Virginia/Wake County, North Carolina)
Confederate States Navy. Resident of Northampton County, Virginia, he enlisted in Company E, 41st Virginia Infantry in Norfolk on April 19, 1861. Served as a volunteer aboard the CSS VIRGINIA and manned a port bow gun during the Battle of Hampton Roads on March 8-9, 1862. Re-enlisted for the war in Company C, 19th Battalion, Virginia Artillery (a.k.a. United Artillery), until detailed to the Navy on October 1, 1864. A post-war teacher, Drake was admitted to the Old Soldier's Home, Raleigh, North Carolina, in November 1902 and died there on August 13, 1930. He was buried in Oakwood Cemetery, Raleigh, North Carolina, and is said to have been the last survivor of the battle between the Monitor and Merrimac (CSS VIRGINIA).
[Source(s): Driver]

Dray, James J. (Canada/New Hanover County, North Carolina)
Landsman, Confederate States Navy. Dray was born in Canada in 1845 (one source shows date of birth as May 13, 1835) and served as a Landsman aboard the CSS NORTH CAROLINA, 1864. His pension application states he enlisted in 1862 in Raleigh, North Carolina, for the war (another source gives his enlistment date as August 8, 1864). He resided as a bar keeper in Wilmington, North Carolina, 1870. The claim for a pension he filed on July 21, 1910 at age 64, post office Wilmington, New Hanover County was approved. His pension states he fought at Fort Fisher and that he marched "through Wilmington with the Army, then carried on to Virginia and [the] command at Drewry's Bluff then captured and paroled at Richmond." States he had "long and severe case of Pneumonia with continued fever in January-February-March 1865, that he convalesced in April 1865, and that his current rheumatism and general debilitation was a result of this. Born in "Canady" [Canada] in 1845 [Source "Foenander" gives date as May 13, 1835]. He died in Mecklenburg County, North Carolina April 24, 1918 at age 73. Buried in Belleview Cemetery, Wilmington, North Carolina, his grave has no marker.
[Source(s): McElroy; Pensions (NORTH CAROLINA); Gravestone Records, v. 6, p. 326; Stepp, "Burials;" NA, RG 45; Foenander]

Drowst [Droust], Wm. L. (New Hanover, North Carolina)
Confederate States Navy. Drowst served aboard the steamer CSS EUGENIE. Registers of Confederate States Army General Military Hospital No. 4, Wilmington, North Carolina, state he was admitted on October 15, 1863, with "feb con com" and returned to duty November 16, 1863. Post office given on records as Wilmington, NORTH CAROLINA
[Source(s): McElroy; NA, RG 109]

Duffy, Edward
Seaman, Confederate States Navy. Wounded slightly in the shoulder at Fort Fisher, December 25, 1864.
[Source(s): McElroy; Daily Confed. (1/2/65)]

Duke, W. [NOTE: May be same as "Washington Duke," q.v.]
Landsman, Confederate States Navy. Enlisted June 13, 1864, in Raleigh for the war.
[Source(s): McElroy; NA, RG 45]

Duke, Washington (Orange [later Durham] County, North Carolina) [NOTE: May be same as "W. Duke," q.v.]
Seaman [Landsman], Confederate States Navy. Born on December 20, 1820, Orange County, North Carolina, Duke died on May 8, 1905, and was buried in Maplewood Cemetery, Durham County, North Carolina. He enlisted from Orange County, North Carolina in 1863 and served in the Guard of Camp Holmes. On May 25, 1864, Duke

transferred to the Confederate States Navy in Charleston, South Carolina, and served aboard the receiving ship CSS INDIAN CHIEF, thence moved to Battery Burk [Source *Cyclopedia* states battery "Brook"] in defense of Richmond. He was captured on the retreat from Richmond, held prisoner at Libby Prison, and freed when peace was declared. Per source *Cyclopedia*, "For his expert management of artillery, he was distinguished, and at Battery Brook, he was promoted to the rank of Orderly Sergeant. After release, [he was] given transportation to New Bern, North Carolina, [and] walked the 134 miles home and resumed farming." Duke's daughter was a Mrs. Angier, 106 Buchanan Bldg., Durham, North Carolina. Washington Duke founded the great Duke tobacco dynasty which later endowed Trinity College which became Duke University. His photo appears on page 565 of *Cyclopedia*. [NOTE: A Washington "Drew" appears on the March - October 1864 CSS NEUSE muster roll.
[Source(s): McElroy; Stepp, "Burials;" *Cyclopedia*; CMACSSN]

Dunbar, Andrew
3rd Assistant Engineer, Confederate States Navy. Dunbar served in the defenses of North Carolina in 1862.
[Source: NCCWSP]

Duncan, F. M.
Boatswain's Mate, North Carolina Navy, Confederate States Navy.
Duncan served upon the NCS FANNY until it was destroyed to prevent capture in the Battle of Elizabeth City on February 10, 1862. He was received aboard the receiving ship CSS UNITED STATES on February 20, 1862 "and shipped with Comm. Hunter for his new command" [NOTE: No further explanation].
[Source: NCCWSP]

Duncan, Thomas M. (also Thomas W.)
Seaman, Quartermaster, North Carolina Navy, Confederate States Navy.
Duncan served aboard the NCS WINSLOW per the ship's muster roll covering the period July 30, 1861 - November 30, 1861. He was paid at Gosport Navy Yard on December 13, 1861. Duncan served as a Seaman with the North Carolina Squadron from December 13, 1861 - March 31, 1862. Records indicate he received a partial payment on February 13, 1862 at the Gosport Navy Yard. Duncan's name appears on a payroll of the receiving ship CSS UNITED STATES with an ending date of March 31, 1862. He appears on the North Carolina Squadron payroll for the 1st quarter of 1862 covering from December 1, 1861 - March 31, 1862. He was listed as having "run" per the payroll ending March 31, 1862. He reenlisted March 25, 1862 for the war as a member of CSS VIRGINIA's crew and was paid a $50 bonus. He served as a Quartermaster aboard the CSS VIRGINIA and appears on that ship's final payroll covering the period June 14, 1862 - September 30, 1862. Duncan served at Drewry's Bluff as a Seaman per that station's April 1, 1863 - June 30, 1863 payroll. Pay records indicate he was paid at Drewry's Bluff for the period October 1, 1863 - January 1864. He is listed as a prisoner of war (POW) of Federal forces at New Berne [sic], North Carolina as of February 2, 1864, following the sinking of the USS UNDERWRITER in a raid under Commander John Taylor Wood, Confederate States Navy. He was sent to the Federal prison at Point Lookout, Maryland on February 27, 1864, thence to Fort Warren in Boston Harbor, Boston, Massachusetts on September 20, 1864.
[Source: NCCWSP]

Dunn, J. L.
Landsman, Confederate States Navy. Enlisted June 22, 1863, in Wilmington for the war.
[Source(s): McElroy; NA, RG 45]

Dunn, Martin
Landsman, Confederate States Navy. Dunn enlisted on February 9, 1864, in Raleigh for the war and served as a Landsman on board the CSS RALEIGH, North Carolina and Virginia waters, 1862-1864.
[Source(s): McElroy; NA, RG 45; *ORN* 2, 1, 302]

Dunn, Nat
Landsman, Confederate States Navy. Enlisted November 27, 1863, in Wilmington for the war.
[Source(s): McElroy; NA, RG 45]

Dunnavant, James (also Donnovant)
Seaman, Confederate States Navy.
Dunnavant received a partial payment on February 13, 1862 at the Gosport Navy Yard. His name appears on a payroll for the North Carolina Squadron covering the 1st quarter of 1862 from January 7, 1862 - February 28, 1862. He is listed as having "run" on the final North Carolina Squadron payroll dated February 28, 1862.
[Source: NCCWSP]

Dunnavant, Joseph (also Joe Donnovant)
Seaman, Confederate States Navy.
Dunnavant received a partial payment on February 13, 1862 at the Gosport Navy Yard. He appears on the North Carolina Squadron payroll for the 1st quarter of 1862 covering from January 10, 1862 - March 31, 1862. Dunnavant's name appears on the payroll of the receiving ship CSS UNITED STATES ending March 31, 1862. He is listed as having "run" per the payroll ending March 31, 1862.
[Source: NCCWSP]

Dunnavant, Michael (also Donovant)
Landsman, Confederate States Navy.
Dunnavant received a partial payment on February 13, 1862 at the Gosport Navy Yard. He appears on a North Carolina Squadron payroll for the 1st quarter of 1862 covering from January 10, 1862 - March 24, 1862. Per a payroll ending March 31, 1862, Dunnavant was aboard the Receiving ship CSS UNITED STATES as of that date. He served aboard the CSS VIRGINIA's final payroll as a Landsman for the period April 1,1862 - September 30, 1862. He was at Drewry's Bluff as a Landsman as confirmed by a payroll covering the period April 1, 1863 - June 30, 1863.
[Source: NCCWSP]

Dunton (Duncan), Edmond S. [C.] (Currituck County, North Carolina)
Seaman, Confederate States Navy. Born circa 1834 in North Carolina, Dunton resided in the Coinjock District of Currituck County, North Carolina in 1860 as a Seaman. He appears as a Seaman on the crew of the CSS ELLIS during the period August 2, 1861 through May 1862. [NOTE: Source NCCWSP indicates Dunston was "moved to Johnston's payroll February 21, 1862," but is no further information]. His name appears on a payroll of the receiving ship CSS UNITED STATES with a date ending March 31, 1862. He received pay for the period February 21, 1862 - April 15, 1862 on the final North Carolina Squadron payroll. Dunton served as a Seaman at Drewry's Bluff from April 1, 1863 - June 30, 1863.
[Sources: Census (NC), 1860; NCCWSP]

Dunton, Joseph S. (Currituck County, North Carolina)
Confederate States Navy. Born in North Carolina in 1843, the son of Caroline Dunton, Dunton lived in the Coinjock District of Currituck County, North Carolina. He enlisted for one year on August 25, 1861 and served aboard the CSS RALEIGH as a Landsman through April 1862. Source NCCWSP states his name appears on a North Carolina Squadron payroll covering the period February 21, 1862 - April 15, 1862, on which date he was transferred to the James River Squadron. The same source shows he served at Drewry's Bluff as a Landsman from at least April 1, 1863 - June 30, 1863, per payroll records. Other sources show he served on Halifax Station, 1862 – 1864, and on the CSS ALBEMARLE where he was wounded in the right eye by a fragment of bursting shell at Plymouth, North Carolina during the naval engagement in Albemarle Sound, June 1864. Dunton resided as a laborer, in 1880, with his wife, Hannah, and six children (eldest child born 1868), at Crawford, Currituck County, North Carolina. He was shown as a fisherman, in 1910, at Crawford. His pension application filed on June 1, 1885, at age 42, listing his post office as Comjock [Coinjock?], Currituck County, North Carolina. A claim was filed by his widow, Hannah Dunton, age not shown, post office not shown, Dare County, on August 18, 1927. The pension application was approved. Her application states she married Joseph J. Dunton on December 31, 1865. He died on September 4, 1925.
[Source(s): McElroy; Pensions (North Carolina); Foenander; Census (NC), Census, 1860, 1880, and 1910; *ORN* 2, 1, 274 & 301; NCCWSP]

Dupree, Obadiah P. (Wake County, North Carolina)
Landsman ("Private"), Confederate States Navy. Enlisted June 10, 1864, in Raleigh for the war. Name appears as a signature to an Oath of Allegiance to the United States, subscribed and sworn to at Point Lookout, Maryland, June 26, 1865, which gives place of residence as Wake County, North Carolina, and description as follows: Complexion- fair; hair-light brown; eyes-red; height- 5 ft. 10¾ in.
[Source(s): McElroy; NA, RG 109; NA, RG 45]

Durham, Thomas S. (Chatham County, North Carolina)
Landsman, Confederate States Navy. Born 1845, Durham enlisted in the Confederate States Navy on May 18 (or 20), 1864, in Raleigh for the war. His claim for a pension filed on July 6, 1913, at age 68, was disallowed for insufficient disability. An additional claim filed on July 13, 1914, post office Riggsbee, Chatham County, was approved. It states he served in the Navy in Charleston, South Carolina, and when it was evacuated, he was sent to the "artillery" at Drewry's Bluff, and later surrendered at Appomattox. Durham died in 1916 and was buried at

Lystra Baptist Church.
[Source(s): McElroy; NA, RG 45; Pensions (NORTH CAROLINA); Lane Society]

Dutton, Nathan Parks (Maryland/North Carolina[?])
Confederate States Navy. Born on April 13, 1816 in Baltimore, Maryland, Dutton served on an unnamed blockade runner.
[Source(s): McElroy; UDC, Southport]

Duvall, Robert Carson (Yadkin County, North Carolina)
Captain (Lieutenant), Confederate States Navy [One source indicates he was a Landsman]. Born in Iredell County, November 15, 1819, Duvall was the stepson of Josiah Cowles, of Yadkin County, North Carolina. A graduate of the United States Naval Academy at Annapolis, Duvall had previous service in the United States Navy from October 19, 1841 to his dismissal from United States Navy, December 12, 1859. He served as a Lieutenant in the North Carolina State Navy, 1861, and was among the first commissioned in the "North Carolina Navy." He took command of the steamer "Beaufort" [later, CSS BEAUFORT, an 85-ton iron propeller vessel] on July 9, 1861 when it was put into commission and sent to Ocracoke Island to act as a commerce raider. Its first naval engagement with the Federal forces was reported to have taken place off Oregon Inlet on July 21, 1861. On July 30, 1861, the "Beaufort" anchored at Portsmouth Island. An 1861 resolution by the General Assembly of North Carolina complimented Duvall on his naval skills, qualifications, and service to the Navy of the State of North Carolina and recommended him for the Confederate States Navy. A further notation in the 1861 North Carolina General Assembly resolution stated Duvall should be paid as a "purser" for the time he acted as such while in the late navy of North Carolina [Note: said act was ratified on September 12, 1861]." Born November 15, 1819, Duvall died in Raleigh, North Carolina, on February 4, 1863, at age 45, of an "incurable" disease. He was buried at Flat Rock Baptist Church, Hamptonville, Yadkin County, North Carolina.
[Source(s): McElroy; People's Press 2/27/63; Casstevens; Stepp, "Burials;" DH Hill; Resolutions (GA of North Carolina); Foenander; *ORN* 1, 6, 21 – 22, 781 & 794; *Fay. Obs. (*February 12, 1863); NCS; McElroy; "Officers, January 1, 1864"]

Dyer (Dwyer), Thomas K. (Massachusetts or Nova Scotia/New Hanover County, North Carolina)
Private, Confederate States Army//Seaman, Confederate States Navy.
Dyer may have served as a Pilot [Source "McElroy" lists his rank and unit as "Private, Naval Battalion," Confederate States Navy]. Dyer was born in 1834 in Massachusetts and resided as a pilot in New Hanover County, North Carolina [NOTE: the 1860 United States Census shows place of birth as Nova Scotia]. He married Sarah E. Reaves in New Hanover County, North Carolina, June 22, 1856. In 1860, he resided as a pilot, with his wife, Sarah, and two children, at Smithville Township, Brunswick County, North Carolina, where he enlisted at age 31, on June 8, 1861, as a Private in Company E, 10th Regiment, North Carolina Troops (1st Regiment North Carolina Artillery). He served aboard the blockade runner *Agnes Fry*. He transferred to the Confederate States Navy on September 26, 1861 and, per payroll records, was a Seaman aboard the CSS BEAUFORT during the period September – November 1861, and later aboard the CSS CASWELL. His name appears on a register of Confederate States Army General Military Hospital Number 4, Wilmington, North Carolina, dated March 15, 1862, which gives his disease as "febris remittens," post office as Smithville, North Carolina, and states that he was returned to duty March 28, 1862.
[Source(s): McElroy; NPS; North Carolina Troops, I; NA, RG 109; *ORN* 2, 1, 281 & 282; Census (North Carolina), 1860; UDC, MC of Svc.; NCCWSP]

Dysart, W. F.
Landsman, Confederate States Navy. Enlisted June 6, 1864, in Raleigh for the war.
[Source(s): McElroy; NA, RG 45]

Dywar, John
Seaman, Confederate States Navy. Enlisted January 26, 1864, in Wilmington for the war.
[Source(s): McElroy; NA, RG 45]

Eakins, John, Sr. (New Hanover County, North Carolina) (Pension application states "Pender County")
Landsman, Confederate States Navy. Born in North Carolina, in December 1820, Eakins enlisted in the Confederate States Navy in August 1863 (or on September 5, 1863) in Wilmington, North Carolina for the war. He resided as a farmer with his wife Martha, and daughter Ethern (born 1866), in Columbia, Pender County, North Carolina, in

1880. He filed a claim for a Confederate pension on July 5, 1909, at age 89, giving his post office as Burgaw, Pender County. His pension was approved. He served as a witness on the widow's application filed by Mrs. A. J. White based on service of William White (q.v.) of Pender County, North Carolina. A claim filed by his widow, Martha Eakins, age 85, post office Rock Point, Pender County, July 4, 1910, was also approved.
[Source(s): McElroy; Pensions (North Carolina); NA, RG 45; MR, 4, p. 445; St. Amand; Foenander]

Eanons (?), Robert (North Carolina?)
(Possibly Black)
"Navy Department."
Listed as "Coloured, overseer Daniel McKnight [?]," Eanons was admitted to the Confederate General Hospital No. 4, Wilmington, North Carolina on May 22, 1862 with "Diarrhea Chron." and listing no post office. He was discharged two days later, on May 24th.
[Source: Hosp. (No. 4), Wilm.]

Earnheart, D. H. (Rowan County, North Carolina)
Confederate States Navy. Enlisted March 10, 1864, at Camp Holmes, near Raleigh, from Colonel Bradshaw's 76th Regiment, North Carolina Militia, from Rowan County, North Carolina. Description: Age-19; eyes-gray; hair-dark; complexion-dark; height-5 ft. 6 in.; place of birth-Rowan County; occupation-farmer.
[Source(s): McElroy]

Earnheart, George H.
Landsman, Confederate States Navy. Enlisted March 11, 1864, in Raleigh for the war.
[Source(s): McElroy; NA, RG 45]

Earnheart, Henry L. (Rowan County, North Carolina)
Confederate States Navy. Conscripted March 10, 1864 (or enlisted March 11, 1864) at Camp Holmes, Raleigh, for the war, from Colonel Bradshaw's 76th Regiment, North Carolina Militia, from Rowan County. Description given as follows: Age-18; eyes-blue; hair-light; complexion-light; height-5 ft. 6½ in.; place of birth-Rowan County; occupation-farmer.
[Source(s): McElroy; NA, RG 45]

Eason, John B. (Anson County, North Carolina)
Private, Confederate States Army//Landsman, Confederate States Navy. Born in North Carolina about 1835, Eason enlisted for the war in Anson County, North Carolina, at age 26 on May 10, 1862, as a Private in Company A, 59th Regiment, North Carolina Troops (4th Regiment, North Carolina Cavalry). Detailed as Commissary Sergeant between October 31, 1862 and February 28, 1863, he transferred to the Confederate States Navy on September 3, 1863 where he served as a Landsman on the CSS CHICORA, 1863–1864. He transferred back to this company and regiment on January 7, 1865. Eason married in 1869 and resided as a farmer, in 1880, with his wife, Clia and children, in Thomas County, Georgia. He was still residing in Thomas County in 1900
[Source(s): McElroy; North Carolina Troops, II; NPS; Census (Ga.), 1880 and 1900; Foenander]

Easters, James E. (Beaufort County, North Carolina) [Possibly same as James Eastis (Eastus) q.v.)]
Carpenter's Mate [and/or Gunner's Mate], Confederate States Navy. Easters was serving aboard the CSS ARCTIC by August 1862. Prisoner of War records indicate he was captured on the Cape Fear River at Wilmington, North Carolina on February 19, 1865, along with five other personnel of the Confederate States Navy, by Union sailors from the USS PEQUOT. He was confined at the military prison, Camp Hamilton, Virginia, until released and sent to Point Lookout, Maryland, March 1, 1865. He was confined at Point Lookout until released on taking the Oath of Allegiance to the United States circa May 12-14, 1865. Place of residence given on records as Beaufort County, North Carolina, occupation Seaman.
[Source(s): McElroy; NA, RG 109; Foenander; "Beaufort County Sailors;" ORN, 1, 23, 703; ORN 2, 1, p.276]

Eastis, James (Hyde County, North Carolina) [Possibly same as James Eastus]
Confederate States Navy. Enlisted in the Confederate States Navy in Wilmington, North Carolina.
[Source(s): MR, IV, 445]

Eastus, James (Beaufort County, North Carolina) [Possibly same as James Easters (Eastus), q.v.]
Confederate States Navy. Born about 1832 in Beaufort County, North Carolina, where he resided as a sailor. Enlisted for the war as a Private in Company C, 40th Regiment, North Carolina Troops (3rd Regiment, North Carolina

Artillery), age 29, on October 21, 1861. Present or accounted for until he transferred to the Confederate States Navy on May 8, 1862.
[Source(s): McElroy; MR, III; North Carolina Troops, I; NPS; NA, RG 109; Foenander; "Beaufort County Sailors"]

Eatman, Avrit
Landsman, Confederate States Navy. Enlisted February 23, 1864, in Raleigh for the war.
[Source(s): McElroy; NA, RG 45]

Edward, E. P. (Edgecombe County, North Carolina)
Landsman, Confederate States Navy. Name appears as signature to an Oath of Allegiance to the United States, subscribed and sworn to at Point Lookout, Maryland, June 12, 1862. Place of residence given on Oath as Edgecombe County, North Carolina, giving description as follows: Complexion-fair; hair-brown; eyes-grayish; height-5 ft. 7¼ in.
[Source(s): McElroy; NA, RG 109]

Edwards, Francis M. (Beaufort County, North Carolina)
Ordinary Seaman and Officer's Steward, Confederate States Navy. Born in North Carolina in 1840, Edwards enlisted on June 5, 1863, in Wilmington for the war and served as a crewman on board the CSS NORTH CAROLINA. His application for a pension dated June 11, 1904 states he is aged 65 and that he enlisted in the Confederate States Navy on December 15, 1862 and served on the CSS NORTH CAROLINA [1864] at Smithville, North Carolina. He was injured on June 15, 1863, "ruptured while raising the anchor." In 1880, Edwards resided as a farmer with his second wife, Francis, in Beaufort County, North Carolina. He married his third wife, Clia, about 1895, and by 1910 resided as a farmer with his family at Richland Township, Beaufort County, North Carolina
[Source(s): McElroy; NA, RG 45; MR, 4, p. 445; Foenander]

Edwards, James
Seaman, Confederate States Navy. Enlisted on June 13, 1863, in Wilmington, for the war.
[Source(s): McElroy; NA, RG 45]

Edwards, Thomas
Seaman, Confederate States Navy.
Edwards' name appears on the North Carolina Squadron's payroll for the 1st quarter of 1862 covering from January 10, 1862 - March 31, 1862. He is listed as having "run" per the payroll ending March 31, 1862.
[Source: NCCWSP]

Eliason, Augustus
Seaman, Confederate States Navy.
Eliason served as a Seaman aboard the CSS BEAUFORT. His name appears on a clothing list for December 1861 and a bounty list dated January 16, 1862. He received a partial payment on February 13, 1862 at the Gosport Navy Yard following having helped man Fort Cobb at Elizabeth City during the battle on February 10, 1862. Eliason appears on clothing lists for the BEAUFORT for February and March 1862. He was aboard the Confederate Receiving ship CSS UNITED STATES per that ship's payroll ending March 31, 1862. He was listed on the North Carolina Squadron payroll for the 1st quarter of 1862 covering from January 10, 1862 - April 15, 1862 on which date he transferred to the James River Squadron.
[Source: NCCWSP]

Elliott, George P.
Landsman, Confederate States Navy. Enlisted April 29, 1864, in Raleigh for the war.
[Source(s): McElroy; NA, RG 45]

Elliott, Charles Gilbert (Pasquotank County, North Carolina)
First Lieutenant, Confederate States Army//Confederate States Navy. Born in Elizabeth City, Pasquotank County, North Carolina, on December 10, 1843, where he resided as a "secretary court clerk" prior to enlisting in Pasquotank County, North Carolina, at age 21 on May 4, 1861 in Company L, 17th Regiment, North Carolina Troops (1st Organization). Mustered in as 1st Sergeant and appointed Second Lieutenant to rank from August 12, 1861. Present or accounted for until captured at Roanoke Island on February 8, 1862. Paroled at Elizabeth City, North Carolina, on February 21, 1862, he was exchanged in August 1862. Present or accounted for until the company was disbanded on or about March 4, 1863. Appointed as Adjutant (First Lieutenant) of the 17th Regiment, North Carolina Troops (2nd Organization) to rank from May 17, 1862. Present or accounted for until he resigned on January 20, 1864. Builder of

the CSS ALBEMARLE at 19 years of age. Elliott died on May 9, 1895 at Station Island, New York.
[Source(s): McElroy; NPS; North Carolina Troops, VI]

Elliot (or Elliott), James B. (Stanly County, North Carolina)
Landsman, Confederate States Navy. Enlisted for the war on February 11, 1864, in Raleigh. He served as a Landsman aboard the CSS ARCTIC, Cape Fear River, North Carolina, 1863 (NOTE: May be the same as "James O. Elliott," q.v.). He later served aboard the CSS RALEIGH, in North Carolina and Virginia waters, 1864. His name appears on registers of Confederate States Army General Military Hospital Number 4, Wilmington, North Carolina, which indicates he was admitted February 22, 1864, with "bronchitis acuta" and returned to duty April 7, 1864. His post office was given as Albemarle, North Carolina, and also as Summersville.
[Source(s): McElroy; NA, RG 45; NA, RG 109; Foenander]

Elliott, James O. (Guilford County, North Carolina)
Landsman, Confederate States Navy (Private, Company A, Naval Battalion.). Enlisted March 3, 1864, in Raleigh for the war. Elliott served as a Landsman aboard the CSS ARCTIC, Cape Fear River, North Carolina, 1863 (NOTE: May be the same as "James B. Elliott," q.v.). His name appears on a roll of Prisoners of War at Point Lookout, Maryland, which states he was captured at High Bridge April 6, 1865. He was confined at Point Lookout April 14, 1865 and released June 12, 1865. His signature appears on an Oath of Allegiance to the United States subscribed and sworn to at Point Lookout, Maryland, June 12, 1865, which give his place of residence as Guilford County, North Carolina, and description as follows: Complexion-dark; hair-brown; eyes-light hazel; height-5 feet 7 inches.
[Source(s): McElroy; NA, RG 109; Foenander]

Elliott, William P. (New Hanover County, North Carolina)
1st Sergeant, Confederate States Army//Paymaster's Clerk, Confederate States Navy. Born in Randolph County, North Carolina in 1830, Elliott resided there until early manhood when he moved to Fayetteville to engage in merchandising. He moved to Wilmington about 1856 where he was engaged in merchandising and the steamboat business, "Elliott and Utley." He was a veteran of the Wilmington Light Infantry. Elliott enlisted in New Hanover County, North Carolina, in 1st Company A, 36th Regiment, North Carolina Troops (2nd Regiment, North Carolina Artillery) on July 3, 1861 for twelve months. Mustered in as a Sergeant, Elliott was appointed Ordnance Sergeant on October 9, 1862. He was appointed 1st Sergeant sometime in November-December 1862. Captured at Kinston, North Carolina, on December 14, 1862, he was paroled the same day. Elliott transferred to the Confederate States Navy on May 27, 1863 on receipt of appointment as Paymaster's Clerk. He served as a Paymaster's Clerk aboard the CSS PALMETTO STATE, Charleston Station, 1863-1864. Elliott died on May 5, 1894 [Source *"Oakdale,"* Davis states May 10, 1894], in or near Fayetteville as a result of severe injuries received in a fall from a train ("Cape Fear and Yadkin Valley Rail Road" [sic]). He was buried in Oakdale Cemetery, Wilmington, New Hanover County, North Carolina.
[Source(s): McElroy; NA, RG 109; NPS; Stepp, "Burials;" North Carolina Troops, I; *Oakdale*, Davis; "Messenger," 5/20/1894; *ORN* 2, 1, 298; Foenander]

Ellis, George W.
Landsman, Confederate States Navy. Enlisted April 29, 1864, in Raleigh for the war.
[Source(s): McElroy; NA, RG 45]

Ellis, John W.
Landsman, Confederate States Navy. Enlisted April 15, 1864, in Raleigh for the war.
[Source(s): McElroy; NA; RG 45]

Ellis, R. M. (Guilford County, North Carolina)
Landsman, Confederate States Navy. Ellis was conscripted on March 29, 1864 (or "enlisted" March 31, 1864) at Camp Holmes, Raleigh for the war from Colonel Amos' 42nd Regiment North Carolina Militia, Granville County. Description: Age-24; eyes-gray; hair-dark; complexion-fair; height-5ft. 9½ in.; place of birth-Granville; occupation-farmer.
[Source(s): McElroy; NA, RG 45]

Ellis, Tohs. [?], H.
Landsman, Confederate States Navy. Enlisted June 24, 1864, at Raleigh for the war.
[Source(s): McElroy; NA, RG 45]

Ellis, William H.
Landsman, Confederate States Navy. Enlisted July 21, 1864, in Raleigh for the war.
[Source(s): McElroy; NA, RG 45]

Else, Henry P.
Seaman, Confederate States Navy. Else enlisted on May 27, 1863 in Wilmington for the war. He served as a Seaman aboard the CSS NORTH CAROLINA, Cape Fear River, North Carolina, 1864 (Henry Else, a Seaman who served aboard the CSS VIRGINIA II, James River, Virginia, 1864 – 1865 [May be the same as "Henry P. Else"].
[Source(s): McElroy; NA, RG 45; Foenander]

Eno, Robert H.
Ordinary Seaman, Confederate States Navy.
Born in North Carolina about 1845, Eno served as an Ordinary Seaman aboard the steamer CSS FANNY circa 8 October 1861- December 1862. He received a partial payment on February 13, 1862 at Gosport Navy Yard, Norfolk, Virginia following the burning of the FANNY at the Battle of Elizabeth City on February 10, 1862. His name appears on a payroll of the receiving ship CSS UNITED STATES ending 31 March 1862.
He served with the North Carolina Squadron from December 1, 1861 through February 28, 1862, and at Drewry's Bluff as an Ordinary Seaman from April 1, 1863 through at least June 30, 1863. One source stated he served aboard the CSS ALBEMARLE, at Halifax Station, 1864. In 1880, he resided in Claiborne County, Mississippi, as a farmer with his wife, Laura A. Eno.
[Source(s): Foenander; ORN 2, 1, 274 & 285; Census (Ms.), 1880; NCCWSP]

Epps, Manuel (Marvel?) (Montgomery County, North Carolina)
Private, Confederate States Army//Confederate States Navy. Born in Montgomery County, North Carolina, about 1841, Epps resided as a farmer prior to enlisting there for the war at age 21 as a Private, in Company F, 44th Regiment, North Carolina Troops, on March 1, 1862. He was listed as present or accounted for until he was reportedly transferred to the Confederate States Navy on or about April 1, 1864. [Source "North Carolina Troops" states it found no evidence of his service in the Confederate States Navy]. He resided as a farmer, in 1870, with his wife Cirona, and four children, at Eldorado Township, Montgomery County, North Carolina. In 1910, he is shown residing with his second wife Nancy (married in 1907) at Eldorado Township.
[Source(s): McElroy; North Carolina Troops, X; NPS; Foenander]

Etheredge [Etheridge], S. Adolphus (Currituck County, North Carolina)
Private, Confederate States Army//Confederate States Navy. Born in Currituck County, North Carolina, in 1844, he resided there as a student prior to enlisting at Oregon Inlet at age 17 on July 28, 1861 as a Private in Company E, 17th Regiment, North Carolina Troops. He transferred to the Confederate States Navy on an unspecified date where he served initially as a Landsman, later as a Seaman, on the CSS FANNY, circa October 8, 1861 – December 20, 1861. He received a partial payment on February 13, 1862 at Gosport Navy Yard, Norfolk, Virginia, following the burning of the FANNY at Elizabeth City, North Carolina on February 10, 1862. According to payroll records, he served with the North Carolina Squadron from December 1, 1861 - February 28, 1862.
[Source(s): McElroy; North Carolina Troops, VI; Foenander; *ORN* 2, 1, 285; Census (North Carolina) 1850 and 1860; NCCWSP]

Etheridge [Ethridge], Walter L. (Pasquotank County, North Carolina)
1st Class Boy, Confederate States Navy. Etheridge enlisted on May 18, 1863, in Wilmington for three years or the war. He died in May of 1919, and was buried in Hollywood Cemetery, Pasquotank County, North Carolina.
[Source(s): McElroy; NA, RG 45; Stepp, "Burials"]

Etheridge, William A. (Currituck County, North Carolina)
Private, Confederate States Army//Landsman, Seaman, Confederate States Navy. He was born in Currituck County, North Carolina, where he resided as a wheelwright or carpenter prior to enlisting at age 17 on May 13, 1861 as a Private in Company E, 17th Regiment North Carolina Troops (1st and 2nd Organizations). He was listed as present or accounted for until he transferred to the Confederate States Navy on or about October 25, 1861. According to payroll records, he served as a Landsman aboard the CSS FANNY as of October 8, 1861 and as a Seaman on the CSS CURLEW November 20, 1861. He is listed on payroll records for the first quarter of 1862 as a Landsman on the CURLEW. His name appears on a payroll of the receiving ship CSS UNITED STATES ending March 31, 1862.
[Source(s): McElroy; North Carolina Troops, VI; NPS; Foenander; NCCWSP]

Evans, Daniel
    Confederate States Navy. Evans served previously as a Private, Company A, 8th Regiment, North Carolina Troops
    [Source(s): McElroy; North Carolina Troops, NPS]

Evans, William E.
    Landsman, Confederate States Navy. Evans enlisted on November 29, 1863, in Wilmington, North Carolina, for the war.
    [Source(s): McElroy; NA, RG 45]

Everitt, William (New Hanover County, North Carolina)
    Confederate States Navy. Everitt appears on a register of Confederate States Army General Military Hospital Number 4, Wilmington, North Carolina, dated February 10, 1862, giving disease as "pneumonia" and post office as Wilmington, North Carolina. He was returned to duty on February 20, 1862.
    [Source(s): McElroy; NA, RG 109]

Exum, James (New Hanover County, North Carolina)
    Private, Confederate States Army//temporarily "detailed" to Confederate States Navy. Exum resided in New Hanover County, North Carolina, but enlisted in Wake County, North Carolina, in Company C, 1st Battalion, North Carolina Heavy Artillery, on April 28, 1862, for the war. He was detailed to the government steamer "John Dawson" [CSS JOHN DAWSON] on April 15, 1863 and reported as absent detailed through February 18, 1864. He was detailed on the Wilmington and Manchester Railroad May-June 1864, and apparently through August 1864.
    [Source(s): North Carolina Troops, I]

Exum [Axsum, Axum], James (County unknown)
    Landsman, Confederate States Navy. Exum enlisted on February 4, 1864, in Raleigh, North Carolina, for the war, and served as a Landsman aboard the CSS ARCTIC, Cape Fear River, North Carolina, 1863.
    [Source(s): NA, RG 45; Card File; Foenander]

Ezzell, John W. (New Hanover County, North Carolina)
    Confederate States Navy. Ezzell enlisted in Company A, 71st Regiment, North Carolina Troops, on April 1, 1864, in Raleigh, North Carolina. He was transferred to the Confederate States Navy "and was in Gunboat the flag ship when Richmond Surrendered [sic]." He made application for a Confederate pension on June 16, 1909, age 63, while living in Wilmington, North Carolina.
    [Source(s): Pensions (North Carolina)]

Fail, Needham (Wayne County, North Carolina)
    Confederate States Navy. Born in North Carolina in 1832, Fail served as a Landsman aboard the CSS ARCTIC, Cape Fear River, North Carolina, 1863. He later served on the CSS RALEIGH in North Carolina and Virginia waters, 1864. In 1880, he resided as a farmer with his wife Pharibee, and seven children (eldest child born 1861), at Saulston, Wayne County, North Carolina.
    [Source(s): Foenander; ORN 2, 1, 278 & 302; Census (NC), 1880]

Faircloth, Blueford (Bluford) (Cumberland County, North Carolina)
    Landsman, Confederate States Navy (also listed as Private, Confederate States Marine Corps). Faircloth enlisted on November 20, 1863, in Raleigh, North Carolina, for the war [another source shows enlistment on November 22, 1863, in Wilmington, North Carolina, for the war]. He apparently served as a Landsman aboard the CSS ARCTIC, 1863, and the CSS RALEIGH in North Carolina and Virginia waters, 1864. His name appears on a roll of prisoners of war at Point Lookout, Maryland, which states he was captured at Piney Grove, North Carolina, on March 8, 1865 and confined at Point Lookout, Maryland, April 3, 1865 until released June 27, 1865. His Oath of Allegiance, sworn at Point Lookout, Maryland, on June 27, 1865, gives his residence as Cumberland County, North Carolina. Description: complexion light; hair brown; eyes hazel; height 5 feet 11 inches. Faircloth filed a pension claim in North Carolina on June 2, 1902, age 80, as a Navy veteran. He listed his post office as Autryville, "Cumberland County" [sic] [Sampson County], North Carolina. Pension approved.
    [Source(s): Foenander; North Carolina Troops, Doc.# 0185, p. 1, and 0299; Card File; NA RG 45; NA RG 109; ORN 2, 1, 277 & 302]

Faircloth, Henry C. (County unknown)
   Landsman, Confederate States Navy. Faircloth enlisted on May 13, 1864, in Raleigh, North Carolina, for the war.
   [Source(s): Card File; NA RG 45]

Faircloth, James (County unknown)
   Landsman, Confederate States Navy. Faircloth enlisted on November 22, 1863, in Wilmington, North Carolina, for the war [an alternate source gives his enlistment date as the 20th and the place as Raleigh]. Faircloth served as a Landsman aboard the CSS ARCTIC, Cape Fear River, North Carolina, 1863, and later aboard the CSS RALEIGH in North Carolina and Virginia waters, 1864.
   [Source(s): Foenander; Card File; NA RG 45]

Faircloth, Samuel (New Hanover County, North Carolina)
   Private, Confederate States Marine Corps. Faircloth was listed as a Prisoner of War, released on April 12, 1865. Transportation records indicate "destination Wilmington."
   [Source(s): NT, Doc. # 0185, p. 1, and 0299; Card File]

Faircloth, Samuel F. (Cumberland County, North Carolina)
   Private, Confederate States Army//Confederate States Navy. Born in North Carolina in 1823 [another source lists his birth as November 20, 1820], he was a workman at the Arsenal in Fayetteville in 1864 when he volunteered for Starr's Battery. There were some "irregularities" in his paperwork, and he was assigned to or enlisted in the Confederate States Navy in 1864 and served aboard the CSS CHICORA at Charleston, South Carolina, through the close of the war. He lost a finger shot off his left hand. In 1880, he resided as a farmer with his wife Eliza, and other relatives (eldest son born 1850), at Flea Hill, Cumberland County, North Carolina. His pension claim filed on June 21, 1901, at age 75, listed his post office as Fayetteville, Cumberland County, North Carolina, was approved. He died on November 13, 1901, and was buried in Cross Creek Cemetery, Fayetteville, Cumberland County, North Carolina.
   [Source(s): Card File; Pensions (North Carolina); Stepp, "Burials;" Foenander]

Fallow ["Fallon"], William A.
   Confederate States Navy//Private, Confederate States Army. Fallow transferred to 2nd Company H, 40th Regiment, North Carolina Troops (3rd Regiment, North Carolina Artillery) from the steamer CSS NORTH CAROLINA on August 10, 1863. He was listed as present or accounted for through December 1864.
   [Source(s): Card File; NA RG 109; North Carolina Troops, I; Foenander]

Falls, Leander M. (Lincoln County, North Carolina)
   Landsman, Confederate States Navy. Falls served as a Landsman, CSS ARCTIC, Cape Fear River, North Carolina, 1863.
   [Source(s): Lincoln Roster; Foenander; *ORN* 2, 1, 277; Foenander]

Fanner [Fauner, Fannon], Valentine ("West Creek, North Carolina")
   Ordinary Seaman, Confederate States Navy. Fanner enlisted on September 5, 1863, in Wilmington, North Carolina, for the war. His name appears on registers of Confederate States Army General Military Hospital Number 4, Wilmington, North Carolina, which state he was admitted on September 28, 1863 with "feb. continu," placed in ward 6, bed number 168. He deserted on October 2, 1863. His post office was listed as "West Creek [Note: "Western Creek" was crossed out], North Carolina."
   [Source(s): Card File; NA RG 45; NA RG 109; Hosp. (No. 4), Wilm.,]

Farrel, William H. (Pasquotank County, North Carolina)
   Private, Confederate States Army//Ordinary Seaman, Confederate States Navy. Born and residing in Pasquotank County, North Carolina, as a farmer, Farrel enlisted there on August 19, 1861 at age 22 as a Private in Company A, 8th Regiment, North Carolina State Troops. He was captured at Roanoke Island on February 8, 1862; paroled at Elizabeth City, North Carolina; and, exchanged in August 1862. He was present or accounted for until he transferred to the Confederate States Navy on April 18, 1863. He is shown as an Ordinary Seaman aboard the CSS CHICORA, 1863-1864 (A "W. H. Farrell," served as an Ordinary Seaman aboard the CSS CHICORA in Charleston Harbor, South Carolina, July 1863 - September 1864).
   [Source(s): Card File; MR, I; North Carolina Troops, IV; Foenander]

Farrell, Michael
2nd Class Fireman, Confederate States Navy. Farrell served as a 2nd Class Fireman aboard the CSS NORTH CAROLINA and CSS TALLAHASSEE, Wilmington Station, 1864.
[Source(s): *ORN* 2, 1, 295, 296 and 307; Foenander; MR, I]

Farrow, Joel E. (New Hanover County, North Carolina [?])
First Class Cabin Boy, Confederate States Navy. Farrow enlisted on June 29, 1864, in Wilmington, North Carolina, for the war. Born on March 22, 1847, he died on April 12 (26?), 1912, and was buried in Bellevue Cemetery, Wilmington, New Hanover County, North Carolina.
[Source(s): Card File; NA RG 45; Stepp, "Burials"]

Farrow, William A. (County unknown)
Confederate States Navy//Confederate States Army. Farrow transferred from the Confederate States Navy to 2nd Company H, 40th Regiment, North Carolina Troops (3rd Regiment, North Carolina Artillery), on August 10, 1863. He was listed as present or accounted for through December 1864.
[Source(s): North Carolina Troops, I]

Faucett, A. H.
Landsman, Confederate States Navy. Faucett enlisted on June 10, 1864, in Raleigh, North Carolina, for the war.
[Source(s): Card File; NA RG 45]

Faust, D. M.
Landsman, Confederate States Navy. Faust enlisted on June 11, 1864, in Raleigh, North Carolina, for the war. A September 25, 1864 letter requesting a transfer from Charleston, South Carolina (CSS INDIAN CHIEF) to either Halifax or Kinston, North Carolina, to North Carolina Governor Zebulon B. Vance, is signed by D. Beck, D. M. Faust, R. Tripp, and J. C. Tripp. Apparently, the transfer was not within Vance's ability to grant. The letter states all four were "Soldiers in Colonel Mallet's [Mallett's] battalion and desired when we entered the navy to serve in North Carolina but were not permitted to do so."
[Source(s): Card File; NA RG 45; Vance Papers]

Fennell, C. N.
Confederate States Navy. Fennell was born in North Carolina (Source "Foenander" shows birthplace as Maryland), appointed from Florida, and served as a Clerk in 1862 on the staff of Confederate Secretary of the Navy Stephen Mallory, and later as Chief Clerk, Office of Medicine and Surgery, Confederate States Navy Department, Richmond, Virginia, 1863 - 1864.
[Source(s): Foenander; Register, 1862; Register, 1863; Register, 1864]

Ferguson, John A.
3rd Assistant Engineer, Confederate States Navy.
Appointed 3rd Assistant Engineer on December 16, 1861 and served as such aboard the CSS CORA, 1861-62 [NOTE: The CSS CORA may have been a blockade runner].
[Source: NCCWSP]

Fergerson, Jon H.
Landsman, Confederate States Navy. Fergerson enlisted on February 29, 1864, in Raleigh, North Carolina, for the war.
[Source(s): Card File; NA RG 45]

Feril [Fail] [Farrell?], Needham
Landsman, Confederate States Navy. Feril enlisted on January 25, 1865, in Raleigh, North Carolina, for the war.
[Source(s): Card File; NA RG 45]

Fesmire, Balaam Walker (Chatham County, North Carolina)
Landsman, Confederate States Navy. Born in 1835, Fesmire enlisted in the Confederate States Navy on August 5, 1863, in Wilmington, North Carolina. He died in 1922 and was buried at Love's Creek Baptist Church, Chatham County, North Carolina.
[Source(s): MR, 4, p. 445; Stepp, "Burials;" Lane Society]

Fields, Charles (Craven County, North Carolina) [NOTE: May be same as "Charles M. Fields," q.v.]
Confederate States Navy. Crewman aboard the CSS NORTH CAROLINA.
[Source(s): MR, 4, p. 443]

Fields, Charles M. (Craven County, North Carolina) [NOTE: May be same as "Charles Fields," q.v.]
Private, Confederate States Army//Ordinary Seaman, Confederate States Navy. Fields resided in Craven County, North Carolina, where he enlisted on June 4, 1861at age 18 in Company K, 2nd Regiment, North Carolina Troops, for the war. Captured at South Mountain, Maryland, on September 14, 1862, he was exchanged at Aiken's Landing, Virginia, on October 6, 1862, and declared exchanged on November 10, 1862. Fields transferred to the Confederate States Navy on June 16, 1863 [NOTE: Sources "Foenander" and "North Carolina Troops, III" give the date as January 29, 1863]. One source shows he "enlisted" for the war in Wilmington, North Carolina.
[Source(s): Card File; Foenander; NA RG 45; North Carolina Troops, III]

Finch, W. C.
Landsman, Confederate States Navy. Finch enlisted on October 16, 1863, at Camp Holmes, near Raleigh, North Carolina, for the war [alternate source lists enlistment October 16, 1863, in Wilmington, North Carolina].
[Source(s): Card file; NA RG 45]

Fincher, Benjamin F. (Union County, North Carolina)
Corporal, Confederate States Army//Confederate States Navy. Born in North Carolina, about 1842, Fincher resided in Union County, North Carolina, where he enlisted at age 23 on March 19, 1862, as a Private in Company A, 48th Regiment, North Carolina Troops. Mustered in as a Corporal, he was reported present or accounted for in September-October 1862, and January-June 1863. He transferred to the Confederate States Navy on or about April 15, 1864. Fincher resided as a farmer, in 1880, with his wife, Matilda, in Monroe, Union County, North Carolina.
[Source(s): Card File; North Carolina Troops, XI; Foenander]

Finney, John
Ordinary Seaman, Confederate States Navy. Finney enlisted on November 10, 1863, in Wilmington, North Carolina, for the war, and served as a Landsman aboard the CSS ARCTIC, Cape Fear River, North Carolina, 1863. He later served as an Ordinary Seaman aboard the CSS YADKIN, Wilmington, North Carolina, 1864.
[Source(s): Card File; NA RG 45; Foenander]

Fisher, E. D.
Landsman, Confederate States Navy. Fisher enlisted on October 5, 1863, at Camp Holmes, near Raleigh, North Carolina, for the war.
[Source(s): Card File; NA RG 45]

Fisher, Joseph (Currituck County, North Carolina)
Seaman/Ship's Cook, Confederate States Navy. Born in North Carolina circa 1833, Fisher lived in the Coinjock District of Currituck County, North Carolina as a sailor in 1860. On 25 July 1861, he shipped as a Seaman aboard the CSS EDWARD, but was listed as "Ship's Cook" on an October 30, 1861 muster roll of the CSS EDWARD. He appears as a "Ship's Cook" on the CSS FORREST circa the first quarter of 1862. Fisher was received aboard the receiving ship CSS UNITED STATES by order of French Forrest on 21 February 1862 and ordered shipped for three years. A payroll for that ship ending 31 March 1862 lists him as still aboard. He appears as a Seaman on the final payroll of the CSS VIRGINIA that covered the period 1 April 1862 through 30 September 1862 and served at Drewry's Bluff as a Seaman from 1 April 1863 through 30 June 1863.
[Sources: Census (NC), 1860; NCCWSP]

Fisher, J. W.
Landsman, Confederate States Navy. Registers of Jackson Hospital, Richmond, Virginia, indicate that Fisher was admitted on April 8, 1865, and died May 11, 1865. Disease not given.
[Source(s): Card File; NA RG 109; ONWR]

Fisher, William
Seaman, Ship's Cook, Confederate States Navy.
Fisher appears in the logbook of the CSS ELLIS in an entry dated August1, 1861. He served as Ship's Cook aboard the CSS ELLIS from November 2, 1861 – May 1862. Fisher was received aboard the receiving ship CSS UNITED STATES by order of Flag Officer French Forrest on February 21, 1862 and ordered shipped for three years. He

appears on that ship's payroll ending March 31, 1862. Fisher served aboard the CSS VIRGINIA appearing on her final payroll as Seaman.
[Source: NCCWSP]

Fiske, James E. (Vermont; North Carolina)
Midshipman, later Lieutenant, Confederate States Navy. Born in Vermont in 1843, he was a citizen of and appointed from North Carolina as an Acting Midshipman, United States Navy. He resigned as an Acting Midshipman, United States Navy, on April 16, 1861, was appointed a Midshipman, Confederate States Navy, on June 14, 1861, and Acting Master, on September 24, 1861. Promoted to Lieutenant for the war, on February 8, 1862, Fiske resigned on December 29, 1863. He served on board the CSS PATRICK HENRY, [Virginia waters], 1861, CSS MOBILE, New Orleans, and Jackson stations, 1861-1862, and the CSS TUSCALOOSA, Mobile Squadron, 1862-1863.
[Source(s): Register; McElroy; Card File; Journal; Foenander; Fold3, USN Resignees]

Fitzgerald, Thomas
Ordinary Seaman, Confederate States Navy. Fitzgerald enlisted on February 13, 1864, in Wilmington, North Carolina, for the war. He served as a Seaman aboard the CSS ARCTIC, Cape Fear River, North Carolina, 1863.
[Source(s): Card File; NA RG 45; Foenander; *ORN* 2, 1, 278]

Flake, Elijah [Elisha] Wilson (Anson County, North Carolina)
Private, Confederate States Army//, Landsman, Confederate States Navy. Born and reared in Anson County, North Carolina, Flake lived there as a farmer until he enlisted at Camp Bee, Virginia, on September 5, 1861 [Source MR, I, gives the date as October 10, 1861] at age 20 in Company C, 14th Regiment, North Carolina Troops. On February 15, 1862, while stationed near Smithfield, Virginia, not far from Portsmouth, Virginia, where the USS MERRIMAC was being transformed into the CSS VIRGINIA, he was transferred to the Confederate States Navy and served aboard her as a Landsman, participating in the famous duel with the USS CUMBERLAND and USS MONITOR. Discharged [date unknown] from the Confederate States Navy after the CSS VIRGINIA was scuttled, he enlisted in Company K, 26th Regiment, North Carolina Troops, in Anson County, North Carolina, on February 1, 1863. He was present or accounted for until wounded at Gettysburg, Pennsylvania, on July 3, 1863. He was reported absent wounded or absent sick until the March-June 1863 muster roll, when he was detailed for hospital duty as a Steward [hospital name and location unknown]. Reported absent on detail through February 1865, Flake rejoined his company prior to April 9, 1865, when he was paroled at Appomattox Court House, Virginia. Flake died at age 77 in 1914.
[Source(s): Smithwick, from the section on the Battle Between the *Merrimack* and the *Monitor*, by Elijah Flake; Card File; Flake; ORN 2, 1, 309; Foenander; North Carolina Troops, V & VII; ORN 2, 1, 309]

Flanagan, William B. (Currituck County, North Carolina)
Private, Confederate States Army//Quartermaster, Seaman, Confederate States Navy. Born in Currituck County, North Carolina, Flanagan resided there as a Seaman prior to enlisting in Pasquotank County, North Carolina, at age 39 on May 4, 1861, as a Private in Company L, 17th Regiment, North Carolina Troops (1st Organization). He was listed as present or accounted for until he transferred to the Confederate States Navy on October 4, 1861. He served as a Quartermaster, and later as a Seaman, aboard the CSS FORREST, in the first quarter of 1862. His name appears on a payroll of the receiving ship CSS UNITED STATES ending March 31, 1862
[Source(s): Card File; North Carolina Troops, VI; Foenander; NCCWSP]

Flanner, Benjamin (New Hanover County, North Carolina)
Confederate States Navy. Crewmember on the privateer "*Mariner*" under command of Captain Benjamin Washington Beery, circa 1861.
[Source(s): Card file of "Benjamin Washington Beery;" *Oakdale*, Davis]

Fleming, Emanuel
2nd Class Fireman, Confederate States Navy. Fleming enlisted on January 1, 1863, in Raleigh, North Carolina, for the war.
[Source(s): Card File; NA RG 45]

Fleming, James (African American)
Confederate States Navy. Fleming enlisted on February 20, 1864, in Wilmington, North Carolina, for the war. A "J. Fleming" served as a 2nd Class Fireman aboard the CSS ARCTIC, Cape Fear River, North Carolina, 1863
[Source(s): Card File; NA RG 45; Foenander]

Fletcher, James W. (North Carolina?)
    Confederate States Navy. Name appears on the March-October 1864 roster of the CSS NEUSE.
    [Source: CMACSSN]

Flowers, John T. (Hyde County, North Carolina)
    Musician, Confederate States Army//Confederate States Navy (crewman on blockade runner). Born in Hyde County, North Carolina, Flowers resided there as a Seaman until he enlisted there at age 17 on May 15, 1861 in Company B, 17th Regiment, North Carolina Troops (1st Organization). Mustered in as a Musician, Flowers was present or accounted for until the company was disbanded on March 26, 1862. He enlisted in Company B, 17th Regiment, North Carolina Troops (2nd Organization) on or about May 1, 1862, but never reported for duty as he was "running blockade from Wilmington…on Gvt Steamer" [possibly the "*Ad-Vance*"].
    [Source(s): Foenander; North Carolina Troops, VI; MR, II]

Floyd, D. A.
    Landsman, Confederate States Navy. Floyd enlisted on March 5, 1864, in Wilmington, North Carolina, for the war.
    [Source(s): Card File; NA RG 45]

Floyd, English G.
    Landsman, Confederate States Navy. Floyd enlisted on February 23, 1864, in Raleigh, North Carolina, for the war, and served as a Landsman, CSS ARCTIC, Cape Fear River, North Carolina, 1863.
    [Source(s): Card File; NA RG 45; Foenander; ORN 2, 1, 278]

Flynn, James (Resided in Louisiana, enlisted in the Confederate States Army in Halifax County, North Carolina).
    Private, Confederate States Army//Confederate States Navy. Resided in Louisiana and enlisted in Halifax County, North Carolina, at age 34, on October 3, 1862, for the war. He enlisted as a Private in Company D, 24th Regiment, North Carolina Troops, as a substitute for Private John L. Ivey. Flynn was listed as present or accounted for until he transferred to the Confederate States Navy Department on April 10, 1864.
    [Source(s): North Carolina Troops, VII; Howard; Foenander]

Foley, Richard Flemming (Brunswick County (?), North Carolina)
    Captain, Confederate States Army//Acting Master//Master, Confederate States Navy. Born on March 18, 1836 in and appointed from North Carolina [Alternate source states he was born in Baltimore, Maryland, March 18, 183_ (?), and was a resident of Baltimore, Maryland]. Foley served as a Master's Mate aboard the United States Coastal Survey schooner "Crawford" in North Carolina waters until his resignation on March 15, 1861. He served as Captain of Engineers on General Whiting's staff until his original entry into Confederate States Navy, as an Acting Master on October 13, 1861 [Source "Driver" states he "enlisted in the Confederate States Navy February 14, 1861"]. He was appointed a Master Not-in-the Line of Promotion on July 24, 1862. Foley served on the CSS ELLIS in North Carolina waters in 1861, and CSS CASWELL and CSS ARCTIC, Wilmington Station, 1861-1863. Ordered to the CSS RICHMOND on June 10, 1862, Foley served with the James River Squadron, 1862-1863. He resigned on April 30, 1863 and was ordered to the blockade runner "*Robert E. Lee*" May 1, 1863. Foley was a post-war steamship captain in Baltimore, and a member of the "Maryland Line," Army and Navy Society, Maryland Line Association. He died on March 3, 1884 at age 84 and was buried in Southport Cemetery, Brunswick County, North Carolina.
    [Source(s): Register, McElroy; Card File; Gravestone Records, v. 8, p. 60; Driver; Stepp, "Burials"]

Foote, George Anderson (Warren County, North Carolina)
    Assistant Surgeon, Confederate States Navy. Foote was born in Warrenton, North Carolina, December 16, 1834, and appointed from North Carolina as an Assistant Surgeon, Confederate States Navy, for the war on January 7, 1864 [NOTE: One source lists the date as March 11, 1862]. Appointed Assistant Surgeon, Provisional Navy, on June 2, 1864, Foote served on the ironclad CSS RALEIGH, Wilmington Station, 1863-1864 (Source "Driver" gives his reporting date as January 7, 1864) and CSS ALBEMARLE in North Carolina waters, reporting June 2, 1864. Captured on January 15, 1865, at Fort Fisher, Foote was sent to Fort Columbus as a Prisoner of War, and exchanged at Boulware's Wharf, Virginia, about March 5, 1865 (Source "Driver" states he was exchanged March 15, 1865). He died in Warrenton, North Carolina, January 25, 1897. His wife was receiving a pension in Portsmouth, Virginia, as late as October 7, 1919.
    [Source(s): Register; McElroy; Card File; CMH, v.4, p. 489; Driver; ORN 1, 10, 718 and 2, 1, 274 & 301; ONWR]

Forbes, Elijah B.
Private, Confederate States Navy. Born in North Carolina in 1827, Forbes worked as a farmer until he enlisted in Company F, 41st Virginia Infantry in Norfolk, Virginia, April 22, 1861. Wounded at Chancellorsville, May 1, 1863, he was wounded again at Mine Run, Virginia, in November 1863. Forbes transferred to the Confederate States Navy on December 30, 1863.
[Source(s): Driver]

Forbes, J. H.
Landsman, Confederate States Navy. Forbes enlisted on October 5, 1863, at Camp Holmes, near Raleigh, North Carolina.
[Source(s): card File; NA RG 45]

Forbes, J. W. (Gaston County, North Carolina)
Landsman, Confederate States Navy ("Naval Battalion"). Forbes enlisted on July 16, 1864, in Raleigh, North Carolina, for the war. His name appears on a Roll of Prisoners at Newport News, Virginia, which states he was captured in Amelia County, Virginia, April 6, 1865. His name also appears on an Oath of Allegiance subscribed and sworn to at Newport News, Virginia, June 26, 1865, giving his place of residence as Gaston County, North Carolina, and stating he was captured at Farmville, Virginia. Description: complexion dark; hair dark; eyes black; height 5 feet 7 inches.
[Source(s): Card File; NA RG 109; Cloninger]

Forcum, W. W.
Landsman, Confederate States Navy. Forcum enlisted on June 11, 1864, in Raleigh, North Carolina, for the war.
[Source(s): Card File; NA RG 45]

Foreman, Ivy (Pitt County, North Carolina)
Midshipman, Master, Second Lieutenant, First Lieutenant, Confederate States Navy. Foreman was born at "Greenwreaeth," Pitt County, North Carolina on December 20, 1843 ["1842" per source Stepp, "Burials," and "1845" per source "Foenander"], and was shown residing with his brother William, in 1850, at the home of Richard H. and Martha E. Lewis, in Pitt County, North Carolina. Resigned as Acting Midshipman, United States Navy, April 24, 1861, he was appointed Acting Midshipman, Confederate States Navy, on October 6, 1861 (Source "Driver" states October 7, 1861) and appears as a Midshipman aboard the CSS FANNY according to a muster roll dated December 12, 1861. Foreman was appointed Master in Line of Promotion on October 15, 1862, and Second Lieutenant, January 7, 1864 [1863], to rank from April 26, 1863. He was promoted to First Lieutenant, Provisional Navy, June 2, 1864 ("Driver" states April 29, 1863) to rank from January 6, 1864. Foreman served on the CSS FANNY from 1861-1862; the CSS BEAUFORT in Virginia waters, 1862, as Midshipman, later Master; and, participated in the battle of Hampton Roads, Virginia, March 8-9, 1862, serving as aide to his commander. He served aboard the CSS BALTIC, Mobile Squadron, 1862-1863, and had service abroad, 1863-1864. He was a passenger on the steamer "Margaret and Jessie" when it was chased ashore by USS RHODE ISLAND, May 30, 1863. Foreman served on the CSS FREDERICKSBURG in the James River Squadron, beginning on or about September 17, 1864. Foreman received temporary commands of the CSS HAMPTON, James River squadron, in October 1864 in the absence of Lieutenant J. S. Maury, who was sick, and CSS TORPEDO, November 1864. He died in Richmond, Virginia, of typhoid fever, the day after his twenty-first birthday, December 21, 1864. His letter describing the fight between the CSS VIRGINIA and USS CONGRESS is in the holdings of the Virginia Historical Society. He was buried at Calvary Episcopal Church, Edgecombe County, North Carolina.
[Source(s): Register; Foenander; McElroy; Card File; Thorpe Roster, p. 133; Driver; Stepp, "Burials;" Journal; *Fay. Obs.* (January 16, 1865); NCCWSP; ONWR; Fold3, Midshipmen]

Foreman (Forman), Michael (Beaufort County, North Carolina)
Private, Confederate States Army//Seaman, Confederate States Navy. Resided in Beaufort County, North Carolina, where he enlisted in Company G, 19th Regiment, North Carolina Troops (2nd Regiment, North Carolina Cavalry) on June 26, 1861, at age 21, "for the war." Present or accounted for until transferred to the Confederate States Navy on February 1, 1862 where he served as a Seaman aboard the CSS RALEIGH, North Carolina, 1862 - 1864. His name appears on a payroll of the North Carolina Squadron for the period February 6, 1861 – April 15, 1862. Foreman served at Drewry's Bluff as Boatswain's Mate from at least April 1, 1863 - June 30, 1863.
[Source(s): Card File; North Carolina Troops, II; Foenander; "Beaufort County Sailors;" NCCWSP]

Forrest, Dulany A.
Confederate States Navy. Forrest died in Oxford, North Carolina, August 10, 1863.
[Source(s): Card File; "TGP"]

Forrest, I. T.
Landsman, Confederate States Navy. Forrest enlisted on September 11, 1863, at Camp Holmes [near Raleigh], for the war.
[Source(s): Card File; NA RG 45]

Forrest, Jesse Tatum (Stanly County, North Carolina)
"Private," Confederate States Navy. Enlisted for the Confederate States Navy August 24 [21] [or, June 22, 1863], 1863 in Wilmington, North Carolina, for the war. He appears on the 1860 North Carolina Census as a farmer with a wife from Missouri, aged 30, and three sons ages 6-11. His census entry reveals he owned an estate valued at $150. Forrest served aboard the CSS NEUSE as of the ship's March – April 1864 muster roll. Aged 38 in 1864, he appears on a register of Confederate States Army General Hospital No. 3, Greensboro, North Carolina, which states he was admitted March 1, 1865, with "catarrhus" and sent to another hospital the same day. The register lists his post office as Albemarle and carries the remark "Transferred from Kinston." Born October 15, 1828, Forrest died in 1885, and was buried at Fork Baptist Church, Davie County, North Carolina.
[Source(s): MR, 4, p. 445; Hill; Census (NC), 1860; Card File; NA RG 45; NA RG 109; Stepp, "Burials;" NEUSE Roster]

Fort, John (Cumberland County, North Carolina) [NOTE: May be same as John W. Fort, q.v.] Confederate States Navy. Fort served as a Seaman on the CSS NORTH CAROLINA.
[Source(s): Oates; MR, 4, p. 443]

Fort [Forte; Fost], John W. [NOTE: May be same as John Fort, q.v.]
Ordinary Seaman [Seaman, per Card File)], Confederate States Navy. Enlisted June 5, 1863, in Wilmington, North Carolina, for the war, and served aboard the CSS NORTH CAROLINA, Cape Fear River, 1864.
[Source(s): Card File; NA RG 45; Foenander; ORN 2, 1, 294]

Fort, Wiley [Wilie] B. (Wayne County, North Carolina)
Paymaster's Clerk [per "Foenander"] [Landsman (per "Stepp")], Confederate States Navy. Born in Pikeville, Wayne County, North Carolina, in 1842 [another source gives the date as "1840"], Fort enlisted in the Confederate States Navy in North Carolina in 1861. He served aboard the receiving ship CSS INDIAN CHIEF and the CSS COLUMBIA, Charleston Station, as well as aboard the blockade runners "Torch," "Henno," and "Stono." His daughter was Mrs. H. B. Parker, Goldsboro, North Carolina. Gravestone Records source states he was "a Hero in the Confederate Navy." He lived fourteen miles north of Goldsboro on Nahunta Swamp. He is buried on the plantation where he lived (Wayne County, North Carolina)." Another source states Fort "enlisted in Wayne County in January 1862 in the Confederate States Navy. He was discharged April 9, 1865 at Appomattox with the Naval Brigade under Admiral Semmes. After the war, Fort was a member of the United Confederate Veterans. He resided as a farmer, in 1910, with his daughter, Pearl, at Pikeville, Wayne County, North Carolina; and, is shown as a widower, in 1910. Fort died in 1926 and was buried in the Fort Cemetery, Wayne County, North Carolina.
[Source(s): McElroy; Foenander; Names-1907; Card File; Gravestone Records, v. 3, p. 247; Ruffin Chap., UDC; Stepp, "Burials"]

Foscue, William F. (Rhode Island/ Craven County, North Carolina)
Private, Confederate States Army//Confederate States Navy. Born in Rhode Island, about 1823, Foscue resided as a sailor in New Bern, North Carolina, in 1850 [resided in Virginia and enlisted at age 36 per "North Carolina Troops, III"]. He enlisted in Craven County, North Carolina on June 24, 1861, as a Private in Company K, 2nd Regiment, North Carolina State Troops. Present or accounted for until he transferred to the Confederate States Navy on May 7, 1862.
[Source(s): North Carolina Troops, III; Census (North Carolina), 1850; Foenander]

Foskey (Fosky), William (Craven County, North Carolina)
Boatswain's Mate/Seaman, Confederate States Navy. Born in North Carolina in 1818, Foskey served aboard the screw steamer CSS FANNY, North Carolina, 1861 – 1862, and as a Seaman (also shown as Boatswain's Mate) aboard the CSS ARCTIC in 1862. He resided as a mariner, in 1870, with his wife Martha and two children in Craven County, North Carolina. Source "MR" states he enlisted in Wilmington, North Carolina.
[Source(s): Foenander; ORN 1, 23, 703 and 2, 1, 276 & 285; Census (North Carolina), 1870; MR, IV, 445]

Foster, Lyman L. [B.] (Maine//Hertford County, North Carolina)

1st Sergeant, Confederate States Army//Confederate States Navy. Born in Maine in 1842, the son of Cony and Caroline Foster, he resided with his parents at Orono, Maine, in 1850. Foster had previous service as a Midshipman in the United States Navy. He resided in Hertford County, North Carolina, where he enlisted for the war at age 20 on July 5, 1861 in Company F, 1st Regiment, North Carolina Troops. He mustered in as 3rd Sergeant and promoted to 1st Sergeant after October 1862. Wounded in action at Chancellorsville, Virginia, on May 3, 1863, Foster was present or accounted for through January-February 1864 muster roll on which he is reported with the remark: "Promoted to Master in the Navy, December 15, 1863." He transferred to the Confederate States Navy on that date. Another source states he was appointed an Acting Master's Mate, December 24, 1863, and Acting Master's Mate, Provisional Navy, June 2, 1864. Another source states he served in the "Confederate States Army" [probably Confederate States Navy] at Drewry's Bluff, Virginia, 1864 and on the Confederate States steamers CSS FREDERICKSBURG and CSS DRURY and in the James River Batteries, 1864-1865. Foster resided as a store clerk in 1880 with his wife Susan A. Foster, and two children (eldest child born 1876), in Richmond, Virginia.
[Source(s): Register; Card File; North Carolina Troops, III; Foenander; ORN 1, 10, 632 & 766 and 2, 1, 322; Census (Va.), 1880; MR, I]

Foster, P. A. [Possible North Carolinian]

Seaman, Confederate States Navy. Wounded in mouth and right shoulder at Fort Fisher, December 24-25, 1864.
[Source(s): Daily Confed. (1/2/65); Card File]

Fountain, Coffield [Cofuld] (Edgecombe County, North Carolina)

Landsman, Confederate States Navy. Born in Edgecombe County, North Carolina, in 1838, he was by occupation a farmer until he enlisted on March 24, 1864, in Raleigh, North Carolina, for the war, in the Confederate States Navy. Another source states Fountain was conscripted on September 17, 1864 at age 23 from Colonel James' 31st Regiment, North Carolina Militia from Edgecombe County, North Carolina. Fountain served as a Landsman aboard the CSS ALBEMARLE, and at Halifax Station, 1864. Description: Age 25 [?]; eyes blue; hair light; complexion florid; height 6 feet; place of birth Edgecombe County, North Carolina; occupation farmer. One source states he appears on a list of conscripts "in yard at Halifax, June 9, 1864." He resided as a farmer, in 1870, with his wife, Laura, at Upper Fishing Creek, Edgecombe County, North Carolina.
[Source(s): Card File; NA RG 45; Foenander; Census (North Carolina), 1870; ORN 2, 1, 274]

Fowler, John W.

Landsman, Confederate States Navy. Enlisted June 11, 1864, in Raleigh, North Carolina, for the war.
[Source(s): Card File; NA RG 45]

Fraley, B. F. (Rowan County, North Carolina)

Confederate States Navy. Fraley signed an Oath of Allegiance at Salisbury, North Carolina, May 29, 1865. His Oath states "a sailor of the County of Rowan, State of North Carolina."
[Source(s): Card File; NA RG 109]

Franklin, Charles M. (Wake County, North Carolina)

Landsman, Confederate States Navy. Born in North Carolina in 1837, Franklin enlisted on February 23, 1864 [Source "Pensions (North Carolina)" states he enlisted in January 1864], in Raleigh, North Carolina, for the war. He served as a Landsman aboard the CSS ARCTIC, Cape Fear River, North Carolina, 1863, and aboard the CSS EQUATOR under Commodore Lynch. He was never wounded, but suffered a rupture jumping from one boat to another. A letter dated April 11, 1903, from B. P. Williamson states that Franklin "was detailed to work with me on C.S. Government Ordinance [sic] work at Raleigh, North Carolina, during the war 1861-1865." Franklin was sent in Janaury1864 to the Navy Department at Wilmington, North Carolina, Commodore Lynch in charge, where he remained till the war ended. Franklin lived as a post war farmer. He married in 1888, and resided in 1910 with his wife, Frances and son William at Swift Creek, Wake County, North Carolina. His pension claim filed May 25, 1901, at age 62, Post office: Massey, Wake County, North Carolina, was disapproved. In his application for admittance to the Soldier's Home, April 11, 1903, Franklin stated he went home on furlough in March 1865 and was there when the war ended. No indication of admittance indicated. Described as having a dark complexion, standing five feet ten inches tall, and a farmer.
[Source(s): Card File; Pensions (North Carolina); NA RG 45; Foenander]

Franklin, Jesse (Haywood County, North Carolina [?])

Landsman, Confederate States Navy. Born on November 17, 1832, Franklin died on February 16, 1911, and was buried at Green Hill, Haywood County, North Carolina. [Source(s): Stepp, "Burials"]

Frazier, Martin (North Carolina)
>Private, Confederate States Marine Corps. A worker at the Confederate States Navy Yard, Charlotte, North Carolina who was likely one of the circa three hundred workmen armed, equipped, and formed into one of three companies of "Marines" for defense purposes in late 1864 or early 1865. He may have been a member of the one company detailed to accompany Confederate Major General Joseph Wheeler as his unit escorted the wife and family of President Jefferson Davis, some government officials, and the gold of the Confederate Treasury south as they attempted to escape Union capture.
>[Source: SHSP (Vol. 40); "Char. Obs.," April 3, 1910 and June 5, 1910; "Char. News," June 5, 1910]

Freeman, Hiram
>Acting Master, Confederate States Navy.
>Freeman was appointed an Acting Master on July 25, 1861 and is listed on payroll records as serving aboard the NCS EDWARDS from July - October 1861 [NOTE: In August 1861 the EDWARDS, the pre-war "Weldon N. Edwards," was "pronounced generally worthless"]. He transferred to the NCS ELLIS on October 8, 1861. Freeman was appointed Master Not in Line of Promotion on December 9, 1861 and served aboard the CSS APPOMATTOX and at Wilmington Station, 1862. His commission was withdrawn on June 19, 1862.
>[Source: NCCWSP]

Freeman, J. M., Jr.
>3rd Assistant Engineer, North Carolina Navy. Served aboard the NCS WINSLOW.
>[Source: NCS]

Freshwater, B. N. [Alamance County, North Carolina]
>Landsman, Confederate States Navy. Freshwater was born in Alamance County, North Carolina. In pre-war years he worked as a machinist until he enlisted in Alamance County on March 6 [1864?], at age 24, in the Confederate States Navy. His name "appears on a list of conscripts in the yard [at Halifax?] and then transferred to Wilmington, North Carolina, June 9, 1864." Another source states he was "conscripted March 6 [7?], 1864, at Camp Holmes [Raleigh, North Carolina] from Colonel Lee's 48th Regiment, North Carolina Militia from Alamance County. Description: Age 24; eyes dark; hair dark; complexion dark; height 6 feet ½ inch; place of birth Alamance [County, North Carolina]; occupation mechanic.
>[Source(s): Card File; NA RG 45]

Freshwater, Henry (Alamance County, North Carolina)
>Landsman, Confederate States Navy. Born in Alamance County, North Carolina, about 1834 where he resided as a carpenter until he enlisted March 28, 1864, in Raleigh, North Carolina, for the war. Other sources state he was conscripted March 9, 1864, at Camp Holmes, from Colonel Lee's 48th Regiment, North Carolina Militia, Alamance County, North Carolina. Source "Foenander" states he enlisted on March 6, [1864?] in the Confederate States Navy. Description: Age 31; eyes grey; hair dark; complexion dark; height 5 feet 3.5 inches; place of birth Alamance County, North Carolina; occupation carpenter. Another source states he "appears on a list of conscripts in the yard [at Halifax?], and then transferred to Wilmington, North Carolina, June 9, 1864." He married in 1884 and resided in 1910 as a farmer with his wife and daughter at Melville, Alamance County, North Carolina, where he was still shown as a resident in 1920. There was a claim filed for a Confederate widow's pension on November 1, 1924 by his widow, Isabella Freshwater, at age 67, listing her post office as Burlington, Alamance County, North Carolina. It was disallowed. Her application claims he enlisted in "1862." On her second application filed on July 14, 1927, which was approved, she stated he enlisted in December 1863. An affidavit (letter) dated October 30, 1924, from E. C. Thompson (q.v.) says Freshwater was in the "C. S. Army, was at Fort Fisher, and was also assigned to the Navy at Charleston, SC. Born January 30, 1833, Freshwater died on December 9, 1921 and was buried at Hawfields Presbyterian Church, Alamance County, North Carolina.
>[Source(s): Card File; NA RG 45; Pensions (North Carolina); Stepp, "Burials;" Census (North Carolina), 1910 and 1920; Foenander]

Freshwater, Thomas [Alamance County, North Carolina]
>Landsman, Confederate States Navy. Freshwater enlisted on June 10, 1864, in Raleigh, North Carolina, for the war. He died on April 10, 1914 and was buried at Hawfields Presbyterian Church, Alamance County, North Carolina.
>[Source(s): Card File; NA RG 45; Stepp, "Burials"]

Freeman, George G. [or, "J"]
>Landsman, Confederate States Navy. Enlisted August 31, 1864, in Raleigh, North Carolina, for the war.
>[Source(s): Card File; NA RG 45]

Freeman, John C.
>Ordinary Seaman, Confederate States Navy. Enlisted June 15, 1863, in Wilmington, North Carolina, for the war.
>[Source(s): Card File; NA RG 45]

Freeze [?], Frederick
>Seaman, Confederate States Navy. Enlisted February 26, 1863, in Wilmington, North Carolina, for three years or the war.
>[Source(s): Card File; NA RG 45]

Friddle (Fiddle), Fred
>Seaman, Confederate States Navy. Enlisted June 15, 1864, in Raleigh, North Carolina, for the war.
>[Source(s): Card File; NA RG 45; Duke Papers]

Fulford, James N. (L.) (Currituck County, North Carolina)
>Landsman, Confederate States Navy.
>Born in North Carolina, circa 1823, and resided in the Court House District of Currituck County, North Carolina, as farmer. He shipped for six months aboard the CSS RALEIGH on December 21, 1861 as a Landsman. His name appears on rosters of the North Carolina Squadron from December 1, 1861 through April 15, 1862. He was transferred to the James River Squadron on April 15, 1862 and served at Drewry's Bluff as a Landsman.
>[Sources: Census (NC), 1860; NCCWSP]

Fulp, George
>Private, Confederate States Army//Confederate States Navy. Transferred from the Confederate States Navy on December 26, 1863 as a Private to Company K, 3rd Regiment North Carolina Cavalry, December 26, 1863. Present or accounted for through October 1864.
>[Source(s): North Carolina Troops, II]

Fulp, George W.
>Landsman ["Private"], Confederate States Navy. Enlisted October 14, 1863, in Wilmington [or, at Camp Holmes, Raleigh, North Carolina], North Carolina, for the war. Prior service Company K, 41st Regiment, North Carolina Troops (3rd North Carolina Cavalry). No further record.
>[Source(s): Card File; NA RG 445; North Carolina Troops, II]

Furgerson, Jessie
>Confederate States Navy. Enlisted August 29, 1864, at Raleigh, North Carolina, for the war.
>[Source(s): Card File; NA RG 45]

Furlow, Aaron (County unknown)
>Confederate States Marine Corps. Wounded (left leg amputated) and captured at Fort Fisher on January 15, 1865.
>[Source(s): "Daily Confed." (2/18/65); Card File]

Furpless, W. F. (Brunswick County, North Carolina)
>Confederate States Navy. Born in North Carolina in 1826, Furpless resided as a pilot, in 1850, with his first wife, Marinda, and two children, at Smithville, Brunswick County, North Carolina. He is shown, in 1860, as a slave owner. Furpless served in the Confederate States Navy. A pension claim was filed by his widow, Mrs. Ella Furpless, age 62, post office Southport, Brunswick County (North Carolina), July 1, 1907. Approved.
>[Source(s): Card File; Pensions (North Carolina); Foenander; Census (North Carolina), 1850]

Gadsby, John E. (New Hanover County, North Carolina)
>Corporal, Confederate States Army//Landsman, Confederate States Navy. Born in Maine in 1839, he enlisted on May 16, 1862 for three years, in 1st Company A, 36th Regiment, North Carolina Troops (2nd Regiment, North Carolina Artillery). Present or accounted for until transferred as a Corporal to 2nd Company I, 10th Regiment, North Carolina State Troops (1st North Carolina Artillery) in November 1863. He was transferred to the Confederate States Navy on February 26, 1864 at Wilmington, North Carolina. Gadsby served as a Seaman on the CSS ARCTIC, 1864. He resided in Duplin County, North Carolina, in 1870. He resided as a farmer, in 1880, with his wife, Annie E., and four children, at Richlands, Onslow County, North Carolina.
>[Source(s): Card File; NA RG 45; North Carolina Troops, I; Foenander; Census (NC), 1880]

Gaffey, R. E. (Rutherford County, North Carolina)
    Confederate States Navy. Enlisted in Wilmington, North Carolina, on October 17, 1863.
    [Source(s): MR, 4, p. 445; BRGS]

Gaither, J. B.
    Confederate States Navy. Enlisted in the Confederate States Navy on June 13 [11], 1864, in Raleigh, North Carolina, for the war.
    [Source(s): Card File; NA RG 45]

Gaither, Burgess
    Confederate States Navy. Listed as on duty with the Navy in Charleston, South Carolina. May have been enlisted for naval service from Mallett's Battalion [See source Hilderman].
    [Source(s): Hilderman]

Gallagher, George T.
    Confederate States Navy. Gallagher served aboard the NCS BEAUFORT as of December 1861 per clothing records. He received a partial payment on February 13, 1862 at the Gosport Navy Yard following his assistance in manning Fort Cobb at the Battle of Elizabeth City on February 10, 1862. His name appears on the payroll ending March 31, 1862 of the receiving ship CSS UNITED STATES. Gallagher appears on the North Carolina Squadron payroll for the 1st quarter of 1862 covering from January 10, 1862 - March 23, 1862. He is listed as having "run" on the March 23, 1862 payroll.
    [Source: NCCWSP]

Gallop, John C. (Currituck County, North Carolina)
    Private, Confederate States Army//Confederate States Navy. Born in Currituck County, North Carolina, Gallop resided there as a farmer prior to enlisting there at age 21 on August 19, 1861 for the war in Company B, 8th Regiment, North Carolina State Troops. Mustered in as a corporal, he was reduced to the ranks prior to March-April 1863 and deserted in June 1863. Source Card File states he later joined the Confederate States Navy.
    [Source(s): Card File; North Carolina Troops, IV]

Gallop, Samuel
    Private, Confederate States Navy. Born in North Carolina circa 1820, Gallop was a ship's carpenter by trade. He enlisted in Company A, 3rd Virginia Infantry, Portsmouth, Virginia, April 20, 1861, at age 41. He was detailed to the Confederate States Navy on April 22, 1862 but discharged as over-aged on July 15, 1862.
    [Source(s): Driver]

Galloway, John
    Ordinary Seaman, Confederate States Navy.
    Per a bounty list for the CSS BEAUFORT dated January 16, 1862, Galloway served aboard that vessel at least as early as that date though March 1862. He appears on the payroll of the North Carolina Squadron for the 1st quarter of 1862 from March 11, 1862 - April 15, 1862 on which date he transferred to the James River Squadron.
    [Source: NCCWSP]

Game, James T. (Cumberland County, North Carolina)
    Confederate States Navy. Game was born in Wayne County, North Carolina, in January 1838 where he resided as a carpenter until he enlisted in the Confederate States Navy on March 16, 1864, at Camp Holmes, Raleigh, North Carolina, from Colonel Pemberton's 53rd Regiment, North Carolina Militia, Cumberland County, North Carolina. He served as a Landsman aboard the CSS ALBEMARLE, and on the Halifax Station, 1864. He was involved in the battle of Plymouth, North Carolina and in the battle with the Union fleet in Albemarle Sound. Game was discharged from naval service on October 3, 1864. He married on August 30, 1880, and was still residing as a carpenter in Florence, South Carolina, in 1900. His wife, Susan Game, applied for a Confederate widow's pension from Marion, South Carolina, in 1919. The pension papers indicate he was wounded three times during the war. Game died on October 29, 1909.
    [Source(s): Card File; NA RG 45; Foenander; Census (SC), 1900]

Game, Joseph T. (Cumberland County, North Carolina)
    Landsman, Confederate States Navy. Enlisted March 18, 1864, in Raleigh, North Carolina, for the war.
    [Source(s): Card File; NA RG 45]

Ganus, Stephen D. (Brunswick County, North Carolina)
Private, Confederate States Army//Confederate States Navy. Born and resided in Brunswick County, North Carolina, as a farmer prior to enlisting in New Hanover County, North Carolina, at age 21 on July 3, 1861, for the war, in Company C, 8th Regiment, North Carolina State Troops. Ganus was captured on Roanoke Island on February 8, 1862, paroled at Elizabeth City, North Carolina, on February 21, 1862, and exchanged in August 1862. He was present or accounted for until captured again at Cold Harbor, Virginia, May 31-June 1, 1864. Confined at Point Lookout, Maryland he was transferred to the federal prison at Elmira, New York, on July 12, 1864. Ganus was released from Elmira on May 19, 1865 after taking the Oath of Allegiance.
[Source(s): Card File; North Carolina Troops, IV]

Gardner, Baldwin P. (Wilson County, North Carolina)
Private, Confederate States Army//Confederate States Navy. Resided in Wilson County, North Carolina, and enlisted in Wayne County, North Carolina, at age 19 on May 30, 1861 (Source MR, I, gives the date as May 30, 1861), for the war, in Company D, 2nd Regiment, North Carolina State Troops. Present or accounted for until he transferred to the Confederate States Navy on February 1, 1862.
[Source(s): Card File; North Carolina Troops, III; MR, I]

Gardner, James
Landsman, Confederate States Navy. Enlisted September 28, 1863, at Camp Holmes, for the war.
[Source(s): Card File; NA RG 45]

Gardner, Joseph M.
Acting Midshipman, Confederate States Navy.
Gardner was born in Virginia and appointed from that state as an Acting Midshipman on July 8, 1861. He served in that capacity aboard the NCS SEA BIRD participating in the Battle of Roanoke Island on February 7-8, 1862 and the Battle of Elizabeth City on February 10, 1862. Ordered to report to Lieutenant Alexander on the CSS RALEIGH for duty by Flag Officer French Forrest on March 4, 1862, he served aboard that ship during 1862. He was aboard the CSS GAINES with the Mobile Squadron, 1862 – 1863. During 1863 he reported for service at Drewry's Bluff. Gardner was promoted for gallant and meritorious conduct in the capture of USS SATELITE and USS RELIANCE on the Rappahannock River on August 23, 1863. Gardner participated in the Johnson's Island Expedition of 1863 and was appointed a 2nd Lieutenant on January 7, 1864 to rank from September 22, 1863. He was appointed to the rank of 1st Lieutenant, Provisional Navy, on June 2, 1864 to rank from January 6, 1864 and served aboard the CSS TALLAHASSEE in 1864. He served for a while on the Served on CSS FREDERICKSBURG, later commanding the CSS BEAUFORT in the James River Squadron, 1863-64. Gardner was captured at the Battle of Sailor's Creek, Virginia, on April 6, 1865 and was held at Johnson's Island, Federal Prisoner of War Camp, until released on June 20, 1865.
[Source: NCCWSP]

Gardner [Gardiner], M. H.
Landsman, Confederate States Navy. Enlisted on October 21 [26], 1863, at Camp Holmes [or, at Wilmington, for the war], Raleigh, North Carolina, and served as a Landsman aboard the CSS ARCTIC, Cape Fear River, North Carolina, 1863. He later served aboard the CSS RALEIGH, in North Carolina and Virginia waters, 1864.
[Source(s): Card File; NA RG 45; Foenander]

Gardner, M. M. (Guilford County, North Carolina)
Confederate States Navy. Enlisted in Wilmington, North Carolina, October 6, 1863.
[Source(s): MR, IV, 445]

Garibaldi, John (North Carolina)
Private, Confederate States Marine Corps. A worker at the Confederate States Navy Yard, Charlotte, North Carolina who was likely one of the circa three hundred workmen armed, equipped, and formed into one of three companies of "Marines" for defense purposes in late 1864 or early 1865. He may have been a member of the one company detailed to accompany Confederate Major General Joseph Wheeler as his unit escorted the wife and family of President Jefferson Davis, some government officials, and the gold of the Confederate Treasury south as they attempted to escape Union capture.
[Source: SHSP (Vol. 40); "Char. Obs.," April 3, 1910 and June 5, 1910; "Char. News," June 5, 1910]

Garner, E. (Moore County, North Carolina)
Private, Confederate States Marine Corps. A resident of Moore County, North Carolina, Garner served in the Confederate States Marine Corps. He was sent to Camp Holmes, where he was instructed for a short time, then

sent on to Charleston to the CSS INDIAN CHIEF, arriving there on Sunday, November 6, 1864, for further drill and instruction as a marine. He later served aboard the CSS CHICORA, Charleston Station. A letter of James C. Davis November 17, 1864, states the group from Camp Holmes, of which Garner was a part, arrived aboard the CSS INDIAN CHIEF, Charleston, SC, Sunday, November 6, 1864, and was designated to serve aboard the ironclad CSS CHICORA.
[Source(s): Davis, November 17, 1864; Foenander]

Garrard, W. B.
Landsman, Confederate States Navy. Enlisted June 11, 1864, in Raleigh, for the war.
[Source(s): card File; NA RG 45]
[Source(s): St. Amand]

Garris, H.B.R. [H.B.S.; H.B.R.)] (New Hanover County, North Carolina)
Confederate States Navy. Enlisted in the Confederate States Navy in Wilmington, North Carolina, August 23, 1863. Franklin County, North Carolina. Enlisted in the Confederate States Navy in Wilmington, North Carolina, October 24, 1863. An "H.B.L." Garris enlisted September 5, 1863, in Wilmington, for the war, per source NA RG 45.
[Source(s): MR, 4, p. 445, Hill; NA RG 45; St. Amand; NEUSE Roster; CMACCSN]

Garris, James (New Hanover County, North Carolina)
Ordinary Seaman, Confederate States Navy. Enlisted September 27, 1863, at Wilmington for the war.
[Source(s): Card File; MR, 4, p. 445; NA RG 45; St. Amand]

Garrison, D. B. (Mecklenburg County, North Carolina)
Landsman, Confederate States Navy. Born in North Carolina in 1832, Garrison enlisted on June 11, 1864, in Raleigh, for the war. Pension claim filed June 29, 1901, age 68, post office Uncas, Mecklenburg County, North Carolina was approved. Pension application states he enlisted in August 1862; served at Battery Meares, Wilmington, North Carolina [NOTE: at or near Fort Fisher?]' and, was wounded on or about February 21, 1865, having his left leg cut off below the knee by a shell. Garrison resided as a farmer, in 1880, with his six children (eldest child born 1862), at Mallard Creek, Mecklenburg, North Carolina. Widowed, he applied for a Confederate pension from Mecklenburg County, North Carolina on June 1, 1885, at age 50, listing his post office as Charlotte, Mecklenburg County, North Carolina. Artificial leg furnished by Jewett's Patent Leg Company, August 30, 1866 (lost left foot).
[Source(s): Card File; NA RG 45; Pensions (North Carolina); Foenander]

Garrison, James
First [Class] Cabin Boy, Confederate States Navy. Enlisted March 12, 1864, in Wilmington, for the war.
[Source(s): Card File; NA RG 445]

Garrison, Thomas C.
Confederate States Navy. Garrison served as a Seaman aboard the CSS CASWELL, a wooden side-wheeled steamer operating as a tender on the Wilmington Station, North Carolina. He served sometime between July 1861 and June 1862 ("Thomas B. Garrison [Garrason]," q.v., may be the same person).
[Source(s): ORN 2, 1, 282; Foenander]

Gaskill, Silas (Carteret County, North Carolina)
Ordinary Seaman, Confederate States Navy. Born circa 1842, Gaskill resided in Beaufort, Carteret County, North Carolina as a fisherman. Though his enlistment date unknown, Gaskill served as a Seaman aboard the CSS EDWARDS per shipping articles dated July 25, 1861. Payroll records indicate he served as an Ordinary Seaman aboard the CSS FORREST at least as early as the first quarter of 1862. His name is found on a payroll of the receiving ship CSS UNITED STATES ending March 31, 1862. His name appears on the final payroll of the CSS VIRGINIA, April 1, 1862 – September 30, 1862. Gaskill served at Drewry's Bluff as an Ordinary Seaman from April 1, 1863 - June 30, 1863.
[Sources: Census (NC), 1860; NCCWSP]

Gaskill, W. (Carteret County, North Carolina)
Ship's Cook, Confederate States Navy. Born circa 1819, Gaskill resided in Portsmouth, Carteret County, North Carolina as a fisherman in 1860. He served as a Ship's Cook aboard the CSS FANNY at least during December 12 – 13, 1861. He is listed on a payroll as a part of the North Carolina Squadron, December 1, 1861 – February 28, 1862.
[Sources: Census (NC), 1860; NCCWSP]

Gaskins, C. G.
Confederate States Navy ("Naval Department"). "Killed on the Tarboro' Branch Railroad, on Wednesday the 18th inst., two men, named John Balt and C. G. Gaskins. They belonged to the Naval Department at Wilmington. Their bodies were brought to Rocky Mount and interred as decently as circumstances would admit."
[Source(s): Card File; "Daily Confederate" (4/23/64)]

Gaskins (Gaskill), Silas (Carteret County, North Carolina)
Seaman, Ordinary Seaman Confederate States Navy.
Born circa 1842, Gaskins resided in Beaufort, Carteret County, North Carolina where he worked as a fisherman. Per his shipping articles, joined the NCS EDWARDS on July 25, 1861 as a Seaman and served with the North Carolina Squadron. He appears as an Ordinary Seaman aboard the CSS FORREST on that ship's payroll for the 1st quarter of 1862, and on the payroll of the receiving ship CSS UNITED STATES ending March 31, 1862. He served aboard the CSS VIRGINIA and appeared as an Ordinary Seaman on that ship's final payroll covering the period April 1, 1862 - 30 September 30, 1862. Payroll records indicate he served at Drewry's Bluff as an Ordinary Seaman from April 1, 1863 - June 30, 1863. Gaskins' application for pension contains his original "Oath and Parole" dated April 17, 1865 from Libby Prison listing him as Confederate States Navy. The pension claim filed by his widow, Mary Gaskins, age 70, post office listed as Wit, Carteret County, North Carolina, on July 9, 1910, states he enlisted in the Confederate States Navy on July 1, 1862 "on Board the *Merrimac* (?)." Her application was approved. His name sometimes appears as "Silas Gaskill" (a Silas Gaskill served as an Ordinary Seaman aboard the CSS VIRGINIA, Hampton Roads, Virginia, 1862, and later as a Landsman aboard the CSS FREDERICKSBURG, James River Squadron, 1865).
[Source(s): Card File; Pensions (North Carolina); Foenander; NCCWSP]

Gaskill, W.
Ship's Cook, Confederate States Navy.
Born circa 1819, Gaskill resided in Portsmouth, Carteret County, North Carolina and was by occupation a fisherman per the 1860 North Carolina census. Per muster and payroll records, he served aboard the CSS FANNY from at least as early as December 12, 1861. His name appears on the North Carolina Squadron payroll for the 1st quarter of 1862 covering from December 1, 1861 - February 28, 1862. He is listed as having "run" on the February 28, 1862.
[Source: NCCWSP; NC Census (1860)]

Gates, Thomas
Pilot, [May have served in the Confederate States Navy]
Gates served as a Pilot aboard the CSS CORA in 1862
[Source: NCCWSP]

Gause, Ephraim DeVaun (Brunswick County, North Carolina)
Pilot ["Blockade Runner"], Confederate States Navy. Born in 1825 in Brunswick County, North Carolina, Gause died on March 30, 1887 and was buried in Old Southport Cemetery, Brunswick County, North Carolina.
[Source(s): Card File; UDC, Southport; Gravestone Records, v. 11, p. 305 and v. 6, p. 306; Stepp, "Burials"]

Gee, David
Landsman, Confederate States Navy. Enlisted December 18 [10], 1863, in Wilmington [Raleigh] for the war. Served as a Landsman aboard the CSS ARCTIC, Cape Fear River, North Carolina, and aboard the CSS NORTH CAROLINA, Cape Fear River, North Carolina, 1864.
[Source(s): Card File; NA RG 45; Foenander; *ORN* 2, 1, 277, 294 & 295]

Geer, Edwin, Jr. (North Carolina)
CSA//Captain's Clerk [Warrant Officer], CSN. Born in Washington, Beaufort County, North Carolina circa 1844, the son of an Episcopal minister named Edwin Geer, Sr. Geer served as a Captain's Clerk under Lieutenant Hoole aboard the CSS FORREST. After the February 7, 1862 battle of Roanoke Island, the ship was burned on February 10th to prevent its capture. Geer was discharged on the next day (11th). He enlisted on July 10, 1862 as a Private in Company K, 10th Regiment, North Carolina Troops (1st North Carolina Artillery). On September 29, 1862 he transferred to Company B, 61st Regiment, North Carolina Troops and was soon promoted to Sergeant. He died at Smithville [now Southport], North Carolina, prior to October 27, 1862 of bilious fever while acting as an aide to Brigadier General Gabriel J. Rains. Following the death of Edwin Geer, Jr., his parents had another son whom they also named Edwin Geer, Jr.
[Source: Foenander; Long Email; Census (NC), 1860; NCCWSP]

George, M. A.
Paymaster's Clerk, Confederate States Navy.
George's name appears as a Paymaster's Clerk on a payroll list for the January - May 1862 period. He served in the North Carolina Squadron.
[Source: NCCWSP]

Gibbons, Robert (Beaufort County, North Carolina)
Private, Confederate States Army//Confederate States Navy. Previously residing in England, Gibbons enlisted in Beaufort County, North Carolina, on June 3, 1861, aged 23, for the war, as a Private in Company E, 4th Regiment, North Carolina State Troops. He was wounded in action at Chancellorsville, Virginia on May 3, 1863. He rejoined the Company prior to September 1, 1863 and was transferred to the Confederate States Navy on September 3, 1863 [Source MR, I lists the date as the 7th].
[Source(s): Foenander; North Carolina Troops, IV; MR, I]

Gibson, D. W.
Landsman, Confederate States Navy. Enlisted in the Confederate States Navy on June 11, 1864 in Raleigh, North Carolina, for the war.
[Source(s): Card File; NA RG 45]

Gibson, Nathaniel N. P.
Landsman, Confederate States Navy. Enlisted on April 15, 1864 in Raleigh, North Carolina, for the war.
[Source(s): Card File; NA RG 45]

Gibson, Robert
"Private," Confederate States Navy. See also Company E, 4th Regiment, North Carolina State Troops.
[Source(s): Card File; NA RG 45]

Gibson, Thomas P. (New Hanover County(?), North Carolina)
Private, Confederate States Marine Corps. While serving with Company H, Confederate States Marine Corps, Gibson was wounded in the left thigh and captured at Fort Fisher on January 15, 1865. He died on January 17 ["19" (see Stepp)], 1865, and was buried in the Confederate Mass Grave, Oakdale Cemetery, Wilmington, New Hanover County, North Carolina.
[Source(s): "Daily Confed." (2/18/65); Stepp, "Burials"]

Gibson, William G.
Landsman, Confederate States Navy. Enlisted August 29, 1864 at Raleigh, North Carolina, for the war.
[Source(s): Card File; NA RG 45]

Gilbert, Philip
Landsman, Confederate States Navy.
Per payroll and muster records, Gilbert served as a Landsman aboard the NCS EDWARDS from July - October 30, 1861. He was transferred to the receiving ship CSS UNITED STATES on August 31, 1861 on detached duty.
[NOTE: In August 1861, the NCS EDWARDS was "pronounced generally worthless."]
[Source: NCCWSP; Moebs]

Gill, Ezra (Izra?) Thomas (Franklin County, North Carolina)
Corporal, Confederate States Army//Landsman [Seaman], Confederate States Navy. Gill was born in Franklin County, North Carolina, in August 1841 and enlisted there at age 21 on May 16, 1861, in Company E, 15th Regiment, North Carolina Troops. Mustered as a Private, he was present or accounted for until captured at or near Crampton's Pass, Maryland, on September 14, 1862. Confined at Fort Delaware, Delaware, until transferred to Aiken's Landing, James River, Virginia, on October 2, 1862, for exchange. Gill was declared exchanged at Aiken's Landing on November 10, 1862 and returned to duty before January 1, 1863. Promoted to Corporal on that date, Gill was present or accounted for until he transferred to the Confederate States Navy on or about February 15, 1864 and served on board the CSS YADKIN, Wilmington Station, North Carolina, 1864. His name appears on a Roll of Prisoners of War at Point Lookout, Maryland, which states he was captured at Sailor's Creek, April 6, 1865, and confined at Point Lookout from April 14, 1865 until released June 27, 1865 upon signing the Oath of Allegiance. On the Oath his place of residence was listed as Franklin County, North Carolina. Description: complexion fair;

hair brown; eyes hazel; height 5 feet 8 inches. Gill died in June 1914 and was buried in the Confederate Section of Oakwood Cemetery, Raleigh, North Carolina. [Source(s): Kearney; Oakwood; NA RG 109; Card File; Stepp, "Burials;" North Carolina Troops, V; Foenander]

Gill, Joseph T.
Landsman and Ship's Steward, Confederate States Navy. Enlisted March 1, 1864 in Raleigh, North Carolina, for the war. Gill served as a Ship's Steward aboard the CSS ARCTIC, Cape Fear River, North Carolina, 1863.
[Source(s): Card File; NA RG 45; Foenander]

Gillen, James (also Gillan)
Ordinary Seaman, Seaman, Confederate States Navy.
Born in Ireland about 1835, Gillen shipped as an Ordinary Seaman aboard the NCS EDWARDS on July 25, 1861, remaining with her through October 30, 1861 during her service with the North Carolina Squadron. According to the payroll of the 1st quarter of 1862, he served aboard the CSS FORREST as a Seaman. His name appears on the payroll of the receiving ship CSS UNITED STATES for the period ending March 31, 1862. Served on the CSS VIRGINIA and is found on that ship's final payroll as Seaman during the period of April 1, 1862 - August 15, 1862 on which date he was listed as discharged.
[Source(s): MR, NCCWSP]

Gilmer, James
Landsman, Confederate States Navy. Enlisted February 4, 1864 at Raleigh, North Carolina, for the war.
[Source(s): Card File]

Gilmore, J. H. (Anson County, North Carolina)
Private, Confederate States Navy. Listed as having served in the "Naval Battalion, Gilmore's name appears on an Oath of Allegiance signed at Point Lookout, Maryland, June 27, 1865. The Oath lists his place of residence Anson County, North Carolina, and description as follows: complexion fair; hair light brown; eyes blue; height 5 feet 8 ½ inches.
[Source(s): Card File; NA RG 109]

Ginn, Thomas P. M. (Craven County, North Carolina)
Landsman, Confederate States Navy. Ginn was born in 1836, died in 1894, and was buried at Cedar Grove, Craven County, North Carolina.
[Source(s): Stepp, "Burials"]

Gleason [Gleeson], James (New Hanover County, North Carolina)
Ordinary Seaman, Confederate States Navy. Gleason enlisted on September 28, 1863 in Wilmington, North Carolina, for the war. He served as an Ordinary Seaman aboard the CSS ARCTIC, 1863, and as a Coal Heaver aboard the CSS NORTH CAROLINA, 1864.
[Source(s): MR, 4, p. 445; Card File; NA RG 45; St. Amand; Foenander]

Gleason, William
Confederate States Navy. Gleason served as a Boatswain's Mate aboard the CSS CASWELL, 1862, and later as Acting Boatswain's Mate aboard the CSS NORTH CAROLINA, 1863-1864. A "William Gleason" also served as a Seaman aboard the CSS ARCTIC, 1863.
[Source(s): St. Amand; Foenander]

Glidwell, N. M.
Landsman, Confederate States Navy. Enlisted April 13, 1864 in Raleigh for the war.
[Source(s): Card File; NA RG 45]

Glover, John T. (Northampton County, North Carolina)
Private, Confederate States Army//Confederate States Navy. Glover resided in Northampton County, North Carolina, where he enlisted at age 30 on May 23, 1861, in Company A, 15th Regiment, North Carolina Troops. He was present or accounted for until transferred to the Confederate States Navy on or about April 1, 1864.
[Source(s): Card File; North Carolina Troops, V; Foenander]

Gooch, Henry S. (Granville County, North Carolina)
    Landsman, Confederate States Navy. Gooch enlisted on March 31, 1864 in Raleigh, North Carolina, for the war. Another source states Gooch was conscripted March 30, 1864 at Camp Holmes, near Raleigh, North Carolina, from Colonel Dolby's 43rd Regiment, North Carolina Militia, Granville County, North Carolina. Description: Age 30; eyes hazel; hair dark; complexion fair; height 5 feet 7 inches; place of birth Granville County, North Carolina; occupation farmer.
    [Source(s): Card File; NA RG 45]

Gooch, Samuel I. [J.] (Granville County, North Carolina) [NOTE: Probably same as "Samuel T. Gooch," q.v.]
    Seaman [Landsman], Confederate States Navy. Born March 7, 1841, Gooch enlisted in Company E, Mallett's Battalion, North Carolina Troops, in 1861. He enlisted in the Confederate States Navy on June 11, 1864 in Raleigh, North Carolina for the war when Mallett's Battalion was disbanded. He served aboard the Confederate States receiving ship CSS INDIAN CHIEF in Charleston, SC, and later transferred to the Confederate States gunboat CSS STONEHO in 1863 [?]. He is also said to have served at Wilmington, North Carolina, and Drewry's Bluff, Virginia. Gooch applied for a pension on September 25, 1908 at age 67 in which he stated he had been bruised by a shell on the leg while serving at Wilmington and that it still bothered him (rheumatism). He further stated he had been captured on April 8, 1865. While living in Raleigh, he applied for and was admitted to the Old Soldier's Home, Raleigh, North Carolina, on November 26, 1912 to which he was admitted at age 72. He died there on February 10, 1922, cause of death not reported. He was a widower whose father was listed as D. S. Gooch (born Granville County, North Carolina), and his mother Polly Bennett (Granville County, North Carolina).
    [Source(s): McElroy; Card File; NA RG 45; Soldier's Home; Pensions (North Carolina); Wake Co. OLS, I]

Gooch, Samuel T. (middle initial also incorrectly shown as "H"]
    [NOTE: Probably same as "Samuel I. Gooch," q.v.] (Granville County, North Carolina).
    Private, Confederate States Army//Confederate States Navy. Gooch was born in Granville County, North Carolina, where he resided as a farmer prior to enlisting in Wake County, North Carolina, at age 28 on July 8, 1862, for the war, in Company E, 23rd Regiment, North Carolina Troops. He was discharged November 1, 1862 after providing Private James A Suit as a substitute. He may have served later in the 43rd Regiment North Carolina Militia, and as landsman in the Confederate States Navy; applied for a post war Confederate pension from Granville County and Wake County, North Carolina; also applied to the Home for the Disabled.
    [Source(s): North Carolina Troops VII, 189 & 683 and VII Addendum; Howard; Foenander]

Gooch, W. N.
    Confederate States Navy. Enlisted June 11, 1864 in Raleigh, North Carolina, for the war.
    [Source(s): Card File; NA RG 45]

Gooding, Matthew R. (Carteret County, North Carolina [?])
    Captain, Confederate States Navy (?)//Blockade Runner. Born in July 1830, Gooding died in January 1863 and was buried in the Old Beaufort Burying Ground, Carteret County, North Carolina. Gooding ran the long, low converted side-wheel steamer blockade runner "*Nashville*" out of Beaufort, NC. It was described as painted "the color of a Hatteras fog."
    [Source(s): Stepp, "Burials"]

Goodnight, Caleb M. B. (Cabarrus County, North Carolina)
    Landsman, Confederate States Navy. A farmer in Cabarrus County, North Carolina prior to enlisting at Camp Hill near Statesville, North Carolina on August 19, 1862 for the war in Company B, Colonel Peter Mallett's Battalion, North Carolina Troops. He was captured at Kinston on or about December 14, 1862 and paroled there on December 11, 1862. He was reported absent sick on the September-October 1863 muster roll. His name appears on clothing receipt rolls dated May 28 and June 3, 1864. Goodnight enlisted in the Confederate States Navy on June 11, 1864 in Raleigh, North Carolina, for the war. His picture as a soldier appears on page 88, Volume XIX, NORTH CAROLINA TROOPS.
    [Source(s): Card File; NA RG 45; Vol. XIX, North Carolina Troops]

Goodson, John Franklin (Lincoln County, North Carolina)
    Confederate States Navy. Source "Hoke Camp" states Goodson was commissioned a Second Lieutenant (Confederate States Army) on June 22, 1861. [NOTE sources North Carolina Troops, VII and XII list a "John F. Goodson" who was elected a Second Lieutenant, Company K, 23rd Regiment, North Carolina Troops, in June 1861, and served until defeated for re-election in April 1862. He may be the say man that served under that name

in Company G, 52nd Regiment, North Carolina Troops. The latter was wounded at Gettysburg and imprisoned, later taking the Oath of Allegiance to the United States in early 1864 and joining the 1st United States Volunteers]. One source shows he "transferred to Confederate States Navy."
[Source(s): Lincoln Roster; Hoke Camp; North Carolina Troops, VII and XII]

Goodson, John W.
Landsman, Confederate States Navy. Enlisted September 28, 1863 at Camp Holmes for the war.
[Source(s): Card File; NA RG 45]

Goodwin, John
Landsman, Confederate States Navy. Enlisted June 6, 1864 in Raleigh, North Carolina, for the war.
[Source(s): Card File; NA RG 45]

Goodwyn, G. A.
Seaman, Confederate States Navy.
Per payroll records, Goodwyn served aboard the NCS BEAUFORT with the North Carolina Squadron from September - November 1861.
[Source: NCCWSP]

Goote, George A.
Assistant Surgeon, Confederate States Navy. Born in and appointed from North Carolina, Goote was appointed Assistant Surgeon for the war on March 1, 1862 (One source gives the date as January 7, 1864) and Assistant Surgeon, Provisional Navy, on June 2, 1864. Goote served aboard the CSS RALEIGH, 1863-1864, and CSS ALBEMARLE 1864.
[Source(s): Card File]

Gorham, Michael
Ordinary Seaman, Confederate States Navy. Enlisted October 31, 1863 in Wilmington, North Carolina, for the war.
[Source(s): Card File; NA RG 45; MR, IV, 445]

Graham, J. M. (Wake County, North Carolina)
Ordinary Seaman, Confederate States Navy. Enlisted in Wilmington, North Carolina, for the war.
[Source(s): MR, 4, p. 445; Card File; NA RG 45]

Graham, James C.
Landsman, Confederate States Navy. Enlisted June 6, 1864 in Raleigh, North Carolina, for the war.
[Source(s): Card File; NA RG 45]

Grary, W. W. (North Carolina?)
Assistant Surgeon, Confederate States Navy. Source "Fold3, USN Resignees" lists a "W. W. Grary" as having joined the Confederate States Navy on April 9, 1862 from civilian life. A search of the 1860 Census of the United States using a variety of name spellings failed to reveal a man by this name.
[Source(s): Census (United States); Fold3, USN Resignees]

Graves, Charles Iverson (Caswell County [?], North Carolina)
Lieutenant, Confederate States Navy. Enlisting from North Carolina, Graves was in command of the Naval Cadets guarding the Confederate States Treasury on the retreat into Georgia. He was married to Maggie R. Lea on December 10, 1862 at the home of the Hon. Calvin Graves, Caswell County, North Carolina.
[Source(s): McElroy; Card File; "NCStndrd," December 19, 1862]

Graves, George W.
Seaman, Landsman, Confederate States Navy//Private, Confederate States Army. Graves served as a Seaman aboard the CSS FANNY, October 8, 1861 – December 20, 1862, and aboard the CSS RALEIGH as a Seaman, January 6, 1862 – April 1862. He was listed as having served in the North Carolina Squadron from December 1, 1861 – April 21, 1862. He is listed as having transferred to the James River Squadron on April 15, 1862 and is known to have served at Drewry's Bluff as a Seaman from at least April 1, 1862 – June 30, 1862. Graves served as a Paymaster's Steward aboard the CSS RALEIGH from at least November 16, 1863 – December 15, 1863. He transferred from the Confederate States Navy, CSS ROANOKE, to Company B, 8th Regiment, North Carolina Volunteers by Special

Order #12/12, Adjutant & Inspector General's Office, dated January 15, 1864, in exchange for Private Lemuel B. Gray. Graves was killed in action at Plymouth, North Carolina on April 20, 1864.
[Source(s): Card File; NA RG 109; North Carolina Troops, IV; Foenander; NCCWSP]

Graves, John F. (Bladen County, North Carolina)
Private, Confederate States Army//Confederate States Navy. Graves was born in Bladen County, North Carolina, where he resided as a farmer prior to enlisting on May 3, 1861 at age 30 in Bladen County, North Carolina, as a Private in Company B, 18th Regiment, North Carolina Troops. He was present or accounted for until transferred to the Confederate States Navy on or about April 3, 1864.
[Source(s): Card File; North Carolina Troops, VI; Foenander]

Graves, William W.
Assistant Surgeon, Confederate States Navy. Born in and appointed from North Carolina as an Assistant Surgeon for the war on April 7, 1862 [another source gives date as May 1, 1863], Graves served at the Naval rendezvous, Mobile, Alabama, 1862 – 1864. He was appointed Assistant Surgeon, Provisional Navy, on June 2, 1864. He served on the Mobile Station, 1862-1865 [1864]. Surrendering on May 4, 1865, he was paroled at Nunna Hubba Bluff, Alabama on May 10, 1865.
[Source(s): McElroy; Register; Card File; Foenander; ONWR]

Graves, John F. (Bladen County, North Carolina)
Private, Confederate States Army//Confederate States Navy. Graves was born in Bladen County, North Carolina, where he lived as a farmer. He enlisted as a Private on May 3, 1861 at 30 years old. He transferred to Confederate States Navy on April 3, 1864 from Company B, 18th Regiment, North Carolina Troops.
[Source(s): North Carolina Troops, 6, p.325; Army to Navy]

Gray, A. G.
Confederate States Navy. Gray enlisted in the Confederate States Navy at the same time as Thomas P. Gray (q.v.). His affidavit on behalf of Thomas P. Gray is in the Thomas P. Gray application for pension, State Archives of North Carolina, Raleigh, North Carolina.
[Source(s): Pensions (North Carolina)]

Gray, B[enjamin?] Franklin (Brunswick County, North Carolina)
Seaman [Landsman], Confederate States Navy. Born in 1845, Gray served on the crew of the CSS CASWELL. Source "Foenander" lists a "B.F. Gray," Seaman, who served aboard the CSS RALEIGH, in North Carolina and Virginia waters, 1862 – 1864. He died in 1926 and was buried in the Chapel Hill Cemetery, Brunswick County, North Carolina.
[Source(s): Card File; Gravestone Records, v. 8, p. 61; Stepp, "Burials;" Foenander]

Gray, Benjamin F.
Seaman, Confederate States Navy.
Gray was a Seaman aboard the CSS RALEIGH, and per bounty, muster, small stores, and clothing records, appears to have served from October of 1861 through at least April of 1862. His name appears on the North Carolina Squadron payroll for the 1st quarter of 1862 covering from January 14, 1862 - April 15, 1862. He and his ship transferred to the James River Squadron on April 15, 1862, where he continued serving as a Seaman aboard the CSS RALEIGH through December 15, 1862. He served at Drewry's Bluff as a Seaman according to that station's payroll for April 1, 1863 - June 30, 1863. Gray again served on the CSS RALEIGH as a Seaman from November 16 - December 15, 1863, still with the James River Squadron.
[Source: NCCWSP]

Gray, Benjamin H. (Negro) (Bertie County, North Carolina)
Powder Boy, Confederate States Navy. Gray enlisted as a powder boy in the Confederate States Navy at age 12 in Wilmington, North Carolina. As a Powder Boy his job was to carry bags of gunpowder from the magazine below decks to the gun deck, which was potentially a dangerous job. He served on and was likely on board the CSS ALBEMARLE when it was destroyed. Following the war, he resided as a pastor and farmer. He appears in the 1880 North Carolina census with his wife, Margaret, and three children (eldest child born 1874), at Whites, Bertie County, North Carolina. His pension claim filed on June 23, 1917, age 65, listing his post office as Windsor, Bertie County, North Carolina was approved. Another claim filed by his widow, Margaret Gray, age 63, post office Windsor, Bertie County, North Carolina, on June 30, 1924, was also approved. Her application states he served as a "powder boy

or 'monkey' on board the Confederate gunboat Ram [ALBEMARLE] [,] regularly enlisted in the Confederate Navy and served until his command was captured by the United States forces, about six months." "Was captured and held for about six months." [NOTE: The term "Powder Monkey" was a commonly used name for the young boys employed on ships to transport powder from the magazines to the guns during combat. Their small size and agility made them ideal for the very hazardous job which required them to run through smokey gundecks and weave between the busy gunners and heavy recoiling guns].
[Source(s): Pensions (North Carolina); Card File; www.navyandmarine.org; NCCWSP]

Gray, Hardy (Hyde or Tyrrell County, North Carolina)
Confederate States Navy. A r in Hyde or Tyrrell County, North Carolina before the war, he was "ordered to the Confederate States Navy by special order of the Adjutant General." (No army record – UDC – Headquarters in Raleigh has a document stating this)
[Source(s): Mrs. Cathy West – 10 June 2003, phone: 919-553-2996, Raleigh]

Gray, I. A. [I. G.]
Landsman, Confederate States Navy. Enlisted June 11, 1864 in Raleigh, North Carolina, for the war.
[Source(s): Card File; NA RG 45]

Gray, James (New Hanover County, North Carolina)
Seaman, Confederate States Navy. Gray's name appears on an Oath of Allegiance sworn to at Fort Monroe, Virginia, November 5, 1863. His place of residence on the Oath was shown as Wilmington, North Carolina, and his description was as follows: complexion light; hair brown; eyes grey; height 5 feet 5 ¾ inches. Oath carries the remark, "Rebel deserter came into our lines at Wilmington, North Carolina." Source "Foenander" lists a "James Grey," who served on the CSS NORTH CAROLINA at New Inlet, North Carolina. He deserted on October 9, 1863 and was taken aboard the USS SHENANDOAH off Beaufort, North Carolina. He was later sent to Hampton Roads, Virginia, for further questioning.
[Source(s): Card File; NA RG 109; Foenander; ORN 1, 9, 235]

Gray, James A. (Iredell County, North Carolina)
Landsman, Confederate States Navy. Gray is said to have served as a member of the Naval Battalion. His name appears on a Roll of Prisoners of War at Point Lookout, Maryland, stating he was captured at Burkeville, Virginia, April 6, 1865, and confined at Point Lookout, Maryland, from April 14, 1865 until released June 27, 1865. He signed an Oath of Allegiance at Point Lookout, Maryland, June 27, 1865, which gives his place of residence as Iredell County, North Carolina. His description was given as follows: complexion dark; hair dark brown; eyes gray; height 5 feet 6 ½ inches.
[Source(s): Card File; NA RG 109]

Gray [Grey], John A. (or, James) (New Hanover County, North Carolina)
Pilot, Confederate States Navy. Born in North Carolina circa 1815, Gray resided in the 1st Ward of New Bern, Craven County, North Carolina as a sea captain in 1860. He was appointed a Pilot on December 30, 1861 and served aboard the Confederate steamer and blockade runner CSS CORNUBIA. Registers of Confederate States Army General Military Hospital Number 4, Wilmington, North Carolina, states he was admitted September 29, 1863, with "dysenteria" and returned to duty October 3, 1863. His post office was given as Wilmington, North Carolina. At some time, he served as a Pilot aboard the CSS BEAUFORT.
[Source(s): Card File; NA RG 109; Library of Virginia; Census (NC), 1860; NCCWSP]

Gray, Spencer (also, Spence) (Currituck County, North Carolina)
Born in North Carolina, circa 1828, he resided in the Poplar Branch District of Currituck County, North Carolina, as of 1860. He enlisted for the war aboard the CSS RALEIGH on 12 November 1861 and served aboard her from October 1861 [Note: Differs from enlistment date] through at least April 1862. He appears on records of the North Carolina Squadron from February 21, 1862 through February 28, 1862, being transferred to the James River Squadron on April 15, 1862. He served at Drewry's Bluff as a Seaman from April 1, 1863 through June 30, 1863.
[Sources: North Carolina Census, 1850 and 1860; NCCWSP]

Gray, Lemuel B [R]. (Currituck County, North Carolina)
Private, Confederate States Army//Confederate States Navy. Born in Currituck County, North Carolina, in 1860 Gray was a resident at a boarding house in Elizabeth City, Pasquotank County, North Carolina. He resided as a sailor in Currituck County until he enlisted at age 28 on August 1, 1861, for the war, in Company B, 8th Regiment, North

Carolina State Troops. He was present or accounted for until transferred to the Confederate States Navy in exchange for Private George W. Graves on or about January 15, 1864.
[Source(s): Card File; North Carolina Troops, IV; Foenander]

Gray, Thomas P. (Caldwell County, North Carolina)
Landsman, Confederate States Navy. Gray enlisted on May 11, 1864 (another source says he enlisted "Spring 1862") in Raleigh, for the war. His pension claim filed July 21, 1924, age 78, post office Granite Falls, Caldwell County, North Carolina, was approved as 4th Class. The application states he "served on a boat and in Fort Sumter" for two years and served "under Lt. Swinson in command of the naval forces around Charleston." An affidavit by A. G. Gray (q.v.) of McDowell County, North Carolina, on behalf of Thomas P. Gray's application states he and Gray enlisted in the Confederate States Navy at the same time.
[Source(s): Card File; Pension (North Carolina); NA RG 45]

Green, David (Richmond County, North Carolina)
Confederate States Navy.
[Source(s): Richmond County Soldiers]

Green, Drury D. (Rutherford County, North Carolina)
Confederate States Navy. Green enlisted on May 27, 1864 in Raleigh, North Carolina, for the war. His pension claim filed on June 28, 1901, age 57, post office Carolina, Rutherford County, North Carolina (disallowed) states he enlisted in "May 1863" and served aboard the CSS INDIAN CHIEF in Charleston, SC, and on the CSS PEE DEE. He filed a second application dated July 3, 1905, age 61, which was approved. A third application dated July 5, 1921, age 77, while a resident of Forrest City, North Carolina, states he enlisted in April 1864 in Charleston, South Carolina, and that he was "struck in the head by [a] fragment of shell." The application was approved at 4th class. His request for an upgrade from one-quarter to one-half disability was later approved.
[Source(s): Card File; Pension (North Carolina); NA RG 45]

Green, E. (New Hanover County, North Carolina)
Confederate States Navy. Appears on a register of Confederate States Army General Military Hospital Number 4, Wilmington, North Carolina, dated May 28, 1862, giving his disease as "febris cont comm." It further states he was returned to duty June 28, 1862. Post office Wilmington, North Carolina.
[Source(s): Card File; NA RG 109]

Green, Isaac N.
Landsman, Confederate States Navy. Enlisted October 29, 1863 at Camp Holmes, near Raleigh, North Carolina.
[Source(s): Card File; NA RG 45]

Green, James F. (New Hanover County, North Carolina) [May be same as James Foy Green(e), q.v.]
Landsman, Confederate States Navy. Green enlisted on November 1, 1863 in Wilmington, North Carolina, for the war. His name appears on a register of Confederate States Army General Military Hospital Number 4, Wilmington, North Carolina, dated May 13, 1864, which gives disease as "rubeola" and post office as Wilmington.
[Source(s): Card File; NA RG 45; NA RG 109; Foenander]

Green(e), James Foy [May be same as James F. Green, q.v.]
Assistant Engineer, Confederate States Navy. Born in and appointed from North Carolina, Green(e) resided in Fayetteville, North Carolina, where he was employed at the Arsenal, prior to his service in the Confederate States Navy. His original entry into the Confederate States Navy as a Second Engineer was on January 29, 1863. Appointed Second Assistant Engineer Provisional Confederate States Navy, June 2, 1864, he served on board the CSS NORTH CAROLINA and CSS RALEIGH, Wilmington Station, 1863-1864, the steamer CSS COQUETTE, 1864, CSS TALLAHASSEE (Olustee), 1864 and was attached as a Lieutenant to Semmes' Naval Brigade, for special service, April 1865. He was paroled at Greensboro, North Carolina, April 28, 1865. Per source Card File, his name appears as Assistant Engineer, CSS TALLAHASSEE in an unidentified newspaper article.
[Source(s): Card File; Register, McElroy; Foenander; *Fay. Obs.* (February 2, 1863); ONWR]

Green, J. N. (Franklin County, North Carolina)
Confederate States Navy. Green enlisted in the Confederate States Navy in Wilmington, North Carolina on October 24, 1863.
[Source(s): MR, 4, p. 445; Smithwick]

Greenhow, James W. B.
Surgeon, Confederate States Navy. Born in Georgia, Greenhow was a former Surgeon in the United States Navy. He resigned his commission upon the secession of the South. And joined the Confederate States Navy on August 2, 1861. Appointed Surgeon, he served as such aboard the NCS SEA BIRD at least until February 1862 with the North Carolina Squadron. He was captured at the Battle of Elizabeth City, taken to Union-controlled Roanoke Island, and paroled on February 12, 1862 at which time he returned to Elizabeth City, North Carolina. He subsequently served on the Wilmington Station and was especially noted for his work during the 1862 Yellow Fever epidemic. He died on May 12, 1866 in Chapel Hill, North Carolina and was buried in the cemetery of the University of North Carolina at Chapel Hill.
[Source(s): Card File; "WWJ" (May 24, 1866); Stepp, "Burials;" NCCWSP]

Greeson, George
Landsman, Confederate States Navy. Enlisted March 1, 1864 in Raleigh, North Carolina, for the war.
[Source(s): Card File; NA RG 45]

Gregory, Fred W.
Confederate States Navy. Signal officer. Gregory served aboard the CSS SUSAN BIERNE.
[Source(s): McElroy; Card File; Clark's Regts.]

Gregory, Iowa (or, Iago) (Pasquotank County, North Carolina)
Ordinary Seaman/Seaman, Confederate States Navy. Born in North Carolina in 1843 and resided with Edward and Nancy Franklin (possibly his adoptive parents), as of 1850 in Pasquotank County, North Carolina. Per a muster roll covering the period July through November 1861, Gregory served as a Landsman aboard the CSS WINSLOW. His name appears on a payroll of the North Carolina Squadron from December 1, 1861 through March 13, 1862 He is listed as having served as an Ordinary Seaman aboard the CSS SEA BIRD as of February 1862. Source "Foenander" states Gregory was captured at Cobb's Point Battery on Roanoke Island, North Carolina on February 10, 1862. He was paroled and returned to Norfolk, Virginia, on February 19, 1862, and sent to Norfolk, Virginia. [Note: Source NCCWSP states he was captured in the Battle of Elizabeth City and carried to Roanoke Island on February 10, 1862; that he was paroled at Roanoke Island on February 12, 1862 and returned to Elizabeth City. He received a partial payment on February 18, 1862 at Gosport following the sinking of the SEA BIRD at Elizabeth City on February 10, 1862]. His name appears on a payroll of the receiving ship CSS UNITED STATES ending March 31, 1862. Payroll records for the 1st quarter of 1862 covering the period from December 1, 1861 - March 13, 1862 indicate he served with the North Carolina Squadron.
[Source(s): Foenander; Census (NC), 1860; NCCWSP]

Gregory, Samuel Stanford (Sampson County, North Carolina)
Acting Midshipman, Passed Midshipman, Lieutenant, Confederate States Navy.
Born 1845 in Turkey Township [Sampson County, North Carolina[?]), Gregory was a student, Class of 1859, United States Naval Academy, Annapolis, Maryland, until he resigned in 1861 as a Midshipman, United States Navy, to join the Confederate States Navy. He was appointed Acting Midshipman, Confederate States Navy, on June 20, 1861 and per source NCCWSP served in that capacity aboard the NCS EDWARDS during the 1st quarter of 1862 [per source NCCWSP as a member of the North Carolina Squadron], and aboard the CSS RALEIGH on an unspecified date. He transferred to the James River Squadron on March 31, 1862 and was made a Passed Midshipman on October 3, 1862 while serving in Virginia waters. Gregory was promoted to Master Not in Line of Promotion, January 7, 1864, and Second Lieutenant Provisional Navy, June 2, 1864. He served on the Confederate States receiving ship CSS UNITED STATES, 1861, CSS RALEIGH, Richmond Station, 1861-1862, and at Drewry's Bluff, Virginia, 1862-1863. He was on "special service abroad," 1863-1864, and served as a Second Lieutenant, Naval Battery, Fort Fisher, Battery Buchanan, North Carolina, 1864. Gregory was paroled on April 9, 1865 at Appomattox Court House, Virginia. Another source states he served aboard blockade runners between Wilmington and France as a Lieutenant. He died in 1868.
[Source(s): Register; McElroy; Card File; Bizzell; Foenander; ONWR; Fold3, Midshipmen]

Gregory, Stephen D. (Pasquotank County, North Carolina)
Private, Confederate States Army//Confederate States Navy. Born in Pasquotank County, North Carolina, Gregory resided there as a farmer prior to enlisting at age 26 [Source "Foenander" gives age as "20"], date and place unknown, as a Private in Company D [Source North Carolina Troops, VI gives company as "E"], 17th Regiment, North Carolina Troops (1st Organization). He transferred to the Confederate States Navy prior to July 28, 1861 and

served on the CSS FANNY from circa October 8, 1861 – December 13, 1861. He received a partial payment on February 13. 1862 at Gosport Navy Yard, Norfolk, Virginia following the burning of the CSS FANNY at Elizabeth City, North Carolina on February 10, 1862. His name appears on a North Carolina Squadron payroll covering the period December 1, 1861 - March 31, 1862 but is listed as having "run" per that final date.
[Source(s): Card File; North Carolina Troops, VI; Foenander; NCCWSP]

Grice, Isaac W. (Sampson County, North Carolina)
Sergeant, Confederate States Army//Confederate States Navy. Grice was born in Sampson County, North Carolina in 1836, where he resided as a farmer and enlisted at age 26 on May 16, 1862 for the war in Company C, 63rd Regiment, North Carolina Troops (5th North Carolina Cavalry). Mustered as a Private and appointed Sergeant on June 4, 1863. Present or accounted for until transferred to the Confederate States Navy on April 21, 1864. He served as a Landsman on the steamer CSS ROANOKE, James River Squadron, and was wounded in action on the James River, January 24, 1865. He resided as a mechanic, in 1880, with his wife, Susan, and two daughters, at Smithfield, Johnston County, North Carolina.
[Source(s): Card File; North Carolina Troops, II; Foenander; Census (NC), 1880]

Griffin, Henry
Seaman, Confederate States Navy. Griffin enlisted on June 13, 1864 in Raleigh, North Carolina, for the war.
[Source(s): Card File; NA RG 45]

Griffin, John (Camden County, North Carolina)
Landsman, Confederate States Navy. Born in Camden County, North Carolina, Griffin enlisted at age 22 on July 7, 1863 as a Private in Company B, 68th Regiment, North Carolina Troops. He transferred to the Confederate States Navy on April 5, 1864 [per source "North Carolina Troops"] [other source lists April 8, 1864] at Halifax or Plymouth, North Carolina for the war.
[Source(s): Card File; NA RG 45; North Carolina Troops, XV]

Griffin, John
Landsman, Confederate States Navy. Enlisted June 11, 1864 in Raleigh, North Carolina, for the war.
[Source(s): Card File; NA RG 45]

Griffis [Grifthis], Henry (New Hanover County, North Carolina)
Confederate States Navy. Griffis served aboard the Confederate steamer "Eugenie" [CSS EUGENIE(?)]. His name appears on a register of Confederate States Army General Military Hospital Number 4, Wilmington, North Carolina, which states that he was admitted November 11 [12], 1863 giving his disease as "feb int quot" and that he was returned to duty November 21, 1863. His post office was listed as Wilmington, North Carolina.
[Source(s): Card File; NA RG 109]

Griffith, John
Ordinary Seaman, Confederate States Navy. Enlisted in the Confederate States Navy on June 8, 1863 in Wilmington, North Carolina, for the war.
[Source(s): Card File; NA RG 45]

Griggs, Samuel (Currituck County, North Carolina)
Private, Confederate States Army//Confederate States Navy. Griggs was born in Currituck County, North Carolina, where he resided as a farmer prior to enlisting there as a Private at age 18 on August 19, 1861, for the war, in Company B, 8th Regiment, North Carolina State Troops. He was captured at Roanoke Island on February 8, 1862, paroled at Elizabeth City, North Carolina, on February 21, 1862, and exchanged at Aiken's Landing, James River, Virginia, on November 10, 1862. He was listed as present or accounted for until he deserted to the enemy at Sullivan's Island, Charleston Harbor, South Carolina, on August 20, 1863. He was reported in confinement at Fort Monroe, Virginia, on September 13, 1863, and at Fort Norfolk, Virginia, on October 2, 1863. Source "North Carolina Troops, IV" states "No further records." Source Card File shows Confederate Navy service.
[Source(s): Card File; North Carolina Troops, IV]

Griggs, William Walbert [Wilbert] (North Carolina)
Assistant Surgeon, Confederate States Navy. Born in North Carolina, 1841, Griggs graduated from Bellevue Hospital, New York City. He enlisted in Company I, 9th Virginia Infantry, Princess Anne County, Virginia, April 20, 1861 at age 20. He transferred to Company A. ("Driver" states: Appointed a Hospital Steward on December 17, 1862, and detailed in Richmond hospitals April 29, 1862-February 1863. Appointed Assistant Surgeon from Virginia

on May 1, 1863). Another source states he was appointed Assistant Surgeon, May 1, 1861, by the Confederate States Congress from North Carolina. He was appointed Assistant Surgeon, Provisional Navy, June 2, 1864. Griggs served on the CSS NORTH CAROLINA (assigned May 19, 1863 ["Driver"]) and CSS ARCTIC (orders on October 1, 1864) on the Wilmington Station, 1863-1864. "Driver" states he was transferred to the CSS BALTIC in January 1864. He served temporarily at Charleston, South Carolina, 1863, and was at Battery Buchanan, Fort Fisher, North Carolina, 1864. Captured on January 15, 1865, at Fort Fisher, he was sent to Fort Columbus as a Prisoner of War. He received a "pass" from the Provost Marshal's Office, Fort Columbus, New York Harbor dated January 24, 1865. Griggs was transferred to City Point, Virginia, February 25, 1865, and exchanged. Griggs was ordered to report to Surgeon James F. Harrison at the Naval Hospital, Richmond, Virginia, on March 6, 1865. He was paroled in Greensboro, North Carolina, April 28, 1865. He practiced medicine in Elizabeth City, North Carolina, postwar, and died there May 16, 1907.
[Source(s): Register; McElroy; Card File; PRCMO (p. 17); Driver]

Grimes, Hezekiah (Wayne County, North Carolina)
Confederate States Navy. Grimes is listed as having served as a "Private," Naval Battery. His name appears as a signature on an Oath of Allegiance to the United States sworn to at Point Lookout, Maryland, June 27, 1865. His place of residence was listed as Wayne County, North Carolina and his description as follows: complexion dark; hair dark brown; eyes hazel; height 5 feet 8 inches.
[Source(s): Card File; NA RG 109]

Grissom [Grisson], Edgar [Edward] A. (New Hanover or Brunswick County, North Carolina) [May be same as "Edgar. Grissom, q.v.]
Private, Confederate States Army//Confederate States Navy. Born in North Carolina in 1840, Grissom's pension application filed July 6, 1908, age 68, states he enlisted on September 1, 1861 "in Howard's Cavalry [sic]." [NOTE: Captain William C. Howard's Company, North Carolina Local Defense Troops, was raised for local defense in the lower Cape Fear River was disbanded on June 7, 1862]. Source "Foenander" states he enlisted for twelve months in New Hanover County, North Carolina, on October 1, 1861, at age 21, as a Private in Captain William C. Howard's Cavalry Company and transferred to the "Naval service" on April 11, 1862. He served as a Seaman and Pilot aboard the CSS ARCTIC, 1862, and as a Pilot aboard the CSS YADKIN at Wilmington, 1863. Jonathan W. Galloway, Southport, North Carolina, appeared on his behalf [for his pension application]. A pension claim filed by his widow, Cassie [Cassey] Grissom, age 67, post office Southport, Brunswick County, North Carolina, July 4, 1910, was approved at 4th Class. Her application states he enlisted on August 1, 1862.
[Source(s): Pensions (North Carolina); North Carolina Troops, II; St. Amand; Foenander]

Grissom, Edgar (New Hanover County, North Carolina) [May be same as "Edgar A. Grissom, q.v.]
Confederate States Navy. Crewman, CSS NORTH CAROLINA.
[Source(s): MR, 4, p. 443]

Grissom, Robert S. [A.] (New Hanover County, North Carolina [?])
Pilot, Confederate States Navy. Born in North Carolina in 1849, Grissom served aboard the blockade runner "Little Hattie." Source "Foenander" states he served in the Confederate States Navy, and that he and his wife Savannah Grissom, lived in Weakley County, Tennessee, after the war, and that he received a Tennessee Confederate pension. He was a farmer in 1910, and still living as of the 1920 Census.
[Source(s): McElroy; Card File; Foenander; *Tennessee Confederate Pension* file #S14047, wife's pension file #W10370; 1920 United States Census].

Grissom [Gressom], Simon [Simeon] S. (New Hanover County, North Carolina).
Pilot, Confederate States Navy. Grissom served aboard the Confederate States steamer "R. E. Lee." His name appears as a signature on an Oath of Allegiance to the United States sworn to at Fort Warren, Boston Harbor, Massachusetts, June 15, 1865. His place of residence was given as Wilmington, North Carolina, and his description as follows: complexion dark; hair grey; eyes hazel; height 5 feet 5 ½ inches. Born December 25, 1811, Grissom died on August 11, 1874 and was buried in the Southport Cemetery, Brunswick County, North Carolina.
[Source(s): Card File; NA RG 109; Stepp, "Burials"]

Grissom [Grissam], Thomas B. [J.] (Brunswick or New Hanover County, North Carolina).
Private, Confederate States Army//Seaman and Pilot, Confederate States Navy. Born either in New Hanover or Brunswick Company, North Carolina about 1837 or 1838, as of 1860, Grissom resided in Smithville District of Brunswick County, North Carolina where he worked as a river pilot. He enlisted in New Hanover County, North Carolina at age 23 [Note: age "18" per source NCCWSP] on June 1, 1861 as a Private in Company E, 10th Regiment,

North Carolina State Troops (1st Regiment, North Carolina Light Artillery) for the war. He transferred to the Confederate States Navy on August 24, 1861 and served as a Seaman aboard the CSS BEAUFORT, circa September through November 1861 [Note: Source Foenander states he served aboard the BEAUFORT into1862]. Grissom served aboard the CSS CASWELL, 1862. Other source(s) state he served aboard the blockade runner "*Lilian*." He died on April 13, 1877 and was buried in the Southport Cemetery, Brunswick County, North Carolina. He resided in Smithville [Southport], Brunswick County, North Carolina, after the war as a Pilot.
[Source(s): Card File; McElroy; North Carolina Troops, I; Stepp, "Burials;" Stepp, "Burials;" Foenander; 1870 Census (NC), 1860; NCCWSP]

Grissom [Grisson], W. J. (Brunswick County, North Carolina)
Ordinary Seaman and Carpenter, Confederate States Navy. Source "Foenander" lists a "W. J. Grisson" as an Ordinary Seaman and Carpenter, CSS ARCTIC, 1862 – 1863. He may have been the "W.J. Grissom" who served as a Pilot aboard the steamer *Vulture*, out of Wilmington, North Carolina, November 1864. His name appears on a register of Confederate States Army General Military Hospital Number 4, Wilmington, North Carolina, dated March 15, 1862, which gives disease as "dyspepsia" and post office as Smithville, North Carolina. A pension claim filed by his widow, Mary Grissom, age 65, post office Southport, Brunswick County, North Carolina, July 5, 1909 (approved) states he enlisted in the Confederate States Navy on or about January 15, 1861. Jonathan W. Galloway appeared on her behalf.
[Source(s): Card File; NA RG 109; Pensions (North Carolina); Foenander]

Grizzard, Henry
Landsman, Confederate States Navy. Enlisted May 20, 1864 in Raleigh, North Carolina, for the war.
[Source(s): Card File; Pensions (North Carolina)]

Groves, Jacob D.
Master's Mate, Confederate States Navy.
[Source(s): Pensions (FL); Card File]

Grubb, Alex
Landsman, Confederate States Navy. Enlisted December 10, 1863 in Raleigh [December 10, 1863, Wilmington], North Carolina, for the war.
[Source(s): Card File; NA RG 45]

Guerard, Charle[s]
Seaman, Confederate States Navy. Enlisted June 22, 1863 in Wilmington, North Carolina, for the war.
[Source(s): Card File; NA RG 45]

Guffey, Robert Enon (Rutherford County, North Carolina)
Landsman, Confederate States Navy. Enlisted October 26 [October 17], 1863 at Camp Holmes, near Raleigh, North Carolina, and was stationed at Wilmington, North Carolina. He served as a Landsman, aboard the CSS ARCTIC. A pension claim filed by his widow, J. A. Guffey, age 66, post office Carolina, Rutherford County, North Carolina, on July 1, 1901 (approved at 4th Class) states he served in "the Navy under 'Captain Bell Irturem' [illegible] [at] Wilmington and Fayetteville." [Source "Pensions (North Carolina)" states he served in "Captain Bell's Company, Confederate States Navy"). Born 1819, Guffey died in 1897 and was buried at Brittain Presbyterian Church Cemetery [Rutherford County, North Carolina?].
[Source(s): Card File; NA RG 45; Pension (North Carolina); Foenander]

Gunter, James A., Jr. (Chatham County, North Carolina)
Private, Confederate States Marine Corps. Enlisted on March 1, 1862 [Another source says March 2, 1862; another 1861]. Gunter stated that he served at Fort Sumter, South Carolina, November 20, 1862, on the ironclad CSS PALMETTO [STATE], and under Commander Tucker. He was not wounded in service, but his hearing was injured by the firing of heavy guns, causing deafness in later years. Gunter was born March 3, 1832, the son of James and Polly Hughes Gunter of Chatham County. A post-war farmer and widower, he filed a claim for a pension on June 28, 1902 at age 70, listing his post office as Jonesboro, Moore [later Lee] County. The pension request was approved. He applied for admission to the Old Soldier's Home, Raleigh, North Carolina, on June 30, 1919 at age 82 and was admitted on July 31, 1919, where he died at 11:45PM on December 7, 1919 of "Exhaustion & Acute Mania."
[Source(s): Soldier's Home; Pensions (North Carolina); Card File]

Gurgamous [Gurganus?], Thomas
> Landsman, Confederate States Navy. Enlisted December 12, 1863 in Wilmington, North Carolina, for the war.
> [Source(s): Card File; NA RG 45]

Gurney, Thomas
> Acting 2nd Assistant Engineer, Confederate States Navy.
> Gurney served as an Acting 2nd Assistant Engineer aboard the NCS CURLEW with the North Carolina Squadron from at least November 20, 1861 through the 1st quarter of 1862, per that ship's payroll list ending on November 20, 1861.
> [Source: NCCWSP]

Guthrie, Archibald M. (Brunswick County, North Carolina [?])
> Pilot, Confederate States Navy. Guthrie served aboard the blockade runner "*R.E. Lee*." He was born January 14, 1821, died on August 17, 1870, and was buried in the Southport Cemetery, Brunswick County, North Carolina.
> [Source(s): McElroy; Stepp, "Burials"]

Guthrie, Benjamin Wilburne (North Carolina)
> Lieutenant, Confederate States Navy. Born circa 1841 in and appointed from North Carolina, Guthrie resided in Portsmouth, Virginia, where he enlisted on August 31, 1861, in the "Old Dominion Guard," Company K, 9th Virginia Infantry at Pinners Point, Virginia. He was described as having a light complexion, dark hair, and hazel eyes. Guthrie transferred to the Confederate States Navy on February 27, 1862 to accept a commission as a Master Not in Line of Promotion, February 24, 1862 [Source "Fold3, Midshipmen" lists him as being appointed a midshipman from civilian life on February 24, 1862 and on another list as being appointed an Acting Master]. He was appointed Master Not in Line of Promotion, Provisional Confederate States Navy, June 2, 1864. Guthrie served on the Richmond Station, 1862; Confederate States floating battery "New Orleans" [CSS NEW ORLEANS(?)], New Orleans Station, 1862 [-1863]; Confederate States receiving ship and floating battery CSS ARCTIC, Wilmington Station, 1862 [1863]-1864; and, CSS PALMETTO STATE, Charleston Station, 1864. He was a post-war Manufacturer's Agent, New York City, in the wallpaper business. Guthrie was a member of the Stonewall Camp, United Confederate Veterans, Portsmouth, Virginia. He died in New York City on May 21, 1895 and was buried in Cedar Grove Cemetery, Portsmouth, Virginia. Son of John J. Guthrie and brother of John J. Guthrie, Jr.
> [Source(s): Register; McElroy; Card File; Driver; Foenander; ONWR; Fold3, USN Resignees]

Guthrie, E. C. (Craven County, North Carolina)
> Captain, Confederate States Navy. Guthrie's name appears as a signature to Roll of Prisoners of War paroled at Fort Delaware, Delaware, April 25, 1863, which states he was captured at "Abaco Bahams," July 12, 1862, and carries the remarks "On schooner Ida," and further states "Capt., New Bern, North Carolina."
> [Source(s): Card File; NA RG 109]

Guthrie, James J. (Carteret County, North Carolina)
> Lieutenant Commander, Confederate States Navy. Born circa 1827 in Carteret County, North Carolina, Guthrie died on September 13, 1884 and was buried in Bellevue Cemetery, Wilmington, North Carolina. His name appears on the roll of the Wilmington Naval Station.
> [Source(s): Stepp, "Burials"]

Guthrie, John Julius [Sr.] [John Julius Guthrie, Jr.] (Washington, Beaufort County, North Carolina)
> Lieutenant, Confederate States Navy. Born in Washington, North Carolina, April 27, 1815. He received an appointment to United States Military Academy at West Point as a Cadet in 1833, but stayed only one year, leaving to accept an appointment to the United States Naval Academy. Guthrie was later a resident of Portsmouth, Virginia. He served in the United States Navy, 1834-1861, beginning as a Midshipman on February 28, 1834. He was elevated to Passed Midshipman on July 16, 1840, to Master on March 22, 1847, and Lieutenant on July 7, 1847. Per source *Reveille*, in 1861, he was a United States Navy "Lieutenant in the squadron then employed in suppressing the slave trade on the African coast. On the night of April 20, 1861, he was detailed in command of two boats to board the ship '*Nightingale*,' of Boston, whose movements had excited suspicion. Lieutenant Guthrie found nine hundred and sixty-one slaves aboard and took the ship as a prize. Commander Taylor, USS SARATOGA, by whose order the capture was made, sent the '*Nightingale*' to the United States in command of Lieutenant Guthrie. He arrived at New York on June 15, 1861 and turned the ship over to the proper authorities. As the War had broken out, Lieutenant Guthrie resigned his United States Navy commission and threw his fortunes with the Confederacy." He was dismissed from the United States Navy on July 13, 1861. Appointed First Lieutenant, Confederate States Navy, from North Carolina, on July 13, 1861, he was with Commodore Lynch's flotilla in Eastern North Carolina [Source

"Fold3, USN Resignees" gives date of appointment as June 8, 1861]. He was promoted to First Lieutenant, July 13, 1861 (another source says he was appointed a First Lieutenant, October 23, 1862, to rank from October 2, 1862). Guthrie served on the Rappahannock River defenses, 1861. He commanded the CSS RED ROVER and Confederate States floating battery "New Orleans" [CSS NEW ORLEANS (?)] on the Mississippi River, New Orleans Station, 1862-1863 (another source says 1861-1862). "Driver" states he served aboard the CSS GENERAL POLK in 1862. Captured at Island No. 10 on April 8, 1862, he was sent to Johnson's Island and exchanged on August 8, 1862. Guthrie was appointed First Lieutenant on October 23, 1862 to rank from October 2, 1862. He was commanding the CSS CHATTAHOOCHEE in Florida waters at the time of a boiler explosion on board, May 27, 1863. He served at the Richmond Naval Station, 1863, and commanded the CSS ALBEMARLE in North Carolina waters, 1863-1864. Records show he was issued clothing, September 27, 1864. On special service, 1864, Guthrie commanded the North Carolina blockade runner "*Ad-Vance*," 1864-1865, with Captain Joe Gaskill for mate. The "*Advance*" was captured returning from Nassau to Wilmington, and her crew sent as prisoners to Fort Lafayette. He was appointed volunteer aide on the personal staff of North Carolina Governor Zebulon B. Vance on March 23, 1865. He was appointed by President U. S. Grant to the Superintendency of the Life-Saving Service with stations stretching from Cape Henry, Virginia, to Hatteras on the North Carolina coast. Captain Guthrie drowned near Nag's Head off the coast of North Carolina on November 27, 1877 while assisting in the rescue of the crew of the United States steamship HURON. He was hailed as a hero for his efforts. Guthrie was buried in Cedar Grove Cemetery, Portsmouth, Virginia. He was the father of Benjamin W. and John J. Guthrie, Jr.

[Source(s): Register; McElroy; Card File; "Roster Document #0392 (pp. 79-80)"; "Raleigh Spirit;" Driver; Journal; *Reveille*; CWDTS; ONWR; Fold3, USN Resignees]

Guy, John J. (Duplin County, North Carolina)

Private, Confederate States Army//Confederate States Navy(?). Born and resided in Duplin County, North Carolina, Guy worked as a as a mechanic or carpenter prior to enlisting there at age 23 on April 15, 1861, as a Private in 1st Company C, 12th Regiment, North Carolina Troops (2nd Regiment, North Carolina Volunteers) for six months. He was present or accounted for until the company was disbanded on November 18, 1861. Guy enlisted as a Private on December 20, 1861, for the war, in Company D, 13th Battalion, North Carolina Infantry, and was present or accounted for until he transferred to Company A, 51st Regiment, North Carolina Troops on April 15, 1862. Mustered in as a Corporal, he was reduced to the ranks in September-October 1862. He was present or accounted for until captured at Cold Harbor, Virginia, on June 1, 1864, and confined at Point Lookout, Maryland, on June 11, 1864. He was transferred to Elmira, New York, on July 12, 1864, and released there on June 21, 1865, after taking the Oath of Allegiance. Source Card File indicates Confederate Naval service.

[Source(s): Card File; North Carolina Troops, V & XII]

Hackett, John

Ordinary Seaman, Confederate States Navy. Hackett enlisted on September 30, 1863, in Wilmington, North Carolina, for the war and served aboard the CSS ARCTIC. He later served aboard the CSS NEUSE as of the ship's March - October 1864 muster rolls. In April 1865 he was attached to Semmes' Naval Brigade, and was surrendered and paroled at Greensboro, North Carolina, April 26, 1865.

[Source(s): MR, 4, p. 445; NA RG 45; Card File; ORN 2, 1, p. 276; NEUSE Roster; CMACSSN]

Haddock, William (Beaufort County, North Carolina)

Private, Confederate States Army//Confederate States Navy. Haddock resided in Beaufort County, North Carolina, where he enlisted "for the war" on July 4, 1861, age 27, as a Private in Company G, 19th Regiment, North Carolina Troops (2nd Regiment, North Carolina). He was present or accounted for until he transferred to the Confederate States Navy in March 1862. Another source indicates he was "discharged by Lieutenant Nelson under Conscript Act, June 1862."

[Source(s): North Carolina Troops, II, p.152; Foenander; "Beaufort County Sailors"]

Haden, Burgess F.

Landsman, Confederate States Navy. Enlisted July 16, 1864 in Raleigh, North Carolina, for the war.

[Source(s): Card File; NA RG 45]

Haden, James H. (Davidson County, North Carolina)
    Landsman, Confederate States Navy. Haden enlisted on July 16, 1864 in Raleigh for the war. Haden served as a Private in Company D, 1st Naval Battalion. He appears on a Roll of Prisoners of war at Newport News, Virginia, which states that he was "captured on SSRR" April 6, 1865, and confined at Newport News, Virginia, April 16, 1865. His name appears as a signature to an Oath of Allegiance to the United States subscribed to and sworn at Newport News, Virginia, June 20, 1865. Haden's place of residence was listed as "Dawson [probably "Davidson"] County, North Carolina. Description: complexion dark; eyes grey; height 5 feet 9 inches. He was buried in an unmarked grave at Jersey Baptist Church, Davidson County, North Carolina.
    [Source(s): Card File; NA RG 45; NA RG 109; Stepp, "Burials"]

Hager, George W. (Lincoln County, North Carolina)
    Private, Confederate States Army//Seaman, Confederate States Navy. Born in North Carolina in 1839, Hager enlisted in Lincoln County, North Carolina, at age 22, on August 18, 1862 for the war, in Company K, 63rd regiment, North Carolina Troops (5th Regiment, North Carolina Cavalry). He was captured in Carteret County, North Carolina on May 4, 1863 and confined at Fort Monroe, Virginia, until paroled and exchanged at City Point, Virginia, on May 28, 1863. He was present or accounted for until transferred to the Confederate States Navy on April 29, 1864. A member of the Naval Battalion, his name appears on a Roll of Prisoners of War at Point Lookout, Maryland, which states he was captured at Chesterfield [Virginia] April 3, 1865, and released June 27, 1865, having been confined at Point Lookout, Maryland, since April 14, 1865. Name also appears as signature to an Oath of Allegiance to the United States subscribed and sworn to at Point Lookout, Maryland, June 27, 1865, which gives place of residence as Lincoln County, North Carolina. Description: complexion dark; hair dark brown; eyes hazel; height 5 feet 9 ½ inches. Hager married in 1867 and was residing as a farmer in 1900 with his wife, Mary Jane, and three children, at Catawba Springs, Lincoln County, North Carolina. He died in Jackson County, North Carolina, July 23, 1916.
    [Source(s): Card File; NA RG 109; North Carolina Troops, II; Foenander]

Hagerty, P. (County unknown)
    Confederate States Navy. Enlisted in Wilmington, North Carolina.

Haggarty [Haggarty], Jeremiah (Brunswick County, North Carolina).
    Private, Confederate States Army; Confederate States Navy. Hagerty enlisted in 2nd Company H, 40th Regt, North Carolina Troops (3rd North Carolina Artillery) in Brunswick County, North Carolina, on June 2, 1861, for the war. The June 24-August 31, 1861 muster roll states he was "Discharged [from the Army] for improper conduct and transferred to the steamer *Yorktown* [CSN]" at Richmond July 23, 1861."
    [Source(s): Card File; North Carolina Troops, I]

Haggerly, John (County unknown)
    Private, Confederate States Marine Corps [also listed as "20 Marines or 3 Bat. North Carolina A"]. Serving as a member of Company A, Confederate States Marine Corps, Haggerly appears on an undated record of prisoners which states he was captured at Fort Fisher on January 15, 1865.
    [Source(s): NA; Card File]

Hagler, Barney
    Landsman, Confederate States Navy. Enlisted August 10, 1864 in Raleigh, North Carolina, for the war.
    [Source(s): Card File; NA RG 45]

Hailey [Haley], W. L. (Richmond County, North Carolina)
    Landsman, Confederate States Navy. Haley enlisted on July 16, 1864 in Raleigh, North Carolina, for the war. Source NA RG 109 states he served on the James River at Battery Mitchell and appeared on a Roll of Prisoners of War at Point Lookout, Maryland, released May 15, 1865 on taking the Oath of Allegiance to the United States which stated he was captured at Richmond County, North Carolina, March 7, 1865. The Oath gives his residence as Richmond County, North Carolina. His occupation was listed as farmer.
    [Source(s): Card File; NA RG 45; NA RG 109]

Halbrook, George
    Landsman, Confederate States Navy. Halbrook enlisted on October 14 [Source MR, 4, p. 445 states "13"], 1863 in Wilmington, North Carolina, [another source says "at Camp Holmes"] for the war.
    [Source(s): Card File; NA RG 45; MR, 4, p. 445]

Roster of North Carolinians in Confederate Naval Service

Hale, Edward (New Hanover County, North Carolina)
Confederate States Navy. Enlisted in New Hanover County, North Carolina, on August 20, 1861 for twelve months in 1st Company A, 36th Regiment, North Carolina Troops (2nd Regiment, North Carolina Artillery). Detailed from 1st Company A, 36th Regiment, North Carolina Troops, November 8, 1861 on the steamer "Ben." Transferred to Confederate States Navy July-August 1862 while still on detail on the "Ben." He served as a Captain's Steward on board the CSS ARCTIC, 1862 – 1863. Source "Foenander" lists an "Edward Hall," Captain's Clerk, who served on the Wilmington Station, North Carolina, 1862 – 1864 [NOTE: May be same as Edward Hale, q.v.].
[Source(s): Card File; NA RG 109; North Carolina Troops, I; Foenander]

Hale, T. C.
Landsman, Confederate States Navy. Enlisted June 11, 1864 in Raleigh, North Carolina, for the war.
[Source(s): Card File; NA RG 45]

Hall, Robert
Landsman, Officer's Cook, Confederate States Navy.
Hall served as a Landsman aboard the NCS WINSLOW according to that ship's muster roll for July - November 1861, and as an Officer's Cook aboard the NCS SEA BIRD, February 1862]
[Source: NCCWSP]

Hall, Samuel P. (Wilkes County, North Carolina)
Private, Confederate States Army/Confederate States Navy. Hall resided in Wilkes County, North Carolina, where he enlisted at age 21 on June 12, 1861 as a Private in Company C, 26th Regiment, North Carolina Troops. He was present or accounted for until wounded in the right thigh at Gettysburg, PA, and captured on or about July 3, 1863. Hall remained in a hospital in Gettysburg until transferred to David's Island, New York Harbor, July 17-24, 1863. Paroled at David's Island and transferred to City Point, Virginia, where he was received on September 16, 1863 for exchange. There is no record of his having returned to duty with his regiment. Hall transferred to the Confederate States Navy on or about April 15, 1864.
[Source(s): Card File; North Carolina Troops, VII; Foenander]

Hallman, Jacob
Landsman, Confederate States Navy. Enlisted September 28, 1863 at Camp Holmes, near Raleigh, for the war.
[Source(s): Card File; NA RG 45]

Hamilton, Oliver Clark [per source "Howard," his first name was "Oscar"] (Randolph County, North Carolina)
Sergeant, Confederate States Army//Landsman, Confederate States Navy. Born in Randolph County, North Carolina in 1839, Hamilton was the son of E. Speaks and Frances Hamilton, and a resident of Oak Grove, North Carolina. He resided as a farmer in Randolph County, North Carolina, where he enlisted at age 22 on November 4, 1861, as a Private in Company H, 38th Regiment, North Carolina Troops. Promoted to the rank of Sergeant on April 28 [source "North Carolina Troops" states April 18], 1862, he was present or accounted for until reportedly transferred to the Confederate States Navy on or about April 3, 1864 by Special Order 89 [Source "North Carolina Troops" states "No evidence of his service in the C. S. Navy was located]. Source "Foenander" reports Hamilton served as a Landsman aboard the CSS FREDERICKSBURG; that he transferred to the CSS PATRICK HENRY sometime after May 19, 1864, and to the CSS VIRGINIA II, September 16, 1864. He returned to North Carolina after the war, where he remained for the rest of his life, as owner and principal of various colleges in and around Union County. In 1880, he married for a second time to his war time female correspondent, Lizzie Garner. He died in Stokes County, North Carolina, on July 31, 1918. His son, Oscar A. Hamilton, donated his war-time letters to the collections of the University of North Carolina.
[Source(s): Card File; Foenander; North Carolina Troops, X; Howard]

Hamlet, Samuel W. (Warren County, North Carolina)
Landsman, Confederate States Navy. Hamlet enlisted on January 25, 1864 in Raleigh, North Carolina, for the war. He served as a Private in Tucker's Naval Battalion. His name appears on a Roll of Prisoners of War at Point Lookout, Maryland, which states he was captured at Harpers Farm April 6, 1865 and confined at Point Lookout, Maryland, April 14, 1865 until released on June 13, 1865. His name appears as a signature on an Oath of Allegiance to the United States subscribed and sworn to at Point Lookout, Maryland, June 13, 1865. Place of residence given on Oath as Warren County, North Carolina. Description: complexion dark; hair dark brown; eyes blue; height 5 feet 8 ¾ inches. Hamlet was born on November 30, 1839, died on July 30, 1918, and was buried in Suncrest Cemetery, Union County, North Carolina.
[Source(s): Card File; NA RG 109; NA RG 45; Stepp, "Burials"]

Hampton, David (Currituck County, North Carolina
 Ordinary Seaman, Confederate States Navy. Born in North Carolina circa 1842, Hampton resided in the Narrow Shores District of Currituck County, North Carolina as a Seaman. He enlisted for one year aboard the CSS RALEIGH on August 24, 1861, serving at least through April 1862. His name appears on a payroll of the North Carolina Squadron from February 21, 1862 through April 15, 1862.
 [Sources: NCCWSP; Census (NC), 1860]

Hampton, William B. (Currituck County, North Carolina)
 Private, Confederate States Army//Landsman, Confederate States Navy. Born in Currituck County, North Carolina, Hampton resided as a farmer prior to enlisting there at age 17 on May 13, 1861 as a Private in Company E, 17th Regiment, North Carolina Troops (1st Organization). He was present or accounted for until he transferred to the Confederate States Navy on or about July 28, 1861 where he served as a Landsman on board the CSS FANNY from at least October 8, 1861 – December 12, 1862. His name appears on a payroll of the North Carolina Squadron covering the period March 11, 1862 - February 28, 1862.
 [Source(s): Card File; North Carolina Troops, VI; Foenander]; NCCWSP]

Hangs, E. (Wilson County, North Carolina[?])
 Confederate States Navy. Hangs appears on an undated Roll of Prisoners of war paroled at Provost Marshal's Office at Goldsboro, North Carolina. Residence given on roll as "Wilson County," however state not listed.
 [Source(s): Card File; NA RG 109]

Hanks, James
 Second Engineer, Confederate States Navy. Possibly born in New York, Hanks served aboard the CSS NORTH CAROLINA. Source "Fold3, Midshipmen" listed him as appointed a Third Assistant Engineer on August 28, 1861, but "Dismissed," no date or reason given].
 [Source(s): Fold3, Midshipmen]

Hanks, Junius (Tyrrell County, North Carolina)
 2nd Assistant Engineer, Confederate States Navy.
 Born in New York in 1830, Hanks resided as a machinist in Tyrrell County, North Carolina in 1860, with his wife, Mary, and three children, at the home of Jeremiah and Mary Swain, in Columbia, Tyrrell County, North Carolina. Appointed an Acting 3rd Assistant Engineer on August 28, 1861, Hanks was appointed a Second Assistant Engineer on August 6, 1863. He was appointed a Second Assistant Engineer, Provisional Confederate States Navy, on June 2, 1864 [Source "Foenander" gives date as April 6, 1863]. Hanks served on the Confederate States receiving ship CSS UNITED STATES, 1861, CSS SEA BIRD, and in the Battle of Roanoke Island, February 7-8, 1862. He was captured and paroled on February 12, 1862. He later served aboard the CSS PATRICK HENRY, 1862-1863, CSS NORTH CAROLINA, 1863 – 1864, CSS YADKIN, Wilmington Station, 1864, and CSS DREWRY and CSS FREDERICKSBURG, James River Squadron, 1864.
 [Source(s): Register, McElroy; Card File; Foenander; ONWR; NCCWSP]

Hanks, Tom H.
 Confederate States Army (?)//Confederate States Navy. Source "Card File" states he served in Company K, 10th Regiments, North Carolina Troops (1st Regiment, North Carolina Artillery), but his name does not appear for said regiment in source *North Carolina Troops*. Name may have been mistakenly copied as "Tom" rather than "William (q. v.)."
 [Source(s): Card File; NCT, Vol. I]

Hanks, William H. (Beaufort County, North Carolina)
 Third Assistant Engineer, Confederate States Navy. Hanks was born in Beaufort County, North Carolina, in 1837, where he resided until enlisting there as a Private in Company K, 10th Regiment, North Carolina Troops (1st Regiment, North Carolina Artillery), age 24, on April 22, 1861 for twelve months. He transferred to the Confederate States Navy in July 1861 and was appointed Third Assistant Engineer, CSS BEAUFORT, September 1861 - April 1862. Said vessel operated in North Carolina and Virginia waters. He served with the North Carolina Squadron. His first marriage was to Catherine Blunt, in Orange County, North Carolina, on December 11, 1867. He resided as a machinist, in 1880, in Durham, Orange [now Durham County] County, North Carolina. He is shown as a widower in 1880 but married again about 1881 and shown residing with his wife, Sarah, and son, at Durham, in 1900.
 [Source(s): Card File; NCCWSP; Foenander; North Carolina Troops, I, p.163; "Beaufort County Sailors;" www.thewashingtongrays.homestead.com; www.ncgenweb.us/nccivwar/rosters/10cok.htm; Census (NC), 1880]

Hanson, Peter (Halifax County, North Carolina)
Ordinary Seaman, Confederate States Navy. Hanson enlisted on November 5, 1863 in Wilmington for the war and served aboard the CSS ARCTIC,1863. Source "MR" gives his home county as New Hanover.
[Source(s): Card File; NA RG 45; MR, 4, p. 446; St. Armand; Foenander]

Harden, John William
"Private," Confederate States Navy. Harden served in Company G, "Navy Battalion." "Discharged June 27, 1865."
[Source(s): Card File; UDC, Recorder]

Harden, William M. (Randolph County, North Carolina)
Landsman, Confederate States Navy. Harden enlisted on April 25, 1864 in Raleigh, North Carolina, for the war, and was stationed in Charleston, South Carolina. His application for a Confederate pension, filed on July 1, 1901, at age 76, listing his post office as Randleman, Randolph County, North Carolina, was approved. Another source states he enlisted in the Confederate States Navy in Charleston, SC, about April 1, 1863.
[Source(s): Card File; NA RG 45; Foenander; Pensions (North Carolina)]

Harder, Alexander (Pitt County, North Carolina)
Landsman, Confederate States Navy. Harder was born in North Carolina in 1845, the son of O. P. Harder. In 1850, he lived with his family in the Greenville District of Pitt County, North Carolina. He served as a Landsman aboard the CSS ARCTIC, 1863.
[Source(s): Foenander; 1850 North Carolina. Census]

Hardin, Alex (Robeson County, North Carolina)
Confederate States Navy. Hardin enlisted in the Confederate States Navy in Wilmington, North Carolina on 24 July 1863.
[Source(s): MR, 4, p. 445]

Hardin, I. W.
Seaman, Confederate States Navy. Hardin enlisted on June 22, 1864 in Raleigh, North Carolina, for the war. [NOTE: May be same as "John W. Harden," q.v.].
[Source(s): Card File; NA RG 45]

Hardin [Harding], John M. [Jno. N.] [John William] (Alamance County, North Carolina)
Seaman, Confederate States Navy. Born on July 22, 1833, Hardin served in the "Naval Battalion," and signed an Oath of Allegiance at Point Lookout, Maryland on June 27, 1865. On the Oath his residence was listed as Alamance County, North Carolina, and his description was as follows: complexion light; hair brown; eyes hazel; height 5 feet 9 inches. Both spellings of name appear on the same Oath. One reference states he "served under Com. Tucker and was in prison at Point Lookout at time of surrender."
[Source(s): Card File; NA RG 109; UDC, Graham; UDC, Recorder]

Hardison, William P. (Craven County, North Carolina)
Corporal, Confederate States Army//Confederate States Navy (?). Born in Craven County, North Carolina, Hardison enlisted there at the age of 19 on November 21, 1861, as a Private in Company K, 31st Regiment, North Carolina Troops. He was captured at Roanoke Island on February 8, 1862, paroled at Elizabeth City on February 21, 1862, and returned to duty on or about September 15, 1862. He was again wounded at White Hall in the shoulder on December 16, 1862 and returned to duty prior to March 1, 1863. He was promoted to Corporal on September 4, 1863 and wounded in the elbow at or near Drewry's Bluff, Virginia, on May 16, 1864, and died in a Richmond hospital on June 7, 1864. Source Card File claims he had Confederate Naval service.
[Source(s): Card File; North Carolina Troops, VIII]

Hardy, Peter
2nd Cabin Boy, Confederate States Navy. Hardy enlisted on April 25, 1864 in Halifax or Plymouth for the war.
[Source(s): Card File; NA RG 45]

Hardy, W. H. (May be the "W. H. Hardy" of Wilmington, NC)
Confederate States Navy. Name appears on the March – October 1864 muster roll of the CSS NEUSE.
[Source: CMACCSN]

Harold, J. J. (Martin County, North Carolina)
"Private," Confederate States Navy. Harold served in the "Naval Battalion," and signed an Oath of Allegiance to the United States at Newport News, Virginia, June 26, 1865. Place of residence listed on the Oath as Martin County, North Carolina, and description as follows: complexion light; hair light; eyes blue; height 5 feet 7 inches. Oath carries remark: "Captured Farmville, Virginia, April 6."
[Source(s): Card File; NA RG 109]

Hargarty, P.
Confederate States Navy. Hargarty enlisted in the Confederate States Navy in Wilmington, North Carolina.
[Source(s): MR, 4, p. 445]

Harnesson, J. H.
Seaman, Confederate Stats Navy.
Harnesson served as a Seaman aboard the NCS SEA BIRD according to that ship's muster roll for July - November 1861. His name appears on the North Carolina Squadron payroll for the 1st quarter of 1862 beginning December 1, 1861. On that payroll he is listed as having "run" as of December 1, 1861.
[Source: NCCWSP]

Harralson [Harallson] [Harrolson], Brice [Price] (Caswell County, North Carolina)
Private, Confederate States Army//Landsman, Confederate States Navy. Born in Caswell County, North Carolina, in 1831, Harralson resided there as a merchant in the home of merchant Albert Stevens, in Milton, Caswell County. He enlisted in Caswell County, North Carolina at age 30 on April 29, 1861, as a Private in Company. A, 13th Regiment, North Carolina Troops. He was present or accounted for until transferred to the Confederate States Navy on February 19, 1862 for service aboard the CSS VIRGINIA [aka CSS MERRIMAC] as a Landsman.
[Source(s): Card File; NA RG 45; North Carolina Troops, V; Foenander; *ORN* 2, 1, 309]

Harrell, A. B.
Landsman, Confederate States Navy. Harrell enlisted on June 28, 1864 in Raleigh, North Carolina, for the war.
[Source(s): Card File; NA RG 45]

Harrell, George J. (Hertford County, North Carolina)
Private, Confederate States Army//Confederate States Navy. Harrell resided in Hertford County, North Carolina, and enlisted at age 21 on September 12, 1861 as a Private in Company G, 31st Regiment, North Carolina Troops. He was captured at Roanoke Island, North Carolina, on February 8, 1862, paroled at Elizabeth City, North Carolina, on February 21, 1862, and returned to duty on or about September 15, 1862. He transferred to the Confederate States Navy on December 30, 1863.
[Source(s): Card File; NA RG 45; North Carolina Troops, VIII; Foenander]

Harrell, Jacob (Duplin County, North Carolina) [NOTE: May be same as "Jacob Harrell, Ordinary Seaman, q.v.]
Landsman, Confederate States Navy. Harrell enlisted on September 11, 1863 at Camp Holmes, near Raleigh, North Carolina, for the war. Source MR states he enlisted on September 9, 1863 in Wilmington, North Carolina.
[Source(s): MR, 4, p. 445; Card File; NA RG 45]

Harrell, Jacob [NOTE: May be same as "Jacob Harrell, Duplin County, q.v.]
Ordinary Seaman, Confederate States Navy. Harrell enlisted on September 22, 1863 in Wilmington, North Carolina, for the war.
[Source(s): Card File; NA RG 45]

Harrington, J. W. (Anson County, North Carolina) [Possibly same as "John Harrington," q.v.]
"Private," Confederate States Navy. Harrington served in the "Naval Battalion" and signed an Oath of Allegiance at Newport News, Virginia, June 30, 1865, which gave his residence as Anson County, North Carolina, and his description as follows: complexion light; hair light; eyes blue; height 5 feet 4 inches. His Oath carries the remark: "Captured at Farmville April 6, 1865.
[Source(s): Card File; NA RG 109]

Harrington, John [POSSIBLY SAME AS "J. W. HARRINGTON," q.v.]
Landsman, Confederate States Navy. Harrington enlisted on February 9, 1864 in Raleigh, North Carolina, for the

war.
[Source(s): Card File; NA RG 45]

Harris [NO FIRST NAME LISTED]
Lieutenant, Confederate States Navy. In command of the schooner "*Black Warrior*," under the fleet of Commodore Lynch that participated in the fight at Roanoke Island, February 8-9, 1862.
[Source(s): McElroy; Card File]

Harris, Alex
Landsman, Confederate States Navy. Enlisted December 15, 1863 in Raleigh, North Carolina, for the war. Another reference states he enlisted on December 18, 1863 in Wilmington for the war.
[Source(s): Card File; NA RG 45]

Harris, Caleb
Landsman, Confederate States Navy. Enlisted August 22, 1864 in Raleigh, North Carolina, for the war.
[Source(s): Card File; NA RG 45]

Harris, Edward C. (Franklin County, North Carolina)
Confederate States Navy. A farmer, Harris was conscripted on March 25, 1864 [or, enlisted March 28, 1864] at Camp Holmes near Raleigh, North Carolina from Colonel Thomas' 41st Regiment, North Carolina Militia, Franklin County, North Carolina. Description: Age 23; eyes black; hair dark; complexion fair; height 5 feet 5 inches; place of birth Franklin County, North Carolina; occupation farmer.
[Source(s): Card File; NA RG 45; Foenander]

Harris, Edward W. (Chatham County, North Carolina)
Private, Confederate States Marine Corps. Harris' name appears on a roll of Prisoners of War at Point Lookout, Maryland. He was captured at Farmville, Virginia, on April 6, 1865 and confined on April 14, 1865. His name appears as a signature to an Oath of Allegiance to the United States, subscribed and sworn to at Point Lookout, Maryland, upon his release on June 27, 1865. Place of residence given on Oath as Chatham County, North Carolina. Description as follows: Complexion light; hair auburn; eyes blue; height 5 feet 9 ½ inches.
[Source(s): North Carolina Troops, Doc.# 0185, p. 1 and 0299; NA; Card File; Donnelly-ENL; Donnelly]

Harris, Frank M.
Midshipman, Confederate States Navy.
Harris appears on payroll and muster rolls of the NCS EDWARDS for the period July – October 30, 1861, serving with the North Carolina Squadron. He was serving in the same rank aboard the NCS FORREST as of the 1st quarter of 1862, and as a Midshipman aboard the NCS CURLEW at an undetermined date. He was "Midshipman Commanding" the CSS BLACK WARRIOR in the Battle of Elizabeth City on February 10, 1862.
[Source: NCCWSP]

Harris, John (Pasquotank County, North Carolina) [NOTE: May be same as "John Harris, Company E, Naval Battalion," q.v.]
Private, Confederate States Army//Confederate States Navy. Harris resided in Pasquotank County, North Carolina, where he enlisted for the war on July 8, 1862, aged 28, as a Private in Company A, 8th Regiment, North Carolina State Troops. He was captured at Roanoke Island, February 8, 1862, paroled at Elizabeth City, North Carolina, on February 21, 1862, and exchanged August 1862. He was present or accounted for until he transferred to the Confederate States Navy on or about April 18, 1863.
[Source(s): Card File; NA RG 45; North Carolina Troops, IV; Foenander; Purser]

Harris, John [NOTE: May be same as "John Harris, Pasquotank County, North Carolina," q.v.]
Confederate States Navy. Harris served in Company E, Naval Battalion. He died on June 30, 1865 as a Prisoner of War at Newport News, Virginia, and was buried in Greenlawn Cemetery, Newport News, Virginia.
[Card File; Document#0314-5-16]

Harris, Leonard C. (Granville County, North Carolina)
Private, Confederate States Army//Confederate States Navy(?). Born in Granville County, North Carolina, Harris resided there as a farmer prior to enlisting at Camp Holmes, near Raleigh, North Carolina, at age 23 on July 22, 1862, for the war, as a Private in Company G, 47th Regiment, North Carolina Troops. He was captured at Falling Waters, Maryland, on July 14, 1863, and confined at Point Lookout, Maryland. Harris was released on January 25, 1865 on taking the Oath of Allegiance and joining the United States Army. He was assigned to the 1st Regiment,

United States Volunteer Infantry, but was rejected for service. He was further rejected for service in the United States Navy. North Carolina pension records indicate he survived the war. Source Card File indicates Confederate Naval service.
[Source(s): Card File; North Carolina Troops, XI; Pensions (North Carolina)]

Harris, Nehemiah Taylor (New Hanover County, North Carolina)
Confederate States Navy. Born in Wilmington, Harris died in Wilmington at age 43 on April 23, 1872 and was buried in Oakdale Cemetery, Wilmington, North Carolina.
[Source(s): "Star," 4/24/1872]

Harris, Richard (Orange County, North Carolina)
Confederate States Navy. Harris' signature appears on an Oath of Allegiance to the United States signed at Knoxville, Tennessee, "during the month ending March 31, 1865." His place of residence was given as Orange County, North Carolina, and his description was as follows: complexion dark; hair dark; eyes blue; height 5 feet 11 inches. The Oath carries the remark: "Deserted at Wilmington, North Carolina, October 14, 1864. Sent north." Another source shows his name appearing on an Oath of Allegiance to the United States sworn to at Louisville, KY, April 5, 1865, giving same place of residence and description. May be the same "Richard Harris" who provided a statement in support of the application for pension of Samuel W. Pitchford (q.v.).
[Source(s): Card File; NA RG 109; Pensions (North Carolina) (see "Sam W. Pitchford" Pension Application)]

Harris, William (possibly William R.)
Ordinary Seaman, Confederate States Navy.
Harris served aboard the NCS FANNY per that ship's muster and payrolls from circa October 8, 1861 – December 20, 1861. His name appears on the payroll of the receiving ship CSS UNITED STATES ending March 31, 1862, and on the payroll of the North Carolina Squadron for the 1st quarter of 1862 covering from December 1, 1861 - 28 February 28, 1862 which noted he had "run" by the latter date.
[Source: NCCWSP]

Harrison (Harrisson), Howell W. (Johnston County, North Carolina)
Private, Confederate States Army//Landsman, Confederate States Navy. Born in Johnston County, North Carolina, where he resided as a cooper, Harrison enlisted in Wake County, North Carolina, on May 1, 1861 at age 21 as a Private in Company E, 14th Regiment, North Carolina Troops. He was present or accounted for until transferred to the Confederate States Navy on February 15, 1862 for duty on the CSS VIRGINIA [MERRIMAC] where he served as a Landsman.
[Source(s): North Carolina Troops, V; ORN 2, 1, 309; Card File; Foenander; MR, I]

Harrison, James L.
Landsman, Confederate States Navy. Enlisted January 18, 1864 in Raleigh, North Carolina, for the war.
[Source(s): Card File; NA RG 45]

Harrison, John
Landsman, Confederate States Navy. Enlisted June 11, 1864 in Raleigh, North Carolina, for the war.
[Source(s): Card File; NA RG 45]

Harrison, Richard (Rowan County, North Carolina [?])
Landsman, Confederate States Navy. Harrison was born in 1826, died on October 19, 1861, and was buried in the Lutheran Cemetery, Rowan County, North Carolina.
[Source(s): Stepp, "Burials"]

Harrison, Thomas [NOTE: This man "may" be the same as Thomas D. Harrison, q. v.]
Ordinary Seaman, 2nd Class Fireman, Confederate States Navy.
Per shipping articles dated July 25, 1861, Harrison served aboard the NCS EDWARDS as an Ordinary Seaman from July – October 30, 1861. Per muster rolls, he served as a 2nd Class Fireman aboard the NCS FANNY from December 12, 1861 – February 10, 1862, when the ship was destroyed to prevent capture. He received a partial payment on February 13, 1862 at the Gosport Navy Yard following burning of Fanny at Elizabeth City, North Carolina. His name appears on a payroll of the North Carolina Squadron for the 1st quarter of 1862 covering from December 1, 1861 - February 28, 1862 whereon he is listed as having "run" on February 28, 1862.
[Source: NCCWSP]

Harrison, Thomas D.
>Seaman, Confederate States Navy.
>Enlisted June 15, 1864 in Raleigh, North Carolina, for the war.
>[Source(s): Card File; NA RG 45]

Harroldson, Brice (Caswell County, North Carolina)
>Confederate States Navy. Harroldson transferred from the Yanceyville Grays, Confederate States Army to the Confederate States Navy and served as a crewmember aboard the CSS VIRGINIA. He was wounded in the arm and later captured. Brothers: P.E. Harroldson, Union Ridge, North Carolina; L.F. Harroldson, Union Ridge, North Carolina. Sister: Laura Baynes, Union Ridge, North Carolina.
>[Source(s): McElroy; Card File]

Hartley, Marion
>Ordinary Seaman, Confederate States Navy. Hartley enlisted in the Confederate States Navy in Wilmington, North Carolina, and served aboard the CSS ARCTIC, 1863.
>[Source(s): MR, 4, p. 445'St Amand; Foenander]

Harts, John R. (New Hanover County, North Carolina)
>Confederate States Navy[?]. Harts enlisted in the Wilmington Light Artillery under Captain S. D. Moore, thence attached to the Navy. ["Card File states "Capt. A.D. Moore's/Attached to Navy-Wilmington Light Artillery"]. His pension claim filed June 5, 1901, age 80, listed his post office as Wilmington, North Carolina, and states he enlisted in May 1864, and that he "was not wounded, but was hurt by falling from a horse in Battery, thence made hospital nurse[.] [I]n about 1864 was detailed to work at Navy Yard at Wilmington under Com. Lynch." Three-quarters disabled (injury in 1863, left testicle in atrophied condition").
>[Source(s): Card File; Pensions (North Carolina)]

Hartsell [Heartsell], Tilmon [Tilman][Tilghman][Filghman] [Possibly Stanly, Rowan, Bertie, or Jackson County, North Carolina]
>Landsman [Private], Confederate States Navy. Born in North Carolina in 1821, Hartsell enlisted on November 1, 1863 in Wilmington, North Carolina, for the war [Source MR states he enlisted October 2, 1863 in Wilmington]. Another source states he enlisted on October 31, 1863 in Raleigh, North Carolina, for the war. He served as a Landsman aboard the CSS ARCTIC, Cape Fear River, North Carolina, 1863, and later aboard the CSS RALEIGH, in North Carolina and Virginia waters, 1864. The name "T. Hartsell" appears on a register of Confederate States Army General Military Hospital Number 4, Wilmington, North Carolina, dated February 16, 1864, which gives disease as "debilitas," returned to duty April 13, 1864 and post office as Black Rock [another source lists residence as "Leo" [Washington County, North Carolina]. Hartsell resided as a farmer, in 1880, with his wife, Mary L. Hartsell, and three children (eldest child born 1867), at Furrs, Stanly County, North Carolina.
>[Source(s): Card File; NA RG 45; NA RG 109; UDC, China Grove; Foenander]

Harstene, Henry Julius (North Carolina)
>Captain, Confederate States Navy. Harstene was born circa 1801 in North Carolina [another source gives state as South Carolina]. One source shows he entered Norwich University, Vermont, from Savannah, GA, circa 1828, and graduated. Harstene entered the United States Navy as a Midshipman on April 1, 1828 and rose to the rank of Commander in 1855. He resigned his commission on January 9, 1861 and was appointed a Commander in the Confederate States Navy, March 26, 1861. He served on the Charleston Station, 1861-1862; as a Naval aide on the staff of Brigadier General W. S. Walker, Confederate Army, during the actions near Pocotaligo, South Carolina, in October 1862, and was later in command of several steamers in support of the CSS CHICORA and CSS PALMETTO STATE, during an action against the blockading squadron off Charleston, South Carolina, January 1863. Later, he served on the Savannah Station, 1863, had service abroad, and was reported as being extremely ill, in Munich, in October 1863. One source shows he served as Commander of Confederate naval forces at Charleston, South Carolina, until late 1862, when he suddenly went insane. He was sent to Paris, France, for treatment, but died there on May 31, 1868.
>[Source(s): Ellis; Foenander]

Hashagan, Henry [NOTE: May be same as "H. G. Hashagan," q.v.]
>Steward, Confederate States Navy. Enlisted from North Carolina. Served aboard the flagship CSS YADKIN on the Cape Fear River.
>[Source(s): McElroy; Card File]

Hashagan, H. G. [NOTE: May be same as "Henry Hashagan," q.v.]
Landsman, Confederate States Navy. Enlisted February 4, 1864 in Raleigh, North Carolina, for the war.
[Source(s): Card File; NA RG 45]

Hasker, Charles H.
Boatswain, Confederate States Navy.
Hasker was appointed a Boatswain on June 11, 1861 and served on the CSS FANNY through at least October 8, 1861. He was promoted to Acting Master while serving on the CSS FANNY. Hasker served on the CSS VIRGINIA appearing on her final payroll as a Boatswain, April 1, 1862 – August 2, 1862.
[Source: NCCWSP]

Haskins, E. M.
Landsman, Confederate States Navy. Enlisted February 4, 1864 in Raleigh, North Carolina, for the war.
[Source(s): Card File; NA RG 45]

Hassel [Hassell] [Hascell], Doran [Dorum] [Douglas] [Durham] (Tyrrell County, North Carolina)
Private, Confederate States Army//Seaman, Ship's Cook, Confederate States Navy.
Born in Tyrrell County, North Carolina., Hassel worked as a Seaman before enlisting as a Private in Company D, 5th Regiment, North Carolina Troops, in Craven County, North Carolina, on June 1, 1861, at age 22. He was present or accounted for until transferred to the Confederate States Navy in December 1861. He served as a Seaman aboard the CSS BEAUFORT, September 1861-March 1862, and aboard the CSS NEUSE as of the ship's March – October 1864 muster roll. He transferred to the James River Squadron on April 15, 1862, serving as a Seaman aboard the CSS BEAUFORT at least during the period October 1, 1863 - December 15, 1863 per payroll records. He was promoted to Ship's Cook aboard the CSS BEAUFORT on November 1, 1863.
[Source(s): North Carolina Troops, IV; Hill; Card File; NA RG 45; Foenander; MR, I; NEUSE Roster; CMACSSN; NCCWSP]

Haste, Henry (Washington County, North Carolina)
Private, Confederate States Army//Confederate States Navy. Haste resided and enlisted in Washington County, North Carolina, on June 26, 1861, at age 19, as a Private in Company G, 1st Regiment North Carolina State Troops. He was present or accounted for until discharged on February 3, 1862 [January 1862, per MR, I)] upon transfer to the Confederate States Navy.
[Source(s): Card File; Foenander; North Carolina Troops, III; MR, I]

Hatch, Thomas I.
Landsman, Confederate States Navy. Enlisted June 10, 1864 in Raleigh, North Carolina, for the war. A "T. G. Hatch," identified as "North Carolina Naval Hospital," is buried in the Seaman's Burial Ground, Ashley River, Charleston, South Carolina, date of death listed as October 11, 1864.
[Source(s): Card File; NA RG 45; SBG]

Hatley [Hatly], Hardy (Stanly County, North Carolina)
Landsman, Confederate States Navy. Born in Stanly County, North Carolina, in 1835, the son of Wiley Hatly. Hatley's name appears on a List of Conscripts "in yard at Halifax," June 9, 1864. Source NA RG 45 states "Hardy Hatley" enlisted March 16, 1864 in Raleigh, North Carolina, for the war. The same source states Hardy "Hatly" was conscripted March 14, 1864 at Camp Holmes [near Raleigh, North Carolina] from Colonel Simpson's 83rd Regiment, North Carolina Militia, Stanly County. He served as a Landsman aboard the CSS ALBEMARLE, and on Halifax Station, 1864. Description: Age 28; eyes hazel; hair dark; complexion fair; height 6 feet; place of birth Stanly County; occupation farmer. He resided as a farmer, in 1880, with his wife, Malinda (maiden name Hartsell), and three children, at Big Lick Township, Stanly County, North Carolina
[Source(s): Card File; NA RG 45; Foenander]

Hatley, William M. [N] (Albemarle, Stanly County, North Carolina)
Landsman, Confederate States Navy. Enlisted February 11, 1864 in Raleigh, North Carolina, for the war. The name "William N. Hatley" appears on a register of Confederate States Army General Military Hospital Number 4, Wilmington, North Carolina, stating he was admitted March 3, 1864 with "Febris typhoides" and returned to duty March 21, 1864. A remark on the register states: "Died but accounted for as returned to duty." Post office given as Albemarle, North Carolina.
[Source(s): Card File; NA RG 45; NS RG 109]

Hatts, William T.
Seaman, Confederate States Navy [Naval Battalion]. Hatts' name appears on a Roll of Prisoners of War at Point Lookout, Maryland, released June 13, 1865 on taking the Oath of Allegiance to the United States. The roll states he was captured at Burkeville, Virginia, April 6, 1865, and confined at Point lookout, Maryland, April 14, 1865.
[Source(s): Card File; NA RG 109]

Hawes, Charles William [Williams] (New Hanover County, North Carolina [?])
Confederate States Navy. Hawes was born circa 1838 in Wilmington, North Carolina. A letter from his daughter, Mrs. Marion H. Noonan, of Columbus, Ohio, (dated July 25, 1915 or February 17, 1955) states that he "… fought for the South in the Civil War and was on a blockade runner, was wounded in the leg." He died at age 55 on July 25, 1893 in Birmingham, Alabama and was buried on July 29, 1893 in Oakdale Cemetery, Wilmington, North Carolina. No marker at grave.
[Source(s): Card File; Oakdale Cemetery Rec., Vol. 2; Morning Star, July 26, 28, and 30, 1893; Gravestone Records, v. 2, p. 307 and v. 6, p. 282; Stepp, "Burials"]

Hawes, William Byrd (Duplin County, North Carolina)
Confederate States Marine Corps. Born on May 25, 1845, Hawes enlisted in the on the Charleston Station. His pension claim filed June 14, 1919 at age 74, listing is post office as Rose Hill, Duplin County, North Carolina was disallowed. He died on May 13, 1923 and was buried in the Hawes Family Cemetery, 6 ¼ miles east of Rose Hill, Duplin County, North Carolina.
[Source(s): Pensions (North Carolina); Card File; Comer, *Rogers*]

Hay, Gilbert [North Carolina??]
Confederate States Navy. Hay joined the Confederate States Navy in Wilmington, North Carolina, served aboard the Confederate privateer "Retribution," and is said to have commanded the privateer "*Beauregard*."
[Source(s): Foenander; ORN 1, 2, 66]

Hayman (Haymond), James M. (Tyrrell County, North Carolina)
Seaman, Confederate States Navy. Born in North Carolina, circa 1839, Hayman lived in Columbia, Tyrrell County, North Carolina, as a mariner. He enlisted as a Seaman on or about January 16, 1862 and served aboard the CSS RALEIGH from January through April 1862. He appears on rolls of the North Carolina Squadron from at least February 7, 1862 through April 15, 1862. Hayman transferred to the James River Squadron on April 15, 1862.
[Source(s): Census (NC), 1860; NCCWSP]

Hayman, Samuel M. B. (Beaufort County, North Carolina)
Private, Confederate States Army//Confederate States Navy. Hayman enlisted in Beaufort County, North Carolina, age 21, as a Private in Company G, 19th Regiment, North Carolina Troops (2nd North Carolina Cavalry) on June 27, 1861 "for the war." He was present or accounted for until he transferred to the Confederate States Navy on February 1, 1862.
[Source(s): Card File; Foenander; "Beaufort County Sailors;" North Carolina Troops, II, p.153]

Haynes, Giles Henry (Connecticut/ Craven County, North Carolina)
1st Class Fireman, Confederate States Navy. Born in Connecticut in 1829, Haynes married Jane H. Wilson on April 24, 1858 in Craven County, North Carolina. He resided as a fisherman, in 1860, with his wife, and son William, at New Bern, Craven County, North Carolina. He served as a First-Class Fireman aboard the CSS BEAUFORT, September 1861 through April 1862 with the North Carolina Squadron. The vessel operated in North Carolina and Virginia waters. He served aboard the CSS NEUSE as of the ship's March - October 1864 muster rolls. Haynes received a partial payment on February 13, 1862 at Gosport Navy Yard, Norfolk, Virginia, following service in manning Fort Cobb at Elizabeth City, North Carolina on February 10, 1862. Haynes served as a 1st Class Fireman, aboard the CSS BEAUFORT per clothing lists from February - March 1862. His name appears on a payroll of the North Carolina Squadron for the 1st quarter of 1862 from December 1, 1862 - April 15, 1862. Haynes transferred to the James River Squadron on April 15, 1862 and continued to serve as a 1st Class Fireman, aboard the CSS BEAUFORT with that squadron for the period October 1, 1863 - 15 December 15, 1863.
[Source(s): ORN 2, 1, 281; Census (North Carolina), 1860; Foenander; NEUSE Roster; NCCWSP; CMACSSN]

Hays, W. R. (Granville County, North Carolina) [NOTE: Possibly same as "W.W. Hays"]
Landsman, Confederate States Navy. Hays' name appears as a signature to an Oath of Allegiance to the United States subscribed and sworn to at Newport News, Virginia, June 27, 1865. Place of residence on the Oath was shown as Granville County, North Carolina. Description: Complexion dark; hair black; eyes black; height 6 feet 6 inches.

Remark on Oath: "Captured at Farmville April 6, 1865."
[Source(s): Card File; NA RG 109]

Hays, W. W. (Granville County, North Carolina)
Confederate States Navy. Appears on a list of conscripts "in the yard at Halifax," June 9, 1864. Source NA RG 45 states he was conscripted at Camp Holmes [near Raleigh, North Carolina] March 30, 1864 from Colonel Dolby's 43rd Regiment, North Carolina Militia. Description: Age 30; eyes hazel; hair dark; height 6 feet 1 inch; place of birth Granville County, North Carolina; occupation farmer.
[Source(s): Card File; NA RG 45]

Hayward, Benjamin
Confederate States Navy, 2nd Cabin Boy. Enlisted April 25, 1864 at Halifax or Plymouth, North Carolina, for the war.
[Source(s): Card File; NA RG 45]

Hayworth, John Franklin III (Davidson County, North Carolina [?])
Seaman, Confederate States Navy. Enlisted June 18, 1864 in Raleigh, North Carolina, for the war. Born April 18, 1830, Hayworth died on March 25, 1902, and was buried at Abbott's Creek Baptist Church, Davidson County, North Carolina.
[Source(s): Card File; NA RG 45; Duke Papers; Stepp, "Burials"]

Hazard [Hazzard], Samuel (Lenoir County, North Carolina)
Private, Confederate States Army//Confederate States Navy. Hazard was born in North Carolina in 1824 and enlisted at age 37 on April 27, 1861 in Company D, 27th Regiment, North Carolina Troops. He transferred to the Confederate States Navy on April 1, 1864. He served as a Landsman and was later attached as a Private in Company K, 2nd Regiment, Semmes' Naval Brigade, April 1865. Hazard surrendered and was paroled in Greensboro, North Carolina, April 26, 1865. In 1870, he resided as a farm laborer with his wife, Harriet, and son, at Kinston, Lenoir County, North Carolina.
[Source(s): Card File; North Carolina Troops; North Carolina Troops, VIII; Foenander; Census (North Carolina), 1870]

Heady, Hamilton D. (Onslow County, North Carolina)
Confederate States Army//Confederate States Navy(?). Born in North Carolina, 1836, the son of Ann Heady, Heady was a "mariner" by trade residing in Swansboro, Onslow County, North Carolina, with a wife and two children, when he enlisted "for the war" in Carteret County, North Carolina, on May 22, 1861, at age 25, as a Sergeant in Company G, 10th Regiment, North Carolina State Troops (1st Regiment, North Carolina Artillery). Reduced to Private sometime between January-February 1862, he was absent when his company was captured at Fort Macon on April 26, 1862. He was temporarily assigned to Company E until Company G was exchanged in August 1862. He was re-appointed Sergeant, March or April 1863. Transferred to Confederate States Navy on September 3, 1863, the order was revoked on December 4, 1863 and he was returned to Company G as a Private. Present or accounted for through February 1865. He lived as a fisherman in Swansboro, North Carolina, after the war.
[Source(s): Card File; UDC, Recorder; Foenander; North Carolina Troops, I]

Healy, M.J.
Seaman, Confederate States Navy. Enlisted September 29, 1863 in Wilmington, North Carolina, for the war.
[Source(s): MR, 4, p. 445; NA RG 45; Card File]

Hean (Heans), David (Scotland/New Hanover County, North Carolina)
Confederate States Navy. A Scottish-born resident of New Hanover County, Hean was a native of Dundee, Scotland, and had been an American citizen for some time. He served as a Seaman and Purser's Steward aboard the CSS ARCTIC, 1862. Hean died at the General Hospital in Wilmington, North Carolina, July 30, 1863, aged 39. Source "WDJ (July 1, 1863)" states he died of unrecorded causes in June 1863 in a Wilmington hotel.
[Source(s): ORN 1, 23, 703 and 2, 1, 276; Fay. Obs. (August 3, 1863); "WDJ" (July 1, 1863)]

Hearn(e), William A. (Craven County, North Carolina[?])
Assistant Paymaster, Confederate States Navy. Source "MR" states he enlisted March 12, 1862 from (or "in") Halifax County, North Carolina, in an unnamed regiment. Discharged on October 3, 1862, he was promoted to "Major and Paymaster" in the Confederate States Navy. He was buried at Cedar Grove, Craven County, North Carolina. [NOTE: Source "Foenander" states Hearne was appointed from Arkansas, as Assistant Paymaster,

Confederate States Navy, and that he was paroled in Alexandria, Louisiana, on June 3, 1865.
[Source(s): Stepp, "Burials;" MR, III; Foenander]

Heath, R. (Goldsboro, Wayne County, North Carolina) [NOTE: Possibly same as "Robert Heath," q.v.]
Seaman, Confederate States Navy. Name appears as signature to an Oath of Allegiance to the United States, subscribed and sworn to at Elmira, New York, July 3, 1865. Place of residence given on Oath as Goldsboro, North Carolina. Description: Complexion florid; hair dark; eyes blue; height 5 feet 10 inches.
[Source(s): Card File; NA RG 109]

Heath, Robert (Greene County, North Carolina) [NOTE: Possibly same as "R. Heath," q.v.]
Confederate States Navy ["Naval Command"]. Born in North Carolina in 1828, Heath filed a claim for a Confederate pension on June 17, 1901, at age 76, listing his post office as Bull Head, Greene County, North Carolina. The pension was approved at the 4th Class level. His pension application states that he served under Captain Poindexter in service on "the Cape Fear River defenses" on or about September 1, 1864, and was at Battery Buchanan, Fort Fisher, North Carolina, when the fort fell. He was made a Prisoner of War. He received a three-quarters disability due to age and disease. No indication of approval or rejection. He resided as a laborer, in 1880, in Bull Head, Greene Company, North Carolina.
[Source(s): Card File; Pensions (North Carolina); Foenander]

Heath, Thomas (England; Greene County [?], North Carolina)
Landsman, Confederate States Navy. Born in England, his pre-war occupation was that of blacksmith. He enlisted in Greene County, North Carolina, March 17, 1864, aged 25, in the Confederate States Navy. His name is crossed out in the *Confederate States Navy Shipping Articles* (possibly because of desertion or non-appearance).
[Source(s): Card File; NA RG 45; Foenander; *Confederate States Navy Shipping Articles*]

Heathcock, Allen
Landsman, Confederate States Navy. Enlisted July 21, 1864 in Raleigh, North Carolina, for the war.
[Source(s): Card File; NA RG 45]

Hedgepeth [Hedgepath], Joseph S. (Edgecombe County, North Carolina)
Private, Confederate States Army// Landsman, Confederate States Navy. Resided as a farmer in Edgecombe County, North Carolina where he enlisted on May 8, 1861[Source MR, I, gives the date as May 1st] at age 18 as a Private in Company G, 13th Regiment, North Carolina Troops. Present or accounted for until he transferred to the Confederate States Navy on February 20, 1862 [Source MR, I, gives the date as February 4, 1862]. Hedgepeth served as a Landsman aboard the CSS VIRGINIA, Hampton Roads, Virginia, 1862; was attached to Semmes' Naval Brigade, April 1865; and, surrendered and was paroled at Greensboro, North Carolina, April 26, 1865.
[Source(s): Card File; North Carolina Troops, V; ORN 2, 1, 309; Foenander; MR, I]

Hedrick(s), Samuel (Chowan County, North Carolina)
Landsman, Confederate States Navy. Born in North Carolina in 1808, Hedrick(s) resided as a carpenter in 1850 with his wife, Margaret, and five children, in the Edenton district, Chowan County, North Carolina. He enlisted in Chowan County on February 15, 1862 as a Private in Company F, 11th Regiment, North Carolina Troops. On April 1, 1864, Hedrick(s) transferred to the Confederate States Navy. Sources Card File and "NA RG 45" state he enlisted August 1, 1864 in Raleigh, North Carolina, for the war.
[Source(s): Card File; NA RG 45; Foenander]

Hedricks, Thomas (Chowan County, North Carolina)
Private, Confederate States Army//Confederate States Navy. Resided in Chowan County, North Carolina, where he enlisted at age 54 on February 15, 1862, for the war, in Company F, 11th Regiment, North Carolina Troops. Present or accounted for until he transferred to the Confederate States Navy on April 1, 1864 [age 56].
[Source(s): Card File; North Carolina Troops, V]

Heflin [Heffron], Stephen
Landsman, Confederate States Navy. Enlisted April 13, 1864 in Kinston, North Carolina, for three years. He served aboard the CSS NEUSE as of the ship's March – October 1864 muster rolls.
[Source(s): Card File; NA RG 45; NEUSE Roster; CMACSSN]

Helms, Gideon B. (Buncombe County, North Carolina)
Private, Confederate States Army//Confederate States Navy[?]. Resided in Buncombe County, North Carolina,

where he was by occupation a farmer prior to enlisting there as a Private at age 20 on May 3, 1861 in Company F, 14th Regiment, North Carolina Troops. Present or accounted for through August 1864, though reported as absent sick or on detail during much of the period.
[Source(s): Card File; North Carolina Troops, V]

Helms, John (Union County, North Carolina) [May be the same as "John Helms, q.v."]
Ordinary Seaman, Confederate States Navy. Born in Union County, North Carolina on November 7, 1837, Helms worked at the Army Gun Shop, Jamestown, North Carolina. He enlisted in the Confederate States Navy in Wilmington, North Carolina, October 31, 1863 [Source "Foenander" gives the date as "August or September 1863"] and served aboard the CSS ARCTIC (under Captain C. B. Poindexter). Helms was on sick furlough at home in Monroe, North Carolina, when the war ended. After the war, he resided in Florida, beginning as early as December 1872. He died on November 3, 1920 [another source gives date as November 2], and is buried at the Good Hope Cemetery, Bunnell, Flagler County, Florida. He died in 1920.
[Source(s): MR, 4, p. 446; Ellis; Foenander]

Helms, John [May be the same as "Helms, John (Union County, North Carolina)," q.v.]
Ordinary Seaman, Confederate States Navy. Enlisted on November 5, 1863 at Wilmington, North Carolina, for the war. Source NA RG 45 states enlisted November 2, 1863 at Raleigh, North Carolina, for the war.
[Source(s): Card File; NA RG 45; Pensions (FL)]

Helms, Lewellen D. (Union County, North Carolina)
Private, Confederate States Army//Confederate States Navy. Born in North Carolina in 1838, the son of Green B. and Nelly Helms, in 1850 Helms resided with his parents in Union County, North Carolina. On November 10, 1854, he married Mary Ann Bass in Union County. He lived in Union County as a farmer until he enlisted there at age 22 on April 8, 1862, in Company I, 53rd Regiment, North Carolina Troops. Reported present on surviving company muster rolls through February 1864, he was listed as a "faithful soldier." He transferred to the Confederate States Navy on April 18, 1864.
[Source(s): Card File; North Carolina Troops, XIII; Foenander]

Henderson, Jackson B. (Caldwell County, North Carolina)
Private, Confederate States Army//Confederate States Navy. Resided and enlisted in Caldwell County, North Carolina, at age 30 on July 26, 1861 as a Sergeant in Company I, 26th Regiment, North Carolina Troops. Present or accounted for until he was wounded and captured at or near Gettysburg, Pennsylvania, sometime between July 1-5, 1863 [Roll of Honor states he "acted badly in Battle of Gettysburg and (was) taken prisoner."]. Confined at David's Island, New York Harbor, until paroled and transferred to City Point, Virginia, where he was received on September 16, 1863 for exchange. Reduced to the ranks on an unspecified date. Transferred to the Confederate States Navy in January-February 1864.
[Source(s): Card File; North Carolina Troops, VII]

Henderson, James
2nd Cabin Boy, Confederate States Navy. Enlisted April 25, 1864 in Halifax or Plymouth, North Carolina, for the war.
[Source(s): Card File; NA RG 45]

Henderson, J. J.
Third Assistant Engineer, Confederate States Navy. Appointed from North Carolina. Henderson was appointed as an Acting Third Assistant Engineer on November 2, 1861 in the Confederate States Navy [Source "Fold3, Midshipmen" lists him as appointed a Third Assistant Engineer on November 20, 1861]. He served on the CSS SEA BIRD, and participated in the Battle of Roanoke Island, North Carolina on February 10, 1862, where he was wounded and captured. He was paroled on February 12, 1862 at Roanoke Island and returned to Elizabeth City, North Carolina. He resigned on November 14, 1862.
[Source(s): Register; <u>ORN</u>, Series I, Vol. 6, p.596; Foenander; Fold3, Midshipmen; NCCWSP]

Henderson, Jones S. (Beaufort County [?], North Carolina)
Private, Confederate States Army//Confederate States Navy. Enlisted in Beaufort County, North Carolina, on July 15, 1861, age 20, as a Private in Company G, 19th Regiment, North Carolina Troops (2nd Regiment, North Carolina Cavalry) on July 15, 1861 "for the war." Wounded in action at Pollocksville, North Carolina, in May 1862, he was wounded again at Brandy Station, Virginia, on June 9, 1863. He was listed as present or accounted for until

he transferred as a Private to Company E, 4th Regiment, North Carolina State Troops on January 16, 1864. He transferred to the Confederate States Navy on April 5, 1864.
[Source(s): Card File; North Carolina Troops, II and IV; Foenander; "Beaufort County Sailors"]

Hendrick, Thomas J. (Perquimans County, North Carolina) [NOTE: May be same as "Thomas Hendricks," q.v.]
Ordinary Seaman, Confederate States Navy. Born in North Carolina in February 1841, the son of Jonah and Mary Hendricks, he resided, in 1850, with his parents, at Up River district, Perquimans County, North Carolina. He enlisted on June 5, 1863 in Wilmington, North Carolina, for the war [Source "Pensions (North Carolina)" states he enlisted on or about May 1863]. He served as an Ordinary Seaman aboard the CSS NORTH CAROLINA [Source(s): Card File states "Gunboat '1st N. C.'"] and the CSS TALLAHASSEE, 1864. Hendrick married in 1868 and was residing as a farmer in 1900 with his wife, Mary, in Belvidere Precinct, Perquimans County, North Carolina. Hendrick filed for a North Carolina Confederate pension on July 1, 1907 at the age of 67. On the application, he listed his post office as Belvidere, Perquimans, County, North Carolina. He served in the North Carolina [Squadron?] at Wilmington and was wounded in the leg by a piece of wood circa June 1864 at Wilmington, North Carolina. "Scar on right leg from splinter wood in Gunboat in 1864." Three-quarters disabled from age and wound. Pension approved at 4th Class. He died in Perquimans County on May 20, 1916.
[Source(s): Card File; NA RG 45; Pensions (North Carolina)]; Foenander; MR, 4, p. 444]

Henly, M. J.
Confederate States Navy. Enlisted in Wilmington, North Carolina.
[Source(s): MR, IV, 445]

Hennessy, Patrick (New Hanover or Rowan County, North Carolina)
Confederate States Navy. Served on the CSS EUGENIE. Appears on registers of Confederate States Army General Military Hospital Number 4, Wilmington, North Carolina, as being admitted September 28, 1863, with "int. feb. tertia" [Card File says "feb. cont."] and returned to duty October 21, 1863. Post office given on register as Wilmington [NA RG 109 states post office as Salisbury].
[Source(s): Card File; NA RG 109]

Henry, Archibald [Archy] [Sampson County, North Carolina]
Landsman, Confederate States Navy. Enlisted January 2, 1864 in Raleigh, North Carolina, for the war. His name appears on a register of Confederate States Army General Military Hospital Number 4, Wilmington, North Carolina, as being admitted January 27, 1864, with "diarrhea chronic" and returned to duty March 21, 1864. Post office listed as Morrison and Harrell's Store, North Carolina. The "Wilmington Daily Journal" of April 27, 186, states Henry was a New Hanover County resident, a member of the Confederate States Navy, and died of unrecorded causes in April 1864.
[Source(s): Card File; NA RG 45; NA RG 109; "WDJ," April 27, 1864]

Henry, William
Landsman, Confederate States Navy. Enlisted June 6, 1864 in Raleigh, North Carolina, for the war.
[Source(s): Card File; NA RG 45]

Henshaw, G. M.
Landsman, Confederate States Navy. Enlisted November 20, 1863 in Raleigh, North Carolina, for the war.
[Source(s): Card File; NA RG 45]

Henshaw, M.
Landsman, Confederate States Navy. Age 21, black eyes, light hair, fair complexion, born in North Carolina.
[Source(s): CSS "Tennessee"]

Hensley, N. L.
Landsman, Confederate States Navy. Enlisted August 10, 1864 in Raleigh, North Carolina, for the war.
[Source(s): Card File; NA RG 45]

Herbert, John J.
Landsman, Confederate States Navy. Enlisted May 9, 1864 in Raleigh, North Carolina, for the war.
[Source(s): Card File; NA RG 45]

Herndon, J. R. [I. R.] (Forsyth County, North Carolina)
> Landsman, Confederate States Navy. Born in Virginia, Herndon's pre-war occupation was that of mariner. He enlisted in the Confederate States Navy on March 18, 1864 at age 29 in Forsyth County, North Carolina [Other sources state he enlisted on March 21, 1864 in Raleigh, North Carolina, for the war]. His name appears on a list of conscripts "in the yard "[at Halifax?]. He was then transferred to Wilmington, North Carolina on June 9, 1864. Source "NA RG 45" states he was conscripted March 18, 1864 at Camp Holmes [near Raleigh, North Carolina] from Colonel Morton's 71st Regiment, North Carolina Militia, Forsyth County, North Carolina. Description: Age 29; eyes grey' hair light; complexion light; height 5 feet 7 inches; place of birth Virginia; occupation farmer.
> [Source(s): Card File; NA RG 45; Foenander]

Herring, Benjamin Sims (Duplin County, North Carolina; appointed from Virginia)
> Assistant Engineer, Confederate States Navy. Born in Duplin County, North Carolina, on March 4, 1837 [Source Card File gives date as March 14, 1837], the son of Bryan Whitfield and Penelope Simms (or Sims) Herring. He was the brother of Confederate Navy officer Robert S. Herring. In June 1860, he resided with his parents and siblings, at Duplin County, North Carolina as an engineer. He was appointed from North Carolina (Source "Lib. of Virginia" states he was appointed from Virginia). Herring formerly served as a Third Assistant Engineer in the United States Navy from August 11, 1860, and may have served in the Virginia Navy, 1861. Herring was appointed an Acting Third Assistant Engineer in the Confederate States Navy on July 23, 1861 and was promoted to Acting Second Assistant Engineer on August 13, 1863 [Source "Fold3, Midshipmen" states he was appointed a Second Assistant Engineer on November 29, 1861 from the United States Navy]. He was subsequently appointed to the rank of First Assistant Engineer on August 20, 1863, and to First Assistant Engineer Provisional Confederate Navy on June 2, 1864. He served on the CSS JAMESTOWN, Richmond Station, 1861, and served as an Assistant Engineer on the CSS VIRGINIA (MERRIMACK). Herring participated in the Battle of Hampton Roads, Virginia, on March 8-9, 1862. He served at the Naval Works, Columbus, GA, 1862-1863. He had further service on the CSS GAINES, Mobile Station, 1863, CSS TENNESSEE, 1863-1864, CSS W. H. WEBB, Red River defenses, 1864, and with the Mobile Squadron, 1864-1865. Herring surrendered on May 4, 1865 and was paroled on May 10, 1865. Same source ["Roster Document #0421] references "a long article" written by or about him.
> [Source(s): Register, McElroy; Card File; Foenander; Roster Document #0421]; Lib. of Virginia; ONWR; Fold3, Midshipmen].

Herring, J. B. (New Hanover County, North Carolina)
> Ordinary Seaman, Confederate States Navy. Herring enlisted 23 August 1863. Source NA RG 45 states he enlisted on September 5, 1863, in Wilmington, North Carolina.
> [Source(s): MR, 4, p. 445; St. Armand]

Herring, J. F.
> Landsman, Confederate States Navy. Enlisted on October 11, 1863 in Wilmington, North Carolina, for the war. Source "NA RG 45" states he enlisted on October 12, 1863 at Camp Holmes [near Raleigh, North Carolina].
> [Source(s): Card File; NA RG 45]

Herring, John (Halifax County, North Carolina) [NOTE: May be same as "John Herring, Carpenter's Mate," q.v.]
> Seaman, Confederate States Navy. Herring enlisted on October 28, 1863 [per various sources: October 30, 1863, in Raleigh, North Carolina, or November 1] in Wilmington, North Carolina [for the war]. Source "Foenander" lists a "John Herring" who served as a Seaman aboard the CSS ARCTIC in Wilmington, North Carolina, 1863." Source "St. Armand" lists his enlistment date in the Confederate States Navy as August 23, 1863.
> [Source(s): MR, 4, p. 446; NA RG 45; Card File; Foenander]

Herring, John [NOTE: May be same as "John Herring, Seaman," q.v.]
> Carpenter's Mate, Confederate States Navy. Source "Foenander" lists a "John Herring" (who may be the same as "John Herring (Halifax County, North Carolina," q.v.) who served as a Carpenter's Mate aboard the CSS RALEIGH, operating in North Carolina and Virginia waters, 1862-1864.
> [Sources): Foenander]

Herring, Joshua J. (Lenoir County, North Carolina)
> Landsman [later as Ordinary Seaman?], Confederate States Navy [Naval Battalion]. Herring enlisted on September 2 [22], 1863 in Wilmington, North Carolina. Source "NA RG 45" states he enlisted as a Landsman September 11, 1863 at Camp Holmes [near Raleigh, North Carolina], for the war]. His name appears on an Oath of Allegiance to the United States subscribed and sworn to at Newport News, Virginia, June 26, 1865. His residence was given as Lenoir County, North Carolina, and his description as follows: complexion light; hair dark; eyes dark; height

5 feet 2 inches. Oath carries the remark: "Captured at Farmville, Virginia, April 6." Source "UDC, Greene" states Herring served as a Landsman on the CSS ARCTIC, Wilmington Station, June 1862 [&] November 1864, and CSS VIRGINIA II November 1864-April 1865.
[Source(s): MR, 4, p. 445; Card File; NA RG 45; NA RG 109; UDC, Greene]

Herring, J. T.
Landsman, Confederate States Navy. CSS ARCTIC, 1863.
[Source(s): Foenander; *ORN* 2, 1]

Herring, Owen F.
Private, Confederate States Army//Confederate States Navy(?). Serving in Captain William S. Devane's Independent Company, North Carolina Troops, Herring transferred as a Private to Company A, 61st Regiment, North Carolina Troops, on or about September 5, 1862. Present or accounted for through April 30, 1864, he was promoted to Corporal on or about April 13, 1864. Captured near Petersburg, Virginia, on or about August 4, 1864, he was confined at Old Capitol Prison, Washington, DC, on August 10, 1864. Herring was transferred to Fort Delaware, Delaware, where he arrived on August 12, 1864. He took the Oath of Allegiance and was released from Fort Delaware on June 17, 1865. Source Card File indicates Confederate Naval service.
[Source(s): Card File; NA RG 45; North Carolina Troops, XIV]

Herring, Robert S. (Duplin County, North Carolina)
Sergeant, Confederate States Army//Acting Second Assistant Engineer, Confederate States Navy. Born in Duplin County, North Carolina in November 1841, the son of Bryan Whitfield and Penelope Simms (Sims) Herring, Herring resided in Duplin County with his parents and siblings as a school student in June 1860. He was the brother of Confederate States Navy officer, Benjamin Simms Herring. Herring resided as a farmer in Duplin County until he enlisted at age 18 on October 16, 1861 for twelve months in 1st Company I, 36th Regiment, North Carolina Troops (2nd Regiment, North Carolina Artillery) [One source indicates he initially served as a Private in Captain William S. Devane's Independent Company, North Carolina Troops]. He mustered in as a Sergeant, but later transferred as a Private to Company A, 61st Regiment, North Carolina Troops between July 8-9, 1862. He was reported on detached duty with the Signal Corps in the Cape Fear District from September 12, 1862 through April 30, 1863, probably as a telegraph operator. Herring transferred to Company F, 36th Regiment, North Carolina (2nd North Carolina Artillery) on May 18, 1863. He transferred to the Confederate States Navy and was appointed a Third Assistant Engineer on August 1, 1863. He is listed as a Third Assistant Engineer, Provisional Confederate Navy as of June 2, 1864, and was appointed Acting Second Assistant Engineer in 1864. Herring served aboard the CSS RALEIGH, CSS YADKIN, CSS NORTH CAROLINA, and CSS EQUATOR, Wilmington Station, North Carolina, 1863-1864. He is said to have served on the Richmond Station, 1864. Herring was paroled in Greensboro, North Carolina on April 28, 1865. He resided as a machinist, in 1900, with his wife, Jennie, and three children, at Water Valley, Yalobusha County, Mississippi.
[Source(s): Register; Card File; NA RG 109; North Carolina Troops I and XIV; Foenander]

Hester, John C.
Ordinary Seaman, Confederate States Navy. Hester enlisted on December 17, 1863 in Wilmington, North Carolina, for the war.
[Source(s): Card File; NA RG 45]

Hester, John Willis (Durham County[?], North Carolina)
Landsman, Confederate States Navy. Enlisted May 5, 1864 in Raleigh, North Carolina, for the war. Born circa 1836, he died on January 27, 1899, and was buried at Cedar Hill Cemetery, Durham County, North Carolina.
[Source(s): Card File; NA RG 45; Stepp, "Burials"]

Hester, Joseph Goodwyn
Master's Mate, Confederate States Navy. Hester was born in North Carolina on August 28, 1840 (other sources incorrectly show him as a native of Georgia or South Carolina). He was a mariner of note prior to the War Between the States, apparently joining the crew of the Confederate cruiser CSS SUMTER from one of her prizes. He later served as an Acting Master's Mate, and possibly a Master's Mate, under its commander Raphael Semmes, 1861-1862. He murdered Acting Midshipman William Andrews who was in command of the ship as it lay off Gibraltar in October 1862 and was subsequently sent to the Bahamas on a British ship. One source indicates he was denied entry into the Confederacy by blockading Union vessels, but obviously gained entry at some point. For some reason, he was never charged for this crime. Hester married in Columbia, South Carolina on June 18, 1864. He was captured on July 8, 1864 while serving as captain of the blockade runner, *Pocahontas*, off Charleston, South Carolina, and

sent north as prisoner of war. In 1870, he is shown as an auctioneer, residing with his wife, Josephine, in Raleigh, North Carolina. Hester applied for a United States passport on March 25, 1873. He was a member of the Methodist Church. Hester served as an agent of the Post office until November 30, 1874, and was employed, as of December 1, 1874, by General Healy "in Alabama" [?] as a Deputy Marshal and government detective engaged in "waging a war on the Ku Klux Klan of North and South Carolina" (NOTE: A newspaper report dated in October 1874, shows him as already being a United States detective. Hester came face to face with his former Confederate Navy commander, Raphael Semmes, at a Klan trial. Semmes described the incident on the CSS SUMTER to the reporter, as "a most foul and brutal murder." Described as "a young, handsome, brave and intelligent man" who was "rapidly achieving an enviable reputation…In the discharge of his duties he has made his name a terror to traitors and assassins." Between 1880 and 1900, Hester resided with his wife Josephine as a real estate dealer in Washington, D.C.
[Source(s): Foenander; Sullivan]

Hewlett, Henry C. (New Hanover County, North Carolina)
Seaman, Confederate States Navy. Hewlett enlisted on March 24, 1864 in Raleigh, North Carolina, for the war. One source shows he was conscripted on March 22, 1864 at Camp Holmes [near Raleigh, North Carolina] from Colonel Strange's 22nd Regiment, North Carolina Militia, New Hanover County, North Carolina. Description: Age 31; eyes black; hair dark; complexion dark; height 5 feet 1 ½ inch; place of birth New Hanover County, North Carolina; occupation machinist. Hewlett served as a Seaman aboard the CSS ARCTIC, Cape Fear River, North Carolina, 1863. Born circa 1833, his death date is unknown. He is buried in an unmarked grave at Masonboro Baptist Church, New Hanover County, North Carolina.
[Source(s): Card File; NA RG 45; Stepp, "Burials;" Foenander]

Hexter, George (Wilmington, New Hanover County, North Carolina)
Petty Officer, Confederate States Navy [Naval Battalion]. Name appears as signature on an Oath of Allegiance to the US subscribed and sworn to at Newport News, Virginia, June 24, 1865. Place of residence given on Oath as Wilmington, North Carolina. Description: Complexion dark; hair black; eyes dark; height 5 feet 8 inches. Oath carries remark, "Captured Drewry's Bluff, Virginia, April 6, 1865.
[Source(s): Card File; NA RG 109]

Hicks, R. (Edgecombe County, North Carolina)
Confederate States Navy. Enlisted in Wilmington, North Carolina. From Edgecombe County, North Carolina. Per WPA Groves Index, "a" Robert Hicks (10 October 1837 – 3 October 1913) is buried in Kemp Family Cemetery, Elizabethtown, Bladen County, North Carolina. Source NA RG 45 says he enlisted October 19, 1863 at Camp Holmes [near Raleigh, North Carolina] [Card File says enlisted at Wilmington, North Carolina]. Hicks served as a Landsman aboard the CSS ARCTIC, Cape Fear River, North Carolina, 1863. An "R. Hicks" served aboard the CSS NEUSE as of the ship's March – October 1864 muster roll.
[Source(s): MR, 4, p. 446; Hill, McElroy; NA RG 45; Card File; Foenander; NEUSE Roster; CMACSSN]

Hicks, William
Landsman, Confederate States Navy. Hicks enlisted in the Confederate States Navy on January 2, 1864 in Raleigh, North Carolina, for the war, and served as a Landsman aboard the CSS ARCTIC, Cape Fear River, North Carolina, 1863.
[Source(s): Card File; NA RG 45; Foenander]

Higgins, J. F. (North Carolina[?])
Seaman, Confederate States Navy. Most of Higgins' right leg was shot off at Fort Fisher, December 24 [24-25], 1864. He then underwent amputation at the upper third of the thigh.
[Source(s): "Daily Confed." (1/2/65); Card File]

Hill, James C. (Halifax County, North Carolina)
Master's Mate [Ensign], Confederate States Navy. Hill enlisted from Scotland Neck, North Carolina and served aboard the CSS ALBEMARLE as Master's Mate in North Carolina waters, 1864. His card listed a cousin, Miss Lena Smith, in Scotland Neck, North Carolina.
[Source(s): McElroy; Card File]

Hill, John
Pilot, Confederate States Navy. Hill served aboard the blockade runner "*Ella*."
[Source(s): McElroy]

Hill, John H.
Landsman, Confederate States Navy. Hill enlisted on May 11, 1864 in Raleigh, North Carolina, for the war.
[Source(s): Card File; NA RG 45]

Hill, Philin
Landsman, Confederate States Navy. Hill enlisted on September 28, 1863 at Camp Holmes [near Raleigh, North Carolina] for the war.
[Source(s): Card File; NA RG 45]

Hill, Robert (Iredell County, North Carolina)
Confederate States Navy [Naval Battalion]. Hill's name appears on a roll of Prisoners of War at Pont Lookout, Maryland, which states he was captured at Burkeville [Virginia] April 6, 1865, and confined at Point Lookout, Maryland, April 14, 1865, until released June 27, 1865. He signed an Oath of Allegiance at Point Lookout, Maryland, June 27, 1865. Hill's place of residence was listed as Iredell County, North Carolina. Description: complexion light; hair dark brown; eyes hazel; height 5 feet 11 inches.
[Source(s): Card File; NA RG 109]

Hill, R. R. (Craven County, North Carolina)
Seaman, Confederate States Navy. Hill enlisted on June 13, 1864 in Raleigh, North Carolina, for the war.
[Source(s): Card File; NA RG 45]

Hill, William
Seaman, Confederate States Navy.
Per clothing lists, Hill serve as a Seaman aboard the CSS BEAUFORT February – March 1862. His name appears on the payroll of the receiving ship CSS UNITED STATES for the period ending March 31, 1862. His name also appears on the payroll of the North Carolina Squadron for the 1st quarter of 1862 covering from January 10, 1862 - April 15, 1862. Hill transferred to the James River Squadron as of April 14, 1862.
[Source: NCCWSP]

Hill, William ("Willis") (Craven County, North Carolina)
Confederate States Navy.
Hill enlisted on January 25, 1864 in Raleigh, North Carolina, for the war. His pension claim filed on June 26, 1901, at age 78, post office Newport, Craven County, North Carolina, was approved. The application states he enlisted in the Confederate States Navy in 1863and served aboard the CSS RALEIGH. It further states he suffered from a hernia resulting "from moving cannon on board the Ram RALEIGH." A doctor's affidavit states Hill "Has large scar on right shin which breaks out into an open sore every summer. This [was] caused by a cut from a piece of copper while dismantling the RALEIGH." One-half disabled, his request for a pension was approved at the 4th Class level. Source "Foenander" lists a "William Hill" that served as a Landsman aboard the CSS ARCTIC, Cape Fear River, North Carolina, 1863, and aboard CSS RALEIGH in North Carolina and Virginia waters, 1864.
[Source(s): Card File; Pension (North Carolina); NA RG 45; Foenander]

Hilton, Cyrus (Davidson County, North Carolina)
Landsman, Confederate States Navy. Born in North Carolina in June 1843, Hilton enlisted on March 1, 1864 in Raleigh, North Carolina, for the war. He served as a Landsman aboard the CSS YADKIN, Wilmington Station, North Carolina, 1864. His pension file contains an original letter dated November 9, 1864, from Fleet Surgeon "Jeff" [illegible] Greenhow, Wilmington, North Carolina, to Flag Officer R. F. Pinkney, Commanding, authorizing Hilton a 20-day furlough due to serious illness. Reverse has note for "One Ration at Way Hospital Number 4, Goldsboro, North Carolina [signature illegible]." Hilton married in 1871 and resided as a farmer in 1880 with his wife Jane and son Mayfield (born 1870) in Thomasville, Davidson County, North Carolina. In his pension claim filed on June 25, 1906, at age 64, post office Thomasville, Davidson County, North Carolina (pension approved at 4th Class), Hilton states he "was hurt by a fall from the deck." In an earlier pension application, filed when Hilton was aged 58, and living in Thomasville, North Carolina, he stated he served at Wilmington, North Carolina. He received a disability of one-half. A pension claim filed by widow, Jane Hilton, age 72, POST OFFICE Rt. #2, Thomasville, Davidson County, North Carolina, on June 5, 1916, was approved.
[Source(s): Card File; Pension (North Carolina); NA RG 45; Foenander]

Hinshaw, G. M. [NOTE: Probably same as "Milton Hinshaw, q.v."]
Landsman, Confederate States Navy. Hinshaw enlisted on November 22, 1863 in Wilmington, North Carolina, for

the war, and served as a Landsman aboard the CSS ARCTIC, Cape Fear River, North Carolina, 1863.
[Source(s): Card File; NA RG 45; Foenander]

Hinshaw, Milton [NOTE: Probably same as "G. M. Hinshaw, q.v."]
Landsman, Confederate States Navy. Hinshaw enlisted on November 22, 1863 in Wilmington, North Carolina, for the war. Source "NA RG 45" states he enlisted on November 20, 1863 in Raleigh, North Carolina, for the war, and served as a Landsman, aboard the CSS ARCTIC, Cape Fear River, North Carolina, 1863
[Source(s): Card File; NA RG 45; Foenander]

Hinson, J. H. (Washington County, North Carolina)
Confederate States Navy. Hinson's name appears on a Roll of Prisoners of War paroled at the Provost Marshal's Office, Goldsboro, North Carolina, May 2, 1865, giving residence as Washington County, North Carolina.
[Source(s): Card File; NA RG 109]

Hinton, James
Landsman, Confederate States Navy. Hinton enlisted on August 8, 1864 in Raleigh, North Carolina, for the war.
[Source(s): Card File; NA RG 45]

Hobbs, Charles L. (Currituck County, North Carolina)
Corporal, Confederate States Army//Confederate States Navy. Hobbs was born, resided in as a sailor, and enlisted in Currituck County, North Carolina prior to enlisting at age 20 on August 1, 1861, for the war, in Company B, 8th Regiment, North Carolina State Troops. He was mustered in as a Private and promoted to Corporal on September 1, 1863. Hobbs was present or accounted for until he transferred to the Confederate States Navy on or about April 1, 1864, where he served as a Seaman aboard the CSS ALBEMARLE and at Halifax Station, mid 1864. Hobbs married Bethana O'Neal on February 9, 1868 in Currituck County, North Carolina. His post war occupations included farmer and waterman. On the 1880 census, Hobbs is indicated as being disabled with dyspepsia.
[Source(s): Card File; North Carolina Troops, IV; Foenander]

Hobbs, George W. (Currituck County, North Carolina)
Confederate States Navy. Quartermaster and Pilot. Hobbs was born circa1843 in Currituck County, North Carolina, where he resided as a sailor. Per Source NCCWSP, clothing records indicate Hobbs served as a Seaman aboard the NCS SEA BIRD from at least July 1861 – February 20, 1862. His name appears on a payroll of the North Carolina Squadron covering the period December 1, 1861 - March 31, 1862 whereon he was listed as having "run" as per the last day of the payroll. Hobbs enlisted at age 18 (another source states age 23) as a Private on August 2, 1861, for the war, in Company B, 8th Regiment, North Carolina State Troops. He is recorded as present or accounted for until he transferred to the Confederate States Navy on April 1, 1864. He served as a Quartermaster and Pilot aboard the CSS ALBEMARLE, and at the Halifax Naval Station, 1864. Source "Driver" states he also claimed service in Company A, 4th Battalion (Naval), Virginia Local Defense Troops, Richmond, Virginia. He was a member of the Pickett-Buchanan Camp, United Confederate Veterans, Norfolk, Virginia. He married Mary E. Dulin on June 21, 1866, in Currituck County, North Carolina, and was receiving a pension in Norfolk as late as July 17, 1908 at age 73.
[Source(s): Sea Bird; Register, 1983 reprint by J. M. Carroll and Company, Mattituck, New York; North Carolina Troops, IV; Driver; Foenander]; NCCWSP]

Hobbs, Julius C. (Sampson County, North Carolina)
Sergeant, Confederate States Army//Confederate States Navy(?). Hobbs served previously as a Musician in Captain William S. Devane's Independent Company, North Carolina Troops. He transferred to Company A, 61st Regiment, North Carolina Troops, on or about September 5, 1862. Mustered as a Musician, he was reduced to the ranks in November-December 1862. Reported present through April 30, 1863, he was reported on duty as a picket guard at Hilton Ferry, near Wilmington, North Carolina, from May 8 through June 30, 1863. He rejoined his company in July-August 1863 and was promoted to Corporal on September 25, 1863. Hobbs was promoted to Sergeant on April 13, 1864 and reported present through April 30, 1864. On October 19, 1864, he transferred as a Private to Company C, 63rd Regiment, North Carolina Troops (5th Regiment, North Carolina Cavalry). Issued clothing on December 28, 1864, he was captured at Aberdeen Church, Virginia, on April 3, 1865. Confined at Point Lookout, Maryland, he was released on June 13, 1865, after taking the Oath of Allegiance. Source Card File indicates Confederate States Navy service.
[Source(s): Card File; North Carolina Troops, II & XIV]

Hodder [Hardder], Humphrey (Bertie County, North Carolina)
Private, Confederate States Army//Ordinary Seaman, Confederate States Navy. Born in Bertie County, North

Carolina in 1840, Hodder was the stepson of William P. and Sarah E. Gurley. He resided and enlisted "for the war" in Washington County, North Carolina, on June 24, 1861, at age 22, as a Private in Company G, 1st Regiment, North Carolina State Troops. He was discharged on February 3, 1862 [January 1862, per source MR, I], and transferred to the Confederate States Navy [date unknown] where he served as an Ordinary Seaman aboard the CSS VIRGINIA, Hampton Roads, Virginia, 1862.

[Source(s): Card File; Foenander; MR, I; North Carolina Troops, III; Census (North Carolina), 1850; North Carolina VR; ORN 2, 1, 309]

Hodges, Henry H.

Landsman, Confederate States Navy. Hodges enlisted on May 27, 1864 in Raleigh, North Carolina, for the war. He was stationed at Battery Brooks, below Drewry's Bluff, Virginia. Hodges was discharged at Lee's surrender.
[Source(s): Card File; UDC, Faison-Hicks; NA RG 45]

Hoffman, Caleb (Gaston County, North Carolina)

Landsman, Confederate States Navy [Naval Battalion]. Hoffman was born on October 25, 1821 in Gaston County, North Carolina. He served as a Landsman aboard the CSS ARCTIC, Cape Fear River, North Carolina, 1863. His name appears as a signature to an Oath of Allegiance to the United States subscribed and sworn to at Newport News, Virginia, June 26, 1865. Place of residence given as Gaston County, North Carolina. Description: complexion dark; hair dark; eyes blue; height 5 feet 10 inches. Oath carries remark: "Captured Farmville, Virginia, April 6." Hoffman died on November 30, 1876 and was buried in Christ's Lutheran Church Cemetery, Stanley, Gaston County, North Carolina.
[Source(s): Card File; NA RG 109; Foenander; Cloninger]

Hoffman, James [North Carolina??]

Confederate States Navy. Served as a Landsman aboard the CSS ARCTIC, Cape Fear River, North Carolina, 1863.
[Source(s): ORN 2, 1, 279; Foenander]

Hoffman, Jonas (Gaston County, North Carolina [?])

Landsman, Confederate States Navy. Born on June 20, 1820, Hoffman served in the Commissary under Captain Poindexter at Wilmington, North Carolina and Drewry's Bluff, Virginia, 1864-1865, and as a member of the Naval Brigade. He died on September 5, 1901, and was buried at Holy Communion Lutheran Church, Dallas, Gaston County, North Carolina. Hoffman was married three times and has fourteen children all totaled. His first was born in 1843 and his last in 1878.
[Source(s): Stepp, "Burials;" Gaston County Veterans; Cloninger]

Holbrook, George

Private, Confederate States Army//Confederate States Navy. Holbrook transferred from the Confederate States Navy on December 26, 1863 to Company I, 41st Regiment, North Carolina Troops (3rd Regiment, North Carolina Cavalry). He transferred to Company G, 18th Regiment, North Carolina Troops (8th Regiment, North Carolina Vols.) on January 17, 1865, and is listed as a deserter as of February 20, 1865.
[Source(s): Card File; North Carolina Troops, II and VI; Foenander]

Holcomb(e), James W. (Robeson County, North Carolina)

Confederate States Navy [Naval Battalion]. Holcomb's name appears as a signature to an Oath of Allegiance to the United States subscribed and sworn to at Point Lookout, Maryland, June 28, 1865. Place of residence given as Robeson County, North Carolina. Description: complexion florid; hair dark brown; eyes hazel; height 5 feet 6 ¾ inches. His claim for a pension, filed on July 2, 1906, at age 61, listed his address as POST OFFICE Purvis, Robeson County, North Carolina. The claim, approved at the 4th Class level, states he enlisted on or about September 1863, and was wounded in the Spring of 1865 at Drewry's Bluff, Virginia, by a piece of timber falling on right shoulder and dislocating it, "More or less disabled ever since."
[Source(s): Card File; NA RG 109; Pension (North Carolina)]

Holder, Abram F.

Landsman, Confederate States Navy. Holder enlisted on April 25, 1864 in Raleigh, North Carolina, for the war.
[Source(s): Card File; NA RG 45]

Holder, Samuel W. (New Hanover County, North Carolina)

Private, Confederate States Army//Confederate States Navy(?). Holder resided in New Hanover County, North Carolina, where he enlisted at age 28, on October 13, 1861, for the war, in 2nd Company D, 36th Regiment, North

Carolina Troops (2nd Regiment, North Carolina Artillery). He was detailed as a carpenter and rafts man at Smithville, North Carolina, August 31, 1863 through August31, 1864.
[Source(s): Howard; North Carolina Troops, I]

Holland, Christopher (New Hanover County(?), North Carolina)
Private, Confederate States Marine Corps. Holland was listed as a prisoner of war, released at Washington, DC, April 12, 1865. He was furnished transportation to Wilmington, North Carolina.
[Source(s): North Carolina Troops, Doc. # 0185, p. 1 and 0299; Card File]

Holland, G. G.
Seaman, Confederate States Navy. Holland enlisted on June 13, 1864 in Raleigh, North Carolina, for the war.
[Source(s): Card File; NA RG 45]

Holland, Simpson Womack (Wake County, North Carolina)
Confederate States Navy. Holland's card reads, "There are no records unless they are in the Navy records in Washington, DC." He was a blacksmith and went to Richmond after September 19, 1864 (date of will). He died in a hospital in Richmond from an infected foot around November 17, 1864. His will was recorded in the Wake County Courthouse in February 1865. He was buried in Section W, grave No. 678, Hollywood Cemetery, Richmond, Virginia, on November 18, 1864.
[Source(s): Card File; North Carolina Troops, Doc. #0077; Trull]

Holland, W. H. (Chatham County, North Carolina)
Landsman, Confederate States Navy [Company F, Naval Battalion]. Holland enlisted on June 30, 1864 in Raleigh, North Carolina, for the war. His name appears on a roll of Prisoners of War at Point Lookout, Maryland, which states he was captured at Harper's Farm [Virginia] April 6, 1865, and confined at Point Lookout, Maryland, until released on taking the Oath of Allegiance to the United States on June 27, 1865. His place of residence was given as Chatham County, North Carolina. Description: complexion light; hair dark brown; eyes grey; height 5 feet 10 inches.
[Source(s): Card File; NA RG 45; NA RG 109]

Hollerman, Griffin
Landsman, Confederate States Navy. Hollerman enlisted on August 3, 1864 in Raleigh, North Carolina, for the war, and served as a Landsman aboard the CSS NORTH Carolina, Cape Fear River, North Carolina, 1864.
[Source(s): Card File; NA RG 45; Foenander]

Hollingsworth, Owen R. (Duplin County, North Carolina)
Private, Confederate States Army//Confederate States Navy. Born in Duplin County, North Carolina, in 1833, Hollingsworth was the son of Guilford Hollingsworth. He resided in Duplin County as a distiller prior to enlisting in New Hanover County, North Carolina at age 28 on June 25, 1861 as a Private in Company I, 18th Regiment, North Carolina Troops. He was listed as present or accounted for until transferred to the Confederate States Navy on or about April 9, 1864 by Special Order # 89. He married Mary Walker on May 2, 1865 in New Hanover County, and resided there as a farmer with his wife in Caswell, as late as 1870.
[Source(s): S. O. # 89; North Carolina Troops, VI; NA RG 109; Foenander]

Hollis, David
Seaman, 2nd Class Fireman Confederate States Navy.
Per bounty, small stores, and payroll records, Hollis served as a Seaman, aboard the CSS BEAUFORT from September 1861 – April 1862. He received a partial payment on February 13, 1862 at the Gosport Navy Yard following his service in manning Fort Cobb at the Battle of Elizabeth City on February 10, 1862. His name appears on a payroll of the North Carolina Squadron for the 1st quarter of 1862 covering from December 1, 1861 - April 15, 1862. He transferred to the James River Squadron on April 15, 1862 and served as a 2nd Class Fireman aboard the CSS BEAUFORT per the James River Squadron payroll covering from October 1, 1863 - December 15, 1863]
[Source: NCCWSP]

Holloman, James
Landsman, Confederate States Navy. Holloman enlisted on February 23, 1864 in Wilmington, North Carolina, for the war. He served as a Landsman aboard the CSS YADKIN, Wilmington, North Carolina, 1864
[Source(s): Card File; NA RG 45; Foenander]

Holloway, James Hugh (Orange [later, Durham] County, North Carolina)
Confederate States Navy. He filed a pension request on June 6, 1908 age 63, post office Gorman, Durham County, North Carolina [NOTE: Durham County, not formed until 1881]. The pension was approved at the 4th Class level. His application states he "enlisted in James River Navy on the late Merrymac [sic] commanded by Captain Pennington (?) under Admiral Simms [Semmes?], October 1864" and "Stayed until the war closed." Source Card File indicates he enlisted on October 1, 1864. A separate note in his pension file dated July 29, 1909 from the Durham County Pension Board to the State Pension board states that Holloway failed to declare on his application that he owned property in Durham County with a tax value of $900.00, and had personal property valued at $286.00 [NOTE: He may not have qualified for a pension at that time due to his level of wealth. Dudley Peed (q.v.), former member of the Confederate States Navy, was witness on his behalf. By 1931, his property valued no more than $2000.00]. He was eventually approved "S.D.P. Fourth Class." His widow Martha Holloway's August 22, 1931 application for a Widow's Pension was approved as "Class B." She stated her age as 74 years and that her husband enlisted in 1864 in Raleigh, North Carolina, in Company D, 11th Regiment, North Carolina Troops [NOTE: No record found to support his enlistment in the 11th Regiment, North Carolina Troops]. She further stated that she married him in 1898, and that he died in Durham County, North Carolina, in 1924.
[Source(s): Card File; Pensions (North Carolina); Foenander]

Holmes, Armstead
Captain's Cook, Confederate States Navy.
Holmes served as a Captain's Cook aboard the NCS CURLEW per payroll records for the 1st quarter of 1862.
[Source: NCCWSP]

Holmes, Cicero K. [R.] (Davidson County, North Carolina)
Ordinary Seaman, Confederate States Navy. Holmes was born in Davidson County, North Carolina on January 19, 1846. He enlisted at age 18 on February 18, 1864 in Raleigh, North Carolina, for the war, and served as a Landsman and Ordinary Seaman aboard the CSS NORTH CAROLINA, Cape Fear River, North Carolina, 1864. He served mostly as the Coxswain of his Captain's gig while in Wilmington. Just prior to the fall of Wilmington, Holmes and his naval comrades evacuated toward Richmond, serving at Drewry's Bluff until Richmond was evacuated. He is said to have fought at Sailor's Creek with Commodore Tucker's Brigade, and that his unit did not surrender until all the others serving under General Ewell had done so. His name appears on a roll of Prisoners of War at Point Lookout, Maryland, which states he was captured at Harper's Farm [Virginia] April 6, 1865, and confined at Point Lookout, Maryland, from April 14, 1865 until released after taking the Oath of Allegiance to the United States on June 27, 1865. He was back home by July 3, 1865. Place of residence given as Davidson County, North Carolina. Description: complexion light; hair dark brown; eyes hazel; height 5 feet 9 inches. A biographical sketch of Holmes appears in *Confederate Military History*, V. 4, p. 550. Born January 19, 1846, he died on November 27, 1913, and was buried at Macedonia Methodist Church, Davidson County, North Carolina.
[Source(s): Card File; NA RG 109; NA RG 45; CMH; Stepp, "Burials;" Foenander; *CMH*, V. 4, p. 550]

Holmes, David [Daniel]
Seaman, Confederate States Navy. Holmes enlisted on January 1, 1863 in Wilmington, North Carolina, "for three years or the war," and served as Coxswain to the flag officer aboard the CSS ARCTIC, Cape Fear River, North Carolina, 1863.
[Source(s): Card File; NA RG 45; Foenander]

Holmes, Harry (Franklin County, North Carolina)
Private, Confederate States Army//Confederate States Navy. Holmes was born in Franklin County, North Carolina, and resided in Granville County, North Carolina, where he was by occupation an engineer prior to enlisting there at age 28 on July 15, 1861, for the war, in Company D, 8th Regiment, North Carolina State Troops. He was listed as present or accounted for until he transferred to the Confederate States Navy on or about April 6, 1863.
[Source(s): Card File; North Carolina Troops, IV]

Holmes, Thomas (Washington County, North Carolina)
Confederate States Navy.
[Source(s): WCL; Darden]

Holmes, Trimigan (Trimagin; Trimagen; Termagent; Tennagant; Trinigan) (Washington County, North Carolina)
Private, Company A, Confederate States Marine Corps. Holmes was born on February 20, 1830, and resided in Washington County, North Carolina when he enlisted on October 20, 1862 [Another source says he enlisted in

Raleigh, North Carolina, on October 6, 1864]. He served on the Charleston, South Carolina, station, and was a Private of the Marine guard on board the ironclad CSS COLUMBIA to February 7, 1865. He transferred to the CSS INDIAN CHIEF on February 8, 1865. His name appears on a roll of Prisoners of War at Point Lookout, Maryland, which states that he was captured on April 6, 1865 at Farmville, Virginia. Holmes was confined at Point Lookout on April 15, 1865 and released on June 28, 1865. His name appears as a signature to an Oath of Allegiance to the United States, subscribed and sworn to at Point Lookout, Maryland, upon release on June 28, 1865. Place of residence given on Oath as Washington County, North Carolina. A claim for pension was filed on July 2, 1917 by his widow Mary Holmes, age 77, post office Creswell, Washington County, North Carolina. The claim was approved. Her pension application shows "he enlisted circa October 20, 1862, but this date cannot be confirmed." He died March 23, 1891, and was buried at the Spruill-Holmes Cemetery, Rt. 1142, at the junction with Rt. 1155, one mile out of Creswell, Washington County, North Carolina.
[Source(s): WCL; NA; North Carolina Troops, Doc. # 0185, p. 1, and 0299; Pensions (North Carolina); Card File; Stepp, "Burials;" Darden; Donnelly-ENL]

Holmes, William
Landsman, Confederate States Navy. Holmes enlisted on April 25, 1864 at either Halifax or Plymouth for the war. He served on the CSS ALBEMARLE [?], and on the Halifax Station, 1864.
[Source(s): Card File; NA RG 45; PCNMC]

Holshouser, Paul (Rowan County, North Carolina)
Confederate States Navy [Naval Battery]. Holshouser's name appears as a signature to an Oath of Allegiance to the United States, subscribed and sworn to at Point Lookout, Maryland, June 27, 1865. Place of residence given as Rowan County, North Carolina. Description: complexion dark; hair dark; eyes blue; height 5 feet 10 inches.
[Source(s): Card File; NA RG 45]

Holsman, James [New Hanover County, North Carolina)
Private, Confederate States Navy. Holsman's name appears on a register of Confederate States Army General Military Hospital Number 4, Wilmington, North Carolina, being admitted February 26, 1864 with "Syphilis primativa" and returned to duty May 27, 1864. Post office given as Wilmington, North Carolina.
[Source(s): Card File; NA RG 45]

Holt, Henry [North Carolina??]
Landsman, Confederate States Navy. Holt served as a Landsman aboard the CSS ARCTIC, Cape Fear River, North Carolina, 1863.
[Source(s): Foenander; ORN 2, 1, 279.]

Holt, John N.
Landsman, Confederate States Navy. Holt enlisted on December 17, 1863 in Raleigh, North Carolina, for the war. He served as a Landsman, CSS ARCTIC, Cape Fear River, North Carolina, 1863.
[Source(s): Card File; NA RG 45; Foenander]

Honeycutt, Alfred B. (Cabarrus County, North Carolina)
Landsman ["Corps mate" (?)], Confederate States Navy. Honeycutt enlisted on June 11, 1864 in Raleigh, North Carolina, for the war. He served on board the CSS INDIAN CHIEF. His name appears as a signature on an Oath of Allegiance to the United States subscribed and sworn to at Point Lookout, Maryland, June 27, 1865. Place of residence given as Cabarrus County, North Carolina. Description: Complexion dark; hair dark brown; eyes dark hazel; height 5 feet 11 ½ inches. Born November 1, 1828, he died on September 25, 1901, and was buried at St. Stephens Lutheran Church, Cabarrus County, North Carolina.
[Source(s): Card File; NA RG 45; NA RG 109; Stepp, "Burials"]

Hooker, Daniel S. (Tyrrell County, North Carolina)
Private, Confederate States Army//Confederate States Navy. Hooker was born in Tyrrell County, North Carolina, where he resided as a farmer prior to enlisting there at age 20 on May 16, 1861 as a Private in Company L, 12th Regiment, North Carolina Troops (2nd Regiment, North Carolina Volunteers). Holmes was listed as present or accounted for until he transferred to Company A, 32nd Regiment, North Carolina Troops, in October 1861. He was present or accounted for until wounded in the shoulder and/or left leg and captured at Gettysburg, Pennsylvania, July 1-5, 1863. He was hospitalized in Gettysburg until September 14, 1863 when he was transferred to a hospital in Baltimore, Maryland. He was paroled in Baltimore on September 25, 1863, and received for exchange at City

Point, Virginia, on September 27, 1863. Reported absent wounded through December 1863, company records do not indicate whether he returned to duty. He transferred to the Confederate States Navy on April 5, 1864. He served as a coal heaver aboard the CSS VIRGINIA II, 1864-1865.
[Source(s): Card File; NA RG 45; North Carolina Troops, V and VIII; *ORN* 2, 1, 311; Foenander]

Hoole, James Lingard
Acting Master, Lieutenant, Confederate States Navy.
Born in Alabama, Hoole commanded the NCS EDWARDS prior to serving as a 2nd Lieutenant Commanding the CSS FORREST as part of the fleet under Commodore Lynch that participated in the fighting at Roanoke Island, February 7-8, 1862.
[Source(s): McElroy; Card File; NCCWSP]

Hooper, Richard W.
Coxswain, Seaman, Quarter Gunner, Confederate States Navy.
Hooper served as a Coxswain aboard the NCS FANNY as of that ship's muster roll dated October 8, 1861. The payroll of the NCS CURLEW dated November 20, 1861 serving as a Seaman. By that ship's 1st quarter of 1862 payroll, he was serving as a Quarter Gunner. His name appears on the receiving ship UNITED STATES' payroll ending March 31, 1862.
[Source: NCCWSP]

Hooten, George
2nd Cabin Boy, Confederate States Navy. Hooten enlisted on April 25, 1864 in Halifax or Plymouth, North Carolina, for the war.
[Source(s): Card File; NA RG 45]

Hope, Alfred (North Carolina?)
Landsman, Confederate States Navy. Hope enlisted on April 13, 1864 in Kinston, North Carolina, for three years or the war. He served aboard the CSS NEUSE as of the ship's March – October 1864 muster rolls.
[Source(s): Card File; NA RG 45; NEUSE Roster; CMACSSN]

Hope, James Barron (Virginia/Pasquotank County, North Carolina)
Commodore's Secretary, Confederate States Navy. Born in Norfolk, Virginia on March 23, 1829, Hope graduated from the College of William and Mary with an A. B. degree in 1847. He practiced law in Elizabeth City, North Carolina, and was elected Commonwealth's Attorney (Virginia) in 1856. Hope enlisted in the United States Navy in 1856 and served until his resignation in 1861. Hope was appointed Commodore's Secretary from North Carolina and served aboard the CSS CONFEDERATE STATES, 1861-1862. Appointed Commandant's Clerk, September 1, 1862, Hope served at the Richmond and Charlotte Naval Stations, 1862. Appointed Captain, Confederate States Army, Hope served on the staff of General Joseph E. Johnston, and was paroled at Greensboro, North Carolina, April 28, 1865. A postwar newspaper editor, in Norfolk, Virginia, Hope died in Portsmouth, Virginia on September 15, 1887. His papers are in the possession of the Virginia Historical Society.
[Source(s): Driver]

Hopkins, James B.
Seaman, Acting Master, Confederate States Navy.
Payroll records for the CSS BEAUFORT indicate Hopkins served aboard that ship as an Acting Master from at least September 1861 – March 1862 as a member of the North Carolina Squadron. Hopkins enlisted on December 5, 1863 in Wilmington, North Carolina, for the war, and served as a Seaman aboard the CSS ARCTIC, Cape Fear River, North Carolina, 1863. Source "Foenander" lists a "J. B. Hopkins" who served as an Acting Master, CSS BEAUFORT, September 1861 - April 1862, operating in North Carolina and Virginia waters ("James Hopkins" and "John B. Hopkins," may be the same person).
[Source(s): Card File; NA RG 45; *ORN* 2, 1, 281; Foenander; NCCWSP]

Hopkins, John B. [North Carolina??] [See "James B. Hopkins"]
Confederate States Navy. Hopkins served as a Pilot aboard the CSS ALBEMARLE, 1864. He was involved in the attack on Plymouth, North Carolina, April 20, 1864. He was highly praised by the CSS ALBEMARLE's commander, J. W. Cooke, for his handling of the vessel during its engagement in May 1864 (Source "Foenander" states "John B. Hopkins," "James Hopkins," and "J.B. Hopkins" may all be the same person). Source also references

an article on the CSS ALBEMARLE, on page 2 of the [Richmond, Virginia] "Sentinel" of Monday, May 23, 1864. [Source(s): Foenander; ORN 1, 9, 657 & 771, ORN 1, 10, 718, and ORN 2, 1, 274; see also article on CSS ALBEMARLE, on page 2 of the [Richmond, Virginia] Sentinel, of Monday, May 23, 1864.]

Hopkins, S. D.
Landsman, Confederate States Navy. Hopkins enlisted on July 25, 1864 in Raleigh, North Carolina, for the war.
[Source(s): Card File; NA RG 45]

Horn, J.
Landsman, Confederate States Navy. Horn enlisted on August 31, 1864 in Raleigh, North Carolina, for the war.
[Source(s): Card File; NA RG 45]

Horn, Jonathan (Wake County, North Carolina [?])
Landsman, Confederate States Navy. Horn enlisted on February 4, 1864 in Raleigh, North Carolina, for the war. His name appears on Registers of Confederate States Army General Military Hospital Number 4, Wilmington, North Carolina, which state he was admitted March 31, 1864 with "diarrhea acuta" and returned to duty April 20, 1864. However, register carries the remark, "Died but accounted for as returned to duty." Post office given as Camp Holmes, North Carolina.
[Source(s): Card File; NA RG 109]

Horne, G. W.
Landsman, Confederate States Navy. Horne enlisted on June 11, 1864 in Raleigh, North Carolina, for the war, serving as a Landsman aboard the CSS ARCTIC, Cape Fear River, North Carolina, 1863, and aboard the CSS ALBEMARLE, and at the Halifax Station, 1864.
[Source(s): Card File; NA RG 45; *ORN* 2, 1, 274 & 279; Foenander]

Horney, Alson G.
Landsman, Confederate States Navy. Horney enlisted on March 1, 1864 in Raleigh, North Carolina, for the war.
[Source(s): Card File; NA RG 45]

Horton, C. R.
Landsman, Confederate States Navy. Horton enlisted on June 6, 1864 in Raleigh, North Carolina, for the war.
[Source(s): Card File; NA RG 45]

Horton, John W.
Seaman, Confederate States Navy.
Records indicate Horton served as a Seaman aboard the CSS SEA BIRD as part of the North Carolina Squadron from July 1861 – February 1862. He was promoted to Ship's Cook on December 2, 1861. He received an overcoat on February 20, 1862. Captured in the Battle of Elizabeth City and carried to Roanoke Island, he was paroled there on February 12, 1862 and returned to Elizabeth City, North Carolina. Horton received a partial payment on February 18, 1862 at Gosport Navy Yard following the sinking of the CSS SEA BIRD at Elizabeth City on February 10, 1862. His name appears on a North Carolina Squadron payroll for the 1st quarter of 1862 covering from December 1, 1861 - April 15, 1862 as of which date he is listed as "on parole."
[Source: NCCWSP]

Hoskins [Hoskin], Ellis Newton (Guilford County, North Carolina).
Confederate States Navy. Hoskins was born on November 29, 1829 in Guilford County, North Carolina, and enlisted in the Confederate States Navy at the age of 32. He saw service as a Landsman aboard the CSS ARCTIC on the Cape Fear River, 1863, and participated in the engagement at Fort Fisher. He died on June 2, 1892 in Winston-Salem, North Carolina.
[Source(s): McElroy; Card File; Foenander]

Hotchkiss, Seth Augustus (York District, South Carolina)
Private, Confederate States Army//Confederate States Navy. Hotchkiss was born in the York District of South Carolina, about 1843 [*1920 United States Census* shows state of birth as Georgia] and resided in South Carolina as a farmer. He enlisted at age 18 in Mecklenburg County, North Carolina on April 3, 1861 as a Private in Company B, 13th Regiment, North Carolina Troops [Source "Foenander" indicates that Hotchkiss' obituary in the *New York Times* of Sunday, April 15, 1934 states that he was a veteran of the 53rd North Carolina Infantry, that he was

captured during the retreat from Gettysburg, in July 1863, and that he spent eighteen months in the Union prison at Fort Delaware]. Hotchkiss transferred to the Confederate States Navy on February 15, 1862, for duty on the CSS VIRGINIA (MERRIMAC). He married in 1878 and resided as a carton maker, in 1910, with his wife, Margaret, in New Haven, Connecticut. Indicated to have been an arms expert, Hotchkiss amassed a fortune as a contractor for the Winchester Repeating Arms Company. He retired about 1914 and died as the result of a fall from a three-story window at the home of his daughter, Mrs. Mary Maher, in New Haven, April 14, 1934. [Source http://hotchkissfamily.lbbhost.com/CWC.html state that when the MERRIMAC "was blown up," Seth went back to the Army and was promoted to 2nd Corporal at age 20 upon reenlistment in Company H, 11th Regiment, North Carolina Troops. While serving in the 11th Infantry, he was captured at Gettysburg after Pickett's Charge and finished the war in the Elmira, New York, POW camp. He was listed as a Private upon discharge from the Elmira. He owned one slave in 1850]. Family # 143-128-4

[Source(s): Card File; MR, I; North Carolina Troops, V; Foenander; Hotchkiss Family]

House, W. R.
Private, Confederate States Marine Corps. House enlisted in Raleigh, North Carolina, on November 14, 1864. He served on the Charleston, South Carolina station, and was a Private of the Marine guard on board the ironclad CSS COLUMBIA to February 7, 1865.
[Source(s): North Carolina Troops, Doc.# 0299; Card File]

Howard, Charles
Seaman, Confederate States Navy.
Per a bounty roll dated January 16, 1862, Howard served as a Seaman aboard the CSS BEAUFORT until his transfer to the CSS RALEIGH on March 18, 1862. His name appears on a payroll of the North Carolina Squadron for the 1st quarter of 1862 covering from February 14, 1862 - April 15, 1862 on which date he transferred to the James River Squadron.
[Source: NCCWSP]

Howard, Henry
Pilot, Confederate States Navy. Served aboard the blockade runner "*Fannie*."
[Source(s): McElroy; Card File]

Howard, James
Landsman, Confederate States Navy. Howard enlisted on June 6, 1864 in Raleigh, North Carolina, for the war.
[Source(s): Card File; NA RG 45]

Howard, W. [William H.?]
Ordinary Seaman, Confederate States Navy. Howard enlisted on June 1, 1863 in Wilmington, North Carolina, for the war. He may be the same "William H. Howard" who served as an Ordinary Seaman and Seaman aboard the CSS NORTH CAROLINA, Cape Fear River, North Carolina, 1864.
[Source(s): Card File; NA RG 45; *ORN* 2, 1, 294 – 296; Foenander]

Howell, J.
Confederate States Navy(?).
A "J. L. Hatch," identified as "North Carolina Naval Hospital," is buried in the Seaman's Burial Ground, Ashley River, Charleston, South Carolina, date of death listed as August 10, 1864.
[Source(s): SBG]

Hubble, Peter
Seaman, Confederate States Navy.
Hubble served previously aboard the EMPIRE in the Virginia Navy. He served as a Seaman aboard the CSS BEAUFORT from September 1861 - March 1862 per clothing, bounty, and small stores lists for the ship. He received a partial payment on February 13, 1862 at Gosport Navy Yard following his service in manning Fort Cobb at Elizabeth City on February 10, 1862. His name appears on a North Carolina Squadron payroll for the 1st quarter of 1862 covering from December 1, 1861 - April 15, 1862 on which date he transferred to the James River Squadron and continued to serve as a Seaman aboard the CSS BEAUFORT, James River Squadron per the squadron's payroll for October 1, 1863 - December 15, 1863.
[Source: NCCWSP]

Hudgins, Steve W. (Mathews County, Virginia)
"Sailor," Confederate States Navy. Source "Driver" states he was "born Mathews circa 1837 County" [sic]. He enlisted in the 36th North Carolina Regiment ("Driver" states "not on muster rolls") and transferred to the Confederate States Navy per pension application. He was receiving a pension in Mathews County, Virginia, on May 26, 1910, at age 73.
[Source(s): Driver]

Hudleson (Huddleson), J. M. (Rutherford County, North Carolina)
Landsman, Confederate States Navy.
Hudleson enlisted on October 17 [26], 1863 in Wilmington, North Carolina. He served aboard the CSS ARCTIC, Cape Fear River, North Carolina, 1863, and aboard the CSS RALEIGH, in North Carolina and Virginia waters, 1864.
[Source(s): MR, 4, p. 446; Card File; NA RG 45; Foenander; BRGS]

Hudleston, J. W. (or "I. W.") [NOTE: May be same as "J. M. Hudleston"]
Landsman, Confederate States Navy. Hudleston enlisted on October 26, 1863 at Camp Holmes [near Raleigh, North Carolina].
[Source(s): Card File; NA RG 45]

Hudson, Henry (Guilford County, North Carolina)
Confederate States Navy. Hudson enlisted on September 15, 1863 and served on the CSS NORTH CAROLINA. His claim for a pension filed July 7, 1902, age 59, post office Greensboro, Guilford County, North Carolina, was disallowed. A claim filed on June 24, 1911, age 66, post office Guilford College, Guilford County, North Carolina, was also disallowed.
[Source(s): Card File; Pensions (North Carolina)]

Huffman, Thomas (Burke County, North Carolina)
Private, Confederate States Army//Confederate States Navy. Huffman resided in Burke County, North Carolina, as a farmer prior to his enlistment in Catawba County, North Carolina, at age 36, on February 2, 1863, for the war, in Company F, 55th Regiment, North Carolina Troops. He was reported absent without leave on October 25, 1863, but apparently returned at an unspecified date. He transferred to the Confederate States Navy on or about April 3, 1864.
[Source(s): Card File; North Carolina Troops, XIII; Foenander]

Hufham, John J.
Landsman, Confederate States Navy. Hufham enlisted on September 5, 1863 in Wilmington, North Carolina, for the war.
[Source(s): Card File; NA RG 45]

Huggins, Cohen H. (Pender County, North Carolina)
Confederate States Navy. Huggins filed a pension application on July 3, 1905, age 74, post office Long Creek, Pender County, North Carolina. He was wounded when "kicked by a cannon while in the war and had an abscess afterwards from the effects of the bruise [,] could not do anything for a long time on account of it." His pension was approved at the 4th Class level. W. W. Larkin was a witness on his application [NOTE: No indication of his service in the Confederate States Navy].
[Source(s): Card file; Pensions (North Carolina); Foenander]

Hullender, D. D. (Cleveland County, North Carolina)
Private, Confederate States Army//Confederate States Navy. Hullender was born in York District, South Carolina, but resided in Cleveland County, North Carolina, as a farmer where he enlisted in at age 21 on October 1, 1861 as a Private in Company H, 34th Regiment, North Carolina Troops. He was reported absent without leave on August 2, 1862 and listed as a deserter and dropped from the rolls in July-August 1863. The Roll of Honor indicates he "joined the Navy contrary to orders while on sick leave;" however, records of the Confederate States Navy do not indicate that he served therein. No further records.
[Source(s): Card File; North Carolina Troops, IX; Foenander]

Humble, Alfred (Guilford County, North Carolina)
Landsman, Confederate States Navy. Humble was born in North Carolina in November 1827, married in 1855, and enlisted on March 5, 1864 in Raleigh, North Carolina, for the war. He served as a Landsman aboard the CSS ALBEMARLE, and on the Halifax Station, 1864. His pension application file contains his original parole dated

May 2, 1865. He was listed as a "Priv [Private] Navy Department." His pension application, dated June 8, 1908, at age 80, post office Liberty, Guilford County, North Carolina, states he enlisted in the Confederate States Navy in February 1864 and "I was a cripple and conscripted and taken to Camp Homes [sic] and sent from there to Halifax to the Navy Yard to work in the Smith Shop then we went Hamilton finished vessel [CSS ALBEMARLE] there then Captain Cook then [sic] the Yanks Blew us up then I was taken Sick and finaly [sic] sent home on Furlough." Doctor's statement with application states Humble had no wounds but is "crippled in feet" and has other health problems. His pension was approved as 4th Class.
[Source(s): Card File; NA RG 45; Foenander]

Hunter, Thomas T., Jr.
Captain's Clerk, Confederate States Navy.
Per ship's payroll documents, Hunter served as a Captain's Clerk aboard the CSS CURLEW (North Carolina Squadron) as early as November 20, 1861 – the 1st quarter of 1862. Per source Moebs, Hunter was appointed from Maryland and discharged on February 12, 1862. He was appointed an Acting Master's Mate, Provisional Navy, on June 2, 1864, and Master's Mate on September 29, 1864. Source Moebs indicates Hunter was stationed aboard the CSS FLORIDA, 1863 - 1864, was captured by the USS WACHUSETT at Bahia, Brazil on October 7, 1864, and imprisoned at Fort Warren prisoner of war camp from where he was released on February 1, 1864.
[Source: NCCWSP; Moebs]

Hunter, Thomas T., Sr.
Commander, Confederate States Navy.
Born in Virginia, Hunter was a Commander, United States Navy until his resignation on June 10, 1861. He was placed in charge of the naval defenses, Norfolk Navy Yard, Virginia, 1861 – 1862. He was placed in command of the expedition for the defense of North Carolina (North Carolina Squadron) 1861 and served as the Captain of the CSS CURLEW per the ship's payroll records for November 20, 1861 - 1st quarter of 1862. From this command he was sent west to command the CSS GAINES, Mobile Squadron, 1862. Hunter was made a Commander in the Confederate States Navy on October 23, 1862, to rank from March 26, 1861. He commanded the CSS CHICORA on the Charleston Station, 1863 – 1865. On June 2, 1864 he was promoted to the rank of Commander, Provisional Navy, to rank from May 13, 1863. Hunter was captured on April 6, 1865 at the Battle of Sailor's Creek, Virginia and imprisoned at Fort Warren Union prisoner of war camp from which he was released after taking the Oath of Allegiance to the Union on July 24, 1865.
[Source(s): NCCWSP; Moebs]

Hunter, William W.
Midshipman, Confederate States Navy.
Hunter was born in Maryland and appointed a Midshipman from Maryland on August 16, 1861. Curlew Ordered to report to Commander Hunter [NOTE: likely his father] by Flag Officer French Forrest on February 20, 1862 for duty on the CSS OLD DOMINION. Per source Moebs, Hunter served aboard the receiving ship CSS UNITED STATES and the CSS CURLEW on the Richmond Station, 1861 – 1862, and the CSS GAINES, Mobile Squadron, 1862 – 1863. He died on February 4, 1863.
[Source(s): NCCWSP; Moebs]

Hurn, Atles
Landsman, Confederate States Navy. Hurn enlisted on August 10, 1864 in Raleigh, North Carolina, for the war.
[Source(s): Card File; NA RG 45]

Hutson [Hudson], Henry
Landsman, Confederate States Navy. Hutson [Hudson] enlisted on December 10, 1863 in Raleigh, North Carolina, for the war, and served as a Landsman aboard the CSS ARCTIC, Cape Fear River, North Carolina, 1863.
[Source(s): Card File; NA RG 45; ORN 2, 1, 277; Foenander]

Hutter, William C.
Midshipman, Confederate States Navy.
Served as a Midshipman aboard the CSS FANNY. He was killed in action on March 8. 1862 while serving aboard the CSS RALEIGH.
[Source: NCCWSP]

Hyde, Wm. C.
Seaman, Confederate States Navy. Hyde enlisted in the Confederate States Navy on June 13, 1864 in Raleigh, for

the war.
[Source(s): Card File; NA RG 45; Duke Papers]

Hyman, Joseph (Martin County, North Carolina)
Private, Confederate States Army//Seaman, Confederate States Navy. Hyman was born in Martin County, North Carolina, where he resided as a carpenter prior to enlisting in Pasquotank County, North Carolina, at age 22 on May 4, 1861 as a Private in Company. L, 17th Regiment, North Carolina Troops (1st org.). He was present or accounted for until transferred to the Confederate States Navy on October 4, 1861. He served as a Seaman aboard the CSS CURLEW from at least November 20, 1861 – first quarter of 1862. His name appears on a payroll of the receiving ship CSS UNITED STATES ending March 31, 1862.
[Source(s): Card File; North Carolina Troops, VI; NCCWSP]

Inglehart, O. S. (North Carolina?)
Assistant Surgeon, Confederate States Navy. "Fold3, USN Resignees" lists Inglehart having served in the United States Navy as an Assistant Surgeon and having been appointed to the same rank in the Confederate States Navy on January 23, 1862. No doctor, physician, or surgeon named "O. S. Inglehart," "Englehard or other variant spelling was found in the Federal Census of 1860.
[Source(s): Fold3, USN Resignees; Census (US), 1860]

Ingold, Francis D.
Landsman, Confederate States Navy. Ingold enlisted on November 15, 1863 (another source says November 9, 1863) as a Landsman in Wilmington, for the war, and served aboard the CSS ARCTIC, Cape Fear River, North Carolina, 1863.
[Source(s): NA, RG 45; McElroy; *ORN* 2, 1, 277; Foenander]

Ingram, James W. (Davidson County, North Carolina)
Private, Confederate States Army//Confederate States Navy. Ingram resided in Davidson County, North Carolina, as a miner until he enlisted there at age 21 on May 14, 1861 as a Private in Company I ("Lexington Wildcats"), 14th Regiment, North Carolina Troops. He was present or accounted for until he transferred to the Confederate States Navy on or about April 5, 1864.
[Source(s): McElroy; North Carolina Troops, V]

Ives, E. H.
Seaman, Confederate States Navy.
Per a ship's log entry of August 1, 1861 of the NCS ELLIS, Ives served as a Seaman aboard that ship beginning of that date through May 1862. His name appears on the payroll of the receiving ship CSS UNITED STATES ending March 31, 1862. Ives served aboard the CSS VIRGINIA and appeared on her final payroll (April 1, 1862 - September 30, 1862) as a Seaman. He served at Drewry's Bluff as a Seaman per that post's payroll for the period April 1, 1863 - June 30, 1863.
[Source: NCCWSP]

Ives, Edward [Edmund] T. (Camden County, North Carolina)
Private, Confederate States Army//Landsman, Confederate States Navy. Ives previously served as a Private in Captain G. G. Luke's Independent Company. He was assigned to 1st Company H, 32nd Regiment, North Carolina Troops, in September 1861, while a Prisoner of War at Fort Columbus, New York Harbor, or at Fort Warren, Boston Harbor, Massachusetts. Ives was paroled at Fort Warren on December 11, 1861 and transferred for exchange. Listed as present or accounted for until the company was disbanded on April 2, 1862, he enlisted in Camden County, North Carolina, at age 55 on July 7, 1863, for the war, in Company B, 68th Regiment, North Carolina Troops. He transferred to the Confederate States Navy on April 5, 1864 and served as a Landsman aboard the CSS ALBEMARLE, and at the Halifax Station, 1864. [Source "North Carolina Troops" states "May have served previously (under the name of Edmond Ives) as Private in 1st Company H, 32nd Regiment, North Carolina Troops].
[Source(s): McElroy; North Carolina Troops, IX and XV; Foenander]

Ivey, Norton
Seaman, Confederate States Navy. Ivey enlisted on September 22, 1863 as a Seaman in the Confederate States Navy in Wilmington, North Carolina (another source says he enlisted on September 9, 1863 at Camp Holmes, near

Raleigh, North Carolina, as a "substitute"). Ivey served as a Seaman aboard the CSS ARCTIC, 1863 and the CSS NORTH CAROLINA, 1864.
[Source(s): MR, 4, p. 446; McElroy; NA, RG 45; St. Armand; Foenander; *ORN* 2, 1, 276 & 294]

Jackson, E. P.
Landsman, Confederate States Navy. Jackson enlisted as a Landsman in the Confederate States Navy on March 21, 1864 in Raleigh, for the war.
[Source(s): McElroy; NA, RG 45]

Jackson, Enoch (New Hanover County, North Carolina)
Confederate States Navy. Jackson enlisted on March 18, 1864 at age 19 in the Confederate States Navy. Another source states he was conscripted on March 18, 1864 at Camp Holmes from Colonel Strange's 22nd Regiment, North Carolina Militia, New Hanover County, North Carolina. Description: Age 19; eyes grey; hair light; complexion light; height 5 ft. 8 in.; place of birth South Carolina; occupation blacksmith.
[Source(s): McElroy; NA, RG 45; Roster, 22nd Regiment, North Carolina Militia]

Jackson, James (New Hanover County, North Carolina)
Private, Confederate States Army/detailed to Confederate States Navy. Jackson enlisted in 2nd Company D, 36th Regiment, North Carolina Troops (2nd Regiment, North Carolina Artillery) at age 29 on October 28, 1861 for the war. Present or accounted for through June 1862 when he was detailed "to work on a gunboat."
[Source(s): North Carolina Troops, I]

Jackson, John D.
Ordinary Seaman, Confederate States Navy. Jackson enlisted on June 22, 1863 in Wilmington as an Ordinary Seaman.
[Source(s): McElroy; NA, RG 45]

Jackson, John W. (Craven County, North Carolina)
Private, Confederate States Army//Ordinary Seaman, Confederate States Navy. Jackson resided in Craven County, North Carolina, where he enlisted at age 30 on November 21, 1861 as a Private in Company K, 31st Regiment, North Carolina troops. He failed to report for duty with his company by reason of having "joined the navy." A "J. W. Jackson" enlisted on June 22, 1864, as an Ordinary Seaman, for the war, and served aboard the CSS FANNY in Wilmington, December 1861. His name appears on North Carolina Squadron payroll covering the period December 1, 1861 - February 28, 1862 on which he is annotated as having "run" at some point during the pay period.
[Source(s): McElroy; NA, RG 45; North Carolina Troops, VIII; Foenander; NCCWSP]

Jackson, W. T.
Confederate States Navy. Jackson served in Company C, 1st Regiment, North Carolina Troops. He was transferred to the Confederate States Navy by Special Order # 89.
[Source(s): S.O. #89]

Jackson, William Congreve
Acting Midshipman, Confederate States Navy.
Born in and appointed from Virginia as an Acting Midshipman, United States Navy, Jackson resigned that position on April 20, 1861. He served in the Virginia Navy, and was appointed an Acting Midshipman in the Confederate States Navy on June 11, 1861. He served on the receiving ship CSS UNITED STATES in 1861 and was serving as an Acting Midshipman aboard the CSS ELLIS when mortally wounded on February 10, 1861 during the Battle of Elizabeth City.
[Source(s): NCCWSP; Moebs]

Jackson, William T. (Rowan County, North Carolina)
Private, Confederate States Army//Confederate States Navy. Jackson resided in Gold Hill, Rowan County, North Carolina, where he enlisted at Camp Hill at age 22 on September 6, 1862, for the war, as a Private in Company C, 18th Regiment, North Carolina Troops. He was listed as present of accounted for until he deserted on August 1, 1863. Jackson returned to duty prior to March 1, 1864 and was transferred to the Confederate States Navy on or about April 3, 1864.
[Source(s): McElroy; North Carolina Troops, VI]

Jacobs, Joseph L. (New Hanover County, North Carolina)
Landsman, Confederate States Navy. Jacobs enlisted from New Hanover County, North Carolina as First Lieutenant in the 18th Regiment, North Carolina Troops. He was wounded and given a furlough. While on furlough, Jacobs enlisted as a Landsman, Confederate States Navy, on July 7, 1864 in Raleigh, for the war, under the name "J. L. Jacobs." He served aboard the CSS PATRICK HENRY. Jacobs died in the Naval Hospital at Charleston, South Carolina, on August 31, 1864. The attending surgeon pronounced his cause of death as a diseased heart. Identified as "North Carolina Naval Hospital," Jacobs is buried in the Seaman's Burial Ground, Ashley River, Charleston, South Carolina.
[Source(s): McElroy; NA, RG 45; SBG; McElroy]

James, H. L. (Warren County, North Carolina)
Landsman, Confederate States Navy. James enlisted in the Confederate States Navy on October 8, 1863 (another source gives date as October 11, 1863) in Wilmington, North Carolina, for the war. He served as a Landsman aboard the CSS ARCTIC, 1863, and aboard the CSS RALEIGH, 1864. Another source gives his date and place of enlistment as October 12, 1863 at Camp Holmes).
[Source(s): MR, 4, p. 446; McElroy; NA, RG 45; Foenander]

James, William H. (Pasquotank County, North Carolina)
Private, Confederate States Army//Landsman, Confederate States Navy.
James was born in Pasquotank County, North Carolina, where he resided as a farmer prior to enlisting in Currituck County, North Carolina, at age 20 on May13, 1861 as a Private in Company E, 17th Regiment, North Carolina Troops (1st Organization). He was present or accounted for until he transferred to the Confederate States Navy prior to July 28, 1861, where he served as a Landsman aboard the CSS FANNY from at least October 8, 1861 – December 20, 1862. His name appears on a North Carolina Squadron payroll covering the period December 1, 1861 - March 31, 1862 on which he is listed as having "run" at some point during the period.
[Source(s): McElroy; North Carolina Troops, VI; Foenander; NCCWSP]

Jarrell, John F. (NC) (County unknown)
Private, Confederate States Navy(?). Jarrell is listed as having served in the "Navy Dept., North Carolina, Naval Battalion, North Carolina Infantry."
[Source(s): USCWS]

Jarvis, W. W. (also W. R.)
Seaman, Confederate States Navy.
Jarvis served aboard the CSS FANNY per its muster roll dated October 8, 1861. According to clothing, muster, and payroll records, he remained aboard the ship through at least December 13, 1861. His name appears on the payroll of receiving ship CSS UNITED STATES ending March 31, 1862. He is shown on the North Carolina Squadron payroll for the 1st quarter of 1862 covering the period from December 1,1861 - February 28, 1862. On this payroll he is listed as having "run" at some time during the pay period.
[Source: NCCWSP]

Jasper, John
Officer's Steward, Confederate States Navy.
Jasper served in the North Carolina Squadron aboard the NCS WINSLOW per that ship's muster roll of July - November 1861. He was discharged on December 1, 1861.
[Source: NCCWSP]

Jenkins, E. (Onslow County, North Carolina)
Confederate States Navy. Jenkins enlisted in the Confederate States Navy on July 1, 1863 in Wilmington, North Carolina.
[Source(s): MR, 4, p. 446]

Jenkins, Edward (New Hanover County, North Carolina [?]) [NOTE: May be same as "E. Jenkins," q.v.]
Landsman, Confederate States Navy. Jenkins died on March 17, 1889, and was buried at Bellevue, New Hanover County, North Carolina.
[Source(s): Stepp, "Burials"]

Jenkins, J. B.
> Landsman, Confederate States Navy. Jenkins enlisted as a Landsman on August 29, 1864 in Raleigh for the war.
> [Source(s): McElroy; NA, RG 45]

Jenkins, Israel B. (Richmond County, North Carolina)
> Confederate States Navy. Born in North Carolina in 1828, Jenkins enlisted in August 1863 in the Confederate States Navy and "served under Capt. Johnson." He resided in 1880 as a farm laborer with his wife Patsy Jane Jenkins and six children (eldest child born 1871) at Mineral Springs, Richmond County, North Carolina. His application for a Confederate pension was filed on July 6, 1905 (1908?) at age 77. He listed his post office as Samson, Richmond County, North Carolina. On his approved pension, he stated he received no wounds during the war.
> [Source(s): McElroy; Pensions (North Carolina); Foenander]

Jenkins, John A. (Halifax County, North Carolina)
> Confederate States Navy. A pre-war fisherman, Jenkins enlisted on January 24, 1862. He was on detached service to Fort Fisher, Brunswick Point, as of April 1, 1862. He was declared unfit for active service and detailed to hospital duty on April 3, 1863. "Soldier has distortion to head of femur from ulceration of the cartilage, also partial dislocation." He was admitted on April 4, 1863, to General Hospital #4, Wilmington, North Carolina, with "erysipelas," but returned to duty on April 19, 1963.
> [Source(s): Edge]

Jenkins, Joseph S. (Brunswick County, North Carolina)
> Private, Confederate States Army//Seaman, Confederate States Navy. Jenkins resided in Brunswick County, North Carolina, and enlisted at age 18 in May 1861 [Source "North Carolina Troops" states July 18, 1861] at Camp Howard in Company C., 30th Regiment, North Carolina Troops. He was present or accounted for until April 5, 1864, when he was transferred to the Confederate States Navy. Jenkins served as a Seaman aboard the tugboat CSS BEAUFORT on the James River.
> [Source(s): North Carolina Troops, VIII; McElroy; Foenander]

Jenkins, Neill
> Landsman, Confederate States Navy. Jenkins enlisted on November 25, 1864 in Raleigh, for the war, and served as a Landsman aboard the CSS RALEIGH in North Carolina and Virginia waters, 1862 – 1864.
> [Source(s): McElroy; NA, RG 45; Foenander]

Jenkins [Jinkins], Paul
> Seaman, Confederate States Navy. Jenkins enlisted on March 25, 1863 as a Seaman in Wilmington for three years, or the war. He served aboard the CSS ARCTIC, Cape Fear River, North Carolina, 1863.
> [Source(s): McElroy; NA, RG 45; Foenander]

Jerry, Waddel (Robeson County, North Carolina)
> Confederate States Navy. Jerry was conscripted on March 18, 1864, at Camp Holmes, from Colonel Morally's 58th Regiment, North Carolina Militia, from Robeson County, North Carolina. Description: Age 44; eyes grey; hair dark; complexion dark; height 5ft. 6 ½ in.; place of birth Robeson County, North Carolina; occupation farmer.
> [Source(s): McElroy; NA, RG 45; Roster, 58th Regiment, North Carolina Militia]

Jiggitts, Lewis M.
> Confederate States Navy. Jiggitts was born in North Carolina, about 1837, and resided in 1860 as a planter in Madison County, Mississippi. He served aboard CSS LIVINGSTON. He married Laura Robinson, in Madison County, Mississippi, on October 1, 1866.
> [Source(s): Foenander]

Johnson, A. J.
> Landsman, Confederate States Navy. Johnson enlisted on November 5, 1863 in Wilmington for the war.
> [Source(s): McElroy; NA, RG 45]

Johnson, A. N.
> Landsman, Confederate States Navy. Johnson enlisted on April 25, 1864 in Raleigh, for the war.
> [Source(s): McElroy; NA, RG 45]

Johnson, David (Pender County, North Carolina)
    Confederate States Navy. Johnson enlisted at the Navy Yard in Wilmington, North Carolina. Pension claim was filed by his widow, Lizzie Jane Johnson, age 70, Post office Willard, Pender County, North Carolina, on July 5, 1926. The pension request was approved.
    [Source(s): McElroy; Pensions (North Carolina)]

Johnson, Evan
    Landsman, Confederate States Navy. Johnson enlisted on March 20, 1864, in Raleigh, for the war.
    [Source(s): McElroy; NA, RG 45]

Johnson, H. B. (Rockingham County, North Carolina)
    Confederate States Navy. Johnson enlisted in the Confederate States Navy on August 2, 1863 in Wilmington, North Carolina.
    [Source(s): MR, 4, p. 446]

Johnson, J. A. (Alamance County, North Carolina)
    Confederate States Navy. Johnson's name appears on a register of Confederate States Army General Military Hospital Number 4 Wilmington, North Carolina, dated February 25, 1864, which gives his disease as "feb cont con" and post office as Snow Camp [Alamance County, North Carolina].
    [Source(s): McElroy; NA, RG 109]

Johnson, J. H. (Northampton County, North Carolina)
    Confederate States Navy. Johnson's name appears as a signature to an Oath of Allegiance to the United States, subscribed and sworn to at Newport News, Virginia, June 30, 1865. Place of residence given on Oath as Northampton, North Carolina, and described as follows: complexion light; hair light; eyes blue; height 5 ft. 6 in. The Oath carries the remark: "Captured at Richmond, April 3, 1865."
    [Source(s): McElroy; NA, RG 109]

Johnson, James
    Confederate States Navy. Formerly a Private, Company D, 32nd Regiment, North Carolina Troops, Johnson may be the same "James Johnson" that served as a Paymaster's Clerk on the Wilmington Station, North Carolina, 1864.
    [Source(s): McElroy; *ORN* 2, 1, 323]

Johnson, James B.
    Acting Master, Confederate States Navy.
    No further information.
    [Source: NCCWSP]

Johnson, Jefferson
    Landsman, Confederate States Navy. Johnson enlisted on February 4, 1864, in Raleigh, for the war.
    [Source(s): McElroy; NA, RG 45]

Johnson, Jesse N. (Northampton County, North Carolina) [Sources "North Carolina Troops" and "Foenander" list middle initial as "H"]
    Private, Confederate States Army//Confederate States Navy. Johnson was born in Northampton County, North Carolina, where he resided as a farmer prior to enlisting at age 35 on February 11, 1862, as a Private in Company D, 32nd Regiment, North Carolina Troops. He was present or accounted for until wounded in the thigh and captured at Gettysburg, Pennsylvania, July 1-5, 1863. He remained in a hospital in Gettysburg until transferred as a Prisoner of War to David's Island, New York Harbor, July 17-24, 1863. Paroled at David's Island, Johnson was received at City Point, Virginia, on August 28, 1863, for exchange. Reported absent sick through December 1863, Johnson transferred to the Confederate States Navy on April 5, 1864.
    [Source(s): McElroy; North Carolina Troops, IX; Foenander]

Johnson, John (Forsyth County, North Carolina)
    Confederate States Navy. Johnson enlisted in the Confederate States Navy on October 2, 1863 in Wilmington, North Carolina.
    [Source(s): MR, 4, p. 446]

Johnson (Johnston), John
Paymaster, Confederate States Navy. Born in Ireland, Johnson was a citizen of and appointed from North Carolina as a Paymaster in the North Carolina Navy from North Carolina. Johnson served in the United States Navy from August 28, 1850, until his resignation as Paymaster, United States Navy on April 20, 1861. He was appointed Paymaster, Confederate States Navy, by the Confederate States Congress on June 21, 1861 (also shown as October 23, 1862) to rank from March 26, 1861. Source ".D. H. Hill" states that he was one of the first officers commissioned as a Paymaster in the North Carolina Navy Johnson served at the Gosport Navy Yard, 1861, and at the Naval Works, Charlotte, 1862-1864. He was paroled on May 3, 1865 in Charlotte, North Carolina.
[Source(s): Foenander; McElroy; Register; Journal; CWDTS; Dudley; OCSN; ONWR]

Johnson, John
Landsman, Confederate States Navy. Johnson enlisted on October 9, 1863 at Camp Holmes, near Raleigh, North Carolina. [NOTE: May be same as "Jno. Johnson" or "John Johnson of Forsyth County, North Carolina."
[Source(s): McElroy; NA, RG 45]

Johnson, John B.
Confederate States Navy. Johnson was appointed from North Carolina as an Acting Third Assistant Engineer on April 13, 1863. He resigned on October 7, 1863. He is said to have served on the CSS NORTH CAROLINA, Wilmington Station, 1863.
[Source(s): Foenander; Register; *ORN* 2, 1, 323]

Johnson, Jno.
Ordinary Seaman, Confederate States Navy. Johnson enlisted on October 11, 1863, in Wilmington, for the war.
[NOTE: May be same as John Johnson of Forsyth County, North Carolina].
[Source(s): McElroy; NA, RG 45]

Johnson, Lindsey
Landsman, Confederate States Navy. Johnson enlisted on August 29, 1864 in Raleigh, North Carolina for the war.
[Source(s): McElroy; NA, RG 45]

Johnson, M. W. (Union County, North Carolina)
Confederate States Navy. Johnson was conscripted on March 25, 1864 at Camp Holmes, near Raleigh, North Carolina, from Colonel McKane's 82nd Regiment, North Carolina Militia, Union County, North Carolina. Description: Age 38; eyes hazel; hair red; complexion florid; height 5 ft. 11 ½ in.; place of birth South Carolina; occupation farmer.
[Source(s): McElroy; NA, RG 45; Roster, 82nd Regiment, North Carolina Militia]

Johnson, Neil(l) A. (Robeson County, North Carolina)
Landsman, Confederate States Navy. Johnson enlisted on October 11, 1863 [Source "Pensions (North Carolina)" states October 8, 1863], in Wilmington, North Carolina, for the war, and served as a Landsman aboard the CSS ARCTIC, 1863. Another source states he enlisted October 12, 1863 at Camp Holmes, near Raleigh, North Carolina. An "N. A. Johnson" served aboard the CSS NEUSE as of the ship's March – October 1864 muster rolls. He filed for a pension on July 2, 1923, at age 78, listing his post office as St. Pauls, Robeson County, North Carolina. Pension approved.
[Source(s): McElroy; NA, RG 45; Pensions (North Carolina); Foenander; NEUSE Roster; CMACSSN]

Johnson, Rufus A.
Landsman, Confederate States Navy. This name canceled on roll with the remark: "Detailed of Army."
[Source(s): McElroy; NA, RG 45]

Johnson, T. H.
Landsman, Confederate States Navy. Johnson enlisted on December 19, 1863, in Wilmington, for the war, and served as a Landsman aboard the CSS ARCTIC, Cape Fear River, North Carolina, 1863. Another source has "T. H. Johnson" as enlisting "November 13, 1863."
[Source(s): McElroy; NA, RG 45; Foenander]

Johnson, Thomas (also Johnston)
Seaman, Gunner's Mate Confederate States Navy.

Johnson served aboard the NCS WINSLOW per its muster roll of July - November 1861 [NOTE: The NCS WINSLOW was lost near Ocracoke Inlet on November 7, 1861 after striking a submerged hull]. He served as a Gunner's Mate aboard the NCS SEABIRD in February 1862. He was captured in the Battle of Elizabeth City and carried to Roanoke Island where he was paroled on February 12, 1862 and returned to Elizabeth City, North Carolina. Johnson was received aboard receiving ship CSS UNITED STATES ON February 17, 1862 as "destitute" while on parole. He received a partial payment on February 18, 1862 at Gosport Navy Yard following the sinking of the NCS SEA BIRD during the Battle of Elizabeth City on February 10, 1862. His name appears on the North Carolina Squadron payroll for the 1st quarter of 1862 (December 1, 1861 - April 15, 1862) on which his name is annotated as "on parole" as of April 15, 1862. [Source(s): NCCWSP; Moebs]

Johnson, Thomas P. (Rowan County, North Carolina)
Paymaster's Clerk, Confederate States Navy. Served aboard the CSS ALBEMARLE. Later transferred to Fort Fisher, North Carolina.
[Source: Rumple]

Johnson, Wiley (Wayne County, North Carolina)
Private, Confederate States Marine Corps. Johnson was a Prisoner of War released at Washington, DC, on April 12, 1865. His place of residence was listed as "Goldsboro." Transportation furnished for him to Goldsboro, North Carolina.
[Source(s): North Carolina Troops, Doc. # 0185, p. 2 and 0299; Card File]

Johnson, William
Confederate States Navy. Johnson enlisted on January 21, 1863 in Wilmington, North Carolina, for three years or the war.
[Source(s): McElroy; NA, RG 45]

Johnson, William F. (New Hanover County, North Carolina)
Private, Confederate States Army//Confederate States Navy. Johnson enlisted in New Hanover County, North Carolina, at age 27 [Source "Foenander" gives age as 30] in 2nd Company D, 36th Regiment, North Carolina Troops (2nd Regiment, North Carolina Artillery) on October 28, 1861 for the war. He was present or accounted for until transferred to the Confederate States Navy on February 18, 1863. Johnson transferred from the Navy back to the Army to 3rd Company B, 36th Regiment, North Carolina Troops (2nd Regiment, North Carolina Artillery) in early 1864, and to Company E of this regiment on July 18, 1864. He was captured at Fort Fisher, January 15, 1865 and confined at Elmira, New York, until exchanged in early March 1865. Records indicate that he was admitted to a hospital in Richmond, Virginia, on March 9, 1865, where he died on March 21, 1865 [Another source says Johnson died in North Carolina on January 15, 1865].
[Source(s): North Carolina Troops, I; McElroy; NA RG 109; Foenander]

Johnson, William R. (Johnston County, North Carolina)
Landsman, Confederate States Navy. Johnson's name appears on a roll of Prisoners of War at Point Lookout, Maryland, which states he was captured at Richmond on April 3, 1865, and confined at Point Lookout on April 14, 1865, until released on June 28, 1865. His name appears as a signature to an Oath of Allegiance to the United States, subscribed and sworn to at Point Lookout, Maryland, June 28, 1865. Place of residence given on Oath as Johnston County, North Carolina. Description: complexion dark; hair brown; eyes hazel, height 5 ft. 8 ½ in.
[Source(s): McElroy; NA, RG 109]

Johnston (Johnson), Bartlett Shipp (Mecklenburg County, North Carolina)
Midshipman, Confederate States Navy. Born in either Baltimore, Maryland (1844) or Charlotte, North Carolina (1845). Johnston was a resident of Baltimore, Maryland, and the brother of Confederate General Robert Daniel Johnston. [NOTE: One source shows he served in the 23rd Regiment, North Carolina Troops, but no record of this is found]. He was appointed Acting Midshipman, Confederate States Navy, from North Carolina, in December 1863 (another source gives date as October 1863), and Midshipman, 1864 (another source gives date as June 2, 1864). He served aboard the CSS VIRGINIA II, James River Squadron, 1864-1865 (another source gives his report date as January 1865). Johnston served in Tucker's Naval Brigade, and was captured at Sailor's Creek, Virginia, April 6, 1865. Sent to Johnson's Island as a Prisoner of War, he was released on taking the Oath on June 18, 1865 at Johnson's Island, Ohio. Place of residence given on Oath as Charlotte, North Carolina, age 18, described as follows: complexion florid; hair red; eyes hazel; height 5 feet 8 inches. A post-war resident of Baltimore, Maryland, Johnston was a member of the Army and Navy Society, Maryland Line Association, in 1905. He died in Riderwood,

Maryland, on June 26, 1927, and was buried at Green Mount Cemetery, Baltimore.
[Source(s): Register; McElroy; NA, RG 109; Driver; Lincoln Roster; Academy; Foenander; Hoke Camp]

Johnston, Henry F. (South Carolina)
Private, Confederate States Army//Confederate States Navy. Johnston was born in South Carolina where he resided as a farmer prior to enlisting at age 17 in Mecklenburg County, North Carolina on April 3, 1861 as a Private in Company B, 13th Regiment, North Carolina Troops. He was present or accounted for until he transferred to the Confederate States Navy on February 15, 1862, for duty aboard the CSS VIRGINIA (MERRIMAC).
[Source(s): McElroy; North Carolina Troops, V; Foenander; MR, I]

Johnston, J. (New Hanover County, North Carolina)
Ordinary Seaman (?), Confederate States Navy. Johnston enlisted in the Confederate States Navy in Wilmington, North Carolina. Source "Foenander" lists "J. Johnston" as "John Johnson," Ordinary Seaman, CSS ARCTIC, 1863.
[Source(s): MR, 4, p. 446; St. Armand; Foenander]

Johnston, Jeff A. (Alamance County, North Carolina)
Landsman, Confederate States Navy. Johnston's name appears on a register of Confederate States Army General Military Hospital Number 4, Wilmington, North Carolina, being admitted February 25, 1864, with "febris contina communis," and returned to duty March 21, 1864. His post office was listed as Snow Camp, North Carolina. He may be the same as "Jefferson Johnston" who served as a Landsman aboard the CSS ARCTIC, Cape Fear River, North Carolina, 1863, and later aboard the CSS RALEIGH, in North Carolina and Virginia waters, 1864 [per source "Foenander"].
[Source(s): Foenander; McElroy; NA, RG 109]

Johnston [Johnson], John (North Carolina)
Confederate States Navy. Johnston was born in and appointed from North Carolina as an Acting Midshipman, Confederate States Naval Academy, on May 2, 1863. He was appointed Midshipman, Provisional Confederate States Navy, June 2, 1864. Johnston served aboard the CSS PATRICK HENRY, 1863, and later the Confederate States steamers CSS RALEIGH and CSS YADKIN, Wilmington Station, North Carolina, 1863 - 1864.
[Source(s): Foenander; Register; Academy]

Johnston, M. Newton (Burke County, North Carolina) [middle initial also incorrectly shown as "W"]
Landsman, Confederate States Navy. Johnston enlisted on July 1, 1864 [Source "Foenander" gives date as "March 25, [1864(?), at age 38." A claim for pension filed by his widow, Mrs. J. B. Johnston, age 63, on June 29, 1903, listing post office at Chesterfield, Burke County, North Carolina (pension approved) states he enlisted on or about July 1, 1864 [Source "NA RG 45" states he enlisted March 28, 1864, at Raleigh, for the war] in Charlotte, North Carolina, and was serving aboard the CSS ALBEMARLE when it was sunk. Also mentions "Captain Poindexter."
[Source(s): McElroy; Foenander; Pensions (North Carolina); NA, RG 45]

Johnston, Neill, A. (New Hanover County, North Carolina)
Johnson enlisted in the Confederate States Navy on October 8, 1863 in Wilmington, North Carolina.
[Source(s): MR, 4, p. 446; St. Armand]

Johnston, S. S.
Landsman, Confederate States Navy. Johnson enlisted on June 11, 1864 in Raleigh, for the war.
[Source(s): McElroy; NA, RG 45]

Johnston, Thomas Pinkney (Rowan County, North Carolina)
Landsman/Paymaster's Clerk/Assistant Paymaster, Confederate States Navy. Born on September 8, 1845, Johnston enlisted on September 15, 1863, in Raleigh, North Carolina. Johns[t]on, of Salisbury, enlisted for the Confederate States Navy at age 16 and was sent to Edwards' Ferry to act as commissary for the builders of the CSS ALBEMARLE. He is also listed by other sources as "Assistant Paymaster" and "Paymaster's Clerk" for the CSS ALBEMARLE. He was honorably discharged in Guilford County, North Carolina, at the close of the war (One source says he surrendered six months after the war in Salisbury, North Carolina). He served as a Ship's Steward aboard the CSS ALBEMARLE, and on Halifax Station, 1864 [per source "Foenander"]. Wife: Mrs. Jennie Kate Johnston, Salisbury, North Carolina; Sons: Thomas Edgar Johnston, Salisbury, North Carolina, and Reb. Thomas Pinkney Johnston, Christiansburg, Virginia; Daughter: Mrs. Anna Miller, Deland, Florida. Johnston was a member of the United Confederate Veterans and resident of Florida as late as September 1929. He died on October 12, 1939,

and was buried in Lutheran Cemetery, Rowan County, North Carolina.
[Source(s): McElroy; "Booker," p.79-80; Rumple; Stepp, "Burials;" Foenander]

Johnston, Thomas (Rowan County, North Carolina)
Landsman, Confederate States Navy. One source states Johnston enlisted on March 7, 1864 in Raleigh, for the war, while another source states he was conscripted on March 7, 1864, at Camp Holmes (near Raleigh), from the 76th Regiment, North Carolina Militia, Rowan County, North Carolina. Description: Age 18; eyes blue; hair light; complexion fair; height 5 ft. 10 in.; place of birth Rowan County, North Carolina; occupation student.
[Source(s): McElroy; NA, RG 45; Roster, 76th Regiment, North Carolina Militia]

Johnston, William (Brunswick County, North Carolina)
Confederate States Navy. Johnston enlisted in the Confederate States Navy in Wilmington, North Carolina.
[Source(s): MR, 4, p. 446]

Johnston, William F. (New Hanover County, North Carolina)
Seaman, Confederate States Navy. Johnston is said to have served aboard the CSS ARCTIC, 1863-1864, and the CSS NORTH CAROLINA. 1864.
[Source(s): MR, 4, p. 443; Foenander; St. Amand]

Joiner, A. (Robeson County, North Carolina)
Confederate States Navy. Joiner's name appears as signature to an Oath of Allegiance to the United States, subscribed and sworn to at Newport News, Virginia, on June 30, 1865. Place of residence given on Oath as "Robinson" County, North Carolina. Described: complexion light; hair light; eyes blue; height 5 ft. 2 in.; Oath also carries the remark: "Captured near Farmville, Virginia, April 6 [1865]."
[Source(s): McElroy; NA, RG 109]

Jolly, W. F. (Bladen County [?], North Carolina)
Seaman, Confederate States Navy. A "W. A. Jolly," born about 1847, appears on the 1860 Census of North Carolina. A newspaper entry states Jolly was burned by the bursting of a gun at Fort Fisher, December 25 [24th, per source "FSW" (12/24/64)], 1864.
[Source(s): Daily Confed. (1/2/65); "FSW" (12/24/64); Census (NC), 1860]

Jolly, William H.
Confederate States Navy. Jolly enlisted on May 27, 1864 in Raleigh, for the war.
[Source(s): McElroy; NA, RG 45]

Jones, Absalom (Person County, North Carolina)
Corporal, Company B, Confederate States Marine Corps. Captured at Harper's Farm, Virginia, on April 6, 1865, Jones' name appears as a signature to an Oath of Allegiance to the United States, subscribed and sworn to at Point Lookout, Maryland, on occasion of his release on June 28, 1865. His place of residence on the Oath was given as Person County, North Carolina. Description as follows: Complexion dark; hair brown; eyes hazel; height 5 feet 4 ½ inches. He was captured at Harper's Farm on April 6, 1865.
[Source(s): NA; North Carolina Troops, Doc. # 0185, p. 1, and 0299; Card File]

Jones, D. C. (Johnston County, North Carolina)
Landsman, Confederate States Navy. Jones enlisted in the Confederate States Navy on October 25, 1863 (October 26, 1863 at Camp Holmes) in Wilmington, North Carolina. He served as a Landsman aboard the CSS ARCTIC, Cape Fear River, North Carolina, 1863 and aboard the CSS RALEIGH in North Carolina and Virginia waters, 1864. His name appears on registers of Confederate States Army General Military Hospital Number 4, Wilmington, North Carolina, being admitted March 31, 1864, with "febris remittens" and returned to duty April 12, 1864. His post office was listed as Smithfield, North Carolina. His card (Source "McElroy") carries the remark: "Furloughed from Navy."
[Source(s): MR, 4, p. 446; McElroy; NA, RG 45, NA, RG 109; RCWV; Foenander]

Jones, E. Holt
Assistant Surgeon, Confederate States Navy.
Jones served as an Assistant Surgeon aboard the NCS SEA BIRD during February 1862. He was captured in the Battle of Elizabeth City, carried to Roanoke Island on February 10, 1862, and paroled there on February 12, 1862.

He returned to Elizabeth City, North Carolina.
[Source: NCCWSP]

Jones, E. J. R. (may be Edwin T.R. Jones)
Seaman, Carpenter's Mate, Confederate States Navy.
Born in Maryland in 1840, Jones resided in Baltimore, Maryland as a carpenter in 1860. His name appears on the North Carolina Squadron payroll dated December 23, 1861. He was promoted from Seaman to "c. mate" (Carpenter's Mate) on December 24, 1861. The promotion warranted a salary of $25.00 a month. He served as a Carpenter's Mate aboard the NCS SEA BIRD as early as February 20, 1862 at which time clothing records indicate he was issued an overcoat. Captured in the Battle of Elizabeth City, Jones was carried to Roanoke Island where he was paroled on February 12, 1862 and returned to Elizabeth City, North Carolina. He received a partial payment on February 18, 1862 at Gosport Navy Yard following the sinking of the SEA BIRD at Elizabeth City on February 10, 1862 [Source Moebs indicates she was sunk after being rammed by the USS COMMODRE PERRY]. Jones was received aboard receiving ship CSS UNITED STATES on February 17, 1862 as "destitute" while on parole. He appears on the North Carolina Squadron payroll for the 1st quarter of 1862 covering from December 23, 1861 - April 15, 1862 on which he is listed as "on parole."
[Source(s): NCCWSP; Moebs]

Jones, Elija
Landsman, Confederate States Navy. Jones enlisted on May 18, 1864 in Raleigh, for the war.
[Source(s): McElroy; NA, RG 45]

Jones, Felix (Camden County, North Carolina[?])
Corporal(?), Confederate States Army//Confederate States Navy. Jones was born in North Carolina in January 1841. He previously served as a Private in Captain G. G. Luke's Independent Company. Assigned to 1st Company H, 32nd Regiment, North Carolina Troops, in September 1861, while a Prisoner of War at Fort Columbus, New York Harbor, or at Fort Warren, Boston Harbor, Massachusetts. Paroled at Fort Warren on December 11, 1861 and transferred for exchange. Present or accounted for until the company was disbanded on April 2, 1862. He enlisted in Camden County, North Carolina at age 22 on July 7, 1863, for the war, as a Private in Company B, 68th Regiment, North Carolina Troops, but was probably mustered in with the rank of Corporal. On April 5, 1864, he transferred to the Confederate States Navy.
[Source(s): McElroy; North Carolina Troops, IX and XV; Foenander]

Jones, G. W. (Craven County, North Carolina) [NOTE: May be same as "George W. and/or George W. N. Jones, q.v.].
Confederate States Navy. Jones enlisted in the Confederate States Navy in Wilmington, North Carolina.
[Source(s): MR, 4, p. 446]

Jones, George
Seaman, Confederate States Navy.
Served aboard the CSS CORA per her payroll of the 1st quarter of 1862. He served from December 21, 1861 - March 31, 1862. Jones' name appears on the North Carolina Squadron payroll for the 1st quarter of 1862 covering from December 31, 1861 - March 31, 1862. [Source: NCCWSP]

Jones, George W. (Craven County, North Carolina) [NOTE: May be same as "George W. and/or George W. N. Jones, q.v.]
Private, Confederate States Army//Seaman, Confederate States Navy. Jones resided and enlisted in Craven County, North Carolina on June 14, 1861, at age 29, in Company K, 2nd Regiment, North Carolina State Troops. [NOTE: May be same as "George W. N. Jones" who served in Company C, 19th Regiment, North Carolina Troops (2nd Regiment., North Carolina Cavalry) and Company L, 17th Regiment, North Carolina Troops (1st Organization), and/or "G. W. Jones" who served in Company K, 2nd Regiment, North Carolina State Troops. A "G. W. Jones" of Craven County, North Carolina enlisted in the Confederate States Navy in Wilmington, North Carolina (per source MR, 4, p. 446)]. Jones transferred to the Confederate States Navy on May 7, 1862, and served as a Seaman on the CSS ARCTIC, 1862 [Foenander].
[Source(s): McElroy; North Carolina Troops, III; MR, 1 and 4; Foenander; *ORN* 1, 23, 703]

Jones, George W. [NOTE: May be same as "George W. and/or George W. N. Jones, q.v.]
Seaman, Confederate States Navy. Jones served aboard the screw steamer CSS FANNY, North Carolina, 1861 – 1862.
[Source(s): Foenander; *ORN* 2, 1, 285]

Jones, George W. [NOTE: May be same as "George W. and/or George W. N. Jones, q.v.]
Ship's Steward, Confederate States Navy. Jones served aboard the steam gunboat CSS YADKIN, Wilmington, North Carolina, 1864.
[Source(s): Foenander; *ORN* 2, 1, 313.]

Jones, George W. N. (Perquimens County, North Carolina) [NOTE: May be same as "George W. and/or George W. N. Jones, q.v.]
Private, Confederate States Army//Confederate States Navy. Born in Perquimans County, North Carolina, in 1837, Jones resided a Private in Company L, 17th Regiment North Carolina Troops (1st Organization). He is listed as present or accounted for until captured at Roanoke Island, February 8, 1862. Jones was paroled at Elizabeth City, February 21, 1862, and exchanged in August 1862. He transferred to Company C [Source "North Carolina Troops, VI" gives the company as "D"], 19th Regiment, North Carolina Troops (2nd North Carolina Cavalry) prior to September 1, 1862. Present or accounted for until he transferred to the Confederate States Navy on April 21, 1864 [Source "Foenander" gives date as April 12, 1864].
[Source(s): North Carolina Troops, II & VI; Census (North Carolina), 1860; Foenander]

Jones, Griffin
Seaman, Quarter Gunner
Confederate States Navy. Jones was born in North Carolina in 1815 and resided in the Narrow Shore District in Currituck County, North Carolina as a "waterman." He enlisted for the war on August 25, 1861 to serve aboard the CSS RALEIGH from approximately September 2, 1861, or before. He appears on documents as a Seaman aboard the CSS RALEIGH through April 1862 and as a member of the North Carolina Squadron from February 21, 1862 through April 15, 1862. Jones transferred to the James River Squadron on April 15, 1862 and served at Drewry's Bluff as a Quarter Gunner from April 1, 1863 through at least June 30, 1863.
[Source: NCCWSP; Census (NC), 1860]

Jones, Henry
Landsman, Confederate States Navy. Enlisting on February 23, 1864 in Raleigh, for the war, Jones served aboard the CSS NORTH CAROLINA, Cape Fear River, North Carolina, 1864.
[Source(s): McElroy; Foenander; NA, RG 45; *ORN* 2, 1, 294, 295 & 297]

Jones, J. Pembroke
First Lieutenant, Confederate States Navy. Jones served on the CSS RALEIGH, an ironclad ship with four guns, on the Cape Fear River under Flag Officer W.F. Lynch.
[Source(s): McElroy]

Jones, James J.
Landsman, Confederate States Navy. Jones enlisted on April 13, 1864 in Raleigh, for the war.
[Source(s): McElroy; NA, RG 45]

Jones, James S. (North Carolina)
Confederate States Navy. Jones was born in Virginia [Source "Foenander" states, "Register 1864 shows place of birth as North Carolina"] and appointed from Florida. He served as Chief Clerk, Office of Orders and Details, Confederate States Navy Department, 1862 – 1863. He served later as Register Clerk, Office of Orders and Detail, Confederate States Navy, 1864.
[Source(s): Foenander]

Jones, John
Officer's Clerk, Confederate States Navy.
Per payroll records, Jones served as an Officer's Clerk aboard the CSS RALEIGH at least during the 1st quarter of 1862.
[Source: NCCWSP]

Jones, John (Jack)
Seaman, Gunner's Mate Confederate States Navy.
A resident of Norfolk County, Virginia, Jones served as a Seaman, aboard the NCS EDWARDS beginning on July 25, 1861, per his shipping articles. From payroll and muster records, he served aboard the NCS EDWARDS from July – October 30, 1861. He transferred to the CSS CURLEW on September 30, 1861 as a Seaman, but by the November 20, 1861 payroll he is listed as a Gunner's Mate, remaining so at least through the 1st quarter of 1862. He

last appears on the payroll of the receiving ship CSS UNITED STATES ending March 31, 1862. He is said to have served on the CSS VIRGINIA.
[Source: NCCWSP]

Jones, John W. (Camden County, North Carolina)
Confederate States Navy. Jones was born in Camden County, North Carolina where he resided as a farmer until he enlisted at age 18 in Company A, 8th Regiment, North Carolina State Troops on July 25, 1861 for the war. Captured at Roanoke Island, North Carolina on February 8, 1862, he was paroled in Elizabeth City, North Carolina on February 21, 1862, and exchanged in August 1862. He was present or accounted for until wounded at Morris Island, Charleston Harbor, South Carolina on August 28, 1863. He rejoined his unit November – December 1863 and was present of accounted for until killed near Drewry's Bluff, Virginia on May 14, 1864. Source "McElroy" indicated a "John W. Jones" served in the Confederate States Navy. There was a significant presence of Confederate sailors and marines at Drewry's Bluff.
[Source(s): McElroy; NCT, Vol. IV]

Jones, Minor S.
Master's Mate, Confederate States Navy.
[Source(s): Pension (FL)

Jones, Nelson
Seaman, Confederate States Navy.
Jones served as a Seaman aboard the CSS JUNALUSKA per a muster roll in the North Carolina State Archives and a payroll for the period June 1861 - August 20, 1861.
[Source(s): NCCWSP; North Carolina Archives]

Jones, Wiley (Wily) (Johnston County, North Carolina)
Landsman, Confederate States Navy. Born in Johnston County, North Carolina, Jones resided there as a farmer until he enlisted on March 24, 1864 in Raleigh, at age 43, for the war. Another source says conscripted March 18, 1864, at Camp Holmes, from Colonel Heath's 41st Regiment, North Carolina Militia, Johnston County, North Carolina. Description: age 43; eyes grey; hair dark; complexion dark; height 5 ft. 8 in.; place of birth Johnston County, North Carolina; occupation farmer. He served as a Landsman, aboard the CSS ALBEMARLE, and on the Halifax Station, 1864.
[Source(s): McElroy; NA, RG 45; Foenander]

Jones, William F. (Perquimans County, North Carolina)
1st Sergeant/Confederate States Navy. Born and resided in Perquimans County, North Carolina, as a draftsman prior to enlisting there on May 16, 1861 in Company F, 27th Regiment, North Carolina Troops. Mustered as First Sergeant and was present or accounted for until discharged February 11, 1862 by reason of "Promotion in the navy." Discharge certificate gives his age as 21. Entered the Confederate States Navy as a 3rd Assistant Engineer on February 2, 1862. He served on the ironclad ram CSS CHICORA (which operated in Charleston Harbor, South Carolina), 1862 – 1864. He was promoted to 2nd Assistant Engineer on May 21, 1863.
[Source(s): McElroy; North Carolina GENWEB; North Carolina Troops, VIII; Foenander]

Jones, William H.
Confederate States Navy. Jones' card (Source "McElroy") reads "Blockade Service Navy(?)." Born September 22 [Source "Stepp" – September 23, 1824], 1827, Jones died on November 2 [Source "Stepp" – November 7, 1875], 1875. He was buried in Cedar Grove Cemetery, New Bern, North Carolina.
[Source(s): McElroy; Gravestone Records, v. I, p. 275; Stepp, "Burials"]

Jordan, John W.
Landsman, Confederate States Navy. Jordan enlisted on May 27, 1864 in Raleigh, for the war.
[Source(s): McElroy; NA, RG 45]

Jordan, Vincent (Wake County, North Carolina/Alabama)
Private, Company C, Confederate States Marine Corps. Conscripted in Talladega County, Alabama on March 6, 1863, Jordan transferred to the Confederate States Marine Corps, March 18, 1863. Records indicate he was paid in Richmond, Virginia, May 8, 1863. He was assigned to schooner "Gallego" on June 17, 1863, and was at the Navy yard opposite Rocketts, Richmond, Virginia, from September 3, 1863 until the 3rd Quarter of 1864. Jordan was discharged on a Surgeon's Certificate of Disability, Naval Hospital, Richmond, Virginia October 27, 1864. He is

listed as paid through November 7, 1864. He was born in Wake County, North Carolina, and was age 52 in 1864. He is described as having been a farmer with hazel eyes, dark hair, fair complexion, and 5' 11" tall.
[Source(s): Donnelly-ENL]

Jourdan, Alvin
Landsman, Confederate States Navy. Jourdan enlisted on June 11, 1864 in Raleigh, for the war.
[Source(s): McElroy, NA, RG 45]

Joyner, A.
Landsman, Confederate States Navy. Joyner enlisted on October 26, 1863, at Wilmington, for the war. Source "Foenander" lists an "Abraham Joyner" who served as a Landsman aboard the CSS ARCTIC, Cape Fear River, North Carolina, 1863, and later aboard the CSS RALEIGH, in North Carolina and Virginia waters, 1864. [NOTE: May be same as Abram Joyner].
[Source(s): McElroy; NA, RG 45; ORN 2, 1, 277, 278 & 302; Foenander]

Joyner, Abram (Robeson County, North Carolina)
Confederate States Navy. Joyner enlisted in the Confederate States Navy on September 4, 1863 in Wilmington, North Carolina.
[Source(s): MR, 4, p. 446]

Joyner, Baram
Landsman, Confederate States Navy. Joyner enlisted on October 21, 1863 at Camp Holmes (near Raleigh).
[Source(s): McElroy; NA, RG 45]

Joyner, Mills (Hertford County, North Carolina)
Confederate States Navy. Born in North Carolina in September 1840, Joyner married in 1864 and enlisted on April 5, 1864. He filed a claim for pension on June 22, 1912 at age 72, listing his post office as Murfreesboro, Hertford County, North Carolina. His approved pension states that he enlisted Confederate States Navy on the CSS FREDERICKSBURG on or about April 5, 1864. He was listed as having partial paralysis amounting to "more than three-fourths." He resided as a blacksmith and wheelwright, from about 1880 to 1910, with his wife Elisabeth, and children, at Murfreesboro, Hertford County, North Carolina
[Source(s): McElroy; Pensions (North Carolina); Foenander]

Kaulke, Elbert
Seaman, Ordinary Seaman, Confederate States Navy.
A member of the crew of the ship "Transit" captured by the NCS WINSLOW who joined NCS WINSLOW's crew at New Bern, North Carolina. He served as a Seaman aboard the NCS WINSLOW from July – November 1861, and as an Ordinary Seaman aboard the CSS SEA BIRD from December 1, 1861 – December 20, 1861. He received a discharge on December 20, 1861.
[Source: NCCWSP]

Keck, Andrew (Alamance County, North Carolina)
Private, Confederate States Army/Confederate States Navy. Keck was born in Alamance County, North Carolina, and resided in Guilford County, North Carolina, as a farmer, prior to enlisting there at age 40 on March 6, 1862 as a Private in Company A, 53rd Regiment, North Carolina Troops. He was discharged in May 1862, by reason of being overage [Source North Carolina Troops" states he "Previously served (rank unknown) in the 68th Regiment, North Carolina Militia (1861)." He was conscripted on March 3 (5), 1864, at Camp Holmes, near Raleigh, North Carolina, from Colonel Coble's 68th Regiment, North Carolina Militia from Guilford County, North Carolina, he served as a Landsman, Confederate States Navy]. Description: Age 43; eyes hazel; hair dark; complexion florid; height 5 ft. 7 in.; place of birth Alamance County, North Carolina; occupation farmer. Served previously as a Private, Company A, 53rd Regiment, North Carolina Troops and 68th Regiment, North Carolina Militia.
[Source(s): McElroy; NA, RG 45; Roster, 68th Regiment, North Carolina Militia; North Carolina Troops, XIII]

Roster of North Carolinians in Confederate Naval Service

Keck, George
Landsman, Confederate States Navy. Keck enlisted on March 5, 1864 in Raleigh, for the war.
[Source(s): McElroy; NA, RG 45]

Kedslie, John M.
Deck Hand, Seaman, Ship's Cook, Confederate States Navy.
Kedslie's name appears on a payroll dated July 29,1861 for the NCS ALBEMARLE on which he served as a deck hand. Per clothing, bounty, and small stores records, he served as a Seaman aboard the CSS BEAUFORT from September - March 1862. Promoted to Ship's Cook on December 2, 1861, his name appears on the North Carolina Squadron payroll for the 1st quarter of 1862 covering from December 1, 1861 - April 15, 1862. He transferred to the James River Squadron on April 15, 1862 and, per payroll records, continued to serve as a Seaman on the CSS BEAUFORT from at least October 1, 1863 - December 15, 1863.
[Source: NCCWSP]

Keen, James (or Joseph) L.
Seaman, Confederate States Navy. Keen enlisted on June 15, 1864 in Raleigh, for the war.
[Source(s): McElroy; NA, RG 45]

Keeter, Elijah
Private, Confederate States Army//Confederate States Navy. Born in North Carolina in 1839, the son of Nehemiah and Delila Keeter, Keeter resided with his parents in 1850 in Brunswick County, North Carolina. He enlisted in New Hanover County, North Carolina, on May 27, 1861 at age 22 as a Private in Company D, 3rd Regiment, North Carolina State Troops. He transferred to the Confederate States Navy on April 18, 1864. He transferred to the Confederate States Navy on April 18, 1864. In 1880, Keeter resided in New Hanover County, North Carolina.
[Source(s): McElroy; North Carolina Troops, III; Foenander]

Keight, D.
Confederate States Navy.
Per clothing and small stores records, Keight served in an unknown rank aboard the CSS RALEIGH from before September 2, 1861 through a date unknown.
[Source: NCCWSP]

Keith, J. F. (New Hanover County, North Carolina)
Ordinary Seaman, Confederate States Navy. Keith enlisted in the Confederate States Navy on August 23, 1863 (or September 5, 1863) in Wilmington, North Carolina.
[Source(s): MR, 4, p. 446; McElroy; NA, RG 45; St. Armand]

Kelher, Daniel
Ordinary Seaman, Confederate States Navy. Per bounty and clothing lists, Kelher served as an Ordinary Seaman aboard the CSS BEAUFORT from January 16, 1862 – April 15, 1862 Ordinary Seaman, Beaufort [Clothing list, Mar. 1862. His name appears on the North Carolina Squadron payroll for the 1st quarter of 1862 covering from March 7, 1861 - April 15, 1862.
[Source: NCCWSP]

Keller, Andrew
Seaman, Landsman, Confederate States Navy. Keller enlisted on June 13, 1864 in Raleigh, for the war.
[Source(s): McElroy; NA, RG 45]

Kelly, James
Seaman, Confederate States Navy. Kelly enlisted on October 23, 1863 in Wilmington, North Carolina, for the war, and served as a Seaman aboard the CSS ARCTIC, Cape Fear River, North Carolina, 1863.
[Source(s): MR, 4, p. 446; McElroy; NA, RG 45; St. Armand; ORN 2, 1, 277; Foenander]

Kelly, L. J. (I?) (Richmond County, North Carolina)
Landsman, Confederate States Navy. Kelly enlisted in the Confederate States Navy on September 10, 1863 (or, September 28, 1863 at Camp Holmes) in Wilmington, North Carolina. Another source lists enlistment date as October 6, 1863 in Wilmington, North Carolina.
[Source(s): MR, 4, p. 446; McElroy; NA, RG 45]

Kelly [Kelley], Oliver
    Landsman, Confederate States Navy. Kelly enlisted on November 14, 1863, in Wilmington, for the war, and served as a Landsman aboard the CSS ARCTIC, Cape Fear River, North Carolina, 1863.
    [Source(s): McElroy; NA, RG 45; *ORN* 2, 1, 277; Foenander]

Kelly (Kelley), Patrick (New Hanover County, North Carolina)
    Confederate States Navy. Kelly's name appears on registers of Confederate States Army General Military Hospital Number 4, Wilmington, North Carolina, which state that he was admitted on August 29, 1863, with "feb int" and returned to duty on September 1, 1863. He served on the steamer CSS PHANTOM. He formerly served in Company K, 11th Regiment, North Carolina Troops. His post office was given on the registers as Wilmington, North Carolina. Note on card says "from information available it couldn't be determined whether or not this person was a native of North Carolina. [Rock Island (IL) Cemetery List]."
    [McElroy; NA, RG 109; Rock Island (IL) Cemetery List]

Kelly (Kelley), Patrick (McDowell County, North Carolina)
    Private, Confederate States Army//Seaman, Confederate States Navy. Kelly resided in McDowell County, North Carolina, and enlisted in Buncombe County, North Carolina, on April 15, 1862, for the war, in Company K, 11th Regiment, North Carolina Troops. He was present or accounted for until he transferred to the Confederate States Navy on April 1, 1864. He served at the Vicksburg, Mississippi, Naval Station and, later served in the Naval Battalion in Virginia at the end of the war. His name appears on a roll of Prisoners of War at Point Lookout, Maryland, which states he was captured at Burkeville [Virginia] on April 6, 1865. He was confined at Point Lookout from April 14, 1865 until released on June 28, 1865. Kelly's name also appears as signature to an Oath of Allegiance to the United States, subscribed and sworn to at Point Lookout on June 28, 1865. His place of residence on the Oath was given as McDowell County, North Carolina. Description: complexion dark; hair black; eyes blue; height 5 ft. 5 in. He was a member of the Army and Navy Society, Maryland Line Association, in 1894.
    [McElroy; NA, RG 109; Driver; North Carolina Troops, V]

Kelly, William W. J.
    Born in North Carolina; commissioned as a Paymaster into the United States Navy from Florida, which state he listed as his home. Resigned from the United States Navy to serve in the Confederate States Navy. He served as the first Lieutenant Governor of the State of Florida, 1865 – 1868 as a Republican. He died in 1878.
    [Source: Dudley; OCSN; Wikipedia]

Kemp, Zebulon W. (Tyrrell County, North Carolina)
    Sergeant, Confederate States Army/Confederate States Navy. Kemp resided in Tyrrell County, North Carolina, where he enlisted at age 25 on May 16, 1861 as a Private in Company L, 12th Regiment, North Carolina Troops (2nd Regiment, North Carolina Volunteers). He was present or accounted for until he transferred as a Private to Company A, 32nd Regiment, North Carolina Troops, in October 1861. Promoted to Corporal on January 27, 1862, and to Sergeant on April 1, 1862, he was present or accounted for until wounded in the left foot and captured at Gettysburg, Pennsylvania, July 1-5, 1863. Hospitalized in Frederick, Maryland, July 25, 1863, he was transferred to a hospital in Baltimore, Maryland, August 10, 1863. On August 22, 1863, he was paroled and transferred for exchange. He was reported in the hospital at Petersburg, Virginia, September-October 1863. Returned to duty in November-December 1863, he transferred to the Confederate States Navy on an unspecified date.
    [Source(s): North Carolina Troops, V and IX; Foenander]

Kenion, John P. (Pasquotank County, North Carolina)
    Ordinary Seaman, Confederate States Navy. Kenion was born in North Carolina circa 1842 and lived in Pasquotank County, North Carolina as a farm hand per the 1860 census. He served aboard the CSS SEA BIRD during the period of July through November 1861, and the North Carolina Squadron from the 1st quarter of 1862.
    [Sources: Census (NC), 1860; NCCWSP]

Kennady, James P.
    Ordinary Seaman, Confederate States Navy. Kennady enlisted on June 1, 1863 in Wilmington for three years.
    [McElroy; NA, RG 45]

Kennedy, Charles H. A. H. (Virginia/Appointed from North Carolina)
    Captain, Confederate States Navy. Born in Virginia, Kennedy began his service in the United States Navy on February 10, 1819 as a Midshipman. He became a Passed Midshipman on June 4, 1831, a Lieutenant on March 3, 1835, and a Commander on September 14, 1855. He was dismissed from the United States Navy on June 14, 1861

and, according to one source, served initially in the Virginia Navy. He was appointed to the Confederate States Navy from North Carolina, apparently at the rank of Commander, June 25, 1861 (another source gives his rank as "Commander, October 23, 1862, to rank from March 26, 1861"). He had duty on the Potomac River, 1861-1862; commanded the CSS MORGAN, Mobile Squadron, 1862; and, served on the Richmond Station, 1864. He was on recruiting service in Macon, Georgia, 1864.
[Source(s): Register; McElroy; Kennedy; Journal; Foenander; CWDTS; ONWR]

Kennedy, D. R. (New Hanover County, North Carolina)
Confederate States Navy. Kennedy enlisted in the Confederate States Navy on July 8, 1863 in Wilmington, North Carolina. Source "St. Armand" gives enlistment date as July 18, 1863.
[Source(s): MR, 4, p. 446; St. Armand]

Kennedy, W. J. R.
Landsman, Confederate States Navy. Kennedy enlisted on August 29, 1864 in Raleigh, for the war.
[McElroy; NA, RG 45]

Kennedy, William
Landsman, Confederate States Navy. Kennedy enlisted on March 1, 1864 in Raleigh, for the war.
[McElroy; NA, RG 45]

Kennedy [Can(n)ady], William (Moore County, North Carolina)
Private, Confederate States Marine Corps. Kennedy resided in Moore County, North Carolina, when conscripted and sent to Camp Holmes, near Raleigh, North Carolina. A letter of James C. Davis, dated November 17, 1864, states the group from Camp Holmes, of which Kennedy was a part, arrived aboard the CSS INDIAN CHIEF, Charleston, SC, on Sunday, November 6, 1864, and was designated to serve aboard the ironclad CSS CHICORA. Per source "McLeod, August 30, 1874," Kennedy left the unit [deserted?] at Jonesboro, North Carolina, on the march to Richmond in 1865.
[Source(s): "Citizen News-Record," July 8, 1987; [*Fayetteville Observer* (Fayetteville,   North Carolina) dated November 24, 1864; Davis, November 17, 1864]

Kennett (Kennet), Augustus S. (Guilford or Randolph County, North Carolina)
Sergeant, Confederate States Army/Confederate States Navy. Kennett resided in Randolph County, North Carolina, where he enlisted at age 22 on June 5, 1861 in Company I, 22nd Regiment, North Carolina Troops. He mustered in as a Sergeant. Kennett transferred to the Confederate States Navy on or about April 3, 1864 and served as a Landsman on board the CSS VIRGINIA II, 1864-1865. One source shows he died at Union Factory, Randolph County, North Carolina, February 12, 1865, while still a Sergeant. The "Greensborough Patriot" of February 23, 1865 listed Augustus S. Kennet [sic] as a Guilford County native, former soldier in the 22nd Regiment, North Carolina Troops who transferred to the Confederate States Navy, as dying of unknown causes in February 1865.
[Source(s): McElroy; "Greensborough Patriot (February 23, 1865)"; North Carolina Troops, VII; Foenander]

Kerney, S. W. [S. H.]
Sergeant, Confederate States Marine Corps. Enlisting in Raleigh, North Carolina, on October 6, 1864, Kerney served on the Charleston, South Carolina, naval station as a Sergeant of the Marine guard on board the ironclad, CSS COLUMBIA to February 7, 1865. He transferred to the CSS INDIAN CHIEF on February 8, 1865.
[Source(s): North Carolina Troops, Doc. # 0299; Card File; Donnelly; McLeod, August 30, 1865]

Kerr, W. H. (Caswell County, North Carolina)
Lieutenant, Confederate States Navy. Kerr received his commission as a Lieutenant in the Confederate States Navy, in 1861, from Caswell County, North Carolina.
[Source(s): MR, 4, p. 404 and 449]

Kerr, William A.
Lieutenant, Confederate States Navy. Born in North Carolina, Kerr served in the United States Navy from September 20, 1854, until he resigned as a Master, United States Navy, on April 24, 1861. He was appointed from North Carolina as a Master, Confederate States Navy, on May 2, 1861. Appointed Acting Lieutenant on Sept 19, 1861, he was promoted to First Lieutenant on October 23, 1862 [Source "Foenander" gives the date as February 8, 1862], to rank from October 2, 1862. He was promoted to First Lieutenant, Provisional Navy, on June 2, 1864 [January 6, 1864 (Foenander)], to rank from January 6, 1864. Kerr served on the Savannah Station, 1861-1862, and on the New Orleans Station, 1862. He served aboard the CSS RALEIGH in North Carolina waters and the CSS

NANSEMOND, James River Squadron, 1862-1863. He commanded the CSS YADKIN, "a one gunner on the Cape Fear River," under Flag Officer W.F. Lynch, 1864, and the CSS NORTH CAROLINA on the Wilmington Station, 1864. One source mentions he was on special duty, 1864. [NOTE: A "W. H. Kerr, Lieutenant, of Caswell County, North Carolina, is listed in Source "MR"].
[Source(s): Register; McElroy; Journal; Foenander; ONWR]

Kight, Dempsey (Currituck County, North Carolina).
Confederate States Navy. Thought to have served aboard the CSS RALEIGH.
[Source: http://civilwarnenc.ning.com]

Kight, Henry C. (Camden County, North Carolina)
Confederate States Navy. Kight enlisted in Camden County, North Carolina, on November 1, 1863, as a Private in Company B, 68th Regiment North Carolina Troops. He transferred to the Confederate States Navy on April 5, 1864 and is probably the "H. C. Hight" who served as a Landsman on board the CSS ALBEMARLE.
[Source(s): McElroy; North Carolina Troops, XV; *ORN* 2, 1, 274; Foenander]

King, George M. (Brunswick County, North Carolina)
Corporal, Company, Coast Guards [SEE NOTE #2]. A fisherman by trade, King enlisted on January 24, 1862 and was detached to the Signal Service on March 25, 1863.
[Source(s): Edge]

King, Joel G. (Franklin County, North Carolina)
Assistant Surgeon, Confederate States Navy. Born in North Carolina in December 1841, the son of Doctor William R. King, and his wife, Tempy W. King, resided with his parents in Franklin County, North Carolina, in 1860. At age 23, he was appointed from North Carolina in the Confederate States Navy as an Assistant Surgeon for the war on January 7, 1864 [another source says served in 1863]. Appointed an Assistant Surgeon, Provisional Navy, June 2, 1864, King served at the naval hospital, Richmond, 1864; at Kinston, North Carolina, 1864; and, aboard the CSS NEUSE, 1864. He married Bettie D. Massenburg in Franklin County, North Carolina, on October 3, 1866, and resided as a physician, in 1900, with his wife, and daughter, Nora, in Warrenton, Warren County, North Carolina. King died in 1913 and was buried in Fairview Cemetery, Warren County, North Carolina.
[Source(s): Register; McElroy; Hill; King; Gravestone Records, v. II, p. 223; Stepp, "Burials;" Foenander; NEUSE Roster; ONWR; CMACSSN]

King, Sewell (Wake County, North Carolina)
Landsman, Confederate States Navy. King's name appears as signature to an Oath of Allegiance to the United States, subscribed and sworn to at Point Lookout, Maryland, June 28, 1865. His place of residence was given on the Oath as Wake County, North Carolina, and he was described as follows: Complexion light; hair light brown; eyes blue; height 5 ft. 9 ½ in.
[Source(s): McElroy; NA, RG 109]

Kirby, D. C.
Seaman, Confederate States Navy. Kirby enlisted on September 4, 1863 in Wilmington for the war.
[Source(s): McElroy; NA, RG 45]

Kirby, Lewis
Ordinary Seaman, Confederate States Navy.
Kirby enlisted on March 20, 1863 in Wilmington, for the war, and served as an Ordinary Seaman aboard the CSS ARCTIC, Cape Fear River, North Carolina, 1863.
[Source(s): Foenander; McElroy; NA, RG 45]

Kirk, W. M.
Landsman, Confederate States Navy.
Kirk enlisted on July 21, 1864 in Raleigh, North Carolina, for the war.
[Source(s): McElroy; NA, RG 45]

Kirkland, William Alexander
Confederate States Navy.
[Source (s): McElroy; DNCB, III, p. 370].

Kirsey, William E.
Landsman, Confederate States Navy.
Kirsey enlisted on May 23, 1864 in Raleigh, North Carolina, for the war.
[Source(s): McElroy; NA, RG 45]

Kite, Noah (Currituck County, North Carolina)
Ordinary Seaman, Confederate States Navy.
Born in North Carolina in 1839, the son of Dempsey and Julia Kite. In 1860, Kite resided as a farmer at Indian Ridge, Currituck County, North Carolina. He married Martha Pool in Currituck County, North Carolina, on January 2, 1861. Kite served as an Ordinary Seaman aboard the side wheeled steam tug CSS ELLIS, North Carolina from at least 1 August 1861 through 2 November 1862. His name appears on a payroll of the receiving ship CSS UNITED STATES ending March 31, 1862. In 1880, he resided as a laborer with his wife, Martha, in Crawford, Currituck County, North Carolina.
[Source(s): Foenander; ORN 2, 1, 285; NCCWSP; Census (NC), 1860]

Klutts (Klutz), R. B.
Seaman, Confederate States Navy.
Klutts enlisted on June 22, 1864 in Raleigh, North Carolina, for the war.
[Source(s): McElroy; NA, RG 45; Duke Papers]

Knight, Valerius A. (Pasquotank County, North Carolina)
1st Class Fireman/Acting Boatswain's Mate, Confederate States Navy.
Born in North Carolina, about 1835, Knight resided as a mariner at the home of merchant B. B. Balance and his wife Margaret in Elizabeth City, Pasquotank County, North Carolina, in 1860. He served as a Fireman but acting as a Boatswain's Mate, aboard the side wheeled steam tug CSS ELLIS, North Carolina from at least August 1,1861 through November 2, 1862 with the North Carolina Squadron. He is listed as a First-Class Fireman aboard the CSS ELLIS from January through May 1862 [Note: Source NCCWSP states Knight's name appears on a payroll of the receiving ship CSS UNITED STATES ending March 31,1862. Knight also performed the duties of Boatswain, Gunner, and Watch Officer, at Roanoke Island circa February 1862 and was described as "efficient."
[Source(s): Foenander; ORN 1, 6, 597 and 781; 2, 1, 285; NCCWSP Census (NC), 1860]

Knight, William D. (Pasquotank County, North Carolina)
Gunner's Mate, Ordinary Seaman, Confederate States Navy.
Knight was born in North Carolina circa 1832 and resided in Elizabeth City, North Carolina as a mariner in 1860. He appears as a Gunner's Mate on a log of the CSS ELLIS dated 2 November 1861, and as an Ordinary Seaman on payrolls for that ship between January through May 1862. His name appears on a payroll of the receiving ship CSS UNITED STATES ending 31 March 1862.
[Sources: North Carolina Census, 1860; NCCWSP]

Knott, A. B. (Forsyth County, North Carolina)
Landsman, Confederate States Navy.
Knott enlisted in the Confederate States Navy on October 13 [or, 14], 1863 in Wilmington, North Carolina [or, at Camp Holmes, near Raleigh]. He served aboard the CSS NEUSE as of the ship's March – October 1864 muster rolls.
[Source(s): MR, 4, p. 446; McElroy; NA, RG 45; NEUSE Roster; CMACSSN]

Knowles, John (New Hanover County, North Carolina)
Private, Confederate States Army//Confederate States Navy(?).
Knowles enlisted for the war at age 31 in New Hanover County, North Carolina, on April 16, 1861 in 2nd Company H, 40th Regiment, North Carolina Troops. Mustered in as a Sergeant and promoted to 1st Sergeant in on September 24, 1861, he was reduced to the ranks when detailed to work on gunboats at Wilmington, North Carolina, on December 1, 1862. He was listed as absent detailed until discharged on August 27, 1864.
[Source(s): North Carolina Troops, I; McElroy]

Kodill, William H.
Seaman, Confederate States Navy.
Per payroll records, Kodill served from December 2, 1861 - 15 April 15, 1862 with the North Carolina Squadron.
[Source: NCCWSP]

Kosler (Rosler?), John
>Ordinary Seaman, Confederate States Navy.
>Per his shipping articles Kosler served aboard the NCS EDWARDS beginning on July 25, 1861. [NOTE: May be same as John A. Rosler, q. v.].
>[Source: NCCWSP]

Kyle, George W.
>Seaman, Confederate States Navy. Kyle enlisted on June 17, 1864 in Raleigh, for the war.
>[Source(s): McElroy; NA, RG 45]

LaHaise, Oliver (Anson County, North Carolina, or Montreal, Canada)
>Confederate States Navy(?). Residing in either Anson County, North Carolina, or Montreal, Canada, La Haise enlisted at age 21 in 1861 (month and day unknown), as a Private in Company B, 24th Regiment, North Carolina Troops (14th Regiment, North Carolina Volunteers). He was apparently discharged and enlisted in Anson County, North Carolina, in Company K, 26th Regiment, North Carolina Troops, on September 17, 1861. He was present or accounted for until wounded at Barrington's Ferry on March 14, 1863. He returned to duty on or about May 1, 1863, where he was present or accounted for until captured at or near Falling Waters, Maryland, on or about July 14, 1863. He was confined at Old Capitol Prison, Washington, DC, until released on or about December 13, 1863 after taking the Oath of Allegiance. LaHaise was apparently transferred to the Confederate States Navy after he was captured and took the Oath of Allegiance; therefore, his transfer may have taken place only on paper, and he may never have actually served in the Confederate States Navy.
>[Source(s): McElroy; North Carolina Troops, VII]

Lamb, George
>3rd Assistant Engineer, Confederate States Navy.
>Per payroll records, Lamb served as a 3rd Assistant Engineer with the North Carolina Squadron. No further information.
>[Source: NCCWSP]

Lamb, Isham [Isam] (Robeson County, North Carolina)
>Private, Confederate States Army/Landsman, Confederate States Navy. Born in North Carolina in 1846, the son of Thomas and Winnie Lamb, Lamb resided with his parents and siblings, in 1860, at Robeson County, North Carolina. Source "Foenander" states that Lamb served as a Landsman aboard the CSS ARCTIC, Cape Fear River, North Carolina, 1863. He enlisted at the age of 18 on February 23, 1864, in Raleigh, North Carolina, for the war, in Company B, 50th Regiment, North Carolina Troops. Source "North Carolina Troops" gives enlistment date as September 1, 1864 and adds that Lamb survived the war. Lamb married Marietta Carter at Robeson County on October 3, 1870.
>[Source(s): Foenander; McElroy; NA, RG 45; North Carolina Troops, XII]

Lamb, Thomas
>Landsman, Confederate States Navy. Lamb enlisted on February 23, 1864, in Raleigh, North Carolina, for the war, and served as a Landsman aboard the CSS ARCTIC, Cape Fear River, North Carolina, 1863.
>[Source(s): Foenander; McElroy; NA, RG 45]

Lamont, Alexander
>Landsman, Confederate States Navy. Lamont enlisted on June 6, 1864 in Raleigh, North Carolina, for the war.
>[McElroy; NA, RG 45]

Lampley, J. R.
>Confederate States Navy. Born in North Carolina, and by trade a merchant, Lampley enlisted at age 47. Records indicate he served aboard the CSS TENNESSEE and had blue eyes, light hair, and a light complexion.
>[Source(s): CSS TENNESSEE]

Lancaster, L. [D.] H. (Franklin County, North Carolina)
>Confederate States Navy. Conscripted on March 2, 1864 at Camp Holmes from Colonel Thomas' 40th Regiment, North Carolina Militia, Franklin County, North Carolina [Source "Foenander" states he "enlisted in Franklin County,

March 2, 1864, aged 29"] Lancaster enlisted in the Confederate States Navy. He was described as age 29, with blue eyes; dark hair; a sallow complexion; and standing 5 feet 9 inches tall. His place of birth was listed as Franklin County, North Carolina, and his occupation as "clerk."
[Source(s): Foenander; McElroy; NA, RG 45; Roster, 40th Regiment, North Carolina Militia]

Lancaster, S. H.
Confederate States Navy. Lancaster's name appears on a list of conscripts "in yard at Halifax" dated June 9, 1864.
[Source(s): McElroy]

Lancaster, S. H.
Landsman, Confederate States Navy. Lancaster enlisted on March 24, 1864 in Raleigh, North Carolina, for the war. [NOTE: Could be same a S. H. Lancaster conscripted June 9, 1864, though entry dates are over two months apart].
[Source(s): McElroy; NA, RG 45]

Lancaster, William A. (Pitt County, North Carolina)
Private, Company, Coast Guards [SEE NOTE #2]. A fisherman before the war, Lancaster enlisted on January 24, 1862.
[Source(s): Edge]

Land, Henry G.
Confederate States Navy. Born in Texas in 1839 [NOTE: 1860 United States Census shows state of birth as Virginia, and 1870 United States Census shows state of birth as North Carolina]. Land resided as a medical student, in 1860, at Princess Anne County, Virginia. His original entry into the Confederate States Navy was August 31, 1863. He was commissioned as an Assistant Surgeon on January 7, 1864, to rank from August 31, 1863. He served aboard the CSS RICHMOND, James River Squadron, Virginia, 1863 – 1864. He was appointed Assistant Surgeon, Provisional Confederate States Navy, on June 2, 1864. Land later served on the CSS SAVANNAH and CSS MACON, Savannah Squadron, Georgia, 1864-1865. He resided as a physician, in 1870, with his wife, Sarah, and two children, at Poplar Branch, Currituck County, North Carolina.
[Source(s): Foenander; ORN 1, 10, 671]

Langford, William
Landsman, Confederate States Navy. Langford enlisted in the Confederate States Navy on January 6, 1864 in Raleigh, North Carolina, for the war. He served as a Landsman aboard the CSS ARCTIC, Cape Fear River, North Carolina, 1863, and later on the CSS RALEIGH in North Carolina and Virginia waters, 1864.
[Source(s): Foenander; McElroy; NA, RG45]

Langhorne, J. C.
Captain's Clerk, Confederate States Navy.
According to clothing and small stores records, Langhorne served as a Captain's Clerk aboard the CSS RALEIGH from September 2, 1861 through the 1st quarter of 1862. He transferred to the James River Squadron on April 15, 1862.
[Source: NCCWSP]

Lanier, Ira (Northampton County, North Carolina) (NOTE: May be same as Ira Laniere, Duplin County" q.v.).
Lanier enlisted in the Confederate States Navy on August 27, 1863 in Wilmington, North Carolina. He served as a Seaman aboard the CSS ARCTIC, Cape Fear River, North Carolina, 1863.
[Source(s): Foenander; MR, 4, p. 446]

Laniere, Ira (Duplin County, North Carolina) (NOTE: May be same as Ira Lanier, Northampton County" q.v.)
Landsman, Confederate States Navy. Laniere enlisted on October 26, 1863 in Wilmington, for the war. His name appears on Registers of Confederate States Army General Hospital Number 4, Wilmington, North Carolina, which indicate he was admitted on November 14, 1863 with "febis typhoides," and assigned to ward 6, bed number 107. He returned to duty on March 21, 1864. His post office was given on the registers as Warsaw, North Carolina.
[McElroy; NA, RG 45; NA, RG 109; Hosp. (No. 4), Wilm.]

Lashly [Lashley], John
Landsman, Confederate States Navy. Lashly enlisted on November 20, 1863 in Wilmington, for the war. Another source states he enlisted on November 17, 1863 in Raleigh, for the war. He served as a Landsman aboard the CSS ARCTIC, Cape Fear River, North Carolina, 1863.

[Source(s): Foenander; McElroy; NA, RG 45]

Laughinghouse, Ajax (North Carolina)
Deck Hand. Steamer "*Albemarle*." Mulatto (per the 1850 Craven County, North Carolina Census).
[Source: NCCWSP; Census (NC), 1850)]

Laughinghouse [Lavinghouse], E. S. [J.] (Edgecombe County, North Carolina)
Landsman, Confederate States Navy. Laughinghouse served as a Landsman aboard the CSS ARCTIC, Cape Fear River, North Carolina, 1863. His name appears as signature to an Oath of Allegiance to the US subscribed and sworn to at Newport News, Virginia, June 27, 1865. Place of residence given on Oath as Edgecombe County, North Carolina, and described as follows: complexion, fair; hair, light; eyes, blue; height, 5 ft. 9 in.; Oath also carries the remark, "Captured at Farmville April 6, 1865."
[Source(s): Foenander; McElroy; NA, RG 109]

Laurance, Yancey S. (Guilford County, North Carolina)
Landsman, Confederate States Navy. Laurance enlisted on June 10, 1864 in Raleigh, North Carolina, for the war. He was a member of a Confederate States Naval Battalion. His name appears as a signature to an Oath of Allegiance to the United States, subscribed and sworn to at Newport News, Virginia, June 26, 1865. His place of residence was given on the Oath as Guilford County, North Carolina. Description: complexion, light; hair, light; eyes, grey; height, 5 feet 9 inches. His oath carries the remark, "Captured Farmville, Virginia, April 6, 1865."
[McElroy; NA, RG 45; NA, RG 109]

Lautenschlager, J. C.
Seaman, Confederate States Navy. Lautenschlager enlisted on June 15, 1864 in Raleigh, North Carolina, for the war.
[McElroy; NA, RG 45]

Lawless (Lollis, Lawley), William Henry [May have been from North Carolina]
Private, Confederate States Marine Corps. Lawless enlisted as a Private with Company B (Van Benthuysen's Company) of the Confederate States Marine Corps, which was organized at Pensacola. Source notes that he probably enlisted in Wilmington, North Carolina, but does not offer a reason for this assumption. He was assigned to the Marine Guard aboard the CSS RALEIGH and served from April 19, 1864-May 31, 1864. The CSS RALEIGH was sunk earlier in May, so he did not serve out this entire assignment. He reported to the CSS ARCTIC on June 1, 1864 and served until September 30, 1864. Captured on January 15, 1865 at Fort Fisher, he was held as a Prisoner of War at "Camp Hoffman Prisoner of War Prison, Point Lookout, Maryland until released upon taking the Oath of Allegiance to the United States on May 13, 1865. He moved from Pickens County to Johnson County, Arkansas about 1880. He was the son-in-law of James Polk Woodard, Company H, 5th Alabama Infantry Regiment.
[Source(s): PCNMC]

Lawley, Thomas (North Carolina?)
Corporal, Confederate States Marine Corps. Per "New York Times" article of January 17, 1865, Lawley served at Battery Buchanan, Fort Fisher until he deserted to the Union Navy with five others.
[Source(s): New York Times," 17 January 1865; Card File]

Lawrence, Alex [Alexander] W. (North Carolina)
Former Professor of Mathematics, Observatory, Washington, DC, United States Navy whose dismissal is annotated with "At the south." Listed as a "Staff Captain" and Assistant Commissary on the staff of North Carolina Governor John W. Ellis, 1861.
[Source: Dudley]

Lawson, Abraham (also Larson)
Seaman, Confederate States Navy.
Per clothing, small stores and payroll records, Lawson served as a Seaman aboard the CSS BEAUFORT from December 1861 – January 1862. His name appears on the payroll of the receiving ship CSS UNITED STATES March 31, 1862, and on the payroll of the North Carolina Squadron for the 1st quarter of 1862 covering from January 10, 1862 - April 15, 1862. He transferred to the James River Squadron on April 15, 1862.
[Source: NCCWSP]

Lawson, Alfred W. (New Hanover County, North Carolina)
Private, Confederate States Army/Landsman, Confederate States Navy. Lawson enlisted for twelve months on April 16, 1861 in New Hanover County, North Carolina in 1st Company C, 36 Regiment (2nd Regiment, North Carolina Artillery). He served as a Corporal prior to the unit's muster into active service. He mustered in as an Artificer but was reduced to ranks July-August 1863. He was listed as present or accounted for until he transferred to Company C, 13th Battalion, North Carolina Light Artillery on November 4, 1863. He was listed as present or accounted for through April 1864 when he transferred to the Confederate States Navy. Another source states he enlisted on April 22, 1864 in Kinston, North Carolina, for three years or the war. Another source states he was "Exchanged with W. Lyerly to C. S. Navy," March-April 1864. He served aboard the CSS NEUSE as of the ship's March – October 1864 muster rolls.
[Source(s): North Carolina Troops, I, p.572; Foenander; Hill; McElroy; NA, RG 109; NA, RG 45; NEUSE Roster; CMACSSN]

Lawson, William S. (Person County, North Carolina)
1st Sergeant, Confederate States Army/Confederate States Navy. Born in Person County, North Carolina, where he resided as a farmer prior to enlisting there at age 18 on September 25, 1861, as a Private in Company E, 35th Regiment, North Carolina Troops. Present or accounted for during January-April 1862. Promoted to 1st Sergeant, May 1862-December 1864. Reported present during November 1864-February 1865. Captured at or near Fort Stedman, Virginia, March 25, 1865, and confined at Point Lookout, Maryland, until released on June 28, 1865, after taking the Oath of Allegiance. [May have also served in the Confederate States Navy].
[Source(s): Foenander; McElroy; North Carolina Troops, IX]

Layton [Laton], John (Guilford County, North Carolina)
Landsman, Confederate States Navy. Layton's name appears as a signature to an Oath of Allegiance to the United States, subscribed and sworn to at Point Lookout, Maryland, June 28, 1865. Place of residence given on Oath as Guilford County, North Carolina. Description: complexion, light; hair, light brown; eyes, blue; height, 5 ft. 9 ¾ in. Another source shows his enlistment as both June 1863 and March 1864 [enlisted March 1, 1864 at Raleigh for the war]. Layton filed a pension claim on August 10, 1912, age 73, post office Kernersville, Guilford County, North Carolina. Claim disallowed. States he "had rendered service to the government then hired a substitute paying the sum of $1,800 then in 8 months he was conscripted and sent to the Navy at Willmington [sic] was captured in battle at Farmville in Virginia was sent to Point Lookout as a prisoner serving about 18 months in the army [sic]…" He was a Prisoner of War for about three months.
[Source(s): Foenander; McElroy; NA, RG 109; NA, RG 45; Pensions (North Carolina)]

Lea (Lee, Charles E. (Brunswick County(?), North Carolina)
Master, North Carolina Navy. Lea served as Master of the "Issabel (Isabel, Isabella)" Confederate States Navy. Born in 1826 in South Carolina, he died in 1864 and was buried in the Morse Cemetery, Southport (Previously Smithville), North Carolina.
[Source(s): Ellis; Stepp, "Burials"]

Lea, W. D. (Pender County, North Carolina)
Confederate States Navy. One source lists his service as "Navy-Ga." Lea filed a claim for a pension on July 1, 1912, age 67, listing his post office as Hampstead, Pender County, North Carolina. The claim was disallowed. His application for pension claims he was "Wounded May 7, 1862 at Shilo [sic], Virginia."
[McElroy; Pensions (North Carolina)]

Lee, Willis
Landsman, Confederate States Navy.
Born in Currituck County, North Carolina, Lee was by occupation a farmer prior to enlisting at age 26 in Currituck County on May 13, 1861 as a Private in Company E, 17th Regiment, North Carolina Troops (1st Organization). He transferred to Confederate States Navy on or about September 11, 1861 and served as a Landsman, aboard the NCS FANNY. According to muster, clothing, and payroll records, he served from at least October 8, 1861 through February 28, 1862 with the North Carolina Squadron. He is listed as having "run" in or before February 28, 1862.
[Source: NCCWSP]

Leach, N. (Moore County, North Carolina) [May be same as "Neill Leach," q.v.]
Private, Confederate States Marine Corps. Leach was a resident of Moore County, North Carolina, and served in the Confederate States Marine Corps. He left Moore County and was sent to Camp Holmes, where he was instructed for a short time, then sent to Charleston, aboard the CSS INDIAN CHIEF, arriving there on Sunday, November 6, 1864,

for further drill and instruction as a marine; later sent aboard the CSS CHICORA, Charleston Station. Letter of James C. Davis, November 17, 1864, states the group from Camp Holmes, of which "N. Leach" was a part, arrived aboard the CSS INDIAN CHIEF, Charleston, SC, Sunday, November 6, 1864, and was designated to serve aboard the ironclad CSS CHICORA.
[Source(s): Foenander; Davis, November 17, 1864]

Leach, Neill (Moore County, North Carolina) [May be same as "N. Leach," q.v.]
Landsman, Confederate States Navy. Leach enlisted on June 10, 1864 in Raleigh, North Carolina, for the war. He is listed as serving in the Naval Battalion. His name appears as a signature to an Oath of Allegiance to the United States, subscribed and sworn to at Point Lookout, Maryland, on June 28, 1865. His place of residence is listed on the Oath as Moore County, North Carolina. Description: complexion, light; hair, brown; eyes, blue; height, 5 ft. 10 inches.
[McElroy; NA, RG 45; NA, RG 109]

Leahey, James (New Hanover County, North Carolina)
Confederate States Navy. Leahey's name appears on a register of Confederate States Army General Military Hospital Number 4, Wilmington, North Carolina, admitted on February 28, 1864, with "pneumonia." Records indicate he was returned to duty on March 26, 1864. His post office was listed on the register as Wilmington, North Carolina.
[McElroy; NA, RG 109]

Leary, John H.
Seaman, Confederate States Navy. Leary enlisted on April 13, 1864 in Kinston, North Carolina, for three years or the war.
[McElroy; NA, RG 445]

Ledwell, David D.
Ordinary Seaman, Confederate States Navy//Private, Confederate States Army. Originally enlisting in the Confederate States Navy on June 1, 1863 in Wilmington for three years, Ledwell transferred from Confederate States Navy to Company K, 10th Regiment, North Carolina State Troops (1st Regiment, North Carolina Artillery) July 19, 1863 by Special Order 164/11, Adjutant and Inspector General's Office, dated July 11, 1863. Deserted on September 21, 1863.
[Source(s): Foenander; McElroy; NA, RG 45; NA, RG 109;www.thewashingtongrays.homestead.com; www.ncgenweb.us/nccivwar/rosters/10cok.htm, North Carolina Troops, I]

Lee, Frank
Engineer, Confederate States Navy. Lee enlisted from North Carolina in 1861 and served aboard the CSS CHICORA.
[Source(s): McElroy]

Lee, Thomas J. (Washington County, North Carolina)
Private, Confederate States Army//Confederate States Navy. Lee resided in Washington County, North Carolina, where he enlisted at age 21 on July 3, 1861 as a Private in Company G, 1st Regiment, North Carolina State Troops. Present of accounted for until discharged on February 1, 1862 upon transfer to the Confederate States Navy (in January 1862 per MR, I) where he served as an Ordinary Seaman on the CSS VIRGINIA, Hampton Roads, Virginia, 1862.
[Source(s): Foenander; McElroy; North Carolina Troops, III; MR, I]

Lee, William R. (Sampson County, North Carolina) [NOTE: May be same as "W. R. Leigh" (q.v.)]
Private, Confederate States Army/Confederate States Navy. Born in Sampson County, North Carolina, Lee was a farmer by occupation when he enlisted in Cumberland County, North Carolina, as a Private in Company I, 51st Regiment, North Carolina Troops, at age 19 on March 31, 1862. Listed as present or accounted for until transferred to the Confederate States Navy on April 23, 1863, where he served as a Landsman aboard the CSS PALMETTO STATE, Charleston Harbor, South Carolina, 1863 - 1864. A "Mary E. Branch" (who married Matthew D. Branch, after the death of William R. Lee, sometime prior to 1877) in a widow's pension claimed her first husband was W. R. Lee of Sampson County.
Source(S): McElroy; North Carolina Troops, XII; Pensions (North Carolina); North Carolina Troops, XII]

Lee, Willis (Currituck County, North Carolina)
Private, Confederate States Army/Confederate States Navy. Born in Currituck County, North Carolina, where he resided as a farmer prior to enlisting there at age 26 on May 13, 1861 as a Private in Company E, 17th Regiment, North Carolina Troops (1st Organization) [Per source "McElroy," he also served in Company C, 61st Regiment, Virginia Infantry]. Present or accounted for until he transferred to the Confederate States Navy on September 11, 1861. Lee served as a Landsman on the CSS FANNY, North Carolina, October 8, 1861 – December 13, 1862. His name appears on a North Carolina Squadron payroll covering the period December 1, 1861 - February 28, 1862.
[Source(s): Foenander; McElroy; North Carolina Troops, VI; NCCWSP]

Lehen [Lehew, Lehue] Samuel
Landsman, Confederate States Navy. Lehen enlisted on January 11, 1864, in Raleigh for the war and served as a Landsman aboard the CSS ARCTIC, Cape Fear River, North Carolina, 1863. In 1864, he served aboard the CSS NORTH CAROLINA, Cape Fear River, North Carolina.
[Source(s): Foenander; McElroy; NA, RG 45]

Lehman, P. T. (Forsyth County, North Carolina)
Confederate States Navy. Lehman enlisted from Forsyth County, North Carolina. He died on February 5, 1924, in Winston Salem, North Carolina. Brother: Seyton Lehman, Winston Salem, North Carolina.
[Source(s): McElroy]

Leigh, W. R. [NOTE: May be same as "William R. Lee" (q.v.)]
Landsman, Confederate States Navy. Leigh enlisted on May 11, 1864, in Raleigh for the war.
[Source(s): McElroy; NA, RG 45]

Leonard, John H. (Maryland//Chowan County, North Carolina)
Private, Confederate States Army//Confederate States Navy. Leonard resided in Maryland and enlisted in Chowan County, North Carolina, at age 25 on May 18, 1861 (May 15, 1861 per MR), for the war, in Company A, 1st Regiment, North Carolina Troops. Discharged on February 1, 1862 and transferred to the Confederate States Navy. Leonard served as a Seaman on board the CSS VIRGINIA (MERRIMAC) where he was wounded in one eye in the Battle of Hampton Roads, Virginia, March 8, 1862. Discharged for disability, he later enlisted in the Surry Light Artillery (Company I, 3rd Virginia Infantry, afterward Captain T. W. Ruffin's Company, Virginia Artillery). Personal description as 6 feet, 10 or 11 inches high, thick set, dark hair; deserted from his camp, near Richmond, Virginia, on December 17 or 19, 1862; reward of $30 offered for his apprehension and delivery to his company captain.
[Source(s): Foenander; North Carolina Troops, III; MR, I]

Leonard, Valentine (Davidson County, North Carolina)
Landsman, Confederate States Navy. Leonard enlisted on July 16, 1864 in Raleigh for the war. He served in Company F, Naval Battalion. His name appears on a roll of Prisoners of War at Point Lookout, Maryland, which states he was captured at Harper's Farm on April 6, 1865, confined at Point Lookout from April 14, 1865 until released June 28, 1865. His name also appears as a signature to an Oath of Allegiance to the US, subscribed and sworn to at Point Lookout, Maryland, June 28, 1865. Place of residence given on Oath as Davidson County, North Carolina. Description: Complexion, light; hair, brown; eyes, hazel; height, 5 ft. 9 in.
[Source(s): McElroy; NA, RG 45; NA, RG 109]

Lessman, August
Landsman, Confederate States Navy. Lessman enlisted on December 12 [5], 1863, at Wilmington [Raleigh] for the war.
[McElroy; NA, RG 45]

Lewis, John (Beaufort County, North Carolina)
Private, Confederate States Army//Confederate States Navy. Lewis enlisted in Beaufort County, North Carolina, on July 3, 1861, age 38, as a Private in Company G, 19th Regiment, North Carolina Troops (2nd Regiment, North Carolina Cavalry). He was present or accounted for until he transferred to the Confederate States Navy on February 1, 1862.
[Source(s): North Carolina Troops, II; McElroy; Foenander; "Beaufort County Sailors"]

Leyerlie, Miley
Ordinary Seaman, Confederate States Navy. Leyerlie enlisted on September 22, 1863, at Wilmington, North

Carolina, for the war. [NOTE: May be same as "W. Lyerly" and "Lyerlie, Wiley"].
[McElroy; NA, RG 45]

Libby [Lebby], Henry Sterlin (North Carolina)
Captain, Confederate States Navy. Originally of South Carolina, Libby enlisted on April 2, 1861 as a Blockade Runner. He was promoted to "Captain of the blockade runner "The Hallie ["Hattie"]," the last vessel running in and out of Charleston Harbor, February 2, 1865. Taken prisoner, he escaped in a mail steamer from New York to Liverpool and then to Nassau."
[McElroy; UDC, Graham Chapter; UDC, Highland Boys]

Ligon, Junius H.
Confederate States Navy(?). Ligon served in Company A, Naval Battalion. From North Carolina (?).
[Source(s): Ancestry.com, CW Soldiers]

Lillard, T. [J.] W.
Ordinary Seaman, Confederate States Navy. Lillard enlisted on June 8, 1863, at Wilmington, North Carolina, for the war, and served as an Ordinary Seaman aboard the CSS NORTH CAROLINA, Cape Fear River, North Carolina, 1864.
[Source(s): Foenander; McElroy; NA, RG 45]

Lindsay (Lindsey), Eugene K. (Rockingham County, North Carolina?) [NOTE: possibly same as "E. H. Lindsay," q.v.].
Landsman, Confederate States Navy. Born in North Carolina, Lindsey enlisted March 24, 1864, at Raleigh, North Carolina for the war [another record states he was conscripted on March 22, 1864, at Camp Holmes from COL Dillon's 70th Regiment, North Carolina Militia from Rockingham County, North Carolina. Description: eyes. Blue; hair, dark; complexion, fair; age, 21 (or 20); place of birth, Rockingham County, North Carolina; occupation, farmer]. Served aboard the "Albemarle." Captured at Fort Fisher, January 15, 1865. Died in prison at Elmira, New York, May 8, 1865, of pneumonia. In his effects was twenty cents. Buried in grave #2846, Woodland Cemetery, Elmira, New York. Brother: T.B. Lindsay, Stoneville, North Carolina.
[Source(s): PCNMC; Foenander; McElroy; NA, RG 45; UDC, Gordon; Roster, 70th Regiment, North Carolina Militia; Purser]

Lindsay, James E.
Assistant Surgeon, Confederate States Navy. Born in 1837 in and appointed from North Carolina. Lindsay served as an Assistant Surgeon, United States Navy, beginning on May 2, 1860. He was appointed an Assistant Surgeon, Confederate States Navy, on January 23, 1862. He was promoted to Passed Assistant Surgeon on April 29, 1863, to rank from October 25, 1862, and to Passed Assistant Surgeon, Provisional Confederate Navy, on June 2, 1864. He was a prisoner at Fort Warren, October 15, 1861, and was exchanged on January 24, 1862. Lindsay served on board the CSS VIRGINIA (MERRIMACK), 1862, and at Drewry's Bluff, Virginia, 1862-1863. He had service abroad, 1863-1865. Lindsay is shown as dean of the faculty of Washington University, 1875 – 1876, and resided as a doctor, in 1880, with his wife Charlotte, and daughter, Margaret (born 1878), in Baltimore, Maryland.
[Source(s): Foenander; Register; McElroy; Journal; ONWR; Fold3, USN Resignees]

Lindsey, E. R.
Confederate States Navy. Lindsey's name appears on a list of conscripts "in yard at Halifax," June 9, 1864. He served on board the CSS ALBEMARLE, and at Halifax Station, 1864 [possibly the same person shown in the previous listing, E.H. Lindsay].
[McElroy; NA, RG 45; PCNMC]

Lindsey, Pinkney
Seaman, Confederate States Navy. Lindsey enlisted on June 13, 1864, at Raleigh for the war.
[McElroy; NA, RG 45]

Linthicum, William H.
Landsman, Confederate States Navy. Born on February 14, 1818, Linthicum died on September 22, 1886, and was buried in Maplewood Cemetery, Durham, North Carolina.
[McElroy; Gravestone Records, v. 3, p. 177; Stepp, "Burials"]

Lipscomb, John P.
Assistant surgeon, Confederate States Navy. Born in and appointed from North Carolina, Lipscomb's original entry into the Confederate States Navy was on March 26, 1863. He was promoted to Assistant Surgeon on May 1, 1863 and served on the Charleston Station, 1862, as well as on the CSS PALMETTO STATE, Charleston Harbor, South Carolina, 1863 – 1864. He was promoted to Assistant Surgeon, Provisional Navy, on June 2, 1864 and served with the Charleston Squadron, 1862-1864 [or, 1863-1864]; CSS PALMETTO STATE, 1864, the CSS FREDERICKSBURG and CSS HAMPTON, James River Squadron, 1865. Serving with Semmes Naval Brigade, 1865, he was paroled at Greensboro, North Carolina, April 28, 1865.
[Source(s): Foenander; McElroy; Register; ONWR]

Litchfield, George D. (Brunswick County, North Carolina [?])
Private, Company, Coast Guards [SEE NOTE #2]. Litchfield enlisted on February 20, 1864.
[Source(s): Edge]

Litchfield, Joseph (Currituck County, North Carolina)
Private, Confederate States Army//Confederate States Navy. Litchfield was born in Currituck County, North Carolina where he resided as a sailor prior to enlisting at age 24 as a Private in Company B, 8th Regiment, North Carolina State Troops on August 1, 1861 for the war. Captured at Roanoke Island, North Carolina on February 8, 1862, he was paroled in Elizabeth City, North Carolina on February 21, 1862, and exchanged at Aiken's Landing, James River, Virginia on November 10, 1862. He was present or accounted for until captured at Cold Harbor, Virginia on June 1. 1864. Initially sent as a prisoner of war to Point Lookout Prison, he was later transferred to Elmira Prison, New York where he was received on July 12, 1864. He died while in prison at Elmire on April 29, 1865 of "variola." Source "McElroy" states a Joseph Litchfield" of North Carolina had Confederate naval service.
[McElroy; NCT, Vol. IV]

Litchfield (Lichfield), Orison (Orson)
Private, Confederate States Army/Private, Confederate States Marine Corps. Litchfield may have been the same person who served in Company G, 61st North Carolina Infantry. Per North Carolina Troops, XIV, an "Orson Litchfield," born in Missouri, by occupation an overseer, enlisted in New Hanover County, North Carolina, at age 23, on August 14, 1862, for the war, in Company G, 61st Regiment, North Carolina Troops. He was reported absent without leave on an unspecified date (probably in the summer of 1862). No further records. [Note: Litchfield may be one of the 51 men who enlisted in Captain Moore's Independent Company whose service terminated prior to September 29, 1862, the date the company was mustered into the 59th Regiment, North Carolina Troops, later re-designated the 61st Regiment, North Carolina Troops]. Litchfield served as a Private in the Confederate States Marine Corps aboard the CSS VIRGINIA, Hampton Roads, Virginia, 1862; absent without leave, September 15, 1862.
[Source(s): PCNMC; North Carolina Troops, XIV; Foenander; *ORN* 2, 1, 311]

Litchfield (Lichfield), Spencer (Spence) (Chowan County, North Carolina)
Private, Confederate States Army//Confederate States Navy. Litchfield was born in North Carolina in 1837 and resided in 1860 in Elizabeth City, Pasquotank County, North Carolina, as a mariner. He enlisted in Chowan County, North Carolina, May 18, 1861 (May 15, 1861 per MR), as a Private, in Company A, 1st Regiment, North Carolina State Troops on February 1, 1862. He was present or accounted for until discharged on February 1, 1862 upon his transfer to the Confederate States Navy. Litchfield served as an Ordinary Seaman aboard the CSS VIRGINIA, Hampton Roads, Virginia, 1862.
[Source(s): McElroy; PCNMC; Foenander; MR, I]

Litchfield, Thomas (Currituck County, North Carolina)
Private, Confederate States Army//Confederate States Navy. Litchfield was initially a Private in Company B, 8th Regiment, North Carolina State Troops. Captured at Roanoke Island, North Carolina on February 8, 1862, he was paroled in Elizabeth City, North Carolina on February 21, 1862, and exchanged in August 1862. He was again captured at Cold Harbor, Virginia on June 1, 1864, sent as a prisoner of war to Point Lookout, Maryland, thence to Elmira Prison and later paroled. He was transferred to Venus Point, Savannah River, Georgia where he was received on November 15, 1864 for exchange. Source "McElroy" listed naval service.
[McElroy; NCT, IV]

Little, Christopher C.
Ordinary Seaman, Confederate States Navy. Little enlisted on June 5, 1863, in Wilmington for the war. He served aboard the CSS NORTH CAROLINA, Cape Fear River, 1863-1864. Little married Sarah E. Atkinson on October

29, 1863 in Fayetteville, North Carolina at the home of her father.
[Source(s): McElroy; NA, RG 45; "Fay. Obs.," November 9, 1863; Foenander; ORN 2, 1, 294, 295 & 297; "Fay. Obs." (5 November 1863); Oates; MR, 4, p. 443]

Little, Isaac (New Hanover County, North Carolina)
Landsman, Confederate States Navy. Little enlisted in the Confederate States Navy on October 8 [or, 12th], 1863 in Wilmington, North Carolina [or, Camp Holmes] for the war. He served aboard the CSS ARCTIC, Cape Fear River, North Carolina 1863, and aboard the CSS RALEIGH, in 1864. Little appears on a register of Confederate States Army General Military Hospital Number 4, Wilmington, North Carolina, which states that he was admitted December 19, 1863, with "rheumatism chronicus" and returned to duty May 9, 1864. His post office was given on the register as Brinkley's Depot, North Carolina.
[Source(s): MR, 4, p. 446; McElroy; NA, RG 45; ORN 2, 1, 276, 278 & 302; NA, RGR 109; St. Armand; Foenander]

Little, Jno. T. (Anson County, North Carolina)
Confederate States Navy. Private, Company F, Naval Battalion. Little's name appears on a roll of Prisoners of War at Point Lookout, Maryland. The roll states he was captured on April 6, 1865, at Amelia Court House, and confined at Point Lookout, USA General Hospital, from April 14, 1865, until released on taking Oath of Allegiance to the US, July 25, 1865. His place of residence is given on his Oath as Anson County, North Carolina. Description: complexion, fair; hair, dark; eyes, dark; height, 5 ft. 8 in.
[McElroy; NA, RG 109]

Little, William (Wake County, North Carolina)
Private, Confederate States Army//Landsman, Confederate States Navy. Little was born in Wake County, North Carolina, where he resided as a laborer until he enlisted in Wake County at age 20 as a Private in Company K, 14th Regiment, North Carolina Troops on May 21, 1861. He was present or accounted for until transferred to the Confederate States Navy for duty as a Landsman aboard the CSS VIRGINIA [MERRIMAC] on February 15, 1862, at Hampton Roads, Virginia.
[Source(s): McElroy; North Carolina Troops, V; Foenander; MR, I; ORN 2, 1, 309]

Littleton (Littlejohn), Amos C. (Jones County, North Carolina)
Private, Confederate States Army/Confederate States Navy. Littleton was born in Jones County, North Carolina, where he lived as a farmer prior to enlisting there on January 22, 1862, aged 35, as a Private in Company C, 61st Regiment, North Carolina Troops. He deserted on August 27, 1862 but returned to duty on February 26, 1863. Reported present through June 30, 1863, he was wounded in the right shoulder at Morris Island, Charleston Harbor, South Carolina, on or about August 26, 1863. He was reported present, but sick on his unit's September-October 1863 muster. He deserted at Kenansville, North Carolina, on November 23, 1863, but is listed as having transferred to the Confederate States Navy on December 30, 1863. His name may have been "Littlejohn."
[Source(s): McElroy; Foenander; MR, III; North Carolina Troops, XIV]

Liverman, Thomas M. (Beaufort County, North Carolina)
Seaman, Confederate States Navy. Liverman resided and enlisted "for the war" in Beaufort County, North Carolina, on November 7, 1861 [October 21, 1861, per "MR, III"], age 20, as a Private in Company C, 40th Regiment, North Carolina Troops (3rd Regiment, North Carolina Artillery). He was present or accounted for until he transferred to the Confederate States Navy on May 8, 1865[sic] [Per source "North Carolina Troops"] [an apparent typo; should probably be 1862] Served as Seaman on the CSS ARCTIC, 1862.
[Source(s): North Carolina Troops, I; ORN 1, 23, 703; ORN, 2, 1, 276; McElroy; NA, RG 109; Foenander; "Beaufort County Sailors;" MR, III]

Livingston, Alexander L. (Anson County, North Carolina)
Corporal, Confederate States Army//Confederate States Navy. Livingston resided in Anson County, North Carolina where he enlisted at age 32 on October 3, 1861 as a Private in Company B, 31st Regiment, North Carolina Troops. Promoted to Corporal between January 1862 and February 1863, he was present of accounted for until captured at Roanoke Island, North Carolina on February 8, 1862 and was paroled in Elizabeth City, North Carolina on February 21, 1862. He returned to duty on or about September 15, 1862 and was captured at Cold Harbor, Virginia on June 1, 1864. Initially sent as a prisoner of war to Point Lookout Prison, Maryland where he arrived on June 11, 1864, Livingston was transferred to Elmira Prison, New York on July 12, 1864. He was paroled on an unspecified date and transferred to "the James River" where he was received on or about February 20, 1865 for exchange. Source

"McElroy" indicates he had Confederate naval service.
[Source(s): McElroy; NCT, Vol. VIII]

Livingstone, George
Captain's Clerk, Confederate States Navy.
According to source "Moebs," Livingstone served aboard the NCS WINSLOW as a Captain's Clerk. He later served in the same capacity aboard the NCS SEA BIRD during the month of February 1862 and took part in the Battle of Elizabeth City at which he was captured. He was carried to Roanoke Island on February 10, 1862 and paroled there on February 12, 1862. He returned to Elizabeth City, North Carolina.
[Source(s): NCCWSP; Moebs]

Lockett, H. C. (NOTE: May be same as "Henry C. Lockheart," q.v.)
Confederate States Navy. Lockett enlisted in the Confederate States Navy in Wilmington, North Carolina.
[Source(s): MR, 4, p. 446]

Lockett, Henry C. (Craven County, North Carolina) (NOTE: May be same as H. C. Lockheart, q.v.)
Private, Confederate States Army//Confederate States Navy. Lockett was born in Craven County, North Carolina where he resided as a laborer prior to enlisting there at age 18 on June 11, 1861, for the war, in Company D, 5th Regiment, North Carolina State Troops. He was present or accounted for until September 17, 1862 when he deserted or was captured at Sharpsburg, Maryland. A list of deserters from the 5th Regiment carries the following remarks: "taken prisoner at Sharpsburg, Maryland. Never returned to company. Thought to be in our Navy at Wilmington, North Carolina." Records of the Federal Provost Marshal do not substantiate the report of his capture.
[Source(s): North Carolina Troops, IV; Foenander]

Lockwood, Thomas J.
Captain, Confederate States Navy. Lockwood served in the Confederate States Navy as captain aboard the privateer "*Gordon*" in South Carolina Waters, 1861. He was a blockade runner, commanding the "*Elizabeth*," "*Kate*," and "*The Colonel Lamb*." He was the brother-in-law of Chief Engineer George C. McDougald (q.v.), who was said to have made 60 voyages through the blockade in four years and was only captured once.
[Source(s): McElroy; Derelicts]

Lockyer, Charles John (England/North Carolina) ([NOTE: Source NCCWSP lists him as Charles W. Lockyer].
Seaman, Confederate States Navy.
Born on November 8, 1830 in Bristol, England, Lockyer served as a Seaman aboard the CSS BEAUFORT from September 1861 - April 1862 in North Carolina and Virginia waters. His name appears on a payroll of the North Carolina Squadron for the 1st quarter of 1862 covering from January 24, 1862 - April 15, 1862. He transferred to the James River Squadron on April 15, 1862. Lockyer died in Beaufort County, North Carolina, on October 13, 1904.
[*ORN* 2, 1, 281.] [Source(s): Foenander; McElroy; Chauncey; NCCWSP]

Lodge, John S.
Landsman, Confederate States Navy. Lodge enlisted on May 27, 1864, in Raleigh, North Carolina, for the war.
[Source(s): McElroy; NA, RG 45]

Lodge, William H.
Landsman, Confederate States Navy. Lodge enlisted May 27, 1864, in Raleigh, North Carolina, for the war.
[Source(s): McElroy; NA, RG 45]

Loflin, H. L.
Landsman, Confederate States Navy. Loflin enlisted on April 25, 1864 in Raleigh, North Carolina, for the war.
[Source(s): Card File; NA RG 45]

Loflin (Loflen), John [NOTE: May be same as "John Loftin (Davidson County, North Carolina), q.v.]
Landsman, Confederate States Navy. Loflin enlisted on November 1, 1863 in Wilmington, North Carolina, for the war. Another Card states he enlisted on October 30, 1863 in Raleigh, North Carolina, for the war.
[Source(s): Foenander; Card File; NA RG 45]

Loftin, John (Davidson County, North Carolina) [NOTE: May be same as "John Loflin, q.v.]
Confederate States Navy. Loftin enlisted in the Confederate States Navy on October 28, 1863 in Wilmington, North

Carolina.
[Source(s): Foenander; MR, 4, p. 446]

Logan, John (New Hanover County, North Carolina)
Confederate States Navy. Served on the Confederate States Steamer PHANTOM. Appears on registers of Confederate States Army General Military Hospital Number 4, Wilmington, North Carolina, which state he was admitted August 29, 1863 with "febis int" and returned to duty September 1, 1863. Post office listed as Wilmington, North Carolina.
[Source(s): Card File; NA RG 109]

Long, C. W.
Landsman, Confederate States Navy. Enlisted March 3, 1864 at Raleigh, North Carolina, for the war.
[Source(s): Card File; NA RG 45]

Long, James Crosby
Midshipman, Confederate States Navy.
The payroll list of the NCS CURLEW for November 20, 1861 lists Long as a Midshipman aboard that vessel.
[Source: NCCWSP]

Longmain, Thomas (possibly resided in New Hanover County, North Carolina)
Seaman, Confederate States Navy. Longmain was born in England (aged 22 in December 1864) and came to Wilmington, North Carolina, on a blockade runner. He served in Confederate service for twelve months, at least part of which was aboard the CSS VIRGINIA II.
[Source(s): Foenander; PCNMC]

Longman, James (England/Beaufort County, North Carolina)
Seaman, Boatswain's Mate, Confederate States Navy.
Born in England circa 1815, he resided in the county prison in Washington, Beaufort County, North Carolina as of 1850. He shipped for one year aboard the CSS RALEIGH on December 14, 1861, serving as a Seaman from circa March 1862 – April 1862. He was promoted to the rank of Boatswain's Mate on February 22, 1862. His name appears on a North Carolina Squadron payroll covering the period February 21, 1862 - April 15, 1862. He transferred to the James River Squadron April 15, 1862.
[Sources: Census (NC), 1850; NCCWSP]

Lord, John Bradley (New Hanover County, North Carolina)
Cabin Boy, Blockade Runner. At age 13, Lord served as a Cabin Boy aboard a Confederate blockade runner. Born and reared in Wilmington, North Carolina, he practiced law in Brooklyn, New York, from 1875-1914. He died in Darien, Connecticut, at the home of a son on January 10, 1835.
[Source(s): *Oakdale*, Davis; "Star," 1/12/1935]

Loughlin (Laughlin), Charles (Warren County, North Carolina)
Musician (Drummer), Confederate States Army/Confederate States Navy. Residing in Warren County, North Carolina, Loughlin enlisted there at age 17 on August 16, 1861 as musician (drummer) in Company B, 30th Regiment, North Carolina Troops. He was present or accounted for until transferred to the Confederate States Navy on or about April 10, 1862.
[Source(s): Card File; NA RG 45; Foenander; MR, II; North Carolina Troops, VIII]

Louis, Manuel
Landsman, Confederate States Navy. Louis enlisted on March 1, 1864, in Raleigh, North Carolina, for the war.
[Source(s): Card File; NA RG 45]

Love, William C. (Bladen County, North Carolina)
Midshipman, Confederate States Navy. Love was appointed from North Carolina, as an Acting Midshipman, Confederate States Naval Academy, December 13, 1864. He served aboard the CSS PATRICK HENRY, 1864-1865, and was paroled May 24, 1865, at Staunton, Virginia.
[Source(s): Register; Academy]

Loving, Jonathan J.
Landsman, Confederate States Navy. Loving enlisted on October 11, 1863, in Wilmington, North Carolina, for the war.
[Source(s): Card File; NA RG 45]

Lowrey, John G. (Henderson County, North Carolina)
Private, Confederate States Army// Officers' Cook, Confederate States Navy. Lowrey resided in Henderson County, North Carolina, where he enlisted as a Private at age 20 on May 5, 1861 in Company I, 16th Regiment, North Carolina Troops. He was listed as present or accounted for until wounded at or near Seven Pines, Virginia, on or about May 31, 1862, and returned to duty on an unspecified date. He was hospitalized in Richmond, Virginia, on December 15, 1862, with a gunshot wound to the left middle finger. Place and date of wound unknown but was likely wounded at Fredericksburg, Virginia, on or about December 13, 1862. He returned to duty on March 9, 1863 and was listed as present or accounted for until transferred to the 13th Regiment, South Carolina Troops. Source Card File claims he had Confederate Naval service. Source "Foenander" states that he served as an Officers' Cook, CSS ARCTIC, Cape Fear River, North Carolina, 1863, and as a Landsman on the CSS RALEIGH in North Carolina and Virginia waters, 1864.
[Source(s): Card File; North Carolina Troops, VI; Foenander; *ORN* 2, 1, 278 & 302]

Lowrie, Samuel J.
Private, Confederate States Army//Landsman, Confederate States Navy. Lowrie enlisted on August 1, 1864, in Raleigh, North Carolina, for the war. He served aboard the CSS INDIAN CHIEF before transferring to Company D, 10th Battalion, North Carolina Heavy Artillery by SO#6/27, A&IGO, dated January 9, 1865. Source "North Carolina Troops, I" states could find no record of his having actually joined Company D.
[Source(s): Card File; NA RG 45; NA RG 109; North Carolina Troops, I; Foenander]

Loyd, Alex.
2nd Class Boy, Confederate States Navy. Loyd enlisted on February 16, 1864 in Wilmington, North Carolina, for the war.
[Source(s): Foenander; Card File; NA RG 45]

Loyd, John
2nd Class Boy, Confederate States Navy. Loyd enlisted on February 16, 1864 in Wilmington, North Carolina, for the war, and served aboard the CSS RALEIGH in North Carolina and Virginia waters, 1862 – 1864.
[Source(s): Foenander; Card File; NA RG 45]

Luark, John (North Carolina)
Seaman, Confederate States Navy. Born in North Carolina in 1842, Luark served as a Seaman aboard the CSS SEA BIRD from at least July through November 1861, and as a member of the North Carolina Squadron as of December 1, 1861. He resided as a fisherman, in 1870, with his wife, Frances, and three children, at Nags Head, Currituck County, North Carolina.
[Source(s): Foenander; ORN 2, 1, 306; Census (North Carolina), 1870; NCCWSP]

Lucas, Sherrod [Sherwood] (Sampson County, North Carolina)
Private, Confederate States Army//Confederate States Navy. Born in Sampson County, North Carolina, where he resided as a farmer until he enlisted there at age 25 on March 3, 1862 [another source says "1861"] and served as a Private in Captain Holmes' Company, Company I, 46th Regiment, North Carolina Troops. Present or accounted for until hospitalized at Charlottesville, Virginia, on September 3, 1862, with a gunshot wound of the hand. Place and date of wound not reported. Reported absent without leave during November 1862 - April 1863 but returned to duty in May - June 1863. Present or accounted for until his transfer to the Confederate States Navy in Richmond, Virginia, on April 1, 1864. Taken sick, he lingered for three months in the hospital in Richmond before dying of "chronic disease and consumption" at the age of 29 on July 15, 1864. Obituary lists a wife, two children, a mother, four sisters, and six brothers (five of whom serving in the Confederate States Army). He had been a member of the Baptist Church for eight years prior to his death.
[Source(s): Card File; "Fay. Obs." (14 November 1864); North Carolina Troops, XI]

Luck, John
Captain, Confederate States Navy. Luck served as a pilot on the *E. Mills*, possibly a civilian transport. He is also said to have served aboard the CSS ALBEMARLE, and on the Wilmington Station, North Carolina, 1862 – 1864, and been involved in the attack on Plymouth, North Carolina, April 20, 1864.

[Source(s): Foenander; Card File; UDC, MC of Svc]

Luck, John (also Lucke)
Gunner's Mate, Confederate States Navy.
Luck shipped for war aboard the CSS RALEIGH on August 6, 1861 and, per payroll, bounty, and clothing records, remained with her through April 1862. His name appears on the payroll of the North Carolina Squadron for the 1st quarter of 1862 covering from February 21, 1862 - April 15, 1862. He transferred to the James River Squadron on April 15, 1862 but is listed as having served at Drewry's Bluff as a Gunner's Mate on that station's payroll for the period from April 1, 1863 - 30 June 30, 1863. He later served as a Gunner's Mate aboard the CSS RALEIGH with the James River Squadron per its payroll covering from November 16, 1863 - December 15, 1863.
[Source: NCCWSP]

Lumsden, Henry C. (New Hanover County, North Carolina)
Private, Confederate States Army// Ordinary Seaman, Confederate States Navy. Born in New Hanover County, North Carolina in December 1842, Lumsden resided as a laborer in Wilmington, North Carolina, where he enlisted at age 18 on June 6, 1861 in Company E, 1st Regiment, North Carolina State Troops. He was discharged at Skinner's Neck, Virginia, on February 11, 1863, for disability, having hurt his back putting a log on a trench. Lumsden was later conscripted at Pisgah Church, Virginia, on February 14, 1864, "for the war ..." (regiment unknown). He was present or accounted for until his transfer to the Confederate States Navy on April 17, 1864, where he served as an Ordinary Seaman. He was attached as a Private to Company H, 2nd Regiment, Semmes' Naval Brigade in April 1865, and was surrendered and paroled at Greensboro, North Carolina on April 26, 1865. He resided, as a widower, in 1900, at Masonboro, New Hanover County, North Carolina, and may have lived in the soldier's home, Raleigh, North Carolina (per Source "Mosley"). Lumsden died in Wilmington, North Carolina. His Compiled Confederate Service Record card states that he "transferred to N." [Navy] by Special Order #95/7. April 23, 1864.
[Source(s): Foenander; Mr. Terry Mosley, Durham, North Carolina; North Carolina Troops, III; Card File]

Luper, Robert S.
Landsman, Confederate States Navy. Enlisted October 5, 1863 at Camp Holmes (near Raleigh, North Carolina).
[Source(s): Card File; NA RG 45]

Luydam (Lysham, Laydam), J. W.
Seaman, Confederate States Navy [NOTE: May be the same as J. N. Lysham]
From clothing and payroll lists, he is known to have served as a Seaman aboard the CSS BEAUFORT from September – December 1861, and likely afterwards. He received a partial payment on February 13, 1862 at Gosport Navy Yard following his service in manning Fort Cobb at the Battle of Elizabeth City on February 10, 1862. Luydam appears on the payroll of the North Carolina Squadron for the 1st quarter of 1862 covering from December 1, 1861 - February 28, 1862 and is listed as having "run" on or by February 28, 1862.
[Source: NCCWSP]

Lyerly [Lyerlie, Lyerlee], **Wiley** (Stanly County, North Carolina)
Landsman, Confederate States Navy. Enlisted for the Confederate States Navy on August 24, 1863 in Wilmington, North Carolina. Some sources state he enlisted September 11, 1863 at Camp Holmes (near Raleigh, North Carolina) for the war. The record of Alfred W. Lawson states that he was "Exchanged with W. Lyerly to C. S. Navy," March-April 1864. Transferred March-April 1864 to Company C, 13th Battalion, North Carolina Light Artillery. Present or accounted for through February 1865. Paroled at Greensboro, North Carolina, May 1, 1865.
[Source(s): MR, 4, p. 446; Card File; Foenander; NA RG 45; North Carolina Troops, I; McElroy; NA RG 109]

Lyerly, W.
Confederate States Navy//Private, Confederate States Army. Transferred from the Confederate States Navy circa March-April 1864, for the war, to Company C, 13th Battalion, North Carolina Light Artillery. Present or accounted for through February 1865. Paroled at Greensboro, North Carolina, on May 1, 1865.
[Source(s): McElroy; Card File; NA RG 109; North Carolina Troops, I]

Lynam (Lymun), Marcus A. (Granville County, North Carolina)
Landsman, Confederate States Navy. Born Granville County, North Carolina, 1845. Conscripted March 30, 1863, at Camp Holmes (near Raleigh, North Carolina) from Colonel Dolby's 43rd Regiment, North Carolina Militia, Granville County, North Carolina. Description: Age 19; eyes blue; hair light; complexion fair; height 5 feet 9 inches; place of birth Granville County, North Carolina; occupation farmer. Another source states he enlisted March 31, 1864 at Raleigh, North Carolina, for the war, while another says his name appears on a list of conscripts "in the yard

at Halifax." He served as a Landsman aboard the CSS ALBEMARLE, and on the Halifax Station, 1864, after the destruction of the CSS ALBEMARLE. Lynam's post-war status was that of a married farmer, residing in Tennessee since 1870. His second marriage was to Alice Measles, in DeKalb County, Tennessee, on August 21, 1878. He resided as a farmer, in 1910, with his wife, and daughter Alia, at Liberty, DeKalb County, Tennessee. His application for a Confederate pension was filed in Tennessee (file number 11450).
[Source(s): Card File; NA RG 45; Foenander]

Lynch, Hugh
Ordinary Seaman, Confederate States Navy. Lynch enlisted on June 13, 1863, in Wilmington, North Carolina, for the war.
[Source(s): Card File; NA RG 45]

Lynch, J. H. (Halifax County, North Carolina)
Confederate States Navy. Lynch enlisted in the Confederate States on Navy August 17, 1863 in Wilmington, North Carolina.
[Source(s): MR, 4, p. 446]

Lynch, John (New Hanover County, North Carolina)
Private, Confederate States Army//Confederate States Navy. Born in Ireland, Lynch worked as a sailmaker in New Hanover County, North Carolina, where he enlisted at age 22 on June 19, 1861, as a Private in Company F, 3rd Regiment, North Carolina State Troops. He transferred to the Confederate States Navy on February 1, 1862.
[Source(s): Card File; North Carolina Troops, III; Foenander; MR, I]

Lynch. Junius J. (Maryland or North Carolina)
Assistant Paymaster, Confederate States Navy. Nephew of Commodore William F. Lynch, Confederate States Navy. Born 1836 in Maryland and lived in Baltimore, Maryland, as a bookkeeper in 1860. Appointed March 18, 1862 as Assistant Paymaster from Virginia (though also reportedly a resident of North Carolina). Served on the Richmond Station, 1861 – 1862. Assigned by letter dated October 25, 1862, from the Confederate Secretary of the Navy to serve aboard the steamer CSS FLORIDA, then in Mobile Bay (1862 – 1863) under Captain John Newland Maffitt, Confederate States Navy. Died on July 13, 1863 of consumption after a short illness while serving aboard the CSS FLORIDA off Bermuda. Buried in Bermuda (probably in Hamilton) in an Episcopal cemetery. Was described as a "zealous officer, respected and esteemed by all on board [CSS FLORIDA]. [One source gives first name as "James"].
[Source(s): Maffitt; Foenander; *ORN*; *Register*; Census (North Carolina) 1860]

Lynch, Rufus (Johnston County, North Carolina)
Confederate States Navy. Born April 1826. In 1900, Lynch applied for a Confederate pension from Johnston County, North Carolina where he resided as a mechanic, at Wilder (Johnston County). He is shown as a widower, residing as a mechanic in 1900, and still living in 1910. His pension application dated July 1, 1901, age 75, Eason's post office, states he was never wounded. The application was disapproved. On a subsequent application dated July 4, 1910, at age 84, Lynch states he enlisted in the Confederate States Navy in 1864. This pension was approved for 4th Class.
[Source(s): Census (North Carolina), 1900; Census (North Carolina), 1910; Foenander; Pensions (North Carolina)]

Lynch, William F.
Flag Officer, Confederate States Navy.
Born in Virginia, Lynch was appointed to the United States Navy from that state and served until he resigned his commission on April 21, 1861 at the rank of Captain. He served in the Virginia Navy and was appointed to the rank of captain in the Confederate States Navy on June 10, 1861 [Source "Moebs" gives the date as October 23, 1861] to rank from March 26, 1861. He commanded several naval batteries along Aquia Creek, Virginia in 1861 and was appointed to command the water defenses of North Carolina and Virginia, 1861 – 1862 using as his flagship the CSS SEA BIRD. He was aboard the CSS SEA BIRD as a member of the North Carolina Squadron as early as July 1861 per that ship's muster roll for the period July – November 1861. He was briefly aboard the CSS RALEIGH per clothing records dated September 2, 1861. Lynch participated in the Battle of Roanoke Island, February 7 – 8, 1862, and temporarily commanded the Mississippi River defenses in 1862. He was placed in command of the naval defenses of North Carolina, 1862 – 1864. He was serving on the Richmond, Virginia Station in 1864, and was paroled om May 3, 1865 following the close hostilities.
[Source(s): NCCWSP; Moebs]

Lynn, John (Wake County, North Carolina)
Confederate States Navy (Naval Battalion). Lynn's name appears on a roll of Prisoners of War at Point Lookout, Maryland, which states he was captured April 7, 1865 in Wake County, North Carolina, and confined at Point Lookout, Maryland, from April 7, 1865 until released June 28, 1865 on taking the Oath of Allegiance. Description: complexion fair; hair light brown; eyes light blue; height 5 feet 6 inches; place of residence Wake County, North Carolina.
[Source(s): Card File; NA RG 109]

Lyon, William Franklin (Caswell County, North Carolina [NOTE: May be same as "William W. Lyon," q.v.]
Landsman, Confederate States Navy. Lyon was born on January 22, 1845; died March 3, 1913; and was buried at Prospect Methodist Church, Caswell County, North Carolina.
[Source(s): Stepp, "Burials"]

Lyon, William W. (Caswell County, North Carolina) [NOTE: May be same as "William Franklin Lyon," q.v.]
Private, Confederate States Army//Confederate States Navy. Lyon was born in Caswell County, North Carolina and resided as a carpenter or mechanic in Rockingham County, North Carolina, where he enlisted on May 30, 1861 at age 25 as a Private in Company A, 13th Regiment, North Carolina Troops. He was listed as present or accounted for until he transferred to the Confederate States Navy for duty as a Landsman aboard the CSS VIRGINIA [MERRIMAC], at Hampton Roads, Virginia, on February 14, 1862.
[Source(s): North Carolina Troops, V; MR, I; ORN 2, 1, 309; Card File; Foenander; NA RG 45]

MacLoughlin, John D.
Landsman, Confederate States Navy. MacLoughlin enlisted on April 13, 1864, at Kinston, North Carolina, for three years or the war.
[Source(s): Card File; NA RG 45]

McAlister, Alexander (Yancey County, North Carolina)
Private, Confederate States Army/Confederate States Navy. McAlister resided in Yancey County, North Carolina, where he enlisted at age 23 on May 1, 1861 as a Private in Company C, 16th Regiment, North Carolina Troops. Promoted to Corporal in January-February 1863, he was present or accounted for until reported missing in action at Falling Waters, Maryland, on July 13-14, 1863. Roll of Honor records indicate he was captured in an unspecified battle and escaped from Point Lookout, Maryland; however, records of the Federal Provost Marshal do not substantiate either report. Source "Foenander" states he escaped from Point Lookout, Maryland at an unspecified date; rejoined his company September or October 1863. He was present or accounted for until he transferred to the Confederate States Navy on April 3, 1864.
[Source(s): Card File; North Carolina Troops, VI; Foenander]

McAllister, John W.
Landsman, Confederate States Navy. McAllister enlisted on December 15 [19], 1863 at Raleigh [at Wilmington], North Carolina, for the war, McAllister served as a Landsman aboard the CSS ARCTIC, Cape Fear River, North Carolina, 1863, and CSS RALEIGH, North Carolina and Virginia waters, 1864.
[Source(s): Card File; NA RG 45; Foenander]

McAnulty [McAnully], Julius A.
Landsman, Confederate States Navy. Enlisting in the Confederate States Navy on January 11, 1864 in Raleigh, North Carolina, for the war, McAnulty served as a Landsman, CSS ARCTIC, Cape Fear River, North Carolina, 1863, and may be the same as "J.A. McAnulty" who served aboard the CSS RALEIGH, North Carolina, and Virginia waters, 1862 – 1864.
[Source(s): Card File; NA RG 45; *ORN* 2, 1, 278; Foenander]

McArthur, Peter (Richmond County, North Carolina) [May BE PETER "Jr." or "Sr."]
Landsman, Confederate States Navy. McArthur enlisted in the Confederate States Navy in Wilmington, North Carolina. NA RG 45 states he enlisted on October 19, 1863 at Camp Holmes (near Raleigh, North Carolina). He served as a Landsman aboard the CSS ARCTIC in 1863, and the CSS YADKIN, Wilmington, North Carolina, 1863 [-1864?]. Source "NA RG 109" states he was a private in the Naval Battalion. His name appears as a signature on an Oath of Allegiance to the US subscribed to and sworn to at Point Lookout, Maryland, on June 29, 1865. Description:

Complexion light; hair brown; eyes dark blue; height 5 feet 11 inches; residence listed as Richmond County, North Carolina.
[Source(s): MR, 4, p. 446; Card File; Foenander; NA RG 45; NA RG 109; Richmond County Soldiers]

McArthur, Peter (Richmond County, North Carolina) [May be Peter "Jr." or "Sr.;" or the same man]
Confederate States Navy.
[Source(s): Richmond County Soldiers]

McBride, A. A. (Robeson County, North Carolina)
Landsman [Sergeant], Confederate States Navy [Naval Battalion]. McBride enlisted on May 5, 1864, in Raleigh, North Carolina, for the war. His name appears as a signature to an Oath of Allegiance to the US, subscribed and sworn to at Newport News, Virginia, June 30, 1865. His place of residence was given on the Oath as "Roberson [sic] County, North Carolina," and his description as follows: Complexion fair; hair dark; eyes blue; height 5 ft. 8 in. The Oath carries the remark: "Captured at Farmville [Virginia] April 6, 1865."
[Source(s): Card File; NA RG 45; NA RG 109]

McBride, Owen (New Hanover County, North Carolina)
Confederate States Navy. McBride served aboard the Confederate Steamer EUGENIE. His name appears on a register of Confederate States Army General Military Hospital Number 4, Wilmington, North Carolina, as being admitted November 4, 1863 with "febris intermittens tertian," and returned to duty November 11, 1863. His post office on the register was listed as Wilmington, North Carolina.
[Source(s): NA RG 109; Card File]

McCahan, J. H. (Washington County, North Carolina)
Seaman, Confederate States Navy. McCahan served on the CSS ALBEMARLE. Name appears as signature to an Oath of Amnesty subscribed and sworn to at Fort Monroe, Virginia, July 2, 1864. Place of residence given on Oath as Plymouth, North Carolina, and description as follows: Complexion light; height 5 ft. 11 in.; hair brown; eyes grey. Oath carries the remark: "Rebel deserter came in Federal lines near Plymouth, North Carolina."
[Source(s): NA RG 109; Card File]

McCall [McColl], Daniel (Cumberland County, North Carolina)
Landsman, Confederate States Navy. McCall enlisted on March 18, 1864, at Raleigh, North Carolina, for the war. NA RG 45 states he was conscripted March 17, 1864 at Camp Holmes [near Raleigh, North Carolina] from Colonel McKay's 54th Regiment, North Carolina Militia from Cumberland County, North Carolina. Description: Age 29; eyes hazel; hair dark; complexion fair; height 5 ft. 9 in.; place of birth Cumberland County, North Carolina; occupation cooper.
[Source(s): NA RG 45; Card File]

McCall [McColl], David (Cumberland County, North Carolina)
Confederate States Navy. Born in Cumberland County, North Carolina, McCall [McColl] worked as a cooper prior to enlisting there on March 17, 1864, aged 29, in the Confederate States Navy. His name appears on a "List of Conscripts in the Yard [at Halifax?]" and then transferred to Wilmington, North Carolina, June 9, 1864.
[Source(s): NA RG 45; Card File; Foenander]

McCall, Edward
Seaman, Confederate States Navy. McCall enlisted in the Confederate States Navy in Wilmington, North Carolina. NA RG 45 lists an "Edward McCall" as having enlisted on October 23, 1863 in Wilmington for the war. He served aboard the CSS ARCTIC, 1863, and the CSS NORTH CAROLINA, 1864.
[Source(s): MR, 4, p. 446; NA RG 45; Card File; St. Armand; Foenander]

McCann, John B. (Duplin County, North Carolina)
Corporal, Confederate States Army/Confederate States Navy. McCann was born and resided in Duplin County, North Carolina, where he resided as a farmer until his enlistment as a Private in Company A, 38th Regiment, North Carolina Troops, at age 18, on October 1, 1861. Promoted to Corporal on July 26, 1862, he was present or accounted for until wounded at the Battle of Second Manassas, Virginia, August 30, 1862, and returned to duty prior to January 1, 1863. He was wounded in the right parietal bone at Chancellorsville, Virginia, May 3, 1863. He returned to duty on July 24, 1863 and was present or accounted for until transferred to the Confederate States Navy on April 3, 1864.
[Source(s): Card File; Hamilton; North Carolina Troops, X; Foenander]

McCarrick, James W.
> Master's Mate, Confederate States Navy. Born in Virginia, circa 1843,
> McCarrick served as a Master's Mate aboard the CSS SEA BIRD as of February 1862.
> [Source: NCCWSP]

McCarrick, Patrick (Ireland/North Carolina [?])
> First Lieutenant, Confederate States Navy.
> Source "Driver" states he was born in Ballina Company, Ireland, on June 16, 1821. McCarrick resided as a steamboat captain in Norfolk at the time of his entry into Confederate service. He was appointed Acting Master, August 25, 1861, from North Carolina; later appointed Master. Source "Driver" states he was "transferred to the Confederate States Navy as Master, from Virginia, not in line for promotion, August 25, 1861, that he was Captain of the steamer CSS NORTHAMPTON, and that he was appointed a First Lieutenant in the North Carolina Navy. "Driver" further states he came in May 1861 to command the CSS WINSLOW (formerly "F. E. Coffee"), after it was purchased by the State of North Carolina [Source NCCWSP gives his dates of command from circa July – November 1861]. He remained aboard until it sank in Ocracoke Inlet, 1861. He was a Lieutenant, commanding the CSS SEA BIRD, Commodore Lynch's flagship, 1861-1862, and participated in the Battles of Roanoke Island, North Carolina, February 7, 1862, and Elizabeth City, North Carolina, February 10, 1862. He was captured on February 10, 1862 [Source "Driver" states that he was paroled at Elizabeth City, North Carolina, February 12, 1862] and exchanged September 1862. McCarrick was listed as a prisoner on parole, Gosport Navy Yard, in 1862. He served on the Mississippi River defenses, 1862-1863, commanding the steamer CSS CHARM, 1863. Source "Driver" states he served on a blockade runner out of Wilmington, 1863, and as a Lieutenant on the Johnson's Island Canadian Expedition in October 1863. He was promoted to Lieutenant, Confederate States Navy, for the war, on March 18, 1864, and First Lieutenant, Provisional Confederate States Navy, on June 2, 1864, to rank from January 6, 1864. His service included the CSS NORTH CAROLINA, Wilmington Station, 1864-1865, and special duty, Wilmington Station, 1864-1865. After the war, McCarrick worked as a Ship's Captain for the Old Dominion Steamship Company, Portsmouth, Virginia. He died in Norfolk, February 3, 1888, and is buried at St. Mary's Cemetery.
> [Source(s): McElroy; Register; Card File; Driver; Foenander]
> [NOTE: Some information on Patrick McCarrick and his son Patrick Henry McCarrick may have been inadvertently interchanged; NCCWSP]

McCarrick, Patrick Henry (North Carolina)
> Midshipman, Confederate States Navy. McCarrick was born in and appointed from North Carolina in the North Carolina Navy, June 1, 1861 as an Acting Midshipman (Midshipman 4th Class), Confederate States Navy. Source Census (Virginia), 1860 shows him as having been born in Virginia about 1845 and living then in Norfolk, Virginia. Per source "Fold3, Midshipmen," he was appointed as an Acting Midshipman, Confederate States Navy, from civilian life on August 31, 1861. One source indicates he served aboard the Confederate States Receiving Ship CSS UNITED STATES, 1861; Acting Midshipman on the CSS FORREST as part of the North Carolina Squadron (Source NCCWSP); the naval defenses of North Carolina, 1861-1862; and, the Gosport Navy Yard, 1862; and, CSS BALTIC, Mobile Squadron, Mississippi River, 1862-1863. Appointed a Midshipman, Provisional Navy, on June 2, 1864, he was promoted to Passed Midshipman, Provisional Navy, on December 19, 1864 and ordered to report to Lieutenant W. L. Bradford, CSN, for duty on the James River shore batteries. He served on the Confederate States steamers CSS PATRICK HENRY, CSS VIRGINIA II, James River Squadron, 1863-1864, the CSS NORTH CAROLINA, Wilmington Squadron, 1863-1864, and the CSS FREDERICKSBURG [Card File source states he was on the CSS FREDERICKSBURG in Virginia waters in 1865] and "Driver" states he participated in the Battle of Sailors Creek, Virginia, and surrendered as a Second Lieutenant, Company C, 1st Regiment, Semmes Naval Brigade, April 1865. Another source states he surrendered at Appomattox. He was paroled at Greensboro, North Carolina, April 28, 1865.
> [Source(s): McElroy; Register; Sea Bird; Card File; Driver; NCCWSP; Journal; Foenander; Academy; ONWR; Fold3, Midshipmen]
> [NOTE: Some sources may have inadvertently interchanged information on Patrick McCarrick and his son Patrick Henry McCarrick]
]
McCauts, G. M. D.
> Landsman, Confederate States Navy. McCauts enlisted on October 15, 1863 in Wilmington, North Carolina, for the war.
> [Source(s): Card File; NA RG 45]

McClawn, Benjamin
> Landsman, Confederate States Navy. McClawn enlisted on April 8, 1864 at Halifax or Plymouth, North Carolina, for

the war.
[Source(s): Card File; NA RG 45]

McClennahan (McClanahan), A.
Landsman, Confederate States Navy. McClennahan enlisted on April 12, 1864 at Kinston, North Carolina, for three years or the war. May be the "A. M. Clanahan" that served aboard the CSS NEUSE as of March – October 1864.
[Source(s): Card File; NA RG 45; NEUSE Roster; CMACSSN]

McClenny, J. (Sampson County, North Carolina)
Crewman, Confederate States Navy. McClenny enlisted at Wilmington, North Carolina and served on the CSS NORTH CAROLINA. [NOTE: May be the same as "Joseph McClenny or James or Josiah McClanney," all of whom served aboard the CSS NORTH CAROLINA, Cape Fear River, North Carolina, 1864].
[Source(s): MR, 4, p. 443; Card File; "Bizzell," p. 236; Foenander]

McCombs, Amos
Landsman, Confederate States Navy. McCombs enlisted on May 27, 1864 at Raleigh, North Carolina, for the war.
[Source(s): Card File; NA RG 45]

McCree, James C. (Mecklenburg County, North Carolina)
Confederate States Navy. McCree enlisted in the Confederate States Navy on October 31, 1863 in Wilmington, North Carolina. His widow Fannie E. McCree's application for pension dated July 25, 1921, age 71, listing her post office as Charlotte, North Carolina, states he enlisted in Wilmington, North Carolina. The pension was approved at 4th Class.
[Source(s): MR, 4, p. 446; Pensions (North Carolina)]

McCumber, Amos
Private, Confederate States Army//Confederate States Navy. Born in New Hanover County, North Carolina, McCumber worked as a bricklayer until he enlisted at age 22 on July 11, 1861 in Company F, 8th Regiment, North Carolina State Troops. Captured at Roanoke Island, North Carolina on February 8, 1862, he was probably paroled in Elizabeth City, North Carolina on February 21, 1862, and exchanged in August 1862. He deserted his unit twice. First, from December 1, 1863 until he rejoined his unit on or about July 28, 1864. He deserted again on August 15, 1864. McCumber is listed in the hospital at Petersburg, Virginia as of September 13, 1864. He was transferred to the Provost Marshal on September 30, 1864 and is listed as having died in the hospital on January 24, 1865. Source "Card File" indicates naval service.
[Source(s): Card File; NCT, Vol. IV]

McCurry, John L. (Cleveland County, North Carolina)
Confederate States Marine Corps. McCurry enlisted at Raleigh, North Carolina, on October 6, 1864 [Source "Pensions (North Carolina)" states he enlisted on September 6, 1864. He served on the Charleston, SC, Station as a Private of the Marine guard on board the ironclad, CSS COLUMBIA to February 7, 1865. Paroled as a Private in Company F, 2nd Regiment, Semmes' Naval Brigade at Greensboro, North Carolina, "circa April 28, 1865" [Source "Foenander" states he was "surrendered and paroled at Greensboro, North Carolina, April 26, 1865." McCurry filed a pension application dated July 1, 1910 at age 66. Application for pension of his widow Nancy N. McCurry of King's Mountain, Cleveland County, North Carolina, dated August 8, 1921 states he entered service on or about September 6, 1864, and that he died on July 8, 1921. Another source lists her address as Shelby, Cleveland County, North Carolina. He was circa age 20 upon enlistment, as he is listed as age 66 in the 1910 Census of North Carolina.
[Source(s): North Carolina Troops, Doc.# 0299; Card File; Pensions (North Carolina); Census (North Carolina), 1910; Donnelly-ENL; Foenander]

McDade, W. H.
Landsman, Confederate States Navy. McDade enlisted on January 27, 1864 in Wilmington, North Carolina, for the war, and served as a coal heaver, steam gunboat CSS YADKIN, Wilmington, North Carolina, 1864.
[Source(s): Card File; NA RG 45; Foenander]

McDaniel, I. W. [NOTE: May be same as "J. W. McDaniel," q.v.]
Landsman, Confederate States Navy. A "J. W. McDaniel" served as a Landsman, CSS ARCTIC, Cape Fear River, North Carolina, 1863.
[Source(s): Card File; NA RG 45; Foenander]

McDaniel, J. W. [J. M.] [I. W.] (Rutherford County, North Carolina) [NOTE: May be same as "I. W. McDaniel," q.v.]
Confederate States Navy. McDaniel enlisted in the Confederate States Navy on October 17, 1863 in Wilmington, North Carolina, for the war [Source NA RG 45 states he enlisted October 26, 1863 at Camp Holmes [near Raleigh], North Carolina.
[Source(s): MR, IV; Card File; NA RG 45; BRGS]

McDaniel, William J. (Halifax County, North Carolina)
Landsman, Confederate States Navy. McDaniel enlisted on March 30, 1864 in Raleigh, North Carolina, for the war. NA RG 45 source states he was conscripted March 29, 1864 at Camp Holmes [Near Raleigh, North Carolina], North Carolina from Colonel Johnson's 34th Regiment, North Carolina Militia from Halifax County, North Carolina. Description: Age 23; eyes blue; hair light; complexion fair; height 5 ft. 5 ½ in.; place of birth Halifax; occupation farmer.
[Source(s): Card File; NA RG 45]

McDonald, M. A. (Moore County, North Carolina)
Private, Confederate States Marine Corps. McDonald enlisted in Raleigh, North Carolina, on November 4, 1864 [NOTE: Letter of James C. Davis, November 17, 1864, states the group from Camp Holmes, of which McDonald was a part, arrived aboard the CSS INDIAN CHIEF, Charleston, SC, Sunday, November 6, 1864, and was designated to serve aboard the ironclad CSS CHICORA]. He served on the Charleston, SC, Station as a Private of the Marine guard on board the ironclad, CSS COLUMBIA. McDonald deserted on January 5, 1865. A Conscript Office (Raleigh) letter dated January 17, 1865 to the Enrolling Officer (Moore County) lists him as a deserter from the "C.S. Navy" and describes him as "30 years old, 5 feet 11 inches high, grey eyes, light hair, light complexion."
[Source(s): North Carolina Troops, Doc. # 0299; Card File; McDonald Papers; Davis, November 17, 1864]

McDonald, William
Seaman, Confederate States Navy.
Muster records indicate McDonald served aboard the NCS SEA BIRD from July - February 1862. Captured in the Battle of Elizabeth City, he was carried to Roanoke Island on February 10, 1862 and took the Oath of Allegiance to the United States on February 12, 1862. His name appears on the payroll of the North Carolina Squadron for the 1st quarter of 1862 (December 1, 1861 - February 12, 1862. His name is annotated with "run" February 12, 1862.
[Source: NCCWSP]

McDonald, W. C. (Richmond County, North Carolina)
Landsman [Private], Confederate States Navy. McDonald enlisted on August 31, 1864 in Raleigh, North Carolina, for the war. His name appears on a Register of Prisoners of War at Hart's Island, New York Harbor, which states he was captured in Richmond County, North Carolina, March 6, 1865, and confined at Hart's Island, April 10, 1865, until released June 18, 1865. Name appears as signature to an Oath of Allegiance to the United States, subscribed and sworn to at Hart's Island, New York Harbor on June 18, 1865. His place of residence was given on the Oath as Richmond County, North Carolina. Description: complexion dark, eyes grey; height 5 ft. 8 in.
[Source(s): Card File; NA RG 45, NA RG 109]

McDougal, George C.
Chief Engineer and blockade runner, Confederate States Navy. Brother-in-law of famed blockade runner Captain Thomas J. Lockwood, McDougal is said to have made 60 voyages through the blockade, being captured only once during his four years of service. He was the Chief Engineer of the Confederate States streamers CSS GORDON, CSS KATE, AND CSS ELIZABETH. Born in 1826, he died on October 20, 1909, and was buried in Oakdale Cemetery, Wilmington, New Hanover County, North Carolina.
[Source(s): McElroy; Card File; Stepp, "Burials;" Derelicts]

McDuffie. Murdock (Richmond County, North Carolina)
Landsman or Seaman, Confederate States Navy. McDuffie enlisted on September 28, 1863 at Camp Holmes [near Raleigh, North Carolina], North Carolina, for the war. His name appears on a roll of Prisoners of War at Point Lookout, Maryland, which states he was captured at Burkeville, Virginia, April 6, 1865, and confined at Point Lookout, Maryland, from April 14, 1865, until released June 29, 1865. His name further appears as a signature to an Oath of Allegiance to the United States subscribed and sworn to at Point Lookout, Maryland, June 29, 1865. The Oath gives his place of residence as Richmond County, North Carolina. Description: Complexion fair; hair brown; eyes hazel; height 6 feet.
[Source(s): Card File; NA RG 45; NA RG 109]

McDuffy, H. E. (New Hanover County, North Carolina)
Confederate States Navy. McDuffy appears on registers of the Confederate States Army General Military Hospital Number 4, Wilmington, North Carolina, dated July 25, 1863, giving his disease as "conjunctiv.," and listing his post office as Wilmington, North Carolina.
[Source(s): Card File; NA RG 45; NA RG 109]

McElwell, Joseph (North Carolina)
1st Class Fireman, Confederate States Navy.
McElwell previously served in the North Carolina Navy aboard the North Carolina Ship NCS WINSLOW as a 1st Class Fireman from at least July through November 1861, and later as a1st Class Fireman aboard the CSS SEA BIRD. His name appears on a payroll of the North Carolina Squadron covering the period December 1, 1861 through March 31, 1862. Yet, according to the order book of Captain French Forrest, CSN, Commander of the Gosport Navy Yard and the James River Squadron, McElwell was discharged by his order on January 3, 1862.
[Source: NCCWSP; Wikipedia (French Forrest)]

McFall[s], Leander (Lincoln County, North Carolina)
Landsman, Confederate States Navy. McFall enlisted on November 4 [or, 5], 1863, in Wilmington, North Carolina, for the war. Source "MR" gives his enlistment date as July 7, 1863. He died on January 27, 1864 and was buried in Oakdale Cemetery, the Confederate mass grave, Wilmington, New Hanover County, North Carolina.
[Source(s): MR, 4, p. 446; Card File; NA RG 45; Stepp, "Burials;" Hoke Camp]

McFarland, D. B.
Landsman, Confederate States Navy. Enlisted December 21, 1863 at Raleigh, North Carolina, for the war. [NOTE: May be Duncan B. McFarland, who served as a Landsman on the CSS ARCTIC, Cape Fear River, North Carolina, 1863, and who was subsequently confined at Point Lookout, Maryland, where he died and is buried (Foenander)].
[Source(s): Card File; NA RG 45]

McFarland, William (New Hanover County, North Carolina)
"Private," Confederate States Navy. Appears on registers of Confederate States Army General Military Hospital Number 4, Wilmington, North Carolina, which state that he was admitted February 27, 1864, with "pneumonia" and returned to duty March 21, 1864. Post office given on registers as Wilmington, North Carolina. [NOTE: Source "Foenander" lists a "W. A. McFarland," who served as a Landsman, CSS ARCTIC, Cape Fear River, North Carolina, 1863; a "William McFarland," who served as a crew member aboard the CSS BOMBSHELL, was captured aboard that vessel during the engagement at Albemarle Sound, North Carolina, May 5, 1864, transferred the same day from the USS CERES to the USS SASSACUS, thence to the steamer USS LOCKWOOD (May 10, 1864) for transportation to Old Capitol Prison, Washington, D.C. (Listed as a resident of New Orleans, Louisiana, but does not state whether this was before or after the war); and, a "William A. McFarland," who was a Landsman aboard the CSS RALEIGH, North Carolina and Virginia waters, 1862 – 1864].
[Source(s): Card File; NA RG 109; Foenander]

McFerrell, _____(?) (New Hanover County, North Carolina)
Private, Confederate States Army/Confederate States Navy. Resided in New Hanover County, North Carolina, where he enlisted as a Private at age 25 on July 1, 1863, "for the war," in Company F, 31st Regiment, North Carolina Troops. Transferred to the Confederate States Navy prior to May 1, 1864.
[Source(s): Card File; North Carolina Troops, VIII; Foenander]

McGary, Charles P. (Maryland/Appointed from North Carolina)
Lieutenant, Confederate States Navy. McGary was born in Maryland and appointed in the Confederate States Navy from North Carolina. Enlisting in the United States Navy on October 19, 1841, McGary became a Passed Midshipman on August 10, 1847, a Master on September 14, 1855, and a Lieutenant on September 15, 1855, and resigned on April 25, 1861. He was appointed as a First Lieutenant, Confederate States Navy, on June 27, 1861 [Another source gives the date as October 23, 1862 to rank from October 2, 1862, while source "Fold3, USN Resignees" gives the date as November 26, 1861]. He was appointed a First Lieutenant, Provisional Navy, on June 2, 1864, to rank from January 6, 1864. He served aboard the CSS JACKSON; commanded the CSS TUSCARORA, New Orleans Station, 1861; commanded the CSS SPRAY, St. Marks, Florida, 1862; and served aboard the CSS STONO, Charleston Station, 1862-1863. He was on leave of absence, 1863. He commanded the CSS TUSCARORA, Mobile Squadron, 1863-1864, and surrendered at Mobile, Alabama, on May 4, 1865. He was paroled on May 10, 1865.
[Source(s): Register; McElroy; Card File; Foenander; CWDTS; ONWR; Fold3, USN Resignees]

McGee, D. (New Hanover County, North Carolina)
    Confederate States Navy. Served on the CSS R. E. LEE. Appears on a Register of Confederate States Army General Military Hospital Number 4, Wilmington, North Carolina, dated June 26, 1863, which gives disease as "debility" and post office as Wilmington, North Carolina.
    [Source(s): Card File; NA RG 109]

McGee, James
    Confederate States Navy. McGee enlisted in New Hanover County, North Carolina, on March 6, 1862, as a Private, 2nd Company D, 2nd Regiment, North Carolina Artillery. He transferred to the Confederate States Navy on February 18, 1863.
    [Source(s): Foenander; North Carolina Troops 1, 242]

McGee, James
    Private, Confederate States Army/Confederate States Navy. Enlisted in New Hanover County, North Carolina, at age 28 on March 6, 1862 in 2nd Company D, 36th Regiment, North Carolina Troops (2nd North Carolina Artillery). Present or accounted for until he transferred to the Confederate States Navy on February 18, 1863.
    [Source(s): Card File; NA RG 109; North Carolina Troops, I]

McGill, Angus
    Landsman, Confederate States Navy. Enlisted July 14, 1864 at Raleigh, North Carolina, for the war.
    [Source(s): Card File; NA RG 45]

McGinn, Thomas
    Enlisted in the Confederate States Navy in Wilmington, North Carolina.
    [Source(s): MR, 4, p. 446]

McGinn [McGuin], T. P. [T. F.] (Craven County, North Carolina)
    Landsman, Confederate States Navy. Enlisted June 1 [5], 1863 in Wilmington, North Carolina. Born 1836, died 1894, buried in Cedar Grove Cemetery, New Bern, Craven County, North Carolina.
    [Source(s): Card File; Gravestone Records, v. I, p. 276; NA RG 45; Stepp, "Burials"]

McGinnis, J. W.
    Landsman, Confederate States Navy. Enlisted June 6, 1864 at Raleigh, North Carolina, for the war.
    [Source(s): Card File; NA RG 45]

McGrath, John J. (born in Philadelphia, PA/New Hanover County, North Carolina)
    Private, Confederate States Army/3rd Assistant Engineer, Confederate States Navy. By occupation, a machinist prior to enlisting. Appears on a receipt roll dated August 20, 1861 which indicates he served from April 17 to May 30, 1861 [Source "Foenander" gives date as May 31, 1861] in the "Wilmington Horse Artillery," which was accepted for state service in June 1861, and mustered into Confederate service as 1st Company A, 36th Regiment, North Carolina Troops (2nd Regiment, North Carolina Artillery) in August 1861. He enlisted in New Hanover County, North Carolina, at age 26, on May 31, 1861 for the war in Company E, 10th Regiment, North Carolina Troops (1st Regiment, North Carolina Artillery). He was detailed on engineer duty at the Fayetteville Arsenal and Armory, Fayetteville, North Carolina, on May 23, 1862. Temporarily attached to Company A, 2nd North Carolina Battalion, Local Defense Troops while at the Arsenal. McGrath was absent, detailed through December 7, 1863 when he was transferred to the Confederate States Navy and promoted to Acting 3rd Assistant Engineer in the Navy Department by Special Order No. 81 dated Fayetteville Arsenal and Armory, North Carolina, December 7, 1863. He served on board the CSS RALEIGH and the CSS ARCTIC, Wilmington, North Carolina, 1864
    [Source(s): Card File; North Carolina Troops, I; Foenander]

McHorney, Benjamin (F.) (Currituck County, North Carolina)
    Seaman/Quarter Gunner, Confederate States Navy. McHorney was born in North Carolina circa 1840 and lived in the Poplar Branch District of Currituck County, North Carolina. He shipped (enlisted) for one year as a Seaman aboard the CSS RALEIGH on 3 October 1861. He remained in that rank aboard the RALEIGH from October 1861 through at least April 1862. He is listed as having served as a member of the North Carolina Squadron from February 21, 1862 through April 15, 1862, transferring to the James River Squadron on April 15, 1862 where he served at Drewry's Bluff as a Seaman from April 1, 1863 through June 30, 1863, and as a Quarter Gunner aboard the CSS RALEIGH with the James River Squadron from November 16, 1863 through at least December 15, 1863.
    [Note: A Benjamin McHorney appears in Vol. III, page 714 of Clarks Regiments as a First Lieutenant, Company G,

8th North Carolina Regiment].
[Sources: NCCWSP; Census (NC), 1850; Clarks]

McHorney, Noah (Currituck County, North Carolina)
Seaman, Confederate States Navy.
McHorney was born in North Carolina in February 1842, the son of Elizabeth McHorney. He resided as a waterman, in 1860, with his mother, and siblings, at Poplar Branch, Currituck County, North Carolina. On September 8, 1861 he shipped for one year as a Seaman aboard the CSS RALEIGH, serving from September 1861 through April 15, 1862. His name appears on rolls of the North Carolina Squadron from February 21, 1862 through April 15, 1862, when he transferred to the James River Squadron. McHorney served at Drewry's Bluff as a Seaman from April 1, 1863 through June 30, 1863. He never married, and resided as a grocer, in 1900, in Norfolk, Virginia. He was still residing in Norfolk in 1910 and boarded as a lodger at the Mansion House in Norfolk.
[Source(s): Foenander; ORN 2, 1, 301; NCCWSP; Census (NC), 1860]

McHorney, R. (Currituck County [?], North Carolina)
Seaman, Confederate States Navy. McHorney served aboard the CSS RALEIGH in North Carolina and Virginia waters, 1862 – 1864.
[Source(s): Foenander; ORN 2, 1, 301; DANFS; NCCWSP]

McHorney, Samuel (Currituck County, North Carolina)
Private, Confederate States Army//Seaman, Confederate States Navy.
McHorney was born in Currituck County, North Carolina where he resided prior to enlisting at age 30 on August 27, 1861 for the war in Company B, 8th Regiment, North Carolina State Troops. He was present or accounted for until wounded in the back and captured at Cold Harbor, Virginia on June 1, 1864. He was reported in the Union Army's 18th Army Corps Hospital, Army of the James, on June 2, 1864. Source NCCWSP states he served as a Seaman aboard the CSS RALEIGH as part of the North Carolina Squadron from at least March through April 1862 and is listed with the North Carolina Squadron from October 15, 1861 through April 14, 1862. He may be the same Samuel McHorney, Company C, 8th North Carolina Regiment that was listed as on detached duty]. Editor's Note: McHorney's name does not show up as a member of Company C, 8th North Carolina Regiment].
[Source(s): Card File; North Carolina Troops, IV; NCCWSP]

McInnis, Neill (Neil) (Cumberland County, North Carolina)
Confederate States Navy. Conscripted March 17 [18], 1864 at Camp Holmes [near Raleigh, North Carolina] [Source "Foenander" states he enlisted in Cumberland County] from Colonel Pemberton's 53rd Regiment, North Carolina Militia from Cumberland County, North Carolina. Description: Age 37; eyes grey; hair red; complexion florid; height 5 ft. 9 in.; place of birth Cumberland County, North Carolina; occupation carpenter. Appears on a List of Conscripts in the Yard [at Halifax, North Carolina?]; transferred to Wilmington, North Carolina, June 9, 1864.
[Source(s): Card File; NA RG 45; Foenander]

McKay, John A. (Robeson County, North Carolina) [May be same as "John A. McKay (McKoy)" (q.v.)]
Seaman [Private], Confederate States Navy. Resided in Robeson County, North Carolina, and enlisted June 5, 1863 at Wilmington, North Carolina, "and subsequently joined C. S. Navy." McKay served as an Ordinary Seaman aboard the CSS NORTH CAROLINA and CSS TALLAHASSEE, North Carolina waters, 1864. He was attached as a Private to Company F, 2nd Regiment, Semmes' Naval Brigade, April 1865 [per Foenander]. "Discharged" from said service by "R. Sims" [sic]["Semmes"?], Rear Admiral, Confederate States Navy at Greensboro, North Carolina, May 1, 1865. McKay resided in Red Springs, North Carolina, per UDC Certificate filed July 25, 1905. Name sometimes incorrectly shown as "McRay (Foenander)"
[Source(s): Card File; UDC, Recorder; NA RG 45; Foenander]

McKay [McKoy], John A. (Robeson County, North Carolina) (Pension application gives county as "Cumberland"] [May be same as "John A. McKay" (q.v.)]
Crewman, Confederate States Navy. Served on the CSS NORTH CAROLINA. His application dated June 29, 1901 at age 66, Alderman post office, states he enlisted in Company C, 10th Regiment, North Carolina Troops (1st Regiment, North Carolina Artillery). He was wounded at Dutch Gap, Virginia, "by minie ball in the head." States a "ball ploughed through right side of scalp." Was left with a painful nervous condition. Further states "I was a member of Company H, 1st North Carolina Vols." [NOTE: No evidence found of service in either army unit]. Enlisted in the Confederate States Navy in 1864 [Source(s): MR, 4, p. 443; Pensions (North Carolina)]

McKay (McCoy), Patrick (Warren County, North Carolina)
    Sergeant, Confederate States Army//Confederate States Navy. McKay resided and enlisted in Warren County, North Carolina, where he enlisted at age 46 on March 5, 1862 in Company C, 46th Regiment, North Carolina Troops as a Private. Promoted to Corporal, November-December 1862; promoted to Sergeant in January-February 1864. Present or accounted for until transferred to the Confederate States Navy on April 1, 1864.
    [Source(s): Card File; North Carolina Troops, XI; MR, III; Foenander]

McKee, Wm. N.
    Seaman, Confederate States Navy. McKee enlisted on June 13, 1864 in Raleigh, North Carolina, for the war.
    [Source(s): Card File; NA RG 45; Duke Papers]

McKellar [McKeller], Archibald
    Seaman and 1st Class Fireman, Confederate States Navy. McKellar enlisted on June 22, 1863 in Wilmington, North Carolina, for the war. He served as a 2nd Class Fireman and 1st Class Fireman aboard the CSS NORTH CAROLINA, Cape Fear River, North Carolina, 1864.
    [Source(s): Card File; NA RG 45; Foenander; *ORN* 2, 1, 294 & 295]

McKellar [McKeller], Michael (North Carolina?) [NOTE: May be brother to Archibald McKeller, q.v., as both appear to have served as Firemen aboard the same ship at the same time]
    1st Class Fireman, Confederate States Navy. McKellar served aboard the ironclad sloop CSS NORTH CAROLINA, Cape Fear River, North Carolina, 1864.
    [Source(s): Foenander]

McKenzie, Robert
    Landsman, Confederate States Navy. Enlisting on February 11, 1864 in Wilmington, North Carolina, for the war, McKenzie served as a Landsman aboard the CSS ARCTIC, Cape Fear River, North Carolina, 1863.
    [Source(s): Card File; NA RG 45; *ORN* 2, 1, 278; Foenander]

McKinney (McKimmey), Joseph (Camden County, North Carolina)
    Private, Confederate States Army//Confederate States Navy. McKinney was born in Camden County, North Carolina, where he resided as a sailor prior to enlisting in Pasquotank County, North Carolina, at age 26, on May 4, 1861, as a Private in Company L, 17th Regiment, North Carolina Troops (1st Organization). He was present or accounted for until he transferred to the Confederate States Navy on October 4, 1861. He served as a Seaman aboard the CSS CURLEW as part of the North Carolina Squadron from circa November 20, 1861 – first quarter of 1862. His name appears on a receiving ship CSS UNITED STATES payroll ending March 31,1862.
    [Source(s): Card File; North Carolina Troops, VI; NCCWSP; Foenander]

McKinnon [McKenon], Neil[l] (Sampson County, North Carolina)
    Landsman, Confederate States Navy. McKinnon enlisted on December 29, 1863 in Raleigh, North Carolina, for the war. One source shows he "Died at the hospital in this town [Fayetteville, North Carolina] after a protracted illness of typhoid fever [1864]," age 43. Per source "Foenander," an "N. McKinnon," served as a Landsman, CSS ARCTIC, Cape Fear River, North Carolina, 1863.
    [Source(s): Card File; NA RG 45; "Fay. Obs." (June 6, 1864); ORN 2, 1, 278; Foenander]

McLaughlin, Samuel W.
    Seaman, Confederate States Navy. McLaughlin enlisted on June 13, 1864 in Raleigh, North Carolina, for the war.
    [Source(s): Card File; NA RG 45; Duke Papers]

McLean, H. B.
    Landsman, Confederate States Navy. McLean enlisted on June 11, 1864 in Raleigh, North Carolina for the war.
    [Source(s): Card File; NA RG 45]

McLellan, E. C.
    Landsman, Confederate States Navy. McLellan enlisted on December 21, 1863 in Raleigh, North Carolina, for the war.
    [Source(s): Card File; NA RG 45]

McLelland, Haynes R. (Columbus County, North Carolina)
Private, Confederate States Army//Confederate States Navy[?]. McLelland enlisted in Columbus County, North Carolina at age 27 on March 1, 1862 in Company E, 36th Regiment, North Carolina Troops (2nd Regiment, North Carolina Artillery) for the war. He was detailed as a boatman at Smithville, North Carolina, December 1863. Absent on detail through December 1864.
[Source(s): North Carolina Troops, I]

McLeod, William (Moore County, North Carolina)
Private, Company B, Confederate States Marine Corps. McLeod enlisted in Raleigh, North Carolina, on November 4, 1864 [NOTE: Letter of James C. Davis, November 17, 1864, states the group from Camp Holmes, of which McLeod was a part, arrived aboard the CSS INDIAN CHIEF, Charleston, SC, Sunday, November 6, 1864]. He served as a Private of the Marine guard on board the ironclad CSS COLUMBIA to February 7, 1865 [Per "Foenander," McLeod was later sent aboard the CSS CHICORA, Charleston Station]. Captured during the Appomattox Campaign, McLeod was paroled at Burkeville, Virginia, between April 14 and April 17, 1865.
[Source(s): North Carolina Troops, Doc. # 0299; Card File; "Citizen News-Record," July 8, 1987; Davis, November 17, 1864; Foenander; "Fay. Obs." (24 November 1864)]

McLeon [McLean?], William A. (Cumberland County, North Carolina)
Landsman, Confederate States Navy. McLeon enlisted on June 6, 1864 in Raleigh, North Carolina, for the war. His name appears as a signature to an Oath of Allegiance to the United States, subscribed and sworn to at Point Lookout, Maryland, on June 29, 1865. Place of residence given on Oath as Cumberland County, North Carolina. Description: Complexion light; hair brown; eyes grey; height 5 ft. 9 ½ in.
[Source(s): Card File; NA RG 109]

McMillen, A. N.
Landsman, Confederate States Navy. McMillen enlisted on August 29, 1864 in Raleigh, North Carolina, for the war.
[Source(s): Card File; NA RG 45]

McPhaul, Milton (Robeson County, North Carolina)
Confederate States Navy. McPhaul's name appears on a roll of Prisoners of War at Point Lookout, Maryland, which states he was captured at Burkesville, Virginia, April 6, 1865, and confined at Point Lookout, Maryland, from April 14, 1865 until released June 29, 1865. His name also appears as signature to an Oath of Allegiance to the United States, subscribed and sworn to at Point Lookout, Maryland, June 29, 1865, which gives place of residence as Robeson County, North Carolina. Description: Complexion fair; hair red; eyes blue; height 5 feet 10 ½ inches.
[Source(s): Card File; NA RG 109]

McQuin, John
Landsman, Confederate States Navy. McQuin enlisted on September 28, 1863 at Camp Holmes [near Raleigh, North Carolina] for the war.
[Source(s): Card File; NA RG 45]

McQuinn, T. F. (Mecklenburg County, North Carolina)
"Private," Confederate States Navy. McQuinn served on a gunboat. His name appears on a register of Confederate States Army General Military Hospital Number 4, Wilmington, North Carolina, which states that he was admitted on September 4, 1863 and returned to duty October 8, 1863. Post office given on register as Charlotte, North Carolina.
[Source(s): Card File; NA RG 109]

McRae, Donald L.
Landsman, Confederate States Navy. Enlisting on February 27, 1864 in Raleigh, North Carolina, for the war, McRae served as a Landsman, CSS NORTH CAROLINA, Cape Fear River, North Carolina, 1864.
[Source(s): Card File; NA RG 45; ORN 2, 1, 294 & 295; Foenander

McRae [McRee], J. C.
Landsman, Confederate States Navy. McRae enlisted in the Confederate States Navy on November 5, 1863 in Wilmington, North Carolina, for the war. He transferred from the Confederate States Navy to 2nd Company I, 10th Regiment, North Carolina Troops (1st Regiment, North Carolina Artillery) circa March-April 1864. He was paroled at Greensboro, North Carolina, May 1, 1865. Source "Foenander" states he "originally enlisted in the Confederate States Navy, date unknown; served as a Landsman aboard the CSS ARCTIC, Cape Fear River, North Carolina, 1863, and, as an Ordinary Seaman aboard the steam gunboat CSS RALEIGH, North Carolina, 1864; transferred

to 2nd company I, 1st Regiment North Carolina Artillery, March or April 1864, as a Private; and was paroled at Greensboro, North Carolina, May 1, 1865.
[Source(s): Card File; NA RG 45; Card File; NA RG 109; North Carolina Troops, I; Foenander]

McSwain, W. R. (Stanly County, North Carolina)
Confederate States Navy. McSwain resided in Tyson Township, Stanly County, North Carolina, circa 1917.
[Source(s): "Stanly Reunions"]

McUne, John (New Hanover County, North Carolina)
Confederate States Navy. McUne enlisted in the Confederate States Navy in Wilmington, North Carolina.
[Source(s): MR, 4, p. 446; St. Armand]

Madden, M. J. (Ireland//Cumberland County, North Carolina)
Landsman, Confederate States Navy. Born in Ireland, Madden worked as a pre-war mason. He enlisted at age 18 on March 18, 1864 in Raleigh, North Carolina, for the war. Another source states he was conscripted on March 16, 1864 at Camp Holmes (near Raleigh, North Carolina) from Colonel Pemberton's 53rd Regiment, North Carolina Militia, from Cumberland County, North Carolina. Description: Age 18; eyes hazel; hair dark; complexion florid; height 5 feet 6 inches; and occupation mason.
[Source(s): Foenander; Card File; NA RG 45]

Maffitt, Eugene Anderson
Lieutenant, Confederate States Navy. There are many discrepancies concerning the birth and appointment to the Confederate States Navy of Eugene Anderson Maffitt. Source "*Oakdale*, Davis" states he was born in Wilmington; source "Foenander" says he was born in North Carolina and appointed from Georgia; source "Driver" states he was born in Baltimore on November 25, 1844; and source "Stepp" gives his birth date as November 6, 1844. He attended Georgetown University, 1858-1861]. He was appointed in the Confederate States Navy on November 16, 1861 as a Midshipman 4th Class from North Carolina [*Register of the commissioned and warrant officers of the Navy of the Confederate States, to January 1, 1864*, published by the Confederate States Navy, published in 1864 by Macfarlane & Fergusson, printers (Richmond) shows entry date as August 29, 1861, "Foenander"]. Served on the Savannah Station, 1861 – 1862 and was in one of the forts at the Battle of Port Royal, South Carolina, in the fall of 1861. He was later appointed a Master's Mate in 1861 ["Foenander"]. He served as Midshipman aboard the Confederate cruiser CSS ALABAMA, 1862-1864 [another source says only 1864]. He was picked up by the "*Deerhound*" after the CSS ALABAMA sank and taken to England where he was subsequently ordered to join his father, Commander John Newland Maffitt, Confederate States Navy, in Nassau, where he made one blockade run on the "*Owl*." Following the end of the war, Maffitt sailed to Liverpool, England, and thence to Boston, Massachusetts, where he was recognized by a detective, arrested, and sent to Portland, Maine, then imprisoned at Fort Warren, Boston Harbor, where he was received December 8, 1865. Released on January 10, 1866, he traveled to Wilmington, North Carolina, and thence traveled to Europe and became an officer on board the steamship "*North Carolina*," trading between Dublin, Ireland, and Odessa, Russia. He returned to Wilmington, North Carolina, and was married on November 6, 1868, and entered business with his father-in-law, Mr. Alfred Martin, with whom he worked until his death. Buried in Oakdale Cemetery, Wilmington, North Carolina after his death on January 14 [another source gives the 12th], 1886, at the age of 41.
[Source(s): McElroy; Mr. Wayne Carver, Wilmington, North Carolina; Card File; Driver; Stepp, "Burials;" *Oakdale*, Driver; Foenander; "Star," 1/14/1886]

Maffitt, John Newland (Cumberland County, North Carolina)
Captain, Confederate States Navy. Maffitt's parents, Methodist Reverend John Newland Maffitt and Ann Carnicke [Carnic] Maffitt, left Ireland in late January or early February of 1819. Maffitt was born at sea before they reached New York on April 21, 1819. They settled in Connecticut and, at about the age of five, Maffitt was adopted by his uncle Dr. William Maffitt, and moved to Fayetteville, North Carolina. In 1832, at the age of 13, Maffitt was commissioned a Midshipman in the United States Navy and entered the service in February of that year. During his career, he served on a variety of ships, including the USS CONTITUTION, and spent fourteen years as part of the United States Coast Survey, serving up and down the eastern coast of the United States. Prior to his resignation, Maffitt was engaged in suppressing the slave trade for several years off the coast of Africa. He resigned as a Lieutenant, United States Navy, May 2, 1861, and was appointed as a First Lieutenant, Confederate States Navy, from North Carolina, on May 8, 1861 [Source "Fold3, USN Resignees" give date as May 5, 1861 and he was appointed from "South Carolina"]. He commanded CSS SAVANNAH, Savannah squadron, 1861-1862, and participated in the Battle of Port Royal, South Carolina, November 7, 1861. He served as a Naval Aide to General

Robert E. Lee until early in 1862 when he was ordered to the civilian steamer "*Cecile*" to run the federal blockade with supplies for the Confederacy. Also, commanded the "*Nassau*" [date unknown]. On August 17, 1862, he became the first commander of the cruiser CSS FLORIDA and took her through her sea trials, during which he and most of the crew contracted yellow fever. Maffitt was promoted to the rank of Commander on April 29, 1863, "… for gallant and meritorious conduct in command of steam sloop '*Florida*' in running blockade in and out of the port of Mobile," etc. He was forced to relinquish his command of the CSS FLORIDA on February 12, 1864, at Brest, France, due to the lingering effects of yellow fever. During the five months in which he commanded the CSS FLORIDA, she captured fourteen Union vessels in the Atlantic Ocean between New York and Brazil. Maffitt was appointed to the rank of Commander, Provisional Navy, June 2, 1864, to rank from May 13, 1864. He took command of the CSS ALBEMARLE, summer 1864. Detached from command of the CSS ALBEMARLE, September 9, 1864, he was ordered to report to flag officer Lynch, at Wilmington, North Carolina, for command of the blockade runner *Owl*, 1864-1865 (also said to have commanded the blockade runners *Gordon*, *Lillian* and the *Florie*, which was named for his daughter ("Florrie") ("Floria"), 1864. Maffitt served on the Wilmington Station, 1864. During his career, he is said to have made several successful runs through the blockade, bringing in desperately needed supplies, and captured and destroyed more than seventy ships worth between ten and fifteen million dollars. He traveled to England following the war, passed the British Naval Examination, and for two years commanded the British merchant steamer "*Widgeon*" running between Liverpool and South America until he returned to a farm on the sound at Wrightsville Beach near Wilmington, North Carolina, in 1868. Maffitt died on May 5 [Source "*Oakdale*, Davis" says the 15th], 1886, and was buried in Oakdale Cemetery, Wilmington, North Carolina.
[Source(s): McElroy; Register; MR, 4, p. 404; Officer's, January1, 1865; Mr. Wayne Carver; Ellis; Card File; CMH, v. 4, p. 630; Driver; Stepp, "Burials;" *Oakdale*, Davis; Foenander; ONWR; Fold3, USN Resignees; "The Asheville Times" (Asheville, North Carolina), November 17, 1917]

Maglenn, James
Chief Engineer, Confederate States Navy ["North Carolina Navy" see Stepp)]. Maglenn was attached to the blockade runner "*Ad-Vance*" at Wilmington, North Carolina and remained with her until captured September 1864. Born February 23, 1833, he died June 10, 1914 and was buried in Oakwood Cemetery, Raleigh, Wake County, North Carolina.
[Source(s): McElroy; Card File; Stepp, "Burials;" Pensions (North Carolina) (Application of "Thomas O. Wooten" (q.v.)]

Maher, John (North Carolina?)
Confederate States Marine Corps. Maher was killed in a personal fight with a sailor in Wilmington in the first week of January 1865.
[Source(s): "WDJ" (January 15, 1865)]

Mallard, Alfred J. (Duplin County, North Carolina)
Landsman, Confederate States Navy. Mallard enlisted for the Confederate States Navy September 9, 1863 in Wilmington, North Carolina, and served as a Landsman, CSS ARCTIC, Cape Fear River, North Carolina, 1863. Other sources state he enlisted on September 11, 1863 at Camp Holmes (near Raleigh, North Carolina) for the war, and September 22, 1863 in Wilmington, North Carolina, for the war. Name appears on Registers of Confederate States Army General Military Hospital Number 4, Wilmington, North Carolina, which states he was admitted November 26, 1863 with "debilitas" and assigned to ward 3, bed number 39. He returned to duty December 8, 1863. Post office listed as Teachy's Depot, North Carolina, and as "Peachy's" Depot, North Carolina.
[Source(s): *ORN* 2, 1, 279; MR, 4, p. 446; UDC, MC of Svc; Card File; NA RG 45; NA RG 109; Foenander]

Mallory, Charles K., Jr.
Acting Midshipman, Confederate States Navy.
Mallory served aboard the CSS BEAUFORT as an Acting Midshipman from September 1861 – March 1862 per payroll and clothing lists. He was transferred to the James River Squadron as of April 15, 1862.
[Source: NCCWSP]

Malpass [Also "Malpaso"], Henry (Probably Pender, but possibly Brunswick, or Guilford County, North Carolina)
Ordinary Seaman, Confederate States Navy. Malpass enlisted on August 23, 1863 and served aboard the CSS ARCTIC and the CSS RALEIGH, 1862 - 1864. Sources include a discharge certificate from CSS RALEIGH before it was scuttled, and a pass issued to him. Other sources state he enlisted on September 5, 1863 in Wilmington, North Carolina, for the war. His name appears on a register of Confederate States Army General Military Hospital Number 4, Wilmington, North Carolina, showing he was admitted on February 10, 1864 with "febris typhoides" and returned to duty March 21, 1864. Post office listed as Moore's Creek, North Carolina.

[Source(s): MR, 4, p. 446; Murray; Card File; NA RG 45; NA RG 109; *ORN* 2, 1, 276 & 302]

Mangum, James R.
Ordinary Seaman, Confederate States Navy. Mangum enlisted June ["1e" (?)], 1863 in Wilmington, North Carolina, for the war.
[Source(s): Card File; NA RG 45]

Manning, Edward Wilson (Virginia or North Carolina?)
Acting Chief Engineer (Chief Engineer), Confederate States Navy. Born on January 4, 1834 in Portsmouth, Virginia, Manning served in the crew of CSS CASWELL. Source "Chronicles" states he was the Chief Engineer of the Wilmington Station, and that "Smith and Manning" were in charge of the machinery of the CSS RALEIGH. Source "Chronicles" states he died December 10, 1900 (other sources state December 7, 190[?]) and was buried in Bellevue Cemetery, Wilmington, New Hanover County, North Carolina.
[Source(s): Card File; Gravestone Records, v.8, p. 61; Gravestone Records, v. 6, p. 322; Stepp, "Burials;" "Chronicles"]

Manning, John, Sr. (Edenton, Chowan County, North Carolina)
Commander, United States Navy//Commander, Confederate States Navy. Born 1803 in Edenton, North Carolina; died 1872, Pittsboro, North Carolina. Appointed Midshipman, United States Navy in 1820, he served continuously on active duty until approximately 1854. He was promoted to the rank of Commander in 1853. During his many years at sea, Manning developed a severe bronchial condition which probably contributed to his decision to leave active service for the United States Naval Reserve. After nearly six years in the Reserve, Manning resigned his commission on 18 May 1861. On 1 June 1861 he was appointed Chief of the Bureau of Ordnance, Clothing, and Provisions at New Bern, North Carolina for the North Carolina Navy. With the adoption of the Ordinance of Secession, the North Carolina Navy was transferred to the Confederate Government and Manning was discharged from his position. He was given the rank of Commander in the Confederate States Navy.
[Source: NCpedia]

Manor, James (Wake County, North Carolina [?])
Landsman, Confederate States Navy. Manor died January 13, 1865 and is buried in the Confederate Section of Oakwood Cemetery, Raleigh, North Carolina.
[Source(s): "Oakwood;" Stepp, "Burials;" Foenander]

Marchant, David
Seaman, Confederate States Navy. According to bounty, clothing, and small stores lists, Marchant was serving aboard the CSS BEAUFORT as early as December 1861 - March 1862. He received a partial payment on February 13, 1862 at Gosport Navy Yard following his service in manning Fort Cobb at the Battle of Elizabeth City on February 10, 1862. His name appears on the payroll of the receiving ship CSS UNITED STATES ending March 31, 1862. Payroll records of the North Carolina Squadron for the 1st quarter of 1862 covering from January 10, 1862 - April 15, 1862 confirm Marchant as a member of that squadron. He was transferred to the James River Squadron as of April 15, 1862 along with his ship. He is listed as a Quartermaster aboard the CSS BEAUFORT for the payroll period October 1, 1863 - December 15, 1863]
[Source: NCCWSP]

Marco, Samuel (New York/Wilson County, North Carolina)
Corporal, Confederate States Army//Confederate States Navy. Born in New York in 1835, Marco resided as a peddler, in 1860, in the Black Creek District of Wilson County, North Carolina. He enlisted at age 23 in Wayne County, North Carolina, on June 3, 1861 as a Corporal, for the war, in Company D, 2nd Regiment, North Carolina State Troops. He was reduced to the ranks August 27, 1862 and listed as present or accounted for until transferred to the Confederate States Navy on December 30, 1863.
[Source(s): Card File; Foenander; NA RG 45; North Carolina Troops, III]

Market, James
Seaman, Confederate States Navy.
Market appears on a clothing list dated December 1861 for the CSS BEAUFORT. His name appears on the payroll of the receiving ship CSS UNITED STATES for the period ending March 31, 1862. He also appears on the payroll of the North Carolina Squadron for the period of the 1st quarter of 1862 covering from January 10, 1862 - March 13,

1862. Records indicate he was discharged at Norfolk, Virginia on March 13, 1862
[Source: NCCWSP]

Maree, James C.
Landsman, Confederate States Navy. Maree enlisted on November 2, 1863 in Raleigh, North Carolina, for the war.
[Source(s): Card File; NA RG 45]

Marshman, James
Surgeon, Confederate States Navy. One source shows he served in Company F, 4th Regiment [Confederate States Navy?].
[Source(s): Card File; UDC, Dunham]

Marrow, William (also Mara)
2nd Class Fireman, Confederate States Navy.
Marrow served aboard the NCS EDWARDS per that ship's muster roll ending October 30, 1861. He then served as a 2nd Class Fireman aboard the NCS FORREST through the 1st quarter of 1862. Captured in the Battle of Elizabeth City, he was carried to Roanoke Island, paroled there on February 12, 1862, and returned to Elizabeth City, North Carolina. His name appears on the payroll of the receiving ship CSS UNITED STATES for the period ending March 31, 1862.
[Source: NCCWSP]

Martin, James H.
Seaman, Confederate States Navy. Martin enlisted on June 17, 1864 in Raleigh, North Carolina, for the war.
[Source(s): Card File; NA RG 45]

Martin, John (Wake County, North Carolina)
Crewman, Confederate States Navy. Martin served on the CSS NORTH CAROLINA.
[Source(s): MR, 4, p. 444]

Martin, John H. [Notation on Card, "writing very faded"]
Landsman, Confederate States Navy. Martin enlisted on June 6, 1864 in Raleigh, North Carolina, for the war.
[NOTE: Source "Foenander" lists a "John Martin," who served as an Ordinary Seaman, CSS NORTH CAROLINA, and quarter gunner, CSS TALLAHASSEE, North Carolina, 1864].
[Source(s): Card File; NA RG 45; ORN 2, 1, 294, 296 and 307; Foenander]

Martin, John M. (Wake County, North Carolina)
Private, Confederate States Army//Confederate States Navy. Martin was born in Wake County, North Carolina, where he resided as a coach maker prior to enlisting there at age 24 on May 1, 1861 in Company E, 14th Regiment, North Carolina Troops. He was present or accounted for until captured at Sharpsburg, Maryland, on September 17, 1862, and confined at Fort Delaware, Delaware, until transferred to Aiken's Landing, James River, Virginia, on October 2, 1862, for exchange. He was declared exchanged at Aiken's Landing on November 10, 1862 and rejoined his company prior to January 1, 1863. He was listed as present or accounted for until he transferred to the Confederate States Navy on or about April 5, 1864.
[Source(s): Card File; North Carolina Troops, V]

Martin, Thomas
Seaman, Confederate States Navy.
Per clothing, bounty, payroll, and small stores records, Martin served as a Seaman aboard the CSS BEAUFORT from at least September 1861 – March 1862. He received a partial payment on February 13, 1862 at Gosport Navy Yard following his service in manning Fort Cobb at the Battle of Elizabeth City on February 10, 1862. His name appears on the payroll of the North Carolina Squadron for the period of the 1st quarter of 1862 from (December 1, 1861 - April 15, 1862). He was transferred to the James River Squadron as of April 15, 1862.
[Source: NCCWSP]

Mashburn [May have also been listed as **"Washburn"**], **J. S.** (Moore County, North Carolina)
Private, Confederate States Marine Corps. Letter of James C. Davis, November 17, 1864, states the group from Camp Holmes, of which Mashburn was a part, arrived aboard the CSS INDIAN CHIEF, Charleston, SC, Sunday, November 6, 1864, and was designated to serve aboard the ironclad CSS CHICORA.
[Source(s): Davis, November 17, 1864; Foenander]

Massey [Massy], Simon (Simeon) (Johnston County, North Carolina)
Landsman, Confederate States Navy. Massey was born in Johnston County, North Carolina in 1843 where he lived as a farmer prior to enlisting there on March 18, 1864, aged 21, in the Confederate States Navy. His name appears on a list of conscripts "in the yard at Halifax" on June 9, 1864. Another source states he was conscripted March 18 [or 24th], 1864 at Camp Holmes (near Raleigh, North Carolina) from Colonel Heath's 41st Regiment, North Carolina Militia, Johnston County, North Carolina. Description: Age 21; eyes grey; hair light; complexion light; height 5 feet 6.5 inches; place of birth Johnston County, North Carolina; occupation farmer. After the war, he lived on Rt. 1, Smithfield, North Carolina. In his first application for pension dated July 3, 1911, age 68, Massey stated that he enlisted in June 1864 and served in the "Navy on ALBEMARLE." His first application for pension disallowed, Massey filed a second application dated June 26, 1916, age 73, in which he stated that he was aboard when the ALBEMARLE blew up. He was then transferred to Wilmington and put on the CSS EQUATOR and sent to Fort Anderson where he remained until the end of the war [Source "Foenander" states that he also served on the Halifax Station, 1864]. The application was approved, though no class was listed. He was shown as a resident of Smithfield, in 1910. His application for admission to the North Carolina Soldier's Home, dated July 15, 1926, at age 84, stated that he enlisted at Camp Holmes in Company C, 5th Regiment, North Carolina Troops [NOTE: No evidence found of service in this unit], then went [no date listed] to the CSS ALBEMARLE where he stayed to the end of the war. He was described as unmarried, fair complexion, five and one-half feet tall, he was a farmer and listed a son, E. W. Massey. His request approved he was admitted on July 26, 1926.
[Source(s): Pensions (North Carolina); Foenander; Card File; NA RG 45]

Mathis, D. C. (New Hanover County, North Carolina)
Ordinary Seaman, Confederate States Navy. Enlisting in the Confederate States Navy on August 23, 1863 [or, September 5] in Wilmington, North Carolina, Mathis served aboard the CSS ARCTIC, 1863.
[Source(s): MR, 4, p. 446; Card File; NA RG 45; St. Armand; Foenander]

Matthews, David C. (Sampson County, North Carolina)
"Private," Confederate States Navy. Matthews' name appears on registers of Confederate States Army General Military Hospital Number 4, Wilmington, North Carolina, stating he was admitted October 22, 1863 with "rheumatism chron" and returned to duty July 23, 1864. Post office listed as Harrell's Store, North Carolina.
[Source(s): Card File; NA RG 109]

Maury, John Soffrien [Sifrien] (North Carolina)
First Lieutenant, Confederate States Navy. Maury, born circa 1824, was appointed to the United States Navy from North Carolina on February 19, 1838 as a Midshipman (another source gives the date as February 10, 1838. Maury became a Passed Midshipman on May 20, 1844, a Master on November 2, 1852, and a Lieutenant on August 1, 1853. While serving as a First Lieutenant, his name was stricken from the rolls of the United States Navy on April 18, 1861. He was appointed a First Lieutenant from North Carolina in the Virginia Navy in May 1861. He was appointed a First Lieutenant, Confederate States Navy on June 10, 1861 [Another source gives the date as October 23, 1862, to rank from October 2, 1862]. He was appointed First Lieutenant, Provisional Navy on June 2, 1864, to rank from January 6, 1864. Maury served at Gosport Navy Yard, 1861-1862, and on the Richmond Station, 1862 – 1864. One source shows he transferred from Charlotte, North Carolina, to Richmond, Virginia, June 7, 1862. He commanded the steamers CSS HAMPTON (1863-1864) and CSS RICHMOND (July 1864-1865) in the James River Squadron. He served in Semmes' Naval Brigade, 1865, surrendered and was paroled at Greensboro, North Carolina, April 28, 1865 [April 26, 1865, per "Foenander"]. Maury resided in Baltimore postwar, and was a member of the Army and Navy Society, Maryland Line Association. He died in Baltimore on February 4, 1893 at the age of 69, and was buried at New Cathedral Cemetery, Baltimore.
[Source(s): Register, McElroy; Card File; Driver; Journal; Foenander; CWDTS; ONWR]

Maury, W. L.
Commander, Confederate States Navy. Maury commanded the CSS NORTH CAROLINA, an ironclad sloop with four guns, on the Cape Fear River under flag officer W.F. Lynch.
[Source(s): McElroy; Card File]

May, C. O.
Landsman, Confederate States Navy. May enlisted on June 11, 1864 in Raleigh, North Carolina, for the war.
[Source(s): Card File; NA RG 45]

May, Joseph A. (Franklin County, North Carolina)
Private, Confederate States Army//Yeoman, Confederate States Navy. Born in North Carolina in 1839, the son

of Elias and Elizabeth May, Joseph resided as a laborer with his parents and siblings in Franklin County, North Carolina in 1860. He enlisted there at age 22 on May 1, 1862, for the war, as a Private in Company G, 47th Regiment, North Carolina Troops [one source states he was a Corporal]. Reported present in January-February 1863, he was mentioned in dispatches for "good conduct" in fighting near Washington, North Carolina, March 30-31, 1863. He was wounded by a piece of shell at Gettysburg, Pennsylvania, on July 1, 1863. May transferred to the Confederate States Navy on December 30, 1863 and served as a Seaman on the CSS ARCTIC, 1863 - 1864, and as a Yeoman on the CSS RALEIGH, North Carolina, 1864. He resided as a farmer, in 1870, with his wife, Elizabeth, in Louisburg, Franklin County, North Carolina.
[Source(s): Card File; NA RG 45; North Carolina Troops, XI; Foenander]

May, William (New Hanover County, North Carolina)
1st Sergeant, Confederate States Army//Boatswain's Mate, Confederate States Navy. May enlisted from New Hanover County, North Carolina at age 32, October 23, 1861, as First Sergeant, 2nd Company D, 36th Regiment, North Carolina Troops (2nd Regiment, North Carolina Artillery). He was listed as present or accounted for until he transferred to the Confederate States Navy, February 18, 1863. May served as a Seaman on the CSS ARCTIC (1863) and a Boatswain's Mate on the CSS NORTH CAROLINA and CSS TALLAHASSEE (1864). Another source states he enlisted as a Seaman on January 24, 1863 in Wilmington, North Carolina, for three years.
[Source(s): MR, 4, p. 444; ORN, 2,1, p.279,294-296; North Carolina Troops, I; NA RG 45; Card File; Foenander; St. Amand]

Maynard, Green J. (Wake or Harnett County, North Carolina)
Confederate States Navy. Maynard filed a pension claim on June 6, 1901, age 66, post office Raleigh, Wake County, North Carolina. Source Card File states he served in the Navy "under Commodore Mitchell (Drewry's Bluff)." Another source states he filed another pension claim on June 21, 1912, age 77, listing his post office as Lillington, Harnett County, North Carolina. His claim was disallowed. A claim filed on June 27, 1913 at age 78 was approved. Buried in City Cemetery, Raleigh, North Carolina (born August 24, 1835; died December 21, 1913).
[Source(s): Card File; NA RG 45; Pensions (North Carolina); Old City Cemetery, Raleigh, North Carolina]

Mayo, Milton S. (Carteret County, North Carolina)
3rd Class Fireman, 2nd Class Fireman, Pilot, Confederate States Navy. Mayo was born in Portsmouth, Carteret County, North Carolina, in 1840 (one source shows 1842), the son of John A. and Susan Mayo. He was a resident of Carteret County, North Carolina when he began his service as a 3rd Class Fireman, later 2nd Class Fireman (January - May 1862), and finally and as a Pilot aboard the side-wheeled steam tug CSS ELLIS (which operated in North Carolina waters), 1861 – 1862. Source NCCWSP shows he was discharged from the ELLIS on March 25, 1862. Described as "efficient" and having performed his "duties with promptness and efficiency," he ran the blockade from Wilmington to Nassau. He moved to Washington, North Carolina, at the close of the war, and married Susan Orall [Orrell?] in 1866 (she died in February 1896). He resided as a widower, in 1910, in Washington, Beaufort County, North Carolina, but died in Avery County, North Carolina, on June 10, 1910.
[Source(s): Foenander; ORN 1, 6, 597 & 2, 1, 285; NCCWSP]

Mayo, Thomas N.
1st Sergeant, Confederate States Army//Confederate States Navy. Born in Craven County, North Carolina, Mayo was by occupation a Seaman prior to enlisting there at age 30 on June 22, 1861, for the war, in Company D, 5th Regiment, North Carolina Troops. Mustered in as a Private, and promoted to Corporal in January-February 1862, he was present or accounted for until wounded at Gaines' Mill, Virginia, on June 27, 1862. He rejoined the company and was promoted to 1st Sergeant prior to December 31, 1862. Mayo was present or accounted for until he transferred to the Confederate States Navy on April 23, 1864.
[Source(s): Card File; North Carolina Troops, IV; Foenander]

Meacham, John
Landsman, Confederate States Navy. Meacham enlisted on October 5, 1863, at Camp Holmes [near Raleigh, North Carolina].
[Source(s): Card File; NA RG 45]

Meadows, John D. (Guilford County, North Carolina)
Private, Confederate States Navy. Meadows' name appears on registers of Confederate States Army General Military Hospital Number 4, Wilmington, North Carolina, which state that he was admitted on February 25, 1864 with "scabies" and returned to duty March 21, 1864. Post office given on register as Jamestown, North Carolina.
[Source(s): Card File; NA RG 109]

Meadows, J. R.
Landsman, Confederate States Navy. Meadows enlisted on November 5, 1863 in Wilmington, North Carolina, for the war. He served as a Landsman, CSS ARCTIC, Cape Fear River, North Carolina, 1863, and aboard the CSS RALEIGH in North Carolina and Virginia waters, 1864.
[Source(s): Card File; NA RG 45; *ORN* 2, 1, 277, 278 & 302; Foenander]

Meadows, J. S. (Guilford County, North Carolina)
Confederate States Navy. Meadows enlisted in the Confederate States Navy on October 7, 1863 in Wilmington, North Carolina.
[Source(s): MR, 4, p. 446]

Meddons, J. D.
Landsman, Confederate States Navy. Meddons enlisted on November 4, 1863 in Raleigh, North Carolina for the war.
[Source(s): Card File; NA RG 45]

Medlin, John
Landsman, Confederate States Navy. Medlin enlisted on January 6, 1864, in Raleigh, North Carolina, for the war. He served as a Landsman, CSS ARCTIC, Cape Fear River, North Carolina, 1863.
[Source(s): Card File; NA RG 45; *ORN* 2, 1, 278; Foenander]

Medlin, M. [NOTE: May be same as "Miles Medlin" (q.v.)]
Landsman, Confederate States Navy. Medlin enlisted on October 5, 1863 at Camp Holmes [near Raleigh, North Carolina].
[Source(s): Card File]

Medlin, Miles [Millas] [Milas] (Union County, North Carolina)
Seaman, Confederate States Navy. Medlin enlisted from Union County, North Carolina, in Wilmington, North Carolina in 1861 [Pension states he enlisted on October 1, 1862 and was assigned to the CSS SAVANNAH, serving aboard that vessel at Savannah, Georgia, until the city fell to Union General Sherman in December 1864. He was afterwards assigned to Company B, 3rd Naval Battalion, Army of Northern Virginia, wherein he served until he surrendered at Appomattox] [Source "Foenander" states he served as a Landsman aboard the CSS ISONDIGA and CSS SAVANNAH, Savannah Squadron, Georgia, 1863 – 1864]. His name appears on a list of those paroled on April 9, 1865. A pension claim filed on June 11, 1907 at age 64 listed his post office as Charlotte, Mecklenburg County, North Carolina. He was judged ¾ disabled and the pension approved at 4th Class. Medlin was born circa 1845 and died February 19, 1931. He was buried at Zion Methodist Church near Unionville, Union County, North Carolina.
[Source(s): McElroy; *Union County Cemeteries*, p. 166; Card File; Pensions (North Carolina); Stepp, "Burials;" Foenander]

Meekins, John W. (Dare County, North Carolina)
Confederate States Navy. Meekins filed a pension claim on July 17, 1905 at age 60, listing his post office as Callington, Dare County, North Carolina. He transferred to the gunboat CSS BOMBSHELL. His pension claim was approved at 4th Class.
[Source(s): Card File; Pensions (North Carolina)]

Meicenheimer, C. [NOTE: May be the same as C. (et al) Meicenhimer (et al)]
Ordinary Seaman, Confederate States Navy. Meicenheimer enlisted on September 22, 1863 in Wilmington, North Carolina, for the war.
[Source(s): Card File]

Meisinheimer [Mercenheimer] [Meicernheimer] [Meicenher], C. [Claborn][Claben] (Stanly County, North Carolina)
Confederate States Navy. Meisinheimer enlisted in the Confederate States Navy on August 24, 1863 in Wilmington, North Carolina [Source NA RG 45 states he enlisted September 11, 1863 at Camp Holmes for the war]. His name appears as a signature to an Oath of Allegiance subscribed and sworn to at Salisbury, North Carolina, May 10, 1865. His unit was listed as "Naval Service of North Carolina." A pension claim was filed on July 1, 1905 by his widow, Mary A. Misenheimer, age 70, listed her post office as Capal Grove, Stanly County, North Carolina. She stated her husband enlisted in "…Confederate Navy at Wilmington, North Carolina. See North Carolina Roster Vol. 4, Page 446." A claim was filed July 5, 1909 by the widow, age 73, showing her post office as Richfield, Stanly County, North Carolina, which was approved as 4th Class.

[Source(s): MR, 4, p. 446; Card File; NA RG 45; NA RG 109; Pensions (North Carolina)]

Melton, George (North Carolina?)
Landsman, Confederate States Navy. Melton served aboard the CSS ARCTIC, Cape Fear River, North Carolina, 1863. He also served on the steam gunboat CSS RALEIGH in North Carolina and Virginia waters, 1864.
[Source(s): Foenander]

Melton, John
Confederate States Navy.
Clothing records indicate Melton served aboard the CSS RALEIGH as part of the North Carolina Squadron from before September 2, 1861.
[Source: NCCWSP]

Melton, Joseph G. (Rutherford County, North Carolina)
"Private," Confederate States Navy. Melton's name appears as a signature to an Oath of Allegiance to the United States, subscribed and sworn to at Point Lookout, Maryland, June 29, 1865. Place of residence given on Oath as Rutherford County, North Carolina. Description: Complexion light; hair dark brown; eyes blue; height 5 feet 9 ½ inches. [Source(s): Card File; NA RG 109]

Mercer, James E (North Carolina?) [NOTE: Served aboard the "Ellis" with Thomas P. Mercer, q.v.]
Seaman, Confederate States Navy. Mercer served aboard the side-wheel steam tug CSS ELLIS in North Carolina waters as part of the North Carolina Squadron between August 1861 - May 1862. His name appears on a payroll of the receiving ship CSS UNITED STATES ending March 31, 1862. He served aboard the CSS VIRGINIA, Hampton Roads, Virginia, 1862, and is listed as discharged on the final CSS VIRGINIA payroll of September 13, 1862.,
[Source(s): Foenander; NCCWSP]

Mercer, Thomas P. (Currituck County, North Carolina)
Seaman, Confederate States Navy. Born in North Carolina in 1828, Mercer resided as a farmer, in 1860, with his wife, Mary, and five children, in Narrow Shore, Currituck County, North Carolina. He served as a Seaman aboard the CSS VIRGINIA, Hampton Roads, Virginia, 1862. Source "Foenander" lists a "T. P. Mercer" who served as a Seaman aboard the side wheeled steam tug CSS ELLIS (which operated in North Carolina waters) as part of the North Carolina Squadron sometime in August - October 1861, or January – May 1862.
[Source(s): Foenander; ORN 2, 1, 310; ORN 2, 1, 285, NCCWSP]

Mercer, W. H. (Brunswick County [?], North Carolina)
Landsman, Confederate States Navy. Mercer enlisted on March 24, 1864 in Raleigh, North Carolina, for the war. Source "NA RG 45" states he enlisted on March 21, 1864 at Camp Holmes [NOTE: Camp Holmes was near Raleigh] from Colonel Leonard's 56th Regiment, North Carolina Militia, Brunswick County, North Carolina. Description: Age 37; eyes grey; hair dark; complexion fair; height 5 feet 6 ½ inches; place of birth Brunswick County, North Carolina; occupation farmer. Mercer's name appears on a List of Conscripts "in the yard" [probably at Halifax, North Carolina] and subsequently transferred to Wilmington, North Carolina, June 9, 1864.
[Source(s): Card File; NA RG 45; Foenander]

Merkin [Meerkin; Merkin; Murkin], Henry A. (Iredell County, North Carolina)
Seaman ["Private"], Confederate States Navy. Merkin enlisted on June 13, 1864, in Raleigh, North Carolina, for the war. His name appears as a signature to an Oath of Allegiance to the United States, subscribed and sworn to at Nashville, Tennessee, April 28, 1865, which states that he entered service November 19, 1863 and deserted April 13, 1865. Place of residence given on Oath as Iredell County, North Carolina. Description: Complexion fair; hair dark; eyes blue; height 6 feet 4 inches.
[Source(s): Card File; NA RG 45; NA RG 109]

Merrell [Merrill], Samuel (Wake County, North Carolina)
Seaman, Purser's Steward [Source NCCWSP records his rank as "Ship's steward"], Confederate States Navy. Merrell served as a Seaman aboard the CSS SEA BIRD as part of the North Carolina Squadron from July - November 1861. He was promoted to the rank of Purser's Steward or Ship's Steward in December 1861 and was serving in that capacity when captured at the Battle of Elizabeth City on February 10, 1862. Merrell was taken to Roanoke Island and paroled on February 19, 1862, after which he traveled to Norfolk, Virginia [Source NCCWSP indicates he returned to Elizabeth City]. His name appears on the payroll of the North Carolina Squadron for the 1st

quarter of 1862 (December 1, 1861 – April 15, 1862). He is listed as "on parole" on this payroll document. Source NCCWSP indicates he was honorably discharged on February 15, 1862 by order of Flag Officer French Forrest. He applied for a post-war Confederate pension from Wake County, North Carolina, and later applied to the Soldier's Home. His application for admission to Soldier's Home in Raleigh, North Carolina, was dated June 8, 1908. The application listed his age as 84 and his post office as Raleigh. The application approved he was admitted on August 10, 1908. Description: Complexion dark; height 5 feet 10 ½ inches; occupation machinist. His nearest relative was listed as Brown Pegram. On the application he states that he enlisted in the Confederate States Navy on November 20, 1861 in Washington, North Carolina and was discharged in 1862 at Suffolk, Virginia.
[Source(s): Card File; Pension (North Carolina); Foenander; "Beaufort County Sailors;" MR, I; North Carolina Troops, III; NCCWSP]

Merrill [Merritt], Daniel P. (New York//Beaufort County, North Carolina)
Private, Confederate States Army//Seaman, Ordinary Seaman, Confederate States Navy. Born about 1834 in New York (resident of Long Island), Merrill resided as a Seaman in and enlisted "for the war" from Beaufort County, North Carolina [source "Foenander" gives place as "Craven County"], on May 10, 1861, at age 27, as a Private in Company I, 3rd Regiment, North Carolina State Troops. He was listed as present or accounted for until he transferred to the Confederate States Navy on January 22, 1862. Received aboard the receiving ship CSS UNITED STATES by order of Commander French Forrest on February 22, 1862, Merrill was ordered shipped for the war. Merrill served as an Ordinary Seaman on the side-wheeled steam tug CSS ELLIS which operated in North Carolina waters sometime in the August - October 1861 time frame, or January - May 1862. His name appears on a North Carolina Squadron payroll covering the period February 24, 1862 - April 15, 1862. He served as a Seaman aboard the CSS RALEIGH in North Carolina waters (circa January 16, 1862 – April 1862) until he deserted on July 16 or 17, 1862. His name appears on the payroll of the North Carolina Squadron 1st quarter of 1862 (February 24, 1862 - April 15, 1862). He was transferred to the James River Squadron on April 15, 1862.
[Source(s): Card File; NCCWSP; Foenander; "Beaufort County Sailors;" MR, I; North Carolina Troops, III]

Merrill, James
Coxswain, Confederate States Navy.
Per muster and payroll records, Merrill served as a Coxswain aboard the CSS FANNY from before October 8, 1861, and as a Seaman on the same ship through at least December 20, 1861. He was reported as unfit for service by a surgeon on March 5, 1862 and discharged from the receiving ship [UNITED STATES?]. He appears on the North Carolina Squadron payroll for the 1st quarter of 1862 (December 1, 1861 - March 6, 1862).
[Source: NCCWSP]

Merrit [Merrick], Elisha
Seaman, Confederate States Navy. Merrit enlisted on January 1, 1864 in Wilmington, North Carolina, for the war. Source "Foenander" lists an "E. Merrick, Coxswain, CSS ARCTIC, Cape Fear River, North Carolina, 1863."
[Source(s): Card File; NA RG 45; Foenander]

Merritt, Daniel
Ordinary Seaman, Confederate States Navy.
Per ship's logs and payroll documents, Merritt served as an Ordinary Seaman as part of the North Carolina Squadron aboard the NCS ELLIS from circa August 1, 1861 – May 1862. He was received aboard the receiving ship CSS UNITED STATES by order of Flag Officer French Forrest on February 21, 1862 and ordered "shipped" for three years.
[Source: NCCWSP]

Merritt, Daniel P. (Craven County, North Carolina)
Corporal, Confederate States Army//Confederate States Navy. Merritt enlisted in Craven County, North Carolina, on March 10, 1862 as a Private in 1st Company H, 40th Regiment, North Carolina Troops (3rd Regiment, North Carolina Artillery). He was present or accounted for until he transferred as a Private to Company F, 13th Battalion, North Carolina Light Artillery, on November 4, 1863. Appointed Corporal, November 20, 1863, he was present or accounted for until he transferred to the Confederate States Navy on April 6, 1864. Source "Foenander" lists a "Daniel Merritt" who served as an Ordinary Seaman aboard the side-wheeled steam tug CSS ELLIS, in North Carolina waters, sometime between August and October 1861, or January and May 1862.
[Source(s): Card File; NA RG 109; North Carolina Troops, I and III; Foenander]

Merritt (Merrill), James (North Carolina?)
Coxswain, Seaman, Confederate States Navy.
Merritt served as a Coxswain aboard the CSS FANNY in North Carolina waters as of October 8, 1861. He served in the rank of Seaman aboard the NCS FANNY sometime during the period September - December 1861 and possibly as late as May 1862. [Source NCCWSP indicates he was reported as unfit for service by a Surgeon on March 5, 1862 and "discharged from the receiving ship." His name appears on a payroll of the North Carolina Squadron for the 1st quarter 1862 (December 1, 1861 - March 6, 1862).
[Source(s): Foenander; MCCWSP]

Messick, Nehemiah M. (Virginia//New Hanover County, North Carolina)
Corporal, Confederate States Army//Ordinary Seaman; Master-at-Arms; and, Quartermaster, Confederate States Navy. Born in Virginia [Source "Foenander" states state of birth may be Maryland], Messick was by occupation a sailor prior to enlisting in New Hanover County, North Carolina, at age 23, in Company E, 10th Regiment, North Carolina State Troops (1st Regiment, North Carolina Artillery) on June 3, 1863 [Source "North Carolina Troops, I" gives date as June 4, 1861] for the war. Mustered in as a Private, he was appointed Corporal circa November-December 1862. Messick transferred to the Confederate States Navy on June 3, 1863. Another source states he enlisted in the Confederate States Navy on June 5, 1863 in Wilmington, North Carolina, for the war. He served as a Master-at-Arms and Quartermaster aboard the CSS NORTH CAROLINA, 1864. He resided as a sailor, in 1880, with his wife Susanna, and five children (eldest child born 1858) at Dames Quarter, Somerset County, Maryland.
[Source(s): Card File; NA RG 45; North Carolina Troops, I; Foenander]

Metters, Henry (also Matters)
Seaman, Confederate States Navy.
Metters served as a Seaman aboard the NCS EDWARDS per his shipping articles dated July 25, 1861 as a part of as part of the North Carolina Squadron. He remained aboard the NCS EDWARDS until sometime in October 1861 when he appears as a Seaman on the payroll 1st quarter of 1862 payroll list for the CSS FORREST. His name appears on the payroll ending March 31, 1862 of the receiving ship CSS UNITED STATES.
[Source: NCCWSP]

Midgett, John S. (Tyrrell County, North Carolina)
Private, Confederate States Army//Seaman, Quarter Gunner, Confederate States Navy.
Midgett was born in Tyrrell County, North Carolina, where he resided as a sailor prior to enlisting in Pasquotank County, North Carolina, at age 22, on May 4, 1861, as a Private in Company L, 17th Regiment, North Carolina Troops (1st Organization). He was present or accounted for until transferred to the Confederate States Navy on October 4, 1861. By November 20, 1861, he was serving as a Seaman aboard the CSS CURLEW, and as a Quarter Gunner on this ship by the first quarter of 1862. His name appears on a receiving ship CSS UNITED STATES payroll ending March 31, 1862. He enlisted in Pasquotank County, North Carolina, as a Private in Company A, 68th Regiment, North Carolina Troops, on April 24, 1863, for the war. He was reported absent on detached duty on April 30, 1864 and reported present on June 30, 1864. No further records.
[Source(s): Card File; North Carolina Troops, VI and XV; Foenander; NCCWSP]

Miles, James
Landsman, Confederate States Navy. Miles enlisted on January 25, 1864, in Raleigh, North Carolina, for the war. He served as a Landsman, CSS ARCTIC, Cape Fear River, North Carolina, 1863.
[Source(s): Card File; NA RG 45; *ORN* 2, 1, 278; Foenander]

Milholen, N. T. (Mecklenburg County, North Carolina?)
Seaman [Private], Confederate States Navy [Company A, 1st Navy Battalion]. Milholen enlisted on June 13, 1864 in Raleigh, North Carolina, for the war. His name appears on a Roll of Prisoners of War at Newport News, Virginia, which states he was "captured on the SSRR April 6, 1865." His name also appears as a signature to an Oath of Allegiance to the United States, subscribed and sworn to at Newport News, Virginia, June 30, 1865. Place of residence given on Oath as Alexandria, North Carolina [probably "Alexandriana, Mecklenburg County, North Carolina]. Description: Complexion light; hair dark; eyes blue; height 5 feet 7 inches; Oath carries the remark "captured Farmville [Virginia] April 6, 1865."
[Source(s): Card File; NA RG 45; NA RG 109]

Miliver, J. [NOTE: May be same as "James L. Millar"] (Wilson County, North Carolina)
Confederate States Navy. Miliver's name appears on a Roll of Prisoners of War paroled at Provost Marshal's Office at Goldsboro, North Carolina. The roll states he was paroled on May 11, 1865, that he "came in for parole," and his

residence was Wilson County, North Carolina.
[Source(s): Card File; NA RG 109]

Millar, James L.
Ordinary Seaman, Confederate States Navy. Millar enlisted on March 27, 1863 in Wilmington, North Carolina, for three years or the war.
[Source(s): Card File; NA RG 45]

Millar [Millen?], W. H.
Confederate States Navy. Millar enlisted on March 28, 1863 in Wilmington, North Carolina, for three years or the war. Source "Foenander" lists a "William H. Millen," who may be the same man, who served as a Landsman, CSS ARCTIC, Cape Fear River, North Carolina, 1863.
[Source(s): Card File; NA RG 45; ORN 2, 1, 279; Foenander]

Miller, Charles (North Carolina?)
Ordinary Seaman, Confederate States Navy. Miller served aboard the CSS ARCTIC, Cape Fear River, North Carolina, 1863, and in 1864, aboard the CSS NORTH CAROLINA, Cape Fear River.
[Source(s): Foenander]

Miller, Felix G.
3rd Assistant Engineer, Confederate States Navy.
Miller was appointed to the rank of 3rd Assistant Engineer on November 2, 1861 and was serving as such aboard the NCS FANNY as part of the North Carolina Squadron per that ship's muster roll dated December 12, 1861 and possibly longer.
[Source: NCCWSP]

Miller, Hiram A. (Catawba County, North Carolina)
Private, Confederate States Army//Confederate States Navy. Born in North Carolina, about 1844, the son of Joel and Harriette Miller, Miller resided in Catawba County, North Carolina, where he enlisted on March 15, 1862, as a Private in Company C., 28th Regiment, North Carolina Troops. Miller was wounded in the head ["Foenander" says "hand"] at Frayser's Farm, Virginia, on June 30, 1862, and returned to duty prior to January 1, 1863. He was wounded at Chancellorsville, Virginia, on May 2-3, 1863, and returned to duty prior to July 1-5, 1863, when he was again wounded at Gettysburg and captured. Hospitalized at David's Island, New York Harbor, July 17-24, 1863, Miller was paroled and transferred to City Point, Virginia, where he was received on September 16, 1863, for exchange. He returned to duty at an unspecified date and was transferred to the Confederate States Navy on April 3, 1864. He is shown residing with his parents and family, in 1870, at Hickory Tavern, Catawba County, North Carolina
[Source(s): North Carolina Troops, VIII; S. O. # 89; Foenander]

Miller, James (New Hanover County, North Carolina)
Seaman, Confederate States Navy. Miller enlisted on June 8, 1863 in Wilmington, North Carolina, for the war. He served aboard the Confederate States Steamer CSS PHANTOM. His name appears on registers of Confederate States Army General Military Hospital Number 4, Wilmington, North Carolina, which state he was admitted on October 31, 1863 with "febris typhoides" and returned to duty November 9, 1863. His post office was given on the register as Wilmington, North Carolina. Source "Foenander" lists a "James Miller," who served as a Seaman, aboard the CSS NORTH CAROLINA, Cape Fear River, North Carolina, 1863 - 1864.
[Source(s): Card File; NA RG 109; NA RG 45; Foenander]

Miller, John
No rate/rank listed, Confederate States Navy. Born in North Carolina and by trade a clerk, at enlistment, Miller was aged 2 with hazel eyes, dark hair, and a dark complexion.
[Source(s): CSS TENNESSEE]

Miller, William H.
Confederate States Navy. Miller enlisted in Wilmington, North Carolina.
[Source(s): MR, 4, p. 446; St. Armand]

Mills, Benjamin B. (Washington County, North Carolina)
Private, Confederate States Army//Landsman, Confederate States Navy. Resided in Washington County, North

Carolina where he enlisted at age 18 on June 24, 1861, for the war, in Company G, 1st Regiment, North Carolina State Troops. He was present or accounted for until discharged on February 3, 1862 upon transfer to the Confederate States Navy where he served as a Landsman aboard the CSS VIRGINIA, Hampton Roads, Virginia, 1862.
[Source(s): Card File; North Carolina Troops, III; Foenander]

Millson, H. J.
Seaman, Confederate States Navy. Millson enlisted on September 5, 1863 in Wilmington, North Carolina, for the war.
[Source(s): Card File; NA RG 45]

Milton, Pinkney (Pinckney) H.
Confederate States Navy. Born in North Carolina in April 1840, the son of physician William H. Milton, and his wife, Elizabeth, Milton resided in 1850 with his parents in Gilmer County, Georgia. He had previous service in Company H, 1st Regiment, Georgia Regulars, beginning March 1861, and was wounded in action at Sharpsburg, Maryland, September 17, 1862. He transferred to the Confederate States Navy on April 4, 1864 and was captured at Charleston, South Carolina. He married in 1866 and resided in 1880 as a tax collector with his wife, Nancy, and five children, at Ellijay, Gilmer County, Georgia. He is still shown residing with his family at Gilmer County, in 1910.
[Source(s): Foenander]

Mintz, John H. (Brunswick County, North Carolina)
Private, Confederate States Army//Confederate States Navy(?). Born in Brunswick County, North Carolina, where he resided as a farmer prior to enlisting in New Hanover County, North Carolina, at age 38 on July 15, 1861 in Company C [Source Card File gives unit as "G"], 8th Regiment, North Carolina State Troops. Captured at Roanoke Island on February 8, 1861, he was paroled at Elizabeth City on February 21, 1862, and exchanged in August 1862. Mintz was listed as present or accounted for until he deserted at Wilmington, North Carolina, on July 21, 1863. "Brought back" on September 25, 1863 and reported "in arrest awaiting his trail for desertion" through February 1864. He is reported to have rejoined his company prior to June 1, 1864, when he was captured at Cold Harbor, Virginia. Confined at Point Lookout, Maryland, he was transferred to the federal prison camp at Elmira, New York, on July 12, 1864, where he died on March 4, 1865 of "diarrhea." Source Card File indicates "John H. Mintz" served in the Confederate Navy.
[Source(s): Card File; North Carolina Troops, IV]

Misenheimer, Clayborn (Stanly County, North Carolina [?])
Landsman, Confederate States Navy. Born in North Carolina in 1820, he is shown in 1860, with his wife Mary and two children, residing in Stanly County. Misenheimer resided as a farmer in 1880 with his wife, Mary A. and three children, at Risenhours, Stanly County, North Carolina. His widow's application for pension dated July 1, 1905 when she was age 70, listed her post office as Cassel(?) (illegible) Grove. Her application states he enlisted in the Navy in Wilmington, North Carolina. A pencil notation on the application states he was in Richmond, Virginia, at the close of the war. The pension was approved at 4th Class. She filed a second application for pension dated July 5, 1909 when she was aged 73 and living at RFD #1, Richfield, Stanly County, North Carolina. He was buried at New Bethel Lutheran Church, Stanly County, North Carolina
[Source(s): Stepp, "Burials;" "Stanly Reunions;" Pensions (North Carolina); Foenander]

Mitchell, A. S. (North Carolina?)
Landsman, Confederate States Navy. Mitchell served as a Landsman aboard the CSS ARCTIC, Cape Fear River, North Carolina, 1863, and aboard the CSS RALEIGH in 1864. He served aboard the CSS BOMBSHELL in North Carolina waters, and was captured thereon during an engagement in Albemarle Sound, North Carolina on May 5, 1864.
[Source(s): Foenander]

Mitchell, Ben B. (Granville County, North Carolina)
Landsman, Confederate States Navy ["20th Company (?)]. Mitchell was conscripted on March 30, 1864 at Camp Holmes [near Raleigh, North Carolina] from Colonel Dolby's 43rd Regiment, North Carolina Militia, Granville County, North Carolina. Another source states he "enlisted" on March 31, 1864 in Raleigh, North Carolina, for the war, while another source states he "appears on a list of conscripts 'in yard at Halifax' June 9, 1864." He served as a Landsman aboard the CSS ALBEMARLE, and at the Halifax Station, 1864. He is shown as being a resident of Wakefield, North Carolina, and aged 66, in July 1909. A pension claim filed by Mitchell on July 4, 1910, showing his age as 66, and his post office as Zebulon, Wake County, North Carolina, stated that he served in the Navy "on

Albemarle Iron Clad." The pension was approved at 4th Class. A claim filed on July 7, 1924 by his widow, Sarah F. Mitchell, age 67, post office Wakefield, Wake County, North Carolina, was approved at 4th Class. She married him on November 4, 1879. A claim for increase was filed on October 23, 1937 by the widow, aged 80, based on a certificate of disability. The claim was approved at Class A.
[Source(s): Card File; NA RG 45; Pensions (North Carolina); Foenander]

Mitchell, Dennis (Ireland//NC?)
Confederate States Navy (?)
A native of Ireland, Mitchell died in Wilmington, North Carolina at age 24 on August 17, 1862 of "Billious Fever (?). He was listed as a "Sailor" and buried in Oakdale Cemetery, Wilmington, North Carolina.
[Source: Oakdale (Davis)]

Mitchell, Edward (Ireland//Chatham County, North Carolina)
Private, Confederate States Army//Confederate States Navy(?). A native of Westmead, Ireland, Mitchell resided in Chatham County, North Carolina, where he resided, oddly enough, as a "sailor." He enlisted there at age 36 on July 7, 1862, for the war, as a Private in Company D, 61st Regiment, North Carolina Troops. Present or accounted for in November-December 1863, he was captured at Morris Island, Charleston Harbor, South Carolina, on August 26, 1863, and confined at Hilton Head, South Carolina, on September 1, 1863. On September 22, 1863, he was transferred to Fort Columbus, New York Harbor, New York, and four days later to Point Lookout, Maryland, arriving there on September 26, 1863 where he was paroled on April 27, 1864. He was received at City Point, Virginia, on April 30, 1864 for exchange. On May 1, 1864, Mitchell was hospitalized in Richmond, Virginia, with a dislocated left shoulder. The place and date of the injury are unknown. He was furloughed for thirty days on May 6, 1864 and retired to the Invalid Corps on December 24, 1864. Source Card File indicates Confederate Naval service.
[Source(s): Card File; North Carolina Troops, XIV]

Mitchell, James (Iredell County, North Carolina)
Landsman (Private), Confederate States Navy. Mitchell's name appears on a register of Confederate States Army General Military Hospital Number 4, Wilmington, North Carolina, which states he was admitted on March 30, 1864 with "febris typhoides," and returned to duty on May 6, 1864. The register gives his post office as Poplar Bridge, North Carolina [County unknown], and carries the remark "Furloughed from Navy." His claim for a pension was filed on June 22, 1912 at age 67, listing his post office as Jennings, Iredell County, North Carolina. The claim was approved at 4th Class. His application states he served in "the Navy department under Captain Poindexter on the receiving ship CSS ARCTIC anchored on the Cape Fear River at Wilmington." R. D. Speaks (q.v.), Confederate States Navy, a witness on Mitchell's application, was in service with him.
[Source(s): Card File; Pension (North Carolina); NA RG 109; Foenander; MR, I]

Mitchell, James [NOTE: May be the same as "James Mitchell" of Iredell County, North Carolina (q.v.)]
Landsman, Confederate States Navy. Mitchell enlisted on January 11, 1864 in Raleigh, North Carolina, for the war. A "James Mitchell," served as a Landsman, CSS ARCTIC, Cape Fear River, North Carolina, 1863 [per Foenander].
[Source(s): Card File; ORN 2, 1, 278; Foenander]

Mitchell, James [NOTE: May be the same as "James Mitchell" of Iredell County, North Carolina (q.v.)]
Landsman, Confederate States Navy. Mitchell served aboard the CSS ARCTIC, Cape Fear River, NC, 1863.
[Source(s): Foenander]

Mitchell, John
Ordinary Seaman, Confederate States Navy.
Mitchell served as an Ordinary Seaman as part of the North Carolina Squadron aboard the NCS EDWARDS beginning with his shipping articles dated July 25, 1861. He was aboard that ship until sometime in October when he appears as an Ordinary Seaman aboard the CSS FORREST, per that vessel's payroll list for the 1st quarter 1862.
[Source: NCCWSP]

Mitchell, John Kirkwood (North Carolina)
Captain, Confederate States Navy. Mitchell was born in North Carolina, circa 1810-1811, and was reportedly related to Admiral David Glasgow Farragut, United States Navy. Mitchell served in the United States Navy from February 1, 1825 until his resignation in 1861. He was appointed from Florida to the rank of Commander in the Confederate States Navy on November 11, 1861. Another source states he was appointed to the rank of Commander on October 23, 1862 to rank from March 26, 1861 (or November 11, 1861). Attached to the New Orleans Station in December 1861, as the subordinate to a Commander Hollins, he later commanded the station from February 1, 1861 – March

1862. Mitchell was commanding the naval forces on the Lower Mississippi River at the time of the surrender of Forts Jackson and St. Philip on April 28, 1862. Mitchell was captured at New Orleans in April 1862; held as a Prisoner of War at Fort Warren, Boston Harbor, Massachusetts; and, exchanged at Aiken's Landing, Virginia, on August 5, 1862. Following his release, he served on the Jackson Station, 1862, and later as aide to the Secretary of the Navy. He commanded the Office of Orders and Detail, Richmond, Virginia, 1863 – 1864 [another source shows the dates as "1862-1864"]. Promoted to Captain in the Provisional Navy, to rank from May 13, 1863, he assumed command of the James River Squadron (except for the CSS PATRICK HENRY) on May 7, 1864, with his flagship as the CSS RICHMOND, until May 18, 1864. He commanded the CSS VIRGINIA II from July through October 1864, and the James River Squadron, 1864-1865. Mitchell was detached from command of the James River Squadron on February 15, 1865, when the command was transferred to Rear Admiral Raphael Semmes on February 18, 1865. Attached to Semmes' Naval Brigade in April 1865, Mitchell surrendered and was paroled at Greensboro, North Carolina, April 26, 1865. Mitchell was a post-war resident of Richmond, Virginia, where he died on December 5, 1889 [another report indicates he died on Thursday, December 6, 1889], and was buried at Hollywood Cemetery.
[Source(s): Foenander; Register; Driver; ONWR]

Mitchell, John [Jno.] W. (Granville County, North Carolina)
Confederate States Army//Landsman, Confederate States Navy. Mitchell was conscripted on March 30, 1864 at Camp Holmes [near Raleigh, North Carolina] from Colonel Dolby's 43rd Regiment, North Carolina Militia, Granville County, North Carolina. Another source states he enlisted on March 31 ["30," per Foenander], 1864. His name appears on a list of conscripts "in yard at Halifax," June 9, 1864. Description: Age 29; eyes grey; hair dark; complexion fair; height 5 feet 10 ½ inches; place of birth Granville County, North Carolina; occupation farmer. He served as a Landsman aboard the CSS ALBEMARLE, and at the Halifax Station, 1864. His first application for a pension, dated July 1, 1901, age 67, listed his post office as Wilton, Granville, County, North Carolina. His application for pension states he enlisted in the Confederate States Navy at Halifax in the summer of 1863, that he had typhoid fever in the summer of 1864, and that he has had a running sore on his leg ever since. He was judged totally disabled and given a pension rated at 4th class. He filed a second application for an increase in benefits on July 4, 1904 which was "referred to the Chairman." His third application, for increase, dated July 3, 1905, was disallowed. A fourth application, again for increase, was filed on July 6, 1908, at age 74, in which he states he enlisted in the Navy and was assigned to the Ram CSS ALBEMARLE. He states he contracted a severe case of typhoid while stationed at Halifax, North Carolina, which settled in his left leg and rendered him permanently lame. A July 5, 1909 letter from Dr. James A. Morris states that Mitchell was discharged from the Navy due to the lameness of his leg. A fifth application for an increase in benefits dated July 5, 1909 was disallowed. His sixth, and final, application for an increase in benefits, dated July 1, 1914, at age 81, listed his post office as Wilton, was disallowed.
[Source(s): Card File; NA RG 45; Pensions (North Carolina); Foenander]

Mitchell, J. L. [NOTE: May be the same as "James Mitchell" of Iredell County, North Carolina (q.v.)]
Seaman, Confederate States Navy. Mitchell enlisted on June 15, 1864 in Raleigh, North Carolina, for the war.
[Source(s): Card File; NA RG 45]

Mitchell, John W. (Granville County, North Carolina)
Landsman, Confederate States Navy. Mitchell resided in Granville County, North Carolina where he enlisted in the Confederate States Navy at age 29 on March 30, [1864?]. He served as a Landsman aboard the CSS ALBEMARLE, and at the Halifax Station, 1864. He applied for a post war Confederate pension from Granville County, NC.
[Source(s): Foenander; Pensions (North Carolina); *ORN* 2, 1, 274]

Mitchell, Richard Alex (Caswell County, North Carolina)
Private, Confederate States Army//Landsman, Confederate States Navy. Mitchell was born in Caswell County, North Carolina, but resided as a laborer in Alamance County, North Carolina, at the time of his enlistment in Company E, 13th Regiment, North Carolina Troops at age 25 on May 8, 1861 [Source "MR" gives the date as May 3, 1861]. When he mustered for service at Garysburg, North Carolina [NOTE: Camp of Instruction] on May 15, 1861, he was described as being six feet tall, sandy hair, fair complexion, and blue eyes He was present or accounted for until he transferred to the Confederate States Navy for duty as a Landsman aboard the CSS VIRGINIA [MERRIMAC] at Hampton Roads, Virginia, on February 19, 1862.
[Source(s): Card File; MR, I; North Carolina Troops, V; Foenander; ORN 2, 1, 310; Quarstein]

Mitchell, Robert
Private, Confederate States Army//Landsman, Confederate States Navy. Mitchell was born in Caswell County, North Carolina, and resided in Alamance Company, North Carolina, where he was by occupation a laborer prior

to enlisting in Alamance County, North Carolina, at age 25 on May 8, 1861, in Company E, 13th Regiment, North Carolina Troops. One source shows he enlisted on December 23, 1863 in Wilmington, North Carolina, for the war. He was present or accounted for until he transferred to the Confederate States Navy for duty on the CSS VIRGINIA [MERRIMAC] on February 19, 1862. He served as a Landsman aboard the CSS ARCTIC, Cape Fear River, North Carolina, and served as Ship's Corporal or Ship's Cook aboard the steam gunboat CSS YADKIN, Wilmington, North Carolina, 1864.
[Source(s): Card File; NA RG 45; Foenander; *ORN* 2, 1, 278 & 313; North Carolina Troops, V]

Mitchell, W. A.
Landsman, Confederate States Navy. Mitchell enlisted on June 10, 1864 in Raleigh, North Carolina, for the war.
[Source(s): Card File; NA RG 45]

Mixon, Langley (Wilson County, North Carolina)
Private, Confederate States Army//Confederate States Navy. Resided in Wilson County, North Carolina, and enlisted in Craven County, North Carolina, at age 22 on June 28, 1861, for the war, in Company F, 4th Regiment, North Carolina State Troops. Wounded in the left thigh and captured at Fredericksburg, Virginia, on May 3, 1863, he was hospitalized in Washington, DC, until transferred to Old Capitol Prison, Washington, DC, on June16, 1863. He was paroled on June 25, 1863 and transferred to City Point, Virginia, for exchange. He rejoined the company prior to September 1, 1863 and was present or accounted for until transferred to the Confederate States Navy on April 5, 1864. The date "April 15, 1864" appears on the card without explanation, which may be his enlistment date.
[Source(s): Card File; North Carolina Troops, IV; Foenander]

Moddling, Alonzo (Appears also as A. Maudling, A. Muddling, Lorenzo Modlin)
Seaman, Boatswain's Mate, Confederate States Navy.
Moddling served as a Seaman aboard the NCS SEA BIRD from July - November 1861, per that vessel's muster roll. He was serving as a Boatswain's Mate aboard the same ship as of February 1862. He was wounded in the arm during the Battle of Elizabeth City on February 10, 1862, captured and carried to Roanoke Island where he was paroled on February 12, 1862. He returned to Elizabeth City. He received a partial payment on February 18, 1862 at Gosport Navy Yard following the sinking of the SEA BIRD at Elizabeth City on February 10, 1862. Records indicate he was ordered to be received by the hospital on orders from Flag Officer French Forrest on February 22, 1862 for wounds received at Elizabeth City, North Carolina. His name appears on a payroll of the North Carolina Squadron for the1st quarter of 1862 (December 1, 1861 - April 15, 1862). According to payroll records, he was listed as "on parole" as of April 15, 1862.
[Source: NCCWSP]

Mode, John O.
Landsman, Confederate States Navy. Mode enlisted on May 27, 1864 in Raleigh, North Carolina for the war.
[Source(s): Card File; NA RG 45]

Moffit, Joshua (North Carolina)
Landsman, Confederate States Navy. Moffit enlisted on November 22, 1863 in Wilmington, North Carolina, for the war [another source states he enlisted November 20, 1863 in Raleigh, North Carolina for the war]. At enlistment, Moffit was aged 23 with blue eyes, dark hair, and a fair complexion. He was born in North Carolina.
[Source(s): North Carolina "Tennessee;" Card File; NA RG 45]

Moffitt, David
Landsman, Confederate States Navy. Moffitt enlisted on April 13, 1864 in Raleigh, North Carolina, for the war.
[Source(s): Card File; NA RG 45]

Monroe, D.
Landsman, Confederate States Navy. Monroe was assigned from Raleigh, North Carolina, in October 1864 as a Landsman, to Battery Brooke, James River, Virginia, October 1864.
[Source(s): PCNMC; *ORN* 1, 10, 805; Foenander]

Monroe, John (Cumberland County, North Carolina)
Confederate States Navy. Monroe was listed as aboard the steamer CSS NORTH CAROLINA.
[Source(s): Oates; MR, 4, p. 444; Foenander]

Monroe, John Archie [A] [H.] (Robeson County, North Carolina)
Seaman/Ordinary Seaman, Confederate States Navy. Monroe enlisted on June 5, 1863 in Wilmington, North Carolina for the war and served as an Ordinary Seaman aboard the CSS NORTH CAROLINA, Cape Fear River, North Carolina, 1864.
[Source(s): Card File; UDC, Highland Boys; NA RG 45; Foenander]

Montague, J. H. (New Hanover County, North Carolina)
Private, Confederate States Navy [Naval Battalion]. Montague's name appears as a signature to an Oath of Allegiance to the United States, subscribed and sworn to at Newport News, Virginia, June 15, 1865. His place of residence was given on the Oath as Wilmington, North Carolina. Description: Complexion light; hair black; eyes blue; height 5 feet 5 inches. The Oath carries the remark, "Captured Richmond April 3."
[Source(s): Card File; NA RG 109]

Moon, Oliver (Moore County, North Carolina)
Landsman, Confederate States Navy. Moon enlisted on December 12, 1863 in Wilmington, North Carolina for the war. Another source states he enlisted on December 10, 1863 in Raleigh, North Carolina for the war. He is listed as a deserter from the Confederate States Navy in a February 8, 1865 letter from the Conscript Office (Raleigh) to the Enrolling Officer (Moore County). No physical description given.
[Source(s): McDonald Papers; NA RG 45; McNeill Papers].

Moore, Alexander
Cook, Confederate States Navy.
Per muster rolls, Moore served as a Cook aboard the CSS JUNALUSKA as part of the North Carolina Squadron at least during the period June 15, 1861 - August 20, 1861.
[Source: NCCWSP]

Moore, Charles
Ordinary Seaman, Confederate States Navy.
Per muster rolls, Moore served as an Ordinary Seaman aboard the CSS JUNALUSKA as part of the North Carolina Squadron at least during the period June 15, 1861 - August 20, 1861.
[Source: NCCWSP]

Moore, Edward Warren [E. W.] (Bladen County, North Carolina)
Confederate States Navy. Moore enlisted in the Confederate States Navy on October 21, 1863 in Wilmington, North Carolina. Another source states he enlisted on October 30, 1863 in Raleigh, North Carolina for the war, while still another says he enlisted on November 1, 1863 in Wilmington, North Carolina for the war. Moore served aboard the CSS ARCTIC, 1863, and the CSS RALEIGH, 1864. His name appears on a roll of Prisoners of War at Point Lookout, Maryland, which states he was captured on April 6, 1865, at "Harpers" and was confined at Point Lookout, Maryland, from April 14, 1865 until released June 15, 1865. His name appears as a signature to an Oath of Allegiance to the United States subscribed and sworn to at Point Lookout, Maryland, June 15, 1865. His place of residence was given on the Oath as Bladen County, North Carolina. Description: Complexion dark; hair black; eyes blue; height 5 feet 10 ¼ inches. His pension claim filed December 19, 1912 at age 70, listed his post office as Kelly, Bladen County, North Carolina, was disallowed. A claim filed on June 23, 1916 by his widow, Rebecca E. Moore, age 73, listing her post office as Kelly, Bladen County, North Carolina was approved. A subsequent claim filed for increase on May 13, 1935 by his widow at age 92, was approved.
[Source(s): Card File; NA RG 109; NA RG 45; Pensions (North Carolina); St. Armand' Foenander; MR, IV, 446]

Moore, Edward
Pilot, Confederate States Navy. Moore served in the Confederate States Navy as a Pilot aboard the CSS PATRICK HENRY in Virginia waters in 1862. He served as a Pilot aboard the CSS BEAUFORT in Virginia waters in 1864 and the CSS VIRGINIA II in Virginia waters in 1865.
[Source(s): Card File; McElroy]

Moore, G. W.
Landsman, Confederate States Navy. Moore enlisted on September 28, 1863 at Camp Holmes [near Raleigh, North Carolina] for the war.
[Source(s): Card File; NA RG 45]

Moore, Henry (Wake County, North Carolina) [NOTE: May be same as "Henry Moore," q.v.]
Private, Confederate States Army//Seaman, Confederate States Navy. Moore enlisted in Wake County, North Carolina, at age 45 on November 10, 1861 in Company A, 19th Regiment, North Carolina State Troops (2nd Regiment, North Carolina Cavalry). He was admitted to the hospital in Richmond, Virginia, on December 24, 1862 with gunshot wound through the right foot. Moore was present or accounted for through October 1863 and transferred to the Confederate States Navy on April 25, 1864.
[Source(s): Card File; NA RG 45; North Carolina Troops, II]

Moore, James O.
Assistant Paymaster, Paymaster, Confederate States Navy. Prior service in the United States Navy. Moore was born in and appointed from North Carolina as an Assistant Paymaster on September 21, 1861 [Source "Fold3, USN Resignees" lists the date as September 21, 1861]. He served as such aboard the CSS ELLIS as part of the North Carolina Squadron from January 1862 – May 1862. He was appointed to Paymaster on February 6, 1863, and Paymaster, Provisional Navy, on June 2, 1864. He served on the Richmond Station, 1861-1863; the CSS RICHMOND, 1862-1863 [1864, per Foenander]; and, participated in the Battle of Roanoke Island, North Carolina, February 7-8, 1862. He served aboard the CSS VIRGINIA II, James River Squadron, 1864. Attached to Semmes' Naval Brigade, he was surrendered and paroled at Greensboro, North Carolina, April 26, 1865 [another source gives the date as April 28, 1865].
[Source(s): McElroy; Register; Card File; Journal; Foenander; ONWR; Fold3, USN Resignees]

Moore, James W.
Seaman, Confederate States Navy. Born in North Carolina in 1846, Moore resided with his mother Martha, and siblings in Apalachicola, Florida in 1860. He resided next door to John Theobald, who was later a fellow sailor aboard the CSS SPRAY. Moore enlisted in 1861 in Thigpen's 2nd Florida Cavalry. He transferred to the Confederate States Navy and served as a Seaman aboard the CSS SPRAY and was surrendered aboard that vessel in May 1865. He resided as a sailor with his mother Martha in Apalachicola, Franklin County, Florida in 1880. Moore married Mary Alice Johnston on April 15, 1884 (or 1883), in Franklin County. He died on January 24, 1891, in Apalachicola.
[Source(s): Foenander]

Moore, Jim
Seaman, Confederate States Navy. Moore enlisted on January 1, 1863 in Wilmington, North Carolina for three years or the war.
[Source(s): Card File; NA RG 45]

Moore, John
Landsman, Confederate States Navy. Moore enlisted on April 18, 1864 in Raleigh, North Carolina for the war.
[Source(s): Card File; NA RG 45]

Moore, John (Negro)
Fireman, NCS WINSLOW. Moore was the slave of Master Patrick McCarrick, and one of seven African American crew members aboard the NCS WINSLOW.
[Source(s): NCS]

Moore, John (Wake County, North Carolina) [NOTE: May be same as "John Moore" who enlisted April 18, 1864]
Private, Confederate States Army//Landsman, Confederate States Navy. Moore resided in Wake County, North Carolina, where he enlisted at age 28 in Company I, 8th Regiment, North Carolina State Troops, on September 23, 1862, for the war. He was present or accounted for until he transferred to the Confederate States Navy, enlisting in Raleigh, North Carolina, on or about April 22, 1863.
[Source(s): Card File; NA RG 45; North Carolina Troops, IV; Foenander]

Moore, Jordan M. (Harnett County, North Carolina)
Confederate States Navy. Moore was born in Harnett County, North Carolina, where he resided as a farmer until his enlistment in that county at age 20 on April 5, 1862 as a Private in Company B, 10th Battalion, North Carolina Heavy Artillery. He was present or accounted for until he transferred to Company D of the same Battalion on May 23, 1863. Present or accounted for through October 1864, he transferred to the Confederate States Navy for service aboard the CSS INDIAN CHIEF at Charleston, South Carolina, on January 9, 1865. He was captured in Harnett County on March 18, 1865 and confined at Point Lookout, Maryland, until released after taking the Oath of Allegiance on June 29, 1865.
[Source(s): Card File; Foenander; MR, IV; North Carolina Troops, I]

Moore, Moses
Landsman, Confederate States Navy. Moore enlisted on October 5, 1863 at Camp Holmes [near Raleigh, North Carolina].
[Source(s): Card File; NA RG 45]

Moore, Oliver (North Carolina?)
Landsman, Confederate States Navy. Moore served aboard the CSS ARCTIC, Cape Fear River, North Carolina, 1863.
[Source(s): Foenander]

Moore, Samuel
Ordinary Seaman, Confederate States Navy.
Per muster rolls, Moore served as an Ordinary Seaman as part of the North Carolina Squadron aboard the CSS JUNALUSKA at least during the period June 15, 1861 - August 20, 1861.
[Source: NCCWSP]

Moore, Scipior (?)
Seaman, Confederate States Navy. Moore enlisted on January 1, 1863 in Wilmington, North Carolina for the war.
[Source(s): Card File; NA RG 45]

Moore, Thomas G. (Halifax County, North Carolina)
Confederate States Navy. Born in North Carolina, Moore enlisted in the Confederate States Navy on October 31, 1863 in Wilmington, North Carolina. Another source states he enlisted on November 5, 1863 in Wilmington, North Carolina, while another says he enlisted November 2, 1863 in Raleigh, North Carolina. He resided as a farmer, in 1880, with his wife, Deacy (maiden name Wood), and three children (eldest child born 1862) at Faucetts, Halifax County, North Carolina. His pension claim filed on March 19, 1904, age 73, listing his post office as Raleigh, North Carolina, Wake County, North Carolina, states he enlisted from Halifax County, North Carolina, on or about October 15, 1863. He served aboard the CSS ARCTIC receiving ship under Commander C. B. Poindexter at Wilmington, North Carolina, 1863. He stated he received no wounds during his service. His claim for pension was approved at 4th Class. A pension claim filed on July 1, 1907 by his widow, Detsey (Decie) Ann Moore (whom he married in 1850), age 72, listing her post office as Raleigh, North Carolina, Wake County, North Carolina was approved at 4th Class. Her husband died on February 13, 1907 and was buried in Oakwood Cemetery, Raleigh, North Carolina.
[Source(s): MR, 4, p. 446; Card File; NA RG 45; Pensions (North Carolina); *ORN* 2, 1, 277; Foenander]

Moore, Thomas Longworth (Hertford County, North Carolina)
Lieutenant, Confederate States Navy. Born at Mulberry Grove plantation, Hertford County, North Carolina, on February 22, 1847 (one source shows year of birth as 1845) the son of Dr. Godwin Cotton Moore, and Julia Munro Wheeler. Moore was educated at home, by private tutors until he entered service on September 30, 1857, in the United States Navy, as a Midshipman. He served in the United State Navy until he resigned on April 19, 1861. He assisted in the organization and drilling of the first company of soldiers raised in Murfreesboro, North Carolina [*"Before the Rebel Flag Fell,"* by F. Roy Johnson]. Moore was appointed an Acting Midshipman in the Confederate States Navy on June 12, 1861 and served aboard the Confederate Receiving Ship CSS UNITED STATES [later CSS CONFEDERATE STATES]. He captained the privateer *Dixie*, in November 1861, and served on the side-wheeled gunboat CSS FLORIDA (which was later re-named CSS SELMA) in the Lake Pontchartrain, Louisiana and Mobile Bay, Alabama areas, 1862 – 1863. Promoted to the rank of Acting Master on October 4 [3], 1862, he was sent overseas in 1863, and assigned to the cruiser CSS TEXAS, which never saw service afloat. Moore was promoted to the rank of Second Lieutenant on January 7, 1864, to rank from April 29, 1863, and to First Lieutenant, Provisional Navy of the Confederate States, on June 2, 1864, to rank from January 6, 1864. He married Rose Standish Ludlam, at Baden, Germany, on August 17 (or 22), 1864 [after her death at Baltimore, Maryland, in 1870, he married Kate Ward, April 14, 1873]. In September 1864, Moore was listed as awaiting duty in Europe. He reported for duty aboard the CSS RAPPAHANNOCK at Calais, France, on December 28, 1864. Following the war, he resided for a time, in Richmond, Virginia, as a businessman. In 1880, Moore was employed as a clerk in the United States House of Representatives in Washington, D.C. In 1910, he was employed as a civil engineer in New York City, and was a member and adjutant of the Confederate Veteran Camp of New York. He was awarded the United Daughters of the Confederacy Cross of Honor. Moore returned to Washington, DC, and ultimately settled in Portsmouth, Virginia, where he died on May 17, 1926.
[Source(s): Foenander; McElroy; Register; MR, IV, 449; Card File; Journal *ORN* 2, 1, 286 & 306; *ORN* 2, 2, 516, & 819-820; Census (Virginia), 1880; ONWR;
Fold3, Midshipmen]

Moore, W. P. (County unknown)
Confederate States Marine Corps. Moore was listed as "Shock[ed]" and captured at Fort Fisher on January 15, 1865.
[Source(s): Card File]

Moore, W. T.
North Carolina Navy. Listed by source "DH Hill" as one of the first officers commissioned as a Midshipman in the North Carolina Navy.
[Source(s): DH Hill; NCS]

Moore, Wesley W. (Onslow County, North Carolina)
Private, Confederate States Army//Confederate States Navy. Moore resided and enlisted for the war in Onslow County, North Carolina, on March 24, 1862, as a Private in Company E, 3rd Regiment, North Carolina State Troops. Moore was wounded in action at Gettysburg, Pennsylvania, July 3, 1863, and captured while in the hospital at Gettysburg, July 4-5, 1863. Moore was incarcerated at DeCamp General Hospital, David's Island, New York Harbor until paroled and exchanged at City Point, Virginia, on August 28, 1863. On April 5, 1864, he transferred to the Confederate States Navy.
[Source(s): Card File; Foenander; North Carolina Troops, III; MR, I]]

Moore, William (Granville County, North Carolina)
Confederate States Navy. Moore was conscripted on March 29, 1864 at Camp Holmes [near Raleigh, North Carolina] from Colonel Amos' 42nd Regiment, North Carolina Militia from Granville County, North Carolina. Description: Age 44; eyes hazel; hair dark; complexion dark; height 5 feet 10 ½ inches; place of birth Halifax County, North Carolina; occupation merchant.
[Source(s): Card File; NA RG 45]

Morehead, James
Ordinary Seaman, Confederate States Navy. Morehead enlisted on April 15, 1863 in Wilmington, North Carolina for three years or the war.
[Source(s): Card File; NA RG 45]

Morris, Aug H.
Landsman, Confederate States Navy. Morris enlisted on April 13, 1864 in Raleigh for the war.
[Source(s): Card File; NA RG 45]

Morris, Elwood
Engineer-in-Chief, Confederate States Navy. Served as Engineer-in-Chief at Ocracoke.
[Source: NCS]

Morris, James
Seaman, Confederate States Navy. Morris enlisted in the Confederate States Navy on September 12, 1863 in Wilmington, North Carolina for the war. Source "Foenander" lists a "James Harris," Seaman, CSS ARCTIC, and a "James Harris," Ship's Cook, CSS NORTH CAROLINA and Seaman aboard the CSS TALLAHASSEE, Cape Fear River, 1864.
[Source(s): MR, 4, p. 446; Card File; NA RG 45; St. Armand; Foenander]

Morris, James H. (Granville County, North Carolina)
Confederate States Navy.
[Source(s): Granville County Troops]

Morris, Joseph H. (Granville County, North Carolina)
Confederate States Navy. Morris served as a Landsman aboard the CSS NORTH CAROLINA, Cape Fear River, North Carolina, 1864. Morris filed a pension claim on July 15, 1915, age 69, listing his post office as RFD #1, Oxford, Granville County, North Carolina, stating that he enlisted in the Navy in 1862 and was "ruptured during the war" and was "now unable to do any work at all from said [illegible]." His claim was disallowed. In a sworn statement by Mitchell, dated July 15, 1915, he states he enlisted "about the year 1862" in the Navy and went on "the old North Carolina iron clad that was sunk." He says he then went aboard "the old RALEIGH and that was sunk also," then "to Fort Fishure [sic]." His claim filed on July 3, 1916 was disallowed.
[Source(s): Card File; Pensions (North Carolina); Granville County Troops; Foenander; ORN 2, 1, 294-296]

Morris, William P. (Tyrrell County, North Carolina)
Private, Confederate States Army//Landsman, Ordinary Seaman, Master-at-Arms, Confederate States Navy. Born Tyrrell County, North Carolina, circa 1835, Morris was a shoemaker until he enlisted in Company G, 1st Regiment, North Carolina Infantry, in Portsmouth, Washington County, North Carolina, on June 24, 1861, at age 25. He was discharged from his regiment on February 3, 1862 due to transfer to the Confederate States Navy and served aboard the CSS VIRGINIA in March 1862. Records indicate he was paid for service on the CSS VIRGINIA for the period April 1 – December 1862. He served at Drewry's Bluff from May 12, 1862 through March 31, 1864, and as an Ordinary Seaman aboard the CSS FREDERICKSBURG, James River Squadron, 1864-1865. He was ordered to the Naval Ordnance Works, Richmond, Virginia, January 13, 1865, and served as Master-at-Arms, Company A, Naval Battalion. Captured at Burkeville, Virginia, on April 6, 1865, Morris was sent to Point Lookout, Maryland, as a Prisoner of War, where he was held until released on June 29, 1865. Description: Height, 5'6;" light complexion; brown hair; blue eyes; residence, Norfolk, Virginia.
[Source(s): Card File; Driver; St. Armand; Foenander; North Carolina Troops, III; MR, IV, 446]

Morris [Morriss], William P. [W. P.] (Wales//Pasquotank County or New Hanover County, North Carolina)
Private, Confederate States Army//Seaman (later Master-At-Arms), Confederate States Navy. A native of Milford, Wales, Morris resided in Pasquotank County, North Carolina, as a miner prior to enlisting on August 14, 1861 at age 24 as a Private in Company A, 8th Regiment, North Carolina State Troops. He was captured at Roanoke Island, North Carolina, on February 8, 1862, was paroled at Elizabeth City, North Carolina on February 21, 1862, and exchanged in August 1862. He was listed as present or accounted for until transferred to the Confederate States Navy on or about February 2, 1863. Morris served as Master-at-Arms aboard the CSS ARCTIC, 1863. Another source states he enlisted in the Confederate States Navy in Wilmington, North Carolina, on January 18, 1863 for the war. He appears on registers of Confederate States Army General Military Hospital Number 4, Wilmington, North Carolina, being admitted on October 31, 1863 with "feb. int. quotidiani," and returned to duty on January 4, 1864. His post office was given on registers as Wilmington, North Carolina.
[Source(s): MR, 4, p. 446; Card File; NA RG 45; NA RG 109; North Carolina Troops, IV; ORN 2, 1; Foenander]

Morris, W. J.
Landsman, Confederate States Navy.
Payroll records indicate Morris served as a Landsman aboard the CSS BEAUFORT from September - November 1861. His name appears on the North Carolina Squadron payroll for the 1st quarter of 1862 (beginning December 1, 1861). He is listed as being "discharged" on the December 1, 1861 payroll.
[Source: NCCWSP]

Morrisett, Asa (Currituck County, North Carolina)
Seaman, Confederate States Navy. Morrisett served as a Seaman aboard the CSS ELLIS as part of the North Carolina Squadron either between August - October 1861, or "January – May" 1862 [NOTE: CSS ELLIS was captured on February 10, 1862], operating in North Carolina waters.
[Source(s): Foenander; ORN 2, 1; *ORN* 2, 1, 285, NCCWSP; Moebs]

Morrison, Benjamin (Negro)
Landsman, Confederate States Navy. Morrison enlisted on February 20, 1864 in Wilmington, North Carolina, "for the war." Another source lists him as a Landsman aboard the CSS ARCTIC, 1863.
[Source(s): Foenander; Card File; NA RG 45; *ORN* 2, 1, 278]

Morrison, George
Captain [?], Confederate States Navy. Morrison served as Chief engineer on the "*Ad-Vance*."
[Source(s): McElroy; Card File]

Morrison, Henry (Ireland//Cumberland County, North Carolina)
Private, Confederate States Army//Confederate States Navy. Born in Ireland, Morrison resided in Cumberland County, North Carolina, as a laborer, where he enlisted, on May 29, 1861, at age 23, as a Private in Company C, 3rd Regiment, North Carolina State Troops. He transferred to the Confederate States Navy on February 1, 1862.
[Source(s): Foenander; North Carolina Troops, III; MR, I; Card File]

Morrison, Samuel N. (Moore County, North Carolina)
Private, Confederate States Marine Corps. Born on December 28, 1828, Morrison enlisted in the Confederate States Navy in Raleigh on October 6, 1864. A letter of James C. Davis, November 17, 1864, states the group from Camp Holmes, of which Morrison was a part, arrived aboard the CSS INDIAN CHIEF, Charleston, South Carolina,

Sunday, November 6, 1864, and was designated to serve aboard the ironclad CSS CHICORA. He served as a Private of the Marine guard on board the ironclad CSS COLUMBIA, Charleston, SC, to February 7, 1865, then assigned to the CSS INDIAN CHIEF. Per source "McLeod, August 30, 1874," Morrison left the unit [deserted?] at Jonesboro, North Carolina, on the march Richmond. He was paroled at Greensboro on May 9, 1865, with his home listed as Eagle Springs, Moore County, North Carolina. Morrison died on October 17, 1907 and was buried at Bensalem Presbyterian Church, Eagle Springs, Moore County, North Carolina.
[Source(s): Foenander; North Carolina Troops, Doc.# 0299; Card File; Stepp, "Burials;" "Citizen News-Record," July 8, 1987; Donnelly; Davis, November 17m 1864; Donnelly-ENL]

Morse, Christopher C. [C.C.]
Pilot, Confederate States Navy ["North Carolina Navy" (see Stepp)]. Morse served as a Cape Fear Pilot on the North Carolina steamer "*Ad-Vance*," and the steamer "*Kate.*" *Chronicles of the Cape Fear* by James Sprunt states he was a pilot of the blockade runner "*Columbia*," afterwards called the "*Lady Davis.*" He was born on June 9, 1829, died on November 21, 1903, and was buried in the Old Southport Cemetery, Southport, North Carolina.
[Source(s): McElroy; Card File; Gravestone Records, v. 6. P.307; "Chronicles;" Stepp, "Burials"]

Morse, Edward Dudley (Middle initial sometimes shown as "W") (North Carolina)
Seaman, Confederate States Navy. Born in North Carolina in August 1836, Morse served as a Seaman aboard the CSS PALMETTO STATE (also possibly as a pilot), and on the "submarine *David.*" He married on November 5, 1868, and in 1900 resided as a pilot in Charleston, South Carolina. His wife, Alice A. Morse, applied for a Confederate widow's pension from Charleston, South Carolina, in 1919, after the death of her husband on October 16, 1912. He was buried in Magnolia Cemetery, 70 Cunnington Avenue, North, Charleston, South Carolina.
[Source(s): Foenander]

Morton, M.
Confederate States Navy.
Morton received a partial payment on February 13, 1862 at Gosport Navy Yard as part of the North Carolina Squadron.
[Source: NCCWP]

Moss, William T. (Granville County, North Carolina)
Landsman, Confederate States Navy. Moss was conscripted on March 30 [31], 1864 at Camp Holmes [near Raleigh, North Carolina] from Colonel Dolby's 43rd North Carolina Militia, Granville County, North Carolina. Description: Age 18; eyes hazel; hair dark; complexion fair; height 5 feet 11 inches; place of birth Granville County, North Carolina; occupation farmer.
[Source(s): Card File; NA RG 45]

Motsinger, J. W.
Landsman, Confederate States Navy. Motsinger enlisted on April 20, 1864 in Raleigh, North Carolina for the war.
[Source(s): Card File; NA RG 45]

Mullins, John [Jno.] (New Hanover County, North Carolina)
Seaman, Confederate States Navy. Mullins is said to have enlisted as a substitute at Camp Holmes [near Raleigh, North Carolina] on September 9, 1863 for the war, while another source says he enlisted on October 28, 1863 in the Confederate States Navy in Wilmington, North Carolina, for the war. Yet another source lists him as enlisting on September 22, 1863 in Wilmington, North Carolina.
[Source(s): MR, 4, p. 446; Card File; NA RG 45]

Mullins, John (North Carolina?)
Seaman, Confederate States Navy. Mullins served aboard the CSS ARCTIC, 1863 and 1864, and aboard the CSS NORTH CAROLINA, 1864.
[Source(s): Foenander]

Mullins, John
Seaman, Confederate States Navy. Mullins served aboard the CSS ALBEMARLE, and at the Halifax Station, North Carolina, 1864.
[Source(s): Foenander; ORN2, 1]

Mullins, John J.
    Seaman, Confederate States Navy. Mullins served aboard the CSS YADKIN at Wilmington, North Carolina, 1864.
    [Source(s): Foenander; ORN 2, 1]

Mullis, John C.
    Landsman, Confederate States Navy. Mullis enlisted on October 5, 1863 at Camp Holmes [near Raleigh, North Carolina].
    [Source(s): Card File; NA RG 45]

Mullis, John P. (Mecklenburg County, North Carolina)
    Confederate States Navy. A pension claim filed on July 4, 1901 by widow, Elizabeth Mullis, age 78, listing her post office as Charlotte, Mecklenburg County, North Carolina, states that her husband enlisted in Savannah, Georgia, in 1863. He went from there to Charleston, South Carolina, thence to Wilmington, North Carolina, and then to Raleigh, where, on account of sickness, he had to be taken home in February 1865. The pension was approved.
    [Source(s): Card File; Pensions (North Carolina); Foenander]

Mulroy, John (also Mulby and Mulbry)
    1st Class Fireman, Confederate States Navy.
    Per shipping articles, payroll, and muster records, Mulroy served as a 1st Class Fireman aboard the CSS EDWARDS from July 1861 through the 1st quarter of 1862. He is listed as a 1st Class Fireman aboard the CSS FORREST, no dates given. His name appears on the payroll of the receiving ship UNITED STATES ending March 31, 1862. He is said to have served on the CSS VIRGINIA.
    [Source: NCCWSP]

Munday [Mundy], Rufus Milton [R. M.] (Lincoln County, North Carolina)
    Landsman [Seaman], Confederate States Navy. Born in North Carolina in 1846, Munday (Mundy) enlisted on June 30, 1864 in Raleigh, North Carolina, for the war. His pension claim filed on July 1, 1912, age 66, listing his post office as Denver, Lincoln County, North Carolina, states "I belonged to the navy in Charleston, SC." The claim was disallowed due to owning too much property ($3,062.00). He served aboard the receiving ship [probably the CSS INDIAN CHIEF] at Charleston, SC. His name appears as a signature to an Oath of Allegiance to the United States, subscribed and sworn to at Point Lookout, Maryland, June 29, 1865. His place of residence on the Oath was listed as Lincoln County, North Carolina. Description: Complexion light; hair dark brown; eyes hazel; height 5 feet 9 ½ inches. Born May 17, 1846, Munday died on January 2, 1922 and was buried at Bethel Methodist Church, Lincoln County, North Carolina. Married in 1868, he applied for a Confederate pension from Lincoln County, North Carolina, where he resided as a farmer in 1910 with his wife Fannie and five children at Catawba Springs, Lincoln County, North Carolina. He was still residing as a widower in Catawba Springs in 1920.
    [Source(s): Card File; NA RG 45; NA RG 109; Pensions (North Carolina); Roster Document #0345; Stepp, "Burials;" Hoke Camp; Foenander]

Murdaugh, W. H.
    Lieutenant, Confederate States Navy. Murdaugh was attached to the CSS ELLIS and lost his left arm during the bombardment at Fort Hatteras, July 29, 1861.
    [Source(s): McElroy; Card File]

Murdock, A. L.
    Landsman, Confederate States Navy. Murdock enlisted on November 22, 1863 in Wilmington, North Carolina, for the war. Another source states he enlisted on November 20, 1863 in Raleigh, North Carolina.
    [Source(s): Card File; NA RG 45]

Murdock, A. S.
    Landsman, Confederate States Navy. Born in North Carolina, at enlistment Murdock was age 24 with blue eyes, light hair, and a fair complexion. He was sent back to the receiving vessel on March 7, 1864.
    [Source(s): CSS TENNESSEE]

Murdock, H. L. (North Carolina?)
    Landsman, Confederate States Navy. Murdock served aboard the CSS ARCTIC, Cape Fear River, North Carolina, 1863.
    [Source(s): Foenander]

Murke (Marke), Fred
> Landsman, Confederate States Navy.
> Murke served as a Landsman aboard the CSS FORREST as a member of the North Carolina Squadron at least as early as the 1st quarter of 1862. His name appears on the payroll of the receiving ship CSS UNITED STATES ending March 31, 1862.
> [Source: NCCWSP]

Murphey, James (Burke County, North Carolina)
> Private, Confederate States Army//Confederate States Navy. Murphey resided in Burke County, North Carolina, where he enlisted at age 30 on May 10, 1861 in Company E, 16th Regiment, North Carolina Troops. He was present or accounted for until he transferred to the Confederate States Navy on April 3, 1864.
> [Source(s): Card File; North Carolina Troops, VI; Foenander]

Murphey [Murphy], Peter Umstead (Orange County, North Carolina)
> Lieutenant, Confederate States Navy. Born on July 10, 1810, in Hillsborough, North Carolina, Murphey was appointed from North Carolina as a Midshipman in the United States Navy on May 12, 1834 (One source gives the date of his original entry into the United States Navy as May 12, 1831). He became a Passed Midshipman on July 8, 1839 and a Lieutenant on May 29, 1846. At the outbreak of the war, he was commanding the receiving ship USS PENNSYLVANIA. His name was stricken from the rolls of the United States Navy on April 21, 1861, upon his resignation. Murphey accepted a Confederate Navy commission as a First Lieutenant on June 10, 1861 ["June 11, 1861, per "Fold3, USN Resignees"]. One source gives his promotion to First Lieutenant as October 23, 1862, to rank from October 2, 1862. Source NCCWSP indicates he served as a Lieutenant Commanding, CSS JUNALUSKA. He was commanded the Confederate States Steamer CSS ARROW, Chesapeake Bay, April 1861; was on Confederate naval defenses in Virginia and North Carolina, 1861; and, at Gosport Navy Yard, 1861-1862. Assigned to the Mobile Squadron, he commanded the gunboat CSS MORGAN, 1862 and the gunboat CSS SELMA, 1862-1864 [Another source gives the dates as "1863-1864"], in Alabama waters. Murphey participated in the Battle of Mobile Bay on August 5, 1864 and was wounded severely in the wrist and made a prisoner of war when his ship was captured. He was confined at Fort Warren and exchanged at Cox Wharf, Virginia, October 18, 1864. He surrendered on May 4, 1865 and was paroled at Nanna Hubba Bluff, Alabama, on May 10, 1865. His sword and sash were surrendered to Lieutenant James E. Jouett of the Union Navy but, these were later returned, at the request of his daughter, Kate Piercy Murphey Chestney. Lieutenant Murphey died on August 13, 1876 of apoplexy (causing him to drown in the bath) in Mobile, Alabama.
> [Source(s): Register; McElroy; Card File; Wikipedia; Journal; PCNMC; NCCWSP; Foenander; CWDTS; ONWR; Fold3, USN Resignees]

Murphy, James
> Confederate States Navy. Murphy enlisted from North Carolina in 1861. He served aboard the CSS CHICORA but deserted to the Federal Fleet in the early part of 1862.
> [Source(s): Unknown]

Murphy, James W. (McDowell County, North Carolina)
> Corporal, Confederate States Army//Confederate States Navy. Murphy resided in McDowell County, North Carolina, where he enlisted at age 30 on May 8, 1861 as a Private in Company B, 22nd Regiment, North Carolina Troops. Mustered in as a Corporal, he was wounded in the right lung and captured near Richmond, Virginia, in the summer of 1862. He was hospitalized in Portsmouth Grove, Rhode Island, July 7, 1862, and transferred to Fort Monroe, Virginia, on September 18, 1862, and paroled there on September 22, 1862. He was transferred to Aiken's Landing, James River, Virginia, where he was received on September 23, 1862 for exchange. He was declared exchanged on November 10, 1862. Listed as reduced to the ranks on an unspecified date, he transferred to the Navy Department at Marion, South Carolina, in March 1863.
> [Sources(s): North Carolina Troops, VII; Foenander]

Murphy, John (North Carolina?)
> Seaman, Confederate States Navy. Murphy served aboard the CSS ARCTIC, Cape Fear River, North Carolina, 1863.
> [Source(s): Foenander

Murphy, John (North Carolina?)
> 1st Class Fireman, Confederate States Navy. Murphy served aboard the CSS RALEIGH, in North Carolina and Virginia waters, 1862 – 1864.
> [Source(s): Foenander]

Murphy, Phillip (also Patrick)
>2nd Class Fireman, Confederate States Navy.
>Murphy served as a 2nd Class Fireman from at least January 15, 1862 - February 28, 1862 (no ship listed). He received a partial payment on February 13, 1862 at Gosport Navy Yard.
>[Source: NCCWSP]

Murphy, Thomas J.
>Landsman, Confederate States Navy. Murphy enlisted on March 1, 1864 in Raleigh, North Carolina, for the war, and served as a Landsman, CSS YADKIN, Wilmington, North Carolina, 1864.
>[Source(s): Card File; NA RG 45; Foenander]

Murphy, William Bailey (Duplin County or New Hanover, North Carolina)
>Signal officer, Confederate States Navy. Per source "North Carolina Troops, I," Murphy resided in Duplin County, North Carolina, and enlisted in Brunswick County, North Carolina, at age 18 on May 11, 1863, in Company A, 36th Regiment, North Carolina Troops (2nd North Carolina Artillery). Another source states he enlisted from New Hanover County, North Carolina, in Wilmington, North Carolina. He was detailed to the Signal Corps through August 1864 and served as a Signal Officer aboard the blockade runners "*Beauregard*" at Wilmington, and on the "*Will of the Wisp*," "*Heroine*," and the "*Mariana*." He was admitted to the hospital in Wilmington, North Carolina, on February 10, 1865 with fever.
>[Source(s): McElroy; Card File; UDC, Singletary; North Carolina Troops, I]

Murphy, W. T. (Sampson County, North Carolina)
>Lieutenant, Confederate States Navy. Murphy was commissioned from Sampson County, North Carolina in 1861.
>[Source(s): MR, 4, p. 404 and 449]

Murray, Alexander
>Seaman, Confederate States Navy. Murray enlisted on December 15, 1862 in Wilmington, North Carolina, for three years or the war.
>[Source(s): Card File; NA RG 45]

Murray, George M. (Pender County, North Carolina)
>Confederate States Navy. Murray enlisted in 1861. A pension claim filed on July 6, 1903 by his widow, A. M. Murray, age 63, listing her post office as Ashton, Pender County, North Carolina, was approved at 4th Class.
>[Source(s): Card File; NA RG 45; Pensions (North Carolina); Foenander]

Murray, James T. (Pender County, North Carolina)
>Confederate States Navy. A pension claim filed on June 14, 1907 by his widow, Hanah [sic] Murray, age 80, listing her post office as "Wasta" [Watha], Pender County, was approved at 4th Class. She states he enlisted in the Navy on May 10, 1862.
>[Source(s): Card File; Pensions (North Carolina); Foenander]

Murray, John
>Seaman, Confederate States Navy. Murray enlisted March 25, 1864 in Wilmington, North Carolina, for the war.
>[Source(s): Card File; NA RG 45]

Murray, Peter
>Landsman, Confederate States Navy. Murray enlisted on December 5, 1863, in Wilmington, North Carolina, for the war, and served as a Landsman aboard the CSS ARCTIC, Cape Fear River, North Carolina, 1863. He later served aboard the CSS RALEIGH in North Carolina and Virginia waters, 1864.
>[Source(s): Card File; NA RG 45; *ORN* 2, 1, 277, 278 & 302; Foenander]

Murray, Spencer (Chatham County, North Carolina)
>Private, Confederate States Army//Confederate States Navy. Born in Chatham County, North Carolina, in 1839, Murray resided there as a laborer prior to enlisting at age 23 on February 25, 1862 in Company G, 48th Regiment, North Carolina Troops. He was reported as present in September-October 1862, and January-June 1863. He transferred to the Confederate States Navy on or about April 1, 1864.
>[Source(s): Card File; North Carolina Troops, XI; Lane Society; Foenander]

Murrell, Isaac (Currituck County, North Carolina)
    Musician, Confederate States Army// Confederate States Navy(?). Born in Currituck County, North Carolina, Murrell resided as a sailor prior to enlisting there at age 19 on August 2, 1861, for the war, in Company B, 8th Regiment, North Carolina State Troops. Mustered in as a Musician (fifer), he was captured at Roanoke Island on February 8, 1862, paroled at Elizabeth City on February 21, 1862, and exchanged in August 1862. He was present or accounted for until captured at Cold Harbor, Virginia, May 31, 1864-June 1, 1864. Confined at Point Lookout, Maryland, he was later transferred to Elmira, New York, on July 12, 1864. Paroled at Elmira, February 9-13, 1865, he was transferred to James River, Virginia, for exchange. Murrell was reported in the hospital at Richmond, Virginia, on February 28, 1865. Source Card File indicates Confederate States Naval service.
    [Source(s): Card File; North Carolina Troops, IV]

Murtle, George (born in Virginia//Pasquotank County, North Carolina)
    Pilot, Confederate States Navy. Born in Virginia in 1816, Murtle resided as a mariner, in 1860, with his wife, Charlotte, and three children, in Elizabeth City, North Carolina. He served as a Pilot aboard the CSS FANNY, 1861 – December 12, 1862.
    [Source(s): Foenander; ORN 2, 1, 285; NCCWSP]

Muse, James B.
    Landsman and Ordinary Seaman, Confederate States Navy. Born in Craven County, North Carolina, Muse resided as a mechanic prior to enlisting in the Confederate States Navy on March 18, 1864, at age 36, at Bowlar [?] County, North Carolina [Another source says he enlisted on March 21, 1864, in Raleigh, North Carolina, for the war]. He served as an Ordinary Seaman aboard the CSS ARCTIC, 1863, and aboard the CSS RALEIGH, 1864.
    [Source(s): Card File; NA RG 45; Foenander; *ORN* 2, 1, 278 & 302]

Muse, John Blount (Virginia//Chowan County, North Carolina)
    Ordinary Seaman, Confederate States Navy. Born in Virginia circa 1842 [Source "Stepp" – 1842], the son of Commodore William T. Muse, and brother of William T. Muse, Muse resided in Fairfax County, Virginia, in 1860. His enlistment date and place are unknown. He served aboard the CSS ARCTIC and CSS RALEIGH, Wilmington Squadron, June 1862-November 1864. Other sources state he died on June 30, 1861["Foenander" and "Stepp"] ["Driver" states he died 1865], aged 19, at Warrenton, North Carolina. Muse was buried in Old Warrenton Cemetery [Source "Stepp" – Fairview Cemetery, Warren County, North Carolina].
    [Source(s): Foenander; Ellis; <u>ORN</u>, 2, 1, p. 278 and 302; Stepp, "Burials"]

Muse, William Templeman, Jr. (Nash County, North Carolina)
    Powder Monkey, Ordinary Seaman, Third Steward, Confederate States Navy. Muse was born in 1849 [Foenander gives date as 1851], the son of Commodore William T. Muse, and brother of John Blount Muse. He resided in Fairfax County, Virginia, in 1860, and enlisted on July 9, 1861, as a "Powder Monkey." Muse served aboard the CSS ELLIS in North Carolina waters, April 1861; aboard the CSS FORT CASWELL, July 1861-June 1862, and the CSS NORTH CAROLINA, January –March 1864. He served as Third Steward on the blockade runner "*Advance*," and was captured on September 19, 1864 and sent to New York as a Prisoner of War. His pension claim filed on February 13, 1907, age 56, listing his post office as Rocky Mount, Nash County, North Carolina was approved at 4th Class. A handwritten card states he "was at the bombardment of Hatteras August 29, 1861, on board the Confederate States steamer "*Gov. Ellis*;" after the capture of Hatteras was transferred to Wilmington with my father Commodore W. T. Muse as Powder Boy Confederate States Navy joined Capt. J. F. [sic] Maffitt, Confederate States Navy, on the Confederate States steamer CSS OWL and remained in service until war closed." In a second claim, filed December 3, 1907 at age 57 and approved, he states he received no wounds while in service.
    [Source(s): Card File; Pensions (North Carolina); Driver; ONWR]

Muse, William Templeton, Sr. (Chowan County, North Carolina)
    Commander [Captain], Confederate States Navy. Born on April 1, 1811 in and appointed from North Carolina, Muse served in the United States Navy beginning on June 1, 1828 as a Midshipman. He was elevated to Passed Midshipman on June 14, 1834, to Lieutenant on December 29, 1840, and to Commander on September 14, 1855. He resided as a naval officer, in 1850, with his wife, Priscilla, and son John Blount Muse, in Fairfax County, Virginia (Muse resided in Fairfax County, Virginia, 1850-1860; owned property at Alexandria, which was occupied by Union forces). His name was stricken from the rolls of the United States Navy on April 2, 1861. Formerly a Commander ["Driver" states "Lieutenant Commander"], United States Navy, until his resignation, he is listed by source "DH Hill" as one of the first officers commissioned as a Lieutenant in the North Carolina Navy [shown as "W. S. Muse"]. Muse enlisted in the Confederate States Navy on July 9, 1861 ["Driver" and "Foenander" state he was appointed

a Commander, Confederate States Navy, from North Carolina, June 24, 1861]. He was ordered by the Naval and Military Board to Norfolk, Virginia to take charge of and fit out the CSS ELLIS as a gunboat at the Navy Yard. Appointed Commander, Confederate States Navy, October 23, 1862, to rank from March 26, 1861 as a member of the North Carolina Squadron (One source says he was appointed "Commander, June 24, 1861" while another source states he was appointed Commander, Provisional Navy, May 13, 1863). His name appears on a register of Confederate States Army General Military Hospital Number 4, Wilmington, North Carolina, dated August 5, 1862, which gives disease as "icterus" and states that he was returned to duty on August 5, 1862, and giving his post office as Wilmington, North Carolina. Muse was appointed to the rank of Commander, Provisional Confederate States Navy, on May 13, 1863. He commanded the CSS ELLIS which sailed from Norfolk, Virginia, August 2, 1861 and arrived off Ocracoke on August 4, 1861. He commanded the CSS ELLIS (August 1861), CSS FORT CASWELL, CSS ARCTIC, and CSS NORTH CAROLINA (which he superintended) as Commander of the Wilmington Station, 1861-1864. Muse died in service in Wilmington, North Carolina, on April 8, 1864 of typhoid fever. He was buried in Fairfax Cemetery [Virginia?] ["Foenander" states he died on Friday, April 8, 1864, and that his remains were escorted to the depot of the Wilmington & Weldon Railroad, Saturday, April 9, 1864, with naval and military honors, to be sent to Warren County for interment]. His name appears on the Confederate Veterans Monument, Fairfax Courthouse, Virginia. He was the father of William T. Muse, Jr., and John Blount Muse. His widow, Priscilla, resided in Rocky Mount, Nash County, North Carolina, in 1880.
[Source(s): MR, 4, p. 404 and 449; Register; McElroy; Officers, January 1, 1864; Card File; NA RG 109; Card File; Driver; Journal; DH Hill; CWDTS; ONWR; Fold3, USN Resignees; NCCWSP]

Musgrove, Calvin
Landsman, Confederate States Navy. Musgrove enlisted on February 6, 1864, in Raleigh, North Carolina, for the war, and served aboard the CSS NORTH CAROLINA, Cape Fear River, North Carolina 1864
[Source(s): Card File; NA RG 45; Foenander]

Myers, Joseph H. (Washington [per MR, I] or Hertford County, North Carolina)
Private, Confederate States Army//Landsman, Confederate States Navy. Myers resided in Washington County, North Carolina, where he was born on December 21, 1844. He enlisted at age 19 on June 24, 1861 (July 24, 1861 per MR, I), for the war, in Company G, 1st Regiment, North Carolina State Troops. He was present or accounted for until discharged on February 20, 1862 upon transfer to the Confederate States Navy. He served as a Landsman on the CSS VIRGINIA, Hampton Roads, Virginia. He died on March 14, 1935 and was buried at Christian Harbor Baptist Church.
[Source(s): Card File; Stepp, "Burials;" North Carolina Troops, III; Foenander; MR, I]

Myrick, Frankling
Landsman, Confederate States Navy. Myrick enlisted on May 20, 1864, in Raleigh, for the war.
[Source(s): Card File; NA RG 45]

Nading, John H. (Forsyth County, North Carolina)
1st Sergeant, Confederate States Army//Confederate States Navy. Born in North Carolina, about 1843, the son of Alexander and Sarah Nading, Nading resided in Forsyth County, North Carolina, as a painter prior to his enlistment at age 21 on May 1, 1862, for the war, as a Private in Company K, 48th Regiment, North Carolina Troops. Reported present in September-October 1862, he was promoted to Sergeant in November 1862-February 1863, and to 1st Sergeant in March-April 1863. Reported as present in January-June 1863, he transferred to the Confederate States Navy on April 15, 1864 [source "North Carolina Troops" states he "May have been wounded slightly at or near Sharpsburg, Maryland, on or about September 17, 1862]. Nading resided as a painter, in 1870, at a hotel in Jackson Township, Clinton County, Indiana. He later returned to North Carolina, and is shown as a painter, residing with his parents in Forsyth County, in 1880.
[Source(s): Card File; North Carolina Troops, XI; Foenander]

Nash, Robert
3rd Assistant Engineer, North Carolina Navy.
Served aboard the NCS WINSLOW.
[Source: NCS]

Nash, Robert S. (Stanly County, North Carolina)
    Private, Confederate States Navy (Company F, Naval Battalion). Nash enlisted on July 21, 1864 in Raleigh, North Carolina, for the war. His name appears on a roll of Prisoners of War at Point Lookout, Maryland, which states he was captured at Amelia Court House, Virginia, April 6, 1865, and confined at Point Lookout, Maryland, until released June 15, 1865. His name appears as a signature to an Oath of Allegiance to the United States, subscribed and sworn to at Point Lookout, Maryland, on June 15, 1865. His place of residence was given on the oath as Stanly County, North Carolina. Description: complexion light; hair gray; eyes hazel; height 5 feet 11 inches.
    [Source(s): Card File; NA RG 45; NA RG 109]

Nawl, D.
    Landsman, Confederate States Navy. Nawl enlisted on June 11, 1864 in Raleigh, North Carolina, for the war.
    [Source(s): Card File; NA RG 45]

Neaham [Needham], George
    Seaman; 1st Class Fireman, Confederate States Navy. Neaham enlisted on November 27, 1863 in Wilmington, North Carolina for the war. Source "Foenander" lists a "George Neaham (surname also shown as Needham), as a Seaman, CSS ARCTIC, Cape Fear River, North Carolina, 1863. He served, later, as a 1st Class Fireman, aboard the CSS YADKIN, Wilmington, North Carolina, 1864. [.]
    [Source(s): Card File; NA RG 45; ORN 2, 1, 277 & 313; Foenander]

Nefant (Neafant), Louis
    Seaman, Carpenter's Mate, Confederate States Navy.
    Nefant served aboard the prizeship *Transit* and joined the crew of the NCS WINSLOW as a member of the North Carolina Squadron at New Bern in 1861. Per payroll, clothing, bounty, and small stores records, he served as a Seaman aboard the CSS BEAUFORT from September – January 16, 1862. He appears on the North Carolina Squadron payroll for the 1st quarter of 1862 (December 1, 1861 - April 15, 1862). Nefant transferred to the James River Squadron on April 15, 1862. He served as a Carpenter's Mate on the CSS BEAUFORT as a member of the James River Squadron per its payroll of October 1, 1863 - December 15, 1863.
    [Source: NCCWSP]

Nelson (Nielson, Neilson), John
    Coal Heaver, Seaman, Confederate States Navy.
    Nelson signed shipping articles on July 25, 1861 and served as a member of the North Carolina Squadron as a Coal Heaver aboard the NCS EDWARDS through that ship's muster roll dated October 30, 1861. He appears as a Coal Heaver on the payroll list of the CSN FORREST for the 1st quarter of 1862. Nelson served on CSS VIRGINIA. He was on duty at Drewry's Bluff as a Seaman from April 1, 1863 - June 30, 1863.
    [Source: NCCWSP]

Nelson, Peter
    Landsman, Confederate States Navy. Nelson enlisted on May 21, 1863, in Wilmington, North Carolina, for the war., and served as a Landsman, CSS NORTH CAROLINA, and later aboard the CSS TALLAHASSEE, 1864.
    [Source(s): Card File; NA RG 45; Foenander; *ORN* 2, 1, 294-296 and 307]

Nelson, William N.
    Coxswain, Seaman, Landsman, Confederate States Navy.
    Nelson served as a Coxswain aboard the CSS FANNY per the ship's muster roll dated October 8, 1861. He was listed as a Seaman on the ship per its muster roll dated December 12, 1861. A payroll dated December 13, 1861 shows him as a Landsman. His name appears on a payroll for the receiving ship CSS UNITED STATES ending March 31, 1862. His name appears on the payroll of the North Carolina Squadron for the 1st quarter of 1862 (December 1, 1861 - February 28, 1862). Nelson's name is annotated on this payroll as having "run" on or by February 28, 1862.
    [Source: NCCWSP]

Newbury, A. J. (County unknown)
    Private, Confederate States Marine Corps. Newberry enlisted in Raleigh, North Carolina on October 6, 1864. He served on the Charleston, South Carolina Station as a Private of the Marine guard on board the ironclad CSS COLUMBIA to February 7, 1865.
    [Source(s): North Carolina Troops, Doc.# 0299; Card File]

Newkirk, T.
Landsman, Confederate States Navy. Newkirk was assigned in October 1864 as a Landsman from Raleigh, North Carolina, to Battery Brooke, James River, Virginia, October 1864.
[Source(s): PCNMC; *ORN* 1, 10, 805; Foenander]

Newton, Christopher Columbus
Private, Confederate States Army//Confederate States Navy(?). Newton served in Captain William S. Devane's Independent Company, North Carolina Troops, before transferring to Company A, 61st Regiment, North Carolina Troops, on September 5, 1862, as a Private. Reported as present or accounted for through June 30, 1864, he was wounded in the arm and shoulder on August 25, 1863, at Morris Island, Charleston Harbor, South Carolina. He was hospitalized in Wilmington, North Carolina, and furloughed for thirty days on September 18, 1863. He returned to duty in November-December 1863. Present or accounted for April 30, 1864, he was promoted to Corporal on April 13, 1864 and again wounded, in the hand, at or near Petersburg, Virginia, on or about June 16-19, 1864. He was reported in the hospital at High Point, North Carolina, on August 17, 1864, furloughed on August 18, 1864, and present for duty September-November 1964. Newton survived the war. Source Card File indicates Confederate Naval service and possible prior service in 20th Regiment, North Carolina Troops (10th Regiment, North Carolina Volunteers.
[Source(s): Card File; North Carolina Troops, XIV]

Newton, J. H. (Brunswick County, North Carolina)
Confederate States Navy. A pension claim filed on July 4, 1910 by his widow, Mrs. J. H. Newton, age 71, listing her post office as Southport, Brunswick County, North Carolina, was approved at 4th Class. She states he enlisted on or about September 1, 1862.
[Source(s): Card File; Pensions (North Carolina); MR, 4, p. 446; Foenander]

Newton, James (New Hanover County, North Carolina) [NOTE: May be same as James M. [N.] Newton, q.v.]
Confederate States Navy. Newton enlisted in the Confederate States Navy in Wilmington, North Carolina.
[Source(s): MR, 4, p. 446]

Newton, James M [N.]. (New Hanover County, North Carolina) [NOTE: May be same as James Newton, q.v.]
Seaman, Quarter Gunner, Confederate States Navy (Company A, Naval Brigade). Newton served aboard the side-wheeled steam tug CSS CASWELL, Wilmington, North Carolina, 1862, and as a Seaman and Quarter Gunner aboard the CSS ARCTIC, Wilmington, North Carolina, 1862. His name appears on a Roll of Prisoners of War at Point Lookout, Maryland, released May 15, 1865, on taking the Oath of Allegiance to the United States. The roll states he was captured on January 15, 1865, at Fort Fisher and gives his residence as Wilmington, North Carolina, and occupation as Seaman. He died on February 12, 1917 and was buried in Bellevue Cemetery, Wilmington, North Carolina.
[Source(s): Card File; NA RG 109; Foenander; Gravestone Records, v. 8, p. 60]

Newton, James (New Hanover County, North Carolina)
Confederate States Navy. Newton enlisted in the Confederate States Navy in Wilmington, North Carolina.
[Source(s): MR, 4, p. 446]

Newton, S. T. (Pender County, North Carolina)
Confederate States Navy. A pension claim filed on July 7, 1902 by his widow, Martha A. Newton, age 67, listing her post office as South Washington, Pender County, North Carolina, was approved at 4th Class. She states he enlisted on or about July 1862.
[Source(s): Card File; Pensions (North Carolina); Foenander]

Newton, T. W.
Pilot, Confederate States Navy. Newton served aboard the blockade runner "*Eugenia.*"
[Source(s): McElroy; Card File]

Newton, Virginius
Midshipman, Confederate States Navy. Born in Virginia [another source states he was born in North Carolina] in October 1844 Newton was appointed from civilian life from North Carolina as an Acting Midshipman in the Confederate States Navy on September 30, 1861, serving with the North Carolina Squadron. He was appointed a Midshipman, Provisional Navy on June 2, 1864. He served on the Confederate States receiving ship CSS UNITED STATES, 1861; Gosport Navy Yard, [Norfolk] 1861; CSS BEAUFORT (by March 1862 as an Acting Midshipman);

and, participated in the battles of Elizabeth City, North Carolina, February 8 [10], 1862 and Hampton Roads, Virginia, March 8-9, 1862. Newton transferred to the James River Squadron on April 15, 1862, but apparently was soon sent west since he was commended by the commanding officer, CSS GAINES, Mobile Squadron, 1862-1863. Newton was engaged in service abroad, 1863-1865, and served aboard the CSS RAPPAHANNOCK, Calais, France, 1864. He was ordered to the CSS STONEWALL, 1864, and reported at Havana, Cuba, 1865. According to a letter written by Newton on March 31, 1899, he was temporarily assigned to the blockade runner "*Richmond*"" (no date or duration specified). He resided as a lawyer, in 1870, at the home of his parents, in Norfolk, Virginia, and as a banker, in 1900, at Richmond, Virginia. He is shown, in 1900, as a widower.
[Source(s): McElroy; Register; Card File; Foenander; ONWR; Fold3, Midshipmen; NCCWSP]

Newton, William Seavey (New Hanover County, North Carolina)
Private, Company C, Confederate States Marine Corps. Newton is said to have enlisted on March 1, 1864 but was not on company roll as of December 31, 1864. He is thought to have been a North Carolina conscript. Newton's name appears on a roll of prisoners of war at Point Lookout, Maryland, which states he was captured at Farmville, Virginia, on April 6, 1865, and was confined at Point Lookout until released on June 29, 1865. His name also appears as a signature to an Oath of Allegiance to the United States subscribed and sworn to at Point Lookout on June 29, 1865. His place of residence was given on the Oath as New Hanover County, North Carolina. Description as follows: Complexion fair; hair brown; eyes hazel; height 5 feet 5 inches. His claim for pension filed on May 22, 1909 at age 63 years, listing his post office as Willard, Sampson County, North Carolina, was approved at 4th class.
[Source(s): NA; North Carolina Troops, Doc. # 0185, p. 2, and 0299; Card File; Pension (North Carolina); Donnelly-ENL].

Nicholson, D. S.
Landsman, Confederate States Navy. Nicholson enlisted on June 11, 1864 in Raleigh, North Carolina, for the war.
[Source(s): Card File; NA RG 45]

Nicholson, John (Moore County, North Carolina)
Private, Confederate States Navy (Naval Battalion). Nicholson's name appears as a signature to an Oath of Allegiance to the United States, subscribed and sworn to at Newport News, Virginia, June 26, 1865. His place of residence is given on the Oath as Moore County, North Carolina. Description as follows: Complexion fair; hair dark; eyes blue; height 5 feet 11 inches. Oath carries the remark: "Captured Farmville, Virginia April 6, 1865."
[Source(s): Card File; NA RG 109]

Nixon, P. H. (New Hanover County, North Carolina)
Ordinary Seaman, Seaman, Confederate States Navy. Nixon enlisted in the Confederate States Navy on September 21, 1863 in Wilmington, North Carolina, for the war. Source "Foenander" states he served as a Seaman aboard the CSS ARCTIC, 1863. He served aboard the CSS NEUSE as of the ship's March – October 1864 muster rolls.
[Source(s): MR, 4, p. 446; Card File; NA RG 45; *ORN* 2, 1, 276; Foenander; St. Armand; NEUSE Roster; CMACSSN]

Nixon, Thomas W. (Beaufort County, North Carolina)
Seaman and Gunner's Mate, Confederate States Navy. Nixon was born in Beaufort County, North Carolina, where he resided as a sailor until he enlisted on November 7, 1861 [October 21, 1861, per "MR, III"], age 35, as a Private in Company C, 40th Regiment, North Carolina Troops (3rd Regiment, North Carolina Artillery). He was listed as present or accounted for until he transferred to the Confederate States Navy on May 8, 1862 [May 5, 1862, per "MR, III"]. Nixon served as a Seaman and Gunner's Mate, CSS ARCTIC, August 1862. He transferred from gunboat CSS ALBEMARLE to Company I, 24th Regiment, North Carolina Troops, by Special Order # 177/27, A & IGO, dated July 28, 1864.
[Source(s): Card File; NA RG 45; NA RG 109; North Carolina Troops, I; Foenander; "Beaufort County Sailors;" MR, III; *ORN* 1, 23, 703]

Noah [Noahe], Amos D. [E.] (Guilford County, North Carolina)
Landsman, Confederate States Navy. Noah was born in North Carolina about 1824 and resided as a farmer in Alamance County, North Carolina, with his wife and three children. He enlisted on March 7 [3], 1864, in Raleigh, North Carolina, for the war. His name appears on a list of conscripts "on Egypt Mills" June 9, 1864. He was conscripted from Colonel Lee's 48th Regiment, North Carolina Militia, Alamance County, North Carolina, March 3, 1864, at Camp Holmes. Description: Age 40 [39]; eyes hazel; hair dark; complexion dark; height 5 feet 8 ½ inches; place of birth Guilford County, North Carolina; occupation farmer. Noah served aboard the CSS ALBEMARLE, and on the Halifax Station, 1864. He resided as a farmer, in 1880, with his wife, Barbara, and children, at Patterson,

Alamance County, North Carolina.
[Source(s): Foenander; Census (NC), 1860 and 1880; ORN 2, 1; Card File; NA RG 45; NA RG 109; Census (North Carolina), 1860 and 1880]

Noble, J. S.
Landsman, Confederate States Navy. Noble served aboard the CSS ARCTIC, Cape Fear River, North Carolina, 1863.
[Sources): Foenander; ORN 2, 1]

Nobles, John A. (Pasquotank County, North Carolina)
Sergeant, Confederate States Army//Confederate States Navy. Nobles resided in and enlisted from Pasquotank County, North Carolina, on July 23, 1861, at age 23, as a Private in Company A, 8th Regiment, North Carolina State Troops. He was captured at Roanoke Island on February 8, 1862, was paroled at Elizabeth City, North Carolina, on February 21, 1862, and exchanged in August 1862. He was promoted to Corporal on March 21, 1863, and to Sergeant on December 22, 1863. He transferred to the Confederate States Navy on April 5, 1864 and served as a Seaman aboard the CSS ALBEMARLE and at Halifax Station, in mid-1864.
[Source(s): North Carolina Troops, IV; Card File; NA RG 45; ORN 2, 1; Foenander]

Noles, J. S.
Landsman, Confederate States Navy. Noles enlisted on August 8, 1864, in Raleigh, North Carolina, for the war, and served aboard the CSS ARCTIC, Cape Fear River, North Carolina, 1863.
[Source(s): Card File; NA RG 45; Foenander]

Norman, Henry Howell (Washington County, North Carolina)
Landsman, Confederate States Navy. Born in Tyrrell County, North Carolina, in October 1834, Norman lived northwest of Creswell, Washington County, North Carolina. He was conscripted into the Confederate States Navy, 1864. He was assigned to the CSS ARCTIC, a floating battery on the Cape Fear River ["Foenander" states that "H. H. Norman" served as a Landsman, CSS ARCTIC, Cape Fear River, North Carolina, 1863]. Norman was said to have been "detailed" to the Beery Shipyard for a time. In early 1865 with the fall of Fort Fisher and the evacuation of Wilmington, he was transferred to Drewry's Bluff, Virginia. He died in the hospital in Richmond on April 1, 1865 and is buried in that city's Hollywood Cemetery. Other references state he died of disease at the hospital in Wilmington, North Carolina, December 20, 1864. A pension claim was filed by his widow, Elizabeth Norman, age 50, who listed her residence as Creswell, Washington County, North Carolina, 1886. She filed a second claim in November 1887 indicating that he died January 1865 in Wilmington, North Carolina in the hospital and that he enlisted on September 1, 1864 in the Navy. One source lists his wife as Elizabeth Julia Ann McCoke.
[Source(s): WCL; *ORN*, II, Vol. I; *Civil War Readers, 1995-2000: A Civil War Reader II, Letters, Reminiscences, and Rosters*, "Newsletter of the Washington Company General Soc.," 1996, Plymouth, North Carolina, p.18 and 22; his name is on a roster of CSS ARCTIC; Mr. Philip Madre, Chocowinity, North Carolina; Card File; Pensions (North Carolina); Darden; Foenander].

Norman, J. S.
Seaman, Ordinary Seaman, Confederate States Navy.
Norman served as a Seaman aboard the CSS SEA BIRD'S muster roll for July - November 1861. By February 1862, he is listed as an Ordinary Seaman aboard the CSS SEA BIRD. He received a partial payment on February 18, 1862 at Gosport Navy Yard following the sinking of the CSS SEA BIRD at Elizabeth City on February 10, 1862. He appears on the North Carolina Squadron payroll for the 1st quarter of 1862 (December 1, 1861 - March 31, 1862). He is listed as having "run" on a March 13, 1862.
[Source: NCCWSP]

Norton, Darling (D. N.) (Richmond County, North Carolina)
Landsman, Confederate States Navy. Born in North Carolina in 1844, the son of Eli and Rachel Norton, Norton resided as a farm hand, in 1860, with his parents, in Richmond, County, North Carolina. He enlisted on September 28, 1863, at Camp Holmes, for the war (his North Carolina pension applications also show dates for entry into service of "April 1, 1863" and "1864"). He served as a Landsman aboard the ironclad floating battery CSS GEORGIA and CSS SAVANNAH, at Savannah, Georgia, about 1863 - 1864. Norton applied for a Confederate pension from Scotland County, North Carolina. In 1910, his occupation was shown as that of a sweeper at a cotton mill in Stewartsville Precinct, Scotland County, North Carolina. He was still living in Scotland County in 1930. His pension claim filed in Scotland Company, (was Richmond County until 1899 creation of Scotland County), North Carolina, on August 5, 1901, age 55, post office Laurinburg, states he enlisted in "Scotland County," was

never wounded, was in service at the end of the war and had been for two years, and states "I was not a deserter." A doctor's examination rated him as half disabled due to old age, but the pension is disallowed. A claim filed on July 14, 1902, age 59 years, was disapproved due to "insufficient disability." A claim filed on July 20, 1903, age 62 [ages do not align on the four applications], states he "enlisted" in 1864 in Savannah, Georgia, and served in the Navy there. The pension was disapproved. In his July 3, 1905 application he states that he "Was conscripted & assigned to Navy…was sent from Wilmington to Navy at Savannah, Georgia, Captain Gorthamy Floating Battery. Thence with James River fleet. Was in no command after Richmond was evacuated"). This claim was approved at 4th Class. Source "Norton" states Darling Norton served aboard the CSS GEORGIA and CSS SAVANNAH while stationed in Savannah; that his wife Rebecca Beasley Norton preceded him in death; and that he was born in 1843 and died in 1932, and is buried behind Laurel Hill Baptist Church, Laurel Hill, North Carolina.
[Source(s): Card File; NA RG 45; Pensions (North Carolina); Norton; Foenander]

Norton, Godfrey
Confederate States Navy. Born in North Carolina in 1832, the son of Reuben and Elizabeth Norton, Norton resided as a laborer, in 1850, at Laurel Hill, Richmond County, North Carolina. By 1860, he was listed as a "waggoner," living with his wife Mary in Williamson, Richmond County, North Carolina. He served as a Landsman, CSS ARCTIC, Cape Fear River, North Carolina, 1863.
[Source(s): Foenander; ORN 2, 1, 279]

Norton, Joshua
Landsman (Private), Confederate States Navy. Norton enlisted on January 2, 1864, in Raleigh, North Carolina, for the war. His name appears on a register of Confederate States Army General Military Hospital Number 4, Wilmington, North Carolina, as being admitted on January 10, 1864 with "pleurodynia" and returned to duty January 21, 1864. His post office was given on the register as Florisville [?], North Carolina.
[Source(s): Card File; NA RG 45; NA RG 109]

Norville [Norvel, Nowell] William A. (Rutherford County, North Carolina)
Private, Confederate States Army/Confederate States Navy. Norville enlisted in Wake County, North Carolina, on October 10, 1862, for the war, as a Private in Company I, 50th Regiment, North Carolina Troops. He was reported as present in September-December 1862 but deserted on an unspecified date. He returned to duty on February 13, 1864. His Widow's application for pension by "Maryan" Norville, age 69, on July 5, 1909, listing her post office as Bostic, states her husband enlisted in Company I, 50th Regiment, North Carolina Troops, and "was transferred to a Confederate gunboat." Says husband was wounded on December 5, 1864 at Fort Fisher and died on December 12, 1864. The application was approved at 4th class. A muster roll for the CSS ARCTIC shows that a "W.E. Norvell" served aboard that vessel as a Landsman, 1863, and aboard the CSS RALEIGH, North Carolina.
[Source(s): Pensions (North Carolina); North Carolina Troops, XII; Foenander]

Norwood, Solomon L. [NOTE: May be same as "S. S. Norwood," 42nd North Carolina Militia]
Landsman, Confederate States Navy. Norwood enlisted on March 30, 1864, in Raleigh, North Carolina, for the war.
[Source(s): Card File; NA RG 45]

Norwood, S. S. (Granville County, North Carolina)
Confederate States Navy. Norwood was conscripted on March 29, 1864, at Camp Holmes, from Colonel Amos' 42nd North Carolina Militia, Granville County, North Carolina. Description: Age 27; eyes grey; hair light; complexion fair; height 5 feet 8 inches; place of birth Granville County, North Carolina; occupation merchant.
[Source(s): Card File; NA RG 45]

Oakley, Bedford S. (Bertie County, North Carolina)
Landsman (Private), Confederate States Navy (Naval Battalion). Oakley enlisted on August 29, 1864, in Raleigh, North Carolina, for the war. His name appears on a Roll of Prisoners of War at Point Lookout, Maryland, which states he was captured on April 7, 1865 at Danville and released on June 29, 1865. His name also appears as a signature to an Oath of Allegiance to the United States, subscribed and sworn to at Point Lookout, Maryland on June 29, 1865. His place of birth was given as Bertie County, North Carolina. Description: Complexion light; hair light brown; eyes light hazel; height 5 feet 7 ½ inches. The name of "B. S. Oakley" also appears on a receipt roll for clothing issued August 30, 1864 giving rank as "conscript." "??mthers as W. Huske, LT. [?]."
[Source(s): Card File; NA RG 109; NA RG 45]

O'Brian, John
Ordinary Seaman, Confederate States Navy. O'Brian enlisted in the Confederate States Navy in Wilmington, North Carolina. He served aboard the CSS ARCTIC. He may be the same as the "John O'Brien who served as an Ordinary Seaman and Officers' Cook aboard the CSS NORTH CAROLINA, 1864.
[Source(s): MR, 4, p. 446; Foenander]

O'Brien, Edward (Ireland//New Hanover County, North Carolina)
Sergeant, Confederate States Army//Confederate States Navy. Source Card File states O'Brien, a native of Ireland, had Confederate Naval service and that he had prior Army service as a 1st Sergeant in Company F, 8th Regiment, North Carolina State Troops. Source "North Carolina Troops, IV" states he resided in New Hanover County, North Carolina as a sailor, where he enlisted in the 8th Regiment at age 33 on August 7, 1861, for the war. He mustered in as a Sergeant and was promoted to 1st Sergeant on March 19, 1863. Listed as present or accounted for until captured at Cold Harbor, on June 1, 1864, he was confined at Point Lookout, Maryland. Transferred to Elmira, New York, he is reported to have died of "pneumonia" on October 2, 1864.
[Source(s): Card File; North Carolina Troops, IV]

O'Brien, Robert
Ordinary Seaman, Confederate States Navy. O'Brien enlisted on June 22, 1863, in Wilmington, North Carolina, for the war. A "Robert O'Brien served as a Landsman aboard the CSS ARCTIC, 1863
[Source(s): Card File; NA RG 45; Foenander]

O'Brien [O'Brian], Thomas (New Hanover County, North Carolina)
Seaman, Confederate States Navy. O'Brien enlisted in the Confederate States Navy on October 29 [November 3], 1863, in Wilmington, North Carolina, for the war. He served aboard the CSS ARCTIC, 1863, and the CSS RALEIGH, 1864. His name appears on a register of Confederate States Army General Military Hospital Number 4, Wilmington, North Carolina, being admitted March 31, 1864 with "bubo syphiliticum" and "died July 12, [1864] but accounted for as returned to duty." A "Thomas O'Brien" served as an Ordinary Seaman and Officers' Cook aboard the CSS NORTH CAROLINA, Cape Fear River, North Carolina, 1864. His post office was given on the register as Wilmington, North Carolina.
[Source(s): MR, 4, p. 446; Card File; NA RG 45; NA RG 109; Foenander; St. Armand]

Oden, George W. (Beaufort County, North Carolina)
Private, Confederate States Marine Corps. Born on October 11, 1841 (*1900 United States Census* shows month of birth as November 1841) in North Carolina, Oden enlisted in Raleigh, North Carolina, on October 6, 1864. He served on the Charleston, South Carolina Station as a Private of the Marine guard on board the ironclad CSS COLUMBIA to February 7, 1865 and transferred to the CSS INDIAN CHIEF on February 8, 1865. Records show he was received at Washington, DC from City Point, Virginia, as a Prisoner of War on April 12, 1865. Transportation furnished to Plymouth, North Carolina. He died on March 1, 1906 and was buried at Athens Chapel Cemetery, Whitepost Community (near Bath), North Carolina. Oden is shown residing as a farmer, in 1900, with his second wife, Mary (whom he married in 1896), and grown children from his first marriage, in Bath Township, North Carolina. [Source(s): Oden; North Carolina Troops, Doc. # 0299; Card File; Donnelly-ENL; Lauderdale; Census (North Carolina), 1900; Foenander]

O'Donnell [O'Donnel], John (Ireland//New Hanover County, North Carolina)
Private, Confederate States Army//Confederate States Navy. O'Donnell resided in New Hanover County, North Carolina, and enlisted in Brunswick County, North Carolina, at age 30 on June 2, 1861, for the war, as a Private in 2nd Company H, 40th Regiment, North Carolina Troops (3rd Regiment, North Carolina Artillery). He was present or accounted for until June 1863 when he appears with the remark: "In confinement for mutinous conduct." O'Donnell was transferred to Company E, 31st Regiment, North Carolina Troops, in July 1863, and transferred to the Confederate States Navy on April 6, 1864. Source "Howard" states O'Donnell was one of 27 mutinous conspirators in his former artillery unit, all Irish immigrants. He may be the same as the "John O'Donnell" who served as a Landsman, aboard the CSS NORTH CAROLINA, Cape Fear River, North Carolina, 1864, and as a 2nd Class Fireman aboard the CSS NORTH CAROLINA, Cape Fear River, North Carolina, 1864
[Source(s): Card File; NA RG 45; North Carolina Troops, I & VIII; Howard; Foenander]

O'Donnell, Patrick (Ireland//NC?)
Confederate States Navy (?).
O'Donnell died at age 34 on September 16, 1862 in Wilmington, North Carolina of "Billious & Yellow Fever (?)"

He was listed as a "Steward."
[Source: Oakdale (Davis)]

O'Kaafe, R. (County unknown)
Confederate States Marine Corps. O'Kaafe was wounded in the left arm and captured at Fort Fisher on January 15, 1865.
[Source(s): "Daily Confed." (2/18/65); Card File]

Olds, Andrew Holstead (Greene County, North Carolina)
Confederate States Navy. Born in Greene County, North Carolina on March 9, 1843, Olds served as a Landsman, CSS CHATTAHOOCHEE, 1863. He later served as a Surgeon's Steward on board the CSS SAVANNAH, 1863. He was later attached to the Naval Brigade at Richmond, Virginia, 1865 and was paroled at Appomattox, Virginia, April 1865. Olds resided as a farm laborer, in 1870, with his wife, Sarah R. Olds, and daughter, in Jackson County, Florida. He moved to Alabama sometime after 1870, and is shown to be residing in Louisville, Barbour County, Alabama, in 1907.
[Source(s): Foenander]

Oliver, Joseph Lafayette (Washington County, North Carolina)
Private, Confederate States Army//Sailor, Confederate States Navy. Born circa 1842 in Washington County, North Carolina, Oliver resided as a laborer in Washington County, North Carolina where he enlisted in Plymouth, North Carolina, at age 20 on June 24, 1861, for the war, in Company G, 1st Regiment, North Carolina State Troops. He was present or accounted for until discharged on February 3, 1862 to enlist in Confederate States Navy (Source MR, I indicates he transferred to the Navy in January 1862). He served aboard the CSS VIRGINIA, March 1862 ["Foenander" states he "served aboard the CSS VIRGINIA; was wounded in the battle at Hampton Roads, Virginia, March 8-9, 1862, and discharged from the service, shortly after]. He re-enlisted for the war, on March 25, 1862, but left before April 1, 1862. He served in the 3rd Virginia Infantry. He stated on his pension that he was wounded. Oliver entered the Old Soldier's Home, Richmond, Virginia, on March 6, 1897, at age 52. He resided, as a carpenter, with his wife, Mary J., and two children, in 1880, in Elizabeth City, Pasquotank County, North Carolina. His post-war occupation is also shown as ship's carpenter. Oliver received a Confederate pension from North Carolina. A letter dated January 19, 1897 states that the wounds he received in action, aboard the CSS VIRGINIA, had never healed. He was admitted to the Robert E. Lee, Camp 1, Confederate Veterans' Home, Richmond, Virginia, in March 1897 at age 52, residence shown as Norfolk, Virginia. He died on April 16, 1897, and was buried in Berkeley, Norfolk County, Virginia.
[Source(s): Card File; NA RG 45; Driver; North Carolina Troops, III; Foenander; MR, I]

O'Neal, Caswell G. (Wake County, North Carolina)
Confederate States Navy. O'Neal's name appears as a signature to an Oath of Allegiance to the United States subscribed and sworn to on June 3, 1865, in Raleigh, North Carolina. His place of residence was given on the Oath as Wake County, North Carolina.
[Source(s): Card File; NA RG 109]

O'Neal, Christopher Thomas, Jr. (Hyde County, North Carolina)
Private, Confederate States Army//Confederate States Navy. Born on Ocracoke Island off the coast of North Carolina, on August 2, 1826, O'Neal married Nancy O'Neal on November 26, 1846 (there were seven children of this marriage, only three of whom survived a typhoid epidemic in the 1860's). He lived on Ocracoke where he worked as a pilot at Ocracoke Inlet. He enlisted in Hyde County, North Carolina as a Private on October 17, 1861 [January 1, 1863, per "MR, II"], at age 44 [North Carolina Troops entry shows his age as 41], in Company H, 33rd Regiment, North Carolina Troops. He was reported absent without leave on March 14, 1862 but returned to duty between March and August 1863. O'Neal transferred to the Confederate States Navy on April 3, 1864. He died circa May 18, 1911, and was buried in the O'Neal Family Cemetery, Ocracoke Island, Hyde County, North Carolina.
[Source(s): North Carolina Troops, IX; Army to Navy; S.O. # 89; Ellen Cloud; MR, II and III; Foenander]

O'Neal, William (Currituck County, North Carolina)
Private, Confederate States Army//Confederate States Navy. O'Neal resided in Currituck County, North Carolina, where he enlisted at age 18 on October 11, 1862, for the war, in Company B, 8th Regiment, North Carolina State Troops. He was present or accounted for until he deserted to the enemy at Sullivan's Island, Charleston Harbor, South Carolina, on August 20, 1863. He was reported in confinement at Fort Monroe, Virginia, on September 13, 1863, but was released the same date. He rejoined his company in November-December 1863 and was present or accounted for until he transferred to the Confederate States Navy on or about April 1, 1864. Source "Foenander"

lists a "William B. O'Neill (O'Neil)," who served as a Landsman aboard the CSS ARCTIC, Cape Fear River, North Carolina, 1863 and as an Ordinary Seaman aboard the CSS RALEIGH in North Carolina and Virginia waters, 1864.
[Source(s): Card File; North Carolina Troops, IV; Foenander]

O'Neill, John
Seaman, Confederate States Navy. O'Neil enlisted on June 8, 1863, in Wilmington, North Carolina, for the war. He may be the same "John O'Neil" that is listed by "Foenander" as a Seaman and Coal Heaver on the CSS NORTH CAROLINA, or the "John O'Neill" that served as a Seaman, aboard the CSS NORTH CAROLINA, Cape Fear River, North Carolina 1864
[Source(s): Card File; NA RG 45; Foenander]

Orrell, Adolphus Lafayete, Sr. (Guilford County, North Carolina)
Private, Confederate States Army//Confederate States Navy. Orrell resided in Guilford County, North Carolina, when he enlisted in Company B, 27th Regiment, North Carolina Troops, at Fort Macon, North Carolina, at age 22, on April 20, 1861. Orrell was wounded at Bristoe Station, Virginia, October 14, 1863. He transferred to the Confederate States Navy on April 1, 1864 [Source "Sloan" gives the date as March 31, 1864, and indicates the records as saying, concerning his transfer to the Confederate States Navy, "or, words to that effect"]. He married Margaret H. Banks, December 14, 1865, at St. Johns Church, Fayetteville, Cumberland County, North Carolina.
[Source(s): Card File; NA RG 45; www.guilfordgreys.com/Original_Greys.htm; Sloan;   North Carolina Troops, VIII; Foenander]

Orrell, John J.
Pilot, Confederate States Navy. Orrell served in the North Carolina militia as a lieutenant. He either deserted or was captured and later served as a pilot in the Union Navy. Acting Rear Admiral Samuel Lee mentions in dispatch dated April 36, 1864 that he was taking both Orrell and Pucket as pilots into government service.
[Source(s): ORN, 1, 9, p. 300 and 672-676; Foenander]

Orrell, R. C.
Landsman, Confederate States Navy. Orrell enlisted on June 28, 1864, in Raleigh, North Carolina, for the war.
[Source(s): Card File; NA RG 45]

Osment, Leonard
Landsman, Confederate States Navy. Osment enlisted on December 18, 1863, in Wilmington, North Carolina, for the war.
[Source(s): Card File; NA RG 45]

Osment [Ozment], Robert L. (Guilford County, North Carolina)
Landsman, Confederate States Navy. Osment enlisted on March 3, 1864, in Raleigh, North Carolina, for the war. He filed a pension claim on July 6, 1908 at age 67, listing his post office as Greensboro, R. F. D. # 1, Guilford County, North Carolina. The claim was disallowed with the notation, "Record of service incomplete." A second claim filed on July 6, 1909 at age 68, same post office as above, was approved at 4th Class. On the claim he states he was in "the Navy, was on board the Yadkin, Flagship" and that he received no wounds. Says he served under "Commodore Lynch, Capt. May being officer of the day." He enlisted in 1864. His pension file contains his original May 23, 1864 letter written from Smithville, North Carolina, to his mother that states "I am at the 'Horsepittle'" and am "bad off with my hip and 'crest…' [illegible].
[Source(s): Card File; NA RG 45; Pensions (North Carolina)]

Osteen [Ostein, Ousten], Reuben (Craven County, North Carolina)
Crewman, Confederate States Navy. Osteen enlisted at age 32 as a Private and substitute, in Company K, 2nd North Carolina Regiment. He was sent on detached service to the Confederate States Navy, per payroll and clothing records, he served as a Seaman aboard the CSS BEAUFORT from September - December 1861. He transferred to the Confederate States Navy on May 7, 1862. He later served on the CSS NORTH CAROLINA. His name appears on a register of Confederate States Army General Military Hospital Number 4, Wilmington, North Carolina, dated August 6, 1862, giving disease as "pneumonia" and post office as New Bern.
[Source(s): MR, 4, p. 444; Card File; NA RG 109; 1860 Census (NC); NCCWSP]

Ostein [Osteen, Oustein, Ouctrin] Robert (Craven County, North Carolina)
Private, Confederate States Army//Seaman/Quarter Gunner, Confederate States Navy. Ostein resided and enlisted as a "substitute," in Craven County, North Carolina, in February of 1862 [January, per MR, I], at age 32, as a Private in

Company K, 2nd Regiment, North Carolina State Troops. He transferred to the Confederate States Navy on May 7, 1862 and served as a Seaman aboard the CSS ARCTIC and CSS FANNY, 1862 as a member of the North Carolina Squadron. He is also indicated to have served as a Seaman aboard the CSS BEAUFORT, 1861 – 1862 [NOTE: entry into service does not corroborate these dates], and as a Quarter Gunner and Seaman aboard the ironclad sloop CSS NORTH CAROLINA, Cape Fear River, North Carolina, 1864.
[Source(s): North Carolina Troops, III; ORN 1, 23, 703 and 2, 1, 279, 281, 285, 293, 295 & 296; Foenander; MR, I; NA RG 45; Card File; Foenander]

Outlaw, William (Bertie County, North Carolina)
Private, Confederate States Army//Landsman, Seaman, Confederate States Navy. Outlaw was born in Bertie County, North Carolina, where he resided as a farmer prior to enlisting in Currituck County, North Carolina, at age 23, on May 13, 1861, as a Private in Company E, 17th Regiment, North Carolina Troops (1st Organization). He transferred to the Confederate States Navy on or prior to July 28, 1861. He served as a Landsman aboard the CSS FANNY during December 1861, and perhaps longer. He received a partial payment on February 13, 1862 at Gosport Navy Yard following the burning of the CSS FANNY at Elizabeth City, North Carolina on February 10, 1862. He appears on the North Carolina Squadron payroll for the 1st quarter of 1862 (December 1, 1861 - February 28, 1862). He was listed as having "run" on or by February 28, 1862.
[Source(s): http://ftp.rootsweb.com/pub/usgenweb/nc/bertie/military/confeds3.txt; Card File; North Carolina Troops, VI; Foenander; NCCWSP]

Overman, James M. (Randolph County, North Carolina)
Landsman, Confederate States Navy [Company F, Confederate States Naval Battalion]. Overman's enlistment date is a point of confusion due to conflicting sources. One source indicates he enlisted in the Confederate States Navy on October 20, 1863 in Wilmington, North Carolina, while others give the date as October 3, 1862, October 26, 1863, and October 21, 1863 at Camp Holmes, North Carolina (near Raleigh)]. His name appears on a roll of Prisoners of War at Point Lookout, Maryland, which states he was captured on April 6, 1865, at Harper's Farm [Virginia] and confined at Point Lookout from April 14, 1865 until released on June 29, 185. His name also appears as a signature to an Oath of Allegiance to the United States subscribed and sworn to at Point Lookout, Maryland, June 28, 1865. His place of residence was given on the Oath as Randolph County, North Carolina. Description: Complexion fair; hair brown; eyes blue; height 5 feet 9 inches. His pension claim filed on July 9, 1903 at age 79, listing his post office as Ramseur, Randolph County, North Carolina was approved at 4th Class. He was wounded near Petersburg, Virginia, and captured on April 1, 1865. His application states that he "Did service at and near Wilmington, North Carolina, near close of war was ordered to Virginia Captain Thomas Poindexter was in Command after being captured was taken to Point Look Out[sic] and not relieved until June 14th 1865 all of which papers he still has in his possession[.]"
[Source(s): MR, 4, p. 446; Card File; NA RG 45; NA RG 109; Pensions (North Carolina); NCCWSP]

Overman, Joseph
Ship's Carpenter, Confederate States Navy. Overman was born in North Carolina. He served at Gosport Naval Yard, 1861-1862 and at the Charlotte Naval Yard 1862-1865. He was a post-war employee of Airline Railroad.
[Source(s): Driver]

Overton, Ben
Seaman, Ship's Cook, Confederate States Navy.
Overton served as a Seaman aboard the CSS CURLEW as a member of the North Carolina Squadron from November 20, 1861 through the 1st quarter of 1862. He appears on the ship's payroll as a Ship's Cook for the 1st quarter of 1862. His name appears on the payroll of the receiving ship UNITED STATES ending March 31, 1862.
[Source: NCCWSP]

Overton, Charles N.
Private, Confederate States Navy. Born in North Carolina, Overton enlisted in Company A, 61st Virginia Infantry, at Washington Point, Norfolk County, Virginia, on July 11, 1861. He was wounded (skull fractured) and captured at Gettysburg, July 3, 1863. Overton was sent to Fort McHenry as a Prisoner of War; transferred to Fort Delaware and exchanged on July 31, 1863. He transferred to the Confederate States Navy on April 6, 1864. He was in Libby Prison, Richmond, Virginia, April 10, 1865. Overton was receiving a pension at Sign Pine, Norfolk County, Virginia, on June 17, 1890, age 58.
[Source(s): Driver]

Owens, Joseph S. (L.) (Currituck County, North Carolina)
Private, Confederate States Army//Quartermaster, Confederate States Navy. Owens enlisted in Currituck County, North Carolina, on May 13, 1861, as a Private in Company E, 17th Regiment, North Carolina Troops (1st Organization). He was present or accounted for until he transferred to the Confederate States Navy on or about September 11, 1861. Source NCCWSP indicates he "shipped for war" on August 31, 1861 and served aboard the CSS RALEIGH as a member of the North Carolina Squadron. Per clothing, bounty, payroll, and small stores records, Owens served aboard the CSS RALEIGH from before September 2,1861 - April 1862. His name appears on the North Carolina Squadron payroll for the1st quarter of 1862 (February 21, 1862 - April 15, 1862. He transferred to the James River Squadron on April 15, 1862
[Source(s): Card File; North Carolina Troops, VI; Foenander; NCCWSP]

Owens, William L.
Seaman, Confederate States Navy.
Per small stores, payroll, and muster records, Owens shipped for one year aboard the CSS RALEIGH on September 8, 1861 and served thereon through April 1862. His name appears on the North Carolina Squadron payroll for the 1st quarter of 1862 (February 21, 1862 - April 15, 1862). He transferred to the James River Squadron on April 15, 1862 and served at Drewry's Bluff as a Quartermaster from March 28, 1863 - April 27, 1863. Owens was listed as discharged on or before April 27, 1863.
[Source: NCCWSP]

Ozment [Osment?], Leven
Landsman, Confederate States Navy. Ozment enlisted on December 12, 1863, in Raleigh, North Carolina, for the war.
[Source(s): Card File; NA RG 45]

Ozment [Osment], Robert L.
Confederate States Navy. Born in North Carolina in 1841, Ozment served as a Landsman aboard the CSS ARCTIC and CSS YADKIN, Cape Fear River, North Carolina, 1863 – 1864. He married Emeline L. Stephenson in Guilford County, North Carolina, on December 25, 1868. A farmer, Ozment applied for a Confederate pension from Guilford County, North Carolina. He died in Gates County, North Carolina, July 13, 1929.
[Source(s): Foenander; ORN 2, 1, 278 & 313]

P

Page, Carroll (Durham's Depot [possibly Orange, now Durham, County, North Carolina])
Confederate States Navy. Page's name appears on a register of Confederate States Army General Military Hospital Number 4, Wilmington, North Carolina, being admitted on September 4, 1863, and returned to duty on October 9, 1863. His post office given as Durham's Depot.
[Source(s): Card File; NA RG 109]

Paine, Matthias (Tyrrell County, North Carolina)
Private, Confederate States Army//Confederate States Navy. Paine was born in Tyrrell County, North Carolina, and resided in Pasquotank County, North Carolina where he worked as a mariner prior to enlisting there at age 26 on July 29, 1861, for the war, in Company A, 8th Regiment, North Carolina State Troops. Captured at Roanoke Island, North Carolina, on February 8, 1862, Paine was paroled at Elizabeth City, North Carolina, on February 21, 1862. Exchanged in August 1862, he was present or accounted for until he transferred to the Confederate States Navy on or about April 15, 1864.
[Source(s): Card File; NA RG 45; North Carolina Troops, IV; Foenander]

Paisley, Hugh S. (Born in North Carolina)
Confederate States Navy. Paisley was born in North Carolina and appointed for the war as an Assistant Surgeon, Confederate States Navy, on April 28, 1864, from Alabama, and as an Assistant Surgeon, Provisional Navy, June 2, 1864. He served at the Naval Station, Marion Court House, South Carolina, 1864 – 1865. In 1870 he resided as a dentist, with his wife, Mollie, and a son, in Selma, Alabama.
[Source(s): Foenander; Confederate States Navy Register; JCC 4, 123; 1870 United States Census.]

Palmer, William A. (Stanly County, North Carolina)
Confederate States Navy. Palmer enlisted in the Confederate States Navy on August 24, 1863 in Wilmington, North Carolina. A "W. A. Palmer" served aboard the CSS NEUSE as of the ship's March – October 1864 muster rolls.

His occupation according to the 1860 census was that of farmer. His census data recorded that he was living with wife, Margaret, age 32, and five children; estimated estate value: $900. He was born December 29, 1822, died on February 26, 1902, and was buried at Bethel Reformed Lutheran Church Cemetery, Mount Pleasant, Stanly County, North Carolina. He was age 41 in 1864.
[Source(s): WPA; Hill; Census (NC), 1860; MR, 4, p. 447; NEUSE Roster; CMACSSN]

Palmer, William A. [NOTE: May be same as "William A. Palmer" of Stanly County, North Carolina, q. v.]
Landsman, Confederate States Navy. Palmer enlisted on September 11, 1863 at Camp Holmes [near Raleigh, North Carolina] for the war. A "W. A. Palmer" served aboard the CSS NEUSE as of the ship's March – April 1864 muster roll.
[Source(s): Card File; NA RG 45; NEUSE Roster]

Palmer, W. M. A.
Ordinary Seaman, Confederate States Navy. Palmer enlisted on September 22, 1863 in Wilmington, North Carolina, for the war.
[Source(s): Card File; NA RG 45]

Paris, Edward
Second Class Fireman, Confederate States Navy.
Paris served aboard the CSS BEAUFORT per a payroll list for the September - November 1861 period. Per clothing, bounty, and small stores records, Paris remained aboard the CSS BEAUFORT as a Second-Class Fireman from December 1861 – March 1862. He received a partial payment on February 13, 1862 at Gosport Navy Yard following his service in manning Fort Cobb at the Battle of Elizabeth City on February 10, 1862. His name appears on North Carolina Squadron payroll for the 1st quarter of 1862 (December 1, 1861 - April 15, 1862). He transferred to the James River Squadron as of April 15, 1862.
[Source: NCCWSP]

Parish, N. G.
Private, Confederate States Marine Corps. Enlisting in Raleigh, North Carolina on October 6, 1864, Parish served on the Charleston, South Carolina Station as a Private of the Marine guard on board the ironclad CSS COLUMBIA to February 7, 1865.
[Source(s): North Carolina Troops, Doc. # 0299; Card File]

Parish [Parrish], Wyatt Washington (Guilford County, North Carolina)
Private, Company B, Confederate States Marine Corps. Born in Guilford County, North Carolina, circa 1846, Parish was a resident of Virginia. He was enrolled as a conscript at age 18 at Camp Lee, Richmond, Virginia, on May 2, 1864, and "assigned" to the Confederate States Marine Corps on May 5, 1864. He served as part of the Marine guard aboard the CSS VIRGINIA II beginning February 18, 1865. Parish deserted from Drewry's Bluff on March 11, 1865 while on liberty but was returned to his ship under arrest on March 16, 1865. No further record. Married his wife Sarah at Round Peak, North Carolina, in 1862. He received a Virginia State Pension. Description: 5" 4," blue eyes, light hair, light complexion; occupation listed as laborer. Parish died at Max, Virginia, on May 16, 1917.
[Source(s): Donnelly-ENL; ORN 2, 1, 314]

Parker, Columbus W. (Davie County, North Carolina)
Landsman, Confederate States Navy. Parker enlisted on August 17, 1864, in Raleigh, North Carolina for the war. His name appears on a roll of Prisoners of War at Point Lookout, Maryland, which states that he was captured at High Bridge April 6, 1865, and confined at Point Lookout, Maryland, from April 14, 1865, until released June 17, 1865. His name also appears as a signature to an Oath of Allegiance to the United States, subscribed and sworn to at Point Lookout, Maryland, on June 17, 1865. His place of residence was given on the Oath as Davie County, North Carolina. Description: Complexion fair; hair dark brown; eyes grey; height 5 feet 7 ¼ inches.
[Source(s): Card File; NA RG 45; NA RG 109]

Parker, Crawford (Forsyth County, North Carolina)
Landsman, Confederate States Navy. Parker was born in North Carolina in May 1826, and enlisted on February 6, 1864 in Raleigh, North Carolina, for the war. He served as a Landsman aboard the CSS ARCTIC, Cape Fear River, North Carolina, 1863, and aboard the CSS RALEIGH in North Carolina and Virginia waters, 1864. Parker resided as a farmer, in 1880, with his wife, Mary A. Parker, and eight children (eldest child born 1857) at Belews Creek, Forsyth County, North Carolina. He resided in 1900 as a widower at the home of his son and family on Belews Creek. He applied for a North Carolina Confederate pension on June 15, 1901, at age 75, listing his post office

as Belew's Creek, Forsyth County, North Carolina. On his pension he states that he "Enlisted on the RALEIGH gunboat" on or about June 15, 1863 and contracted chronic diarrhea at Wilmington on or about May 1, 1864 and never fully recovered. His claim was approved at 4th Class.
[Source(s): Card File; Pensions (North Carolina); Foenander]

Parker, F. R. (Halifax County, North Carolina)
1st Sergeant, Confederate States Army//Confederate States Navy(?). Parker was born and resided in Halifax County, North Carolina, where he resided as a constable prior to enlisting there at age 22 on April 25, 1861, as a Private in Company G, 12th Regiment, North Carolina Troops. He was present or accounted for until he transferred as a Private to Company I of this regiment on March 30, 1862. He was promoted to Sergeant prior to June 1, 1862, on which date he was promoted to 1st Sergeant. He was present or accounted for until he died at Guinea Station, Virginia, on May 10, 1863, of wounds. The place and date he was wounded was not reported. Note on source Card File reference states he "Died prior to date he was supposedly transferred [to Confederate States Navy], which was September 3, 1863."
[Source(s): Card File; North Carolina Troops, V]

Parker, Gilbert (Wilson County, North Carolina)
Confederate States Navy. Parker was born in North Carolina, in January 1833. Pension claim filed July 1, 1901, age 68 years, no town or county listed. States he served in the Confederate States Navy and was not wounded and does not give any dates of service. Approved 4th Class. Widow's pension filed on October 17, 1958 by Mary Long Parker, Rt. 1, Elm City, North Carolina, age 82, states she married him in 1897 and lived with him for six years until his death on June 3, 1904. She further states that he drew a pension while a resident of Nash County, North Carolina. Her application was approved as Class A. A 1958 copy of their marriage certificate lists him as age 63 and her age 21 when they married on March 7, 1897, in Wilson, North Carolina.
[Source(s): Card File; Pensions (North Carolina); Foenander]

Parker, H. N. (Davidson County, North Carolina; born Wake County, North Carolina)
Landsman, Confederate States Navy. Parker enlisted on March 17, 1864 at Camp Holmes [near Raleigh, North Carolina] from Colonel Crouse's 65th Regiment, North Carolina Militia, Davidson County, North Carolina. One source indicates he enlisted March 21, 1864 at Raleigh, North Carolina, for the war, while another source states his name appeared on a list of conscripts "in yard at Halifax" November 9, 1864. Description: Age 35; eyes blue; hair light; complexion fair; height 6 feet ½ inch; place of birth Wake County, North Carolina; occupation farmer.
[Source(s): Card File; NA RG 45]

Parker, Jesse L. (Union County, North Carolina)
Private, Confederate States Army//Confederate States Navy. Parker was born in Union County, North Carolina, in 1834, the son of Matthew and Marina Parker. He resided in Union County, North Carolina, as a farmer until he enlisted there at age 27 on March 14, 1862, in Company F, 48th Regiment, North Carolina Troops. He mustered in as a Corporal and was reported as present in September-October 1862. Promoted to Sergeant in November 1862 - February 1863 and reported present in January-June 1863. He was wounded in the left foot at Bristoe Station, Virginia, on October 14, 1863, and hospitalized at Richmond, Virginia. He was furloughed for forty days on October 30, 1863. He was reduced to the ranks prior to January 1, 1864, but company records do not indicate whether he had returned to duty. He transferred to the Confederate States Navy on or about April 1, 1864. North Carolina Confederate Pension Application records indicate he was wounded in the left eye at Richmond, Virginia, on an unspecified date [Source(s): Card File; Pensions (North Carolina); North Carolina Troops, XI; Foenander]

Parker, John (Columbus County, North Carolina)
Landsman [Seaman], Confederate States Navy. Parker enlisted on February 23, 1864 in Raleigh, North Carolina, for the war. His name appears on registers of Confederate States Army General Military Hospital Number 4, Wilmington, North Carolina, which state he was admitted on March 3, 1864, with "febris remittens" and returned to duty March 31, 1864. His post office was listed on the hospital registers as Cerra Gordo, [Columbus County], North Carolina.
[Source(s): Card File; NA RG 45; NA RG 109]

Parker, John Henry
3rd Assistant Engineer, Confederate States Navy.
Parker served aboard the CSS FORREST as a 3rd Assistant Engineer, as well as aboard the CSS RALEIGH. He transferred to the James River Squadron on April 15, 1862 and is listed as a 3rd Assistant Engineer aboard the

CSS RALEIGH with the James River Squadron payroll, for November 16, 1863 - December 15, 1863.
[Source: NCCWSP]

Parker, William Harwar
Lieutenant Commander, Confederate States Navy.
Parker was born in New York City on October 8, 1826. He commanded the CSS BEAUFORT in the mouth of the Neuse River, and participated in the fight at Roanoke Island on February 7-8, 1862, under Commodore Lynch. He served aboard the ship from at least September 1861 – March 1862.
[Source(s): McElroy; Card File; NCCWSP]

Parker, W. W.
Landsman, Confederate States Navy. Parker enlisted on September 28, 1863 at Camp Holmes [near Raleigh, North Carolina] for the war.
[Source(s): Card File; NA RG 45]

Parker (Parks), J. W.
Chief Engineer, North Carolina Navy. J. W. Parker is listed by source "DH Hill" as one of the first officers commissioned as a Chief Engineer aboard the NCS ELLIS in the North Carolina Navy.
[Source(s): DH Hill; NCS]

Parks, Marshall
"Naval Agent," North Carolina Navy. Marshall Parks is listed by source "DH Hill" as one of the first officers commissioned as a "naval agent" in the North Carolina Navy.
[Source(s): DH Hill; NCS]

Parks, William Calvin (Surry County, North Carolina)
Private, Confederate States Army//Confederate States Navy. Born in North Carolina about 1830, Parks resided in Surry County, North Carolina, where he enlisted at age 32 on March 18, 1862, as a Private in Company A, 28th Regiment, North Carolina Troops. He was present or accounted for until captured at Hanover Court House, Virginia, on May 27, 1862. Parks was confined at Fort Monroe, Virginia, and at Fort Columbus, New York Harbor. He was transferred to Aiken's Landing, James River, Virginia, where he was received on July 12, 1862 for exchange. Declared exchanged at Aiken's Landing on August 5, 1862, he returned to duty prior to August 27-30, 1862, when he was wounded in the thigh at or near Manassas, Virginia. Reported absent without leave in January-February 1863, company records do not indicate whether he returned to duty. He transferred to the Confederate States Navy on or about April 3, 1864 by Special Order.
[Source(s): Card File; NA RG 45; Foenander; S.O. # 89; North Carolina Troops, VIII; Army and Navy]

Parrish (Parish), Hillsman (Hinsman) (Beaufort County, North Carolina)
Private, Confederate States Army//Ordinary Seaman, Confederate States Navy. Born in Raleigh, Wake County, North Carolina, circa 1842, the son of William and Charity Parrish. He resided in Beaufort County, North Carolina, as a Seaman where he enlisted, age 20, as a Private in Company I, 3rd Regiment, North Carolina State Troops on May 10, 1861 [May 16, 1861, per MR, I]. Present or accounted for until he transferred to the Confederate States Navy on January 29, 1862 where he served aboard the CSS VIRGINIA, at Hampton Roads, Virginia. A muster roll of this vessel, dated in 1862, shows his name as "Hinsman Parrish." Reenlisting for the war on March 25, 1862, Parrish (Parish) served at Drewry's Bluff, Virginia, May 12-24, 1862. He enlisted in Company B, 39th Battalion Virginia Cavalry, Charlottesville, Virginia, August 25, 1862. Source MR, I indicates he was a former "courier for General Ewell." He was ordered transferred to the Maryland Line on April 1, 1864, but the order was revoked on April 6, 1864. Captured at Petersburg, West Virginia, July 28, 1864, he took the Oath of Allegiance at Berlin, Maryland, November 14, 1864. Description: 5'4;" dark complexion; dark hair; dark eyes; residence New Bern, North Carolina. Transportation provided to Norfolk, Virginia.
[Source(s): Card File; MR, I; Driver; Foenander; "Beaufort County Sailors;" North Carolina Troops, III; ORN, 2, 1, 310; Census (North Carolina), 1850]

Parsons, Duncan (Montgomery County, North Carolina)
Landsman/Seaman/Acting Master's Mate, Confederate States Navy. Parsons enlisted on December 17, 1863 in Raleigh, North Carolina, for the war, and served as a Seaman aboard the CSS ARCTIC, Cape Fear River, North Carolina, 1863. He was appointed an Acting Master's Mate on July 24, 1863 and served on the Wilmington Station, North Carolina, 1863 – 1864. He served aboard the CSS NEUSE, 1864, and was appointed an Acting Master's

Mate, Provisional Navy, on June 2, 1864. His name appears on registers of Confederate States Army General Military Hospital, Number 4, Wilmington, North Carolina, which state he was admitted January 21, 1864, with "febris typhoides" and returned to duty April 12, 1864. His post office was given on the registers as "Basadonia, North Carolina [?] [probably Macedonia, Montgomery County, North Carolina]."
[Source(s): Card File; NA RG 45; Foenander; NA RG 109; 1860 North Carolina Census]

Parsons [Parson], Edgar O. (New Hanover County, North Carolina)
Private, Confederate States Army//Confederate States Navy. Parsons enlisted in New Hanover County, North Carolina, on May 16, 1862 for the war as a Private in Company G, 41st Regiment (3rd Regiment, North Carolina Cavalry). He was present or accounted for until he transferred to the Confederate States Navy on July 16, 1863. He served aboard the CSS NEUSE as of the ship's March – October 1864 muster rolls.
[Source(s): Card File; *North Carolina Troops, II*; Hill; Foenander; NEUSE Roster; CMACSSN]

Parsons [Person], William (Cumberland County, North Carolina)
Private, Confederate States Army//Confederate States Navy. Parsons enlisted from Cumberland County, North Carolina, on December 15, 1862, as a Private in 2nd Company B, 36th Regiment, North Carolina troops (2nd North Carolina Artillery). He was present or accounted for until transferred to Company B, 13th Battalion, North Carolina Light Artillery on November 4, 1863. He was present or accounted for until he transferred to the Confederate States Navy on May 18, 1864. A "William Parsons" served aboard the CSS NEUSE as of the ship's March – October 1864 muster rolls.
[Source(s): Card File; NA RG 109; *North Carolina Troops, I*; Hill; NEUSE Roster; CMACSSN]

Parsons, William Thomas (Carteret County, North Carolina)
Private, Confederate States Army. Parsons resided in Carteret County, North Carolina as a farmer prior to enlisting in Company G, 10th Regiment, North Carolina Troops (1st Regiment, North Carolina Artillery) at age 29 on April 13, 1861. His NCT, Vol. I entry carries the notation "killed by explosion of steam boiler on boat March 9, 1862." Though no listing was found tying him to the Confederate States Navy, the coincidence of the date of his death and type of death noted may be an indicator of naval service.
[Source: NCT, I]

Partridge [Partriage], William H. (Currituck County, North Carolina)
Private, Confederate States Army//Seaman, Quartermaster, Master-at-Arms, Confederate States Navy. Born in Currituck County, North Carolina, where he resided as a Seaman until he enlisted "for the war" in Company B, 8th Regiment, North Carolina State Troops, on August 9, 1861 at age 23. Promoted to Corporal October 27, 1862, he was present or accounted for until he transferred to the Confederate States Navy on or about February 9, 1863 in Wilmington, North Carolina, enlisting for "three years or the war." Partridge served as a Seaman on the CSS SEA BIRD (July – August 1861; as Quartermaster, circa February 1862), the CSS ARCTIC as a Landsman, and the CSS YADIN as a Master-at-Arms. His name appears on a North Carolina Squadron payroll covering the period December 1, 1861 – March 31, 1862. He is listed as having "run" on this payroll ending March 31, 1862.
[Source(s): MR, 4, p. 447; *North Carolina Troops, IV*; Sea Bird; Foenander; "Beaufort County Sailors;" Card File; NA RG 45; NCCWSP; North Carolina Troops, IV]

Parvin, William H. (Beaufort County, North Carolina)
Confederate States Navy. Parvin enlisted in Beaufort County, North Carolina, on May 8, 1861 at age 22 for twelve months in Company K, 10th Regiment, North Carolina State Troops (1st North Carolina Artillery). He was captured at Fort Hatteras on August 29, 1861 and confined at Fort Warren, Massachusetts until paroled for exchange on February 3, 1862. Parvin was detailed from Company K, 10th Regiment, North Carolina State Troops (1st Regiment, North Carolina Artillery) as a crew member of the Confederate government transport CSS SAMUEL HINES on June 5, 1863. Absent detailed through October 1864.
[Source(s): Card File; North Carolina Troops, I]

Paschall, I. A.
Seaman, Confederate States Navy. Paschall enlisted on June 29, 1864, at Wilmington, North Carolina for the war.
[Source(s): Card File; NA RG 45]

Pate, John A.
Landsman, Confederate States Navy [Company A, Confederate States Naval Battalion]. Pate enlisted on August 29, 1864 in Raleigh, North Carolina for the war. He signed a prisoner's parole at Alvin's Ferry, North Carolina, April 27,

1865, giving above unit and states that he was captured in Chatham County, North Carolina.
[Source(s): Card File; NA RG 109; NA RG 45]

Pate, Joseph W. (Beaufort County, North Carolina)
Private, Confederate States Army//Ship's Cook, Seaman, Confederate States Navy. Pate was born in Beaufort County, North Carolina, and worked there as a Seaman until he enlisted for twelve months as a Private in Company K, 10th Regiment, North Carolina Troops (1st Regiment, North Carolina Artillery) at age 21 years on May 8, 1861. He was temporarily attached to Company B, 61st Regiment, North Carolina Troops when Company K was captured at Fort Hatteras, August 29, 1861. He was returned to Company K when it was exchanged in February 1862. Card reference states he was detailed from Company K, 10th Regiment, North Carolina State Troops as a crew member of the government transport CSS SAMUEL HINES on June 5, 1863. He transferred to the Confederate States Navy on July 19, 1863 and served as ship's cook aboard the CSS NORTH CAROLINA. He later served as a Seaman aboard CSS TALLAHASSEE.
[Source(s): MR, IV; ORN, 2, 1, pp. 294-296; North Carolina Troops, I; Card File; Foenander; "Beaufort County Sailors;" *North Carolina Troops, I*, p.166-167;
www.thewashingtongrays.homestead.com; www.ncgenweb.us/nccivwar/rosters/10cok.htm]

Patrick, Joel
Seaman, Confederate States Navy. Patrick enlisted on June 13, 1864 in Raleigh, North Carolina for the war.
[Source(s): Card File; NA RG 45]

Patrick, William H. (Currituck County, North Carolina)
Confederate States Navy. Patrick enlisted in Currituck County, North Carolina, in the Confederate States Army on August 26, 1861. He transferred to the Confederate States Navy in January 1863.
[Source(s): MR, I]

Patterson, Edward (Rowan County, North Carolina)
Private, Confederate States Army//Landsman, Confederate States Navy. A resident of Rowan County, North Carolina, Patterson enlisted in Brunswick County, North Carolina, at age 28 on May 31 [May 30, per source Rumple], 1861, for the war, in Company K, 4th Regiment, North Carolina State Troops. He was hospitalized in Richmond, Virginia, on June 5, 1863 with "debility from wounds" (place and date of wounding not recorded) [Wounded at Sharpsburg and on May 19, 1864, per source Rumple; NOTE month and year conflicts]. Present or accounted for until transferred to the Confederate States Navy on April 5, 1864 where he served as a Landsman aboard the CSS VIRGINIA II, 1864 - 1865.
[Source(s): Card File; North Carolina Troops, IV; Foenander; Rumple]

Patterson, Michael William
Confederate States Navy or Coast Guard. "Was in the Navy or Coast Guard, stationed at Wilmington, North Carolina. He died of yellow fever during the Civil War."
[Source(s): Card File; North Carolina Troops, doc. #0139]

Patterson, William
Landsman, Confederate States Navy. Patterson enlisted on March 3, 1864 in Raleigh, North Carolina for the war. Source "Foenander" lists a "W. W. Patterson" who served as a Landsman aboard the CSS ARCTIC, Cape Fear River, North Carolina, 1863.
[Source(s): Card File; NA RG 45; Foenander]

Patterson, W. M. (North Carolina?)
Confederate States Navy. A "W. M. Patterson" served aboard the CSS NEUSE per its March - October 1864 muster roll.
[Source: CMACSSN]

Patton, Henry D. (Wilson County, North Carolina)
Musician, Confederate States Army//Confederate States Navy. A resident of Wilson County, North Carolina, Patton enlisted in Craven County, North Carolina at age 33 on June 28, 1861, for the war, in Company F, 4th Regiment, North Carolina State Troops. Mustered in as a Musician, he was present or accounted for until transferred to the Confederate States Navy on October 2, 1863.
[Source(s): Card File; North Carolina Troops, IV; Foenander]

Patton, R. E. (McDowell County, North Carolina)
    Landsman, Confederate States Navy. Patton enlisted on June 6, 1864 in Raleigh, North Carolina for the war. Patton's name appears on a prisoner's parole from Libby Prison dated April 21, 1865. He was given permission to go to his home in McDowell County, North Carolina.
    [Source(s): Card File; NA RG 45; NA RG 109]

Payne, John A.
    Master's Mate, Confederate States Navy.
    Payne was serving aboard the CSS RALEIGH as of March 25, 1862. He transferred to the James River Squadron on April 15, 1862.
    [Source: NCCWSP]

Paysour, Jacob A.
    Landsman, Confederate States Navy. Paysour enlisted on September 28, 1863, at Camp Holmes [near Raleigh, North Carolina] for the war.
    [Source(s): Card File; NA RG 45]

Pearce, Silvester
    Landsman, Confederate States Navy. Enlisted October 26, 1863, at Camp Holmes [near Raleigh, North Carolina]. Source RCWV gives enlistment date as October 25, 1863.
    [Source(s): Card File; NA RG 45; RCWV]

Pearce, William C. (County unknown)
    Private, Confederate States Navy(?) ("Company A, Navy Battalion, North Carolina Infantry")
    [Source(s): Unknown]

Pearson, James M.
    Midshipman, Confederate States Navy.
    Pearson served as a Midshipman aboard the CSS FANNY per that ship's muster roll, dated October 8, 1861.
    [Source: NCCWSP]

Pedrick, William J. (Beaufort County, North Carolina)
    Private, Confederate States Army//Confederate States Navy. Enlisted in Beaufort County, North Carolina, in Company K, 10th Regiment, North Carolina State Troops (1st Regiment, North Carolina Artillery) at age 22 on April 22, 1861 for twelve months. Present or accounted for until detailed as a member of the crew of the Confederate government transport CSS SAMUEL HINES on June 5, 1863. Absent detailed through October 1864.
    [Source(s): Card File; North Carolina Troops, I]

Peed, Dudley (Wake County, North Carolina)
    Confederate States Navy. Peed was born in North Carolina in 1825. On his application for a North Carolina Confederate pension, filed June 15, 1907, at age 82, he listed his post office as Roger's Store, Wake County, North Carolina. He further states that he enlisted in the Navy and served on the flagship CSS VIRGINIA II under Captain Denning [Dunningham?], Commanding, under Admiral Semmes in October 1864 in the James River Fleet. He stated he "was a member of the same command" as James Hugh Holloway (q.v.), for whom he served as a witness in his quest for a pension. He also stated that he served until the surrender. The pension was approved at 4th Class.
    [Source(s): Card File; Pensions (North Carolina); Foenander]

Peadon [Peadon, Peden], Henry (Johnston County, North Carolina)
    Landsman, Confederate States Navy. Peadon was born in Johnston County, North Carolina, in 1832, the son of William and Celia Peadon, of Guilford County, North Carolina. He enlisted in the Confederate States Navy October 8, [11 or 12] 1863 in Wilmington, North Carolina. His brother John Peadon, q.v., also served in the Confederate States Navy. In 1860, Peadon resided as a farmer with his wife, Susan, and three children, in Guilford County, North Carolina. He served as a Landsman aboard the CSS NORTH CAROLINA, Cape Fear River, North Carolina, 1864.
    [Source(s): Foenander; Census (North Carolina), 1860; MR, 4, p. 446; Card File; NA RG 45]

Peadon [Peadon, Peden], John (Johnston County, North Carolina)
    Landsman, Confederate States Navy. Peadon was born in Johnston County, North Carolina, about 1835, the son of William and Celia Peadon, of Guilford County, North Carolina. He enlisted in the Confederate States Navy on October 10 [11or 12], 1863 at Camp Holmes] 1863, in Wilmington, North Carolina. His brother Henry Peadon,

q.v., also served in the Confederate States Navy. Peadon resided as a farmer, in 1860, with his wife, Polly Capps Peadon, and daughter, Celia, in Guilford County, North Carolina. He served as a Landsman aboard the CSS NORTH CAROLINA, Cape Fear River, North Carolina, 1864.
[Source(s): Foenander; Census (North Carolina), 1850 and 1860; MR, 4, p. 446; Card File; NA RG 45]

Peel, William R. (Gates County, North Carolina)
Private, Confederate States Army//Confederate States Navy. Peel was born in Gates County, North Carolina, where he resided as a carpenter prior to enlisting there at age 33 on February 27, 1862, as a Private in Company C, 52nd Regiment, North Carolina Troops. Reported present on surviving company muster rolls through February 1864, he transferred to the Confederate States Navy on April 1, 1864.
[Source(s): Card File; North Carolina Troops, XII; Foenander]

Peeling [Pealing, Peling], Alonzo (Rowan County, North Carolina)
Private, Confederate States Army / Ordinary Seaman, Confederate States Navy. Peeling enlisted in Rowan County, North Carolina, on July 7, 1862, as a Private in Company K, 57th Regiment, North Carolina Troops. He was wounded at Fredericksburg, Virginia, on December 13, 1862, was hospitalized in Richmond, Virginia, and returned to duty on or about February 28, 1863. He enlisted in the Confederate States Navy on April 11, 1864, in Kinston, North Carolina for "three years or the war." Records indicate he transferred to steamer Neuse" [CSS NEUSE] prior to May 1, 1864. Records indicate he was aboard the CSS NEUSE as of the ship's March – October 1864 muster rolls.
[Source(s): Foenander; North Carolina Troops XIV; Hill; CR; Card File; NA RG 45; NEUSE Roster; CMACSSN]

Pence, John H.
Ordinary Seaman, Confederate States Navy. Pence enlisted on June 8, 1863, in Wilmington, North Carolina for the war and served aboard the CSS NORTH CAROLINA, Cape Fear River, North Carolina, 1864.
[Source(s): Card File; NA RG 45; Foenander]

Pengillay [Pengally], John [H.] (New Hanover County, North Carolina)
Ship's Cook, Confederate States Navy. Pengillay enlisted in the Confederate States Navy in Wilmington, North Carolina. He served aboard the CSS CASWELL, and on the Wilmington Station, North Carolina, 1861 – 1862, and as a Ship's Cook on the CSS ARCTIC, 1862. His name appears on a register of Confederate States Army General Military Hospital Number 4, Wilmington, North Carolina, dated July 19, 1862 diagnosed with "bubo sippiliticum." His post office was given as Wilmington, North Carolina. He returned to duty on August 11, 1862.
[Source(s): MR, 4, p. 447; Card File; NA RG 109; Foenander]

Penny, Benjamin F. (Brunswick County, North Carolina)
Musician (Drummer), Confederate States Army//Landsman, Confederate States Navy. Penny was born in North Carolina about 1845, the son of William and Elizabeth Penny. He resided in Brunswick County, North Carolina, and enlisted at Camp Howard, North Carolina, on July 18, 1861, as a Musician (Drummer), in Company C, 30th Regiment, North Carolina Troops. Penny was reported absent without leave in December 1862 but returned to duty prior to July 1, 1863. He transferred to the Confederate States Navy on September 3, 1863 where he served as a Landsman aboard the CSS CHICORA, 1863-1864, and later aboard the CSS NORTH CAROLINA, 1864. He married about 1868, and was listed as residing as a dry goods merchant, in 1900, with his wife, Mary F. Penny, and four children, in Wilmington, North Carolina. He died in February 1918 in Northampton County, North Carolina.
[Source(s): Card File; North Carolina Troops, VIII; Foenander]

Penny, John
Landsman, Confederate States Navy. Penny enlisted on February 4, 1864 in Raleigh "for the war" and served aboard the CSS ARCTIC, Cape Fear River, North Carolina, 1863.
[Source(s): Card File; Foenander]

Pepper, Joseph H. [A.?] (New Hanover County, North Carolina)
Landsman [Private], Confederate States Navy [Naval Battalion]. Pepper was born in North Carolina in January 1845 and enlisted on November 18, 1863, in Wilmington, North Carolina for the war. He served in the Confederate States Navy as a Landsman aboard the CSS ARCTIC, Cape Fear River, North Carolina, 1863. His name appears on a roll of Prisoners of War at Point Lookout, Maryland, which states that he was captured April 6, 1865, at High Bridge [Virginia] and released on June 17, 1865. His name appears on an Oath of Allegiance to the United States subscribed and sworn to at Point Lookout, Maryland, June 17, 1865 on which his place of residence was given as Wilmington, North Carolina and his description as follows: Complexion, fair; hair, brown; eyes, hazel; height, 5 feet

10 ½ inches. Pepper married in 1870 and resided as a pilot with his wife Ann and son, Elijah, at Federal Point, New Hanover County, North Carolina. He was residing as a fisherman in 1900 with his family in Masonboro Township, New Hanover County, North Carolina. His June 5, 1909 application for pension, age 65, from Wilmington, states he served in the Navy under Captain Poindexter in 1863, served at Drewry's Bluff, Virginia, was captured at Drewry's' Bluff in 1865, and was taken to Point Lookout, Maryland where he was held "until [sic] the surrender." James W. Craig (q.v.) served as a witness on behalf of Pepper's application which was approved at 4th class. Widow's application by Ann E. Pepper, June 19, 1913, age 64, of Wilmington, states he died on September 2, 1913.
[Source(s): Card File; NA RG 45; NA RG 109; Pensions (North Carolina); Foenander]

Pepper, J. N. (New Hanover County, North Carolina)
Confederate States Navy. Pepper filed a pension claim on June 15, 1909, age 65 years, post office Wilmington, New Hanover County, North Carolina which states he served under Captain Poindexter. It was approved at 4th Class. A claim was filed on June 19, 1913 by his widow, Ann E. Pepper, age 64 years, post office Wilmington, New Hanover County, North Carolina wherein she states her husband died on September 2, 1913. The claim was approved.
[Source(s): Card File; Pensions (North Carolina)]

Perkins, John J. (Gaston County, North Carolina)
Private, Confederate States Army//Confederate States Navy. Perkins resided in Gaston County, North Carolina, where he enlisted on July 30, 1861, at age 22, as a Private in Company D (Source *North Carolina Troops* indicates Company B), 28th Regiment, North Carolina Troops. He was present or accounted for until his desertion on April 27, 1863. He returned to duty on an unspecified date and transferred to the Confederate States Navy on April 3, 1864, possibly by authority of S.O. # 89.
[Source(s): North Carolina Troops, VIII; Army to Navy; Card File; Foenander; Cloninger]

Perry, Elisha R. (Perquimans County, North Carolina)
Private, Confederate States Army//Confederate States Navy. Perry was born in Perquimans County, North Carolina, where he resided as a farmer prior to enlisting there at age 25, on May 8, 1861, as a Private in Company I, 17th Regiment, North Carolina Troops (1st Organization). He was present or accounted for until reportedly transferred to the Confederate States Navy prior to July 30, 1861. However, records of the Federal Provost Marshal indicate he was captured at Roanoke Island on February 8, 1862, and paroled at Elizabeth City, North Carolina, on February 21, 1862. He was exchanged in August 1862. No further military records were found. He resided as a farmer in 1870 with his wife Mary A. Perry, and three children, at Hertford Township, Perquimans County, North Carolina.
[Source(s): Card File; North Carolina Troops, VI; Foenander]

Peters, _____ [North Carolina (?)]
Confederate States Navy. Peter's name appears as overseeing the Confederate States Naval Store located at the corner of East Trade St. and South College St, Charlotte, North Carolina.
[Source(s): McElroy; Card File]

Peters, James A.
Midshipman, Confederate States Navy.
Peters served aboard the CSS ELLIS as a Midshipman per an entry in that ship's logbook dated November 2, 1861. Per payroll records, he served aboard the CSS ELLIS from January - May 1862. He is on the rolls of the CSS SEA BIRD as a Midshipman as of February 1862. Captured in the Battle of Elizabeth City, he was carried to Roanoke Island on February 10, 1862 where he was paroled on February 12, 1862 and returned to Elizabeth City, North Carolina.
[Source: NCCWSP]

Peterson, Fleet (New Hanover County, North Carolina)
Ordinary Seaman, Confederate States Navy. Born in North Carolina in 1833, Peterson lived as a farm laborer in the Little Coharie District, Sampson County, North Carolina, in 1860, with his wife, Matilda, and two daughters. He enlisted in the Confederate States Navy on August 23, 1863 [or September 5, 1863] in Wilmington, North Carolina, and served aboard the CSS ARCTIC, 1863.
[Source(s): MR, 4, p. 447; Card File; NA RG 45; Foenander; St. Armand; Census (North Carolina), 1860]

Peterson [Petterson], William H. (New York//Craven County, North Carolina)
Private, Confederate States Army//Confederate States Navy. Born in Rockland County, New York, Peterson was a dentist when he enlisted on May 14, 1862 for twelve months in Craven County, North Carolina, in Company I, 41st

Regiment, North Carolina Troops (3rd North Carolina Cavalry). He transferred to the Confederate States Navy on December 26, 1863. A "W. M. Petterson" served aboard the CSS NEUSE as of the ship's March – April 1864 muster roll.
[Source(s): Card File; North Carolina Troops, II; Foenander]

Pevie, Levie (Leir) (New Hanover County, North Carolina)
Private, Confederate States Army//Confederate States Navy. Pevie enlisted in New Hanover County, North Carolina at age 18 on April 16, 1861 in 2nd Company H, 40th Regiment, North Carolina Troops (3rd North Carolina Artillery) for the war. He was present or accounted for until transferred to the Confederate States Navy on August 10, 1863.
[Source(s): Card File; North Carolina Troops, I; Foenander]

Phelps, Amariah (Amory, Amari, Amri) (Washington County, North Carolina)
Private, Confederate States Navy [Company A, Confederate States Naval Battalion]. Prisoner of War records indicate he was captured at Sailor's Creek or Amelia Court House on April 6, 1865 and confined at Point Lookout, Maryland, until released on taking the Oath of Allegiance to the United States on June 17, 1865. His place of residence was listed on the Oath as Washington County, North Carolina, and his description as follows: Complexion, fair; hair, brown; eyes, grey; height, 5 feet 6 ½ inches.
[Source(s): WCL; Card File; NA RG 109; Darden]

Phelps, John (Washington County, North Carolina)
Confederate States Navy.
[Source(s): WCL; Darden]

**Phelps, Timothy (Brunswick County, North Carolina)
Corporal, Company, Coast Guards [SEE NOTE #2]. Phelps worked as a fisherman until his enlistment on January 24, 1862.
[Source(s): Edge]

Phillips, B. C.
Confederate States Navy. Phillips may have served in the Confederate States Navy. His widow, Martitia M. Waddill (who later married Confederate States Navy veteran, Edmund Waddill), applied for a post war Confederate pension from Moore County, North Carolina.
[Source(s): Foenander]

Phillips, John
Pilot, Confederate States Navy.
Phillips served as a Pilot aboard the CSS RALEIGH from at least January 1, 1862 – March 1, 1862 per a payroll covering the 1st quarter of 1862.
[Source: NCCWSP]

Phillips, John C.
3rd Assistant Engineer, Confederate States Navy. Phillips was born in and appointed from North Carolina as a Third Assistant Engineer on June 20, 1863. He served aboard the CSS GEORGIA, Savannah Squadron, 1863-1864. Phillips was detached on April 30 [20], 1864 and ordered to report to Flag Officer J. R. Tucker, at Charleston Station, 1864-1865. He was appointed a Third Assistant Engineer, Provisional Navy, on June 2, 1864. Phillips was paroled in Greensboro, North Carolina on April 28, 1865.
[Source(s): Register; McElroy; Card File; Foenander; ONWR]

Phillips, John W.
Quartermaster, Confederate States Navy.
Phillips was promoted to Quartermaster, on December 17, 1862 and served in that capacity aboard the CSS SEA BIRD as early as February 1862. He was captured in the Battle of Elizabeth City and carried to Roanoke Island on February 10, 1862 where he was paroled on February 12, 1862 and returned to Elizabeth City, North Carolina. He a partial payment on February 18, 1862 at Gosport Navy Yard following the sinking of the SEA BIRD at Elizabeth City on February 10, 1862. His name appears on the North Carolina Squadron payroll for the 1st quarter of 1862 (December 16, 1861 - April 15, 1862). He is listed as "on parole" per a payroll dated April 15, 1862. Phillips transferred to the James River Squadron on April 15, 1862.
[Source: NCCWSP]

Phipps, W. H.
    Seaman, Quartermaster, Confederate States Navy. Phipps enlisted on November 14, 1863, in Wilmington, North Carolina, for the war, and served aboard the CSS ARCTIC, Cape Fear River, North Carolina, 1863. He later served as a crew member aboard the CSS BOMBSHELL and was captured aboard that vessel during the engagement in Albemarle Sound, North Carolina, on May 5, 1864. He was transferred the same day from the USS CERES to the USS SASSACUS, then to the steamer USS LOCKWOOD, on May 10, 1864, for transportation to a prisoner of war facility. Source "Foenander" lists a "William H. Phillips" as serving as a Landsman aboard the CSS ARCTIC, Cape Fear River, North Carolina, 1863. He also served as a Quartermaster aboard the CSS RALEIGH in North Carolina and Virginia waters, 1864. Phillips may be the same person as W. H. Phipps.
    [Source(s): Card File; NA RG 45; Foenander]

Pickett, Thomas J. (Orange County, North Carolina)
    Private, Confederate States Army//Confederate States Navy. Pickett resided in Orange County, North Carolina, where he enlisted at age 22 on September 10, 1861 for the war in Company K, 19th Regiment, North Carolina Troops (2nd North Carolina Cavalry). He was present or accounted for until he transferred to the Confederate States Navy on May 21, 1864.
    [Source(s): Card File; North Carolina Troops, II; Foenander]

Pickney (Pinkney), Roger (Hodge) (Richmond County, North Carolina)
    Confederate States Navy. Pickney served as a Midshipman in the Confederate States Navy.
    [Source(s): McElroy; Card File]

Pierce, E. E. (Pender County, North Carolina)
    Carpenter's Mate, Confederate States Navy. A pension claim filed on July 1, 1901 by Pierce's widow Sarah Pierce, age 75 years, post office Burgaw, Pender County, North Carolina, was approved. It states he enlisted in the spring of 1862 and served as a carpenter in the Confederate States Navy. It further states that he died "about 25 years ago."
    [Source(s): Card File; Pensions (North Carolina); Foenander]

Pierce, Frederick [F. S.] (Halifax County, North Carolina)
    Landsman, Confederate States Navy. Pierce was conscripted on March 29, 1864, at Camp Holmes [near Raleigh, North Carolina] from Colonel Johnston's 34th Regiment, North Carolina Militia, Halifax County, North Carolina. Another source says he "enlisted" March 30, 1864, in Raleigh. His description was given as follows: Age, 23; eyes, black; hair, dark; complexion, fair; height, 5 feet 7 ½ inches; place of birth, Halifax County, North Carolina; occupation farmer.
    [Source(s): Card File; NA RG 45]

Pierce, John (Wake County, North Carolina)
    Private, Confederate States Army//Confederate States Navy. Born in Wake County, North Carolina, Pierce resided in Moore County, North Carolina, as a farmer prior to enlisting there at age 44 as a Private on March 11, 1862 in Company H, 46th Regiment, North Carolina Troops. He was present or accounted for until transferred to the Confederate States Navy on April 1, 1864.
    [Source(s): Card File; North Carolina Troops, XI; Foenander]

Pierce, Richard (Hertford County, North Carolina)
    Private, Confederate States Army//Confederate States Navy (?). Residing in Hertford County, North Carolina, Pierce enlisted at age 18 on September 12, 1861 as a Private in Company G, 31st Regiment, North Carolina Troops. He was captured at Roanoke Island, North Carolina, on February 8, 1862, and paroled at Elizabeth City on February 21, 1862. He returned to duty prior to May 14, 1863. Pierce was hospitalized in Richmond, Virginia, on May 14, 1864, with a gunshot wound to the larynx received on a date and at a place unknown and died there on May 16, 1864. Source Card File claims Pierce had Confederate Naval service.
    [Source(s): Card File; North Carolina Troops, VIII]

Pierce (Pearce), Sylvester (Johnston County, North Carolina)
    Landsman, Confederate States Navy. Born in North Carolina in 1818, Pierce enlisted as a Landsman, in the Confederate States Navy on 21, 24, or 26 October 1863 in Wilmington, North Carolina and served aboard the CSS ARCTIC, Cape Fear River, North Carolina, 1863. His name appears on a register of Confederate States Army General Military Hospital, No.4, Wilmington, North Carolina, as being admitted on November 22, 1863, with "debilitas" and returned to duty February 3, 1864. His post office was given on the register as Boon Hill [now

Princeton], North Carolina. He resided as a farmer in 1880 with his wife, at Boon Hill, Johnston County, North Carolina.
[Source(s): MR, 4, p. 446; Card File; NA RG 45; North Carolina RG 109; Foenander]

Pigford, J. E. (New Hanover County, North Carolina)
Landsman, Confederate States Navy. Pigford enlisted on November 3, 1863 in Wilmington, North Carolina, for the war (per source "MR" he enlisted in the Confederate States Navy on October 27, 1863, in Wilmington, North Carolina) and served aboard the CSS ARCTIC, 1863.
[Source(s): Card File; NA RG 45; MR, 4, p. 446; Pensions (North Carolina); Foenander; St. Armand]

Pigford, William J. (New Hanover County, North Carolina)
Private, Confederate States Army// Confederate States Navy (?) [Detailed to Confederate Shipyard]. Pigford enlisted in New Hanover County, North Carolina, for twelve months on April 16, 1861 in 2nd Company C, 36th Regiment, North Carolina Troops (2nd Regiment, North Carolina Artillery). He was detailed on special duty to the "C. S. Ship Yard, Wilmington, April 24, 1862." Pigford was reported absent detailed when transferred to Company C, 13th Battalion, North Carolina Light Artillery on November 4, 1863.
[Source(s): North Carolina Troops, I]

Piner, Lawrence M. (New Hanover County, North Carolina)
Private, Confederate States Army//Confederate States Navy (?). Source "Card File" lists Confederate Naval service. Source "North Carolina Troops, IV" states he was born in New Hanover County, North Carolina, where he resided as a mechanic prior to enlisting there at age 23 on June 22, 1861, for the war, in Company C, 8th Regiment, North Carolina Troops. Captured at Roanoke Island on February 8, 1862, and paroled at Elizabeth City on February 21, 1862, he was exchanged in August 1862. He is listed as present or accounted for until transferred to the Engineer Corps on or about June 24, 1863. Source "Card File" indicates naval service.
[Source(s): Card File; North Carolina Troops, IV]

Pinkney, R[obert] F.
Commander, Confederate States Navy. Commander of the Inland Waters of North Carolina, April 30, 1864. Pinkney also served as commander of the fleet at New Orleans and abroad the CSS SAVANNAH. An "R. F. Pinkney" served aboard the CSS NEUSE as of the ship's March - October 1864 muster roll.
[Source(s): McElroy; CR, V, p .296; CW North Carolina, III, p.153; IV, p.50; VI, p.234 and 298; Hill; Card File; NEUSE Roster; CMACSSN]

Pipkin, Isaac (Craven County, North Carolina)
Private, Confederate States Army//Confederate States Navy(?). Residing in Craven County, North Carolina, Pipkin enlisted there at age 18 on November 21, 1861, as a Private in Company K, 31st Regiment, North Carolina Troops. Captured at Roanoke Island, North Carolina, on February 8, 1862, he was paroled at Elizabeth City on February 21, 1862 and returned to duty on or about September 15, 1862. After suffering a gunshot fracture of the left arm, Pipkin was hospitalized in Richmond, Virginia, on May 17, 1864. The date and place of the wound are unknown. He is listed as having deserted on or about August 15, 1864. Source Card File or "NA RG 45" lists him as having enlisted in the Confederate States Navy on October 29, 1863, at Camp Holmes [near Raleigh, North Carolina].
[Source(s): Card File; NA RG 45; North Carolina Troops, VIII]

Pitchford, J.
Landsman, Confederate States Navy. Pitchford enlisted on June 6, 1864 in Raleigh, North Carolina, for the war.
[Source(s): Card File; NA RG 45]

Pitchford, Samuel "Sam" W. (Warren County, North Carolina)
Confederate States Navy. Born in North Carolina in 1847, Pitchford served in the Confederate States Navy. He resided as a farmer in 1880 with his wife Emma, and three children (eldest child born 1870) at Fork, Warren County, North Carolina. His widow, Emma Pitchford, applied for a North Carolina Confederate pension from Littleton, Warren County, North Carolina, on July 6, 1925, at age 76. The pension was initially denied but approved at 4th class after a clerk annotated the pension application with the word "Navy." Deponent Richard Harris states Pitchford was "sworn into the Confederate Army [sic] at Raleigh" in 1864 when his father was a member of the North Carolina State Legislature. Pitchford died on July 15, 1923 at 76 years of age.
[Source(s): McCaslin, p.54 and 370; Pensions (North Carolina); Foenander]

Pitman, J. W.
Landsman, Confederate States Navy. Pittman enlisted on January 11, 1864 in Raleigh, North Carolina, for the war; however, his name was cancelled on the roll with the remark: "Deserted from camp."
[Source(s): Card File; NA RG 45]

Pitman, Sion
Landsman, Confederate States Navy. Pitman enlisted on February 23, 1864 in Raleigh, for the war.
[Source(s): Card File; NA RG 45]

Pitman, Stephen
Landsman, Confederate States Navy. Pitman enlisted on February 23, 1864 in Raleigh, North Carolina, for the war and served aboard the CSS ARCTIC, Cape Fear River, North Carolina, 1863.
[Source(s): Card File; NA RG 45; Foenander]

Pittman, F. W.
Seaman, Confederate States Navy. Pittman enlisted on April 12, 1864 in Kinston, North Carolina for three years or the war. He served aboard the CSS NEUSE as of the ship's March – October 1864 muster roll.
[Source(s): Card File; NA RG 45; NEUSE Roster; CMACSSN]

Pittman, Randolph (Robeson County, North Carolina [?])
Corporal, Confederate States Army//Confederate States Navy (?). Pittman served as a Private, 1st Company D, 12th Regiment, North Carolina Troops (2nd Regiment, North Carolina Volunteers). He enlisted in Company K, 10th Regiment, North Carolina Troops (1st Regiment, North Carolina Artillery) in Robeson County, North Carolina, on February 28, 1862 and mustered in as a Corporal. Present or accounted for through April 1863, he was reported absent on detached service at Wilmington (probably with the Confederate States Navy) from May 1863 through February 1864. Rejoining the company in March-April 1864, he was present or accounted for until wounded in the right leg at Drewry's Bluff, Virginia on May 16, 1864. Hospitalized in Richmond, Virginia, he was furloughed for sixty days on June 8, 1864 and returned to duty in November-December 1864. Pittman was present or accounted for through December 1864.
[Source(s): www.freepages.military.rootsweb.com/.../index2.htm]

Pitts, John
Seaman, Confederate States Navy. Pitts enlisted on December 9, 1862 in Wilmington, North Carolina, for three years or the war and served aboard the CSS ARCTIC, Cape Fear River, North Carolina, 1863.
[Source(s): Card File; NA RG 45; Foenander]

Piver, J. L.
Seaman, Landsman, Confederate States Navy.
Piver's name appears on the Curlew payroll list of the CSS CURLEW dated November 20, 1861. On the ship's payroll for the 1st quarter of 1862, Piver is listed as a Landsman aboard the CSS CURLEW. Landsman, Curlew [Payroll list, 1st quarter 1862. His name appears on the payroll list of the receiving ship CSS UNITED STATES ending March 31, 1862.
[Source: NCCWSP]

Plana (Plane), Thomas
Purser, Blockade Runner (probably Civilian). Per source "WDJ" (September 20, 1864), Plana served as the Purser of the steamer "*Let Her Rip*." He died in Bermuda in August 1864 of yellow fever at the age of 33. He was an officer on said blockade runner.
[Source(s): "WDJ" (Sept. 20, 1864)]

Platt(e), Samuel P. (Brunswick County, North Carolina)
Confederate States Navy. Platte was born in North Carolina in 1839, the son of William and Margaret Platt. He was a resident of Smithville District, Brunswick County, North Carolina, where he worked as a mariner. He served as pilot aboard the CSS ARCTIC, 1863. In 1870, he resided as a steamboat captain in Wilmington, North Carolina, with his wife Josephine, and two children. He enlisted in the Confederate States Navy in Wilmington, North Carolina.
[Source(s): MR, 4, p. 447; Foenander]

Plyler [Plyer], Tobias A. (Stanly County, North Carolina)
Landsman, Seaman, Confederate States Navy. Born about 1823, Plyler lived in Stanly County, North Carolina, as a farmer with his wife Mary, age 45, and seven children, ages 2 – 18; real estate value: $4,000. He enlisted on September 22, 1863 [another source gives the date as August 24, 1863 in Wilmington, North Carolina, for the war. Another source states he enlisted on September 11, 1863, at Camp Holmes [near Raleigh, North Carolina]. Plyler served as a Seaman aboard the CSS ARCTIC 1864 and the CSS NEUSE, March - October1864. He transferred [one source says "Exchanged from C.S. Navy"] as a Private sometime between September-October 1864 to Company C, 13th Battalion, Light Artillery [Another source says he also served in 1st Company C, 36th Regiment, North Carolina Troops (2nd North Carolina Artillery), but he does not appear in source North Carolina Troops, I]. He was present or accounted for through February 1865 and paroled at Greensboro on May 1, 1865. He was 41 years old in 1864.
[Source(s): Card File; NA RG 45; NA RG 109; MR, IV; Census (North Carolina), 1860; Hill; North Carolina Troops, I; Foenander; NEUSE Roster; CMACSSN]

Poe, Harper [Possibly John Harper Poe] (Guilford County, North Carolina).
Private, Confederate States Army//Landsman, CSS DREWRY. Per source "NCT," Poe enlisted at age 22 on February 22, 1862 in Company E, 23rd Regiment, North Carolina Troops. He was wounded at or near Gaines Mill, Virginia on or about June 27, 1862 and returned to duty on June 30, 1862. He was reported on duty as a nurse at a hospital in Richmond, Virginia for the pay period January-February 1863. Back in his regiment, Poe was again wounded at Chancellorsville between May 1 – 3, 1863. He was court-martialed on or about September 10, 1863 for some unreported reason. No further Army records were found. However, from a document dated July 28, 1864 from source www.history.navy.mil/library/manuscript/confed.htm, a "Harper Poe," Landsman aboard the CSS DREWRY, allotted $8.00 of his monthly pay to his wife Elizabeth Poe. There is some question as to whether the Army and Navy "Harper Poes" are the same man. The Guilford County "Harper Poe" born on May 28, 1841 and died on May 14, 1927 at the age of 85. He was buried at Salem Cemetery, Winston-Salem, North Carolina.
[Source: http://www.history.navy.mil/library/manuscript/confed.htm; Vol. VII, NCT; find-a-grave.com; http://www.poegen.net/Images/Harper Poe_CSSdrewry.jpg]

Poindexter, C. B.
First Lieutenant, Confederate States Navy. Poindexter served aboard the CSS ARCTIC, a floating battery with three guns on the Cape Fear River under Flag Officer W. F. Lynch.
[Source(s): Card File; McElroy]

Poiner (Poyner), E. D. (Currituck County, North Carolina)
Seaman, Confederate States Navy. Born in North Carolina circa 1832, Poiner lived in the Coinjock District of Currituck County, North Carolina in 1860. He shipped for a year aboard the CSS RALEIGH on September 8, 1861 and served through April 1862. His name appears on a payroll of the North Carolina Squadron covering the period February 21, 1862 through April 15, 1862, on which date he was transferred to the James River Squadron.
[Sources: Census (NC), 1860; NCCWSP]

Pool, Joseph C.
Landsman, Confederate States Navy. Pool enlisted on May 11, 1864 in Raleigh, North Carolina, for the war.
[Source(s): Card File; NA RG 45]

Poole, Henry
Landsman, Confederate States Navy. Poole enlisted on April 7, 1863 in Wilmington, North Carolina, for three years or the war.
[Source(s): Card File; NA RG 45]

Poole, Luke (Currituck County, North Carolina)
Landsman, Confederate States Navy. Poole was born in North Carolina and lived in the Coinjock District of Currituck County, North Carolina in1860. He appears as a Landsman serving aboard the CSS FANNY from October 8, 1861 through December 20, 1861. He appears on a payroll of the North Carolina Squadron covering the period from December 1, 1861 through February 28, 1862, on which he is listed as having "run" by the end of the period.
[Sources: NCCWSP; Census (NC), 1860]

Pope, W. H. (Cumberland County, North Carolina) [NOTE: May be same as "William H. Pope," q.v.]
Confederate States Navy. Pope served aboard the CSS NORTH CAROLINA.
[Source(s): MR, IV, p. 444; Oates]

Pope, William H. [NOTE: May be same as "W. H. Pope," q.v.]
Seaman, Confederate States Navy. Pope enlisted on June 5, 1863 in Wilmington, North Carolina, for the war.
[Source(s): Card File; NA RG 45; MR, 4, p. 444]

Porter, Charles E.
Confederate States Navy. Porter enlisted in the Confederate States Navy in Wilmington, North Carolina. He served aboard the CSS NEUSE as of the ship's March – October 1864 muster rolls.
[Source(s): MR, 4, p. 447; NEUSE Roster; CMACSSN]

Porter, John L.
Chief Constructor, Confederate States Navy. Porter prepared the plans and specifications of the "Ram ALBEMARLE."
[Source(s): Card File]

Portlocke, Anthony
Seaman, Confederate States Navy.
Portlocke served as a Seaman aboard the CSS JUNALUSKA per that ship's muster roll and a payroll for June 18, 1861 - August 20, 1861.
[Source: NCCWSP]

Potter, J. W.
Pilot, Confederate States Navy. Potter served aboard the blockade runner "*Beauregard*."
[Source(s): Card File; McElroy]

Potter, Richard (Perquimans County, North Carolina)
Private, Confederate States Army//Confederate States Navy. Born in Perquimans County, North Carolina, Potter resided there as a farmer where he enlisted at age 21 on May 20, 1861 as a Private in Company I, 17th Regiment, North Carolina Troops (1st Organization). Company records indicate he was transferred to the Confederate States Navy prior to July 30, 1861; however, records of the Federal Provost Marshal indicate he was captured at Roanoke Island on February 8, 1862, and paroled at Elizabeth City, North Carolina, on February 11, 1862. No further records.
[Source(s): Card File; North Carolina Troops, VI; Foenander]

Potter, Samuel (New Hanover County, North Carolina)
Confederate States Navy. Potter was a crew member on the privateer "*Mariner*" under command of Captain Benjamin Washington Beery, circa 1861.
[Source(s): Card file of "Benjamin Washington Beery;" *Oakdale*, Davis]

Poulson, G. B.
Hospital Steward, Confederate States Navy.
Poulson's name appears on the North Carolina Squadron payroll for the 1st quarter of 1862 (September 25, 1861 - January 20, 1862).
[Source: NCCWSP]

Powell, Daniel
Officer's Cook, Confederate States Navy.
Powell served as an Officer's Cook aboard the CSS RALEIGH from at least December 4, 1861 - 1st quarter 1862 as a member of the North Carolina Squadron.
[Source: NCCWSP]

Powell, William
Ordinary Seaman, Confederate States Navy. Per "Moore's Roster," Powell enlisted in the Confederate States Navy in Wilmington, North Carolina. He served aboard the CSS ARCTIC, 1863. Source "Driver" states he "may have served in a North Carolina regiment," and that he served in Company A, Naval Brigade. He was captured at High Bridge, April 6, 1865, and sent to Point Lookout, Maryland, where he was released on April 16, 1865. His description was as follows: 5'7" in height; fair complexion; light hair; blue eyes; residence, Nansemond County, Virginia." [NOTE: May not have been a North Carolinian] [Source(s): MR, 4, p. 447; Driver; Foenander; St. Armand]

Powell, William H. (Hertford County, North Carolina)
"Sailor," Confederate States Navy (?).
Powell died in Wilmington, North Carolina at age 22 of typhoid fever on August 7, 1862. He was buried in the Confederate Section, Oakwood Cemetery, Raleigh, North Carolina.
[Source: Oakwood]

Powell, William John
Ordinary Seaman, Confederate States Navy.
Powell served aboard the CSS JUNALUSKA per a muster roll and her payroll for June 15, 1861 - August 20, 1861.
[Source: NCCWSP]

Powers, Cornelius (Currituck County, North Carolina)
Private, Confederate States Army//Confederate States Navy. Powers was born and lived in Currituck County, North Carolina, where he worked as a farmer and enlisted as a Private at age 23 on May 13, 1861, in Company E, 17th Regiment, North Carolina Troops (1st Organization). He was listed as present or accounted for until captured at Roanoke Island on February 8, 1862 and paroled at Elizabeth City on February 21, 1862. He was present or accounted for until the company was disbanded on or about April 2, 1862. Source Card File states he had Confederate Navy service.
[Source(s): Card File; North Carolina Troops, VI]

Powers, William Riley (Buncombe County, North Carolina)
Private, Confederate States Army//Seaman [Landsman], Confederate States Navy. Born, resided as a farmer, and enlisted in Buncombe County, North Carolina, at age 21 on May 3, 1861 [Source MR, I gives the date as May 4, 1861] under Zebulon Vance as a Private in what became Company F ("Rough and Ready Guards"), 14th Regiment, North Carolina Troops. Present or accounted for until he transferred to the Confederate States Navy on February 18, 1862 by order of Gen. Benjamin Huger to serve as a Landsman aboard the CSS VIRGINIA ("MERRIMACK"). He received a wound on his head during the battle between the CSS VIRGINIA and the USS MONITOR. One source indicates he was aboard her "when she sank." He drew a pension from the state of North Carolina. Daughter: Mrs. J.P. West, Skyland, North Carolina.
[Source(s): McElroy; Card File, Pensions (North Carolina); Howard; North Carolina Troops, V; Foenander; MR, I; ORN 2, 1, 309]

Pratt, William (Charleston, SC)
Private, Confederate States Army//Gunner's mate, Confederate States Navy. Pratt was a resident of South Carolina where he worked as a Seaman until his enlistment at age 38 on August 4, 1861, in New Hanover County, North Carolina, in Company C, 8th Regiment, North Carolina State Troops. Captured at Roanoke Island, North Carolina, on February 8, 1862, and paroled at Elizabeth City, North Carolina, on February 21, 1862, he was exchanged in August 1862. He was present or accounted for until transferred to the Confederate States Navy on or about May 24, 1864 where he served as Gunner's Mate aboard the CSS ALBEMARLE and at Halifax Station, 1864.
[Source(s): Card File; North Carolina Troops, IV; Foenander]

Preddy [Priddy], Alexander A. (Granville County, North Carolina)
Private, Confederate States Army//Confederate States Navy. Preddy resided in Granville County, North Carolina, where he enlisted at age 37 on February 16, 1863, for the war, as a Private in Company G, 47th Regiment, North Carolina Troops. Reported present or accounted for in January-March 1864, he was transferred to the Confederate States Navy on April 3, 1864 and served aboard the CSS COLUMBIA and another Confederate States Navy ship in 1864. Preddy was a relative of source "Kearney."
[Source(s): Kearney; Army to Navy; S.O. # 89; North Carolina Troops, XI; Card File; Foenander]

Price, B. T.
Ordinary Seaman, Confederate States Navy. Price enlisted on June 20, 1863 in Wilmington, North Carolina, for the war.
[Source(s): Card File; NA RG 45]

Price, F. D. (Brunswick County, North Carolina)
Confederate States Navy. Price enlisted in the Confederate States Navy on April 15, 1864. His pension application filed on July 5, 1909 at age 64 years, listed his post office as Southport, Brunswick County, North Carolina was approved at 4th Class.
[Source(s): Card File; NA RG 45; Pensions (North Carolina)]

Price, Fred J. (Rutherford County, North Carolina)
Confederate States Navy. Price was born in North Carolina about 1825. In 1860, he resided at Flint Hill, Rutherford County, North Carolina, where he enlisted on July 10, 1862, for the war, at age 35 in Company I, 56th Regiment, North Carolina Troops. Source "North Carolina Troops" states he was present through December 1864 and was captured at Five Forks, Virginia, April 1, 1865. He was confined at Point Lookout, Maryland, April 6, 1865, and released on June 16, 1865, after taking the Oath of Allegiance. He is said to have served in the Confederate States Navy. He applied for a Confederate pension from Rutherford County, North Carolina, though his pension application is marked "Navy," it makes no mention of service in the Navy, only in Company I, 56th Regiment, North Carolina Troops.
[Source(s): Pensions (North Carolina); North Carolina Troops, XIII; Foenander]

Price, James
Ship's Cook, Confederate States Navy.
Source NCCWSP gives his date of enlistment as August 17, 1861. He served as a Ship's Cook aboard the CSS RALEIGH in North Carolina waters from September 2, 1862 – April 1864. His name appears on a North Carolina Squadron payroll covering February 21, 1862 - April 15, 1862. Price was transferred to the James River Squadron on April 15, 1862 and served at Drewry's Bluff as a Ship's Cook (April 1, 1863 - June 30, 1863). Payroll records indicate Pugh served as a Ship's Cook aboard the CSS RALEIGH in the James River Squadron (November 16, 1863 - December 15, 1863].
[Source(s): Card File; North Carolina Troops, III; Foenander; NCCWSP]

Price, J. B.
Landsman, Confederate States Navy. Price enlisted on April 12, 1864 in Kinston, North Carolina, for three years or the war. He served aboard the CSS NEUSE as of the ship's March – October 1864 muster rolls.
[Source(s): Card File; NA RG 45; NEUSE Roster; CMACSSN]

Price, Joseph H. (Duplin County, North Carolina)
First Lieutenant, Confederate States Army//Commander] [Captain?], Confederate States Navy. Price was born in Duplin County, North Carolina, October 26, 1835, but was reared from infancy in Wilmington, North Carolina. He enlisted in 1854 and served for five years as a Second Lieutenant in the United States Revenue Marine Service aboard the cutter JOSEPH LANE with service in the Pacific. Price resigned his commission in the United States service at the outbreak of war, April 1861, and enlisted at age 25 in 2nd Company H, 40th Regiment, North Carolina Troops (3rd Regiment, North Carolina Artillery) on April 16, 1861 for the war. Appointed First Lieutenant to rank from May 16, 1861 [?] [One source shows he served as a First Lieutenant, 2nd Regiment, North Carolina State Troops, which was an infantry regiment in the Army of Northern Virginia]. He resigned his commission on September 16, 1861 and returned to Wilmington. He commanded the schooner-rigged privateer "Retribution" [formerly the United States steamer USS UNCLE BEN (engines removed at Wilmington for other purposes)] out of Wilmington, North Carolina, for several months, making many successful trips. Appointed First Lieutenant Provisional Confederate Navy, June 2, 1864 to rank from January 6, 1864, and assigned to the gunboat CSS GEORGIA at Savannah, Georgia. As second in command [later first in command], Price took part in the June 4, 1864 capture of the United States Navy side-wheel gunboat USS WATER WITCH in Ossabow Sound, Georgia, as second–in-command. He took command of the expedition after the commander, Thomas Pelot, was killed. Price received a severe saber wound to the head during the action. He was appointed Commander, Provisional Navy on July 12, 1864 for gallant and meritorious conduct during the attack on the USS WATER WITCH. Further service included CSS GEORGIA, temporary command of the CSS SAMPSON (Savannah Squadron, 1863-1864) on August 29, 1864 [?], and the CSS NEUSE (as Commander, as of August 24, 1864 (Ellis), replacing Lt. Benjamin Loyall). He served under Commander R. F. Pinckney who was in command of inland waters in North Carolina. After the war he served for five years as conductor on the Wilmington and Manchester Railroad, then as an inspector of naval stores, and finally as Harbor Master in Wilmington. Price died at the age of 60 on May 15, 1895 at his home in the northwest corner of 7th and Princess Streets, Wilmington, North Carolina, and was buried in Oakdale Cemetery, Wilmington, North Carolina.
[Source(s): Ellis; Bright, et al; Register; McElroy; Wayne Carver; "Chronicles;" CR, V, p. 296; Hill; Card File; "Messenger," 5/16/1895; North Carolina Troops, I; *Oakdale*, Davis; Foenander; NEUSE Roster; ONWR; CMACSSN]

Price, William Crapon (Brunswick County(?), North Carolina)
Captain, Confederate States Navy ["North Carolina Navy" (see Stepp)]. Price was born in 1846, died in 1932, and was buried in Morse Cemetery near the yacht basin in Southport (formerly Smithville), North Carolina. His

headstone states he was a "Capt. in the Confederate Navy when 18 years of age," but there is no official record of this.
[Source(s): Ellis; Card File; Foenander; Gravestone Records, v. 6. P. 301; Stepp, "Burials;" St. Amand]

Price, William M. (Edgecombe County, North Carolina)
Private, Confederate States Army//Landsman, Confederate States Navy. Born in and resided as a carpenter or cabinetmaker in Edgecombe County, North Carolina, where he enlisted on May 8, 1861 [Source MR, I, lists the date as May 1st] at age 24, as a Private in Company G, 13th Regiment, North Carolina Troops. He was present or accounted for until he transferred to the Confederate States Navy on February 20, 1862 [Source MR, I, gives the date as February 4, 1862]. Price served as a Landsman on the CSS VIRGINIA, Hampton Roads, Virginia, 1862.
[Source(s): North Carolina Troops, V; Card File; ORN 2, 1, 309; Foenander; MR, I]

Prickett, J. H.
Landsman, Confederate States Navy. Prickett served aboard the CSS ARCTIC, Cape Fear River, North Carolina, 1863.
[Source(s): Foenander; *ORN* 2, 1, 278]

Pridgen, David (New Hanover County, North Carolina)
Landsman, Confederate States Navy. Pridgen enlisted in the Confederate States Navy on October 12, 1863, at Camp Holmes [near Raleigh, North Carolina] and served aboard the CSS NORTH CAROLINA. Another source states he enlisted on October 14, 1863 in Wilmington, North Carolina. He also served aboard the CSS ARCTIC, Wilmington Station, North Carolina, 1863 - 1864.
[Source(s): MR, 4, p. 444; Card File; NA RG 45; Foenander; St. Amand; *ORN* 2, 1, 276]

Pridgen, William E.
Landsman, Confederate States Navy. Pridgen enlisted on April 22, 1864 in Raleigh, North Carolina, for the war.
[Source(s): Card File; NA RG 45]

Priest, J. (Richmond County[?], North Carolina)
Confederate States Navy [Confederate States Naval Battalion]. Priest's name appears as a signature to an Oath of Allegiance to the United States subscribed and sworn to at Newport News, Virginia on June 26, 1865. His place of residence was given on the Oath as "Richland County, North Carolina" [probably "Richmond County"], and place of capture as Farmville, Virginia, April 6, 1865. His description was given as follows: Complexion, light; hair, grey; eyes, grey; height, 5 feet 5 inches.
[Source(s): Card File; NA RG 109]

Pritchet (Pritchard), Adam (Aaron per MR, I) (Washington County, North Carolina)
Private, Confederate States Army//Ordinary Seaman, Confederate States Navy. Pritchet resided in Washington County, North Carolina where he enlisted as a Private at age 25 on June 24, 1861, for the war, in Company G, 1st Regiment, North Carolina State Troops. He was listed as present or accounted for until discharged on February 3, 1862 upon transfer to the Confederate States Navy (Source MR, I, gives the date as January 1862) where he served as an Ordinary Seaman on the CSS VIRGINIA, Hampton Roads, Virginia, 1862.
[Source(s): Card File; North Carolina Troops, III; Foenander]

Pritchett, Asa (Craven County, North Carolina)
Private, Confederate States Army//Confederate States Navy. Born in Craven County, North Carolina about 1834 and resided as a coach mechanic in Greenville, Pitt County, North Carolina, in 1860 with his wife Georgeanna and son. He enlisted in Pitt County at age 28 on January 27, 1862, in Company D, 44th Regiment, North Carolina Troops. He mustered in as a Private and was promoted to Corporal on March 24, 1862. Promoted to Sergeant on July 1, 1862, he was reduced to the ranks between September 1862 and February 1863. Pritchett was listed as present or accounted for until he was reportedly transferred to the Confederate States Navy on or about April 1, 1864 [source "North Carolina Troops" states "No evidence of his service in the C.S. Navy was located"]. He was employed in a coach shop in Greenville, where he resided with his family after the war.
[Source(s): Card File; North Carolina Troops, X; Foenander; Census (North Carolina), 1850 and 1870]

Pritchett, Peter G. (Person County, North Carolina)
Confederate States Navy. Pritchett was born in North Carolina in 1846 and enlisted in the Confederate States Navy on or about November 15, 1862. In 1880, he resided with his wife, Lizie, and daughter Nancy (born 1878) at Allensville, Person County, North Carolina, as a practicing physician. He applied for a North Carolina Confederate

pension from Person County, North Carolina on July 5, 1924, at age 80, listing his post office as Timberlake, Person County, North Carolina. His application was approved at 4th class.
[Source(s): Card File; Pensions (North Carolina); Foenander]

Proctor, H. B. (Edgecombe County, North Carolina)
Confederate States Navy. Proctor signed a prisoner's parole on April 22, 1865 at Manchester, Virginia, and was given permission to go to his home in Edgecombe County, North Carolina.
[Source(s): Card File; NA RG 109]

Proctor, Wiley S. (Rutherford County, North Carolina)
Landsman, Confederate States Navy. Proctor enlisted on May 27, 1864, in Raleigh, North Carolina, for the war. A pension claim filed on July 6, 1903 by his widow S. A. Proctor, age 65 years, listing his post office as Forrest City, Rutherford County, North Carolina. Mrs. Proctor stated her husband served on the gunboat CSS PEEDEE. The claim was approved at 4th Class.
[Source(s): Card File; NA RG 109; NA RG 45; Pensions (North Carolina)]

Propst, J. H.
Landsman, Confederate States Navy. Propst enlisted on May 3, 1864, in Raleigh, North Carolina, for the war.
[Source(s): Card File; NA RG 45]

Provanger, Marie (North Carolina?)
Seaman, Confederate States Navy. Provanger received a laceration wound in left breast at Fort Fisher on December 25, 1864.
[Source(s): Daily Confed. (1/2/65); Card File]

Provo, John (Onslow County, North Carolina)
Seaman [Landsman [see Stepp]), Confederate States Navy. Hospital records indicate Provo was admitted to Confederate States Army General Military Hospital Number 4, Wilmington, North Carolina on January 20, 1864 with "pneumonia" where he died on January 22, 1864. He was buried in the Confederate Mass Grave, Oakdale Cemetery, Wilmington, North Carolina. Hospital records listed his post office as Swansboro, North Carolina.
[Source(s): Card File; NA RG 109; Stepp, "Burials"]

Provo, John D. [NOTE: May be same as "John Provo"]
Landsman, Confederate States Navy. Provo enlisted on January 11, 1864 in Raleigh, North Carolina, for the war. However, his name was canceled on the roll with the remark "Deserted from camp."
[Source(s): Card File; NA RG 45]

Pucket, John H.
Landsman, Confederate States Navy. Born in and a resident of North Carolina, he originally served as a Landsman aboard the CSS RALEIGH. He deserted in March 1864 and was taken aboard the USS NIPHON on April 7, 1864 with other "refugees," where he volunteered much information about salt works, personnel, and sounds in the vicinity of Masonboro, North Carolina. About a month later he, along with another pilot (John J. Orrell) guided the Union expedition against salt works at Masonboro with the proviso that the workers be allowed to leave with the Union forces to avoid Confederate conscription. Pucket applied for a position as "Pilot" through United States Navy Captain Benjamin F. Sands. Acting Rear Admiral S. P. Lee appointed him an "Acting ensign and pilot," United States Navy, on April 26, 1864 [per Source Foenander] [another source gives date as "Sept. 1864"]. Pucket served aboard the USS MONTICELLO. He resigned his commission on March 8, 1865.
[Source(s): ORN, 1, 9, p.561 and 672-676; ORN, 2, 1, p. 302; Navy Register; Callahan; Foenander]

Puckett, J. H. D. [NOTE: May be same as "John H. Pucket"]
Landsman, Confederate States Navy. Puckett enlisted on January 11, 1864 in Raleigh, North Carolina, for the war.
[Source(s): Card File; NA RG 45]

Pugh, James (Currituck County, North Carolina)
Private, Confederate States Army//Confederate States Navy. Pugh resided in Currituck County, North Carolina and enlisted in Chowan County, North Carolina at age 27 on June 1, 1861, for the war in Company A, 1st Regiment, North Carolina State Troops [Volunteers] (Source NCCWSP gives his period of service as "for three months"). Wounded at Gettysburg, Pennsylvania on July 3, 1863, he was present or accounted for in his unit until transferred to the Confederate States Navy on April 18, 1864.

Pugh, William J. (Northampton or Gaston County, North Carolina)
First Lieutenant, Confederate States Army//Confederate States Navy (?). Pugh resided as a merchant in either Northampton or Gaston County, North Carolina, prior to enlisting in Warren County, North Carolina at age 17, on March 30, 1861, as a Private in Company A, 14th Regiment, North Carolina Troops. He was elected Second Lieutenant to rank from October 1, 1862 and was present or accounted for until wounded at Chancellorsville, Virginia, on May 3, 1863. He rejoined his company in July-August 1863 and was promoted to First Lieutenant on March 1, 1864. He was present or accounted for until captured in the hospital at Petersburg, Virginia, on April 3, 1865, and transferred to Norfolk, Virginia, on April 22, 1865. He was subsequently transferred to Old Capitol Prison, Washington, DC, on April 28, 1865, and then to Johnson's Island, Ohio, on May 11, 1865. He took the Oath of Allegiance and was released there on June 19, 1865. Source Card File claims he had Confederate Naval service.
[Source(s): Card File; North Carolina Troops, V; Cloninger]

Pullee, G. (New Hanover County, North Carolina)
Confederate States Navy. Pullee's name appears on registers of Confederate States Army General Military Hospital Number 4, Wilmington, North Carolina, which indicate that he was admitted on September 12, 1863, with "febris intermit" and listing his post office as Wilmington, North Carolina. He served on the Confederate States Navy Steamer CSS EUGENIE.
[Source(s): Card File; NA RG 109]

Purdy, Alexander (Granville County, North Carolina)
Confederate States Navy. Purdy's name appears on a Roll of Prisoners of War at Newport News, Virginia, which states that he was captured in Richmond, Virginia on April 3, 1865. His name also appears as signature to an Oath of Allegiance to the United States subscribed and sworn to at Newport News, Virginia, June 30, 1865. His place of residence was given on the Oath as Granville County, North Carolina, and his description as follows: Complexion, dark; hair, light; eyes, grey; height, 5 feet 9 inches.
[Source(s): Card File; NA RG 109]

Putnam, Edward H.
Mate, Confederate States Navy. Putnam served aboard the steamer CSS LIZZIE. His name appears as signature to an Oath of Allegiance to the United States subscribed and sworn to at Fort Warren, Boston Harbor, Massachusetts, June 15, 1865. His place of residence was given on the Oath as Washington, North Carolina and his description as follows: Complexion, light; hair, light; eyes, blue; height, 5 feet 5 inches.
[Source(s): Card File; NA RG 109]

Puttick, James A. (Wake County, North Carolina)
Musician, Confederate States Army//Confederate States Navy. Puttrick was born in Wake County, North Carolina, where he resided as a printer prior to enlisting as a Musician in Company K, 14th Regiment, North Carolina Troops at age 18, on May 21, 1861. Mustered as a Private, he was promoted to Musician circa July-August 1861. He was present or accounted for until his transfer to the Confederate States Navy for duty aboard the CSS VIRGINIA [MERRIMAC] on February 15, 1862.
[Source(s): Card File; North Carolina Troops, Vol. V; Foenander]

Quidley, Lorenzo F. (Hyde County, North Carolina)
Ordinary Seaman, Confederate States Navy.
Quidley was born in North Carolina, in 1843, the son of Reddin and Elvy Quidley. In 1850, he resided with his parents and siblings at "Cape Hatteras Banks," Hyde County, North Carolina. He enlisted for one year and served as an Ordinary Seaman aboard the steam gunboat CSS RALEIGH in North Carolina and Virginia waters from December 4, 1861 through April 1862. He served with the North Carolina Squadron from February 21, 1862 through April 15, 1862, transferring on this date to the James River Squadron. He served at Drewry's Bluff as an Ordinary Seaman from April 1, 1863 through at least June 30, 1863. He appears on payroll documents of the James River Squadron as a crew member on the CSS RALEIGH from October 1, 1863 through December 15, 1863. Source "Foenander" states he served with the James River Squadron into 1864.
[Source(s): Foenander; ORN 2, 1, 301; Census (NC), 1850 and 1860; NCCWSP]

Quinn, William (North Carolina?)
Private, Company B, Confederate States Marine Corps. Wounded ("amputation of leg") and captured at Fort Fisher

on January 15, 1865, he died on January 22 ["24" (see Stepp)], 1865 and was buried in the Confederate Mass Grave, Oakdale Cemetery, Wilmington, New Hanover County, North Carolina.
[Source(s): "Daily Confed." (2/18/65); Card File]

Raddon, James L.
Landsman, Confederate States Navy. Raddon enlisted on October 5, 1863, at Camp Holmes [near Raleigh, North Carolina].
[Source(s): Card File; NA RG 45]

Rafferty, Patrick
Seaman/1st Class Fireman, Confederate States Navy. Rafferty enlisted on June 22, 1863, in Wilmington, North Carolina, for the war. He served as a 1st Class Fireman aboard the CSS NORTH CAROLINA, Cape Fear River, North Carolina, in 1864. He later served on the CSS TALLAHASSEE, 1864.
[Source(s): Card File; NA RG 45; Foenander]

Rainey, H. P.
Landsman, Confederate States Navy. Rainey enlisted on June 24, 1864 in Raleigh, North Carolina, for the war. An "H. P. Rainey," identified as "North Carolina Naval Hospital" is buried in the Seaman's Burial Ground, Ashley River, Charleston, SC, date of death listed as August 10, 1864.
[Source(s): Card File; NA RG 45; SBG]

Rainey, V. M. [V. U.] (Forsyth ["Foenander" states Caswell] County, North Carolina)
Landsman, Confederate States Navy. Rainey enlisted in the Confederate States Navy on March 21, 1864 in Raleigh, North Carolina, for the war. Source "Foenander" states he enlisted in Forsyth County, while one indicates he was conscripted on March 18, 1864 at Camp Holmes [near Raleigh, North Carolina] from Colonel Morton's 71st Regiment, North Carolina Militia, Forsyth County, North Carolina. His description was as follows: Age, 26 years; hair, light; height, 5 feet 8 inches; place of birth, Caswell County, North Carolina; occupation, farmer. Another source states that he appeared on a list of conscripts "in the yard at Halifax" June 9, 1864. Source "Foenander" gives his pre-war occupation as "mariner."
[Source(s): Card File; NA RG 45; Foenander]

Ralph, Doss (Pasquotank County, North Carolina)
Confederate States Navy. Ralph enlisted from Elizabeth City, North Carolina in Company C, 56th Regiment, North Carolina Troops, Ransom's Brigade. He transferred about February 1864 to the Confederate States Navy and served aboard the Confederate States ram CSS ALBEMARLE.
[Source(s): McElroy]

Ramseur (Ramsour, Ransom), Melvin V. C. (Lincoln County, North Carolina)
Private, Company A, Confederate States Marine Corps. Ramseur enlisted on September 1, 1864 [another source says "October 6, 1865"]. He is listed as a Marine on the flagship CSS COLUMBIA under the command of Commodore Tucker from October 6, 1864-February 7, 1865. Ramseur transferred to the CSS INDIAN CHIEF on February 8, 1865 and is listed as having been captured at Burkeville, Virginia, on April 6, 1865 and sent as a Prisoner of War to Point Lookout, Maryland. He was released on June 30, 1865. Source "Donnelly-ENL states he was a resident of Lincoln County, North Carolina, when he filed a claim for pension on July 4, 1910 at age 65 years, though he listed his post office as Maiden, Catawba County, North Carolina. In his pension application, which was approved, Ramseur stated he enlisted when he was about age 19. Another claim was filed on July 4, 1921 by his widow, Mattie E. Ramseur at age 63, listing her post office as Newton, Catawba County, North Carolina. The claim was disallowed as having been "married too late." The claim states that "M. V. Ramseur enlisted in Confederate States Navy on February 12, 1864 and was a Marine on the gunboat CSS COLUMBIA in Charleston till the evacuation in February 1865, [and] was then transferred as infantry to Virginia, being captured at Salem, Virginia [another source says "Burkeville, Virginia] on April 6, 1865." His name appears as a signature to an Oath of Allegiance to the United States subscribed and sworn to at Point Lookout on June 30, 1865 [another source says "July 3, 1865"], at which time he was released. His place of residence was listed on the Oath as Lincoln County, North Carolina and his description as follows: Complexion, light; hair, dark brown; eyes, blue; height, 5 feet 7 inches.
[Source(s): NA; Card File; Pension (North Carolina); North Carolina Troops, Doc. # 0185, p. 1, and 0299; Donnelly-ENL; Donnelly]

Ramsay, Talcot W. (Carteret County, North Carolina)
Private, Confederate States Army//Confederate States Navy (?). Ramsay was born in Carteret County, North Carolina, about 1839, the son of Nancy Ramsay. He resided in Beaufort County as a fisherman prior to enlisting at age 19 on May 25, 1861 for the war in Company. H, 10th Regiment, North Carolina State Troops (1st Regiment, North Carolina Artillery). He was captured at Fort Macon, North Carolina, on April 26, 1862 and paroled until exchanged in August 1861. Ramsay transferred to the Confederate States Navy on September 3, 1863; however, his transfer was revoked on December 4, 1864. He was present or accounted for with Company H through February 1865.
[Source(s): Card File; North Carolina Troops, I; Foenander]

Ramsay, T. N.
Landsman, Confederate States Navy. In a December 4, 1864, letter to Governor Zebulon B. Vance from Charleston, South Carolina, Ramsay claimed he had been enlisted in the Confederate States Navy by fraud as a "common sailor," having been led to believe he would receive a "senior situation." He was seeking Vance's aid in being transferred to the "Provisional Army," but Vance's notation on the back states, "Nothing about his case and any effort of mine could do no good as I have tried a dozen times. ZBV."
[Source(s): Vance Papers [1864 Correspondence File]

Ramsey, F. P.
Landsman, Confederate States Navy. Ramsey enlisted on April 18, 1865 in Raleigh, North Carolina, for the war.
[Source(s): Card File; NA RG 45]

Ramsey, Francis (Person County, North Carolina)
Confederate States Navy. Per *Heritage of Person County, Volume II*, p. 287, "France [sic] P. served in the Navy due to lameness.
[Source(s): *Heritage of Person County, Volume II*; Goss]

Ramsey, Robert McGrea[?] (Mecklenburg County, North Carolina)
Second Lieutenant, Company C, Confederate States Marine Corps. Born in 1832, Ramsey died on June 4, 1890 and was buried at Huntersville Presbyterian Church, Mecklenburg County, North Carolina.
[Source(s): Stepp, "Burials"]

Randolph, Jesse (Pitt County, North Carolina)
Private, Confederate States Army//Confederate States Navy (?). Randolph was born in North Carolina in 1824, the son of Assenor Randolph. He resided and enlisted in Pitt County, North Carolina, at the age of 40 on January 25, 1863, for the war, as a Private in Company C, 44th Regiment, North Carolina Troops. He was present or accounted for until April 15, 1864, when he was reportedly transferred to the Confederate States Navy [source "North Carolina Troops" state "No evidence of his service in the Confederate States Navy was located"].
[Source(s): Card File; NA RG 45; North Carolina Troops, X; Foenander]

Rayfield, John Berry [Berry] [J. B.] (Bladen County, North Carolina).
Landsman, [Source Dowless states he was a "Hospital Steward"], Confederate States Navy. Rayfield enlisted on April 1, 1862 in Charleston, South Carolina, and served there. Born circa July 5, 1845, he died on October 30 ["29" [see Stepp], 1931 and was buried in the Hall-Rayfield Family Cemetery, Bladen County, North Carolina. Post-war he lived in the "White Oak" District of Bladen County, North Carolina. He married Sarah A. Rayfield on March 19, 1901. Another source states he enlisted on April 29, 1864 in Raleigh, North Carolina for the war. Pension records state he filed a claim on May 25, 1914 at age 69 years, listing his post office as White Oak, Bladen County, North Carolina, claiming that he served in the Confederate States Navy in South Carolina. His claim was annotated "Disallowed S. C." A second claim filed on February 29, 1924 at age 78 years, listing his post office as White Oak, North Carolina, was approved as 4th class. In his claim he stated he was in the Navy in Charleston, South Carolina, and enlisted in 1863. A claim filed on April 16, 1934 by his widow, Sarah A. Rayfield at age 67 years, listing her post office as White Oak, North Carolina, was "Disallowed." It states John B. Rayfield died on October 30, 1931 in Bladen County, North Carolina. A letter from the State Auditor of North Carolina says her March 19, 1901 marriage to Rayfield is "beyond the limit" [NOTE: State law dictated that marriages had to have been before 1880 but could make exceptions for marriages before January 1, 1899].
[Source(s): Pensions (North Carolina); Dowless; Card File; NA RG 45; Stepp, "Burials;" Foenander]

Rayl, William Q. (Guilford County, North Carolina)
Landsman, Confederate States Navy. Rayl's name appears on a roll of Prisoners of War at Point Lookout, Maryland,

which states he was captured at Harper's Farm, April 6, 1865, and confined at Point Lookout, Maryland, until released on June 19, 1865. His name appears as a signature to an Oath of Allegiance to the United States subscribed and sworn to at Point Lookout, Maryland on June 19, 1865. His place of residence was given on the Oath as Guilford County, North Carolina and his description as follows: Complexion, dark; hair, dark brown; eyes, hazel; height, 5 feet 8 ½ inches.
[Source(s): Card File]

Read, William Watkins
Midshipman, Master, Lieutenant, Confederate States Navy. Born in 1845 in and appointed from North Carolina [Other sources give "Virginia" for both]. Read had previous service in the United States Navy as a Midshipman from September 27, 1858 until he resigned as Acting Midshipman, United States Navy on April 23, 1861. He served as a Midshipman in the Virginia Navy until appointed an Acting Midshipman, Confederate States Navy, on June 11, 1861. Promoted to Passed Midshipman, October 3, 1862, he reported for duty aboard the CSS HARRIETT LANE in Galveston Bay, Texas, in February 1863. Promoted to Master in Line of Promotion on January 7, 1864, records indicate he was appointed "Second Lieutenant," Provisional Navy, on June 2, 1864. He served aboard the Confederate States receiving ship CSS UNITED STATES, 1861; at the James River batteries, 1862; Gosport Navy Yard, 1862; aboard the CSS PATRICK HENRY, 1862, the CSS HARRIET LANE, 1863, and the CSS MISSOURI, Red River defenses, 1863. Read commanded the CSS NANSEMOND and was on board the CSS RICHMOND, James River Squadron, 1863-1865 [1862-1865]. He was attached, as a Captain, commanding Company F, 2nd Regiment, to Semmes' Naval Brigade, in April 1865; and, was surrendered and paroled at Greensboro, North Carolina, April 26, 1865 [Other sources give the date as April 28, 1865]. Read was a member of the Confederate Veterans Camp of New York, until he died at his home on 97th Street and Fort Hamilton Avenue, Brooklyn, New York, on Monday, August 15, 1910.
[Source(s): Register; McElroy; Card File; Foenander; ONWR]

Redditt, W. (William) H. (Craven County, North Carolina)
Seaman, Confederate States Navy.
Per clothing, bounty, and muster roll records, Redditt served aboard the CSS RALEIGH January 1, 1861 – April 1, 1862. He transferred to the James River Squadron on April 15, 1862. He was promoted to "boson's mate" [Boatswain's Mate] on October 16, 1862 [NOTE: Per a James River Squadron payroll, he was promoted to Boatswain's Mate on November 16, 1863]. He served at Drewry's Bluff as a Seaman per a payroll covering April 1, 1863 - June 30, 1863. He was back aboard the CSS RALEIGH as a Seaman as part of the James River Squadron during the period October 1,1863 - December 15, 1863. A pension claim filed on June 30, 1885 by Redditt's widow, Winnie J. Redditt, age 51 years, listing her post office as New Bern, Craven County, North Carolina, states her husband served on the gunboat CSS NEUSE and died January 1865 in North Carolina. The claim carries the notation: "Need proof as to identity." Redditt served aboard the CSS NEUSE as of the ship's March – October 1864 muster rolls.
[Source(s): Card File; Pension (North Carolina); NEUSE Roster; CMACSSN; NCCWSP]

Redmon, John
Confederate States Navy [?]. Redmon's pension claim filed on August 7, 1922, age 71 years, listing his post office as Lumberton, Robeson County, North Carolina, stated he engaged in blockade running. The claim was approved as 4th Class.
[Source(s): Card File; Pensions (North Carolina)]

Reed, Lawrence (Wayne County, North Carolina) [Free colored man]
Fireman, Confederate States Navy. Served aboard the Confederate States steamer CSS ARROW. Reed's name appears on a roll of Prisoners of War at Elmira, New York, desirous to take the Oath of Allegiance to the United States, which he did on September 30, 1864. The roll states he was captured at Gatesville, North Carolina on July 28, 1864 and carries the remark: "Is a free colored man and resided in Wayne County, North Carolina. Was never in the Confederate Service. Was compelled to act as a fireman on the rebel propeller the [CSS] ARROW. Desires to remain North." Other Prisoner of War records carry some information on his capture. His name appears as a signature (by mark) to a parole of prisoners of war paroled at Elmira, New York, March 10, 1865, and sent to James River and exchanged.
[Source(s): Card File]

Reeves, W. R. [NOTE: May be same as "Wright Reeves"]
Landsman, Confederate States Navy. Reeves enlisted on June 11, 1864 in Raleigh, North Carolina, for the war.
[Source(s): Card File; NA RG 45]

Reeves [Reaves] [Rives], Wright (Iredell County, North Carolina) (Pension application states "Davie" Company)
Landsman, Confederate States Navy. Born in North Carolina in 1847, Reeves is said to have served on a "Charleston Ram." His name appears on a roll of Prisoners of War at Point Lookout, Maryland, which states he was captured on April 6, 1865 at Burkesville [Virginia], and confined at Point Lookout, Maryland, until released on June 17, 1865. His name appears as a signature to an Oath of Allegiance (signed by his mark) subscribed and sworn to at Point Lookout, Maryland, June 17, 1865. His place of residence was given on the Oath as Iredell County, North Carolina, and description as follows: Complexion, light; hair, dark brown; eyes, dark brown; height, 5 feet ¼ inch. His first application for a pension, filed July 4, 1904, age 66, County Line post office, states he served in the Navy on the gunboat CSS CHARLESTON, but knew no one who could act as a corroborating witness of his service. The claim was disallowed for "Insufficient evidence." In a second pension application, dated July 31, 1905, age 67, Reeves states he enlisted in Captain James McRae's Company of Mallett's Battalion, saying, "I received no wound, but had my clothes shot in holes, and my hat brim shot off, the last year of the war I was taken with piles [in the last months of the war] … bloody piles since the war … he has hemmorrhoides [sic]." Also blind in his left eye from a cataract he says started while in the service, the examining doctor rated his disability at three-quarters. His application was approved at 4th class. His accompanying statement (transcript of statement of service and Oath of Allegiance, Point Lookout, Maryland), dated June 17, 1865, states he enlisted on August 8, [illegible], with Captain James McRae at Statesville, North Carolina, ('the first call for conscripts') … and placed in Mallett's battalion. It further states that after the Battle of Kinston he was "sent to Charleston and placed on board gun boat CSS CHARLESTON, Captain Brown, Commander, the boat was burned to prevent its falling in the enemies [sic] hands, was then sent to Richmond and had charge of a battery below Drewry's Bluff and remained there until the fall of Petersburg, stayed with Lee on the retreat until three days before the surrender then I was captured and carried to prison." His widow Nancy Reaves' approved application for pension dated July 31, 1917 gives her age as 80, her post office as Harmony [?], and mentions her husband's service in Mallett's Battalion, but not the Navy.
[Source(s): Card File; NA RG 109; Pensions (North Carolina); Foenander]

Register, Henry B.
Landsman, Confederate States Navy. Register enlisted on December 5, 1863 in Wilmington, North Carolina, for the war, and served as a Landsman aboard the CSS ARCTIC, Cape Fear River, North Carolina, 1863. He later served aboard the CSS RALEIGH in North Carolina and Virginia waters, 1864.
[Source(s): Card File; NA RG 45; Foenander; ORN 2, 1, 277 & 302]

Register, John R. (Sampson County, North Carolina)
Private, Confederate States Army//Confederate States Navy [?]. Register resided in Sampson Company, North Carolina, and served in Captain William S. Devane's Independent Company, North Carolina Troops. Records indicate he was transferred to Company A, 61st Regiment, North Carolina Troops as a Private on or about September 5, 1862. He was reported as present through December 1862, then as detailed for duty in the medical department, probably as an ambulance driver, on February 27, 1863. He rejoined his company on October 14, 1863 and was reported as present through April 30, 1864. On October 19, 1864, Register transferred to Company C, 63rd Regiment, North Carolina Troops (5th North Carolina Cavalry). He was captured at Aberdeen Church, Virginia, on April 3, 1865, and confined at Point Lookout, Maryland until released on June 17, 1865 after taking the Oath of Allegiance. Source "Card File: indicates Confederate Naval service.
[Source(s): Card File; North Carolina Troops, II & XIV]

Register, John W.
Landsman, Confederate States Navy. Register enlisted on February 18, 1864, in Raleigh, North Carolina, for the war, and served aboard the CSS ARCTIC, Cape Fear River, North Carolina, 1863.
[Source(s): Card File; NA RG 45; Foenander; ORN 2, 1, 278]

Register, N. G.
Landsman, Confederate States Navy. Register enlisted on November 30, 1863, in Raleigh, North Carolina, for the war.
[Source(s): Card File; NA RG 45]

Reid (Reids), A. G. (Mecklenburg County, North Carolina)
Landsman, Confederate States Navy. Reid enlisted on August 8, 1864, in Raleigh, North Carolina, for the war and served as a Landsman aboard the CSS ARCTIC, Cape Fear River, North Carolina, 1863. Source "NA RG 109" states he was part of Tucker's Naval Battalion. His name appears on a roll of Prisoners of War at Point Lookout, Maryland, which states he was captured at Burkesville [Virginia] April 6, 1865 and confined until released June 17, 1865. His name appears as a signature to an Oath of Allegiance to the United States subscribed and sworn to at Point

Lookout, Maryland, June 17, 1865. His place of residence was given on the Oath as Mecklenburg County, North Carolina and his description as follows: Complexion, dark; hair, grey; eyes, hazel; height, 6 feet 3 inches.
[Source(s): Card File; NA RG 45; NA RG 109; Foenander]

Reid, Alfred (also Albert Reed)
Landsman, Wardroom Steward, Commander's Cook, Confederate States Navy.
Reid was promoted from Landsman to Wardroom Steward on November 17, 1861. He served as a Commander's Cook aboard the SEA BIRD as of February 1862. He was captured in the Battle of Elizabeth City and carried to Roanoke Island on February 10, 1862 where he was paroled on February 12, 1862 and returned to Elizabeth City, North Carolina. His name appears on a payroll of the receiving ship CSS UNITED STATES ending March 31, 1862. He is listed on the North Carolina Squadron payroll for the 1st quarter of 1862 (November 16, 1861 - April 15, 1862). Reid is listed as "on parole" on the ship's April 15, 1862 payroll.
[Source: NCCWSP]

Reilly (Riebly), John (Ireland//Warren County, North Carolina)
Private, Confederate States Army//Confederate States Navy. Born in Ireland, Reilly resided in Warren County, North Carolina, as a laborer prior to enlisting in New Hanover County, North Carolina, as a Private at age 32 on August 7, 1861, for the war, in Company F, 8th Regiment, North Carolina State Troops. Company muster roll dated October 31, 1862 – July 2, 1862 states he "enlisted in Lamb's Artillery [?] 34 [th] Reg[imen]t" (?); however, he was present or accounted for until he transferred to the Confederate States Navy in March-April 1863.
[Source(s): Card File; MR, I; NA RG 45; North Carolina Troops, IV; Foenander]

Remmington, Ed
Ordinary Seaman, Confederate States Navy.
Remmington's name appears on the payroll of the North Carolina Squadron for the 1st quarter of 1862 (January 10, 1862 - March 31, 1862). He is listed as having "run" on this payroll.
[Source: NCCWSP]

Renalds, John
Landsman, Confederate States Navy. Renalds enlisted on December 17, 1863 in Raleigh, North Carolina, for the war.
[Source(s): Card File; NA RG 45]

Renn, William Z. (Granville County, North Carolina)
Confederate States Navy. Born in North Carolina in 1828, Renn served in the Confederate States Navy. In 1880, he resided as a millwright with his wife, Mary E. and their four children (the eldest born in 1862) at "E.D. 108, Fishing Creek, Granville County, North Carolina." His widow applied for a Confederate pension, which was approved, on May 23, 1901, at age 70, listing her post office as Watkins, Granville County, North Carolina. Her husband died in 1891. She stated that he enlisted in the Navy about October 1, 1864.
[Source(s): Card File; Pensions (North Carolina); Foenander]

Respass, John R. (Washington County (?), North Carolina)
Landsman, Confederate States Navy. Respass was born in North Carolina, in 1838, the son of Langly R. and Nancy Respass. In 1860, he resided as a farmer with his wife Harriet and three children, in Washington County, North Carolina. Respass enlisted on August 3, 1864, in Raleigh, North Carolina, for the war, and served as a Landsman aboard the CSS NORTH CAROLINA, Cape Fear River, North Carolina, 1864.
[Source(s): Card File; NA RG 45; Foenander]

Rey [Ray?], W. T.
Landsman, Confederate States Navy. Rey enlisted on April 13, 1864 in Kinston, North Carolina, for three years or the war.
[Source(s): Card File; NA RG 45]

Reyburn [Ryburn], William E. (County unknown)
Private, Company A, Confederate States Marine Corps. Born on June 22, 1832, Ryburn enlisted in Raleigh, North Carolina on October 6, 1864 as a Private in Company A, Confederate States Marine Corps. He served on the Charleston, South Carolina, station as a Private of the Marine guard aboard the CSS COLUMBIA until February 7, 1865. He transferred to the CSS INDIAN CHIEF on February 8, 1865. Ryburn surrendered as a member of the Naval Battalion at Appomattox Court House, Virginia on April 9, 1865. Ryburn died on June 30 ["20," per

PCNMC], 1892 [1893, per "Foenander"], and was buried in Sunset Cemetery, Shelby, Cleveland County, North Carolina. His last name is spelled "Reyburn" on his grave marker.
[Source(s): North Carolina Troops, Doc. # 0299; Card File; Donnelly-ENL; PCNMC; Foenander]

Reynolds. Isaac R. ["Doil," see Stepp] (Brunswick County, North Carolina)
Private, Confederate States Army//Crewman ["Coxswain" [see Stepp], Confederate States Navy. Reynolds was born in Brunswick County, North Carolina, in 1833, and was residing there when he enlisted on April 16, 1862, at age 29, as a Private (Fifer) in 3rd Company G, 36th Regiment, North Carolina Troops (2nd North Carolina Artillery) for the war. Transferring to the Confederate States Navy on August 5, 1863, he served aboard the CSS NORTH CAROLINA. Per his headstone in Bellevue Cemetery, Wilmington, North Carolina, Reynolds was born on May 30, 1833 and died on June 30, 1914.
[Source(s): MR, 4, p. 444; Wayne Carver; Card File; Gravestone Records, v. 6, p. 322-A; NA RG 109; Stepp, "Burials;" North Carolina Troops, I; Foenander]

Reynolds, John W. (Cumberland County, North Carolina)
Landsman, Confederate States Navy. Born in Wake County, North Carolina, Reynolds worked as a mason prior to enlisting on March 18, 1864, in Raleigh, North Carolina, for the war. Source NA RG 45 states he was enlisted on March 17, 1864, at Camp Holmes [near Raleigh, North Carolina] from Colonel Pemberton's 53rd Regiment, North Carolina Militia, Cumberland County, North Carolina. His description was as follows: Age, 29; eyes, grey; hair, dark; complexion, florid; height, 5 feet 4 inches; place of birth, Wake County, North Carolina; occupation, mason. A "John Reynolds" served aboard the CSS NEUSE as of the ship's March – October 1864 muster rolls.
[Source(s): Card File; NA RG 45; Foenander; NEUSE Roster; CMACSSN]

Reynolds, Murdock C. (Brunswick County, North Carolina)
Private, Confederate States Army//Ordinary Seaman, Confederate States Navy. Reynolds resided in and enlisted from Brunswick County, North Carolina, at age 26 on April 16, 1862 in 3rd Company G, 36th Regiment, North Carolina Troops (2nd North Carolina Artillery) for the war. He was present or accounted for until transferred to the Confederate States Navy on August 5, 1863, where he served as an Ordinary Seaman aboard the CSS NORTH CAROLINA.
[Source(s): MR, 4, p. 444; NA RG 109; Card File; North Carolina Troops, I; Foenander]

Reynolds, Thomas (New Hanover County, North Carolina)
Private, Confederate States Navy. Reynolds served aboard the Confederate States steamer CSS EUGENIE. His name appears on a register of Confederate States Army General Military Hospital Number 4, Wilmington, North Carolina, which states he was admitted on October 2, 1863, with "feb remittens" and returned to duty October 10, 1863. His post office was given on the register as Wilmington, North Carolina.
[Source(s): Card File; NA RG 109]

Reynolds, William
Seaman, Confederate States Navy.
Reynolds served as a Seaman aboard the CSS CURLEW at least during the 1st quarter of 1862. He appears on the payroll of the receiving ship CSS UNITED STATES ending March 31, 1862.
[Source: NCCWSP]

Rhea, Andrew B.
Landsman, Confederate States Navy. Rhea enlisted on April 13, 1864 in Raleigh, North Carolina, for the war.
[Source(s): Card File; NA RG 45]

Rhodes, A. G. (Wilson County, North Carolina)
Ordinary Seaman, Confederate States Navy. Rhodes enlisted on September 1, 1863 in Wilmington, North Carolina, for the war. Reference "NA RG 109" states his name appeared on a role of Prisoners of War paroled at the Provost Marshal's Office in Goldsboro, North Carolina, May 9, 1865, with the remark: "Came in for parole." The residence given for him on the parole was Wilson County, North Carolina.
[Source(s): Card File; NA RG 45; NA RG 109]

Rhodes, James M. (Jesse)
Pilot, Confederate States Navy.
Born in Elizabeth City, North Carolina, circa 1828, Rhodes resided in that city where he lived as a mariner. He

served as a Pilot aboard the CSS CURLEW from November 20, 1862 – February 10, 1862 when he was discharged. [Source(s): 1860 Census (NC); NCCWSP]

Rhodes, Jesse (James) M. (Pasquotank County, North Carolina)
Pilot, Confederate States Navy. Born in Elizabeth City, North Carolina, in 1828, Rhodes took up a seafaring career at the age of 12 and occupied every position from cabin boy to captain. He was living in Elizabeth City, North Carolina in 1860 as a mariner. He served as a Pilot in the Confederate States Navy, and was at Roanoke Island, at its capture. He served as the Pilot aboard the CSS CURLEW, 1861 – 1862, and was discharged February 10, 1862 (Source NCCWSP quotes a payroll showing him as being paid as the Pilot of the CSS CURLEW as late as November 20, 1862. Post-war, Rhodes was employed as a Pilot for the Old Dominion Company. In 1880 he was residing as a sailor with his wife Mary and two children in New Bern, North Carolina. He died in New Bern, North Carolina, on December 17, 1882. [Source(s): Foenander; NCCWSP]

Rhodes, Julius
Landsman, Confederate States Navy. Rhodes enlisted on March 1, 1864 in Raleigh, North Carolina, for the war. He served at Wilmington and Drewry's Bluff, Virginia under Captain Poindexter, Confederate States Navy. Source "Foenander" lists a "Julius J. Rhodes" who served aboard the CSS NORTH CAROLINA on the Cape Fear River, North Carolina, in 1864.
[Source(s): Card File; NA RG 45; Gaston County Veterans; Foenander; Cloninger]

Rhodes, William B. (Camden County, North Carolina)
Private, Confederate States Army//Confederate States Navy (?). Source Card File indicates Rhodes had Confederate Naval service. Source "North Carolina Troops, IV" states he was born and resided in Camden County, North Carolina, as a farmer where he enlisted at age 29 on July 24, 1861, for the war, in Company A, 8th Regiment, North Carolina State Troops. He was captured at Roanoke Island on February 8, 1862, paroled at Elizabeth City on February 21, 1862 and exchanged at Elizabeth City in August 1862. Present or accounted for until captured at Cold Harbor, Virginia, on June 1, 1864, he was confined at Point Lookout, Maryland until transferred to Elmira, New York, on July 9, 1864, where he died on May 24, 1865 of "pneumonia."
[Source(s): Card File; North Carolina Troops, IV]

Rhyne, Jacob Moses (Gaston County, North Carolina)
Landsman, Confederate States Navy. Born in 1838, Rhyne died in 1905 and was buried at the Lutheran Chapel, Gaston County, North Carolina. [Source(s): Stepp, "Burials;" Cloninger]

Rich, W. C. (Davie County, North Carolina)
Confederate States Navy. Rich enlisted in the Confederate States Navy on August 3, 1863 in Wilmington, North Carolina. He was age 25 in 1850; 35 in 1860. One source indicates he "Lives with brother David Rich."
[Source(s): MR, 4, p. 447; Census (NC), 1850 and 1860]

Richardson, James M.
Landsman, Confederate States Navy. Richardson enlisted on January 25, 1864 in Raleigh [Camp Holmes], North Carolina, for the war, and served as a Landsman aboard the CSS ARCTIC, Cape Fear River, North Carolina, 1863.
[Source(s): Card File; NA RG 45; Foenander]

Richardson, Thomas W. (New Hanover County, North Carolina)
Landsman/Seaman, Confederate States Navy. Richardson enlisted in the Confederate States Navy on October 8 [or, 12], 1863 in Wilmington, North Carolina. He served aboard the CSS ARCTIC, 1863.
[Source(s): MR, 4, p. 447; Card File; NA RG 45; St. Armand; Foenander]

Ricketts, George W. (Anson County, North Carolina)
Landsman, Confederate States Navy. Born in Anson County, North Carolina, Ricketts was a farmer prior to enlisting on March 28, 1864, in Raleigh, North Carolina, for the war. Another reference states he enlisted on March 20, 1864, at Camp Holmes [near Raleigh, North Carolina] from Colonel Smith's 80th Regiment, North Carolina Militia, Anson County, North Carolina. His description was as follows: Age, 22; eyes, hazel; hair, dark; complexion, dark; height, 5 feet 3 ½ inches; place of birth, Anson County, North Carolina; occupation farmer.
[Source(s): Card File; NA RG 45; Foenander]

Ricks, William R. (Edgecombe County, North Carolina)
Midshipman, Confederate States Navy. Appointed from North Carolina, one source states he enlisted from Tarboro,

Edgecombe County, North Carolina, in September 1864 at the age of 14 years. Appointed an Acting Midshipman on December 2, 1864, he served aboard the CSS PATRICK HENRY in 1864. He was one of the Corps of Cadets of the Naval Brigade appointed to escort Mrs. Jefferson Davis and the Confederate Treasury from Richmond, Virginia when it was evacuated. He reported at Danville, Virginia and accompanied them to Charlotte, North Carolina, then across country to Newberry and Abbeville, South Carolina and then to Washington and Augusta, Georgia. He then went back over the same route to Abbeville, South Carolina at which place the Naval Brigade was disbanded and he received $27.50 in gold for the services rendered to the time of disbandment in April 1865. He was paroled on May 11, 1865 in Charlotte, North Carolina. His pension request filed on June 28, 1927, age 76, listing his post office as Rocky Mount, Nash County, North Carolina was approved as Class A. A statement dated May 21, 1927 from John L. Bridger, Jr., states "Ricks was a Cadet in the Confederate States Navy. I was tendered the appointment, but could not go on account of my mother, and Ricks was appointed." Ricks' statement: "October 1863, when only 13 years old, was employed by the Quarter Master Department to assist in collecting and guarding supplies for the army at Joyner's Depot and at Tarboro under my uncle David Pender, District Quarter Master at Tarboro for the Confederate States. September 1864 was appointed Midshipman in the Navy and went aboard steamer CSS PATRICK HENRY at Richmond. Upon [the] fall of Richmond we were appointed guard for the Treasury and government archives and left for Danville, Virginia. Upon surrender of General Lee, we commenced our meandering going as far south as Augusta, Georgia, returning to Abeville [sic], South Carolina. On May 3, 1865 President Davis with his cabinet and escort arrived and we turned our charge to them. At Chester, South Carolina, Mrs. Davis was added to our charge. We were disbanded May 4, 1865."
[Source(s): Register; McElroy; Card File; Pensions (North Carolina); Thorpe Roster; Academy; Foenander]

Riddick, Jacob
Seaman, Confederate States Navy.
Riddick served as a Seaman aboard the CSS CURLOW at least for the 1st quarter of 1862. His name appears on the payroll of the receiving ship CSS UNITED STATES ending March 31, 1862.
[Source: NCCWSP]

Ridgen, Josiah
Landsman, Confederate States Navy. Ridgen enlisted on February 4, 1864 in Raleigh, North Carolina, for the war.
[Source(s): Card File; NA RG 45]

Riggan (Riggan, Riggans, Regan, Rigan), Joseph R. (Alamance County, North Carolina)
Landsman ("Private"), Confederate States Navy. [NOTE: This man's entry may be a mix of several men with similar names]. Riggan/Regan enlisted on December 17, 1863 in Raleigh, North Carolina, for the war. Source "Foenander" lists a "J. R. Regan," a "J. R. Rigon," and a "J. W. Regan" (who may all be the same man) as having served as a Landsman aboard the CSS ARCTIC, Cape Fear River, North Carolina, 1863. A "J. R. Regan" served aboard the CSS NEUSE as of the ship's March – October 1864 muster rolls. His pension file claimed on July 7, 1913 at age 70, listing his post office as Burlington, Alamance County, North Carolina, says he enlisted "on the Boat CSS ARCTIC at Wilmington, North Carolina, on or about February 13, 1863." He received a sprained ankle at Kinston, North Carolina, December 1, 1863, while working on the CSS NEUSE, on which he served from March – October 1864, per ship's muster roll. Said ankle remained stiff and gave trouble. He received no wounds in service. His pension request was disallowed, insufficient disability. Another claim filed July 1, 1914, age 71, listing his post office as #9, Burlington, says he enlisted in August 1863. This disallowed application was annotated with "not in army." In a third claim filed on July 5, 1915, "age 68 to 70," he re-states his service on the CSS ARTIC, and adds service "on the 'Ironclad' at Kinston." This application was approved. His attached statement reads "Volunteered November 1863 went to Camp Mangum and I wint [sic] from thre [sic] to the Navey [sic] and was put on the Iron Clad and then served there until [sic] the Iron Clad was sunk at Kinston Capt. Sharp and then Capt. Price and after Iron [Clad] was sunk I was sent to Halafax [sic] Navey [sic] Yard and there untill [sic] General Lee surrendered at Alamast [sic] Court House."
[Source(s): Card File; NA RG 45; Foenander; NEUSE Roster; Pension (North Carolina); UDC, Recorder; CMACSSN]

Riggs, Alpheus B. (Camden County, North Carolina)
Private, Confederate States Army//Landsman, Confederate States Navy. Residing in Camden County, North Carolina, Riggs enlisted there on May 30, 1861 at age 22 as a Private in Company M, 12th Regiment, North Carolina Troops (2nd Regiment, North Carolina Volunteers). He was present or accounted for until he transferred to 2nd Company B, 32nd Regiment, North Carolina Troops, in October 1861. He was listed as "present or accounted for" until he transferred to the Confederate States Navy on December 30, 1863 and served as a Landsman on the

CSS ARCTIC, 1864, and the CSS RALEIGH, 1864.
[Source(s): Card File; Foenander; North Carolina Troops, V and IX; MR, I]

Riggs, James T.
Landsman, Confederate States Navy. Riggs served aboard the CSS ARCTIC, Cape Fear River, North Carolina, 1863, and aboard the steam gunboat CSS RALEIGH in North Carolina and Virginia waters, 1864.
[Source(s): Foenander; MR, I]

Riggs, Joseph (Pasquotank County, North Carolina]
Private, Confederate States Army//Seaman, Confederate States Navy. Born in Camden County, North Carolina, Riggs resided in Pasquotank County, North Carolina, as a mariner, prior to enlisting there at age 27 on April 23, 1861 [one source gives date as July 31, 1861] as a Private in Company A, 17th Regiment, North Carolina Troops (1st Organization). Riggs was present of accounted for until transferred as a Private to Company A, 8th Regiment, North Carolina State Troops. Captured at Roanoke Island, North Carolina on February 8, 1862, he was paroled at Elizabeth City on February 21, 1862 and exchanged in August 1862. He was present or accounted for until transferred to the Confederate States Navy on or about January 20, 1863 and served as a Seaman aboard the CSS ARCTIC. One source states Riggs enlisted on January 23, 1863 in Wilmington, North Carolina, for three years or the war. Another source states he "served on a gunboat." His name appears on registers of Confederate States Army General Military Hospital Number 4, Wilmington, North Carolina, dated June 29, 1863, which gives his disease as "debility" and post office as Elizabeth City, North Carolina. No date for return to duty was indicated.
[Source(s): North Carolina Troops, IV & VI; Card File; NA RG 109; NA RG 45; Foenander; MR, I]

Riggs, Marshall P.
Landsman, Confederate States Navy. Riggs served aboard the CSS ARCTIC, Cape Fear River, North Carolina, 1863.
[Source(s): MR, I; Foenander]

Riggs, R.W.
Landsman, Confederate States Navy. Riggs served aboard the CSS ARCTIC, Cape Fear River, North Carolina, 1863.
[Source(s): MR, I; Foenander]

Rigler, John (North Carolina)
Private, Confederate States Marine Corps. A worker at the Confederate States Navy Yard, Charlotte, North Carolina who was likely one of the circa three hundred workmen armed, equipped, and formed into one of three companies of "Marines" for defense purposes in late 1864 or early 1865. He may have been a member of the one company detailed to accompany Confederate Major General Joseph Wheeler as his unit escorted the wife and family of President Jefferson Davis, some government officials, and the gold of the Confederate Treasury south as they attempted to escape Union capture.
[Source: SHSP (Vol. 40); "Char. Obs.," April 3, 1910 and June 5, 1910; "Char. News," June 5, 1910]

Riley, John (Ireland//Cumberland County, North Carolina)
Private, Confederate States Army//Confederate States Navy. Riley was born in Ireland and resided as a laborer in Cumberland County, North Carolina, where he enlisted at age 19 as a Private in Company C, 3rd Regiment, North Carolina State Troops, on May 29, 1861. He transferred to the Confederate States Navy on January 29, 1862.
[Source(s): Card File; Foenander; North Carolina Troops, III]

Rimer, Milton F. (Rowan County, North Carolina)
Private, Confederate States Army//Confederate States Navy. Rimer was born and resided in Rowan County, North Carolina, where he enlisted "for the war" at age 14 on November 17, 1861, as a Private in Company K, 8th Regiment, North Carolina State Troops. Captured at Roanoke Island on February 8, 1862, he was paroled at Elizabeth City on February 21, 1862 and exchanged in August 1862. He was present or accounted for until killed at Morris Island, Charleston Harbor, South Carolina, on August 31, 1863. Source Card File contains a note that states "it appears he was killed before his transfer [to the Confederate States Navy] could be carried out."
[Source(s): Card File; North Carolina Troops, IV]

Rittenberry, J. R.
Landsman, Confederate States Navy. Rittenberry enlisted on September 28, 1863 at Camp Holmes [near Raleigh,

North Carolina] for the war.
[Source(s): Card File; NA RG 45]

Rivenbark, John V. (New Hanover County, North Carolina)
Private, Confederate States Army//Confederate States Navy. Born in New Hanover County, North Carolina, Rivenbark resided in the same county as a farmer prior to enlisting there at age 20 on July 5, 1861, for the war, as a Private in Company F, 8th Regiment, North Carolina State Troops. Wounded in the head and captured at Roanoke Island on February 8, 1862, he was paroled at Elizabeth City on February 21, 1862 and exchanged in August 1862. He was present or accounted for through January 11, 1865. Source Card File states he had Confederate Naval service.
[Source(s): Card File; North Carolina Troops, IV]

Robbins, L.
First Cabin Boy, Confederate States Navy. Robbins enlisted on June 17, 1863 in Wilmington, North Carolina, for the war.
[Source(s): Card File; NA RG 45]

Robbins, McDonald
Landsman, Confederate States Navy. Robbins enlisted on January 11, 1864 in Raleigh, North Carolina for the war. However, his name was canceled on roll with remark: "Deserted from camp."
[Source(s): Card File; NA RG 45]

Robbins, Major T.
Landsman, Confederate States Navy. Robbins enlisted on May 27, 1864 in Raleigh, North Carolina, for the war.
[Source(s): Card File; NA RG 45]

Robbins, Thomas W.
Landsman, Confederate States Navy. Robbins enlisted on May 27, 1864 in Raleigh, North Carolina, for the war.
[Source(s): Card File; NA RG 45]

Robbins, William (New Hanover County, North Carolina)
Ordinary Seaman, Confederate States Navy. Robbins enlisted in the Confederate States Navy in Wilmington, North Carolina and served as an Ordinary Seaman aboard the CSS ARCTIC, 1863.
[Source(s): MR, 4, p. 447; Foenander; St. Armand]

Roberts, Daniel (Carteret County, North Carolina)
Mate, Confederate States Navy. Roberts served on the schooner "Duroe." His name appears on an Oath of Allegiance to the United States subscribed and sworn to at Fort Warren, Boston Harbor, Massachusetts, June 15, 1865, whereon his residence was listed as Portsmouth, North Carolina. His description was as follows: Complexion, light; hair, brown; eyes, blue; height, 5 feet 7 ¾ inches.
[Source(s): Card File; NA RG 109]

Roberts, Daniel L. (Craven County, North Carolina) [may be same as "Roberts, Daniel (Carteret County, NC," q.v.]
Landsman, Confederate States Navy. Born on April 19, 1837, Roberts died on May 16, 1919 and was buried in the Cedar Grove Cemetery, Craven County, North Carolina.
[Source(s): Stepp, "Burials"]

Roberts [Robert], Henry H. [C.]
Assistant Engineer [Source NCCWSP records his rank as Acting 3rd Assistant Engineer], Confederate States Navy. Born in and appointed from North Carolina, Roberts was appointed Acting Third Assistant Engineer on October 13, 1861, and Third Assistant Engineer on February 19 [or 10], 1863. Promoted to Third Assistant Engineer, Provisional Navy on June 2, 1864. Roberts served aboard the CSS SEA BIRD, 1861, on the Wilmington Station, North Carolina, 1861[1862] – 1864; aboard the CSS RALEIGH, 1863-1864; the CSS TALLAHASSEE, 1864; and, the CSS YADKIN, 1864.
[Source(s): Register; McElroy; Card File; Foenander; ONWR; NCCWSP]

Roberts, J. H.
Landsman, Confederate States Navy. Roberts enlisted on June 1, 1864 in Raleigh, North Carolina, for the war.
[Source(s): Card File; NA RG 45]

Roberts, John DeBerniere (Craven County, North Carolina//South Carolina)
Second Lieutenant, Confederate States Marine Corps. Born in Craven County, North Carolina, on July 4, 1843, Roberts was the son of Rev. John Jones Roberts of New Bern, North Carolina, Professor of Modern Languages, University of North Carolina, 1841-1842, who became an Episcopal minister in 1846. John DeBerniere Roberts was a resident of South Carolina when the war broke out. At the outbreak of war, Roberts enlisted as a Private at Columbia, South Carolina, on July 15, 1861, and mustered in on August 19, 1861, at age 18, in Company G (Infantry), Hampton Legion. He was promoted to Corporal sometime between September-October 1861, and to Sergeant on February 28, 1863. He was hospitalized for a wounded arm and shoulder in September 1862. Roberts was nominated to the Confederate Senate for a commission on June 7, 1864, under the name "J. DuBose Roberts," which was confirmed on June 9, 1864. He accepted his appointment as a Second Lieutenant, Confederate States Marine Corps on June 16, 1864. At age 20, upon his discharge from the Confederate States Army, he was described as a student, 6 feet 2 inches tall, with dark eyes and hair, and a fair complexion. He served initially with Company C, Confederate States Marine Corps, at Drewry's Bluff, Virginia, and accompanied the Marine battalion to Wilmington during the summer of 1864, for the projected expedition to release the Confederate prisoners at Point Lookout, Maryland. Unfortunately, he fell down a hatchway on the ship "Let-Her-B" and had to drop out of the expedition. On September 22, 1864, he was assigned to Wilmington, North Carolina, for "command of one of the Marine Guards attached to the Cape Fear River squadron." He reported to Captain A. C. Van Benthuysen on September 30, 1864, and on November 4, 1864, took over command of the Marine detachment sent to the Naval battery known as Battery Buchanan [Fort Fisher]. He participated in the defense of Fort Fisher and was captured at the fall of the fort on January 15, 1865. First sent as a Prisoner of War to Fort Monroe, Virginia, he was later transferred to Fort Columbus, New York Harbor, arriving there on January 26, 1865. Roberts was treated in the prison hospital from February 15-20, 1865 for an injury caused by a pocketknife. He was paroled and sent to City Point, Virginia, for exchange on February 25, 1865. He was back in Virginia on March 5, 1865 and presumably exchanged about the same time. He died on April 28, 1880, in Charleston, South Carolina, and was buried the next day in St. Phillip's Churchyard, Lot 3078, West Cemetery. He was survived by his father and his wife, Mary Lapham Roberts, and a son, John Lapham Roberts. His uncle, Johnson Jones Hoper, was editor of the Montgomery, Alabama, newspaper the "Mail" and served as secretary of the Provisional [Confederate] Congress.
[Source(s): North Carolina Troops, Doc. # 0299; Card File; Donnelly-RL; Donnelly-BS]

Roberts, S. (North Carolina)
Lieutenant, Confederate States Navy. Roberts' name appears on a Morning Report of 6th Division, General Hospital, Camp Winder, Richmond, Virginia, which states he was admitted on November 25, 1864, with the remark: "Reported as a N. Carolinian."
[Source(s): Card File; NA RG 109]

Roberts, Thomas (North Carolina)
Private, Confederate States Marine Corps. A worker at the Confederate States Navy Yard, Charlotte, North Carolina who was likely one of the circa three hundred workmen armed, equipped, and formed into one of three companies of "Marines" for defense purposes in late 1864 or early 1865. He may have been a member of the one company detailed to accompany Confederate Major General Joseph Wheeler as his unit escorted the wife and family of President Jefferson Davis, some government officials, and the gold of the Confederate Treasury south as they attempted to escape Union capture.
[Source: SHSP (Vol. 40); "Char. Obs.," April 3, 1910 and June 5, 1910; "Char. News," June 5, 1910]

Roberts, William (Pasquotank County, North Carolina)
Private, Confederate States Army//Seaman, Confederate States Navy. Roberts resided as a mariner in Pasquotank County, North Carolina, before enlisting in Company A, 8th Regiment, North Carolina State Troops, on August 17, 1861, at age 24. Captured on Roanoke Island, February 8, 1862, he was paroled at Elizabeth City, North Carolina, February 21, 1862, and exchanged in August 1862. He was present or accounted for till transferred to the Confederate States Navy on or about January 20, 1863. Another source states he enlisted in the Confederate States Navy in Wilmington, North Carolina, while another source notes he enlisted on January 29, 1863, at Wilmington, North Carolina, for the war. One source shows he served in "Company D, 6th Regiment, North Carolina Independent Cavalry," but there is no record of such unit or service. Source "Foenander" states he may have served in the 32nd Regiment, North Carolina Troops. Source North Carolina Troops IV lists a "William Roberts, Cook" on the May-June 1862 muster roll of the 32nd Regiment, North Carolina Troops.
[Source(s): MR, 4, p. 447; Card File; NA RG 45; North Carolina Troops, IV; Foenander]

Roberts, W. L.
Landsman, Confederate States Navy. Roberts enlisted in the Confederate States Navy on February 13, 1864 in Wilmington, North Carolina, for the war. He served as a Landsman, CSS ARCTIC, Cape Fear River, North Carolina, 1863 (NOTE: Per source "Foenander," may be the same as "William L. Roberts, quartermaster, steam gunboat CSS RALEIGH, North Carolina and Virginia waters, 1862 – 1864.
[Source(s): Card File; NA RG 45; Foenander; ORN, 2, 1, pgs. 278 and 302].

Roberts, William W.
First Lieutenant ["Captain," (see Stepp)], Confederate States Navy. Born in and appointed from North Carolina, Roberts resigned as a Lieutenant, United States Navy, on May 19, 1860. Listed by source "DH Hill" as one of the first officers commissioned as a Lieutenant in the North Carolina Navy, 1861, he was appointed Lieutenant, Confederate States Navy, August 26, 1863 and Lieutenant for the war, January 7, 1864, to rank from August 26, 1863. He was appointed First Lieutenant Provisional, Navy on June 2, 1864 to rank from January 6, 1864. He served on the CSS CHARLESTON, Charleston Station, 1863-1864; Wilmington Station, 1864; CSS ALBEMARLE, 1864; Battery Buchanan, 1864 and as First Lieutenant commanding CSS TORPEDO, James River Squadron, 1865. Roberts was captured on April 6, 1865, Sailors Creek, Virginia, and released on oath, May 19, 1865, from Johnson's Island. He was buried in Cedar Grove Cemetery, Craven County, North Carolina.
[Source(s): Register; McElroy; Card File; Stepp, "Burials;" DH Hill; Foenander; ONWR]

Robinett[e], George M. (Alexander County, North Carolina)
Landsman, Confederate States Navy. Born on September 19, 1825, Robinette died on July 10, 1900 and was buried at Three Forks Baptist Church, Alexander County, North Carolina. [Source(s): Stepp, "Burials;" Foenander]

Robinson, T. [Possible North Carolinian]
Seaman, Confederate States Navy. Robinson received a slight wound to the head at Fort Fisher on December 25, 1864. [Source(s): Daily Confed. (1/2/65); Card File]

Robinson, William
Gun Captain, Confederate States Navy.
Born in England, Robinson previously served in the British Navy. He served aboard the CSS BEAUFORT per that ship's payroll, bounty, and clothing records from September 1861 - February 16, 1862. He received a partial payment on February 13, 1862 at Gosport Navy Yard following his service in manning Fort Cobb at the Battle of Elizabeth City on February 10, 1862. He was killed in action at the Battle of Hampton Roads, March 8, 1862. His name appears on the payroll of the North Carolina Squadron for the 1st quarter of 1862 December 1, 1861 - March 8, 1862). [Source: NCCWSP]

Robinson, William F. (North Carolina)
Resigned his position as Professor of Mathematics, United States Navy, to go south and join the Confederate States Navy. The record of his dismissal" from the United States Navy is annotated with "In the Rebel navy."
[Source: Dudley]

Robinson, William G. (Wake County, North Carolina)
Lieutenant Colonel, Confederate States Army//Detailed to the Confederate Navy Department. Robinson resided in Wake County, North Carolina where he was appointed to the rank of Lieutenant Colonel to rank from September 1, 1861. He was wounded and captured at Gillett's Farm, Jones County, North Carolina, on April 13, 1862; date of exchange unknown. Promoted to Colonel on September 9, 1863 to rank from July 23, 1863, he was present or accounted for until dropped from the rolls of the regiment on May 25, 1864 by reason of his being detailed in the Navy Department by order of the Secretary of War.
[Source(s): North Carolina Troops, II]

Rochelle, M. S. (New Hanover County, North Carolina)
Private, Confederate States Marine Corps. Rochelle enlisted in Raleigh, North Carolina on October 6, 1864, and served on the Charleston, South Carolina Station as a Private of the Marine guard on board the ironclad CSS COLUMBIA to February 7, 1865. He transferred to the CSS INDIAN CHIEF on February 8, 1865. Rochelle signed an Oath of Allegiance in Wilmington, North Carolina, on July 28, 1865. He was described as 6" 1," with blue eyes, dark hair, fair complexion, age 26, a farmer, born and resided in New Hanover County, North Carolina. Rochelle was in the Marine Corps five months.
[Source(s): North Carolina Troops, Doc. # 0299; Card File; Donnelly-ENL]

Rodes, G. W. N. (Gates Company [?], North Carolina)
    Private, Confederate States Army//Confederate States Navy. Transferred from Company C, 19th Regiment, North Carolina Troops (2nd Regiment, North Carolina Cavalry) to the Confederate States Navy "by orders dated April 23, 1864 and May 21, 1864." No further record.
    [Source(s): North Carolina Troops, II; Foenander]

Rodman, John F. (T. J.) (Davidson County, North Carolina)
    Midshipman, Confederate States Navy. Born in North Carolina and appointed from there as a Midshipman on August 24, 1861. Rodman served on the Mississippi defenses, 1862 – 1863. Source "Foenander" lists a "John F. Rodman, Jr." with the following information: "Acting Midshipman; served on the Richmond Station, 1861 – 1862; later aboard the stern-wheeled gunboat CSS ISONDIGA (which operated around Savannah, Georgia and St. Augustine Creek, Florida), sometime between January 1863 and September 1864." Source "Fold3, Midshipman" lists a "John F. Rodman," while the 1860 Federal Census for Davidson County, North Carolina shows him living there. Born 1845.
    [Source(s): McElroy; Card File; Foenander; ONWR; Fold3, Midshipmen; Census (North Carolina), 1860]

Roe, W. F. (Washington County, North Carolina)
    Confederate States Navy.
    [Source(s): WCL; Darden]

Roff, Michael
    Seaman, Confederate States Navy. Roff enlisted on March 30, 1863 in Wilmington, North Carolina, for three years or the war.
    [Source(s): Card File; NA RG 45]

Rogers, Bryant (Beaufort County, North Carolina)
    Private, Company A, Confederate States Marine Corps. Rogers' name appears on a roll of prisoners of war at Point Lookout, Maryland, which states he was captured on April 6, 1865 at Farmville, Virginia and confined at Point Lookout until released on June 17, 1865. His name also appears as a signature to an Oath of Allegiance to the United States subscribed and sworn to at Point Lookout on June 17, 1865. Rogers' place of residence was given on the Oath as Beaufort County, North Carolina and his description as follows: Complexion, fair; hair, brown; eyes, hazel; height, 5 feet 6 ½ inches.
    [Source(s): Card File; NA; North Carolina Troops, Doc. # 0185, p. 2, and 0299; Donnelly]

Rogers, William
    Seaman ["Landsman" [see Stepp], Confederate States Navy. Registers and Report of Sick and Wounded at Confederate States Army General Military Hospital Number 4, Wilmington, North Carolina, state he was admitted on January 27, 1864, with "febris typhoides" and died February 8, 1864. He was buried in the Confederate Mass Grave, Oakdale Cemetery, Wilmington, North Carolina. His post office was listed as Popular (or Poplets) Hill, North Carolina [County?].
    [Source(s): Card File; NA RG 109; Stepp, "Burials"]

Rogers, Willis C.
    Landsman, Confederate States Navy. Rogers enlisted on February 29, 1864 in Raleigh, North Carolina, for the war.
    [Source(s): Card File; NA RG 45]

Rogers, W. T. (NOTE: May be same as "William Rogers," q.v.)
    Landsman, Confederate States Navy. Rogers enlisted on December 12 [or, 8th] in Raleigh, North Carolina, 1863 (or in Wilmington, North Carolina), for the war.
    [Source(s): Card File; NA RG 45]

Rooker, George
    Landsman, Confederate States Navy. Enlisting on December 17, 1863 in Raleigh, North Carolina, for the war, Rooker served as a Landsman aboard the CSS ARCTIC, Cape Fear River, North Carolina, 1863. He served aboard the CSS NEUSE as of the ship's March – October 1864 muster rolls.
    [Source(s): Card File; NA RG 45; Foenander; NEUSE Roster; CMACSSN]

Rosler ("Rosser" [?]), John A. (Pasquotank County, North Carolina)
    Private, Confederate States Army//Seaman, Landsman, Coxswain, Master's Mate, Confederate States Navy. Rosler

enlisted in Pasquotank County, North Carolina, as a Private "for twelve months" in Company K, 10th Regiment, North Carolina State Troops (1st Regiment, North Carolina Artillery) on April 22, 1861 at age 21. He transferred to the Confederate States Navy in July 1861 for service on the CSS FORREST. His name appears on a payroll of the receiving ship CSS UNITED STATES ending March 31, 1862. He served as a Landsman aboard the CSS ARCTIC; as a Coxswain on board the CSS VIRGINIA in the Battle of Hampton Roads, Virginia in 1862; and, was sent from his duty station at Drewry's Bluff to Saffold, Georgia in November 1862 to serve as the Coxswain on board the CSS CHATTAHOOCHIE, August 1862. He was appointed Master's Mate [Source NCCWSP gives his appointment rank as "Acting Master's Mate") on July 7, 1863 (Source NCCWSP gives the date as July 17, 1863) and served aboard the CSS SAMPSON at the Savannah Station, 1863 - 1864. Rosler participated in the expedition to capture the USS WATER WITCH, June 3, 1864. He was based in Savannah, Georgia, in June 1864.
[Source(s): Card File; Foenander; "Beaufort County Sailors;" North Carolina Troops, I, p.168; ORN 1, 15, p. 499; 1, 17, p.864; ORN 2, 1, pp.279, 303 & 309; Confederate States Navy Register; NCCWSP; www.thewashingtongrays.homestead.com; www.ncgenweb.us/nccivwar/rosters/10cok.htm]

Ross, James E.
Seaman, Confederate States Navy.
Ross served as a Seaman aboard the CSS BEAUFORT per clothing, bounty, and payroll lists from at least December 1861 - January 1862. Records indicate he received a partial payment on February 13, 1862 at Gosport Navy Yard following his service in manning Fort Cobb at the Battle of Elizabeth City on February 10, 1862. His name appears on the receiving ship CSS UNITED STATES payroll ending March 31, 1862. He served aboard the CSS VIRGINIA He is found on the payroll of the North Carolina Squadron for the 1st quarter of 1862 (January 10, 1862 - April 15, 1862). He transferred to the James River Squadron on April 15, 1862, serving at Drewry's Bluff as a Seaman at least during the period April 1, 1863 - June 30, 1863.
[Source: NCCWSP]

Ross, James (Norfolk, Virginia//Wilson County, North Carolina)
Corporal, Confederate States Army//Confederate States Navy. Born in Norfolk County, Virginia, and a caulker by trade, Ross enlisted in Wilson County, North Carolina, at age 27 on June 26, 1861, for the war, in Company G, 5th Regiment, North Carolina State Troops. Mustered in as a Private, he was promoted to Corporal in January-February 1862. He was present or accounted for until wounded and captured at Williamsburg, Virginia on May 5, 1862. Hospitalized in Baltimore, Maryland, he was exchanged at Aiken's Landing, James River, Virginia on August 5, 1862. He rejoined his company in November-December 1862 and was transferred to the Confederate States Navy on or about February 2, 1863.
[Source(s): Card File; North Carolina Troops, IV; Foenander]

Ross, James E.
Seaman, Confederate States Navy.
Ross served as a Seaman aboard the CSS BEAUFORT per clothing, bounty, and payroll lists from at least December 1861 - January 1862. He is found on the payroll of the North Carolina Squadron for the 1st quarter of 1862 (January 10, 1862 - April 15, 1862). Records indicate he received a partial payment on February 13, 1862 at Gosport Navy Yard following his service in manning Fort Cobb at the Battle of Elizabeth City on February 10, 1862. His name appears on the receiving ship CSS UNITED STATES payroll ending March 31, 1862. He served aboard the CSS VIRGINIA. He transferred to the James River Squadron on April 15, 1862, serving at Drewry's Bluff as a Seaman at least during the period April 1, 1863 - June 30, 1863.
[Source: NCCWSP]

Ross, John
Confederate States Navy.
Served aboard the CSS FANNY before being discharged from the hospital (sick) to the care of his mother by order of Flag Officer French Forrest January 17, 1862. His name appears on the payroll of the North Carolina Squadron for the 1st quarter of 1862 (February 7, 1862 - April 15, 1862).
[Source: NCCWSP]

Ross, John
Landsman, Confederate States Navy. Ross enlisted on May 27, 1864 in Raleigh, North Carolina, for the war.
[Source(s): Card File; NA RG 45]

Rosser, Joseph A.
Landsman, Confederate States Navy. Rosser enlisted on August 10, 1864 in Raleigh, North Carolina, for the war.
[Source(s): Card File; NA RG 45]

Rouark, John (Lenoir County, North Carolina)
Sergeant, Confederate States Army//Confederate States Navy (?). Rouark was born in Lenoir County, North Carolina, where he resided as a painter prior to enlisting in Wake County, North Carolina at age 28 on August 27, 1862, for the war. He served as a Private in Company C, 61st Regiment, North Carolina Troops. He was detailed as a hospital nurse in Wilson on December 1, 1862 but rejoined the company in May-June 1863. Reported as on duty as a provost guard at Magnolia in July-October 1863. He was promoted to Corporal on October 18, 1863, then to Sergeant on January 18, 1864. Rouark was reported present through April 30, 1864, but was killed in action at Bermuda Hundred, Virginia, on May 18, 1864. Source Card File indicates Confederate Naval service.
[Source(s): Card File; North Carolina Troops, XIV]

Roulley, George (New Hanover County, North Carolina)
Confederate States Navy. Served on the steamer CSS EUGENIE. His name appears on registers of Confederate States Army General Military Hospital Number 4, Wilmington, North Carolina, which states he was admitted on November 9, 1863 with "febris intermittens tertian," but his date of return to duty was not given. His post office was listed as Wilmington, North Carolina,
[Source(s): Card File; NA RG 109]

Rowe, William J. (Washington County, North Carolina)
Private, Confederate States Marine Corps. Rowe enlisted in Company A, Confederate States Marine Corps in Raleigh, North Carolina on November 4, 1864. Source "Pensions (North Carolina)" lists his enlistment date as 1863. He served on the Charleston, South Carolina Station and served as a Private of the Marine guard on board the ironclad CSS COLUMBIA until it was blown up on February 7, 1865. Afterwards, he was transferred to the CSS INDIAN CHIEF (February 8, 1865), thence to Richmond, Virginia. His name appears on a roll of prisoners of war at Point Lookout, Maryland, which states he was captured at Farmville, Virginia on April 6, 1865 and confined at Point Lookout until released on June 17, 1865. His name also appears as a signature to an Oath of Allegiance to the United States subscribed and sworn to at Point Lookout on June 17, 1865. His place of residence was listed on the Oath as Washington County, North Carolina and his description as follows: Complexion, light; hair, "I. Gray;" eyes, blue; height, 5 feet 6 ¼ inches. Per source "McLeod, August 30, 1874," Rowe was referred to by McLeod as "little Rowe." A claim for pension filed on July 1, 1901 by his widow Mary E. Rowe age 64, listing her post office as Creswell, Washington County, North Carolina was approved. He died at age 47 and was buried on "Furlough Farm" near Creswell, Washington County, North Carolina.
[Source(s): NA; Card File; North Carolina Troops, Doc. # 0185, p. 2, and 0299; Pensions (North Carolina); McLeod, August 30, 1874]

Rowzee (Rouzee), Claudius (Rowan County, North Carolina)
Private/Musician, Confederate States Army//Surgeon's Steward, Confederate States Navy. Rowzee was born and resided in Rowan County, North Carolina, where he worked as a physician and where he enlisted as a Private at age 25 in Company K, 8th Regiment, North Carolina Troops. He was captured at Roanoke Island, North Carolina, August 27, 1861; paroled at Elizabeth City, North Carolina, on February 21, 1862; and, exchanged in August 1862. Promoted to Musician between July and October 1863, he was present of accounted for until promoted to "Surgeon's Steward" on July 22, 1864. Source "MR" states he transferred to the Confederate States Navy on an unknown date. Source "Foenander" states he served as a Surgeon's Steward aboard the CSS ALBEMARLE and at Halifax Station, 1864.
[Source(s): MR, I; North Carolina Troops, IV; Foenander]

Royals [Royall], A. H.
Landsman, Confederate States Navy. Royals enlisted on August 10, 1864 in Raleigh, North Carolina, for the war, and served as a Landsman aboard the CSS ARCTIC, Cape Fear River, North Carolina, 1863.
[Source(s): Card File; NA RG 45; Foenander]

Rue, Alexander M. (Beaufort County, North Carolina)
Private, Confederate States Army//Seaman, Confederate States Navy. Rue enlisted in Beaufort County, North Carolina, on June 27 [26], 1861, age 27, "for the war," as a Private in Company G, 19th Regiment, North Carolina Troops [2nd Regiment, North Carolina]. He was present or accounted until he transferred to the Confederate States Navy on February 1, 1862 [Source NCCWSP indicates Rue's name appears on a clothing list for the CSS RALEIGH

dated January 16, 1862] where he served as a Seaman aboard the CSS RALEIGH through at least April 1862. Rue's name appears on a North Carolina Squadron payroll covering the period February 7, 1862 - April 15, 1862. He was transferred to the James River Squadron on April 15, 1862.
[Source(s): Card File; ORN 2, 1, p.301; North Carolina Troops, II; Foenander; "Beaufort County Sailors;" NCCWSP]

Rue, John G. (Beaufort County, North Carolina)
Private, Confederate States Army//Quartermaster/Seaman, Confederate States Navy. Rue enlisted "for the war" in Beaufort County, North Carolina at age 30 on July 10 [11], 1861 as a Private in Company G, 19th Regiment, North Carolina Troops [2nd Regiment, North Carolina Cavalry]. He was present or accounted for until he transferred to the Confederate States Navy on February 1, 1862. Rue was a Quartermaster aboard the CSS RALEIGH from January 16, 1862 [per source NCCWSP] through 15 December 15, 1863. He transferred to the James River Squadron on April 15, 1862. Rue served at Drewry's Bluff, Virginia as a Seaman from at least April 1, 1863 through June 30, 1863. He is listed as a Quartermaster aboard the CSS RALEIGH from November 16, 1863 through December 15, 1863. He married about 1876 and resided as a sailor, in 1880, with his wife Lilia, at Washington, Beaufort County, North Carolina. He was later employed as a house painter.
[Source(s): Card File; NA RG 45; North Carolina Troops, II; Foenander; "Beaufort County Sailors;" NCCWSP]

Runnells (Runnell), John (Washington County, North Carolina)
Private, Confederate States Army//Seaman, Confederate States Navy. Runnells resided in Washington County, North Carolina where he enlisted at age 26 on June 25, 1861 (Source MR, I, gives the date as June 24, 1861), for the war, in Company G, 1st Regiment, North Carolina State Troops. He was present or accounted for until discharged from his regiment on February 3, 1862, upon being transferred to the Confederate States Navy where he served as a Seaman aboard the CSS VIRGINIA, Hampton Roads, Virginia, 1862.
[Source(s): Card File; North Carolina Troops, III; Foenander; MR, I]

Russell, B. R. (Pasquotank County, North Carolina)
Assistant Engineer: "Captain" [rank appears on Card source], Confederate States Navy. Though listed as a crewman on the CSS NORTH CAROLINA, Russell's name does not appear in the Confederate States Navy officer register. Source "Foenander" lists a "B. R. Russell" who served as a "2nd class fireman, CSS ARCTIC, Cape Fear River, North Carolina, 1863." Russell died on December 15, 1906 and was buried in the Bellevue Cemetery, New Hanover County, North Carolina.
[Source(s): MR, 4, p. 444; Wayne Carver; Gravestone Records, v. 6, p. 323; Stepp, "Burials;" "Chronicles;" Foenander]

Russell, Benjamin R. (NOTE: May be same as "B. R. Russell," q.v., though rank is incorrect)
Seaman, Confederate States Navy. Russell enlisted on June 5, 1863 in Wilmington, North Carolina, for the war.
[Source(s): Card File; NA RG 45]

Russell, Robert M. [NOTE: May be same as "R. W. Russell," q.v.]
Ordinary Seaman, Confederate States Navy. Russell enlisted on September 22, 1863 in Wilmington, North Carolina, for the war. His name appears on registers of Confederate States Army General Military Hospital Number 4, Wilmington, North Carolina, which states he was admitted on October 22, 1863 with "feb int tert" and returned to duty on December 22, 1863. His post office was listed as "Morristown," North Carolina, and "Morristown Yard [or, "Morrison Tan Yard" (see "Russell, R. W." entry) North Carolina [County?].
[Source(s): Card File; NA RG 109]

Russell, R. W. (Mecklenburg County, North Carolina) [NOTE: May be same as "Robert M. Russell," q.v.]
Seaman, Confederate States Navy. Russell enlisted on September 9, 1863 in Wilmington, North Carolina [or, September 11th, at Camp Holmes, near Raleigh, North Carolina], and served as a Seaman aboard the CSS ARCTIC, North Carolina, 1863, and as an Ordinary Seaman aboard the CSS YADKIN, Wilmington, North Carolina, 1864. His name appears on registers of Confederate States Army General Military Hospital Number 4, Wilmington, North Carolina, being admitted January 28, 1864, with "abscessus" and returned to duty on March 26, 1864. His post office was listed as "Morrison Tan Yard, North Carolina [County?]." A pension claim filed on June 10, 1901 by his widow Sarah Russell, age 68, listed her post office as Mill Bridge, Rowan County, North Carolina. It states her husband enlisted in the Confederate States Navy in Wilmington on or about September 9, 1863 and served there." He died at home after the war. The pension was approved.
[Source(s): MR, 4, p. 447; Card File; NA RG 109; NA RG 45; Pensions (North Carolina); Foenander]

Russell, Stephen E. (Cumberland County, North Carolina)
Private, Confederate States Army//Confederate States Navy. Russell enlisted in Cumberland County, North Carolina at age 21 for six months on April 17, 1861 in Company H ("Fayetteville Independent Light Infantry"), 1st Regiment, North Carolina Infantry (6 Months) ("Bethel Regiment"). He was present or accounted for until mustered out on November 12-13, 1861. He enlisted in Cumberland County, North Carolina, in Company I, 51st Regiment, North Carolina Troops on April 29, 1862, for the war. Reported absent sick in July-August 1962, he returned to duty in September-October 1862. He was present or accounted for until transferred as a Private to 2nd Company B [Source "North Carolina Troops, I" lists him in "3rd" Company B], 36th Regiment (2nd, North Carolina Artillery) on September 24, 1863. Transferred to Company B, 13th Bn., North Carolina, Light Artillery on November 3 [Source "North Carolina Troops, I" gives the date as November 4], 1863, he was present or accounted for until transferred to the Confederate States Navy on May 16, 1864. Source NEUSE Roster states he served aboard the CSS NEUSE as of the ship's March – October 1864 muster rolls. He married Mary Ann Howell in Cumberland County, North Carolina on September 2, 1865.
[Source(s): North Carolina Troops I, III, and XII; Marriage Bonds, North Carolina Div. of Historical Res.; Hill; Card File; NA RG 109; Foenander; NEUSE Roster; CMACSSN]

Ruth, Solomon (Randolph County, North Carolina)
Landsman, Confederate States Navy. Ruth enlisted on October 20 (21, 26, or, 29), 1863 at Camp Holmes, near Raleigh, North Carolina (or, in Wilmington, North Carolina). Source "Foenander" lists an "S. Ruth, Landsman, CSS ARCTIC, Cape Fear River, North Carolina, 1863."
[Source(s): MR, 4, p. 447; Card File; NA RG 45; Foenander]

Ryan, James [May be same as "James H. Ryan," q.v.]
Seaman, Confederate States Navy. Ryan enlisted on September 22, 1863 in Wilmington, North Carolina, for the war [or, September 9, 1863, at Camp Holmes, near Raleigh, North Carolina, for the war as a substitute]. He may be the same as the "James Ryan" who served aboard the CSS ARCTIC, 1863, and the "James Ryan" who served as a Seaman and Ordinary Seaman aboard the CSS NORTH CAROLINA, 1864.
[Source(s): Card File; NA RG 45; MR, 4, p. 447; Foenander; St. Armand]

Ryan, James H. (New Hanover Company (?), North Carolina) [May be same as "James Ryan," q.v.]
Seaman, Confederate States Navy. Born 1824, Ryan died on February 13, 1869 and was buried in Oakdale Cemetery, Wilmington, New Hanover County, North Carolina. [Source(s): Stepp, "Burials"]

Rymer, Pleasant A. (Rowan County, North Carolina)
Seaman, Confederate States Navy. Rymer enlisted on June 15, 1864 in Raleigh, North Carolina, for the war. He served aboard the Confederate States steamer "P. D." [likely the CSS PEEDEE]. Signed a parole at Salisbury, North Carolina, May 17, 1865. His name appears on an Oath of Allegiance to the United States dated July 8, 1865 signed at Salisbury, North Carolina. His residence was listed as Rowan County, North Carolina.
[Source(s): Card File; NA RG 45]

Safley, Paul (Rowan County, North Carolina)
Confederate States Navy. His name appears on a prisoner's parole at Libby Prison, Richmond, Virginia, dated April 21, 1865. Granted permission to go to his home is "Salisburg" [sic] (Salisbury), North Carolina."
[Source(s): Card File; NA RG 109]

Saintsing [St. Sing], Robert (Wake Company [?], North Carolina)
Landsman, Confederate States Navy. Born in North Carolina in 1843, Saintsing [St. Sing] enlisted on August 11, 1864 in Raleigh, North Carolina, for the war, and served as a Landsman aboard the CSS ARCTIC, Cape Fear River, North Carolina, 1863. He resided as a farmer, in 1880, with his wife Lucy H. St. Sing, and three children (eldest child born 1870) at Oak Grove, Wake County, North Carolina. [Source(s): Card File; NA RG 45; Foenander]

St. George, William
Pilot, Confederate States Navy. St. George served aboard the blockade runner "*Don*."
[Source(s): McElroy]

Salling, Sterling (New Hanover County, North Carolina)
Seaman [Landsman], Confederate States Navy. Salling enlisted on October 5, 1863 at Camp Holmes [near Raleigh,

North Carolina]. Prisoner of war records indicate that as a "rebel deserter [he] came on board the Gun Boat of [at?] New Inlet." Date of desertion not given, however, records state he was received at Fort Monroe, Virginia, January 29, 1864, from Newbern [sic]. Confined at Fort Monroe, Virginia, until released on taking the Oath of Allegiance to the US, February 10, 1864. His residence was listed as Masonboro, North Carolina. Description: Complexion light; hair dark; eyes blue; height 5 feet 9 ½ inches.
[Source(s): Card File; NA RG 45; NA RG 109]

Salyer, Samuel (Currituck County, North Carolina)
Private, Confederate States Army//Landsman, Seaman, Pilot, Confederate States Navy. Salyer resided in Currituck County, North Carolina, where he enlisted on May 13, 1861, as a Private in Company L, 17th Regiment, North Carolina Troops. He deserted or was transferred to the Confederate States Navy prior to July 28, 1861. One source indicates he transferred to the Confederate States Navy prior to July 28, 1861 as his name appears on a payroll dated July 29, 1861 for the NCS ALBEMARLE on which he served as a Pilot [per source NCCWSP]. However, by October 8, 1861 he is listed as a Landsman aboard the CSS FANNY, with which he stayed at least until December 1, 1861. By the ship's December 12, 1861 payroll, he is listed as a Seaman. Records indicate he served with the North Carolina Squadron from December 1, 1861 through at least March 24, 1862. Salyer is said to have served as a Landsman on the CSS FANNY, 1861-1862, and aboard the CSS VIRGINIA, Hampton Roads, Virginia, 1862. He enlisted in Camden County, North Carolina, on July 7, 1863, for the war, as a Private in Company B, 68th Regiment, North Carolina Troops. He is reported present on April 30, 1864, and on guard duty on June 30, 1864. His name appears on a receipt roll for clothing dated September 30, 1864. He was paroled at the office of the Federal Provost Marshal for the District of Eastern Virginia on April 30, 1865. [Source "North Carolina Troops, XV" entry states he "May have served previously as Private in Company, 17th Regiment, North Carolina Troops (1st Organization), and the Confederate States Navy. If so, the information in 6:758 of this series is incorrect, and the correct date of his death is May 23, 1865 (not 1862)].
[Source(s): Card File; North Carolina Troops, VI; Foenander; NCCWSP]

Sampson, N.
Confederate States Navy. Sampson's name appears on a register of Confederate States Army General Military Hospital Number 4, Wilmington, North Carolina dated June 15, 1863, which gives his disease as "dysentery" office as "Mount Pellis, North Carolina."
[Source(s): Card File; NA RG 109]

Sanders, Charles
Ordinary Seaman, Confederate States Navy.
Sanders serve aboard the CSS SEA BIRD as an Ordinary Seaman. His name appears on the payroll of the North Carolina Squadron for the 1st quarter of 1862 (December 1, 1861 - March 31, 1862). He is listed as having "run" as of March 31, 1862.
[Source: NCCWSP]

Sanders, James A.
Confederate States Navy. Sanders originally served as a Private in Captain McDugald's Company, North Carolina Infantry. He transferred to the Confederate States Navy at an unspecified date.
[Source(s): Foenander]

Sanders, J. T. [NOTE: Possibly same as "James T. Sanders," q.v.]
Landsman, Confederate States Navy. Sanders enlisted on March 18, 1864 in Raleigh, North Carolina, for the war.
[Source(s): Card File; NA RG 45]

Sanders, James T. (Wake County, North Carolina; born in Franklin County, North Carolina)
Confederate States Navy. Sanders resided as a farmer in Wake County, North Carolina prior to being conscripted [per "Foenander," he enlisted] there on February 15, 1864, at Camp Holmes [near Raleigh, North Carolina], from Colonel Ivey's 38th Regiment, North Carolina Militia from Wake County, North Carolina. His description was as follows: Age, 23; eyes, blue; hair, light; complexion, fair; height, 5 feet 11 inches; place of birth, Franklin County, North Carolina; occupation farmer.
[Source(s): Card File; NA RG 45; Foenander]

Sanford, Douglas (Mecklenburg County, North Carolina?)
Private, Confederate States Army//Confederate States Navy. Sanford enlisted at Gaines' Mill, Virginia, on June 5, 1864 in Company C, 10th Regiment, North Carolina State Troops (1st Regiment, North Carolina Artillery), for

the war. He was dropped from the rolls July-August 1864 because he "belongs to Navy," and was ordered to his command.
[Source(s): Card File; NA RG 109; North Carolina Troops, I; Foenander]

Sandford, James
Landsman, Confederate States Navy. Sandford enlisted on March 11, 1864 in Wilmington, North Carolina, for the war.
[Source(s): Card File; NA RG 45]

Sandford [Sanford John W., Jr.
Surgeon, Confederate States Navy. Born in Fayetteville, North Carolina, on November 5, 1834, Sandford graduated from the University of North Carolina, Chapel Hill, North Carolina in 1854. He also graduated from the Jefferson Medical College, in 1857. Appointed as an Assistant Surgeon from North Carolina, Sandford entered the United States Navy on May 28, 1857 and was dismissed on May 29, 1861. His original appointment in the Confederate States Navy as a Passed Assistant Surgeon came on June 26, 1861 [June 11, 1861, per "Fold3, USN Resignees." Another source gives his appointment to Passed Assistant Surgeon as September 17, 1862, to rank from September 13, 1862, while yet another indicates he was elevated to Passed Assistant Surgeon Provisional Navy, June 2, 1864]. He served on the Savannah Station, 1861-1862; served under Captain James D. Johnston at Mobile Bay aboard the CSS BALTIC, Mobile Squadron, 1862; the CSS PALMETTO STATE, Charleston Station, 1862; the CSS SAVANNAH, Savannah Squadron, 1863-1864; at Smithville, North Carolina; and, on the Wilmington Station, 1864. He practiced medicine in Fayetteville for a short time after the war, but removed to Mobile, Alabama, about 1870, and held the position of bookkeeper and cashier in the Western Union Telegraph office. He died of disease at Mobile, Alabama, in December 1881.
[Source(s): Register; McElroy; Card File; Journal; Foenander; CWDTS; ONWR; Fold3, USN Resignees]

Satterthwaite [Salterthwaite], C. W. B. (Beaufort County, North Carolina)
Landsman [Seaman], Confederate States Navy. Enlisted on August 8, 1864, in Raleigh, North Carolina, for the war, Satterthwaite's name appears on a Register of Pettigrew General Hospital No. 13, Raleigh, North Carolina being admitted on December 27, 1864, with "phthisis pulmonalis" and transferred to "Kittrells" January 1, 1865. His post office was listed as Leechville, Beaufort County, North Carolina.
[Source(s): Card File; NA RG 45; NA RG 109]

Saunders (Sanders), John
Seaman, Ordinary Seaman, Confederate States Navy.
Per the payroll list of July-September 1861, Saunders is recorded as a Seaman aboard the NSC EDWARDS and a Seaman aboard the CSS FORREST muster roll dated October 30, 1861. He transferred to the CSS SEA BIRD on October 26, 1861 and served as an Ordinary Seaman from July 1861 - February 1862. He received a partial payment on February 13, 1862 at Gosport Navy Yard following Battle of Elizabeth City on February 10, 1862.
He appears as an Ordinary Seaman on an overcoat issue list dated February 20, 1862 for the CSS SEA BIRD [NOTE: The names "Sanders" and "Saunders" may have been used interchangeably for John and Thomas O., q. v. Both served in Company B, 8th Regiment, North Carolina Troops and are recorded as transferring to the Confederate States Navy on or about February 9, 1863].
[Source: NCCWSP]

Saunders, Daniel
Landsman, Confederate States Navy. Saunders enlisted on April 13, 1864, in Raleigh, North Carolina, for the war.
[Source(s): Card File; NA RG 45]

Saunders, James T.
Confederate States Navy. Saunders' name appears on a list of conscripts "in the yard at Halifax" June 9, 1864.
[Source(s): Card File; NA RG 45]

Saunders [Sanders], John (Currituck County, North Carolina)
Private, Confederate States Army//Seaman, Ordinary Seaman, Confederate States Navy.
[Note: Given the discrepancy in dates and other conflicting information, there is a possibility that "John Sanders" and "John Saunders" were two different men from the same area]. Saunders was born in and resided as a farmer in Currituck County, North Carolina. Saunders is listed as having served as a Seaman aboard the NCS EDWARDS (later renamed the CSS FORREST) payroll list for July-September 1861. He is shown as a Seaman on the muster

roll of the CSS FORREST dated October 30, 1861 but was transferred to the CSS SEA BIRD on October 26, 1861. Per muster and clothing records, he appears as an Ordinary Seaman aboard the CSS SEA BIRD from July 1861 – February 1862 with the North Carolina Squadron. He received a partial payment on February 13, 1862 at Gosport Navy Yard following the Battle of Elizabeth City on February 10, 1862. Other records show a man by this name enlisted in the Confederate States Army at age 20 on August 19, 1861 in Company B, 8th Regiment, North Carolina Troops. He transferred to the Confederate States Navy on January 30, 1863 [Sources "North Carolina Troops, IV" and "Foenander" give the date as "on or about" February 9, 1863]. He served as a Seaman aboard the CSS ARCTIC and CSS NORTH CAROLINA in 1864, the CSS TALLAHASSEE in late 1864. He may have been the brother of Thomas O. Saunders, q. v.

[Source(s): MR, I & IV, p. 444; SEA BIRD; North Carolina Troops, IV, p. 540 (Broadfoot ed., name shown as "Saunders"); Card File; NA RG 45; Foenander; *ORN* 2, 1, 279, 294-296, 306 & 307; NCCWSP]

Saunders (Sanders), Thomas O. (Currituck County, North Carolina)

[Note: Given the discrepancy in dates, there is a possibility that "Thomas O. Sanders" and "Thomas O. Saunders" were two different men from the same area].

Seaman, Confederate States Navy//Private, Confederate States Army.

Born in Currituck County, North Carolina, Sanders resided there as a farmer. Muster and clothing records indicate he served as a Seaman aboard the CSS SEA BIRD from July 1861 – February 1862. He is listed as having received a partial payment at Norfolk Navy Yard on February 13, 1862 following the Battle of Elizabeth City on February 10, 1862. His name appears on the receiving ship CSS UNITED STATES per its payroll ending March 31, 1862. He is listed as having served with the North Carolina Squadron according to the Squadron's payroll for the 1st quarter of 1862 (December 1, 1861 - March 31, 1862 on which he is listed as having "run" on or before March 31, 1862. A Thomas O. Saunders enlisted in Company B, 8th Regiment, North Carolina State Troops on August 19, 1861 at 18 years of age. He transferred to the Confederate States Navy on or about February 9, 1863 [Source "MR I" gives date as January 1863, while another source indicates he enlisted in the Confederate States Navy on January 21, 1863, in Wilmington, North Carolina, for three years or the war]. [Records used by source NCCWSP indicate a "Thomas O. Saunders (Sanders)" served aboard the CSS SEA BIRD from at least July 1861 – February 1862, and that he received a partial pay on February 13, 1862 at Gosport Navy Yard, Norfolk, Virginia following the Battle of Elizabeth City, North Carolina on February 10, 1862. His name appears on a payroll of the receiving ship CSS UNITED STATES ending March 31, 1862. He is listed as having served with the North Carolina Squadron during the period December 1, 1861 – March 31, 1862, and perhaps earlier or later]. He is listed as having "run" on or before March 31, 1862. Other records indicate he served as a Seaman aboard the CSS ARCTIC and CSS NORTH CAROLINA in 1864 and aboard the CSS TALLAHASSEE in late 1864. He may have been the brother of John Saunders, q. v.

[Source(s): MR, I & IV, p. 444; SEA BIRD; *North Carolina Troops*, IV, p. 540, 596 (Broadfoot edition, name shown as "Saunders"); Card File; NA RG 45; Foenander; ORN 2, 1, 279, 293, 295, 296, 306 & 307; NCCWSP; Census (NC), 1850]

Savage, John P. (New Hanover County, North Carolina [Source "North Carolina Troops, I" gives county as Brunswick County, North Carolina).

Private, Confederate States Army//Seaman and Pilot, Confederate States Navy. Born in Brunswick County, North Carolina, Savage was by occupation a pilot prior to enlisting in New Hanover County, North Carolina at age 25 on June 3, 1861 in Company E, 10th Regiment, North Carolina State Troops (1st Regiment, North Carolina Artillery). He was transferred to the Confederate States Navy on May 5, 1862, and served as Seaman and Pilot on the CSS ARCTIC, 1862. His name appears on a register of Confederate States Army General Military Hospital Number 4, Wilmington, North Carolina, dated May 19, 1862, which gives disease as "parotitis" and post office as Wilmington, North Carolina. He returned to duty on May 20, 1862.

[Source(s): Card File; NA RG 109; North Carolina Troops, I; Foenander]

Savage, Joseph P.

Pilot, Confederate States Navy. Savage transferred to the Confederate States Navy on May 5, 1862 from Company E, 10th Regiment, North Carolina State Troops (1st Regiment, North Carolina Artillery).

[Source(s): Card File]

Savage, L. P. [NOTE: See "Lewis P. Savage"]

Ordinary Seaman, Confederate States Navy. Savage enlisted on September 5, 1863, in Wilmington, North Carolina, for the war.

[Source(s): Card File; NA RG 45]

Savage, Lewis T. [P.] (New Hanover County, North Carolina) [NOTE: See "L. P. Savage"]
Ordinary Seaman, Confederate States Navy//Private, Confederate States Army. Savage enlisted in the Confederate States Navy on August 23, 1863 in Wilmington, North Carolina, and served as an Ordinary Seaman aboard the CSS ARCTIC, 1863. Savage transferred as a Private to Company C, 13th Battalion, North Carolina Artillery on March 21, 1864. He was paroled at Greensboro, North Carolina, May 1, 1865. His name appears on a Muster Roll for March-April 1864 of Company C, 13th Battalion, North Carolina Artillery, with the remark: "Exchanged from C. S. Navy for W. R. [Whitford Robert] Beery, April 19, 1864." He served aboard the CSS NEUSE as of the ship's March – October 1864 muster rolls. Present or accounted for until February 1865, he is listed as having been paroled at Greensboro, North Carolina, May 1, 1865.
[Source(s): MR, 4, p. 447; Card File; NA RG 109; North Carolina Troops, I; Foenander; NEUSE Roster; CMACSSN]

Sawyer, Ebenezer W. (Born in Portsmouth, Virginia//Pasquotank County, North Carolina)
Corporal, Confederate States Army//Ordinary Seaman, Confederate States Navy. Sawyer was born in Portsmouth, Virginia, and was by occupation a clerk. He enlisted in Pasquotank County, North Carolina, at age 21, on April 23, 1861, as a Private or Corporal in Company A, 17th Regiment, North Carolina Troops (1st Organization). He was present or accounted for until he transferred to the Confederate States Navy on October 4, 1861 and per payroll records served as an Ordinary Seaman aboard the CSS CURLEW from November 1861 – 1st quarter of 1862. His name appears on a roll of the receiving ship CSS UNITED STATES ending March 31, 1862. He enlisted in Portsmouth County, North Carolina, on April 24, 1863, for the war, as a Private in Company A, 68th Regiment, North Carolina Troops. Captured at the "Big Black River," Virginia, on August 18, 1863, Sawyer was sent to Fort Norfolk, Virginia, and then transferred to Point Lookout, Maryland, arriving on September 22, 1863. He died at Point Lookout on March 26, 1864, cause of death not reported. Federal Provost Records identify this man as a member of the 66th Regiment, North Carolina Troops. In reality he was a member of a regiment in the process of organizing that was tentatively designated the 66th Regiment, North Carolina Troops, but eventually became the 68th Regiment, North Carolina Troops (per "Foenander": "service also shown as being in Company B, 32nd North Carolina Infantry").
[Source(s): Card File; NA RG 45; North Carolina Troops, VI and XV; Foenander; NCCWSP]

Sawyer, Joseph (Currituck County, North Carolina)
Private, Confederate States Army//Landsman, Confederate States Navy. Sawyer was born in Currituck County, North Carolina, where he resided as a farmer until enlisting there at age 31 on May 13, 1861 as a Private in Company E, 17th Regiment, North Carolina Troops (1st Organization). He was present or accounted for until he transferred to the Confederate States Navy on or about December 15, 1861 where he served as a Landsman aboard the CSS FANNY from at least October 8, 1861 – December 20, 1861. His name appears on a North Carolina Squadron payroll covering the period from December 1, 1861 - February 28, 1862.
[Source(s): Card File; NA RG 45; North Carolina Troops, VI; Foenander; NCCWSP]

Sawyer, Samuel (Currituck County, North Carolina)
Private, Confederate States Army//Landsman, Confederate States Navy. Born in 1838, Sawyer enlisted in Currituck County, North Carolina, on May 13, 1861, as a Private in Company E, 17th Regiment, North Carolina Troops (1st Organization), and transferred to the Confederate States Navy prior to July 28, 1861 where he served as a Landsman aboard the CSS FANNY from at least October 8, 1861-December 20, 1862. His name appears on a payroll document of the North Carolina Squadron covering the period December 1, 1861 - February 28, 1862 on which date he is listed as having "run." Sawyer died on October 2, 1894 and was buried in the Sawyer Family Cemetery, Camden County, North Carolina.
[Source(s): Card File; NA RG 45; Stepp, "Burials;" North Carolina Troops, VI; Foenander; NCCWSP]

Scersey (Scerscey, Scersey), Jasper H.
Landsman, Confederate States Navy. He enlisted on November 5, 1863, in Wilmington, North Carolina, for the war [Another source cites his enlistment as November 2, 1863, in Raleigh, North Carolina, for the war] and served as a Landsman aboard the CSS ARCTIC, Cape Fear River, North Carolina, 1863, and later as a Landsman aboard the CSS NORTH CAROLINA, Cape Fear River, North Carolina, 1864.
[Source(s): Card File; NA RG 45; Foenander]

Schafer, B.
Landsman, Confederate States Navy. Schafer enlisted on October 11, 1863, in Wilmington, North Carolina, for the war.
[Source(s): Card File; NA RG 45]

Scharer [Shaver, Schaver], Jacob
> Landsman, Confederate States Navy. Scharer enlisted on November 15, 1863, in Wilmington, North Carolina, for the war, and served as a Landsman aboard the CSS ARCTIC, Cape Fear River, North Carolina, 1863. He also served aboard the steam gunboat CSS RALEIGH, in North Carolina and Virginia waters, 1864.
> [Source(s): Card File; NA RG 45; Foenander]

Schisano, Stephen P. (Virginian; served in North Carolina unit)
> Sergeant, Confederate States Army//Gunner, Confederate States Navy.
> Schisano resided in Virginia and enlisted at Camp Bee, Virginia at age 25 on October 6, 1861, for the war, in Company K, 1st Regiment, North Carolina State Troops. Mustered in as a Sergeant, he was present or accounted for until discharged on October 27, 1862 by reason of his "having been appointed an officer of the Confederate States Navy" (one source shows original entry into Confederate States Navy, as Acting Gunner, October 3, 1862, while source MR, I lists the date as October 6, 1862). He served as an Acting Gunner on the CSS ARCTIC, 1863 and Gunner at the Richmond Station, and at Drewry's Bluff, Virginia, 1862 - 1864.
> [Source(s): Card File; NA RG 45; North Carolina Troops, III; Foenander]

Schroeder, John Albert (New Hanover County, North Carolina [?])
> First Class Fireman ["Fireman" (see Stepp)], Confederate States Navy. Schroeder served on the CSS SELMA. Born in 1841, he died in 1901 and was buried in Bellevue Cemetery, Wilmington, New Hanover County, North Carolina.
> [Source(s): Card File, Gravestone Records, v.8, p. 41; Stepp, "Burials"]

Schulkin, M.
> Landsman, Confederate States Navy. Schulkin enlisted on August 12, 1864, in Raleigh, North Carolina, for the war.
> [Source(s): Card File; NA RG 45]

Schwartzman, Adolphus J. (North Carolina)
> Engineer (Second Lieutenant), Confederate States Navy. Born in North Carolina in 1844, the son of Gus and Carrie Schwartzman, Schwartzman was appointed from North Carolina as a Third Assistant Engineer, Confederate States Navy, on April 30, 1863. He was appointed a Third Assistant Engineer, Provisional Navy, on June 2, 1864, and was later promoted to Second Assistant Engineer. He served aboard the CSS JUNO and CSS CHICORA, Charleston Station, 1863-1864; the CSS FREDERICKSBURG, James River Squadron, 1865; and was detached on February 15, 1865 and ordered to the CSS NANSEMOND. Source "Driver" states he served at Drewry's Bluff as of February 1865. He was captured on April 6, 1865, at Painesville, Virginia. Initially sent to Old Capitol Prison, he was transferred to Johnson's Island, and released on taking the Oath of Allegiance to the United States on June 1, 1865. Description: Age 22; height, 5'10;" complexion dark; hair brown; eyes hazel; residence Richmond, Virginia.
> [Source(s): Register, McElroy; Card File; Driver; Foenander; ONWR]

Scoggin, John S.
> Landsman, Confederate States Navy. Scoggin enlisted on May 27, 1864, in Raleigh, North Carolina, for the war.
> [Source(s): Card File; NA RG 45]

Scott, Edward W.
> Landsman, Confederate States Navy. Scott enlisted on December 15, 1863, in Raleigh, North Carolina, for the war [another source cites his enlistment as occurring on December 18, 1863 in Wilmington, North Carolina, "for the war]." He served as a Landsman aboard the CSS ARCTIC, Cape Fear River, North Carolina, 1863, and later aboard the CSS YADKIN, Wilmington, North Carolina, 1864.
> [Source(s): Card File; NA RG 45; Foenander]

Scott, Henry H. (North Carolina)
> Assistant Ordnance Officer, Confederate States Navy. Scott was born in and appointed from North Carolina as an Acting Midshipman, "3rd Class," January 10, 1862, and served on the Richmond station, 1862. He served at the Evansport Battery, 1862; in the Mobile Squadron, 1862-1863; aboard the Confederate States steamers CSS MORGAN (1863-1864) and CSS TUSCALOOSA; CSS PATRICK HENRY, 1864; CSS VIRGINIA II, and CSS RICHMOND, James River Squadron, 1864-1865. Appointed Midshipman, Provisional Navy, June 2, 1864, and later, Passed Midshipman [no date], he was appointed Assistant Ordnance Officer, James River Squadron, November 1864, and subsequently assigned to the CSS W. H. WEBB which was abandoned below New Orleans on April 24, 1865. Captured on April 25, 1865, he was sent aboard the USS LACKAWANNA, and then the USS RICHMOND, as a prisoner of war, on the same day. He was sent to Florida for transfer north on April 27, 1865, and later to Fort Columbus, New York Harbor. He was later sent to Fort Warren, Boston Harbor, where he was received May 20,

1865 and released on June 13, 1865 upon taking the Oath of Allegiance there. [NOTE: Source "Foenander" gives Scott's date and place of birth as 1844 or 1845 in Virginia or Kentucky, and states he was a citizen of California. Other sources indicate he could have been from or resided in Alamance or Orange County, North Carolina. Foenander gives his entry into Confederate Naval Service as July 10, 1862 vice January 10, 1862, and states further that Scott survived the war and resided as a stockbroker in San Francisco, California].
[Source(s): Register; McElroy; Card File; Academy; Foenander; ONWR]

Scott, William
Ordinary Seaman, Confederate States Navy. Scott enlisted on March 26, 1863, in Wilmington, North Carolina, for three years or the war. He served aboard the CSS ARCTIC, Cape Fear River, North Carolina, 1863; and later aboard the CSS RALEIGH in North Carolina and Virginia waters, 1864.
[Source(s): Card File; NA RG 45; Foenander]

Scott, W. M.
Landsman, Confederate States Navy. Scott enlisted on July 16, 1864, in Raleigh, North Carolina, for the war.
[Source(s): Card File; NA RG 45]

Scusey, Jasper (Mecklenburg County, North Carolina)
Confederate States Navy. Scusey enlisted in the Confederate States Navy on October 31, 1863 in Wilmington, North Carolina.
[Source(s): MR, 4, p. 447]

Seachrist, Conrad
Landsman, Confederate States Navy. Seachrist enlisted on June 30, 1864, in Raleigh, North Carolina, for the war.
[Source(s): Card File; NA RG 45]

Seawell, James A.
Lieutenant, North Carolina Navy.
Served aboard the NCS WINSLOW.
[Source: NCS]

Sebastian, Samuel
Quarter Gunner, Confederate States Navy.
Clothing, payroll, and small stores records indicate Sebastian served aboard the CSS RALEIGH as a Quarter Gunner serving with the North Carolina Squadron from September 2, 1861 - 1st quarter 1862.
[Source: NCCWSP]

Seitz, Abel
Landsman, Confederate States Navy. Seitz enlisted on June 8, 1864, in Raleigh, North Carolina, for the war.
[Source(s): Card File; NA RG 45]

Selby, Samuel C. S.
Landsman, Confederate States Navy. Selby enlisted on April 20, 1864, in Raleigh, North Carolina, for the war.
[Source(s): Card File; NA RG 45]

Sellars, R.
Pilot, Confederate States Navy. Sellars served aboard the blockade runner "*Venus*."
[Source(s): McElroy; Card File]

Sellers, Alfred
Landsman, Confederate States Navy. Sellers enlisted on October 5, 1863, at Camp Holmes [near Raleigh, North Carolina].
[Source(s): Card File; NA RG 45]

Senter, Randall J. [Source "Howard" gives name as "Richard"] (Harnett County, North Carolina)
Private, Confederate States Army//Landsman, Confederate States Navy. Born in Harnett County, North Carolina about 1827, Senter resided as a laborer in Duplin County, North Carolina prior to enlisting in Wayne County, North Carolina, at age 27 on June 24, 1861, for the war, in 2nd Company C, 2nd Regiment, North Carolina State Troops. He was present or accounted for until transferred to the Confederate States Navy on April 10, 1864 where he served as

a Landsman. He was attached as a Private to Company B, Semmes' Naval Brigade, April 1865, and was surrendered and paroled at Greensboro, North Carolina, on April 26, 1865. In 1880, he resided as a farmer with his wife, Martha, at Indian Springs, Wayne County, North Carolina.
[Source(s): Card File; Howard; North Carolina Troops, III; Foenander]

Sessoms (Sessans; Sessman), Albert (Sampson County, North Carolina)
Landsman, Confederate States Navy. Born in 1839, Sessoms enlisted at age 25 on March 17, 1864 at Camp Holmes [near Raleigh, North Carolina] from Colonel McKay's 24th Regiment, North Carolina Militia from Sampson County, North Carolina. His description was as follows: Age 25; eyes, grey; hair, light; complexion, florid; height, 5 feet 9 inches; place of birth, Sampson County, North Carolina; occupation, farmer. Another source states he enlisted on March 18, 1864, in Raleigh, North Carolina, for the war. Sessoms enlisted in the Confederate States Navy and served as a Landsman aboard the CSS ARCTIC, Wilmington Station, North Carolina, 1863. In 1880, he resided as a farmer with his wife Mary and six children at Dismal, Sampson County, North Carolina.
[Source(s): Card File; NA RG 45; Foenander]

Sessums, M.
Confederate States Navy. Sessums appears on a list of "Conscripts in the yard" [at Halifax?] subsequently transferred to Wilmington, North Carolina, June 9, 1864.
[Source(s): Card File; NA RG 45]

Sevier, Charles T.
Midshipman, Confederate States Navy.
Sevier served with the North Carolina Squadron as a Midshipman aboard the CSS CURLEW per that ship's payroll list for the 1st quarter of 1862.
[Source: NCCWSP]

Sexpy, Edward (New Hanover County, North Carolina)
Confederate States Navy. Sexpy served aboard the steamer CSS PHANTOM. His name appears on registers of Confederate States Army General Military Hospital Number 4, Wilmington, North Carolina, which state he was admitted on October 22, 1863, with "feg int tertiana" and deserted October 26, 1863. His post office was listed as Wilmington, North Carolina.
[Source(s): Card File; NA RG 109]

Shackelford, John F. (Alabama// New Hanover County, North Carolina)
Confederate States Navy. Born in Lowndes County, Alabama, on August 1, 1846, Shackelford resided in New Hanover County, North Carolina, and was educated at the Hillsborough Military Academy. He enlisted, rank unknown, in Company K, 61st Regiment North Carolina Troops, on an unspecified date and was discharged on an unspecified date. He later served in the Confederate States Navy.
[Source(s): North Carolina Troops XIV; Foenander]

Shafer, R. [B.] (New Hanover County, North Carolina)
Ordinary Seaman, Confederate States Navy. Shafer enlisted on August 10, 1863 in Wilmington, North Carolina and served aboard the CSS ARCTIC, 1863.
[Source(s): MR, 4, p. 447; Foenander; St. Armand]

Sharer, Jacob
Landsman, Confederate States Navy. Sharer enlisted on November 12, 1863, in Raleigh, North Carolina, for the war.
[Source(s): Card File; NA RG 45]

Sharp, John W. (Orange County, North Carolina)
Private, Confederate States Army//Confederate States Navy. Sharp resided as a farmer in Orange County, North Carolina, where he enlisted as a Private at age 27 on March 11, 1862 for the war in 2nd Company G, 40th Regiment (3rd Regiment, North Carolina Artillery). He was present or accounted for until transferred to Company E, 13th Bn., North Carolina Light Artillery on November 4, 1863. Sharp was present or accounted for until he transferred to the Confederate States Navy on May 25, 1864. A "J. W. Sharp" served aboard the CSS NEUSE per its March – October 1864 muster roll. Sharp married Sarag [sic] C. Roark in Orange County, North Carolina on May 14, 1867. He was age 29 in 1864.
[Source(s): North Carolina Troops, I; Marriage Bonds, North Carolina Div. of Historical Res.; Hill; Card File]

Sharp, William
Lieutenant, Confederate States Navy. While attached to the CSS ELLIS, he participated in the battle of July 29, 1861 at Fort Hatteras.
[Source(s): McElroy; Card File]

Sharpe, William Feimster (Iredell County, North Carolina)
Private, Confederate States Marine Corps. Born on April 20, 1839, Sharpe died on January 1, 1923, and was buried at Concord Presbyterian Church, Iredell County, North Carolina.
[Source(s): Stepp, "Burials"]

Sheffield, James M. (Henry County, Virginia//Mecklenburg County, North Carolina)
Private, Confederate States Army//Landsman, Confederate States Navy. Born in 1827 in Henry County, Virginia, Sheffield resided in Mecklenburg County, North Carolina, as a "tobacconist" where he enlisted at age 34 as a Private in Company B, 13th Regiment, North Carolina Troops on June 23, 1861. He was present or accounted for until discharged and transferred to the Confederate States Navy on February 15, 1862 for duty as a Landsman on board the CSS VIRGINIA (CSS MERRIMAC). His height was given as 6'3." Documents indicate he was paid for service at Drewry's Bluff for the period February 15-June15, 1862. Sheffield was discharged by September 30, 1862, and re-enlisted in Hardwicke's Virginia Artillery, Richmond, Virginia, on December 13, 1863. He was wounded in action (right lung) and captured at Winchester, Virginia, September 29, 1864. He remained in a field hospital at Winchester until transferred to a hospital in Frederick, Maryland, on November 9, 1864. He was transferred to Hammond Hospital, Point Lookout, Maryland, on January 28, 1865, and remained a patient in said hospital until April 7, 1865. He was released on June 21, 1865. Sheffield died on October 9, 1895 and was buried in the Confederate Section of Oakwood Cemetery, Raleigh, North Carolina.
[Source(s): Ellis; Oakwood; Card File; Driver]; Stepp, "Burials;" MR, I; North Carolina Troops, V; Foenander; *ORN* 2, 1, 309]

Shell, Moses
Landsman, Confederate States Navy. Shell enlisted on February 6, 1864, in Raleigh, North Carolina, for the war.
[Source(s): Card File; NA RG 45]

Shelton, Rufus (North Carolina)
Landsman, Confederate States Navy. Shelton enlisted on May 11, 1864, in Raleigh, North Carolina, for the war and served aboard the CSS INDIAN CHIEF. His name appears on a report by Captain Pratt, Provost Marshal, of "rebel deserters and refugees" reported at "Nor. Dist., Dept. South," for the 16 days ending March 31, 1865. The report dated March 28, 1865 states he was born in and resides in North Carolina. His description was as follows: age, 16; eyes, dark; hair, dark; complexion, light; height, 5 feet 2 inches. A remark on the report states "taken the oath and discharge." [Source(s): Card File; NA RG 45; NA RG 109]

Shepard, W. R.
Landsman, Confederate States Navy. Shepard enlisted on July 16, 1864, in Raleigh, North Carolina, for the war.
[Source(s): Card File; NA RG 45]

Shepherd, Edward
Landsman, Confederate States Navy. Shepherd enlisted on December 10, 1863, at Raleigh, North Carolina, for the war. Another source states he enlisted on December 12, 1863, in Wilmington, North Carolina, for the war.
[Source(s): Card File; NA RG 45]

Shepherd, John F. (Pennsylvania//New Hanover County, North Carolina)
Private, Confederate States Army//Confederate States Navy. Shepherd was born in Pennsylvania and resided as a Seaman in New Hanover County, North Carolina. He enlisted there at age 28 on December 9, 1861, for the war, in Company F, 3rd Regiment, North Carolina State Troops. He transferred to the Confederate States Navy on February 20, 1862.
[Source(s): Card File; North Carolina Troops, III]

Sheppard (Shepard), John (Beaufort County, North Carolina)
Seaman, Ordinary Seaman, Confederate States Navy. Sheppard resided in Beaufort County, North Carolina, where he enlisted as a Private at age 27 on May 10, 1861, in Company I, 3rd Regiment, North Carolina State Troops, for the war. Present or accounted for until he transferred to the Confederate States Navy on February 20, 1862. One source mentions he enlisted on November 5, 1863, at Wilmington, North Carolina, for the war. Another source lists

him as from New Hanover County, North Carolina [NOTE: see also "John Sheppard (New Hanover County, North Carolina)" entry]. He served as a Seaman aboard the CSS RALEIGH from at least January 16, 1862 – April 1862. His name appears on a payroll of the North Carolina Squadron covering the period February 28, 1862 - April 15, 1862, on which date he transferred to the James River Squadron.
[Source(s): MR, 4, p. 447; Card File; NA RG 45; North Carolina Troops, III; Foenander; "Beaufort County Sailors;" St. Armand; NCCWSP]

Sheppard, John (New Hanover County, North Carolina)
[Note: May be the same as "John Sheppard" of Beaufort County, North Carolina, q. v.]
Confederate States Navy. Sheppard enlisted in Wilmington, North Carolina.
[Source(s): MR, IV, 447]

Sheppard, William R. (Cleveland County, North Carolina)
Landsman, Confederate States Navy.
Sheppard's name appears on a roll of Prisoners of War at Point Lookout, Maryland, which states he was captured at Burkeville, Virginia, April 6, 1865, and confined at Point Lookout, Maryland, until released on June 20, 1865. His name appears as a signature to an Oath of Allegiance to the United States subscribed and sworn to at Point Lookout, Maryland, on June 20, 1865. His place of residence was given as Cleveland County, North Carolina and his description as follows: Complexion, dark; hair, black; eyes, hazel; height, 5 feet 10 ¼ inches.
[Source(s): Card File; NA RG 109]

Shepperd [Shepherd], Francis Edgar
Lieutenant, Confederate States Navy. Born in North Carolina, the son of Augustin Shepperd, Congressman from Forsyth district, North Carolina, Shepperd served in the United States Navy beginning on October 16, 1849 as a Midshipman. He became a Passed Midshipman on June 12, 1855, a Master on September 16, 1855, and a Lieutenant on January 1, 1857. Shepperd was dismissed from the United States Navy on July 8, 1861 and appointed a First Lieutenant in the Confederate States Navy from North Carolina on July 15, 1861. Another source states he was appointed a First Lieutenant on October 23, 1862 to rank from October 2, 1862. He was appointed a First Lieutenant, Provisional Confederate States Navy, on June 2, 1864, to rank from January 6, 1864. Shepperd commanded the CSS FLORIDA (Selma) and CSS MOBILE, Mississippi River defenses, 1861-1863. He served on board the CSS CHARLESTON and commanded the CSS PALMETTO STATE and CSS TORCH, Charleston Station, 1863-1864. He commanded the CSS FREDERICKSBURG, CSS HAMPTON, and CSS VIRGINIA II, James River Squadron, 1864-1865. Another source states he was a "LT and Executive Officer aboard the CSS FREDERICKSBURG in Virginia waters in 1864."
[Source(s): Register; McElroy; Francis E. Shepperd Papers, Box # 912, Private Collections, State Archives of North Carolina (orders for him to report to CSS FORUM); Card File; Foenander; CWDTS; OCSN; ONWR; Fold3, USN Resignees; USCWSRP]

Sherrill, Moses O. (Osborne) (Catawba or Rowan County, North Carolina)
Private, Confederate States Army//Fireman, Confederate States Navy. Sherrill was born in Catawba County, North Carolina, and resided there as a farmer prior to enlisting in Cabarrus County, North Carolina, at age 28 on September 13, 1861 as a Private in Company C, 33rd Regiment, North Carolina Troops, as per S.O. # 89. He was present or accounted for until wounded in the right thigh at Fredericksburg, Virginia, on or about December 13, 1862. Returning to duty nearly a year later (November-December 1863), he was present or accounted for until he transferred to the Confederate States Navy on or about April 16, 1864. Other sources state he was transferred to the Confederate States Navy in January 1864 and was discharged at the close of the war. He served aboard the Confederate States steamer CSS STROPMAN as a Fireman. His name appears on a roll of Prisoners of War at Point Lookout, Maryland, which states he was captured in Richmond, Virginia on April 4, 1865, and confined at Point Lookout, Maryland, until released after subscribing and swearing to an Oath of Allegiance to the United States on June 20, 1865. Said Oath lists his residence as Rowan County, North Carolina, and description as follows: Complexion, light; hair, brown; eyes, hazel; height, 5 feet 10 inches.
[Source(s): North Carolina Troops, IX; S. O. # 89; Army to Navy; Card File; UDC Recorder; NA RG 109]

Sherron [Sherran, Sherrin], Buck L. (Granville County, North Carolina)
Confederate States Navy. Sherron was born in North Carolina in 1829 and served in the Confederate States Navy. He resided as a farmer, in 1880, with his wife Sally K. Sherrin, and six children (eldest child born 1855) at Dutchville, Granville County, North Carolina. He applied for a Confederate pension from Granville County, North Carolina on July 1, 1901, at age 72, listing his post office as Wilton, Granville County, North Carolina. The pension application states he was first sent to Government Shops and stayed there two years, then volunteered and went

into the Navy. He was captured at Drewry's Bluff but was in the hospital at Jacksons (North Carolina?) at the close of war. The application was approved at 4th class. A second claim filed July 5, 1921, age 93, Rt. #2, Oxford, North Carolina was also approved at 4th Class. He served as a witness on the pension application of John C. Usry (q.v.).
[Source(s): Card File; Pensions (North Carolina); Foenander]

Shields, B. W. [NOTE: May be "Bryant W. Shields," Moore County, North Carolina,
Mallett's Battalion (Camp Guard, Camp Mangum)]
Landsman, Confederate States Navy. Shields enlisted on June 10, 1864, in Raleigh, North Carolina, for the war. A "B. W. Shields," identified as "North Carolina Naval Hospital," is buried in the Seaman's Burial Ground, Ashley River, Charleston, South Carolina, date of death listed as August 30, 1864.
[Source(s): Card File; NA RG 45; Census (NC), 1860; SBG]

Shipley, Walter (North Carolina?)
1st Class Fireman, Confederate States Navy.
Shipley shipped for the war aboard the CSS RALEIGH ON August 6, 1861. Per a variety of records for this ship, he served aboard the CSS RALEIGH since before September 2, 1861 - April 1862. His name appears on the North Carolina Squadron payroll for the 1st quarter of 1862 from February 21, 1862 - April 15, 1862 on which date he transferred to the James River Squadron. He served at Drewry's Bluff as a 1st Class Fireman from at least April 1, 1863 - June 30, 1863. From October 1, 1863 - 15 December 15, 1863 he again served aboard the CSS RALEIGH with the James River Squadron.
[Source: NCCWSP]

Shofer, B.
Landsman, Confederate States Navy. Shofer enlisted on October 5, 1863, at Camp Holmes [near Raleigh, North Carolina]. Lines are drawn through his name on the Card File list, but with no explanation.
[Source(s): Card File; NA RG 45]

Sholar, William H. (born New Hanover County, North Carolina) (resided Cumberland County, North Carolina)
Confederate States Navy. A pre-war mason by trade, Sholar was conscripted on March 18 [or, 21], 1864, at Camp Holmes [near Raleigh, North Carolina] from Colonel McCoy's 54th Regiment, North Carolina Militia, Cumberland County, North Carolina. Description: Age, 30; eyes, black; hair, dark; complexion, dark; height, 5 feet 7 ½ inches; place of birth, New Hanover County, North Carolina; occupation mason.
[Source(s): Card File; NA RG 45; Foenander]

Sholanbarrer (Shullanbarrier), David [NOTE: See "Shullenbarrier [Shullenbaner]"]
Landsman, Confederate States Navy. Scholanbarrer enlisted on October 14, 1863, at Camp Holmes [near Raleigh, North Carolina]. Another source states he enlisted on that day in Wilmington, North Carolina. He served aboard the CSS NORTH CAROLINA.
[Source(s): Card File; NA RG 45; MR, IV, 444]

Showalter, John
Seaman, Confederate States Navy. Showalter enlisted on June 8, 1863, in Wilmington, North Carolina, for the war, and served aboard the CSS NORTH CAROLINA. He later served as a Seaman aboard the CSS TALLAHASSEE, 1864.
[Source(s): Card File; NA RG 45; Foenander]

Shugars, Charles H. (Washington County, North Carolina)
Private, Confederate States Army//Confederate States Navy. Shugars resided in Washington County, North Carolina where he enlisted for the war at age 19 on July 3, 1861 in Company G, 1st Regiment, North Carolina State Troops. He was present or accounted for until discharged on February 3, 1862 (Source MR, I shows the date as January 1862) upon transfer to the Confederate States Navy.
[Source(s): Card File; North Carolina Troops, III; MR, I]

Shugart, Isaac L. (Yadkin County, North Carolina)
Corporal, Confederate States Army//Landsman, Confederate States Navy. Born on March 17, 1843, Shugart was the son of Enoch and Carolina Davis Shugart. He enlisted in Yadkin County, North Carolina, on May 12, 1861 and was present until transferred as a Corporal from Company B, 21st Regiment (11th Regiment, North Carolina Volunteers) to Company A, 1st Battalion, North Carolina Sharpshooters on April 26, 1862. Wounded at Hazel Run,

Virginia, on August 22, 1862, he was present until transferred to the Confederate States Navy on April 19, 1864. The muster roll of the CSS NEUSE lists him as aboard March - October 1864. Shugart married Emma Johnson in Mount Airy Township, North Carolina, on January 1, 1876 and, as late as 1880 resided as a farmer with his wife and four children, at Fall Creek, Yadkin County, North Carolina. He died on January 17, 1915 and was buried at Boonville Baptist Church, Boonville, Yadkin Company, North Carolina.
[Source(s): Hill, North Carolina Troops, III and VI; Stepp, "Burials;" Casstevens; Foenander; CMACSSN]

Shugart, James L.
Confederate States Navy. Shugart enlisted on April 1, 1864, in Kinston, North Carolina, for three years or the war.
[Source(s): Card File; NA RG 45]

Shullenbarrier [Shullenbaner], David (Cabarrus County, North Carolina) [NOTE: See Sholanbarrer (Shullanbarrier)]
Landsman, Confederate States Navy. Shullenbarrier served as a crewman aboard the CSS NORTH CAROLINA, as well as the CSS ARCTIC, 1863.
[Source(s): MR, 4, p. 444; Cruse; Foenander]

Shults, E. J.
Seaman, Confederate States Navy. Shults enlisted on June 18, 1864, in Raleigh, North Carolina, for the war.
[Source(s): Card File; NA RG 45]

Shultz, B. T.
Landsman, Confederate States Navy. Shultz enlisted on June 11, 1864, in Raleigh, North Carolina, for the war.
[Source(s): Card File; NA RG 45]

Sigmon, J. F.
Seaman, Confederate States Navy. Sigmon enlisted on June 13, 1864, in Raleigh, North Carolina, for the war.
[Source(s): Card File; NA RG 45]

Sikes, D. D. (Sampson County, North Carolina)
Confederate States Navy. Sikes enlisted on or about September "1865" [sic] [1864?] and served till the surrender. His application for a pension, filed on July 12, 1904, at age 80, listing his post office as Salemburg, Sampson County, North Carolina, was approved at 4th Class. It states he served on board the CSS INDIAN CHIEF and later aboard the CSS PEE DEE on the Pee Dee River at Mars (?) Bluff, South Carolina. It further states "I was not wounded in the war" and "I was not in actual service long. I was in the home guard, etc."
[Source(s): Card File; Pensions (North Carolina)]

Sikes, Franklin
Seaman, Confederate States Navy. Sikes enlisted on April 8, 1864, in Halifax or Plymouth, North Carolina, for the war.
[Source(s): Card File; NA RG 45]

Siler, T. (Moore County, North Carolina)
Private, Confederate States Marine Corps. Siler served in the Confederate States Marine Corps. Along with several others, he left Moore County and was sent to Camp Holmes, where he was instructed for a short time, then sent to Charleston, to serve aboard the CSS INDIAN CHIEF, arriving there on Sunday, November 6, 1864, for further drill and instruction as a marine. He was later sent aboard the CSS CHICORA, Charleston Station. A letter from James C. Davis, dated November 17, 1864, states that a group from Camp Holmes, of which "T. Siler" was a part, arrived aboard the CSS INDIAN CHIEF, Charleston, South Carolina, Sunday, November 6, 1864, and was designated to serve aboard the ironclad CSS CHICORA.
[Source(s): Davis, November 17, 1864; Foenander]

Siler, Thompson (Chatham County, North Carolina)
Private, Confederate States Army//Landsman, Confederate States Navy. Siler enlisted on June 10, 1864, in Raleigh, North Carolina, for the war. He was listed in Mallet's Battalion (North Carolina Troops, Broadfoot edition). He transferred from the Confederate States Army to the Confederate States Navy at Charleston, South Carolina in 1864 from the State of North Carolina. Attached to the receiving ship CSS INDIAN CHIEF, he saw service on Sullivan Island, James Island, Morris Island, and Drewry's Bluff, and surrendered at Appomattox on April 9, 1865. He was not listed in the 1860 Census. Sons: Percy T. Siler, Union St., Greensboro, North Carolina; Guy W. Siler, Silver Run

Ave., Greensboro, North Carolina. Daughters: Mrs. Ida P. Kine, W. Market St., Greensboro, North Carolina and Mrs. Bertie E. Coble, Greensboro, North Carolina.
[Source(s): McElroy; North Carolina Troops (Broadfoot Ed.); Card File; NA RG 45; Census (NC), 1860]

Silivant (Sillevent), Larry
Landsman, Confederate States Navy. Silivant enlisted on December 12, 1863, in Wilmington, North Carolina, for the war. Another source states he enlisted on December 10, 1863, in Raleigh, North Carolina, for the war.
[Source(s): Card File; NA RG 45]

Silva, Antonio (probably Portugal//New Hanover County, North Carolina)
Seaman, Confederate States Navy.
Per the muster roll of the CSS SEA BIRD for July - November 1861, Silva served as a Seaman. His name appears on the North Carolina Squadron's payroll for the 1st quarter of 1862 from (December 1, 1861 - January 19, 1862).
[Source: NCCWSP]

Silva, Jno. E., Sr. (Portugal//New Hanover County, North Carolina)
Confederate States Navy. A native of Portugal, Silva resided in Wilmington, North Carolina, most of his life. He died circa February 19, 1892, and was buried in Bellevue Cemetery, Wilmington, North Carolina).
[Source(s): Card File; "Messenger," 2/19/1892]

Simmonds, D. D. (also Simmons)
Acting Master, Confederate States Navy.
Simmonds served as an Acting Master aboard the CSS CORA, a possible blockade runner, from December 14, 1861 - March 31, 1862.
[Source: NCCWSP]

Simmons, Miles
Seaman, Confederate States Navy.
Simmons served as a Seaman aboard the NCS ELLIS as of an August 1, 1861 entry into her logbook. He was aboard her from at least November 2, 1861 - May 1862.
[Source: NCCWSP]

Simmons, M. W. [NOTE: May be same as "Simmons, Mitchell W.," q.v.]
Ordinary Seaman, Confederate States Navy. Simmons enlisted on June 8, 1863, in Wilmington, North Carolina, for the war.
[Source(s): Card File; NA RG 45]

Simmons, Mitchell W. (Currituck County, North Carolina)
Hospital Steward, Confederate States Navy. Simmons was born in Currituck County, North Carolina in 1825, and enlisted in Company B, 6th Virginia Infantry in Norfolk, Virginia on May 10, 1861. Discharged for disability on August 21, 1862, he was appointed a Hospital Steward, Confederate States Navy, date unknown. Simmons was captured at Harper's Farm [Virginia] on April 6, 1865, and sent to Point Lookout, Maryland, where he was released on June 19, 1865. Description: height 5'10;" complexion light; hair brown; eyes gray; residence Norfolk, Virginia.
[Source(s): Driver]

Simmons, William
Seaman, Confederate States Navy.
Simmons served as a Seaman aboard the NCS ELLIS beginning on August 1, 1861 per a logbook entry through May 1862.
[Source: NCCWSP]

Simmons (Simmonds), William H. (Currituck County, North Carolina)
Private, Confederate States Army//Seaman, Confederate States Navy. Born in Currituck County, North Carolina [Source "North Carolina Troops, IV" gives his birthplace as Norfolk, Virginia], Simmons resided in Pasquotank County, North Carolina, as a mariner. He enlisted on August 17, 1861, in Pasquotank County, North Carolina, at age 27, "for the war," in Company A, 8th Regiment, North Carolina State Troops. Captured at Roanoke Island, North Carolina, on February 8, 1862, Simmons was paroled at Elizabeth City, North Carolina on February 21, 1862 and exchanged in August 1862. He was present or accounted for until he enlisted in the Confederate States Navy on or about January 9, 1863, for "three years or the war" in Wilmington, North Carolina. He served as a Seaman aboard

the CSS NORTH CAROLINA, mid-1864. His name appears on registers of Confederate States Army General Military Hospital Number 4, Wilmington, North Carolina, dated June 27, 1863, giving his disease as "debility," and listing his post office as Elizabeth City, North Carolina, and that he was returned to duty July 10, 1863.
[Source(s): MR, I & IV; Card File; NA RG 109; North Carolina Troops, IV; Foenander]

Simmons, W. S.
Landsman, Confederate States Navy. Simmons served aboard the CSS ALBEMARLE, and on the Halifax Station, 1864.
[Source(s): Foenander]

Simms, C. C.
Lieutenant Commander, Confederate States Navy. Simms commanded the CSS APPOMATTOX as part of the fleet under Commodore Lunch that participated in the battle at Roanoke Island, February 8-9, 1862.
[Source(s): McElroy; Card File]

Simpson, Isaac (Pasquotank County, North Carolina)
Private, Confederate States Army//Ordinary Seaman, Confederate States Navy. Born in Pasquotank County, North Carolina, where he resided as a farmer prior to enlisting there at age 22 on April 23, 1861, as a Private in Company A, 17th Regiment, North Carolina Troops (1st Organization). He was present or accounted for until he was reportedly transferred to Company E, 8th Regiment, North Carolina Troops between September 1861 and February 1862. However, records of the 8th Regiment, North Carolina Troops, do not indicate he served in that unit. Payroll records of the CSS CURLEW used by source NCCWSP indicate Simpson served aboard that ship from at least November 20, 1861 – first quarter 1862. The same source states he later served aboard the CSS ALBEMARLE. Other records indicate he enlisted in Company C, 56th Regiment, North Carolina Troops, in Camden County, North Carolina, on April 2, 1862. Reported present through December 1862, he was reported absent sick at Rocky Mount, North Carolina, on January 15, 1863. He returned to duty in March-April 1863 and was detailed as a bridge guard at Goldsboro, North Carolina, on May 27, 1863, after he was disabled. The circumstances of his disablement are not reported. He rejoined the company in July-August 1863 and was reported present through February 1864. He transferred to the Confederate States Navy on April 12, 1864.
[Source(s): Card File; North Carolina Troops, VI and XIII; NCCWSP]

Simpson, S. L.
1st Cabin boy, Confederate States Navy. Simpson enlisted on November 23, 1863, in Wilmington, North Carolina, for the war.
[Source(s): Card File; NA RG 45]

Sims, Willy
Confederate States Navy. Sims' name appears on a list of conscripts "in yard at Halifax," June 9, 1864.
[Source(s): Card File; NA RG 45]

Sinclair, Arthur, Jr.
Master's Mate, Confederate States Navy.
Sinclair served as a Master's Mate aboard the CSS SEA BIRD.
[Source: NCCWSP}

Sinclair, Arthur, Sr.
Commander, Confederate States Navy. Sinclair assumed command of the CSS WINSLOW on July 9, 1861, succeeding LT T. M. Crossan.
[Source(s): Card File; McElroy; NCCWSP]

Sirmond, David D.
Master (Commanding), Confederate States Navy. Sirmond was appointed a Master Not-in-Line-of-Promotion on December 18, 1861 from North Carolina. He commanded the steamer CSS CORA, 1862. He was captured by the USS DAYLIGHT off Masonboro Inlet, North Carolina, December 3, 1862, while in command of the blockade runner "*Brilliant*." His card states he was "Captured in prize 'Merrimac' and sent to US Hospital, August 1863 [?]."
[Source(s): Card File; ONWR]

Sisk, Robert
Landsman, Confederate States Navy. Sisk enlisted on December 12, 1863, in Wilmington, North Carolina, for the

war. Another source states he enlisted on December 5, 1863, in Raleigh, North Carolina, for the war.
[Source(s): Card File; NA RG 45]

Skillen, Jos. (New Hanover County, North Carolina)
Confederate States Navy. Skillen appears on registers of Confederate States Army General Military Hospital Number 4, Wilmington, North Carolina, dated June 27, 1863, which give his disease as "diarr chron" and post office as Wilmington, North Carolina.
[Source(s): Card File; NA RG 109]

Skiner, William [NOTE: May be same as "W. M. Skiner," q. v.]
Landsman, Confederate States Navy. Skiner enlisted on August 5, 1864, in Raleigh, North Carolina, for the war.
[Source(s): Card File; NA RG 45]

Skinner, L. T.
Landsman, Confederate States Navy. Skinner enlisted on April 27, 1864, in Raleigh, North Carolina, for the war.
[Source(s): Card File; NA RG 45]

Skinner, W. M. [NOTE: May be same as "William Skiner," q. v.] (Mecklenburg County, North Carolina)
Confederate States Navy. Skinner enlisted on or about August 1, 1863 in the Confederate States Navy and served on board the CSS NORTH CAROLINA for about twelve months. He was sent to Fort Fisher after the ship sank. He was subsequently sent to Danville, Virginia, where he remained until the close of the war. He filed a pension claim on July 2, 1903, age 59 years, post office Charlotte, Mecklenburg County, North Carolina, which was approved at 4th Class (a pencil note states "3rd class"]. A second pension claim filed June 22, 1908, age 65 years old, Mecklenburg County, North Carolina, states he served in "Company A, Navy" and that "I served on the Gun Boat (in the Navy) at Smithville about 18 months and from there to Fort Fisher until it was taken then we went with Hoke's Brigade to Danville…"
[Source(s): Card File; Pensions (North Carolina); Foenander]

Skinner, William W. (New Hanover County, North Carolina)
Confederate States Army//Confederate States Navy. Skinner's pension claim filed on July 14, 1902, age 71, post office Wilmington, North Carolina, states his first enlistment was in the "Infantry." He then transferred to the Confederate States Navy on the James River and, at the fall of Richmond, was sent to Danville and thence to Greensboro at the surrender. No date of enlistment is shown. A statement by Captain A. B. Williams on this application says Skinner was a Pilot in the James River Squadron. "Claimant states he injured his back during the war." His pension was approved at 4th Class.
[Source(s): Card File; Pension (North Carolina)]

Skipper, Peter (New Hanover County, North Carolina)
Landsman, Confederate States Navy. Born in North Carolina in 1828, Skipper enlisted on November 20, 1863, in Raleigh, North Carolina, for the war and served as a Landsman aboard the CSS ARCTIC. Another source states he enlisted on November 22, 1863, in Wilmington, North Carolina, for the war. His name appears on registers of Confederate States Army General Military Hospital Number 4, Wilmington, North Carolina, which state he was admitted on November 26, 1863, with "rheumatismus chronicus" and returned to duty on January 22, 1864. The post office given on the registers was listed as Wilmington, North Carolina. Registers show he was again admitted on February 17, 1864, with "subluxatio" and returned to duty May 24, 1864. His post office was listed as both Wilmington and Black Rock, North Carolina (possibly Bertie or Jackson County, North Carolina). Skipper and his family lived at Carvers Creek, Bladen County, North Carolina in 1880, where he worked as a "house carpenter." A pension claim filed July 7, 1902 by his widow Mary Skipper, age 72, post office Abbottsburg, Bladen County, North Carolina was approved at 4th class.
[Source(s): Card File; NA RG 45; NA RG 109; Pensions (North Carolina); Foenander; Census (NC), 1880]

Small, Daniel W.
Landsman, Confederate States Navy.
Small began serving as a Landsman aboard the NCS EDWARDS (later, renamed the CSS FORREST) per his shipping articles signed on July 25, 1861. He served as a member of the North Carolina Squadron aboard her through September 1861 when he was transferred to the receiving ship CSS UNITED STATES on September 17, 1861 on detached duty.
[Source: NCCWSP]

Small, James [NOTE: May be same as "James M. Small" (q.v.)]
Landsman, Confederate States Navy. Small enlisted on August 17, 1864, in Raleigh, North Carolina, for the war.
[Source(s): Card File; NA RG 45]

Small, James M. (Rockingham County, North Carolina) [NOTE: May be same as "James Small" (q.v.)]
Confederate States Navy. Small enlisted on or about February 1, 1864 and "served on the Flag ship CSS INDIAN CHIEF." His pension claim filed July 17, 1924, age 84, post office Wentworth, Rockingham County, North Carolina was approved at 4th Class. A second pension claim filed January 23, 1925, age 84 was also approved at 4th Class.
[Source(s): Card File; Pension (North Carolina); Foenander]

Small, William A.
Seaman, Confederate States Navy.
Small shipped aboard the NCS ELLIS [Source NCCWSP lists the ship as the CSS EDWARDS] per shipping articles signed on July 25, 1861 and remained on the ship until he transferred to the receiving ship CSS UNITED STATES on September 17, 1861 on detached duty. He appears on the muster roll of the CSS FORREST (formerly the CSS EDWARDS) ending October 30, 1861.
[Source: NCCWSP]

Smart, John Carson (Rutherford or McDowell County, North Carolina)
Confederate States Navy. Smart enlisted on October 15, 1863 in Wilmington, North Carolina. Another source states he enlisted on October 26, 1863, at Camp Holmes [near Raleigh, North Carolina]. His name appears on a register of Confederate States Army General Military Hospital Number 4, Wilmington, North Carolina, as being admitted on December 19, 1863, with "febris remittens," and returned to duty on January 15, 1864. His post office given as "Dizersville, North Carolina" [Dysartsville, McDowell County, North Carolina].
[Source(s): MR, IV, p. 447; Card File; Smart, H. J., Letter; Card File; NA RG 45; NA RG 109; BRGS]

Smaw, F. D., Jr.
Landsman, Confederate States Navy. Smaw enlisted on September 28, 1863, at Camp Holmes [near Raleigh, North Carolina] for the war.
[Source(s): Card File; NA RG 45]

Smith, _____ (Cumberland County, North Carolina)
Engineer, Confederate States Navy. James Sprunt, in "Chronicles," states that Engineer Smith was from Fayetteville, Cumberland County, North Carolina, and was, along with Engineer Edward Wilson Manning, "in charge of the machinery of the CSS RALEIGH."
[Source(s): "Chronicles"]

Smith, A. L. (Mecklenburg County, North Carolina)
Seaman/Messenger Boy, Confederate States Navy. Smith served as a messenger boy at Edwards Ferry on the Roanoke River while the CSS ALBEMARLE was being built on his father's farm in North Carolina. Source Foenander states he "served as a Seaman aboard the CSS ALBEMARLE and was involved in the engagements at Plymouth and in Albemarle Sound, North Carolina." He resided in Charlotte, North Carolina, in 1907. Wife: Mrs. Lou Young Smith, Charlotte, North Carolina; son: Burton H. Smith, Norfolk, Virginia.
[Source(s): McElroy; Names-1907; Card File; Foenander]

Smith, C. (Wake County, North Carolina)
Confederate States Navy. Smith enlisted in the Confederate States Navy in Wilmington, North Carolina.
[Source(s): MR, 4, p. 447]

Smith, C. A. D. (Rutherford County, North Carolina)
Landsman, Confederate States Navy. Smith enlisted on October 14, 1863 in Wilmington, North Carolina. Another source states he enlisted on October 26, 1863, at Camp Holmes [near Raleigh, North Carolina].
[Source(s): MR, IV, p. 447; Card File; NA RG 45; BRGS]

Smith, C. C.
Landsman, Confederate States Navy. Smith enlisted on June 11, 1862, in Raleigh, North Carolina, for the war.
[Source(s): Card File; NA RG 45]

Smith, Charles
Seaman, Ordinary Seaman, Confederate States Navy.
Smith served aboard the CSS BEAUFORT from November 1861 – March 1862 per clothing, bounty, and small stores records. He received a partial payment on February 13, 1862 at the Gosport Navy Yard following his service manning Fort Cobb at the Battle of Elizabeth City on February 10, 1862. He was court-martialed and reduced in rank to Ordinary Seaman on March 16, 1862. His name appears on the North Carolina Squadron payroll for the 1st quarter of 1862 from December 1, 1861 - April 15, 1862 on which date he transferred to the James River Squadron. He is listed as an Ordinary Seamanserving at Drewry's Bluff as a Seaman from April 1, 1863 - June 30, 1863 per that station's payroll for the period.
[Source: NCCWSP]

Smith, D. A. [may be same as "D. A. Smith" who enlisted on November 12, 1863]
Landsman, Confederate States Navy. Smith enlisted on June 20, 1863, in Wilmington, North Carolina, for the war.
[Source(s): Card File; NA RG 45]

Smith, D. A. [May be same as "D. A. Smith" who enlisted June 20, 1863]
Landsman, Confederate States Navy. Smith enlisted on November 12, 1863, in Raleigh, North Carolina, for the war.
[Source(s): Card File; NA RG 45]

Smith, George (Brunswick County, North Carolina [?])
"1st C. F." [May be 1st Class Fireman"] (Seaman), Confederate States Navy. Born on July 24, 1803 or 1804, Smith enlisted on May 9, 1863, in Wilmington, North Carolina, for three years or the war and served on the crew of the CSS CASWELL. A "George Smith" is listed on the March – October 1864 muster roll of the CSS NEUSE. He died on December 1, 1882 and was buried in the Grimes Cemetery in Brunswick County, North Carolina.
[Source(s): Card File; Gravestone Records, v. 8, p. 61; NA RG 45; CMACSSN]

Smith, Henry A. (Columbus County, North Carolina)
Private, Confederate States Army//Landsman, Seaman, Confederate States Navy. Smith enlisted in Beaufort County, North Carolina, on July 4, 1861 for the war at age 38 as a Private, in Company G, 19th Regiment, North Carolina Troops (2nd Regiment, North Carolina Cavalry). He transferred to the Confederate States Navy on February 1, 1862. Another source states he enlisted [Confederate States Navy?] on September 28, 1863, at Camp Holmes [near Raleigh, North Carolina] "for the war." Bounty Payroll, Clothing, and Muster roll records used by source NCCWSP indicate he served as a Seaman aboard the CSS RALEIGH from at least January 16, 1862 – April 1862. His name appears on a payroll of the North Carolina Squadron for the period February 7, 1862 - April 15, 1862, on which date he transferred to the James River Squadron. Smith served at Drewry's Bluff as a Seaman from at least April 1, 1863 - June 30,1863. A James River Squadron payroll for the period November 16, 1863 - December 15, 1863 show Smith as a Gunner's Mate aboard the CSS RALEIGH. Smith's pension claim filed on July 7, 1908, age 74, listing his post office as Bolton, Columbus County, North Carolina, states he contracted rheumatism while in service. His claim was approved at 4th Class. A second claim filed June 7, 1909, age 75, states he enlisted on September 24, 1863 in Savannah, Georgia, and became physically disabled on or about December 19, 1864. He was sent to the hospital in Charleston, South Carolina, with rheumatism that same day and was subsequently sent home on furlough where he was when the war ended. He served under Captain Ravand" ["Ravenal"?] on the gunboat CSS ISONDIGA.
[Source(s): Card File; NA RG 45; Pension (North Carolina); Foenander; "Beaufort County Sailors;" North Carolina Troops, II; NCCWSP]

Smith, James
Landsman, Confederate States Navy. Smith enlisted on October 30, 1863, in Raleigh, North Carolina, for the war. [NOTE: another source states he enlisted November 1, 1863, in Wilmington, North Carolina, for three years or the war.
[Source(s): Card File; NA RG 45]

Smith, James (Davidson County, North Carolina)
Confederate States Navy. Smith enlisted on October 8, 1863 in Wilmington, North Carolina [another source gives the date as on or about October 10, 1862]. His pension claim filed May 23, 1902, age 73, listing his post office as Versailles, Davidson County, North Carolina, states he lost his health due to chronic diarrhea on or about July 7, 1863. His claim was approved at 4th Class. A claim filed June 25, 1904 by his widow Mary A. Smith, age 72, whose post office was listed as Versailles, Davidson County, North Carolina, states he enlisted on September 1, 1863. Her claim was approved.
[Source(s): MR, 4, p. 447; Card File; NA RG 45; Pensions (North Carolina)]

Smith, James
> Boatswain, Confederate States Navy. Smith enlisted on September 26, 1863. He was promoted to Boatswain's Mate, Provisional Confederate States Navy on June 2, 1864 while serving with the Charleston Squadron, 1863-1864. He served on the gunboat "*Huntress*" from Savannah, Georgia.
> [Source(s): McElroy; Card File]

Smith, J. E. (Admitted to the Wake County, North Carolina Old Soldiers Home from Durham County, North Carolina)
> Confederate States Navy. Wake Co., NC Old Soldier's Home records indicate Smith served in the Confederate States Navy, was from North Carolina, and was admitted to the home on November 14, 1905, age not given. No further information.
> [Source: Wake Co. OLS, I]

Smith, John (New Hanover County, North Carolina)
> Private, Confederate States Army//Confederate States Navy. Smith enlisted in New Hanover County, North Carolina, on December 31, 1861 for twelve months in Captain William C. Howard's Cavalry Company (North Carolina Local Defense Troops). He was present or accounted for until he transferred to the Confederate States Navy on May 3, 1862.
> [Source(s): Card File; North Carolina Troops, II; Foenander]

Smith, John (Virginia)
> Private, Confederate States Army//Confederate States Navy. Smith resided in Virginia and enlisted in Petersburg, Virginia, at age 36 on July 17, 1862, for the war, as a substitute for Private John W. Patillo of Company G, 43rd Regiment, North Carolina Troops. [Per source "North Carolina Troops," he was present or accounted for until he was reportedly transferred to the Confederate States Navy on January 10, 1865, but no evidence of his service in the Confederate States Navy was located].
> [Source(s): Card File; North Carolina Troops, X]

Smith, John
> Private, Confederate States Army//Confederate States Navy. Smith enlisted in New Hanover County, North Carolina, in 2nd Company H, 40th Regiment, North Carolina Troops (3rd North Carolina Artillery) at age 21 on April 16, 1861, "for the war." "Discharged for improper conduct," he was transferred to the steamer CSS YORKTOWN at Richmond, Virginia, July 23, 1861.
> [Source(s): Card File; NA RG 45; North Carolina Troops, I]

Smith, John
> Ordinary Seaman, Confederate States Navy. Smith enlisted on April 11, 1864, in Kinston, North Carolina, for three years or the war. A "John Smith" is listed on the March -October 1864 muster roll of the CSS NEUSE.
> [Source(s): Card File; NA RG 45; CMACSSN]

Smith, John Baptist (Caswell County, North Carolina)
> Signal Officer, Confederate States Navy. A native of Caswell County, North Carolina, Smith served aboard the Confederate blockade runner "*Ad-Vance*" and was the originator of the flashing light signal system. He died near Guilford College, North Carolina.
> [Source(s): McElroy; Card File]

Smith, John E. (Granville County, North Carolina)
> Seaman ["Landsman" (per source Stepp)], Confederate States Navy. Born in 1845, Smith enlisted in Wilmington, North Carolina, under Captain Muse and "Com. Lynch" in the spring of 1862 and served as a crewman aboard the CSS NORTH CAROLINA. Records indicate he was on "iron clad vessels at Wilmington and Charleston, South Carolina." He was captured at Battery Sims at the fall of Richmond, Virginia. His application to the North Carolina Soldier's Home on March 15, 1905, age 61, post office Oxford, Granville, County, North Carolina, lists him as a widower with dark complexion, 5 feet 9 inches, and a salesman. He was admitted on November (December?) 14, 1905, died on January 11, 1914, and was buried in Grave #97 of the Confederate Section of Oakwood Cemetery, Raleigh, North Carolina. He served as a witness on the pension application of "Thomas O. Wooten" (q.v.).
> [Source(s): MR, 4, p. 444; Oakwood; Card File; Pensions (North Carolina); Stepp, "Burials;" Foenander]

Smith, John H. (Martin County, North Carolina)
> Private, Confederate States Army//Confederate States Navy. Smith was born in Martin County, North Carolina,

where he resided as a farmer prior to enlisting there at age 19 on April 16, 1862, for the war, as a Private in Company E, 55th Regiment, North Carolina Troops. Reported present in June 1862, he was hospitalized at Richmond, Virginia, on July 19, 1863 with dyspepsia and furloughed for thirty days on August 16, 1863. Reported present in May-June 1864. Hospitalized in Richmond, Virginia, on June 15, 1864, with dyspepsia, and furloughed for thirty days on June 30, 1864. Reported at home on sick furlough in September-October 1864. Hospitalized at Richmond, Virginia, on October 25, 1864, with an unspecified complaint. Returned to duty on November 9, 1864. Source "North Carolina Troops" states he "may have been transferred to the Confederate States Navy. Source Foenander states he was hospitalized several times in Richmond, mainly for dyspepsia," and may have been transferred to the Confederate States Navy.
[Source(s): Card File; North Carolina Troops, XIII; Foenander]

Smith, Joseph C. (Rutherford County, North Carolina)
Sergeant, Confederate States Army//Confederate States Navy. Smith was born in Rutherford County, North Carolina, where he resided as a farmer prior to enlisting there at age 23 on October 6, 1861 as a Sergeant in Company I, 34th Regiment, North Carolina Troops. Reduced to the ranks in March-April 1862, he was promoted to Sergeant between May 1862 and February 1863. Reduced to the ranks again in September-October 1863, he was reported absent without leave on October 5, 1863 but returned to duty on an unspecified date. Smith transferred to the Confederate States Navy on or about April 3, 1864.
[Source(s): Card File; North Carolina Troops, IX; Foenander]

Smith, Joseph
Seaman, Confederate States Navy.
Smith served aboard the NCS WINSLOW per that ship's muster roll, for the July - November 1861 period. By February 1862, he was serving as a Seaman aboard the CSS SEA BIRD. Captured in the Battle of Elizabeth City, he was carried to Roanoke Island where he took the Oath of Allegiance to the United States on February 12, 1862. His name appears on the North Carolina Squadron payroll for the 1st quarter of 1862 (December 1, 1861 - February 12, 1862). Smith is listed as having "run" on February 12, 1862.
[Source: NCCWSP]

Smith, Captain Joseph William (Carteret County, North Carolina)
Confederate States Army//Confederate States Navy. Smith was wounded in the leg while serving in Virginia with the Confederate States Army. He later served as Captain of the blockade runner "*Old Dominion*," converted in Bristol, England, with which he smuggled goods into Confederacy from Bermuda and the Caribbean.
[Source(s): *North Carolina's Coastal Carteret County During the Civil War*, Ed. By Jean Brugers Kell, 1999 (located in the Search Room of the North Carolina Archives)]

Smith, Joshua (Columbus County, North Carolina)
Landsman, Confederate States Navy (Hunter's Naval Battalion). His name appears on a roll of Prisoners of War at Point Lookout, Maryland, which states he was captured at "Sailors Creek" April 6, 1865, and confined at Point Lookout, Maryland, where he was held until released on June 20, 1865 after taking the Oath of Allegiance to the United States. His place of residence was given as Columbus County, North Carolina, and his description was as follows: Complexion, fair; hair, light; eyes, blue; height, 6 feet 3 inches.
[Source(s): Card File; NA RG 109]

Smith, L. B.
Landsman, Confederate States Navy. Smith enlisted on June 24, 1864, in Raleigh, North Carolina, for the war.
[Source(s): Card File; NA RG 45]

Smith, R. H.
Landsman, Confederate States Navy. Smith enlisted on June 10, 1864, in Raleigh, North Carolina, for the war.
[Source(s): Card File]

Smith, Reubin
Landsman, Confederate States Navy. Smith enlisted on January 25, 1864, in Raleigh, North Carolina, for the war. A "Reubin Smith" is listed on the March -October 1864 muster roll of the CSS NEUSE.
[Source(s): Card File; NA RG 45; CMACSSN]

Smith, Rufus
Landsman, Confederate States Navy. Smith is buried in Cedar Grove Cemetery, New Bern, Craven County, North

Carolina.
[Source(s): Card File; Gravestone Records, v. I, p. 256; Stepp, "Burials"]

Smith, Samuel W. (Wake County, North Carolina)
Private, Confederate States Army//Seaman/Landsman, Confederate States Navy. Smith was born and resided as a farmer in Wake County, North Carolina, where he enlisted on July 12, 1861 ["May 24, 1861" (per source MR, I)], at age 23, as a Private in Company K, 14th Regiment, North Carolina Troops. He was present or accounted for until he transferred to the Confederate States Navy on February 15, 1862 for duty aboard the CSS VIRGINIA (CSS MERRIMAC). He later served as a Seaman on board the CSS ISONDIGA, 1863-1864, and as a Landsman aboard the CSS NORTH CAROLINA, 1864.
[Source(s): North Carolina Troops, V; ORN 2, 1, 289 & 297; Card File; MR, I; Foenander]

Smith, Simon (Beaufort County, North Carolina)
Private, Confederate States Army//Confederate States Navy. Smith enlisted in Beaufort County, North Carolina, on July 4, 1861 for the war as a Private in Company G, 19th Regiment, North Carolina Troops (2nd Regiment, North Carolina Cavalry). He transferred to the Confederate States Navy in March 1862.
[Source(s): Card File; Foenander; "Beaufort County Sailors;" North Carolina Troops, II; MR, III]

Smith, S. W. [NOTE: May be the same as "Samuel W. Smith, q.v.]
Landsman, Confederate States Navy. Smith enlisted on August 5, 1864, in Raleigh, North Carolina, for the war.
[Source(s): Card File; NA RG 45]

Smith, Thomas C.
Private, Confederate States Army//Seaman, Carpenter's Mate, Confederate States Navy. Smith's place and date of enlistment were not reported in Company E, 17th Regiment, North Carolina Troops (1st Organization). He transferred to the Confederate States Navy prior to July 28, 1861. Per payroll records, Smith served as a Seaman aboard the CSS CURLEW from November 20, 1861 – 1st quarter of 1862. He was promoted to Carpenter's Mate April 2, 1862. His name appears on the payroll for the receiving ship CSS UNITED STATES ending March 31, 1862. He appears on the North Carolina Squadron payroll for the 1st quarter of 1862 (April 1, 1862 - April 12, 1862 (?).
[Source(s): Card File; North Carolina Troops, VI; Foenander; NCCWSP]

Smith, William E. (Union County, North Carolina)
Private, Confederate States Army//Confederate States Navy. Smith was born in Union County, North Carolina, where he resided as a farmer prior to enlisting there at age 23 on June 5, 1861 as a Private in Company B, 26th Regiment, North Carolina Troops. He was present or accounted for until he transferred to the Confederate States Navy on April 1, 1864.
[Source(s): Card File; North Carolina Troops, VII]

Smith, William M.
Landsman, Confederate States Navy. Smith enlisted on February 29, 1864, in Raleigh, North Carolina, for the war.
[Source(s): Card File; NA RG 45]

Smithson, Miles (Pasquotank or Davidson County, North Carolina]
Private, Confederate States Army//Ordinary Seaman, Confederate States Navy (and with the Naval Battalion). Smithson resided in Pasquotank County, North Carolina, where he enlisted at age 19 on May 4, 1861 for the war in Company A, 8th Regiment, North Carolina State Troops. He was present or accounted for until he transferred to the Confederate States Navy on April 22, 1863, where he served as an Ordinary Seaman aboard the CSS PALMETTO STATE, 1863-1864. His name appears [by mark] to an Oath of Allegiance to the United States subscribed and sworn to at Point Lookout, Maryland, on June 20, 1865. His place of residence was listed as Davidson County, North Carolina [Source "North Carolina Troops, IV" gives his place of residence at enlistment as Pasquotank County, North Carolina] and his description as follows: Complexion, dark; hair, black; eyes, blue; height, 5 feet 11 inches.
[Source(s): Card File; Card File; NA RG 109; North Carolina Troops, IV; Foenander]

Smithson, William
Ordinary Seaman, 2nd Class Fireman, Confederate States Navy.
Smithson served with the North Carolina Squadron as an Ordinary Seaman aboard the CSS SEA BIRD per the ship's muster roll for July - November 1861. He appeared as a 2nd Class Fireman aboard the same ship as of February 1862.
[Source: NCCWSP]

Smithwick, James Robert (Warren County, North Carolina)
Ordinary Seaman, Confederate States Navy. Born on March 25, 1822 to Jimmie and Frances Smithwick, Smithwick served as a crewman on board the CSS VIRGINIA (CSS MERRIMAC), CSS ALBEMARLE; and, Halifax Station, 1864. He died on May 30, 1872 and was buried in Brown's Baptist Church Cemetery, Warrenton, Warren County, North Carolina. His nickname was "Smitty."
[Source(s): Smithwick; *ORN*, 2, 1, p. 274; Grissom; Census (NC), 1860; Stepp, "Burials;" Foenander]

Snider (Snyder), William L. (Davidson County, North Carolina)
Landsman, Confederate States Navy (Company A, "Navy Battalion"). Snider enlisted on December 10, 1863, in Raleigh, North Carolina, for the war, and served as a Landsman aboard the CSS ARTIC and CSS YADKIN. Another source states he enlisted on December 12, 1863, in Wilmington, North Carolina, for the war. His name appears as a signature to an Oath of Allegiance to the United States subscribed and sworn to at Point Lookout, Maryland, June 20, 1865, giving his place of residence as Davidson County, North Carolina, and his description as follows: Complexion, light; hair, auburn; eyes, blue; height, 5 feet 5 ½ inches. His pension claim filed on June 17, 1912, age 67, listed his post office as Jubilee, Route 1, Davidson County, North Carolina. The application was marked "deserter" in pencil yet approved. The application has letters attached attesting to his service and a letter from War Department with his military history. A letter dated April 6, 1912, from L. F. Snider (brother of William L. Snider) to "the Honorable Military Secretary, Washington, DC" requesting information states that William L. Snider served as a Landsman, Confederate States Navy, was captured at Burkeville [sic], Virginia, April the 6th 1865 and took the Oath of Allegiance at Point Lookout, Maryland, April 20th [sic] ["June"?] 1865." A letter dated March 11, 1912 from the Adjutant General, Washington, DC states that Snider was received from City Point, Virginia on April 14, 1865 at Point Lookout, Maryland, and released on June 20, 1865. A letter from Andrew Jackson Young, dated April 11, 1902, states he was with Snider at Point Lookout and returned home with him.
[Source(s): Card File; Pensions (North Carolina); NA RG 45; NA RG 109; Foenander]

Snowden, James B. (Currituck County, North Carolina)
Sergeant, Confederate States Army//Confederate States Navy. Snowden was born and resided in Currituck County, North Carolina, as a farmer prior to enlisting there at age 25 on August 1, 1861, for the war, in Company B, 8th Regiment, North Carolina State Troops. Mustered in as a Sergeant, he was captured at Roanoke Island on February 8, 1862, paroled at Elizabeth City on February 21, 1862 and exchanged at Aiken's Landing, James River, Virginia, on November 10, 1862. He was again captured in Currituck County, North Carolina, on September 14, 1864, and confined at Fort Monroe, Virginia, until transferred to Point Lookout, Maryland, where he arrived on September 30, 1864. Snowden was paroled at Point Lookout and transferred to Bouleware's Wharf, James River, Virginia, where he was received on March 19, 1865, for exchange. Source Card File claims he had Confederate Naval service.
[Source(s): Card File; North Carolina Troops, IV]

Sorrell, W. M.
Landsman, Confederate States Navy. Sorrell enlisted on June 11, 1864, in Raleigh, North Carolina, for the war.
[Source(s): Card File; NA RG 45]

Southall, John
Ordinary Seaman, NCS WINSLOW. Southall was a slave of Master Patrick McCarrick, and one of seven African American crew members aboard the NCS WINSLOW.
[Source(s): NCS]

Sowers, J. A.
Landsman, Confederate States Navy. Sowers enlisted on July 25, 1864, in Raleigh, North Carolina, for the war.
[Source(s): Card File; NA RG 45]

Sowers, J. S.
Landsman, Confederate States Navy. Sowers enlisted on July 16, 1864, in Raleigh, North Carolina, for the war.
[Source(s): Card File; NA RG 45]

Sparks, Rufus
Landsman, Confederate States Navy. Sparks enlisted on April 13, 1864, in Raleigh, North Carolina, for the war.
[Source(s): Card File; NA RG 45]

Speak(e)s, Richard E. (Iredell County, North Carolina)
Landsman, Confederate States Navy. Speaks was born in 1841 in Iredell County, North Carolina, the son of M. and

Aladelpha Speaks. His pension claim filed July 2, 1904, age 65, post office Evalin, Iredell County, North Carolina was approved at 4th Class. The pension application states he enlisted on the "receiving Ship CSS ARCTIC" under command of Captain Poindexter, on or about December 1, 1863, at Wilmington. He was taken with "typhoid pneumonia" on or about February 15, 1864 that wrecked his health. A widow's application filed June 24, 1916 by Nancy Speaks, age 69 years (who he married about 1870), post office Jennings, Iredell County, North Carolina was approved. Richard Speak(e)s died in Haywood County, North Carolina, on March 8, 1916.
[Source(s): Card File; Pensions (North Carolina); ORN, Census (North Carolina) (1860); Foenander]

Speakes, Washington M.
Landsman, Confederate States Navy. Speakes enlisted on April 13, 1864, in Raleigh, North Carolina, for the war.
[Source(s): Card File; NA RG 45]

Speaks, Aswell
Landsman, Confederate States Navy. Speaks enlisted on January 11, 1864, in Raleigh, North Carolina, for the war.
[Source(s): Card File; NA RG 45]

Speaks, Richmon [sic]
Landsman, Confederate States Navy. Speaks enlisted on January 11, 1864, in Raleigh, North Carolina, for the war.
[Source(s): Card File; NA RG 45]

Spears, Robert
Confederate States Navy. Spears' name appears on a register of Confederate States Army General Military Hospital Number 4, Wilmington, North Carolina, as being admitted on January 21, 1864, with "febris typhoides" and giving his post office as "Zenerran" or "Zinivan," North Carolina.
[Source(s): Card File; NA RG 109]

Spence, John (Camden County, North Carolina)
Private, Confederate States Army//Confederate States Navy. Spence resided in Camden County, North Carolina, and enlisted in Pasquotank County, North Carolina, at age 28 on March 4, 1861, for the war, as a Private in Company A, 8th Regiment, North Carolina State Troops. He was present or accounted for until he deserted near Petersburg, Virginia, on July 19, 1864. Source Card File states he had Confederate Naval service.
[Source(s): Card File; NA RG 45; North Carolina Troops, IV]

Spikes, William B. (Wake County, North Carolina)
Ordinary Seaman, Confederate States Navy. Spikes enlisted on June 1, 1863, in Wilmington, North Carolina, for the war. He served as a crewman on board the CSS NORTH CAROLINA.
[Source(s): MR, 4, p. 444; Card File; NA RG 45]

Springs, Joseph
Pilot, Confederate States Navy. Springs served aboard the blockade runner "*Alice*."
[Source(s): McElroy]

Spruill, Charles Henry (Washington County, North Carolina)
Confederate States Marine Corps. Spruill enlisted at Camp Holmes, near Raleigh, North Carolina in September 1862. His pension claim filed on July 3, 1905, age 69, listing him from [post office not given], Washington County, North Carolina was approved at 4th Class. His application states he "Enlisted in the marine service while at Camp Holmes near Raleigh." An attached doctor's letter states that Charles H. Spruill is 69, paralyzed and about to become a charge of the county. He served "…in the Marine service on the Ship CSS YADKIN, Captain Kerr, under Commodore Pinkney…" A pension claim filed on July 4, 1910 [1905(?)] by widow, Laura Spruill, age 64, listing her post office as Creswell, Washington County, North Carolina, was approved.
[Source(s): WCL; Card File; Pensions (North Carolina); UDC, Dunham; Darden]

Spruill, E. H. (Washington County, North Carolina)
Confederate States Navy.
[Source(s): Darden]

Spruill, Noah (Tyrrell County, North Carolina) (Source "Darden" lists "Washington County, North Carolina)
Confederate States Navy. Spruill was born in North Carolina in 1841, the son of Charles and Martha Spruill. He served aboard the CSS CHICORA stationed at Charleston, South Carolina, beginning about September 1, 1864. In

1870, he resided as a farmer with his wife Mary Ann Spruill and four children in Cool Spring Township, Washington County, North Carolina. He later resided as a farmer in Scuppernong Township, Tyrrell County, North Carolina [1880]. A pension claim filed July 5, 1909 by his widow Mary A. Spruill, age 72, post office Columbia, Tyrrell County, North Carolina, was approved at the 4th Class rate.
[Source(s): Card File; Pension (North Carolina); Darden; Foenander]

Sprunt, James (Scotland//New Hanover County, North Carolina)
Purser, Blockade Runner. Born in Glasgow, Scotland, on June 9, 1846, Sprunt arrived in Wilmington with his parents Alexander and Jane Dalziel Sprunt in 1854. His parents settled in Kenansville, Duplin County, North Carolina, where it is said James occupied a pulpit on Sundays and taught school on weekdays. After two years, James and his parents moved to 9th and Princess Streets, Wilmington, North Carolina, where James continued his own education. At age 14, Sprunt left school to assume some unspecified family responsibilities. He studied navigation at night and after three years secured the purser's berth aboard the blockade runners "*North Heath*" and "*Lillian*." Captured and imprisoned at Fort Macon, North Carolina, and afterwards at Fort Monroe, Virginia, he made his escape and returned to Wilmington via Boston, Halifax (Nova Scotia), and Cape Canaveral, Florida, surviving a shipwreck en route. After his return, he was made purser aboard the blockade runner "*Susan-Bierne*," until the fall of Fort Fisher on January 15, 1865. As he had during the war, Sprunt continued in the lucrative cotton and naval stores trade in the post-war years with his father as a member of the firm Alexander Sprunt and Son. When his father died in 1884, James succeeded him as British vice-counsel. Sprunt went on to have a very distinguished career, both commercially and philanthropically. He died at Greenville Sound on July 9, 1924 and was buried in Oakdale Cemetery, Wilmington, New Hanover County, North Carolina.
[Source(s): McElroy; Card File; Gravestone Records, v. 6, p. 316; "Chronicles," p. 352; Stepp, "Burials;" *Oakdale*, Davis]

Stack, Harvey (Union County, North Carolina)
Confederate States Navy. The "Fayetteville Observer Semi-Weekly" of December 18, 1863 lists an obituary for Stack stating he was a Union County native and member of the Confederate States Navy who died "at the naval yards" in December 1863 of unrecorded causes.
[Source(s): "Fay. Obs." (December 18, 1863)]

Stacy (Stacey), John (Montgomery County, North Carolina)
Landsman, Confederate States Navy. Stacy's name appears on a record of paroled prisoners, Provost Marshal's Office, Middle Military Department which states he took the Oath of Allegiance to the United States and was paroled in Wilmington, North Carolina on April 9, 1865, and was sent to Baltimore County, Maryland. His former residence was listed as "Montgomery, North Carolina." His application for a pension filed on July 5, 1902 at age 57, listing his post office as Wadeville [sic], Montgomery County, North Carolina, was disapproved for insufficient disability. He served on the CSS ARCTIC under Captain Poindexter beginning in the fall of 1864. His pension claim filed on July 4, 1904 at age 59, listing the same post office, was approved at 4th Class. In his pension request, Stacy recounts his service aboard the CSS ARCTIC at Wilmington, North Carolina.
[Source(s): Card File; Pensions (North Carolina); NA RG 109; Foenander]

Stafford, James M. (North Carolina)
Midshipman, Confederate States Navy.
Born in and appointed Acting Midshipman, United States Navy, from North Carolina. He resigned from the United States Navy on April 25, 1861 and was appointed Acting Midshipman, Confederate States Navy, on July 16, 1861 and served aboard the NCS ELLIS as a part of the North Carolina Squadron from December 1, 1861 – February 5, 1862. One source indicates he resigned on May 24, 1862 while source NCCWSP lists him as having "run" on February 5, 1862.
[Source: OCSN; Fold3, Midshipmen; NCCWSP]

Stag (Stagg), Goodman
Landsman, Confederate States Navy. Stag enlisted on December 10, 1863, in Raleigh, North Carolina, for the war. Another source states he enlisted on December 12, 1863, in Wilmington, North Carolina, for the war.
[Source(s): Card File; NA RG 45]

Staley, Henry C.
Landsman, Confederate States Navy. Staley enlisted on November 5, 1863, in Wilmington, North Carolina, for the war. Another source states he enlisted on November 2, 1863, in Raleigh, North Carolina, for the war.
[Source(s): Card File; NA RG 45]

Stallings, Sterling (New Hanover County, North Carolina)
Ordinary Seaman, Confederate States Navy. Stallings enlisted in the Confederate States Navy on August 6, 1863 in Wilmington, North Carolina, and served aboard the CSS ARCTIC.
[Source(s): MR, 4, p. 447; Foenander; St. Armand]

Stalling[s], W[ylie] M.
Landsman, Confederate States Navy. Stallings enlisted on June 11, 1864, in Raleigh, North Carolina, for the war.
[Source(s): Card File; NA RG 45]

Stamper, Meridith D. (Ashe County, North Carolina)
Private, Confederate States Army//Confederate States Navy. Stamper resided in Ashe County, North Carolina, where he enlisted at age 19 on May 17, 1861 as a Private in Company A, 26th Regiment, North Carolina Troops. Source "Foenander" states Stamper killed another Private of his company, one H. D. Wagoner, in camp near Kinston, on April 20, 1862 (further details of this killing not known). He was reported present or accounted for until he transferred to the Confederate States Navy on or about April 1, 1864.
[Source(s): Card File; North Carolina Troops, VII; Foenander]

Stancil (Stancel), Moses (Johnston County, North Carolina)
Private, Confederate States Army//Confederate States Navy. Stancil was born in Johnston County, North Carolina, in August 1841, the son of William and Salley Stancil. Moses Stancil was a farmer prior to enlisting in Company B, 10th Bn., North Carolina Heavy Artillery, serving later in Companies C and E, 24th North Carolina Troops. He enlisted in the Confederate States Navy on March 18, 1864, at Camp Holmes [near Raleigh, North Carolina] from Colonel Heath's 41st Regiment, North Carolina Militia, Johnston County, North Carolina. His description was as follows: Age, 22; eyes, hazel; hair, dark; complexion, dark; height, 5 feet 9 ½ inches. Other sources state he enlisted on March 24, 1864, in Raleigh, North Carolina, for the war, and was on a list of conscripts "in yard at Halifax" June 9, 1864. He was a crewman on the CSS ALBEMARLE according to the muster roll for July- September 1864. [NOTE: Source "North Carolina Troops" does not list him as either a member of Company B, 10th Battalion, North Carolina Heavy Artillery, or the 24th Regiment, North Carolina Troops]. He was paroled at Appomattox with Company C., 53rd North Carolina Troops ("No mention of naval service [?]).".
[Source(s): ORN; his daughter; *The Daily Record*, Dunn, North Carolina, March 19-21, 1999; Card File; NA RG 45; Foenander]

Stanland, Joseph
Landsman, Confederate States Navy. Stanland enlisted on September 12, 1863, in Wilmington, North Carolina, for the war.
[Source(s): Card File; NA RG 45]

Stanland, Lorenzo (Brunswick County, North Carolina)
Confederate States Navy. A pension claim filed on July 5, 1909 by widow Jennie Stanland, age 64, listing her post office as Southport, Brunswick County, North Carolina, was approved at 4th Class. In it she states her husband served in the Confederate States Navy beginning on or about December 15, 1864.
[Source(s): Card File; Pensions (North Carolina)]

Stanley, Daniel K. (Lenoir County, North Carolina)
Private, Confederate States Army//Confederate States Navy (?). Born in Lenoir County, North Carolina, Stanley was a farmer prior to enlisting at age 17 in Company D, 13th Battalion, North Carolina Infantry, in Wayne County, North Carolina on January 3, 1862, for the war. He was present or accounted for until he transferred to Company K, 66th Regiment, North Carolina Troops on October 2, 1863. However, he failed to report, probably because he was on detached duty. He transferred to Captain Guilford W. Cox's Independent Company (Kinston Provost Guard), North Carolina Local Defense Troops, prior to March 1, 1864. Source Card File indicates naval service but gives no details. A "D. R." Stanley is listed on the March – October 1864 muster roll of the CSS NEUSE.
[Source(s): Card File; North Carolina Troops, XV; CMACSSN]

Stanley, Fredrick (also Shadrick)
Seaman, Ship's Cook, Confederate States Navy.
Stanley served as a Seaman aboard the CSS CORA from December 21, 1861 - December 31, 1861, and as a rated Ship's Cook from January 1, 1862 - March 31, 1862. He appears on the North Carolina payroll for the 1st quarter of 1862 from December 31, 1861 - March 31, 1862.
[Source: NCCWSP]

Stanley, I. R.
Landsman, Confederate States Navy. Stanley enlisted on June 10, 1864, in Raleigh, North Carolina, for the war.
[Source(s): Card File; NA RG 45]

Stanly, Calim
Landsman, Confederate States Navy. Stanly enlisted on October 26, 1863, in Wilmington, North Carolina, for the war.
[Source(s): Card File; NA RG 45]

Stanly (Stanley), Calvin (Guilford County, North Carolina)
Landsman, Confederate States Navy. Stanly enlisted on October 10, 1863 in Wilmington, North Carolina. Another source states he enlisted on October 19, 1863, at Camp Holmes [near Raleigh, North Carolina]).
[Source(s): MR, 4, p. 447; Card File; NA RG 45]

Stanly, Henry C. (Chatham County, North Carolina)
Confederate States Navy. Stanly enlisted in the Confederate States Navy on October 31, 1863 in Wilmington, North Carolina.
[Source(s): MR, 4, p. 447]

Staunton, William B. (Cumberland County, North Carolina)
Private, Confederate States Army//Confederate States Navy. Staunton enlisted in Cumberland County, North Carolina, on March 1, 1862 in 2nd Company [Source Foenander lists "3rd Company"] B, 36th Regiment, North Carolina Troops (2nd North Carolina Artillery) for the war. He transferred to the Confederate States Navy on May 5, 1862.
[Source(s): Card File; NA RG 45; NA RG 109; North Carolina Troops, I; Foenander]

Staysey, John
Landsman, Confederate States Navy. Staysey enlisted on February 18, 1864, in Raleigh, North Carolina, for the war.
[Name may be "Stacey"]
[Source(s): Card File; NA RG 45]

Steel, Henry A. (Randolph County, North Carolina)
Confederate States Navy. Steel enlisted in the Confederate States Navy on August 10, 1863 in Wilmington, North Carolina.
[Source(s): MR, 4, p. 447]

Steely, J. W.
Seaman, Confederate States Navy. Steely enlisted on February 3, 1864 in Halifax or Plymouth, North Carolina, for the war.
[Source(s): Card File; NA RG 45]

Sterling, Niel Howison (Guilford County, North Carolina)
Midshipman, Confederate States Navy. Born in 1844, the son of Fort Sterling of Greensboro, North Carolina, and the nephew of R. R. Howison of Richmond, Virginia, Sterling was appointed to the Confederate States Navy from North Carolina. Appointed an Acting Midshipman 4th Class, Confederate States Navy, on August 24, 1861, he served aboard the CSS JAMESTOWN, James River Squadron, 1861; on the Richmond Naval Station, 1862, and at Drewry's Bluff, Virginia, 1862-1863. Sterling served aboard the CSS HARRIETT LANE at Galveston, Texas, 1863, and aboard CSS GAINES, Mobile Squadron, 1863. He attended the Confederate States Naval Academy at age 17, serving aboard the CSS PATRICK HENRY 1863-1864. Information secured September 1924, from J. G. Sterling confirms Sterling was a Midshipman, and states that he enlisted from Richmond, Virginia, and died in service at Richmond, Virginia, on April 17, 1864 at the age of 17 years, 3 months, and 9 days. His funeral service was held on Tuesday, April 19, 1864, at the home of his uncle, R. R. Howison, in Richmond. His name appears on a Prescription Book of Hospital, Steamer GAINES, Confederate States Navy, being admitted July 9, 1863, with "inter fever" and discharged July 11, 1863, age given as 16, stating he was from North Carolina. He appears on another Prescription Book of the same ship stating he was admitted August 16, 1863, with "inter fever, chill" and was discharged August 22, 1863. This book gives his age as 18 and carries the comment: "North Carolina." Source "Driver" states he died in Richmond on April 14, 1865, and was buried in the Confederate Cemetery, Fredericksburg, Virginia.
[Source(s): McElroy; Register; Sterling; Card File; NA RG 45; Driver; Academy; Foenander; ONWR]

Stevens, G. K. (Mecklenburg County, North Carolina)
Confederate States Navy. Stevens filed a claim for pension on July 1, 1903, at age 73, listing his post office as Charlotte, Mecklenburg County, North Carolina. On the application he states he enlisted on or about August 1, 1863 and served on the CSS NORTH CAROLINA, and that he was ruptured while handling heavy iron on the ship. The pension was approved at 4th Class.
[Source(s): Card File; Pensions (North Carolina)]

Stevenson, C. H.
Ordinary Seaman, Confederate States Navy. Stevenson enlisted on October 5, 1863, in Wilmington, North Carolina, for the war.
[Source(s): MR, 4, p. 447; Card File; NA RG 45]

Stewart, Henry C. (Beaufort County, North Carolina)
Confederate States Navy (Confederate States Naval Battalion). Stewart's name appears as a signature on an Oath of Allegiance to the United States subscribed and sworn to at Point Lookout, Maryland June 20, 1865. His place of residence was given on the Oath as Beaufort County, North Carolina. Description: Complexion, light; hair, brown; eyes, blue; height, 5 feet 5 inches.
[Source(s): Card File; NA RG 109]

Stewart, James (Alias: "James Sullivan)
Seaman, Confederate States Navy. Stewart enlisted from North Carolina in 1861 and served aboard the CSS CHICORA.
[Source(s): McElroy; Card File]

St. George, William
Pilot, Confederate States Navy. St. George served aboard the blockade runner "*Don.*"
[Source(s): Card File]

Stoakley, William S.
Assistant Surgeon, Confederate States Navy. Born in and appointed from North Carolina, Stoakley was commissioned Assistant Surgeon for the war, May 1, 1863, by the Confederate Congress. He was elevated to Assistant Surgeon, Provisional Navy, on June 2, 1864. He served on the Savannah Station, 1863-1864.
[Source(s): McElroy; Register; Card File; ONWR; USCWSRP]

Stokely, Henry C. (Pasquotank County, North Carolina)
Corporal, Confederate States Army//Confederate States Navy. Stokely was born and resided in Pasquotank County, North Carolina, as a farmer prior to enlisting there at age 19 on July 24, 1861, for the war, as a Private in Company A, 8th Regiment, North Carolina Troops. He was captured at Roanoke Island on February 8, 1862, paroled at Elizabeth City on February 21, 1862 and exchanged in August 1862. He was promoted to Corporal on December 22, 1863. Stokely was present or accounted for until killed at Plymouth on April 20, 1864. Source Card File claims he had Confederate Naval service.
[Source(s): Card File; NA RG 45]

Stoke, J. A.
Landsman, Confederate States Navy. Stoke enlisted on June 8, 1864, in Raleigh, North Carolina, for the war. [Note: writing on card very faded]
[Source(s): Card File; NA RG 45]

Stokes, John (Beaufort County, North Carolina)
Private, Confederate States Army//Cook, Captain's Cook, Ordinary Seaman, Confederate States Navy. Stokes resided and enlisted in Beaufort County, North Carolina, on July 3, 1861, aged 29, as a Private in Company G, 19th Regiment, North Carolina Troops (2nd North Carolina Cavalry) [Source NCCWSP gives his age as "38"]. Present or accounted for until he transferred to the Confederate States Navy on February 1, 1862. He was promoted to the rank of "Cook" on February 8, 1862 while serving aboard the CSS RALEIGH and served as an Officer's Cook, James River Squadron, from at least November 16, 1863 - December 15, 1863, as a Captain's Cook aboard the CSS ARCTIC from at least January 16, 1862 – April 1862, and as an Ordinary Seaman on the CSS SAVANNAH, 1862-1863. His name appears on a payroll of the North Carolina Squadron covering the period February 7, 1862 - April 15, 1862. He transferred to the James River Squadron on April 15, 1862 and served at Drewry's Bluff as an Officer's

Cook from at least April 1, 1863 - June 30, 1863. Officer's cook, Raleigh [James River Squadron payroll, November 16 - December 15, 1863]
[Source(s): Card File; "Beaufort County Sailors;" North Carolina Troops, II; Foenander; NCCWSP]

Stokes (Stoker), John J. (Rowan County, North Carolina; possibly Rockingham or Rutherford County, North Carolina)
Landsman, Confederate States Navy. Stokes enlisted on December 5, 1863, in Raleigh, North Carolina, for the war. His name appears on a register of Confederate States Army General Military Hospital Number 4, Wilmington, North Carolina, being admitted March 30, 1864, with "febris typhoides." Register states he was returned to duty on April 24, 1864; however, it also carries the remark: "Died but accounted for as returned to duty." His post office was given as Gold Hill, North Carolina. Another source states he enlisted on December 12, 1863, in Wilmington, North Carolina, for the war.
[Source(s): Card File; NA RG 45; NA RG 109]

Stokes, Thomas
1st Cabin Boy, Confederate States Navy. Stokes enlisted on June 19, 1863, in Wilmington, North Carolina, for the war.
[Source(s): Card File; NA RG 45]

Stone, Benjamin F. (Nash County, North Carolina)
Private, Confederate States Army//Confederate States Navy. Stone resided in Nash County, North Carolina, and enlisted at Camp Magnum, near Raleigh, North Carolina, at age 23 [Source Foenander gives age as "32"] on May 2, 1862, for the war, in Company D, 47th Regiment, North Carolina Troops. Stunned by a shell and captured at Gettysburg, Pennsylvania, July 1-5, 1863, he was hospitalized at David's Island, New York Harbor, on or about July 17, 1863. He was paroled at David's Island on August 24, 1863, and received at City Point, Virginia, on August 28, 1863, for exchange. Reported present in January-February 1864, he transferred to the Confederate States Navy on April 15, 1864.
[Source(s): Card File; North Carolina Troops, XI; Foenander]

Stone, Joseph (Staffordshire, England; Currituck County, North Carolina)
Private, Confederate States Army//Confederate States Navy. Born in Staffordshire, England, Stone worked as a laborer in Currituck County, North Carolina, prior to enlisting there at age 40 on May 13, 1861 as a Private in Company L, 17th Regiment, North Carolina Troops (1st Organization). He was present or accounted for until he transferred to the Confederate States Navy on or about July 28, 1861. Stone served as a Seaman aboard the CSS CURLEW from at least November 20, 1861 – the 1st quarter of 1862. His name appears on the payroll of the receiving ship CSS UNITED STATES with an end date of March 31, 1862.
[Source(s): Card File; North Carolina Troops, VI; Foenander; NCCWSP]

Stone, J. W.
Seaman, Confederate States Navy. Stone enlisted on June 13, 1864, in Raleigh, North Carolina, for the war.
[Source(s): Card File; NA RG 45]

Stone, Young
Landsman, Confederate States Navy. Stone enlisted on June 11, 1862, in Raleigh, North Carolina, for the war.
[Source(s): Card File; NA RG 45]

Stowe, J. A. (Ashe County, North Carolina)
Confederate States Navy. Stowe's name appears as a signature (by mark) to an Oath of Allegiance to the United States, subscribed and sworn to at Point Lookout, Maryland, June 30, 1865. His place of residence was given on the Oath as Ashe County, North Carolina. Description: Complexion light; hair red; eyes blue; height 5 feet 11 inches.
[Source(s): Card File; NA RG 109]

Street, Jessy R. (Cleveland County, North Carolina)
Landsman, Confederate States Navy. Street enlisted on May 27, 1864, in Raleigh, North Carolina, for the war. The pension claim Street filed on June 28, 1901 at age 63, listing his post office as Cliffdale, Rutherford County, North Carolina, was disallowed. Street served aboard the CSS INDIAN CHIEF; no dates given. A second application dated July 6, 1908, age 70, listing his home as Lattimore, North Carolina (Cleveland County, North Carolina), states he served aboard the CSS PEE DEE. D. D. Green's statement of support says he served with Street on the PEE DEE and that they enlisted at Charleston, South Carolina, together on "the CSS INDIAN CHIEF receiving vessel for the purpose of Drilling and then transferred to PEE DEE Gun Boat in A.D. 1864." His claim was disallowed due to

insufficient disability.
[Source(s): Card File; NA RG 45; Pensions (North Carolina); Foenander]

Street, William T.
Landsman, Confederate States Navy. Street enlisted on May 11, 1864, in Raleigh, North Carolina, for the war.
[Source(s): Card File; NA RG 45]

Strickland (Strickling), H.
Landsman, Confederate States Navy. Strickland enlisted on October 11, 1863, in Wilmington, North Carolina, for the war. Another source states he enlisted on October 12, 1863, at Camp Holmes [near Raleigh, North Carolina].
[Source(s): Card File; NA RG 45]

Strickland, James (Columbus County, North Carolina)
Confederate States Navy. Strickland was a crewman on the CSS NORTH CAROLINA.
[Source(s): MR, 4, p. 444; Lyon]

Strickland, James B.
Landsman, Confederate States Navy. Strickland enlisted on December 15, 1863, in Raleigh, North Carolina, for the war. Another source states he enlisted December 18, 1863, in Wilmington, North Carolina, for the war.
[Source(s): Card File; NA RG 45]

Strickland (Strickling), Nathaniel (Cumberland County, North Carolina)
Landsman, Confederate States Navy. Strickland enlisted in the Confederate States Navy on October 12, 1863, at Camp Holmes [near Raleigh, North Carolina]. Another source states he enlisted on October 12, 1863, in Wilmington, North Carolina, for the war. Strickland served as a crewman on the CSS NORTH CAROLINA. He transferred from the Confederate States Navy, where he had served under Captain Muse, to Company E, 36th Regiment, North Carolina Troops (2nd Regiment, North Carolina Artillery) on February 29, 1864. Present or accounted for through August 1864, Strickland was captured at Fort Fisher, North Carolina, on January 15, 1865, and confined at Elmira, New York, where he died on March 12, 1865 of pneumonia. He was buried in Woodlawn National Cemetery, Elmira.
[Source(s): MR, 4, p. 444; Oates; Card File; NA RG 45; NA RG 109; North Carolina Troops, I; Foenander]

Stringer, George W.
Landsman, Confederate States Navy. Stringer enlisted on August 8, 1864, in Raleigh, North Carolina, for the war.
[Source(s): Card File; NA RG 45]

Strong, George W.
Landsman, Confederate States Navy. Strong enlisted on June 6, 1864, in Raleigh, North Carolina, for the war.
[Source(s): Card File; NA RG 45]

Stroup, Alford [Alfred] A. (Born Gaston Company, North Carolina [NOTE: 1860 Census of North Carolina shows birthplace as Buncombe County, North Carolina]; resided in Cleveland County, North Carolina)
Private, Confederate States Army//Landsman, Confederate States Navy. Stroup was a farmer prior to enlisting in Surry County, North Carolina, at age 22 on April 26, 1861 in Company D, 14th Regiment, North Carolina Troops. He was present or accounted for until he transferred to the Confederate States Navy on February 19, 1862 for service aboard the CSS VIRGINIA (CSS MERRIMAC).
[Source(s): Card File; North Carolina Troops, V; Foenander; Cloninger]

Stuart, W. E. (County unknown)
Private, Confederate States Marine Corps. Stuart enlisted in Raleigh, North Carolina on October 6, 1864. He served on the Charleston, South Carolina Station as a Private of the Marine guard on board the ironclad CSS COLUMBIA. He deserted on January 5, 1865.
[Source(s): North Carolina Troops, Doc. # 0299; Card File]

Sturdivant, A. J. (Wake County, North Carolina)
Landsman, Confederate States Navy. Sturdivant enlisted on October 25, 1863 in Wilmington, North Carolina, for the war. Another source states he enlisted October 26, 1863, at Camp Holmes [near Raleigh, North Carolina].
[Source(s): MR, 4, p. 447; Card File; NA RG 45]

Suggs, J. S.
>Landsman, Confederate States Navy. Suggs enlisted on November 20, 1863, in Raleigh, North Carolina, for the war. Another source states he enlisted on November 22, 1863, in Wilmington, North Carolina, for the war.
>[Source(s): Card File; NA RG 45]

Suit, Edmund (Edmond) F. (Granville County, North Carolina)
>Landsman, Confederate States Navy. Suit enlisted on March 31, 1864, in Raleigh, North Carolina, for the war. Another source states he was conscripted on March 29, 1864, at Camp Holmes [near Raleigh, North Carolina] from Colonel Dolby's 43rd Regiment, North Carolina Militia, Granville County, North Carolina. Description: Age, 28; eyes, blue; hair, light; complexion, fair; height, 5 feet 9 ½ inches; place of birth, Granville County, North Carolina; occupation farmer.
>[Source(s): Card File; NA RG 45]

Suit, M. H. (Granville County, North Carolina)
>Landsman, Confederate States Navy. Conscripted on March 30, 1864, at Camp Holmes [near Raleigh, North Carolina] from Colonel Dolby's 43rd Regiment, North Carolina Militia, Granville County, North Carolina. Description: Age, 30; eyes, blue; hair, dark; complexion, fair; height, 5 feet 6 ½ inches; place of birth, Granville County; occupation, farmer. Another source states he enlisted on March 31, 1864, in Raleigh, North Carolina, for the war.
>[Source(s): Card File; NA RG 45]

Sullivan, Alexander (New Hanover County, North Carolina)
>Private, Confederate States Army//Confederate States Navy. Born in New Hanover County, North Carolina, Sullivan resided as a laborer and enlisted there at age 20 on July 20, 1861, for the war, as a Private in Company F, 8th Regiment, North Carolina Troops. Captured at Roanoke Island on February 8, 1862, he was paroled at Elizabeth City on February 21, 1862 and exchanged in August 1862. Sullivan was present or accounted for until he was transferred to the Engineer Corps in June 1863. Source Card File claims he had Confederate Naval service.
>[Source(s): Card File; North Carolina Troops, IV]

Sullivan, James [alias of **"James Stewart,"** q.v.]

Sullivan, James T.
>Ordinary Seaman, Confederate States Navy.
>Sullivan served as an Ordinary Seaman aboard the NCS WINSLOW per the ship's muster roll and other records from at least July - November 1861 and in the same rank aboard the CSS SEA BIRD as late as February 20, 1862. He received a partial payment on February 18, 1862 at Gosport Navy Yard following the sinking of the CSS SEA BIRD at the Battle of Elizabeth City on February 10, 1862. His name appears on the North Carolina Squadron payroll for the 1st quarter of 1862 (December 1, 1861 - April 15, 1862. Sullivan was listed as "on parole' as of April 15, 1862.
>[Source: NCCWSP]

Sullivan, John
>Seaman, Boatswain's Mate, Confederate States Navy.
>Sullivan served aboard the CSS BEAUFORT as a Seaman per the ship's payroll list for September - November 1861. According to the ship's bounty, payroll, and small stores records, he served aboard her from September 1861 through circa February 1862. He was captured in the Battle of Elizabeth City, carried to Roanoke Island on February 10, 1862, and paroled there on February 12, 1862 after which he returned to Elizabeth City. He received a partial payment on February 13, 1862 at the Gosport Navy Yard following his service in manning Fort Cobb at the Battle of Elizabeth City on February 10, 1862. His name appears on the North Carolina Squadron payroll for the 1st quarter of 1862 (December 1, 1861 - April 15, 1862). He was listed as a Boatswain's Mate on December 1, 1861. Sullivan transferred to the James River Squadron on April 15, 1862 as Boatswain's Mate.
>[Source: NCCWSP]

Summers, J. C.
>Seaman, Confederate States Navy. Summers enlisted on June 13, 1864, in Raleigh, North Carolina, for the war.
>[Source(s): Card File; NA RG 45]

Summers, John L.
Landsman, Confederate States Navy. Summers enlisted on November 12, 1863, in Raleigh, North Carolina, for the war.
[Source(s): Card File; NA RG 45]

Summers [Somers, Sommers], Perry Melmout (Iredell County, North Carolina)
Seaman, Confederate States Navy. A "P. M. Sommers" enlisted as a Landsman on June 11, 1864, in Raleigh, North Carolina, for the war, and served aboard the CSS INDIAN CHIEF. He may have been enlisted for naval service from Mallett's Battalion [See source Hilderman]. Union records indicate that he escaped from Confederate receiving ship CSS INDIAN CHIEF in Charleston Harbor, South Carolina, January 26, 1865. He appears on a list of deserters from the enemy turned over to the Provost Marshal General, Department of the South, to be furnished transportation to New York, New York, per steamer USS FULTON in February 1865. The list further states he was born in North Carolina and gives his last residence as North Carolina. Description: Age, 22; eyes, blue; hair, light; height, 5 feet 7 inches. It states he deserted on January 26, 1865, and came into Union lines at Morris Island, SC. He died on October 16, 1917, and was buried at Bethany Presbyterian Church, Iredell County, North Carolina.
[Source(s): Card File; Stepp, "Burials;" NA RG 45; Hilderman]

Summers, Sid
Confederate States Navy. Listed as on duty with the Navy in Charleston, South Carolina, Summers may have been enlisted for naval service from Mallett's Battalion [See source Hilderman].
[Source(s): Hilderman]

Summers, W. H.
Landsman, Confederate States Navy. Summers enlisted on June 11, 1864, in Raleigh, North Carolina, for the war.
[Source(s): Card File; NA RG 45]

Sumner, Joseph J. (Hertford County, North Carolina)
Private, Confederate States Army//Fireman, Confederate States Navy (?). Born in Hertford County, North Carolina, Sumner lived as a farmer or mechanic prior to enlisting at age 21 on May 22, 1861 as a Private in Company D, 17th Regiment, North Carolina Troops (1st Organization). He was present or accounted for until captured at Fort Hatteras, North Carolina, on August 29, 1861. He was confined at Fort Columbus, New York Harbor, New York and at Fort Warren, Boston Harbor, Massachusetts, until paroled on or about January 30, 1862, and transferred for exchange. Declared exchanged on February 20, 1862, Sumner was present or accounted for until the company was disbanded on or about March 20, 1862. He enlisted as a Private in Company C, 17th Regiment, North Carolina Troops, on March 24, 1862, for the war and was present or accounted for until captured while detailed as a Fireman on board the CSS BOMBSHELL at Plymouth, May 5 [One source gives the date as the 8th], 1864. He was transferred the same day, from the USS CERES to the USS SASSACUS, then to the steamer USS LOCKWOOD, on May 10, 1864, for transportation to a prisoner of war facility, and never returned to duty. [North Carolina pension records indicate he survived the war].
[Source(s): North Carolina Troops, VI; Foenander]

Surrat, A. G. (County unknown)
Private, Confederate States Marine Corps. Surrat enlisted in Raleigh, North Carolina on October 6, 1864 and served on the Charleston, South Carolina Station as a Private of the Marine guard on board the ironclad CSS COLUMBIA. He deserted on January 5, 1865.
[Source(s): North Carolina Troops, Doc. # 0299; Card File]

Sussdorf, Gustavus E.
Assistant Surgeon, Confederate States Navy. Sussdorf enlisted from North Carolina and was commissioned in 1864 by the Confederate States Congress.
[Source(s): McElroy; Card File; "Officers, January 1, 1864"]

Suttle, John H. (Cleveland County, North Carolina)
Confederate States Navy. Suttle's name appears on a register of Confederate States Army General Military Hospital No. 4, Wilmington, North Carolina, being admitted April 7, 1864, with "diarrhea chronic" and returned to duty May 18, 1864. His post office was listed as Polkville, North Carolina. Suttle appears again on a register of the same hospital shown as admitted September 8, 1864, with "febris typhoides" and returned to duty September 28, 1864.
[Source(s): Card File; NA RG 109]

Sutton, B. L.
Landsman, Confederate States Navy. Sutton enlisted on December 29, 1863, in Raleigh, North Carolina, for the war.
[Source(s): Card File; NA RG 45]

Sutton, John Caleb, Jr.
Ordinary Seaman, Confederate States Navy//Private, Confederate States Army. Sutton was born in 1845 in Robeson County, North Carolina, the son of John Calem [Caleb?] Sutton and Marinda Boyette. He enlisted in the Confederate States Navy on June 13, 1863, in Wilmington, North Carolina, for the war [Another source indicates he enlisted at Camp Holmes near Raleigh, North Carolina on June 10, 1863]. He transferred from the Confederate States Navy on August 5, 1863 to 3rd Company G, 36th Regiment, North Carolina Troops (2nd Regiment, North Carolina Artillery), where he was present or accounted for through August 1864. He was captured at Fort Fisher, North Carolina, on January 15, 1865 and confined at Elmira, New York, where he died on April 16, 1865 of pneumonia and was buried in Woodlawn National Cemetery, Elmira, New York.
[Source(s): Card File; NA RG 45; North Carolina Troops, I]

Sutton, John L.
Landsman, Confederate States Navy. Sutton enlisted on November 15, 1863, in Wilmington, North Carolina, for the war.
[Source(s): Card File; NA RG 45]

Sutton, William T. (Bertie County, North Carolina)
Assistant Surgeon, Confederate States Navy. Born at Elmwood, Bertie County, North Carolina, on March 5, 1839, Sutton graduated from the University of North Carolina at Chapel Hill, North Carolina, in 1858, and from the University of Pennsylvania Medical School in 1860. He practiced medicine in Windsor, North Carolina. Source "Driver" lists him as "Surgeon, Confederate States Navy." He was practicing medicine in Norfolk, Virginia, as of 1878.
[Source(s): Driver]

Swain, Benjamin F. (Brunswick County, North Carolina)
Corporal, Confederate States Army//Landsman/Seaman, Confederate States Navy (Confederate States Naval Battalion). Swain resided in Brunswick County, North Carolina, where he enlisted at Camp Howard in May 1861 [Source "North Carolina Troops" gives date as July 18, 1861] in Company C., 30th Regiment, North Carolina Troops. Mustered in as a Sergeant, he was reduced to the ranks in May-December 1862. Swain was wounded in the left arm at Gaines' Mill, Virginia, on or about June 27, 1862, and returned to duty prior to January 1, 1863. He was promoted to Corporal in January-June 1863 and was present or accounted for until he transferred to the Confederate States Navy on April 5, 1864. He served as a Seaman on the Confederate States tugboat CSS BEAUFORT in the James River for about two months then transferred to the CSS YADKIN, 1864, the flag ship of Commodore Lynch on the Cape Fear River. He participated in an engagement at Drewry's Bluff, and was later captured at Burkeville Junction on April 8, 1865, and sent to prison at Point Lookout, Maryland. Another record states his name appears on a roll of Prisoners of War at Point Lookout, Maryland, stating he was captured at Sailor's Creek, Virginia, on April 6, 1865, and confined until taking the Oath of Allegiance to the United States and released on June 20, 1865. His residence on the Oath was listed as Brunswick County, North Carolina. Description: Complexion, light; hair, brown; eyes, grey; height, 5 feet 9 ½ inches. Daughter: Mrs. Margarette Clarke, 414 Orange St., Wilmington, North Carolina; son: G. C. Swain, 510 N. 4th St., Wilmington, North Carolina.
[Source(s): McElroy; Card File; NA RG 109; North Carolina Troops, VIII; Foenander]

Swain, James
Ordinary Seaman, Confederate States Navy. Swain enlisted on January 1, 1863, in Wilmington, North Carolina, for the war.
[Source(s): Card File; NA RG 45]

Swain, James (Perquimans County, North Carolina) [NOTE: May be same as "James Swain, Ordinary Seaman, q.v.]
Confederate States Navy. Swain deserted on June 15, 1863 from Wilmington, North Carolina.
[Source(s): "Absentees"]

Swan, Henry Greenwood
"Blockade Runner." Swan was born on December 10, 1830 in Southport, North Carolina.
[Source(s): Card File; UDC, Southport]

Sweat, James G. (born in North Carolina)
Confederate States Navy. Born in North Carolina in 1833, Sweat enlisted in Captain A. B. Noyes' Coast Guard Company (Florida) on March 14, 1862 at Camp Leon, Florida. He died of pneumonia on January 7, 1863 in Lynchburg, Virginia.
[Source(s): www.Confederate States Navyavy.org/stmarks.htm]

Swicegood, J. C. (Rowan County, North Carolina)
Confederate States Navy.
Served at Charleston, South Carolina.
[Source: Rumple]

Swicegood, "Step." (Stephen?) J.
(Davidson County, North Carolina)
Landsman, Confederate States Navy (Confederate States Naval Battalion). Swicegood enlisted on July 16, 1864, in Raleigh, North Carolina, for the war. His name appears as a signature to an Oath of Allegiance to the United States, subscribed and sworn to at Point Lookout, Maryland, June 20, 1865. His place of residence was given as Davidson County, North Carolina. Description: Complexion, light; hair, brown; eyes, hazel; height, 5 feet 5 ¾ inches.
[Source(s): Card File; NA RG 45; NA RG 109]

Swing, John J. (Guilford County, North Carolina)
Landsman, Confederate States Navy. Swing enlisted on October 1, 1863, in Wilmington, North Carolina. Another source states he enlisted on October 12, 1863, at Camp Holmes [near Raleigh, North Carolina].
[Source(s): MR, 4, p. 447; Card File; NA RG 45]

Tabb, M. L.
Captain's Clerk, Confederate States Navy.
Tabb served in the North Carolina Squadron aboard the CSS BEAUFORT for at least the payroll period September 1861 - November 1861.
[Source: NCCWSP]

Tait (Taite), Spencer
Landsman, Confederate States Navy. Tait enlisted on December 17, 1863, in Raleigh, North Carolina, for the war. Appears on the March – October 1864 muster roll of the CSS NEUSE.
[Source(s): Card File; NA RG 45; CMACSSN]

Tarleton, A. B. (Cabarrus County, North Carolina)
Landsman, Confederate States Navy. Tarleton enlisted on October 5, 1863, at Camp Holmes [near Raleigh, North Carolina], and served as a Landsman aboard the CSS ISONDIGA and CSS SAVANNAH. His pension claim filed on July 20, 1901, at age 57, listing his post office as Clear Creek, Cabarrus County, North Carolina, states he enlisted in September 1862 [Source Foenander states he also made application from Mecklenburg County, North Carolina)]. The pension request was disallowed. A claim filed on July 6, 1908, at age 63, listed his address as RFD #11, Charlotte, Mecklenburg County, North Carolina, and states he enlisted in the Confederate States Navy at Savannah, Georgia, September 1863. This request was also disallowed due to "Record too meager." A third pension claim filed June 12, 1909, at age 64 states he enlisted on or about September 15, 1862 and was approved at 4th Class. A claim filed on June 13, 1931 by his widow, Mattie Tarleton, age 62, listed her post office as Oakboro, Stanly Company, North Carolina. Her application states that her husband enlisted in Union County, North Carolina, and that she married him in 1888. He died on June 29, 1930. A claim filed for increase on June 29, 1938 by his widow, age 67 and listing "1889" as marriage date, was approved for Class B.
[Source(s): Card File; Pensions (North Carolina); NA RG 45; Foenander]

Tarleton, James A.
Confederate States Navy (?), Bookkeeper. Tarleton served as a Bookkeeper on the North Carolina Steamer "*Advance.*"
[Source(s): Bradley, 2]

Tatum, James W. (Durham County, North Carolina)
>Confederate States Navy. Tatum was listed as being at the "Navy Yard." His pension claim filed on February 17, 1931, at age 83, listed his post office as Durham, Durham County, North Carolina. It states he enlisted at "the Navy Yard" on October 20, 1863 and served at Edward's Ferry, Halifax County, North Carolina and that his captain was Gilbert Elliot. The pension was approved as Class A. An attached affidavit from Tatum states, "I enlisted in the Navy Yard at Edward's Ferry in October 1863. Mr. Peter Smith was the Chief Manager of the Navy Yard…Mr. Gilbert Elliott worked under Mr. Smith and was called Captain Elliott." [CSS ALBEMARLE construction]. He states he "worked as courier for the yard about 18 months and worked in the shop when not delivering messages." "I was underage [sic] and the government paid my father for my services." Peter E. Smith was Chief of Construction on the CSS ALBEMARLE per Smith's daughter Lena H. Smith, Historian, Scotland Neck Chapter, UDC (1931) (Statement in Tatum's application file) says Elliott wanted the [CSS] ALBEMARLE christened by Mrs. Nannie Hill (whom he later married) and who was Lena H. Smith's mother's sister. It was christened by Miss Mary Spottswood of Virginia. A 1931 letter in the file mentions Tom and Jim Willcox, Halifax, North Carolina [NOTE: Not seen on Foenander's list].
>[Source(s): Card File; Pensions (North Carolina); Foenander]

Tatum, Washington A. (Person County, North Carolina)
>Confederate States Navy. Born in North Carolina in 1822, Tatum enlisted on or about April 1, 1862 in the Confederate States Navy. In 1880, he resided as a blacksmith with his wife Emily F. Tatum, and daughter, Selonia F. Tatum (born 1859) at Holloways, Person County, North Carolina. His widow Emily F. Tatum, age 79, post office Moriah, Person Company, North Carolina, applied for a North Carolina Confederate pension on July 20, 1901, which was approved.
>[Source(s): Card File; Pensions (North Carolina); Foenander]

Tayloe, James Langhorne
>Master, Lieutenant, Confederate Statse Navy.
>Tayloe was Master Commanding the NCS FANNY per this ship's muster roll ending October 8, 1861. Other records indicate he commanded the NCS FANNY through circa February 8, 1862, serving with the North Carolina Squadron. Lieutenant Commanding. He was mortally wounded aboard the CSS RALEIGH during the battle of Hampton Roads on March 8, 1862 and died of his wounds on March 10, 1862.
>[Source: NCCWSP]

Taylor, _____ [?] [North Carolina (?)]
>Midshipman, Confederate States Navy. Taylor is said to have commanded the CSS FANNY, one of the fleet under Commodore Lynch "that participated in the fight" at Roanoke Island, February 7-8, 1862.
>[Source(s): McElroy; Card File]

Taylor, A. E. [NOTE: May be same as Archibald E. Taylor, q.v.]
>Confederate States Navy. Taylor's name appears on a list of conscripts in the yard (at Halifax?) and then transferred to Wilmington, North Carolina, June 9, 1864.
>[Source(s): Card File; NA RG 45]

Taylor, Andrew (Louisiana//Beaufort County, North Carolina)
>Private, Confederate States Army//Confederate States Navy. Born in Louisiana, Taylor worked as a mechanic in Beaufort County, North Carolina, where he enlisted on May 10, 1861, at age 23, as a Private in Company I, 3rd Regiment, North Carolina State Troops. He was present or accounted for until he transferred to the Confederate States Navy on January 22, 1862.
>[Source(s): Foenander; MR, I; Card File; "Beaufort County Sailors;" North Carolina Troops, III]

Taylor, Archibald E. (Cumberland or New Hanover County, North Carolina)
>Landsman, Confederate States Navy. Taylor was a pre-war carpenter who enlisted on March 18 [or, 21], 1864, at Camp Holmes [near Raleigh, North Carolina] [Edgecombe County, North Carolina, per "Foenander"] in Company F, 2nd Battalion, North Carolina Local Defense Troops, from Colonel McKoy's 54th Regiment, North Carolina Militia, Cumberland County, North Carolina. Description: Age, 30 [age 29, per "North Carolina Troops, III"]; eyes, blue; hair, red; complexion, light; height 5 feet 6 ½ inches; place of birth, New Hanover Company, North Carolina; occupation, carpenter.
>[Source(s): Card File; NA RG 45; Foenander]

Taylor, D.
> Landsman, Confederate States Navy. Taylor enlisted on March 23, 1864, in Wilmington, North Carolina, for the war.
> [Source(s): Card File; NA RG 45]

Taylor, Edward
> Confederate States Navy. Taylor was a Quartermaster on the Ironclad CSS ALBEMARLE, 1864, and on Halifax Station, North Carolina. He signed a testimony relative to the pension claim of Jos. S. Dunston, Confederate States Navy, Currituck County, North Carolina.
> [Source(s): Card File; Pensions (North Carolina); *ORN* 2, 1, 274]

Taylor, Edward (Camden County, North Carolina)
> Private, Confederate States Army//Confederate States Navy. Taylor enlisted in Camden County, North Carolina, on November 1, 1863, for the war, as a Private in Company B, 68th Regiment, North Carolina Troops. He transferred to the Confederate States Navy on April 5, 1864.
> [Source(s): Card File; Foenander; North Carolina Troops, XV]

Taylor, James (New Hanover County, North Carolina)
> Seaman, Confederate States Navy. Taylor enlisted on January 26, 1864, in Wilmington, North Carolina, for the war. His name appears on registers of Confederate States Army General Military Hospital Number 4, Wilmington, North Carolina, which state he was admitted February 16, 1864, with "contusio" and returned to duty February 23, 1864. His post office was listed as Wilmington, North Carolina.
> [Source(s): Card File; NA RG 45; NA RG 109]

Taylor, James B. (Halifax County, North Carolina)
> Private, Confederate States Army//Confederate States Navy. Taylor enlisted in Halifax County, North Carolina, at age 24 on April 19, 1861, for six months, in Company I, 1st Regiment, North Carolina Infantry (6 Months, 1861). He was present or accounted for until mustered out November 12-13, 1861. He enlisted as a Private on February 20, 1862 in Company I [Source Foenander gives the company as "D"], 43rd Regiment, North Carolina Troops. Per source "North Carolina Troops," he was present or accounted for until reportedly transferred to the Confederate States Navy on April 10, 1864, to serve on the CSS PATRICK HENRY. No evidence of his service in the Confederate States Navy was located.
> [Source(s): Card File; North Carolina Troops, III and X; Foenander]

Taylor, J. D.
> Landsman, Confederate States Navy. Taylor enlisted on June 8, 1864, in Raleigh, North Carolina, for the war.
> [Source(s): Card File; NA RG 45]

Taylor, James Fauntleroy (Wake County, North Carolina)
> Petty Officer, blockade runner "*Advance*." Born September 21, 1821, Taylor died on August 31, 1903, and was buried in Oakwood Cemetery, Raleigh, Wake County, North Carolina. He was a University of North Carolina at Chapel Hill graduate and served post-war as North Carolina's first full-time State Librarian.
> [Source(s): Powell]

Taylor, William Alfred (Nash County, North Carolina)
> Private, Confederate States Army//Confederate States Navy. Born in Nash County, North Carolina, Taylor resided there as a farmer prior to enlisting in Cumberland County, North Carolina, at age 46 on April 9, 1862, as a Private in Company I, 51st Regiment, North Carolina Troops. Present or accounted for until hospitalized at Wilmington, North Carolina, on or about December 18, 1862, with "hemoptysis," he returned to duty on January 27, 1863. He was hospitalized again in Wilmington, North Carolina, on February 16, 1863. Taylor transferred to the Confederate States Navy on April 18, 1863.
> [Source(s): Card File; North Carolina Troops, XII; Foenander]

Taylor, William B. (New Hanover County, North Carolina)
> Confederate States Navy. Taylor's name appears on a register of Confederate States Army General Military Hospital Number 4, Wilmington, North Carolina, which states he was admitted on January 11, 1864, with "anasarca" and returned to duty on January 16, 1864. His post office was listed as Wilmington, North Carolina.
> [Source(s): Card File; NA RG 109]

Taylor, W. B.
Seaman, Confederate States Navy. Taylor enlisted on May 19, 1863, in Wilmington, North Carolina, for three years or the war.
[Source(s): Card File; UDC, Recorder]

Teague, F. M.
Landsman, Confederate States Navy. Teague enlisted on June 11, 1864, in Raleigh, North Carolina, for the war.
[Source(s): Card File; NA RG 45]

Tebby, Henry Sterling [SEE "Libby (Lebby), Henry Sterlin"]
Captain, Blockade Runner (Confederate States Navy?). Tebby states he "Enlisted April 2, 1861, at Charleston," South Carolina. He was said to be the last runner in and out of Charleston, South Carolina. Tebby served on the "*Hattie*" and "Was also in command of the "*Lillian*" (from "Tales of the Cape Fear" by Dr. James Sprunt, who was the purser on the 'Lillian' and gave an oil painting of this boat to Hall of History, Raleigh, North Carolina)."
[Source(s): Card File; UDC, Recorder]

Telfair, David Alexander (Johnston County, North Carolina)
Midshipman, Master, Lieutenant, Confederate States Navy. Telfair was born in 1844 in and appointed to the United States Naval Academy from North Carolina. Per the 1850, Smithfield, Johnston County, North Carolina, Telfair lived with his father (Dr. Alexander Telfair), mother, siblings, and several boarders in Smithfield. Per the 1860 US Census (Maryland), Telfair was a Midshipman, United States Naval Academy by age 16. He served as an Acting Midshipman, United States Navy from September 23, 1858 until he resigned on March 18, 1861. Appointed Acting Midshipman, Confederate States Navy on May 23, 1861, he was raised to Passed Midshipman on October 3, 1862, and to Master Not in Line of Promotion on January 7, 1864. Records indicate he was appointed to the rank of Second Lieutenant, Provisional Navy, on June 2, 1864. He served on Confederate States steamers CSS JACKSON and CSS CARONDELET, New Orleans Station, 1861-1862; CSS GEORGIA, Savannah Station, 1862-1863; Jackson Station, 1862; and, on the Richmond Station aboard the CSS RAPPAHANNOCK as a Master, 1863. Promoted to Master in Line of promotion [Source Foenander says "not in line of promotion,"], January 7, 1864, he was appointed Second Lieutenant, Provisional Confederate Navy on June 2, 1864. He served on special service in Calais, France, 1863-1864, and aboard the CSS PEE DEE, in 1864. He was attached to Semmes' Naval Brigade, April 1865, and was surrendered and paroled at Greensboro, North Carolina, April 26 [28], 1865. Telfair was involved in politics after the war and served as a representative of North Carolina.
[Source(s): McElroy; Register; Card File; Foenander; Boyd; Census (Maryland) 1860; Census (North Carolina) 1850; Census (North Carolina) 1860; ONWR; Fold3, Midshipmen]

Temple, Wilson S. (Pasquotank County, North Carolina)
Acting Assistant Surgeon, Confederate States Army//Crewman, Confederate States Navy. Temple was born in Pasquotank County, North Carolina, where he worked as a doctor prior to enlisting at age 24 on May 4, 1861, in, per source "North Carolina Troops, VI," Company L, 17th Regiment, North Carolina Troops (1st Organization). He served as Acting Assistant Surgeon of the 17th Regiment, North Carolina Troops (2nd Organization), May – December 1862. He was present or accounted for until the company was disbanded on or about March 4, 1863. Later, Temple served as a Private in Company A, 8th Regiment, North Carolina State Troops. [NOTE: Source "North Carolina Troops" makes no mention of his serving in the Confederate States Navy]. Source "MR" states he was "detailed," that he enlisted in the Confederate States Navy on March 25, 1863 and served aboard the CSS NORTH CAROLINA.
[Source(s): MR, 4, p. 444; North Carolina Troops, VI]

Tennent, John C.
First Assistant Engineer, Confederate States Navy. Appointed from North Carolina, as a First Assistant Engineer on May 18, 1864, Tennent served aboard the CSS FREDERICKSBURG, James River Squadron, 1864. He resigned late in 1864 and went into the Confederate States Army as a chaplain.
[Source(s): Register]

Terrell, Jonathan R. (Caswell County, North Carolina)
Sergeant, Confederate States Army//Confederate States Navy. Terrell resided and enlisted in Caswell County, North Carolina, on July 1, 1861 at age 25 as a Private in Company D, 13th Regiment, North Carolina Troops. He was promoted to Sergeant on August 1, 1862, and wounded at Sharpsburg, Maryland, September 17, 1862. He rejoined the company in November-December 1862 and was present or accounted for until wounded again in the hand at Chancellorsville, Virginia, May 3, 1863. Rejoining the company in September-October 1863, he was present or

accounted for until he transferred to the Confederate States Navy on April 3, 1864.
[Source(s): Foenander; Card File; North Carolina Troops, V]

Terrell (Terrill) (Tyrell), Thomas (Rowan County, North Carolina)
Private, Confederate States Army//Landsman [Fireman?], Confederate States Navy. Terrell resided in Rowan County, North Carolina, where he enlisted on June 15, 1861 [March 19, 1862 per source MR, I] as a Private in Company D (Rowan Artillery), 10th Regiment, North Carolina State Troops (1st North Carolina Artillery). He was present or accounted for until he transferred to the Confederate States Navy on April 6, 1864. [May have served in a unit designated as "1st Regiment, Engineers, Artillery, and Ordnance of North Carolina" per source Rumple]. He is shown as having served as a Landsman aboard the CSS VIRGINIA II. His name appears as a signature to an Oath of Allegiance to the United States, subscribed and sworn to at Point Lookout, Maryland, June 26, 1865. His place of residence was listed as Rowan County, North Carolina. Description: Complexion, fair; hair, fair; eyes, blue; height, 5 feet 5 ½ inches.
[Source(s): Card File; NS RG 109; MR, I; Foenander; North Carolina Troops, I; Rumple]

Terry, C. F. (Burke County, North Carolina)
Purser's Steward, Confederate States Navy. Terry's name appears on a roll of Prisoners of War at Point Lookout, Maryland, which states he was captured at Farmville, Virginia on April 6, 1865, and released on June 21, 1865. His name also appears as a signature to an Oath of Allegiance to the United States, subscribed and sworn to at Point Lookout, Maryland on June 21, 1865. Terry's place of residence was listed as Morganton, North Carolina. Description: Complexion fair; hair auburn; eyes blue; height 5 feet 9 inches.
[Source(s): Card File; NA RG 109]

Tetter (Teter), George H. (Mecklenburg County, North Carolina)
Ordinary Seaman, Confederate States Navy. Tetter enlisted on September 9, 1863, at Camp Holmes [near Raleigh, North Carolina] for the war, as a substitute and served as a crewman on the CSS NORTH CAROLINA. Another source states he enlisted September 22, 1863, in Wilmington, North Carolina, for the war.
[Source(s): MR, 4, p. 444; Card File; NA RG 45]

Tetterton, Robert (Washington County, North Carolina)
Confederate States Navy.
[Source(s): WCL; Darden]

Tetterton [Tittleton and Tittenton], William Roff (Washington County, North Carolina) (Pension states "Beaufort County, North Carolina)
Private, Confederate States Army//Landsman, Confederate States Navy. Tetterton enlisted "for the war" as a Private on July 29, 1861 in Washington County, North Carolina, in Company H, 1st Regiment, North Carolina State Troops. He was present or accounted for until discharged to enter the Confederate States Navy on February 3, 1862. He served as a Landsman aboard the CSS VIRGINIA (MERRIMAC). A widow's application for pension dated July 1, 1907 from Marinda [Melinda] Tetterton, age 56, of Washington, North Carolina, states her husband was in Company H, 1st Regiment, North Carolina Troops. The application was approved as a Class "A" pension on June 24, 1907. A letter from D. P. Sallinger states Tetterton volunteered to go onto the steamer "Mary Mack" [Merrimac]. His name appears on the March – October 1864 muster roll of the CSS NEUSE.
[Source(s): Card File; North Carolina Troops, III; Pensions (North Carolina); MR, I; *ORN* 2, 1, 309; Foenander; Bright et al, p.141; CMACSSN]

Tew, Meila Kenne (Sampson County, North Carolina)
Ordinary Seaman, Confederate States Navy. Born 1826, Tew was a farmer by occupation until he enlisted on August 21, 1863 in Wilmington, North Carolina. Per source "Sills," he served at the Norfolk, Virginia, Station.
[Source(s): MR, 4, p. 447; Card File; Bizzell; NA RG 45; Sills]

Thagard, Captain _____ (Cumberland County, North Carolina)
Confederate States Navy. Thagard resigned from the militia, Cedar Creek District, Cumberland County, North Carolina, to enter upon three years of "naval service."
[Source(s): Militia Letter Book, 1862-1864]

Thomas, Edmund (Granville County, North Carolina)
Private, Confederate States Army//Confederate States Navy. Thomas was born and resided in Granville County, North Carolina, where he lived as a blacksmith prior to enlisting there at age 22 on July 6, 1861, in Company D, 8th

Regiment, North Carolina State Troops. Captured at Roanoke Island, North Carolina, on February 8, 1862, he was paroled at Elizabeth City, North Carolina, on February 21, 1862. He was exchanged in August 1862 and was present or accounted for until transferred to the Confederate States Navy on or about April 6, 1863.
[Source(s): Card File; North Carolina Troops, IV; Foenander]

Thomas, George (Wayne County, North Carolina)
Private, Confederate States Army//Landsman, Confederate States Navy. Thomas resided in Wayne County, North Carolina where he enlisted at age 21 on May 29, 1861, for the war, in Company D, 2nd Regiment, North Carolina State Troops. Another source lists his enlistment date as September 28, 1863 at Camp Holmes, near Raleigh, North Carolina. He was discharged on January 28, 1862 upon transfer to the Confederate States Navy.
[Source(s): Card File; NA RG 45; North Carolina Troops, III]

Thomas, Isaiah (Edgecombe County, North Carolina)
Landsman, Confederate States Navy. Thomas enlisted on August 22, 1863 in Wilmington, North Carolina from Edgecombe County, North Carolina.
[Source(s): MR, 4, p. 447; McElroy; Card File; NA RG 45; Thorpe Roster]

Thomas, James G.
Surgeon, Confederate States Army//Surgeon, Confederate States Navy. Thomas enlisted from North Carolina and served as a Surgeon in the Confederate Army in 1862 and was commissioned by the Confederate States Congress as an Assistant Surgeon for the war, Confederate States Navy, to rank from April 28, 1864, and Assistant Surgeon, Provisional Navy, June 2, 1864. He served at the Naval Ordnance Works, Selma, Alabama, 1864 – 1865, and was paroled on May 27, 1865. [Source(s): McElroy; Card File; Foenander]

Thomas, J. J.
Landsman, Confederate States Navy. Thomas enlisted on October 26, 1863, at Camp Holmes [near Raleigh, North Carolina]. Another source states he enlisted on October 28, 1863, at Wilmington, North Carolina, for the war.
[Source(s): Card File; NA RG 45]

Thomas, Richard (Edgecombe County, North Carolina)
Landsman, Confederate States Navy. Thomas enlisted on May 18, 1863, in Wilmington, North Carolina, for the war, from Edgecombe County, North Carolina.
[Source(s): MR, 4, p. 447; McElroy; NA RG 45; Thorpe Roster]

Thomas, William G.
Seaman, Confederate States Navy.
Per clothing, bounty, payroll, and small stores records, Thomas served as a Seaman aboard the CSS BEAUFORT during the September 1861 - March 1862 time period. Thomas was promoted to the rank of Quartermaster on April 1, 1862 and appears as such on the North Carolina Squadron payroll for the 1st quarter of 1862 (December 1, 1861 - April 15, 1862). He transferred to the James River Squadron as of April 15, 1862 and was serving as a Quartermaster aboard the CSS BEAUFORT per that squadron's payroll for the October 1, 1863 - 15 December 1862 period.
[Source: NCCWSP]

Thompson, C. F. (Bladen County, North Carolina)
Confederate States Navy. Thompson enlisted and served in Wilmington, North Carolina, "on or about September 1864." His pension claim filed July 15, 1907, at age 60, listing his post office as Abbotsburg, Bladen County, North Carolina, was approved as 4th Class. The claim filed on July 1, 1912 by his widow, Mrs. C. F. Thompson, at age 64, post office at Abbottsburg, Bladen County, North Carolina, which was approved, states he enlisted in March 1863.
[Source(s): Card File; Pension (North Carolina); Foenander]

Thompson, David
Landsman, Confederate States Navy. Thompson enlisted on October 5, 1863, at Camp Holmes [near Raleigh, North Carolina].
[Source(s): Card File; NA RG 45]

Thompson, E. C.
Landsman, Confederate States Navy. Thompson enlisted on June 11, 1864, in Raleigh, North Carolina, for the war.
[Source(s): Card File; NA RG 45; Pensions (North Carolina) (see application of "Henry Freshwater")]

Thompson, Edmond
    Ordinary Seaman, Confederate States Navy. Thompson enlisted on June 1, 1863, in Wilmington, North Carolina, for the war.
    [Source(s): Card File; NA RG 45]

Thompson, Henry A.
    Landsman, Confederate States Navy. Thompson enlisted on August 17, 1864, in Raleigh, North Carolina, for the war.
    [Source(s): Card File; NA RG 45]

Thompson, Isaiah
    Seaman, Confederate States Navy.
    Thompson served as a Seaman aboard the CSS CEA BIRD during the period July - November 1861 per that ship's payroll. His name appears on the North Carolina Squadron payroll for the 1st quarter 1of 862 (December 1, 1861 - December 14, 1861).
    [Source: NCCWSP]

Thompson, James (Bladen County, North Carolina)
    Private, Confederate States Army//Confederate States Navy. Thompson resided and enlisted in Bladen County, North Carolina, on December 12, 1861, at age 22, for twelve months as a Private in the 3rd Company B, 36th Regiment, North Carolina Troops (2nd Regiment, North Carolina Artillery). He was present or accounted for until he transferred to the Confederate States Navy, February 11, 1864.
    [Source(s): Card File; NA RG 109; Foenander; North Carolina Troops, I]

Thompson, J. W. [May be the same as J. W. Thompson of Edgecombe or New Hanover County, North Carolina]
    Ordinary Seaman, Confederate States Navy. Thompson enlisted on June 8, 1863, in Wilmington, North Carolina, for the war.
    [Source(s): Card File; NA RG 45]

Thompson, J. W. (Edgecombe County, North Carolina)
    Confederate States Navy. Thompson enlisted on August 22, 1863 in Wilmington, North Carolina, from Edgecombe County, North Carolina. [Source(s): McElroy]

Thompson, John W. (New Hanover County, North Carolina)
    Ordinary Seaman, Confederate States Navy//Private, Confederate States Army. Thompson enlisted in the Confederate States Navy on August 1, 1863 in Wilmington, North Carolina, and served aboard the CSS ARCTIC, 1863. He transferred on August 5, 1863 as a Private to 3rd Company G, 36th Regiment, North Carolina Troops (2nd Regiment, North Carolina Artillery). He was present or accounted for through August 1864. Thompson was wounded and captured at Fort Fisher, North Carolina, on January 15, 1865. Born 1830, Thompson died in 1889, and was buried in Willow Dale Cemetery, Goldsboro, Wayne County, North Carolina.
    [Source(s): MR, 4, p. 447; Card File; Gravestone Records, v. 3, p. 273; Stepp, "Burials;" Foenander; St. Armand; North Carolina Troops, I]

Thompson, Joseph (Brunswick County, North Carolina)
    Confederate States Navy. A widow's application for pension by Mariah Thompson, age 81, of Southport, Brunswick County, North Carolina, dated July 1, 1912, states her husband Joseph Thompson enlisted in the Confederate States Navy on or about June 15, 1862.
    [Source(s): Pensions (North Carolina)]

Thompson, Joseph T. (Brunswick County, North Carolina)
    Confederate States Navy. Thompson's application for pension dated July 6, 1908, living in Southport, North Carolina, states he enlisted in the Confederate States Navy on or about January 15, 1862 was approved as 4th class. A widow's application for pension, dated July 10, 1910, from Mrs. Emma Thompson, age 64, of Southport, North Carolina, states he enlisted on or about July 1, 1863 was approved at 4th class.
    [Source(s): Pensions (North Carolina)]

Thompson, Josiah (Alamance County, North Carolina) [Source MR, I shows Orange County, North Carolina]
    Landsman, Confederate States Navy. Thompson was born in Alamance County, North Carolina, and resided as a farmer in Orange County, North Carolina at the time he enlisted at age 21, for the war, in Warren County, North

Carolina, on August 26, 1861 [Source MR, I indicates the date as August 20, 1861]. He enlisted as a Private in Company I, 8th Regiment, North Carolina State Troops; transferred to the Confederate States Navy in September 1861. Born 1836, he died in1915, and was buried at Salem Methodist Church, Alamance County, North Carolina.
[Source(s): Stepp, "Burials;" North Carolina Troops, IV; Foenander; MR, I]

Thompson, Robert G. (Orange County, North Carolina)
Confederate States Navy. The "Hillsborough Recorder" of September 28, 1864 lists Thompson, an Orange County resident and member of the Confederate States Navy, as having died at his home in Hillsborough of disease in September 1864.
[Source(s): "HR" (Sept. 28, 1864)]

Thompson, Thomas A.
Pilot, Confederate States Navy. Thompson served aboard the blockade runner "*Atlanta*."
[Source(s): McElroy]

Thompson, Thomas M. (Brunswick County (?), North Carolina)
Captain, North Carolina Navy. Born 1831, Thompson died in 1907, and was buried in the Southport Cemetery, Brunswick Company, North Carolina.
[Source(s): Stepp, "Burials"]

Thorent[on?], John (Pasquotank County, North Carolina) [NOTE: May be same as "Thornton, John," q.v.]
Seaman, Confederate States Navy. Thorent[on] is buried in Hollywood Cemetery, Pasquotank County, North Carolina.
[Source(s): Stepp, "Burials"]

Thornton, James
Confederate States Navy. Thornton enlisted in the Confederate States Navy in Wilmington, North Carolina.
[Source(s): MR, 4, p. 447]

Thornton, James (Pasquotank County, North Carolina) [May be same as "James Thornton, CSS BOMBSHELL, q.v.]
Seaman, Confederate States Navy. Thornton was born in Pasquotank County, North Carolina where he resided as a mariner. He enlisted at 18 years old on August 1, 1861 in Company A, 8th Regiment, North Carolina State Troops and transferred to the Confederate States Navy on or about January 9, 1863. Thornton served aboard the CSS NORTH CAROLINA.
[Source(s): MR, 4, p. 444; Sea Bird; *North Carolina Troops*, IV, p. 532 (Broadfoot Ed.); Scharf, p.391 (in notes there was a "John Thornton," Ordinary Seaman, amongst the Confederate Naval personnel captured at Roanoke Island, North Carolina, February 1862)]

Thornton, James [May be same as "James Thornton, CSS NORTH CAROLINA, q.v.]
Confederate States Navy. Thornton served aboard the CSS BOMBSHELL, on which he was captured during the engagement in Albemarle Sound, North Carolina, May 5, 1864. He was transferred the same day from the USS CERES to the USS SASSACUS, thence to the steamer USS LOCKWOOD, on May 10, 1864, for transportation to a prisoner of war facility.
[Source(s): Foenander; ORN 1, 9]

Thornton, John [May be same as "John Thornton," Pasquotank County, North Carolina, q.v.] (Currituck County, North Carolina)
Seaman, Ordinary Seaman, Confederate States Navy. Thornton resided in Currituck County, North Carolina and served as a Seaman and later an Ordinary Seaman aboard the CSS SEA BIRD from at least July – November 1861, and as an Ordinary Seaman through February 1862. He was captured in the Battle of Elizabeth City, North Carolina on February 10, 1862 and taken to Roanoke Island, North Carolina where he was paroled on February 12, 1862. Thornton received a partial payment on February 18, 1862 at Gosport Navy Yard, Norfolk, Virginia following the sinking of the CSS SEA BIRD at Elizabeth City on February 10, 1862. His name appears on a payroll of the North Carolina Squadron covering the period December 1, 1861 - April 15, 1862, on which date he is carried on a payroll as "on parole." One source indicates he may have served in Company A, 8th Regiment, North Carolina Troops.
[*Scharf*, 391; Foenander; MR, IV, 444; NCCWSP]

Thornton, John (Pasquotank County, North Carolina) [May be same as "John Thornton, captured at Roanoke Island, North Carolina," q.v.]

Private, Confederate States Army//Seaman, Confederate States Navy. Thornton was born and resided as a mariner in Pasquotank County, North Carolina where he enlisted on August 1, 1861, aged 18, as a Private in Company A, 8th Regiment, North Carolina State Troops. He transferred to the Confederate States Navy on or about January 9, 1863, and later served aboard the CSS NORTH CAROLINA. He served aboard the CSS SEA BIRD, 1861, prior to enlistment in the Army. Note: A "John Thornton," Currituck County, North Carolina, is listed in MR, IV, p. 444.
[Source(s): North Carolina Troops, IV; ORN 2, 1; Foenander; MR, IV, 444]

Thornton, John (Pasquotank County, North Carolina)
Landsman, Confederate States Navy. Thornton is buried in Hollywood Cemetery, Pasquotank County, North Carolina. Note: A "John Thornton," Currituck County, North Carolina, is listed in MR, IV, 444.
[Source(s): Stepp, "Burials;" MR, IV, 444]

Thrower, Oliver P. (Halifax County, North Carolina)
Private, Confederate States Army//Confederate States Navy. Thrower resided as a farmer in Halifax County, North Carolina, prior to enlisting at age 30 as a Private in Company F., 43rd Regiment, North Carolina Troops, on February 14, 1862. He was present or accounted for through February 1864. He reported on detached duty "on gunboat" at Kinston, July-December 1864. Thrower was "officially" transferred to the Confederate States Navy on January 10, 1865 [Per source "North Carolina Troops," "No evidence of his service in the Confederate States Navy was located"]. He married Margaret Lewis in Halifax County, North Carolina, February 18, 1867.
[Source(s): North Carolina Troops, X; Marriage Bonds, North Carolina Div. of Historical Res.; Hill; Census (NC), 1860; CMACSSN]

Tillman, Daniel (Chatham County, North Carolina)
Confederate States Navy. His application for pension dated July 8, 1912, age 78, listing Bynum as his post office, states he enlisted in the Confederate States Navy in 1862. His application was disallowed due to "property."
[Source(s): Pensions (North Carolina); Foenander]

Tiner, James J. (Johnston County, North Carolina)
Private, Confederate States Army//Confederate States Navy//Confederate States Army. Tiner resided in Johnston County, North Carolina, where he enlisted on June 12, 1861 at age 18 as a Private in Company I, 24th Regiment, North Carolina Troops. He was present or accounted for until July 28, 1864, when he transferred to the CSS ALBEMARLE. He transferred back to Company I, 24th Regiment, North Carolina Troops, on an unspecified date and was paroled at Raleigh, North Carolina, on or about May 6, 1865.
[Source(s): North Carolina Troops, VII; Foenander]

Tiner, Joseph (Johnston County, North Carolina)
Confederate States Navy. Tiner enlisted in the Confederate States Navy on August 12, 1863 in Wilmington, North Carolina.
[Source(s): MR, 4, p. 447]

Tolson (Toleson), Valentine (Carteret County, North Carolina)
Ordinary Seaman, Seaman, Confederate States Navy.
Tolson resided in Portsmouth, Carteret County, North Carolina. He served as an Ordinary Seaman aboard the CSS EDWARDS from at least July 25, 1861 – circa October 1861, when he appears on payroll records of the CSS FORREST (formerly the EDWARDS) from at least October 30, 1861 –through the first quarter of 1862. His name appears on a payroll of the receiving ship CSS UNITED STATES ending March 31, 1862. He is listed as having served on the CSS VIRGINIA, as well as at Drewry's Bluff as a Seaman from at least April 1, 1863 - June 30, 1863.
[Sources: Census (NC), 1860; NCCWSP]

Tomb, A. M.
Seaman, Confederate States Navy. Tomb enlisted from North Carolina in 1863 and served until 1865 aboard the Confederate States torpedo boat *"Little David."*
[Source(s): McElroy]

Tooker, Charles (Beaufort County, North Carolina)
Sergeant, Confederate States Army//Confederate States Navy. A resident of Beaufort County, North Carolina, Tooker enlisted at 44 years of age on May 10, 1861 in Company I, 3rd Regiment, North Carolina State Troops. He was mustered as a Sergeant but was reduced to the ranks when transferred to the Confederate States Navy on February

11, 1862. He may have deserted or been captured, but he is shown as being appointed "Acting master and pilot," October 1, 1864, United States Navy. Tooker served on the USS MATTABESETT and was the commander of the vessel. John C. Febiger in a dispatch dated at Albemarle Sound, North Carolina on May 6, 1864, stated "our pilot, Mr. Tooker, deserves mention for coolness and attention to his duties during our constant maneuverings." Tooker was honorably discharged on September 16, 1865.
[Source(s): ORN, 1, 9, p. 748; North Carolina Troops, III, p. 587; Callahan; "Beaufort County Sailors"]

Tredwell, Adam
Captain's Clerk/Secretary, Assistant Paymaster, Confederate States Navy.
Born in and appointed from North Carolina, Tredwell served with the North Carolina Squadron as a Captain's Clerk/Secretary to Commodore William T. Muse; as an Assistant Paymaster as of October 20, 1862 under Commodores Lynch and Pinkney; and, as an Assistant Paymaster, Provisional Navy, June 2, 1864. He served aboard two Confederate steamers, the CSS ELLIS and CSS CASWELL, 1861-1862. He participated in the battle at Hatteras Inlet, North Carolina, February 7-8, and in the engagement at Elizabeth City, North Carolina, February 10, 1862. He served on the Wilmington Station, 1862-1865, and was paroled at Greensboro, North Carolina, April 28, 1865. He died on March 27, 1912 in Norfolk, Virginia at age seventy-two.
[Source(s): Register; McElroy; "Times-Dispatch;" ONWR; NCCWSP]

Tripp, Joshua C. (Pitt County, North Carolina)
Landsman, Confederate States Navy. A September 25, 1864 letter requesting a transfer from Charleston, South Carolina (CSS INDIAN CHIEF) to either Halifax or Kinston, North Carolina, to North Carolina Governor Zebulon B. Vance, is signed by D. Beck, D. M. Faust, R. Tripp, and J. C. Tripp. Apparently, the transfer was not within Vance's ability to grant. The letter states that all four were "Soldiers in Colonel Mallet's [Mallett's] battalion and desired when we entered the navy to serve in North Carolina but were not permitted to do so." Tripp's July 9, 1903 application for a North Carolina Confederate pension, at age 75, states he served in "Major Peter Mallett's command of Conscripts." He was transferred to the Confederate Navy at Charleston, South Carolina, and served there until the surrender. His application was approved at 4th Class.
[Source(s): Vance Papers; Census (North Carolina), 1860; Pensions (North Carolina)]

Tripp, Redding [Reading] (Pitt County, North Carolina)
Landsman, Confederate States Navy. A September 25, 1864 letter requesting a transfer from Charleston, South Carolina (CSS INDIAN CHIEF) to either Halifax or Kinston, North Carolina, to North Carolina Governor Zebulon B. Vance, is signed by D. Beck, D. M. Faust, R. Tripp, and J. C. Tripp. Apparently, the transfer was not within Vance's ability to grant. The letter states that all four were "Soldiers in Colonel Mallet's [Mallett's] battalion and desired when we entered the navy to serve in North Carolina but were not permitted to do so." His May 10, 1909 application for a North Carolina Confederate pension, filed at age 78, from Winterville, Pitt County, North Carolina, states he was then disabled, and mentions that he had between two and three years of service as a "soldier at Raleigh" and eight months at Charleston, South Carolina till it fell, thence to Wilmington, North Carolina. His application was annotated with "This application is especially recommended by the Board," and was approved at the 4th Class level.
[Source(s): Vance Papers; Census (North Carolina), 1860; Pensions (North Carolina)]

Troutman, M. [Monroe?] (Stanly County, North Carolina)
Confederate States Navy. Troutman enlisted in the Confederate States Navy August 21 and 24, 1863 in Wilmington, North Carolina.
[Source(s): MR, 4, p. 447]

Troutman, Monroe
Landsman/Ordinary Seaman, Confederate States Navy. Troutman enlisted on September 11, 1863, at Camp Holmes for the war. Another source states he enlisted on September 22, 1863, in Wilmington for the war.
[Source(s): McElroy; NA, RG 45]

Troutman, N. M (M. M.)
Seaman, Confederate States Navy. Troutman enlisted on June 13, 1864, in Raleigh for the war.
[Source(s): McElroy; NA, RG 45; Duke Papers]

Troutman, Samuel (Rowan County, North Carolina)
Landsman, Confederate States Navy. Born in Rowan County, North Carolina, Troutman lived there as a farmer until enlisting there at age 36 in the Confederate States Navy. He served as a Landsman aboard the CSS ALBEMARLE, and

on the Halifax Station, 1864. Another source states he was conscripted March 10, 1864 (or enlisted March 11, 1864), at Camp Holmes, Raleigh for the war from the 76th Regiment, North Carolina Militia, under Colonel Bradshaw, from Rowan County. Description given as follows: Age-36; eyes-hazel; hair-light; complexion-light; height-5 ft. 9½ in; place of birth-Rowan County; occupation-farmer. He appears on a list of conscripts "in the yard at Halifax."
[Source(s): McElroy; NA, RG 45; Foenander]

Troxter, John (Alamance County, North Carolina)
Crewman, Confederate States Navy. Troxter served aboard the CSS NORTH CAROLINA.
[Source(s): MR, 4, p. 444]

Truesdell (Truesdale), Stephen Picket
Private, Confederate States Army//Confederate States Navy. Born in Beaufort, North Carolina, on December 25, 1840, Truesdell resided in Mount Pleasant, South Carolina. He enlisted in Richmond, Virginia, July 20, 1861, as a Private, in Company I, 1st South Carolina (Gregg's) Volunteer Infantry (other accounts indicate he enlisted April 8 or 22, 1861, in Charleston, South Carolina, and was stationed on Morris Island, South Carolina before transferring to Richmond, Virginia). He transferred to the Confederate States Navy on January 17, 1862 and served aboard the CSS VIRGINIA, Hampton Roads, Virginia, 1862. He was wounded in the back of the head and left arm by fragments of a bursting gun on board the CSS VIRGINIA. Transferred to the CSS CHARLESTON, his name appears on a list of Confederate refugees and deserters released March 16, 1865, in Charleston, South Carolina, upon taking the Oath of Allegiance. He applied, unsuccessfully, for a Confederate pension. Truesdell resided in Florida as of May or June 1904.
[Source(s): Foenander]

Tuck, Goe
Confederate States Navy. Tuck was conscripted on March 3, 1864, at Camp Holmes from Colonel Lee's 48th Regiment Militia from Alamance County. His description was given as follows: Age, 40; eyes hazel; hair dark; complexion, dark; height, 5 ft. 8 in.; place of birth, Alamance County; occupation, farmer.
[Source(s): McElroy; NA, RG 45]

Tucker, David (Duplin County, North Carolina)
Sailor ["Landsman" (see Stepp)], Confederate States Navy (Naval Battalion). Tucker enlisted on September 20, 1863 and served aboard the CSS SAVANNAH. He served until "near Appomattox, March 1865." Another source states he was wounded when knocked over by a shell at Appomattox Court House, Virginia, 1865. His name appears as a signature to an Oath of Allegiance to the United States, subscribed and sworn to at Newport News, Virginia, June 26, 1865. His place of residence was given on the Oath as Duplin County, North Carolina. Description: Complexion-dark; hair-dark; eyes-dark; height-5 ft. 11 in. The oath also states he was captured at Farmville, Virginia on April 6 [1865]. His claim for a pension filed on July 16, 1901, at age 70 years, listed his post office as Warsaw, Duplin County. A doctor's note states he was "knocked some twenty feet by an exploded shell and was unconscious for some hours." Tucker's request for pension was approved as 4th Class. Born on August 1, 1832, he died on October 11, 1918, and was buried in Pinecrest Cemetery, Duplin County, North Carolina.
[Source(s): McElroy; UDC, Warsaw; NA, RG 109; Pensions (N.C); Stepp, "Burials"]

Tucker, Francis
Officer's Steward, Confederate States Navy.
Tucker served with the North Carolina Squadron aboard the CSS FORREST (formerly the NCS EDWARDS) per that ship's payroll for the 1st quarter of 1862.
[Source: NCCWSP]

Tucker, Frank
Seaman, NCS WINSLOW. Tucker was a slave of Master Patrick McCarrick, and one of seven African American crew members aboard the NCS WINSLOW.
[Source(s): NCS]

Tucker, J. B.
Landsman, Confederate States Navy. Tucker enlisted on June 11, 1864, in Raleigh for the war. A "J. T(?)" Tucker appears on the March – October 1864 muster roll of the CSS NEUSE.
[Source(s): McElroy; NA, RG 45; CMACSSN]

Turner, Alexander [May be same as "Alex Turner" (q.v.)] (Sampson County, North Carolina)
Seaman, Confederate States Navy. Turner enlisted on September 21, 1863. His name appears on a roll of Prisoners of War at Point Lookout, Maryland, which states he was captured as Jetersville April 6, 1865 and confined at Point Lookout until released on June 30, 1865. His name also appears as a signature (by mark) to an Oath of Allegiance to the United States, subscribed and sworn to at Point Lookout June 30, 1865. His place of residence was given on the Oath as Sampson County, North Carolina. Description: Complexion-light; hair-dark; eyes-hazel; height-5 ft. 10½ in. An application for a pension filed on June 14, 1901 by his widow, Josephine Turner, age 70 years, listing her post office as Clinton, Sampson County, North Carolina, states her husband enlisted in the Confederate States Navy on board the CSS PEE DEE under Captain Johnston on or about September 21, 1863. In her claim she stated he was never wounded, and that he has been dead about ten years. The pension was approved.
[Source(s): McElroy; NA, RG 109; Pensions (North Carolina)]

Turner, Alex [May be same as "Alexander Turner" (q.v.)]
Landsman, Confederate States Navy. Turner enlisted on June 11, 1864, in Raleigh for the war.
[Source(s): McElroy; NA, RG 45]

Turner, J. D.
Landsman, Confederate States Navy. Turner enlisted on June 11, 1864, in Raleigh for the war.
[Source(s): McElroy; NA, RG 45]

Turner, J. L.
Private, Confederate States Army//Landsman, Confederate States Navy. Turner enlisted on April 11, 1864, in Kinston for three years or the war. His name appears on the March – October 1864 muster roll of the CSS NEUSE.
[Source(s): McElroy; NA, RG 45; CMACSSN]

Turner, M. V. (Cleveland County, North Carolina)
Private, Confederate States Army//Landsman, Confederate States Navy. Residing in Cleveland County, North Carolina, Turner enlisted there at age 18 on April 27, 1861 as a Private in Company C, 15th Regiment, North Carolina Troops. He was present or accounted for until he transferred to 2nd Company D, 15th Regiment, North Carolina Troops on April 8, 1863. Turner was present or accounted for until he transferred to the Confederate States Navy on April 1, 1864. Born in 1824, Turner died on August 6, 1907, and was buried at Friendship Methodist Church, Cleveland County, North Carolina.
[Source(s): McElroy; NPS; Stepp, "Burials;" North Carolina Troops, V]

Turner, William J. (also William P.)
Ordinary Seaman, Confederate States Navy.
Turner shipped for one year aboard the CSS RALEIGH on August 17, 1861 and, per various records, served through April 1862. His name appears on the North Carolina Squadron payroll for the 1st quarter of 1862 from February 21, 1862 - April 15, 1862. Turner transferred to the James River Squadron on April 15, 1862 and served at Drewry's Bluff as an Ordinary Seaman from April 1, 1863 through June 30, 1863 per payroll records.
[Source: NCCWSP]

Turner, Wm. W. (Iredell County, North Carolina)
Landsman, Confederate States Navy. Turner enlisted in the Confederate States Navy on June 13, 1864, probably at Camp Holmes near Raleigh, North Carolina. He served aboard the CSS INDIAN CHIEF. His name appears as a signature to an Oath of Allegiance to the United States, subscribed and sworn to at Point Lookout, Maryland, June 20, 1865. His place of residence was given on the Oath as Iredell County, North Carolina, and description as follows: Complexion-light; hair-brown; eyes-gray; height-5 ft. 9¼ in.
[Source(s): McElroy; NA, RG 109; NA, RG 45; Duke Papers]

Turrentine, W. H. (Orange or Alamance County, North Carolina)
Confederate States Army//Mechanist, Confederate States Naval Yard (Confederate States Navy?). Turrentine was transferred from the Confederate States Army to the Confederate States Naval Yard at Portsmouth, Virginia in 1862. He helped build the CSS VIRGINIA.
[Source(s): McElroy]

Tyler, Clarence W. (New Hanover County, North Carolina)
Acting Midshipman / Midshipman, Confederate States Navy. Born in New Hanover County, North Carolina, Tyler was a student prior to enlisting on April 15, 1861, at age 17 as a Private in Company I, 18th Regiment, North

Carolina Troops (formerly, 8th Regiment, North Carolina Volunteers). The regiment was organized at Camp Wyatt, near Carolina Beach, North Carolina, in July 1861. Tyler transferred to the Confederate States Navy on or about September 20, 1861 (original entry into Confederate States Navy, as Acting Midshipman, 4th class, also shown as September 12, 1861). Tyler served at the Savannah Station, 1861 – 1862; aboard the CSS CAPITAL, on the Mississippi River, 1862; and, aboard the CSS RESOLUTE, Savannah Squadron, 1861-1862. He served at the Jackson Station, 1862. Source "Academy" states he served aboard the CSS ARCTIC and the CSS NORTH CAROLINA, Wilmington Station, 1862-1863. Another source states he served on the Richmond Station, 1862-1863. He was wounded in the head on July 15, 1862, aboard the CSS ARKANSAS, Yazoo River, during that ram's passage through the Federal fleet above Vicksburg. He was awaiting orders, 1862-1863, and later served aboard the CSS PATRICK HENRY, 1863-1864, the ship serving as the Confederate States Naval Academy. Tyler resigned on January 9, 1864.
[Source(s): McElroy; Register; NPS; Academy; Foenander; North Carolina Troops, VI; ONWR; Fold3, Midshipmen]

Tyner, Joseph (Johnston County, North Carolina)
Confederate States Navy. Tyner enlisted in the Confederate States Navy on or about April 15, 1862, under Captain Muse and Commodore Lynch. A claim for pension was filed on June 19, 1901 by his widow, Polly [Pollie] Tyner, age 63 years, listing her post office as Princeton, Johnston County. No action was indicated.
[Source(s): McElroy; Pensions (NORTH CAROLINA)]

Underwood, J. B.
Landsman, Confederate States Navy. Underwood enlisted on October 31, 1863, in Wilmington for the war.
[Source(s): McElroy; NA, RG 45]

Upchurch, Nathan (Nathaniel) (Wake County, North Carolina)
Landsman, Confederate States Navy. Born in North Carolina, in 1829, Upchurch enlisted on December 9, 1863, at Raleigh for the war [NOTE: Another source states he enlisted on December 12, 1863, in Wilmington for the war]. His widow's pension claim states he enlisted on December 1, 1863. He served as a Landsman aboard the CSS ARCTIC and CSS RALEIGH. His name appears on a register of Confederate States Army General Military Hospital, Number 4, Wilmington, North Carolina, being admitted on December 30, 1863, with "febris remittens" and returned to duty on May 24, 1864. Upchurch's post office was given on the register as Cary, North Carolina. A claim filed on June 15, 1901 by widow, Martha A. Upchurch, age 68 [69] years, listing her post office as Raleigh, Wake County, was approved.
[Source(s): McElroy, NA, RG 45; NA, RG 109; Pensions (NORTH CAROLINA)]

Usry, John C. (Granville County, North Carolina)
Confederate States Navy. Born in 1830 in North Carolina, Usry served in the Confederate States Navy. His application for a pension dated June 27, 1914, at age 84, while living on Rt. 1, Hester, Granville County, North Carolina, states he enlisted in the Confederate States Navy at "Batines (?) Sp…" [illegible], on or about November 1, 1864 in the company of Captain Hillary. Witness B. L. Sherron (q.v.) states he was in the same company with Usry. The claim was approved.
[Source(s): Pensions (North Carolina); Foenander]

Utter, Nicholas
Seaman, Quartermaster, Confederate States Navy.
Utter served with the North Carolina Squadron aboard the CSS BEAUFORT as a Seaman per the ship's payroll for September – November 1861. He served as a Quartermaster aboard the NCS FANNY from December 1861 through February 1862 when she was burned to prevent capture during the Battle of Elizabeth City. He received a partial payment on February 13, 1862 at the Gosport Navy Yard. His name appears on the payroll of the North Carolina Squadron for the 1st quarter of 1862 (December 1, 1861 – April 15, 1862). Utter was reduced in rank from Quartermaster to Seaman on February 11, 1862. He transferred to the James River Squadron on April 15, 1862.
[Source: NCCWSP]

Valentine, B. S.
Confederate States Navy. Valentine enlisted on January 2, 1864, in Raleigh for the war.
[Source(s): McElroy; NA, RG 45]

Valentine, Penner (Randolph County, North Carolina)
    Confederate States Navy. Valentine enlisted in the Confederate States Navy in Wilmington, North Carolina.
    [Source(s): MR, 4, p. 447]

Vanderburg (Vanderberg), M.
    Seaman, Confederate States Navy. Vanderburg enlisted on June 22, 1865, in Raleigh for the war.
    [Source(s): McElroy; NA, RG 45; Duke Papers]

Varner, Ransom
    Landsman, Confederate States Navy. Varner enlisted on December 29, 1863, in Raleigh for the war.
    [Source(s): McElroy; NA, RG 45]

Varnum, R. (Guilford County, North Carolina)
    Landsman, Confederate States Navy. Varnum died on December16, 1864, and was buried in Green Hill Cemetery (Confederate Section), Guilford County, North Carolina.
    [Source(s): Stepp, "Burials"]

Vernon, William H.
    Acting Midshipman, Confederate States Navy.
    Vernon served as an Acting Midshipman aboard the CSS EDWARDS (later the CSS FORREST) and aboard the CSS ELLIS.
    [Source: NCCWSP]

Vick, J. G. W.
    Landsman, Confederate States Navy. Vick enlisted on February 19, 1864, in Raleigh for the war.
    [Source(s): McElroy; NA, RG 45]

Vick, James P. (Nash County, North Carolina)
    Private, Confederate States Army//Confederate States Navy. Vick resided in Nash County, North Carolina, where he enlisted on March 1, 1862, at age 22 as a Private in 2nd Company H, 12th Regiment, North Carolina Troops (2nd Regiment, North Carolina Volunteers). He was present or accounted for until he transferred as a Private in 2nd Company H, 32nd Regiment, North Carolina Troops, on July 22, 1862. He was present of accounted for until wounded in the hip and captured at Gettysburg, Pennsylvania, July 1-5, 1863. Vick was hospitalized at Gettysburg until transferred to the hospital at David's Island, New York Harbor, on or about July 23, 1863. Paroled at David's Island, Vick was transferred to City Point, Virginia, where he was received on September 27, 1863, for exchange. He was reported absent on parole through December 1863. Vick transferred from the Army to the Confederate States Navy on April 5, 1864 [one source gives date as "1863"]. Another source states records exist of a James P. Vick as a Prisoner of War throughout the war.
    [Source(s): McElroy; NPS; North Carolina Troops, V and IX]

Vick, Jesse
    Landsman, Confederate States Navy. Vick enlisted on February 12, 1864, in Wilmington for the war.
    [Source(s): McElroy; NA, RG 45]

Waddell [Waddill], Edmund "Ed" (Moore County, North Carolina)
    Private, Confederate States Marine Corps. Waddell enlisted in Raleigh, North Carolina on November 4, 1864 [NOTE: Letter of James C. Davis, November 17, 1864, states the group from Camp Holmes, of which Waddell was a part, arrived aboard the CSS INDIAN CHIEF, Charleston, South Carolina, Sunday, November 6, 1864, and was designated to serve aboard the CSS CHICORA]. He served on the Charleston, South Carolina station as a Private of the Marine guard on board the ironclad CSS COLUMBIA until February 7, 1865 [NOTE: May be the same "Edmund Waddill" listed as having been in the "Confederate States Navy" in the widow's pension application of Martilda [sic] M. Waddill of Carthage, Moore County, North Carolina, based on service of B. C. Phillips, her first husband, who served in the 48th Regiment, North Carolina Troops. Per source "McLeod, August 30, 1874," Waddell left the unit [deserted?] at Jonesboro, North Carolina, on the march to Richmond. She married Waddell in 1885 and he died on August 18, 1889 [Ralph W. Donnelly states 1899]. No pension application was found for "Edmund Waddill." Source "Citizen News-Record," July 8, 1987 states he was from Prosperity, Moore County, North

Carolina, and had a brother named John J. Waddell who was also a Confederate Marine. Source "McLeod, August 30, 1874," states "Ed. Waddill [sic] is in my county [i.e. Moore County, North Carolina] [.] I see him often, he is well & doing well at farming, he has a wife and lots of children and is nearly as good a Methodist [as] he was when on the Indian Chief [CSS INDIAN CHIEF]. He keeps his white head shingled as close as ever and has that big broad open grin and laugh when anything goes well with him; for a [while] after [the] war Waddill [sic] was half Radical, that is he did not vote at all, but he [finally] fell into line with the Conservatives and is a very good one now."
[Source(s): North Carolina Troops, Doc.# 0299; Card File; Pensions (North Carolina); *"Donnelly – RL;"* "Citizen News-Record," July 8, 1987; Donnelly; Davis, November 17, 1864]

Waddell, James Iredell (Chatham County, North Carolina)
Captain, Confederate States Navy. Born on July 13, 1824 in Pittsboro, North Carolina and appointed from there, Waddell was formerly a Lieutenant in the United States Navy, from which he was dismissed in January 1862. He was appointed a Lieutenant on March 27, 1862 in the Confederate States Navy, and First Lieutenant, October 23, 1862, to rank from October 2, 1862. Waddell was appointed a First Lieutenant, Provisional Confederate Navy on June 2, 1864, to rank from January 6, 1864. He served mainly on shore duties until promoted to the rank of Commander in command of the CSS SHENANDOAH in October 1864. He served on the Richmond Station, 1862, and aboard the CSS MISSISSIPPI on the New Orleans Station, 1862. He participated in the Battle of Drewry's Bluff, May 15, 1862, and served on the Charleston Station, 1862-1863. One source listed him as having had service abroad, 1863-1864. Another source lists him (likely erroneously) as a Midshipman on the CSS ALABAMA. Waddell commanded the CSS SHENANDOAH for twelve and half months, 1864 – 1865, during which he wrought havoc with the New England whaling fleet in the northern Pacific. During that time, Waddell and the CSS SHENANDOAH captured, sank, or bonded some thirty-eight Union vessels, mostly whalers engaged in harvesting whales for the whale oil so vital to the Union war effort. Isolated as he was, it was six months after the war before Waddell knew of its end. Fearing he and his crew would be arrested as pirates, he sailed the ship to Liverpool, England where he turned it over to British authorities on November 6, 1865. The CSS SHENANDOAH has the distinction of having taken the Confederate flag completely around the world, having fired the last shot of the War Between the States (fired over the bow of a Yankee whaler off the Aleutians), being the last Confederate unit to engage the enemy, and the last to furl its flag. Waddell worked post-war for the Pacific Mail Line, in California. He resided as a mariner, in 1880, with his wife, Anne S. Waddell, at Annapolis, Anne Arundel County, Maryland. He died in 1886 and was buried in St. Anne's Cemetery, Annapolis, Maryland.
[Source(s): McElroy; Register; Journal; Lane Society; Foenander; ONWR]

Waddell [Waddill], John J. (Beaufort County, North Carolina [?]) [NOTE: Possibly brother of Edmund Waddell, q.v.; or, perhaps same as "John J. Womble," q.v.)
Confederate States Marine Corps. Per source "Citizen News-Record," July 8, 1987, John Waddell was a brother of Edmund Waddell, Confederate States Marine Corps. He was captured at Farmville, Virginia, April 6, 1865, and died as a Prisoner of War at Point Lookout, Maryland, May 17, 1865.
[Source(s): "Citizen News-Record," July 8, 1987]

Wainwright, William
Ordinary Seaman, Confederate States Navy. Wainwright enlisted on October 31, 1863, in the Confederate States Navy in Wilmington, North Carolina for the war. Wainright's name appears on the March – October 1864 muster rolls of the CSS NEUSE.
[Source(s): McElroy; NA, RG, 45; MR, 4, p. 447; St. Armand; CMACSSN]

Walcott, Stephen F. (Washington County, North Carolina)
Ship's steward, Confederate States Navy. Walcott originally enlisted as a Private in Company K, 1st Regiment, North Carolina Artillery, in Beaufort County, North Carolina on August 10, 1861. Captured at Fort Hatteras on August 29, 1861 and confined at Fort Warren, Massachusetts, he was exchanged on February 3, 1862. Walcott transferred to the Confederate States Navy on July 19, 1863 and served as a Seaman, Coxswain, and Ship's Steward on the CSS NORTH CAROLINA, 1864, and as Ship's Steward on the CSS TALLAHASSEE.
[Source(s): WCL; ORN,2,1,p.295-296; North Carolina Troops, I (where his surname is listed as "Wallcott"); MR, 4,p. 444; www.thewashingtongrays.homestead.com; "Beaufort County Sailors;" Darden; www.ncgenweb.us/nccivwar/rosters/10cok.htm]

Walker, C. W.
Landsman, Confederate States Navy. Walker enlisted on July 11, 1864, in Raleigh for the war.
[Source(s): McElroy; NA, RG 45]

Walker, E. D., Jr.
Landsman, Confederate States Navy. Walker enlisted on January 27, 1864, in Wilmington for the war.
[Source(s): McElroy; NA, RG 45]

Walker, Emerson
Ordinary Seaman, Confederate States Navy.
Walker served as a member of the North Carolina Squadron as an Ordinary Seaman aboard the CSS ELLIS per a logbook entry dated August 1, 1861 and appears to have remained with the ship through May 1862. His name appears on the receiving ship CSS UNITED STATES payroll ending March 31, 1862.
[Source: NCCWSP]

Walker (Walke), Frank. A. (Virginia)
Assistant Surgeon, Confederate States Army//Assistant Surgeon, Confederate States Navy. Walker resided in Virginia and enlisted there on May 16, 1861, at the age of 29. Appointed Assistant Surgeon, Field and Staff, 13th Regiment, North Carolina Troops, he transferred to the Confederate States Navy on February 16, 1863.
[Source(s): McElroy; NPS; Foenander; MR, I; North Carolina Troops, V; PRCMO]

Walker, George W. (Pasquotank County, North Carolina)
Corporal, Confederate States Army//Seaman, Confederate States Navy. Born in Tyrrell County, North Carolina, Walker resided in Pasquotank County, North Carolina as a mariner. He enlisted in Pasquotank County, North Carolina, at age 18 on July 22, 1861 as a Corporal in Company A, 8th Regiment, North Carolina State Troops. He transferred to the Confederate States Navy on an unspecified date and served aboard the CSS SEA BIRD from July 1861 – February 1862. Walker's name appears on the March – October 1864 muster rolls of the CSS NEUSE. Source NCCWSP indicated he served aboard the CSS VIRGINIA. His name appears on the payroll of the North Carolina Squadron for the 1st quarter of 1862 (December 1, 1861 – March 31, 1862). Payroll records indicate he served at Drewry's Bluff as a Seaman from April 1, 1863 – June 30, 1863. Walker married Elizabeth Hill in Randolph County, North Carolina on 19 April 1866. Age 21 in 1864.
[Source(s): McElroy; Sea Bird; North Carolina Troops, IV; Hill; Marriage Bonds, North Carolina Div. of Historical Res.; MR, I; CMACSSN; NCCWSP]

Walker, John W.
Pilot, Acting Master, Confederate States Navy.
Walker served with the North Carolina Squadron aboard the CSS ELLIS as early as an August 1, 1861 logbook entry. Per a logbook entry dated November 2, 1861 and payroll records, he was serving on the CSS ELLIS as an Acting Master through May 1862. Walker was discharged on January 23, 1862.
[Source: NCCWSP]

Walker, J. T.
Landsman, Confederate States Navy. Walker enlisted on April 12, 1864, in Kinston for three years or the war. His name appears on the March – October 1864 muster rolls of the CSS NEUSE.
[Source(s): McElroy; NA, RG 45; CMACSSN]

Walker, Nathaniel
Seaman, Confederate States Navy.
Walker served as a member of the North Carolina Squadron as a Seaman aboard the CSS ELLIS per a logbook entry dated November 2, 1861 and remained aboard through at least May 1862. His name appears on the receiving ship CSS UNITED STATES payroll ending March 31, 1862. He served at Drewry's Bluff as a Seaman from April 1, 1863 - June 30, 1863 per that station's payroll for the period.
[Source: NCCWSP]

Walker, Pealedge P. (Pasquotank County, North Carolina)
Ordinary Seaman, Quartermaster, Confederate States Navy.
Walker was born in North Carolina circa 1839 and resided in Elizabeth City, Pasquotank County, North Carolina as a mariner per the 1860 Census of North Carolina. He served as a member of the North Carolina Squadron as an Ordinary Seaman aboard the CSS ELLIS per a logbook entry dated August 1, 1861. He is listed as a Quartermaster aboard the CSS ELLIS per a logbook entry dated November 2, 1861 where he served through May 1862. His name appears on the receiving ship CSS UNITED STATES payroll ending March 31, 1862.
[Source(s): 1860 Census (NC); NCCWSP]

Walker, William
Seaman, Confederate States Navy. Walker was mortally wounded in the [battle?] at Elizabeth City on February 11, 1862. He was attached to the CSS ELLIS.
[Source(s): McElroy]

Walker, William
Ordinary Seaman, Confederate States Navy. Walker enlisted on March 26, 1863, in Wilmington for three years or the war.
[Source(s): McElroy; NA, RG 45]

Walker, William A. (Craven Company [Carteret County], North Carolina)
Sergeant, Confederate States Army// "Crewman," Confederate States Navy. Walker resided as a mariner prior to enlisting for the war in Carteret County, North Carolina, at age 21 on April 14, 1861 in Company G, 10th Regiment, North Carolina Troops (1st Regiment, North Carolina Artillery). Absent when his company was captured at Fort Macon on April 26, 1862, he was temporarily assigned to Company E of this regiment on June 2, 1862 until his unit was exchanged in August 1862. Back with Company G, he was appointed to the rank of Sergeant in August 1862 but was reduced to the ranks on September 20, 1862. Walker transferred to the Confederate States Navy on February 23, 1863 by Special Order Number 45, Paragraph 16, Adjutant and Inspector General's Office, and served aboard the CSS NORTH CAROLINA.
[Source(s): McElroy; NPS; North Carolina Troops, I; MR, 4, p. 444]

Walker, William A.
Confederate States Navy. Walker was a former Private, Company I, 2nd Regiment, North Carolina Troops, as well as a Private in Companies G and F, 3rd Regiment, Maryland Cavalry.
[Source(s): McElroy; NPS]

Walker, William L. (Currituck County, North Carolina)
Private, Confederate States Army//Confederate States Navy. Walker enlisted in Currituck County, North Carolina, on September 30, 1863, for the war, as a Private in Company G, 68th Regiment, North Carolina Troops. His name appears on a bounty payroll dated February 11, 1864. He transferred to the CSS ALBEMARLE on April 7, 1864.
[Source(s): McElroy; North Carolina Troops, XV]

Walker, William S. (or J.)
Ordinary Seaman, Confederate States Navy.
Walker served as an Ordinary Seaman as a member of the North Carolina Squadron aboard the CSS ELLIS per a logbook entry dated August 1, 1861 and remained aboard through May 1862. His name appears on the receiving ship CSS UNITED STATES payroll ending March 31, 1862.
[Source: NCCWSP]

Wallace, S. Washington (Cabarrus County, North Carolina)
Landsman/Ordinary Seaman, Confederate States Navy. Walker enlisted on November 4, 1863 in Raleigh for the war. Another source states he enlisted on November 5, 1863, in Wilmington for the war). Moore's Roster states he enlisted in the Confederate States Navy on October 28, 1863 in Wilmington, North Carolina.
[Source(s): McElroy; NPS; NA, RG 45; North Carolina Troops; MR, IV, 447; Cruse]

Wallace, Washington (Richmond County, North Carolina)
Private, Confederate States Army//Confederate States Navy. Wallace resided in Richmond County, North Carolina where he enlisted at "McLaurin's" on February 4, 1863 at age 38 as a Private in Company D, 46th Regiment, North Carolina Troops. He was present or accounted for until he transferred to the Confederate States Navy on April 1, 1864.
[Source(s): North Carolina Troops, XI; Foenander]

Wallace, William A. (Mecklenburg County, North Carolina)
Private, Confederate States Army//Confederate States Navy. Wallace resided as a farmer in Mecklenburg County, North Carolina, where he enlisted at age 18 as a Private on July 23, 1861 in Company C, 10th Regiment, North Carolina Troops (1st Regiment, North Carolina Artillery). He transferred to the Confederate States Navy on April 6, 1864.
[Source(s): McElroy; NPS; CWSSI; North Carolina Troops, I; Foenander]

Wallcott (Walcott), Stephen F. (Beaufort County, North Carolina)
Private, Confederate States Army//Seaman, Coxswain, Ship's Steward, Confederate States Navy. Wallcott enlisted in Beaufort County, North Carolina, as a Private in Company K, 10th Regiment, North Carolina Troops (1st Regiment, North Carolina Artillery) on August 10, 1861. Captured at Fort Hatteras on August 29, 1861, he was confined at Fort Warren, Massachusetts and exchanged on February 3, 1862. Wallcott was listed as present or accounted for until he transferred to the Confederate States Navy on July 19, 1863 where he served as a Seaman, Coxswain and Ship's Steward on board the CSS NORTH CAROLINA, 1864. He also served as a Ship's Steward aboard the CSS TALLAHASSEE, 1864.
[Source(s): McElroy; NPS; North Carolina Troops, I; NA, RG 109; thewashingtongrays.homestead.com; Foenander]

Waller, Lawrence (Stanly County, North Carolina)
Confederate States Navy. Waller enlisted in the Confederate States Navy in Wilmington, North Carolina.
[Source(s): MR, 4, p. 447]

Wallis, M. L.
Landsman, Confederate States Navy. Wallis enlisted on August 10, 1864, in Raleigh for the war.
[Source(s): McElroy; NA, RG 45]

Walmsley, [First name unknown] (North Carolina?)
Confederate States Navy. Per source "Foenander," Walmsley was indicated to have been a sailor in the Confederate States Navy who resided, prior to 1885, at 407 Fayetteville Street, Raleigh, North Carolina, as an agent for Fairbanks' Scales. He left the city sometime in December 1884. His wife was charged with infanticide, committed in Wilson County, North Carolina, and was taken into custody, January 2, 1885.
[Source(s): Foenander; "N & O" (4 January 1885)]

Walser, Britton
Landsman, Confederate States Navy. Walser enlisted on December 10, 1863, in Raleigh for the war. Another source states he enlisted on December 12, 1863, in Wilmington for the war. [Source(s): McElroy; NA, RG 45]

Walston, John J.
Landsman, Confederate States Navy. Walston enlisted on May 11, 1864, in Raleigh for the war.
[Source(s): McElroy; NA, RG 45]

Walters, Charles
Seaman, Confederate States Navy. Walters enlisted on January 23, 1963, in Wilmington for three years or the war.
[Source(s): McElroy; NA, RG 45]

Walton, John
Landsman, Confederate States Navy. Walton enlisted on December 10, 1863, in Raleigh for the war. Another source states he enlisted on December 12, 1863, in Wilmington for the war.
[Source(s): McElroy; NA, RG 45]

Ward, A. J. (Onslow County, North Carolina)
Confederate States Navy. Ward enlisted in the Confederate States Navy in Wilmington, North Carolina.
[Source(s): MR, 4, p. 448]

Ward, Benjamin J.
Landsman, Confederate States Navy. Ward enlisted on January 25, 1864, in Raleigh for the war.
[Source(s): McElroy; NA, RG 45]

Ward, James (New Hanover County, North Carolina)
Private, Confederate States Army//Seaman, Confederate States Navy. A pre-war Seaman residing in Beaufort County, North Carolina, Ward enlisted at age 27 as a Private on July 18, 1861 [July 28, 1861, per MR, I], in Company I, 3rd Regiment, North Carolina State Troops. Ward was present or accounted for until he transferred to the Confederate States Navy on January 22, 1862. Per clothing, bounty, and muster records, Ward served as a Seaman aboard the CSS RALEIGH from January 16, 1862 – April 15, 1862 as a member of the North Carolina Squadron. He transferred to the James River Squadron as of April 15, 1862 and served at Drewry's Bluff as a Seaman from April 1, 1863 - June 30, 1863.
[Source(s): McElroy; NPS; "Beaufort County Sailors;" North Carolina Troops, III; NCCWSP]

Ward, James H. (Pasquotank County, North Carolina)
    Private, Confederate States Army//Seaman, Confederate States Navy. Born in Pasquotank County, North Carolina, Ward resided in Beaufort County, North Carolina, as a Seaman. He enlisted on May 10, 1861 [July 18, 1861, per MR, I], at age 34, as a Private in Company I, 3rd Regiment, North Carolina State Troops. He was present or accounted for until he transferred to the Confederate States Navy on January 22, 1862. He served as a Seaman aboard the CSS RALEIGH from January through April 15, 1862 as a member of the North Carolina Squadron. He served as an Ordinary Seaman with the James River Squadron from November 16, 1862 – December 15, 1862. He served at Drewry's Bluff as a Seaman from April 1, 1863 – June 30, 1862
    [Source(s): McElroy; NPS; "Beaufort County Sailors;" North Carolina Troops, III; Foenander; MR, I; NCCWSP]

Ward, James M.
    Landsman, Confederate States Navy. Ward enlisted on April 29, 1964, in Raleigh for the war.
    [Source(s): McElroy; NA, RG 45]

Ward, John (New Hanover County, North Carolina)
    Seaman, Confederate States Navy. Ward served on the ironclad sloop CSS NORTH CAROLINA, New Inlet, North Carolina. He deserted on October 9, 1863 and was taken aboard the USS SHENANDOAH, off Beaufort, North Carolina. Later he was sent to Hampton Roads, Virginia, for further questioning. His name appears on a register under the following heading: "Descriptive list of rebel deserters and refugees received at Fort Monroe, Va." The register states he was received on October 25, 1863, from Wilmington, as a "deserter from the Rebel Navy" and was released on October 31, 1863 for "govt. employ." His place of residence was given as North Carolina, his place of birth as New Hanover County, and his occupation as mason. His description was given as follows: Age, 20; eyes, blue; hair, brown; complexion, light; height, 5 feet 10½ inches. His name appears on an Oath of Allegiance to the United States, sworn to at Fort Monroe, Va., on November 5, 1863, which gives his residence as Wilmington, North Carolina. The oath also carries this remark: "Rebel deserter came into our lines off Wilmington, North Carolina"
    [Source(s): McElroy; NA, RG 109; Foenander; *ORN* 1, 9, 235]

Ward, John (New Hanover County, North Carolina)
    Seaman ["Landsman" (see Stepp)], Confederate States Navy. Ward appears on Registers of Confederate States Army General Military Hospital Number 4, Wilmington, North Carolina, as being admitted on January 12, 1864, with "febris typhoides." He died on January 17 [18], 1864. His post office was given on the register as Wilmington, North Carolina. His name also appears on the report of sick and wounded in General Hospital Number 4, and in a book containing the consolidated report of sick and wounded in hospitals which gives his date of death as January 18, 1864. His name appears on the List of Deaths of Confederate Soldiers in Confederate General Hospital #4, Wilmington, which states he died on January 18, 1864. He was buried in the Confederate Mass Grave, Oakdale Cemetery, Wilmington, New Hanover County, North Carolina.
    [Source(s): McElroy; NA, RG 109; Roster Document #0314-52; Stepp, "Burials"]

Ward, John H.
    Ordinary Seaman, Confederate States Navy. Ward served aboard the CSS ARCTIC, 1863.
    [*ORN* 2, 1, 276; Foenander]

Ward, John W. (New Hanover County, North Carolina) [NOTE: May be same as John W. Ward, who died January 18, 1864, q.v.]
    Ordinary Seaman, Confederate States Navy ("Gunboat"). Ward enlisted on February 5, 1863 (or February 28, 1863), in Wilmington for three years or the war. He appears on registers of Confederate States Army General Military Hospital Number 4, Wilmington, North Carolina, being admitted September 4, 1863, with "dysenteria" and returned to duty September 16, 1863. His post office was given on the registers as Wilmington, North Carolina. Source "MR" lists a "J. W. Ward" of Onslow County, North Carolina that may be this man.
    [Source(s): McElroy; NA, RG 45; NA, RG 109]

Ward, John W. [NOTE: May be same as John W. Ward, New Hanover County, North Carolina, q.v.]
    Confederate States Navy. Ward served in the Confederate States Navy, 1864, and died of typhoid pneumonia at the General Hospital, Fayetteville, North Carolina, January 18, 1864. Source "MR" lists a "J. W. Ward" of Onslow County, North Carolina that may be this man.
    [Source(s): Foenander; "Fay. Obs. (February 1, 1864]

Ward, Robert (Alamance County, North Carolina)
Ordinary Seaman, Confederate States Navy. Ward enlisted in the Confederate States Navy in Wilmington, North Carolina, and served on the CSS ARCTIC, 1863.
[Source(s): MR, IV, 448; *ORN* 2, 1, 276; Foenander]

Ward, William H. (Alamance County, North Carolina)
Private, Confederate States Army//Confederate States Navy. Ward was born and resided in Alamance County, North Carolina, where he worked as a laborer until his enlistment on May 1, 1861 [Source MR, I shows the date as May 2nd] at the age of 20. He volunteered as a Private in Company E, 13th Regiment, North Carolina Troops (3rd North Carolina Volunteers), the first company entering the Confederate service from that county. He transferred to the Confederate States Navy on February 19, 1862 and served as a member of the crew on the CSS VIRGINIA [MERRIMAC] when she participated in the naval battle at the mouth of the James River. Stepdaughter: Miss. Dixie Ward, Dixie St., Burlington, North Carolina.
[Source(s): McElroy; NPS; North Carolina Troops, V; Pensions (NORTH CAROLINA); Foenander; MR, I; *ORN* 2, 1, 310]

Wark(s), Isaac (Ireland/Rowan County, North Carolina)
Private, Confederate States Army//Confederate States Navy. Born in Ireland, Wark(s) resided in Rowan County, North Carolina, as a stone cutter until he enlisted "for the war" at age 53 on June 15, 1861 in Company D, 10th Regiment, North Carolina Troops (1st Regiment, North Carolina Artillery). He was discharged at Camp Taylor, near Lindsay's Turnout, Virginia, January 31, 1864, by reason of rheumatism. Source "MR" states he transferred to the Confederate States Navy (date unknown).
[Source(s): MR, I; North Carolina Troops, I]

Warren, Drury (Caswell County, North Carolina)
Private, Confederate States Army//Confederate States Navy. Born in Caswell County, North Carolina, Warren resided there as a farmer prior to enlisting in Orange County, North Carolina, at age 21 on March 6, 1862 as a Private, Company I, 45th Regiment, North Carolina Troops. He was present or accounted for until April 18, 1864, when he was transferred to the Confederate States Navy.
[Source(s): McElroy; NPS; North Carolina Troops, XI]

Warren, Edward
Surgeon, North Carolina Navy. Born in Tyrrell [Chowan County, per source "medicalantiques"] County, North Carolina the son of Dr. William and Harriet Warren of Edenton, North Carolina. Doctor Warren's family moved to New Bern, North Carolina where his father practiced medicine until after the War Between the States. He attended the University of Virginia, the Jefferson Medical College of Philadelphia, and worked and studied in Paris before the war. Doctor Warren is listed by source "DH Hill" as one of the first officers commissioned as a Surgeon in the North Carolina Navy. Warren served during the War Between the States briefly in the field as a Surgeon with North Carolina and Virginia troops. During this time, he is said to have met General Robert E. Lee who offered him the position of Medical Director of the Army of Northern Virginia, which he declined, but provided the name of a suitable substitute. He prepared a manual on military surgery [*An Epitome of Practical Surgery for Field and Hospital*, Richmond, VA, 1863], and was Surgeon General of North Carolina from 1863 until the end of the war. A personal friend of Governor Zebulon Vance, Dr. Warren played a key role in the surrender of Raleigh in 1865. Following the war, he returned to active practice in Baltimore, Maryland and held a teaching position there. Between 1867 and 1871 he helped establish two hospitals in Baltimore as well as the nucleus of the Johns Hopkins Medical School. He served for two years as Chief Surgeon in the Egyptian Army (recommended by none other than Major General William T. Sherman). In later years he counted General Ulysses S. Grant as a friend and sometime companion. After performing a successful operation on the Minister of War, Warren was awarded the title of "Bey." Dr. Warren moved to Paris, France in the early 1870s for an eye treatment but decided to stay. Because of his work there he was made a Chevalier d'Legion d' Honneur awarded the Cross of the Legion of Honor. Returning to the United States, Dr. Warren served as a professor at the "College of Physicians and Surgeons" of Baltimore, Maryland which was incorporated in 1872. In 1878 it was merged with the Washington University School of Medicine. In 1884, the University of North Carolina at Chapel Hill conferred on him Doctor of Laws degree in absentia. The following year, he wrote and published his autobiography, *A Doctor's Experiences in Three Continents*. His titles included M.D., C.M. (Surgery Master), LL.D (law degree), Commander of the Order of Osmanisch of Turkey, Knight of the Order of Isabella the Catholic of Spain, Redemption of the Holy Sepulchre of Jerusalem, the White Cross of Italy, Medal of Victor Emmanuel, and Bey by Khedival Firman [roughly corresponding to an English knight], Warren is listed by source "DH Hill" as one of the first officers commissioned as a Surgeon in the North

Carolina Navy. Doctor Warren died in Paris, France on September 16, 1895; the location of his grave is unknown. RDW Connor, former State Archivist of North Carolina and the first ever National Archivist said of Warren he was the best North Carolina biographer of the Nineteenth Century.

[Source(s): DH Hill; "Our State" (June 6, 1940); medicalantiques].

Warren, H. J. ["Henry" or "Harry"?]

Midshipman, Confederate States Navy. Born in and appointed a Midshipman from North Carolina on July 21, 1863, Warren was appointed a Midshipman, Provisional Navy on June 2, 1864. He served on the CSS PATRICK HENRY, 1863; CSS NORTH CAROLINA, Wilmington Station, 1863-1864, and was ordered to join the Confederate States cruiser CSS FLORIDA via Bermuda on June 14, 1864. He is shown to have been in Bermuda in December 1864, serving as a Midshipman.

[Source(s): McElroy; Register; ONWR]

Warren, James R. (Wake County, North Carolina)

Landsman, Confederate States Navy. Warren enlisted on August 12, 1864 in Raleigh for the war. His claim for pension filed on June 3, 1901, age 65 years (NOTE: If truly age 65 in 1901, would have been born circa 1836, therefore hardly "underage"], post office Cary, Wake County, North Carolina, states he enlisted in August 1864 under Commodore Pinkney and served aboard the CSS ARCTIC [with] Captain Poindexter, and that he was never wounded. W. J. Howle was a witness. The application was denied. Warren's subsequent claim for pension filed on June 29, 1905 at age 69 years, listing his address as RFD #1, Cary, North Carolina, states he served aboard the CSS ARCTIC and later the CSS CHICKAMAUGA. Sidney Partin served as a witness. An accompanying doctor's statement references Warren's being "underage" in the service. This application was approved at 4th Class. A claim filed on July 17, 1911 by his widow Susan A. Warren age 69 years, post office Cary, Wake County, North Carolina, states her husband died in November 1910. This claim was approved at 4th Class.

[Source(s): McElroy; Pensions (NORTH CAROLINA); NA, RG 45]

Warren, Max

Seaman, Confederate States Navy.

Warren served as a member of the North Carolina Squadron as a Seaman aboard the CSS CURLEW per her payroll list for the 1st quarter of 1862. His name appears on the receiving ship CSS UNITED STATES payroll ending March 31, 1862.

[Source: NCCWSP]

Warren, Watkins L.

Assistant Surgeon, Confederate States Navy. Commissioned by the Confederate States Congress and enlisting from North Carolina, Warren was nominated as Assistant Surgeon for the war in February 1864 and Assistant Surgeon, Provisional Confederate States Navy on June 2, 1864. He was ordered to the CSS ISONDIGA, Savannah Squadron, on April 30, 1864; the CSS SAVANNAH, in May 1864; and the CSS GEORGIA, temporarily, on June 13, 1864. He was detached on July 4, 1864 and ordered to the CSS MACON. Detached again on November 19, 1864 and ordered to the CSS SAVANNAH, Warren was detached a final time on November 24, 1864 and ordered to CSS GEORGIA.

[Source(s): McElroy]

Warrick, Alpheus (Wayne County, North Carolina)

Ordinary Seaman, Confederate States Navy. Born in North Carolina in 1838, Warrick enlisted in the Confederate States Navy on July 26, 1863 in Wilmington, North Carolina, and served as an Ordinary Seaman aboard the CSS ARCTIC, 1863. He appears on a Register of Prisoners of War at Hart's Island, New York Harbor, which states he was captured in Wayne County, North Carolina, March 19, 1865, and confined to Hart's Island from April 10, 1865 until released on June 19, 1865. His name also appears as a signature to an Oath of Allegiance to the United States subscribed and sworn to at Hart's Island, New York Harbor, June 19, 1865 giving his place of residence as Wayne County, North Carolina. His description was given as follows: Complexion-dark; hair-dark; eyes-blue; height- 5 ft. 5 in. Warrick resided as a farmer in 1880 with his wife Sarah Warrick and daughter Octavia (born 1863) at Grantham, Wayne County, North Carolina.

[Source(s): McElroy; NA, RG 109; MR, 4, p. 447; Foenander; 1880 (North Carolina) Census]

Waters, James R. (possibly from Columbus County, North Carolina)

Private, Confederate States Army//Confederate States Navy. Waters enlisted on December 4, 1862 at age 31 for the war in Company E, 36th Regiment, North Carolina Troops (2nd Regiment, North Carolina Artillery). He transferred to the Confederate States Navy on February 19, 1864 [Source "North Carolina Troops, I" gives the date as the February

29, 1864].
[Source(s): McElroy; NA, RG 109; NPS; North Carolina Troops, I]

Waters (Warters), Roderick (Lenoir County, North Carolina)
Corporal, Confederate States Army//Confederate States Navy. Waters resided in Lenoir County, North Carolina where he enlisted at age 23 on April 17, 1861 as a Private in Company C [Source Foenander gives the company as "D"], 27th Regiment, North Carolina Troops. Promoted to Corporal on July 20, 1861, he was reduced to the ranks in May-June 1862. He is listed as present or accounted for until his transfer to the Confederate States Navy on or about April 6, 1864.
[Source(s): McElroy; NPS; North Carolina Troops; www.ncgenweb.us/nccivwar/rosters/27coc.htm; North Carolina Troops, VIII]

Watkins, David (North Carolina)
Landsman, Confederate States Navy. Watkins enlisted on November 17, 1863, in Raleigh for the war. Another source states he enlisted on November 20, 1863, in Wilmington for the war). He appears on a register of Confederate States Army General Military Hospital Number 4, Wilmington, North Carolina, which states he was admitted December 19, 1863, with "pneumonia" and returned to duty May 9, 1864. His post office was given on register as Bear Swamp, North Carolina.
[Source(s): McElroy; NA, RG 45; NA, RG 109]

Watkins, John
Seaman, Confederate States Navy.
Watkins received a partial payment on February 13, 1862 at Gosport Navy Yard, probably after service in the Battle of Roanoke Island or Elizabeth City. His name appears on the North Carolina Squadron payroll for the 1st qtr. of 1862 (January 7, 1862 - February 28, 1862. He is listed as having "run" on the payroll ending on February 28, 1862.
[Source: NCCWSP]

Watson, E. (Moore County, North Carolina)
Private, Confederate States Marine Corps. A letter of James C. Davis dated November 17, 1864 states the group from Camp Holmes, of which Watson was a part, arrived aboard the CSS INDIAN CHIEF, Charleston, South Carolina on Sunday, November 6, 1864, and was designated to serve aboard the ironclad CSS CHICORA.
[Source(s): Davis, November 17, 1864]

Watson, A. L.
Landsman, Confederate States Navy. Watson enlisted on June 10, 1864 in Raleigh for the year.
[Source(s): McElroy; NA, RG 45]

Watson, Henry Bulls (Johnston County, North Carolina) [NOTE: May be same as H. D. Watson, q.v.]
Private, Confederate States Army//Landsman/Ordinary Seaman, Confederate States Navy. Watson enlisted as a substitute on October 5, 1863, at Camp Holmes, Raleigh. Another source states he enlisted in the Confederate States Navy in Wilmington, North Carolina. He served aboard the CSS NORTH CAROLINA and was discharged by reason of ill health on March 16, 1864. Had served previously as Commandant of Camp Mangum near Raleigh, North Carolina. He served as an Ordinary Seaman aboard the CSS ARCTIC in 1863. [ORN 2, 1, p.276.]. Source RCWV states "he was our drillmaster while we were at Smithfield in May 1861, i.e., if he is the man we think of." Born October 16, 1812, Watson died on January 25, 1869 and was buried in the Watson Family Cemetery, Johnston County, North Carolina.
[Source(s): McElroy; NA, RG 45; MR, 4, p. 444 and 447; Stepp, "Burials;" ORN, 2, 1, p.276; RCWV]

Watson, H. D. [NOTE: May be same as Henry Bulls Watson, q.v.]
Ordinary Seaman, Confederate States Navy. Watson enlisted on October 9, 1863, in Wilmington for the war.
[Source(s): McElroy; NA, RG 45]

Watson, John (Onslow County, North Carolina)
Private, Confederate States Army//Confederate States Navy. Watson enlisted in Onslow County, North Carolina on May 13, 1861 in Company E, 3rd Regiment, North Carolina Troops. He transferred to the Confederate States Navy, date unknown.
[Source(s): MR, I]

Watson, James J.
>Landsman, Confederate States Navy. Watson enlisted on July 29, 1864 in Raleigh for the war.
>[Source(s): McElroy; NA, RG 45]

Watson, Nelson
>Landsman, Confederate States Navy. Watson enlisted on June 6, 1864 in Raleigh for the war.
>[Source(s): McElroy; NA, RG 45]

Watson, Wm.
>Landsman, Confederate States Navy. Watson enlisted on June 10, 1864 in Raleigh for the war.
>[Source(s): McElroy; NA, RG 45]

Watson, Wm. C. (Robeson County, North Carolina)
>Landsman, Confederate States Navy (Naval Battalion). Watson enlisted on November 30, 1863 in Raleigh for the war. Another source states he enlisted on December 5, 1863 in Wilmington for the war). His name appears on a roll of Prisoners of War at Point Lookout, Maryland stating that he was captured at "Sailors Creek" on April 6, 1865. His name also appears as a signature to an Oath of Allegiance to the United States, subscribed and sworn to at Point Lookout on June 21, 1865. His place of residence was given on the Oath as "Robinson" County, North Carolina, and his description as follows: Complexion-fair; hair-light; eyes-blue; height-5 ft. 7½ in.
>[Source(s): McElroy; NA, RG 45; NA, RG 109]

Watt, Nicholas Porter (Alexander County, North Carolina)
>Landsman/Seaman, Confederate States Navy. Watt enlisted on June 13, 1864 in Raleigh for the war. His name appears on a roll of Prisoners of War at Point Lookout, Maryland stating that he was captured at Burkeville on April 1, 1865 and confined at Point Lookout until released on June 21, 1865. His name also appears as a signature to an Oath of Allegiance to the United States, subscribed and sworn to at Point Lookout, Maryland, June 21, 1865 showing his place of residence as Alexander County, North Carolina, and his description as follows: Complexion-fair; hair-black; eyes-blue; height-5 ft. 11¾ in. He died on May 11, 1920 and was buried in Oakwood Cemetery, Iredell County, North Carolina.
>[Source(s): McElroy; NA; RG 45; NA, RG 109; Stepp, "Burials"]

Watt, W. T.
>Seaman, Confederate States Navy. Watt enlisted on June 13, 1864 in Raleigh for the war.
>[Source(s): McElroy; NA, RG 45]

Watters, Charles
>Confederate States Navy. Watters enlisted in the Confederate States Navy in Wilmington, North Carolina and served aboard the CSS ARCTIC, 1863. He was born on April 6, 1825, died on November 2, 1905, and was buried in Lebanon Chapel Cemetery, located on the Arlie Estate on Wrightsville Sound in New Hanover County, North Carolina.
>[Source(s): McElroy; MR, 4, p. 447; Gravestone Records, v. 6, p.297]

Watters, John
>Gunner, Confederate States Navy. Watters served aboard the CSS ARCTIC, 1863.
>[Source(s): Foenander; *ORN* 2, 1]

Watts, William G. (Mecklenburg County, North Carolina)
>Ordinary Seaman, Confederate States Navy. Watts enlisted on June 1, 1863 in Wilmington for the war and served aboard the CSS NORTH CAROLINA. His name appears on registers of Confederate States Army General Military Hospital Number 4, Wilmington, North Carolina, which state he was admitted on January 11, 1864, with "anasarca," and returned to duty on February 10, 1864. His post office was listed on the registers as Charlotte, North Carolina.
>[Source(s): McElroy; MR, 4, p. 444; NA, RG 45; NA, RG 109]

Wayne, William Anderson (Born in Georgia; died in Warrenton, Warren County, North Carolina) [NOTE: May not have been a resident of North Carolina]
>Lieutenant, Confederate States Navy. Wayne was born on March 21, 1819 in Georgia, died on August 4, 1863, and was buried in Fairview Cemetery, Warren County, North Carolina [Source "Foenander" lists "Old Warrenton Cemetery"].
>[Source(s): Stepp, "Burials;" Foenander]

Wayne, William Wright
    Landsman, Confederate States Navy. Wayne enlisted on September 28, 1863 at Camp Holmes for the war. He transferred from CSS SAVANNAH to CSS ISONDIGA on November 1, 1863. He was a Landsman and later served as a Quartermaster, December 1, 1863-September 20, 1864. He served throughout the war.
    [Source(s): Card File; NA, RG 45; UDC, MC of Svc.]

Waynick, Lewis Marion (Born in Alamance County, resided in Rockingham County, North Carolina)
    Private, Confederate States Army//Confederate States Navy. Born in Alamance County, North Carolina, Waynick resided in Rockingham County, North Carolina, where he was a farmer prior to enlisting in Guilford County, North Carolina, at age 20 on March 5, 1862 as a Private in Company B, 45th Regiment, North Carolina Troops. Present or accounted for through April 1863, he was reported under arrest during May-August 1863, reason not listed. He returned to duty in September-October 1863 and was present or accounted for until transferred to the Confederate States Navy on May 4, 1864.
    [Source(s): Card File; NPS; North Carolina Troops, XI; Foenander]

Weaver, Joseph (Black)
    Officer's Steward, Confederate States Navy.
    Weaver served as an Officer's Steward aboard the CSS SEA BIRD as early as February 1862.
    He was captured in the Battle of Elizabeth City, carried to Roanoke Island where he took the Oath of Allegiance to the United States February 12, 1862. His name appears on the North Carolina Squadron's payroll list for the 1st quarter of 1862 (November 16, 1861 - February 12, 1862). He is listed as having "run" on 12 February 12, 1862.
    [Source: NCCWSP]

Weaver, Joseph F.
    Carpenter, Confederate States Navy.
    Weaver resided in Portsmouth, Virginia, prior to enlisting as a Private in the "Portsmouth Rifle Company," Company G, 9th Virginia Regiment. He served as a Carpenter aboard the CSS SEA BIRD as of February 1862 as a member of the North Carolina Squadron. He was captured in the Battle of Elizabeth City, carried to Roanoke Island on February 10, 1862, and paroled there on February 12, 1862 after which he returned to Elizabeth City, North Carolina.
    [Source: NCCWSP]

Weaver, Thomas (Black)
    Ordinary Seaman, Confederate States Navy.
    Weaver served first as an Ordinary Seaman aboard the CSS SEA BIRD until promoted to Captain's Steward on October 10, 1861. By February 1862 he was serving as the Commander's Steward aboard the CSS SEA BIRD. Captured in the Battle of Elizabeth City, Weaver was carried to Roanoke Island where he took the Oath of Allegiance to the United States on February 12, 1862. His name appears on the North Carolina Squadron payroll for the 1st quarter of 1862 (October 9, 1861 - February 12, 1862). He is listed as having "run" on February 12, 1862.
    [Source: NCCWSP]

Webb, Joseph L.
    Landsman, Confederate States Navy. Webb enlisted on April 15, 1864 in Kinston for three years, or the war. A "Joseph Webb" appears on the March – October 1864 muster rolls of the CSS NEUSE.
    [Source(s): Card File; NA, RG 45; CMACSSN]

Weeks, T. P.
    Landsman, Confederate States Navy. Weeks enlisted on October 15, 1863 at Camp Holmes (near Raleigh, North Carolina), for the war. Another source states he enlisted on October 19, 1863, in Wilmington for the war). He served aboard the CSS ALBEMARLE, and on the Halifax Station, 1864.
    [Source(s): Card File; NA, RG 45; MR, 4, p. 447; Foenander; St. Armand]

Welborn, David Lindsay (Randolph County, North Carolina)
    Confederate States Navy. Born in Randolph County, North Carolina, Welborn lived as a farmer on his father Joseph's farm in a county where Union sentiment was widespread and could lead to violence between neighbors. He served in the 63rd Regiment, North Carolina Militia, not necessarily voluntarily, until he transferred to active service in the Confederate Navy in 1863 at the age of twenty. He had submitted two petitions to the local conscription authorities requesting deferment, but to no avail. Once in the Navy he was assigned to the crew of the CSS FREDERICKSBURG patrolling on the James River south of Richmond.
    [Source: civilwarodyssey.com (author B.J. Welborn's Civil War Odyssey blog)]

Welburn, A.
Landsman, Confederate States Navy. Welburn enlisted on August 10, 1864 in Raleigh for the war.
[Source(s): Card File; NA, RG 45]

Welch, James
Landsman, Confederate States Navy. Webb enlisted on October 29, 1863 in Wilmington for the war.
[Source(s): Card File; NA, RG 45; MR, 4, p. 447; St. Armand]

Welch, John
Ordinary Seaman, Confederate States Navy. Welch enlisted on June 17, 1863 in Wilmington for the war.
[Source(s): Card File; NA, RG 45]

Wells, Marcus (Rutherford County, North Carolina)
Fireman, Confederate States Navy. Wells' name appears on a roll of Prisoners of War at Point Lookout, Maryland, which states he was captured at Farmville [Virginia] on April 6, 1865 and confined at Point Lookout until released on June 21, 1865. His name also appears as a signature to an Oath of Allegiance to the United States, subscribed and sworn to at Point Lookout, Maryland on June 21, 1865 giving his place of residence as Rutherford County, North Carolina, and his description as follows: Complexion-fair; hair-brown; eyes-blue; height-5 ft. 6 ½ in.
[Source(s): Card File; NA, RG 109]

Wells, Marshal Teachey (Duplin County, North Carolina)
Confederate States Navy. A claim for pension filed on June 25, 1928 by his widow, Mary Katherine Wells, listing her post office as Wallace, Duplin County, states her husband died on October 31, 1916. The claim was approved.
[Source(s): Card File; Pensions (NORTH CAROLINA)]

Welson, W. E. (New Hanover County, North Carolina)
Confederate States Navy. Welson's name appears on registers of Confederate States Army General Military Hospital Number 4, Wilmington, North Carolina stating he was admitted on September 3, 1863, with "debilitas." His post office was given on the registers as Wilmington, North Carolina.
[Source(s): Card File; NA, RG 109]

Wescott, Henry A. (Brunswick County, North Carolina)
Private, Confederate States Army//Seaman, Confederate States Navy. Wescott resided in Brunswick County, North Carolina, where he enlisted at age 20 on July 18, 1861, as a Musician (Fifer) in Company C, 30th Regiment, North Carolina Troops. He was present or accounted for until reported absent without leave in December 1862. Returned to duty on an unspecified date, he was promoted to Sergeant in March,1863, and listed as present or accounted for until he transferred to the Confederate States Navy on April 5, 1864.
[Source(s): Card File; McElroy; NPS; North Carolina Troops, VIII]

Wescott, John L. [Jack" (?)] (Brunswick County, North Carolina)
Seaman ["Landsman" (see Stepp)], Confederate States Navy. Wescott enlisted from Brunswick County, North Carolina. After the war he worked as a pilot on the Cape Fear River. Born 1826, he died on August 5, 1896, and was buried in the Southport Cemetery, Brunswick County, North Carolina.
[Source(s): Stepp, "Burials"]

Wescott, James (Brunswick County, North Carolina)
Seaman, Confederate States Navy. Wescott enlisted from Brunswick County, North Carolina. After the war he was a pilot on the Cape Fear River.
[Source(s): McElroy]

Wescott, John L. (Brunswick County, North Carolina)
Seaman, Confederate States Navy. Wescott served on the crew of the CSS CASWELL. He died on August 5, 1896 at age 76 and was buried in the Old Cemetery at Southport. His name appears on a register of Confederate States Army General Military Hospital Number 4, Wilmington, North Carolina, dated July 21, 1862, listing his disease as "cholera morbus" and post office as Smithville.
[Source(s): Card File; Gravestone Records, v. 8, p. 60; NA, RG 109]

Westcott, W. F. (Brunswick County, North Carolina)
Confederate States Navy. Wescott served aboard the CSS NORTH CAROLINA.
[Source(s): MR, IV, p. 444]

Wescott, William T. (Brunswick County, North Carolina)
Private, Confederate States Army//Confederate States Navy. Wescott enlisted in New Hanover County, North Carolina on April 16, 1861 for twelve months as a Private in 1st Company C, 36th Regiment, North Carolina Troops (2nd Regiment North Carolina Artillery). He was detailed as Captain of the schooner *Samuel Hines*, January-February 1862, and transferred to the Confederate States Navy on May 6, 1862. His name appears on registers of Confederate States Army General Military Hospital Number 4, Wilmington, North Carolina, dated July 14, 1863, which give his disease as "dysentery" and state that he was returned to duty on July 25, 1863. His post office was given as Smithville.
[Source(s): Card File; NA, RG 109; North Carolina Troops, I; NPS]

*Wesson, Isaac D. (Brunswick County, North Carolina [?])
Confederate States Navy. Wesson enlisted on February 16, 1863 and was detached to the Signal Service, date unknown.
[Source(s): Edge]

West, Frederick (New Hanover County, North Carolina)
First Officer, Confederate States Navy. West served on the steamer CSS PHANTOM. His name appears on registers of Confederate States Army General Military Hospital Number 4, Wilmington, North Carolina, which state he was admitted on September 28, 1863 with "feb int tertia" and returned to duty on October 1, 1863. Post office given on registers as Wilmington, North Carolina.
[Source(s): Card File; NA, RG 109]

Westcott, W. F. (Brunswick County, North Carolina)
Crewman, Confederate States Navy. Westcott served aboard the CSS NORTH CAROLINA.
[Source(s): MR, 4, p. 444]

Westmorland, J. S.
Seaman, Confederate States Navy. Westmorland enlisted on June 13, 1864, in Raleigh for the war.
[Source(s): Card File; NA; RG 45; Duke Papers]

Westly, John (Dare County, North Carolina)
Fireman (?), Confederate States Navy. Westly's name appears on a Roll of Prisoners of War released at Point Lookout, Maryland from May 12 to 14, 1865 upon taking the Oath of Allegiance. The roll states he was captured at Albemarle [sic] County on May 5, 1864 and giving his occupation as sailor, his residence as Roanoke Island, North Carolina, and carrying the remark: "Regd. Fireman."
[Source(s): Card File; NA, RG 109]

Whaley, George
Landsman, Confederate States Navy. Whaley's name appears on a roll of Prisoners of War at Point Lookout, Maryland which states he was captured at Harpers Farm April 7, 1865 and confined at Point Lookout until released on June 21, 1865. His name also appears as a signature to an Oath of Allegiance to the United States subscribed and sworn to at Point Lookout, Maryland on June 21, 1865. Whaley's place of residence was given on the Oath as Sampson County, North Carolina, and his description as follows: Complexion-dark; hair-dark; eyes-hazel; height-5 ft. 8 in.
[Source(s): Card File; NA, RG 109]

Whalin, Thomas (New Hanover County, North Carolina)
Ordinary Seaman, Confederate States Navy. Whalin enlisted on November 5, 1863, in Wilmington for the war.
[Source(s): Card File; MR, 4, p. 447; St. Armand]

Wheeler, B. H.
Landsman, Confederate States Navy. Wheeler enlisted on August 8, 1864 in Raleigh for the war.
[Source(s): Card File; NA, RG 45]

Wheeler, John (New Hanover County, North Carolina)
Confederate States Navy. Wheeler enlisted in the Confederate States Navy on October 8, 1863, in Wilmington, North Carolina.
[Source(s): MR, 4, p. 447; St. Armand]

Wheeler, John [Probably same as "John Wheeler, who enlisted in Wilmington, North Carolina, q.v.]
Landsman, Confederate States Navy. Wheeler enlisted on October 12, 1863 at Camp Holmes as a substitute.
[Source(s): Card File; NA, RG 45; Foenander]

Wheeler, John [Probably same as "John Wheeler, who enlisted at Camp Holmes, North Carolina, q.v.]
Seaman, Confederate States Navy. Wheeler enlisted on October 12, 1863, in Wilmington for the war.
[Source(s): Card File; NA, RG 45; Foenander]

Whit, Henderson (Davidson County, North Carolina)
Confederate States Navy. Henderson enlisted in the Confederate States Navy on August 13, 1864 in Wilmington, North Carolina.
[Source(s): MR, IV, 448]

Whitaker, William C. M. (Chowan County, North Carolina)
Private, Confederate States Army//Ordinary Seaman, Confederate States Navy. Whitaker resided in Chowan County where he enlisted at age 30 on May 18, 1861 (May 15, 1861 per MR) for the war as a Private in Company A, 1st Regiment, North Carolina Troops. He was present or accounted for until discharged on February 1, 1862 and transferred to the Confederate States Navy where he served as an Ordinary Seaman aboard the CSS VIRGINIA, 1862.
[Source(s): Card File; North Carolina Troops, III; NPS; Foenander; MR, I]

White, Benjamin
Ordinary Seaman, Confederate States Navy. White enlisted on April 6, 1863, in Wilmington for three years or the war. Records indicate a "Benjamin J. White," Quartermaster, CSS ARCTIC, 1863. He was attached as a Private to Semmes' Naval Brigade, April 1865, and surrendered and was paroled at Greensboro, North Carolina, April 26, 1865. [.]
[Source(s): Card File; NA, RG 45; MR, 4, p. 447; Foenander; St. Armand; *ORN* 2, 1, 276; *M1091*]

White, Charles
Landsman, Confederate States Navy. White enlisted on April 25, 1864, in Halifax or Plymouth for the war.
[Source(s): Card File; NA, RG 45]

White, Clark (Bladen County, North Carolina)
Landsman, Confederate States Navy. White enlisted on September 28, 1863, at Camp Holmes (near Raleigh, North Carolina) for the war. He served aboard the steamer "*Iseneger*" (sic) [ISONDIGA?]. He appears on a roll of Prisoners of War at Point Lookout, Maryland, which states he was captured near Savannah on December 21, 1864, and confined at Point Lookout, until released June 21, 1865. His name also appears as a signature to an Oath of Allegiance to the United States subscribed and sworn to at Point Lookout, Maryland June 21, 1865 giving his place of residence as Bladen County, North Carolina and his description as follows: Complexion-dark; hair-black; eyes-brown; height 5 ft. 6 ½ in.
[Source(s): Card File; NA, RG 109; NA, RG 45]

White, E. H.
Landsman, Confederate States Navy. White enlisted on August 5, 1864 in Raleigh for the war.
[Source(s): Card File; NA, RG 45]

White, George (New Hanover County, North Carolina)
Seaman, Confederate States Navy. White enlisted from Wilmington, North Carolina in Cumming's Battery which was the 1st Company C, 36th Regiment, North Carolina Troops (2nd Regiment, North Carolina Artillery). He was later transferred to the Confederate States Navy.
[Source(s): Card File; McElroy; North Carolina Troops, I]

White, George W. (Stanly County, North Carolina)
    Landsman, Confederate States Navy. White enlisted on December 15, 1863, in Raleigh for the war. Another source states he enlisted on December 18, 1863, in Wilmington for the war). He appears on registers of Confederate States Army General Military Hospital Number 4, Wilmington, North Carolina which state he was admitted on January 9, 1864 with "parotitis" and returned to duty February 12, 1864. His post office given on the registers as Bloomington, North Carolina (Stanly County). His name appears on the same registers stating he was admitted on March 23, 1864 with "rheumatismus chronicus" and transferred to the Smallpox Hospital April 4, 1864.
    [Source(s): Card File; NA, RG 45; NA, RG 109]

White, Henderson (Forsyth County, North Carolina)
    Confederate States Navy. His claim for a pension filed on July 7, 1902 age 64, listing his post office as Winston-Salem, Forsyth County was approved at 4th Class.
    [Source(s): Card File; Pensions (North Carolina)

White, J. C.
    Ordinary Seaman, Confederate States Navy. White enlisted on June 13, 1863 in Wilmington for the war.
    [Source(s): Card File; NA, RG 45]

White, John
    Seaman, Confederate States Navy.
    White resided on Knotts Island, Currituck County, North Carolina as a schoolteacher prior to serving in the North Carolina Navy aboard the NCS WINSLOW from July - November 1861. He served as a Seaman aboard the CSS FORREST (formerly the CSS EDWARDS) during the 1st quarter of 1862 as a member of the North Carolina Squadron. His name appears on the payroll of the receiving ship CSS UNITED STATES ending March 31, 1862.
    [Source: NCCWSP]

White, John
    Seaman, Confederate States Navy. White enlisted on March 16, 1863 in Wilmington for the war.
    [Source(s): Card File; NA, RG 45]

White, John
    Landsman, Confederate States Navy. White enlisted on April 10, 1864 in Kinston for three years or the war.
    [Source(s): Card File; NA, RG 45]

White, John Johnston
    Private, Confederate States Army//Landsman, Confederate States Navy. White enlisted for twelve months in New Hanover County, North Carolina, on April 16, 1861 as a Private in 1st Company C, 36th Regiment, North Carolina Troops (2nd Regiment North Carolina Artillery). He was present or accounted for until transferred to Company C, 13th Battalion, (North Carolina) Light Artillery on November 4, 1863. He transferred to the Confederate States Navy on April 9, 1864. Born on October 31, 1837, White died on January 17, 1918, and was buried in Pineview Cemetery, Edgecombe County, North Carolina.
    [Source(s): Card File; NA, RG 109; North Carolina Troops, I; Stepp, "Burials"]

White, Malachi/Malicha (Washington, North Carolina)
    Seaman, Confederate States Navy. A widow's pension application dated July 23, 1904, from Mrs. Frances M. "Fannie" White, age 75, post office Cherry, Washington County, North Carolina, states that White enlisted on September 10, 1863 and served as a "Seaman" on the Confederate States steamer CSS YADKIN with Captain Whitehead. The request was approved at 4th Class. Her application lists her as living about thirty miles from Plymouth, North Carolina. Benjamin Woodley (Creswell, North Carolina) and Eli J. Spruill (Creswell, North Carolina) served as witnesses.
    [Source(s): Card File; Pensions (NORTH CAROLINA); WCL; Darden]

White, Redmond (Residence listed as "Bertie," Hertford County, North Carolina).
    Confederate States Navy (?) White died in Wilmington, North Carolina at age 28 on August 21, 1862 of "Conti' Fever(?)." He was listed as a "Sailor."
    [Source: Oakdale (Davis)]

White, Samuel W. (Born in Tennessee, or possibly from Washington County, North Carolina)
    Seaman, Confederate States Navy. White enlisted on March 27 [20th, per source Foenander], 1864 at Camp Vance.

His description was given as follows: Age 18; eyes-hazel; hair-sandy; complexion-fair; height-5 ft. 6 in.; place of birth-Tennessee; occupation-farmer. Records indicate he was enlisted from Washington County, "Tenn." (North Carolina?) His name appears on a list of conscripts "in yard at Halifax" June 9, 1864. Source Foenander states he served aboard the CSS ALBEMARLE.
[Source(s): Card File; NA, RG 45; Foenander]

White, Samuel [Possibly same as White, Samuel W.]
Landsman, Confederate States Navy. White enlisted on March 30, 1864 in Raleigh for the war.
[Source(s): Card File; NA, RG 45]

White, Thomas (Wayne County, North Carolina)
Private, Company A, Confederate States Marine Corps. White enlisted in Raleigh, North Carolina on November 4, 1864. White served on the Charleston, South Carolina Station as a Private of the Marine guard on board the ironclad CSS COLUMBIA to February 7, 1865. He transferred to the CSS INDIAN CHIEF on February 8, 1865. His name appears on a roll of prisoners of war at Point Lookout, Maryland which states he was captured at Harper's Farm [another source says "Farmville"], Virginia on April 6, 1865. He was confined at Point Lookout until released on June 21, 1865. His name also appears as a signature (by mark) to an Oath of Allegiance to the United States subscribed and sworn to at Point Lookout on June 21, 1865. His place of residence was given on the Oath as Wayne County, North Carolina and his description as follows: Complexion, dark; hair, black; eyes, hazel; height 5 feet 5 inches.
[Source(s): NA; Card File; North Carolina Troops, Doc. # 0185, p. 1, and 0299; Donnelly-ENL]

White, Thomas (Edgecombe County, North Carolina)
Confederate States Navy. White resided in Edgecombe County.
[Source(s): Card File; Thorpe Roster]

White, W. (New Hanover County, North Carolina) [NOTE: All or some of the "W." and "William" Whites may be the same person]
Confederate States Navy. White enlisted in the Confederate States Navy on August 23, 1863 in Wilmington, North Carolina.
[Source(s): MR, 4, p. 447; St. Armand]

White, William
Landsman, Confederate States Navy.
White served aboard the CSS CURLEW as a member of the North Carolina Squadron during the 1st quarter of 1862. His name appears on the payroll list of the receiving ship CSS UNITED STATES ending March 31, 1862.
[Source: NCCWSP]

White, William (Pender County [?], North Carolina)
Confederate States Navy. A claim for pension filed on July 2, 1906 by White's widow, Ann J. White, age 66 years, post office Watha, Pender County, North Carolina, states he enlisted in the Confederate States Navy on or about May 10, 1863. John Eakins (q.v.), former Confederate States Navy, of Atkinson, North Carolina, served as witness. The application was approved.
[Source(s): Card File; Pensions (North Carolina); Foenander]

White, William
Landsman, Confederate States Navy. White enlisted on September 5, 1863, in Wilmington for the war.
[Source(s): Card File; NA, RG 45]

White, William
Landsman, Confederate States Navy. White enlisted on November 12, 1863, in Raleigh for the war. Another source states he enlisted on November 15, 1863 in Wilmington for the war.
[Source(s): Card File; NA, RG 45]

White, William
Landsman, Confederate States Navy. White served as a Landsman aboard the CSS ARCTIC, 1863.
[Source(s): Foenander; ORN 2, 1]

White, William H. (Camden County, North Carolina)
    1st Sergeant, Confederate States Army//Confederate States Navy. White resided in Camden County, North Carolina, where he enlisted at age 20 on May 3, 1861 as a Private in Company M, 12th Regiment, North Carolina Troops. He was present or accounted for until transferred to 2nd Company B, 32nd Regiment, North Carolina Troops, in October 1861. He held the rank of Private until promoted to Sergeant in May-August 1862. Promoted to 1st Sergeant on February 21, 1863, he was reduced to the rank of Sergeant on May 1, 1863. He was present or accounted for until he transferred to the Confederate States Navy on December 30, 1863.
    [Source(s): Card File; North Carolina Troops, V and IX; Foenander]

White, William H. (Hertford County, North Carolina)
    Private, Confederate States Army//Confederate States Navy. Born in Hertford County, North Carolina, White was by occupation a farmer prior to enlisting in Lincoln County, North Carolina, at age 33 on October 19, 1863, for the war, in Company H, 52nd Regiment, North Carolina Troops. He transferred to the Confederate States Navy on or about April 1, 1864.
    [Source(s): Card File; North Carolina Troops, XII; NPS; Foenander]

Whitehead, William
    Landsman, Confederate States Navy.
    Whitehead shipped for one year aboard the CSS RALEIGH on November 11, 1861 and served as a Landsman from October 1861 – April 1862. His name appears on the North Carolina Squadron payroll for the 1st quarter of 1862 (February 21, 1862 - April 15, 1862. He transferred to the James River Squadron, as of April 15, 1862. He served at Drewry's Bluff as a Landsman from April 1, 1863 - June 30, 1863). He served as a Landsman aboard the CSS RALEIGH with the James River Squadron during the period November 16 - December 15, 1862.
    [Source: NCCWSP]

Whiteheart, W. (Davidson County, North Carolina)
    Confederate States Navy. Whiteheart enlisted in the Confederate States Navy on August 13, 1863 in Wilmington, North Carolina.
    [Source(s): MR, 4, p. 448]

Whitenell, Hayes K.
    Landsman, Confederate States Navy. Whitenell enlisted on March 31, 1864, in Raleigh for the war.
    [Source(s): Card File; NA, RG 45]

Whitfield, J. E.
    Landsman, Confederate States Navy. Whitfield served as a Landsman on board the CSS VIRGINIA II. Born in 1822, Whitfield died in 1877 and was buried in Bellevue Cemetery, Wilmington, New Hanover County, North Carolina.
    [Source(s): Gravestone Records, vol. 8, p. 41; North Carolina CGVL; Stepp, "Burials"]

Whitley, Josiah
    Landsman, Confederate States Navy. Whitley enlisted on January 2, 1864 in Raleigh for the war.
    [Source(s): Card File; NA, RG 45]

Whitley, Samuel
    Landsman, Confederate States Navy. Whitley enlisted on September 28, 1863 at Camp Holmes (near Raleigh, North Carolina) for the war.
    [Source(s): Card File; NA, RG 45]

Whitlock, James D.
    Landsman, Confederate States Navy. Whitlock enlisted on November 25, 1864 in Raleigh for the war. A "J. D. Whitlock" appears on the March – October 1864 muster rolls of the CSS NEUSE.
    [Source(s): Card File; NA, RG 45; CMACSSN]

Whitney, Eli Gedding [Born in South Carolina/resided in North Carolina (?)]
    Landsman, Confederate States Navy. Whitney was discharged from the Confederate States Navy on April 7, 1865. Born on May 2, 1842, Whitney died on September 2, 1890, and was buried in Bellevue Cemetery, Wilmington, New Hanover County, North Carolina. Source "PCNMC" states he was born in Charleston, South Carolina.
    [Source(s): Stepp, "Burials;" PCNMC]

Whitt, Henderson W. ["W. Henderson" (see Stepp)] (Forsyth County, North Carolina)
Confederate States Navy. Whitt enlisted on August 13, 1864. He was captured on April 6, 1865, imprisoned at Point Lookout, Maryland, and paroled on June 22, 1865. His pension application filed on July 1, 1902, age 64, listing his residence as Winston-Salem, North Carolina, states he enlisted in the Confederate States Navy in August 1862 and was not wounded, "but my eyes are injured by powder from the explosion of a gun on board ship." D. [?] W. Jones of Winston-Salem, North Carolina, served as a witness on his application, which was approved as 4th class. An accompanying doctor's letter refers to Whitt as having been in the "Naval Department" and mentions a "Capt. Brown." His claim for increase, filed on July 1, 1907, at age 69, from Forsyth County, was disapproved. He was buried in Woodlawn Cemetery, No. 3214 Indiana Ave., Winston-Salem, Forsyth County, North Carolina.
[Source(s): Card File; Gravestone Records, vol. 8, p. 170; Pensions (North Carolina); Stepp, "Burials"]

Whittington, Calvin (Guilford County, North Carolina)
Private, Confederate States Army//Ordinary Seaman, Confederate States Navy. Whittington was born in Guilford County where he resided as a farmer prior to enlisting in Wake County at age 22 on September 19, 1861, for the war, as a Private in 2nd Company E, 2nd Regiment, North Carolina Troops. He was present or accounted for until transferred to the Confederate States Navy in January 1862 [Note: Another source states he enlisted on October 5 or 9, 1863, at Camp Holmes (near Raleigh, North Carolina); another source states he enlisted on October 11, 1863, in Wilmington for the war]. He served as an Ordinary Seaman aboard the CSS ARCTIC and CSS NORTH CAROLINA.
[Source(s): Card File; NPS; North Carolina Troops, III; NA, RG 45; MR, 4, p. 444; Foenander]

Whomsley, John P.
3rd Assistant Engineer, Confederate States Navy. Whomsley was born in North Carolina and appointed from the state as a 3rd Assistant Engineer on July 31, 1861. He served aboard the CSS ELLIS, from at least August 1861 – November 1862, in North Carolina waters as part of the North Carolina Squadron. He was captured in the Battle of Roanoke Island and paroled on February 12, 1862.
[Source(s): ELLIS Crew List; Fold3, Midshipmen; NCCWSP]

Wicks, James A. (North Carolina)
Confederate States Navy. Wicks was born somewhere in North Carolina, sometime between 1819 and 1830. He was serving in New York City in the United States Navy circa 1850 and was married to an English girl named Catherine Kelly. When his ship the USS CONGRESS was sunk by the CSS VIRGINIA off Hampton Roads, Wicks supposedly swam ashore and joined the Confederate States Navy. Wicks served on the CSS HUNLEY's third crew and drowned on February 17, 1864 after the HUNLEY sank the USS HOUSATONIC. His family is said to have resided in Florida at the time Wicks drowned,
[Source(s): Internet sites and genealogist with Lasch Laboratory, Charleston, SC]

Wiles, Samuel
Private, Confederate States Army//Detached service in the Confederate States Navy. Wiles transferred as a Private from the Confederate States Signal Corps on December 1, 1862 to 2nd Company A, 36th Regiment, North Carolina Troops (2nd Regiment, North Carolina Artillery), and was detailed as a telegraph operator on the Cape Fear River on January 1, 1863. Listed as "absent, detailed" [duty and location not listed] when transferred to Captain Abner A. Moseley's Company North Carolina Troops (Sampson Artillery), on December 1, 1863. Wiles was appointed to the rank of Sergeant on February 5, 1864 but reduced to ranks upon appointment as Surgeon's Steward and detailed to the Confederate States Navy, September 12, 1864. Absent "detailed" [duty and location not listed] through December 1864. His name appears on a roll of men paroled at Greensboro, North Carolina, on April 28, 1865, and noted as being on "detached service in the Confederate States Navy.
[Source(s): Foenander; North Carolina Troops, I]

Wilkinson (Wilkenson), Allen
Landsman, Confederate States Navy. Wilkinson enlisted on December 5, 1863, in Raleigh for the war. Another source states he enlisted on December 12, 1863, in Wilmington for the war.
[Source(s): Card File; NA, RG 45]

Wilkinson, John P.
Seaman, Confederate States Navy. Records indicate Wilkinson enlisted on June 13, 1864, in Raleigh for the war in [from?] Mallett's Battalion. Another source states he enlisted in the Confederate States Navy, June 13, 1864, in Raleigh, North Carolina. He served as Seaman.
[Source(s): Card File; NA, RG 45; Foenander]

Wilkinson, William A.
Private, Confederate States Army//Confederate States Navy. Wilkinson enlisted in New Hanover County, North Carolina on April 16, 1861 for twelve months as a Private in 1st Company C, 36th Regiment North Carolina Troops (2nd Regiment North Carolina Artillery). He was present or accounted for until he transferred as a Private to Company C, 13th Battalion North Carolina Light Artillery on November 4, 1863. He transferred to the Confederate States Navy by authority of the Secretary of War on September 21 (or October 21), 1864. He served aboard the CSS NEUSE per the ship's March - October 1864 muster rolls.
[Source(s): Card File; North Carolina Troops, I; NA, RG 109; Hill; CMACSSN]

Wilhelm, G. L. (Stanly County, North Carolina)
Confederate States Navy.
[Source(s): "Stanly Reunions"]

Willaby (Willeby), Freeman
Ordinary Seaman, Confederate States Navy.
Willaby served aboard the CSS RALEIGH per clothing and small stores records as a member of the North Carolina Squadron beginning before September 2, 1862.
[Source: NCCWSP]

Willard, Henry (Beaufort County, North Carolina)
Private, Company A, Confederate States Marine Corps. Willard enlisted in Raleigh, North Carolina on October 6, 1864. He served on the Charleston, South Carolina Station. As a Private of the Marine guard on board the ironclad CSS COLUMBIA to February 7, 1865. He was captured at Farmville, Virginia on April 6, 1865 and held as a prisoner of war at Point Lookout, Maryland until released on June 3, 1865.
[Source(s): North Carolina Troops, Doc. # 0299; Card File]

Willcox, Jim
Confederate States Navy. Willcox served at Edward's Ferry, Halifax County, North Carolina circa October 1863 [CSS ALBEMARLE construction].
[Source(s): Pensions (NC) (1931 letter in "James W. Tatum" file]

Willcox, Tom
Confederate States Navy. Willcox served at Edward's Ferry, Halifax County, North Carolina circa October 1863 [CSS ALBEMARLE construction].
[Source(s): Pensions (NC) (1931 letter in "James W. Tatum" file]

Williams, Charles
Ordinary Seaman, 2nd Class Fireman, Coal Heaver, Seaman, Confederate States Navy.
Williams served as an Ordinary Seaman aboard the CSS EDWARDS beginning with his shipping articles signed on July 25, 1861. He served aboard the CSS EDWARDS through October 31, 1861, then as a 2nd Class Fireman aboard the CSS FORREST (formerly the CSS EDWARDS) in December 1861. He received a partial payment on February 13, 1862 at Gosport Navy Yard following his service in manning Fort Cobb at the Battle of Elizabeth City on February 10, 1862. He is listed as a Coal Heaver aboard the CSS BEAUFORT on a bounty list dated January 16, 1862. He was aboard through March 1862 per a clothing record. His name appears on a North Carolina Squadron payroll for the 1st quarter of 1862 (December 1, 1861 - April 15, 1862). He was promoted from Coal Heaver to Seaman on February 10, 1862 and transferred to the James River Squadron on April 15, 1862.
[Source: NCCWSP]

Williams, Daniel W.
Seaman, Confederate States Navy.
Williams served aboard the CSS BEAUFORT as a member of the North Carolina Squadron as a Seaman per the ship's bounty list dated January 16, 1862. He received a partial payment on February 13, 1862 at Gosport Navy Yard following his service manning Fort Cobb at the Battle of Elizabeth City on February 10, 1862. Clothing records indicate he was aboard the CSS BEAUFORT as late as March 1862. His name appears on a payroll of the North Carolina Squadron for the 1st quarter of 1862 (January 10, 1862 - April 15, 1862). He transferred to the James River Squadron as of April 15, 1862. Williams is also said to have served aboard the CSS PATRICK HENRY.
[Source: NCCWSP]

Williams, Eames
Landsman, Confederate States Navy.
Williams served as a Landsman aboard the CSS SEA BIRD in the North Carolina Squadron as early as February 1862. He was captured in the Battle of Elizabeth City and carried to Roanoke Island on February 10, 1862 where he was paroled February 12, 1862 and returned to Elizabeth City, North Carolina.
[Source: NCCWSP]

Williams, Edward
Ordinary Seaman, Confederate States Navy.
Per clothing, bounty, and small stores records, Williams served as an Ordinary Seaman aboard the CSS RALEIGH from September 2, 1862 through at least October 1861 with the North Carolina Squadron.
[Source: NCCWSP]

Williams, Elias (Currituck County, North Carolina)
Quartermaster, Seaman, Confederate States Navy.
Williams worked as a teacher on Knotts Island, North Carolina prior to enlisting as a Quartermaster aboard the NCS WINSLOW per the ship's muster roll for July - November 1861. He served as a Seaman aboard the CSS SEA BIRD as of February 1862. He was captured in the Battle of Elizabeth City and carried to Roanoke Island on February 10, 1862 where he was paroled on February 12, 1862 and returned to Elizabeth City. He received a partial payment on February 18, 1862 at Gosport Navy Yard following the sinking of the CSS SEA BIRD at Elizabeth City on February 10, 1862. His name appears on the North Carolina Squadron payroll for the 1st quarter of 1862 (Dec. 1, 1861 - April 15, 1862).
[Source: NCCWSP]

Williams, Eugene M. (Craven County, North Carolina)
Acting Gunner, Gunner, Confederate States Navy.
Williams resided in Craven County and enlisted in Wayne County at age 18 on May 1, 1862, for the war, as a Private in Company K 2nd Regiment, North Carolina Troops. He was present or accounted for until transferred to the Confederate States Navy on October 13, 1862 where he served as an Acting Gunner as of October 16, 1862 on board the CSS RICHMOND. He served at Drewry's Bluff, Virginia, 1862-1863 and on the Richmond Station (1864) as part of the James River Squadron, 1862-1865. He was promoted to Gunner, Provisional Navy, on June 2, 1864. He was paroled on May 5, 1865 at Greensboro, North Carolina. His widow, Mrs. Mary A. Williams, age 68, a resident of New Bern, North Carolina, applied for a pension on July 14, 1913.
[Source(s): Card File; North Carolina Troops, III; Pensions (NORTH CAROLINA); Register]

Williams, Ezekiel
Seaman, Confederate States Navy.
Williams served as a Seaman aboard the NCS WINSLOW per that ship's muster roll for July - November 1861. He served as a Seaman aboard the CSS SEA BIRD as of February 1862. He was received aboard the receiving ship CSS UNITED STATES by order of Flag Officer French Forrest on March 24, 1862. His name appears on the North Carolina Squadron payroll for the 1st quarter of 1862 (December 1, 1861 - March 31, 1862).
[Source: NCCWSP]

Williams, George
Captain's Clerk, Confederate States Navy.
Born in New York, Williams resided in New Orleans as a sailor. He enlisted at Camp Moore, Louisiana as a Private in Company G, 10th Louisiana Infantry on June 22, 1861. He transferred to the Confederate States Navy in November 1861 and served as a Captain's Clerk in the North Carolina Squadron aboard the NCS WINSLOW per that ship's muster roll for July - November 1861.
[Source: NCCWSP]

Williams, Henry [Henri] S. H. (K.) (North Carolina)
Acting midshipman, Confederate States Navy. Williams was born in and appointed from North Carolina. He served as an Acting Midshipman, United States Navy, from September 27, 1860 to March 18, 1861, when he resigned. He was appointed an "Acting Midshipman, 3rd Class," Confederate States Navy, on September 14, 1861 [July 8, 1861, per source "Fold3, Midshipmen") and ordered to proceed to New Bern, North Carolina, and report to flag officer Lynch for duty; on September 26, 1861, he was ordered by Lieutenant William H. Parker, aboard the CSS BEAUFORT at New Bern, to proceed to Norfolk, Virginia, and report to flag officer French Forrest, for

transportation aboard the CSS WINSLOW to Roanoke Island, where he was to assume duty. Williams served aboard two steamers, the CSS ELLIS at Roanoke Island in 1861 and the CSS EDWARDS (later renamed the CSS FORREST) from July through October 1861. The Confederate States receiving ship CSS UNITED STATES, Gosport Navy Yard, Norfolk, Virginia, 1861-1862; the CSS BALTIC, Mobile Squadron, 1862; the CSS PALMETTO STATE and the steamers CSS CHICORA and CSS STONO, Charleston Station, 1862-1863; on the Wilmington Station, 1862-1863 [?]; and, aboard the CSS PATRICK HENRY, 1863. He resigned on January 14, 1864. [NOTE: Williams' dates of service as provided by the sources conflict].
[Source(s): Card File; McElroy; Register; Foenander; ONWR; NCCWSP]

Williams, Jacob
Seaman, Landsman, Confederate States Navy.
Williams served as a Seaman aboard the CSS EDWARDS (later renamed the CSS FORREST) per shipping articles he signed on July 25, 1861. He is found serving as a Landsman aboard the CSS EDWARDS per that ship's payroll list for July - September 1861. He appears as a Landsman aboard the CSS FORREST (the former CSS EDWARDS) as of the ship's muster roll dated October 30, 1861. He transferred to the CSS BEAUFORT on October 30, 1861 and, according to various records, served on that ship as a Landsman from September- December 1861. His name appears on the North Carolina Squadron payroll for the 1st quarter of 1862 (December 1, 1861 - January 8, 1862).
[Source: NCCWSP]

Williams, John (New Hanover County, North Carolina)
Seaman, Confederate States Navy. Williams served aboard the CSS ALBEMARLE. His name appears as a signature to an Oath of Allegiance subscribed and sworn to at Fort Monroe, Virginia, July 2, 1864. Place of residence given on Oath as Wilmington, North Carolina, and description as follows: Complexion-light; hair-brown; eyes-brown; height-5 ft. 9 in. Oath carries the remark: "Rebel deserter came in Federal lines near Plymouth, North Carolina.
[Source(s): Card File; NA, RG 109]

Williams, John R. (Martin County, North Carolina)
Private, Confederate States Army//Confederate States Navy. Williams was born in Pitt County and resided in Martin County as a laborer prior to enlisting in Martin County at age 19, March 21, 1862, for the war, in Company A, 17th Regiment North Carolina Troops (2nd Organization). He was present or accounted for until he transferred to Company F, 31st Regiment North Carolina Troops, January 1, 1863, in exchange for Private John D. Biggs. He was hospitalized in Richmond, Virginia, May 16, 1864, with a gunshot wound. Place and date of gunshot not reported. He died in the hospital in Richmond, Virginia, on May 20, 1864 of wounds. He was buried in Oakwood (Richmond?) in Henrico County, Virginia (Confederate States Navy reference found in Card File).
[Source(s): Card File; North Carolina Troops, Vols. 6 and 8; North Carolina CVGL]

Williams, L. A.
Seaman, Coal Heaver, Confederate States Navy.
Williams served aboard the CSS SEA BIRD as a Seaman from July – February 20, 1862 per muster and clothing records. He appears as a Coal Heaver aboard this same ship in February 1862. His name appears on a North Carolina Squadron payroll for the 1st quarter of 1862 (December 1, 1861 - April 15, 1862). His listed as "on parole" as of April 15, 1862.
[Source: NCCWSP]

William(s), Lewis
Landsman, Confederate States Navy. Williams enlisted on April 25, 1864, in Halifax or Plymouth for the war.
[Source(s): Card File; NA, RG 45]

Williams, Reuben
Landsman, Confederate States Navy. Williams enlisted on April 14, 1864, in Raleigh for the war.
[Source(s): Card File; NA, RG 45]

Williams, William A.
Landsman, Confederate States Navy. Williams enlisted on August 17, 1864, in Raleigh for the war.
[Source(s): Card File; NA, RG 45]

Williams, William H.
Private, Confederate States Army//Confederate States Navy. Williams enlisted as a Private in 2nd Company G, 36th Regiment, North Carolina Troops (2nd Regiment, North Carolina Artillery) in Beaufort County at age 18 on

September 23, 1861 for twelve months. He deserted on August 16, 1862. (Confederate States Navy reference found on source Card File).
[Source(s): Card File; North Carolina Troops, I]

Williams, William T. (Nash County, North Carolina)
Assistant Surgeon, Confederate States Navy. Williams was born on June 25, 1840, was a resident of Nash County, North Carolina, and a physician by trade. Originally appointed as Captain, Company H., 12th North Carolina Troops on May 1, 1861, then Lieutenant Colonel, 1st North Carolina Battalion (later 32nd Regiment, North Carolina Troops) on November 29, 1861. Williams gave his resignation on June 18, 1863 with the unusual reason of wanting to serve the Confederacy as a Private. Soon after his resignation, he was appointed as an Assistant Surgeon in the Confederate States Navy. The April 18, 1864 issue of *Daily Confederate* (Raleigh) recorded that Williams died in Nash County on March 9 at the home of his brother, Henry G. Williams, at the age of 23. However, a letter, dated April 28, 1864 written by W. A. W. Spotswood, Surgeon in Charge, Confederate State Navy Department, Office of Medicine and Surgery to S. R. Mallory, Confederate Secretary of the Navy, states that "Dr. W. T. Williams, of Oxford, North Carolina, who had received his appointment, died on the 15th of March, before receiving his orders to Charleston." His exact death date may never be known. After his death he was buried in the Arrington Family Cemetery, Hwy 43, in the Hilliardston community in northern Nash County, North Carolina.
[Source(s): Card File; McElroy; *North Carolina Troops*, V, p. 204; *Lee's Colonels*, Robert K. Krick, p.372 gives death state as 7 March 1864 as opposed to that in *ORN*, as well as the "Journal of the Confederate Congresses;" Daily Confed. (4/18/64) ORN, 2, 2, 647; Gravestone Records, v. 1, p. 104; ONWR; "Officers, January 1, 1864"]

Williamson, A. M. (Columbus County, North Carolina)
Ordinary Seaman, Confederate States Navy. Williamson enlisted on June 5, 1863, in Wilmington for the war. He served aboard the CSS NORTH CAROLINA. His name appears on Registers of Confederate States Army General Military Hospital, Number 4, Wilmington, North Carolina, dated June 24, 1863, which gives his disease as "feb typh" and states that he returned to duty on August 3, 1863. Post office given as "Bug Hill Colum." (Columbus County). He again appears on registers of Confederate States Army General Military Hospital Number 4, Wilmington, North Carolina, which state he was admitted September 4, 1863, with "rheumatismus" and returned to duty December 2, 1863.
[Source(s): Card File; NA, RG 45, NA, RG 109; MR, 4, p. 447; St. Armand]

Williamson, A. P. [Possibly same as Williamson, A. M.]
Ordinary Seaman, Confederate States Navy. Williamson enlisted on June 5, 1863, in Wilmington for the war.
[Source(s): Card File; NA, RG 45]

Williamson, B. P.
Confederate States Navy (?). A letter dated April 11, 1903, from B. P. Williamson stated Charles M. Franklin, Confederate States Navy (q.v.) "was detailed to work with me on C. S. Government Ordinance [sic] work at Raleigh, North Carolina, during the war 1861-1865."
[Source(s): Pensions (North Carolina) (see application of "Charles M. Franklin")

Williamson, Eli (Hertford County, North Carolina) (Black)
Pilot, Seaman, Confederate States Navy. Williamson, a free Negro from a third generation free Murfreesboro family, was born on December 23, 1824. In his youth he lived with a Quaker family who taught him to read and write, tie fishing nets, and rig seines for large fisheries. He enlisted in the United States Navy but left prior to the Civil War to enter the merchant service where he worked, eventually becoming the Chief Pilot for the steamer *"Curlew."* Williamston enlisted on September 25, 1861 and was listed as a Seaman, on the November 20, 1861 muster roll for the CSS CURLEW. At the time of his wounding in action at the Battle of Roanoke Island on February 7, 1862, he was acting in his pre-war position as Pilot. Following the CSS CURLEW's sinking, he accompanied the crew to Gosport Navy Yard where he re-enlisted. He was placed on board the receiving ship CSS UNITED STATES by Commander T. T. Hunter per its muster roll dated March 31, 1862 and was said to have served as a crewmember on Hunter's new command, the gunboat CSS OLD DOMINION, but the unfinished ship was destroyed when Gosport Navy Yard was abandoned in May of 1862. Records indicate he was discharged from service by order of Flag Officer French Forrest on March 15, 1862. Williamson's claim for a pension filed on July 3, 1905, age 81, post office Ahoskie, Hertford County, North Carolina, confirms he enlisted in the Confederate States Navy on September 25, 1861. He mentions service at Roanoke Island, North Carolina, on or about February 17, 1862 where his "right arm was broken by the wheel of the steamer [CSS] CURLEW the said wheel having been broken by a shell from the enemy's ship. The arm was broken between the elbow and the wrist." His pension was approved at 4th Class.

Jno. E. Vann of Winston-Salem, North Carolina, was a witness on Williamson's application. Per source Foenander, said pension was from Hertford County, North Carolina. Williamson had four daughters which grew into maturity, naming each for a ship which he had served prior to the war: Curlew, Katherine, Sea Bird, and Emma. He died in 1915 at the home of a daughter in Washington, North Carolina at the age of ninety-one following a five-day illness.
[Source(s): Pensions (NORTH CAROLINA); Foenander; NCS; NCCWSP]

Williamson, James (Randolph County, North Carolina)
Landsman, Confederate States Navy. Williamson enlisted in the Confederate States Navy on October 20, 1863 (date from source "MR") in Wilmington, North Carolina. Other sources state he enlisted on October 21, 1863, at Camp Holmes (near Raleigh, North Carolina) or October 26, or 27, 1863, in Wilmington for the war.
[Source(s): NA, RG 45; MR, 4, p. 447]

Williamson, P. D. (Cleveland County, North Carolina)
Confederate States Navy (Naval Battalion). Williamson enlisted on March 1, 1864. His claim for pension filed on January 31, 1925, age 80 years, post office Shelby, Cleveland County, North Carolina was approved as 4th Class. J. M. Walker served as a witness. Mr. Williamson's handwritten statement of service states he "went to Raleigh joined the Navy [,] stationed on James River [sic] at Fork [Fort?] Brooks twelve miles from Richmond, Virginia [;] served under Captain Bradford. Captured April 6, 1865[;] in prison at NewPort [sic] News." His name appears as a signature to an Oath of Allegiance to the United States, subscribed and sworn to at Newport News, Virginia, June 25, 1865. Place of residence given on as Cleveland County, North Carolina, and description as follows: Complexion-dark; hair-dark; eyes-grey; height-5 ft. 7 in. Oath also carries the remark: "Captured at Farmville, Va., April 6."
[Source(s): Card File; Pensions (NORTH CAROLINA); NA, RG 109]

Willis, J. (Bladen County [?], North Carolina)
Confederate States Navy (Naval Battalion). Willis' name appears as a signature to an Oath of Allegiance to the United States, subscribed and sworn to at Newport News, Virginia, June 15, 1865. Place of residence given on Oath as "Laden County, North Carolina," [probably Bladen County] and description as follows: Complexion-light; hair-dark; eyes-hazel; height-5 ft. 8 in. Oath carries the remark: "Captured at Farmville, Va., April 6, 1865."
[Source(s): Card File; NA, RG 109]

Willis, Reuben F. (Carteret County [?], North Carolina)
Pilot, Confederate States Navy. Born in North Carolina, in 1820, Willis served as a Pilot, Confederate States Navy. He was captured at the Battle of Elizabeth City on February 10, 1862 and paroled on February 12, 1862 at Roanoke Island and returned to Elizabeth City, North Carolina. As of 1880, he resided as a sailor with his wife, Aumariah Willis, and other relatives at Straits, Carteret County, North Carolina.
[Source(s): Foenander; NCCWSP]

Willis, William B. (Beaufort County, North Carolina)
Confederate States Navy. Willis enlisted in Beaufort County, North Carolina, at age 22 on April 22, 1861 for twelve months. He was captured at Fort Hatteras, August 29, 1861 and confined at Fort Warren, Massachusetts until paroled for exchange in November 1861. Willis was present until detailed to the Confederate Navy Yard at Wilmington, September 4, 1862. He was absent "detailed" through October 1864.
[Source(s): www.thewashingtongrays.homestead.com; www.ncgenweb.us/nccivwar/rosters/10cok.htm]

Willoughby (Willerbee, Willerby), Kedar (Cader)
Landsman, Confederate States Navy//Private, Confederate States Army. Willoughby (Willerbee) enlisted on December 18 [or on December 14 and 15], 1863, in Wilmington for the war [or, in Raleigh for the war] and served aboard the CSS NEUSE per the ship's March - October 1864 muster rolls. He transferred from "Lt. Loyall's command, C. S. Navy" at Kinston, North Carolina to Captain Cumming's battery, by S. O. #88.14, A&IGO, April 15, 1864 (Card File states see also Company C, 13th Battalion North Carolina Light Artillery).
[Source(s): Card File; NA, RG 109; NCCWSP; NA, RG 45; CMACSSN]

Willson, John
Landsman, Confederate States Navy. Willson enlisted on October 5, 1863, at Camp Holmes (near Raleigh, North Carolina).
[Source(s): Card File; NA, RG 45]

Wilson, Charles (Beaufort County, North Carolina)
Seaman, Confederate States Navy.

Wilson enlisted in Beaufort County, North Carolina, on May 8, 1861, aged 23, for twelve months, as a Private in Company K, 10th Regiment North Carolina Troops (1st Regiment, North Carolina Artillery). He transferred to the Confederate States Navy sometime between May 8 and July 25, 1861. Wilson served as a Seaman with the North Carolina Squadron aboard the CSS EDWARDS (later renamed the CSS FORREST) from July 25, 1861, the date he signed his shipping articles, through the 1st quarter of 1862 per payroll records. He is listed as a Seaman as of November 20, 1861 and served as such until the 1st quarter of 1862 when he appears as a Quartermaster aboard the CSS CURLEW. He was received aboard the receiving ship CSS UNITED STATES on February 20, 1862 and shipped with Commander Hunter for service aboard his new command. He appears again on the receiving ship CSS UNITED STATES per its payroll ending March 31, 1862 and is said to have served aboard the CSS VIRGINIA.
[Source(s): Card File; North Carolina Troops, I; NA, RG 109; www.thewashingtongrays.homestead.com; "Beaufort County Sailors;" www.ncgenweb.us/nccivwar/rosters/10cok.htm; NCCWSP]

Wilson, Daniel (New Hanover County, North Carolina)
Confederate States Navy. Wilson enlisted in the Confederate States Navy on October 21, 1863 in Wilmington, North Carolina.
[Source(s): MR, 4, p. 447; St. Armand]

Wilson, Daniel [Possibly the Daniel Wilson of New Hanover County]
Landsman, Confederate States Navy. Wilson enlisted on October 30, 1863, in Raleigh for the war. Another source states he enlisted on November 1, 1863, in Wilmington for the war.
[Source(s): Card File; NA, RG 45]

Wilson, H. J.
Ordinary Seaman, Confederate States Navy. Wilson enlisted in the Confederate States Navy in Wilmington, North Carolina, and served aboard the CSS ARCTIC, 1863. An "H. J." Wilson is listed on the March – October 1864 muster rolls of the CSS NEUSE.
[Source(s): MR, 4, p. 447; St. Armand]; ORN 2, 1; CMACSSN]

Wilson, James L. (Born Sampson County, North Carolina; resided in Wake County, North Carolina)
Landsman, Confederate States Navy. Wilson was conscripted on March 15, 1864, at Camp Holmes from Colonel Ivey's 38th Regiment North Carolina Militia from Wake County. Description as follows: Age 27 ["29," per Foenander]; eyes-hazel; hair-dark; complexion-sallow [sic]; height-5 ft. 8 ½ in.; place of birth-Sampson County; occupation-shoemaker. Another source states he enlisted on March 18, 1864, in Raleigh for the war.
[Source(s): Card File; NA, RG 45]

Wilson, John (Born in Germany//Onslow County, North Carolina)
Confederate States Navy. Wilson served as a Private, Company E, 3rd Regiment North Carolina Troops. Born in Germany, Wilson resided as a bridge carpenter in Onslow County where he enlisted at age 34, May 13, 1861, for the war. He was discharged on January 29, 1862 and transferred to the Confederate States Navy.
[Source(s): Card File; North Carolina Troops, Vol. 3]

Wilson, John A.
Seaman, Confederate States Navy.
Wilson served as a Seaman aboard the CSS SEA BIRD from July – February 1862 per that ship's muster rolls. Captured in the Battle of Elizabeth City, Wilson was carried to Roanoke Island on February 10, 1862, paroled there on February 12, 1862 and returned to Elizabeth City. Records indicate he received a partial payment on February 18, 1862 at Gosport Navy Yard following the sinking of the CSS SEA BIRD at the Battle of Elizabeth City on February 10, 1862. His name appears on the receiving ship CSS UNITED STATES payroll ending March 31, 1862, and on that of the North Carolina Squadron payroll for the 1st quarter of 1862 (December 1, 1861 - April 15, 1862). He is listed as "on parole" as of April 15, 1862.
[Source: NCCWSP]

Wilson, John R. (Granville County, North Carolina)
Landsman, Confederate States Navy. Wilson was conscripted at Camp Holmes (near Raleigh, North Carolina) on March 29, 1864, from Colonel Amos' 42nd Regiment North Carolina Militia, Granville County. Description: Age 23; eyes-blue; hair-dark; complexion-fair; height-5 ft. 8 in.; place of birth-Granville County; occupation-farmer. Another source states he enlisted on March 31, 1864, in Raleigh for the war.
[Source(s): Card File; NA, RG 45]

Wilson, Robert
Landsman, Confederate States Navy. Wilson enlisted on April 15, 1864, in Kinston for three years.
[Source(s): Card File; NA, RG 45]

Wilson, Thomas
Seaman, Confederate States Navy. Wilson received a flesh wound in the face at Fort Fisher, December 25, 1864.
[Source(s): Card File; Daily Conf. (1/2/65)]

Wilson, Thomas H. (Hertford County, North Carolina)
Confederate States Navy. Wilson served as a Private, Company F, 1st Regiment North Carolina Troops. He resided in Hertford County where he enlisted at age 18, July 5, 1861, for the war. He was present or accounted for until transferred to the Confederate States Navy on April 18, 1864, to take effect from April 5, 1864.
[Source(s): Card File; North Carolina Troops, Vol. 3]

Wilson, William
Confederate States Navy. Wilson's name appears on a list of conscripts "in yard at Halifax" June 9, 1864.
[Source(s): Card File; NA, RG 45]

Wilson, William (Born in Caswell County, North Carolina; enlisted from Forsyth County, North Carolina)
Confederate States Navy. Wilson enlisted on March 18, 1864, at Camp Holmes (near Raleigh, North Carolina) from Colonel Mastin's 71st Regiment North Carolina Militia, Forsyth County. Description given as follows: Age 30; eyes-blue; hair-light; complexion-fair; height-5 ft. 4 ½ in.; place of birth-Caswell County; occupation a farmer.
[Source(s): Card File; NA, RG 45]

Wilson, William
Landsman, Confederate States Navy. Wilson enlisted on March 21, 1864, in Raleigh for the war.
[Source(s): Card File; NA, RG 45]

Winbey/Winley, Thomas (Beaufort County, North Carolina)
Landsman, Confederate States Navy. Winbey enlisted on May 27, 1864, in Raleigh for the war. He served as a Landsman in Company F, Confederate States Navy (Navy Battalion). His name appears on a roll of Prisoners of War at Point Lookout, Maryland, which states he was captured on April 6, 1865, at Harpers Farm and confined at Point Lookout until released June 22, 1865. His name also appears as a signature (by mark) to an Oath of Allegiance to the United States, subscribed and sworn to at Point Lookout, Maryland, June 21, 1865. Place of residence given on Oath as Beaufort Co, North Carolina. Description: complexion fair, hair dark brown, eyes hazel, height 5'5.
[Source(s): NA, RG 109; NA, RG45]

Winborn/Winbun/Winburn, Augustus (Edgecombe County, North Carolina)
Landsman/Seaman, Confederate States Navy. Winborn enlisted on May 13, 1864, in Raleigh for the war. His name appears on a roll of Prisoners of War at Point Lookout, Maryland, which states he was captured at Burkeville [Virginia] on April 1, 1865 and confined at Point Lookout until released June 14, 1865. His name also appears as a signature (by mark) to an Oath of Allegiance to the United States, subscribed and sworn to at Point Lookout, Maryland, June 14, 1865 listing his place of residence given as Edgecombe County, North Carolina. Description: eyes-blue; height-5 ft. 1 ¾ in. His claim for a pension filed on August 3, 1901, listing his age as 55 years and his post office as Scotland Neck, Halifax County was approved at 4th Class.
[Source(s): Card File; NA, RG 45; NA, RG 109; Pensions (North Carolina)]

Windens, H.
Landsman, Confederate States Navy. Windens was assigned from Raleigh, North Carolina to Battery Brooke, James River, Virginia in October 1864.
[Source(s): PCNMC; Foenander]

Winsted, Burt
Landsman, Confederate States Navy. Winstead enlisted on May 27, 1864 in Raleigh for the war.
[Source(s): NA, RG 45]

Winstead, Wiley W. (Wilson County, North Carolina)
Ordinary Seaman, Confederate States Navy. Winstead enlisted on September 25, 1863, in Wilmington, North Carolina. [Source(s): MR, 4, p. 447; NA, RG 45]

Wise, John H.
Confederate States Navy. Wise "did service in the Schooner '*Guard*' around Roanoke Island and Hatteras," North Carolina, during the war.
[Source(s): UDC, Neuse]

Wise, Lawson (Gaston County, North Carolina)
"Private," Confederate States Navy. Born in Lincoln County, North Carolina, May 1838, Wise resided in Gaston County, North Carolina, as a carriage maker, prior to enlisting in Lincoln County, North Carolina, on September 11, 1861, as a Private, in Company E, 34th Regiment, North Carolina Troops. He was wounded sometime between May 1-4, 1863 in the left thigh at Chancellorsville, Virginia. He was transferred to the Confederate States Navy on April 3, 1864. Wise married Ann Odum in Marshall County, Mississippi, August 8, 1868, and resided there as a widowed farmer in 1900 with his five children. Wise died in 1906 and was buried in Chewalla Primative Baptist Church Cemetery, Potts Camp, Marshall County, Mississippi.
[Source(s): Card File; Foenander; Cloninger; Find-a-Grave]

Wise, Samuel A.
Landsman, Confederate States Navy. Wise enlisted on February 18, 1864, in Raleigh for the war.
[Source(s): NA, RG 45]

Wohmsley, John P. (North Carolina)
[3rd] Assistant Engineer, Confederate States Navy. Wohmsley was born in and appointed from North Carolina as a Third Assistant Engineer on July 31, 1861. He served aboard the CSS ELLIS, 1861-1862. He resigned but was captured at the Battle of Roanoke Island, North Carolina on February 7-8, 1862 before his resignation could be accepted [Source NCCWSP records he was captured at the Battle of Elizabeth City on February 10, 1862]. He was paroled on February 12 on Roanoke Island and returned to Elizabeth City. He was exchanged on August 5, 1862.
[Source(s): Register; McElroy; ONWR; NCCWSP]

Womble, Alfred (Guilford County, North Carolina)
Confederate States Navy. Womble enlisted on March 3, 1864, at Camp Holmes (near Raleigh, North Carolina) from Colonel Coble's 68th Regiment, North Carolina Militia from Guilford County. Description given as follows: Age, 37, eyes, hazel; hair, dark; complexion, florid; height, 5'5 ½;" place of birth, Guilford [County, North Carolinaoccupation farmer.
[Source(s): NA, RG45]

Womble, John J. (Chatham County, North Carolina) [NOTE: May be same as "John J. Womble," q.v.)
Private, Confederate States Marine Corps. Womble was captured at Farmville, Virginia on April 6, 1865. He was sent from City Point, Virginia, to and held as a prisoner of war at Point Lookout, Maryland until he died there on May 17, 1865 of typhoid fever.
[Source(s): North Carolina Troops, Doc. # 0299; Card File; Donnelly; Purser]

Womble, John S.
Landsman, Confederate States Navy. Womble enlisted on June 11, 1864, in Raleigh for the war.
[Source(s): NA, RG45]

Womble, S.
Landsman, Confederate States Navy. Womble enlisted on June 11, 1864, in Raleigh for the war.
[Source(s): Na, RG 45]

Womble (Wimbold, Wambold), Samuel T. (Chatham County, North Carolina)
Private, Company B, Confederate States Marine Corps. Womble appears on a roll of prisoners of war at Point Lookout, Maryland, which states he was captured at Farmville, Virginia on April 6, 1865. He was hospitalized April 12-14, 1865, in Petersburg, Virginia, and confined at Point Lookout until released on June 22, 1865. His name appears as a signature to an Oath of Allegiance to the United States subscribed and sworn to at Point Lookout on June 22, 1865 listing his place of residence as Chatham County, North Carolina. Description as follows: Complexion, light; hair, "L. Gray;" eyes, "L. hazel;" height, 6 feet 2 3/4 inches.
[Source(s): NA; Card File; North Carolina Troops, Doc. # 0185, p. 1, AND 0299; Donnelly]

Wood (Wook), James ["John," per Foenander] **Knight** (Granville County, North Carolina)
>Ordinary Seaman, North Carolina Navy ["Landsman, Confederate States Navy" (see Stepp)]. Born in Oxford, Granville County, North Carolina, on July 31, 1844, Wood enlisted in the Confederate States Navy in 1862 (other sources say 1861 and June 17, 1863) in Wilmington, North Carolina. He served on the CSS NORTH CAROLINA for two years. Per Source CMH (North Carolina), he subsequently served aboard the CSS RALEIGH under the command of Lieutenant Pembroke Jones. Wood was aboard the CSS RALEIGH when she steamed out of the Cape Fear River in May 1864 to escort blockade runners. It drove several Union vessels out to sea but ran aground on a sand bar on its return upriver and its keel was broken as the tide went down. Wood then served with a battery below Fort Fisher; was on the CSS NORTH CAROLINA until she sank; served at Battery Cameron near Wilmington, and after the evacuation of Wilmington, was on duty at Drewry's Bluff until it was abandoned. He was with John Taylor Wood in early February 1864 and took part in the night assault on the USS UNDERWRITER in the Neuse River near New Bern, North Carolina. He signed a Parole of Honor as a Prisoner of War in Richmond, Virginia, April 20, 1865. Wood was given permission to go to his home in Oxford, North Carolina. A claim for pension was filed on July 15, 1915 by his widow, Fannie J. Wood, age 70, of Oxford, Granville County, North Carolina, which states he was born July 11, 1844, that they married in the fall of 1865. It further states he died on November 2, 1907, and was buried in Elmwood Cemetery, Granville County, North Carolina. The pension was approved as 4th class. A notation on her application states that his photograph is found on page 298 of Volume V of *Histories of the Several Regiments and Battalions From North Carolina in the Great War, 1861-1865 (a.k.a. Clark's Regiments)*, by Walter Clark, 1905. [Source(s): UDC, MC of Svc.; NA, RG 45; NA, RG 109; CMH; Pensions (North Carolina); Names-1907; MR, 4, p. 444; McElroy; Stepp, "Burials;" Granville County Troops]

Wood, John S.
>1st Class Boy, Confederate States Navy. Wood enlisted on February 16, 1864, in Wilmington for the war. [Source(s): NA, RG 45]

Wood, Levin H. (Leven) (Caswell County, North Carolina)
>Seaman/Private, Confederate States Navy [Source "Stepp" gives his rank as "Landsman"]. Born in 1834 in Alamance County, North Carolina, Wood resided as a grocer in Caswell County, North Carolina, where he enlisted on April 29, 1861 at age 27 as a Private in Company A, 13th Regiment, North Carolina Troops. He transferred to the Confederate States Navy on February 19, 1862 for duty on the CSS VIRGINIA [CSS MERRIMAC]. One source shows that after the CSS VIRGINIA was blown up, he was attached to Company B, Virginia Rifles (Company A, 13th Regt North Carolina Troops) and participated in engagements at Drewry's Bluff. He died on January 17, 1888, and was buried in Linwood Cemetery, Alamance County, North Carolina.
>[Source(s): McElroy; Card File; Stepp, "Burials;" MR, I; Foenander; North Carolina Troops, V; *ORN* 2, 1, 310]

Woodall, Troy
>Ordinary Seaman, Confederate States Navy. Woodall enlisted on June 13, 1864 in Wilmington for the war. [Source(s): NA, RG 45]

Woodcock, J. C. (Pender County, North Carolina)
>Confederate States Navy. Woodcock was born in North Carolina in 1825. His claim for a pension filed on July 3, 1905, at age 82 years, listing his post office as Rooks, Pender County, North Carolina, states he enlisted in the Confederate States Navy in Wilmington, North Carolina [no date], and that his foot was mashed while in service in Wilmington, North Carolina. Doctor's statement says he "had his foot and ankle severely mashed at navy yard and cannot walk at times. [Has] one arm." His claim was approved as 3rd Class.
>[Source(s): Pensions (North Carolina)]

Woodell, Jerry (May be same as "Jerry Woodell, Robeson County, North Carolina," q.v.)
>Landsman, Confederate States Navy. Woodell enlisted on March 21, 1865, in Raleigh for the war. [Source(s): NA, RG 45]

Woodell (Woodel), Jerry (Robeson County, North Carolina) (May be same as "Jerry Woodell, enlisted March 21, 1865," q.v.)
>Landsman, Confederate States Navy. Born in Robeson County, North Carolina, Woodell resided there as a yeoman prior to enlisting in the Confederate States Navy in Robeson County on March 18, 1864 at age 44. He served as a Landsman, CSS ALBEMARLE, and on the Halifax Station, 1864. [Source(S): Foenander]

Woodhouse, Samuel
> Seaman, Landsman, Confederate States Navy.
> Woodhouse was born in North Carolina circa 1840 and resided in the Narrow Shore District, Currituck County, North Carolina. He served as a Seaman aboard the CSS FANNY per that ship's muster rolls from circa October 8, 1861 through at least November and as a Landsman aboard the ship as of December 20, 1861. He appears on the North Carolina Squadron payroll for the 1st quarter of 1862 (December1, 1861 - February 28, 1862. He is listed as having "run" on or before the payroll dated 28 February 28, 1862.
> [Source(s): 1860 Census (NC), NCCWSP]

Woodward, J. (Brunswick County, North Carolina)
> Landsman/Ordinary Seaman, Confederate States Navy. Woodward served aboard the wooden side-wheeled steamer tender CSS CASWELL on the Wilmington Station, North Carolina during, or sometime between, the period July 1861 to June 1862. Later, Woodward served on the CSS ARCTIC, Cape Fear River, North Carolina, 1862 -1863, and in 1864, as an Ordinary Seaman aboard the CSS NORTH CAROLINA, Cape Fear River, North Carolina.
> [Source(s): MR, 4, p. 444; Foenander]

Woolard (Wollard, Willard), Aaron (Beaufort County, North Carolina)
> Private, Company A, Confederate States Marine Corps. Born on February 11, 1845, Woolard enlisted in Raleigh, North Carolina on October 6, 1864 [Source "Pensions (North Carolina)" lists enlistment date as October 1, 1864]. He served on the Charleston, South Carolina station as a Private of the Marine guard on board the ironclad CSS COLUMBIA to February 7, 1865. Woolard transferred to the CSS INDIAN CHIEF on February 8, 1865. His name appears on a roll of prisoners of war at Point Lookout, Maryland which states he was captured at Amelia Court House, Virginia on April 6, 1865. His name appears as a signature to an Oath of Allegiance to the United States subscribed and sworn to at Point Lookout on June 21, 1865 listing his place of residence as Beaufort County, North Carolina. Description as follows: Complexion, fair; hair, light; eyes, blue; height 5 feet 8 inches. His application for pension dated June 28, 1901 states he is aged 56, that he served in the "Marine Core" [sic], and that he "was hurt by a heavy gun in February 1865." Woolard married Sarah E. McKeel in Beaufort County, North Carolina, on February 24, 1875. He died on January 20, 1904 and was buried in the Asbury Methodist Church Cemetery, Bunyon [sic] (Bunyan), North Carolina east of Washington, North Carolina.
> [Source(s): Donnelly-ENL; Card File; NA; North Carolina Troops, Doc. # 0185, p. 1; Pensions (North Carolina); "Beaufort County Sailors"]

Woolard, William Henry (Beaufort County, North Carolina)
> Confederate States Marine Corps. Enlisting on October 6, 1864 [Source "Pension (North Carolina)" lists his enlistment date October 9, 1864], Woolard served as a Private in the Marine guard aboard the CSS COLUMBIA, October 6, 1864 – February 7, 1865. He transferred to the CSS INDIAN CHIEF on February 8, 1865 and was captured at Harper's Farm, Virginia, on April 6, 1865. Sent as a Prisoner of War to Point Lookout, Maryland, he was released as a "sick Prisoner of War" on oath on June 3, 1865. He died on his farm at Hunter's Bridge on March 10, 1892 while working in the fields [NOTE: this information is contradicted by the following]. His pension claim filed on July 1, 1901 at age 60, listing his post office as Hunter's Bridge, Beaufort County, North Carolina was approved at "Class 4."
> [Source(s): Pensions (North Carolina); Card File; Donnelly-ENL; Donnelly]

Woolvin, John J.
> Landsman, Confederate States Navy. Born in North Carolina, 1823, Woolvin enlisted on October 25, 1864 in Raleigh for the war. He served as a Landsman on the CSS ARCTIC, Cape Fear River, North Carolina, 1863, and the CSS RALEIGH, in North Carolina and Virginia waters, 1864. He transferred from the Confederate States Navy to 2nd Company I, 10th Regiment, North Carolina State Troops (1st Regiment, North Carolina Artillery) on February 26, 1864.
> [Source(s): Card file; NA, RG 45; NA, RG 109; Foenander]

Wooster, Emmond[?]
> Seaman, Confederate States Navy. Wooster enlisted on January 1, 1864, in Wilmington for the war.
> [Source unknown]

Worth, J. M.
> Commander's Clerk, North Carolina Navy. Served aboard the NCS WINSLOW.
> [Source: NCS]

Wright, George
Pilot, North Carolina Navy. Served aboard the NCS WINSLOW.
[Source: NCS]

Wright, John A. (Camden County, North Carolina)
"Private," Confederate States Navy. Wright served previously as a Private in Captain G. G. Luke's Independent Company. He was assigned to 1st Company H, 32nd Regiment, North Carolina Troops, in September 1861, while a prisoner of war at Fort Columbus, New York Harbor, New York, or Fort Warren, Boston Harbor, Massachusetts. He was paroled at Fort Warren on December 11, 1861 and transferred for exchange. Reported to be "acting with the enemy at Hatteras" when the company was disbanded on April 2, 1865[?]. He enlisted in Camden County, North Carolina, on July 7, 1863, for the war, as a Private in Company B, 68th Regiment, North Carolina Troops. He transferred to the Confederate States Navy on April 5, 1864. He was said to have served aboard the CSS ALBEMARLE. Wright signed a testimony relative to the Pension Claim of Jos. S. Dunton (q.v.), Confederate States Navy, Currituck County, North Carolina.
[Source(s): Card File, Pension (North Carolina); North Carolina Troops, IX]

Wright, Joshua Creacy (Norfolk, Virginia)
Private, Confederate States Army//Midshipman, Confederate States Navy. Wright enlisted in Chowan County, North Carolina on April 25, 1863 "for the War" in Company B, 3rd Battalion, North Carolina Artillery. He was detailed and attached to the staff of General W. H. C. Whiting as post courier, in December 1863. Wright was absent detailed through December 1864. On the recommendation of General Whiting, Wright was appointed by President Davis as a Midshipman in the Confederate States Navy. He served aboard the side wheeled steamer CSS PATRICK HENRY, James River, Virginia, 1864, but resigned from Naval service in early 1865 and joined the 15th Battalion, North Carolina Cavalry, serving in the company of Captain Thomas S. Capeheart [NOTE: No "Captain Capeheart" seen in North Carolina Troops, I]. One source indicates he was paroled at Greensboro, North Carolina, April 28, 1865 with the remark: "Courier on General Whiting's staff," while another states his unit was disbanded in the trans-Mississippi Department, at the close of the war and that he made his way back to his old home at Norfolk, Virginia. He was a resident of Houston, Texas in 1899.
[Source(s): *ORN* 2, 1, 300; *News and Observer* (Raleigh, North Carolina) dated May 28, 1899, page 8; Foenander]

Wright, Milton (Richmond County, North Carolina)
Confederate States Navy. Wright was born in North Carolina in 1846, enlisted in 1864, and served in Company F, Naval Battalion, Confederate States Navy. His name appears on a roll of Prisoners of War at Point Lookout, Maryland., which states he was captured at Harpers Farm on April 6, 1865 and confined at Point Lookout until released Jun 22, 1865. Name appears as a signature (by mark) to an Oath of Allegiance to the United States, subscribed and sworn to at Point Lookout June 22, 1865 listing his place of residence as Richmond County, North Carolina. Description: Complexion light; hair yellow; eyes blue; height 5'7 ½." His original certificate of release and Oath of Allegiance from Point Lookout prison, dated June 22, 1865, are in his pension file. He resided as a farmer, in 1880, with his wife, Eliza, and five children (eldest child born 1871) at Smiths, Robeson County, North Carolina. His pension application filed on August 1, 1921, at age 76 years, listing his post office as Parkton, Robeson County, North Carolina, states he enlisted in the Confederate States Navy in 1864. It was approved at 4th class. A claim filed on June 29, 1930 by his widow, Eliza J. Wright, at age 80 years, and listing her post office as Parkton, Robeson County, North Carolina, states she married Mr. Wright on April 6, 1871, and that her husband died on February 10, 1930. It was approved as Class B. A claim filed for increase in 1937 [possibly December 1936] by Mrs. Wright at age 88 years in Wake County was approved as Class A.
[Source(s): NA, RG 109; Pension (North Carolina); Foenander; *North Carolina State Archives*; Census North Carolina), *1880*]

Wright, P. J.
Landsman, Confederate States Navy. Wright served aboard the CSS ARCTIC, Cape Fear River, North Carolina, 1863.
[Source(s): Foenander; *ORN* 2, 1, 279.]

Wright, Sidney Robert (middle initial sometimes incorrectly shown as "W") (Caswell County, North Carolina)
Private, Confederate States Army// Landsman, Confederate States Navy. Wright was born and resided as either a painter or carpenter in Caswell County, North Carolina, where he enlisted on May 1, 1861 at age 25 as a Sergeant in Company D, 13th Regiment, North Carolina Troops, but was reduced to Private on October 31, 1861. He transferred to the Confederate States Navy on February 15, 1862 for duty as a Landsman on the CSS VIRGINIA (CSS

MERRIMAC), Hampton Roads, Virginia.
[Source(s): Card File; North Carolina Troops, V; *ORN* 2, 1, 310; Foenander; MR, I; Quarstein]

Wright, Thomas
Pilot, North Carolina Navy. Wright served as a Pilot aboard the NCS WINSLOW.
[Source: NCS]

Wroton [Wroten, Wooten], Thomas O. (Beaufort County, North Carolina)
Ship's Steward; Seaman; Captain of Afterguard, Confederate States Navy ["Landsman" (see Stepp)]. Born in New Bern, Craven County, North Carolina, on December 3, 1841 [Another source gives the date as 1842], Wroten enlisted from Beaufort County, North Carolina, at age 22 on April 22, 1861 for twelve months in Company K, 1st Regiment, North Carolina Troops (1st Regiment, North Carolina Artillery). Captured at Fort Hatteras on Aug 29, 1861, he was confined at Fort Warren, Massachusetts, until paroled for exchange on February 3, 1862. He was present or accounted for until transferred to the Confederate States Navy on July 19, 1863. He served as a Ship's Steward and Seaman aboard the CSS NORTH CAROLINA, Cape Fear River, North Carolina, 1864. He was highly commended by his commander, J. W. Cooke, in a dispatch from Plymouth, North Carolina, dated May 7, 1864 while serving abroad CSS ALBEMARLE. He later served as Captain of the Afterguard on the CSS TALLAHASSEE. Wroten died in Winston (now Winston-Salem), North Carolina, on August 15, 1887 and was buried in Cedar Grove Cemetery in New Bern, Craven County, North Carolina. A claim for pension filed July 16, 1909 by his widow, Virginia Wroten, listing her post office as Durham, Durham County, states her husband served on the steamer CSS NORTH CAROLINA. The claim was approved at 4th class. The witnesses for the claim were J. E. Smith and James Maglenn (q.v.) of Raleigh, North Carolina.
[Source(s): MR, I & IV; ORN, 1, 9, p. 771 (Listed as an Ordinary Seaman); ORN, 2, 1, p. 294-296; North Carolina Troops, I; North Carolina CVGL ; Foenander; Pensions (North Carolina); www.thewashingtongrays.homestead.com; "Beaufort County Sailors;" www.ncgenweb.us/nccivwar/rosters/10cok.htm; UDC CGR; Card File; NA, RG 109]

Wyatt, T. C.
Landsman/Confederate States Navy. Wyatt enlisted on February 18, 1864 in Raleigh for the war.
[Source(s): NA, RG 45]

Wyatt, Thomas
Ordinary Seaman, Confederate States Navy.
Wyatt served as an Ordinary Seaman aboard the CSS EDWARDS (later renamed the CSS FORREST) per his shipping articles signed on July 25, 1861. Muster and payroll records indicated he served aboard the CSS FORREST as an Ordinary Seaman per that ship's muster roll dated October 30, 1861, and as late as the 1st quarter of 1862. He received a partial payment on February 13, 1862 at Gosport Navy Yard following the burning of the CSS FORREST at Elizabeth City on February10, 1862 to prevent her capture. His name appears on the receiving ship CSS UNITED STATES payroll ending March 31, 1862. Wyatt was reported unfit for service by a surgeon on March 5, 1862 and discharged from the receiving ship.
[Source: NCCWSP]

Wyatt, Wyley A. (Gaston County, North Carolina)
Private, Confederate States Army//Landsman, Confederate States Navy. Born on August 27, 1836 [1839, per source "Cloninger"], Wyatt resided and enlisted in Gaston County, North Carolina, on July 30, 1861, at age 21, as a Private, in Company B, 28th Regiment, North Carolina Troops (North Carolina Troops entry shows Company B). Captured at Hanover Court House, Virginia, May 27, 1862, he was confined at Fort Monroe, Virginia and at Fort Columbus, New York Harbor. Exchanged at Aiken's Landing, James River, Virginia, August 5, 1862, he rejoined his unit and was again captured at Fredericksburg, Virginia, December 13, 1862, and exchanged later that same month. Wyatt transferred to the Confederate States Navy, on April 3, 1864 where he served as a Landsman aboard the CSS VIRGINIA II, James River, Virginia, 1864-1865. He was later attached as a Private to Company E, 1st Regiment, Semmes' Naval Brigade in April 1865. He surrendered and was paroled at Greensboro, North Carolina, April 26, 1865. He died on September 23, 1907 and was buried in the West Salem Cemetery, Attala, Mississippi.
[Source(s): North Carolina Troops, VIII; Army to Navy; Card File; Foenander; Cloninger]

Y - Z

Yonce, E. F.
Landsman, Confederate States Navy. Yonce enlisted in Wilmington for the war.
[Source(s): NA, RG 45]

York, Franklin (Forsyth County, North Carolina)
Landsman, Confederate States Navy. Born in Randolph County, North Carolina, in 1840, the son of Adam York, York resided there with his father and siblings, in 1850, but at some time prior to the war worked as a Seaman, location unknown. He enlisted in the Confederate States Navy on March 18 (another source lists the date as the 21st), 1864, in Raleigh (Camp Holmes) from Colonel Maston's 71st Regiment, North Carolina Militia, Forsyth County. Description given as follows: Age "18" [NOTE: age does not match birth year]; eyes grey; hair light; complexion fair; height 5'10;" born in Randolph County, shoemaker. York served as a Landsman, CSS ALBEMARLE, and on the Halifax Station, 1864.
[Source(s): NA, RG 45; Card File; Foenander]

York, W. J.
Landsman, Confederate States Navy. York enlisted on August 29, 1864 in Raleigh for the war.
[Source(s): NA, RG 45]

Yost, John (Jno) (Rowan County, North Carolina)
Landsman, Confederate States Navy. Born in North Carolina in 1824, Yost enlisted in the Confederate States Navy on October 12, 1862 (another source states Oct 14, 1863 at Camp Holmes, near Raleigh) in Wilmington, North Carolina. He served as a Landsman, CSS ARCTIC, 1863. A claim for pension filed May 30, 1901 by his widow, Elizabeth Yost, at age 74, listing her post office as China Grove, Rowan County, North Carolina, states he enlisted in the Confederate States Navy in Wilmington, North Carolina, on or about October 12, 1862. Note reads, "Husband died since the war." The pension claim was approved.
[Source(s): MR, 4, p. 447; Pension (North Carolina); NA, RG 45; Foenander]

Young, Andrew Jackson (L. F.)
Landsman, Confederate States Navy. Young enlisted on December 10 (12), 1863, in Wilmington (Raleigh) for the war, and served as a Landsman, CSS ARCTIC, Cape Fear River, North Carolina, 1863. He signed an April 11, 1902 affidavit for William L. Snider [q.v.], Confederate States Navy veteran of Davidson County, North Carolina.
[Source(s): NA, RG 45; Pensions (North Carolina); Foenander]

Young, James R. (Wake County, North Carolina)
Landsman/Confederate States Navy (Naval Battalion) Young's name appears on a roll of Prisoners of War at Point Lookout, Maryland, which states that he was captured at Appomattox April 7, 1865, and confined at Point Lookout until released Jun 22, 1865. His name also appears as a signature to an Oath of Allegiance to the United States, subscribed and sworn to at Point Lookout, Maryland, Jun 22, 1865, listing his place of residence as Wake County. Description: complexion fair; hair brown; eyes hazel; height 5'4 ¾."
[Source(s): NA, RG 109]

Young, John W.
Seaman, Confederate States Navy.
Young served as a Seaman aboard the CSS ELLIS per an August 1, 1861 entry in her logbook. Payroll records indicate he served aboard the CSS ELLIS as a member of the North Carolina Squadron from at least August 1, 1861 through May 1862. Captured at the Battle of Elizabeth City, he was carried to Roanoke Island on February 10, 1862 where he was paroled on February 12, 1862 and returned to Elizabeth City. His name appears on the receiving ship CSS UNITED STATES payroll ending March 31, 1862.
[Source: NCCWSP]

Young, William
Confederate States Navy.
Young's name appears on the receiving ship CSS UNITED STATES payroll ending March 31, 1862. His name appears on the North Carolina Squadron payroll for the 1st quarter of 1862 (January 10, 1862 - March 6, 1862).
[Source: NCCWSP]

Young, William H. (Granville County, North Carolina)

Confederate States Army//Confederate States Navy. No pension found. Young was an attorney from Granville County, North Carolina. He enlisted at 24 years of age in April 1861 as a Private in Company D., 12th Regiment, North Carolina Troops. He was promoted to Corporal, but "Quit" in June 1861 to join the Confederate Navy. He left the Confederate States Navy to become Adjutant of the 55th Regiment, North Carolina Troops in November 1862, and was appointed a Lieutenant in Company F (Stonewall Boys), 54th Regiment, North Carolina Troops in August 1863. He served only three months before being captured with most of his unit at Rappahannock Bridge, Virginia on November 7, 1863. Young was sent to Old Capitol Prison, then to Johnson's Island from which he was released on June 13, 1865.

[Source(s): McCaslin, p.153; Card File]

Young, W. S.

Landsman, Confederate States Navy. Young enlisted on June 11, 1864, in Raleigh for the war.

[Source(s): NA, RG 45]

Younts, E. F. (Ashe County, North Carolina)

Confederate States Navy. Younts enlisted in the Confederate States Navy on August 19, 1863 in Wilmington, North Carolina.

[Source(s): MR, 4, p. 448]

APPENDIX I: NOTES

NOTE #1: The annotation "Disallowed" on a North Carolina application for Confederate pension did not necessarily mean the individual's service was not proven. It often indicated that there was either insufficient evidence of a qualifying disability, as was true in the case of some subsequent applications for pension upgrades, or that the applicant did not meet the other requirements to qualify for the state-funded pension, perhaps, for example, due to having too much money or property.

NOTE #2: Entries identified as serving with the "North Carolina Squadron," but listing no North Carolina connection may or may not be North Carolinians.

NOTE: Dates of entrance into Confederate Naval service may vary due to differences in dates of enlistment or conscription and actual swearing-in to the Navy.

NOTE: Personnel hailing from foreign countries or states other than North Carolina are listed if they served in a military unit from North Carolina prior to or following their naval service or had some other substantial link to North Carolina (e. g. born in North Carolina).

NOTE: Contradictory records from sources may indicate inaccurately transcribed information, confusion resulting from the mixing of records from two different persons, or both.

NOTE: Special thanks to Josh Howard, Research Branch, North Carolina Department of Cultural Resources, Raleigh, North Carolina, for his invaluable assistance in locating entries for this roster. Because of Josh's hard work and dedication, the names of four hundred and seventeen Confederate States Army soldiers who transferred to the Confederate States Navy were identified and included in the roster. A simple "thank you" does not seem enough.

NOTE: The letters NCS before a ship's name designates "North Carolina Ship."

APPENDIX II: CITATION ABBREVIATIONS FOR SOURCES CITED

"Absentees" "Absentees and Deserters from Various Companies Lurking in Those Counties of the 1st Congressional District Over Which Colonel J. W. Hinton Has Control,"Folder #13, Box 65 "Miscellaneous," Civil War Collection, North Carolina Division of Historical Resources, Raleigh, North Carolina.

Academy *Academy on the James, The Confederate Naval School*, by R. Thomas Campbell, Shippensburg, Pa., Burd Street Press, c. 1998.

"Army to Navy" "Confederate States Army to Navy Transfers" by Terry Foenander [http://home.ozconnect.net/tfoen/transfers.htm]

Ashe Family www.ashefamily.info/ashefamily/4188.htm

"Asheville Times" "Asheville Times" (November 18, 1917) (November 18, 1917)

Beall   Report by Confederate States Marine Corps Commandant Colonel Lloyd J. Beall dated October 30, 1864.

"Beaufort County Sailors" "Beaufort County Sailors Who Served in the Confederate States Navy and Marine Corps," www.ncgenweb.us/beaufort/mil/boConfederate States Navy.htm

Bizzell *Sampson County Heritage, North Carolina*, by O. M. Bizzell.

Booker *Historical and Traditional Tar Heel Stories from the Colorful Central Coastal Plain* by Louise R. Booker, (Johnson Publishing Company, Murfreesboro, North Carolina).

Roster of North Carolinians in Confederate Naval Service

Booth *Records of Louisiana Confederate Soldiers and Louisiana Confederate Commands*, 3 volumes, by Andrew B. Booth, Compiler, 1920.

Boyd Boyd, Henry P. "Hank," Chattanooga, TN, August 2010.

Bradley, Vol. 1 *North Carolina Confederate Militia and Home Guard* Bradley, Vol. 1, Records, Volume 1, Militia Letter Book, *1862-1864,* abstracted by Dr. Stephen E. Bradley, Jr.

Bradley, Vol. 2 *North Carolina Confederate Militia and Home Guard* Records, Volume2, Militia Letter Book, *1864-1865, and Home Guard Orders,* abstracted by Dr. Stephen E. Bradley, Jr.

BRGS *Cleveland and Rutherford Counties, North Carolina, Confederate Soldiers, 1861-1865*, by Broad River Genealogical Society, Shelby, North Carolina (1981)

Bright, et al *CSS NEUSE: A Question of Iron and Time*, Bright, Leslie S., William H. Rowland, and James C. Bordon, Raleigh Division of Archives and History, 1981.

BrunswickVets (1908) /www.usgwarchives.net/nc/brunswick/vets/vets1908.html.

Callahan *List of Officers of the Navy of the United States and of the Marine Corps from 1775 to 1900*, ed. by Edward W. Callahan; (originally published by R. R. Hamersly & Company, New York (1901); reprinted by Olde Soldier Books, Inc., Gaithersburg, Maryland, no date).

Card File Card File, North Carolinians in Confederate Service, Historical Publications Branch, North Carolina Division of Historical Resources, Raleigh, North Carolina [copied from cards on file at the National Archives, Washington, DC].

Casstevens *The Civil War and Yadkin County, North Carolina, A History,* by Frances H. Casstevens, McFarland & Company Jefferson, North Carolina (1997).

Chauncey Mr. James E. Chauncey, Norfolk, Virginia. Letter to the Search Room, North Carolina State Archives, received February 10, 1978.

Census (GA), 1870 Census (GA), 1870

Census (Maryland), 1860 Census (Maryland), 1860

Census (Neb.), 1880 Census (Neb.), 1880

Census (NC), 1910 Census (North Carolina), 1910

Census (NC), 1900 Census (North Carolina), 1900

Census (NC), 1870 Census (North Carolina), 1870

Census (NC), 1860 Census (North Carolina) 1860

Census (NC), 1850 Census (North Carolina), 1850

Census (North Carolina) United States Census, North Carolina, 1790 (Ancestry.com) 1890 (Ancestry.com)

Census (TN), 1860 Census (Tennessee), 1860

Census (US), 1860 Census (United States), 1860

Census (VA), 1860 Census (Virginia), 1860

"Chronicles" *Chronicles of the Cape, 1660 Fear River -1916*, by James Sprunt, Edwards and Broughton Company, Raleigh, North Carolina, 1916.

"Char. News" (June 5, "Charlotte News" (Charlotte, North Carolina), June 5, 1910 (1910)

"Char. Obs." (April 3, "Charlotte Observer" (Charlotte, North Carolina), April 3, 1910) 1910

"Citizen News-Record," "Citizen News-Record" (Moore County, July 8, 1987 North Carolina), July 8, 1987.

Clark *Histories of the Several Regiments and Battalions From North Carolina in the Great War, 1861-1865, (a.k.a. Clark's Regiments)*, by Walter Clark, 1905.

Cloninger Bruce Cloninger (Cherryville, North Carolina)

CMACSSN "Crew Members Aboard the CSS Neuse, March-October 1864," CSS NEUSE Historic Site, NC Historic Sites

CMH *Confederate Military History* (Volume 4, page 377) edited by General Clement A. Evans (Volumes I-XII), The Confederate Publishing Company, Atlanta, GA, 1899.

CN Subj. Files Fold3, Confederate Navy subject file N - Personnel; NA – Complements, rolls, lists of persons, etc., CSS Alabama – CSS Neuse]

Cooke Wild, Wicked Wartime Wilmington (2009) by Robert J. Cooke

Cruse *Cabarrus Confederate Veterans, In Alphabetical Order*, complied by Bernard W. Cruse, Jr., Cabarrus Genealogical Society, Concord, North Carolina (2001).

"CSMC Officer Burials" "Alphabetical List of Confederate States Marine Officers' Process of Burial" [www.Confederate States Navyavy.org/Confederate States Marine Corps/Confederate States Marine Corps, alpha, name.htm]

CN Subj. Files Fold3, Confederate Navy subject file N - Personnel; NA – Complements, rolls, lists of persons, etc., CSS Alabama – CSS Neuse]

CSS North Carolina, 3rd Qtr., Roster, CSS NORTH CAROLINA, 3rd Quarter, 1864. 1864

CSS TENNESSEE "Crew List of the Confederate States Steamer TENNESSEE" Terry Foenander [http://hub.dataline.net.au/~tfoen/tennessee.htm].

"CSR" "Compiled Service Records," National Archives Microfilm Copy, North Carolina Division of Historical Resources.

CVM *Confederate Veteran Magazine*, S. A Cunningham, Editor, 1893 – 1932, Nashville, Tennessee CVM.

CWC Civil War Collection, Box 41, North Carolina Division of Historical Resources, North Carolina Department of Cultural Resources, Raleigh, North Carolina CWDTS Civil War Days and Those Surnames http://civilwarthosesurnames.blogspot.com/2010/12/united-states-confederate-navy-of.html

"CW-E," April 19, 1979 "Charlotte Weekly-East," April 19, 1979, p. 29. CWNavalChron. *Civil War Naval Chronology, 1861-1865*," Naval History Division, 1966.

CWSSI Civil War Soldier Surname Index, Civil War Soldier Records of North Carolina "Wall" www.censusdiggins.com/nc_civil_war_wall.html

Cloninger Cloninger, Bruce (Cherryville, NC)

Comer, *Rogers Rogers: Our Common Bond*, compiled by James Vann Comer (1990)

Cyclopedia Cyclopedia of Eminent and Representative Men of the Carolina of the Nineteenth Century, Vol. II, by Edward McGrady and Samuel A'Court Ashe, Madison, Wisconsin, 1892.

"Daily Confed." (4/18/64) "Daily Confederate" (Raleigh), April 18, 1864

"Daily Confed." (12/25/64) "Daily Confederate" (Raleigh), December 25, 1864

"Daily Confed." (4/23/64) "Daily Confederate" (Raleigh). May 23, 1864

"Daily Confed." (1/2/65) "Daily Confederate" (Raleigh), January 2, 1865

"Daily Confed." (2/18/65) "Daily Confederate" (Raleigh), February 18, 1865

"Daily Confed." (5/23/65) "Daily Confederate" (Raleigh), May 23, 1865

"Daily Dispatch," February "Daily Dispatch" (Richmond, Virginia), February 19, 19, 1862 1862)

Dallas   Dallas, John T. e-mail to author, dated January 17, 2005.

DANFS   *Dictionary of American Navy Fighting Ships*   www.hazegray.org/danfs/csn/c.txt)

Darden   Major Louis Charles Latham Chapter, UDC, Chapter Historian Mrs. J. W. Darden, Plymouth, North Carolina.

Davis, November 17, 1864 Davis, James C., Letter, November 17, 1864, "Fayetteville Observer," [no date].

Derelicts *Derelict: an account of ships lost at sea in general commercial traffic and a brief history of blockade runners stranded along the North Carolina coast, 1861-1865*, by James Sprunt. Wilmington, N. C., 1920.

DNCB, III, p.370   *Dictionary of North Carolina Biography,* III, p. 370.

Document #0314-5-16 Document #0314-5-16 [No explanation on card]

Donnelly   Letter from Ralph W. Donnelly to James Vann Comer,   Donnelly July 29, 1987 [Copy on file in the "North Carolinians in Confederate Naval Service" Materials, Vertical File, Military Collection, State Archives of North Carolina].

Donnelly – ENL   *Service Records of Confederate Enlisted Marines* (1974) by Ralph W. Donnelly.

Donnelly – RL   *The Confederate States Marine Corps: The Rebel Leathernecks* (1989) by Ralph W. Donnelly.

Donnelly-BS   *Biographical Sketches of the Commissioned Officers of the   Confederate States Marine Corps*, by Ralph W. Donnelly.

Dowless   Mr. Layton Dowless, Whiteville, North Carolina.

"DR," March 19, 1889 "Daily Review" (Wilmington, North Carolina), March 19, 1889.

Driver   *Confederate Sailors, Marines, and Signalmen from   Virginia and Maryland*, by Robert J. Driver, Jr. (Heritage Books, 2007).

Dudley   "Going South: United States Navy Officer Resignations & Dismissals" on the Eve of the Civil War, by William S. Dudley, Washington, D.C.: Naval Historical Foundation © 1981

Duke Papers   "Shipping Articles [Confederate States Navy], June 13-22, 1864, Raleigh, North Carolina" (Xerographic copy in the Washington Duke Papers, Perkins Library, Duke University, Durham, North Carolina).

Ellis   John E. Ellis, "Confederate States Navy Research Library, Mobile, AL [www.Confederate States Navyavy.org]

ELLIS Crew List   CSS Crew List www.rblong.net/ncsquadron/Ellis%20Lists.htm)

"Ellis, W. A." *Norwich University, 1819-1911: Her History, Her Graduates, Her Roll of Honor*, William Arba Ellis, Editor,

Published by Major Grenville M. Dodge, Montpellier, VT, 1911.

Evans *Confederate Military History*, Vol. VI, Clement Anselm Evans, Published by Evans' Confederate Publishing Company, Atlanta, GA (1899).

"Fay. Obs." (Nov. 5, 1863) "Fayetteville Observer" (Fayetteville, North Carolina, November 5, 1865).

"Fay. Obs." (Dec. 18, 1863) "Fayetteville Observer" (Fayetteville, North Carolina, December 18, 1863).

"Fay. Obs." (Nov. 14, 1864) "Fayetteville Observer" (Fayetteville, North Carolina, November 14, 1864).

"Fay. Obs." (Nov. 24, 1864) "Fayetteville Observer" (Fayetteville, North Carolina, November 14, 1864.

Findagrave WWW.findagrave.com

Flake "Elijah Wilson Flake's History," by Michael Flake, posted February 15, 2006 on www.genforum.genealogy.com/flake/messages/438.html.

Foenander Foenander, Terry, Toowoomba, Queensland, Australia. [http://home.ozconnect.net/tfoen.htm]

Fold3, Midshipmen Fold3, Acting Midshipmen Appointed from Civilian Life, CSN.

Fold3, USN Resignees "List of Officers in the Navy of the Confederate States Who Resigned Their Positions in the United States Navy"
(Fold3)

"FSW" (12/24/64) "Fayetteville Semi-Weekly" (December 24, 1864)

Gaines *Encyclopedia of Civil War Shipwrecks: Poems*, by Craig Gaines

Gaston County Veterans "Roster of Confederate Veterans of Gaston County, North Carolina," Civil War Collection, Box 64 (Misc. Records), Folder #3, State Archives of North Carolina.

Georgia Roster Roster of the Confederate Soldiers of Georgia, 1861-1865, by Lillian Henderson

Goss Mildred Goss, Creedmore, North Carolina.

Granville County Troops "Roster of Granville County Troops," Civil War Collection, Box 64 (Misc. Records), Folder #3, State Archives of North Carolina.

Gravestone Records Confederate Gravestone Records, v. X, p. X, North v. X, p. X Carolina Division, United Daughters of the Confederacy, North Carolina Department of Archives and History, Raleigh, North Carolina.

Grissom Grover Grissom, 236 Sweetwater Hills Dr., Hendersonville, North Carolina 28791.

Hamilton Hamilton, Oliver C., and Calier G. Hamilton Papers, Private Collection #1215, North Carolina Division of Historical Resources (Archives), Raleigh, North Carolina.

Hardy *Beaufort's Old Burying Ground, North Carolina*, by Diane Hardy, Marilyn Collins, and Mamré Wilson (1999)

Hasty and Winfree *The Civil War Roster of Davie County, North Carolina, Biographies of 1,147 Men Before, During, and After the Conflict*, by Mary Alice Hasty and Hazel M. Winfree (2009).

Hilderman *They Went into the Fight Cheering*, by Walt Hilderman

Hill, DH *Bethel to Sharpsburg* (In Two Volumes), by Daniel Harvey Hill, Edwards and Broughton Company, Raleigh, North Carolina, 1926.

Hill, M. "The Crew of the CSS NEUSE: A Revised Roster" by Michael Hill, Research Branch Division of Archives and History, August 12, 1986.

Hoke Camp   *Roster of Confederate Soldiers in the War Between the States Furnished by Lincoln County, North Carolina, 1861-1865*, by W. J. Hoke Camp, UCV (ca. 1902).

Hollywood Cem. "Register of the Confederate Dead, Interred in Hollywood Cemetery," Richmond, Virginia, p. 52.

H and P Records   "Hospital and Prison Records for C. S. Marines and Navy," federally produced microfilm in the collection of the North Carolina State Archives, Raleigh, North Carolina.

Hosp. (No. 4), Wilm. "Registers of Confederate States Army General Military Hospital Number 4, Wilmington, North Carolina," Microfilm Collection, North Carolina State Archives, Raleigh, North Carolina.

Howard   Howard, Josh (Historian, Research Branch, North Carolina Division of Historical Resources, Raleigh, North Carolina.

"HR" (Sept. 28, 1864)   "Hillsborough Recorder" (September 28, 1864)

HSC   *Heritage of Sampson County*, by O. M. Bizzell

http://civilwarnenc.ning.com   http://civilwarnenc.ning.com

Jackson   *The Big Book of the Cape Fear River*, by Claude V. Jackson, III, and Jack E. Fryar, Jr., Editor

Journal   *Journal of the Congress of the Confederate States of America, 1861-1865, Vol. II*, Washington, DC, US Government Printing Office, 1904.

http://hotchkissfamily.lbbhost.com/CWC.html Hotchkiss Family

Kearney   Timothy Kearney (6 Sept. 2002).

King   Joel King Papers, Manuscript Dept., Duke University.

Labree   *The Confederate Soldier in the Civil War*, edited by Ben Labree, The Courier-Journal Job Printing Company, Publisher, Louisville, KY, 1895.

Lane Society   *Roster of Confederate Veterans from Chatham County, North Carolina*, by the Colonel John Randolph Lane Society, Siler City, North Carolina.

Lauderdale   "Confederate Burials," Vol. XV. Published by Lauderdale County Dept. of Archives and History, Inc., 1994.

Lib. of Virginia   Library of Virginia (www.lva.lib.va.us/whatwehave/milconnavy/ship_results.asp?page=5&ship

Lincoln Roster   *A Civil War Roster for Lincoln County, North Carolina, Lest We Forget*, by Beatties Ford Rifles Chapter, UDC, 1991.

LocateGrave   www.locategrave.org/l/4589279/Diggs

Long   Long, R. Bruce, "The Civil War in North Eastern North Carolina" [http://civilwarnenc.ning.com/]

Long -Email   Long, Bruce (Email dated 29 NOV 2013)

Lostcolleges   www.lostcolleges.com/college-of-physicians-and-surgeonsofba#:~:text=College%20of%20Physicians%20and%20Surgeons%20was%20incorporated%20in%201872%20with,336%20students%20from%2023%20states.

Lyon   "A Roster of Confederate Veterans of Columbus County, North Carolina," by Mrs. Homer L. (Kate Burkhead) Lyon, Jefferson Davis Chapter, #657, Whiteville, North Carolina [n.d.]

McCaslin *Portraits of Conflict: A Photographic History of North Carolina in the Civil War* by Dr. Richard B. McCaslin, University of Arkansas Press, 1997.

McDonald Papers McDonald Papers, Alexander Hamilton (PC#1761.1, State Archives of North Carolina).

McElroy McElroy, Captain W. H., Naval Department, United Confederate Veterans (UCV) (information drawn from several sources circa 1924-25. Card file in State Archives of North Carolina). [Source(s): North Carolina Division of Historical Resources, Archives and Records Section, Military Collection, Civil War Collection, Miscellaneous Records, Box #66, Folder #8 "Card File Roster of North Carolina Officers and Enlisted Men in Confederate States Navy."]

McLeod, April 24, 1871 Letter from William McLeod to Aaron Woolard, April 24, 1871 [Transcription in Donnelly to Comer letter, July 29, 1987].

McLeod, August 30, 1874 "Letter from William McLeod to Aaron Woolard, August 30, 1874" [Transcription in Donnelly to Comer letter, July 29, 1987].

McNeill Papers "McNeill Papers," Alexander Hamilton, Confederate Bureau of Conscription, Richmond, Virginia, January 17, 1865, Moore County, North Carolina, Civil War Collection.

Madre Mr. Philip Madre, Chocowinity, North Carolina.

Maffitt *The Life and Services of John Newland Maffitt,* by Emma Martin Maffitt (His Widow), The Neale Publishing Company, New York, and Washington, 1906.

Margaret Carter Carter, Ms. Margaret (Granddaughter of LT Jonathan Hanby "Margaret Carter" Carter, Confederate States Navy). E-mail dated June 23, 2009 including information extracted from the following sources: RIVER OF YEARS, book by Glenna W. Wilding and Sister Mary S. Carter; National Archives Pension Records (Mexican War) and National Archives (Old Army Records Branch), Washington, DC; OFFICIAL RECORDS: WAR OF THE REBELLION, Series I, Volumes 26 and 48; SKETCHES OF NORTH CAROLINA, book by Humphrey Hunters; and, a handwritten biographical sketch of the life of Jonathan H. Carter, thought to have been written by his youngest daughter, Kate G. Carter.

medicalantiques http://www.medicalantiques.com/civilwar/Medical_Authors_Faculty/Warren_Edward.htm

"Messenger," 2/19/1892 "Wilmington Messenger," February 19, 1892

"Messenger," 4/20/1892 "Wilmington Messenger," April 20, 1892

"Messenger," 5/16/1895 "Wilmington Messenger," May 6, 1895.

"Messenger," 5/20/1894 "Wilmington Messenger," May 20, 1894.

"Messenger," 3/25/1900 "Wilmington Messenger," March 25, 1900.

"MI," May-June 1994 "Military Images Magazine" (May-June 1994).

Moebs *Confederate States Navy Research Guide: Confederate Naval Imprints Described and Annotated, Chronology of Naval Operation and Administration, Marine Corps and Naval Officer Biographies, Description of Vessels, [and] Subject Bibliography*, by Thomas Truxton Moebs, Moebs Publishing Company, Williamsburg, Virginia, 1991.

Mosley Terry Mosley, Durham, North Carolina.

MR Moore's Roster (*Roster of the North Carolina Troops, In the War Between the States During the Years 1861, 1862, 1863, 1864, and 1865*, 4 Vols., Maj. John W. Moore).

Murray Murray, Will, Papers in possession of, 10055 Point Caswell Rd., Watha, North Carolina 28471 (Malpass was his wife's great, great, grandfather)]

NA, RG 109 National Archives War Department Collection of Confederate Records, Record Group 109, Carded Naval Records

NA, RG45 National Archives, Records of the Navy Department, Record Group 45, Shipping Articles, Confederate States Navy

"Names-1907" "Names and Locations of Confederate States Navy Veterans Published by the 'Richmond Examiner' Newspaper in 1907," Confederate States Navy Research Library, Mobile, AL [www.ConfederateStatesNavyavy.org].

Navy Gray *Navy Gray: Engineering the Confederate Navy on the Chattahoochee River*, by Maxine T. Turner

"Navy Register – 1865" "Registers of the Commissioned, Warrant, and Volunteer Officers of the Navy of the United States Including Officers of the Marine Corps and others to January 1, 1865," published by US Government Printing Office, Washington, DC, 1865.

NCpedia www.NCpedia.org/biography/manning-john]

NCCWSP "North Carolina Civil War Sailor's Project," NC Squadron, http://rblong.net/sailor/index.html

NCStndard "North Carolina Standard" (Raleigh, North Carolina), December 19, 1862.

NEUSE Roster Master Rolls of the Confederate Navy Department, Record   Group 45, National Archives, Washington, DC [CSS NEUSE, March - April 1864]

North Carolina Archives North Carolina Division of Historical Resources, Archives and Records Section, Raleigh, North Carolina.

North CarolinaCVGL *North Carolina Confederate Veteran Grave Locations* By Charlotte Carrere and Robert McAllister, Raleigh, NORTH CAROLINA: Carolina Abstractors, 1996.

North Carolina Death Coll. *North Carolina Death Collection, 1908 – 1996*   (Ancestry.com)

North CarolinaGENWEB /www.ncgenweb.us/nccivwar/rosters/27coc.htm

North CarolinaGENWEB www.ncgenweb.us/nccivwar/rosters/27cof.htm

North CarolinaGENWEB www.ncgenweb.us/nccivwar/rosters/37coh.htm

NC Gaz *The North Carolina Gazetteer, A Dictionary of Tar Heel Places*, by William S. Powell.

NCS   North Carolina Squadron [http://ncsquadron.wordpress.com] (Blog by R. B. Long)

NCSquadron   North Carolina Squadron   www.rblong.net/ncsquadron)

"NCStndrd" "North Carolina Standard" (Raleigh, North Carolina), December 9, 1862.

North Carolina *North Carolina Troops, 1861-1865: A Roster,* by Louis Troops, [Vol.]   Manarin and Weymouth T. Jordan.

NCT, Vol. [ ] Addenda *North Carolina Troops, 1861-1865: A Roster Vol. [ ]Addenda*, by Louis Manarin and Weymouth T. Jordan.

NCT, Doc. #xxxx   *North Carolina Troops, 1861-1865: A Roster,* by Louis Manarin and Weymouth T. Jordan, Letters Received Pertaining to Individual Service Records, Document No. xxxx, p. x.

North CarolinaVR *North Carolina Vital Records, 1720 – 1880* at   Ancestry.com.

"News-Argus" "News-Argus" [Goldsboro, North Carolina], September 10, 2008.

"N & O" [4 January 1885] "News and Observer" [Raleigh, North Carolina], January 4, 1885.

NPS   National Park Service, Civil War Soldiers and Sailors System, www.itd.nps.gov/cwss/

Norton   Norton, Edward, Winston-Salem, North Carolina, 26 August 08.

NUMA   National Underwater and Marine Agency (www.NUMA.net/expeditions/lost-confederate-fleet/)

"NYT"   "New York Times," 17 January 1865.

Oakdale, Davis   *Oakdale Cemetery: A Roster of Confederate Soldiers at   Rest*, compiled by J. Kenneth Davis, Jr., privately published (February 1, 2008).

Oakdale Cem. Rec. Vol 2 *Oakdale Cemetery Records, 1880-1919*, Vol. 2 by Delmas D. Haskett and William M. Reaves, Wilmington, NORTH CAROLINA: New Hanover Public Library, 1990.

Oakwood   "Confederate Burials at Oakwood Cemetery," created by the Olivia Raney Library, Charles Purser Compiler (Raleigh, North Carolina).

Oates   *The Story of Fayetteville and the Upper Cape Fear* by John Oates (1950) – "Cumberland Company Men on the Steamer NORTH CAROLINA," p. 408.

OCSN   *Officers in the Confederate States Navy, 1861 – 1865,* Office of Naval War Records, US Government Printing Office, Washington, DC (1898).

Oden   John Oden, Pinetown, North Carolina.

O-Donnell-Rosales   *Hispanic Confederates*

OCSN   *Officers in the Confederate States Navy, 1861-65*,   Officers Naval War Records Office, United States, US Government Printing Office, Washington, DC (1898).

"Officers, January 1, 1864" "Officers of the Navy of the Confederate States, January 1, 1864," www.Confederate States Navyavy.org/cmdrlist.jpg.

ONWR   Office of Naval War Records, Memorandum #8, Officers of the Confederate States Navy, 1861-1865, United States Navy Department, 1898.

ORN   *Official Records of the War of the Rebellion (Navy)*

Old City Cem., Raleigh,   Old City Cemetery, Raleigh, North Carolina

Pensions (FL)   Confederate Pension Applications, Florida State Archives, File No. A02854.

Pensions (North Carolina) "Confederate Pension Applications, North Carolina Div. of Historical Resources, Archives and Records Section, Raleigh, North Carolina.

Pensions (TN) (RD 1788) Tennessee [Confederate] Pension Applications, Tennessee State Archives, Nashville, TN.

PCNMC   Personnel Confederate Naval Marine Corps   www.http://membres.multimania.fr/confederatestatearmy/repertoire/p/0p.html

Powell   Powell, William S., *Dictionary of North Carolina Biography*, Volume 6 (T-Z)

PRCMO (page) Provisional Record of Confederate Medical Officers, Offered by the Confederate Veterans Committee, Medical Society, North Carolina, for corrections and additions, (page).

Purser, Charles Charles Purser, Garner, North Carolina

Quarstein   The CSS VIRGINIA: Sink Before Surrender, by John V. Quarstein (2012)

"Raleigh Spirit" "Raleigh Spirit of the Age," August 7, 1861 (p. 3, Col. 2)

RCWV "Record of Civil War Veteran, 1861-1865: List of Ex-Confederates (Soldiers/Widows" [Johnston County, North Carolina], C.056, 90003, North Carolina State Archives Microfilm.

"Register" *Register of Officers of the Confederate States Navy, 1861 – 1865*, As compiled by The Office of Naval Records and Library, United States Navy Dept., 1931, from all available data – United States Government Printing Office, Washington, DC, 1931.

Resolutions (GA of North "Resolutions of A Private Nature Passed by The of North Carolina General Assembly Of North Carolina At Its Second Extra Session, 1861"

Reveille The Confederate Reveille (Centennial Edition), published by The Pamlico Chapter of the Daughters of the Confederacy, Washington, North Carolina, May 10, 1898 (re-published 1964).

Richmond County Soldiers "Roster of Richmond County Soldiers," Civil War   Collection, Box 64 (Misc. Records), Folder #4, State Archives of North Carolina.

Rock Island (IL)   Rock Island (IL) Cemetery List Cemetery List

Roster Document   "Roster Document #0392 (pp. 79-80)"   [No explanation of this source listed on Card File]

Roster Doc. #0421   "Roster Document #0421   [No explanation of this source listed on Card File]

Roster, ("X") Regiment, Roster, ("X") Regiment, North Carolina Militia, Civil War North Carolina Militia Collection, Military Collection, North Carolina Division of Historical Resources, Raleigh, North Carolina.

Ruffin Chap., UDC   North Carolina Division, United Daughters of the Confederacy, Thomas Ruffin Chapter 349, Goldsboro, North Carolina

Rumple   *History of Rowan County* by Rumple, page 588.(North Carolina Division, UDC, Laura Wesson Chapter 1965, High Point, North Carolina)

St. Amand   "New Hanover County Roster of Confederate Troops, Including Confederate Pensioners and Roster of Cape Fear Camp. U.C.V.," compiled and by Jeannette Cox St. Amand, Wilmington, North Carolina, 1960.

Salter   Bryan Salter, Sea Level, North Carolina.

SBG   Seaman's Burial Ground, Ashley River, Charleston, SC.

"Sea Bird"   *ORN, 2, 1*, p.306 (CSSSea Bird, Muster Roll, July – November 1861).

Scharf *History of the Confederate States Navy* by J. Thomas Scharf, 1996 edition, Random House, NJ.

SHSP (Vol. 40) *Southern Historical Society Papers (Vol. 40)*

Shuford Chapt., UDC Abel A. Shuford Chapter (Records), UDC, Hickory, North Carolina

Sills   Milton Johnson Sills, Southern Pines, North Carolina.

Sloan   *Reminiscences of the Guilford Grays, Company B, 27th Regiment, North Carolina Troops*, by John A. Sloan (1883)

Smart, H. J., Letter Smart, H. J., (420 McGraw St., Healdon, OK 73438) Letter dated August 8, 1984.

Smithwick   "Roster of Franklin County Servicemen Who Participated in All Wars to Present Date, April 15, 1945" by Dr. D. T. Smithwick [unpublished, typed manuscript in Military Collection, misc. materials (various dates), State Archives of North Carolina].

Soldier's Home State Auditor's Papers, Soldier's Home, Record of Inmates, 1896-1924 (Aud. 7.5).

S.O. # 89 Special Order # 89, dated April 16, 1864, Army of N. Virginia [authorized transfer of Army personnel to Confederate States Navy]

S.O. # 92 Special Order # 92, dated April 3, 1864, Army of N. Virginia [authorized transfer of Army personnel to Confederate States Navy].

SoThndr Southern Thunder, Exploits of the Confederate States Navy by R. Thomas Campbell (1996)

Stanly Reunions "Stanly County Annual Reunions of Old Confederate Veterans, 1898-1928 (Camp 1369), Folder 1A, Box #65 "Miscellaneous," Civil War Collection, North Carolina Division of Historical Resources, Raleigh, North Carolina.

"Star," 1/14/1886 "Wilmington Star," January 14, 1886

"Star," 1/12/1935 "Wilmington Star," January 12, 1935

"Star," 6/2/1916 *"Wilmington Star,"* June 2, 1916

"State Auditor" State Auditor's Records, North Carolina Division of Historical Resources, North Carolina Department of Cultural Resources, Raleigh, North Carolina.

Stepp, "Burials" Burial locations of Confederate States Navy, Marine, and North Carolina Navy Personnel within North Carolina, compiled by Jeff Stepp (E-mail received July 15, 2009)

Sterling Sterling, J. G., 1602 Patterson Avenue, Winston-Salem, North Carolina, (1924).

Sullivan David Sullivan, Historian, Rutland, Massachusetts

"Tallahassee": ORN, Series 2, Vol. 1, p. 307 – "CSS TALLAHASSEE. Crew Roster."

"TGP" "The Greensborough Patriot" (Weekly), September 3, 1863, Greensboro, North Carolina.

"TGP" "The Greensborough Patriot" (Weekly), February 23, 1863, Greensboro, North Carolina.

"The State" "The State" magazine.

Thorpe Roster "Roster of Nash County Confederate Soldiers and Copy of   Edgecombe County Roster," by John H. Thorpe

"Times-Dispatch" "Times-Dispatch" (Richmond, VA), March 27, 1912 To Bear Arms *To Bear Arms, Civil War Information from Local Folks,* Chatham County and Adjacent Counties, by Zeb D. and Martha Harrington, Moncure, North Carolina, 1984.

Tomblin *Life in Jefferson Davis' Navy*, by Barbara Brooks Tomblin (2019), Naval Institute Press, Annapolis, Maryland.

Trull Letter on file from Mabel Holland Trull, Rt. 6, Creedmoor Road, Raleigh, North Carolina, North Carolina Troops Roster Project.

UDC, MC of Svc. United Daughters of the Confederacy, North Carolina Division, Application for a Military Cross of Service, North Carolina Division, U.D.C., Records of the Recorder of Crosses.

UDC, Bladen Starlets United Daughters of the Confederacy, North Carolina Division, Bladen Starlets Chapter 603, Elizabethtown, North Carolina. Records of chapter.

UDC, Dunham United Daughters of the Confederacy, North Carolina Division, John W. Dunham Chapter, 374, Wilson, North Carolina.

UDC, Cape Fear United Daughters of the Confederacy, North Carolina Division, Cape Fear Chapter 3, Wilmington, North Carolina. Records of chapter.

UDC, China Grove United Daughters of the Confederacy, North Carolina Division, China Grove Chapter, China Grove, North Carolina. Records of chapter.

UDC, Faison-Hicks United Daughters of the Confederacy, North Carolina Division, Faison-Hicks Chapter, Faison, North Carolina. Records of chapter.

UDC, Gordon United Daughters of the Confederacy, North Carolina Division, James B. Gordon Chapter, 211, Winston-Salem, North Carolina. Records of chapter.

UDC, Graham United Daughters of the Confederacy, North Carolina Division, Graham Chapter, 944, Graham, North Carolina. Records of chapter.

UDC, Greene United Daughters of the Confederacy, North Carolina Division, Greene Chapter, 1709, Snow Hill, North Carolina. Records of chapter.

UDC, Highland Boys United Daughters of the Confederacy, North Carolina Division, Highland Boys Chapter, St. Pauls, North Carolina. Records of chapter.

UDC, Recorder United Daughters of the Confederacy, Certificate of Eligibility for the Military Cross of Honor, North Carolina Division, UDC Records in possession of the Recorder of Crosses.

UDC, Singletary United Daughters of the Confederacy, North Carolina Division, Singletary Chapter, 313, Greenville, North Carolina. Records of chapter.

UDC, Southport United Daughters of the Confederacy, North Carolina Division, Southport Chapter, Southport, North Carolina. Records of chapter.

UDC, Waddell United Daughters of the Confederacy, North Carolina Division, Alfred Moore Waddell Chapter, 382, Kinston, North Carolina. Records of chapter.

Union Company Cemeteries *Union County Cemeteries 1710-1914 and Roster of Confederate and Revolutionary Soldiers (1958).*

USCWS United States Civil War Soldiers, 1861-1865, AncestryLibrary.com.

USCWSRP https://www.ancestry.com (U.S., Civil War Soldier Records and Profiles, 1861 - 1865

USNHC *Confederate Ships Afloat*, by US Naval Historical Center (2011)

USSCONSTITUTION http://captainsclerk.info/clerk/clerk.html (USS CONSTITUTION

Vance Papers Governor Zebulon B. Vance Papers, Correspondence (1864)

Wake Co. OLS Wake County, NC - Old Soldiers' Home Inmate Register, 1890-1917, Auditor's Office, Soldiers' Home Association Register, 1890-1917, Aud.7.4.

WCL Washington County Library, List of Washington County men in C.S. Navy, A Civil War Reader III, Reports, Reminiscences, and Rosters, Journal, Washington County Genealogical Society (Vol. 5, No.1, April 1997), Plymouth, North Carolina.

"Weekly Raleigh Register" "Weekly Raleigh Register" (Raleigh, North Carolina), (March 12, 1862) March 12, 1862.

Welborn civilwarodyssey.com (author B.J. Welborn's Civil War Odyssey blog)]

"WD," July 2, 1864 "Western Democrat" (Charlotte, North Carolina), July 12, 1864.

"WDJ" (April 24, 1863) "Wilmington Daily Journal" 4/24/63

"WDJ" (July 1, 1863) "Wilmington Daily Journal," July 1, 1863
"WDJ" (October 14, 1863) "Wilmington Daily Journal," October 14, 1863

"WDJ" (April 27, 1864) "Wilmington Daily Journal," April 27, 1864

"WDJ" (August 13, 1864) "Wilmington Daily Journal," August 13, 1864

"WDJ" (Sept. 7, 1864) "Wilmington Daily Journal," September 7, 1864.

"WDJ" (January 15, 1865) "Wilmington Daily Journal," January 15, 1865

Wikipedia   https://en.wikipedia.org/wiki/List_of_ships_of_the_Confederate_States_Navy

Wikipedia   Wikipedia (Subjects Vary)   "WPA": Resources. WPA Groves Index, North Carolina Division of Historical

"WWJ" (date)   "Wilmington Weekly Journal"

www.ashefamily.info/ashefamily/4188.htm   Ashe Family

www.Confederate States Navyavy.org/stmarks.htm

www.couchgenweb.com/arkansas/jackson/biog-c.htm

WWW.findagrave.com   Findagrave

www.freepages.military.rootsweb.com/.../index2.htm

www.guilfordgreys.com/Original_Greys.htm

www.navyandmarine.org   www.navyandmarine.org

www.ncgenweb.us/nccivwar/rosters/10cok.htm

www.thewashingtongrays.homestead.com

www.http://membres.multimania.fr/confederatestatearmy/repertoire/p/0p.html   www.http://membres.multimania.fr/confederatestatearmy/repertoire/p/0p.html

CSS EAGLE   www.https://wrecksite.eu/wreck.aspx?220507 (CSS EAGLE)   Yopp   "Incidents Connected with the Surrender of Wilmington, North Carolina, to the Yankees on February the 22nd 1865," by William Harriss Yopp (Originally appeared as a serial in the "Wilmington Sunday Star" on August 16, 23, 30, and September 13 and 20, 1936).

APPENDIX III: SOURCES CITED WITH ABBREVIATIONS

Abel A. Shuford Chapter (Records), UDC, Hickory,   Shuford North Carolina Chapt., UDC"

"Absentees and Deserters from Various Companies   Absentees Lurking in Those Counties of the 1st Congressional District Over Which Colonel J. W. Hinton Has Control," Folder #13, Box 65 "Miscellaneous," Civil War Collection, North Carolina Division of Historical Resources, Raleigh, North Carolina.

Academy on the James, The Confederate Naval School, by Academy R. Thomas Campbell, Shippensburg, Pa.: Burd Street Press, c. 1998.

"Alphabetical List of Confederate States Marine   CSMC Officer Officers' Process of Burials,"   Burials [www.ConfederateStatesNavy.org/Confederate States Marine Corps/Confederate States Marine Corps, alpha, name.htm]

"Asheville Times" (November 18, 1917) "Asheville Times" (November 18, 1917)

"Beaufort County Sailors Who Served in the Confederate   Beaufort County States Navy and Marine Corps,"   Sailors www.ncgenweb.us/beaufort/mil/boConfederate States Navy.htm

Beaufort's Old Burying Ground, North Carolina   Hardy by Diane Hardy, Marilyn Collins, and Mamré Wilson (1999)

Bethel to Sharpsburg (In Two Volumes), by Daniel Harvey Hill, DH Hill, Edwards and Broughton Company, Raleigh, North Carolina, 1926.

Biographical Sketches of the Commissioned Officers of the   Donnelly-BS *Confederate States Marine Corps*, by Ralph W. Donnelly.

Boyd, Henry P. "Hank," Chattanooga, TN, August 2010.   Boyd

"Burial locations of Confederate States Navy, Marine,   Stepp, "Burials" and North Carolina Navy Personnel within North Carolina," compiled by Jeff Stepp (E-mail received July 15, 2009)

Cabarrus Confederate Veterans, In Alphabetical Order,   Cruse complied by Bernard W. Cruse, Jr., Cabarrus Genealogical Society, Concord, North Carolina (2001).

Card File, North Carolinians in Confederate Service,   Card File Historical Publications Branch [North Carolina Troops PROJECT Files], North Carolina Division of Historical Resources, Raleigh, North Carolina [copied from cards on file at the National Archives, Washington, DC].

Carter, Ms. Margaret (Granddaughter of LT Jonathan Hanby Margaret Carter Carter, Confederate States Navy). Email dated June 23, 2009 including information extracted from the following sources: RIVER OF YEARS, book by Glenna W. Wilding and Sister Mary S. Carter; National Archives Pension Records (Mexican War) and National Archives (Old Army Records Branch), Washington, District of Columbia; OFFICIAL RECORDS: WAR OF THE REBELLION, Series I, Volumes 26 and 48; SKETCHES OF NORTH CAROLINA, book by Humphrey Hunters; and a handwritten biographical sketch of the life of Jonathan H. Carter thought to have been written by his youngest daughter, Kate G. Carter.

Census (GA), 1870   Census (GA), 1870

Census (Maryland), 1860   Census (Maryland), 1860

Census (Neb.), 1880   Census (Neb.), 1880

Census (North Carolina), 1910   Census (NC), 1910

Census (North Carolina), 1900   Census (NC), 1900

Census (North Carolina), 1870   Census (NC), 1870

Census (North Carolina) 1860   Census (NC) 1860

Census (North Carolina), 1850   Census (NC), 1850

Census (United States), 1860   Census (US), 1860

Census (Tennessee), 1860   Census (TN), 1860

Census (Virginia), 1860   Census (VA), 1860

"Charlotte News" (Charlotte, North Carolina), June 5, 1910 "Char. Obs." (June 5, 1910)

"Charlotte Observer" (Charlotte, North Carolina), April 3, 1910 "Char. Obs. (April 3, 1910)

"Charlotte Weekly-East" (Charlotte, North Carolina) "CW-E," April 19,1979 April 19, 1979, p. 29.

Chauncey, Mr. James E., Norfolk, Virginia. Letter to the   Chauncey Search Room, North Carolina State Archives, received February 10, 1978.

Chronicles of the Cape Fear River, 1660-1916, by James   Chronicles Sprunt, Edwards and Broughton Company, Raleigh, North Carolina, 1916.

"Citizen News-Record" (Moore County,   Citizen News-Record, North Carolina), July 8, 1987.   July 8, 1987

civilwarodyssey.com (author B.J. Welborn's Civil War   Welborn Odyssey blog)]

A Civil War Roster for Lincoln County, North Carolina,   Lincoln Roster *Lest We Forget*, by Beatties Ford Rifles Chapter, UDC, 1991.

The Civil War Roster of Davie County, North Carolina,   Hasty and Hasty *Biographies of 1,147 Men Before, During, and After the Conflict*, by Mary Alice Hasty and Hazel M. Winfree   (2009).

Civil War Collection, Box 41, North Carolina Division of   CWC Historical Resources, North Carolina Department of Cultural Resources, Raleigh, North Carolina

Civil War Days and Those Surnames   CWDTS http://civilwarthosesurnames.blogspot.com/2010/12/united-states-confederate-navy-of.html

Civil War Naval Chronology, 1861-1865, Naval History Division, 19665.   CWNavalChron.

Civil War Soldier Surname Index, Civil War Soldier   CWSSI Records of North Carolina "Wall" *www.censusdiggins.com/nc_civil_war_wall.html*

Cleveland and Rutherford Counties, North Carolina,   BRGS *Confederate Soldiers, 1861-1865*, by Broad River Genealogical Society, Shelby, North Carolina (1981)

Cloninger, Bruce (Cherryville, NC)   Cloninger

Compiled Service Records, National Archives Microfilm   ConfederateStatesR Copy, North Carolina Division of Historical Resources.

"Confederate Burials," Vol. XV. Published by Lauderdale   Lauderdale County Dept. of Archives and History, Inc., 1994.

"Confederate Burials at Oakwood Cemetery," created by   Oakwood the Olivia Raney Library, Charles Purser Compiler (Raleigh, North Carolina).

Confederate Navy subject file N - Personnel; NA – Complements, rolls, lists of persons, etc.; CSS Alabama – CSS Neuse.

Confederate Military History, Vol. VI, Clement Anselm Evans Evans, Published by Evans' Confederate Publishing Company, Atlanta, GA (1899).

Confederate Records, v. X, p. X, North Carolina Gravestone Records Division, United Daughters of the Confederacy, North Carolina Division of Historical Resources, Raleigh, North Carolina.

Confederate Pension Applications, Florida State Archives, Pensions (FL) File No. A02854.

Confederate Pension Applications, North Carolina Div. Pensions (North of Historical Resources, Archives and Records Carolina) Section, Raleigh, North Carolina.

Confederate Military History, edited by General Clement A. CMH (North Evans (Volumes I-XII), The Confederate Publishing Carolina) Company, Atlanta, GA, 1899

Confederate Sailors, Marines, and Signalmen from Virginia Driver *and Maryland*, by Robert J. Driver, Jr. (Heritage Books, 2007).

Confederate Ships Afloat, by US Naval Historical Center (2011) USNHC

"Confederate States Army to Navy Transfers" by Terry Army to Navy Foenander [http://home.ozconnect.net/tfoen/transfers.htm].

The Confederate States Marine Corps: The Rebel Donnelly – RL *Leathernecks* (1989) by Ralph W. Donnelly.

Confederate States Navy Research Library, ELLIS Ellis, John E., Mobile, AL [http://www.ConfederateStates Navyavy.org]

Confederate States Navy Research Guide: Confederate Naval Moebs Imprints Described and Annotated, Chronology of Naval Operation and Administration, Marine Corps and Naval Officer Biographies, Description of Vessels, [and] Subject Bibliography, by Thomas Truxton Moebs, Moebs' Publishing Company, Williamsburg, Virginia, 1991

CSS Crew List www.rblong.net/ncsquadron/Ellis%20Lists.htm) ELLIS Crew List

CSS NEUSE: A Question of Iron and Time, Bright, Leslie Bright, et al S., William H. Rowland, and James C. Bordon, Raleigh Division of Archives and History, 1981.

CSS SEA BIRD, Muster Roll, July – November 1861, *ORN, 2, 1*, SEA BIRD p.306.

"CSS TALLAHASSEE Crew Roster," *ORN*, Series 2, TALLAHASSEE Vol. 1, p. 307.

Confederate Veteran Magazine, S. A Cunningham, Editor, 1893 – 1932, Nashville, Tennessee CVM (Vol. __)

"Crew List of the Confederate States Steamer CSS TENN. TENNESSEE" Terry Foenander [http://hub.dataline.net.au/~tfoen/tennessee.htm].

"(The) Crew of the CSS NEUSE: A Revised Roster," Hill, M by Hill, Michael, Research Branch, Division of Archives and History, August 12, 1986.

"Crew Members Aboard the CSS Neuse, March-October CMACSSN 1864," CSS NEUSE Historic Site, NC Historic Sites

"Cumberland Company Men on the Steamer NORTH Oates CAROLINA," *The Story of Fayetteville and the Upper Cape Fear* by John A. Oates (1950) p. 408.

Cyclopedia of Eminent and Representative Men of the Carolina Cyclopedia of the Nineteenth Century, Vol. II, by Edward McGrady and Samuel A-Court Ashe, Madison, Wisconsin, 1892

"Daily Confederate" (Raleigh), April 18, 1864 "Daily Confed." (4/18/64)

"Daily Confederate" (Raleigh), December 25, 1864   "Daily Confed." 12/25/64)

"Daily Confederate" (Raleigh), May 23, 1864   "Daily Confed."   (5/23/64)

"Daily Confederate" (Raleigh), January 2, 1865   "Daily Confed."   (1/2/65)

"Daily Confederate" (Raleigh), February 18, 1865   "Daily Confed."   (2/18/65)

"Daily Confederate" (Raleigh), May 23, 1865   "Daily Confed."   (5/23/65)

"Daily Dispatch" (Richmond, Virginia), February 19,1862) "Daily Dispatch,"   February 19, 1862

"Daily Review" (Wilmington, North Carolina), March 19, 1889 "DR," March 19, 1889

Dallas, John T. -email to author, dated January 17, 2005. Dallas

Davis, James C., Letter, November 17, 1864, "Fayetteville   Davis, November 17, Observer," [no date].   1864

Derelicts: an account of ships lost at sea in general commercial traffic and a brief history of blockade runners stranded along the North Carolina coast, 1861-1865, by James Sprunt. Wilmington, N. C., 1920.   Derelicts

Dictionary of North Carolina Biography, III, p. 370. DNCB, III, p.370

Dictionary of American Navy Fighting Ships www.hazegray.org/danfs/csn/c.txt)   DANFS

Document #0314-5-16 [No explanation on card] Document#0314-5-16

Dowless, Mr. Layton, Whiteville, North Carolina   Dowless

"Elijah Wilson Flake's History," by Michael Flake, posted   Flake February 15, 2006 on www.genforum.genealogy.com/flake/messages/438.html

"Fayetteville Observer" (Fayetteville, North Carolina) "Fay. Obs." (November 9, 1863).   (November 9, 1863)

"Fayetteville Observer" (North Carolina, North Carolina) "Fay. Obs. (February 1, 1864   (February 1, 1864

"Fayetteville Observer" (Fayetteville, North Carolina) "Fay. Obs." (November 14, 1864)   (November 14, 1864).

"Fayetteville Semi-Weekly" (December 24, 1864)   "FSW" (12/24/64)

Foenander, Terry, Toowoomba, Queensland, Australia.   Foenander [http://home.ozconnect.net/tfoen.htm]

Fold3, Confederate Navy subject file N - Personnel; NA –   CN Subj. Files Complements, rolls, lists of persons, etc., CSS Alabama – CSS Neuse]

Fold3, Acting Midshipmen Appointed from Civilian Life, CSN Fold3, Midshipmen

"Going South: United States Navy Officer Resignations & Dismissals On the Eve of the Civil War," by William S. Dudley, Washington, D.C.: Naval Historical Foundation © 1981 Dudley

Goss, Mildred, Creedmore, North Carolina.   Goss

Governor Zebulon B. Vance Papers, Correspondence Vance Papers (1864)

"The Greensborough Patriot" (Weekly), September 3,   TGP (Sept. 3, 1863) 1863, Greensboro, North Carolina.

"The Greensborough Patriot" (Weekly), February 23,   TGP (Feb. 23, 1865, Greensboro, North Carolina.   1863)

Grissom, Grover, 236 Sweetwater Hills Dr., Grissom Hendersonville, North Carolina 28791.

Hamilton, Oliver C. and Calier G. Hamilton Papers, Private Hamilton Collection #1215, North Carolina Division of Historical Resources (Archives), Raleigh, North Carolina. *Heritage of Sampson County*, by O. M. Bizzell HSC, p. (__)

"Hillsborough Recorder" (September 28, 1864) HR (Sept. 28, 1864)

Hispanic Confederates (1997) O'Donnell-Rosales

Historical and Traditional Tar Heel Stories from the Booker *Colorful Central Coastal Plain* by Louise R. Booker, (Johnson Publishing Company, Murfeesboro, North Carolina).

Histories of the Several Regiments and Battalions Clark *From North Carolina in the Great War, 1861-1865, (a.k.a. Clark's Regiments)*, by Walter Clark, 1905

History of Rowan County by Rumple, page 588. Rumple (North Carolina Division, UDC, Laura Wesson Chapter 1965, High Point, North Carolina)

History of the Confederate States Navy by J. Thomas Scharf Scharf, 1996 edition, Random House, NJ.

"Hospital and Prison Records for C. S. Marines and Navy," H and P Records federally produced microfilm in the collection of the North Carolina State Archives, Raleigh, North Carolina. Hotchkiss Family http://hotchkissfamily.lbbhost.com/CWC.html

Howard, Josh (Historian, Research Branch, North Carolina Josh Howard Division of Historical Resources, Raleigh, North Carolina).

http://captainsclerk.info/clerk/clerk.html (USS USSCONSTITUTION CONSTITUTION

http://civilwarnenc.ning.com http://civilwarnenc.ning.com

http://www.usgwarchives.net/nc/brunswick/vets/ BrunswickVets (1908) vets1908.html

www.locategrave.org/l/4589279/Diggs LocateGrave

www.ncgenweb.us/nccivwar/rosters/27coc.htm North CarolinaGENWEB

www.ancestry.com (U.S., Civil War Soldier USCWSRP Records and Profiles, 1861 - 1865

https://en.wikipedia.org/wiki/List_of_ships_of_the_Confederate_States_Navy Wikipedia

https://www.NCpedia.org/biography/manning-john NCpedia

"Incidents Connected with the Surrender of Wilmington, Yopp North Carolina, to the Yankees on February the 22nd 1865," by William Harriss Yopp (Originally appeared as a serial in the "Wilmington Sunday Star" on August 16, 23, 30, and September 13 and 20, 1936).

Journal of the Congress of the Confederate States of America, Journal *1861-1865, Vol. II,* Washington, DC, US Government Printing Office, 1904.

Kearney, Timothy (6 Sept. 2002). Kearney

King, Joel, Papers, Manuscript Dept., Duke University. King

Letter from Ralph W. Donnelly to James Vann Comer, Donnelly July 29, 1987 [Copy on file in the "North Carolinians in Confederate Naval Service" Materials, Vertical File, Military Collection, State Archives of North Carolina].

Letter from William McLeod to Aaron Woolard, April 24, 1871 McLeod, April 24, [Transcription in Donnelly to Comer letter, July 29, 1987]. 1871

Letter from William McLeod to Aaron Woolard, August 30, 1874 [Transcription in Donnelly to Comer letter, July 29, 1987]. McLeod, August 30, 1874

Letter on file from Mabel Holland Trull, Rt. 6, Creedmoor Trull Road, Raleigh, North Carolina. North Carolina Troops Roster Project.

Library of Virginia   Lib. of Virginia (www.lva.lib.va.us/whatwehave/milconnavy ship_results.asp?page=5&ship

Life in Jefferson Davis' Navy by Barbara Brooks Tomblin (2019), Naval Institute Press, Annapolis, Maryland. Tomblin

"List of Officers in the Navy of the Confederate States Who Resigned Their Positions in the United States Navy" (Fold3) Fold3, USN Resignees

List of Officers of the Navy of the United States and of the Marine Corps from 1775 to 1900, ed. By Edward W. Callahan; (originally published by R.R. Hamersly & Company, New York (1901); reprinted by Olde Soldier Books, Inc., Gaithersburg, Maryland, no date). Callahan

"List of Washington County Men in the C.S. Navy, A Reader III, Reports, Reminiscences, and Rosters, Journal," Washington County Library, Washington County Genealogical Society (Vol. 5, No.1, April 1997), Plymouth, North Carolina. WCL Civil War

Long, Bruce, "The Civil War in North Eastern North Carolina" [http://civilwarnenc.ning.com/] Long

Long, Bruce (Email dated 29 NOV 2013)   Long E-mail

www.lostcolleges.com/college-of-physicians-and-surgeonsofba#:~:text=College%20of%20Physicians%20and%20Surgeons%20was%20incorporated%20in%201872%20with,336%20students%20from%2023%20states.   Lostcolleges

McDonald Papers, Alexander Hamilton ("Soldiers Against Whom Letters of Investigation and Arrest Were Issued," PC#1761.1, State Archives of North Carolina). McDonald Papers

McElroy, Captain W. H., Naval Department, United Confederate Veterans (UCV)(information drawn from several sources circa 1924-25. Card file in State Archives of North Carolina). [Source(s): North Carolina Division of Historical Resources, Archives and Records Section, Military Collection, Civil War Collection, Miscellaneous Records, Box #66, Folder #8 "Card File Roster of North Carolina Officers and Enlisted Men in Confederate States Navy."] McElroy

McNeill Papers, Alexander Hamilton, Confederate Bureau of Conscription, Richmond, Virginia, January 17, 1865, Moore County, North Carolina, Civil War Collection. McNeill Papers

Madre, Mr. Philip, Chocowinity, North Carolina.   Madre

Major Louis Charles Latham Chapter, UDC, Historian Mrs. J. W. Darden, Plymouth, North Carolina.   Chapter Darden

Master Rolls of the Confederate Navy Department, Record Group 45, National Archives, Washington, DC [CSS NEUSE, March - April 1864]   NEUSE Roster

www.medicalantiques.com/civilwar/Medical_Authors_Faculty/Warren_Edward.htm   medicalantiques

"Military Images" Magazine (May-June 1994). MI, May-June 1994

Milton Johnson Sills, Southern Pines, North Carolina. Sills

Moore's Roster (*Roster of the North Carolina Troops, In the War Between the States During the Years 1861, 1862, 1863, 1864, and 1865*, 4 Vols., Maj. John W. Moore).   MR

Mosley, Terry, Durham, North Carolina.   Mosley

Murray, Will, Papers in possession of, 10055 Point Caswell Murray Rd., Watha, North Carolina 28471 (Malpass was his wife's great, great, grandfather)]

"Names and Locations of Confederate States Navy Veterans Names-1907 Published by the 'Richmond Examiner' Newspaper in 1907," Confederate States Navy Research Library, Mobile, AL [www.Confederate States Navyavy.org].

National Archives, War Department Collection of Confederate NA RG 109 Records, Record Group 109, Carded Naval Records

National Archives, Records of the Navy Department, NA RG 45 Record Group 45, Shipping Articles, Confederate States Navy

National Park Service, Civil War Soldiers and Sailors NPS System, www.itd.nps.gov/cwss/

National Underwater and Marine Agency (www.NUMA.net/expeditions/lost-confederate-fleet/) NUMA

Navy Gray Engineering the Confederate Navy on the Navy Gray *Chattahoochee River*, by Maxine T. Turner

New Hanover County Roster of Confederate Troops, St.Amand Including Confederate Pensioners and Roster of Cape Fear Camp. UCV, compiled and by Jeannette Cox St. Amand, Wilmington, North Carolina, 1960.

"New York Times," 17 January 1865. "New YorkT"

"News-Argus" [Goldsboro, North Carolina] "News-Argus"

"News and Observer" [Raleigh, North Carolina], January 4, 1885. "N & O" [4 January 1885]

"North Carolina Civil War Sailor's Project," NC Squadron, http://rblong.net/sailor/index.html NCCWSP

North Carolina Confederate Militia and Home Guard Bradley, Vol. 1, *Records, Volume 1, Militia Letter Book, 1862-1864,* abstracted by Dr. Stephen E. Bradley, Jr.

North Carolina Confederate Militia and Home Guard Bradley, Vol. 2 *Records, Volume2, Militia Letter Book, 1864-1865, and Home Guard Orders,* abstracted by Dr. Stephen E. Bradley, Jr.

North Carolina Confederate Veteran Grave Locations North CarolinaCVGL By Charlotte Carrere and Robert McAllister, Raleigh, NORTH CAROLINA: Carolina Abstractors, 1996.

North Carolina Death Collection, 1908 – 1996 North Carolina Death Coll. *(*Ancestry.com)

North Carolina Division of Historical Resources, North Carolina Archives Archives and Records Section, Raleigh, North Carolina.

North Carolina Division, United Daughters of the Ruffin Chap., UDC Confederacy, Thomas Ruffin Chapter, 349, Goldsboro, North Carolina

(The) North Carolina Gazetteer, A Dictionary of Tar Heel Places, by William S. Powell. NC Gaz

North Carolina Squadron [http://ncsquadron.wordpress.com/] (Blog by R. B. Long) NCS

"North Carolina Standard" (Raleigh, North Carolina), December 19, 1862 NCStndrd, December 19, 1862.

North Carolina Troops, 1861-1865: A Roster, by Louis NCT, Vol. ___ Manarin and Weymouth T. Jordan.

North Carolina Troops, 1861-1865: A Roster NCT, Vol.___, Addenda *Vol. [ ], Addenda,* by Louis Manarin and Weymouth T. Jordan.

North Carolina Troops, 1861-1865: A Roster, by Louis   NCT, Doc. #xxxx Manarin and Weymouth T. Jordan, Letters Received Pertaining to Individual Service Records, Document No. xxxx, p. x.

North Carolina Vital Records, 1720 – 1880 at   North CarolinaVR Ancestry.com.

Norton, Edward, Winston-Salem, North Carolina,   Norton 26 August 08

Norwich University, 1819-1911: Her History, Her Graduates,   Ellis *Her Roll of Honor,* William Arba Ellis, Editor, Published by Major Grenville M. Dodge, Montpellier, VT, 1911.

Oakdale Cemetery: A Roster of Confederate Soldiers at Rest, Oakdale, Davis compiled by J. Kenneth Davis, Jr., privately published (February 1, 2008).

Oakdale Cemetery Records, 1880-1919, Vol. 2 by Delmas D. Oakdale Cem. Rec., Haskett and William M. Reaves, Wilmington, North   Vol. 2 Carolina: New Hanover Public Library, 1990.

Oden, John, Pinetown, North Carolina.   Oden

Office of Naval War Records, Memorandum #8,   ONWR
Officers of the Confederate States Navy, 1861-1865, United States Navy Department, 1898.

Officers in the Confederate States Navy, 1861 – 1865,
Office of Naval War Records, US Government Printing Office, Washington, DC (1898).   OCSN
"Officers of the Navy of the Confederate States, January 1, 1864," www.ConfederateStatesNavyavy.org/cmdrlist.jpg.
"Officers, January 1,1864"

Official Records of the War of the Rebellion (Navy)   ORN

Old City Cem., Raleigh, North Carolina   Old City Cemetery, Raleigh, North Carolina

"Our State" Magazine (June 6, 1940)   "Our State" (June 6, 1940)

Personnel Confederate Naval Marine Corps   PCNMC
 www.http://membres.multimania.fr/confederatestatearmy/repertoire/p/0p.html

Portraits of Conflict: A Photographic History of North Carolina in the Civil War by Dr. Richard B. McCaslin, University of Arkansas Press, 1997. McCaslin

Powell, William S., *Dictionary of North Carolina Biography*, Powell Volume 6 (T-Z)

Provisional Record of Confederate Medical Officers, Offered PRCMO By the Confederate Veterans Committee, Medical Society of the State of North Carolina, circa 1890.

Purser, Charles, Garner, North Carolina   Purser

"Raleigh Spirit of the Age," August 7, 1861 (p. 3, Colonel 2) "Raleigh Spirit"

"Record of Civil War Veteran, 1861-1865: List of   RCWV
 Ex-Confederates (Soldiers/Widows" [Johnston County, North Carolina], C.056, 90003, North Carolina State Archives Microfilm

Records of Louisiana Confederate Soldiers and Louisiana Confederate Commands, 3 volumes, by Andrew B. Booth, Compiler,1920. Booth

Register of Officers of the Confederate States Navy, 1861 – 1865, As Compiled by The Office of Naval Records and Library, United States Navy Dept., 1931, from all available data – United States Government Printing Office, Washington, DC, 1931. Register

Registers of the Commissioned, Warrant, and Volunteer Officers of the Navy of the United States Including Officers of the Marine Corps and others to January 1, 1865, published by US Government Printing Office, Washington, DC, 1865. "Navy Register – 1865"

"Register of the Confederate Dead, Interred in Hollywood Cemetery," Richmond, Virginia, p. 52. Hollywood Cem

"Registers of Confederate States Army General Military Hosp. (No.4), Wilm.
Hospital Number 4, Wilmington, North Carolina," Microfilm Collection, North Carolina State Archives, Raleigh, North Carolina.

Reminiscences of the Guilford Grays, Company B, 27th Regiment, North Carolina Troops, by John A. Sloan (1883)   Sloan

"Report by Confederate States Marine Corps Commandant   Beall
Colonel Lloyd J. Beall, dated October 30, 1864."

"Resolutions of A Private Nature Passed by The General Assembly Of North Carolina At Its Second Extra   (GA of North Session, 1861."   Carolina) Rock Island (IL) Cemetery List   Rock Island (IL) Cemetery List   Resolutions

Rogers: Our Common Bond, compiled by James Vann   Comer, *Rogers*   Comer (1990)

Roster, CSS NORTH CAROLINA, 3rd Quarter, 1864. CSS North Carolina, 3rd Qtr., 1864

"Roster Document #0392 (pp. 79-80)"   Roster Document [No explanation of this source listed on Card File]

"Roster Document #0421   Roster Doc. #0421 [No explanation of this source listed on Card File]

Roster of Confederate Soldiers in the War Between the States Furnished by Lincoln County, North Carolina, 1861-1865, by W. J. Hoke Camp, UCV (ca. 1902) Hoke Camp

Roster of the Confederate Soldiers of Georgia,   Georgia Roster   *1861-1865*, by Lillian Henderson

Roster of Confederate Veterans from Chatham County, North Carolina, by the Colonel John Randolph Lane Society, Siler City, North Carolina.   Lane Society

"A Roster of Confederate Veterans of Columbus County, North Carolina," by Mrs. Homer L. (Kate Burkhead) Lyon, Jefferson Davis Chapter, 657, Whiteville, North Carolina [n.d.]   Lyon

"Roster of Confederate Veterans of Gaston County, North   Gaston County
Carolina, Civil War Collection, Box 64 (Misc.   Veterans Records), Folder #3, State Archives of North Carolina.

"Roster of Confederate Veterans of Granville County Troops,   Granville County County Civil War Collection, Box 64 (Misc. Records),   Troops Folder #3, Veterans State Archives of North Carolina.

"Roster of Franklin County Servicemen Who Participated   Smithwick in All Wars to Present Date, April 15, 1945" by Dr. D. T. Smithwick [unpublished, typed manuscript in Military Collection, misc. materials (various dates), State Archives of North Carolina].

"Roster of Granville County Troops," Civil War   Granville County Collection, Box 64 (Misc. Records), Folder #4, State Troops Archives of North Carolina.

"Roster of Nash County Confederate Soldiers and Copy of   Thorpe Roster Edgecombe County Roster," by John H. Thorpe

"Roster of Richmond County Soldiers," Civil War   Richmond County Collection, Box 64 (Misc. Records), Folder #4, State Soldiers Archives of North Carolina.

Roster of the North Carolina Troops, In the War Between the States During the Years 1861, 1862, 1863, 1864, and 1865, 4 Vols., by Maj. John W. Moore.   MR

Roster, (X) Regiment, North Carolina Militia, Civil Roster, (X) Regiment
War Collection, Military Collection, North Carolina Division of Historical Resources, North Carolina Militia Raleigh, North Carolina

Salter, Bryan, Sea Level, North Carolina. Salter

Sampson County Heritage, North Carolina, by O. M. Bizzell Bizzell

Seaman's Burial Ground, Ashley River, Charleston, SC. SBG

Service Records of Confederate Enlisted Marines (1974) by Donnelly – ENL
Ralph W. Donnelly.

"Shipping Articles [Confederate States Navy], June 13-22, 1864, Raleigh, North Carolina" (Xerographic copy in the Washington Duke Papers, Perkins Library, Duke University, Durham, North Carolina). Duke Papers

Smart, H. J., (420 McGraw St., Healdon, OK 73438) Smart, H. J., Letter Letter dated August 8, 1984.

Southern Historical Society Papers (Vol. 40) SHSP (Vol. 40)

Special Order # 89, dated, 16 April 1864, Army of N. Virginia S.O. # 89
[authorized transfer of Army personnel to Confederate States Navy]

Special Order # 92, dated, 3 April 1864, Army of N. Virginia S.O. # 92
[authorized transfer of Army personnel to Confederate States Navy]

"Stanly County Annual Reunions of Old Confederate Veterans, Stanly Reunions
 1898-1928 (Camp #1369), Folder 1A, Box #65
 "Miscellaneous," Civil War Collection, North Carolina Division of Historical resources, Raleigh, North Carolina.

State Auditor's Records, North Carolina Division of Historical State Auditor Resources, North Carolina Department of Cultural Resources, Raleigh, North Carolina.

State Auditor's Papers, Soldier's Home, Record of Inmates, Soldier's Home 1896-1924 (Aud. 7.5).

Sterling, J. G., 1602 Patterson Avenue, Winston-Salem, Sterling North Carolina (1924).

Sullivan, David, Historian, Rutland, Massachusetts Sullivan

Tennessee [Confederate] Pension Applications, Tennessee Pensions (TN) (RD
State Archives, Nashville, TN. 1788)

The Big Book of the Cape Fear River, by Claude V. Jackson, III, and Jack E. Fryar, Jr., Editor Jackson

The Civil War and Yadkin County, North Carolina, A History... Casstevens by Frances H. Casstevens, McFarland & Company, Jefferson, North Carolina (1997).

The Confederate Reveille (Centennial Edition), published by "Reveille"
 The Pamlico Chapter of the Daughters of the Confederacy, Washington, North Carolina, May 10, 1898 (re-published 1964).

The Confederate Soldier in the Civil War, edited by Ben Labree
Labree, The Courier-Journal Job Printing Company, Publisher, Louisville, KY, 1895.

The CSS VIRGINIA: Sink Before Surrender, by John V. Quarstein (2012)

The Life and Services of John Newland Maffitt, by Emma Maffitt
Martin Maffitt (His Widow), The Neale Publishing Company, New York and Washington, 1906.

The Story of Fayetteville and the Upper Cape Fear by John Oates (1950) – "Cumberland Company Men on the Steamer NORTH CAROLINA."   Oates

"The State" (Magazine)   "The State"

They Went Into the Fight Cheering, by Walt Hilderman Hilderman

"Times-Dispatch" (Richmond, VA), March 27, 1912 "Times-Dispatch"

To Bear Arms, Civil War Information from Local Folks, Chatham County and Adjacent Counties, by Zeb D. and Martha Harrington, Moncure, North Carolina, 1984. To Bear Arms

Union County Cemeteries 1710-1914 and Roster of Confederate and Revolutionary Soldiers (1958).   Union County Cemeteries

United Daughters of the Confederacy, Certificate of UDC, Recorder Eligibility for the Military Cross of Honor, North Carolina Division, U.D.C. Records in possession of the Recorder of Crosses.

United Daughters of the Confederacy, Application for a UDC, MC of Svc. Military Cross of Service, North Carolina Division, UDC, Records of the Recorder of Crosses.

United Daughters of the Confederacy, North Carolina   UDC, Bladen Starlets Division, Bladen Starlets Chapter 603, Elizabethtown, North Carolina. Records of chapter.

United Daughters of the Confederacy, North Carolina   UDC, Cape Fear Division, Cape Fear Chapter 3, Wilmington, North Carolina. Records of chapter.

United Daughters of the Confederacy, North Carolina Division, UDC, China Grove China Grove Chapter, China Grove, North Carolina. Records of chapter.

United Daughters of the Confederacy, North Carolina Division, UDC, Dunham John W. Dunham Chapter, 374, Wilson, North Carolina.

United Daughters of the Confederacy, North Carolina Division, UDC, Faison-Hicks Faison-Hicks Chapter, 539, Faison, North Carolina. Records of chapter.

United Daughters of the Confederacy, North Carolina Division, UDC, Gordon James B. Gordon Chapter, 211, Winston-Salem, North Carolina. Records of chapter.

United Daughters of the Confederacy, North Carolina Division, UDC, Graham Graham Chapter, #944, Graham, North Carolina. Records of chapter.

United Daughters of the Confederacy, North Carolina Division, UDC, Singletary Singletary Chapter, 313, Greenville, North Carolina. Records of chapter.

United Daughters of the Confederacy, North Carolina Division, UDC, Greene Greene Chapter, 1709, Snow Hill, North Carolina. Records of chapter.

United Daughters of the Confederacy, North Carolina Division, UDC, Highland Boys Highland Boys Chapter, St. Pauls, North Carolina. Records of chapter.

United Daughters of the Confederacy, North Carolina Division, UDC, Southport Southport Chapter, Southport, North Carolina. Records of chapter.

United Daughters of the Confederacy, North Carolina Division, UDC, Waddell Alfred Moore Waddell Chapter, 382, Kinston, North Carolina. Records of chapter.

United States Census, North Carolina, 1790-1890 Census (North (Ancestry.com)   Carolina) (Ancestry.com)

United States Civil War Soldiers, 1861-1865,   USCWS AncestryLibrary.com.

Wake County, NC - Old Soldiers' Home Inmate Wake Co. OLS Register, 1890-1917, Auditor's Office, Soldiers' Home Association Register, 1890-1917, Aud.7.4.

"Weekly Raleigh Register" (Raleigh, North Carolina), "Weekly Raleigh Register" March 12, 1862)   (March 12, 1862)

"Western Democrat" (Charlotte, North Carolina),   "WD," July 12, 1864 July 12, 1864.

Wikipedia (Subjects Vary)   Wikipedia

Wild, Wicked Wartime Wilmington (2009) by   Cooke Robert J. Cooke

"Wilmington Daily Journal," July 1, 1863   "WDJ" (July 1, 1863)

"Wilmington Daily Journal" 4/24/63   "WDJ" (April 24, 1863)

"Wilmington Daily Journal," October 14, 1863 "WDJ" (October 14, 1863)

"Wilmington Daily Journal," April 27, 1864   "WDJ" (April 27, 1864)

"Wilmington Daily Journal," August 13, 1864 "WDJ" (August 13, 1864)

"Wilmington Daily Journal," September 7, 1864. "WDJ" (Sept. 7, 1864)

"Wilmington Daily Journal," September 20, 1864. "WDJ" (Sept. 20, 1864)

"Wilmington Daily Journal," January 15, 1865 "WDJ" (January 15, 1865)

"Wilmington Messenger," April 20, 1892 "Messenger," 4/20/1892

"Wilmington Messenger," February 19, 1892 "Messenger," 2/19/1892

"Wilmington Messenger," March 25, 1900. "Messenger," 3/25/1900

"Wilmington Messenger," May 6, 1895. "Messenger," 5/16/1895

"Wilmington Messenger," May 20, 1894. "Messenger," 5/20/1894

"Wilmington Star," January 12, 1935   "Star," 1/12/1935

"Wilmington Star," January 14, 1886   "Star," 1/14/1886

"Wilmington Star," June 2, 1916   "Star," 6/2/1916

"Wilmington Star," January 28, 28, & 30, 1893 "Star," 1/26, 28, 30/1893

"Wilmington Weekly Journal"   "WWJ" (date)

WPA Graves Index, North Carolina Division of Historical   WPA Resources.

www.Confederate States Navyavy.org/stmarks.htm   www.Confederate States Navyavy.org/stmarks.htm

WWW.findagrave.com   Findagrave

www.freepages.military.rootsweb.com/.../index2.htm

www.https://wrecksite.eu/wreck.aspx?220507 (CSS EAGLE) CSS EAGLE

www.guilfordgreys.com/Original_Greys.htm

www.navyandmarine.org   www.navyandmarine.org

www.thewashingtongrays.homestead.com   www.thewashingtongrays.homestead.com

Appendix IV: Ranks/Rates and Special Terms Mentioned in the Roster

Armorer: Maintained all small arms aboard ship.

Armorer's Mate: Junior petty officer who assisted the Armorer in maintaining the ship's small arms.

Boatswain's Mate (Boatswain): Supervises ship's maintenance on external structure, rigging, deck equipment and boats. An all-purpose rating encompassing a variety of deck force duties. Pronounced and sometimes spelled "bo-sun."

Bounty List: List of personnel who received a cash amount as an inducement to enlist.

Boy/Cabin Boy: Attended ship's officers. Position similar in nature to that of steward.

Captain: Both a naval rank equivalent to a Colonel in the Army or Marine Corps, and a generic term used for the commander of a naval vessel.

Captain's Clerk: The captain's clerk was a junior "civil officer" in the Navy who was required to have a decent command of the English language, could copy the Captain's out-going letters in a "fair round hand," and maintained files of all his employer's correspondence [Source: http://captainsclerk.info/clerk/clerk.html]. Administrative assistant to the ship's Captain.

Captain's Cook: Self-explanatory.

Captain's Steward: Charged with taking care of the Captain. This included preparing and delivering his meals.

Carpenter's Mate (Carpenter): General carpentry work; maintained the integrity of the ship's hull. During battle, would fight fires and use plugs to patch holes in the hull of wooden ships.

Clothing List: List of various clothing items available on shore or aboard ship available for issue to naval personnel.

Commander's Clerk: See "Captain's Clerk"

Cook: Prepared meals for the ship's crew.

Engineer (1st, 2nd, 3rd Assistant Engineer): Officers charged with the operation and maintenance of boilers on steam-driven vessels.

Fireman (1st Class; 2nd Class): On steam-powered vessels, the fireman or stoker fueled and tended the boiler which created the steam to power the engine. It was hard physical work shoveling coal into the boiler's firebox.

Gunner's Mate: A rating established in the United States Navy in 1794 (one of the first eight chief petty officer positions).

	The Gunner's Mates had charge of the cannon on board ship, saw to their maintenance, to the training of the assistant gunners and gun crews, and prepared all artillery rounds.
Landsman:	Person unskilled in Seamanship. New recruits were often rated as Landsmen. They primarily performed duties on a ship not requiring detailed knowledge of Seamanship.
Lieutenant (2nd; 1st) (CSN/CSMC):	Officer rank below that of Lieutenant Commander in the Navy and Captain in the Marines Corps. Navy Lieutenants could command ships and in that capacity were referred to as "Captain," regardless of their actual rank.
Lieutenant, Commanding:	An officer in the rank of Lieutenant in command of a vessel.
Master (In Line of Promotion):	The Master's main duty was navigation, taking the ship's position at least daily and, on sailing ships, setting the sails as appropriate for the required course and conditions. The Master was responsible for obtaining all required sailing supplies, stowing materials in the hold, and, through his subordinates, hoisting and lowering the anchor, and docking and undocking the ship. In addition, he inspected the ship daily for problems with the anchors, sails, masts, ropes, or pulleys, and was charged with making daily entries on the weather, ship's position, and expenditures into the ship's official log. The "Master (In line of Promotion) was eligible for promotion. Later, this position was made a commissioned officer's billet. Some masters were commissioned as officers, formally to distinguish them from the warrant masters who would not be promoted.
Master (Not in Line of Promotion):	(SEE: Master (In Line of Promotion). A Warrant, rather than commissioned, position without promotion potential.
Master-at-Arms:	Ship's senior police officer, charged with maintaining order aboard ship. Often assisted by one or more Ship's Corporals.
Master's Mate:	Sailor, ordinarily a petty officer, who assisted the Master, a naval officer trained in and responsible for the navigation of a sailing vessel, the condition of sails, rigging, and anchors. Usually selected from senior warrant officers and senior midshipmen who are unlikely to pass the examination for lieutenant.
Master's Mate (Acting)	See "Master's Mate." Sailor temporarily assigned to this duty.
Naval Department:	The administrative and body that controlled all aspects of the Navy including recruiting, personnel, training, supplying, and directing naval operations. The Confederate States Navy Department was headquartered in Richmond, Virginia.
Officer's Clerk	See "Captain's Clerk"
Officer's Steward:	(See Steward)
Ordinary Seaman:	A skilled sailor ranking between a Landsman and Seaman.
Paymaster:	Officer charged with payment of crew members and other financial matters. In earlier times, these functions, as well as keeping the Captain's records, correspondence, and financial accounts were fulfilled by a "Purser."
Paymaster (Assistant):	Junior officer ranking below the Paymaster who assisted him with his duties. On ships whose size did not warrant a Paymaster, those duties would be assigned to an Assistant Paymaster.
Pilot:	Skilled helmsman, especially one qualified to sail a vessel through local waters.
Private (CSMC or Naval Battalion):	Term sometimes applied to sailors below the rank of petty officer, especially when serving as infantry as many did in the Spring of 1865. Most personnel listed as "Private" were either Marines, or Soldiers who had been transferred from the Army into the Navy. The latter often retained their Army uniforms in total or in part until naval uniforms became available, if ever.

Provisional Navy: Embodied by the Confederate States Congress on May1, 1863, its "object being, without interfering with the rank of the officers in the Regular Navy, to cull out from that navy list, younger and more active men, and put them in the Provisional Navy, with increased rank. The Regular Navy became thus, a kind of retired list, and the Secretary of the Navy was enabled to accomplish his object of bringing forward younger officers for active service, without wounding the feelings of the older officers, by promoting their juniors over their heads, on the same list." [Source: Moebs]

Quartermaster: A sailor, often a petty officer, qualified to man the helm and assist with ship's navigation.

Quarter-Gunner: A petty officer whose duty was to assist the ship's Gunner in keeping the guns and their carriages in proper order, scaling (calibrating) the barrels when necessary, filling the cartridges with powder, and other associated duties. Quarter-gunners were appointed in each ship at the rate of one for every four guns.

Receiving Ship: A ship or land station used for receiving new recruits or naval personnel intransit. It was at a receiving ship where recruits received their initial naval training.

Seaman: Skilled, experience sailor ranking above an Ordinary Seaman.

Ship's Corporal A junior petty officer who assisted the Master-at-Arms.

Small Stores: Any number of smaller items available for purchase or issue to naval personnel aboard ship or ashore. Included but not limited to items such as needles and thread and personal care items.

Steward: Sailor whose responsibility it was to see to the needs of the ship's officers.

Surgeon: Ship's medical officer. On ships that did not warrant a Surgeon, those duties would be assigned to an Asst. Surgeon.

Surgeon (Assistant): Medical doctor ranking beneath and assistant to the senior medical officer.

Surgeon's Steward: Surgeon's stewards assisted the ship's doctor and ranked second in seniority among the ship's petty officers, next only after the master-at-arms. He was expected to have some knowledge of pharmacy.

Yeoman: Petty officers, clerks, who assisted the Paymaster who were also responsible for storage and issue of provisions.

[Source: Mr. Andrew Duppstadt; author knowledge; various miscellaneous sources]

Appendix V: Confederate Ships and Floating Batteries Mentioned in the Roster

[**NOTE:** Information varies depending on information available]

"Advance" (a.k.a. "*A.D. Vance*"): Blockade runner owned by the State of North Carolina. A 902-ton side-wheel steamer built in Scotland in 1862 as a River Clyde packet. Purchased in 1863 and put to work running the Federal blockade. She was one of the most successful Confederate blockade runners, making more than twenty voyages before her capture by USS *Santiago de Cuba* off Wilmington, North Carolina, on September 10, 1864. Taken into the United States Navy soon thereafter, she served as USS *Advance* until June 1865, when she was renamed *Frolic*. [Source: https://americancivilwar.com/tcwn/civil_war/Navy_Ships/blockade_runner_Advance.html]

CSS ALABAMA: Screw Sloop-of-War built in England for the Confederacy under the name of *Enrica*. Fitted out as a cruiser by CAPT Raphael Semmes, CSN, in August 1862, she was commissioned CSS Alabama on August 24, 1862 while at sea. During her 21-month career, the CSS Alabama roamed the seas disrupting commerce and capturing and burning more than sixty ships. She was sunk in combat action off Cherbourg, France on June 11, 1864 by the **USS Kearsarge**.
Specifications:
Length: 220'
Beam: 31' 8"
Speed: 13 knots
Complement: 145
Armament: six 32-pdrs, one 110-pdr rifle, one 68-pdr
Propulsion: sail and steam
[Source: www.navsource.org/archives]

NCS ALBEMARLE: The *Albemarle* was chartered and later purchased by the State of North Carolina. She was never armed; her name was never changed; and she was not sold to Confederate States Navy. The NCS ALBEMARLE was turned over to the Confederate States Army quartermaster and, at some point, commanded by Lieutenant W. W. Roberts.
[Source: NCS]

CSS ALBEMARLE: Steam powered ironclad ram, built on the Roanoke River at Edwards Ferry, North Carolina, 1863-64. Commissioned CSS Albemarle, April 10, 1864. Torpedoed and sunk while undergoing repairs on the Roanoke River, October 27 – 28, 1864 by LIEUTENANT William B. Cushing, USN, with a crew of 14.
Specifications:
Length 152'
Beam 34'
Complement: unknown
Speed: 4 knots
Armament: two 6.4" Brooke rifles
Propulsion: steam.
[Source: www.navsource.org/archives]

CSS ALERT: Lighthouse tender, schooner rigged.
[Source: https://en.wikipedia.org/wiki/List_of_ships_of_the_Confederate_States_Navy]

CSS APPOMATTOX: Gunboat; former tugboat, burned: February 10, 1862. [Source: https://en.wikipedia.org/wiki/List_of_ships_of_the_Confederate_States_Navy]

CSS ARCTIC: Ironclad floating battery, scuttled: December 24, 1864.
[Source: https://en.wikipedia.org/wiki/List_of_ships_of_the_Confederate_States_Navy; Jackson]

CSS ARKANSAS: Arkansas Class ironclad ram. Construction began in 1861 in Memphis, Tennessee, completed on the Yazoo River after the fall of Memphis in May 1862. Saw much combat during the war. Was burned on August 5, 1862 to prevent capture.
Specifications:
Length: 165'
Beam: 35'
Speed: 8 knots
Complement: 200
Armament: two 9" smoothbore cannon, two 9" 64-pdrs, two 9" shell guns; two 6" rifled cannon; two 32-pdr smoothbore

cannon
Propulsion: two low pressure 900 hp steam engines twin screws
[Source: www.navsource.org/archives]

CSS ARROW: Screw steamer. Burned by the Confederates on June 4, 1862 to prevent its capture.
Specifications:
Armament: one 32-pounder cannon.
[Source: *Encyclopedia of Civil War Shipwrecks: Poems*, by Craig Gaines]

CSS ATLANTA: Iron-clad ram built 1861 as an iron-hulled, schooner-rigged, screw steamer ("*SS Fingal*") in Scotland. Purchased for blockade running in September 1861 for use as a Confederate blockade runner ("SS *Fingal*"). Converted to an iron-clad ram in 1862 at the Confederate Navy Yard, Savannah, GA. Surrendered to USS WEEHAWKEN on June 17, 1863 at Wassaw Sound, GA after attempting to run the Union blockade at Savannah, GA. Temporarily commissioned as USS ATLANTA, de-commissioned and condemned, repaired at the Philadelphia Navy Yard, re-commissioned USS ATLANTA on February 2, 1864. Decommissioned June 21, 1865 and placed in reserve.
Specifications:
Length 204'
Beam 41'
Armor, Casemate 4," Deck .5," Hull 2," Pilothouse 4;" Speed 13 knots;
Complement 162
Armament, two 7" Single Banded Brooke rifles, one mounted fore and one aft; two 150-pdr rifles; two 100-pdr smoothbores.
Propulsion, Screw Steamer.
[Source: www.navsource.org/archives]

CSS BALTIC: Ironclad ram built in 1860 as the sidewheel river tow boat SS Baltic. Purchased by the State of Alabama and converted to an armored ram. Turned over to the Confederate Navy in 1863 and commissioned CSS Baltic. Operated in and around Mobile Bay, AL. Reported unfit for service in 1863. Dismantled by July 1864 and her armor transferred to the CSS Nashville.
Specifications:
Length: 186'
Beam: 36'
Complement: 86
Armament: two Dahlgren guns, two 32-pdrs, two smaller pieces,
Propulsion: steam.
[Source: www.navsource.org/archives]

"Banshee": A side-wheel steamship, was built in Liverpool, England, in 1862 for running the Federal blockade. Her trans-Atlantic maiden voyage in April 1863 was a "first" for a steel-hulled ship. During her seven-month career, *Banshee* made seven round-trip voyages between Bermuda or the Bahamas and Wilmington, North Carolina. She was captured by USS *Grand Gulf* and the United States Army Transport *Fulton* on November 21, 1863, while en route to Wilmington. Purchased in March 1864 by the United States Navy, she was converted to a gunboat and, in June 1864, commissioned as USS *Banshee*. In December 1864 she took part in the abortive attempt to capture Fort Fisher, North Carolina. Decommissioned after the war, she was sold in November 1865. [Source: https://americancivilwar.com/tcwn/civil_war/Navy_Ships/CSS_Banshee.html]

CSS BEAUFORT: Iron-hulled, screw steamer gunboat that served in North Carolina and Virginia waters. Originally named the "Caledonia," she was purchased by the State of North Carolina, armed with a long 32-pounder, and commanded by Lieutenant Robert C. Duval. She was sold to the Confederate States Navy and turned over to them on August 20, 1861. Captured by the United States Navy on April 3, 1865.
[Source: NCS; https://en.wikipedia.org/wiki/List_of_ships_of_the_Confederate_States_Navy]

CSS BOMBSHELL: Believed to have been a former Erie Canal steamer, date of construction unknown. Acquired by the United States Army, date unknown, and sunk by Confederate batteries in Albemarle Sound, N.C., April 18, 1864. Raised by the Confederate forces and taken into their navy. *Bombshell* was recaptured in Albemarle Sound USS MATTABESETT and USS SASSACUS on May 5, 1864 and sent to New York. Final Disposition, fate unknown.
Specifications:
Length 90'
Beam unknown
Speed 13 knots
Complement unknown
Armament: three howitzers, one 20-pdr gun
Propulsion steam
[Source: www.navsource.org/archives]

CSS CAPITAL: Government side-wheel river steamer, burned June 28, 1862 [Source: https://en.wikipedia.org/wiki/List_of_ships_of_the_Confederate_States_Navy]

CSS CARONDELET: Sidewheel steamer gunboat, destroyed April 1862 [Source: https://en.wikipedia.org/wiki/List_of_ships_of_the_Confederate_States_Navy]

CSS CASWELL (aka CSS FORT CASWELL [?]): Side-wheel wooden steamer that operated as a tender on the Wilmington Station, 1861-62. Complement 32. Acting Master W. B. Whitehead, CSN, commanding. She was burned to avoid capture when Wilmington, N.C., fell in February 1865.
[Source: https://en.wikipedia.org/wiki/List_of_ships_of_the_Confederate_States_Navy; DANFS]

CSS CHAMELION [a.k.a. CAMELION] [SEE: CSS OLUSTEE; CSS TALLAHASSEE] Screw Steamer built (date unknown) as the twin-screw ferry "*Atlanta*" in London, England. Purchased in Wilmington, N. C. in 1864 by the Confederate States Navy and commissioned CSS TALLAHASSEE. In a 19-day raid commencing on August 6, 1864, CSS TALLAHASSEE destroyed 26 vessels and captured 7 others which were bonded or released. Renamed CSS OLUSTEE, she ran the blockade off Wilmington on October 29, 1864 capturing and destroying six ships before returning to Wilmington on November 7, 1864. CSS OLUSTEE's battery was removed and she was renamed **CSS *Chameleon***, date unknown. After running the blockade on December 24, 1864, and finding it impossible to re-enter a southern port, CSS CHAMELION was sailed to Liverpool, England, to be turned over to CDR J. D. Bullock, CSN, financial agent of the Confederate Navy Department. Arriving on April 9, 1865, she was seized and sold by British authorities. They sued, won, and was handed over to the United States consul at Liverpool, April 26, 1866. Sold to a Japanese Shipping company in March 1867 and renamed ***SS Haya Maru***, she sank June 27, 1869.
Specifications:
Length 220'
Beam 24'
Speed 17 knots.
Complement 120
Armament: one 32-pdr rifled cannon, forward; one 100-pounder rifled cannon, amidships; one 30-pdr heavy Parrot gun, aft; and one brass howitzer.
Propulsion: two 100 hp steam engines, twin propellers
[Source: www.navsource.org/archives]

CSS CHARLESTON: Steam-powered, casemate ironclad ram or battery, built in Charleston, SC, and funded by the State of South Carolina and donations by patriotic women's associations in the city. She defended the city until destroyed on February 18, 1865 when advancing Union troops threatened Charleston. [Source: https://en.wikipedia.org/wiki/List_of_ships_of_the_Confederate_States_Navy

CSS CHARM: Side-wheel transport steamer of 223 tons, built in 1860 in Cincinnati, Ohio. She served the Confederacy as an ammunition and gun carrier and troop transport in the Mississippi River area, serving with great distinction in the Battle of Belmont, Missouri, on November 7, 1861. Later lashed to the CSS PAUL JONES, both were scuttled by the Confederates on May 17, 1863 in the Big Black River in Mississippi to prevent capture.
[Source: *Encyclopedia of Civil War Shipwrecks: Poems*, by Craig Gaines; DANFS]

CSS CHATTAHOOCHEE: Twin-screw steamer built 1862-1863 in Georgia. Scuttled in December 1864.
Specifications:
Length: 150'
Beam: 25'
Speed: 12 knots
Complement: 120
Armament: 4 X 32-pounder smoothbore cannon, a 32-pounder rifled cannon and a 9-inch smoothbore cannon
[Source: https://en.wikipedia.org/wiki/CSS_Chattahoochee]

CSS CHICKAMAUGA (former blockade runner "Edith"): Wooden steam cruiser, originally built as the blockade runner *Edith*. Purchased by the Confederate States Navy at Wilmington, North Carolina in September 1864. She put to sea on October 28, 1864 for a cruise north to the entrance of Long Island Sound, thence to St. George, Bermuda, for repairs and coal. She took several prizes before returning to Wilmington on November 19, 1864. In December 1864, a portion of her crew served the guns at Fort Fisher, as well as transported ammunition. She lent support to the fort when it was bombarded again on January 15, 1865. After the evacuation of Wilmington, CHICKAMAUGA sailed up the Cape Fear River where she was burned to prevent capture on 25 February 1865.
Specifications:
Complement: 120
Armament: 3 rifled cannons
Propulsion: Steam
[Source: https://en.wikipedia.org/wiki/List_of_ships_of_the_Confederate_States_Navy]

CSS CHICORA: Richmond class ironclad ram built in 1862 at Charleston, S.C., and commissioned in November 1862. Before dawn on January 31, 1863, CSS CHICORA and her sister ram CSS PALMETTO STATE attacked blockading Union vessels off Charleston, disabling the USS KEYSTONE STATE and USS MERCIDETA. CHICORA participated in the defense of Charleston during 1863 and 1864 and provided the first volunteer officer and crew for the Confederate Submarine Torpedo Boat H. L. Hunley. CHICORA was burned by the Confederates upon the evacuation of Charleston on February 18, 1865.
Specifications:
Length: 150'
Beam: 35'
Speed: 5 knots
Complement: 150
Armament: two 9" guns; four 32-pdr rifles
Propulsion: steam
[Source: www.navsource.org/archives]

CSS COLUMBIA: Iron-clad ram built at Charleston, S.C. in 1864 of yellow pine and white oak with iron fastenings and 6-inch iron plating. COLUMBIA was damaged on January 12, 1865 coming out of Charleston when she ran onto a sunken wreck. When Charleston was seized by Union forces on February 18, 1865, COLUMBIA was found to have had her guns and some armor plating removed and ship worms already destroying her hull. Raised by the Federals on April 26, 1865 and towed to Hampton Roads, VA. Final Disposition, fate unknown
Specifications:
Length 215'
Beam 51' 4"
Speed unknown
Complement 50
Armament: four pivot guns and two broadside guns
Propulsion: two steam engines; twin propellers
[Source: www.navsource.org/archives]

CSS CONFEDERATE STATES [SEE CSS UNITED STATES]: Wooden-hulled, three-masted sail powered, heavy frigate built in 1797 as one of the first six frigates authorized for construction. Served in the United States Navy until captured at Norfolk in 1861 by the Confederates. She was subsequently commissioned in to Confederate service as the CSS UNITED STATES (though apparently sometimes referred to as the CSS CONFEDERATE STATES) and used for harbor defense. She was later scuttled by Confederate forces to prevent capture but raised by Union forces which retained control of the ship until she was broken up in 1865.
Specifications:
Length: 175'
Beam: 43 ½'
Propulsion: Sail
Speed: 11 kts.
Complement (/When in US service): 400-600 officers and sailors, plus 50 Marines)
Armament (when in US service): 323 X long 24 pdrs; 24 X
42 pounder caronade (during the War of 1812)
[Source: Wikipedia]

CSS COQUETTE (blockade runner): According to the *Dictionary of American Fighting Ships* (DANFS), there were two ships named CSS COQUETTE. The COQUETTE operating as a blockade runner based in Wilmington, N.C. was built in 1859 at Mobile, Alabama. In the spring of 1864, while under command of Lieutenant Robert R. Carter, CSN, she imported two marine engines past the Federal blockade into Wilmington.
Specifications:
Length: 220'
Beam: 25'
Propulsion: Steam
[Source: DANFS]

CSS CORA: Schooner. Specifics on her size, armament, crew complement, and military use are unknown.
[Source: Gaines]

CSS CORNUBIA [aka: LADY DAVIS] (blockade runner): A long, fast, and powerful, white-painted, iron steamer with a low silhouette. Constructed in Cornwall, England in 1858. Purchased by the Confederacy circa 1862 and made twenty-two successful trips through the Union blockade. On November 11, 1863, as the CORNUBIA tried to run into Wilmington, NC, on her 23rd attempt to run the blockade, the ship was being pursued closely by the USS NIPHON and beached by her captain, Lieutenant Richard H. Gayle, CSN. Within half an hour, the ship was towed to sea by the USS JAMES ADGER.

The loss of her desperately needed cargo paled in comparison to papers found on board and had an important impact on the conduct of the naval war by the United States Government in relation to foreign nationals captured aboard Confederate States vessels. The United States Government decided since blockade runners owned or commanded by Confederate Navy officers belonged to the Confederacy. Because of this revelation, a tougher policy toward British seamen caught engaging in blockade running was enacted. Secretary of the United States Navy, Gideon Welles, determined that "… persons captured on the boats mentioned and others in like cases [were] to be detained as prisoners."
Specifications:
Length: 190';
Beam: 24' 6"
Draft: 9';
Speed: 18 knots.
[Source: DANFS; USNHC]

CSS CURLEW: Sidewheel Steamer built at Wilmington, Del., in 1856 as a tug. Purchased in Norfolk, Va., in 1861 by the Confederate Government for operations in North Carolina waters. *Curlew* participated in the battle of Roanoke Island on February 7, 1862 but was sunk in shoal water by the Confederates the following day to prevent capture by United States forces.
Specifications:
Length: 150'
Beam: unknown
Speed: 12 knots
Complement: Unknown
Armament: 1 X 32-pounder and 1 X 12 pounder brass smoothbore aft
Propulsion: Steam
[Source: www.navsource.org/archives]

CSS DAVID: Steam torpedo boat built as a private venture by T. Stoney at Charleston, S.C., in 1863. Designed to operate very lowly in the water, CSS DAVID resembled a submarine, but was a surface vessel. The fate of the CSS DAVID is uncertain. Several torpedo boats of this type fell into Union hands when Charleston was captured in February 1865 and CSS DAVID may well have been among them. The term "David" came to be the generic term for any torpedo boat resembling CSS DAVID, the prototype of others built in Charleston. The names, if any, that were given to these other boats are not known. Their existence caused some concern among Union naval officers, but they were never a serious threat to the blockade. The exact number of "David's" built is not known.
Specifications:
Length: 50'
Beam: 6'
Draft: 5'
Speed: unknown
Complement: 4
Armament: one 60 to 70 lbs. spar torpedo
Propulsion: steam
[Source: www.navsource.org/archives]

CSS DRURY (CSS DREWRY): A Steam powered wooden gunboat and tender commissioned in 1863 that featured a foredeck protected by an iron V-shaped shield. Classed as a tender, she was attached to the James River Squadron in 1863. In addition to transporting troops and other routine service, she took part in several engagements along the river prior to January 24, 1865, when she was destroyed by two shots from a 100-pounder rifle from a battery of the 1st Connecticut Artillery. The second shot exploded her magazine as she assisted CSS Richmond to get afloat. All but two of her crew had reached safety before the explosion.
Specifications:
Length: 106'
Beam: 21'
Propulsion: Steam
Armament: 1 X 6.4" rifled cannon; 1 X 7" rifled cannon
[Source: https://en.wikipedia.org/wiki/CSS_Drewry]

CSS EDWARDS: Built in 1855, converted to steam in 1856, she was a former canal boat (the *J. A. Smith*) purchased in Norfolk in May 1861 by the State of North Carolina. Renamed the *Weldon N. Edwards* after the President of the State of North Carolina's Secession Convention, she operated as a Confederate States Navy gunboat beginning on July 21, 1861 under the command of James Wallace Cooke. Renamed the CSS FORREST in late December 1861. She was "worn out" and burned in Elizabeth City to prevent capture while under repairs.
[Source: Wikipedia (CSS FORREST) https://en.wikipedia.org/wiki/CSS_Forrest; NCCWSP; NCpedia; NCS]

CSS ELIZABETH: Confederate States steamer.
[Source(s): McElroy; Card File; Stepp, "Burials." Derelicts]

"Ella and Annie" (*William G. Hewes*): Iron side-wheel steamship, built as the *William G. Hewes* in Wilmington, Delaware, in 1860 for commercial service between the United States East Coast and the Gulf of Mexico. She made her maiden voyage early in 1861 and was seized by the State of Louisiana in late April 1861. Initially intended as a gunboat, she became a blockade runner operating out of New Orleans. After the fall of the lower Mississippi River to the Federals in April 1862, she was moved to the Carolina ports. At some point thereafter, *William G. Hewes* was transferred to private ownership and renamed *Ella and Annie*. She continued to run the Federal blockade on behalf of the Confederacy until November 9, 1863, when USS *Niphon* captured her off New Inlet, North Carolina, as she tried to enter the port of Wilmington. *Ella and Annie* was purchased by the United States Navy and commissioned as the USS *Malvern*. Sold at auction in October 1865, she reentered civil employment under her original name until wrecked off Cuba on February 20, 1895.
[Source: www.greyriderfordixienet.com/css-ella--annie.html]

CSS ELLIOTT: No information.

CSS ELLIS: Sidewheel steamer built in 1860, Wilmington, Delaware, originally named the *Fairfield*. Purchased at Norfolk, Virginia, in 1861 by the State of North Carolina, turned over to the Confederacy on July 21, 1861. CSS ELLIS fought in the defense of Forts Hatteras and Clark in Hatteras Inlet, N.C., August 28 – 29, 1861, of Roanoke Island, February 7 – 8, 1862, and of Elizabeth City, N.C. February 10, 1862. CSS ELLIS was captured at Elizabeth City, February 10, 1862 by USS CERES after a fierce battle. She was taken into the Union Navy as the USS ELLIS and assigned to the North Atlantic Blockading Squadron serving in the sounds and rivers of North Carolina. On November 24, 1862, on a mission under command of Lieutenant W. B. Cushing, USN, up the New River Inlet CSS ELLIS ran aground and was set afire to prevent her falling back into Confederate hands.
Specifications:
Displacement 100 tons
Length unknown
Beam unknown
Depth of Hold unknown
Draft 6'
Speed unknown
Complement 28
Armament: one 32-pdr rifle; one 12-pdr howitzer
Propulsion steam
[Source: www.navsource.org/archives]

EMPIRE: Steamship purchased by the State of Virginia soon after that state's secession for use on the James River.

CSS EQUATOR: Source "Gaines" states CSS EQUATOR was a wooden, side-wheel or screw steamer tug, 64 tons, built in 1854 in Philadelphia, Pennsylvania. Armed with one gun. Source www.cfhi.net/IroncladDefendersoftheCapeFear.php indicates she was a lightly armed gunboat steamer; burned in 1865.
[Source: www.cfhi.net/IroncladDefendersoftheCapeFear.php; Gaines]

CSS EUGENIE (blockade runner):
EUGENIE was captured off Mobile Bay May 6, 1863 and purchased from the Key West, Florida, Prize Court by the United Government. She was commissioned into United service on July 9, 1863 and assigned to the West Gulf Blockading Squadron where she served as a dispatch boat and supply ship between Mobile Bay and Pensacola, Florida. USS EUGENIE was renamed USS GLASGOW on January 21, 1864. The ship saw active service until she struck an obstruction and sank in shoal water off Mobile May 8, 1865. The GLASGOW was raised on June 19, 1865, taken to Pensacola, Florida, for repairs, and returned to duty July 1, 1866.
Specifications:
Length: Unknown
Beam: Unknown
Draft: 6 ft. 9 in.
Propulsion: Steam, side-wheel propelled
Speed: Unknown
Complement: Unknown
Armament: 1 X 12-pounder howitzer 1 X 12-pounder
[Source: Wikipedia]

CSS FANNY: Screw Steamer, iron hull. Built as the United States Army steamer FANNY. The date and location of construction are unknown. Captured by the Confederates in Loggerhead Inlet, N.C., on October 1, 1861 and commissioned the CSS *Fanny*. CSS *Fanny* participated in the battles of Roanoke Island, N.C., February 7 – 8, 1862, and Elizabeth

City, N.C. on February 10, 1862, on which date she ran aground and was blown up to prevent her capture. Per source CWNavalChron., on August 3, 1861, John La Mountain made first ascent in a balloon from Union ship FANNY at Hampton Roads to observe Confederate batteries on [Sewall's] Point, Virginia.
Specifications:
Length: unknown
Beam: unknown
Speed: unknown
Complement: 49
Armament: one 32-pdr; one 8" Parrott rifle
Propulsion: steam
[Source: www.navsource.org/archives; Gaines; Wikipedia]

CSS FINGAL (CSS ATLANTA): A casemate ironclad converted from a Scottish-built blockade runner named *Fingal* by the Confederacy after she made one run to Savannah, Georgia. After conversion to an ironclad, CSS ATLANTA made several unsuccessful attempts to attack Union blockading vessels until the ship was captured by two Union monitors on June 17, 1863 when she ran aground. CSS ATLANTA was captured, repaired, and rearmed and commissioned into the United States Navy in February 1864 and served the Union for the rest of the war, primarily on the James River. She was decommissioned in 1865 and placed in reserve. USS ATLANTA was sold to Haiti on May 4, 1869 but was lost at sea in December 1869 on her delivery voyage.
Specifications:
Length: 204 ft.
Beam: 41 ft.
Draft: 15 ft. 9 in.
Propulsion: Steam
Speed: 7-10 knots
Complement: 145 Officers and Men
Armament: 2 X 7 in. Brooke 2 X 6.4 in. Brooke Rifles

CSS FLORIDA: Sidewheel gunboat built as the civilian coastal steamer (SS *Florida*) in Mobile, Alabama in 1856. Acquired by the Confederacy in June 1861 cut down, strengthened, and armed as the gunboat CSS FLORIDA. Renamed CSS SELMA in July 1862, and served in the New Orleans, Lake Ponchartrain, Mississippi Sound and Mobile Bay areas throughout her career. During the Battle of Mobile Bay, CSS SELMA was forced to surrender to USS METACOMET on August 5, 1864. She was immediately taken into United States Navy service as USS SELMA. Decommissioned on 16 July 1865, she was sold in New Orleans and redocumented for merchant service on August 17, 1865. On June 24, 1868, she foundered off the mouth of the Brazos River, TX.
Specifications:
Length: 252'
Beam: 30'
Speed: 9 knots
Complement: 65 to 94
Armament: two 9" smoothbores, one 8" smoothbore, one 6.4" rifle
Propulsion steam
[Source: www.navsource.org/archives]

CSS FORREST: Gunboat; steamer; former tugboat; burned: February 10, 1862.
[Source: https://en.wikipedia.org/wiki/List_of_ships_of_the_Confederate_States_Navy]

CSS FORUM: No information.

CSS FREDERICKSBURG: Ironclad ram built at Richmond, Virginia, 1862-63, and outfitted at Drewry's Bluff in March 1864. CSS FREDERICKSBURG engaged Federal forces in the James River from mid-1864 until the end of the war. Destroyed by Confederate forces to avoid capture by Federal forces with the evacuation of Richmond, April 3, 1865.
Specifications:
Displacement unknown
Length 188'
Beam 40' 3"
Draft 9' 6"
Speed unknown
Complement 150
Armament: one 11" gun, one 8" rifle, two 6.4" rifles
Propulsion steam
[Source: www.navsource.org/archives]

CSS GAINES: Sidewheel Steamer built 1861-1862 at Mobile, Alabama. CSS GAINES served in the waters of Mobile Bay and participated in the Battle of Mobile Bay on August 5, 1864 when she was run aground during the battle by her own officers to avoid surrender to the Union forces. Her final disposition is unknown.
Specifications:
Length: 202'
Beam: 38'
Speed: 10 knots
Complement: 130
Armor: partially covered with 2" iron plating
Armament: one 8" rifle, five 32-pdrs
Propulsion steam
[Source: www.navsource.org/archives]

CSS GENERAL POLK: Originally a side-wheel river steamer built in 1852 and named either *Ed Howard* or merely *Howard*, she was purchased for $8,000 by the Confederacy in 1861 and outfitted for service as a timber-clad river gunboat. She served on the Mississippi and Missouri Rivers before returning to New Orleans. Following the Union victory there she was burned near Yazoo City, Mississippi on June 26, 1862 to prevent capture.
Specifications:
Length: 280'
Beam: 35'
Propulsion: Side-wheeled steamer
Armament: 2 × 1 - 32-pounder Muzzle-loading rifles; 1 × 1 x smoothbore 32-pounder gun
[Source: https://en.wikipedia.org/wiki/Main_Page and http://www.wikiwand.com/en/CSS_General_Polk]

CSS GEORGIA: Screw steamer built in 1862 as the iron-hull fast merchantman, SS *Japan*. Purchased by the Confederate Government at Dumbarton, Scotland, in March 1863 and commissioned CSS GEORGIA on April 8, 1863 at sea. Between April 8 and October 28, 1864 CSS GEORGIA captured nine prizes. She was decommissioned on an unknown date and sold on June 1, 1864, at Liverpool, England. Captured on August 15, 1864 by USS NIAGRA off Portugal, she was sent to Boston where she was condemned and sold as a prize of the United States. On August 5, 1865, she was re-documented as a US Merchant vessel in New Bedford, MA. Her final disposition is unknown.
Specifications:
Length: 212'
Beam: 27'
Speed: unknown
Complement: unknown
Armament: two 24-pdrs, one 32-pdr
Propulsion: steam
[Source: www.navsource.org/archives]

CSS GEORGIA [Floating Battery]: Iron-clad floating battery built in 1862 in Savannah, GA as the CSS GEORGIA, also known as the STATE OF GEORGIA and the LADIES' RAM since it was paid for by the Ladies' Gunboat Association which raised $115,000 for her construction. Her launch and commissioning dates as CSS GEORGIA are unknown. CSS GEORGIA served in the defense of Savannah, GA, anchored in the Savannah River as a floating battery, protecting both the city and Fort Jackson until scuttled by her crew on December 21, 1864 as General Sherman captured the city.
Specifications:
Length: unknown
Beam: 27'
Speed: unknown
Complement: unknown
Armament: unknown
Propulsion: None
[Source: www.navsource.org/archives]

CSS [?] GORDON: Privateer, which captured the USA Brigandine *William McGilvery* on July 25, 1861, the USA Schooner *Protector* on July 28, 1861.
[Source: https://en.wikipedia.org/wiki/List_of_ships_of_the_Confederate_States_Navy]

CSS GRIST: No information.

CSS HAMPTON: A steam-powered wooden gunboat, one of the few Hampton class gunboats to be built. CSS HAMPTON was built at Norfolk Navy Yard in 1862 and based there until May 1862, when the yard was abandoned and the fleet moved up the James River. HAMPTON participated in several significant river actions before being burned by the Confederates as they evacuated Richmond, Virginia on April 3, 1865. The flag from the CSS HAMPTON was taken from the ship as it sank in the James River by Lieutenant William Ladd, a Union soldier. It is housed in the Hampton Roads Naval Museum.

Specifications:
Length: 106'
Beam: 21'
Propulsion: Steam
Armament: 1 X 9" cannon, 1 X 32-pounder cannon
[Source: https://en.wikipedia.org/wiki/CSS_Hampton]

CSS H.L. Hunley (1863-1864): H. L. HUNLEY was a small, hand-powered submarine, privately built at Mobile, Alabama, in 1863. Following trials in Mobile Bay, she was transported to Charleston, South Carolina, in August 1863 to serve in the defense of that port. On August 29, while moored to a steamer, the submarine was accidentally pulled over on its side and sank, drowning five members of her crew. After salvage, she was given a new crew and began a series of tests. However, during diving trials on October 15, 1863, she failed to surface. Horace Lawson Hunley, its designer, who was directing her operation, and the rest of her men were drowned. H. L. HUNLEY was again raised and repaired. With a third crew, and under orders to only operate on the surface, she began a series of attempts to attack United Navy ships on blockade duty off Charleston. On February 17, 1864, these efforts were successful. H. L. HUNLEY approached the steam sloop of war USS HOUSATONIC and detonated a spar torpedo against her side. The Federal ship sank rapidly, becoming the first warship to be lost to a submarine's attack. However, the H. L. HUNLEY did not return from this mission and was presumed lost with all hands.
[Source: https://americancivilwar.com/tcwn/civil_war/Navy_Ships/Submarine_Hunley.html]

CSS HARRIET LANE (later, LAVINIA): Built in 1859 as a cutter of the United States Revenue Cutter Service (USRCS), she had a hull sheathed and fastened with copper. In September 1860, USRC HARRIETT LANE embarked Edward Albert, the Prince of Wales, on the first trip to the United States by a member of the British Royal Family, for passage to Mount Vernon where he placed a wreath on the tomb of George Washington. On March 30, 1861 USS HARRIETT LANE was transferred to the United States Navy for service in an expedition to supply besieged Fort Sumter, in Charleston Harbor. She arrived off Charleston on April 11 and is credited with firing the first naval shot of the Civil War. In August 1861, USS HARRIETT LANE assisted with the first combined amphibious operation of the war during the capture of Forts Clark and Hatteras on the Outer Banks of North Carolina. She supported Admiral Farragut's operations to take control of New Orleans and the entire Mississippi River. The USS HARRIETT LANE was part of a small squadron that bombarded and captured Galveston, Texas on October 3, 1862. On January 1, 1863, the Confederates counter-attacked, sinking several of the Navy ships and heavily damaging and capturing the HARRIETT LANE. After serving some months as the CSS HARRIETT LANE, the ship was sold and converted into a blockade runner named *Lavinia*. The ship sailed to Havana on April 30, 1864, where she was interned for the duration of the war. When she was recovered in 1867, it was determined that she was unfit for government service. She was sold, converted to a bark rig, and renamed *Elliott Richie*. After 17 years of commercial service, she was abandoned at sea off Pernambuco, Brazil on May 13, 1884 after a major fire broke out in her cargo holds.
Specifications:
Length: 177.5'
Beam: 30.5'
Propulsion: a double-right-angled marine engine with two side paddles supported by two masts.
Speed: 13 knots
Complement: 95
Armament: Initial armaments were described as "light guns." After joining the West Gulf Squadron (1862) firepower upgraded to one four-inch rifled Parrott gun to the forecastle, one nine-inch Dahlgren gun before the first mast, two eight-inch Dahlgren Columbiads and two 24-pounder brass howitzers.
[Source: www.maritimeprofessional.com/blogs/post/usrc-harriet-lane-13534 and https://en.wikipedia.org/wiki/USRC_Harriet_Lane_(1857)]

CSS HUNTSVILLE (aka CSS HUNTERSVILLE [?]): Steam-powered ironclad floating battery built at The Confederate Naval Works, Selma Alabama,1862 - 1863 ironclad steam battery, scuttled in Spanish River on April 12, 1865 to prevent capture.
Specifications:
Length: 152'
Beam: 32'
Propulsion: Steam
Speed: 4 knots
Complement: 40
Armament: 1 X 6.4-inch muzzle-loading rifle; 3 or 4 X 32-pounder smoothbores
[Source: https://en.wikipedia.org/wiki/CSS_Huntsville]

CSS HUNTRESS (SS *Tropic*): Sidewheel Steamer (Mail Packet). Built in 1838 in New York City and purchased by the State of Georgia at New York City in March 1861, she was turned over to the Confederate States Navy, date unknown. CSS HUNTRESS served on the Charleston Station 1861-1862, acting as a transport in Charleston Harbor during the summer of 1862. Sold in October 1862 to some Charleston merchants, she was converted to a blockade runner and renamed SS *Tropic*. She was accidentally burned off Charleston while attempting to escape to sea with a load of turpentine and cotton on January

18, 1863.
Specifications:
Length 230'
Beam 24' 6"
Speed 16-20 knots
Complement unknown
Armament 1 to 3 guns
Propulsion steam
[Source: www.navsource.org/archives]

CSS INDIAN CHIEF: Receiving ship moored on the Cooper River, above the CSS CHICORA, at Charleston, SC, 1861-1865. Receiving ships were generally the first stop for newly enlisted sailors whereon they received their initial Seamanship training. In 1863 she assumed the additional duty as a torpedo (mine) operation support vessel. On August 21, 1863, Flag Officer J. R. Tucker, CSN wrote to her commander, Lieutenant W. G. Dozier, CSN, "You will be pleased to have as many boats fitted with torpedoes as you can hoist up to the davits of the INDIAN CHIEF." Obviously, it was thought the torpedo boat might be the answer to breaking the blockade. The ship was burned by the Confederates on February 18, 1865 as they evacuated Charleston.
[Source: Wikipedia; DANFS; ORN]

"ISABELLA"
"Isabel," Isabell": Privateer or blockade runner. British screw steamer captured on the night of May 28, 1864 as she attempted to enter the port of Galveston, Texas with a cargo of arms and powder. She sank on June 2, 1864 as a result of battle damaged suffered during her capture.
[Source: Wikipedia; Gaines]

CSS ISONDIGA: Small wooden steam gunboat without masts that operated in the waters around Savannah, Georgia and those of Saint Augustine Creek, Florida, from April 1863 to December 1864. She accompanied the ironclad ram CSS ATLANTA in the engagement in which the CSS ATLANTA was captured on June 17, 1863. She escaped from Savannah on December 21, 1864 before the city fell to the forces of United States. General William T. Sherman. She was later burned by her commanding officer and crew to prevent seizure by Union forces.
Specifications:
Propulsion: Steam
Speed: 5 knots
Complement: 60
Armament: 1 X 9" shell gun, 1 X 6.4" rifled cannon
[Source: https://en.wikipedia.org/wiki/CSS_Isondiga]

CSS JACKSON (*Muscogee*): Ironclad ram screw steamer constructed in 1862 at Columbus, GA under the name MUSCOGEE. She was commissioned on December 22, 1864 as the CSS JACKSON. Delays in completion prevented the ship's entering active Naval service. Still awaiting outfitting, CSS JACKSON was set ablaze, then scuttled by Wilson's Raiders during the Battle of Columbus.
Specifications:
Length: 56' 5"
Beam: 8'
Speed: unknown
Complement: unknown
Armor: 4 inches of plate iron over 20 inches of
White Oak
Armament: four 7-inch Brooke Rifles; two 6.4 inch
Brooke Rifles; two 12-pdr boat howitzers
Propulsion: steam
[Source: www.navsource.org/archives]

CSS JAMESTOWN (CSS THOMAS JEFFERSON): Brigantine-rigged sidewheel steamer constructed in 1853 as a passenger steamer, the SS *Jamestown* at New York. She was seized at Richmond, VA in 1861 for the Commonwealth of Virginia Navy and commissioned by the Confederate Navy the following July, renamed CSS THOMAS JEFFERSON, but was generally referred to as CSS JAMESTOWN. She participated in the battle of Hampton Roads, March 8-9, 1862 assisting CSS VIRGINIA in her attack USS CONGRESS and USS CUMBERLAND. CSS JAMESTOWN was sunk on the James River as an obstruction in the channel at Drewry's Bluff on May 15, 1862.
Specifications:
Length: 250'
Beam: 34'
Speed: unknown
Complement: unknown

Propulsion: steam
Armament: two guns
[Source: www.navsource.org/archives and https://americancivilwar.com/tcwn/civil_war/Navy_Ships/CSS_Jackson.html]

CSS JOHN DAWSON: No information.

NCS JUNALUSKA: The *Junaluska* was chartered by the State of North Carolina. Her name was never changed, nor was she sold to the Confederate States Navy. The NCS KAKUKEE was turned over to the Confederate States Army quartermaster and, at some point, commanded by Lieutenant Peter U. Murphy.

CSS JUNO (Later renamed CSS HELEN): A fast, iron-framed, side paddle-wheel steamer built in Scotland in 1860. Sailed as a British blockade runner into Charleston in the spring of 1863 and was purchased by the Confederate States Navy Department for use as a dispatch ship, picket ship, flag-of-truce ship, and torpedo boat. CSS HELEN is said to have served as a Charleston harbor gunboat. The ship saw considerable action until it was sunk on March 10, 1864. The CSS JUNO is not to be confused with another ship named the "*Juno*" that was captured trying to reach Wilmington, North Carolina.
Specifications:
Complement: 35 to 50
Armament: Spar torpedo mounted under her bow.
[Source: Wikipedia]

NCS KAKUKEE: The *Kakukee* was chartered and later purchased by the State of North Carolina. She was never armed; her name was never changed; and she was not sold to Confederate States Navy. The NCS KAKUKEE was turned over to the Confederate States Army quartermaster and, at some point, commanded by Lieutenant Peter U. Murphy.
[Source: NCS]

CSS KATE (a.k.a. KATE L. BRUCE). A wooden sidewheel steamer blockade runner. The outbreak of yellow fever in Wilmington, North Carolina in August 1862 was precipitated by the arrival of the blockade-runner Kate from Nassau. The fever slowed traffic in the port and resulted in quarantines. On September 26, 1862, the *Kate* sailed from Nassau, Bahamas to Charleston. The *Kate* made twenty successful trips through the blockade. On November 18, 1862, she ran aground and was scuttled.
Specifications:
Length: 165'
[Source: https://en.wikipedia.org/w/index
php?search=CSS+Kate+Dale&title=Special:Search&fulltext=1&searchToken=cogcsu23j4b8j94zpcbg1to57 and http://www.rfrajola.com/blockade/blockades.pdf]

CSS LIVINGSTON: Gunboat, side-wheel steamer; destroyed: June 26, 1862 [Source: https://en.wikipedia.org/wiki/List_of_ships_of_the_Confederate_States_Navy]

CSS (?) LIZZIE (blockade runner[?]): No information.

CSS MACON (SS *Ogeechee*): Sternwheel gunboat built as the wooden steamer SS *Ogeechee*, date and location unknown. Outfitted for Confederate naval service at Savannah, Georgia, in early 1864, and her name was changed to CSS MACON on August 3, 1864. She reported for duty although lacking a full crew complement. Three days after Savannah capitulated on 21 December 1864, CSS MACON departed for Augusta, Georgia, where she remained until the end of the war. Macon's final disposition is unknown.
Specifications:
Length: 150'
Beam: 25'
Speed: unknown
Complement: 40
Armament: 6 guns
Propulsion: steam
[Source: www.navsource.org/archives]

CSS MAUREPAS: Wooden hull, side paddle-wheel steamer built in 1858 as the GROSSE TETE, a civilian vessel for river commerce and passenger transportation. Confederate authorities purchased her in November 1861 for conversion as a river gunboat. She was commissioned as the CSS MAUREPAS and operated on the Mississippi, Missouri, and White Rivers. She was scuttled on June 16, 1862, along with steamers *Mary Patterson* and *Eliza G.* to create an obstruction to the Federal navy's navigation of the White River.
Specifications:
Length: 180'
Beam: 34'
Armament: 5 guns (32 pounders & 24 pounders) [Source: https://wrecksite.eu/wreck.aspx?218968]

CSS MISSISSIPPI: Projected ironclad warship, 3-screw steamer; Her design was unusual, as she was built according to house building techniques. Whether this would have proved to be feasible cannot be known, as she was not complete when New Orleans fell. She was burned on April 25, 1862.
 [Source: https://en.wikipedia.org/wiki/CSS_Mississpi]

CSS MISSOURI: Center-wheel steam sloop, launched on April 14, 1863 at Shreveport, Louisiana.
[Source: USNHC]

CSS MOBILE: Ironclad screw steamer, burned May 21, 1863 before launching.
[Source: https://en.wikipedia.org/wiki/List_of_ships_of_the_Confederate_States_Navy]

CSS MORGAN: Schooner built at Mobile, AL in 1861-62 (one reference of October 1862 lists her name as CSS ADMIRAL). CSS MORGAN operated in the waters around Mobile from the time of her completion early in 1862 to the close of hostilities. She was surrendered to the United States Navy on May 4, 1865 and sold in December 1865. Final disposition unknown.
Specifications:
Length: unknown
Beam: unknown
Speed: unknown
Complement: unknown
Armament: 3 guns
Propulsion: sail
[Source: www.navsource.org/archives]

CSS NANSEMOND: Hampton Class screw gunboat constructed and launched in Norfolk, Virginia in 1862. Commissioned the CSS NANSEMOND circa May 1862, she was assigned to the James River Squadron where she remained until the end of the war. She was destroyed on April 3, 1865 to avoid capture by Union forces upon evacuation of Richmond.
Specifications:
Length: unknown
Beam: 21'
Speed: 11.5 knots
Complement: unknown
Armament: two 8" guns
Propulsion: two steam engines; twin propellers
[Source: http://www.navsource.org/archives]

CSS NEUSE: Twin-screw, steam-powered ironclad ram built in North Carolina and launched in November 1863. She was commissioned in April 1864. Her career was spent mostly as a floating fortress guarding Kinston and the upper Neuse River. She was burned on March 14, 1865 to prevent capture.
Specifications:
Length: 152'
Beam: 34'
Complement: 94 (March – October 1864)
Armament: 2 × 6.4 in (160 mm) Brooke rifles.
[Source: https://en.wikipedia.org/wiki/CSS_Neuse.]

CSS NEW ORLEANS: Floating battery fitted out at New Orleans, Louisiana in 1861. The craft featured two small boilers with pump connections for repelling boarders. Operated primarily in the Mississippi River, participating in joint army-navy operations at Island Number 10 and New Madrid, Missouri, from March 12 to April 7, 1862. On the final day of the Battle of Island Number Ten (April 7, 1862), the Confederates sank the NEW ORLEANS.
Specifications:
Armament: 1 x 9 in. gun; 17 x 8 in. guns; 2 x 32 pounder rifles.

CSS NORTH CAROLINA: Richmond Class ironclad sloop constructed in Wilmington, North Carolina in 1863 by Beery & Brothers Shipyard (On the approximate site of the current World War II Battleship NORTH CAROLINA Memorial). Commissioned CSS NORTH CAROLINA late in 1863, she was structurally weak, under-powered, and unable to cross a sand bar on the lower Cape Fear River bar. NORTH CAROLINA remained in the Cape Fear River, until she sank on September 27, 1864 from extensive leaks due to her having been constructed of green timber and the lack of a copper sheathing for the hull as protection from wood-eating teredo worms.
Specifications:
Displacement unknown
Length 150'
Beam 32'
Depth of Hold 14'

Draft 12'
Speed unknown
Complement 150
Armament four guns
Propulsion steam
[Source: www.navsource.org/archives]

CSS NORTHAMPTON: A sidewheel steamer used by the Confederates as a cargo ship. Sunk in the James River as an obstruction at Drewry's Bluff in 1862. She lies along the shore under the bluff.
[Source: NUMA]

CSS OLUSTEE [SEE CSS CHAMELION (a.k.a. CAMELION); CSS TALLAHASSEE]
A twin-screw steamer and cruiser purchased in 1864 by the Confederate States Navy. Operated as a commerce raider off the Atlantic coast. She later sailed under the name CSS OLUSTEE and CSS CHAMELEON.
Specifications:
Length: 220 ft.
Beam: 24 ft.
Draft: 14 ft.
Propulsion: Steam; two screws
Speed: 14 knots
Complement: 120
Armament: 1 X Rifled 32-pounder forward
1 X Rifled 100-pounder amidships
1 X heavy Parrot aft
[Source: Wikipedia]

CSS OWL: Confederate government blockade runner built in Liverpool, England and launched on June 21, 1864. Owl was commanded by Commander John Newland Maffitt, CSN, the "Prince of Privateers" as of about September 9. The ship had a successful career as a blockade runner and was delivered to Fraser, Trenholm, & Co. in Liverpool after war's end.
Specifications:
Length: 230'
Beam: 26'
Propulsion: steam
Speed: 14 – 16 knots
[Source: https://en.wikipedia.org/wiki/CSS_Owl]

CSS PALMETTO STATE: Richmond Class ironclad ram built in January 1862 at Charleston, S.C, and commissioned in September 1862. PALMETTO STATE participated in the defense of Charleston. She was burned by the Confederates during the evacuation of Charleston on February 18, 1865.
Specifications:
Length: 150'
Beam: 34'
Speed: 8 knots
Complement: unknown
Armament: two 7" rifles; two 9" smoothbores
Propulsion steam
[Source: www.navsource.org/archives]

CSS PATRICK HENRY: Sidewheel steamer, built in 1859 as the brigantine-rigged passenger and freight steamer SS *Yorktown* at New York. Seized by the state of Virginia, April 17, 1861 and subsequently turned over to the Confederate Navy. Assigned to the James River Squadron and converted to a lightly protected ship-of-war and renamed CSS PATRICK HENRY. After seeing combat action, she was designated as an academy ship in May 1862 to serve as the floating Confederate States Naval Academy. In October 1863 she was stationed at Drewry's Bluff. The CSS PATRICK HENRY was burned by the Confederates when Richmond was evacuated on April 3, 1865.
Specifications:
Length: 250'
Beam: 34'
Speed: unknown
Complement: 150
Armament: one 64-pdr gun; six 8" guns; two 32-pdr rifles
Propulsion: steam
[Source: www.navsource.org/archives]

CSS PEE DEE: Steam screw sloop configured as a wooden gunboat, built in late 1862 at Mars Bluff near Marion Courthouse, South Carolina on the Great Pee Dee River. She is believed to have been completed and in commission as early as April 20, 1864. She served on the Pee Dee River and was destroyed on February 18, 1865 by the Confederates 110 miles above Georgetown after the evacuation of Charleston to prevent her capture.
Specifications:
Length: 26'
Beam: 17'2"
Speed: 9 knots
Complement: 91
Armament: one 7" Brooke rifle; one 6.4" Brooke rifle; one 9" Dahlgren smoothbore
Propulsion: steam and sail; two steam engines, twin propellers
[Source: www.navsource.org/archives]

CSS PHANTOM: Steamer steel screw drive. CSS PHANTOM was custom-built as a blockade runner in 1862, in Liverpool, England. Used to pick up lead ingots from Bermuda which could be made into cannon shot and bullets. She apparently made two successful trips from Bermuda to Wilmington and back before being spotted at dawn on 23 September 1862 by the USS CONNECTICUT. During a four-hour chase, CSS PHANTOM stuck close to the shoreline trying to avoid the USS CONNECTICUT. Eventually, the USS CONNECTICUT was able to catch up. CSS PHANTOM'S crew ran the boat aground and set it on fire to avoid capture and destroy the ship's cargo. She was believed lost on the shoals of Topsail Inlet just off the coast of Topsail Island, North Carolina. [NOTE: A blockade runner named the "PHANTOM," captained by Piento Peso, operated out of Mariel, Cuba until captured off the Suwanee River, Florida on 2 March 1865. Source: *Hispanic Confederates*, by John O'Donnell-Rosales].
Specifications:
Length: 190'
[Source: https://portcitydaily.com/local-news/2017/11/13/the-phantom-does-topsails-little-known-shipwreck-hide-a-multi-million-dollar-treasure-nws/]

CSS PONCHARTRAIN: The elegant side-wheel steamboat Lizzie Simmons was built in 1859 and ran the Mississippi River between Memphis and New Orleans until purchased by the Confederate Navy on October 12, 1861 for conversion into a gunboat s the CSS PONCHARTRAIN during January and February 1862. She served on the Arkansas and White Rivers and affected Union strategy in 1862 and 1863. One source indicates she never saw combat, while another reported "the vessel fought on the Mississippi River until ordered to serve on Arkansas rivers. Her crew fought at St. Charles and Arkansas Post, but the Pontchartrain remained at Little Rock, a threat to Union sailors." She was burned to prevent her capture on 10 September 1863 when Little Rock fell.
[Source: www.arkansascivilwar150.com/historical-markers/c-s-s-pontchartrain; http://www.encyclopediaofarkansas.net/encyclopedia/entry-detail.aspx?entryID=5914]

CSS RALEIGH: A small, iron-hulled, propeller-driven Richmond Class ironclad steam sloop built in Wilmington, North Carolina in 1863 - 1864 and commissioned on April 30, 1864. Fitted with a spar torpedo instead of an iron ram, CSS RALEIGH served in coastal waters of North Carolina and Virginia and in the James River. She was active in the defense of Roanoke Island, N.C., against an amphibious assault, February 7 – 8, 1862 and at Elizabeth City, N.C., two days later. CSS RALEIGH escaped the North Carolina sounds through Dismal Swamp Canal to Norfolk, VA and served as tender to CSS VIRGINIA, March 8 – 9, 1862, during the historic battle of ironclads at Hampton Roads. With the Federal recapture of Norfolk Navy Yard in May 1862, CSS RALEIGH steamed up the James River but a shortage of crew rendered her unable to continue the fight. Renamed CSS ROANOKE near the end of the war, she was destroyed by the Confederates on April 4, 1865 upon the evacuation of Richmond.
Specifications:
Length: 172'
Beam: 32'
Speed: unknown
Complement: 197 Officers and crew, plus a 24-man marine complement.
Armament: four guns 6" guns; a spar torpedo.
Propulsion: steam
[Source: www.navsource.org/archives; www.cfhi.net/IroncladDefendersoftheCapeFear.php]

CSS RALEIGH (1861): Government steamer. Originally a small, iron-hulled, propeller-driven towing steamer operating on the Albemarle and Chesapeake Canal. She was purchased by the State of North Carolina in May 1861, and transferred to the Confederate States July 21, 1861. She was armed with one to four guns [Source NCS indicates she was never armed]. Her entire service was in the coastal waters of North Carolina and Virginia and in the James River as part of the James River Squadron. RALEIGH supported Fort Hatteras and Fort Clark on August 28–29, 1861; took part in an expedition on October 1 to capture United Army steamer *Fanny* with valuable stores on board; and accompanied CSS SEA BIRD when she reconnoitered Pamlico Sound on January 20, 1862. She was also active in the defense of Roanoke Island against an amphibious assault by overwhelming Federal forces on February 7–8, 1862, and was at Elizabeth City, North Carolina two days later. RALEIGH escaped through Dismal Swamp Canal to Norfolk, Virginia. On March 8–9, 1862, RALEIGH served as tender to CSS VIRGINIA during the historic Battle of Hampton Roads, for which she received the thanks of the Confederate Congress. With the Federal recapture of Norfolk Navy Yard in May 1862, RALEIGH steamed up the James River, but thereafter a shortage of crew members restricted her to flag-of-truce or patrol service. RALEIGH was renamed ROANOKE near the end of the war and destroyed by the Confederates on April 4, 1865 upon the evacuation of Richmond, Virginia.

CSS Raleigh (1864): A steam-powered Civil War casemate ironclad, one of two Richmond class ironclads designed for harbor defense. She was fitted with a spar torpedo instead of an iron ram and was built in 1863-64 for the Confederate States Navy by J. L. Cassidey and Sons Shipyard at Wilmington, North Carolina. Commissioned on April 30, 1864, the RALEIGH was launched later in 1864. On May 6, 1864, the CSS RALEIGH was ordered to leave the Cape Fear River and venture into the midst of the blockading squadron to break it. She engaged six blockading vessels in a night-long running battle but returned to the Cape Fear River by 7:15 on the morning of May 7, 1864. In maneuvering in the lower Cape Fear, she ran aground south of Wilmington, and while stuck on the bar known locally as "the Rip." As the tide receded, her keel could not support the immense weight of her cannon, armor, and machinery and her keel was subsequently broken. She was lost to the Confederacy after only one week of service.
Length: 150'
Beam: 32 ft.
Draft: 12 ft.
Propulsion: Steam
Complement: 188 officers and enlisted men
Armament: 2 x 6 in. Brooke rifled cannons
2 x smoothbore cannons
Construction started: 1863
Launched: 1864
[Source: Wikipedia; https://en.wikipedia.org/wiki/List_of_ships_of_the_Confederate_States_Navy; NCS]

CSS R. E. LEE: Blockade runner. An iron-hulled side-wheel gunboat built in 1860 at Glasgow, Scotland, as the commercial steamer GIRAFFE. In 1862 she became the Confederate blockade runner ROBERT E. LEE and, during the next year successfully penetrated the Federal blockade of the South more than twenty times. While attempting to reach Wilmington, North Carolina, on 9 November 1863, the ship was captured by the United States Navy. Purchased in January 1864, she was converted to a warship and placed in commission in June 1864, as the USS FORT DONELSON. She was stationed off the North Carolina coast as part of the North Atlantic Blockading Squadron where she participated in the January 1865 captured Fort Fisher, eliminating Wilmington as a blockade-running port. In poor condition, USS FORT DONELSON was decommissioned at Philadelphia, Pennsylvania, in August and sold in October 1865.
[Source:https://americancivilwar.com/tcwn/civil_war/Navy_ShipsUSS_Fort_Donelson.html]

CSS RAPPAHANNOCK: Steam sloop-of-war launched 2 November 1855 in London as the steam sloop-of war HMS VICTOR for the British government. She was sold to R. Gordon Coleman as the SCYLLA in November 1863 and resold later in the month to the Confederacy. Suspecting she was destined to be a Confederate commerce raider, she was detained by the British government, but successfully escaped from Sheerness, England, 24 November 1861. Commissioned as a Confederate man-of-war while under way, her bearings burned out in the Thames Estuary and was taken across to Calais for repairs. She was detained on various pretexts by the French Government causing CSS RAPPAHANNOCK to never get to sea. She was turned over to the United States at the close of the war. Final disposition unknown.
Specifications:
Length: 200'
Beam: 30 '2"
Speed: 11.6 knots
Complement: 100
Armament: one 68-pdr muzzle-loading rifle; four 32-pdr
(25 cwt) muzzle-loading smoothbore guns; one 7"
/110-pdr breech loader; one 40pdr breech loader; four 20-pdr breech loaders.
Propulsion: Barque rigged sails and one 2-cylinder horizontal single-expansion steam engine; 1,166 IHP
[Source: www.navsource.org/archives]

CSS RED ROVER: Side-wheel river steamer built in 1859 at Cape Girardeau, Missouri. Purchased by the Confederacy on November 7, 1861 and initially used as a barracks ship for the floating battery at New Orleans, Louisiana. Serving from March 15, 1862, at Island No. 10, near New Madrid, the ship was severely damaged by Union fire during a bombardment of that island sometime before March 25, 1865 leading the Confederates to abandon her as a barracks ship. She was captured by the Union gunboat USS MOUND CITY on April 7, 1862. She was repaired by Union forces who fitted her out as a summer hospital ship.
[Source: https://en.wikipedia.org/wiki/USS_Red_Rover_(1859)]

CSS RESOLUTE: Sidewheel steamer built as the tug RESOLUTE in 1858 at Savannah, Georgia. She entered Confederate service in 1861 as a tow boat, transport, receiving ship, and tender to CSS SAVANNAH. On 12 December 1864 CSS RESOLUTE accompanied the gunboats CSS MACON and CSS SAMPSON in their attempt to destroy the Charleston and Savannah Railway Bridge spanning the Savannah River. Following an unsuccessful attack, she was disabled in a collision with the two gunboats during their retreat. CSS RESOLUTE was run aground on Argyle Island on the Savannah River, captured by Union soldiers, and taken into Federal service.
Specifications:
Length: unknown
Beam: unknown
Speed: unknown
Complement: 35
Armament: unknown [Source: www.navsource.org/archives]

CSS RICHMOND: Richmond Class ironclad ram constructed in 1862 at the Gosport (Norfolk) Navy Yard. She was launched on 6 May 1862, completed in Richmond in July 1862, and commissioned in July 1862. After an active combat career on the James River, CSS RICHMOND was destroyed by order of RADM Raphael Semmes, CSN, to prevent capture by Federal forces when the Confederate capital was evacuated on 3 April 1865.
Specifications:
Length: 172' 6"
Beam: 34'
Speed: 5 knots
Complement: 150
Armament: four rifled guns, two on each side; two shell guns, on each side; one spar torpedo
Propulsion: steam
[Source: www.navsource.org/archives]

CSS ROANOKE: Screw steamer, destroyed: April 4, 1865. Formerly, the CSS RALEIGH (q. v.).
[Source: https://en.wikipedia.org/wiki/List_of_ships_of_t he_Confederate States_Navy]

CSS SAMPSON: Sidewheel steamer employed as a tug before entering Confederate Government service in 1861. She participated in operations at Port Royal Sound, S.C., helped evacuate the garrison of Port Royal's to Savannah, resupplied Fort Pulaski while under fire, and served as receiving ship at Savannah until 16 November 1863 when she was reassigned to combat duty, patrolling the Savannah River. In December 1864 she participated with CSS MACON and CSS RESOLUTE in an expedition to destroy the Charleston and Savannah Railway bridge spanning the Savannah River. CSS SAMPSON was taken up the river to Augusta, GA prior to Sherman's capture of Savannah on 21 December 1864 and remained there until the end of the war. Final disposition unknown.
Specifications:
Length: unknown
Beam: unknown
Speed: unknown
Complement: 49
Armament: one 32-pdr smoothbore; one 12-pdr
Propulsion: steam
[Source: www.navsource.org/archives]

CSS SAMUEL HINES: No Information found.

CSS SAVANNAH I: Sidewheel steamer, gunboat, constructed in 1856 as the SS EVERGLADE in New York. She was purchased by the State of Georgia in early 1861 and converted into a gunboat for coast defense. She was commissioned CSS SAVANNAH by the Confederate States Navy, circa 18 January 1861. The SAVANNAH I took part in actions against Union forces preparing to attack Port Royal Sound, S.C., the defense of Forts Walker and Beauregard, and aided in the attack on Union vessels at the mouth of the Savannah River, 26 November 1861, and assisted in the attempted defense of Fort Pulaski on 10-11 April 1862. She was reassigned as a receiving ship at Savannah in 1862 with her name being changed to SS OCONEE, 28 April 1863. In June SS OCONEE sailed for England loaded with cotton with which to pay for badly needed supplies. She foundered in bad weather on 18 August 1863 and a boat with four officers and 11 men was captured 2 days later. The remainder of her crew escaped.
Specifications:
Length: unknown
Beam: unknown
Speed: unknown
Complement: unknown
Armament: one 32-pdrs
Propulsion: steam
[Source: www.navsource.org/archives]

CSS SAVANNAH II Richmond-type ironclad ram built in 1863 as an ironclad steam sloop in Savannah, GA. Commissioned in 1863, she was assigned to naval forces in the Savannah River. The CSS SAVANNAH II was burned by the Confederates on 21 December 1864 upon the approach of Gen. William T. Sherman's Union forces.
Specifications:
Length 150'
Beam 34'
Speed 6 to 7 knots.
Complement 180
Armament: two 7" rifles; two 6.4" rifles
Propulsion steam
[Source: www.navsource.org/archives]

CSS SEA BIRD: Sidewheel steamer built in 1854 in Keyport, New Jersey. She was purchased by the State of North Carolina at Norfolk, VA., in 1861 and fitted for service with the Confederate States Navy for duty along the coasts of Virginia and North Carolina. CSS SEA BIRD served as the flagship of Confederate Flag Officer W. F. Lynch's "Mosquito Fleet" during the battles in defense of Roanoke Island on February 7-8, 1862, and Elizabeth City, N.C. She was rammed and sunk by the USS COMMODRE PERRY on 10 February 1862.
Specifications:
Length: unknown
Beam: unknown
Speed: unknown
Complement 42
Armament: one 32-pdr smoothbore: one 30-pdr rifle
Propulsion: steam
[Source: www.navsource.org/archives]

CSS SELMA [SEE CSS FLORIDA (1861 - 1862)]: Sidewheel steam-powered gunboat originally constructed as the civilian coastal steamer SS FLORIDA in 1856 at Mobile, AL. Acquired by the Confederacy in June, she was cut down and strengthened for use as a gunboat. On active service as of 12 November 1861, she operated in the New Orleans, Lake Ponchartrain, Mississippi Sound and Mobile Bay areas throughout her career. She was renamed CSS SELMA in July 1862. During the Battle of Mobile Bay, CSS SELMA was forced to surrender USS METACOMET on 5 August 1864 and was immediately taken into US Navy service as the USS SELMA. Decommissioned on 16 July 1865, she was sold at New Orleans on 17 August 1865 and redocumented for merchant service. SS SELMA foundered off the mouth of the Brazos River, TX., 24 June 1868.
Specifications:
Length: 252'
Beam: 30'
Speed: 9 knots
Complement: 65 to 94
Armament: two 9" smoothbores; one 8" smoothbore; one 6.4" Rifle.
Propulsion: steam
[Source: www.navsource.org/archives]

CSS SHENNANDOAH: Armed Cruiser. Built on the River Clyde in Scotland as the SS SEA KING as an iron-framed, teak-planked, full-rigged ship, with auxiliary steam power. Launched on 17 August 1863, she was purchased by the Confederate Government in 1864 and converted to an armed cruiser. She began operations on 8 October 1864, departing London for Bombay, India on a "trading voyage." Off Funchal, Madeira, SEA KING was converted to a ship-of-war and commissioned the CSS SHENANDOAH on 19 October 1864 under the command of Lieutenant. James I. Waddell, CSN. Short-handed the cruiser headed for Australia, capturing nine prizes en route. On departing Melbourne, CSS SHENANDOAH headed for the North Pacific whaling grounds, burning four whalers in the Caroline Islands in April 1864, an additional ship in Sea of Okhotsk, and twenty-one more in the Arctic Ocean. On Learning on 2 August 1865 of the end of the war, Captain Waddell lowered his Confederate flag. The SHENANDOAH then underwent a physical alteration, dismantling and storing her guns below deck and painting her hull to resemble an ordinary merchant vessel. She sailed to Liverpool where she surrendered to the Royal Navy on 6 November 1865, marking the last surrender of the War. During her service as a Confederate commerce raider CSS SHENANDOAH captured an amazing 38 vessels. Seized by the United government in 1866, she was sold to the first Sultan of Zanzibar, who renamed her after himself EL MAJIDI. She was severely damaged by a hurricane in Zanzibar on 15 April 1872.
Specifications:
Length: 81' 6"
Beam: 18' 9"
Speed: 14 knots
Complement: 19
Armament: one 20-pdr Parrot Rifle; one heavy 12-pdr
Propulsion: sail and auxiliary steam engine [Source: www.navsource.org/archives]

CSS SPRAY: Side paddle-wheel steamer built in New Albany, Indiana as a merchant tugboat. She was purchased in 1850 and operated along the Florida coast as far north as Georgia and as far west as New Orleans. She entered Confederate service in 1863 commissioned as the CSS SPRAY. CSS SPRAY saw combat action and was said to be the only Confederate States Navy vessel to operate exclusively in Florida waters. CSS SPRAY surrendered to the Federal forces on 12 May 1865.
Specifications:
Complement: 25
Armament: two guns
[Source: www.navsource.org/archives]

CSS STONO [may be same as CSS STONE/CSS STONEHO]: Former passenger and cargo ship the USS ISAAC SMITH. After being wrecked, she was captured by the Confederates on 30 January 1863, becoming the only US Navy warship to be captured by enemy land forces during the War Between the States. She was burned in 1865.
Specifications:
Length: 171' 6"
Beam: 31' 4"
Complement: 56
Armament: one 30-pounder Parrott rifle; eight 8" Dahlgren smoothbores.
Propulsion: Steam, screw propeller.
[Source: https://en.wikipedia.org/wiki/Main_Page]

CSS STONEWALL: Ironclad ram built in Bordeaux, France in 1863-64 for the Confederate States Government. However, the French Government refused to permit her delivery. She was sold to Denmark, via a Swedish intermediary, for use in the Schleswig-Holstein War and named the SPHINX. SPHINX failed to reach Copenhagen before end of the Schleswig-Holstein War and was returned to her builders and resold to the Confederate States Government in December 1864. Renamed CSS STONEWALL, she departed Copenhagen to load supplies in France. In order to throw off suspicion of her actual ownership, she was renamed STAERKODDER and OLINE. CSS STONEWALL reached Nassau, New Providence on 6 May 1865, but because of the war's end, she sailed for Cuba where she was turned over to the Captain General of Cuba, who in turn transferred it to the US Government in July 1865. The US Government sold STONEWALL to Japan in 1867, where she was renamed KOTESU and later AZUMA.
Specifications:
Length: 171' 10"
Beam: 32' 8"
Speed: 10 knots
Complement: unknown
Armament: unknown
Propulsion steam
[Source: www.navsource.org/archives]

CSS STROPMAN: No information found.

CSS SUMTER: Screw steamer constructed as the bark-rigged steamer SS HABANAOF NEW ORLEANS at Philadelphia, PA. She was purchased by the Confederate States Navy at New Orleans in April 1861 and converted to a cruiser by CAPT Raphael Semmes, CSN. Commissioned as the CSS SUMTER on 3 June 1861, she cruised the West Indies and as far south as Brazil capturing eighteen prizes in six months. Forced to run for Gibraltar in December 1861, she was disarmed and laid up at Gibraltar in January 1862. Sold at auction on 19 December 1862 to the Fraser-Trenholm interests, SUMTER quietly continued her service to the Confederacy under British colors as the blockade runner SS GIBRALTER. Her final disposition is unknown.
Specifications:
Length: 184'
Beam: 30'
Speed: 10 knots
Complement: unknown
Armament: one 8" shell gun; four 32-pdrs
Propulsion: steam
[Source: www.navsource.org/archives]

"Susan Bierne": Blockade runner from Glasgow, Scotland that operated out of Wilmington, North Carolina.
[Source: www.electricscotland.com/history/america/capefear.htm]

CSS TALLAHASSEE [SEE: CSS OLUSTEE]

CSS TENNESSEE: Casemated, ironclad ram constructed in Selma, Alabama in 1862 - 1863. Launched in late February 1863, she was commissioned the CSS TENNESSEE on 16 February 1864 at Mobile, Alabama and was assigned to the defense of Mobile Bay. During the Battle of Mobile Bay on 5 August 1864 CSS TENNESSEE was forced to surrender to

a superior federal naval force under the command of Rear Admiral David Farragut. Re-commissioned USS TENNESSEE on the same day as her capture, 5 August 1864, she joined the Mississippi Squadron after repairs at New Orleans. She was decommissioned on 19 August 1865 and laid up at New Orleans until sold at auction on 27 November 1867 for scrap.
Specifications:
Length: 209'
Beam: 48'
Speed: 6 knots.
Complement: unknown
Armament: two 7" Brooke rifles; four 6" Brooke rifles
Propulsion: steam
[Source: www.navsource.org/archives]

CSS TEXAS: Ironclad ram built in Richmond, VA in 1864 and launched in 1865. She was unfinished but intact in an outfitting berth in the Richmond Navy Yard when that city fell on 4 April 1865. She was taken into the United States Navy but saw no service. The TEXAS was kept in Norfolk, VA until sold in 1867.
Specifications:
Length: 217'
Beam: 48' 6"
Speed: unknown
Complement: 50
Armament: four pivot guns; two broadside guns
Propulsion: two steam engines; twin propellers
[Source: www.navsource.org/archives]

CSS TORPEDO: Gunboat, screw steamer, tug/tender, iron; burned: April 4, 1865.
[Source: https://en.wikipedia.org/wiki/List_of_ships_of_the_Confederate_States_Navy#Government_steamers]

CSS TORCH: Small case-mated steamer with no cannon, but three spars to which 70 to 100-pound torpedoes (mines) were attacked. A Confederate deserter in January 1864 described CSS Torch as "built like the other ironclads, with a casemate, but very small." She was launched in Charleston, South Carolina, in the Summer of 1863, and was operational by 1863. On night of 20 August 1863 she left her moorings with a volunteer crew of Charlestonians to foray against the blockade. She attempted to engage the USS NEW IRONSIDES, despite the fact she was surrounded by five Union ironclads, but the tides kept her from closing to use her torpedoes. She returned to Charleston amid a hail of Union cannon fire. Transferred to the James River Squadron, she was partially burned and sank on 3 April 1865 to prevent capture by Union forces entering Richmond.
[Source: www.lva.virginia.gov/public/guides/connavy/ship_results.asp?page=4&ship; ORN]

CSS TUSCALOOSA: Ironclad steam battery constructed in 1862 at the Confederate Naval Works at Selma and launched on 7 February 1863. She was scuttled in the Spanish River on 12 April 1865. To prevent capture.
Specifications:
Length: 152'
Beam: 34'
Speed: 3 knots
Propulsion: Steam
Complement: 40
Armament: 1 x Brooke 6.4-inch muzzle-loading rifle; 4 x
32 pounder smoothbores. [Source: https://en.wikipedia.org/wiki/CSS_Tuscaloosa_(ironclad)]

CSS UNITED (a.k.a. CSS CONFEDERATE STATES): Wooden-hulled, three-masted heavy frigate of the United Navy, the first of the six original frigates authorized for construction by the Naval Act of 1794. Built at Humphrey's shipyard in Philadelphia, Pennsylvania and launched on 10 May 1797. Immediately saw action in the Quasi-War with France. Saw additional service in the War of 1812 and the Second Barbary War. De-commissioned in 1844, she was re-commissioned in 1846 and detailed to the African Squadron to suppress the illicit slave trade. Returned to Norfolk on 17 February 1849 and was again decommissioned on 24 February and placed again in ordinary [reserve]. She sat rotting away in Norfolk until 20 April 1861 when the navy yard was captured by Confederate troops deemed too far gone and not worth burning by the retreating Federals. She was pumped out, repaired, and commissioned the CSS UNITED STATES [sometimes referred to as the CSS CONFEDERATE STATES], outfitted with a battery of nineteen deck guns and used for harbor defense. When the Confederates abandoned the navy yard in May 1862, the USS UNITED was ordered sunk in the Elizabeth River, Virginia, to form an obstruction to Union vessels. The old timbers of the frigate were so strong and well-preserved they ruined one whole box of axes when attempts were made to scuttle her, and it was necessary to bore through the hull from inside before she would sink. Shortly after the destruction of ironclad ram CSS VIRGINIA on May 11, 1862 and the surrender of the Norfolk Navy Yard to Union troops, USS UNITED was raised and towed to the yard by federal authorities. She remained there until March 1864, when the Bureau of Construction and Repair decided to break her up and sell the wood. This was delayed until the Bureau ordered on 18 December that the frigate be docked at Norfolk and finally broken up.
[Source: https://en.wikipedia.org/wiki/USS_United_Stat es_(1797)]

CSS VIRGINIA (aka CSS MERRIMAC[K]): Merrimack Class Screw Frigate, converted into an ironclad ram. Launched on June 15, 1855 at Boston Navy Yard, she was commissioned US Frigate MERRIMACK on February 20, 1856. She was burned by Federal troops to prevent capture by Confederate forces at Norfolk Navy Yard, Portsmouth, VA, but raised by the Confederates and rebuilt as an ironclad ram commissioned the CSS VIRGINIA on February 17, 1862. On March 8, 1862, CSS VIRGINIA engaged and sank the USS CUMBERLAND and the USS CONGRESS off Newport News in Hampton Roads. The following morning, she encountered and engaged the USS MONITOR in what would be the first battle between ironclad vessels. The results of the battle were inconclusive. After repairs and drydocking CSS VIRGINIA returned to Hampton Roads on April 11, 1862 and captured several Union transports. When Confederate forces were forced to evacuate Norfolk, CSS VIRGINIA was destroyed on May 11, 1862 to prevent her falling into Union hands.
Specifications (CSS VIRGINIA):
Length: 281'
Beam: 52' 2"
Speed: 9 knots
Complement: 320
Armament: two 7" rifles; two 6" rifles; six 9" guns; two
12-pounder howitzers
Propulsion: steam
[Source: www.navsource.org/archives]

CSS VIRGINIA II: Ironclad steam sloop built in 1863 in Richmond, VA. She saw action against Federal ships at Trent's Reach, June 21, 1864; exchanged fire with the enemy at Dutch Gap 13 August and October 22, 1864; and, participated in the capture of Signal Hill, August 17, 1864. She was destroyed in the James River before the evacuation of Richmond, VA on April 3, 1865
Specifications:
Length: 197'
Beam: 47' 6"
Speed: 10 knots
Complement: 150
Armament: one 11" gun; one 8" rifle; two 6.4" rifles
Propulsion: steam [Source: www.navsource.org/archives]

CSS WELDON E. EDWARDS (CSS FORREST): Wooden-hulled steam tug converted into a gunboat. The CSS FORREST was originally named the J. A. SMITH when launched in 1855. Designed as a canal boat, she was converted to steam in 1856. The SMITH was bought at Norfolk in 1861 and renamed the WELDON N. EDWARDS in honor of the President of the North Carolina Secession Convention. In late 1861 her name was changed to CSS FORREST. She saw action in the North Carolina sounds in 1861 to 1862 and, despite being considered "worn out," she saw continuous service. CSS FORREST served with the "Mosquito Fleet" in the waters around Roanoke Island. She was involved in towing schooners and performing patrolling duties until burned to prevent capture after the Battle of Elizabeth City in February 1862.
Specifications:
Length: 93'
Beam: 17'
Propulsion: Steam engine, one propeller
Armament: 1 x 32 pounder Gun on the bow and 1 x howitzer on the stern

CSS W. H. WEBB: Screw tug built in New York in 1856 as the WILLIAM H. WEBB. She arrived in New Orleans in May 1861 from Havana and was issued a privateer's commission, although never used in that capacity. She was pressed into service by the Confederacy in mid-January 1862 and converted into a ram which participated in the sinking of the USS INDIANOLA near New Carthage, MS on February 24, 1863. Early in 1865 the W. H. WEBB was transferred to the Confederate Navy and ran the Union blockade on April 23, 1865 at the mouth of the Red River. Closely pursued by Union vessels, she was run ashore and set on fire by her crew to prevent capture.
Specifications:
Length: 206'
Beam: 32'
Speed: unknown
Complement: unknown
Armament: one 130-pdr rifle; two 12-pdr howitzers
Propulsion steam [Source: www.navsource.org/archives]

CSS WINSLOW (North Carolina-owned ship): Side-wheel river steamer built in New York City in 1846 as the JOSEPH E. COFFEE. Originally named the "J.E. Coffee," she was purchased by the State of North Carolina and armed with a short 32-pounder cannon and one rifled 6-pounder brass cannon. Initially commanded by Lieutenant Thomas M. Crossan, the ship was sold to the Confederate States Navy and turned over to them on August 20, 1861. On November 7, 1861 she struck a sunken hulk en route to aid a French corvette at the entrance to Ocracoke Inlet. She was set afire to prevent capture.

[Source: https://en.wikipedia.org/wiki/CSS_Winslow; https://books.google.com/books?id=90d2LcmfpCcC&pg=PA131&lpg=PA131&dq=CSS+WINSLOW.confederate&source=bl&ots=ff_NzIJ9vZ&sig=BQz0sflISskPb9PiB1vF-KMgnU&hl=en&sa=X&ved=0ahUKEwjY5vDNzp3cAhVoRN8KHeSLDJYQ6AEIPjAG#v=onepage&q=CSS%20WINSLOW.confederate&f=false; NCS]

CSS YADKIN: Wooden, screw steam gunboat. Armed with one or two cannons (size unknown). Built in 1863-1864 in Wilmington, North Carolina. She was scuttled to make an obstruction in the Cape Fear River off the CSS Arctic, a floating battery near Fort Campbell in February 1865.
[Source: www.cfhi.net/IroncladDefendersoftheCapeFear.php;https://books.google.com/books?id=90d2LcmfpCcC&pg=PA131&lpg=PA131&dq=CSS+WINSLOW.confederate&source=bl&ots=ff_NzIJ9vZ&sig=BQz0sflISskPb9PiB1vFiKMgnU&hl=en&sa=X&ved=0ahUKEwjY5vDNzp3cAhVoRN8KHeSLDJYQ6AEIPjAG#v=onepage&q=CSS%20WINSLOW.confederate&f=false]

CSS YORKTOWN: (Same as CSS PATRICK HENRY, q.v.) Brigantine-rigged side-wheel steamer built in New York City in 1859 as the civilian steamer Yorktown. She carried passengers and freight between Richmond, Virginia and New York City. Yorktown was anchored in the James River when Virginia seceded from the Union on April 17, 1861 and was seized by the Virginia Navy and later turned over to the Confederate Navy on June 8, 1861. Commander John Randolph Tucker, who commanded the ship, directed that Yorktown be converted into a gunboat and renamed CSS PATRICK HENRY in honor of that revolutionary patriot. She also served as the first flagship of the James River Squadron and is probably the same ship as served as the floating Confederate States Naval Academy.
[Source: https://en.wikipedia.org/wiki/Main_Page

Appendix VI: CONFEDERATE NAVAL STATIONS, YARDS, AND ACTIVITIES MENTIONED IN THE ROSTER:

Beery Brothers Shipyard (AKA "The Navy Yard")

Confederate Ordnance Works (Raleigh, North Carolina)

Charleston Naval Station (South Carolina)

Charlotte Navy Yard (North Carolina) (1862 – 1865): A Confederate marine engineering works and naval ordnance depot located at the Mecklenburg Iron Works and using some of the machinery previously located at the Norfolk Navy Yard in Virginia.

Confederate Shipyard, Wilmington, North Carolina (aka Benjamin W. Beery Shipyard)

Drewry's Bluff (Virginia): An earthen fortification and camp for Confederate sailors and Marines, Drewry's Bluff was also known as "Camp Beall," for Colonel Lloyd J. Beall, former United States Army officer and paymaster, who was the Confederate States Marine Corps' first and only commandant. The camp was located on the James River below Richmond and defended the river approaches. It was known as Fort Darling by the Union forces.

Edward's Ferry (North Carolina) Naval Station/Shipyard: Established in 1862 along the Roanoke River near Scotland Neck, North Carolina

Fayetteville Naval Ordnance Depot: A short-lived (1865) Confederate Naval Ordnance Depot located near the Cape Fear River. It has been moved from Augusta, Georgia.

Gosport Naval Station (Virginia)

Halifax Naval Station (Halifax, North Carolina)

Jackson Naval Station (Mississippi)

"Kingston" [Kinston] (North Carolina)

Marion Court House Station (South Carolina) Naval: 1864-1865

Mobile Naval Station (Alabama)

New Orleans Naval Station (Louisiana)

Portsmouth Naval Station (Virginia)

Richmond Naval Station (Virginia)

Savannah Naval Station (Georgia)

Vicksburg Naval Station (Mississippi)

Washington (Naval) Shipyard (Washington, North Carolina): Established 1861 – 1862, the shipyard was either a Confederate Naval Shipyard or private yard under contract to the Confederacy.

Whitehall Shipyard: A Confederate Naval Shipyard established in 1862 near Seven Springs, North Carolina, it was located along the Neuse River at the Cliffs of the Neuse.

Wilmington Naval Station/Shipyard (Wilmington, North Carolina): In operation from 1862 – 1865, it was either a Confederate Naval Shipyard or a private yard under contract to the Confederacy. Operated as the Beery Shipyard of pre-war days, located on the southern end of Eagle's Island across from the town of Wilmington.

[Source: www.geocities.com/naforts/ships/yards.html; Mr. Andrew Duppstadt; author knowledge]

Appendix VII: THE ODD, THE STRANGE, AND THE NOTEWORTHY: NOTES ON NORTH CAROLINIANS IN CONFEDERATE NAVAL SERVICE

Alderman, Ira H.: Whether Ira Alderman was superstitious or just did not wish to press his luck is unknown. What we do know is that he was wounded three different times (Fredericksburg, Chancellorsville, and Gettysburg) before transferring from the Army to Confederate naval service.

Battle, Richard Henry, Sr.: The motives of the individual Confederate service members for "wearing the gray" were many and varied. Richard Henry Battle, Sr. did not record his reason "for" fighting, but he left no doubt as to that for which did "not" fight. Putting his money, or lack thereof, where his mouth was, Battle chose to never apply for a Confederate pension, stating he "did not fight for pay(!)"

Bishop, Richard: Bishop's wife's pension application stated her husband fell into the Cape Fear River and drowned. Sadly, his body was never found.

Bolt, John: Born in England, Bolt appears to have been a restless soul. He first served in the Confederate Army, transferred to the Confederate Navy, then transferred back to the Confederate Army, and finally transferred back to the Confederate Navy!

Boudinot, William Elias: Boudinot was a graduate of the United States Naval Academy and served as a Lieutenant in the United States Navy prior to casting his lot with his native state. Commissioned a Captain in the Confederate Navy, it was said "His active brain first originated the signal service and if his suggestions had been heeded it would have been adopted years before the war."

Bowen, Henry Hunter: Along with his brother George W. Bowen and a several others, Henry Hunter Bowen was conscripted into Confederate service in 1864 and placed in the Confederate States Marine Corps. The eighteen letters he wrote, plus the one his brother wrote on the back of one of his, are held by the North Carolina State Archives and are thought to be the largest collection of enlisted Confederate Marine correspondence known to exist. A collection of Confederate Army correspondence of that size would not be considered so unique but given the incredibly small size of the Confederate States Marines Corps during the war, the Bowen collection is most valuable. Strangely, Bowen died on his eighty-fourth birthday, February 11, 1907.

Burroughs, Thomas G.: Thomas Burroughs was not happy in the Confederate Navy, so he deserted and joined the Union Navy. Life there was apparently no better for he deserted back to the Confederate Navy!

Cameron, Lieutenant Francis Hawkes: One of the two North Carolinians to serve in the Confederate States Marine Corps as an officer, Cameron served in several engagements including forming part of the rear guard of Lee's army as it retreated from Richmond and Petersburg. He survived the fierce battle of Sailor's Creek, Virginia, on April 6, 1865 and was paroled in May in Richmond. Returning to his home state, he eventually engaged in the insurance business, but kept his hand in the military. He was influential in reforming the North Carolina militia as the State Guard, eventually rising to the post of Adjutant General with the rank of Brigadier General.

Confederate "Sailors of Color": Seven men and boys of color served in the Confederate States Navy from North Carolina. **Jerry Bowden** was described as "a colored boy" who served as a Cabin Boy (Cabin Boys were young boys of both races who served the ship's officers in a role similar to that of a ship's Steward). **Benjamin Gray** was said to have been "regularly enlisted' and served aboard the famous CSS ALBEMARLE as a Powder Boy until it was sunk (The term "Powder Monkey" was commonly used for the young boys of both races employed on ships to transport powder from below decks powder magazines to the guns during combat. Their small size and agility made them ideal for the very hazardous job which required them to run through smokey gundecks, weaving between the many busy gunners and heavily recoiling guns). Their small size and quick movements caused them to be dubbed "monkeys." Gray became a minister in Bertie County following the war. **Benjamin Morrison** served as a Landsman who enlisted "for the war" and served aboard the CSS ARCTIC. **William Course** was a free Negro who served as an Officer's Steward in the short-lived North Carolina Navy, which was absorbed into the Confederate Navy beginning in late 1861. Course served aboard the NCS RALEIGH and deserted in 1862 to join the United States Navy. **John Moore** was a Fireman aboard the North Carolina Ship (NCS) WINSLOW. He was the slave of Master Patrick McCarrick and one of seven African American crew members aboard the NCS WINSLOW most of whose names are sadly unknown. (The term "Master" was a naval rank held by officers tasked with navigation, setting the sails, obtaining all required sailing supplies, stowing materials in the hold, hoisting and lowering the anchor, making daily entries on the weather, ship's position, and expenditures into the ship's official log, and docking and undocking the ship, among other duties).

Eli Williamson served as both a Seaman and Pilot in the Confederate States Navy. Williamson was a free Negro from a third generation free Murfreesboro family. He served in the United States Navy but left prior to the War Between the States to enter the merchant service where he become the Chief Pilot for the steamer "Curlew." He enlisted in1861 and continued to serve aboard the now "North Carolina Ship." His service entry in this roster details his wounding at the Battle of Roanoke Island long and subsequent discharge in 1862, likely from his wound. His service was decidedly voluntary and honorable.

Lawrence Reed of Wayne County was listed as a "free colored man" who served as a Fireman aboard the CSS ARROW. Taken prisoner in 1864 and sent to the Union prisoner of war camp at Elmira, New York, Reed took the Oath of Allegiance to the United States. His oath carried the remark: "Is a free colored man and resided in Wayne County, North Carolina. Was never in the Confederate Service. Was compelled to act as a fireman on the rebel propeller the [CSS] ARROW. Desires to remain North."

Cooke, Captain James Wallace: Cook became North Carolina's highest ranking Confederate naval officer at the rank of Captain (A naval Captain is equal in rank to an Army Colonel). Cooke was born in 1812 in the town of Beaufort, North Carolina. At an early age, he lost his seafaring merchant father in a hurricane off the coast of North Carolina. Orphaned, Cooke and his sister were taken in by their uncle who also lived in Beaufort. Age the age of fifteen in 1828, he was given an appointment as a Midshipman in the United States Navy. The highlight of his many years of service was accompanying Commodore Perry on his expedition to open Japan to trade. In May 1861, Cooke resigned his commission and cast his lot with the Confederacy. His service was both active and varied. He fought in the Battle of Roanoke Island and was wounded and captured in the Battle of Elizabeth City in February 1862. Exchanged, he returned to duty with the Confederate States Navy which included more battles, more promotions, and assignment to the Wilmington Station where he first commanded the CSS BALTIC and later was placed in charge of building the CSS ALBEMARLE. Promoted to the rank of Captain in May 1864, Cooke was given command of all Confederate ships in North Carolina waters, a position he held till the end of the war.

CSS ALBEMARLE Crewmen: Few North Carolina ships of the War Between the States-era are more famous than the ironclad CSS ALBEMARLE. Several North Carolinians served as members of her crew, including **Benjamin Gray** (African American), **M. Newton Johnston, Eugene K. Lindsay, Simon Massey, Hillsman (Hinsman) Parrish (Parish), and Joseph Morris.** Several of these men were aboard the ship when it was sunk by Union Navy Lieutenant William B. Cushing in a daring October 27, 1864 nighttime attack in a small steam launch armed with an explosive spar "torpedo."

Duke, Washington: This tobacco farmer from Orange (now Durham) County entered service, reluctantly, in 1863, becoming a guard at Camp Holmes near Raleigh. In May 1864 he transferred to the Confederate States Navy ultimately serving as a naval artilleryman at Battery Brook in defense of Richmond. He was commended for his skilled handling of the guns and promoted to the rank of Orderly Sergeant (an Army rank!). Captured during the withdrawal from the capital in April 1865, Duke was imprisoned briefly in Richmond's Libby Prison. He was provided transportation to New Bern and walked the entire one hundred and thirty-four miles back to his farm to resume his pre-war life. In the same year, he founded the "W. Duke, Sons & Co.," becoming a tobacco manufacturing company that would eventually merge with other companies to form the highly profitable conglomerate "American Tobacco Company" in 1890. Through his hard work, smart decisions, and a lot of luck, Duke created a tobacco dynasty that made him and his two sons one of the wealthiest families in America. With a massive donation to Trinity College in Randolph County in 1892, the school moved to Durham becoming Duke University. In 1924, James B. Duke, one of Washington's sons, donated $40 million as an endowment to the school, worth $430 million in today's dollars!

Freshwater, Henry: To be perfectly honest, Alamance County carpenter Henry Freshwater did not do anything extraordinary during his Confederate Navy service as a Landsman. But I simply could not resist adding him to this list because of his appropriately (inland sounds and rivers) nautical name: "Freshwater!"

Graves, Charles Iverson: As a Midshipman at the Confederate States Naval Academy housed in the CSS PATRICK HENRY on the James River near Richmond, Graves was one of the "cadets" ordered to accompany the wife of President Jefferson Davis, members of the Confederate cabinet, and the gold in the Confederate treasury as they made their way south to Georgia following the fall of Richmond.

"Gray Beards and No Beards": Several Tar Heels are known to have served in Confederate naval service at advanced ages. **Edward Ives** enlisted at the age of fifty-five to fight for North Carolina and the Confederacy. **Thomas Hedricks** enlisted in 1862 in Company F, 11th Regiment, North Carolina Troops, at fifty-four years of age. Two years later, at the advanced age of fifty-six, he transferred to the Confederate Navy. **George Smith** was born in 1803 and enlisted in Confederate naval service at the ripe old age of sixty, serving as a First-Class Fireman in his ship's engine room. But the winner of the "Oldest Tar Heel Confederate Sailor" contest goes to **Joseph William Boner** who was born in 1798 and enlisted in the Navy at the "ancient" age of sixty-six! On the other end of the extreme was **Thomas Pinkney Johnston** who entered naval service at the tender age of just sixteen years. **William James Harriss Bellamy** enlisted at the age of seventeen and was wounded in the shoulder and knee at the Battle of Gaines' Mill, Virginia, on June 27, 1862. He was discharged on July 16, 1862, by reason of being "underage." He enlisted in the Confederate States Navy a year and six days later on June 22, 1863 in Wilmington, North Carolina, but provided a substitute the next day and returned to the University of North Carolina at Chapel Hill. **William Routh Ricks** of Edgecombe County takes the prize as the youngest in this roster. He began working with the Confederate Quartermaster Department at the age of thirteen and was appointed a "Cadet" in 1864 to attend the Confederate Naval Academy. These young men were far from the only ones to serve at a very young age. Many young men of stout heart and tender years were to be found in the ranks of the Army.

Guthrie, Lieutenant John Julius: After nearly thirty years of service in the United States Navy, Guthrie resigned to follow the flag of his native State. He served in the Confederate States Navy at New Orleans, aboard the blockade runner AD-VANCE, as well as other assignments. Following the war, he was pardoned by President Andrew Johnson, being the "first" officer of the regular service to receive such clemency. Any hindrances to federal employment due to his former Confederate service were removed by a unanimous act of Congress. He was appointed by President U. S. Grant to the Superintendency of the Life-Saving Service with stations stretching from Cape Henry, Virginia, to Hatteras on the North Carolina coast. Captain Guthrie drowned near Nag's Head off the coast in November 1877 while assisting in the rescue of crew members of the United States steamship HURON. He was hailed as a hero for his efforts.

Harstene, Henry Julius: One of the saddest stories uncovered during the compiling of this roster was that of Captain Julius Harstene, born in North Carolina in 1801. After extended service in the Union Navy, Harstene resigned his commission and entered Confederate naval service. After commanding several vessels, he was posted to duty overseas where he was reported as extremely ill in October 1863 while in Munich. One roster source indicated he served as the Commander of Confederate naval forces at Charleston, South Carolina until late 1862, when he suddenly went insane. He was sent to Paris, France, for treatment, but died there on May 31, 1868.

Hoffman, Jonas: Born in 1820, Gaston County's Jonas Hoffman served initially as a Landsman in the Confederate States Navy. He later served in the Navy's Commissary Department at Wilmington, North Carolina and at Drewry's Bluff, Virginia, 1864 -1865. Hoffman also served as a member of the Naval Brigade that fought as infantry covering the retreat of part of General Lee's army. He was married three times and fathered "fourteen" children all totaled. His first was born in 1843 and his last in 1878, born just four days before his father's fifty-ninth birthday! Hoffman died in 1901, but not before likely capturing the record for the most progeny produced by a North Carolina Confederate sailor!

Hotchkiss, Seth Augustus: Said to have been a firearms expert, Hotchkiss served first in the Confederate States Army, was captured on the retreat from Gettysburg and imprisoned for eighteen months. Exchanged, Hotchkiss joined the Confederate Navy, then transferred back to the Army. He is said to have amassed a considerable fortune following the war while working as a contractor for the Winchester Arms Company. He retired about 1914 and died as the result of a fall from a three-story window at the home of his daughter in New Haven, Connecticut on April 14, 1934.

"Less Than Honorable Service": Not all men who volunteered or were conscripted to serve in the Confederate ranks served with honor, and the Confederate Navy had its share. **Jeremiah Haggerty** enlisted in the Army in 1861 but was soon discharged "for improper conduct and transferred to the steamer "Yorktown" at Richmond July 23, 1861." Accompanying Haggarty to the CSS YORKTOWN was another soldier discharged for "improper conduct," **John Smith**. What their "improper conduct" consisted of is unknown but was obviously enough to make the Army wish to sever its ties with the two. The Army was able to rid itself of several of its bad apples by sending them to the Navy who was always short of manpower. **Jackson B. Henderson** was a member of the Confederate Army who "acted badly [at the] Battle of Gettysburg, was wounded and captured." When he was released from prison and exchanged, he was sent to the … where else … the Navy! It was not only enlisted men who behaved badly. **Master's Mate Joseph Goodwyn Hester** murdered an Acting Midshipman while at sea aboard the CSS SUMTER off Gibraltar in October 1862. He was removed from the ship and sent to the Bahamas aboard a British ship. For some reason, he was never charged for this crime. He later commanded a blockade runner and was captured while serving as its Captain. Hester was employed in late 1874 as a Deputy Marshal and government detective and engaged in "waging a war on the Ku Klux Klan of North and South Carolina." His former Confederate Navy commander, Raphael Semmes, described the incident aboard the CSS SUMTER as "a most foul and brutal murder." Brawling was not uncommon among sailors of any nation, and that of the Confederacy was no exception. **John Maher** was killed by another sailor in a fight in Wilmington in the first week of 1865. There are no details to explain the circumstances, but the rough nature of the riverfront and tough sailor's haunts like Paddy's Hollow were hotbeds of drunkenness and violence. According to Robert J. Cooke's 2009 book Wild, Wicked Wartime Wilmington, during the War Between the States, "'Paddy's Hollow' was one of the most lawless sections of Wilmington. Located generally along the riverfront north of Red Cross Street, it was home to no less than 39 saloons" and "streetwalkers were also known for plying their trade in the vicinity." **Private John O'Donnell**, born in Ireland, was one of twenty-seven men convicted of "mutinous conduct" while serving in the 40th Regiment, North Carolina Troops (3rd North Carolina Heavy Artillery). Like so many Army troublemakers, he was transferred to the Confederate Navy. Finally, there was **Meridith D. Stamper** of Ashe County. Stamper enlisted in the Army in 1861 at the age of nineteen. In April 1862, less than a year later, Stamper killed a fellow soldier while his unit was camped near Kinston. Records indicate he was "present or accounted for" until transferred to the Confederate Navy on or about April 1, 1864, two years later! Was the killing in self-defense, or was his transgression covered by the old adage that the victim "needed killing?"

Maffitt, Lieutenant John Newland: Maffitt was born at sea on the voyage that brought his parents from Ireland to New York. At the age of five, Maffitt was adopted by his uncle in Fayetteville, North Carolina, and at the incredibly young age of thirteen was appointed as a Midshipman, United States Navy. His distinguished career included service aboard the famous USS CONSTITUTION in operations off the west coast of Africa helping suppress the slave trade. When war came in 1861, Maffitt resigned and offered his sword to the Confederate States Navy as a "First Lieutenant." In his colorful career serving the Confederacy, Maffitt served as a naval aide to General Robert E. Lee, the captain of several blockade runners, commander of the CSS ALBEMARLE, and the first commander of the commerce raider CSS FLORIDA, during which time he and his crew captured or destroyed over seventy Union vessels and their cargoes in the Atlantic Ocean between New York and Brazil. The value of the ships and cargoes lost to the Union war effort has been estimated at ten to fifteen million dollars. Unwilling to surrender at war's end, Maffitt escaped to Great Britain where he worked as a ship's captain until returning to North Carolina.

Parker, Gilbert: Incredibly, one of the last applications for a Confederate Widow's Pension came ninety-three years after the end of the War Between the States. It was filed in 1958 by the widow of Gilbert Parker, whom she had married on March 7, 1897, in Wilson, North Carolina when he was sixty-three and she a mere twenty-one. Such "May to December" relationships were not uncommon in the post-war South. Poverty tends to breed practicality. Thus, older veterans receiving even the paltry pension awarded them for Confederate service were sometimes preferable to younger men with no monthly income at all!

Parrish, Hillsman: Standing a mere five feet four inches tall, Parrish was another of those who bounced from branch of service and unit to branch of service. Enlisting in the 3rd Regiment, North Carolina Troops at the age of twenty, he soon transferred to the Confederate Navy where he served aboard the famous CSS VIRGINIA (MERRIMACK) at Hampton Roads, Virginia. Later he received a transfer back to the Army, this time to the 39th Battalion of Virginia Cavalry. He was listed in the records as a former courier for General Richard S. Ewell.

Ricks, William Routh: Tarboro, Edgecombe County native William R. Ricks may have been the last surviving member of the Confederate States Navy. He was enlisted into the Navy in September 1864 at the age of 14 years and appointed an Acting Midshipman to attend the Confederate States Naval Academy aboard the ship CSS PATRICK HENRY. He was one of the school's cadets ordered to assist in escorting Mrs. Jefferson Davis, members of the Confederate cabinet, and the Confederate Treasury from Richmond, Virginia when it was evacuated. He began his Confederate service at the incredibly young age of thirteen working for the local Confederate Quartermaster Department. His November 8, 1934 obituary in the Raleigh "News and Observer" indicated he had died on that day and was the "last known" Confederate Navy veteran and had been North Carolina's sole surviving Confederate veteran.

Roberts, Second Lieutenant John DeBerniere: One of only two North Carolinians who served as officers in the Confederacy's Marine Corps, Roberts was serving at the Marines' primary east coast location, Drewry's Bluff, Virginia, when he received orders to report to Wilmington, North Carolina. He soon discovered he was to be part of an audacious plan to travel north by boat and attempt to free the thousands of Confederates imprisoned by the Federals at Point Lookout, Maryland. The plan was not just audacious, it was downright risky with what many might consider a slim chance of success and a huge chance for disaster. Shortly before the expedition was to venture forth, Roberts took a tumble down the hatchway of the blockade runner "Let-Her-B." Although the expedition never came to pass, Roberts' injuries caused him to be struck from the list. His injuries did not, however, prevent his capture on January 15, 1865 while fighting at Fort Fisher's Battery Buchanan.

Serving on the CSS MERRIMACK (A.K.A. CSS VIRGINIA): North Carolinians were counted among the crew of one of the most famous Confederate ships ever, the CSS MERRIMACK (VIRGINIA), the first armored combat ship in America to sink an enemy vessel. Serving at varying periods of time were **Brice Harralson**, **Howell W. Harrison**, **Humphrey Hodder**, **Joseph S. Hedgepeth**, **Seth Augustus Hotchkiss**, and **J. B. Cunningham** who is said to have acted as the ship's pilot during its fateful encounter with the USS MONITOR.

Smith, John Baptist: According to his entry in Wikipedia, Caswell County's John Baptist(e) Smith's invention of the flashing light signal system "is believed by some to have provided the most lasting contribution made by either side during the American Civil War." Born in 1843, he enlisted in a local company of the Confederate Army at seventeen. He transferred to the Confederate Signal Corps and was placed in charge of the signal station on the James River at Newport News with the rank of sergeant. While there he witnessed the CSS VIRGINIA's sinking of the USS CUMBERLAND and USS CONGRESS, and the subsequent battle between the MONITOR and the MERRIMACK (VIRGINIA), the first battle between ironclad ships.

With the evacuation of Norfolk, Smith and his signal men were ordered to take charge of the signal station at Petersburg on the Appomattox River where they were tasked with observing the movements of the Union fleet and land forces. Smith and his men rendered valuable service during the Seven Day's fighting around Richmond, including monitoring the retreat of McClellan's army.
In 1862 he was ordered to Fort Fisher where the idea of substituting flashing lights for torch signaling came to his creative mind. Using white light and red lightship's lanterns, Smith invented a lantern light system of naval signaling which greatly aided blockade runners as they signaled for entry instructions into protective harbors.

Because of his important contribution, the Secretary of War assigned Smith to General W. H. C. Whiting at Wilmington for special duty. Smith was given the opportunity to serve as a Signal Officer aboard the swift and sleek North Carolina-owned blockade runner "Ad-Vance," possibly the fastest ship afloat at the time. Smith served with distinction in this capacity until February 1864, when he received a commission as a lieutenant in the Confederate States Army's Signal Corps. With his promotion came orders to report back to Petersburg for duty.
In recognition of his bravery and proven signal skills, Smith was placed in command of General P. G. T. Beauregard's headquarters signal lines. Just days later Lieutenant Smith was ordered to report in person to General Robert E. Lee. Because of the faith Lee had in this young lieutenant of signals, he placed Smith in command of the signal lines between his own headquarters and the different points around Petersburg.

In 1865 Lieutenant Smith's men were said to have been the last Confederate troops to leave Petersburg, literally crossing the last bridge as it was being burned. Acting as infantry, as they had at times in the trenches around Petersburg, Smith and his small command served as part of the rear guard for General Lee's army. Smith's Signal Corps unit was present for the surrender at Appomattox Court House where the young lieutenant released some Federal prisoners who had been brought along during the retreat from Petersburg. After securing paroles for himself and his men, Smith returned home to Caswell County, arriving on April 15, 1865, exactly four years to the day of his initial his enlistment! He died in 1923.

Stokes, John: Military record keeping has been the brunt of jokes probably since Hannibal crossed the Alps. Sometimes the mistakes are small, but such was not the case with the mistake made on the record of John Stokes who enlisted in the Confederate Navy on December 5, 1863 in Raleigh, North Carolina. Only three and a half months later, his name appeared on a register of Confederate States Army General Military Hospital Number 4, Wilmington, North Carolina, as having been admitted on March 30, 1864 with "febris typhoides." Typhoid was just one of many diseases that took the lives of so many men serving in the military during this time. It was particularly devastating for new recruits, most of whom had lived relatively isolated lives on farms with little opportunity for public interaction. Therefore, diseases to which many "city folks" had acquired a degree of immunity hit those who had no exposure in a bad way. The hospital register states he was returned to duty on April 24, 1864; however, it also carries the remark: "Died but accounted for as returned to duty." One can only hope his lived ones were not given both bits of news.

Tebby, Henry Sterling: By his own account, Tebby stated he enlisted in the Confederate States Navy in Charleston, South Carolina on April 2, 1861. He served as the Captain of at least two different blockade runners, the "Hattie" and the "Lillian." He was said to have been the last blockade runner in and out of the harbor at Charleston.

Tucker, David: Tucker left his Duplin County home to enlist in the Confederate States Navy on September 20, 1863 and served aboard the CSS SAVANNAH. He served for a year and a half without suffering any known serious injuries. The advance of Union Major General William T. Sherman's army in the spring of 1865 forced the abandonment of coastal forts and the scuttling of many Confederate vessels. Their former garrisons and crews were "voluntold" to take up muskets and join the great retreat of Confederate forces as infantry. The "web-footed infantry" trudged alongside their infantry compatriots eventually ending up at Appomattox. Tucker's application for pension states he was "knocked over by a shell near Appomattox Court House." A doctor's note confirmed this stating Tucker "was knocked some twenty feet by an exploding shell and was unconscious for some hours." No mention is made of the lasting medical effects of his "explosive" experience. Tucker survived to his eighty-sixth year, dying on October 11, 1918 as the First World War raged on.

The Confederate Navy "Basketball Team": Now, obviously, the Confederate States Navy did not have a basketball team (at least, not that is known). However, if they had they would certainly have recruited Landsman **W. R. Hays** who stood a healthy six feet six inches in height. Hays could have competed well as a point or shooting guard, but for the heavy work under the basket the Confederate Navy needed the services of Army transfer **John H. Leonard** who stood an incredible six feet ten or eleven inches. Unfortunately, Leonard entered the transfer portal through desertion shortly after his transfer to the Navy.

The Submarine H. L. HUNLEY: The Confederacy launched the first submarine to sink an enemy vessel in combat. But this remarkable achievement did not come without cost. In its short eight-month career between July 1863 and February 1864, the submarine sank three times, killing nearly 30 men, including its inventor and chief financial backer, Horace L. Hunley. It was recovered twice. It is not unusual even today for men to be lost as experimental weapons, vehicles, aircraft, or ships are being tested. It was not unusual that sailors stood along the gunnels of the Confederate receiving ship CSS INDIAN CHIEF in Charleston Harbor and watched as the strange looking craft submerged with its crew ... but did not come back up, drowning all, or most, of those on board. What WAS unusual was that THREE times the call went out for volunteers to man this dangerous, experimental boat, and each time, volunteers stepped forward! One of those who stepped forward was **James W. Cannon**. Cannon enlisted from North Carolina in 1861 and was serving aboard the CSS INDIAN CHIEF when he answered the fateful call for men to crew the HUNLEY in 1863. Whether he died on the first or second descent is unknown. All that is known is that he was willing risked his life to help find a way to break the strangle hold of the Federal blockade of Southern ports. Another North Carolina volunteer was **James Wickes**. Wickes had been a former member of the United States Navy who left his sinking ship at Hampton Roads to offer his services to the fledgling Confederate Navy. He was a member of the third and final HUNLEY crew that sailed into naval history on the night of February 17, 1864. The long-lost submarine and the remains of the eight brave men on board were discovered in 1995. Among the remains were those of James Wickes. Through the miracle of science, forensic sculptors have been able to reconstruct the face of Wickes. This image can be viewed by doing an internet search under his name.

Waddell, Lieutenant James Iredell: A native of Chatham County, Waddell served as a Lieutenant in the United States Navy before being "dismissed" in January 1862 (Fearing possible disloyalty among its land and naval officer corps, the United States government involuntarily dismissed many). Joining the Confederate States Navy in March 1862, Waddell served in a variety of assignments until appointed commander of the commerce raider CSS SHENANDOAH in October of 1864. Serving primarily in the northern Pacific, Waddell and the CSS SHENANDOAH severely damaged the Union's main source of whale oil by capturing, sinking, or bonding some thirty-eight ships, mostly of the New England whaling fleet. The CSS SHENANDOAH holds the distinction of firing the last shot of the War Between the States (a shot fired across the bow of a whaler off the Aleutians), having carried the Confederate flag completely around the world, being the last Confederate unit to cease fighting (Isolated in the northern Pacific for much of the late war, Waddell did not learn of the war's end in April until nearly six months later. Fearing he and his crew might be arrested as pirates, Waddell sailed his ship to Liverpool, England where he turned it over to British authorities on November 6, 1865, thus becoming the last Confederate combat unit to furl its flag).

CSS *Albemarle*, Raised For Salvage

Confederate States Navy "Jack"
[Flown from the bow of a ship
while anchored or moored]

Flag of Captain William F. Lynch,
flown as ensign of his flagship
CSS *Seabird*, 1862

Seal of the Confederate States Navy

"Help Yourself, and God Will Help You"

Confederate States Navy Button

Confederate States Navy Serving Platter

Last Confederate Naval Jack

Index

A

Abaco Bahams 131
Abbeville 265
Abbotsburg 310
Abbottsburg 288
Abbott's Creek Baptist Church 143
Aberdeen Church 151, 261
Adam York 348
Adelaide 97
Advance 227, 305, 307
Ad-Vance 78, 110, 132, 204, 222, 223, 291
Agnes Fry 100
A. H. Dorsey 39
Ahoskie 339
Aiken's Landing 15, 93, 96, 108, 120, 128, 186, 206, 216, 225, 241, 271, 294, 347
Aikens Landing 36
Alabama 6
Alamance Count 61
Alamance County 3, 36, 50, 60, 62, 66, 79, 114, 136, 165, 168, 173, 216, 217, 231, 232, 265, 311, 315, 316, 324, 328, 344
Albemarle 103, 112, 141
Albemarle Sound 13, 37, 38, 40, 72, 84, 93, 99, 116, 198, 214, 248, 289, 312, 314
Aleutians 319
Alexander and Sarah Nading 228
Alexander County 82, 86, 269, 327
Alexandria 144, 212
Alice 295
Alice A. Morse 223
Alice Measles 192
Allensville 255
Alvin's Ferry 242
Amaryllis Pride Hall 9
Amelia County 111
Amelia Court House 187, 229, 247, 345
A. M. Murray 226
Anna Miller 168
Annapolis 29, 32, 90, 100, 127, 319
Ann Baker 12
Ann Carnicke [Carnic] Maffitt 203
Ann Eliza Williams 22
Ann E. Pepper 246
Anne S. Waddell 319
Ann J. White 333
Ann Mitchell Ball 13
Anson County 101, 109, 121, 137, 179, 187, 264
Apalachicola 219
Appomattox 99, 112, 195, 209, 235, 262, 285, 297, 315, 348
Appomattox Court House 53, 109, 127
Aquia Creek 72, 192
Army of Tennessee 8
Arrington Family Cemetery 339
Asbury Methodist Church Cemetery 345
Ashe County 297, 300, 349
Asheville 64, 84
Ashley Rive 91
Ashley River 50, 58, 141, 158, 163, 258, 284
Ashton 226
Athens Chapel Cemetery 234
Atkinson 333
Atlanta 19, 312
Atlantic 19
Atlantic Coast Line 29
Attala 347
Augusta 265
Aumariah Willis 340
Australia 96
Autryville 105
Avent's Ferry 48
Avery County 208

B

Bahamas 148
Bahia 160
Baldwin 91
Baldwin County 64
Ballina Company 195
Baltimore 100, 110, 155, 167, 170, 175, 185, 192, 207, 220, 271, 324
Baltimore County 296
Banshee 49
Barbados 62
Barbour County 235
Barrington's Ferry 179
Barry County 38
Basco 89
Bath 234
Battery Brooke 3, 30, 56, 217, 230, 342
Battery Brooks 152
Battery Buchanan 127, 129, 144, 181, 269
Battery Burk 98
Battery Cameron 344
Battery Meares 118
Battery Mitchell 133
Battery Sims 291
Battle of Bentonville 30
Battle of Roanoke Island 135
Battle of the Crater 30
Bear Swamp 326
Beaufort 49, 71, 72, 119, 122, 125, 315, 323
Beaufort Count 135
Beaufort County 1, 13, 16, 18, 28, 29, 31, 33, 34, 37, 44, 51, 60, 61, 76, 83, 85, 91, 95, 101, 111, 119, 120, 131, 132, 142, 145, 184, 187, 188, 189, 208, 211, 231, 234, 241, 242, 243, 244, 259, 270, 271, 272, 273, 276, 282, 283, 290, 293, 299, 306, 309, 313, 319, 322, 336, 338, 340, 342, 345, 347

Beauregard 142, 252
Beery Shipyard 232
Belews Creek 239
Belhaven 85
Belleview Cemetery 97
Bellevue 163
Bellevue Cemetery 107, 131, 205, 230, 263, 273, 279, 286, 334
Bellevue Hospital 128
Belvidere 146
Benjamin Washington Beery 109
Bensalem Presbyterian Church 223
Bering Straits 56
Berkeley 235
Berlin 241
Bermuda 48, 192, 250, 292, 325
Bermuda Hundred 272
Bertie County 62, 124, 151, 233, 237, 304
Bertie E. Coble 286
Bethana O'Neal 151
Bethany Presbyterian Church 303
Bethel Baptist Church 1
Bethel Reformed Lutheran Church Cemetery 239
Bethphage Presbyterian Church Cemetery 67
Bettie D. Massenburg 177
Big Rockfish Presbyterian Church 46
Birmingham 81, 142
Black Creek District 205
Black Rock 140, 288
Black Warrior 138
Bladenboro 46
Bladen County 37, 42, 69, 73, 85, 124, 149, 169, 189, 218, 259, 288, 310, 311, 331, 340
Bloomington 332
Bolton 290
Boone County 96
Boon Hill 249
Boonville 285
Boonville Baptist Church 285
Bostic 233
Boston 4, 203, 296
Boston Harbor 21, 40, 85, 98, 129, 161, 170, 203, 216, 257, 267, 279, 303, 346
Bouleware's Wharf 294
Boulware's Wharf 25, 110
Bowen Family Cemetery 33
Brandy Station 145
Brazil 160, 204
Brinkley's Depot 187
Bristoe Station 236, 240
Bristol 188, 292
Brittain Presbyterian Church Cemetery 130
Brittania I. Dixon 91
Brooklyn 52, 189, 260
Brown Pegram 211
Brown's Baptist Church Cemetery 294
Brunswick 85
Brunswick Company 75
Brunswick County 2, 7, 12, 22, 24, 25, 36, 40, 45, 49, 61, 64, 76, 82, 91, 100, 110, 115, 117, 119, 124, 129, 130, 131, 133, 164, 169, 174, 177, 182, 186, 210, 214, 226, 230, 234, 243, 245, 247, 250, 253, 254, 263, 277, 290, 297, 304, 311, 329, 330, 345
Brunswick Point 164
Bryan Whitfield 148
Bull Head 144
Buncombe County 75, 84, 144, 175, 253, 301
Bunnell 145
Bunyan 345
Burgaw 30, 33, 101
Burke County 2, 60, 65, 66, 87, 159, 168, 225, 309
Burkesville 64, 72, 261
Burkeville 46, 53, 125, 142, 175, 197, 202, 222, 258, 283, 294, 304, 327, 342
Burlington 324
Burton H. Smith 289
Buxton 16

C

Cabarrus County 30, 67, 89, 122, 155, 283, 285, 305, 321
Calais 220, 231, 308
Caldwell County 126, 145
Callington 209
Calvary Episcopal Church 111
Calvin Betts 27
Calvin Graves 123
Camden 47
Camden County 7, 41, 57, 128, 161, 170, 172, 177, 201, 264, 265, 266, 278, 287, 295, 307, 334, 346
Camp Bee 109, 279
Camp Bragg 60
Camp Clark 77, 88
Camp Hamilton 80, 101
Camp Hill 122, 162
Camp Hoffman 181
Camp Holmes 3, 9, 10, 13, 15, 19, 20, 21, 27, 32, 34, 36, 40, 41, 42, 48, 51, 52, 53, 54, 56, 58, 60, 62, 63, 64, 65, 67, 68, 73, 75, 76, 77, 85, 86, 87, 89, 90, 97, 101, 103, 108, 111, 112, 114, 115, 116, 117, 118, 122, 123, 126, 130, 133, 134, 137, 138, 141, 143, 147, 149, 150, 157, 159, 161, 162, 163, 164, 166, 169, 172, 173, 174, 176, 178, 179, 182, 185, 191, 193, 194, 197, 200, 202, 203, 204, 206, 207, 208, 209, 214, 216, 218, 220, 221, 222, 223, 224, 231, 232, 233, 237, 239, 240, 241, 244, 248, 251, 255, 258, 263, 264, 266, 273, 274, 280, 281, 284, 285, 289, 295, 298, 301, 302, 304, 305, 306, 309, 310, 314, 315, 316, 318, 326, 328, 331, 334, 335, 340, 341, 342, 343, 348
Camp Homes 160
Camp Howard 164, 245, 304
Camp Lee 239
Camp Leon 305
Camp Magnum 300
Camp Mangum 78, 265, 284, 326
Camp Moore 39, 337
Camp Taylor 324
Camp Vance 332

Camp Winder 268
Camp Wyatt 24, 85, 317
Canada 97
Capal Grove 209
Cape Canaveral 296
Cape Fear River 1, 3, 5, 7, 10, 11, 15, 18, 20, 21, 22, 23, 24, 25, 28, 30, 32, 34, 35, 36, 37, 39, 40, 42, 43, 45, 47, 48, 49, 53, 55, 56, 58, 60, 61, 62, 66, 67, 69, 70, 71, 73, 74, 76, 79, 80, 81, 82, 84, 87, 88, 90, 93, 97, 101, 103, 104, 105, 106, 108, 109, 113, 117, 119, 121, 140, 144, 149, 150, 151, 152, 153, 154, 155, 156, 157, 158, 159, 160, 161, 164, 166, 168, 169, 171, 173, 174, 175, 177, 179, 180, 181, 184, 185, 186, 187, 190, 193, 196, 198, 201, 202, 204, 207, 209, 210, 211, 212, 213, 214, 215, 217, 218, 220, 221, 224, 225, 226, 228, 229, 232, 233, 234, 236, 237, 238, 239, 241, 243, 244, 245, 248, 250, 251, 255, 258, 261, 262, 264, 265, 266, 268, 269, 270, 272, 273, 274, 278, 279, 280, 304, 329, 335, 344, 345, 346, 347, 348
Cape Hatteras Banks 257
Cape Henry 132
Captain William Devane 35
Carolina Beach 317
Caroline Dunton 99
Carrie E. Dismukes 91
Carrie M. Smith 85
Carteret County 59, 84, 85, 91, 118, 119, 122, 131, 133, 143, 208, 242, 259, 267, 292, 313, 321, 340
Carthage 318
Carvers Creek 288
Cary 317, 325
Cassie [Cassey] Grissom 129
Castanea Presbyterian Church Cemetery 29
Caswell County 5, 123, 137, 140, 176, 193, 216, 258, 291, 308, 324, 342, 344, 346
Catawba County 15, 85, 159, 213, 258, 283
Catawba Springs 133, 224
Catherine Kelly 335
Cedar Grove 47, 121, 143
Cedar Grove Cemetery 29, 72, 131, 132, 172, 199, 267, 269, 292, 347
Cedar Hill Cemetery 148
Celia T. Pugh 83
Cerra Gordo 240
Chancellorsville 3, 6, 13, 60, 111, 113, 120, 194, 213, 251, 257, 308, 343
Chapel Hill 24, 56, 69, 75, 127
Charles and Martha B. Dismukes 91
Charles and Martha Spruill 295
Charleston 4, 12, 15, 21, 24, 30, 32, 33, 37, 39, 43, 47, 48, 50, 52, 58, 62, 63, 64, 66, 67, 75, 77, 82, 85, 87, 89, 91, 92, 93, 98, 99, 106, 107, 114, 116, 118, 122, 126, 129, 136, 140, 141, 148, 155, 158, 163, 176, 182, 196, 197, 202, 206, 214, 219, 222, 223, 224, 229, 234, 239, 258, 259, 261, 262, 268, 269, 284, 285, 290, 291, 295, 300, 301, 303, 305, 308, 314, 315, 318, 326, 333, 334, 336, 339, 345
Charleston Harbor 54, 70, 93, 106, 128, 172, 183, 185, 186, 187, 215, 230, 235, 266, 303
Charleston Naval Station 77
Charleston Squadron 19, 186, 291
Charleston Station 34, 81, 85, 87, 103, 112, 118, 131, 140, 142, 160, 183, 186, 198, 202, 247, 269, 276, 279, 283, 285, 319, 338
Charlotte 1, 17, 22, 29, 39, 40, 63, 67, 83, 114, 117, 156, 166, 167, 168, 196, 202, 207, 224, 246, 265, 266, 268, 288, 289, 299, 305, 327
Charlottesville 190, 241
Chatham 32
Chatham County 10, 21, 32, 33, 48, 89, 91, 99, 107, 130, 138, 153, 215, 226, 243, 285, 298, 313, 319, 343
Cheraw 70
Cherbourg 6
Cherry 332
Chesapeake Bay 225
Chester 265
Chesterfield 168
Chewalla Primitive Baptist Church Cemetery 343
CHICORA 197
China Grove 348
Chocowinity 95
Chowan County 55, 91, 144, 184, 186, 205, 227, 256, 324, 331, 346
Christian Harbor Baptist Church 228
Christiansburg 168
Christ's Lutheran Church Cemetery 152
Cincinnati 28
City Cemetery 208
City of Petersburg 25
City Point 4, 7, 10, 16, 62, 71, 73, 81, 129, 133, 134, 145, 155, 165, 213, 215, 217, 221, 234, 268, 294, 300, 318, 343
Claiborne County 104
Clarendon Iron Works 28
Clark County 39
Clarksville 51
Clayton 89
Clear Creek 305
Cleveland 283
Cleveland County 2, 31, 55, 159, 196, 263, 300, 301, 303, 316, 340
Cliffdale 300
Clinton 3, 43, 316
Clinton County 228
Cloninger Cemetery 65
Cobb's Point 72
Cobb's Point Battery 127
Cocke County 86
Coinjock 13, 99, 108, 251
Coinjock District 76
Cold Harbor 94, 117, 132, 186, 187, 200, 214, 227, 234, 264
Colfax 8
College of William and Mary 156
Colleton County 30
Colonel Ellwood Morris 2
Colonel Joseph Thompson 38
Colonel Roger Moore 22

Columbia 100, 135, 142, 148, 268, 296
Columbus 142, 147
Columbus County 22, 61, 202, 240, 290, 292, 301, 325, 339
Colvin's Creek 9
Comjock 99
Commander John K. Mitchell 39
Company Shops 79
Concord 28
Concord Presbyterian Church 282
Condor 40
Confederate States Marine Corps 1, 2
Confederate States Naval Academy 189, 298, 317
Confederate States Navy Yard 1, 39, 266, 268
Cool Spring 296
Coquette 83
County 4, 238, 283
Cox Wharf 225
Crampton's Pass 120
Craney Island 70
Craven Company 31
Craven County 1, 9, 17, 30, 37, 58, 59, 60, 71, 80, 86, 108, 112, 121, 125, 131, 136, 141, 142, 143, 150, 162, 170, 181, 188, 199, 208, 211, 227, 236, 246, 249, 255, 260, 267, 268, 269, 292, 337
Crawford 94, 99, 110, 178
Crawford Township 96
Creswell 155, 232, 272, 295, 332
Cross Creek Cemetery 106
CSN FORREST 229
CSS 4, 21
CSS Alabama 39
CSS ALABAMA 203, 319
CSS ALBEMARLE 6, 7, 10, 11, 13, 22, 23, 26, 27, 30, 33, 38, 46, 51, 56, 65, 68, 72, 77, 78, 82, 83, 86, 92, 99, 103, 104, 110, 113, 116, 123, 124, 132, 141, 149, 151, 155, 156, 157, 159, 160, 161, 167, 168, 172, 177, 185, 190, 192, 194, 204, 207, 214, 216, 223, 231, 232, 253, 258, 269, 272, 287, 289, 294, 297, 306, 307, 313, 314, 321, 328, 333, 336, 338, 344, 346, 347, 348
CSS APPOMATTOX 86, 114, 287
CSS ARCTIC 1, 3, 5, 7, 10, 11, 12, 13, 14, 15, 16, 18, 19, 20, 21, 23, 24, 25, 26, 27, 28, 29, 31, 32, 34, 36, 37, 38, 39, 40, 42, 43, 44, 45, 47, 48, 49, 50, 51, 52, 53, 55, 56, 58, 59, 60, 61, 62, 63, 66, 67, 68, 70, 71, 73, 74, 76, 79, 81, 82, 84, 87, 88, 90, 92, 93, 97, 101, 103, 105, 106, 108, 109, 110, 112, 113, 115, 117, 119, 121, 129, 130, 131, 132, 134, 136, 140, 143, 145, 147, 148, 149, 150, 151, 152, 154, 155, 156, 157, 159, 160, 161, 162, 163, 164, 166, 168, 169, 170, 173, 174, 175, 177, 179, 180, 181, 184, 187, 190, 193, 194, 196, 198, 199, 201, 202, 204, 207, 208, 209, 210, 211, 212, 213, 214, 215, 217, 218, 220, 221, 222, 223, 224, 225, 226, 227, 228, 229, 230, 231, 232, 233, 234, 236, 237, 238, 239, 241, 242, 243, 245, 246, 248, 249, 250, 251, 252, 255, 261, 264, 265, 266, 267, 269, 270, 272, 273, 274, 277, 278, 279, 280, 281, 285, 288, 295, 296, 297, 299, 311, 317, 323, 324, 325, 326, 327, 331, 333, 335, 341, 345, 346, 348
CSS ARKANSAS 317

CSS ARROW 225, 260
CSS ARTIC 265, 294
CSS ATLANTA 4, 34, 52
CSS BALTI 72
CSS BALTIC 64, 81, 111, 129, 195, 338
CSS BEAUFORT 4, 7, 11, 16, 18, 32, 43, 45, 50, 59, 84, 94, 96, 100, 102, 111, 116, 117, 125, 130, 135, 141, 142, 150, 153, 156, 158, 164, 174, 181, 188, 191, 204, 205, 206, 218, 222, 229, 230, 236, 237, 239, 241, 269, 271, 290, 302, 304, 305, 310, 317, 336, 337, 338
CSS BLACK WARRIOR 138
CSS BOMBSHELL 13, 37, 38, 40, 84, 93, 198, 209, 214, 248, 303, 312
CSS CAPITAL 317
CSS CARONDELET 308
CSS CASWELL 2, 7, 8, 23, 26, 54, 56, 68, 76, 82, 100, 110, 118, 121, 124, 130, 205, 230, 245, 290, 314, 329, 345
CSS CEA BIRD 311
CSS CHAMELEON 49
CSS CHARLESTON 33, 44, 261, 269, 283, 315
CSS CHARM 195
CSS Chattahoochee 39
CSS CHATTAHOOCHEE 4, 19, 81, 132, 235
CSS CHATTAHOOCHIE 77, 271
CSS CHICKAMAUGA 11, 325
CSS CHICORA 19, 21, 52, 62, 85, 87, 101, 106, 118, 140, 160, 172, 176, 183, 202, 206, 223, 225, 245, 279, 285, 295, 299, 318, 326, 338
CSS COLUMBIA 31, 33, 34, 52, 66, 83, 87, 112, 155, 158, 176, 196, 197, 202, 223, 229, 234, 239, 253, 258, 262, 269, 272, 301, 303, 318, 333, 336, 345
CSS CONFEDERATE STATES 42, 77, 156, 220
CSS COQUETTE 126
CSS CORA 42, 107, 119, 170, 286, 287, 297
CSS CORNUBIA 125
CSS CURLEW 26, 41, 44, 56, 63, 74, 91, 96, 104, 160, 161, 171, 201, 212, 237, 250, 263, 264, 278, 281, 287, 293, 300, 325, 333, 339, 341
CSS CURLOW 265
CSS DREWRY 135, 251
CSS DRURY 113
CSS EDWARDS 18, 26, 49, 108, 118, 224, 289, 313, 318, 332, 336, 338, 341, 347
CSS ELIZABETH 197
CSS ELLIOTT 76
CSS ELLIS 13, 21, 49, 95, 99, 108, 110, 162, 178, 208, 210, 211, 219, 222, 224, 227, 228, 246, 282, 314, 318, 320, 321, 335, 338, 343, 348
CSS EQUATOR 113, 148, 207
CSS EUGENIE 89, 97, 128, 146, 257, 263, 272
CSS FANNY 22, 34, 43, 57, 71, 74, 93, 95, 96, 104, 111, 112, 118, 119, 123, 128, 135, 141, 160, 162, 163, 170, 184, 211, 212, 227, 229, 237, 244, 251, 271, 275, 278, 306, 345
CSS FINGAL 52
CSS FLORIDA 11, 160, 192, 204, 220, 283, 325
CSS FORREST 25, 26, 45, 49, 91, 108, 109, 118, 119, 121, 156, 195, 212, 215, 224, 225, 240, 271, 276, 288, 289,

313, 315, 318, 332, 336, 338, 341, 347
CSS FORT CASWELL 227, 228
CSS FORUM 283
CSS FREDERICKSBURG 27, 90, 111, 113, 117, 119, 134, 135, 173, 186, 195, 222, 279, 283, 308, 328
CSS GAINES 29, 117, 147, 160, 231, 298
CSS GENERAL POLK 57, 132
CSS GEORGIA 4, 19, 39, 81, 232, 233, 247, 254, 308, 325
CSS GORDON 197
CSS GRIST 15
CSS HAMPTON 111, 186, 207, 283
CSS HARRIETT LANE 260, 298
CSS HUNLEY 54, 335
CSS HUNTERSVILLE 61
CSS HUNTRESS 52
CSS INDIAN CHIEF 21, 31, 33, 52, 54, 62, 66, 69, 83, 85, 87, 91, 98, 107, 112, 118, 122, 126, 155, 176, 182, 190, 197, 202, 206, 219, 222, 224, 234, 258, 262, 269, 272, 282, 285, 289, 300, 303, 314, 316, 318, 319, 326, 333, 345
CSS ISONDIGA 19, 81, 209, 270, 290, 293, 305, 325, 328
CSS JACKSON 198, 308
CSS JAMESTOWN 147, 298
CSS JOHN DAWSON 105
CSS JUNALUSKA 41, 59, 172, 218, 220, 225, 252, 253
CSS JUNO 279
CSS KATE 197
CSS LIVINGSTON 81, 164
CSS LIZZIE 257
CSS MACON 180, 325
CSS MASSACHUSETTS 14
CSS MAUREPAS 14
CSS MISSISSIPPI 319
CSS MISSOURI 57, 260
CSS MOBILE 109, 283
CSS MORGAN 176, 225, 279
CSS NANSEMOND 58, 90, 176, 260, 279
CSS Neuse 39, 44
CSS NEUSE 5, 6, 9, 23, 42, 49, 55, 61, 63, 64, 72, 76, 85, 90, 95, 98, 110, 112, 132, 136, 141, 142, 144, 149, 156, 166, 177, 178, 182, 196, 231, 238, 239, 241, 242, 243, 245, 247, 249, 250, 251, 252, 254, 260, 263, 265, 270, 274, 278, 281, 285, 290, 291, 292, 297, 305, 309, 315, 316, 319, 320, 328, 334, 336, 340, 341
CSS NEW ORLEANS 131, 132
CSS NORTHAMPTON 195
CSS North Carolina 11, 45
CSS NORTH Carolina 61, 153, 201
CSS NORTH CAROLINA 1, 2, 3, 7, 8, 14, 15, 18, 22, 24, 26, 28, 29, 30, 31, 32, 35, 36, 37, 39, 40, 44, 47, 49, 54, 55, 56, 59, 64, 65, 67, 68, 69, 79, 80, 82, 87, 92, 93, 95, 97, 102, 104, 106, 107, 108, 112, 119, 121, 125, 126, 129, 135, 146, 148, 158, 159, 162, 166, 169, 171, 177, 184, 185, 186, 194, 195, 196, 200, 201, 202, 206, 207, 208, 212, 213, 217, 218, 221, 223, 227, 228, 229, 234, 236, 237, 243, 244, 245, 251, 255, 258, 262, 263, 264, 273, 274, 277, 278, 284, 285, 287, 288, 291, 293, 295, 299, 301, 308, 309, 312, 313, 315, 317, 319, 321, 322, 323, 325, 326, 327, 330, 335, 339, 344, 345, 347

CSS OLD DOMINION 160, 339
CSS OLUSTEE 49
CSS OWL 227
CSS PALMETTO [STATE] 130
CSS PALMETTO STATE 14, 30, 48, 50, 103, 131, 140, 183, 186, 223, 276, 283, 293, 338
CSS Patrick Henry 57
CSS PATRICK HENRY 31, 73, 83, 84, 91, 109, 134, 135, 163, 168, 189, 195, 216, 218, 260, 265, 279, 298, 307, 317, 325, 336, 338, 346
CSS PEE DEE 70, 86, 126, 285, 300, 308, 316
CSS PEEDEE 256, 274
CSS PHANTOM 70, 175, 213, 281, 330
CSS PONTCHARTRAIN 14
CSS Raleigh 125
CSS RALEIGH 5, 7, 8, 9, 12, 13, 15, 19, 20, 22, 24, 25, 26, 27, 28, 36, 43, 45, 46, 51, 53, 57, 59, 60, 69, 70, 76, 79, 81, 84, 88, 89, 90, 93, 94, 97, 98, 99, 103, 105, 106, 110, 111, 115, 117, 123, 124, 126, 127, 135, 140, 142, 147, 150, 158, 159, 160, 163, 164, 168, 169, 171, 173, 174, 176, 177, 180, 181, 187, 189, 190, 191, 192, 193, 198, 199, 200, 202, 204, 205, 208, 209, 210, 211, 214, 218, 225, 226, 227, 233, 234, 236, 238, 239, 240, 241, 244, 247, 248, 251, 252, 254, 256, 257, 260, 261, 266, 267, 269, 272, 273, 279, 280, 283, 284, 289, 290, 299, 306, 316, 317, 322, 323, 334, 336, 337, 344, 345
CSS RAPPAHANNOCK 220, 231, 308
CSS RED ROVER 132
CSS R. E. LEE 199
CSS RESOLUTE 317
CSS RICHMOND 24, 81, 110, 180, 207, 216, 219, 260, 279, 337
CSS ROANOKE 123, 128
CSS SAMPSON 81, 254, 271
CSS SAMUEL HINES 242, 243, 244
CSS SAVANNAH 52, 77, 180, 203, 209, 232, 233, 235, 249, 276, 299, 305, 315, 325, 328
CSS SEA BIRD 14, 16, 19, 21, 26, 35, 36, 45, 50, 77, 86, 94, 127, 135, 145, 157, 173, 175, 190, 192, 195, 198, 210, 232, 242, 246, 247, 267, 275, 276, 277, 286, 287, 292, 293, 302, 312, 313, 320, 328, 337, 338, 341
CSS SEABIRD 91
CSS Selma 85
CSS SELMA 91, 220, 225, 279
CSS SHENANDOAH 319
CSS SPRAY 37, 198, 219
CSS STONE 91
CSS STONEHO 122
CSS STONEWALL 231
CSS STONO 92, 198, 338
CSS STROPMAN 283
CSS SUMTER 96, 97, 148, 149
CSS Susan Bierne 127
CSS TALLAHASSEE 18, 26, 29, 49, 68, 69, 107, 117, 126, 146, 200, 206, 208, 221, 229, 243, 258, 267, 277, 284, 319, 322, 347
CSS TALLAHSSEE 14
CSS TENNESSEE 16, 147, 179, 213, 224

Roster of North Carolinians in Confederate Naval Service

CSS TEXAS 220
CSS TORCH 283
CSS TORPEDO 111, 269
CSS TUSCALOOSA 81, 109, 279
CSS TUSCARORA 198
CSS UNITED STATES 13, 63, 70, 74, 77, 84, 90, 91, 96, 98, 99, 102, 104, 108, 109, 116, 118, 119, 120, 121, 127, 135, 139, 150, 160, 161, 162, 163, 167, 170, 172, 178, 181, 195, 201, 205, 206, 210, 211, 212, 220, 225, 229, 230, 250, 260, 262, 263, 265, 271, 277, 278, 288, 289, 293, 300, 313, 320, 321, 325, 332, 333, 337, 339, 341, 347, 348
CSS Virginia 6, 69
CSS VIRGINIA 4, 5, 12, 13, 23, 42, 43, 47, 55, 67, 75, 77, 78, 79, 80, 81, 86, 88, 91, 97, 98, 99, 108, 109, 111, 118, 119, 121, 137, 139, 140, 141, 144, 147, 152, 158, 161, 168, 172, 183, 184, 185, 186, 187, 193, 210, 214, 216, 217, 222, 224, 228, 229, 235, 241, 253, 255, 257, 271, 273, 275, 282, 293, 294, 301, 309, 313, 315, 316, 320, 324, 331, 335, 341, 344, 346
CSS VIRGINIA II 3, 4, 62, 73, 84, 88, 104, 134, 148, 156, 167, 176, 189, 195, 216, 218, 219, 239, 243, 244, 279, 283, 309, 334, 347
CSS W. H. WEBB 147, 279
CSS WINSLOW 14, 35, 36, 78, 127, 195, 287
CSS YADIN 242
CSS Yadkin 58, 108
CSS YADKIN 6, 8, 19, 22, 48, 51, 79, 84, 86, 120, 129, 135, 140, 148, 150, 153, 168, 171, 177, 193, 196, 217, 224, 226, 229, 238, 267, 273, 279, 294, 295, 304, 332
CSS YORKTOW 291
Culpepper Courthouse 47
Cumberland and Tennessee Rivers 17
Cumberland County 7, 8, 20, 27, 40, 46, 78, 79, 86, 105, 112, 116, 194, 200, 202, 203, 217, 222, 236, 242, 263, 266, 274, 284, 289, 298, 301, 306, 307, 309
Cumming's Battery 331
Currituck County 13, 14, 15, 16, 19, 20, 21, 26, 34, 57, 74, 76, 82, 83, 89, 93, 95, 96, 99, 104, 108, 109, 115, 116, 125, 128, 135, 151, 163, 171, 177, 178, 180, 182, 184, 186, 190, 199, 200, 210, 227, 235, 237, 238, 242, 243, 251, 253, 256, 275, 276, 277, 278, 286, 294, 300, 307, 312, 313, 321, 332, 337, 345
Cynthia Wheeler 90

D

D. A. C. Mansfield 4
Dallas 152
Dallas Family Cemetery 80
Dames Quarter 212
Danville 265, 288
Dare County 15, 16, 83, 99, 209, 330
Darien 189
David 223
David Glasgow Farragut 215
David's Island 73, 81, 134, 145, 165, 213, 221, 300, 318
Davidson County 31, 133, 143, 150, 154, 161, 184, 188, 240, 270, 290, 293, 294, 305, 331, 334, 348

Davie County 51, 52, 72, 112, 239, 264
Dayton 69
DeCamp General Hospital 73, 221
DeKalb County 192
Deland 168
Dentonville 12
Denver 19, 224
Detroit 28
Detsey (Decie) Ann Moore 220
Dismal 281
Dixie 220
Dixie Ward 324
Don 299
Drewry's Bluff 8, 11, 13, 20, 22, 28, 29, 36, 45, 51, 52, 53, 64, 66, 73, 76, 77, 84, 88, 92, 97, 98, 99, 104, 108, 111, 113, 115, 117, 118, 119, 122, 123, 124, 125, 127, 136, 149, 152, 154, 161, 171, 172, 185, 191, 199, 200, 208, 222, 229, 232, 238, 239, 241, 246, 250, 254, 257, 260, 261, 264, 268, 271, 273, 279, 282, 284, 285, 290, 298, 299, 304, 313, 316, 319, 320, 322, 323, 334, 337, 344
Dr. Fred. J. Hill 32
Dr. Hayward Butt 50
Dr. Nathan Bright and Olive Vestal Dozier 96
Dr. William Maffitt 203
D. S. Gooch 122
Dublin 203
Duke University 98
Dundarrach 79
Dundee 143
Dunfermline 28
Duplin County 18, 46, 63, 115, 132, 137, 142, 147, 148, 153, 180, 194, 204, 226, 254, 280, 296, 315, 329
Durham 31, 98, 135, 185, 238, 306, 347
Durham County 65, 97, 135, 148, 154, 291, 306, 347
Dutch Gap 200
Dutchville 283
Dysartsville 289

E

Eagle's Island 22
Eagle Springs 223
Eaton's Baptist Church 52
Edenton 144, 205, 324
Edgecombe County 19, 67, 102, 111, 113, 144, 149, 181, 255, 256, 264, 306, 310, 311, 332, 333, 342
Edgefield Courthouse 57
EDWARDS 21
Edward's Ferry 19, 336
Edwards Ferry 289
Egyptian Army 324
Egypt Mills 15
Eli and Rachel Norton 232
Elias and Elizabeth May 208
Eliza Ann Barwick 18
Elizabeth City 9, 13, 14, 16, 17, 21, 35, 36, 43, 44, 45, 50, 57, 59, 73, 74, 80, 82, 86, 87, 92, 94, 95, 98, 102, 104, 106, 116, 117, 125, 127, 128, 129, 136, 137, 138, 139, 142, 145, 153, 156, 157, 158, 162, 167, 169, 170, 171, 172,

178, 186, 187, 188, 191, 195, 196, 197, 205, 206, 210, 214, 217, 222, 227, 231, 232, 235, 237, 238, 239, 246, 247, 248, 249, 252, 253, 258, 262, 263, 264, 266, 267, 268, 269, 271, 272, 276, 277, 286, 287, 290, 292, 294, 299, 302, 310, 312, 314, 317, 321, 326, 328, 336, 337, 340, 341, 343, 347, 348
Elizabeth Hill 320
Elizabeth J. Barnhill 17
Elizabeth Julia Ann McCoke 232
Elizabeth McHorney 200
Elizabeth Mullis 224
Elizabeth Norman 232
Elizabeth Poe 251
Elizabethtown 34, 149
Elizabeth Yost 348
Eliza J. Wright 346
Ella 149
Ella and Annie 2
Ella Furpless 115
Elm City 240
Elminor [Elmina] Giles Clonts 65
Elmira 13, 37, 90, 93, 94, 117, 132, 144, 158, 167, 185, 186, 187, 214, 227, 234, 260, 264, 301, 304
Elmira Prison 37, 77
Elmwood 304
Elmwood Cemetery 77, 344
Elon College 50, 66
Emily F. Tatum 306
Emma Johnson 285
Emma Pitchford 249
Emma Thompson 311
England 31, 63, 120, 144, 269, 300
Enoch and Carolina Davis Shugart 284
Ephesus Baptist Church 72
Essex County 34
Esther Daniel 82
Eugenia 230
EUGENIE 42, 194
Europe 17
Evalin 295
Evans Farm 10
Evansport Battery 279

F

Fairfax Cemetery 228
Fairfax County 227
Fairfax Courthouse 228
Fairview Cemetery 177, 327
Falling Waters 138, 179, 193
Fannie 158
Fannie E. McCree 196
Fannie J. Wood 344
Farmville 12, 13, 28, 48, 61, 67, 70, 71, 88, 89, 91, 111, 137, 138, 148, 152, 155, 169, 181, 182, 194, 231, 255, 270, 272, 309, 315, 319, 329, 333, 336, 340, 343
Faucetts 220
Fayetteville 27, 51, 59, 73, 79, 103, 106, 126, 130, 187, 199, 201, 203, 236, 276, 289, 323

Fayetteville Arsenal and Armory 199
Federal Point 246
First Presbyterian Church 28
Fishing Creek 31, 262
Five Forks 254
Flagler County 145
Flamingo 48
Flat Rock Baptist Church 100
Flea Hill 106
Flint Hill 254
Florence 116
Florie 204
Florisville 233
Fork Baptist Church 112
Forrest City 126, 256
Forsyth 283
Forsyth County 3, 6, 32, 38, 40, 64, 147, 165, 166, 178, 184, 228, 239, 240, 258, 332, 335, 342, 348
Fort Anderson 207
Fort Cemetery 112
Fort Cobb 43, 94, 95, 102, 142, 158, 191, 206, 239, 269, 271, 290, 302, 336
Fort Columbus 15, 21, 96, 110, 129, 161, 215, 241, 268, 279, 303, 346, 347
Fort Delaware 55, 62, 76, 120, 131, 148, 158, 206, 237
Fort Fishe 39
Fort Fisher 2, 12, 22, 33, 58, 68, 69, 73, 87, 92, 97, 110, 113, 114, 115, 118, 120, 127, 129, 133, 144, 149, 157, 164, 167, 169, 181, 185, 221, 232, 233, 235, 256, 257, 268, 269, 288, 296, 301, 304, 311, 342
Fort Hatteras 17, 224, 242, 282, 303, 319, 322, 340, 347
Fort Holmes 38
Fort Lafayette 4, 75, 132
Fort Macon 9, 59, 143, 236, 259, 296, 321
Fort McHenry 237
Fort Monroe 13, 15, 37, 96, 125, 128, 133, 194, 225, 235, 241, 268, 275, 294, 296, 323, 338, 347
Fort Norfolk 128
Fort Powhatan 72
Fort Pulaski 76
Fort Stedman 182
Fort Sumter 81, 126, 130
Fort Warren 4, 21, 40, 81, 85, 98, 129, 160, 161, 170, 185, 203, 216, 225, 242, 257, 267, 279, 303, 319, 322, 340, 346, 347
France 127
Frances E. Cable 50
Frances M. "Fannie" White 332
Francis B. Gault 22
Franklin County 11, 18, 39, 55, 63, 65, 69, 70, 92, 118, 120, 126, 138, 154, 177, 179, 180, 207, 275
Franklinsville 47
Franklinton 63
Franklinville 12
Frayser's Farm 213
Frederick 175, 282
Fredericksburg 3, 30, 42, 46, 57, 64, 190, 217, 245, 283, 298, 347

Roster of North Carolinians in Confederate Naval Service   415

French Forrest 4, 108, 160, 198, 211, 271, 337
Friendship Methodist Church 316
FULTON 93
Fulton County 19

G

Gabriel J. Rains 119
GAINES 29, 298
Gaines Mill 251
Gaines' Mill 24, 208, 275, 304
Gainesville 57
Gallego 172
Galveston 9, 57, 298
Galveston Bay 260
Garysburg 216
Gaston Company 301
Gaston County 29, 64, 65, 73, 74, 111, 152, 246, 257, 264, 343, 347
Gates Company 270
Gates County 80, 238, 245
Gatesville 260
General Benjamin Huger 75
General John C. Pemberton 57
General Robert E. Lee 53
General William J. Hardee 4
George C. McDougald 188
Georgetown 56
Georgetown University 203
Germany 341
Gettysburg 3, 55, 62, 68, 73, 81, 109, 123, 134, 145, 155, 158, 165, 175, 208, 213, 221, 237, 256, 300, 318
Gibraltar 148
Gibsonville 50
Gillett's Farm 269
Gilmer County 214
Glasgow 296
Glen Alpine 65
Glen Alpine Methodist Church 65
Globe Tavern 25
Gold Hill 97, 162, 300
Goldsboro 7, 9, 50, 56, 71, 82, 84, 112, 135, 144, 150, 151, 167, 212, 263, 287, 311
Goldston Methodist Church 10
Good Hope Cemetery 145
Gordon 204
Gorman 154
Gosport Naval Yard 237
Gosport Navy Yard 21, 29, 35, 39, 40, 43, 50, 59, 72, 86, 87, 90, 94, 95, 98, 99, 102, 104, 116, 128, 139, 142, 153, 157, 158, 166, 167, 170, 191, 195, 198, 205, 206, 207, 217, 223, 225, 226, 230, 232, 237, 239, 247, 260, 269, 271, 276, 277, 290, 302, 312, 317, 326, 336, 337, 338, 339, 341, 347
Granite Falls 126
Grantham 325
Granville County 13, 20, 27, 29, 31, 38, 46, 68, 75, 77, 103, 122, 138, 142, 154, 191, 214, 216, 221, 223, 233, 253, 257, 262, 283, 291, 302, 309, 317, 341, 344, 349

Green B. and Nelly Helms 145
Greene County 144, 235
Green Hill 113
Green Hill Cemetery 318
Greenlawn Cemetery 138
Green Mount Cemetery 168
Greensboro 8, 18, 19, 27, 38, 52, 62, 66, 70, 84, 90, 112, 126, 129, 132, 143, 144, 148, 156, 186, 191, 195, 196, 200, 202, 203, 207, 216, 219, 223, 236, 247, 251, 260, 278, 281, 285, 288, 298, 308, 314, 331, 335, 337, 346, 347
Greenville 255
Greenville Sound 296
Griffin 10
Grimes Cemetery 290
Gritt 77
Guard 343
Guilford College 159, 291
Guilford County 3, 6, 8, 28, 48, 50, 62, 65, 68, 90, 103, 117, 157, 159, 160, 168, 173, 176, 181, 182, 204, 208, 231, 236, 238, 239, 244, 245, 251, 259, 260, 298, 305, 318, 328, 335, 343
Guinea Station 240
Gus and Carrie Schwartzman 279
Guy W. Siler 285

H

Halifax 10, 11, 13, 18, 21, 30, 31, 38, 40, 56, 62, 63, 73, 75, 77, 82, 107, 128, 136, 141, 143, 145, 147, 155, 156, 160, 180, 185, 192, 194, 195, 197, 200, 207, 210, 214, 216, 240, 258, 276, 281, 287, 296, 297, 298, 306, 314, 315, 331, 333, 338, 342
Halifax County 8, 24, 40, 41, 82, 110, 136, 143, 147, 149, 164, 192, 197, 220, 221, 240, 248, 307, 313, 336
Halifax Station 10, 22, 23, 26, 30, 47, 65, 68, 78, 83, 86, 99, 104, 113, 116, 141, 151, 155, 157, 159, 161, 168, 172, 185, 192, 207, 214, 216, 223, 231, 232, 253, 272, 287, 294, 307, 315, 328, 344, 348
Hall-Rayfield Family Cemetery 259
Hammond Hospital 282
Hampstead 182
Hampton Roads 4, 5, 11, 23, 47, 49, 55, 77, 78, 79, 81, 91, 97, 111, 119, 125, 144, 147, 152, 183, 184, 186, 193, 210, 214, 216, 228, 231, 235, 241, 255, 269, 271, 273, 275, 306, 315, 323, 335, 347
Hamptonville 100
Hanah [sic] Murray 226
Hancock County 85
Hannah Dunton 99
Hanover Court House 15, 96, 241, 347
Hansa 49
HANSER 28
Harnett County 60, 208, 219, 280
Harper's Farm 18, 31, 33, 39, 66, 81, 154, 169, 184, 237, 260, 286, 333, 345
Harpers Farm 74, 89, 134, 330, 342, 346
Harrell's Store 146
Hart's Island 197, 325
Hatteras 68, 132, 227, 343, 346

Hatteras Inlet 7, 314
Hattie 308
Havana 231
Hawes Family Cemetery 142
Hawfields Presbyterian Church 114
Hayes Chapel Christian Church 11
Haywood County 27, 113, 295
Hebe 49
Henderson County 190
Henrico County 338
Henrietta G. Tompkins Carter 56
Henry County 282
Henry Hunter Bowen 33
Henry Marchant Cooke 71
Hertford 246
Hertford County 113, 137, 173, 220, 228, 248, 253, 303, 332, 334, 339, 340, 342
Hester 317
Hickory Tavern 213
Hiddenite 86
High Bridge 7, 16, 103, 239, 252
High Point 230
Hilliardston 339
Hillsborough 4, 52, 53, 225, 312
Hillsborough Military Academy 281
Hilton Ferry 35, 151
Hilton Head 215
HISPANIC CONFEDERATES 15
Holden 38
Holloways 306
Hollywood Cemetery 104, 153, 216, 232, 312, 313
Holt's Chapel 68
Holy Communion Lutheran Church 152
Houston 346
H. R. Marshall 82
Hunley 70
Hunter's Bridge 345
Huntersville Presbyterian Church 259
HURON 132
Hyde County 16, 51, 101, 110, 235, 257

I

Ida P. Kine 286
INDIAN CHIEF 34
Indian Ridge 178
Indian Springs 18, 281
Iredell County 13, 53, 100, 125, 150, 210, 215, 216, 261, 282, 294, 303, 316, 327
Ireland 80, 91, 121, 166, 192, 195, 215, 222, 234, 266
Isaac N. Brown 4
Isabella Battle 19
Isabella Bowen 34
Isabella Freshwater 114
Isaiah P. Breedlove 92
Iseneger 331

J

Jackson County 133, 140, 235

Jackson Hospital 9, 54, 108
Jackson Station 81, 216, 308, 317
J. A. Guffey 130
James and Polly Hughes Gunter 130
James C. Davis 87, 118, 197, 202
James Island 93, 285
James Jennette Barnette 16
James Polk Woodard 181
James River 3, 14, 15, 25, 30, 31, 56, 72, 84, 93, 96, 120, 128, 133, 164, 186, 187, 206, 217, 225, 227, 230, 233, 241, 260, 271, 288, 294, 304, 328, 340, 342, 346, 347
James River Fleet 244
James River Squadron 4, 8, 11, 21, 22, 24, 32, 45, 51, 52, 58, 59, 60, 69, 73, 76, 81, 88, 90, 94, 95, 96, 99, 110, 111, 116, 117, 119, 123, 124, 125, 127, 128, 135, 141, 142, 150, 153, 158, 167, 171, 174, 177, 180, 181, 186, 188, 189, 191, 195, 198, 199, 200, 204, 205, 206, 211, 216, 219, 222, 229, 231, 238, 239, 240, 244, 247, 251, 254, 257, 260, 269, 271, 273, 279, 283, 284, 288, 290, 298, 299, 302, 308, 310, 316, 317, 322, 323, 334, 336, 337
Jamestown 145, 208
James W. Cooke 26
Jane B. Travis 81
Jane Hilton 150
Jane H. Wilson 142
Japan 56, 72
Jefferson County 4
Jefferson Davis 56, 114, 117, 265, 266, 268
Jefferson Medical College 276, 324
Jennie Kate Johnston 168
Jennie Stanland 297
Jersey Baptist Church 133
Jerusalem 324
Jessie and Emanitha Aldridge 4
Jetersville 71, 316
Jimmie and Frances Smithwick 294
John A. and Susan Mayo 208
John Blount Muse 228
John J. Guthrie 131
John Lapham Roberts 268
John M. Davidson 66
John Newland Maffitt 192
Johns Hopkins Medical School 324
Johnson County 38, 181
Johnson Grove Cemetery 53
Johnson Jones Hoper 268
Johnson's Island 117, 132, 167, 195, 257, 269, 279, 349
Johnston County 10, 15, 37, 41, 42, 66, 89, 139, 167, 169, 172, 192, 207, 244, 248, 297, 308, 313, 317, 326
John Taylor Wood 98
John W. Ellis 181
John W. Galloway 82
Jonesboro 52, 130, 176, 318
Jonesboro Guards 7
Jones County 187, 269
Joseph E. Johnston 156
Josephine Turner 316
JOSEPH LANE 254

Joseph Wheeler 114, 266
J.P. West 253
J. S. Maury 111
Jubilee 294
Julia A. Carter 56
J. W. Cooke 156

K

Kate 59
Kate Piercy Murphey Chestney 225
Kelly 218
Kemp Family Cemetery 149
Kenansville 187, 296
Kenyon 75
Kernersville 182
King's Mountain 196
Kinston 5, 21, 23, 24, 49, 55, 63, 64, 68, 72, 84, 85, 95, 103, 107, 112, 122, 143, 144, 156, 177, 182, 183, 193, 196, 245, 250, 254, 261, 262, 265, 285, 291, 297, 313, 314, 316, 320, 328, 332, 340, 342
Kizzy Braswell 37
Knotts Island 20, 332, 337
Knoxville 9, 27, 139

L

Lake Pontchartrain 220
Lake Waccamaw 22
Lamar County 38
Langley R. Bowen 33
Langly R. and Nancy Respass 262
Latimore and Nancy Doxey 95
Lattimore 300
Laura A. Eno 104
Laura Baynes 140
Laura F. Smith 31
Laura Spruill 295
Laurel Hill 233
Laurel Hill Baptist Church 233
Laurinburg 52, 232
Lebanon Chapel Cemetery 327
Leechville 276
Lee County 10
Lena H. Smith 306
Lena Smith 149
Lenoir County 3, 68, 70, 81, 95, 143, 147, 272, 297, 326
Let Her Be 49
L.F. Harroldson 140
Libby Prison 33, 34, 79, 98, 237, 244, 274
Liberty County 19
Lilian 130
Lillian 204, 308
Lillington 208
Lincoln County 4, 65, 88, 90, 106, 122, 133, 198, 224, 258, 334, 343
Lincolnton 4
Lindsay's Turnout 324
Linwood Cemetery 344
Little Buffalo Creek 48

Little David 313
Little Hattie 129
Littleton 249
Liverpool 96, 185, 203, 204, 319
Lizzie Garner 134
London 97
Longacre 83
Long Creek 159
Long Island 211
Los Angeles 81
Louisa J. Clifford Davis 64
Louisa J. Davis 64
Louisburg 92, 208
Louisiana 306
Louisville 139, 235
Lou Young Smith 289
Love's Creek Baptist Church 107
Lowndes County 281
Lucia 29
Lucy Gary Daniel 82
Lucy H. St. Sing 274
Luke Barco 15
Lumberton 260
Lutheran Cemetery 139, 169
Lutheran Chapel 264
Lynchburg 305
Lynch's Flotilla 72
Lynox 75
Lystra Baptist Church 100

M

Macedonia 242
Macedonia Methodist Church 154
Macon 12, 24, 176
Madison County 79, 81, 164
Maggie R. Lea 123
Magnolia 272
Magnolia Cemetery 223
Magnolia Clark 62
Maiden 258
Maine 28, 113, 115
Major A. M. Lewis 2
Major General Joseph Wheeler 1
Major General Leonidas Polk 57
Mallard Creek 118
Mallett's Battalion 303, 335
Manassas 241
Manchester 27, 256
Maplewood Cemetery 97, 185
Margaret Carter 57
Margaret Cole 52
Margaret Gray 124
Margaret H. Banks 236
Margaret Lewis 313
Margaret McMillan 81
Margarette Clarke 304
Mariah Thompson 311
Marietta Carter 179

Marinda Boyette 304
Marinda [Melinda] Tetterton 309
Mariner 109
Marion 24, 116, 225
Marion Court House 238
Marshall County 343
Martha A. Newton 230
Martha Ann Dent 89
Martha A. Upchurch 317
Martha Holloway 154
Martha Jane (Forbes) Russell 15
Martilda [sic] M. Waddill 318
Martin County 23, 137, 161, 291, 338
Martindale-Biddle Cemetery 26
Martitia M. Waddill 247
Mary A. Deans 87
Mary A. Misenheimer 209
Mary Ann Bass 145
Mary Ann Howell 274
"Maryan" Norville 233
Mary Ann Spruill 296
Mary A. Parker 239
Mary A. Perry 246
Mary A. Smith 290
Mary A. Williams 337
Mary Blunt Brewer 39
Mary Celeste 7
Mary E. Branch 183
Mary E. Curtis 79
Mary E. Dulin 151
Mary Elizabeth O'Brien 16
Mary Elizabeth Oden 33
Mary E. Rowe 272
Mary F. Penny 245
Mary Gaskins 119
Mary Grissom 130
Mary J. Ball 13
Mary Katherine Wells 329
Mary Lapham Roberts 268
Mary L. Hartsell 140
Mary Long Parker 240
Mary Maher 158
Mary "Polly" Wescott 83
Mary Skipper 288
Mary Spottswood 306
Mary Walker 153
Masonboro 191, 246, 256, 275
Masonboro Baptist Church 149
Masonboro Inlet 287
Massey 113
Mathews County 159
Matthew and Marina Parker 240
Matthew D. Branch 183
Mattie E. Ramseur 258
Mattie Tarleton 305
Max 239
McDowell County 126, 175, 225, 244, 289
Mecklenburg County 4, 12, 28, 29, 30, 39, 43, 47, 66, 74, 86, 87, 97, 118, 157, 167, 168, 196, 202, 209, 212, 224, 259, 261, 273, 275, 282, 288, 289, 299, 305, 309, 321, 327
Meriwether County 43
Mexican War 32
Milford 222
Milton 5, 137
Mineral Springs 164
Mine Run 111
Mississippi River 192, 195, 216, 317
Mobile 61, 64, 81, 124, 198, 204, 225, 276
Mobile Bay 16, 85, 91, 192, 220, 225, 276
Mobile Squadron 29, 61, 64, 81, 91, 109, 111, 117, 147, 160, 176, 195, 198, 225, 231, 279, 298, 338
Mobile Station 124, 147
Mocksville 51, 52
Moncure 48
Monroe 42, 108, 145
Monroe County 81
Montgomery 52, 268, 296
Montgomery County 104, 241, 242, 296
Montreal 179
Moore County 12, 36, 52, 53, 62, 67, 85, 86, 117, 176, 182, 183, 197, 202, 206, 218, 222, 231, 247, 248, 284, 285, 318, 326
Moore's Creek 88, 204
Morganton 64, 65, 87, 309
Moriah 306
Morris Island 77, 172, 187, 215, 230, 266, 285, 315
Morrison 146
Morristown 273
Morse Cemetery 182
Mount Airy 285
Mount Olive 18
Mount Pellis 275
Mount Pleasant 239, 315
Mrs. A. J. White 101
Mrs. Angier 98
Mrs. G. M. Kirkman 52
Mrs. Hayward Butt 50
Mrs. J.A. Fore 22
Mrs. W.A. Willson 22
Mt. Airy 56, 72
Mt. Holly Baptist Church Cemetery 33
Mulberry Grove 220
Munich 140
Murfreesboro 173, 220, 339
Murphy's Hotel 84

N

Nag's Head 83, 132
Nags Head 190
Nahunta Swamp 112
Nancy Gamiel 15
Nancy N. McCurry 196
Nancy O'Neal 235
Nancy Reaves 261
Nancy Speaks 295
Nanna Hubba Bluff 225

Nannie Hill 306
Nansemond County 83, 252
Narrow Shore 210
Narrow Shore District 171
Nash County 10, 68, 87, 227, 228, 240, 265, 300, 307, 318, 339
Nashville 31, 122, 210
Nassau 15, 58, 132, 185, 203, 208
Nassau County 12, 24
Nathan C. Dozier 96
NCS ALBEMARLE 33, 174, 275
NCS BEAUFORT 116, 123
NCS Curlew 154
NCS CURLEW 131, 138, 156, 189
NCS EDWARDS 6, 69, 70, 79, 114, 119, 120, 127, 138, 139, 156, 171, 179, 206, 215, 229, 276, 288, 315
NCS ELLIS 5, 14, 72, 114, 161, 211, 241, 286, 289, 296
NCS FANNY 98, 139, 156, 182, 212, 213, 306, 317
NCS FORREST 5, 6, 55, 70, 72, 79, 138
NCS JUNALUSKA 17
NCS RALEIGH 59, 69, 74
NCS SEA BIRD 55, 59, 80, 117, 127, 134, 137, 151, 167, 169, 170, 188, 197, 217
NCS SEABIRD 167
NCS WELDON E. EDWARDS 72
NCS WINSLOW 24, 54, 59, 78, 80, 98, 114, 134, 163, 167, 173, 188, 198, 219, 228, 229, 280, 292, 294, 302, 315, 332, 337, 345, 347
Nehemiah and Delila Keeter 174
Neuse 27
Neuse River 241, 344
New Bern 37, 59, 80, 86, 98, 112, 125, 131, 142, 172, 173, 199, 205, 229, 236, 241, 260, 264, 268, 292, 324, 337, 344, 347
New Berne 23
Newberry 265
New Bethel Lutheran Church 214
New Cathedral Cemetery 207
New England 319
New Hanover 48, 97, 146
New Hanover County 7, 9, 18, 22, 24, 26, 28, 33, 35, 36, 40, 42, 44, 45, 48, 53, 55, 56, 58, 59, 63, 67, 68, 71, 72, 73, 75, 76, 77, 82, 85, 87, 91, 93, 97, 100, 103, 105, 106, 107, 109, 115, 117, 118, 120, 121, 125, 126, 128, 129, 134, 139, 140, 142, 143, 146, 147, 149, 152, 153, 155, 162, 163, 167, 168, 169, 174, 175, 176, 178, 182, 183, 187, 189, 191, 192, 194, 196, 197, 198, 199, 203, 205, 207, 208, 212, 213, 218, 222, 223, 226, 230, 231, 234, 242, 245, 246, 247, 249, 252, 253, 255, 257, 258, 262, 263, 264, 267, 269, 272, 273, 274, 277, 278, 279, 281, 282, 283, 284, 286, 288, 291, 296, 297, 302, 306, 307, 311, 316, 322, 323, 327, 329, 330, 331, 332, 333, 334, 336, 338, 341
New Haven 158
New Inlet 49, 125, 323
New Orleans 23, 39, 91, 109, 198, 216, 249, 279, 337
New Orleans Station 57, 131, 132, 176, 198, 215, 308, 319
Newport 150

Newport News 12, 57, 61, 67, 70, 74, 79, 111, 133, 137, 138, 142, 147, 149, 152, 165, 169, 181, 194, 212, 218, 231, 255, 257, 315, 340
Newton 258
New York 68, 93, 203, 205, 303, 337
New York City 128, 131, 220, 335
New York Harbor 4, 21, 75, 81, 96, 134, 145, 161, 165, 197, 213, 215, 221, 241, 268, 279, 300, 303, 318, 325, 346, 347
Nightingale 131
Norfolk 8, 29, 39, 40, 42, 53, 56, 57, 59, 87, 94, 104, 111, 127, 128, 142, 151, 156, 195, 200, 206, 210, 222, 228, 230, 231, 235, 241, 257, 277, 286, 289, 304, 309, 312, 314, 337, 346
Norfolk County 171, 235, 237, 271
Norfolk Navy Yard 160
Northampton County 15, 97, 121, 165, 180, 245
North Carolina 1
North Carolina Navy 166
North Carolina Old Soldiers Home 291
North Carolina Soldier's Home 207
North Carolina Squadron 4, 11, 14, 16, 17, 18, 19, 20, 21, 22, 26, 35, 36, 41, 42, 43, 45, 50, 56, 58, 59, 60, 70, 71, 76, 77, 80, 83, 84, 86, 88, 89, 93, 94, 95, 96, 98, 99, 102, 104, 111, 115, 116, 118, 119, 120, 123, 124, 125, 127, 128, 131, 135, 137, 139, 142, 150, 151, 153, 156, 157, 158, 160, 162, 163, 170, 171, 174, 175, 178, 179, 182, 184, 188, 189, 191, 192, 197, 198, 199, 201, 205, 206, 210, 211, 212, 215, 217, 218, 220, 222, 223, 225, 228, 229, 230, 232, 237, 238, 239, 242, 247, 251, 252, 254, 257, 262, 269, 271, 273, 275, 277, 278, 280, 283, 284, 286, 288, 290, 292, 293, 296, 299, 302, 310, 312, 314, 316, 317, 320, 322, 323, 325, 326, 328, 332, 333, 334, 335, 336, 337, 338, 345, 348
North Heath 92
Norwich University 140
Nova Scotia 100, 296
NSC EDWARDS 276
Nunna Hubba Bluff 124

O

Oakboro 305
Oakdale Cemeter 24
Oakdale Cemetery 20, 22, 23, 24, 33, 48, 63, 75, 85, 92, 103, 120, 139, 142, 197, 198, 203, 204, 215, 254, 256, 258, 270, 274, 296, 323
Oak Grove 19, 134, 274
Oak Grove Church 85
Oakgrove Methodist Church 57
Oakwood Cemetery 1, 79, 90, 97, 121, 204, 205, 220, 253, 282, 291, 307, 327
Ocracoke 68, 221, 228
Ocracoke Inlet 167, 195, 235
Ocracoke Island 100, 235
Odessa 203
OHIO 32
Old Beaufort Burying Ground 122
Old Capitol Prison 148, 179, 198, 217, 257, 279, 349

Old Cemetery 329
Old Dominion 92, 292
Old Settler's Cemetery 29
Old Southport Cemetery 25, 64, 92, 119, 223
Old Stone 27
Old Warrenton Cemetery 227
Olive Frances Gray 16
Olustee 126
Omaha 48
O'Neal Family Cemetery 235
Onslow County 69, 115, 143, 163, 221, 256, 323, 326, 341
O. P. Harder 136
Orange County 1, 47, 52, 56, 75, 76, 97, 135, 139, 225, 248, 280, 281, 311, 312, 324
Orange Court House 91
Oregon Inlet 96, 100, 104
Orono 113
Ossabow Sound 254
Owl 204
Oxford 38, 112, 221, 284, 291, 339, 344

P

Painesville 279
Paris 140, 324, 325
Parkersburg 37
Parkton 346
Pasquotank Company 62
Pasquotank County 9, 13, 14, 41, 44, 47, 56, 59, 73, 83, 92, 102, 104, 106, 109, 125, 127, 138, 156, 161, 163, 175, 178, 186, 201, 212, 222, 227, 232, 235, 238, 258, 264, 266, 268, 270, 273, 278, 286, 293, 295, 299, 308, 312, 313, 320, 323
Patsy Jane Jenkins 164
Peachy's Depot 204
Pee Dee River 285
P.E. Harroldson 140
Pender County 17, 30, 33, 77, 88, 100, 101, 159, 165, 182, 226, 230, 248, 333, 344
Penelope "Penny" Baum 26
Penelope Simms 148
Pensacola 52, 181
Percy T. Siler 285
Perquimans County 11, 15, 16, 59, 60, 80, 146, 172, 246, 252, 304
Perquimens County 171
Person County 169, 182, 255, 256, 259, 306
Pet 75
Peter and S. Parker Ballance 14
Petersburg 30, 35, 36, 41, 53, 55, 79, 92, 96, 148, 175, 196, 230, 237, 241, 257, 261, 291, 295, 343
Pettigrew General Hospital No. 13 72
PHANTOM 189
Philadelphia 28, 34
Philadelphia Lutheran Church 74
Pickens County 181
Pickett-Buchanan Camp 151
Pikeville 112
Pilot 83

Pinecrest Cemetery 315
Pine Level 37
Pineview Cemetery 332
Piney Grove 105
Pinners Point 131
Pisgah Church 191
Pitt County 76, 111, 136, 180, 255, 259, 314, 338
Pittsboro 32, 91, 205, 319
Pittsylvania County 81
Plymouth 18, 51, 62, 63, 72, 77, 99, 116, 124, 128, 136, 143, 145, 155, 156, 190, 194, 195, 232, 234, 235, 285, 289, 298, 299, 303, 331, 332, 338, 347
Pocahontas 148
Pocotaligo 140
Point Lookout 2, 4, 7, 10, 13, 15, 16, 18, 25, 28, 31, 33, 35, 36, 38, 39, 41, 43, 46, 47, 48, 51, 53, 59, 66, 67, 69, 71, 72, 74, 75, 80, 81, 84, 88, 89, 91, 92, 94, 98, 99, 101, 102, 103, 105, 117, 120, 121, 125, 129, 132, 133, 134, 136, 138, 142, 150, 151, 152, 153, 154, 155, 167, 169, 175, 177, 181, 182, 183, 184, 186, 187, 193, 197, 198, 202, 210, 214, 215, 218, 219, 222, 224, 227, 229, 230, 231, 233, 234, 237, 239, 245, 246, 247, 252, 254, 258, 259, 261, 264, 268, 270, 272, 278, 282, 283, 286, 292, 293, 294, 299, 300, 304, 305, 309, 316, 319, 327, 329, 330, 331, 333, 335, 336, 342, 343, 345, 346, 348
Polkville 303
Pollocksville 145
Polly Ann Daniels 83
Polly Bennett 122
Polly Capps Peadon 245
Polly [Pollie] Tyner 317
Poplar Branc 94
Poplar Branch 180, 199, 200
Poplar Bridge 215
Portland 203
Port Royal 52, 203
Portsmouth 29, 72, 91, 109, 110, 116, 118, 119, 131, 132, 156, 195, 205, 208, 220, 222, 267, 278, 316, 328
Portsmouth Grove 225
Portsmouth Island 100
Portugal 286
Potomac River 72, 176
Potts Camp 343
President Jefferson Davis 1
Prince George's County 7
Princess Anne County 128, 180
Princeton 249, 317
Prospect Methodist Church 193
Purvis 152

Q

Quidley Cemetery 16

R

Raleigh 3, 4, 5, 6, 7, 9, 10, 11, 12, 13, 16, 18, 19, 20, 21, 23, 25, 27, 29, 30, 31, 32, 33, 34, 36, 37, 38, 39, 40, 41, 42, 46, 47, 49, 50, 51, 52, 53, 54, 56, 58, 60, 61, 62, 63, 64, 65, 66, 67, 68, 70, 71, 72, 73, 74, 75, 77, 78, 79, 80, 83,

85, 87, 88, 89, 90, 91, 92, 97, 98, 99, 100, 101, 102, 103, 105, 107, 109, 110, 111, 112, 113, 114, 115, 116, 117, 118, 119, 120, 121, 122, 123, 124, 125, 126, 127, 128, 130, 132, 133, 134, 136, 137, 138, 139, 140, 141, 143, 144, 145, 146, 147, 148, 149, 150, 151, 152, 153, 155, 157, 158, 159, 160, 162, 163, 164, 166, 168, 169, 170, 171, 172, 173, 174, 176, 177, 178, 179, 181, 183, 184, 185, 188, 189, 191, 193, 194, 196, 197, 198, 199, 201, 202, 203, 204, 205, 206, 207, 208, 210, 212, 214, 216, 217, 218, 219, 220, 221, 222, 223, 224, 226, 227, 228, 229, 230, 231, 232, 233, 235, 236, 237, 238, 239, 240, 241, 242, 243, 244, 248, 249, 251, 253, 255, 256, 258, 259, 260, 261, 262, 263, 264, 266, 267, 269, 270, 271, 272, 274, 275, 276, 278, 279, 280, 281, 282, 284, 285, 288, 289, 290, 292, 293, 294, 295, 296, 298, 299, 300, 301, 302, 303, 305, 306, 307, 309, 310, 313, 314, 315, 316, 317, 318, 319, 321, 322, 324, 326, 327, 328, 330, 331, 333, 334, 335, 338, 339, 340, 341, 342, 343, 344, 347, 348, 349

RALEIGH 4
Ramseur 47, 237
Randleman 28, 136
Randolph County 12, 28, 42, 47, 57, 74, 76, 79, 85, 103, 134, 136, 176, 237, 274, 298, 318, 320, 328, 340, 348
Raphael Semmes 96, 148, 149, 216
Rappahannock Bridge 349
Rappahannock River 117, 132
Rebecca Beasley Norton 233
Rebecca E. Moore 218
Reb. Thomas Pinkney Johnston 168
Reddin and Elvy Quidley 257
Red River 57, 147
Red River County 38
Red Springs 200
R. E. Lee 129
R.E. Lee 131
R. E. LEE 40
Retribution 142
Reuben and Elizabeth Norton 233
Rev. John Jones Roberts 268
Rhode Island 3, 112
Richard H. and Martha E. Lewis 111
Richfield 209, 214
Richlands 115
Richmond 8, 9, 23, 32, 34, 36, 38, 39, 45, 46, 51, 52, 53, 54, 57, 64, 67, 69, 71, 74, 78, 79, 81, 84, 88, 97, 98, 105, 107, 108, 111, 113, 129, 136, 151, 153, 154, 156, 157, 165, 167, 172, 177, 184, 190, 192, 203, 207, 214, 215, 216, 219, 220, 222, 223, 225, 227, 231, 232, 233, 235, 237, 239, 240, 243, 245, 248, 249, 250, 257, 265, 268, 272, 274, 279, 282, 283, 288, 291, 292, 298, 315, 318, 328, 338, 344
Richmond County 40, 52, 126, 133, 164, 174, 193, 194, 197, 232, 233, 248, 255, 321, 346
Richmond Naval Station 132, 298
Richmond Station 61, 127, 147, 148, 160, 176, 192, 207, 219, 270, 279, 308, 317, 319, 337
Riderwood 167

Riggsbee 99
Risenhours 214
Roanoke 31
Roanoke Island 14, 16, 17, 19, 21, 33, 35, 36, 43, 44, 45, 50, 72, 73, 80, 82, 83, 86, 93, 102, 106, 117, 119, 127, 128, 137, 138, 145, 156, 157, 167, 169, 170, 171, 172, 178, 186, 187, 188, 192, 195, 196, 197, 206, 214, 217, 219, 222, 227, 238, 241, 246, 247, 248, 249, 252, 253, 262, 264, 266, 267, 268, 272, 286, 287, 292, 294, 299, 302, 306, 310, 312, 326, 328, 330, 335, 337, 338, 339, 340, 341, 343, 348
Roanoke River 72, 289
Robert E. Lee 110, 204, 324
Robert Hunter and Jane Martin Henderson Dalton 81
Robert Vance 64
Robert W. Dallas 80
Robeson County 11, 12, 35, 39, 136, 152, 164, 166, 169, 173, 179, 194, 200, 202, 218, 250, 260, 304, 327, 344
Rockingham County 6, 42, 51, 67, 68, 80, 165, 185, 193, 289, 328
Rock Island 175
Rockland County 246
Rock Point 101
Rocky Mount 14, 81, 119, 227, 228, 265, 287
Rocky Point 17
Roger's Store 244
Roseboro 43
Rose Hill 142
Rose Standish Ludlam 220
Round Peak 239
Rowan County 3, 42, 67, 89, 97, 101, 113, 139, 146, 155, 162, 167, 168, 169, 243, 245, 266, 272, 273, 274, 283, 300, 305, 309, 314, 324, 348
Rutherford County 53, 83, 116, 126, 130, 159, 197, 210, 233, 254, 256, 292, 300, 329

S

Saffold 271
Sailor's Creek 53, 92, 117, 120, 154, 160, 167, 247, 304
Sailors Creek 195, 269, 292, 327
Salem 258
Salemburg 285
Salem Cemetery 32, 251
Salem Methodist Church 60, 312
Salem United Methodist Church 38
Salisbury 78, 113, 146, 168, 209, 274
Sallie W. Stone 27
Sally K. Sherrin 283
Salome J. Dailey 16
Sampson County 3, 25, 30, 43, 46, 57, 58, 71, 127, 128, 146, 151, 183, 190, 196, 201, 207, 226, 231, 246, 261, 281, 285, 309, 316, 330, 341
Samuel and Anne Bracy 35
Samuel Hines 330
Samuel W. Pitchford 139
Sandy Point 89
Sanford 10
San Francisco 280

S. A. Proctor 256
Sarag [sic] C. Roark 281
Sarah Anne and James Oscar Young 38
Sarah A. Rayfield 259
Sarah Cone 69
Sarah Core 73
Sarah Daniel 83
Sarah E. Atkinson 186
Sarah E. Daniels 82
Sarah E. McKeel 345
Sarah E. Reaves 100
Sarah F. Mitchell 215
Sarah Pierce 248
Sarah R. Olds 235
Sarah Russell 273
Sarah Warrick 325
Saulston 105
Savannah 52, 140, 209, 224, 232, 233, 254, 270, 271, 290, 291, 305, 331
Savannah Grissom 129
Savannah River 186
Savannah River Squadron 77
Savannah Squadron 4, 19, 39, 81, 180, 209, 247, 254, 276, 317, 325
Savannah Station 140, 203, 271, 276, 299, 308, 317
Sawyer Family Cemetery 278
Scotland 28, 143
Scotland County 232
Scotland Neck 149, 342
Scuppernong 296
S. D. Moore 140
Seaman's Burial Ground 50, 58, 91, 141, 158, 163, 258, 284
Seattle 81
Second Gum Swamp 7
Second Manassas 194
Selma 238, 283, 310
Selonia F. Tatum 306
Semmes Naval brigade 186
Semmes Naval Brigade 195
Semmes' Naval Brigade 8, 18, 19, 66, 70, 84, 126, 132, 143, 144, 191, 196, 200, 207, 216, 219, 260, 281, 308, 331, 347
Seven Days 53
Seven Pines 190
Seyton Lehman 184
Shallow Ford Christian Church 50
Sharpsburg 188, 206, 214, 228, 243, 308
Shelby 196, 263, 340
Shilo 182
Ship Island 16
Sign Pine 237
Skinner's Neck 191
Skyland 253
Smallpox Hospital 3
Smithfield 66, 128, 169, 207, 308, 326
Smiths 346
Smithville 49, 64, 76, 80, 100, 102, 115, 119, 129, 130, 153, 182, 202, 236, 250, 254, 276, 288, 329, 330

Snow Camp 165, 168
Society Hill Baptist Church 53
Soldier's Home 27, 51
Somerset County 212
Somerville Cemetery 78
South Mountain 13, 108
Southport 2, 25, 40, 64, 75, 82, 92, 115, 119, 129, 182, 223, 230, 253, 254, 297, 304, 311, 329
Southport Cemetery 110, 129, 130, 131, 312, 329
Spain 324
Spruill-Holmes Cemetery 155
Staffordshire 300
Stan Hope 87
Stanley 152
Stanly Company 305
Stanly County 6, 41, 63, 68, 103, 112, 140, 141, 191, 203, 209, 214, 229, 238, 251, 314, 322, 332, 336
St. Anne's Cemetery 319
Statesville 13, 122, 261
Station Island 103
Staunton 189
St. Bartholomew's Episcopal Church 32
Stewartsville 232
St. Georges 48
St. Johns Church 236
St. Louis 81
St. Marks 198
St. Matthew's Episcopal Church 53
Stokes County 32, 38, 83, 134
Stoneville 185
Stovall 38
St. Pauls 166
St. Phillip's Churchyard 268
Straits 340
St. Stephens Lutheran Church 15, 155
Stumpy Point 16
Suffolk 211
Sugar Grove 20
Sullivan Island 285
Sullivan's Island 128, 235
Summersville 103
Suncrest Cemetery 134
Sunset Cemetery 263
Supply 91
Surry County 56, 72, 73, 83, 241, 301
Susan Adkins 2
Susan A. Foster 113
Susan A. Warren 325
Susan-Bierne 296
Susan C. Berry 23
Susan Game 116
Susan Mary Butler 50
Susan Orall 208
Swansboro 143, 256
Swepsonville 36
Swift Creek 113

T

Talladega County 172
Tampa 4
Tarboro 119, 264
Tatemville 64
Taylorsville 82
T. C. Brooks 41
Teachy's Depot 204
Tempy W. King 177
Thomas and Julia Dowdy 93, 94
Thomas County 101
Thomas Crossan 78
Thomas Edgar Johnston 168
Thomas P. Gray 124
Thomas Ros Daniels 83
Thomasville 150
Three Forks Baptist Church 269
Timberlake 256
Tobias and Peggy Clapp 61
Torrens River 97
Trinity College 98
Tucker's Naval Battalion 134
Tucker's Naval Brigade 167
Turkey 324
Tyrrell County 16, 17, 76, 84, 125, 135, 141, 142, 155, 175, 212, 222, 232, 238, 295, 320

U

Ulysses S. Grant 324
Uncas 118
Union County 42, 66, 108, 134, 145, 166, 209, 240, 293, 296, 305
Union Factory 176
Union Ridge 140
Unionville 209
United States Military Academy 131
United States Naval Academy 56, 100, 127, 308
University of North Carolina 75, 127, 134, 268, 276, 304, 307, 324
University of Pennsylvania 29
University of Pennsylvania Medical School 304
University of Virginia 324
USS Ceres 198
USS CERES 13, 38, 40, 84, 248, 303, 312
USS COMMODORE PERRY 36
USS COMMODRE PERRY 170
USS CONGRESS 111, 335
USS CONTITUTION 203
USS CUMBERLAND 109
USS DAYLIGHT 287
USS FORT JACKSON 80
USS FULTON 303
USS HOUSATONIC 335
USS LACKAWANNA 279
USS LOCKWOOD 13, 38, 40, 84, 198, 248, 303, 312
USS MATTABESETT 314
USS MIAMI 64
USS MINNESOTA 49
USS MONITOR 109
USS MONTICELLO 256
USS NIPHO 256
USS PENNSYLVANIA 225
USS PEQUOT 101
USS Port Royal 85
USS PORT ROYAL 91
USS RELIANCE 117
USS RHODE ISLAND 111
USS RICHMOND 279
USS SARATOGA 131
USS SASSACUS 13, 38, 40, 84, 198, 248, 303, 312
USS SATELITE 117
USS SHENANDOAH 49, 125, 323
USS SHOKOKON 49
USS SOUTHFIELD 72
USS UNCLE BEN 254
USS UNDERWRITER 98, 344
USS WACHUSETT 160
USS WATER WITCH 254, 271
USS WEEHAWKI 4

V

Venus 280
Venus Point 186
Vermont 109
Versailles 290
Vicksburg 175, 317
Virginia McDonald 24
Virginia Navy 17
Virginia Wroten 347

W

Wadeville 296
Wake Company 274
Wake County 11, 27, 55, 60, 72, 75, 79, 81, 97, 99, 105, 113, 122, 123, 139, 153, 157, 172, 177, 187, 193, 204, 205, 206, 208, 210, 219, 220, 233, 235, 240, 241, 244, 248, 257, 263, 269, 272, 275, 289, 291, 293, 295, 301, 307, 317, 325, 335, 341, 346, 348
Wakefield 214
Wakulla County 37
Wales 222
Wallace 33, 329
Walter and Nancy Aldred 6
Warren County 11, 56, 72, 110, 134, 163, 177, 189, 201, 228, 249, 257, 262, 294, 311, 327
Warrenton 72, 78, 82, 110, 177, 227, 294, 327
Warsaw 180
Washington 76, 91, 119, 131, 149, 153, 167, 179, 181, 189, 198, 208, 211, 217, 220, 234, 257, 265, 273, 294, 309, 332, 340
Washington County 2, 5, 9, 15, 16, 33, 34, 42, 51, 63, 78, 93, 141, 151, 152, 154, 155, 183, 194, 213, 222, 228, 232, 235, 247, 255, 262, 270, 272, 284, 295, 309, 319, 332
Washington Point 237
Washington University 185

Washington University School of Medicine 324
Wassaw Sound 4
Watauga County 20
Water Valley 148
Watkins 262
Watson Family Cemetery 326
Wayne County 18, 35, 49, 50, 56, 82, 84, 86, 105, 112, 116, 117, 129, 144, 167, 205, 260, 280, 297, 310, 325, 333, 337
Weakley County 129
Weekly Raleigh Register 81
Weldon 22, 41
West Creek 106
Westmead 215
West Salem Cemetery 347
White Hall 136
White Oak 259
White Oak Baptist Church Cemetery 73
Wilder 192
Wilkes County 7, 54, 57, 134
Willard 165, 231
William and Celia Peadon 244
William and Charity Parrish 241
William and Elizabeth Penny 245
William and Margaret Platt 250
William and Salley Stancil 297
William H. Bowen 33
William H. Bryan Cemetery 46
William H. Milton 214
William McLeod 36
William P. and Sarah E. Gurley 152
William R. King 177
William Robert Dalton 81
Williamsburg 271
Williamson 233
William T. Muse 227
William T. Sherman 324
Willow Dale Cemetery 311
Wilmington 3, 5, 6, 8, 9, 12, 14, 15, 17, 18, 19, 22, 24, 25, 27, 28, 29, 31, 32, 33, 37, 39, 40, 42, 43, 44, 45, 47, 48, 49, 52, 53, 54, 55, 56, 58, 60, 61, 63, 64, 65, 66, 67, 68, 69, 70, 72, 73, 74, 75, 79, 80, 82, 84, 86, 87, 88, 89, 90, 91, 92, 93, 97, 98, 100, 101, 103, 104, 105, 106, 107, 109, 110, 112, 113, 114, 115, 117, 118, 119, 120, 121, 123, 124, 125, 126, 128, 129, 130, 131, 132, 133, 136, 137, 138, 139, 140, 141, 142, 143, 145, 146, 147, 148, 150, 151, 153, 154, 156, 157, 158, 159, 161, 162, 163, 164, 165, 166, 168, 169, 170, 173, 174, 175, 176, 177, 178, 180, 183, 184, 186, 187, 188, 189, 190, 191, 192, 193, 194, 195, 196, 197, 198, 199, 201, 203, 204, 208, 209, 211, 212, 213, 215, 217, 218, 219, 220, 221, 222, 223, 224, 226, 227, 228, 229, 230, 232, 233, 234, 236, 237, 238, 240, 242, 243, 244, 245, 246, 248, 250, 251, 253, 254, 256, 257, 258, 261, 263, 264, 267, 268, 270, 272, 273, 276, 277, 278, 279, 281, 282, 284, 286, 287, 288, 289, 290, 291, 294, 295, 296, 297, 298, 300, 301, 303, 304, 306, 307, 309, 310, 311, 313, 314, 317, 318, 319, 321, 322, 323, 325, 326, 327, 328, 329, 331, 332, 333, 334, 335, 339, 340, 342, 344, 345, 348, 349
Wilmington and Manchester Railroad 19
Wilmington Light Infantry 103
Wilmington Squadron 227
Wilmington station 46
Wilmington Station 19, 24, 49, 72, 76, 82, 90, 107, 110, 114, 118, 120, 126, 127, 129, 131, 135, 148, 150, 165, 166, 168, 177, 190, 195, 204, 205, 228, 241, 245, 267, 269, 276, 281, 314, 317, 325, 338, 345
Wilmington & Weldon Railroad 228
Wilson 34, 40, 50, 63, 82
Wilson County 6, 47, 48, 117, 135, 205, 212, 217, 240, 243, 263, 271, 322, 342
Wilton 13, 216, 283
Winchester 282
Windsor 62, 124, 304
Winnie J. Redditt 260
Winnsboro 34
WINSLOW 78
Winston Salem 184
Winston- Salem 157
Winston-Salem 31, 251, 332, 335, 340, 347
Winterville 314
Wolfscrape 18
Woodlawn Cemetery 77, 90, 335
Woodlawn National Cemetery 37, 301, 304
Wrightsville Beach 204
Wrightsville Sound 327
W. S. Thompson 12
W. S. Walker 140
W. W. Larkin 159

Y

Yadkin County 58, 71, 96, 100, 284
Yalobusha County 148
Yancey County 193
Yazoo River 317
York District 157, 159
Yorktown [CSN] 133

Z

Zebulon 214
Zebulon B. Vance 21, 75, 107, 132, 259, 314
Zebulon Vance 253, 324
Zion Methodist Church 209

"Aide Toi Et Dieu T'Aidera"
("Help Yourself, and God Will Help You")

[Motto on the ship's wheel of the Confederate commerce raider CSS ALABAMA, commanded by Admiral Raphael Semmes]

"Deo Vindice"
["With God, our Defender/Protector"]
(Translations vary)
Defactor Confederate States Motto

www.ingramcontent.com/pod-product-compliance
Lightning Source LLC
Chambersburg PA
CBHW080501240426
43673CB00006B/255